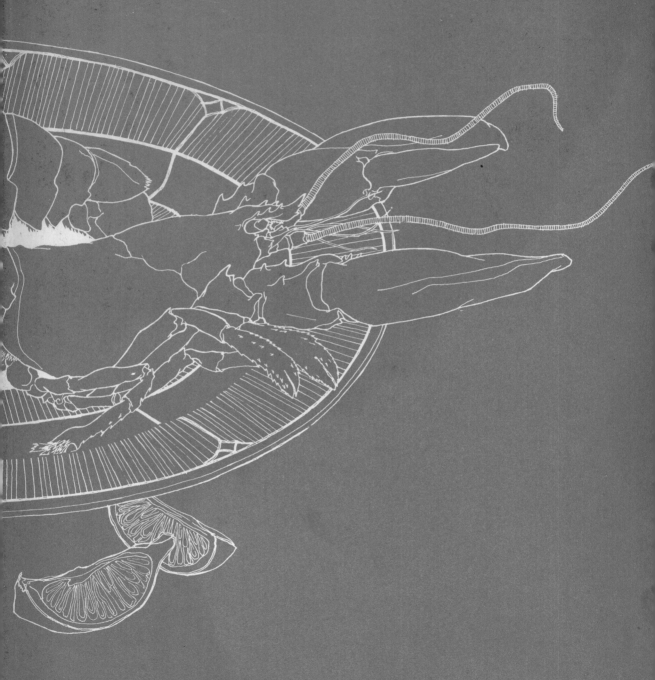

THE

GOOD HOUSEKEEPING COOKBOOK

THE
GOOD HOUSEKEEPING
COOKBOOK

Edited by DOROTHY B. MARSH

Director of Foods and Cookery, Good Housekeeping Institute

Illustrations by Bill Goldsmith

GOOD HOUSEKEEPING BOOK DIVISION, N.Y., N.Y. 10019

Color photographs facing pages 502 and 535 by Paul D'Ome;
all other color photographs by James Viles

Diagrams by Joan Blume

FOREWORD

A cookbook can be many things — depending on its author and its purpose. The only *one* element all are sure to possess is recipes.

This cookbook almost defies classification. It is so many things. It is years of *Good Housekeeping*'s knowledge of and respect for food — its preparation, its serving, its role in family life.

It is a loving compilation of favorite recipes from our famous cookbook series, a complete chapter of our teenage Susan's cherished step-by-step directions to fabulous dishes, more quick-and-easy recipes than ever before. It is what to do to make those ever-present leftovers seem new and exciting. It is how to cook for that magic number — two. It is cooking with utmost confidence because the recipes have been tested and proved beyond any question.

It is the tremendous contribution of the food industry to our country — and the zealous care and protection of our governmental agencies.

Overwhelmingly, it is American women. It is the grandmother who writes from a small town in Montana to say: "My grandchildren's birthday cakes have made me famous. I owe it all to *Good Housekeeping*."

It is the young bride who valiantly copes with the complexities of a new marriage, an outside job, no knowledge of cooking, and who says to us: "Dear *Good Housekeeping*, what would I ever do without you!"

It is the "older" woman who says: "Now that my children are grown, now that our budget is bigger, I can truly enjoy and use all those wonderful ideas for gourmet dishes. Thank you for your food pages."

It is the young high school or college graduate who writes to us: "Dear *Good Housekeeping*: I'm being married in June. My mother says you taught her to cook. Please, will you teach me too?"

It is a Foods and Cookery staff that almost defies belief in its dedication and devotion, its enthusiasm and creativity.

But perhaps more than anything else, this cookbook is the spirit — the *caring* — the untiring *giving* of a magnificent food editor and a great and gracious lady, Dorothy B. Marsh.

It comes to you with the gratitude and best wishes of all of us at *Good Housekeeping*.

WILLIE MAE ROGERS
Director, The Institute

FOREWORD

A cookbook can be many things — depending on its author and its purpose. The only one... all are sure to possess is recipes.

This cookbook almost defies classification. It is so many things. It is years of Good House... knowledge of and respect for food — its preparation, its serving, its role in family life...

It is a loving compilation of favorite recipes from our famous cookbook series, a comple... ter of our teenage Susan's cherished step-by-step directions to fabulous dishes, more... recipes than ever before. It is what to do to make those ever-present leftovers tempting appeal... ing. It is how to cook for that magic number — two. It is cooking with unusual...

the recipes have been tested and proved beyond any question.

Overwhelmingly, it is American women. It is the grandmother who... Montana to say: "My grandchildren's birthday cakes have mad...

It is the "older" women who says: "Now that my... bigger, I can truly enjoy and use all those won... your food pages."

CONTENTS

HOW TO USE OUR INDEX

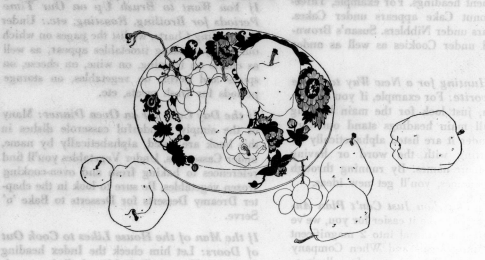

Learn to use our Index freely. It will guide you to a wealth of information and save you many precious minutes.

If a very basic recipe, such as Macaroni and Cheese, seems to be missing from a chapter, it probably is one of Susan's recipes. If you go to the Index first thing, you will be guided to the right page at once.

We tried to think of every way in which you might look for recipes or food information. Here's how it works!

If You're a Beginner Cook: We've a whole chapter of The Best of Susan. Our teen-age Susan's wonderful recipes and many other step-by-step basic dishes will guide you to perfect results every time. Turn to the heading Susan's in the Index. Under it are listed wonderful basic, as well as special-occasion, dishes, all in easy-to-understand, step-by-step form. Be sure to consult the chapters Family Meals, Cook's Vocabulary, and When You Go Marketing.

If You're Cooking for Two: Look under For Two in the Index. Some of our recipes have For Two directions at end.

If Reducing or Gaining Weight Is a Pressing Problem in Your Family: Let our Index headings Weight-Watching and Low-Calorie Recipes direct you to information tailored to your needs. (If you must lose weight, see our chapter on Family Weight-Watching. Our Keep-Young Guide to Happy Eating will lend a hand, too.) And we've a section for teen-age dieters.

If You're Interested in Foreign Recipes: Don't travel any farther than Foreign Flavor in the Index. Under that heading, find the country you'd like to "visit"; you'll find, listed, the dishes that are that land's favorite fare.

If Leftovers Are a Problem: Turn to Leftovers, which will tell you where to look for recipes using leftover meat and turkey.

If You Want to Try a New Fruit: There's a whole chapter on Wonderful Ways with Fruit. Look under the listing for Fruits or under the name of the fruit you are interested in using.

If You're Looking Up a Recipe by Name: The recipes in this book (there are more than 3500) are listed by name, alphabetically. You'll find Three-Layer Coconut Cake in the Ts, Pizza in the Ps, Susan's Brownies under Susan's in the Ss, etc.

Many of our recipes are also listed under other pertinent headings. For example, Three-Layer Coconut Cake appears under Cakes. Pizza appears under Nibblers. Susan's Brownies is listed under Cookies as well as under Brownies.

If You're Hunting for a New Way to Serve an Old Favorite: For example, if you're serving chicken, just look for the main heading Chicken (all main headings stand out very clearly). Under it are listed alphabetically all recipes starting with the word or having chicken in their names. By running through these recipe names, you'll get new ideas.

If You Feel That You Just Can't Plan Another Menu: To make it easier for you, we've combined all our material into 2 magnificent chapters, Family Meals and When Company Comes. There you'll find menus for all situations from cooking for two to gourmet and budget meals. Take time to read through these chapters. Both you and your family will be headed for happier eating. At the end of many of our recipes you will find serving and "go-with" suggestions.

If Any Cookery Term or Method Used in Our Recipes Is New to You: Our Index will tell you where to find what the term means. For example, if the term "bottled sauce for gravy" puzzles you, just turn to Bottled in the Bs, or Sauces in the Ss, for the page on which its explanation will be found.

If Company's Coming: You'll find many answers in the chapter When Company Comes. Turn to it for help with such details as seating guests for dinner, serving buffet style, how to be both cook and hostess. You may want to turn to the chapter When There Is Wine for the correct beverage to serve. Or if it's a huge crowd, turn to Cooking for a Crowd.

If You Have a New Home Freezer or Want to Know Up-to-the-Moment Techniques of

Freezing: The listing under Freezing in the Index will help you. You'll find how-tos on freezing cooked foods, meats, vegetables, etc., plus information on storing frozen foods, refreezing thawed foods, etc.

If You Want to Brush Up on Our Time Periods for Broiling, Roasting, etc.: Under the heading Charts, we list the pages on which our many cooking timetables appear, as well as charts on freezing, on wine, on cheese, on spices and herbs, on vegetables, on storage periods for fresh meats, etc.

If the Day Calls for an Oven Dinner: Many of the simply wonderful casserole dishes in this book are listed, alphabetically by name, under Casseroles. Under Vegetables you'll find references to baking fresh and oven-cooking frozen vegetables. Be sure to look in the chapter Dreamy Desserts for Desserts to Bake 'n' Serve.

If the Man of the House Likes to Cook Out of Doors: Let him check the Index heading Barbecue. There he'll find listed all the superb recipes in this book specially tailored for cooking outdoors.

If You Long to Be a Better Shopper: In the chapter When You Go Marketing, and in those on meats, poultry, vegetables, fruits, etc., shopping tips are covered most thoroughly and helpfully. In The Story of Meats, you will find many photographs of meat cuts—a big boost to beginner shoppers.

If You Must Spend Less on Food: To cut corners safely, check under Meal Planning in the Index, where you'll be directed to safe ways to make food pennies go farther in shopping, cooking, and meal planning.

If You're Chairman of the Food Committee and Need Help in Buying and Cooking for Large Groups: Under the Index heading For a Crowd are listed recipes, plus page references for the many helpful pointers in our chapter Cooking for a Crowd (includes amounts to buy for 25, 50, or 100 persons; marketing in quantity; figuring what to charge, etc.).

THE
GOOD HOUSEKEEPING COOKBOOK

HOW TO USE OUR RECIPES

TO ASSURE SUCCESS WITH OUR RECIPES

No recipe, even *Good Housekeeping*'s, can rate raves if you fail to follow it with meticulous care. So please, please, put these few pointers into practice *from the start*.

Read Every Word of the Recipe First. Never start a dish until you have read the recipe from beginning to end and are completely familiar with it. Then do *exactly* what it tells you — and when!

Follow Our Do-Aheads. Many of our recipes tell you when and how much of the making you can do ahead. A wonderful time-saver, whether it's family or company you're cooking for.

Be Sure Your Pans Are the Right Size. A too-small pan or dish is sure to cause the mixture to run over. A too-large one will leave it underbrowned, skimpy, or flat. So *always* use the size called for. Make Measuring Secrets, pp. 13–16, your guide.

Be Fussy When You Measure. In perfecting our recipes, we use the same measuring cups and spoons as those described in Measuring

Secrets, p. 13. We always measure level. So, to duplicate our results, you must do likewise.

Never Alter Key Ingredients. Vary spices and seasonings if you will. But never, never alter the amounts of flour, sugar, liquid, or shortening we call for. Never substitute other ingredients, either. If we call for sifted cake flour, use cake flour — *not* something else. It makes a difference!

Don't Double a Recipe, Unless We Say To. We can't guarantee success! Rather, make up the recipe exactly as given, then repeat it as many times as needed.

Our Serve-It-With's. Who doesn't run out of menu ideas! So you will often find a hint at the close of our recipes.

Just for the Records! Our recipes tell you how many servings each makes. But remember that *doesn't* mean people. A dish that makes 4 servings, serves only 2, if you plan on seconds.

We are indebted to the National Live Stock and Meat Board for the pictures of meat cuts in the chapter on Meats.

3

COOK'S VOCABULARY

HOW TO USE

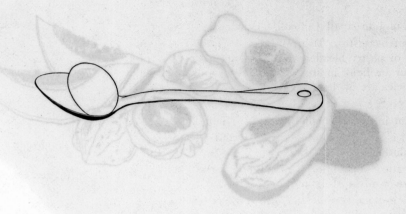

TO ASSURE SUCCESS

COOKERY METHODS

If any of the cookery methods and terms used in our recipes are new to you, read below and you'll find directions telling you what to do.

BAKE: Cook in heated oven. Called roasting when applied to meat.

BASTE: Moisten food, while it is cooking, by spooning on liquid or fat.

BEAT: With electric mixer, hand beater, or spoon, make mixture smooth.

BEAT WITH SPOON: With mixing spoon (or wire whip), lift mixture rapidly, over and over, bringing under part to surface and mixing ingredients evenly. Tilt bowl while beating.

BLANCH: See To Blanch Almonds, p. 99.

BLEND: Combine two or more ingredients well — usually with spoon or electric mixer.

BOIL: Cook food in boiling liquid, in which bubbles constantly rise to surface and break. At sea level, water boils at 212°F. Once liquid boils, lower heat till just high enough to keep liquid boiling. *Slow boiling is just as effective as rapid boiling.*

BRAISE: In a little hot fat, brown meat slowly and *well* on all sides — about 15 to 20 min. Season, add a little water or other liquid. Cover, simmer over *low* heat till tender. (Use this method for less tender meat.)

BROIL: Cook under the heat of a broiler, or over hot coals, or between 2 heated surfaces.

BRUSH WITH: With pastry brush or crumpled wax paper, cover lightly with melted fat, salad oil, cream, beaten egg white, etc.

CARAMELIZE: In large skillet over medium heat, melt granulated sugar, stirring constantly, until sugar caramelizes into a golden-brown syrup. Superfine sugar caramelizes in less time.

CHILL: Place in refrigerator or other cold place until cold.

CHOP: Using knife, chopper, or chopping bowl with knife, cut up food as recipe directs.

CHOP NUTS: See p. 99.

COAT: Using shaker-top can or sifter, sprinkle with flour, sugar, etc., until coated. Or roll

4

in flour, sugar, etc., until coated. Or shake with flour, etc., in paper bag until coated.

COOL: Let stand at room temperature until no longer warm to touch.

CREAM: With spoon, rub or work soft shortening, or soft shortening and sugar, against sides of bowl until creamy. Or use electric mixer.

CUBE: Cut into small (about ½″) cubes.

CUT IN SHORTENING: Using 2 knives, scissor-fashion, or pastry blender, cut soft shortening into flour or flour mixture until flour-coated fat particles are of desired size.

DEEP-FRY: See p. 6.

DICE: Cut into very small (about ¼″) cubes.

DISSOLVE: Mix dry substance with liquid until in solution.

DOT: Scatter small bits, as of butter or margarine, over surface of food.

DOUBLE BOILER, COOK IN: Fill bottom of double boiler with about 2″ water; bring to boil. Set double-boiler top, containing food, in place. Then cook over hot or boiling water as recipe directs.

DREDGE: Coat or sprinkle lightly with flour, sugar, etc.

FOLD IN (BEATEN EGG WHITES, WHIPPED CREAM, ETC.): Heap on top of mixture. Pass wire whip, rubber spatula, or spoon down through mixture and across bottom; bring up some of mixture; place on top of egg whites (or cream). Repeat until egg whites (or cream) are evenly combined with mixture.

GRATE: Rub on grater to produce fine, medium, or coarse particles. When grating lemon rind, use only colored part of rind.

GREASE: Rub lightly with butter, margarine, shortening, or salad oil.

GRIND: Put through meat grinder.

KNEAD: See How To Knead (p. 500), steps 1 through 3.

LARD: Lay strips of salt pork or bacon on top of, or in gashes in, fish or meat. Prevents dryness.

MARINATE: Let stand in a mixture, usually French dressing, for indicated time.

MELT CHOCOLATE: Place in small bowl or custard cup; melt over hot, *not boiling,* water. Or melt, stirring, in saucepan over lowest heat. Or melt, in original wrapping, on piece of foil placed in oven while oven is heating or cooling off. Remove chocolate as soon as melted.

MINCE: Chop fine with chopper. Or, with onion, try this: Cut in half; cut surface of half into tiny squares as deep as you like. Holding onion firmly on cutting surface, slice off ⅛″ slices. Minced onion drops off as you slice. Repeat till all is used.

PAN-BROIL: Cook, uncovered, in ungreased or *lightly* greased hot skillet, pouring off fat as it accumulates.

PAN-FRY: Cook in small amount of hot fat in skillet.

PARBOIL: Boil in water or other liquid until partially cooked, preliminary to another form of cooking.

PARE: With knife, remove outer covering, as of apples.

PEEL: Pull off outer covering, as of bananas or oranges.

PIT: Remove pit or seed, as from prunes.

PREHEAT: Turn on oven; heat to desired baking temperature before putting in food.

PUREE: Press through fine sieve or food mill.

SAUTE: Cook in small amount of hot fat or salad oil in skillet.

SCALD: Heat to just under boiling point (e.g., heat milk in double boiler until tiny bubbles gather at sides).

SCALLOP: Bake in layers with sauce. If desired, top with crumbs.

SCORE: With knife or fork, make shallow slits or gashes.

SEAR: Brown surface quickly over high heat, as in hot skillet.

SEASON: Add, or sprinkle with, salt (or onion, celery, or garlic salt, or seasoned salt), monosodium glutamate, or pepper (or seasoned pepper) to taste.

SHALLOW-FRY: See p. 7.

SIFT: Put through flour sifter or fine sieve.

SIMMER: Cook just below the boiling point — about 185°F. at sea level.

SINGE (POULTRY): Hold over heat to burn off all hairs.

SKEWER: Hold in place by means of metal or wooden skewers.

SLIVER: Cut or split into long, thin pieces.

SNIP: With kitchen shears, cut into small pieces.

STEAM: Cook in steam.

STEEP: Let stand in hot liquid.

STIR: With spoon, blend with circular motion, widening circles until all ingredients are well mixed.

THICKEN: Measure liquid to be thickened. For each cupful, mix 1½ tablesp. flour with 3 tablesp. water till smooth. Stir into hot liquid, cook until thickened.

TOAST: Brown in broiler, oven, toaster, or over hot coals.

TOSS: Mix lightly with 2 forks or with fork and spoon.

TRY OUT: Fry bits of solid fat or fat meat in skillet until fat separates from membrane.

UNMOLD: See Gelatin Dishes, p. 7.

WHIP: Beat rapidly, usually with electric mixer or hand beater, to incorporate air and increase volume.

When You Deep-Fry

Fried foods will be delicious and nutritious prepared this way:

What You Need:

FRYER: You can buy deep-fat fryers that are light and easily handled, with a removable
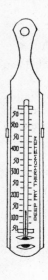
wire basket for lowering food into fat and draining. Such fryers can also be used as saucepans.

DEEP-FAT-FRYING THERMOMETER: With a deep-fat fryer like that described above, you should use a deep-fat-frying thermometer or combination deep-fat-frying-and-candy thermometer (a candy thermometer alone will not do) to determine the exact temperature of fat or salad oil. (See line drawing.) No other method of checking the temperature is as reliable.

AUTOMATIC DEEP-FAT FRYER: An electric fryer simplifies frying because it automatically maintains the temperature you select and insures perfectly fried food. These fryers also do a fine job of cooking casserole dishes, soups, stews, pot roasts, etc. In using them, be sure to follow manufacturer's directions and timetable closely.

FAT OR SALAD OIL: Use any shortening or salad oil except butter, margarine, or olive oil.

PAPER TOWELS OR BROWN PAPER: Arrange on baking pan or in colander to drain fried foods as soon as they are removed from fat.

How to Deep-Fry:

1. Use enough fat or salad oil to cover food completely. There should be at least 3″ between surface of fat and top of kettle, so fat will not bubble over during frying.

2. Gradually heat fat or salad oil to desired temperature, following Deep-Fat-Frying Chart, p. 7, and using deep-fat-frying thermometer or Bread Test for Frying, below.

3. When fat reaches desired temperature (keep thermometer in fat during frying), promptly lower food *gently* into heated fat, using wire basket, spoon, or tongs. Do not try to fry too much at a time; too much cold food reduces temperature of fat so that food may become grease soaked before it browns.

4. Watch fat thermometer and, if necessary, adjust heat to maintain desired temperature as nearly as possible. Don't let fat overheat. Turn food as recipe directs.

When fried food is done, remove to paper towels or brown paper arranged on baking pan or in colander to absorb excess fat from surface. If fried food should be kept hot, set baking pan in 300°F. oven while frying rest of food.

5. Always bring fat back to desired temperature before putting in second batch of food. Skim off loose food particles to prevent smoking.

Bread Test for Frying: If you do not have a deep-fat-frying thermometer to determine temperature of fat or oil, the bread test is the next best thing. Drop 1″ square of day-old bread into hot fat or oil, then count time it takes to brown.

At 370°F., a 1″ square of bread will brown in 60 sec.; at 375°F., in 40 sec.; at 390°F., in 20 sec.

DEEP-FAT-FRYING CHART

KIND OF FOOD	THERMOMETER READING	APPROXIMATE FRYING TIME
Croquettes and other cooked foods	390°F.	2 min.
Doughnuts, fritters	370°F.	2 to 5 min.
French fries (p. 414)	370°F.; then drain and fry at 390°F.	5 to 7 min. Until crisp and brown
Fish:		
Small whole fish	370°F.	3 min.
Fillets	370°F.	4 min.
Oysters, clams	370°F.	2 min.

Care of Fat or Salad Oil After Use: After each use, cool fat a little, then ladle into strainer, lined with cheesecloth, over container kept for the purpose. Cool, cover, store in refrigerator. (Some automatic deep-fat fryers have drain spouts to make emptying easier.)

After frying strong-flavored foods, partially cool fat, then clarify it: Add a few slices of raw potato; reheat slowly, stirring occasionally. Discard potato, strain as above.

A certain amount of fat or oil is absorbed by the food fried in it. So replenish with fresh fat or oil when reusing.

Shallow-Frying

Shallow-frying is an easy substitute for deep-frying croquettes, French fries, doughnuts, fish, etc.

Into *deep* saucepan, put only enough fat or salad oil (see Fat or Salad Oil, p. 6) to make 1½″ when heated. Heat to same temperatures on deep-fat-frying thermometer as in Deep-Fat-Frying Chart, above. Then fry food and drain as in How to Deep-Fry, p. 6. There will be less fat left over for reuse than in deep-frying, but this fat will generally be of higher quality.

To Remove Fat From Broth or Stock

1. Skim off fat with metal spoon gently lowered to surface of liquid.
2. Or lay piece of blotting paper or paper towel on surface of fat. When saturated, remove and replace with fresh piece.
3. Or wrap piece of ice in piece of paper towel and draw lightly across surface of fat. Change paper as needed.
4. Or refrigerate broth overnight. Next day remove congealed fat with spoon.

Gelatin Dishes

UNFLAVORED GELATINE: Today's unflavored gelatine comes 4 env. to the box, and 32 env. in the economy size. Generally 1 env. (about 1 tablesp.) gelatine is sufficient to set 2 cups of liquid.

Dishes made of fresh or frozen pineapple will not set with unflavored gelatine unless the pineapple is first brought to a boil. Cooked or canned pineapple presents no problem.

FRUIT-FLAVOR GELATINS: Fruit-flavor gelatins come in regular and large sizes in a dozen or more delectable fruit flavors (see p. 561).

To Make: Follow recipes on label or those that are given in this book. If fruit (except fresh or frozen pineapple) or vegetables are to be added, chill dissolved gelatin mixture until slightly thickened — not set — before adding. Otherwise ingredients will sink or rise.

To Set: Refrigerate gelatin mixture for several hr. or overnight, covering to prevent evaporation.

To Hasten Setting: Set mold or bowl of gelatin in a pan of ice water, then refrigerate. If to have ingredients like fruit, vegetables, or meat added when slightly thickened, watch carefully to avoid setting too long.

To Unmold: Moisten both chilled serving plate and surface of molded gelatin with wet fingers (it will be easier to slide gelatin into center of plate after unmolding). Dip small pointed knife in warm water and use to loosen gelatin around edge of mold. Then quickly dip mold, just to rim, in warm water, remove, and shake mold gently to loosen gelatin. Cover with inverted serving plate, then invert plate and mold together. Lift off mold carefully. Repeat if necessary.

COOKERY TERMS

BATTER: A mixture, of pouring consistency, of flour, liquid, and other ingredients.

BOTTLED THICK MEAT SAUCE: Any bottled meat or steak sauce, such as A. 1, Heinz Beefsteak Sauce, etc., of rather thick consistency.

BOTTLED SAUCE FOR GRAVY: A sauce, such as Kitchen Bouquet, Gravy Master, etc., that gives rich brown color and flavor to gravies and sauces.

BREAD CRUMBS, BUTTERED: Fresh bread crumbs prepared as follows: To each ½ cup fresh bread crumbs, add 1 tablesp. melted butter, margarine, or shortening, or salad oil; toss with fork. Nice, too, with a little grated cheese added.

BREAD CRUMBS, DRIED: Bread crumbs prepared as follows: Dry out bread slices in 250°F. oven until crisp but not brown. Or let stand at room temperature until thoroughly dry.

Then place in clean, strong paper bag; roll with rolling pin to make fine crumbs. Or put through food chopper, using fine blade. (Tie paper bag to blade end of chopper to receive crumbs.) Refrigerate crumbs. Use to coat croquettes, etc.

Or buy packaged dried bread crumbs.

BREAD CRUMBS, FRESH: Fresh bread slices crumbled between fingers. If you're using unsliced loaf, cut off end crust; pull out small crumbs with fork. Use crusts or not, as you like.

BUTTER BALLS: Butter prepared as follows: Scald, then chill in ice water, pair of wooden butter paddles. Into ice water, drop ¼" pats of butter or margarine. When each piece is cold, roll between paddles to form ball, dipping paddles often into ice water to chill.

To make cylinders, flatten and roll balls between paddles.

Drop balls or cylinders onto chilled plate or into ice water. You may make several days'

supply ahead and refrigerate it in cold water, covered.

BUTTER MOLDS: Butter prepared as follows: Scald, then chill in ice water, fancy butter molds. Pack well with butter; level off with knife; press out; chill.

COCONUT MILK: In saucepan, combine about 1½ cups flaked coconut and 1⅓ cups milk. Simmer over low heat, stirring occasionally, until mixture foams, about 2 min. Strain off milk. Use in curry sauce or other recipes that call for coconut milk. Or serve chilled as beverage. Makes 1 cup coconut milk.

COMMERCIAL SOUR CREAM: See p. 92.

CROUTONS: Bread prepared as follows: Butter bread slices (add bit of garlic if desired). Toast in a little hot fat in skillet or in 300°F. oven. Trim, then cut into small squares.

Or cut bread slices into ½" squares; toss in melted butter or margarine. Toast under broiler. Serve as garnish for soups or salads.

DRIPPINGS: Fat and juices that cook out of roast or poultry into shallow open pan.

DRY INGREDIENTS: Flour, baking powder, baking soda, salt, spices, etc.

EGG WHITES, BEATEN STIFF: Egg whites beaten until they stand in peaks when beater is lifted from surface, with points of peaks drooping over a bit and surface still moist and glossy.

EGG WHITES, BEATEN VERY STIFF: Egg whites beaten until points of peaks stand upright, without drooping, when beater is lifted from surface. Surface should look dry.

EGG YOLKS, WELL BEATEN: Egg yolks beaten until thick and lemon-colored.

EGGS, SLIGHTLY BEATEN: Eggs beaten just enough to blend yolks and whites.

EGGS, WELL BEATEN: Eggs beaten until light and frothy.

FAGGOT: Tie together 2 stalks celery, 4 sprigs parsley, ½ bay leaf, sprig thyme.

FILET OR FILLET: Strip of lean, boneless meat or fish.

GARLIC CLOVE: One of 10 to 15 bulblets, or cloves, found in a root of garlic.

A peeled clove may be added whole or halved to a dish (if toothpick is inserted in clove, it is easy to remove after cooking). Or it may be sprinkled with a little salt, then crushed to a paste with back of spoon. Or it may be crushed in a garlic press. Or you may rub a garlic clove on inside of salad bowl or other bowl used for mixing ingredients.

HALF-AND-HALF: See p. 92.

HEAVY, OR WHIPPING, CREAM: See p. 92.

LIGHT, COFFEE, OR TABLE CREAM: See p. 92.

MEAT-EXTRACT PASTE: Extract of meat, concentrated to a paste, with seasoning added; comes in a jar.

MELTED FAT: Fat heated in small saucepan over low heat until melted. Salad oil may be used in recipes that call for melted fat.

MOUND: Spoonful of mixture dropped onto remaining mixture. A "mound" forms a definite heap and does not blend into the original mixture.

NONFAT DRY MILK: See p. 97.

ONION JUICE: Juice scraped with teaspoon from center of halved onion.

PACKAGED DRIED BREAD CRUMBS: Tiny dried bread crumbs of uniform size, packaged in airtight containers.

SALAD OIL: See p. 99.

SCALLIONS (SPRING OR GREEN ONIONS): A member of the lily family, with characteristic onion flavor. The entire scallion can be eaten. May be served cooked or as raw relish. (See Scallions, p. 119.)

SEASONED FLOUR: Flour mixed with seasonings in the proportions of ¼ cup flour to ¾ teasp. salt, plus ¼ teasp. each pepper and paprika.

SHORTENINGS: See p. 100.

SILVER DRAGEES: Tiny edible, ball-shaped, silver-colored candies.

SKIM MILK: See p. 97.

STOCK OR BROTH: Liquid in which meat, poultry, etc., has simmered till tender.

TENDER OR FORK-TENDER: Softened by cooking until fork pierces easily.

TINTED COCONUT: Flaked coconut, delicately colored as follows: Blend 1 teasp. milk or water with drop or so of desired food color. Add 1⅓ cups flaked (or 1 cup fine grated) coconut, also a little peppermint, almond, or vanilla extract if desired. Toss with fork until blended.

TOAST POINTS: Toast slices, cut diagonally from one corner to opposite corner.

TOP MILK: Top cream layer removed from bottle of whole, nonhomogenized milk.

WHOLE MILK: See p. 97.

KITCHEN TOOLS YOU'LL NEED

If you are checking your supply of pots and pans, or if you are equipping your first kitchen, use the following list as a guide. Buy enough good utensils to start with, then add others as you need them.

The choice of electrical appliances is wide and not included here. However, if you have such appliances as an electric skillet, mixer, coffee maker, toaster, etc., your kitchen will be an easier place in which to work.

It is often a puzzle what size and how many items are needed. We have included suggestions in our following guide list. In addition, be certain that the cookware is sturdy and flat-bottomed, with comfortable, heat-resistant handles.

Equipment Guide

ONE LARGE COVERED PAN — 6- to 10-qt. size. This may be a kettle, saucepan, or Dutch oven, to be used for meats, soups, or spaghetti for a crowd.

ONE DOUBLE BOILER — with 2- or 3-qt. bottom. Use bottom as an extra saucepan. Top can sometimes be used as a casserole.

TWO SAUCEPANS — 1- and 2-qt. sizes.

TWO SKILLETS (FRYING PANS) — 10" size with a cover, for braising and preparing skillet meals; 7" size for small-quantity cooking. Both can be used as griddles.

ONE PRESSURE SAUCEPAN — 4-qt. size is most useful. A must for quick cooking of stews, pot roasts, soups, and vegetables.

ONE LARGE ROASTING PAN — uncovered, with

a rack. Good size is 12″ to 15″ long, 10″ to 12″ wide, and 2″ or 3″ deep.

ONE OR TWO CASSEROLES — at least. The 2-qt. size is a good beginning piece. Some have pie-plate covers.

ONE LOAF PAN — 2-qt. size is a good starter; it's a help if you have only 1 casserole.

CAKE PANS — Two 8″ or 9″ round layer-cake pans; some have removable bottoms. Also 8″ x 8″ x 2″ or 9″ x 9″ x 2″ cake pan.

ONE OR TWO PIE PANS — 8″ or 9″ size. For best results with both cake pans and pie pans, buy aluminum or glass.

ONE TEAKETTLE — 2- or 3-qt. size. The type with a top lid is easy to clean. The enclosed type has a wide spout with a lid raised by a lever in the handle.

ONE OR TWO COOKIE SHEETS — large size. Fine for warming up rolls.

MEASURING CUPS — see Choosing Measuring Cups, p. 13.

MIXING BOWLS — graduated sizes, from 2 cups to 4 qts. Some can double as ovenware and may be used for refrigerator storage.

KNIVES — starter set of 6, including large chef or butcher knife, carving knife, slicer, utility knife (medium-sized), and 2 paring knives.

FLOUR SIFTERS — 1-cup and 5-cup capacities are handy.

GRATERS — single or in a set, for cheese, chocolate, raw vegetables, etc.

STRAINERS — 1 tea-size, 1 large enough to double as a colander.

CANISTER SET WITH SCOOP — graduated sizes for staples.

ROLLING PIN — a great help in making pie. Pastry cloth is nice to have, too.

CUTTING BOARDS — 1 large for slicing meat, 1 small for cheese or vegetables.

HAND BEATER — 1 with heavy-duty gear construction; don't economize. Portable electric mixer can replace this.

FOOD GRINDER — newest kind does not need to be clamped down, so it can be used on any surface.

FRUIT JUICER — 1 small reamer for lemon juice. If you have a juicer attachment for your electric mixer, or are a frozen-orange-juice fan, you won't need a larger juicer for oranges.

TOOL SET — 2 metal spatulas, 1 long and narrow, 1 short and wide (also called a pancake turner); 1 ladle; 1 cooking fork; 1 large spoon, solid or perforated; 1 potato masher (portable electric mixer can do this also).

CAN OPENER — an electric can opener or a wall type, with bracket that will hold other tools; choose solid construction. It must be cleaned often and thoroughly, and oiled.

OTHER FREQUENT NEEDS — rubber spatulas, available in 2 sizes; pastry or blending fork, with many uses besides blending pastry; kitchen shears; wooden spoons for mixing and beating without scratching utensils; all-purpose brush; glass or plastic refrigerator dishes. Peeler for vegetables and fruits.

SINK ACCESSORIES — 1 drainboard, 1 sink mat, 1 dish drainer, 1 sink strainer, 1 dishpan, 2 sponges, 1 soap dish, 1 towel rack, 1 waste pail, 2 garbage pails (1 small and 1 large).

STORAGE ACCESSORIES — vegetable bins; stationary, pull-out drawer, or turn-table type dinnerware racks. Utensil trays give order and efficiency to work space.

Shopping for Pots and Pans

When you embark on a shopping trip for pots and pans, you may find a matched set that's exactly what you want. By and large, however, you will do better to buy assorted wares to suit your needs.

ALUMINUM is practically unbeatable for all-round use. It requires a bit more than average care to keep it clean and shiny (polishing with a steel-wool soap pad), but will more than compensate by giving even heat distribution, especially important in frying (sautéing).

STAINLESS STEEL falls into a somewhat more expensive category, but it is easy to clean and practically indestructible. If you select stainless-steel pans, be sure they have copper, aluminum, or laminated-steel bottoms, or are clad in aluminum (bottom and sides), to give an even distribution of heat. The second metal may or may not be visible, so check tags and labels for construction.

COPPER utensils are handsome but seldom used. They should be plated with tin on the inside for easier cleaning, but eventually the tin wears through and the pan must be replated to restore it.

ENAMELWARE is not used as much today as it once was. Enamelware is glass fused on metal and, consequently, needs careful handling to prevent cracking, chipping, or discoloring. The widest use is in teakettles, double boilers, and saucepans because the heat distribution of this ware is spotty, not even.

CAST IRON is sturdy ware for skillet or Dutch-oven use. It may be used for top-of-the-range or oven cooking. It must be kept seasoned to prevent rust. The seasoning is retained longer by washing with soap rather than a detergent. To season cast iron, spread melted shortening or salad oil on inside of utensil and on its cover. (Do not use any fat that contains salt.) Place in warm oven or over low heat for several hours, swabbing sides and cover occasionally with more fat. When cool, wipe off excess fat or oil with paper towels. The utensil is then ready to use.

PORCELAIN-ENAMELED WARE handsomely combines bright color with sturdy, heavy cast iron or lighter cast aluminum. Porcelain on cast iron is applied inside and out and eliminates the need for seasoning. Porcelain on cast aluminum is applied on the outside only; the inside surface is aluminum and requires the same care as all aluminum utensils. The shiny porcelain surface should be protected against abrasives to avoid scratching.

TEFLON is a useful, safe coating applied to the cooking surface of some utensils — skillets particularly, but also glass and aluminum ovenware. It is possible to cook with or without fat and to expect practically no sticking and surprisingly easy cleanup. The Teflon surface is easily damaged and must be protected against scratching. Use no metal tools, only a wooden spatula or a special Teflon turner.

PYROCERAM is a special ceramic which may be stored in the freezer or refrigerator, go directly to the range (either top of stove or oven), and from there to the table. It presents no cleaning problem and may be washed in an electric dishwasher or by hand.

Treat Your Pots and Pans Right

1. Keep food boiling gently (it cooks just as fast as when it's boiling hard) so it won't boil over and leave burned food to be scoured off later. Gentle boiling also reduces chances of the pan's boiling dry and getting scorched.
2. Preheat griddles and skillets over low-to-medium heat; do not let them get hotter than necessary before use.
3. Reduce the heat under all utensils after cooking has started.
4. To soak pans after emptying them, fill with warm sudsy water.
5. Wash utensils in hot sudsy water; rinse; dry.
6. Cast iron which is not porcelain-enameled needs thorough drying, which can be done by heating over a slow heat about 5 min., to prevent rusting.
7. To remove baked- or burned-on food particles from utensils, or to scour aluminum and cast iron, use steel-wool soap pads, copper or bronze sponges, plastic balls, or nonwoven nylon scouring pads.
8. If you keep your utensils in good condition, you need not hesitate to use any of them — skillet, Dutch oven, or attractively designed saucepan, as well as casseroles — for both cooking and serving. This makes it easy to serve food deliciously hot, saves dishwashing, too.
9. We are still asked whether aluminum utensils are safe. Foods cooked in aluminum utensils may absorb very minute quantities of aluminum, but minute quantities also occur naturally in many foods. Authorities agree that these small amounts have no harmful effect. And good aluminum utensils do not destroy the flavor or nutritive value of the foods cooked in them.

Stain Removal

Stubborn stains on cooking utensils can often be removed in the following ways:

ALUMINUM: To remove dark (water or food) stains, boil a solution of 2 tablesp. cream of tartar in 1 qt. water in the utensil for 5 to 10 min. Then scour with a steel-wool soap pad to restore shine. Anodized (colored) aluminum needs no special cleaning care, but avoid abrasives and do not wash in an automatic dishwasher because the color may fade.

STAINLESS STEEL: To remove heat marks, use a small amount of household cleanser and scour with brisk rubbing motion. Rainbow-type heat marks can be removed with household cleanser, but severe discoloration of a pan that has burned dry requires buffing by the manufacturer.

ENAMELWARE: Soak a solution of 3 tablesp. of chlorine bleach to 1 qt. of warm water in the pan about 5 min.

PORCELAIN-ENAMELED CAST IRON: Soak a solution of liquid or powdered dishwashing detergent and warm water in the utensil for 30 min. or more. If food is badly burned on, boil the solution gently for 15 min. or so, or scrape burned-on food with a wooden spoon.

TEFLON-coated pans should not be cleaned with abrasives. A sponge, water, and warm suds are all that's needed to clean them.

HOW WE MEASURE

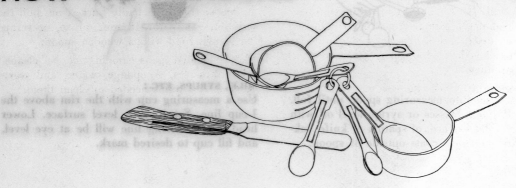

MEASURING SECRETS

Correct measuring of ingredients is essential if you would follow our recipes with consistent success. *All measurements should be level.*

In following the recipes in this cookbook, remember that "cup" means cupful, "teasp." means teaspoonful, and "tablesp." means tablespoonful.

CHOOSING MEASURING CUPS:
When buying measuring cups, choose one type for dry ingredients, another for liquids, as suggested below.

FOR DRY INGREDIENTS:
Buy a set of 4 graduated measuring cups consisting of a ¼-cup, ⅓-cup, ½-cup, and 1-cup measure. Such a set of cups makes accurate measuring easy.

FOR LIQUID INGREDIENTS:
Buy a 1-cup measuring cup whose rim is above the 1-cup line to avoid spilling. The 2-cup and 1-quart measuring cups are also very convenient.

CHOOSING MEASURING SPOONS:

When buying measuring spoons, choose one or more of the sets that come attached to a ring or hang on a special holder (see illustration), including ¼ teasp., ½ teasp., 1 teasp., and 1 tablesp. In a good set, 16 tablesp., or 48 teasp., should equal 1 cup.

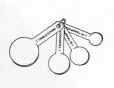

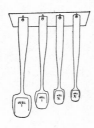

MEASURING LIQUIDS

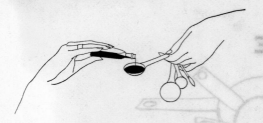

VANILLA, ETC.:
Pour extract into measuring spoon until full. If thick, like molasses or syrup, level off with edge, not flat surface, of spatula or knife, taking care that none coats outside of spoon.

MILK, SYRUPS, ETC.:
Use a measuring cup with the rim above the 1-cup line. Set it on a level surface. Lower head, so measuring line will be at eye level, and fill cup to desired mark.

MEASURING DRY INGREDIENTS

Use a set of 4 graduated measuring cups. Use a set of measuring spoons. Measure as below.

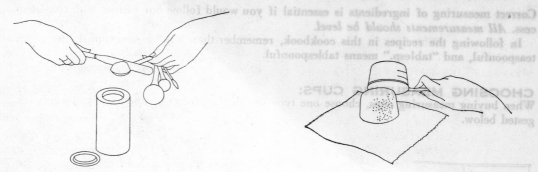

BAKING POWDER, SALT, ETC.:
Dip measuring spoon of correct size into dry ingredient until full; then lift out and level off with edge, not flat surface, of knife or spatula.

If it is necessary to measure half spoonfuls, first measure a level spoonful. Then divide contents lengthwise with knife and push off half.

BROWN SUGAR:
If brown sugar is lumpy, roll out lumps with a rolling pin; then sift. Then spoon the brown sugar into measuring cup, packing it down with back of spoon just enough so it holds when turned out.

GRANULATED OR CONFECTIONERS' SUGAR:
If sugar is at all lumpy, sift first. Then spoon lightly into graduated measuring cup, leveling off with edge, not flat surface, of spatula or knife.

FLOUR:

1. *Just before measuring flour,* sift it once through sifter onto a square of wax paper or into a bowl. Do not sift directly into measuring cup.

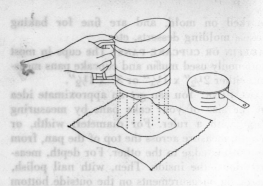

2. Then spoon sifted flour lightly into graduated measuring cup until cup is full.

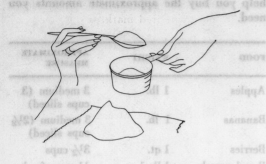

3. Level off flour with edge, not flat surface, of spatula or knife, *without packing it down.*

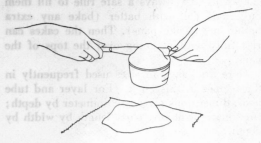

MEASURING SHORTENINGS

SHORTENING: Scoop shortening from can or package, and pack it firmly into a graduated measuring cup up to the top. Then level off with edge, not flat surface, of knife or spatula; remove from cup. This method is preferred to old-fashioned water displacement method (add enough shortening to ½ cup water to push water level up to 1-cup line; pour off water; ½ cup shortening remains).

BUTTER OR MARGARINE: Measure as for shortening, above. Or if you're using a 1-lb. print of butter or margarine, remember that each ¼-lb. stick equals ½ cup, or 8 tablesp. Half a ¼-lb. stick equals ¼ cup, or 4 tablesp. To measure 2 tablesp., cut off one fourth of a ¼-lb. stick.

MELTED FAT: If a recipe calls for melted fat, it doesn't matter whether you measure it before or after melting — the amount will be the same. However, if the fat is hard, it's simpler to measure it after melting.

Salad oil, often used as melted fat, is easily measured in a measuring cup or spoon.

MEASURING PAN SIZES

Recipes in this book suggest the size and type of cake pan, pie plate, casserole, or baking dish we have found best for each particular dish. If you would duplicate our results, it is most important that you use a pan of identical size, or as nearly identical size as possible.

Fortunately, more and more manufacturers of cooking utensils are stamping the inch size or cup capacity of their baking utensils either on the utensil itself, or on a sticker attached to it. So if your pans are hand-me-downs — bigger, smaller, or shallower than our recipes specify — buy yourself some modern pans.

If your pans carry no markings and you are in doubt as to their size, these pointers will help you:

SPRING-FORM PAN: This pan consists of a rim (with or without a clamp) and 2 insets — a flat bottom inset for cheesecake, etc., and a tube inset for angel cake. It is 9″ x 3″ in size.

RING MOLDS: These molds range in capacity from 3⅓ to 11 cups, or 1¼ qt. to 3 qt., as marked on mold, and are fine for baking cakes, molding desserts, etc.

MUFFIN OR CUPCAKE PANS: The cups in most commonly used muffin and cupcake pans measure either 2½″ x 1¼″ or 3″ x 1½″.

CAKE PANS: You can get an approximate idea of the size of your cake pans by measuring them with a ruler. For diameter, width, or length, measure across the top of the pan, from one inside edge to the other. For depth, measure down the inside. Then, with nail polish, mark the measurements on the outside bottom of the pan.

If you have any doubts about the size of your cake pans, it's always a safe rule to fill them only half full with batter (bake any extra batter in cupcake pans). Then the cakes can rise fully without going over the tops of the pans.

Here are cake-pan sizes used frequently in the recipes in this book. (For layer and tube pans, dimensions given are diameter by depth; for square or oblong pans, length by width by depth.)

CAKE-PAN SIZES

LAYER:	8″ x 1¼″	OBLONG OR LOAF:	9″ x 5″ x 3″
	8″ x 1½″		10″ x 5″ x 3″
	9″ x 1½″		10″ x 6″ x 2″
	10″ x 2″		11″ x 7″ x 1½″
			12″ x 8″ x 2″
TIER:	4″ x 2″		13″ x 9″ x 2″
	6″ x 2″		15½″ x 10½″
	8″ x 2″		x 1″ (called
	10″ x 2″		"jelly-roll pan")
TUBE:	9″ x 3½″	SQUARE:	8″ x 8″ x 2″
	10″ x 4″		9″ x 9″ x 2″
	9″ x 9″ x 4″		

PIE PLATES: Pie plates range in size from 4″ to 10″. Our recipes call for 8″, 9″, or 10″ pie plates. Also nice to have is a deep 9″ pie plate, 2″ deep, with a fluted edge.

CASSEROLES AND BAKING DISHES: Casseroles range from 1-qt. to 3-qt. capacity and even larger; if they're of oven glass, the capacity is very plainly marked.

To check the capacity of your casseroles, fill them to the brim with water, measuring the water as you add it.

Baking dishes called for in many of our recipes are the same size as the oblong cake pans listed.

EQUIVALENT AMOUNTS

Many foods are sold by weight, but most recipes designate amounts to be used in terms of measuring cups and spoons. This table will help you buy the approximate amounts you need.

FOOD	WEIGHT	APPROXIMATE MEASURE
Apples	1 lb.	3 medium (3 cups sliced)
Bananas	1 lb.	3 medium (2½ cups sliced)
Berries	1 qt.	3½ cups
Bread crumbs, fresh	1-lb.-1-oz. loaf	11 cups fresh bread crumbs (with crusts)
Butter or margarine	¼-lb. stick	½ cup
	1 lb.	2 cups
Cheese, Cheddar	½ lb.	2 cups grated
Cheese, cream	3-oz. pkg.	6 tablesp.
Cheese, cottage	½ lb.	1 cup
Coffee, ground*	1 lb.	80 tablesp.
Cream, heavy	½ pt.	2 cups whipped
Dates, pitted	8-oz. pkg.	1¼ cups cut up
Dates, chopped and sugar coated	7½-oz. pkg.	1⅓ cups
Egg whites, fresh	about 8 to 11 whites	1 cup
Egg yolks, fresh	about 12 to 14 yolks	1 cup
Flour:		
All-purpose	1 lb.	4 cups sifted
Cake	1 lb.	4¾ to 5 cups sifted

Makes about 40 to 45 serving cups of beverage (1 approved coffee measure per ¾ cup water).

Whole-wheat	1 lb.	About 3½ cups unsifted
Lemon juice	1 medium lemon	3 tablesp. juice
Lemon rind	1 medium lemon	1 tablesp. grated rind
Milk:		
Evaporated	14½-oz. can	1⅔ cups
	6-oz. can	¾ cup
Sweetened condensed	14-oz. can	1¼ cups
	15½-oz. can	1⅓ cups
Nuts in shell:		
Almonds	1¼ lb.	1 to 1¾ cups nut meats
Brazil nuts	1 lb.	1½ cups nut meats
Peanuts	1 lb.	2 cups nut meats
Pecans	1 lb.	2¼ cups nut meats
Walnuts	1 lb.	1⅔ cups chopped
Nuts, shelled:		
Almonds	1 lb. 2 oz.	4 cups
Pecan meats	1 lb.	4 cups
Walnut meats	1 lb.	4 cups
Brazil-nut meats	1 lb.	3 cups
Orange juice	1 medium orange	⅓ cup juice
Orange rind	1 medium orange	2 tablesp. grated rind
Potatoes:		
White	1 lb.	3 medium (2⅓ cups sliced)
Sweet	1 lb.	3 medium (3 cups sliced)
Raisins	15-oz. pkg.	3 cups (not packed)
Sugar:		
Brown	1 lb.	2¼ to 2⅓ cups (firmly packed)
Confectioners'	1 lb.	About 4½ cups unsifted
Granulated or superfine	1 lb.	2¼ to 2½ cups
Tomatoes	1 lb.	3 medium

EQUIVALENT MEASURES

This table is designed to help you translate amounts stated in terms of one measuring device into those of another, perhaps more convenient one, and to do the mathematics for you when you want to divide an ingredient.

Speck	Less than ⅛ teasp.
⅓ of ¼ teasp.	Pinch*
⅓ of ½ teasp.	Pinch*
½ of ¼ teasp.	⅛ teasp.
3 teasp.	1 tablesp.
⅓ of 1 tablesp.	1 teasp.
⅓ of 2 tablesp.	2 teasp.
⅓ of 5 tablesp.	1 tablesp. + 2 teasp.
⅓ of 7 tablesp.	2 tablesp. + 1 teasp.
½ of 1 tablesp.	1½ teasp.
½ of 3 tablesp.	1 tablesp. + 1½ teasp.
½ of 5 tablesp.	2 tablesp. + 1½ teasp.
½ of 7 tablesp.	3 tablesp. + 1½ teasp.
2 tablesp.	⅛ cup
4 tablesp.	¼ cup
5 tablesp. + 1 teasp.	⅓ cup
8 tablesp.	½ cup
10 tablesp. + 2 teasp.	⅔ cup
12 tablesp.	¾ cup
16 tablesp.	1 cup
⅓ of ¼ cup	1 tablesp. + 1 teasp.
⅓ of ⅓ cup	1 tablesp. + 2⅓ teasp.
⅓ of ½ cup	2 tablesp. + 2 teasp.
⅓ of ⅔ cup	3 tablesp. + 1⅔ teasp.
⅓ of ¾ cup	¼ cup
½ of ¼ cup	2 tablesp.
½ of ⅓ cup	2 tablesp. + 2 teasp.
½ of ½ cup	¼ cup
½ of ⅔ cup	⅓ cup
½ of ¾ cup	6 tablesp.
2 cups	1 pt.
2 pt.	1 qt.
1 qt.	4 cups
4 qt.	1 gal.
8 qt.	1 peck
4 pecks	1 bushel
16 oz. (dry measure)	1 lb.

Pinch is as much as can be taken between tip of finger and thumb.

FAMILY MEALS

Meal planning can be a real adventure instead of a gruesome chore. In fact —

MEAL PLANNING CAN BE FUN

Collect Recipes

Index them. Clip and paste your favorites on 3″ x 5″ cards or in a loose-leaf notebook, under headings — casseroles, quick-dinner dishes, etc. Or, if they're in a cookbook or magazine, jot down the page number and title on a card.

Serve at least one brand-new dish each week. Check the recipes in this book as you try them. See if you can eventually check almost all.

Change the pattern. Don't serve meat-and-potato dinners every day. Everyone enjoys a change — the cook most of all. So try all-in-one casserole, Dutch-oven, or skillet meals; hearty soups; the main dish salads. Choose a luscious hot bread and dessert to go with them, and the most militant male will be pleased.

Look for new inspiration. No matter how easy it is for you to plan menus, you always need new ideas. Send for manufacturers' book-

lets; look over a magazine or two each month. *Make holidays special.* To keep family dinners exciting, play up holidays — cherry pie for Washington's Birthday, corned beef and cabbage for St. Patrick's Day, etc.

How to Plan a Menu

And do it in the easiest, pleasantest way.

Choose the main dish first. What will it be? A casserole, stew, main dish salad, serving of meat, hearty soup?

Vegetables come next. Usually it's potatoes and a nonstarchy vegetable, or two nonstarchy ones.

Or instead of potatoes, serve buttered macaroni, spaghetti, noodles, or rice. (Never serve two starchy vegetables at the same meal.)

And if you'd like a starchy dessert, such as rice, cornstarch, or tapioca pudding, it's wiser to serve only nonstarchy vegetables.

Vary the seasonings as in Serve with a Flair, p. 392.

Then select a dessert. If the main course is to be salad or soup, you'll want a hearty dessert

18

— pie à la mode, a cobbler with rich sauce, or chocolate-frosted layer cake, etc.

But if you're having goulash with noodles or mashed potatoes, you'll want something light, such as fruit gelatin and cookies.

Also ask yourself, would a cold or hot dessert taste better?

Now which salad will you choose? The tossed green salad is the perfect answer almost any time. But for variety's sake, consider raw relishes, a jellied salad, fruit or vegetable salad, etc.

What about bread? Does your meal need a hot bread or will a cold one do? Often the choice is plain bread and butter or margarine; now and then it's no bread at all.

Other times you may crave the crispness of toast or French bread, or the glamour of hot muffins, biscuits, or rolls.

Take another look at your menu, for the job isn't done. Consider color, texture, flavor. The dishes of a well-planned meal do not clash in color, flavor, or texture, but do include contrasts.

How much time and effort is involved in getting the meal on the table? Will the cooking be on the top of the range or in the oven? Can you manage it all?

P.S. Consider the day's three meals as a unit — breakfast, lunch, and dinner — and they'll be better in taste, looks, and nutrition.

FAMILY MEALS, FALL AND WINTER

SIMPLY DELICIOUS

ORANGE PORK CHOPS, p. 110
BUTTERED SQUASH   GREEN BEANS
CHEESE-STUFFED CELERY
HEATED BRAN MUFFINS
SUSAN'S RICE CUSTARD PUDDING, p. 132
COFFEE

SPANISH STYLE

ARROZ CON POLLO, p. 276
HARD ROLLS OR CRACKERS
CELERY   PICKLES
FRUITCAKE A LA MODE
COFFEE   TEA   MILK

THIS IS NICE

CURRIED VEAL PAPRIKA, p. 228, ON RICE OR NOODLES
WALDORF SALAD, p. 464
HOT CORN-BREAD SQUARES
(made from mix)
ICE-CREAM PUFFS, p. 608
COFFEE

SOUTHERN STYLE

SMOKED BUTT, SOUTHERN STYLE, p. 213
BROILED TOMATO HALVES
LIMAS AND WATER CHESTNUTS
FRENCH BREAD
LEMON PARFAIT PIE, p. 129
COFFEE

MOTHER'S FAVORITE

POT ROAST OF TURKEY, p. 284, ON MUSHROOM RICE
SOUR-CREAM GRAVY
PEAS WITH CELERY
HOT BISCUITS
PINEAPPLE TIDBITS AND GREEN-GRAPE COMPOTE
COFFEE

WHEN YOU GET BACK FROM SHOPPING

BROWNED RICE-AND-PORK CASSEROLE, p. 204
TOSSED GREEN SALAD
WITH ORANGE SECTIONS AND AVOCADO
BROWN 'N' SERVE ROLLS
GRAPES TO NIBBLE
COOKIES
HOT CHOCOLATE

LIKE MY MOTHER MADE

SALMON LOAF SUPREME, p. 313
MASHED POTATOES
SUMMER SQUASH WITH GREEN PEAS
SLICED, CHILLED CUCUMBERS IN WINE VINEGAR
AND OIL
JELLY ROLL, p. 631   COFFEE

MAKE DESSERT NIGHT BEFORE; SERVE LEFTOVERS AS SNACK

PAN-FRIED THIN HAM SLICE AND CANNED
PINEAPPLE CHUNKS
QUICK-CANDIED SWEET POTATOES, p. 410
GREEN BEANS SEASONED WITH CURRY POWDER
INDIVIDUAL SPANISH CREAMS, p. 573
SALTED PEANUTS
COFFEE OR TEA

A WEIGHT-WATCHING DINNER
VEAL SCALOPPINE, p. 228
FROZEN SQUASH   RYE BREAD
SLICED-CUCUMBER SALAD
TANGERINES
TEA

AND THE DESSERT . . .
SUSAN'S BROWN BEEF STEW, p. 107
BUTTERED BROAD NOODLES WITH POPPY SEEDS
TOSSED SALAD WITH APPLE AND PINEAPPLE CHUNKS
WHITE- OR WHOLE-WHEAT-BREAD FINGERS
TOP-STOVE HOT CHOCOLATE SOUFFLE, p. 582
MILK OR COFFEE

EASY CLEANUP SUPPER
SUSAN'S WAFFLE DEVILS, p. 114
SKILLET CARROTS AND ZUCCHINI
CHILLED STEWED TOMATOES
CRISP CELERY HEARTS
SPICED FRUIT COMPOTE
CHOCOLATE COOKIES   COFFEE

WEDNESDAY DINNER
BRAISED OXJOINTS, p. 198
GREEN PEA SLAW, p. 455
PICKLED BEETS
HOT ROLLS, SKILLET STYLE
AMBROSIA, p. 552
COFFEE

MIXED GRILL TONIGHT
MIXED GRILL, p. 180, OF LAMB PATTIES,
TOMATO HALVES, ZUCCHINI SLICES
QUICK BUTTERED RICE
SO-EASY GOLDEN PUFFS, p. 490, WITH
SOFT VANILLA ICE CREAM
COFFEE (instant) OR TEA

OR TRY
SUSAN'S MEAT LOAF, p. 105
BUTTERED ZUCCHINI
QUICK SCALLOPED POTATOES, p. 414
PINEAPPLE AND AVOCADO SLICES
TAPIOCA, PARFAIT FASHION
MELTAWAYS, p. 660
COFFEE

OVEN DINNER
MEXICALI MEAT PIE, p. 108
ONIONS IN CREAM
ORANGE-AVOCADO-AND-GRAPEFRUIT SALAD
BRAN MUFFINS OR
SPICED APPLE MUFFINS, p. 481
COFFEE

FLAVORFUL
PARMESAN TOASTIES   TOMATO JUICE
SIMMERED SMOKED BONELESS BUTT, p. 212
CURRIED PEARS, p. 437
MASHED SWEET POTATOES
PEAS TOSSED WITH FEW COCKTAIL ONIONS
GINGERBREAD A LA MINCEMEAT
HOT COFFEE

VERY GOOD: VERY EASY TO DO
SUSAN'S CREAMED CHICKEN DE LUXE, p. 122
BUTTERED SUCCOTASH
SLICED TOMATOES
WARM RYE-BREAD SLICES
TOPAZ TAPIOCA, p. 568
COFFEE (instant)

HOMEY GOODNESS
ONION SOUP
BREADED PORK TENDERLOIN, p. 205
BAKED POTATOES
CABBAGE SCRAMBLE, p. 398
DUTCH PLUM CAKE, p. 566
TEA

LAZY DAY
BREADED VEAL CUTLETS WITH HERBS
CREAMED NEW POTATOES AND PEAS, p. 412
CANNED-BEET-AND-ONION SALAD
COCONUT-TOPPED ORANGE SLICES
SUSAN'S BROWNIES, p. 137

GIVE HIM STEAK
BRAISED STEAK, p. 181
RICE, IF YOU WISH
NUTMEG BUTTERED SQUASH
ASPARAGUS   BREAD AND BUTTER
CHERRY-SHERRY JUBILEE, p. 562
MILK OR COFFEE (instant)

Frozen vegetables are often bargains. See p. 389.

Buy foods in the more economical large sizes, and plan to serve them a second or third time. For instance, leftover fruits can be used in salad, vegetables in mixed-vegetable dishes, salads, soups, etc.

But don't buy more food than you'll need. Check ingredient amounts in recipes you'll be using, so you'll know exactly what to buy and how much. Replenish staples as needed, of course.

Have you lots of storage space? Buy staples that keep well, and that you use often, in as large a quantity as your storage space and pocketbook permit.

Read labels carefully. When you buy breads, flours, and cereals, be sure "enriched," "restored," or "whole grain" is printed on the label. You'll get more B-vitamins, minerals. See Cereals, p. 90, for further information.

Out of sight, out of mind. If you buy enough for 2 meals, set half aside so you won't nibble. To make a package of frozen vegetables do for 2 days, divide it in two and keep half frozen until you're ready to use it.

Buy only graded, cartoned eggs kept under refrigeration in the store. Eggs deteriorate rapidly at room temperature. See Eggs — Plain and Fancy, p. 356.

Use grade B eggs in puddings, custards, and baking. They furnish just as much food value as grade A eggs. Brown eggs and white eggs are equally fine and nutritious.

Choose enriched or whole-grain breads and cereals for the extra vitamins and iron they'll give you.

When choosing cereals, remember, hot cereals such as oatmeal, enriched farina, and dark wheat cereal are somewhat less expensive than the ready-to-eat kind. However, the ready-to-eat cereals are still an inexpensive food and a wonderful time-saver.

Use milk, instead of cream, on cereals. It's a saving for sure — and has even higher food value.

Store wisely. At the beginning of several chapters in this book, we give details on best storing methods. Also check When You Go Marketing, p. 88.

Good things to know. Many foods can be used to provide the same amount of specific nutrients. For example:

These foods have practically the same food value, but differ in price:

Fresh milk	Evaporated milk and nonfat dry milk
Sharp Cheddar cheese	Mild Cheddar cheese
Out-of-season fresh vegetables	Canned, frozen, or in-season fresh vegetables
Fresh tomatoes	Canned tomatoes
Calf liver	Beef or pork liver
Porterhouse steak	Chuck steak
Loin chops	Shoulder chops
White eggs	Brown eggs (in some areas)
Ready-to-eat cereal	Hot cereal
Butter	Margarine
Olive oil	Salad oil

These foods give about the same amount of calcium:

1 cup milk (whole, reliquefied nonfat, or diluted evaporated)	2 servings ice cream (⅓-pt. servings)
1 serving cheese (1¼ oz.)	3 servings cottage cheese (½-cup servings)

These foods give about the same amount of high-quality protein:

½ cup cottage cheese	3 oz. Cheddar cheese
2¼ cups milk (whole, reliquefied nonfat, or diluted evaporated)	3 oz. cooked lean meat, fish, or poultry
	3 medium eggs

Always Cook It Right

Make everything look and taste so good that everyone cleans his plate without urging. Use recipes in this book and follow them to the letter. Serve food in pretty ways. (A gay garnish takes more imagination than money. See p. 441.)

Know your family's appetite. Take time to look up the amount to cook for your size family, so there'll be enough food with little or nothing left over. Or plan just how you are going to serve the remaining food.

You can afford gourmet touches. Canned tomatoes; onion; garlic; snipped parsley; celery; green peppers in season; herbs such as thyme, basil, orégano; shaker seasonings like monosodium glutamate, seasoned salt or pepper, etc. (p. 99), cost little, add much.

Don't cheat your family of flavor and food values. First of all, don't overcook vegetables. Secondly, use the vegetable-cooking water (or liquids from canned vegetables) to:

1. Add to vegetable or cream soups.
2. Mix with tomato juice for drinking.
3. Serve as liquid in gravies, molded salads.

Be sparing when paring. Cook vegetables with skins on if possible. To pare potatoes, carrots, apples, pears, etc., use a vegetable parer or sharp knife so you'll lose as little food value as possible.

Don't be ruthless in trimming such vegetables as asparagus, cauliflower, cabbage, lettuce, broccoli. Use outer stalks and leaves of celery in soups, mixed-vegetable dishes, casseroles, gravies, cream sauce, etc.

Make every bit count. Add bits of cooked fish, chicken, or meat, or pieces of cheese, to a tossed salad, casserole, or omelet. Leftovers needn't mean waste or dreary repetition of exactly the same meal. They can easily be worked into dishes that are deliciously different from the food's first appearance. See Last of the Meat, p. 252, and Last of the Bird, p. 288.

Don't forget you can freeze that leftover bird, roast, etc. Give the family a rest by wrapping and freezing bird; bring it out a week or two later, when the family's all enthused again.

Maybe it's not too old. You can use some foods even when past their freshest stage. Stale cake and cookies can be crumbled and served over ice cream, used in puddings, etc. A slice of soft bread put in a jar of dried-out cookies softens them.

A penny saved is a penny earned. Use fats from cooking meats and poultry. Chicken fat is grand for gravies; beef fat for browning onions, for casseroles or spaghetti sauce, etc.; ham or bacon fat for frying eggs, seasoning beans or cabbage, or flavoring soups or gravy, etc.

Make good use of your oven. When planning a casserole as a main dish, choose a vegetable, bread, and/or dessert that bakes at the same temperature as the casserole. See: Market-Fresh or Garden Vegetables In Oven, p. 391; Oven-Cooked Frozen Vegetables, pp. 391–392; Desserts to Bake 'n' Serve p. 566.

Cook on one burner. All-in-one main dishes are thrifty. Use Dutch oven, deep covered skillet, etc. Or use a pressure cooker.

Thrifty Milk: Both evaporated and nonfat dry milk are important penny savers (just turn to p. 97 for the use and care of each milk). For drinking, try mixing whole milk and reliquefied nonfat dry milk in equal amounts.

BUDGET-MINDED MENUS

HEARTY

INDIVIDUAL LAMB-SHANK ROASTS, p. 225
PARSLEYED NOODLES
SLICED CARROTS WITH CELERY SEEDS
TOSSED GREEN SALAD   TOASTED ENGLISH MUFFINS
BANANA CREAM PIE (from packaged mix)
COFFEE

WONDERFUL DINNER-IN-A-DUTCH-OVEN

MOTHER'S POT ROAST WITH VEGETABLES, p. 185
ORANGE MUFFINS
(made from a mix, of course)
VANILLA ICE CREAM WITH NUTMEG
COFFEE

ALL IN FAVOR SAY AYE

FRANKS ITALIAN, p. 245
SPINACH SALAD
HOT, CANNED CLING PEACHES   OATMEAL COOKIES
PITCHER OF MILK

SPARE THE EXPENSE
BUT NOT THE PLEASURE

CHILLED TOMATO JUICE
LINDA'S BRAISED VEAL SHANKS, p. 234
PICKLED-BEET-AND-CELERY RELISH
APPLE BROWN BETTY, p. 567   COFFEE

THRIFTY FOR COMPANY

FISHERMAN'S CHOWDER, p. 168
WARM RYE-BREAD FINGERS
RADISH ROSES, CELERY AND CARROT STICKS
APPLE PIE AND CHEESE   HOT COFFEE

MORE THAN YOUR MONEY'S WORTH
SALMON LOAF SUPREME, p. 313
HEATED CORN MUFFINS   TOSSED SALAD
COCONUT-FROSTED CANNED FRUIT COCKTAIL
HOT TEA

BUDGET MINDED
FRESH CABBAGE GARNI, p. 251
CANNED, STEWED TOMATOES   PUMPERNICKEL BREAD
APPLESAUCE-TOPPED SPICE CAKE
COFFEE

MAXIMUM ENJOYMENT AT MINIMUM COST
CHICKEN SANTA FE, p. 275
WARMED FRENCH BREAD   TOSSED ESCAROLE SALAD
CONCORD GRAPES OR STEWED PRUNES
COFFEE

WEALTH OF GOOD EATING
CREAMED DRIED BEEF, p. 252
CRISP FRENCH FRIES   TOSSED TOMATO SALAD
CANNED PINEAPPLE CHUNKS   GINGERSNAPS
TEA

TALK OF THE TOWN
HAMBURGER STROGANOFF, p. 193
PARSLEYED RICE WITH GRATED CARROT ADDED
BUTTERED CAULIFLOWER
AMBROSIA   NUTTY CHOCOLATE COOKIES
MUGS OF ICY MILK

SUPER-FLAVOR!
LONDON BROIL, p. 182
INSTANT MASHED POTATOES
A NEW-AND-DIFFERENT SALAD
(tossed grapefruit, grated carrots,
and raisins)
CHOCOLATE PUDDING A LA MODE
COFFEE

WHOEVER SAID SAUSAGES WERE ONLY FOR BREAKFAST?
SAUSAGE CASSEROLE DE LUXE, p. 207
GREEN-BEAN-AND-CABBAGE SLAW
SHERBET GLASSES OF PRUNES,
SAUCED WITH VANILLA PUDDING
TEA

JUST THE MEAL TICKET
BAVARIAN SUPPER, p. 244
SLICED TOMATOES   RYE BREAD
CINNAMONED CANNED PEARS
COFFEE

A HAPPY ENDING
CHICKEN CORN SQUARES, p. 275
GREEN BEANS   RAW-CARROT STRIPS
MELON A LA MODE
TEA

SPECIAL AND UNUSUAL
SUPERB SKILLET BURGER LOAF, p. 196
BAKED-BEAN CASSEROLE, p. 401
MELBA-TOAST SLICES   MARINATED TOMATOES
COCONUT CAKE
INSTANT COFFEE

FRANKS WITH STYLE
FRANK CURRY BAKE, p. 246
COLESLAW
(in sour cream or vinaigrette dressing)
HOT REFRIGERATED BISCUITS
GRAPEFRUIT HALVES   BEVERAGE OF YOUR CHOICE

LUSCIOUS MAIN DISH
HAMBURGER POT ROAST, p. 196
FAVORITE GREEN VEGETABLE   CRISP ROMAINE SALAD
BLACKBERRY GELATIN DESSERT
WITH WHIPPED TOPPING
COFFEE

GET ALONG BEAUTIFULLY
FLOUNDER FLORENTINE, p. 300
CANNED WHOLE-KERNEL CORN
INDIVIDUAL TOMATO-ASPIC SALADS, p. 463
CRUSTY RYE BREAD
SLICED ORANGES
TEA

A TASTE-TANTALIZER
VEGETABLE-JUICE COCKTAIL AND LEMON WEDGES
FRICASSEE OF LIVER FRANCOISE, p. 235
BROCCOLI
SPLIT-LAYERED CAKE,
CHOCOLATE FILLED AND FROSTED
TEA

A FEAST
BAKED SAUSAGE LINKS, p. 207
BRUSSELS SPROUTS   BUTTERED SLIVERED CARROTS
A BIG TOSSED SALAD
BUTTER-PECAN ICE CREAM   COOKIES
COFFEE

LIKE A ROYAL DISH
BEEF-KIDNEY STEW, p. 241
ITALIAN BREAD   CELERY AND OLIVES
TOASTED SPONGECAKE SLICES
WITH HOT, CANNED FRUIT COCKTAIL
SPRINKLED WITH NUTMEG
COFFEE

MARVELOUS!
CHILI-SPAGHETTI, p. 379
GARLIC-BUTTERED TOAST
TOSSED SALAD WITH YOUR SPECIAL DRESSING
MARSHMALLOW-TOPPED BAKED APPLES
TEA OR COFFEE

SUPERB PARTNERS
RICE-BOLOGNA HALF SHELLS, p. 243
FROZEN OR CANNED MIXED VEGETABLES
CURLY-ENDIVE SALAD
WARM BAKED PEARS   CHOCOLATE CAKE
TEA

LOVELY TO LOOK AT
SALAMETTI, p. 379
BUTTERED BROCCOLI
TOMATO WEDGES   RIPE OLIVES
GOLDEN-CRUSTED APPLE TURNOVERS
TEA

EAST-WEST ALLIANCE
EAST-WEST CHILI BAKE, p. 250
PINEAPPLE COLESLAW   LOTS OF TOAST
COFFEE JELLY, p. 574, WITH CUSTARD SAUCE
COFFEE

BEAUTIFUL FOR COMPANY
CHICKEN-SPAGHETTI PLATTER, p. 275
SAUTEED PINEAPPLE SLICES   BUTTERED SPINACH
FRENCH BREAD
FRUIT TAPIOCA   HOT TEA

JOHN'S FAVORITE
SKILLET HASH, p. 251
OLD-FASHIONED LETTUCE BOWL, p. 119   RYE BREAD
NUTMEG-TOPPED CANNED APRICOTS
COFFEE

A NICE CHANGE
LAMB WITH LENTILS, p. 225
KALE, BROCCOLI, OR SPINACH
CRUSTY ROLLS
STRAWBERRY GELATIN DESSERT
TOPPED WITH SOFT VANILLA ICE CREAM
COFFEE

SOUTHWESTERN STYLE
CORN-AND-CHILI CASSEROLE, p. 251
BUTTERED PEAS AND CELERY
CHILLED STEWED TOMATOES
PRIZE PRUNE PIE, p. 591   COFFEE

A REGAL REPAST
LIVERWURST AU GOURMET, p. 243
CHOPPED BROCCOLI
LETTUCE WEDGES WITH SHREDDED-CARROT DRESSING
CHOCOLATE ICE CREAM
COFFEE

SOMEWHAT CHINESE
CHINESE EGGS FOO YOUNG, p. 367
SLICED BANANAS
TOPPED WITH CANNED CRUSHED PINEAPPLE
TEA

A CURRY, BUT DIFFERENT
CURRIED EGGS, p. 367, WITH CORN
QUICK-COOKED CABBAGE, p. 397
GRAPEFRUIT-AND-CELERY SALAD
COOKIE SANDWICHES WITH
ICE CREAM BETWEEN
TEA

A FEED
NANCY'S CURRIED SPAGHETTI, p. 381
SWISS CHARD OR ZUCCHINI   BEET SALAD
TOASTED ROLLS IN LOAF, p. 492
SPICED CANNED FRUIT COCKTAIL
MOLASSES COOKIES
TEA

STAND-BY

MACARONI LOAF WITH MEAT SAUCE, p. 383
STUFFED-OLIVE COLESLAW
TOASTED CORN MUFFINS
GRAPEFRUIT SECTIONS IN GRAPE JUICE
TEA OR COFFEE

SPECIAL

BARBECUED SHORT RIBS, p. 186
POPPY-SEED NOODLES   TOSSED RADISH SALAD
CRISP RYE WAFERS
TANGERINES   CHOCOLATE CUPCAKES
MILK AND COFFEE

COMPLETE DINNER

EGGPLANT PARMESAN, p. 402
BREAD STICKS
FRESH FRUIT   FAVORITE CHIFFON CAKE
MILK OR COFFEE

SURPRISE

.LAMB SHANKS WITH PARSLEY POCKETS, p. 224
CRISP CRACKERS
BAKED CUSTARDS WITH A JAM "SURPRISE"
(With spoon, lift up top of each
custard; drop in jam, then
replace top.)
COFFEE

PANTRY-SHELF SPECIAL

LEE'S SPANISH CHILI WITH EGGS, p. 360
TOSSED GREEN SALAD
COMPOTE OF CANNED PINEAPPLE CHUNKS
WITH SLICED BANANAS
MILK

ONE-DISH MEAL

HERB-DUMPLING CHICKEN PIE, p. 279
SWEET-AND-SOUR COLESLAW, p. 454
CHILLED CANNED FRUIT COCKTAIL PLUS
LEMON JUICE OVER SPLIT BANANAS
COFFEE

BOWLING TONIGHT

MUGS OF HOT VEGETABLE-JUICE COCKTAIL
TUNA CORN-BREAD PIE, p. 310
ASSORTED RAW RELISHES
DUNKED IN FRENCH DRESSING
FRESH PEARS   TEA

FRIDAY SPECIAL

CHILLED STEWED TOMATOES IN SHERBET GLASSES
CHEESE STRATA, p. 347
SPINACH SALAD   CRACKERS
LEMON CHIFFON PIE, p. 597
COFFEE

COMPANY COMING

TUNA TETRAZZINI, p. 308
ROMAINE SALAD, p. 448
TOASTED FRENCH BREAD WEDGES, p. 493
VANILLA PUDDING
FLAVORED WITH ALMOND, TOPPED WITH
CHOCOLATE ICE CREAM

OUR VERY BEST

LIVER AND ONIONS AU FROMAGE, p. 235
BAKED WHITE OR SWEET POTATOES
CUT WAX AND GREEN BEANS
YOUR FAVORITE HOT ROLLS
RASPBERRY-LEMON GELATIN DESSERT
SERVED WITH CREAM OR DESSERT TOPPING
COFFEE

EASY DOES IT

BAKED TUNA SANDWICHES, p. 310
BIG BOWL OF TOMATO-AND-PARSLEY COLESLAW
GINGERBREAD SQUARES
TOPPED WITH APPLESAUCE
COFFEE

LOW IN CALORIES AND COST

CRANBERRY-JUICE COCKTAIL
OVEN-FRIED DRUMSTICKS, p. 272
SLICETTES, p. 494
TOSSED GREEN SALAD   LEMON JUICE
CANNED PEACH HALVES
TEA OR COFFEE

QUICK-AND-EASY FRIDAY DINNER

CHEESE-SALMON BAKE, p. 312
GREEN PEAS WITH ONION RINGS
CELERY STALKS   STUFFED OLIVES
VANILLA PUDDING TOPPED WITH ORANGE SECTIONS
COFFEE

OLD-TIME BOILED DINNER

CHILLED TOMATO JUICE
TWENTY-MINUTE BOILED DINNER, p. 247
PARSLEY POTATOES
SUSAN'S SNOW PUDDING, p. 132
COFFEE

YOU'LL APPLAUD

CUBE STEAKS
WITH HASTY-TASTY SAUCE, p. 180
BAKED SWEET POTATOES
BUTTERED PEAS AND CELERY   DILL PICKLES
CHOCOLATE ICE CREAM WITH CHOCOLATE SAUCE
COFFEE OR TEA

CASSEROLE COOKERY

CHEESE AND TUNA SOUFFLE, p. 346
BUTTERED LIMAS
TOSSED GREEN SALAD WITH CELERY TOPS
RYE BREAD
LEMON-COCONUT PUDDING
ICED TEA

DINNER

BREAD STICKS AND BUTTER
SPOON BREAD TAMALE BAKE, p. 196
LEAF LETTUCE, SWEET-SOUR DRESSING
CHOCOLATE FROSTED PEARS, p. 553
INSTANT ICED COFFEE

SING FOR YOUR SUPPER

TUCKER SALMON PIE, p. 313
CREAMED POTATOES, p. 412
BAKED TOMATO HALVES
CRISP LETTUCE WEDGES   DRESSING
HEATED ROLLS
DEEP-DISH FRUIT PIE   MILK OR COFFEE

BUFFET SUPPER

CORNED-BEEF HASH AND TOMATO BAKE, p. 254
SAUTEED EGGPLANT SLICES, p. 402
CELERY, OLIVES, SCALLIONS, AND CHEESE CUBES
CRISP FRENCH BREAD
LIME-SNOW PIE, p. 599
COFFEE

WARM EVENINGS

YANKEE PORK-AND-BEAN PIE, p. 217
CUCUMBERS AND RADISHES VINAIGRETTE
RAISIN BREAD AND BUTTER
CHEDDAR CHEESE AND CRACKERS
A FAT FRUIT BOWL
MILK BY THE PITCHERFUL

MORE, PLEASE

CRANBERRY-RAISIN TONGUE, p. 240
FLUFFY HOT RICE   BUTTERED SQUASH
CHEESE-STUFFED CELERY
CHERRY COBBLER, p. 569, A LA MODE
ICED TEA

"...NOT A PARTY, JUST US FOUR"

BRAISED PORK CHOPS WITH GLAZED APPLES, p. 203
FROZEN POTATO PATTIES   SPINACH-RADISH SALAD
MELBA TOAST
FRESH PINEAPPLE WEDGES
COFFEE

FIFTY MINUTES

GRETCHEN'S CASSEROLE, p. 250
TINY NEW POTATOES   CRISP CARROT STICKS
PRETZELS
CHOCOLATE ICE CREAM   MACAROONS
COFFEE

FRIDAY SPECIAL

CRISP-COATED FISH FILLETS, p. 302
STEWED TOMATOES   POTATO PATTIES
LETTUCE SALAD
DOUBLE FUDGE CAKE, p. 621, A LA MODE
COFFEE (instant)

FAMILY LUNCH ON SATURDAY

INDIAN POWWOW

BIG-CHIEF SOUP
(tomato soup with popcorn garnish)
WIGWAM SANDWICHES
(Cut each sandwich into 4 triangles; then
arrange all 4 triangles, in stand-up style,
to look like wigwams.)
SQUAW-BERRY (STRAWBERRY) SHORTCAKE

BY SEA OR LAKE OR APPLE TREE

ORANGE AND GRAPEFRUIT JUICES
(if you like)
CHEESY SCRAMBLED EGGS, p. 360
SKILLET CUSTARD CORN BREAD, p. 483
CHERRY JAM
POTS OF COFFEE

LADIES AND GENTLEMEN

BROILED OPEN-FACE SANDWICHES, p. 519
TOSSED GREEN SALAD
WITH DRESSING (bottled or mix)
VANILLA ICE CREAM WITH SUGARED BLUEBERRIES
COFFEE (instant)

RODEO DAY

COWBOY CHOWDER
(beef soup with cereal lassos)
WESTERN EGG SANDWICHES, p. 520
FRUIT BASKET
BAR X CHOCOLATE COOKIES
(branded with white frosting)
MILK

WONDERFUL LUNCH!

FROZEN CREAM-OF-SHRIMP SOUP
LETTUCE SLICES WITH PARMESAN FRENCH DRESSING
CRUSTY FRENCH BREAD
PEARS, CRACKERS, AND CREAM CHEESE
COFFEE

FOR MOLLY AND ME

TUNA SPAGHETTI, p. 379
TOASTED, SPLIT ENGLISH MUFFINS
CRANBERRY SAUCE   CARROT STICKS
CANNED-PEACH HALVES
TOPPED WITH QUICK CUSTARD SAUCE
(use packaged instant pudding)
HOT TEA

PIRATES' PICNIC

HIDDEN-TREASURE SOUP IN MUGS
(chicken-with-rice soup, garnished
with chopped peanuts)
TREASURE-CHEST SANDWICHES
(Parkerhouse rolls with egg salad)
JELLY GEMS
(cubes of fruit-flavor gelatin)
NUGGET COOKIES
MILK

ON THE SOUTHERN SIDE

MUGS OF CHICKEN-CORN SOUP, p. 161
SPICED PEACH SALAD
PEANUT-BUTTER COOKIES
MILK OR COFFEE

PANCAKES TODAY

LUNCHEON PANCAKES, p. 258
CRANBERRY-TOPPED PEACHES
ORANGE SHERBET WITH CHOCOLATE SAUCE
MILK OR TEA

SAILORS' CHOICE

NEPTUNE'S NECTAR WITH FLOATING ISLANDS
(clam chowder with slices of hard-cooked egg)
TOP-DECK SANDWICHES
(open-face cheese and bacon)
BANANA-BOAT SUNDAE

FUN FOR LUNCH

GREEN-PEA SOUP (can or mix)
HOT BUTTERED TOAST
BEET, CUCUMBER, CARROT,
TURNIP STICKS, p. 119
MILK OR ICED COFFEE

FOURTH-OF-JULY BRUNCH

TOMATO JUICE WITH OLIVE KABOBS
FRENCH-TOASTED SANDWICHES, p. 519, WITH BACON
CHOICE OF SYRUPS
MILK   COFFEE

HOT AND COLD

CANNED VEGETABLE SOUP
BACON AND EGG SALAD, p. 458
BOSTON BROWN BREAD (baker's or canned)
FROZEN LEMONADE WITH SHERBET FLOATS

NICE FOR COMPANY, TOO

STUFFED LETTUCE, p. 449   POTATO CHIPS
COLD SLICED HAM (if you wish)
HELPINGS AND HELPINGS OF WATERMELON

PERFECT FOR LUNCH

FROZEN POTATO SOUP
TOASTED CHEESE SANDWICHES
PINEAPPLE SOPHISTICATE
(fruit in fresh pineapple shells)
LOTS OF HOT COFFEE

SUSIE'S BACK-YARD PICNIC

CREAM-OF-CHICKEN SOUP

HAM SANDWICHES ON RAISIN BREAD

CELERY CURLS   RADISH ROSES

PEACHES WITH CREAM

ANGEL-FOOD CAKE

LUNCH ON A TRAY

STUFFED ROLLS, p. 516   CUCUMBER STICKS

CRUSHED PINEAPPLE WITH RASPBERRY SHERBET

SPICE COOKIES

MILK OR TEA

VIVE LA DIFFERENCE

HOT BAKED-POTATO SALAD, p. 454

THICK TOMATO SLICES   CRISP RYE WAFERS

CRAN-PINEAPPLE SUNDAE

(whole-cranberry sauce with crushed pineapple)

MILK OR COFFEE

LUNCH ON A PLATE

THREE-FRUIT SALAD, p. 465

WEDGES OF SHARP CHEDDAR CHEESE

TOASTED ENGLISH MUFFINS

ICED TEA

EVERYONE'S STARVING

DIFFERENT EGG SALAD, p. 459

CHERRY TOMATOES   CELERY FANS

BUTTERED ROLLS

HOT CANNED PEACHES   COOKIES

MILK OR TEA

MONDAY LUNCH

FROSTED GREEN-BEAN SALAD, p. 451

TOASTED ENGLISH MUFFINS
SPREAD WITH BLUE CHEESE

FRUITFUL COBBLER, p. 569

MILK OR COFFEE

BLUEBERRIES ARE IN

CHILLED JUICE

BLUEBERRY PANCAKES, p. 488

SYRUP HEATED WITH BUTTER

CRISP BACON

MILK OR COFFEE

AUTUMN SONG

PINEAPPLE JUICE

BROILED OPEN-FACE SANDWICHES, p. 519

(deviled-ham spread, unsalted
scrambled eggs, cheese)

FRIED APPLE RINGS, p. 436

MILK   COFFEE

WHEN MEALS MUST BE QUICK

There are days in every woman's schedule when the time available for preparing dinner is limited. But that doesn't mean dinner can't be a triumph.

Plan Shortcuts

Here are suggestions for making preparations in advance and for quick cooking.

Take stock of the tools you work with. If they're easy to get at, they can speed your chores. See Kitchen Tools You'll Need, p. 9.

Choose two-act dishes like stew; serve it as stew the first day, as meat pie the second.

Plan all-broiled, all-baked, or all-pressure-cooked main courses. They're easy, save time.

Choose dishes that can be made early in the day or night before, or readied in advance.

Serve more of one food so you can cut down on the number of dishes to cook.

Make Saturday's or Sunday's meal an occasion, with all the frills, but eliminate frills Monday through Friday.

On Saturday, cook and bake for the next week.

Shortcuts Begin with Marketing

For easy list making, keep pad and pencil in a handy kitchen spot; jot down what you need as you use it up. Here are some of the quick-to-fix foods that make sure-to-please dinners.

If There's to Be a First Course:

1. Canned soups. Vary as on p. 158. Or use frozen soups, or packaged soup mixes, p. 159.

2. Canned and frozen fruits and fruit juices.

3. Canned tomato or vegetable juice.

For the Main Course:

1. Canned meats — corned beef, corned-beef hash, chili con carne, luncheon meats, stews (beef and chicken), etc. They're ready to serve, or to heat and serve. See p. 248.

2. Frozen meats — pan-ready hamburger patties, pork chops, veal cutlets, sliced liver, etc. Look for trusted brands.

3. Frozen meat pies, chicken pies, and dinners just need heating and eating.

4. Ready-cooked meats — franks, ham, sausages, Canadian-style bacon, bologna, tongue, etc. See p. 242 for delightfully quick and easy ways to use them.

5. Fresh meats — hamburgers, sliced liver, veal cutlet, ham slices, kidneys, chops, etc.

6. Fish and shellfish — canned tuna, sardines, King-crab meat, salmon, etc.; frozen fish fillets, fish sticks, etc.; shrimp, oysters, scallops, crab meat, rock-lobster tails, etc.

7. Chicken and turkey. Buy them fresh or frozen, and cleaned, all ready to sauté, roast, broil, oven-fry, etc. Or buy fresh or frozen cut-up chicken and turkey, or parts by the piece. Or choose canned or frozen cooked chicken, p. 261, or turkey products, p. 280.

8. Cheese. Use packaged slices to save slicing, shredded cheese to save shredding. Use cheese spread, sauce in jars, or cheese-sauce mix to save making sauce. Buy ready-to-use cheese dips.

9. Canned or frozen chow mein, chop suey, Chinese dinners, etc.

10. Spaghetti or macaroni dinners, packaged, frozen, or canned; pizza, frozen or a mix; spaghetti sauces, canned, frozen, or a mix.

11. Eggs. Scrambled, in omelets, etc. See Eggs — Plain and Fancy, p. 356.

For Vegetables:

1. Fresh vegetables. Sliced, slivered, or diced, they take less time to cook than those that are whole.

Shredded cabbage, corn on the cob, sliced summer squash, tomatoes, slivered green beans, okra, all greens, and zucchini are especially quick cooking.

All fresh vegetables are quick, easy, and tasty cooked in a pressure cooker, p. 390.

2. Canned vegetables. They're more delicious than ever. Just heat and season. See Serve with a Flair, p. 392.

3. Frozen vegetables. They're all ready to cook and take half as much time as fresh vegetables. There are many delightful vegetable combinations, too — some with sauces, some already cooked. See p. 391.

4. Packaged precooked rice — ready to eat in minutes, needs no watching as it cooks. For other speedy rice and rice mixtures, see Rice, p. 369.

5. Potatoes. Fine cooked sweets or tiny white potatoes come in cans. Whipped white ones come frozen, mashed ones in instant dehydrated form. Or use frozen French fries, frozen tiny potatoes, canned shoestring potatoes, etc. Don't forget packaged au gratin, cottage fries, hashed brown, scalloped, etc. And potato pancakes from mix or frozen are great.

6. Canned stewed tomatoes, or tomatoes and zucchini. They're all seasoned.

For Salads and Relishes:

1. Fruit-flavor gelatin. It makes short work of molded fruit salads; or look for ready-made jellied salads at the dairy counter.

2. Ready-to-use salad dressings or salad-dressing mixes — a variety of flavors.

3. Canned cranberry sauce or jelly. See No-Cook Cranberry Relishes, p. 440, for delightful variations.

4. Also see Relishes and Garnishes, p. 433. Check grocer's shelves, too.

For Seasonings, Sauces, Additions:

1. Onion salt, dried minced onions, garlic salt, etc. These eliminate the need to mince onion or garlic.

2. Bouillon cubes, instant beef or chicken bouillon, canned bouillon or consommé. Use to step up meat flavor; or use in In-a-Pinch Gravy, p. 177.

3. Parsley, onion, or mint flakes.

4. Canned beef gravy, brown or light gravy mix. It's all ready to heat.

5. Canned tomato sauce. It comes expertly seasoned; or vary it with your own seasonings.

6. Canned cream-of-mushroom, cream-of-chicken, tomato, Cheddar-cheese soup, etc., make fine quick sauces. Also the soup and

sauce mixes. See Extra-Easy Main Course Sauces, p. 527.

7. Canned mushrooms. They come broiled or plain: whole, sliced, chopped, etc.

8. Nuts — shelled, blanched, chopped. Turn to p. 98.

9. Preserved fruits. They're diced, ready to add.

For Hot Breads, etc:

1. Superb mixes. Take your pick: biscuits; hot rolls; muffins — plain, corn, date, etc.; pancakes; popovers; waffles, etc.

2. Frozen waffles or French Toast. Just heat in toaster.

3. Refrigerated biscuits in cans. Make them your own, as on p. 478.

4. Canned breads. They're good warm or cold.

5. Bakers' breads, rolls, muffins, brown 'n' serves, etc. They needn't be humdrum; see Breads and Rolls You Buy, p. 491.

6. A superb collection of new packaged crisp crackers — with appropriate seasonings for use as nibblers, with soup, or with salad, awaits you.

For Desserts:

1. Wonderful mixes. Take your pick: brownies, cakes, cookies, cupcakes, frostings, fruit-flavor gelatin, gingerbread, ice cream, piecrust, pie fillings, puddings — instant or regular, tapioca, etc., rennet-custard desserts, sherbets, etc.

2. Bakers' cakes, pies, cream puffs, etc.

3. Cookies — many kinds. They come packaged.

4. Cheese. Buy individual portions, slices, spreads, etc.

5. Fruits — fresh, frozen, or canned. All are delicious time-savers. Extra-tender dried fruits cook quickly, are good as is, too.

6. Ice creams and sherbets. For glamorous ways to serve them, see Ways to Serve Ice Cream You Buy, p. 605.

7. Frozen dessert treats: turnovers, pies, cakes, escalloped apples, apple cobbler, cherry cobbler, Dutch apple pie, plantation cake, etc.

For Beverages:

1. Instant coffee, cocoa, tea, and iced-tea mix with sugar and lemon already added. They can be made up, hot or cold, in a jiffy.

2. Frozen or canned lemonade, limeade, fruit juices. See Off-the-Shelf Coolers, p. 682.

For the Baby: From breakfast juice to dinner's dessert, baby's foods are ready to use, packed to save Mother time and energy.

Shortcut Cooking

Plan trips to the refrigerator so you can take out all the things you'll need at one time.

Use trays to collect things on — saves extra steps.

Keep a can of your favorite fruit in refrigerator. It will be cold and ready any time.

Grate a large piece of cheese. Refrigerate it, tightly wrapped, and it will be ready to top or add to casseroles, creamed dishes, etc. (Cheddar comes shredded — Parmesan and Romano, grated.)

If you use buttered bread crumbs often, keep a batch on hand, ready to use, in the refrigerator.

Or instead of buttered bread crumbs, try cornflakes, crisp rice cereal, or wheat germ, tossed with melted butter or grated cheese. Nice and quick, to top casseroles, etc.

Hasten the chilling or setting of sauces, puddings, gelatin desserts, salads, etc., by placing them in an empty special tray for ice cubes, p. 610, in the freezing compartment a few minutes. Just watch and stir the mixture occasionally; remove when just right.

Mince an extra amount of onions or green peppers; then wrap and freeze for future use. Or buy frozen minced onions to keep on hand in the freezer.

If a recipe calls for both rind and juice, grate rind first; then squeeze juice.

Stick the garlic clove on a toothpick before dropping it into a mixture. Then you'll find it easily when you want to remove it.

Chop hard-cooked eggs with a pastry blender. It's quick.

MEAT

Serve roasts on the weekend. Then you can use leftovers at several weekday meals. (See Last of the Meat, p. 252.)

If canned corned-beef hash is a favorite in

your household, keep a can on hand in the refrigerator. To open it, remove both ends from can; push hash out about 1″ and cut off a slice. Repeat, cutting off the number of slices needed; refrigerate the rest.

If you're planning to serve hamburger as patties, see To Use Within a Week, p. 189, for a time-saving way to store it.

If dinner calls for meat loaf, bake it in muffin-pan cups as on p. 106. It's quicker.

Deviled ham comes in large and small cans. Keep both on hand, so you won't have to open 2 small cans when 1 large one is just right.

VEGETABLES

When only 2 servings of a frozen vegetable are needed, use part of package one night (divide block with ice pick if necessary); return what's left, wrapped, to freezer. Use part of another frozen vegetable the next night. Combine the two leftovers for third dinner.

Frozen or canned mixed vegetables make time-saving additions for stews, casseroles, etc.

Scalloped vegetables, etc., will bake in less time if they're arranged in one layer in a 9″ or 10″ pie plate rather than a deep casserole.

You can season a vegetable quickly, without making a special sauce, by adding a little chili sauce, prepared mustard, Worcestershire, soy sauce, sour cream, canned tomato sauce, pasteurized process cheese spread, or cream-of-mushroom or Cheddar-cheese soup. Also see Sauce Mixes, p. 102.

Try our Chinese Asparagus, p. 395, and Chinese Cauliflower, p. 399. They're speedy and superb.

An egg slicer makes quick work of slicing cooked or canned beets.

To cut up celery stalks quickly, hold several on board; then slice crosswise on a slant, using very sharp knife.

Canned small boiled onions make fine creamed onions in no time. Or they can be rolled in melted butter, seasoned with salt, then sautéed or broiled until golden.

If potatoes are a dinner must, cook a quantity at one time — enough for 2 or 3 days; then promptly refrigerate them. They can reappear fried, creamed, hash-browned, scalloped with cheese, etc. Or turn to the wonderful packaged potato products now on the market (turn to p. 392).

Canned tiny white potatoes are nice brought to a boil in water to cover, then drained and mashed. Or bring to a boil; drain; roll in melted butter; then brown under broiler. Or slice thin; fry or hash-brown in skillet.

Heat canned shoestring potatoes in butter or margarine in skillet, adding a little cream, then chili sauce if desired.

Use canned sweet potatoes. Glaze, mash, or broil them.

Skin tomatoes quickly by first holding them on a fork over flame until skin cracks.

SALADS AND SALAD DRESSINGS

Wash and store salad greens in the refrigerator, so they're ready to break into bite-size pieces.

Keep a can of tuna, sardines, tiny white potatoes, or luncheon meat on hand in refrigerator, so it will be already chilled for salad.

See Quick-and-Easy Dressings, p. 468.

SAUCES

Canned tomato sauce is a must for many dishes. Or you can use canned tomato soup diluted with ½ can water and seasoned with minced onion, curry, etc.

For speedy gravies, sauces, etc., blend equal parts of butter or margarine and flour. Refrigerate. Stir 3 tablesp. of this paste into each 1 cup hot mixture you wish to thicken; cook until thickened.

Stir a few tablespoonfuls of sour cream into melted butter or margarine; add seasoned salt, lemon juice. Fine on vegetables.

Canned onion soup or onion-soup mix, thickened a little, makes a speedy sauce for hamburgers, cube steaks, etc.

Use canned beef, mushroom, or chicken gravy. Or keep a supply of gravy mix on hand; see p. 102.

Freeze or refrigerate a supply of barbecue sauce. Or use one of the bottled kind.

Try the several sauce mixes described on p. 102.

BREADS

Wrap party rye bread in foil; heat at 375°F. about 10 min.

For the crowd, toast split English or corn muffins, bread slices, or chunks of French bread

under broiler — you can do a lot at one time.
Don't roll and cut out biscuits. Make dropped
ones instead; sprinkle with grated cheese.
Or use the refrigerated biscuits, crescents, etc.,
that come in cans, all ready to bake.
Packaged crisp rye wafers come seasoned now,
too.

DESSERTS

Instead of whipped cream, use slightly soft ice
cream or dessert topping in pressure can.
There's no whipping, no beater to wash.
*Make and refrigerate enough Speedy Custard
Sauce, p. 535,* to last several days. Luscious
on fruit, cake, jellied fruit, etc.
For wonderful speedy cupcakes, use cake mix.
You can mix and bake them in about 35 min.
Bake 2 cake layers with cake mix. Freeze one;
top the other with ice cream or hot sauce.
For freshly baked cookies on short order, use
cookie or brownie mix. Or keep a pkg. of re-
frigerated-cookie dough in refrigerator, ready
to slice and bake.
As an ice-cream topping, keep in your refrigerator an 8-oz. can or a package of frozen
fruit or berries. One can or package is just
enough for 4.
For extra-quick pie or cake fillings, use today's pudding and pie-filling mixes.
Unbaked crumb crusts save time when making
chiffon, cream, and ice-cream pies. See p. 594.
For shortcakes and cobblers, let biscuit mix
give you a head start.
*Look in your market's frozen-food depart-
ment* for many desserts ready to thaw and eat,
or bake and eat, such as large or individual
pies, turnovers, cakes, strudel, homey desserts
like escalloped apples, apple cobbler and
cherry cobbler, etc.

"K.P." Shortcuts

Line muffin and cupcake cups with paper baking cups. Makes dishwashing easier.
Line broiler pan with foil. To simplify cleaning a broiler pan, line the bottom with foil to
catch drippings. Cover the rack, too, but be
sure to slash the foil along the rack's grooves
or slits to allow fat to drip into the pan. To
clean, cool pan a bit; remove foil; sprinkle a
few drops of liquid detergent on the rack; fill
pan with hot water.
  If you have no foil, before you sit down to
dinner, pour off hot fat from broiler; wipe out
pan and rack well with paper towel; then
sprinkle with detergent and fill with warm
water. Steel-wool soap pads remove stubborn
grease.
*Use paper napkins and paper or plastic mats
and tablecloths; serve on paper plates.* Their
quality today makes them socially acceptable
for many meals.
Make it a habit to wipe up immediately anything spilled on work surfaces, floor, etc.
Wash up cooking utensils as you go along. If
you can't wash all the pots and pans before
dinner, let them soak — in cool water, if eggs,
starch, or milk have been cooked in them,
otherwise in hot water. Fill above cooking
line.
Pare vegetables and fruit onto a newspaper
or paper towel for speedy transfer to garbage
can.
Sift flour onto a piece of wax paper, instead of
into a bowl.
A dish drainer allows you to rinse a whole
batch of dishes at one time instead of piece
by piece. Plates and glasses dry by themselves.

QUICK AND EASY
FALL AND WINTER MENUS

IF YOU PLEASE
MUSHROOM CHICKEN LIVER SAUTE, p. 275,
ON ENGLISH MUFFINS
TOSSED ROMAINE SALAD WITH
DANISH BLUE CHEESE
FRUIT LAYERS, p. 543
CRISP COOKIES
COFFEE

A BIT PENNSYLVANIA DUTCH
CHICKEN-PEPPER-POT, p. 161
SEVEN SWEETS AND SOURS
(pickled beets, coleslaw,
sweet and dill pickles, cottage
cheese, jelly, olives)
RYE BREAD
APPLE PIE   COFFEE

IN THIRTY MINUTES

THIRTY-MINUTE GLAZED HAM PATTIES, p. 257
PEAS, LIMAS, AND CELERY
CANNED STEWED TOMATOES
CRISPY SLICETTES, p. 494
CHARLOTTE RUSSE, p. 563

CAN OPENER SPECIAL

QUICK SALMON PLATTER, p. 313
TOSSED GREEN SALAD
WITH THAWED FROZEN PEAS
TOASTED ENGLISH MUFFINS WITH
CARAWAY SEEDS
TRIFLE, p. 561
COFFEE

STARRING A FAVORITE RECIPE

HERB-STUFFED PEPPERS WITH SAUSAGES, p. 208
TOSSED SALAD WITH GRATED
CARROTS
ORANGES, DATES, AND
SLICED BANANAS
LEMON-FILLED COOKIE SANDWICHES
COFFEE

FOR COMPANY, TOO

BROILED DUCKLING, p. 286
HOT FLUFFY RICE WITH PEAS
TOSSED SALAD WITH PINEAPPLE
CHUNKS
RYE BREAD
BERRY-LAYER ICE-CREAM
SHORTCAKES, p. 607
COFFEE

BRING ON THE MENFOLKS

SKILLET-COOKED HAMBURGERS, p. 190
JAMAICAN YAM CASSEROLE, p. 410
TOSSED GREEN SALAD
WITH GRATED ORANGE RIND
BROWNIES TOPPED WITH COFFEE ICE CREAM
COFFEE

"WE'RE HUNGRY, MOM"

SWISS HOT POT, p. 160
BOSTON LETTUCE SALAD BOWL
TOASTED ENGLISH MUFFINS WITH CHILI POWDER
LEMON CHIFFON PIE
(from the freezer)
COFFEE

EASY DOES IT

WASHINGTON-SQUARE SPECIAL, p. 384
BIG FRUIT SALAD, p. 465
CANNED REFRIGERATED BISCUITS
CHOCOLATE ICE CREAM WITH CHOCOLATE SAUCE
AND PRETZELS
TEA

AFTER FOOTBALL PRACTICE

PAN-BROILED HAM SLICES
GNOCCHI U.S.A., p. 347
BUTTERED SPINACH
CRANBERRY SAUCE
COFFEE ICE CREAM WITH COCONUT
COFFEE

FOR HALLOWEEN, MAYBE

GOLDEN-TOPPED BAKED BEANS, p. 218
COLESLAW WITH GREEN PEPPER
BOSTON BROWN BREAD AND
CORN MUFFINS
APPLESAUCE A LA MODE
CHOCOLATE COOKIES
COFFEE

LAST OF THE BIRD

SOUP TO SIP
HAM-CHICKEN SUPREME, p. 257
TOSSED ROMAINE SALAD
WITH APPLE SLICES
CRISP SALTED CRACKERS
SPEEDY PEACH CAKE, p. 563
COFFEE

THE CHILDREN GO FOR IT

TOMATO JUICE
FISH STICKS AND CHIPS IBERIA, p. 302
GREEN BEANS PARMESAN, p. 451
MELBA TOAST
BLACK AND WHITE ICE-CREAM CUPCAKES, p. 607

I'LL BE HOME AT SEVEN

MIXED FISH GRILL, p. 304
GREEN BEANS WITH A BIT OF CURRY
MARINATED TOMATOES
TOASTED CORN MUFFINS
STREAMLINED BANANA SPLIT, p. 607
COFFEE

TRY THIS

SPECIAL LAMB STEAKS, p. 224
FROZEN POTATO PATTIES
SPINACH SALAD BOWL
TOASTED ENGLISH MUFFINS
CARAMEL PEACH CRUNCH, p. 568
COFFEE

INDOOR PICNIC

SLICED READY-TO-EAT MEAT
AND TOMATO PLATTER
GERMAN HOT POTATO SALAD, p. 454
RYE BREAD
BAKED APPLE PANCAKE, p. 579
TEA or COFFEE

DAD'S FAVORITE

TOMATO JUICE
CHEESE-STUFFED CELERY
SKILLET-BOILED DINNER, p. 250
HARD ROLLS
HURRY-UP APPLE "PIE," p. 568
COFFEE

REMEMBER THE TRIP
TO THE CARIBBEAN

BROILED HAMBURGERS
HAITIAN RICE AND MUSHROOMS, p. 374
AVOCADO AND PINEAPPLE SALAD
FRENCH BREAD
COFFEE ICE CREAM WITH
RUM BUTTER-CARAMEL SAUCE, p. 536
COFFEE

THEY LOVE IT THIS WAY

BARBECUED BEEF LIVER, p. 236
INSTANT MASHED POTATOES
BUTTERED PEAS
WARM CORN MUFFINS
BRAZIL BETTY, p. 569
TEA

WHEN GRANDMA WENT TO EUROPE

CUTLET OF VEAL A LA SUISSE, p. 231
SPINACH AND PEAS
SLICED TOMATOES WITH DILL DRESSING
MELBA TOAST
TWO-TONE PLUM BOWL, p. 555
COFFEE

CAN'T GET ENOUGH OF CHOP SUEY

SHRIMP COCKTAIL
BACON CHOP SUEY, p. 217
FROZEN FRUIT FROST, p. 542
TEA AND COOKIES

FRIDAY SPECIAL AT OUR HOUSE

CHEESE-BAKED HADDOCK, p. 301
BROILED TOMATOES
FROZEN FRENCH FRIES
TOSSED GREEN SALAD WITH PICKLE RELISH
CHOCOLATE ICE CREAM WITH
BUTTERSCOTCH SAUCE
COFFEE

ON SUNDAY

VEAL DE LANUX, p. 233
BUTTERED LIMAS WITH CHIVES
ROMAINE SALAD BOWL
PARMESAN FRENCH BREAD
RAINBOW PARFAITS, p. 609
TEA or COFFEE

ON MONDAY

BROWN 'N' SERVE SAUSAGES
MACARONI SAUTE, p. 382
TOSSED GREEN SALAD
HARD ROLLS
ORANGE-JELLY BAGATELLE, p. 562
TEA OR COFFEE
(hot or iced)

IT'S COLD OUTSIDE

FLANK STEAK — BLUE-CHEESE TOPPED, p. 182
ACORN SQUASH RINGS WITH PEAS
TOSSED GREEN SALAD
APPLE SNOW, p. 545
COFFEE

THEY'LL EAT ANYTHING
WITH HAMBURGER

HAMBURGER MIXED GRILL, p. 191
TOSSED GREEN SALAD
TOASTED CORN MUFFINS
WITH POPPY SEEDS
RIPPLE-STYLE TAPIOCA SPECIAL, p. 561
COFFEE

CAN WE HAVE IT AGAIN?

MEAT AND NOODLES, BOHEMIAN STYLE, p. 254
TOSSED SALAD WITH CELERY AND PIMENTO
GRAPEFRUIT SECTIONS AND PINEAPPLE CHUNKS
IN GRAPE JUICE
COFFEE

TASTES LIKE FALL

PAN-BROILED HAM STEAKS
SKILLET MACARONI MEDLEY, p. 382
SLICED LETTUCE
POPPY SEED FRENCH DRESSING
JIFFY JELLIED FRUIT, p. 562
TEA

TRES ELEGANT FOR SUNDAY

VEAL ROMAN STYLE, p. 230
FLUFFY RICE   BUTTERED GREEN BEANS
MELBA TOAST
PEACH FLAMBE, p. 547   DEMITASSE

THIS GOES OVER BIG

GOLDEN SCALLOPS, p. 325
FROZEN FRENCH FRIES WITH A BIT OF CHILI
BUTTERED BROCCOLI
TOSSED SALAD
ORANGE SHERBET TOPPED WITH WHIPPED CREAM
COFFEE

A REAL QUICKIE

BROILER-FRIED OYSTERS, p. 324
BUTTERED LIMAS AND CARROTS
COLESLAW or PINEAPPLE SLICES
ITALIAN BREAD STICKS
CHOCOLATE ICE CREAM
WITH A SHAKE OF CINNAMON
COFFEE

NICE COMBINATION

SOUTHERN CRAB CAKES, p. 318
BUTTERED PEAS AND LIMAS
TOMATO SLICES ON LETTUCE SLICES
WITH CURRY MAYONNAISE, p. 470
BRAN MUFFINS (bought)
STRAWBERRY-CHEESE COUPE, p. 573

FAMILY SPECIAL

STEAK — HIS WAY
VENETIAN RICE AND PEAS, p. 373
TOSSED GREEN SALAD WITH CUCUMBERS
HOT BUTTERED TOAST PARMESAN
VANILLA ICE CREAM WITH HEATED
ORANGE MARMALADE
SPICE COOKIES   COFFEE

GOOD FOR OCTOBER

BEAN BURGERS, p. 191
GREEN BEANS WITH MUSHROOMS
CORN RELISH   CELERY STICKS
EASY BREAD STICKS
BUTTER-NUT PANDOWDY, p. 569
COFFEE

OH BOY, SPAGHETTI

SPAGHETTI-STUFFED PEPPERS, p. 387
TOSSED SALAD WITH OLIVES
AND SALAMI STRIPS
FRENCH BREAD
COFFEE ICE CREAM WITH HOT MINCEMEAT
TOASTER-TOASTED POUNDCAKE
COFFEE

VERY NICE

BROWN 'N' SERVE SAUSAGES
SAVORY RICE AND CHEESE, p. 374
TOSSED GREEN SALAD WITH
AVOCADO AND PINEAPPLE CHUNKS
FRENCH BREAD
BAKED APPLES (bought)
COFFEE

HOMEY GOODNESS

MACARONI-TUNA BAKE, p. 387
BIG TOSSED SALAD WITH CAULIFLOWERETS
PUMPERNICKEL BREAD AND BUTTER
VANILLA PUDDING WITH
CRANBERRY SAUCE
ICED TEA

QUICK AND EASY
SPRING AND SUMMER MENUS

A FAVORITE
CAPER-BUTTERED STEAK SANDWICHES, p. 182
TOSSED GREEN SALAD
TOP HAT ICE-CREAM CUPCAKES, p. 607
COFFEE (hot or iced)

SOMEWHAT ITALIAN
BROWN 'N' SERVE SAUSAGES, p. 207
VAL'S PEPPER AND EGGS, p. 366
MARINATED TOMATOES (with anchovies, perhaps)
CRISP BREAD
PEACHES IN WINE
COFFEE

WHEN YOU'RE THE ONE WHO IS LATE
CHARLESTON SHRIMP SAUTE, p. 330
GNOCCHI U.S.A., p. 347
TOSSED SALAD WITH EGG AND TOMATO
GOURMET GRAPES, p. 549
COFFEE

TOP STOVE STYLE
SKILLET TUNA CASSEROLE, p. 311
DILL PICKLES   CELERY STICKS
TOASTED ENGLISH MUFFINS
FRUIT SALAD WITH WHIPPED CREAM
COFFEE

WHAT'S FOR DESSERT
PIMENTOS FILLED WITH COLESLAW
CAN-OPENER MINESTRONE, p. 162
LOTS OF FRENCH BREAD
LAYER CAKE A LA MODE WITH
FROZEN STRAWBERRIES
COFFEE

"LET THEM NEITHER STARVE
NOR STUFF"
CHICKEN A LA KING SURPRISE, p. 280
SPINACH AND BACON AND RADISH
SALAD BOWL
CINNAMON APRICOTS, p. 545
CHOCOLATE-CAKE SQUARES
COFFEE

EGGS TASTE DIFFERENT AT NIGHT
BUFFET SCRAMBLED EGGS, p. 360
COLD MARINATED ASPARAGUS OR BROCCOLI
SPUR-OF-THE-MOMENT SHORTCAKES, p. 563
COFFEE

MORE, PLEASE
CRAB AND CORN A LA CREME, p. 319
BUTTERED SPINACH
TOSSED SALAD WITH PICKLE RELISH
MELBA TOAST
PEAR-BUTTERSCOTCH CRISP, p. 567
COFFEE

FANCY FIXIN'S
CHEESE STRATA, p. 347
TOMATO DECKERS (coleslaw filled), p. 452
FRUITED MELON
TEA

BEFORE YOU GO TO THE RINK
SHRIMP BROIL, p. 329
CORN ON THE COB
SLICED TOMATOES AND CUCUMBERS
TOASTED ENGLISH MUFFINS WITH CHEESE
COFFEE-MARSHMALLOW REFRIGERATOR CAKE, p. 575
COFFEE

SUPPER IS SERVED
SALMON SCALLOP DIVAN, p. 313
CUCUMBERS IN FRENCH DRESSING WITH DILL
MELBA TOAST
WARM CHOCOLATE PUDDING A LA MODE
ICED COFFEE

FOR A WARM DAY
JUNIOR ANTIPASTO
SOUP ITALIAN, p. 161
BASKET OF MIXED CRACKERS
ICE-CREAM SHORTCAKE, p. 607
ICED COFFEE
(or perhaps demitasse)

SECOND TIME ROUND
COLD ROAST BEEF
MACARONI SAUTE, p. 382
HOT BUTTERED BROCCOLI   QUICK BREAD STICKS
PEACHES AND GRAPES
TOPPED WITH RASPBERRY SHERBET
COFFEE

TOPS

TOP-HATTER FRANKS, p. 247
BROCCOLI VINAIGRETTE
VANILLA ICE CREAM
TOPPED WITH BLUEBERRIES
TEA

DELIGHTFULLY DIFFERENT

CHICKEN A LA KING, p. 123, CORN TOPPED
TOSSED GREEN SALAD WITH SLICED STUFFED OLIVES
PINEAPPLE AND GRAPES
IN APRICOT NECTAR
COFFEE

I'LL TAKE SECONDS

GOLDEN FISH FILLETS WITH ONIONS, p. 305
BUTTERED ZUCCHINI
MARINATED TOMATOES   RYE BREAD
SCOTCH PEACHES, p. 552
COFFEE

LET'S EAT OUTDOORS

BURGER SOUP, p. 159
TOASTED CORN MUFFINS
BIG FRUIT SALAD
FULL COOKIE JAR   COFFEE

PLENTY OF TIME FOR THE SHOW

FRANKFURTERS AND HAMBURGERS
SPAGHETTI AND MUSHROOMS PARMESAN, p. 388
FRUITED GELATIN (bought) ON COLESLAW
CHOCOLATE FROSTED CAKE
(from the freezer)
ICED COFFEE A LA MODE

THE LAST OF THE ROAST

COLD ROAST BEEF
HOT FRENCH FRIES WITH BARBECUE SAUCE
ZUCCHINI WITH PEAS AND OLIVES
HOT BUTTERED SEEDED FRENCH BREAD
RICE CHANTILLY, p. 560
COFFEE

AT YOUR LEISURE

NOODLE STROGANOFF, p. 386
HERB COLESLAW   PUMPERNICKEL BREAD
RASPBERRY PEACHES
HOT TEA

TWO-IN-ONE

BARBECUED FRANKS AND BEANS, p. 247
TOSSED GREEN SALAD WITH PARMESAN CHEESE
PUMPERNICKEL BREAD
PEACHES WITH SOUR CREAM
COCONUT MACAROONS
ICED COFFEE

AFTER THE SWIM

COLD ROAST PORK
MACARONI-AND-BEAN CASSEROLE, p. 388
CRANBERRY JELLY   SPICED PEACHES
WARM FRENCH BREAD
WATERMELON AND BLUEBERRIES WITH SHERBET
FROZEN COFFEECAKE   COFFEE

COOKING FOR ONE OR TWO

To be successful, cooking for just one person requires careful planning, smart shopping, and skillful food preparation. But it can be fun.

Twosomes include young couples, older couples whose children are away, and pairs of career men or women. They go to their jobs, hurry home at the day's end, then work together to get a good dinner in double-quick time. If you count yourself among these twosomes, read on.

Plan Carefully

Plan menus ahead of time, to provide variety and to use leftovers in interesting ways. You can prepare part of tomorrow's dinner as you cook tonight's. For instance:

Serve tonight	*Serve tomorrow*
Mashed potatoes	Potato cakes
Boiled rice	Rice custard
Stewed apricots	Upside-down cake

Plan a roast for the weekend. The leftovers will be a wonderful help the next week. See Last of the Meat, p. 252, and Last of the Bird, p. 288.

Plan streamlined menus. Just serve a few items, but have plenty of each.

Plan to serve plate or plates from the kitchen, dividing the food proportionately. This cuts down dishwashing and eliminates unmanageable leftovers.

How much to buy? That all-important question is answered in the Amount to Buy paragraphs in The Story of Meats, p. 171; Poultry, p. 260; Fish, p. 299; and in the Vegetable Chart, p. 420. Also see recipes throughout book for For 2 directions.

If you go to business, market for staples on weekends, or a late shopping night. If you are a twosome, divide up daily shopping chores.

Use tools that fit. In cooking, it's important to have the right equipment in the right sizes. You'll want regular-size equipment when you cook for company. A few items especially suitable for your small-scale cooking would be:

> Small 7″ Teflon skillet
> 3-cup to 1-qt. saucepans
> 2- or 4-cup coffee server for instant coffee
> Small automatic or conventional coffee maker
> Set of mix-measure bowls (3)
> Electric toaster-oven
> Electric portable broiler
> 2- to 3-cup teapot
> 2½-qt. teakettle
> 1-qt. oven-glass casserole, with cover for pie use
> Individual baking dishes to double as salad bowls

If you both work, let the first one home start the cooking. Agree ahead of time who will start what.

See To Vary and To Serve hints at the ends of our recipes. With a few changes, a dish can seem brand-new when you make it again.

For an unhurried breakfast:
1. Set the table the night before.
2. Keep these breakfast work-savers on hand:
   Canned or frozen fruit juices
   Frozen waffles or coffeecake; pancake, biscuit, muffin, corn-bread, coffeecake, or popover mix
   Individual packages of ready-to-eat cereal
   Quick-cooking hot cereals
   Brown-and-serve pork sausages or bacon
   Instant coffee, instant cocoa mix, etc.
   Powdered cream, etc.
3. Don't dry breakfast dishes; let drain until dinner. Remember to use paper cups and plates (some are plastic-coated).

Shop For and Use Food Wisely

So many foods are made to order for 1 or for 2! They come as single portions, or in small quantities. Or you can use part of a food and save the rest for later.

Bread and Crackers:
1. Packaged biscuit, muffin, or popover mix.
2. Brown 'n' serve rolls. Heat what you need; store rest for next day as label directs.
3. Canned breads. Use for sandwiches.
4. Cans of refrigerated biscuits. Reheat leftovers as in Leftover Biscuits, p. 478.
5. Small packages of crisp crackers.
6. Frozen biscuits, doughnuts, coffeecakes. Heat what you need; keep rest frozen until later.

Cheese: Keep several kinds on hand, to add heartiness to salads, sandwiches, etc. Also see Cheese as Dessert, p. 348.

Chicken:
1. Chicken parts. Fry, broil, or simmer.
2. Frozen chicken pie, à la king, dinners, creamed chicken, etc.
3. Canned chicken stew, fricassee, chow mein, etc.
4. Broiler-fryers. Sauté as on p. 266. Or cook half a chicken as directed in Oven-Easy Chicken, p. 265, and broil the rest next day, p. 263. Or broil it all!

Desserts:
1. Cookies. Keep the cookie jar filled. Use packaged cookies or cookie, brownie, or other mixes. Or make dough for Susan's Refrigerator Cookies, p. 138; refrigerate it; slice off and bake as many cookies as you wish. Or keep a roll of refrigerated slice 'n' bake cookie dough on hand in your refrigerator; turn to p. 667.
2. With today's fine cake and gingerbread mixes, you can have cake when you like. You can freeze part of a cake for later use, p. 707. There are several frosting mixes. Be sure, also, to check on the variety of frozen cakes, pies, turnovers, etc., at your grocer's; they're excellent!
3. Ice cream. Be sure to see Ice Creams and Sherbets, p. 604.
4. Cheese and fruit. This is gourmet fare! Try dates, cheese, and crackers. See Cheese as Dessert, p. 348.

5. Canned fruit (including purple plums). Use as dessert or breakfast fruit.

6. Fresh fruit. Keep a variety on hand — berries, grapefruit, cantaloupe, oranges, bananas, watermelon, etc.

7. Fruit-flavor gelatins, rennet custards.

8. Packaged puddings. See p. 559 for ways to serve them.

Eggs: Serve them scrambled, poached, hard-cooked, creamed, in omelets, etc. See Eggs — Plain and Fancy, p. 356.

Fish and Shellfish:

1. Frozen fish sticks, fish fillets, King-crab meat, rock-lobster tails, scallops, etc.

2. Canned tuna, salmon, King-crab meat, minced clams, etc.

3. Fresh fillets, small whole fish, oysters, shrimp, scallops, etc.

Meats:

1. Canned meats. See p. 248 for ways to serve them.

2. Ready-cooked meats. See p. 242 for ways to serve them.

3. Chops, small steaks. See The Story of Meats, p. 171.

4. Franks. Broil, simmer, or pan-broil. Or use right from the package in sandwiches, etc.

5. Frozen beef pie or dinners — ready to heat and eat; see p. 102.

6. Frozen meats — packaged hamburger patties, veal cutlets, grill steaks, liver, etc.

7. Ham slice. Pan-fry, broil, or bake.

8. Hamburger. Buy just enough for one meal. Or buy enough for two meals; use part for patties, rest in some other favorite way. See p. 189.

9. Lamb and veal kidneys.

10. Pork sausage. Buy fresh or brown 'n' serve kind.

11. Pork tenderloin. Stuff, for special treat.

12. Smoked boneless butt (a fine small ham). Simmer; then finish as you like it.

13. Canned beef stew, chicken stew, or chili con carne.

Salad Makings: Keep salad makings on hand.

1. Greens. See Salad Greens, p. 445.

2. Tomatoes, etc. See Salad Extras, p. 446.

3. Fruit-flavor gelatin. Use it to make molded fruit salads quickly; serve as salad today, dessert tomorrow.

Salad Dressings: Personalize ready-to-use salad dressings or the mixes, as on pp. 468–471.

Sauces and Gravies:

1. Pasteurized process-cheese spread. This makes a wonderful cheese sauce for vegetables, meats, sandwiches.

2. Canned beef gravy or brown- or light-gravy mix. They're fine top-offs for chops, hamburgers, etc., or to add to stew, meat pie, and the like.

3. Canned tomato sauce — it's so delightfully seasoned.

4. Canned cream soups or soup mixes; use as sauce. Or use the sauce mixes.

5. Packaged sauce mixes, p. 102.

Seasonings:

1. Monosodium glutamate. Seasoned, garlic, celery, and onion salt, seasoned pepper, etc. They step up flavors.

2. Herbs and spices. These give new flavor to old favorites.

3. A little wine. Does wonders for a soup, main dish, or dessert. Turn to Cook with Wine, p. 692.

Soups:

1. Canned and frozen soups and soup mixes.

2. Canned and frozen chowders.

3. Chowders. They're so easy to make from canned minced clams, corn, or tuna or frozen fish fillets.

4. Oyster stew — it comes frozen, too.

Vegetables:

1. Frozen vegetables. Cook ½ pkg. at a time. Some come cooked and seasoned, others mixed, still others in sauces.

2. Canned vegetables. Serve part hot, the rest in salad the next day.

3. Potatoes. Frozen French fries or canned white or sweet potatoes eliminate paring and shortcut the cooking process. The instant potato family saves time, too; see p. 392.

4. Canned macaroni and spaghetti dishes, baked beans, etc. They pinch-hit for potatoes.

5. Rice. It's so easy to cook in a small quantity, and there are so many variations! See Rice, p. 369.

How to Tailor Recipes

Recipes for Two: Many recipes in this book may be made as directed for 4; then they'll provide second helpings for 2.

Under some of our recipes you'll find a For 2 paragraph with special directions given. In the chapters on basic cooking methods, those given apply to For 2 amounts as well as to larger quantities. Be sure to check Amount to Buy paragraphs.

If You Make Full Recipe For:

1. SOUPS AND CHOWDERS: Refrigerate leftovers, covered; reheat next day in double boiler.
2. MOLDED SALADS AND DESSERTS: Leftovers keep beautifully till a day or so later.
3. SALAD DRESSINGS: Most dressings keep well in refrigerator. (For those that don't — sour-cream, cream-cheese, and cottage-cheese dressings, etc. — halve ingredients.)
4. QUICK BREADS: Serve part fresh and hot; next day, serve rest warmed or toasted. See Leftover Biscuits, p. 478; To Reheat Muffins, p. 481; Leftover Corn Bread or Corn Muffins, p. 482; Toasted Afternoon Tea Scones, p. 480; Leftover Coffeecake, p. 492.
5. YEAST BREADS: Refrigerator rolls are especially nice for two. See Susan's Refrigerator Rolls, p. 116.

Bakers' bread and rolls need not always be the same; see Breads and Rolls You Buy, p. 491, for wonderful things to do with them.
6. DESSERTS: Serve leftovers a different way the second time; check Dreamy Desserts, p. 559, and To Sauce the Dish, p. 527, for ideas.

Frozen desserts such as escalloped apples, apple cobbler, cherry cobbler, Dutch apple pie, ice cream, and cakes keep handsomely in the freezer.

Dining Alone

The girl who eats alone should adopt the same techniques of dining as the family of two. In fact, for her the setting is even more important. She will want to make a firm, fast resolution never to eat a morsel unless the entire meal is ready, and to sit down at a set table or an attractively set tray. There's nothing to be gained by eating "on the wing."

Music, the type you like best, is a fine background, and occasionally candlelight adds the perfect just-for-one touch.

It's a good idea to save the mail as a treat after dessert. Do cook a real dinner at least a few nights a week. It may seem like a lot of fuss and bother for a person living alone, but dining out on a steady basis palls. And just slicing off some cold ham to eat with potato salad from the delicatessen will do nothing for building morale, the way a good hot dinner can.

COOKING FOR TWO, FALL AND WINTER

CAREER-GIRL SPECIAL

PAN-BROILED HAM STEAK

CUSTARD CORN PUDDING, p. 400

TOSSED GREEN SALAD

MELBA TOAST   CURRANT JELLY

ORANGE SHERBET WITH COCONUT

COFFEE

CLUB MEETING TONIGHT

TOMATO JUICE

CHINESE EGGS FOO YOUNG, p. 367

WITH RICE

CELERY STICKS   RIPE OLIVES

VANILLA ICE CREAM WITH PURPLE PLUMS

TEA

SATISFYING

CURRY-POTATO SOUP, p. 162

SHRIMP, SAILOR STYLE, p. 327

TOSSED GREEN SALAD   FRESH RYE BREAD

ORANGE GELATIN WITH CRUSHED
PINEAPPLE

TEA

TEMPTING

AVOCADO COCKTAIL, p. 140

HAM-AND-MUSHROOM OMELET

COLESLAW ON SLICED CRANBERRY SAUCE

COFFEE ICE CREAM
ON TOASTED POUNDCAKE WITH CHOCOLATE SAUCE

ICED COFFEE

BACHELOR'S CHOICE

ONION SOUP, FRENCH-MARKET STYLE, p. 160

TOSSED GREEN SALAD

FRUIT TART

COFFEE

LIKE MOTHER MADE

SUSAN'S BROWN BEEF STEW, p. 107

TOSSED GREEN SALAD WITH PARMESAN

BAKED APPLE

COFFEE

SOMEWHAT ITALIAN

VEAL SCALOPPINE, p. 228, ON RICE

TOSSED ROMAINE SALAD

BREAD STICKS

VANILLA PUDDING WITH MANDARIN ORANGES

DEMITASSE

NOW THAT THE CHILDREN ARE GONE

BROILED FILLETS AU GRATIN

CHINESE CAULIFLOWER, p. 399

TOSSED SALAD   HARD ROLLS

ORANGE SHERBET   BROWNIES

COFFEE

TETE-A-TETE

CHICKEN CACCIATORE, p. 269

HOT FLUFFY RICE   BREAD STICKS

BIG TOSSED SALAD

WITH FROZEN PEAS ADDED

(partially thawed, not cooked)

SKILLET GRAPEFRUIT FOR TWO, p. 549

DEMITASSE

FRIDAY FARE

CREAMED TUNA SUPREME, p. 311

GREEN-PEA SLAW   BRAN MUFFINS

APPLE TURNOVERS

TEA (hot or iced)

FOR THE FIRESIDE

PORK-CHOP-LIMA SUPPER, p. 203

TOSSED GREEN SALAD   HARD ROLLS

GREEN GRAPES IN GRAPE JUICE

GINGERSNAPS

COFFEE

TASTY TOUCHES

LINDA'S BRAISED VEAL SHANKS, p. 234

TOSSED GREEN SALAD   ZESTY BEETS, p. 395

CHEESECAKE (frozen)

COFFEE

FROSTY EVENINGS

VENETIAN LIVER, p. 235

BUTTERED SPINACH   HI'S CAESAR SALAD, p. 448

GRAPEFRUIT HALVES ROYAL

(fill centers with grape juice)

COFFEE

A NEW TWIST

FLOUNDER FLORENTINE, p. 300

HEATED FROZEN POTATO PATTIES

TOSSED SALAD   WHOLE-WHEAT BREAD

APPLESAUCE A LA MODE

FIX AHEAD

GOURMET CHICKEN SALAD, p. 460

FRESH ASPARAGUS

TOAST   CRANBERRY JELLY

CHOCOLATE ICE CREAM WITH CHOCOLATE SAUCE

ICED COFFEE

ELEGANTLY SIMPLE

TOMATO JUICE   STUFFED CELERY

CHICKEN LIVERS WITH RICE, p. 274

WHOLE GREEN BEANS

BUTTER-PECAN ICE CREAM, BUTTERSCOTCH SAUCE

COFFEE

A SPECIAL GUEST

SCALLOPED HAM, POTATOES, AND CARROTS, p. 213

TOSSED GREEN SALAD

WHOLE-WHEAT BREAD AND BUTTER

QUICK ALMOND-PEACH SHORTCAKE

(spongecake, thawed frozen peaches,

almond whipped cream)

TEA

FUN FARE

MARDI GRAS MACARONI AND CHEESE, p. 382

COLD MARINATED BROCCOLI

CANNED PURPLE PLUMS WITH SOUR CREAM

COCONUT MACAROONS

COFFEE

STICKS-TO-THE-RIBS
BOHEMIAN VEAL, p. 232
RED CABBAGE   CELERY STICKS
RYE BREAD
VANILLA ICE CREAM WITH SLICED PEACHES
COFFEE (hot or iced)

FRANKS WITH A FILLIP
HOT BARBECUED FRANKS, p. 245
KRAUT-NOODLE CASSEROLE, p. 415
BREADSTICKS AND BUTTER
BAKED APPLES (bought) A LA MODE
COFFEE

ALWAYS WELCOME
YOUR FAVORITE HAMBURGERS
JOHN J. LIMAS, p. 404   MARINATED TOMATOES
CUSTARD BREAD PUDDING, p. 131
COFFEE

A NEW BEAU
ROAST ROCK-CORNISH HENS, p. 263
COMPANY WILD RICE, p. 376
MARINATED TOMATOES
MELBA TOAST
STRAWBERRIES IN RED WINE
COFFEE

COOKING FOR TWO, SPRING AND SUMMER

LET'S HAVE IT AGAIN
FROSTED TOMATOES, p. 141
GARLIC-BROILED SHRIMP, p. 327
BUTTERED ZUCCHINI
CANTALOUPE WITH VANILLA ICE CREAM
DEMITASSE

TO IMPRESS
LAMP CHOPS HARBERT, p. 224
BUTTERED PEAS
WILTED LETTUCE, p. 449
MELBA TOAST
CHOCOLATE PUDDING WITH GRATED CHOCOLATE
ICED COFFEE

A NICE LITTLE DINNER
CHICKEN MARENGO, p. 267
HOT FLUFFY RICE   BOSTON-LETTUCE BOWL
CHEESE AND CRACKERS
COFFEE

NEW ENGLAND STYLE
DOWN-EAST CORN CHOWDER, p. 162
BLUEBERRY MUFFINS
CHOCOLATE ICE CREAM
WITH SALTED PEANUTS
COFFEE

CELEBRATE THE RAISE
LOBSTER, OLD-FRENCH STYLE, p. 322
BIG TOSSED SALAD
LOTS OF FRENCH BREAD
HOT SOUFFLE GRAND MARNIER, p. 582
COFFEE

HARVEST TWOSOME
CHUNKY EGG SALAD, p. 458
HARD ROLLS
GINGERBREAD WITH ORANGE SAUCE
ICED COFFEE

SUMMER SPECIAL
STEAK
PEAS AND MUSHROOMS
LETTUCE WEDGE   ROQUEFORT DRESSING
FRENCH BREAD
QUICK CREME BRULEE, p. 543
COFFEE

NORTH-SOUTH
CANADIAN BACON
JAMAICAN YAM CASSEROLE, p. 410
BUTTERED GREEN BEANS   FRENCH BREAD
SNOW PUDDING, p. 132
COFFEE

FOR SISTER SUSIE
EGGS MORNAY, p. 365
ICEBERG CHUNKS WITH SALAD DRESSING
MELBA TOAST
CHOCOLATE-FROSTED CHOCOLATE CUPCAKE
BUNCHES OF GREEN GRAPES
ICED TEA

SOUP TO SAUCE

BOUILLON-ON-THE-ROCKS, p. 163

GOLDEN SCALLOPS, p. 325

BUTTERED SPINACH
(with a bit of horse-radish)

CORN MUFFINS

COFFEE ICE CREAM
(chocolate sauce optional)

COFFEE

WHEN HE COMES

A MAN'S BARBECUED CHICKEN, p. 271

CORN AND LIMAS WITH CHIVES

WHOLE-WHEAT BREAD

VANILLA PUDDING WITH SLICED PEACHES

COFFEE (hot or iced)

INDOOR—OUTDOOR

BARBECUED SPARERIBS, p. 206

BAKED BEANS

PICKLED PEACHES   TOSSED SALAD

STRAWBERRY ICE CREAM

ICED TEA

VIA BELGIUM

FRIEDA'S HAM AND ENDIVES AU GRATIN, p. 214

FRENCH BREAD

PEACH MELBA, p. 606   MACAROONS

COFFEE

DE LUXE

SWEETBREADS EN BROCHETTE, p. 238

TOSSED GREEN SALAD   FRENCH BREAD

PINEAPPLE SOPHISTICATE, p. 555

TEA OR COFFEE

NICE COMBINATION

CURRIED EGGS AND MUSHROOMS, p. 364

SPINACH SALAD BOWL   CORN MUFFINS

HONEYDEW MELON WEDGES WITH ORANGE SHERBET

ICED COFFEE

AND WAIT TILL YOU TASTE THE SLAW

ITALIAN VEAL ROLLS, p. 230

CREAMY CELERY SLAW, p. 456   HARD ROLLS

WATERMELON AND BLUEBERRIES

NUT COOKIES

ICED COFFEE

HIS FAVORITE FRENCH MEAL

JELLIED MADRILENE

MINUTE STEAKS AU POIVRE, p. 180

PETITS POIS A LA FRANCAISE
(peas cooked with lettuce,
onions, and herbs)

SALADE VERTE (green salad)

PECHES SULTANES, p. 579

COFFEE

SOUFFLE FOR TWO

MUSHROOM-CHEESE SOUFFLE, p. 346

ASPARAGUS TOPPED WITH PEAS

RYE BREAD

STRAWBERRY ICE CREAM WITH STRAWBERRIES

ICED TEA

EVERYBODY LIKES CHICKEN

OVEN-EASY CHICKEN, p. 265

LIMAS WITH A DASH OF CURRY

CHEESE-STUFFED CELERY   CARROT STICKS

CORN MUFFINS

CHOCOLATE RENNET-CUSTARD

COFFEE (instant)

CHANGE OF PACE

DILLED TONGUE SALAD, p. 461

BUTTERED PEAS   RYE BREAD

SLICED BANANAS IN CRANBERRY JUICE

COFFEE (hot or iced)

MEALS CAN TASTE GOOD, BE GOOD

All of our chapters are full of recipes to tempt appetites all through the day.

You can practice good nutrition on your family without their even realizing that they are "eating because it's good for them." Consult the following pyramids for good nutrition.

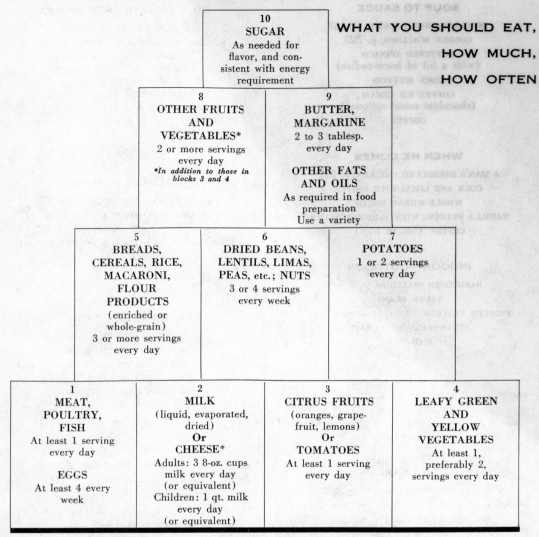

10
SUGAR
As needed for flavor, and consistent with energy requirement

8
OTHER FRUITS AND VEGETABLES*
2 or more servings every day
*In addition to those in blocks 3 and 4

9
BUTTER, MARGARINE
2 to 3 tablesp. every day

OTHER FATS AND OILS
As required in food preparation
Use a variety

5
BREADS, CEREALS, RICE, MACARONI, FLOUR PRODUCTS
(enriched or whole-grain)
3 or more servings every day

6
DRIED BEANS, LENTILS, LIMAS, PEAS, etc.; NUTS
3 or 4 servings every week

7
POTATOES
1 or 2 servings every day

1
MEAT, POULTRY, FISH
At least 1 serving every day

EGGS
At least 4 every week

2
MILK
(liquid, evaporated, dried)
Or
CHEESE*
Adults: 3 8-oz. cups milk every day (or equivalent)
Children: 1 qt. milk every day (or equivalent)

3
CITRUS FRUITS
(oranges, grapefruit, lemons)
Or
TOMATOES
At least 1 serving every day

4
LEAFY GREEN AND YELLOW VEGETABLES
At least 1, preferably 2, servings every day

*See list under: These foods give about the same amount of calcium, p. 25.

How to Use These Pyramids

Everyone knows about calories. But some of us forget that calories are by no means the whole story on food values. It's possible to eat 1500 calories a day and feel marvelous, and to "starve" on 2000.

We meal planners should know about calories. But we also need the rest of the story on food values — which foods provide necessary proteins, minerals, vitamins, and other diet essentials.

This section supplies this information. Read it carefully — and you're on your way to sound menu planning.

We lucky Americans have very little excuse for not eating well and wisely. What a wealth of foods we have to choose from! And a need to be budget-conscious is really no hindrance — either to eating enjoyment or to a sound diet. A well-seasoned meat loaf with a tasty

WHY YOU
SHOULD SELECT
THESE FOODS

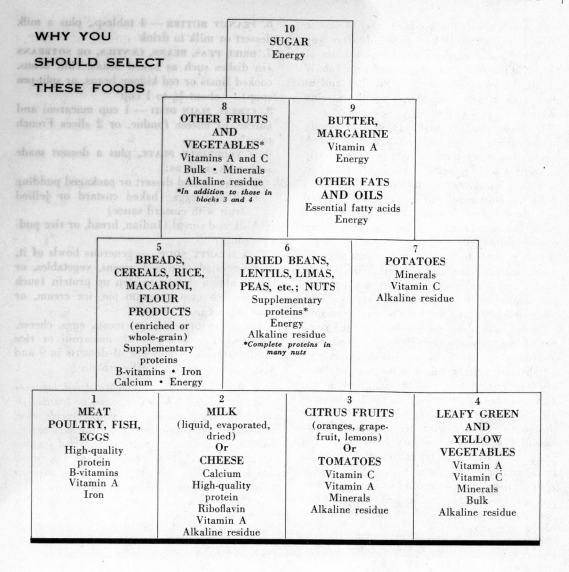

10
SUGAR
Energy

8
**OTHER FRUITS
AND
VEGETABLES***
Vitamins A and C
Bulk • Minerals
Alkaline residue
*In addition to those in
blocks 3 and 4*

9
**BUTTER,
MARGARINE**
Vitamin A
Energy

**OTHER FATS
AND OILS**
Essential fatty acids
Energy

5
**BREADS,
CEREALS, RICE,
MACARONI,
FLOUR
PRODUCTS**
(enriched or
whole-grain)
Supplementary
proteins
B-vitamins • Iron
Calcium • Energy

6
**DRIED BEANS,
LENTILS, LIMAS,
PEAS, etc.; NUTS**
Supplementary
proteins*
Energy
Alkaline residue
*Complete proteins in
many nuts*

7
POTATOES
Minerals
Vitamin C
Alkaline residue

1
**MEAT
POULTRY, FISH,
EGGS**
High-quality
protein
B-vitamins
Vitamin A
Iron

2
MILK
(liquid, evaporated,
dried)
Or
CHEESE
Calcium
High-quality
protein
Riboflavin
Vitamin A
Alkaline residue

3
CITRUS FRUITS
(oranges, grape-
fruit, lemons)
Or
TOMATOES
Vitamin C
Vitamin A
Minerals
Alkaline residue

4
**LEAFY GREEN
AND
YELLOW
VEGETABLES**
Vitamin A
Vitamin C
Minerals
Bulk
Alkaline residue

sauce provides as high-quality protein as prime ribs of beef. Pie fillings, puddings, and sauces made with evaporated milk or nonfat dry milk need make no apology for either flavor or food value. The preparation of delicious and nutritious low-cost meals challenges our skill and ingenuity.

The above pyramids are divided into the following ten blocks:
1. Meat, poultry, fish, and eggs
2. Milk (liquid, evaporated, dried) or cheese
3. Citrus fruits or tomatoes
4. Leafy green and yellow vegetables
5. Breads, cereals, rice, macaroni, and flour products (enriched or whole grain)
6. Dried beans, peas, other legumes, and nuts
7. Potatoes
8. Fruits and vegetables (in addition to those in 3 and 4)
9. Butter, margarine, and other fats and oils
10. Sugar

After you have studied the "What" pyramid, which shows the kinds of food to choose from, turn to the "Why" pyramid. Here you find the special contribution of each class of food. Isn't it really easy to assure your family of all the essentials of a sound diet and at the same time serve them mouth-watering meals?

Whether you are planning normal family meals, trying to reduce, or attempting to collect a few extra pounds, you will be vitally concerned with calories. What is a calorie? It is a unit of energy — the energy needed to stoke the engines of our bodily processes and provide the fuel for our physical activities. Some foods, such as pure fat and pure sugar, supply principally calories, or energy units. Others contribute, in addition, vitamins, minerals, proteins, and other values, vital to our health and well-being. The latter are what we call protective foods, and they are the four blocks which form the base of the pyramids.

We all have a calorie requirement: the number of energy units needed daily for physical activities. If the food we eat supplies this number, we neither gain nor lose weight. Anyone needing to lose weight must reduce the daily number of calories, but not too drastically and never at the expense of the necessary protective foods. Fortunately, many of these essential foods are not too high in energy units (for example, fruits, vegetables, skim milk, and lean meat and fish). *Don't reduce calories to a level where you lose more than two pounds a week.* (This means 1200-1300 calories for most of us.) *Always consult your doctor about weight reduction.*

6. PEANUT BUTTER — 4 tablesp., plus a milk dessert or milk to drink

7. DRIED PEAS, BEANS, LENTILS, OR SOYBEANS (in dishes such as baked beans, chili beans, cooked limas or red kidney beans, or split-pea soup) — about ¾ to 1 cup*

8. CEREAL MAIN DISH — 1 cup macaroni and cheese, or cheese fondue, or 2 slices French toast*

9. A VEGETABLE PLATE, plus a dessert made with milk, such as:

Rennet-custard dessert or packaged pudding

Milk and eggs (baked custard or jellied fruit with custard sauce)

Milk and cereal (Indian, bread, or rice pudding)

10. A HEARTY SOUP — generous bowls of it, with a salad of tossed greens, vegetables, or fruit, plus a dessert to step up protein (such as Spanish cream, cream pie, ice cream, or any dessert in 9, above)

11. A MAIN DISH SALAD (meats, eggs, cheese, or poultry combined with macaroni or rice and vegetables), plus one of desserts in 9 and 10 to round out the meal's protein

A Reminder: When serving dried legumes (soybeans, dried beans or peas, or lentils) or cereal products (bread, breakfast cereals, rice, macaroni, etc.) as a main dish, be sure to:
a. Choose a recipe in which the dried legume or cereal product is combined with a small amount of high-quality protein food, such as milk, cheese, eggs, fish, meat, or poultry.
b. Or serve with it a milk or milk-and-egg dessert, or milk beverage, or a salad containing cheese, or a dessert of cheese and crackers.

Alternates for a Serving of Meat

When planning menus, keep this table beside you. It lists foods — and amounts — that may alternate for a small serving of meat.

1. FISH, SHELLFISH, POULTRY, GAME, OR VARIETY MEATS (liver, kidney, heart, etc.) — a serving

2. EGGS — 2 medium, cooked any way

3. MILK — 1 pt. whole or skim

4. COTTAGE CHEESE — 6 tablesp. (about 3 oz.)

5. CHEDDAR CHEESE — ½ cup grated (about 2 oz.)

A Good Day Starts with a Good Breakfast

There's no substitute for a good breakfast. The most nutrition-packed lunch in the world won't compensate for a skipped morning meal. And the best-balanced dinner won't carry you through in peak form till the following noon. It's been proved: People who eat a good breakfast work better, think better, react faster, and are altogether pleasanter, happier people.

GOOD BREAKFAST PATTERNS

Choose one of these patterns, and your breakfast will be a good nutritious one.

PATTERN NO. 1

Fruit or fruit juice

Ready-to-eat or hot cereal with milk

Enriched white or whole-grain bread, rolls, or toast; butter or margarine

Coffee; milk for children

PATTERN NO. 2

Fruit or fruit juice

Eggs and bacon

Enriched white or whole-grain bread, rolls, or toast; butter or margarine

Coffee; milk for children

PATTERN NO. 3

Your growing son or daughter and your husband (if his work is heavy) needs:

Fruit or fruit juice

Ready-to-eat or hot cereal with milk

Eggs (and breakfast meat, if budget allows)

Enriched white or whole-grain bread, rolls, or toast; butter or margarine

Coffee; milk for children

BREAK THOSE BAD BREAKFAST HABITS!

Develop an appetite! It's possible. Our eating patterns are very much a matter of habit, and with just a little self-discipline, we can adjust and improve them.

If you are eating 50, 60, or even 70 per cent of the day's food at dinnertime, try this experiment: Eat a little more at lunch, a little less at dinner. Go easy on high-calorie desserts, etc.; then make yourself eat your "good breakfast," hungry or not. Keep this up for a week or 10 days, and you'll find you are looking forward to breakfast and are automatically eating less for dinner.

Take Time for Breakfast. Aren't several hours of feeling happily energetic worth getting up 15 min. earlier?

Send a Good Lunch Along

The same food for lunch, day after day, will make anyone's appetite lag, particularly if he must take his lunch with him to school or work. Here's how to keep him always eager.

WHEN YOU PLAN

Plan ahead — not just for tomorrow, but for several days if you can.

Think first of what your lunch toter should have and would like to find in his lunch box, bag, or brief case.

For the sake of his good health, see that each lunch box includes:

1. MEAT, EGGS, POULTRY, CHEESE, OR FISH in sandwiches, salad, or main dish.

2. VEGETABLES — at least one — in sandwiches, salad, or main dish, or as raw relish.

3. FRUIT — at least one — raw, cooked, frozen, or canned, as is or in salad or dessert.

4. BREADS — varied from day to day.

5. MILK — to fill out the day's quota — as is, as a milk drink, in soup or dessert, etc. To pack in extra nourishment, add a beaten egg or tablesp. of nonfat dry milk or molasses to a milk drink.

Keep a list of box-lunch menus so you can rotate them. See Pack-and-Carry Sandwiches, p. 521.

Stock up on paper napkins, wax paper, foil, saran, sandwich bags, paper or plastic containers, spoons, forks, etc.

Maybe a new bag or lunch box would boost the luncher's morale. Today's jaunty bags — big enough to hold both books and lunch — also boast a vacuum bottle in a hideaway compartment.

Buy one of the new widemouthed and/or regular vacuum bottles. They make it safe to pack soups, salads, baked beans, beverages, etc.

Keep the box lunch in mind when planning dinner the night before. Oftentimes you can prepare enough soup, main dish, bread, or dessert to take care of tomorrow's lunch.

Speed lunch-box packing by doing all you can while cleaning up dinner the night before.

1. Unpack, wash, and scald lunch box and vacuum bottle. Dry thoroughly. Let lunch box air.

2. Wash and refrigerate raw vegetables, salad greens, and fruits.

3. Make up, wrap, and refrigerate or freeze sandwiches the night before. Then pack into lunch box at the last possible moment — especially if lunch box cannot be refrigerated.

4. Plan servings as generous as those at home.

VITAMINS, MINERALS, AND YOU

(why you need them, and foods that supply them)

WHY YOU NEED THEM	RICHEST NATURAL SOURCES	WHY YOU NEED THEM	RICHEST NATURAL SOURCES

VITAMIN A

Helps resist nose and throat infections (colds)

Helps prevent night blindness and other eye diseases

Promotes normal growth

Apricots (fresh and dried), butter or margarine, cream, egg yolk, liver, milk (whole, evaporated), yellow and leafy green vegetables (carrots, beet greens, spinach, sweet potatoes, etc.), whole-milk cheese

VITAMIN B1 (THIAMINE)

Necessary for functioning of nerve tissues

Proper utilization of carbohydrates, fats

Promotes normal growth

Stimulates appetite and good muscle tone

Brewers' yeast, chicken, dried beans, dried peas, fish, lean meats, lentils, milk (whole, skim, evaporated, nonfat dry), peanuts, variety meats (liver, kidneys, sweetbreads), wheat germ, whole-grain or enriched breads, cereals, and flours

VITAMIN B2 (RIBOFLAVIN)

Necessary for healthy skin and hair, good digestion, sound nerves

Increases resistance to infection, general weakness, and some eye conditions

Brewers' yeast, chicken, dried peas, eggs, fish, green and leafy vegetables (turnip greens, beet greens, kale, green limas, collards, mustard greens, etc.), kidney, lean meats, liver, milk (whole, skim, evaporated, nonfat dry), wheat germ

VITAMIN C (ASCORBIC ACID)

Prevents and cures scurvy

Increases strength of capillary walls, lessening the possibility of hemorrhages

Increases resistance to infection

Necessary for sound teeth and gums

Cantaloupe, citrus fruits (oranges, grapefruit, lemons, tangerines), green and leafy vegetables (green peppers, mustard greens, Brussels sprouts, kale, parsley, etc.), pineapple, potatoes, raw cabbage, strawberries, tomatoes

VITAMIN D

Aids in utilizing calcium and phosphorus in building bones, teeth

Prevents rickets in children

Egg yolk, fresh and canned oily fish, liver, sunshine action, vitamin-D-enriched cereals, vitamin-D-enriched milk and evaporated milk

NIACIN

Factor in cure and prevention of pellagra

Helps maintain a healthy skin condition

Brewers' yeast, fish, green and leafy vegetables (green beans, broccoli, kale, cabbage, etc.), green peas, heart, kidney, lean meat, liver, milk (whole, skim, evaporated, non-fat dry), wheat germ, whole-grain or enriched breads, cereals, and flours

VITAMINS, MINERALS, AND YOU

(why you need them, and foods that supply them)

WHY YOU NEED THEM	RICHEST NATURAL SOURCES	WHY YOU NEED THEM	RICHEST NATURAL SOURCES
IRON		**PHOSPHORUS**[*]	
Necessary to formation of red blood corpuscles, which carry oxygen in blood Aids in tissue respiration Prevents nutritional anemia	Dried apricots, egg yolk, green and leafy vegetables (green beans, broccoli, kale, cabbage, etc.), liver, molasses, oysters, potatoes, whole-grain or enriched breads, cereals, and flours	Builds bones and teeth Necessary for utilization of fats and carbohydrates by the body	Brewers' yeast, cereals, cheese, eggs, fish, green and leafy vegetables (green beans, broccoli, kale, cabbage, etc.), liver, meats, milk (whole, skim, evaporated, nonfat dry), shellfish, wheat germ
CALCIUM[*]			
Builds strong bones and teeth Necessary for lactation; coagulation of blood; heart, nerve, and muscle functions Helps maintain alkalinity of the blood	Cheese, cream, green and leafy vegetables (green beans, broccoli, kale, cabbage, etc.), milk (whole, skim, evaporated, nonfat dry), sardines		

The correct functioning of both calcium and phosphorus depends on sufficient amount and proper proportion of both, as well as of vitamin D.

WHEN COMPANY COMES

Many of us must be cooks and hostesses, too. For a smooth unflurried occasion, bone up on the numerous different ways to handle a dinner, big or little. And at the same time learn how to cut down on steps and dishes and, most important of all, have everything ready at the right time.

A SIMPLE SIT-DOWN DINNER

Planning the *right* menu is half the battle.
1. Plan dinners with not more than two or three easy-to-serve courses. It's correct, smart. Have you read How to Plan a Menu, p. 18?
2. Eliminate last-minute chores. Choose dishes that can be completely cooked in advance or can be made ready for cooking early in day and kept in refrigerator.
3. Choose dishes that can wait if dinner is delayed or that can be cooked at last minute.
4. Instead of serving the first course at the table, serve it in the living room — fruit, tomato, clam, or vegetable juice; or a hot soup served in mugs or punch glasses. Then you can

slip out of the room and put main course on table. (See Good Beginnings, p. 139; Soups and Chowders, p. 158.)
5. Or serve first course with main course: Place glass of fruit, tomato, clam, or vegetable juice to right of each water glass.
6. If you're serving hors d'oeuvres, choose from Dips, Dunks, and Nibblers, p. 144.
7. Serve course-in-one main dishes, such as casseroles, stews, hearty soups, hearty salads, etc.
8. Choose foods that can be cooked and served in the same dish — casserole main dishes, bread puddings, brown Betty, biscuits baked in oven-glass pie plates or baking dishes, etc.
9. Choose a salad that can be *tossed* in salad bowl and served at table, rather than one that must be *arranged* on individual plates. It saves arranging time. Or if you prefer individual salads, serve them with main course, placing salad plate to left of each dinner plate just before guests sit down. Or make a "do ahead" molded salad.
10. Or instead of salad, serve crisp raw relishes — celery, radishes, raw carrot sticks, coleslaw, etc. — with main course.

54

Everything Ready at the Right Time

Beginners' butterflies are not unusual. Everybody's gone through an agonizing session of seeing the roast done to medium-rare perfection while the potatoes were still hard as rocks. And here's how to wave those butterflies good-by:

Make out a work schedule on paper. Write out your menu. (And of course you've already checked your cupboard and refrigerator to see that you have all the necessary ingredients on hand.)

Gauge your meal by checking the preparation and cooking time for the longest-cooking dish first. For example, if it takes 2 hr. 15 min. to prepare and bake a casserole, and dinner is to be at 6:30, start preparing the casserole at 4:15. If you do this with each dish, you'll know just what to start when. Jot down the time in red pencil beside each recipe—that way you won't have to figure it as you start each dish.

Keep in mind that each and every recipe should be followed with loving care.

Read every word of the recipe first. Make sure all utensils are the right size. Be fussy about measuring (p. 13). When you've become familiar with a recipe, you may change the seasonings to suit your taste, but never increase or decrease the essential ingredients. Preliminary instructions clear? Good. Now you're ready for action.

Set the Dinner Table Correctly

And it's possible to set it correctly and still incorporate easy-on-the-hostess ideas.

The Table Linen: Use easy-to-wipe-off or cloth place mats. Or choose a simple, attractive, easy-to-launder linen cloth.

Fold dinner napkins into oblongs. Place on dinner plate. Or if you are serving a first course, place napkin to left of fork.

Placing Silver, China, etc.:
1. Place dinner plate in center of each place, 1″ in from edge of place mat or table.
2. Set each place with flat silver, 1″ in from edge of place mat or table, as in diagram, right. Notice that the dessertspoon is to right

of knife. If dessert requires a fork, place to right of dinner fork. Or if preferred, place spoon or fork on each dessert plate and serve dessert from kitchen. (Spoons for coffee or tea belong on saucers, never on table.) Arrange plates and glasses as shown. Or adopt the continental way and place the dessert fork and spoon horizontally above the dinner plate, spoon handle to right, fork to left.
3. If you prefer a fruit cup or soup as the first course, place teaspoon or soupspoon to right of dessertspoon.
4. Place salad plates as in diagram below.

If you're serving fruit cup, place filled sherbet glass on small plate on dinner plate. If you're having soup, place filled cream-soup cup on saucer, or attractive soup bowl on small plate, on dinner plate.

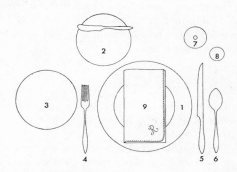

GUEST DINNER SETTING

1. Dinner plate
2. Bread-and-butter plate, with butter spreader across it
3. Salad on 7″ or 8″ plate
4. Dinner fork to be used for both main dish and salad (or place salad fork to right of dinner fork)
5. Dinner knife
6. Dessertspoon
7. Water glass
8. Glass of fruit juice to be enjoyed during main course
9. Dinner napkin, folded into oblong, on dinner plate

P.S. On Setting the Table

Simplicity, not convention, makes the rules today. Don't be afraid to adopt compromises like these when you're cook and hostess, too.
1. Place carving set, if any, before host, with fork to left, and knife and serving spoon to right of space reserved for platter.
2. Place serving silver near serving dishes.
3. Use tray or tea wagon for setting and clearing table, etc.

4. Set tea wagon or small table at hostess' right, for serving salad, dessert, and tea or coffee, or for making waffles.

5. If table is narrow, at host's right place small table from which he can serve vegetables.

6. Let individual salad plates double as bread-and-butter plates.

Who'll Sit Where

As family and guests come into the dining room, the hostess tells each one where he or she is to sit. (Plan your seating arrangement beforehand.)

Usually, the host sits at one end of table, the hostess at the other. To host's immediate right is lady guest of honor, with female guest of next importance to his left.

To hostess' immediate right sits gentleman guest of honor, with male guest of next importance to her left. Remaining places are filled as hostess suggests.

To Serve the Guests

You and the host will put on an A-1 performance if you have also read Maid for the Occasion, p. 66.

1. Serve hot food hot. Check cooking time for each food on your menu; start food cooking so all is done at same time. This way, you will avoid having to keep part of dinner warm while waiting for rest to cook.

2. Incidentally, a double boiler is useful for keeping food hot. But if you have more than one food to keep warm, pour boiling water into large shallow pan over low heat; set covered utensils of food in pan.

3. An automatic coffee maker can keep coffee hot indefinitely.

4. Dovetail meat and vegetables. If meat is sliced or in individual portions, arrange one or more vegetables around it on platter. Or put vegetables in center, meat around them.

5. Or, if possible, arrange vegetables on one platter. For example, place peas in center and broiled tomatoes around them. Or use a compartmented vegetable dish that holds 2 vegetables.

6. Plan to let host serve the main course — meat, vegetables, gravy. You, as hostess, may serve salad, dessert, and beverage.

7. Host arranges a main course serving on plate in front of him. This is passed to hostess. She exchanges it for her empty dinner plate, which is returned to host for next serving. Person to her right is served next, and so on around the table (see The ABCs of Serving, 1, p. 67).

8. Let the children help take dishes to and from the table.

9. If you want to eliminate all at-table serving, arrange entire main course on heated individual dinner plates in kitchen.

10. Hot breads — popovers, muffins, corn bread, biscuits, hot rolls, gingerbread — seem all the more tempting if served right from pan in which they were baked. But don't forget a table pad under the hot dish. Of course you may use a napkin-lined basket.

11. The beverage may be poured by hostess at table — at dessert time or immediately after dessert has been cleared. Bring in tray with coffeepot or coffee maker (or teapot), sugar bowl, creamer (or plate of lemon), etc., as well as cups and saucers with spoons in place (each spoon is placed at back of saucer, with handle parallel to cup handle).

12. Or fill coffee cups in kitchen; place cup, with spoon in place on saucer, to right of each guest.

13. Or serve coffee in living room after dessert. Carry coffee tray to living room; place on low table where beverage can be poured comfortably. Or pass tray with filled demitasse or regular coffee cups, sugar bowl, and creamer.

14. Or omit dessert at table and, with coffee in living room, pass cookies, special candy, or finger fruit.

LITTLE DINNERS — FALL AND WINTER

A COMMUNITY VENTURE — EACH COOK CONTRIBUTES A DISH

ROAST DUCKLING WITH ORANGE GLAZE, p. 286

MEDLEY OF WILD AND FLUFFY WHITE RICE

BEANS TRES BIEN, p. 403

TOSSED GREEN SALAD

MUSHROOM FAN-TANS, p. 495

COFFEE BAVARIAN CREAM, p. 574

STUFFED DATES   SALTED ALMONDS

COFFEE

ELITE

ROAST BEEF TENDERLOIN, p. 177
BORDELAISE SAUCE, p. 531
BAKED ACORN SQUASH WITH PEAS
SPEEDY PICKLED PEACHES, p. 433
WATERMELON RIND
ENDIVE SALAD, p. 448
COLD MARBLE-BAVARIAN SOUFFLE, p. 582
COFFEE

HOMEY GOODNESS

HUNGARIAN GOULASH, p. 188, ON BUTTERED NOODLES
BUTTERED PEAS
WILTED LETTUCE, p. 449
COLOSSAL CORN BREAD, p. 506
CRANBERRY-FLUFF PIE, p. 600, OR
PEACH OF A PIE, p. 597
COFFEE

CONTINENTAL

VEAL PARMIGIANO, p. 233
ZUCCHINI, ITALIAN STYLE, p. 419
MARINATED TOMATOES
TOASTED FRENCH BREAD WEDGES
QUICKIE FRENCH TARTS, p. 603
DEMITASSE

ROYAL HOLIDAY DINNER

HERB CHEESE MELBA ROUNDS, p. 155
HOLIDAY CROWN ROAST OF PORK, p. 200
PEAS WITH CELERY
CAULIFLOWER SUPREME, p. 399
CARROT CURLS AND RIPE OLIVES
COFFEE JELLY WITH HOLIDAY CUSTARD SAUCE, p. 537
BLACK COFFEE
ROASTED WALNUTS
BOWL OF GRAPES FOR NIBBLING

IN BELOVED TRADITION

ROAST TURKEY WITH DOWN-SOUTH STUFFING, p. 339
LOTS OF GRAVY
CANDIED SWEET POTATOES, p. 410
BRUSSELS SPROUTS WITH PEAS
CREAMED ONIONS
RELISH TRAY: OLIVES, CELERY, CRANBERRY SAUCE,
WATERMELON PICKLE, SPICED PEACHES
PUMPKIN OR SQUASH CHIFFON PIE, p. 599
(For the Children: Ice-Cream Pumpkins,
Cookies, Milk)
COFFEE
BOWL OF FRUITS AND NUTS

HEARTY GOODNESS

CRANBERRY-PINEAPPLE FRUIT JUICE
SWEDISH BRAISED SHORT RIBS, p. 186
SWEET-POTATO SOUFFLE, p. 410
BRUSSELS-SPROUTS MEDLEY, p. 396
WARM RYE-BREAD FINGERS, p. 494
SNOW-PEAK BAKED APPLES, p. 544
COFFEE

DELIGHTFUL DINING

CHICKEN DELLA ROBBIA, p. 268,
WITH FLUFFY RICE
BUTTERED PEAS   ENDIVE SALAD, p. 448
BROWN 'N' SERVE BRIOCHES
TOASTED SNOW SQUARES, p. 574
HOT TEA

ROBUST FARE

BEEF BIRDS WITH OLIVE GRAVY, p. 188
BAKED ACORN SQUASH, p. 415
BROCCOLI, CALIFORNIA STYLE, p. 396
DILL PICKLE STRIPS
PUMPERNICKEL AND RYE BREAD
(bought or homemade)
CHEESECAKE DIVINE, p. 580
COFFEE

DELICIOUSLY DIFFERENT

CHICKEN A LA KING ON
MASHED SWEET POTATOES
PEAS AND SCALLIONS
JELLIED CRANBERRY SAUCE
BUTTER DIPS, p. 477
FLUFFY STEAMED FIG PUDDING, p. 570
COFFEE or TEA

A NEW MAN AT THE OFFICE

BEEFSTEAK, PIZZA STYLE, p. 181
CASSEROLE RYE BATTER BREAD, p. 507
CRISP ONION RELISH, p. 439
SKY-HIGH CHOCOLATE CREAM CAKE, p. 637
COFFEE (instant)

OCTOBER SPECIAL

PORK CHOPS ITALIANO, p. 204
BAKED POTATOES
SPINACH SALAD BOWL
CHOCOLATE FROSTED PEARS, p. 553
ORANGE-COCONUT BARS, p. 667
COFFEE WITH A TWIST OF LEMON

SOMEWHAT SOUTHERN

CREAM-OF-SHRIMP SOUP (frozen)
BAKED BROILERS SAUTERNE, p. 270
FRIED SWEET POTATOES, p. 410
PEAS AND SCALLIONS
CREAMY CELERY SLAW, p. 456
WALNUT MERINGUE PIE, p. 592
DEMITASSE

STARRING SAUERBRATEN

GREEN TURTLE SOUP
SAUERBRATEN, p. 184   BUTTERED NOODLES
CARROTS VICHY, p. 398
RIPE OLIVES   MARINATED ARTICHOKES
RYE TOASTIES, p. 494
BUTTERY BAKED PEACHES OR PEARS, p. 553
HOT TEA

FOR THE SLENDER GOURMET

HOT TOMATO JUICE
CHICKEN LIVER SAUTE, CURRIED, p. 275
BAKED POTATOES   BROCCOLI
BROILED GRAPEFRUIT, p. 549
COFFEE or TEA

BRING YOUR PARTNER

ITALIAN PORK-AND-RICE CASSEROLE, p. 201, or
BAKED PORK CHOPS WITH MIXED BEANS, p. 204
SPINACH SALAD A LA GRECQUE, p. 448
TOASTED CHEESE-TOPPED ENGLISH MUFFINS
SUSAN'S SLIPPED CUSTARD PIE, p. 127
COFFEE

BACHELOR'S TREAT

SAVORY LIMA-BEAN POT, p. 401
MAX'S SPINACH-BACON SALAD BOWL, p. 447
CRANBERRY CHUTNEY, p. 440
SAVORY FRENCH BREAD, p. 493
CHOCOLATE-ALMOND DEVIL'S-FOOD CAKE, p. 623
MILK or COFFEE

AFTER BUSINESS DINNER PARTY

BIG BURGER, p. 191
SKILLET CHINESE CABBAGE, p. 397
BEET AND HORSE-RADISH RELISH, p. 439
ONION-RYE ROLLS IN LOAF, p. 492
FROZEN CHOCOLATE RUSSE, p. 610
COFFEE or TEA

FESTIVE FARE

CREAMY GARLIC-CHEESE DIP, p. 156
ITALIAN BREAD STICKS
RIPE OLIVES
TWIN ROAST CHICKENS
GREEN LIMAS AND SCALLIONS, p. 404
WILLIE MAE'S CRANBERRY SHERBET
(instead of cranberry sauce)
RUM-PUMPKIN CREAM CUSTARDS, p. 564
DEMITASSE

A FESTIVE FEAST IN LIMITED SPACE

CRANBERRY-GLAZED HAM ROLLS, p. 214
HOT BUTTERED SQUASH
BUTTERED BROCCOLI
MIXED CRISP CRACKERS
ROQUEFORT SALAD BOWL
BRANDIED APRICOTS, p. 545
with
OLD-DOMINION POUNDCAKE, p. 624
(or frozen poundcake)
COFFEE
BUTTER MINTS

LITTLE DINNERS— SPRING AND SUMMER

HOT MEAL FOR A COOL NIGHT

CUTLET OF VEAL A LA SUISSE, p. 231
HOT TOSSED PEAS WITH RICE
ORANGE-SPINACH SALAD BOWL
WITH HORSE-RADISH DRESSING
HARD ROLLS
CREME DE CACAO ANGEL FOOD, p. 637
ICED COFFEE

"... AND AFTERWARD A BRIDGE GAME"

PIQUANT LAMB STEW, p. 221
FLUFFY PARSLEY RICE
HOT ASPARAGUS or ASPARAGUS VINAIGRETTE
THE BREAD — FRENCH HALF-AND-HALF, p. 493
MOONLIGHT CAKE WITH STRAWBERRIES, p. 632
COFFEE

PATIO PICNIC SUPPER

BROILED DUCKLING, p. 286
CRUSHED PINEAPPLE RELISH, p. 437
WATER-CRESS SANDWICHES
CHOCOLATE-SUNDAE CAKE, p. 622
LEMONADE

ITALIAN DINNER PARTY

TRAY OF FINOCCHI or CELERY AND RIPE OLIVES
TAGLIARINI WITH CHICKEN LIVERS, p. 380
BREAD STICKS   FRENCH BREAD
GREEN BEANS PARMESAN, p. 451
FRUIT COMPOTE WITH CHIANTI
(peaches, apricots, grapefruit)
MERINGUES or MACAROONS
ESPRESSO, p. 679

FAVORITE FEAST

ROAST LAMB WITH CHILI MUSTARD SAUCE, p. 219
BAKED SWEET POTATOES
TOSSED GREEN SALAD
WHOLE-WHEAT BREAD
(homemade or bought)
SWEET BUTTER
FRUITED CREME BRULEE, p. 565
COFFEE   MILK

AFTER THE BOAT RACES

CHILLED COCKTAILS AND CANAPES
BOEUF BOURGIGNON I, p. 189
GNOCCHI, p. 347
MELBA TOAST
FRENCH-STYLE GREEN BEANS
CARAMEL-CUSTARD MOLD, p. 563
COFFEE

DINING DECK SUPPER

BOUILLON-ON-THE-ROCKS, p. 163
or
SHRIMP TO DIP IN SPICY DUNK SAUCE, p. 530
LAMB SHANKS WITH PARSLEY POCKETS, p. 224
VENETIAN RICE AND PEAS, p. 373
CARROTS VICHY, p. 398
QUICK FRENCH BREAD, p. 479
CHERRY-SHERRY JUBILEE, p. 562
COFFEE

LAST MINUTE INVITE

SEA-FOOD COCKTAIL, LIVING ROOM STYLE
ITALIAN VEAL ROLLS, p. 230
GOLDEN RICE, p. 371
ASPARAGUS WITH ALMONDS
FRESH FIGS or BUNCHLETS OF GRAPES
CAMEMBERT CHEESE
SHREDDED WHEAT WAFERS
COFFEE

YOUNG IN FEELING

CHICKEN TETRAZZINI, p. 121
BROILED CANDIED APRICOTS
GARLICKY MIXED GREEN SALAD
TOASTED ENGLISH MUFFINS
PEPPERMINT-VANILLA ICE CREAM, p. 609
BIG CUPS OF COFFEE

A POLISHED PERFORMANCE

CHICKEN IN WINE, p. 269
TOSSED GREEN SALAD BOWL
WHOLE-WHEAT FRENCH BREAD
FRESH PINEAPPLE AND STRAWBERRY SUPREME, p. 555
SUPERB DANISH COFFEE TWIST, p. 508
DEMITASSE

CONNECTICUT SUPPER

SPAGHETTI WITH ITALIAN WHITE CLAM SAUCE, p. 381
(as an introduction)
BARBECUED SPARERIBS, p. 206
TOSSED GREEN SALAD
BROWN 'N' SERVE FRENCH BREAD
WATERMELON SCOOPS, p. 557
STRONG BLACK COFFEE

A SUNDAY DINNER IN SPRING

STANDING RIB ROAST
NEW POTATOES AND SLICED GREEN ONIONS
WATER-CRESS SALAD WITH FRENCH DRESSING
CORN CRISPS, p. 115
FROSTED-DAIQUIRI PIE, p. 599
DEMITASSE

A TOUCH OF ELEGANCE

BOUILLON-ON-THE-ROCKS, p. 163
CHICKEN MARENGO, p. 267
GREEN BEANS AND SAUTEED MUSHROOMS
BAKED POTATOES WITH HERB BUTTER
(Add dried marjoram and basil to melted butter.)
TOSSED GREEN SALAD
COLD RASPBERRY-CREAM SOUFFLE, p. 583
DEMITASSE

A DINNER TO REMEMBER

INDIVIDUAL LAMB-SHANK ROASTS, p. 225
BROILED BANANA HALVES, p. 438
GREEN SALAD BOWL
FRENCH ONION-CHEESE LOAF, p. 493
PEAR ELEGANCE, p. 554

STEAK TONIGHT
BROILED STEAK, p. 178
HELP-YOURSELF TRAY OF SEASONINGS, p. 179
COUNTRY OR COTTAGE-FRIED POTATOES, p. 413
(optional)
ZUCCHINI, ITALIAN STYLE, p. 419
GREEN SALAD BOWL
CHOCOLATE-FLAKE BAVARIAN PIE, p. 600
COFFEE

FOR VISITING FIREMEN
CUPS OF PEA SOUP
MIXED GRILL, p. 180
TOMATO DECKERS, p. 452
TOASTED ROLLS IN LOAF, p. 492
(celery)
CHERRY-GLAZED CHEESE PIE, p. 592
COFFEE

A LOVELY COMBINATION
JELLIED CONSOMME WITH A LIME WEDGE
RADISHES, CELERY, CRACKERS, CHEESE
CHICKEN PIE (with biscuit topping), p. 109
ZUCCHINI, CHINESE STYLE, p. 419
RHUBARB-STRAWBERRY DELIGHT WITH
PINEAPPLE, p. 556
COFFEE or TEA

A MAN'S MEAL
LONDON BROIL, p. 182
BROCCOLI WITH LEMON HOLLANDAISE, p. 531
BUTTERED CORN AND LIMAS
LETTUCE-CUCUMBER-AND-DILL SALAD
TOASTED ENGLISH MUFFINS or
BEST BRAN MUFFINS, p. 481
PICCADILLY TRIFLE, p. 560
ICED TEA

FAVORITES ALL
BROILED CHICKEN PIQUANT, p. 264
CORN FRITTERS, p. 400
BROCCOLI TOPPED WITH PEAS
BOSTON LETTUCE WITH
CREAMY DANISH BLUE CHEESE DRESSING
SEMISWEET-COFFEE CUSTARDS, p. 564
COFFEE

SERVE PROUDLY
FRANKURTERS GARNI, p. 246
GNOCCHI AU GRATIN, p. 412
OLD-FASHIONED LETTUCE BOWL, p. 119
BREAD STICKS
FROSTED PINEAPPLE, p. 555
COFFEE

STANDBY SUPPER
A MAN'S BARBECUED CHICKEN, p. 271
POTATO SALAD WITH
SAUERKRAUT DRESSING, p. 454
RAW-RELISH TRAY
TOASTED FRENCH BREAD
LIME-SNOW PIE, p. 599
COFFEE — HOT or COLD

EXTRA NICE
SPECIAL LAMB STEAKS (BARBECUE), p. 224
BROILED PEACH HALVES WITH CURRANT JELLY
CHINESE ASPARAGUS, p. 395
TOASTED ENGLISH MUFFINS or CORN CRISPS, p. 115
FROSTED COFFEE BAVARIAN PIE, p. 600
DEMITASSE

BACKYARD DINING
CHARCOAL-GRILLED TURKEY, p. 735
CUSTARD CORN PUDDING, p. 400, or
GARLIC-BUTTERED CORN
WHOLE TOMATOES, CUCUMBER FINGERS,
OLIVES, ROMAINE LEAVES
BREAD STICKS
CHERRIES ON STEMS or PEACHES
WEDGE OF CHEDDAR CHEESE
LEMONADE
(made from concentrate)

BUFFET-STYLE SUPPERS

You may want to serve from a sideboard, dining table, living room table (pulled out from, or pushed against, a wall), or top of a low bookcase or chest of drawers.

It's Easy If ...

1. All dishes are completely or partly made ahead.

2. A light first course is served in living room while you handle last-minute details.

3. The food is all fork food — no large pieces that require knife cutting, nothing unmanageable on plates.

4. Whole main course fits on one large dinner plate.

5. Bread is buttered, ready to eat.

6. Casseroles are part of the menu. (You can cook and serve in same dish — and keep food hot longer, as well.)

7. You replenish food when necessary and invite guests to come again for seconds.

8. Water and glasses, coffee and cups, spoons, etc., wait on a side table, where guests may help themselves at any time during meal.

9. A friend removes main course dishes while you clear buffet table for dessert.

How to Route Traffic

At a buffet supper, guests should be able to move easily around the serving table and to serve themselves in logical order, as below. To set the buffet table you may want to use one of the arrangements shown in diagrams A, B, and C.

Arrange plates and food (each dish with its own serving silver), etc., so they can be picked up in this order: napkins, dinner plates, hot dishes, cold dishes (or cold dishes, hot dishes), salad, bread, relishes, forks.

If you can, leave enough room between serving dishes so guests can put down their plates while serving themselves.

If The Crowd is Large

If you have invited quite a large group, you will expedite proceedings if you can arrange duplicate services and let guests form two lines instead of one. (See diagram C.) Guests help themselves; or for extra-speedy service, let two friends serve main dishes and let guests help themselves to salad, bread, relishes.

Where Shall They Sit?

Set up bridge or folding tables in dining or living room. (If space is short, have someone do this while guests serve themselves.)

Or serve, buffet style, from sideboard, and seat guests at dining table just as you would for a sit-down supper.

Or provide trays already set with silver, napkins, etc. Let guests eat from trays on their laps.

Or let guests use end tables, coffee table, desktop, nest of tables, etc. — any surface they can find — to accommodate their coffee, glasses, etc.

Or (especially for a young crowd) let guests sit on stairs, floor, or anywhere they like.

What to Do About Dessert

When the main course is over, ask a friend to remove dinner plates to kitchen while you clear buffet table and reset it with dessert, dessert plates, silver, and coffee service.

Or use a combination centerpiece-dessert — a basket of fruit or a decorated cake — and let guests help themselves whenever they're ready.

Or serve dessert yourself in kitchen and simply pass filled dessert plates.

Or set up dessert on side table.

If coffee accompanies the main course but the buffet table won't accommodate it, put it on a side table, with cups, cream, sugar, etc., plus water pitcher and glasses, if you like. If it's to be served only with dessert, put it on the buffet table or a side table.

A. WHEN THE BUFFET TABLE IS AGAINST A WALL

B. FOR A BUFFET TABLE IN THE CENTER OF THE ROOM

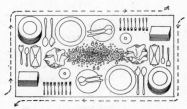

C. FOR A CROWD, DUPLICATE SERVICE AT EITHER END

BUFFETS

GALA BUFFET FOR V.I.P.'S

BEEF STROGANOFF, p. 180, WITH WILD RICE, p. 375

GREEN BEANS WITH HERB SAUCE, p. 403

HELEN'S TOSSED GREEN SALAD, p. 446

RADISH-ROSE TOWER

PETITE DINNER ROLLS

AMBROSIA SHELLS, p. 552

LOTS OF COFFEE

THE MORE THE MERRIER
(smart thrift that doesn't show)

MEAT-BALL STEW EN CASSEROLE, p. 193

ROMAINE SALAD, p. 448

CORN CRISPS (seeded), p. 115

WINTER BREAD PUDDING, p. 571
or RICE-PEACH MELBA, p. 572

HOT COFFEE

BUFFET FEAST WITHOUT FLUSTER

SHRIMP RELISH, p. 146

SPOONBREAD TAMALE BAKE, p. 196

BREAD STICKS

TOSSED SALAD OF GREENS, ONION RINGS,
ORANGE SEGMENTS

LIME MILK SHERBET, p. 612

PRALINE COOKIES, p. 668

COFFEE or TEA

VIENNESE STYLE

VEAL PAPRIKA, p. 228

TOSSED GREEN SALAD BOWL

RAW RELISH PLATTER
(carrot curls, celery fans, assorted olives,
avocado slices, green-and-red-pepper relish)

WARM RYE-BREAD FINGERS, p. 494

WALNUT-MERINGUE TORTE, p. 616

COFFEE

TWO-CASSEROLE BUFFET

SUSAN'S CHICKEN TETRAZZINI, p. 121

COLONEL'S LADY'S SALAD BOWL, p. 449

WATERMELON PICKLE   HEATED BUTTERED ROLLS

CHERRIES FLAMBE, p. 547

COFFEE (instant)

FOR THOSE WHO LIKE THE CONTINENTAL

LOBSTER THERMIDOR WITH PILAF, p. 320

CRISP ARTICHOKE SALAD, p. 450

GREEN AND RIPE OLIVES

BREAD STICKS   CHEESE CUBES

LARGE BABA AU RHUM, p. 580

TEA

GATHERING OF THE CLAN

ROAST ROCK-CORNISH HENS ON COMPANY RICE, p. 371

POLISH MUSHROOMS WITH SOUR CREAM, p. 407

PARSLEYED PEAS

SALAD RUSSE
(tossed salad with grated raw beets)

BRAIDED BREAD (bought)
or SWISS LEMON-TWIST BREAD, p. 511

PINEAPPLE SOPHISTICATE, p. 555   SWEETMEATS

DEMITASSE

COLLEGIANS HOME FOR THE HOLIDAYS

HONEYED PINEAPPLE-HAM LOAF, p. 109

MASHED-POTATO CAKES, p. 412

GREEN BEANS PARMESAN, p. 451

CORN STICKS, p. 482

RICH, REAL FRENCH CHOCOLATE, p. 681

JUST A LITTLE BIT DIFFERENT

CURRIED-LAMB STEW
WITH POPPY-SEED NOODLES, p. 378

HELEN'S TOSSED GREEN SALAD, p. 446

EASY BREAD STICKS, p. 494

PEACH GLACE PIE, p. 598

HOT TEA

CELEBRATION BUFFET

THIN VEAL FORESTIER, p. 232

RING OF BUTTERED CARROTS WITH
ARTICHOKE HEARTS IN CENTER

OUR GIANT POPOVERS, p. 481

DANISH PORCUPINE APPLES, p. 544

HOT TEA

SATURDAY NIGHT BUFFET

BEANS AND BURGERS, p. 194

SLAW SAVOY, p. 455

A BASKET OF BLUEBERRY CORN MUFFINS

A BOWL OF PRETZELS

SPANISH CREAM, p. 573   WALNUT CLUSTERS

COFFEE

SIMPLE BUT SUMPTUOUS

MAZZETTI, p. 195

BUTTERY PEAS AND GREEN BEANS

CHEESE CRESCENTS, p. 479

HOT FRUIT COMPOTE A LA MODE, p. 555

COFFEE
(instant)

INEXPENSIVE AND LUSCIOUS
MEAT BALLS STROGANOFF, p. 193
HOT FLUFFY RICE FLECKED WITH DILL
PICKLED BEETS   CELERY STICKS
POPPY-SEED-BUTTERED MELBA TOAST
DELECTABLE TURNOVERS, p. 603
CAMEMBERT CHEESE
HOT TEA

BUFFET BOUILLABAISSE
BOUILLABAISSE, BUFFET STYLE, p. 168
TOSSED ALL-GREEN SALAD
FRESH PEARS AND BEL PAESE
or
FRENCH STRAWBERRY PIE, p. 597
HOT COFFEE
(steaming, please!)

NEIGHBORS ALL
ROAST BONELESS TURKEY ROLL, p. 283
LUSCIOUS FRUITED WALDORF SALAD, p. 465
BASKETFUL OF HOT BREADS
(Corn-Bread Sticks, Gingerbread Squares,
Toasted Seeded English Muffins,
Mushroom Fan-Tans, p. 495)
CAFE DIABLE, p. 679

A COMPANY SPECIAL
BEEF CURRY DELICIOUS, p. 187
PICKLED CANNED PINEAPPLE CHUNKS
ON ROMAINE
CORN CRISPS, p. 115
SMALL FRENCH-CHOCOLATE CUSTARDS, p. 564, or
CHOCOLATE-MOUSSE PIE, p. 598
HOT TEA

A TOUCH OF NEW ENGLAND
GOOD DRY SHERRY
BAKED-BEAN CASSEROLE, p. 401
DELICIOUS WALNUT-RAISIN BREAD, p. 483
SWEET BUTTER
TOMATO JUICE
(instead of water)
FRUIT DISH
(cut-up oranges, avocados,
bananas, and canned figs)
RICH, DELICIOUS FROZEN COFFEECAKE
LOTS OF COFFEE

DOUBLE-BILL PIZZA BUFFET
MEAT-BALL PIZZAS, p. 111
HARRIET'S SPECIAL TOSSED SALAD, p. 448
COLA DRINKS ON ICE
(Later on:)
QUICK BISCUIT TORTONI, p. 609
(from the freezer)
A BASKET OF PEACHES
COFFEE WITH A TWIST OF LEMON

BUFFET SERVING — SIT-DOWN DINING
DOUBLE TOMATO-ASPIC RINGS WITH
TUNA SALAD, p. 458
MARINATED-VEGETABLE MELANGE, p. 452
DEVILED HAM-FILLED BUTTER FLAKE ROLLS
FINGER FRUITS   ESPRESSO
CHOCOLATE-TIPPED CRESCENTS, p. 667
AND ASSORTED SWEETMEATS

SOME SUMMER BUFFETS

ROUND THE TREE BUFFET LUNCH
MEXICAN BEAN SOUP, p. 161
SEASONED POPCORN, p. 152
HAM AND CHICKEN SALAD, p. 460
RING OF ASSORTED SANDWICHES
FINGERS OF WATERMELON
CHOCOLATE HALFWAY BARS, p. 663
ICED TEA

MEDITERRANEAN FLAVOR
PEAS AND RICE PROVENCALE, p. 461
ITALIAN WHOLE-WHEAT BREAD
FRESH FRUIT HEAPED WITH LEMON ICE
MARBLE ANGEL FOOD, p. 637
HOT COFFEE

SUMMER-SKY BUFFET
CRANBERRY-HAM LOAF, p. 216
CURRIED RICE AND PEA SALAD, p. 452
CHEESE BISCUITS, p. 476
PINEAPPLE RING, p. 555
GOLDEN COCONUT MOUNDS, p. 654
COFFEE

PATIO LUAU PARTY

ICE-COLD PUNCH IN PINEAPPLE SHELLS
(served all through party)
SALTED PEANUTS
BARBECUED SHRIMP, p. 328
BARBECUED SPARERIBS II, p. 206,
WITH GRILLED BANANAS
AND BAKED SWEET POTATOES, p. 409
THREE-LAYER COCONUT CAKE
VANILLA ICE CREAM AND ORANGE SHERBET
COFFEE

FEATURING FISH

TUNA PARTY PILAF, p. 311
GREEN BEANS DE LUXE, p. 403
HERB CABBAGE SLAW ON CANNED JELLIED
CRANBERRY SLICES
WHOLE-WHEAT-BREAD-AND-BUTTER SANDWICHES
LEMON ICE CREAM   PECAN CAKE, p. 622
COFFEE or TEA

SUNDAY BRUNCH ON THE PORCH

GRAPEFRUIT or ORANGE JUICE
FRUIT FROM A BASKET
DEVILED EGGS AND BACON MORNAY, p. 364
BROILED TOMATOES
TOASTED CORN-BREAD SQUARES, p. 483
ORANGE MARMALADE
ENGLISH TEACAKES, p. 664
COFFEE

CABANA BUFFET

TAKE-YOUR-PICK PITCHER SOUPS
(frozen split pea, canned madrilene)
CHILI CON CARNE, p. 194, ON TOASTED CORN BREAD
AVOCADO-SWISS-CHEESE-AND-ONION SALAD
CHOCOLATE-CHIP-WALNUT PIE, p. 591
COFFEE A LA MODE
(ice cream floated on coffee)

INFORMAL FARE

OVEN-FRIED DRUMSTICKS, p. 272
CHIVE-BUTTERED CORN ON THE COB
DILLED PEAS WITH ARTICHOKE HEARTS
SOUR-CREAM SLAW, p. 455
ASSORTED BREAD TRAY
(Pumpernickel Sandwiches, Toasted English
Muffins, p. 496, and
Sesame Crackers)
VANILLA ICE-CREAM AND ORANGE-SHERBET BALLS,
CHOCOLATE-SAUCE-TOPPED
COFFEE

FROM BASKETS OR BOWLS

CHILLED CURRY-AVOCADO SOUP, p. 162
(in paper cups)
FRIED CHICKEN SUPERB, p. 265
OLD-FASHIONED POTATO SALAD, p. 453
BOUQUET OF RAW RELISHES
CRANBERRY-FILLED CLING PEACHES
HELP-YOURSELF COOKIE TRAY   COFFEE

BARBECUE BUFFET

PINEAPPLE-SPARERIB BARBECUE, p. 206
OLD-TIME SCALLOPED POTATOES, p. 413
SESAME-SEED WAFERS
SPINACH SALAD A LA GRECQUE, p. 448
CHERRY TOMATOES
FRUITFUL COBBLER, p. 569, A LA MODE
ICED TEA

FAVORITE SUMMER BUFFET

CREAMY AVOCADO DIP, p. 156, WITH CRACKERS
GLAZED BONELESS SHOULDER BUTT, p. 212
EGGPLANT PARMESAN, p. 402
HELEN'S TOSSED GREEN SALAD, p. 446
GARLIC FRENCH BREAD
WALNUT SQUARES, p. 662   FRESH FRUIT
COFFEE

COUNTRY-HOME BUFFET BREAKFAST

FINGER FRUITS, p. 139
PUNCH-CUP ORANGE JUICE
CEREAL TO MUNCH
BROILED-HAM SLICE
(with brown sugar and mustard)
OVEN-EASY CHICKEN, p. 265 (served cold)
GRILL-TOASTED CORN BREAD
HOT BUTTERED SYRUP
COFFEE

SPUR-OF-THE-MOMENT BUFFET LUNCH

MUGS OF CURRY-POTATO SOUP, p. 162
HAM LOAF, SALAMI, GOUDA CHEESE
KIDNEY-BEAN SOPHISTICATE, p. 401
LONG, THIN FRENCH BREAD
A BIT OF SPICE: SWEET PICKLES, DILL PICKLES,
PICKLED PEACHES
TOMATO WEDGES, CUCUMBER FINGERS, YOUNG
SCALLIONS, ROSY RADISHES WITH CURRY
MAYONNAISE
PRALINE ICE-CREAM RING, p. 616
or PRALINE CRUNCH, p. 616
COFFEE — HOT or COLD

THE COOL DISH AND THE WARM

DOWN-EAST CORN CHOWDER, p. 162

MELANGE OF HOT AND COLD MEATS

TWIN VEGETABLE SALAD, p. 452

APPLE-CHEESE PIE, p. 588

COFFEE

BARBECUES WITH, FOR, AND BY MEN

AD MAN SWEARS BY...

GEOFF'S BARBECUED CHUCK ROAST, p. 732

GEOFF'S ROSIN-BAKED POTATOES, p. 737

SWEET CORN

BIG SALAD

(tossed cucumbers laced with
French dressing plus a whiff of anchovy paste)

FRUIT, CRACKERS, CHEESE

HOT COFFEE

EXPERT ON FOOD RECOMMENDS...

SHORT RIBS OONA LOA, p. 732

SPUDS BAKED IN FOIL, p. 736

(topped with gobs of butter
or with sour cream and chives)

HEARTS-OF-ROMAINE SALAD

TOASTED FRENCH or ITALIAN BREAD

ANGEL or CHIFFON CAKE WITH ICE CREAM

LEMONADE

(if you wish)

LOS ANGELES SALESMAN COOKS...

LEMON-BARBECUED ROCK-LOBSTER TAILS, p. 736

BEANS TRES BIEN, p. 403

OVEN-BAKED POTATOES or
GEOFF'S ROSIN-BAKED POTATOES, p. 737

TRAY OF HELP-YOURSELF TOPPINGS

A SUNDAE

(oh, any kind)

ICED TEA

YOUNG ENGINEER MAKES SUPPER OF...

PINEAPPLE-BARBECUED CHICKS, p. 735

FOIL-WRAPPED SWEET POTATOES (baked in coals)

RIPE RED TOMATOES

BUTTERED FRENCH BREAD

ICE CREAM

SOFT DRINKS

MIDWESTERN BUSINESSMAN SPECIALIZES IN...

SALT-GRILLED STEAK — NAVIN, p. 731

MUSHROOM-TOPPED TOMATOES

AVOCADO SALAD WITH CHOPPED SCALLIONS

MELON A LA MODE

(ice cream spooned right
from electric freezer)

TOASTED MARSHMALLOWS

(the children toast them)

ART DIRECTOR SERVES...

BARBECUED FLAPJACKS, p. 732

ASPARAGUS VINAIGRETTE

or

A SPECIAL COLESLAW

COFFEE ICE CREAM (with a sprinkling of
ground coffee or coffee liqueur)

COFFEE

ARTIST AND PHOTOGRAPHER MAKES...

The Introduction

MUGS OF HOT PEA SOUP or

CHILLED TOMATO JUICE

HOT BITS OF GRILLED LOBSTER TAIL

The Main Course

BARBECUED SPARERIBS, p. 733

NEW POTATOES BAKED IN FOIL

AVOCADO SALAD WITH LIME FRENCH DRESSING

The Dessert

SOUR-CREAM-TOPPED BLUEBERRIES

ENGINEER FROM TURKEY CONSTRUCTS...

TURKISH SHISH KEBAB, p. 735

RAISIN PILAF, p. 373

GREEN-BEAN SALAD

FRENCH BREAD

WATERMELON or SLICED PEACHES IN RED WINE

DEMITASSE

P.R. MAN PREPARES THIS ELEGANT...

FILET OF BEEF AFLAME, p. 731

FRESH PLUCKED CORN

(roasted over the coals)

HANDSOME BEEFSTEAK-TOMATO SLICES

("dressed to taste")

RAISIN OR ONE OF THE CRISP BREADS

QUARTERS OF FRESH PINEAPPLE

CHOCOLATE FROSTED COOKIES

A LONG, COOL DRINK

C.P.A. COUPLES TWO FAVORITES IN...

CHILI-FRANK BURGERS, p. 733
CRISP BREAD FROM A BASKET
GREEN-PEPPER COLESLAW
(surrounded by avocado quarters in shells
topped with lime wedges)
LEMON SHERBET
(garnished with Bing cherries, stems on)
ICED TEA

EX-ARMY COLONEL MAKES...

MINTED LAMB, ROTISSERIE STYLE, p. 734
GRILL-BAKED POTATO IN FOIL
(topped with butter and chopped sweet onion)
GREEN SALAD WITH CREAMY ROQUEFORT DRESSING
HERB-BUTTERED ITALIAN BREAD
HOLLOWED-OUT WATERMELON
(filled with the cut-up melon and other fruits
plus a dash of Cointreau, if desired)
HOT COFFEE
MILK SHAKES FOR THE YOUNG FOLKS

MANHATTANITE, WITH SKYLINE TERRACE, FIXES...

BARBECUED LAMB SHANKS, p. 734
DEMI CORN ON THE COB (half ears of corn)
WATER CRESS AND CUCUMBER SALAD
ITALIAN DRESSING (from mix)
GRILL-TOASTED ENGLISH MUFFINS
HONEYDEW AND CANTALOUPE TRAY
CRISP CHOCOLATE COOKIES
ICED TEA or COFFEE

STYLIST PRODUCES...

AVOCADO AND HEART OF PALM SALAD
(first course à la California)
GRILLED ROCK-LOBSTER TAILS, p. 736
WITH GARDEN PILAF, p. 373
BERRY-TOPPED LEMON-CHIFFON PIE
INSTANT ICED TEA

IF YOU GO FORMAL

There are times when you will want to have a more formal dinner and know exactly how to go about it.

THE TABLE LINEN: For formal use, it's still linen, lace, organdy, a fine synthetic in white or pastel, or an embroidered cloth. Use linen or fine rayon damask over a table pad (for protection); or use a lace, embroidered, or organdy cloth on a bare table. (Cloth overhang should be about 15″ to 18″.) Or use fine lace or embroidered organdy place mats.

Fold each napkin into an oblong. Place on service plate. Or if you are serving a first course, place to left of fork.

PLACING SILVER, CHINA, ETC.:
1. Place service plate in center of each place, 1″ in from edge of place mat or table. Bread-and-butter plates are not used.
2. Set up each place with flat silver, 1″ in from edge of place mat or table, as in diagram, below. Arrange plate, goblet, and wineglasses as shown. Dessert silver is placed just before dessert course, as in Serving Dessert, p. 68.

If you're serving soup, use bouillon cups or rimmed soup plates; place as in Dinner Is Served, p. 67. Also see Who'll Sit Where, p. 56, and Maid for the Occasion, below.

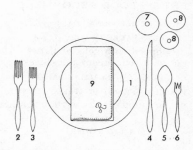

FORMAL DINNER SETTING

1. Service plate
2. Dinner fork
3. Salad fork
4. Dinner knife
5. Cream-soup spoon or dessertspoon for soup
6. Oyster fork for sea-food cocktail
7. Water goblet
8. Wineglasses
9. Dinner napkin, folded into oblong, on dinner plate

MAID FOR THE OCCASION
(basic information every hostess should have)

Smooth service at the table is the ambition of every hostess. Whether you have employed a full-time or part-time maid, she can make a dinner or luncheon party a real joy or a complete nightmare. Everything depends on the training and instructions the maid gets.

Until your maid is letter-perfect, it's helpful to write out for her the menu plus a set of detailed directions. Plan to practice beforehand so she knows exactly what is expected of her. Here are the directions to give her.

The ABCs of Serving

1. Serve hostess first, unless otherwise directed, then person to her right, and so on around table to her right. Exception: When serving 4 persons, skip host; then step back and serve him last, so guest at hostess' left will not be last.
2. Stand at left of each person to place, remove, and offer dishes. Exceptions: To place beverages and dessert silver, stand at right, to avoid reaching in front of guest.
3. To exchange plates, remove used plate with left hand; place new one with right hand, standing at left side of each person, as above.
4. To offer food, hold platter or serving dish flat on palm of left hand. If platter or dish is especially heavy, it may be steadied with right hand. Always offer side of platter or serving dish. See that handles of serving fork (at left) and spoon or knife (at right) are pointed toward person being served. (Rearrange, if necessary, after each guest has helped himself.) Offer dish low enough and close enough to guest to make serving easy.
5. What about service napkins and tray? Fold service napkin (like table napkin, if possible) into square. Place on left hand; use, like a tray, under all serving dishes; do not use when exchanging plates, removing salad or bread-and-butter plates, or carrying two plates. Napkin protects hand from warm and cold dishes, hides hand under glass dishes. For small dishes, use small tray (with napkin under it).
6. Refill water goblets when they're empty, but do not lift them from table. Keep napkin in left hand to catch stray drops.
7. Before starting to serve, have everything ready for that course.
8. Serve hot food on heated plates; serve cold food on chilled dishes.
9. Move quietly and unobtrusively. In emergencies, or if you are uncertain, do the thing that least disturbs a guest.
10. Do not touch guests when serving.
11. Handle lower part of goblets, never top.
12. Do not let thumb extend over rim of plates.

13. Do not start to remove a course until all persons have finished eating.
14. To remove dishes, remove all serving dishes and platters first; then used plates, glasses, silver, etc.; then unused silver, salts and peppers, etc.

Just before Dinner is Served

1. Fill goblets three quarters full of water.
2. If you're using bread-and-butter plates, place individual butter pat or ball on each plate.
3. Set chair at each place, with front of seat flush with table edge.
4. Light candles.
5. If fruit, fruit or sea-food cocktails, or oysters are being served as the first course, place service on service plates on table before dinner is announced.

If soup is the first course, place service on table just before or after guests are seated.
6. Announce dinner: Stand in doorway; catch hostess' eye; say softly, "Dinner is served."
7. During first course, pass crackers, etc.

Serving the Main Course

1. Bring heated dinner plates from kitchen, one at a time; exchange for first course service and service plates. Or bring two dinner plates from kitchen at a time; leave one on serving table while exchanging other for first course service. Take out two first course services and service plates together.
2. Offer platter of meat, then vegetables, gravy, bread, and relishes.
3. Take meat platter and vegetable serving dishes back to the kitchen; rearrange for second servings, ready to pass.
4. Or if host carves or serves meat, after exchanging first course for heated dinner plates, as in step 1 above, bring in carving set on tray or napkin. Place carving fork (at left) and knife and serving spoon (at right) in front of host. Then place meat platter before host.
5. Stand at host's left, with extra heated dinner plate in right hand. When he has arranged meat on dinner plate in front of him, pick it up with left hand and replace it with extra dinner plate in right hand. Take filled plate to hostess, removing her heated plate with right hand and placing filled dinner plate with left

hand. Take this heated plate back to host, and proceed as before. Repeat until everyone is served. Then pass vegetables, gravy, bread, relishes.

6. Serve additional butter; refill water goblets when empty.

Serving Salad

1. Remove meat platter and carving set or serving silver, if used at table.
2. Bring in individual salads (one or two at a time) as in Serving the Main Course, 1, p. 67, exchanging them for dinner plates.
3. Or replace dinner plates with empty individual salad plates; then pass salad bowl.
4. Or place salad fork and spoon, then salad bowl and pile of salad plates, in front of, or a little to left of, hostess. As hostess fills each salad plate, place it before guest, from left.
5. Sometimes a simple salad of tossed greens is served with the main course. In this case, when setting table, place salad plate to left of service plate at each place. Then after meat, vegetables, and gravy have been served, salad bowl should be passed.

Clearing the Table for Dessert

1. Remove salad bowl. From each place, remove salad plate with right hand and bread-and-butter plate with left hand. Or if salad was served with main course, remove dinner plate with right hand and salad plate with left. Then remove bread-and-butter plates, two at a time.
2. Remove salts, peppers, and unused silver onto small tray.
3. Crumb table if necessary, using small napkin and plate.
4. Refill water goblets.

Serving Dessert

1. At each place, place dessert plate, with dessert fork on left side of plate and dessertspoon on right side, parallel to each other. (Guest removes fork and spoon to table, placing fork to left and spoon to right of dessert plate.) Pass dessert, then sauce or cakes.
2. Or put dessert silver on small tray — 1 dessert fork and dessertspoon or teaspoon for each person — and place to right of each place. Then

place dessert, which has been arranged on individual dessert plates in kitchen.
3. Or for a very simple meal, arrange dessert on individual serving dishes in kitchen, with necessary silver — fork or spoon — in place on each plate. Then place.

If Finger Bowls Are Used

1. If finger bowls are used, fill one third full with lukewarm water. Place bowl, with small doily under it, on each dessert plate, with dessert fork to left and dessertspoon to right of finger bowl on plate. Place before each guest from left.
2. Then pass dessert. (Guest removes fork and spoon to table, placing fork to left and spoon to right of dessert plate. He places finger bowl with doily a little to left, just above dessert plate.)

If A Fruit Course Follows Dessert

1. If fruit is to be served after dessert, do not serve finger bowls on dessert plates. Instead, place dessert plate, with silver in place, at each cover; then pass dessert.
2. When dessert has been completed, exchange each dessert plate for fruit plate, with finger bowl and doily in center, and fruit fork to left and fruit knife to right of bowl on plate. (Guest removes silver and finger bowl, as in If Finger Bowls Are Used, 2 above.) Pass bowl of fruit.

Serving Coffee

Serve at table, as in To Serve the Guests, 11, 13, or 14, p. 56.

FORMAL DINNERS

IN THE FRENCH MANNER

PATE DE MAISON, p. 150

CREME VICHYSSOISE, p. 169, WATER CRESS GARNI

CANETON MONTMORENCY, p. 286, WITH WILD RICE

BROCCOLI HOLLANDAISE

ROMAINE SALAD WITH ITALIAN DRESSING

BASKET OF ASSORTED BREADS

PETITE BABAS WITH FRUIT, p. 580

POT OF COFFEE

SOPHISTICATION PERSONIFIED

ITALIAN PROSCIUTTO WITH MELON
GREEN-TURTLE SOUP
BREAST OF CHICKEN PERIGOURDINE, p. 273
PETITS POIS
SALAD OF AVOCADO AND BIBB LETTUCE
FRENCH BREAD
MERINGUES GLACEES, p. 578
BRANDIED STRAWBERRIES, p. 535
PETITS FOURS
DEMITASSE

TO PLEASE HIM

CAVIAR
(or Lobster, Green-Goddess Dressing, p. 470)
FRESH PINEAPPLE-AND-STRAWBERRY SUPREME
FILET OF BEEF BEARNAISE, p. 179,
WITH POMMES SOUFFLES
DILLED PEAS WITH ARTICHOKE HEARTS
SALAD OF TOSSED GREENS
WARM FRENCH BREAD
HOT SOUFFLE GRAND MARNIER, p. 582
CAFE ESPRESSO

TO PLEASE HER

HONEYDEW WEDGE WITH LIME
BISQUE OF LOBSTER AND SHRIMP
(frozen shrimp soup, sherry, and lobster)
LAMB CHOPS HARBERT, p. 224
BROWNED NEW POTATOES   FRESH ASPARAGUS
GRILLED TOMATOES AND MUSHROOM CAPS
WATER-CRESS AND ENDIVE SALAD
CRUSTY HOT ROLLS
RUM CAKE DE MAISON, p. 627
COFFEE

HOLIDAY FEASTING

BAKED LIVER PATE, p. 147
and/or
SHRIMP RELISH, p. 146
ROAST TURKEY, MUSHROOM-RICE STUFFING,
WITH LOTS OF GRAVY
STUFFED BAKED SWEET POTATOES, p. 409
ONIONS PARMESAN   GREEN BEANS WITH HERB SAUCE
RELISH BOUQUET:
CRANBERRY SAUCE, OLIVES, CELERY FANS
CRANBERRY-CRUNCH, p. 568,
WITH SOFT VANILLA ICE CREAM OR GOUDA CHEESE
or
HEAVENLY HONEY-WALNUT PUMPKIN PIE, p. 591
or
LEMON SHERBET WITH MINTED PINEAPPLE
COFFEE, OF COURSE

ITALIAN-SOUTHERN SPECIALTY

MARINATED CRABMEAT, p. 142
BLACK-BEAN SOUP
LASAGNA, p. 122
CHICKEN HICKMANO, p. 272
GARLIC BREAD
ENDIVES WITH ROQUEFORT DRESSING
MOCHA-NUT TORTONI, p. 611
GOLDEN FRUITCAKE, p. 635
DEMITASSE

WHEN IT'S A LUNCHEON

Simplicity, not convention, should determine the rules if you want a serene but maidless luncheon. Don't be afraid to adopt the several compromises suggested below.

A Lovely Luncheon Table

THE TABLE LINEN: Use an attractive cloth or place mats of rayon, linen, organdy, cotton, a blend of fibers, or lace. Or use easy-to-wipe-off plastic, straw, reed, or paper mats.

Fold each napkin into oblong. Lay on luncheon plate. Or if you are serving a first course, place napkin to left of fork.

PLACING THE SILVER AND CHINA:
1. Place 9″ luncheon plate in center of each place, 1″ in from edge of table or mat.
2. Set each place with flat silver, 1″ in from edge of table or mat, as in diagram, p. 70. Place dessert silver as in Serving Dessert, 2, p. 68. Also arrange plates, glasses, etc., as shown.

To Save Yourself Energy

1. Instead of serving a first course at table, serve it in the living room or with the main course, as in A Simple Sit-Down Dinner, 4 or 5, p. 54.
2. Dispense with bread-and-butter plates. Set 7″ or 8″ plate to left of each napkin, to hold both salad and bread. Serve bread-and-butter sandwiches, or buttered hot breads, to eliminate need for butter.
3. Dispense with salad forks and let guests use luncheon forks for both main course and salad.

4. Serve coffee, tea, or cocoa, as in To Serve the Guests, 11, 12, 13, or 14, p. 56.

5. Candles are not used at a luncheon unless the room is dark.

6. See Who'll Sit Where, p. 56.

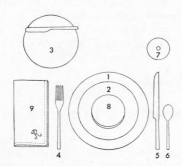

LUNCHEON SETTING WITH FIRST COURSE IN PLACE

1. 9″ luncheon plate for main course
2. 7″ or 8″ plate
3. Bread-and-butter plate with butter spreader across it
4. Luncheon fork to be used for both main dish and salad
5. Luncheon knife
6. Teaspoon for fruit cocktail (substitute soupspoon if first course is soup)
7. Water glass
8. Fruit-cocktail glass
9. Luncheon napkin, folded into oblong

COMPANY LUNCHEONS

THEY ALWAYS ASK FOR THE RECIPE

VENETIAN LIVER, p. 235
BROCCOLI SPEARS   BUTTERED SPAGHETTI
GREEN GODDESS SALAD, p. 449   BREAD STICKS
CHERRY-ORANGE MEDLEY, p. 542
AND ASSORTED CHEESES
COFFEE

COME FOR LASAGNA

LASAGNA, p. 122
TOSSED GREEN SALAD   WARM ITALIAN BREAD
CHRISTMAS PEAR PYRAMID, p. 553
INSTANT CAFFE ESPRESSO

SOME SUMMER DAY

CHERRY TOMATOES TO DUNK IN ITALIAN DRESSING
SWITZERLAND CHEESE-AND-ONION PIE, p. 345
FROZEN CAFE PIE, p. 614
COFFEE

NORDIC AND NICE

DANISH GOULASH, p. 187
TOSSED GREEN-GRAPE SALAD
WITH ROQUEFORT DRESSING
MELBA TOAST
RUM-MOCHA RENNET CUSTARD, p. 561
COFFEE

LUNCH AT ONE

JANE'S COMPANY LOBSTER, p. 323
TOSSED GREEN SALAD WITH ONION AND
GREEN-PEPPER RINGS
BROWN 'N' SERVE SALT STICKS
RASPBERRY-CREAM TARTS, p. 602
ICED COFFEE

BIRTHDAY CELEBRATION

CHICKEN CHASSEUR, p. 269
HERB PEAS WITH ONIONS
CRISP ARTICHOKE SALAD
RYE WAFERS
DOUBLE-CHOCOLATE MINIATURE CAKES, p. 639
COFFEE

YEAR ROUND

BOHEMIAN BURGERS, p. 191
CREAMED MUSHROOMS, p. 406,
ON HOT BUTTERED RYE
GREEN-BEAN-AND-RADISH SALAD
RASPBERRY RIPPLE, p. 547
COFFEE

". . . HEAR ALL ABOUT YOUR TRIP"

POULET A LA CREME JOUBINE, p. 270
BUTTERED ASPARAGUS
PINEAPPLE-CUCUMBER SALAD
GARLIC RYE TOASTIES, p. 494
LITTLE BAKED ALASKAS, p. 614
COFFEE (instant)

"FRIDAY IT'S OUR TURN"

SHRIMP CASSEROLE HARPIN, p. 327
GREEN AND YELLOW SQUASH
(zucchini and summer squash)
TOSSED GREEN SALAD
SAVORY SLICETTES, p. 494
PEACH MELBA, p. 606
TEA — HOT or ICED

SIMPLE BUT SUMPTUOUS

JOSIE'S LEMON SCAMPI, p. 328
PLATTER OF ASPARAGUS
BUTTERED-TOAST FINGERS
EASY CREME BRULEE, p. 560
DEMITASSE

DELIGHTFULLY DIFFERENT

WILD-RICE-AND-TURKEY CASSEROLE, p. 288
MOLDED MANDARIN CRANBERRY RELISH, p. 438
CHEESE BISCUITS
ICE-CREAM AND SHERBET SNOWBALLS, p. 608
COFFEE (instant)

LET'S HAVE OYSTERS

CORN-SCALLOPED OYSTERS, p. 324
BIG GREEN-SALAD BOWL
CRUSTY FRENCH BREAD
ORANGE CRYSTAL CAKE, p. 611
COFFEE or TEA

LIGHT AND LOVELY

FROSTED TOMATOES, p. 141
FRIEDA'S HAM AND ENDIVES AU GRATIN, p. 214
PULLED BREAD, p. 495
FRUIT-WINE JELLY, p. 562
ESPRESSO, p. 679

EVERYBODY'S FAVORITE

FRIED CHICKEN CURRY, p. 265
BROILED TOMATOES   ROMAINE SALAD
SESAME-SEED CRACKERS
STRAWBERRIES ROMANOFF, p. 605
COFFEE WITH A TWIST OF LEMON

DINING BY THE COOL POOL

HI'S CAESAR SALAD, p. 448
(first course à la California)
BARBECUED ROCK-LOBSTER TAILS, p. 322,
WITH GARDEN PILAF, p. 373
BERRY-TOPPED ORANGE CHIFFON PIE, p. 597
ICED TEA

TALK OF THE TOWN

SCALOPPINE OF VEAL MARSALA, p. 232
BUTTERED ZUCCHINI   HOT FLUFFY RICE
ICE-CREAM ECLAIRS, p. 125
COFFEE

COME ON FRIDAY

SHRIMP SAILOR STYLE, p. 327
(Scampi alla Marinara)
GREEN BEANS PARMESAN, p. 451   CRISP ROLLS
ITALIAN FENNEL SALAD
GREEN-GRAPE BUNCHLETS   COCONUT MACAROONS
COFFEE

SIMPLICITY ITSELF

POLENTA WITH TOMATO SAUCE, p. 347
COLD MARINATED BROCCOLI
ITALIAN BREAD STICKS
FRUIT-FILLED ORANGE SHELLS, p. 552
DEMITASSE

FRIDAY DINNER

CHEESE-AND-RICE SOUFFLE, p. 112
MARINATED ASPARAGUS or
MARINATED TOMATOES
MELBA TOAST   CURRANT JELLY
FRUITED MELON, p. 551
FAVORITE ICED DRINK

SOUP, OR SALAD, OR SANDWICH LUNCHEONS

LOBSTER, LADIES?

PINEAPPLE-LEMON-FOAM COCKTAIL
LOBSTER-ARTICHOKE SALAD, p. 457
SKILLET CUSTARD CORN BREAD, p. 483
CHERRY-JUBILEE PIE, p. 597
TEA

APPETIZING COMBINATION

PINEAPPLE-SHELL SALAD, p. 467
TINY WHOLE-WHEAT AND WHITE-BREAD TEA
SANDWICHES FILLED WITH
DEVILED HAM, CHICKEN, OR CREAM CHEESE
MACADAMIA NUTS FOR NIBBLERS
HOT TEA

WINTER OR SUMMER

OLD-COUNTRY BORSCH, p. 166, WITH SOUR CREAM
CORN-BREAD FINGERS
TOSSED GREEN SALAD
FRESH PEAR PIE, p. 588
COFFEE

SANDWICH AND DESSERT

CHICKEN-CHEESE SANDWICHES, p. 517
BARBECUED BAKED APPLES, p. 434
COCOA-CREAM RING, p. 616
ICED COFFEE

SHERBET-CENTERED LUNCHEON PLATE

SHERBET-ICED FRUIT SALAD
TINY CHEDDAR CHEESE SANDWICHES
WILLIAMSBURG BUNS, p. 502
HOT TEA

NAUTICAL

FISHERMAN'S CHOWDER, p. 168
MIXED-GREEN SALAD WITH
GRATED RAW BEETS AND FRENCH DRESSING
HOT FRENCH GARLIC BREAD
TANGERINE DELIGHT, p. 556
DEMITASSE

CARIBBEAN STYLE

LOBSTER SALAD, p. 458
FRENCH BREAD
GUAVA JELLY, PRESERVED KUMQUATS, OR
MANDARIN ORANGES WITH CREAM CHEESE AND
CRACKERS
SMALL CUPS OF BLACK COFFEE

BLISSFUL EATING

JUICE OR SOUP, LIVING-ROOM STYLE
CRUNCHY TUNA SALAD, p. 456
BROILED TOMATOES   SPICED APRICOTS
COFFEE CREAM, p. 575
COFFEE

CHIC

COLD VICHYSSOISE, p. 161
SMALL CLUB SANDWICHES OF DEVILED
HAM AND CHICKEN
TOMATO ASPIC, p. 463
CAFFE ESPRESSO

". . . PLAN THE BAZAAR OVER LUNCH?"

CURRY-VEGETABLE SALAD, p. 451
JELLY-GLAZED SMOKED SHOULDER BUTT, p. 212
PARMESAN-BUTTERED ROLLS
CREAM PUFFS, p. 125, FILLED WITH
COFFEE ICE CREAM
CHOCOLATE SAUCE
COFFEE (instant)

OLD-FASHIONED GOODNESS

PRESSED CHICKEN, p. 464
HOT ASPARAGUS   TOASTED CORN MUFFINS
THIN CANTALOUPE RINGS FILLED WITH
PEACH SLICES
COFFEE — HOT or ICED

SOUTHERN STYLE

SHRIMP SALAD NEW ORLEANS, p. 458
HOT CORN-BREAD SQUARES (from a mix)
LANE CAKE, p. 624
ICED TEA

SURPRISE

HONEYDEW SALAD SUPPER, p. 466
SPICY GINGERBREAD
ICED TEA

SPECIAL

BRAZIL-NUT CRAB SALAD, p. 457
WITH FRENCH ENDIVE, QUARTERED LENGTHWISE
HOT BUTTERED PEAS   SPICED PEACHES
CHOCOLATE-RIPPLE ICE-CREAM-CAKE SUNDAES, p. 607
COFFEE

COMPANY FOR BREAKFAST OR BRUNCH

THE TABLE LINEN: Use easy-to-wipe-off place mats of plastic, straw, reed, or novelty fabric, or use paper place mats. Or use attractive cotton, cotton-and-rayon, or linen table cloth or place mats.

Fold each breakfast napkin into oblong. Place to left of luncheon fork.

PLACING SILVER, CHINA, ETC.:
1. Place 9″ luncheon plate in center of each place, 1″ in from edge of place mat or table.
2. Set up each place with flat silver, 1″ in from edge of place mat or table, as in diagram on p. 73. Arrange plates and glasses as shown.
3. Just before family sits down, place butter pat on each bread-and-butter plate. Or place plate of butter pats on table, to be passed.

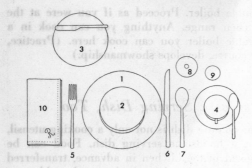

BREAKFAST OR BRUNCH SETTING
WITH CEREAL IN PLACE

1. 9" luncheon plate
2. Bowl of cereal
3. Bread-and-butter plate, with butter spreader across it
4. Cup of coffee, tea, or cocoa, with teaspoon in place

5. Luncheon fork
6. Luncheon knife
7. Dessertspoon or teaspoon for cereal
8. Water glass
9. Glass of fruit juice
10. Breakfast napkin, folded into oblong

BRUNCH

(and a few breakfasts)

MELON AND PINEAPPLE CHUNKS ON PICKS
CRISP BACON
CINNAMON-PUFF TOAST, p. 497
TEA or COFFEE

❖

GRAPEFRUIT SECTIONS WITH POMEGRANATE SEEDS
BROWN-AND-SERVE SAUSAGES
GINGERBREAD or IRISH SODA BREAD, p. 484
COFFEE

❖

TANGERINE OR ORANGE SLICES
WITH CINNAMON SUGAR
DOUGHNUTS, p. 489
A POT OF COCOA

❖

GRAPEFRUIT HALVES WITH SHERRY
(or fruit cup of orange and grapefruit
sections with seedless grapes)
DOUBLE-CORN PANCAKES, p. 489
(with butter and brown sugar, or syrup)
CANADIAN BACON, TINY SAUSAGES, or
CRISP BACON STRIPS
PLENTY OF HOT COFFEE

PINEAPPLE SOPHISTICATE, p. 555
WONDERFUL HASH, p. 253
TOASTED ENGLISH MUFFINS   STRAWBERRY JAM
TEA or COFFEE

❖

APPLE CIDER IN APPLE CUPS
BAKED BEANS AND CRISP BACON
DATE-AND-NUT BREAD, p. 484
COFFEE

❖

BAKED APPLES or
SLICED ORANGES WITH NUTMEG
SCRAMBLED EGGS AND CANADIAN BACON
OUR GIANT POPOVERS, p. 481   APRICOT JAM
CAFE AU LAIT, p. 679

❖

MIXED BERRIES — RIGHT FROM BUSH
SCRAMBLED EGGS
CHEESE-TOMATOES WITH BACON, p. 417
TOAST AND COFFEE

❖

CHILLED GRAPEFRUIT JUICE
MINIATURE PIZZA PIES, p. 151
FRENCH OMELET, p. 361
PITCHERS OF COLD MILK
COFFEE (instant)

❖

BASKET OF TANGERINES
OVEN CINNAMON FRENCH TOAST, p. 497, or
HEATED SWEET ROLLS
CANADIAN BACON
EGGNOG

❖

PAN-BROILED HAM STEAKS
or
HOT BARBECUED FRANKS, p. 245
FROZEN FRENCH FRIES
BANANA MILK SHAKES, p. 685

❖

CRANBERRY PUNCH
COCKTAIL HASH, p. 151
ON-YOUR-OWN BUFFET
(cold ham, turkey, sliced cheese,
sliced white and rye breads)
PEACH-PEAR HALVES, COMPOTE DE LUXE, p. 543
COFFEE

COMPANY MEALS WITH A CHAFING DISH

It adds glamour to every occasion and it's easier than you think.

Almost everything that can be made in a skillet or double boiler can also be made in many chafing dishes. It's that simple!

The upper pan, called the blazer, usually has a long handle and can be used over direct heat, alone, without the lower (hot-water) pan, just as you use a skillet.

Put water in the hot-water pan, set the blazer in it, and you have a double boiler!

Chafing-Dish Technique

With a chafing dish, you can cook and serve right before your guests' very eyes. But, like an actor who is going to perform, you must set the scene and do a bit of rehearsing.

1. *Know your recipe thoroughly.* Have a dress rehearsal if you're new at it.
2. *Collect pretty bowls and pitchers of different sizes* for spices and condiments.
3. *Have your props ready beforehand.* Arrange all ingredients and utensils on one tray. Set up the chafing dish on another tray.
4. *Plan on a first course* to keep your guests busy while you play chef.
5. *Cook noiselessly.* Use a long wooden spoon.

Cook as in a Skillet

There's nothing complicated about chafing-dish cookery. Of course you'll study the manufacturer's directions on how to use and regulate the heat. And you'll reread the hints above on technique.

To cook, place blazer (skillet) of chafing dish over direct heat — and pretend it's just an ordinary skillet on the kitchen range. Anything you can cook in a skillet, you can cook in a chafing dish.

Cook as in a Double Boiler

Set the hot-water pan of your chafing dish in place. Top with the blazer, and you have a double boiler. Proceed as if you were at the kitchen range. Anything you can cook in a double boiler you can cook here. (Practice, of course, develops showmanship.)

Use as a Serving Dish, Too

The chafing dish is not only a cooking utensil, but a handsome serving dish. Food can be cooked in the kitchen in advance, transferred to the chafing dish, and taken to the table.

Besides being glamorous, a chafing dish keeps food hot and appetizing even unto the second helpings. To keep food hot for short periods of time, use just the blazer (skillet). For longer periods, keep it warm over hot-water pan.

AFTERNOON TEA

Enjoy tea time even if you're busy. So pleasant if you're having a few friends in.

The Tea Tray for a Few

Place tray — before or after guests arrive — on table at which you can sit comfortably and located so you can answer doorbell easily. On nearby table, place dessert plates and tea napkins — plus Tea Snacks, p. 75, if there's room. Or put tea snacks on another table. On tray, place:

> Pot of hot tea (p. 680)
> Jug or pitcher of hot water
> Bowl of lump sugar
> Pitcher of milk or light cream
> Plate of lemon or orange slices, with fork
> Rosebud in tiny pitcher or vase, if desired
> Teacups (no saucers), teaspoons (if preferred, use saucers as well as dessert plates)

Place teapot and jug of hot water, with handles toward you, on right side of tray. Place sugar, creamer, lemon, cups (in piles of two each), and spoons on tray so they can be reached easily.

Tea, Properly Poured

To serve each guest, set teacup on dessert plate. Pour tea, adding lemon, milk or cream, and sugar as guest prefers. Place spoon on plate at back of cup, with its handle parallel to handle of cup; pass to guest, with napkin beneath plate. Let guests help themselves to the tea snack; or have a guest pass it; or pass it yourself after all have been served tea.

IN SUMMER: In warm weather, you may wish to serve a choice of hot or iced tea. If so, arrange a tray near tea table. On it, place iced-tea glasses, iced-tea spoons, plate of mint sprigs, bowl of ice cubes, tongs, plate of lemon wedges, and bowl of fruit sugar. Pour hot tea from pot into ice-filled glasses.

The Tea Table for a Crowd

1. The dining table (or large table set in living room) is spread with your prettiest cloth — lace, organdy, or even chintz in a tiny floral design.
2. At one end of table, place tea tray with pot of hot tea, jug of hot water, bowl of lump sugar, creamer (have all handles pointing toward pourer), and plate of lemon slices. At back and sides of tray, or beside tray, arrange cups on saucers, with spoons in place. (You can put extra cups and saucers on sideboard or side table.) If possible, set up one cup and saucer ready for tea.
3. At other end of table, set up a similar tray for coffee. (In warm weather, punch, sherbet, or ice cream may replace tea or coffee.)
4. On table, attractively arrange dessert plates, napkins, and 2 or 3 kinds of Tea Snacks, right.

The Pourers

The hostess asks two friends to pour for her, and two or more friends to be "relief pourers." (Hostess, with guest of honor nearby, greets guests.) Guests pick up dessert plates and napkins, are passed cups of tea, then help themselves to snacks.

TEA SNACKS
(bite size is the right size)

Nothing sticky or moist should be served at a large tea. Everything should be easily eaten with fingers. Choose from these:

Cookies of all kinds
Tiny cupcakes or petits fours
Miniature Danish pastries or tarts
Dainty sandwiches
Petite cream puffs, filled, frosted if desired
Mints or nuts, or both
Thin bread and butter
Doughnut "holes"
Toasted English muffins with jam
Candied fruit
Tiny squares of gingerbread or cake
Tiny cheese-topped baking-powder biscuits

Fruitcake slices filled with butter-frosting
Chocolate cookies filled with cream cheese
Bite-size turnovers or tarts
Nut-bread slices and jelly, jam, or cream cheese
Strawberries dipped into melted jelly
Orange, cinnamon, or honey toast
Lettuce or cucumber sandwiches
Layer cake, to eat with fork

MORE COMPANY MENUS

For menus for all occasions — evening refreshments, showers, club doings, and weddings, as well as more luncheons, dinners, and buffets, see the 278-page *Good Housekeeping Party Book*.

FAMILY WEIGHT-WATCHING

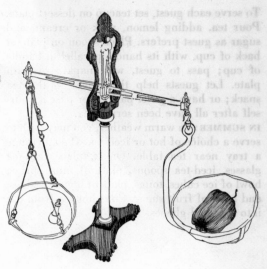

The subject of weight-watching threatens to crowd more interesting subjects out of many conversations today. *Good Housekeeping*'s advice is to do it and don't talk about it — and in this chapter doing it is made easy and as nearly painless as it can be.

There are suggestions for general family meals to maintain the right weight, low-calorie diets for those who must lose weight, and special help for dieting teen-agers and for those who need to gain weight.

DO'S AND DON'T'S

We think you'll find that nothing could be simpler (or more appetite-pleasing) than following *Good Housekeeping*'s Keep-Young Guide, pp. 77–82. If you like, nobody need know that you're ever-so-slightly, ever-so-deliciously changing your family eating pattern — it's that easy. What we've done for you is to divide familiar foods into five groups. They are your keys to happy meal planning, without sacrificing well-loved dishes or making drastic changes in your habits. The portion's the thing!

Do start with the reassuring fact that the foods we list in Groups 1, 2, 3, and 4 allow for a wide variety of the nourishing "musts," such as milk, meat, fruit, vegetables, breads, and cereals.

Do bear in mind that your children's lifelong food habits are set while they're very young — and it's you who set them. Encouraging a real liking for the foods in Groups 1, 2, and 3 is one of the greatest gifts in your power.

Do take our word that it *is* possible to shift the food habits of the grownups in your family painlessly. Give them smaller portions, tempt them with eye-catching, mouth-watering combinations from the foods we list in Groups 1, 2, and 3.

Do mix liquid whole milk with reliquefied nonfat dry milk for drinking. We call this half-and-half combination "slim milk"; it tastes good and is economical — and adds up to the *trim* way to milk-generous meals.

Don't abandon family favorites in Group 5 (the watch-your-step category). But discover the joys of the single-crust or deep-dish pie, the delightfulness of desserts and pie fillings, etc., made with nonfat or evaporated milk instead of heavy cream. And don't overlook dessert toppings (packaged or pressure-canned), with their added bonus of convenience.

All these secrets are yours to keep — or to share.

Don't hesitate to cut the pie, or dish out the dessert, into 10 or 12 portions instead of the customary bigger servings. Use smaller plates, put a little bunch of grapes beside the slimmer-than-usual portion — and if the table talk is going along happily, most likely no one will even notice the difference.

Don't deprive your family of bread and potatoes, if they love them. The plain fact is, it's what you put *on* bread and potatoes that plumps up the menu. So be wise about spreads and go-alongs.

Don't give up in despair over teen-age food habits — those of the fashion-conscious young ladies who starve themselves, or those of either gender who eat the wrong foods in between and at meals, with gay abandon. Be firm with youngsters in the first group; remind them they're preparing for marriage and motherhood. A girl who enjoys being a girl, who looks like a girl and not like a clothes pole, stands the best chance of having a whirl. As to the second group: *You* provide the food, don't you? At least at mealtime. And perhaps you can even influence the choice of in-between snacks!

Do keep on hand a lovely assortment of fresh, good-for-you, and dazzlingly appetizing things for them to nibble when the mood strikes them, such as celery fans, cherries, grapes, pineapple cubes on picks, carrot sticks, orange wedges, strawberries, radishes. (Shiny apples aren't the *only* things that help keep the doctor at his proper distance today!)

KEEP-YOUNG GUIDE TO HAPPY EATING

To help you unlock the door to happy, trim, day-by-day meal planning for your whole family, we have divided a vast array of familiar foods into the following five groups. In

making your choice from these, be sure also to keep in mind the Do's and Don't's we've listed on pp. 76–77.

Group 1
FREE-CHOICE FOODS
(all they can eat, any time they like)

VEGETABLES:

asparagus	mushrooms
beet greens	okra
broccoli	peppers
cabbage	radishes
cauliflower	salad greens
celery	sauerkraut
collards	spinach
cucumbers	summer squash
green beans	tomatoes
kale	zucchini
kohlrabi	

TOMATO OR VEGETABLE JUICE
CONSOMME OR BOUILLON
SEASONERS, RELISHES, ETC.:

catchup	lemon juice
chili sauce	lime juice
cocktail sauce	mustard
bottled meat	sour pickles
sauces	vinegar, etc.

BEVERAGES: coffee or tea; little sugar, no cream

Group 2
BIG, BIG PORTION FOODS
(seconds, too, if they like)

SKIM MILK (REGULAR OR RELIQUEFIED DRY)
BUTTERMILK
PLAIN YOGHURT
FRUIT OR VEGETABLE SALADS
EGGS: soft- or hard-cooked or poached
FRUIT JUICES: apple, grapefruit, orange, pineapple, or blends of these
FRUITS (FRESH):

apples	oranges
bananas	peaches
berries	pineapple
cantaloupe	tangerines
grapefruit	

VEGETABLES:

artichokes or
  artichoke hearts
Brussels sprouts
carrots

green peas
onions
rutabagas
white turnips

SOUPS (EXCEPT CREAM SOUPS AND CHOWDERS)
MELBA TOAST; RYE WAFERS
OLIVES: green, ripe, stuffed

Group 3

GENEROUS-PORTION FOODS

FISH AND SHELLFISH:

bass
cod
flounder
haddock
ocean perch
sardines, drained
  if oil pack

tuna, drained,
  or broth-and-
  water pack
whitefish
shellfish, any

POULTRY: chicken, game hens, turkey (except breaded or fried)
CHEESE: cottage (all varieties and flavors), farmer, pot, ricotta
FRUITS (FRESH):

cherries
grapes
honeydew

pears
watermelon

VEGETABLES:

beets
corn
limas

parsnips
pumpkin
winter squash

FRUIT JUICES: grape, prune
GELATIN DESSERTS (PLAIN OR FRUITED); FRUIT WHIPS
FRUIT DRINKS AND NECTARS

Group 4

REGULAR-SIZE-PORTION FOODS
(not king-size)

FISH: bluefish, halibut, mackerel, salmon, swordfish
MEATS:

lean, well-trimmed cuts of: beef, ham, hamburger, lamb, pork, veal
bacon, crisp
beef, corned
beef, dried
canned meats

cold cuts
frankfurters
liver
organ meats (kidney, heart, etc.)

POULTRY: duck, goose
WHOLE MILK (REGULAR, EVAPORATED)
CHEESE: any not in Group 3
FLAVORED MILK DRINKS
EGGS: any form not listed in Group 2
CREAM SOUPS AND CHOWDERS
DRIED BEANS, PEAS, LENTILS, LIMAS (HOME-COOKED OR CANNED)
CEREALS: ready-to-eat or cooked
POTATOES: sweet or white
BREAD: any variety
BISCUITS, CRACKERS, MUFFINS, ROLLS, ETC.
MACARONI, SPAGHETTI, NOODLES, ETC.
RICE
FRUITS: canned, dried, frozen, stewed
BAKED CUSTARD, CUSTARD SAUCE
PUDDINGS (REGULAR OR INSTANT)
SHERBETS, ICES, ICE MILKS
COOKIES
PANCAKES, WAFFLES
ANGEL FOOD, SPONGECAKE, UNICED CAKES OR CUPCAKES
SALAD DRESSINGS
COCONUT
HONEY, JAMS, JELLIES, MARMALADE
TABLE SYRUPS
HARD CANDY
SOFT DRINKS (PLAIN OR CARBONATED)

Group 5

BE-CAREFUL-OF-PORTION-SIZE FOODS

UNTRIMMED OR FAT MEATS
NUTS AND NUT BUTTERS
BREADED AND FRIED FOODS
CREAM: light, heavy, commercial sour
ICE CREAM
EGGNOG, MALTED-MILK DRINKS
BUTTER, MARGARINE
RICH SAUCES AND GRAVIES
PIES, PASTRIES, FROSTED CAKES, RICH DESSERTS
CANDY (EXCEPT HARD CANDY)
POTATO CHIPS, OTHER "CHIP" SNACKS

Note the omission from these lists of the "ingredient" foods: flour, sugar, shortenings, salad oils. However, typical dishes made with these ingredients are included.

A REDUCING PLAN

If you are already overweight, here's a basic, 1200-calorie plan to guide you. But first talk to your doctor.

General Instructions:

1. Use only skim milk on this diet, both for drinking and food preparation. You may, of course, use either reliquefied nonfat dry milk or liquid skim milk. Skim milk for drinking may be flavored with coffee, flavoring extracts, or a dash of spice.

2. Black coffee or tea may be added to any meal pattern, or be taken between meals, if your doctor does not restrict the use of them. You may always reserve part of your milk "ration" to use in these beverages if you like. A nonnutritive sweetener may be used if you prefer them sweetened.

3. If you wish to broil or roast the less tender and less expensive cuts of meat, try using a powdered instant meat tenderizer, p. 101.

4. Spices and herbs add flavor interest to many dishes — they can be used freely.

Flexible Reducing Pattern
(1200 CALORIES)

BREAKFAST

CHOOSE	HOW MUCH TO EAT
JUICE	4-oz. glass orange, grapefruit, blend of grapefruit and orange, or pineapple (fresh, frozen, or canned unsweetened), *or* 8-oz. glass tomato juice.
or FRUIT	½ cup blueberries, strawberries, or raspberries, or unsweetened applesauce; *or* ½ melon or grapefruit; *or* 1 orange, apple, or peach.

and

EGG, TOAST, AND MILK	1 soft-cooked, hard-cooked, or poached egg; 1 thin slice enriched white or whole-wheat toast; ½ pat butter or margarine; 8-oz. glass skim milk.
or FRENCH TOAST AND MILK	1 slice French toast (using 1 egg and a few tablesp. of your milk); ½ pat butter or margarine; 8-oz. glass skim milk.
or CEREAL, EGG AND BACON, AND MILK	¾-cup ready-to-eat cereal *or* ½ cup cooked cereal; 1 soft-cooked, hard-cooked, or poached egg; 1 slice crisp bacon; 4-oz. glass skim milk (use part on cereal).

MID-MORNING AND MID-AFTERNOON SNACKS

CRACKERS AND MILK	8-oz. glass skim milk; 1 graham cracker *or* 2 saltines.
or SANDWICH AND MILK	1 thin slice enriched white or whole-wheat bread spread with one of the following: 1 teasp. jelly or jam; 2 tablesp. cottage cheese; 2 teasp. honey; 4-oz. glass skim milk or buttermilk.
or JUICE, CRACKERS, AND COTTAGE CHEESE	8-oz. glass tomato or vegetable juice, *or* 4-oz. glass orange, grapefruit, or blended juice; 1 graham cracker *or* 2 saltines; 2 tablesp. cottage cheese.
or FRUIT WITH COTTAGE CHEESE	½ cup orange and grapefruit sections or mixed fresh fruit cup, *or* ½ medium banana, sliced; ⅓ cup cottage cheese.

or
COCOA AND CRACKERS
½ cup cocoa (made with skim milk) ; 2 saltines *or* 1 graham cracker.

LUNCH
Menu No. 1

MEAT BALLS OR OMELET
2 small meat balls (1 oz. each) *or* 1 omelet (2 eggs) ; ½ cup spaghetti, noodles, or mashed potatoes.

and
VEGETABLE
1 serving asparagus, broccoli, or Brussels sprouts with 1 pat butter or margarine.

and
DESSERT
½ cup unsweetened applesauce *or* ½ grapefruit or melon.

and
MILK
4-oz. glass skim milk or buttermilk.

Menu No. 2

SOUP
½ cup cream soup, any variety (made with skim milk).

and
FRUIT OR VEGETABLE SALAD PLATE
½ cup fresh fruit (orange and grapefruit sections, apples, grapes) on lettuce leaves, *or* ½ cup mixed, raw vegetables (lettuce, carrots, green pepper, cucumber) ; ⅓ cup cottage cheese; 2 tablesp. French dressing.

Menu No. 3

FISH
1 serving (3 oz.) broiled or boiled fish (bass, cod, flounder, haddock, halibut) with lemon juice.

---

and
VEGETABLE
1 large serving spinach, turnip greens, or cabbage with lemon juice or vinegar.

and
RELISHES
Celery and carrot sticks.

and
BREAD
1 thin slice enriched white or whole-wheat bread; 1 pat butter or margarine.

and
DESSERT
½ cup vanilla or chocolate pudding (made with skim milk).

Menu No. 4

SOUP
½ cup vegetable soup.

and
HAMBURGER OR FRANKFURTER
1 frankfurter *or* 1 small broiled hamburger patty; 1 roll, lightly buttered; pickle relish, mustard, or catchup.

and
SALAD
Sliced tomatoes on lettuce; 2 tablesp. cottage cheese; 1 tablesp. French dressing or 2 tablesp. low-calorie dressing.*

and
MILK
4-oz. glass skim milk or buttermilk.

Menu No. 5

FISH SALAD PLATE
½ cup crab meat, lobster, water- or broth-packed tuna, *or* 10 to 12 cooked medium shrimp; ½ cup diced celery; a few tomato slices; lettuce; 1 teasp. mayonnaise or 1 tablesp. French dressing.

*See pp. 473–474 for Low-Calorie Salad Dressings.

and
BREAD

3 slices of Melba toast or 1 slice enriched white or whole-wheat bread; 1 pat butter or margarine.

and
MILK

8-oz. glass skim milk or buttermilk.

Menu No. 6
(if you must carry lunch)

SANDWICH

2 thin slices enriched white or whole-wheat bread, buttered; 1 oz. (1 thin slice) Cheddar cheese, bologna, liverwurst, or luncheon loaf.

and
HARD-COOKED EGG

1 egg (*or* an extra slice of meat or cheese).

and
RELISHES

Celery and carrot sticks.

and
MILK

8-oz. glass skim milk or buttermilk.

DINNER
Menu No. 1

APPETIZER

4-oz. glass tomato juice or vegetable juice.

and
BROILED CHOP

2 small lean broiled lamb chops *or* 1 medium pork or veal chop (eat none of the fat).

and
VEGETABLE AND A SALAD OR 2 VEGE-TABLES

½ cup cooked beets, carrots, or peas with 1 teasp. butter or margarine, plus 1 serving mixed green salad with low-calorie dressing* *or* 1 serving asparagus, bróccoli, Brussels sprouts, cabbage, or greens (with lemon juice).

and
DESSERT

½ cup custard or tapioca pudding (made with skim milk).

Menu No. 2

MEAT OR FISH

2-oz. serving roast or broiled beef, lamb, veal, chicken, turkey, or liver, or fish (bass, cod, flounder, haddock, halibut, or perch).

and
POTATO OR BREAD

½ medium baked potato *or* 1 thin slice enriched white or whole-wheat bread; 1 pat butter or margarine.

and
VEGETABLE

1 average serving green beans, stewed tomatoes, summer squash, sauerkraut, or spinach.

and
SALAD

Canned peach or pear half (no syrup) *or* ½ medium banana; 1 oz. grated Cheddar cheese; lettuce; 1 tablesp. low-calorie dressing.*

and
DESSERT

½ cup dietetic gelatin or pudding dessert (latter made with skim milk).

Menu No. 3

APPETIZER

5 small cooked shrimp *or* ¼ cup crabmeat; 2 tablesp. cocktail sauce.

and
STUFFED GREEN PEPPER OR

1 pepper stuffed with 2 oz. chopped beef; 2 tablesp. tomato sauce; *or* 2 oz. roast, broiled, or

See pp. 473–474 for Low-Calorie Salad Dressings.

CHICKEN WITH RICE	boiled chicken with ¼ cup cooked rice, moistened with broth.
and VEGETABLE OR SALAD	Large serving of any green, leafy vegetable *or* mixed green salad; 1 pat butter or margarine *or* 1 tablesp. French dressing.
and DESSERT	1 small sector (1″) angel-food cake *or* small cupcake (1¾″ diameter) *or* ½ cup mixed fresh fruit.

IS THERE AN OVERWEIGHT TEEN-AGER IN YOUR FAMILY?

Here's a plan that makes reducing easy for teen-agers. No fads — no going hungry — this is a pleasant, adequate diet. If it's followed steadily, gradual loss in weight and improved health should result. It may be continued until satisfactory weight is reached. Before starting this diet, have an examination by your physician and get his approval. After you start, have him check up regularly on your teen-ager's weight and health.

TEEN-AGE REDUCING DIET
(about 1500-1600 calories per day)

BREAKFAST

FRUIT — PREFERABLY ½ GRAPEFRUIT OR 1 ORANGE
1 SOFT- OR HARD-COOKED OR POACHED EGG
THIN SLICE TOAST
or MEDIUM SERVING CEREAL
GLASS OF SKIM MILK

LUNCH AT HOME

SMALL SERVING OF MEAT, FISH, OR CHICKEN
or 2 EGGS *or* ¾ CUP COTTAGE CHEESE
LARGE SERVING OF COOKED VEGETABLE
LARGE SERVING OF RAW VEGETABLE
SERVING OF FRUIT   GLASS OF SKIM MILK

LUNCH TO BE CARRIED

SANDWICH OF 2 THIN SLICES OF BREAD FILLED
WITH MEAT, CHOPPED EGG, LIVER SPREAD,
OR COTTAGE CHEESE
RAW VEGETABLES   SERVING OF FRUIT
GLASS OF SKIM MILK
(in vacuum bottle or after school)

DINNER

¾ CUP APPETIZER SOUP (p. 84) OR
JELLIED BOUILLON *or*
¾ CUP HOT OR CHILLED TOMATO
OR VEGETABLE JUICE
GENEROUS SERVING OF LIVER, KIDNEY, HEART,
MEAT, FISH, OR CHICKEN
or 2 MEDIUM FRANKFURTERS
or CHILI CON CARNE (p. 85)
or CRAB-CHEESE PILAF (p. 85)
LARGE SERVING OF 2 COOKED VEGETABLES
(omit vegetables if Chili Con Carne or Crab-Cheese Pilaf is served)
RAW VEGETABLE SALAD
LOW-CALORIE SALAD DRESSING*
SERVING OF FRUIT AND GLASS OF SKIM MILK
or RASPBERRY PARFAIT (p. 86)

BEDTIME

GLASS OF SKIM MILK

Use only the vegetables in the following list. Avoid monotony. Use as many as possible; try those with which you are not familiar. Vegetables are a very important part of a good reducing diet, not only because of their vitamins and minerals, but because the bulk they provide gives a feeling of appetite satisfaction.

Cook vegetables carefully and quickly in a small amount of boiling water, to avoid excessive loss of vitamins and minerals. Salt lightly and serve plain or with lemon juice. *Do not add butter, margarine, cream, etc.*

Because raw vegetables require more chewing and take longer to eat, they are especially valuable. Use them generously both plain and as salads with low-calorie dressings or with

*See pp. 473–474 for Low-Calorie Salad Dressings.

lemon juice. Have them crisp and delicious. Learn to enjoy them with little or no salt. If they are carried in a lunchbox, take a generous serving of several kinds. Wrap in wax paper, foil, or plastic wrap.

VEGETABLES FOR THIS DIET

Asparagus, beet greens, broccoli, Brussels sprouts, cabbage, carrots, cauliflower, celery, chard, chicory, collards, cucumbers, dandelion greens, eggplant, endive, fennel, kale, kohlrabi, lettuce, mushrooms, mustard greens, okra, onions, peppers, radishes, sauerkraut, snap beans, spinach, summer squash, tomatoes, turnip greens, turnips, water cress, zucchini.

No one will complain when dessert is a cool and appetizing serving of one of the fruits listed below. If you had citrus fruit (orange, tangerine, or grapefruit) for breakfast, serve another fruit for dessert. But be sure to have one serving of citrus fruit each day. It is better to use whole fruit than juice; it is more filling for the same calories. *Serve fresh fruit with no sugar.*

If you must use canned or cooked fruit, have smaller servings with no syrup. Or use special dietetic-pack brands.

FRUITS FOR THIS DIET

1 medium apple	1 medium orange
5 medium apricots	1 medium peach
1 medium banana	1 medium pear
¾ cup blackberries	¾ cup pineapple
¾ cup blueberries	4 medium plums
½ large cantaloupe	¾ cup raspberries
20 cherries	1 cup strawberries
½ grapefruit	1 large tangerine
35 small seedless grapes	1 slice (¾" thick, 6" diameter) watermelon
¼ medium honeydew	

Ten Tips for Teens

1. Reducers must have vitamin D. Teen-age youngsters are making bones and teeth and need adequate vitamin D. Most children can get this from vitamin-D milk; but because such milk usually is homogenized and contains the cream, youngsters following this reducing diet cannot have it. So, to make the diet adequate, you should have 400 to 500 International Units of vitamin D daily from other sources. Consult your doctor for the right supplement.

2. Skim milk has only half the calories of whole milk, because the cream (fat) has been removed. Buttermilk makes a welcome change if you like it. Most folks like milk better when it is chilled. Teen-agers need a quart of skim milk daily because of its calcium for bones and teeth. For variety, occasionally use part of the day's quart of skim milk to make desserts (see recipes). You can prepare your own skim milk, easily and economically, by using nonfat dry milk.

3. Liver in some form is wise at least twice a week, for either lunch or dinner. If texture and flavor are not well liked, they can be changed by seasoning and chopping and grinding. And don't think you have to use calf liver only. Any liver is excellent food — beef, pork, lamb, calf, chicken. All supply valuable protein, iron, copper, vitamin A, and riboflavin and other vitamins of the B-complex group. Don't overlook liver sausage, either. It is a good source of these essentials, too.

4. Use no more bread than allowed. You can have any kind you like — enriched white, rye, cracked wheat, or whole wheat. Use it thinly sliced. Toast has the same number of calories as untoasted bread.

5. Remove fat and skin from meat and poultry. Eat no fried foods, gravy, or drippings. They are high in calories.

6. Don't hurry your meal. Don't bolt your food. Chew well for more satisfaction and more pleasure.

7. Drink 6 to 8 glasses of water a day. Drinking a glass of water slowly helps that hungry feeling. Water at meals is all right, but don't use it to wash down food.

8. Constipated? This diet provides bulk from fruits and vegetables, and you should not be constipated. Be sure to have a regular time each day for this function, and allow sufficient time. To stimulate the bowels, drink 2 glasses of water on arising. If this fails, consult your doctor. Do not use cathartics.

9. Avoid those little tidbits between meals. Just one soft drink means from 75 to 100 calories. One five-cent candy bar can undo a whole day

of careful eating. And if you backslide once, it is easy to do it again.

10. That drugstore snack: If the crowd is going to get sodas, you go right along. Ask the clerk to squeeze the juice of a lemon and a lime into a tall glass with tinkling ice and a scant teaspoon of sugar, and fill with plain or charged water. It's fun to drink, is low in calories, and has vitamin C, too.

Adults Can Reduce on This Diet, Too

This teen-age reducing diet is good for adults. They need only 3 cups of skim milk daily and may have tea or coffee, without cream and sugar, if desired.

Warning! When you have lost enough weight, don't go back to old eating habits. Continue to check your weight frequently.

RECIPES FOR DIETERS

Here are a group of recipes especially adapted to the needs of dieters. So good, nondieters will love them, too. All of them were developed and checked in our Bureau Kitchen.

APPETIZER SOUP
(60 calories per serving)

3 cups water
2 beef bouillon cubes
2 chicken bouillon cubes
1 1-lb.-3-oz. can tomatoes
1 medium onion, chopped
½ cup thinly sliced carrots
2 stalks celery, in ½" slices
3 whole peppercorns
½ teasp. dried sage
1 teasp. salt
¼ cup grated Parmesan cheese

In a 2-qt. saucepan, with a well-fitting cover, combine water, beef and chicken bouillon cubes, tomatoes, onion, carrots, celery, peppercorns, sage, and salt; simmer, covered, 1 hr. Serve sprinkled with grated Parmesan cheese. Makes 5 servings.

CHICKEN LIVERS IN WINE
(170 calories per serving or 205 calories per serving on toast)

½ lb. chicken livers
1 tablesp. butter or margarine
¼ cup thinly sliced celery
½ teasp. dried minced parsley
½ teasp. dried minced chives
2 whole cloves
¾ cup dry sherry
1 large red-skinned cooking apple, cored, thinly sliced, then quartered (about 2 cups)
1 teasp. all-purpose flour
Salt
Toast points prepared from 1½ slices of bread (optional)

Wash livers; remove connective tissue. In butter or margarine in medium skillet, sauté livers, celery, parsley, and chives until celery is light brown; remove mixture from pan; add cloves, sherry, and apples; simmer, covered, 5 min., or until apples are almost tender. Make paste of flour and a few drops of water; stir into apple mixture; simmer until thickened; return livers to pan; heat until warm; add salt to taste. Serve on toast points, if desired. Makes 3 servings.

BOEUF BOURGUIGNON II
(290 calories per serving)

1 lb. round steak
All-purpose flour
2 tablesp. butter or margarine
3 tablesp. cognac
1 clove garlic, minced
2 carrots, thinly sliced
2 cups thinly sliced celery
1 cup chopped onions
1 tablesp. dried parsley flakes
1 bay leaf, crumbled
½ teasp. dried thyme
3 cups water
2 teasp. bottled sauce for gravy
Salt
½ teasp. hickory-smoked salt
1 lb. small white onions
1 lb. mushrooms
1 teasp. lemon juice

Day before, if desired: Start heating oven to 350°F. Trim fat from beef; cut beef into 1" cubes; roll cubes in flour until completely covered. In 1 tablesp. butter or margarine, in a Dutch oven, brown beef on all sides. Add cognac and ignite; when flames have subsided, add garlic, carrots, celery, chopped onions, parsley flakes, bay leaf, thyme, 2 cups water, sauce, 2 teasp. salt, and hickory salt. Stir to distribute spices; simmer 2 to 3 min.; cover tightly, then bake 2 hr., or until meat is tender. *One half hour before meat is done:* Wash and peel small white onions (halve those more than 1" in diameter); boil, in salted water to cover, until tender — about 20 min. Wash and stem mushrooms (halve caps more than 1½" in diameter); sauté caps and stems in 1 tablesp. butter or margarine and lemon juice until brown — about 15 min. Make a smooth paste from 2 tablesp. flour and ¼ cup water. To meat mixture, add drained onions, mushrooms, paste, and ¾ cup water; simmer until gravy has thickened, stirring to prevent sticking. Refrigerate until 20 min. before serving time, then reheat over low heat until hot. Makes 6 servings.

CHILI CON CARNE
(270 calories per serving)

1 tablesp. salad oil	ground
1 clove garlic, thinly sliced	1 1-lb. can kidney beans, drained
1 cup chopped onion	2 1-lb. cans tomatoes
2 cups sliced celery	½ teasp. salt or
½ cup chopped green pepper	hickory-smoked salt
1 lb. beef round,	Chili powder

Prepare the day before, if desired: In a 4-qt. kettle, in salad oil, sauté garlic, onion, celery, and green pepper until onion is light brown; add beef, then cook until it is brown. Stir in kidney beans, tomatoes, salt, and 1½ teasp. chili; simmer all, uncovered, at least 45 min. to blend flavors. If prepared in advance, cool, then refrigerate until 20 min. before serving time. To serve, heat slowly. A few min. before serving, stir in enough chili powder to give desired "hotness." Makes 7 servings.

PALOS VERDES STEW
(210 calories per serving)

1 tablesp. butter or margarine	1½ teasp. salt
1 medium onion, minced	1 1-pt.-3-oz. can tomato juice
1 cup chopped celery	1 6½- or 7-oz. can water- or broth-packed tuna, flaked
3 cups quartered, then thinly sliced, pared white potatoes	Dry packaged instant mashed potatoes (optional)
1 cup water	
1½ teasp. whole orégano	

In butter or margarine, in large skillet with tight cover, sauté onion and celery until onion is light brown; add potatoes, water, orégano, and salt; cover tightly, then simmer 10 min., or until potatoes are almost tender. Add tomato juice and tuna; simmer 10 min.; then stir in 1 to 3 tablesp. dry instant mashed potatoes for a bit of thickening, if desired. Serve in soup bowls. Makes 4 servings.

BAKED SWORDFISH AU GRATIN
(210 calories per serving)

1 lb. fresh swordfish steaks, ½" to ¾" thick (or frozen swordfish steaks, thawed)	6 peppercorns
	1 small onion, thinly sliced
	⅓ cup dried bread crumbs
½ cup salad oil	⅓ cup grated Parmesan cheese
½ cup sauterne	
1 teasp. dried parsley flakes	¼ teasp. dried orégano
¼ teasp. dried thyme	½ teasp. salt
1 bay leaf, crumbled	

Cut swordfish steaks into 4 portions. In a shallow baking pan, combine marinade of salad oil, sauterne, parsley, thyme, bay leaf, peppercorns, and onion; lay swordfish on top; refrigerate for at least 2 hr., occasionally spooning marinade over fish.

Now start heating oven to 350°F. Combine bread crumbs, cheese, orégano, and salt; coat fish steaks with this mixture, then place in a shallow covered baking dish (or cover dish with foil). Bake 20 min., then uncover and bake 15 min. longer, or until fish flakes but is still moist. If a browner surface is desired, place under broiler until light brown. Makes 4 servings.

CRAB-CHEESE PILAF
(240 calories per serving)

2 tablesp. salad oil	1 teasp. salt
1 cup chopped onion	1 bay leaf, crumbled
1 cup sliced celery	1 tablesp. granulated sugar
¼ cup diced green pepper	2 1-lb. cans tomatoes
¼ lb. fresh mushrooms, sliced, or 1 3- or 4-oz. can mushrooms (optional)	¾ cup packaged pre-cooked rice
	2 6- to 7-oz. cans King-crab meat, drained
½ cup thinly sliced carrots	½ cup grated natural Cheddar cheese

Start heating oven to 350°F. In salad oil, in a large ovenproof skillet, sauté onion, celery, green pepper, mushrooms, and carrots until onion is golden brown; add salt, bay leaf, sugar, and tomatoes; simmer 5 min. Stir rice and crab meat into tomato mixture; sprinkle cheese on top; bake 20 to 25 min. Serve in soup bowls, if desired. Makes 5 servings.

ZUCCHINI PARMIGIANA
(70 calories per serving)

Salt	2 medium tomatoes,
2 medium zucchini	cut in eighths
cut in ½″ slices	½ cup grated Parme-
½ teasp. dried	san cheese
orégano	

In salted water to cover, simmer zucchini slices and orégano 10 min., or until tender. Preheat broiler 10 min., or as manufacturer directs. Arrange drained zucchini and tomatoes, cut side up, in a shallow baking pan; sprinkle with salt, then cheese. Broil, 4″ from heat, for 3 to 5 min., or until cheese melts and turns light brown. Serve immediately. Makes 4 servings.

DIET DESSERTS

DIETETIC GELATIN DESSERTS

Fruit-flavor gelatin is sweetened with a non-nutritive sweetener instead of sugar. One serving, plain, has only 10 calories.

DIETETIC PUDDINGS

These delicious puddings — chocolate, butterscotch, and vanilla — are sweetened without sugar. A single serving supplies about 54 calories when made with skim milk.

RASPBERRY PARFAIT
(130 calories per serving)

2 10-oz. pkg. frozen	milk
raspberries, thawed	1 pkg. vanilla rennet-
2 cups liquefied non-	custard dessert
fat dry milk or skim	

Drain juice from raspberries; divide half of raspberries among 6 5- to 6-oz. parfait glasses or custard cups. In a small saucepan, heat milk

to lukewarm; remove from heat; stir in rennet custard until completely dissolved. Gently pour ⅓ cup of custard mixture down sides of each glass onto raspberries; let stand undisturbed until firm — about 10 min. Top with remaining raspberries and juice. Refrigerate until chilled, but do not freeze. Makes 6 servings.

PINEAPPLE PARFAIT: Substitute 1 1-lb. can crushed pineapple for the raspberries, then prepare as directed above; garnish each with a maraschino cherry. This parfait provides only 105 calories per serving.

LEMON SNAP COOKIES
(30 calories per cookie)

½ cup butter or mar-	lemon rind
garine	2¼ cups sifted all-
¾ cup granulated	purpose flour
sugar	½ teasp. double-
1 egg	acting baking
2 tablesp. lemon juice	powder
1½ teasp. grated	¼ teasp. salt

In a medium bowl, cream together butter or margarine and sugar until light and fluffy; beat in egg, lemon juice, and lemon rind. Sift together flour, baking powder, and salt; add gradually to shortening mixture; mix until smooth. Refrigerate dough until firm — 1 to 2 hr.

Start heating oven to 400°F. Roll chilled dough to ⅛″ thickness on a well-floured pastry cloth or board. Cut out cookies with a 2″ round or designed cutter; transfer to lightly greased cookie sheet; bake 6 to 8 min., or until edges are a golden brown. Makes about 6 or 7 dozen.

A half-cup serving of canned or frozen fruit, plus 2 cookies, will still hold you under 150 dessert calories.

SLIM-JIM TOPPING
(6 calories per tablespoon)

¾ teasp. unflavored	skim milk)
gelatine	2 tablesp. cold water
1½ teasp. cold water	2 tablesp. instant non-
Granulated sugar	fat dry milk
Pinch salt	½ teasp. vanilla ex-
¼ cup liquefied non-	tract
fat dry milk (or	¾ teasp. lemon juice

Soften gelatine in 1½ teasp. water; dissolve over hot water. Add 1 tablesp. sugar, salt, milk;

stir until dissolved. Chill until as thick as un-beaten egg whites. Meanwhile, on 2 tablesp. water in medium bowl, sprinkle nonfat dry milk. With electric mixer at high speed, or hand beater, beat until mixture holds stiff peaks. Gradually beat in 1 tablesp. sugar. Add vanilla, lemon juice, and gelatine mixture; continue beating until mixture is stiff enough to hold soft peaks — 5 to 10 min. Allow 2 tablesp. per serving. Makes 2 cups.

COFFEE: Substitute 1½ teasp. instant coffee, dissolved in ¼ cup hot water, for ¼ cup milk; omit vanilla.

ORANGE: Substitute ¼ cup orange juice for ¼ cup milk and ¼ teasp. grated orange rind for vanilla.

NOTE: This topping should be used within 3 to 4 hr.

OR ARE YOU UNDERWEIGHT?

Here are seven tips for tipping the scales:

Be Sure that there is no physical (and probably correctable) disturbance which is responsible for your underweight. Check with your doctor!

Be Patient. "Crash" programs are no more sensible in gaining weight than losing it. You probably couldn't stick with it, so why start? Be satisfied with a slow, gradual gain.

Be Sensible. Select your foods with careful thought to a balanced diet. Don't go overboard on any one food, or class of foods. Just as reducing sensibly means an overall *reduction* in quantity, so does gaining mean an overall *increase*.

Be Relaxed. Plenty of sleep is a *must*. Eight hours at least — more is better. Don't hurry your meals, especially breakfast.

Be a Snacker. The road to success in weight-gaining is often paved with frequent, small meals.

Be Active. Fresh air and exercise are nature's own appetite pepper-uppers. (Lack of appetite could be your only problem — try sprinkling dried brewer's yeast on cereals, putting it in hamburgers, meat loaves, etc. Its high thiamin (vitamin B_1 content is a wonderful appetite stimulator.)

Be Glad. You can (and should) indulge yourself in high-calorie dishes. Choose your favorites — everyone eats a little more of the things they especially like.

NOTE: You may send 15¢ for
Good Housekeeping's Complete Calorie Guide
Good Housekeeping Bulletin Service
959 Eighth Avenue
New York 19, New York

WHEN YOU GO MARKETING

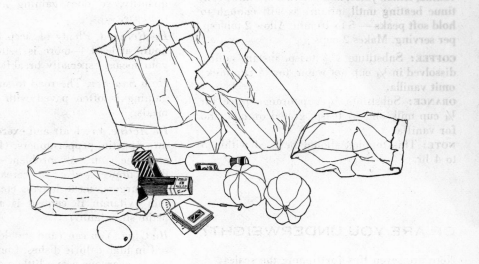

If you would be a thrifty shopper and know your way around today's serve-yourself food stores, don't wait until you get to market to decide what you're going to buy.

Develop some marketing know-how. Read the pages that follow here for marketing tips. Then take time out to leaf through the To Market and To Buy sections of the chapters on Meats, Poultry, Fish, Shellfish, Vegetables, Fruits, etc.

MARKETING TIPS

1. Make a shopping list according to the "route" you will follow in the store, so you don't have to do a lot of backtracking. Take a pencil along to scratch off things as they go into the shopping cart.
2. Check the ads in your local newspaper.
3. Remember that you can often save by purchasing a large, rather than a small, package

of a food that you use frequently, providing it keeps well.
4. Hurry fresh and frozen food home. If the package label calls for storing the food in the refrigerator, *be sure to do so.*

WHEN YOU BUY CANNED FOODS

You Get Fine Cooked Food. Canned foods are delicious just as they come from the can or jar; they are all cooked, too, saving you many hours of preparation and assuring no waste.

The fruits and vegetables used are specially grown, picked at just the right point of maturity, sealed in cans, and cooked in the briefest time after harvesting. So, like other quality canned foods, they retain a high degree of the food value of the fresh food.

The Label Is Your Buying Guide. In this age of self-service food stores, we have all become

CAN SIZES

INDUSTRY TERM	CONSUMER DESCRIPTION		CHIEF USES	NUMBER OF SERVINGS
	APPROX. NET WEIGHT OR FLUID MEASURE (CHECK LABEL)	APPROX. CUPS		
6 oz.	6 oz.	¾	Frozen concentrates, natural-strength juice.	1½ pt.
8 oz.	8 oz.	1	Fruits, vegetables, *specialties for small families.	2
Picnic	10½ to 12 oz.	1¼	Mainly condensed soups. Some fruits, vegetables, meat, fish, *specialties.	3
12 oz. (vacuum)	12 oz.	1½	Principally for vacuum-pack corn.	3 to 4
12 oz.	12 oz.	1½	Family-size frozen juice concentrate.	3 pt.
No. 300	14 to 16 oz.	1¾	Pork and beans, baked beans, meat products, cranberry sauce, blueberries, *specialties.	3 to 4
No. 303	16 to 17 oz.	2	Principal size for fruits and vegetables. Some meat products, ready-to-serve soups, *specialties.	4
No. 2	1 lb. 4 oz. or 1 pt. 2 fl. oz.	2½	**Juices, ready-to-serve soups, some *specialties, pineapple, apple slices. No longer in popular use for most fruits and vegetables.	5
No. 2½	1 lb. 13 oz.	3½	Fruits, pumpkin, sauerkraut, spinach, other greens, tomatoes.	7
No. 3 cyl. or 46 fl. oz.	3 lb. 3 oz. or 1 qt. 14 fl. oz.	5¾	"Economy family-size" fruit and vegetable juices, pork and beans, whole chicken. Institutional size for condensed soups, some vegetables.	10 to 12
No. 10	6½ lb. to 7 lb. 5 oz.	12-13	Institutional size for fruits, vegetables, and some other foods.	25

Meats, fish, and sea food are almost entirely advertised and sold under weight terminology.

Strained and homogenized foods and chopped junior foods come in small jars and cans, suitable for the smaller servings used. The weight is on the label.

*Specialties—Food combinations prepared by special manufacturer's recipe.

**Juices are now being packed in a number of other can sizes, including the 1-qt. size.

increasingly dependent on labels to guide our buying.

For this reason, well-known canners are wording labels to give you a clear picture of what's inside the can. The can size, variety, style, color, maturity, and amount of food in the can (the ingredients in the can are listed according to the amount present — the most first); the number of servings; kind of syrup; uses, etc., are noted right on the label. This helps you buy what you want and the amount you need. Of course, you must judge flavor for yourself. If certain brands satisfy you, remember their names. Canned tuna comes in several styles. Of course, a swelled or bulging can should never be used.

Canned Fruits Are of the Best. Your grocer has a wonderful assortment of canned fruits that come not only in larger sizes but also in 8-oz. cans, which are made to order for the family of one or two. Look for pineapple, peaches, fruit cocktail, pears, grapefruit, cherries, etc. Then refer to Wonderful Ways with Fruits, p. 539, Dreamy Desserts, p. 559, Relishes and Garnishes, p. 433, Salads, p. 445, etc., for ways to serve them.

Canned Vegetables Are Tasty Time-Savers. Today's canned vegetables, such as green peas, green limas, green beans (Blue Lake, etc.), whole-kernel corn, asparagus, etc., are unusually fine in flavor. So it is more important than ever to preserve their flavor and food value when you heat them for the table. For the best heating methods, see Canned Vegetables, p. 389.

Never rinse canned vegetables under cold water; you'll lose food value and flavor. Don't turn them out of the can to be aerated before using them; that simply adds work, does not improve their flavor.

There Are Dietetic Packs, Too. For those who must count calories, watch their sodium intake, or are diabetic, there are increasing numbers of fine dietetic-pack canned foods, including fruits, vegetables, tuna, soups, juices, chicken, meats, prepared dishes, salad dressings, etc.

Know How to Open a Can or Jar Easily. Of course, a good can opener is indispensable, and many fine ones are available today — either electrically or manually operated.

For safety's sake, completely remove can top and discard. Many can openers have a magnet that lifts off the cut top.

For glass jars and tumblers that have pry-off caps, there is now an inexpensive, efficient opener that easily lifts caps without bending or bursting them. The caps may be resealed by pressing with the heels of both hands.

Don't Hesitate to Store Leftovers in Opened Cans. Canned foods may be safely left in the opened can if they're covered and kept in the refrigerator. Of course any leftover cooked food, stored in any type of container, should be refrigerated.

For safety's sake, discard without tasting any opened can of food that has an off odor.

CEREALS

Keep a Variety on Hand. And what a variety there is — more than three dozen kinds of whole-grain, enriched, or restored breakfast cereals, including both hot and ready-to-eat varieties. The hot cereals include instant, quick-cooking, and regular kinds. Ready-to-eat cereals include regular and presweetened.

WHOLE-GRAIN CEREAL is a grain product which has retained the specific nutrients of the whole, unprocessed grain and contains natural proportions of bran, germ, and endosperm.

ENRICHED CEREAL is one to which vitamins or minerals (or both) have been added beyond the whole-grain levels, or to which other nutrients, such as vitamin D, which were not significantly present in the grain of origin, have been added.

RESTORED CEREAL is made from either entire grain or portions of one or more grains to which have been added sufficient amounts of thiamine, niacin, and iron to attain the accepted whole-grain levels of these 3 nutrients found in the original grain (or grains) from which the cereal is prepared.

To Use: Treat your family to exciting new discoveries in food-flavor enjoyment: Combine cereal with coconut, coffee nogs, exotic spices, flavored sugars, fruit or fruit juice, jellies, and sliced fruit.

Or discover many recipes using the special qualities of breakfast cereals — appetizers, breads, cakes, confections, cookies, entrées, frozen desserts, fruit crisps, muffins, piecrusts, puddings, salads, soups, sundaes, and vegetables.

If you've a family of breakfast skimpers and skippers, be sure to see A Good Day Starts with a Good Breakfast, p. 50.

To Store: Store all cereals in a cool, dry, convenient spot. Packages and inner wrappings should be carefully opened so that they may be resealed after each use. This is particularly important with ready-to-eat cereals, which are only at their best when crisp.

Cereals that require cooking should be kept in the original packages so that label directions may be followed.

CHOCOLATE AND COCOA

UNSWEETENED CHOCOLATE comes in squares, 8 1-oz. squares to a package. It is pure chocolate, a special blend of finest cocoa beans.

SEMISWEET-CHOCOLATE SQUARES (once known as candy-making chocolate) come 8 1-oz. squares to a package. It is a rich chocolate, vanilla flavored and sweetened, that's fine for candy making, frostings, sauces, baking, etc.

SEMISWEET-CHOCOLATE PIECES (some have a glazed finish) come in 6-oz. and 12-oz. cellophane bags. To melt, use dry double-boiler top or small bowl, set over hot, *not boiling*, water. If chocolate should stiffen, add 1 to 2 tablesp. vegetable shortening and stir smooth.

GERMAN SWEET COOKING CHOCOLATE, which comes in 1/4-lb. bars, is sweetened, light, rich, smooth. It is used for cooking and eating.

UNSWEETENED COCOA is prepared from cocoa beans by removing varying amounts of cocoa butter.

DUTCH CHOCOLATE COCOA is made from cocoa beans that have been alkalized to give the cocoa a richer, darker color and accent the chocolate flavor.

SWEETENED COCOA MIX is a blend of cocoa, sugar, and flavoring that dissolves readily in cold or hot milk.

INSTANT SWEET MILK COCOA is a blend of cocoa, whole milk, and sugar, for instant home use in hot water or hot milk.

COCONUT

Packaged Coconut comes flaked, fine grated, or toasted:

FLAKED COCONUT is in thin, short flakes, slightly sweetened, and needs neither cutting nor chopping when used as an ingredient in recipes. It is available in a 3½-oz. can or carton (about 1⅓ cups), 7-oz. tray pack (about 2⅔ cups), and 14-oz. polyethelene bag (about 6⅛ cups).

FINE GRATED COCONUT is finely grated and slightly sweetened. It's available in a 7-oz. tray pack (about 2 cups). One cup of packaged fine grated coconut equals 1⅓ cups of flaked coconut; so adjust recipes accordingly when using.

TOASTED COCONUT. Toasting coconut need bother you no longer, for now it comes in a tray pack, moist and lightly browned, with a toasty, nutty flavor. A real time-saver as a topping on cakes, pies, fruit salads, sundaes, etc., or in candies, cookies, desserts, pancakes or unbaked piecrust. Delicious, too, as an accompaniment for curried dishes, creamed chicken, shrimp, etc.

To Store: All packaged coconut, once opened, should be stored in an airtight container in either the refrigerator or the freezer until used up — it's a perishable fruit!

FRESH COCONUT: It's easy to open a fresh coconut this way: With a long nail, puncture the 3 indentations at the end of the coconut. Drain milk out of these holes. Then, in a shallow pan, bake whole coconut at 350°F. 15 min.; this will crack shell. Complete cracking with hammer; then pry out white meat in as large pieces as possible. With knife or vegetable parer, cut brown skin from white meat; then grate meat, rubbing each piece the full length of the grater.

CREAM

HEAVY OR WHIPPING CREAM: Cream containing not less than 30 per cent butterfat.

LIGHT, COFFEE, OR TABLE CREAM: Cream containing not less than 18 per cent butterfat.

HALF-AND-HALF CREAM: Mixture of half milk and half cream containing 10 to 12 per cent butterfat, according to where it is sold.

COMMERCIAL OR DAIRY SOUR CREAM: Light pasteurized cream, of custardlike consistency, with characteristic tangy flavor produced by the addition of a culture or starter. Comes in ½-pt. and 1-pt. containers.

INSTANT POWDERED CREAM: A 100-per-cent pure dairy product — all fresh cream and other milk products — in instant powdered form, that stays fresh and never needs refrigeration. Not only dissolves instantly in hot coffee, tea, or cocoa, but can replace cream or milk in many recipes if manufacturer's directions are followed. Do try it!

DESSERT TOPPING

Low in calories and cost, this light, lovely, wholesome dessert topping comes in two forms:

DESSERT-TOPPING MIX: The kind that comes in a box, to which you add milk and a dash of vanilla and then whip. In this form, it keeps well in the refrigerator without wilting.

INSTANT DESSERT TOPPING: This comes in pressure cans — all ready to whoosh onto favorite desserts, just before serving. Keep refrigerated.

EXTRACTS

Since we use extracts to lend a pleasing flavor to our food, buy well-known, quality brands to insure full, uniform flavor. You may save by buying a medium-to-large, rather than a small, bottle. Keep bottle tightly closed and as far away from the oven heat as possible.

Don't stick to just one or two flavors. Try new ones. Or plan to combine flavors, such as vanilla and almond, lemon and orange. And add the extract to mixtures, after cooling, whenever possible.

PURE VANILLA EXTRACT is an extract of the vanilla bean, conforming to required standards.

IMITATION VANILLA is a solution of synthetic flavorings that yields a product simulating pure vanilla extract.

FLOURS

In cake, cookie, bread, and similar recipes in this book, we indicate the kind of flour to be used. *Never substitute another kind.* The following descriptions will guide you in buying the right flour. Don't buy more than you can use in a reasonable length of time.

All-Purpose Flour is sometimes referred to as general-purpose, or family, flour. It comes in bags and gives good results in all types of home baking.

It may be a blend of hard wheats, soft wheats, or both. It is generally enriched, and this is indicated on the label of the bag. Enriched flour contains thiamine, niacin, riboflavin, and iron, in addition to excellent, energy-yielding carbohydrates and supplementary protein. In following our recipes, always sift all-purpose flour just before measuring.

Bread Flour, which also comes in bags, is excellent for yeast breads but is not as satisfactory for general use. It is made from hard wheats and has a higher gluten content than all-purpose flour. It is not as generally available as all-purpose and cake flours.

Cake Flour comes in packages and makes especially delicate cakes. It is made from selected soft wheats and is specially milled to give a very fine flour. In following our recipes, always sift cake flour just before measuring.

Self-Rising Flour is all-purpose or cake flour to which leavening and salt have been added in proper amounts for most home baking except yeast breads. To use, follow the recipes which appear on the label.

Whole-Wheat, Entire-Wheat, and Graham Flours are synonymous terms. Such flour contains, in natural proportions, all the constituents of the entire cleaned wheat grain. Do not sift these flours before measuring.

FOOD COLORS

Food colors available to the homemaker are limited to those which have been certified as safe for use in foods by the Food and Drug Administration. They come in liquid and paste forms and in a variety of colors.

LEAVENING AGENTS

Baking Powder: Baking powders are classified according to the acid ingredients they contain. There are 3 types, as listed below, but double-acting baking powder is likely to be most widely available. Nationally known brands clearly indicate the type on the label; look for it.

DOUBLE-ACTING BAKING POWDER: Reacts very slowly, releasing about one fifth to one third of its leavening in the cold mixture, the rest in the heat of the oven.

PHOSPHATE BAKING POWDER: Reacts slowly and requires heat to liberate about one third of its leavening.

TARTRATE BAKING POWDER: Reacts rapidly and begins its action at room temperature as soon as liquid is added.

In following our recipes *be sure* to use the kind of baking powder the recipe calls for.

Baking Soda: Baking soda is used alone or with baking powder to leaven cakes made with buttermilk, sour milk, chocolate, molasses, fruit juices, etc. The acid from these ingredients reacts with the soda to release leavening. When using soda, don't delay mixing or baking.

DRIED HERBS AND SPICES

Children, as well as adults, should become familiar with seasoned foods. Herbs and spices add new interest and delightful flavor to your everyday cooking. But when you introduce a new seasoning, do it with a light hand. Remember, herbs and spices should enhance, not overpower, food flavors.

Tips on Using Dried Herbs and Spices

1. Buy only in small containers; a little dried herb or spice goes a long way; also, they lose flavor with time. Store them away from heat and sunlight.
2. Note date of buying on label; then renew them at least once a year, even if not used up. Don't make antiques of spices and herbs. Smell them occasionally — once the scent is gone, they're worthless.
3. If you aren't following a specific recipe, start with a little herb or spice; taste to decide whether to add more. A good rule of thumb: Add $\frac{1}{4}$ teasp. to a dish that makes 4 servings.
4. If it's a stew or soup you're making, add herb or spice during the last hour of cooking.
5. If the soup is canned or frozen, add the herb or spice as you heat the soup.
6. If it's a roast you're preparing, add herb or spice toward end of roasting.
7. If it's a steak or chops, sprinkle with herb during broiling. Or, about one hour ahead, brush with salad oil, sprinkle with herbs, then refrigerate until needed.
8. If it's meat loaf, hamburgers, or stuffings, etc., add herb when mixing.
9. It it's a vegetable or sauce, add herb or spice while cooking.
10. If it's a dish that calls for no cooking, like vegetable or tomato juice, salad dressing, a dip, dunk, or spread, let herb or spice stand in it a while.

FRESH HERBS

Many adventurous cooks and gardeners, in the country or city, enjoy fresh herbs from their gardens. It's a delight to pluck and sniff a leaf of rosemary, tarragon, parsley, or dill, to name a few.

DRIED HERBS AND SPICES

ALLSPICE
(resembles blend of cinnamon, nutmeg, and cloves)

Use whole in:

Pickling, gravies, meats, fish dishes, etc.

Use ground in or on:

Cakes, cookies, puddings, relishes, preserves, tomato sauce, steak, etc.

ANISE SEED
(licoricelike flavor)

Sprinkle on:

Coffeecakes, sweet rolls, fruit, etc.

Use ground in:

Cookies, sweet pickles, candies.

BASIL
(an herb of west Europe)

Sprinkle on:

Green beans, lamb chops, meats, peas, potatoes, sauces, soups. Or on egg, poultry, salad, and tomato dishes.

BAY LEAVES
(an herb from a laurel tree grown in eastern Mediterranean countries)

Use whole in:

Fish dishes, pickling, sauces and gravies, stews and soups.

CARAWAY SEEDS
(from Holland)

Sprinkle (whole or ground) over, or use in:

Sauerkraut, cabbage, asparagus, noodles, French fries, soups, cookies, breads and rolls, cheese spreads, pork, liver, kidneys, loaf cake, etc.

CARDAMOM SEEDS
(small pod of brown seeds)

Use whole in:

Demitasse, pickling, curries, etc.

Use ground in or on:

Cookies, coffeecakes, grape jelly, melon, etc.

CAYENNE PEPPER
(blend of most pungent chili peppers)

Use in:

Sauces, meat and egg dishes, sea food, curries, etc.

CELERY SEEDS
(tiny seedlike fruit)

Use whole or ground in:

Cheese dishes, fish dishes, salad dressings, sauces, soups, stews, tomato, egg, or potato dishes, vegetables, etc.

CHERVIL
(resembles parsley; herb is slightly peppery)

Delicious in:

Egg, fish, poultry, tomato dishes. Or in peas and carrots, salads, summer squash, and salad dressing.

CHILI POWDER
(blend of chilies and spices)

Use in:

Chili con carne, cocktail sauces, egg dishes, gravies, sea food, stews.

CINNAMON
(spicy bark of Oriental tree)

Use whole in:

Pickling, preserving, canned or stewed fruits, etc.

Use ground in or on:

Mashed sweet potatoes, toast, blueberries, apple or pineapple dishes, broiled grapefruit, bananas, cakes, ice cream, cookies, puddings, hot biscuits.

CLOVES
(nail-shaped flower bud of clove tree)

Use whole in or on:

Pork and ham roasts, pickling peaches, pineapple, etc.

Use ground in:

Baked dishes, stews, chocolate puddings, vegetables (beets), broiled grapefruit, potato soup, etc.

DRIED HERBS AND SPICES

CORIANDER SEED
(dried, ripe fruit of an herb of the parsley family; tastes like combination of lemon peel and sage)

Use ground in: Buns, pastry, cookies, cakes.

CUMIN
(a seed with distinctive salty-sweet flavor, a flavoring ingredient of chili powder)

Use whole in: Cream, cottage, or Cheddar cheese, cabbage.

Use ground in: Deviled eggs, meat loaf, hamburgers, chili con carne, rice, sauerkraut, fish.

CURRY POWDER
(blend of spices)

Use in: Sauce for eggs, fish, meats, poultry, vegetables; in tomato juice, etc.

DILL SEEDS
(small seeds of dill plant, imported from India)

Use whole or ground in: Pickling, gravies, apple pie, soups (borsch), potato salad, any cheese spread or dunk, salads, sauerkraut, cabbage, turnips, cauliflower, spaghetti and tomato dishes, cream- or cottage-cheese mixtures, etc.

GINGER
(root of Oriental plant)

Use cracked in: Chutneys, conserves, pickling, stewed dried fruits, applesauce, etc.

Use ground in: Gingerbread, pumpkin pie, Indian pudding, summer squash, melon, canned fruit, chicken dishes, etc.

MACE
(dried pulp around nutmeg kernel; has flavor similar to nutmeg)

Use whole or ground, in or on: Cherries, chocolate dishes, whipped cream, jellies, canned fruit, gingerbread, poundcake, broiled grapefruit, fish sauces, etc.

MARJORAM
(herb of the mint family from France or Chili)

Use sparingly in or on: Roast lamb, meat pies, hash, stews, stuffings, asparagus, carrots, greens, limas, squash, cheese and egg dishes, fish or vegetable sauces.

NUTMEG
(kernel of nutmeg fruit)

Use ground in: Cakes, breads, cabbage, cauliflower, broiled fruit, green beans, greens, puddings, sauces,

Use as topping for: Eggnog, custards, whipped cream, sauces, etc.

OREGANO
(herb imported from Italy and Mexico)

Good in or on: Pork, hamburgers, chili con carne, pizzas, omelets, stews, spaghetti sauce, vegetables, cheese dishes. Or in melted butter served with sea food.

PAPRIKA
(mild member of pepper family; adds color, flavor)

Sprinkle on or use in: Canapés, fish, gravies, meats, salad dressings, shellfish, vegetables, etc.

PARSLEY FLAKES
(green herb, distinctive mild flavor)

Sprinkle on: Soups, salads, stews, sauces, all vegetables, omelets, potatoes.

DRIED HERBS AND SPICES

PEPPER
(world's most popular spice, from East Indies)

Use whole peppercorns in: — Pickling, soups, pepper grinders, etc.

Use ground (black or white) or coarsely ground or cracked black pepper in: — Eggs, gravies, meats, salads, sauces, soups, many vegetables—in fact, most foods.

POPPY SEEDS
(fragrant seeds from Holland)

Sprinkle on: — Breads, rolls, cookies, etc.

Use in: — Salads, noodles, etc.

POULTRY SEASONING
(fragrant herbs combined with sage)

Delicious in: — Biscuit dough, stuffings.

ROSEMARY
(an herb — looks like a pine needle)

Delectable in, with, or on: — Biscuit dough, boiled potatoes, roasts, stews, vegetables, lamb or poultry dishes, sauces for meat or fish, or tossed in vegetable, orange, pear, grapefruit, or peach salad.

SAGE
(a favorite herb with distinctive, positive flavor)

Use lightly in or on: — Cheese, fish, pork, veal, ham, poultry, sausage, or tomato dishes, salads.

SAFFRON
(hand-picked dried stigmas of a plant of crocus family; it takes 225,000 to make a pound. World's most expensive spice; a little goes a long way)

Use whole stigmas. Rub, and use in: — Baked goods, rice, etc.

SAVORY
(herb of the mint family from France and Spain)

Use in or on: — Baked beans, green limas, vegetable soup, meat loaf, roasts, hamburger, egg or rice dishes, potato or squash dishes.

TARRAGON
(leaf with anise flavor)

Good in: — Salads, sauces, sea food, beets, greens, mushrooms, peas, egg and poultry dishes, tomato dishes.

THYME
(many varieties of this herb)

Use sparingly in or with: — Veal, pork, carrots, eggplant, peas, tomatoes, breads, stews, chowders, stuffings, cheese or fish dishes.

TURMERIC
(mild, slightly bitter flavor)

Use ground in: — Mustards, curries, pickling mixtures, chicken, eggs, fish, etc.

MILK

Everyone needs some form of milk every day, so *never* skimp on that daily quota!

When It's Milk

Check Milk Source: Be sure that the milk you buy comes from a supply which is subject to public health inspection by state or local authorities.

Insist That Milk Be Pasteurized: The health of your family is being endangered constantly if you are using raw milk or dairy products made from it. Undulant fever and many streptococcal infections may be carried by raw milk. Pasteurization is a sure way to make milk safe.

Homogenized Milk: This is pasteurized fluid whole milk, now available in nearly all areas of the U.S., in which the fat globules have been reduced in size so they remain evenly distributed throughout the milk. All portions of the milk thus have the same butterfat content. This product is usually available with 400 International Units of vitamin D added.

Skim Milk: This is whole milk from which the butterfat has been removed, without the loss of other significant nutritive qualities of whole milk.

Skim milk fortified with nonfat dry milk is also available, often with added vitamins.

2% Milk: This product is available in many markets as a low-fat milk. It is of the same high quality as pasteurized whole milk except that the fat content has been standardized at 2 per cent. It may or may not be fortified with added nonfat milk solids.

To Care for Milk:
1. *Take delivered milk in promptly* and store at once in coldest part of refrigerator. Refrigerate continuously until used.
2. *Always keep milk covered.*
3. *Never mix new and old milk or cream* except for immediate use.

When It's Condensed Milk

Canned, sweetened, condensed milk is a mixture of pure, whole cow's milk and sugar, from which about 60 per cent of the water is removed before it is put into cans and sealed. This thick milk product is heat-sterilized in the can and has excellent keeping quality. It is used to sweeten coffee and to make ice cream, lemon and other pie fillings, cookies, etc. Keep refrigerated after opening.

When It's Evaporated Milk

Canned evaporated milk is pure, fresh, whole cow's milk of uniform quality, with nothing removed except about half the natural water content. And nothing but vitamin D (the sunshine vitamin) is added. It is homogenized to distribute the cream evenly throughout the milk. It is pasteurized before it is put into the can, then sterilized after the can is sealed.

To Use: Evaporated milk offers one of the best ways to cut down your food bills. Just as it comes from the can (undiluted), or with an equal amount of water added (diluted), it may be used in preparing many dishes, such as cheese sauce, meat loaf, mashed potatoes, scrambled eggs, casseroles, desserts, 5-minute fudge, etc. It's economical, too, used as cream in coffee, or for whipping.

To Store After Opening: Keep evaporated milk refrigerated after opening; cover top with food cover or piece of foil pressed close against top edge. It has excellent keeping quality.

When It's Instant Nonfat Dry Milk

Instant nonfat dry milk is skim milk in granular form. This dairy product is top-quality milk with only the fat and water removed. In reliquefied form, it provides the valuable whole-milk amounts of protein, B-vitamins, and calcium and other protective milk minerals. It's a wonderfully thrifty type of milk. Be sure to keep it in its protective package on a cool, dry pantry shelf; close the package carefully after each use.

To Reliquefy It: Carefully follow the simple label directions. One cup of instant nonfat dry milk makes 3 cups fluid skim milk. Once it's reliquefied, refrigerate it as you would fresh fluid milk. Mixing and holding overnight improves the flavor and palatability of the product.

Or, for use in sauces, soups, and gravies, it may be reliquefied with mild-flavored vegetable liquors or meat or poultry stock.

Or, for use in desserts or fruit drinks, it may be reliquefied with fruit juices.

To Use in Reliquefied Form: No special recipes are needed for using instant nonfat dry milk. After reliquefying it as on p. 97, use in identical amounts, in any recipe calling for milk. Whole milk mixed with an equal amount of reliquefied instant nonfat dry milk is excellent and saves ⅓ on milk bills.

To Use in Dry Form: If you prefer to use nonfat dry milk in its dry form in biscuits, muffins, etc., mix it with the sifted dry ingredients; then add water in approximately the same amount as was called for of fresh fluid milk — consult the label.

Instant nonfat dry milk whips up well for low-calorie desserts; see Slim-Jim Topping, p. 86.

For Extra Nourishment: Oftentimes you can step up the food value of a dish by adding some nonfat dry milk before the dish is baked. See Two-Day Caramel Ham Loaf, p. 216.

MOLASSES

Molasses is an important source of iron, so use it often.

DARK MOLASSES: Has a full, tangy flavor and deep color, and is excellent for all cooking in which many spices are present — gingerbread, Indian pudding, etc.

LIGHT MOLASSES: Has a more delicate flavor than dark molasses, a lower iron content, and a golden color, and is excellent for general cooking purposes.

MONOSODIUM GLUTAMATE

A white crystalline seasoning that comes in a shaker and brings out the natural flavors of many foods. Especially nice for meats, poultry, vegetables, fish, gravy, soup, and salads.

Add it before or during cooking, along with other seasonings, in these approximate amounts:

  1 teasp. per lb. of ground beef
  ½ teasp. per lb. for roasts
  ½ teasp. over each side of individual steaks
  ¾ teasp. per 4 servings of vegetables
  1 teasp. per chicken

NUTS

Let reliable brand name on the nut shell or package be your guide in buying plump, meaty, fresh, sweet nut kernels.

Kinds You Can Buy

IN-THE-SHELL* *(in bags or bulk):*

Almonds	Pistachio nuts
Black walnuts	California walnuts
Brazil nuts	(top-quality, large
Chestnuts	ones likely to carry
Filberts	red brand stamp on
Peanuts	shell; medium ones,
Pecans	blue brand stamp)

SHELLED* *(in clear bags, vacuum cans, or jars):*

Almonds	Cashews
Blanched, whole or	Coconut chips
sliced	Dry toasted nuts, sev-
Roasted, diced	eral varieties
Toasted, blanched,	Filberts
slivered	Macadamias
Smokehouse cocktail	Pecans
Unblanched, whole	Salted pecans, peanuts,
or sliced	mixed nuts, etc.
Black walnuts	California walnuts

For number of cupfuls per lb., see p. 17.

How to Store Nuts

In-the-Shell: Store at room temperature except for prolonged periods. Keep in nut bowl, or in cool, dry place — preferably main section of refrigerator.

Kernels: For best protection, freeze kernels you shell yourself. Store unopened *bags* or *cans* of kernels in main section of refrigerator (or freeze). After opening, keep unused kernels in refrigerator (or freeze).

To Freeze: Put kernels in tightly covered freezer container or plastic bag. Thaw and allow moisture to dry out before using or refreezing.

When You Use Nuts

Almonds:

TO BLANCH: Cover shelled almonds with cold water. Bring to boil; then remove from heat at once and drain. Slip off skins by pressing each almond between thumb and forefinger. Then dry almonds on paper towels.

TO TOAST: Use 300°F. oven for 20 to 25 min. for whole almonds, less for slivers. Remove nuts before they are quite as dark as desired (they continue to brown after removal from oven).

TO ROAST: Toss nuts in a shallow pan with 1 teasp. salad oil per cup of nuts. Roast at 300°F. Stir occasionally to insure even browning.

Brazil Nuts:

TO SHELL: Freeze in-shell nuts a few hours or overnight; then use nutcracker to shell.

Or boil in-shell nuts, in water to cover, 3 min.; drain. Let stand in cold water, to cover, 1 min.; drain. Now they'll crack easily.

TO SLICE: Cover shelled Brazil nuts with water; simmer 2 to 3 min.; drain. Now they'll slice easily. Or use a vegetable parer to make curls.

Walnuts and Pecans:

TO CRACK: If you haven't a nutcracker, place each nut on end, holding by seam. Strike with hammer on pointed end.

TO CHOP:

1. Spread nuts on wooden board. Hold tip of long, sharp knife close to surface of board with one hand, then move knife handle up and down, and around in semicircle, with other hand, so blade contacts uncut nuts.
2. Today's nut choppers do a good job, too.
3. So does the electric blender, especially when you have a large quantity of nuts to chop.
4. Or place kernels inside plastic bag; roll lightly with a rolling pin.

TO TOAST WALNUTS: Boil walnut kernels in rapidly boiling water 3 min., then drain. Spread nuts in shallow pan. Bake at 350°F. 10 to 20 min., or until lightly toasted, stirring often. While hot, brush with butter and sprinkle generously with seasoned, or garlic, or regular, salt. Cool, then refrigerate.

SALAD AND OLIVE OILS

SALAD OILS: When buying salad oil, choose one of the many brands of corn, cottonseed, peanut, safflower, or soy oils, or a blend of two or more oils. They're excellent for sautéing, deep or shallow frying, making salad dressings, preparing dishes that call for melted fat, etc. All of these oils are excellent sources of polyunsaturated fatty acids.

OLIVE OIL: Olive oil, with its unique flavor, is popular for salad dressings, Italian-style dishes, etc.

To Store: After pouring what you need from a bottle of salad or olive oil, before screwing cap back on again, be sure to wipe off neck of bottle and inside of cap with paper towel or tissue.

Salad oils do not require refrigeration, although they may be so stored if you wish. Olive oil should be refrigerated.

SHAKER SEASONINGS

Seasoned salt, celery salt, garlic salt, onion salt, salt, paprika, grated cheese, seasoned pepper, cinnamon-sugar mixture, and others are available for your use in convenient shakers. They are quick, delightful seasoners for meat dishes, vegetables, sauces, salads. They also add glamour and flavor sprinkled on crackers, breads, and rolls before heating.

SEASONED OR SEASONING SALT: A flavorful blend of many spices with salt — just perfect for so many everyday foods!

CELERY SALT: Mixture of ground celery seeds with salt. Gives zest to such dishes as:

Fish	Salad dressings
Oyster stew	Soups
Potato salads	Tomato juice, etc.

GARLIC SALT: Mixture of garlic powder with salt. Use with, or instead of, salt on or in:

Ground meats	spaghetti sauce
Salad dressings	Soups
Salads	Steaks or chops
Sauces such as	Tomato juice

ONION SALT: A blend of dehydrated onion and salt. Adds a delicate onion flavor to:

Meats	Spaghetti sauce
Salad dressings	Vegetables (add to
Salads	cooking water)

SEASONED PEPPER: A blend of imported and domestic pepper with rare spices — slightly mild, mellow in flavor. Excellent with:

Meats	Fish
Eggs	Vegetables
Salads	Soups
Poultry	Gravies

SHORTENINGS

Butter: Butter has always been a favorite because of its popular flavor and its ability to enhance the texture and flavor of so many of our everyday dishes.

It gives us important amounts of vitamin A, as well as a high energy value of 100 calories per tablespoonful. Refrigerate, covered, or in a butter conditioner.

Margarine: Most of today's fine margarine is made entirely from vegetable oils processed to give them desirable spreading and cooking properties. A culture of skim milk used in the manufacturing process is largely responsible for its appetizing flavor.

Margarine has the same energy value as butter, and since it is fortified with a minimum of 15,000 units of vitamin A per lb., it is nutritionally comparable to butter and is uniform in food value throughout the year. Many brands are also fortified with vitamin D.

There are available today new types of margarine, specifically processed to retain the original properties of the basic oils; some require frozen storage, but most, only refrigeration. Also, unsalted margarines are now available. Nationally known, quality brands are excellent and economical for table and cooking use. Buy margarine only from a store

that keeps it refrigerated. Store, covered, in refrigerator.

Shortenings: When we call for "shortening" in a recipe, we have reference to those shortenings which come in 1-lb. and 3-lb. cans. Whether these shortenings are all-vegetable, as many of them are, or a combination of meat fat and vegetable oils, they are specially adapted for the richer, quick-method cakes, as most labels indicate. They're wonderful, too, for pastry and other forms of baking, sautéing, frying, etc. Creamy in texture, bland in odor and flavor, they are light, workable, easy to blend with other ingredients. They require no refrigeration. Also see How-Tos, 2, p. 627.

Some well-known brands of shortening are now processed to retain more of the original values of the basic oils.

Lard: It's quick-blending properties make lard excellent for pastry. It is also used in sautéing, frying, bread making, etc. The majority of brands contain small amounts of antioxidants to improve the keeping properties. Such brands do not require refrigeration. Refrigerate, covered, any lard whose label does not indicate the presence of an antioxidant.

SUGARS

Brown Sugar: Brown sugar, which comes in 1-lb. and 3-lb. packages, gets its color from its molasses content. There are two kinds, each with its own uses. Do not interchange in our recipes.

LIGHT-BROWN SUGAR: Has a delicate molasses flavor, desirable for general cookery.

DARK-BROWN SUGAR: Contains more molasses and is therefore darker, with more molasses flavor. It is excellent for baked beans, baked hams, and other cookery.

TO KEEP BROWN SUGAR SOFT: An airtight container is needed to keep brown sugar soft. So transfer brown sugar from its package to a glass jar having a large opening and a lid with a rubber edging. In this way, it may be kept soft whether on the pantry shelf or in the refrigerator.

For a less satisfactory, but somewhat effective, method of storing brown sugar, store box of sugar directly in vegetable compartment of refrigerator where the normal moisture content of the air will keep sugar moist for some time.

In the event of an emergency, you can place hardened brown sugar in a shallow pan in the oven at low temperature and heat until pliable — *then use at once.* On cooling, sugar becomes harder than before.

Granulated Sugar: There are two kinds: commonly used granulated, and superfine (or very fine) sugar. Superfine sugar has tiny crystals which, because they're smaller, make it especially excellent for:
a. filling sugar bowls
b. easier creaming with shortening in cookies and cakes
c. combining with the eggs in angel and sponge cake and meringues
d. combining with eggs and whipped cream in Bavarian cream and chiffon pies
e. caramelizing to use in brittles or as flavoring

Confectioners' Sugar: Called "powdered" by some, this is a very finely pulverized sugar with a soft, perfectly smooth, fluffy texture.

Cube and Tablet Sugar: A convenient sweetening for hot drinks. The cubes are especially dainty in demitasse, tea, etc. Use the tablets wherever you wish.

SYRUPS

Corn Syrup: Corn syrup, used widely in cooking and as a table syrup, comes in 3 styles:
DARK: Deep-amber in color
WHITE OR LIGHT: Colorless
MAPLE-FLAVORED: Golden

Maple-Blended Syrup: This is a blend of maple and cane syrups. Delightful on pancakes, ice-cream sundaes, etc.

Maple Syrup: This is the pure boiled-down sap from the maple tree. A favorite on pancakes, in candies, on ice cream, etc.

Buttered Syrup: Top-quality maple-blended syrup with butter added to it. Perfect on pancakes, waffles, hot biscuits, and French toast.

POWDERED INSTANT MEAT TENDERIZERS

When powdered instant meat tenderizer — it comes in shaker-top jars, seasoned or unseasoned — is used, the less tender cuts of meat may be cooked as you do the more expensive tender cuts. This powdered tenderizer may be used on steaks, roasts, pot roasts, chops, ground meats, in stews, on fish, variety meats, game birds and poultry. It also helps seal in juices, cuts down shrinkage, and reduces cooking time. Used in cooking dried beans, peas, and limas, it cuts the cooking time.

How to Tenderize Meat: Prepare all surfaces of meat, *one side at a time,* as follows: With your fingers pat cold water from the faucet over the surface of the meat till thoroughly moistened. Then sprinkle it evenly with powdered instant meat tenderizer, allowing about ½ teasp. per lb. *Use no salt.* Now, with fork, pierce meat at ½" intervals, so tenderizer can penetrate. Repeat on all surfaces. Then cook immediately; or, if preferred, refrigerate until ready to cook. Cooking time will be approximately 25% less.

How to Tenderize Poultry and Game Birds: Rinse bird inside and out; drain well. Sprinkle powdered tenderizer evenly over entire cavity, using about ½ teasp. per lb. of bird. *Use no salt.* Then, with kitchen fork, pierce bird deeply from cavity side — under breast and into thigh and leg flesh, but without going through outer skin. Cook immediately. Cooking time and shrinkage are reduced.

VINEGARS

Today you can buy any number of delightfully flavored vinegars to use in cooking. Here are some of them:
CIDER: This fine, all-purpose vinegar is a stand-by for salads and salad dressings.
DISTILLED WHITE: This clear, colorless vinegar is ideal for pickling, preserving.
MALT: Its rich flavor gives zest to salad dressings, meat and fish sauces, sea foods.
TARRAGON: Its herb fragrance is wonderful in salad dressings, salads, sauces, pot roasts.

WINE: Made from a select table wine, it adds zest to sauces, salad dressings, etc.

BASIL, HERB AND SPICE, OR MIXED HERB: Use lightly in or on cooked greens, slaw, sauces, salad dressings, etc.

GARLIC WINE: Use instead of garlic in hamburgers, stews, salads, sauces, etc.

LUSCIOUS TIME-SAVERS

Sauce Mixes: You can add the expertly blended flavors and seasonings of these new-comers to a wide variety of dishes without the time-consuming task of preparing the sauce from scratch. With milk or water added, as each envelope directs, you have luscious brown or light gravy, or cheese, curry, sour-cream, white, meat-loaf, à-la-king, chili, or spaghetti sauce in minutes. Do try them and see!

Barbecue and Hickory-Smoke-Flavored Barbecue Sauces: Both of these are on the grocer's shelves today. They give everyday foods an exciting lift and add a different flavor accent to baked beans and franks, stews, beefburgers, meat loaf, fish dishes, meats, poultry, and shellfish.

Canned Tomato Sauce: Made from the solids of red-type tomatoes, with salt, spices, and sugar added, this ever-popular sauce is prized for its luscious flavor at reasonable cost and is used in endless dishes.

Canned White Sauce, Etc.: In some localities, you can buy canned white sauce, as well as cheese sauce and Hollandaise, all ready to open and heat.

Frozen Prepared Dinners: High on the list of meat dishes that will save you precious minutes at mealtime are quick frozen dinners. Each meat comes with its accompanying potatoes and vegetables — all ready on a tray, for you to heat and serve.

SOME FAVORITE FROZEN DINNERS you're likely to find in your markets are:

Sliced Beef, Meat Loaf, Chopped Sirloin Beef, Loin of Pork, Ham, Swiss Steak, Three Course Dinner (includes soup and dessert, etc.).

SEVERAL OTHER FROZEN DINNERS AND ENTRÈES feature poultry, shellfish, etc., too, including:

Fried Chicken (with whipped potatoes),

Fillet of Haddock, Turkey (with whipped potatoes), Fried Shrimp, Macaroni and Cheese, etc.

And don't forget that, before heating these dinners as the label directs, you may add your special touch to each — a spoonful of whole-cranberry sauce, a sprinkle of a favorite herb, some grated cheese, etc. Or you may prefer to add the gay garnish, chili sauce, catchup, a spiced peach, watermelon circles, a favorite relish, or coleslaw just before each dinner goes to the table.

Other Frozen Hearties

FROZEN MEAT PIES: These come in one or two serving portions and include Beef, Chicken, and Turkey.

FROZEN MAIN DISHES: Your family and guests are sure to enjoy these:

Roast-Beef Hash; Creamed Chicken; Baked Breasts of Chicken, Southern Style; Lobster Newburg; Barbecued Chicken Legs; Shrimp Curry; Turkey Tetrazzini; Swiss Steak with Sauce; Escalloped Chicken and Noodles; Welsh Rarebit; Alaska King Crab in Wine Sauce; Supreme Sauce on Sliced Turkey Breast; Macaroni and Beef with Tomatoes; Tuna-Noodle Casserole, etc.

Oriental Good Things

THESE COME CANNED AND FROZEN, TOO! Discover their delights by trying:

Canned chow mein — chicken, mushroom, vegetable or meatless. Chop suey — beef or mushroom. Chow-mein noodles, soya sauce, sweet and pungent sauce, etc.

IN THE FREEZER, TOO, YOU'RE LIKELY TO FIND:

Frozen shrimp or chicken chow mein. Beef, shrimp, or chicken chop suey. Chicken chow mein with noodles. Fried rice, etc. For dessert — Chinese fruit rolls. A feast of quick, easy Oriental foods!

Fix-and-Serve Macaroni Dishes: Keep a variety of these on hand in your freezer or on the pantry shelf. You can be proud to serve any of them.

IN CANS OR JARS:

Macaroni with Beef in Tomato Sauce
Lasagna
Italian-Style Spaghetti
Ravioli with Beef or Cheese Filling
Spaghetti with Meat Balls in Tomato Sauce

Spaghetti with Ground Beef
Spaghetti with Tomato-Cheese Sauce
Spaghetti in Tomato Sauce with Cheese
Spaghetti Sauce with Mushrooms; with Meat; with Meat Balls
Marinara Sauce
Etc.

PACKAGED:
Macaroni-and-Cheese Dinner
Macaroni-and-Cheese-Deluxe Dinner
Noodle-with-Chicken Dinner
Noodles Italiano
Noodles Almondine
Spaghetti Dinner
Complete Spaghetti Dinner with Meat, Mushrooms, or Meat Balls
Noodles Romanoff
Savory Noodles
Spaghetti-Sauce Mix
Etc.

FROZEN:
Macaroni-and-Cheese Dinner
Ravioli
Lasagna
Chicken with Noodles
Etc.

Freeze Dry Products

This is a field in which extensive research is being conducted and several pantry-shelf items are now available for camping and boating "chefs."

VERSATILE WHEAT GERM

Because wheat germ contains significant amounts of important iron, B-vitamins, natural vitamin E, etc., as well as protein, it is an excellent product to work into your everyday cookery. It comes in glass jars. Here are eight delightful ways to use it.

1. For breading, as you do crumbs, on meats, fish, etc.

2. Mixed with melted butter or margarine as a casserole topping.

3. Mixed with brown sugar, melted butter or margarine, and cinnamon. As a crunchy dessert or coffeecake topping.

4. As part of the crumbs used in making meat loaves or stuffings.

5. As a sprinkle over dry or cooked cereal, cookies that are ready for the oven, etc.

6. Two or three tablesp. in each batch of pancake, waffle, or biscuit-mix batter.

7. In the dough or batter for yeast bread, quick bread, cookies or muffins, made from scratch.

8. As part of crumbs called for in crumb crusts for pies and cheesecakes.

THE BEST OF SUSAN

"Who is Susan? What is she? That all our readers love her?" is *Good Housekeeping's* paraphrase of the famous old song. Susan is our perennial teen-age cook. For nineteen years she has led by the hand, not only teenagers, but cooks and would-be cooks of all ages, through her step-by-step recipes that make cooking a creative joy with dependable results.

Here, in her easy-to-follow style, is a collection of Susan's fabulous recipes designed to turn out to perfection.

FAMILY FAVORITES

When the dish is prepared to perfection, every family meal becomes a sumptuous banquet. Any one of Susan's dishes could be company fare.

FISH CHOWDER

¼ lb. salt pork	thawed frozen haddock or cod fillets
3 medium onions, sliced	1 qt. milk, scalded
5 medium potatoes, pared, sliced or diced	1 cup evaporated milk, undiluted
4 teasp. salt	3 tablesp. butter or margarine
¼ teasp. pepper	Common crackers
3 cups boiling water	Snipped parsley
1½ lb. fresh or	

1. Cut pork into ½" cubes; cook in large kettle till crispy brown, turning often; remove bits; reserve.
2. To hot pork fat, left in kettle, add onions; cook till just tender, stirring occasionally with a fork. Top with potatoes, sprinkle with salt, pepper; pour on boiling water.
3. Top with fish, cut into medium pieces; cover; simmer 25 min., or until potatoes are just tender. Remove any skin from fish.
4. Now add milk, evaporated milk, butter,

crisp pork bits; heat. Arrange split crackers (they're round and hard — especially nice for chowders) on top. Sprinkle with parsley. Makes 6 servings.

To Vary: Sprinkle a little nutmeg over chowder. Or substitute 3 tablesp. butter or margarine for salt pork.

RICE-CRUSTED TUNA PIE

2 tomatoes	1¾ cups finely grated
French dressing	Swiss cheese
2⅔ cups cooked rice	¾ cup scalded milk
1½ tablesp. melted	¼ teasp. salt
butter or margarine	⅛ teasp. pepper
3 eggs	⅛ teasp. nutmeg
1 6½- or 7-oz. can	Snipped scallions
tuna	

1. Cut each tomato into 6 wedges, then let them stand in French dressing to cover.
2. In bowl, combine cooked rice, melted butter or margarine, and 1 egg, slightly beaten. Turn into 9″ pie plate. Using back of tablespoon, press mixture firmly against side and bottom of pie plate, being careful to heap it high on rim of plate.
3. Start heating oven to 400°F. In bowl, flake tuna. Sprinkle ¾ cup grated cheese over rice crust, then top it with a scant half of the tuna, then rest of cheese, piling it high in center.
4. Combine milk, 2 eggs, salt, pepper, and nutmeg until well blended. Pour over cheese in rice-lined pie plate. Sprinkle remaining tuna on top.
5. Bake pie 25 min., or until silver knife inserted in center comes out clean. Then place tomato wedges all around inner edge and bake 10 min. longer.
6. Sprinkle scallions around tomatoes. Then serve pie in wedges. Makes 8 servings.

TUNA TREAT

1 10-oz. pkg. frozen	undiluted
peas or 2 cups	1 6½- or 7-oz. can
canned peas	tuna
⅓ cup milk	4 eggs
1 10½-oz. can con-	¼ lb. process
densed cream-of-	Cheddar cheese,
mushroom soup,	grated (¼ cup)

1. Start heating oven to 400°F. Cook frozen peas as label directs, omitting salt called for.

2. In 1½-qt. casserole combine milk, soup; then drained peas. Next empty tuna — oil and all — into casserole. With fork, toss tuna with soup mixture. Pop casserole in oven for 12 min.
3. Separate eggs — yolks in one bowl, whites in another. Beat whites till they stand in peaks when beater is raised. Beat yolks till lemon-colored. Fold cheese into yolks. Then carefully fold egg-yolk mixture into beaten whites.
4. When tuna has baked 12 min., turn egg mixture on top of it. Bake just 20 min. longer.
5. Serve this dish with its soufflé-like topping at once. Makes 4 servings.

SCALLOPED OYSTERS

2 cups coarse toast	¼ teasp. pepper
crumbs	2 tablesp. light cream
¼ cup melted butter	1 teasp. Worcester-
or margarine	shire
2 doz. shucked raw	Dash cayenne pepper
oysters, drained	2 tablesp. sherry or
¼ cup oyster liquid	light cream
½ teasp. salt	

1. To make toast crumbs, toast 4 white-bread slices. With kitchen scissors, snip into pieces.
2. Start heating oven to 425°F. Combine crumbs and butter; use one third of mixture to cover bottom of greased 12″ x 8″ x 2″ baking dish.
3. Arrange half of oysters on crumbs. Combine oyster liquid with salt, pepper, cream, Worcestershire, cayenne, sherry; spoon half of this sauce over oysters.
4. Sprinkle with one third of crumbs; top with rest of oysters, then rest of sauce, then crumbs. Bake, uncovered, 30 min. Makes 4 servings.

MEAT LOAF

2 cups fresh bread	2 tablesp. horse-radish
crumbs	2½ teasp. salt
¾ cup minced onion	1 teasp. dry mustard
¼ cup minced green	¼ cup milk or
pepper	evaporated milk
2 eggs	¾ cup catchup
2 lb. chuck, ground	

1. When it's convenient, prepare bread crumbs, minced onion, green pepper.

2. *About 1 hr. before serving:* Start heating oven to 400°F.

3. In large bowl, with fork, beat eggs slightly. *Lightly* mix in chuck, then crumbs, onion, pepper. (Meat will be juicier and more tender if you handle it as little as possible.) Add horse-radish, salt, mustard, milk, ¼ cup catchup; combine lightly but well.

4. In bowl, shape meat into oval loaf; transfer to shallow baking dish or broil-and-serve platter; smooth into shapely loaf. Spread top with ½ cup catchup. Bake 50 min.

5. Serve from baking dish or broil-and-serve platter, pouring off excess juices. Or, with 2 broad spatulas, lift loaf out of baking dish onto heated platter. Spoon some of juices over meat. (Nice chilled, then served sliced, too.) Makes 8 servings.

P.S. If you prefer a soft, moist exterior, bake meat loaf as directed, in 9″ x 5″ x 3″ loaf pan. Pour juices from pan after baking. Unmold meat loaf onto cake rack; then place, right side up, on heated platter. Use juices for making gravy if desired.

MEAT-LOAF RING: Place ½ cup catchup in bottom of 1½-qt. ring mold. Turn meat mixture into ring mold. Bake at 400°F. 45 min. Unmold, pouring off excess juice. Fill center with hot buttered or creamed vegetables.

SPEEDY, ONE-APIECE LOAVES: Form meat mixture into 6 oval-shaped loaves; arrange in greased baking pan. Bake at 400°F. ½ hr.

LAST-MINUTE MEAT CUPS: Halve ingredients. If desired, fold in 1 cup grated raw carrot. Bake in 8 3″ cupcake cups at 400°F. 25 min.

OLD-FASHIONED MEAT LOAF: For 2 lb. chuck, substitute ½ lb. pork shoulder, ground; ½ lb. veal round or shoulder, ground; and 1 lb. chuck, rump, or round, ground. Make as directed, omitting ½ cup catchup for topping. Bake at 400°F. 1 hr. 10 min. Makes 6 servings.

VEAL LOAF: For chuck, substitute 2 lb. veal breast, shoulder, or round, ground. Omit ½ cup catchup for topping. Bake at 350°F. 1½ hr. Makes 6 servings.

CHEESEBURGER LOAF: Use ½ lb. process-Cheddar-cheese slices. Into 10″ x 5″ x 3″ loaf pan, lightly press enough of meat-loaf mixture to cover bottom; on top place 2 cheese slices. Repeat until both are used, ending with 2 cheese slices on top. Omit ½ cup catchup on top. Best served hot.

FROSTED MEAT LOAF: Omit ½ cup catchup for topping. When loaf is baked, pour off all juices. Thickly frost top with well-seasoned, creamy mashed potatoes (add some grated cheese or snipped chives if you like). Sprinkle with paprika. Broil till golden.

ITALIAN-STYLE LOAF: To seasonings for meat loaf, add ¼ teasp. each dried rosemary, orégano, and basil. Substitute ½ cup canned tomato sauce, tomato juice, or diluted canned condensed tomato soup for both milk and ¼ cup catchup.

MUSHROOM MEAT LOAF: Substitute ½ cup well-drained, chopped canned mushrooms for green pepper. Add 1 tablesp. grated lemon rind. Omit ½ cup catchup for topping.

BACON-DILL LOAF: Substitute ¼ cup chopped dill pickle and 6 slices chopped crisp bacon for green pepper.

RAINBOW LOAF: For ½ cup onion, substitute ¼ cup minced celery; add ½ cup grated, pared carrots and ¼ cup snipped parsley. Substitute 1 cup canned tomatoes for both milk and ¼ cup catchup. Omit ½ cup catchup for topping. Bake in and serve from shallow baking dish.

BARBECUED-BEEF BUNS

¼ cup vinegar	garine
1½ cups water	1 cup catchup or chili
¼ cup granulated sugar	sauce
4 teasp. prepared mustard	3 tablesp. Worcestershire
¼ teasp. pepper	4 cups 2″ strips cooked beef (leftover pot roast)
¼ teasp. cayenne pepper	
1 tablesp. salt	Celery, sliced on an angle
2 thick lemon slices	Pitted ripe olives
2 medium onions, sliced	About 20 hamburger buns, split and
½ cup butter or mar-	toasted

1. *Early on the day:* In Dutch oven, combine vinegar, water, sugar, mustard, peppers, salt, lemon slices, onion slices, and butter and simmer, uncovered, 20 min. Add catchup, Worcestershire, and pot-roast strips, then refrigerate.

2. *About 45 min. before serving:* Let beef mixture simmer slowly until heated. Then, for a bright touch, sprinkle top with celery and olives.

3. Guests spoon this savory barbecued beef between split, toasted buns. Makes enough for 8 hearty teen-age appetites.

HAMBURGER STROGANOFF BUNS

¼ cup butter or margarine	1 10½-oz. can condensed cream-of-chicken soup, undiluted
½ cup minced onion	
1 lb. chuck, ground	
1 clove garlic, minced	
2 tablesp. flour	6 hard rectangular bakers' or baked brown 'n' serve club rolls
2 teasp. salt	
¼ teasp. monosodium glutamate	
¼ teasp. pepper	1 cup commercial sour cream
¼ teasp. paprika	
1 lb. mushrooms, sliced	Snipped parsley, chives, or fresh dill

1. In hot butter in skillet, sauté onions till golden. Stir in chuck, garlic, flour, salt, monosodium glutamate, pepper, paprika, mushrooms; sauté 5 min. Add soup; simmer, uncovered, 10 min.

2. Meanwhile, cut thin slice from top of each of 6 rolls; hollow out rolls.

3. Into meat mixture, stir cream. Fill rolls with this Stroganoff; sprinkle with parsley, chives, or dill.

4. Serve rolls with spiced peaches. Makes 6 servings.

BROWN BEEF STEW

⅓ cup flour	paste, or 4 beef bouillon cubes
¼ teasp. pepper	
½ teasp. celery salt	½ teasp. salt
1¾ lb. boned chuck or bottom round, cut into 1½″ cubes	½ teasp. Worcestershire
¼ cup fat or salad oil	1 doz. small white onions
¼ cup minced onion	
1 clove garlic, minced (optional)	1 doz. pared small carrots, whole or halved lengthwise
3¾ cups boiling water	½ pkg. frozen peas
4 teasp. meat-extract	5 hot boiled potatoes
	Snipped parsley

1. In bowl, combine flour, pepper, celery salt. Drop in meat, a few pieces at a time; toss until well coated. Reserve leftover flour.

2. Heat fat in Dutch oven or deep kettle; in it, slowly brown floured meat, a few pieces at a time, on all sides — 15 to 20 min. Remove pieces as they brown.

3. To fat in Dutch oven, add minced onion, garlic; simmer until just tender. Stir in reserved flour until blended.

4. Slowly stir in boiling water, meat-extract paste, salt, Worcestershire. Add meat. Simmer, covered, over low heat about 2 hr., or until meat is fork-tender.

5. Add whole onions, carrots; simmer, covered, about 15 min. Add peas; simmer, covered, about 5 min., or until vegetables are tender.

6. Meanwhile, mash, then season potatoes as on p. 412.

7. Serve stew right in Dutch oven or turn into casserole. Heap potatoes in ring on top of stew. Or serve stew on heated platter with vegetables heaped around it. Sprinkle with parsley. Makes 4 to 6 luscious servings.

To Vary: Substitute canned tomato sauce for part of water. Corn may replace peas.

Or, in place of potatoes, make Dumplings for Stew, p. 478. Or serve stew in ring of boiled noodles.

Or make Rice Ring, p. 371. Fill center with meat from stew; group vegetables from stew around it.

Or substitute ½ to 1 cup Burgundy wine for equal amount of water.

Or substitute ½ lb. fresh mushrooms, sliced, for carrots.

♣ FOR 2: Serve stew one day. With leftovers make this meat pie: Place heated leftovers in greased 1-qt. casserole; top with half the recipe for Hot Baking-Powder Biscuits, p. 475. Bake at 450°F. 20 to 25 min., or until biscuits are done.

IRISH STEW: Make stew, omitting flouring and browning of meat.

BEEF PIE: Turn Brown Beef Stew, or any heated leftover stew, into casserole; top with Flaky Pastry, p. 584, or Hot Baking-Powder Biscuit dough, p. 475, rolled ⅛″ to ¼″ thick. Bake at 450°F. 20 to 25 min., or until done.

MEXICALI MEAT PIE

2 lb. beef round, ground	parsley
½ lb. smoked ham, ground	2 eggs, beaten
¼ lb. calf liver, ground	⅓ cup catchup
1 teasp. salt	2 tablesp. Worcestershire
⅛ teasp. pepper	Few drops Tabasco
1 cup fresh white bread crumbs	2 tablesp. prepared mustard
1 tablesp. minced green pepper	¼ cup melted butter or margarine
2 tablesp. snipped	2 12-oz. cans whole-kernel corn, Mexican style

1. *In early afternoon:* In large bowl, combine beef, ham, liver, salt, pepper, crumbs, green pepper, parsley, eggs, catchup, Worcestershire, Tabasco. With large two-tined fork, mix all these ingredients together.

2. Use this meat mixture to line a 10″ pie plate, making sides 2″ thick, and even. With thumb and forefinger, pinch meat to form rope edge around top, 16 "ropes" in all. Refrigerate pie 1 hr. or longer.

3. *One hour before dinner:* Start heating oven to 350°F. Bake pie 30 min.; drain off liquid; then bake 15 min. and drain again.

4. Meanwhile, blend mustard with butter. Heat corn, then heap in center of baked meat pie. Serve pie in wedges, passing mustard butter. Makes 6 to 8 servings.

CORNED BEEF AND CABBAGE

Corned-beef brisket	1 clove garlic
3 onion slices	2 green-pepper rings
4 cloves	1 stalk celery
6 whole black peppers	1 carrot, pared
1 bay leaf	Few sprigs parsley
½ teasp. dried rosemary	1 head green cabbage

1. Buy a half brisket (4 to 5 lb.) or whole brisket (9 to 10 lb.). Place in large deep kettle; cover with cold water.

2. Add onion slices, studded with cloves; whole peppers; bay leaf; rosemary; garlic; pepper rings; and celery, carrot, and parsley, tied together with string. Bring to boil, covered; reduce heat. Simmer half brisket 4 to 5 hr., whole brisket 5 to 6 hr., or until fork-tender.

3. Wash cabbage; cut into quarters or sixths;

trim off core, leaving enough to hold cabbage intact.

4. About ½ hr. before meat is done, skim excess fat from top of liquid; arrange cabbage on meat; simmer, covered, 25 to 30 min., or until cabbage is tender-crisp.

To Serve: Slice meat; put on platter, with cabbage around it. If desired, pour Quick Mustard Sauce, p. 528, over cabbage and meat. A 4- to 5-lb. half brisket makes 4 servings for at least two meals.

SIMMERED CORNED BEEF: Omit cabbage. When meat is tender, remove from liquid; serve it hot, sliced, with Horse-Radish Sauce I or II, p. 532.

Or remove meat from liquid; cool meat and liquid quickly; return meat to liquid; refrigerate. Serve cold, thinly sliced, with Old-Fashioned Potato Salad, p. 453.

Or remove meat from liquid to plate. Cover meat with second plate; weigh down with heavy object, so meat will be well pressed. Cool. Then refrigerate 24 hr. Meat will slice nicely.

BARBECUED CORNED BEEF: Omit cabbage. About 30 min. before meat is done, remove it to shallow open pan. Dot with whole cloves. Heat, until blended, 2 tablesp. butter or margarine; 1 tablesp. prepared mustard; ⅓ cup brown sugar, packed; 5 tablesp. catchup; and 3 tablesp. vinegar. Pour over corned beef. Bake at 350°F., basting occasionally, 30 min., or until brown.

NEW ENGLAND BOILED DINNER: Use half brisket. About 45 min. before meat is done, skim excess fat from top of liquid. To liquid, add 6 pared medium potatoes, 6 pared carrots, 6 pared white turnips. Simmer, covered, 15 min. Add cabbage as above. Simmer until all vegetables are just tender-crisp. (You may cook beets separately to serve with corned beef.) Serve sliced meat on platter, with vegetables. Pass chili sauce, mustard pickles, or horse-radish.

PAN-FRIED LIVER AND BACON

1. For 4 servings, buy ¾ lb. veal or calf liver, sliced ¼″ thick, and ½ lb. bacon slices. Place liver slices on wax paper; sprinkle both sides with Seasoned Flour, p. 9. Never soak or scald liver.

2. In 10″ skillet, over low heat, place overlapping bacon slices, just as they come from package. While they heat, separate them with 2 forks so they lie flat. Cook slowly over low heat, turning with 2 forks or tongs, until crisp but not brittle — about 5 to 8 min. — spooning off all fat as it accumulates. Don't let fat smoke, or bacon flavor will be affected. Remove each slice as it browns; drain on paper towels; keep hot.

3. Now, to skillet, return ¼ cup bacon fat or enough to cover bottom. Using tongs, place liver in skillet; cook quickly, turning once, till crisp brown on both sides and delicate pink inside (medium done) — about 4 min. in all. *Overcooking* makes liver tough and hard.

4. When liver is done, remove to heated platter. Pour all fat from skillet. Place skillet over low heat and add 2 tablesp. butter or margarine; heat slowly until butter is golden brown.

5. Squeeze a few drops of lemon juice onto each liver slice; then pour on browned butter. Top with 2 tablesp. snipped parsley. Serve on heated platter with bacon.

P.S. You may sauté a few thin onion slices with liver; or rub skillet with a cut clove of garlic before sautéing liver.

WITH A FRENCH TOUCH: After cooking liver and pouring fat from skillet, sauté ¼ cup minced onion in 2 tablesp. butter or margarine about 1 min. Add ⅓ cup white wine; bring to boil; cook about 2 min., or until half original volume. Pour over liver; garnish with snipped parsley.

CHICKEN PIE

1 4-lb. stewing chicken	½ teasp. Worcestershire
12 small onions	Pinch dried tarragon
7 tablesp. butter, margarine, or chicken fat	1 cup light cream
	2 cups chicken broth
7 tablesp. flour	2 tablesp. sherry (optional)
Speck pepper	2 cups drained cooked or canned peas (optional)
Dash mace	

1. *Day before:* Cook chicken as in Simmered Chicken, p. 277. Slice meat from bones in large pieces. Refrigerate meat and broth.

2. *About 1 hr. before serving:* Boil onions till tender as on p. 427; drain.

3. In saucepan, melt butter; stir in flour, pepper, mace, Worcestershire, tarragon. Then stir in cream and chicken broth; cook over medium heat, stirring, until thickened. Add sherry.

4. In 2-qt. casserole, arrange chicken meat and onions; pour sauce over them. On top, attractively arrange any of Smart Toppings, below. Bake, uncovered, at 425°F. 25 to 30 min., unless otherwise directed.

5. Serve pie, garnished with hot peas if desired. Makes 6 servings.

Smart Toppings:

BISCUIT WHEELS: Pat baking-powder biscuit dough (Hot Baking-Powder Biscuit, p. 475) ½″ thick; cut out 9 2½″ rings. Brush with light cream.

CORN CRISP: Split 3 or 4 packaged corn muffins crosswise into thirds. Brush with melted butter or margarine. Bake on pie until golden.

PIE CRUSTIES: Make ½ recipe any Flaky Pastry, pp. 584–586. Cut pastry dough into diamonds, squares, or circles; or, with cookie cutter, cut into fancy shapes. Brush lightly with cream. Bake on pie until golden.

TOPPERS: Brush 2″ bread rounds with melted butter or margarine. Bake on pie until golden.

FLUFFY POTATOES: Heap fluffy mashed white or sweet potatoes on top of pie. Brush with melted butter or margarine. Bake on pie at 350°F. about 25 min., or until golden.

CRUNCHY: Use corn or potato chips, corn flakes, or crisp round scalloped crackers. Use as is, or coarsely crumble and mix with grated cheese. Bake on pie 15 min.

CHICKEN-AND-HAM PIE: Arrange a few thin cooked ham slices with chicken in casserole.

HONEYED PINEAPPLE-HAM LOAF

1 9-oz. can crushed pineapple	2 tablesp. brown sugar
2 cans luncheon meat	2 tablesp. honey
	Whole cloves

1. Start heating oven to 425°F. Drain crushed pineapple.

2. Remove luncheon meat from cans. Cut loaves into 4 slices each, not quite through to

bottom. Place them in greased 8" x 8" x 2" baking dish.

3. Mix crushed pineapple with brown sugar and honey, then spoon this mixture between slices and over top of meat.

4. Stud meat with whole cloves. Then bake it 20 to 25 min. Makes 4 servings.

TURKETTI

1¼ cups 2" spaghetti pieces (not thin)
1½ to 2 cups cooked or canned turkey or chicken, in 1" chunks
½ cup diced, cooked ham (optional)
¼ cup minced canned pimento
¼ cup minced green pepper
1 10½-oz. can con-
densed cream-of-mushroom soup, undiluted
½ cup turkey or canned chicken broth
⅛ teasp. celery salt
⅛ teasp. pepper
½ grated small onion
1½ cups grated natural or process sharp Cheddar cheese (6 oz.)

1. *Early in day or night before:* Cook spaghetti until barely tender as label directs; drain.

2. Add rest of ingredients except ½ cup grated cheese. Toss lightly; taste; add more seasonings if needed.

3. Pour into 1½-qt. casserole. Sprinkle with ½ cup grated cheese. Refrigerate.

4. *About 1 hr. before dinner:* Start heating oven to 350°F. Bake casserole, uncovered, 45 min., or until hot. Makes 4 servings.

P.S. Twice the above recipe may be baked in a 3-qt. casserole at 350°F. about 1 hr.

ORANGE PORK CHOPS

4 center-cut loin pork chops, 1" thick
Salt and pepper
Paprika
2 to 4 tablesp. water
5 tablesp. granulated sugar
1½ teasp. cornstarch
¼ teasp. salt
¼ teasp. cinnamon
10 whole cloves
2 teasp. grated orange rind
½ cup orange juice
4 orange slices, halved

1. Trim some of fat from chops. In skillet over low heat, heat a piece of fat; then remove.

2. Generously sprinkle both sides of chops with salt, pepper, paprika.

3. With tongs, arrange chops in skillet. Cook over medium-high heat till a rich golden brown on both sides — 15 to 20 min. (As fat accumulates, tilt pan and spoon off fat.)

4. When chops are well browned, turn heat low. Add water. Cover skillet tightly. Cook chops 45 min. to 1 hr., or until fork-tender and all pink has disappeared, turning them several times during cooking.

5. *About 20 min. before chops are done:* Make this *Orange Glaze:* In saucepan, cook sugar, cornstarch, ¼ teasp. salt, cinnamon, cloves, and orange rind and juice, stirring, until thickened and clear. Add orange slices; cover pan; remove from heat.

6. Serve chops with a spoonful of Orange Glaze on each; garnish with orange slices. Nice with corn bread, peas, and coleslaw. Makes 4 servings.

PINEAPPLE-HAM LOAF

3½ cups ground cooked or canned ham or luncheon meat
½ lb. veal shoulder, ground
½ lb. beef round, ground
2 cups day-old bread crumbs
¼ teasp. poultry seasoning
½ teasp. salt
¼ teasp. pepper
1 egg, slightly beaten
¼ cup catchup
2 celery stalks, finely snipped
¾ cup milk
1 medium onion
2 tablesp. snipped parsley
½ cup brown sugar, packed
4 canned pineapple slices

1. Start heating oven to 350°F. When grinding ham, use medium blade of food grinder.

2. In large mixing bowl put ground ham, veal, and beef. Add crumbs, poultry seasoning, salt, pepper, egg, catchup, celery, milk.

3. Mince onion onto meat (p. 5). Add parsley. With 2-tined fork, lightly mix meat with other ingredients in bowl.

4. Sprinkle bottom of 9" x 9" x 2" baking dish with brown sugar. Arrange pineapple slices on top of sugar. With spoon and spatula, carefully press some of meat mixture around pineapple slices; then pat rest on top. Bake 1 hr.

5. When loaf is done, carefully pour off all drippings. To unmold, place platter or board on top of baking dish; invert so loaf rests, with pineapple side up, on platter or board; lift off baking dish. Spoon some of drippings over top. Makes 6 to 8 servings.

HASHED BROWN POTATOES

4 peeled, chilled, cooked medium potatoes	1 teasp. salt
	Dash pepper
	3 tablesp. butter or margarine
1 tablesp. grated onion	3 tablesp. bacon fat

1. Using medium grater, grate potatoes onto wax paper till you have 4 cups. With same grater, grate onion, then toss with potatoes, salt, pepper.
2. In 10″ skillet, over medium-high heat, heat butter with bacon fat. Add potatoes, pressing down well with turner and shaping into circle, leaving ½″ trough of fat around edge.
3. Sauté about 20 min., or until crisp and brown on underside. (After 12 to 15 min., lift edge to test brownness.)
4. When potatoes are golden on bottom, hold skillet with one hand; with turner, cut through them from far edge to center. Then, with turner, fold these 2 cut quarters, in turn, toward you, onto uncut half.
5. Carefully run turner under potatoes, so they'll slide out of skillet easily. Then, using turner and holding skillet firmly in one hand, turn potatoes onto platter, with uncut side on top. Makes 4 servings.

MEAT-BALL PIZZAS

1 pkg. active dry, or cake, yeast	1 1-lb.-1-oz. can Italian tomatoes
5 cups sifted all-purpose flour	¼ teasp. pepper
Salt	1 tablesp. dried orégano
Olive oil	½ teasp. dried basil
½ lb. chuck, ground	½ teasp. thyme
2 tablesp. instant minced onion	½ teasp. dried crushed red pepper
1 to 2 cloves garlic, crushed	1 teasp. dried minced parsley
2 6-oz. cans tomato paste	1 lb. Mozzarella cheese, sliced

About 2 hr. 15 min. before serving:
1. In large bowl, dissolve yeast in ½ cup warm water; next, mix in about 3 cups flour, 1 teasp. salt, and ½ cup warm water; then stir in ½ cup more warm water and rest of flour. On floured board knead dough until it is well blended, then place it in large oiled bowl, turning it over to oil top. Set dough, covered, in warm place until doubled in bulk — about 1 hr. 15 min.
2. Shape meat into marble-size balls. In large skillet, in ⅓ cup olive oil, brown meat balls, then stir in onion, garlic, tomato paste, tomatoes, 1½ cups water, 2 teasp. salt, pepper, orégano, basil, thyme, red pepper, and parsley. Cook sauce, covered, 1 hr., stirring occasionally.
3. Start heating oven to 450°F. When dough has doubled, punch it down, divide it in half. Roll out each half on its own oiled large cookie sheet to 13″ circle. Pinch up edges of each and brush rims with oil.
4. Next, pour the tomato sauce over the 2 circles, spreading it to the rims. Dot the sauce with cheese slices.
5. Bake about 25 min., or until pastry rims and cheese are golden. Cut each pie in 8 wedges.
P.S. Packaged pizza mix, with cheese or sausage and cheese, or frozen pizza take care of those unexpected gatherings of the gang.

SCALLOPED POTATOES

2 tablesp. snipped parsley	3 teasp. salt
1½ cups thinly sliced onions	3 tablesp. butter or margarine
4½ cups thinly sliced, pared white potatoes	7 teasp. flour
	⅛ teasp. pepper
	⅛ teasp. paprika
	1¾ cups milk

1. Start heating oven to 400°F. Bring 1″ water to boil in covered saucepan. Grease 1½-qt. casserole. Prepare parsley, onions, potatoes.
2. To boiling water, add onions, potatoes, 2 teasp. salt; boil, covered, 5 min. Drain.
3. Meanwhile, in double boiler or skillet, over very low heat, melt butter. Stir in flour, 1 teasp. salt, pepper, paprika, then milk. Cook, stirring constantly, until smooth and thickened.
4. In casserole, arrange one third of potatoes and onions; sprinkle with half of parsley; pour on one third of sauce. Repeat with another third of potatoes and onions, rest of parsley, and half of remaining sauce. Now add rest of potatoes and sauce. Bake, uncovered, 35 min., or until tender and brown. Makes 4 or 5 servings.

♣ FOR 2: Use 4 teasp. flour, 1 cup milk. Halve rest of ingredients; use 1-qt. casserole. Bake 25 min.

PICCALILLI

8 qt. green tomatoes	½ cup salt
12 sweet red peppers	1 cup mustard seeds
12 green peppers	3 tablesp. celery seeds
1 qt. small onions	1 tablesp. cinnamon
3 qt. cider vinegar	1 tablesp. ground all-
7 cups granulated	spice
sugar	Paraffin

1. Place 12 pint preserve jars on wire rack in deep kettle with cold water to cover their tops by at least 1″. Cover; boil jars 20 min., caps, 5 min. Keep in boiling water until ready to be filled.
2. Wash tomatoes; cut out stem ends; quarter lengthwise. Wash and seed peppers; halve, then quarter them lengthwise. Peel and quarter onions.
3. Put all vegetables through grinder, using medium-fine blade; then pour vegetables into colander; drain off liquid and discard it.
4. Turn drained vegetables into large kettle; add 2 qt. vinegar; boil, uncovered, 30 min., stirring often. Again drain vegetables, discarding liquid.
5. Into vegetables, stir 1 qt. vinegar, sugar, and rest of ingredients except paraffin. Simmer, uncovered, 3 min.
6. Pack at once into sterilized jars to within 1″ of top. Pour ½ layer of hot new paraffin into each. Then seal jars at once as manufacturer directs; cool. Makes about 12 pt.

SUSAN'S WAYS WITH CHEESE

Susan has some very special cheese dishes — perfect for brunch, lunch, or a supper main dish.

CHEESE-AND-RICE SOUFFLE

1 cup cooked rice	½ lb. process sharp
2 tablesp. butter or	Cheddar cheese
margarine	4 eggs
3 tablesp. flour	½ teasp. salt
¾ cup milk	Dash cayenne pepper

1. Prepare cooked rice. Start heating oven to 325°F. In double boiler, melt butter; stir in flour till smooth, then milk. Cook, stirring, until thickened. Slice cheese thinly, right into sauce; cook, stirring occasionally, until cheese is melted and sauce thickened.
2. Separate eggs, placing whites in large bowl, yolks in small one. To yolks, add salt and cayenne; beat with fork; slowly add to cheese sauce, stirring constantly. Remove sauce from heat; fold in rice.
3. With electric mixer or hand beater, beat whites until stiff but not dry. Gently fold in cheese-rice mixture. Turn into a 1½-qt. greased casserole. To form crown, with spoon, make shallow path in cheese-rice mixture about 1″ in from edge all the way around. Bake, uncovered, 40 min.
4. Serve at once. Or, if dinner is delayed a bit, leave in oven, with heat turned down to 250°F., just a few min. Makes 5 servings.

VEGETABLE STYLE: Just before folding in egg whites, add 1 cup chopped, cooked broccoli or cooked green beans.

BAKED MACARONI AND CHEESE

½ lb. macaroni, in	¾ teasp. salt
2½″ pieces, or	Speck pepper
elbow macaroni	2 cups milk
(about 2 cups)	½ lb. process Ched-
1 small onion	dar cheese
2 tablesp. butter or	¾ cup fresh bread
margarine	crumbs
1 tablesp. flour	4 teasp. melted but-
¼ teasp. dry mustard	ter or margarine

1. Cook macaroni as label directs. Start heating oven to 400°F. Grease 1½-qt. casserole.
2. Meanwhile, mince onion (about 4 teasp.); put in double boiler with 2 tablesp. butter or margarine. When butter is melted, stir in flour, mustard, salt, pepper. Slowly stir in milk; cook until smooth and hot, stirring often.
3. Slice about three fourths of cheese right into sauce; stir until cheese is melted. (If preferred, grate cheese ahead, using medium grater, or slice it.)
4. When macaroni is tender, drain into colander; turn into casserole. Pour cheese sauce over macaroni, tossing lightly with fork so

that all macaroni gets nicely coated. Top with rest of cheese.

5. Toss bread crumbs with 4 teasp. melted butter. Sprinkle over cheese.

6. Bake, uncovered, 20 min. Makes 4 servings as main dish, or 6 servings when served instead of potatoes. Nice with crisp bacon.

✤ FOR 2: Use following ingredients: ⅓ lb. cheese, 1⅓ cups raw macaroni in 2½" pieces, 1 tablesp. minced onion, 4 teasp. butter or margarine, 2 teasp. flour, ¼ teasp. dry mustard, ½ teasp. salt, speck pepper, 1⅓ cups milk, ½ cup fresh bread crumbs, and 1 tablesp. melted butter or margarine. Bake in 1-qt. casserole at 400°F. 20 min.

BAKED-TOMATO MACARONI: Arrange 2 or 3 sliced, peeled tomatoes in layers with macaroni and sauce.

BAKED MACARONI WITH GREEN BEANS: With cheese in step 4, add 2 cups cooked green beans.

BAKED MACARONI WITH HAM: With sauce in step 4, add ½ to 1½ cups slivered, cooked ham, tongue, chicken, or luncheon meat. (If tongue or ham, reduce salt to ½ teasp.)

CHEESE SOUFFLE FOR SIX

1½ cups milk; or	garine
¾ cup evaporated	¼ cup flour
milk plus ¾ cup	1 teasp. salt
water	Speck cayenne pepper
6 eggs	½ lb. process sharp
¼ cup butter or mar-	Cheddar cheese

1. Start heating oven to 300°F. In saucepan, heat, but do not scald, milk. Separate eggs, putting whites in large bowl, yolks in smaller one.

2. In double boiler, melt butter or margarine. Stir in flour, then heated milk, salt, cayenne; cook, stirring, until smooth and thickened. Thinly slice cheese right into sauce. Stir until cheese melts completely and sauce is velvety smooth; remove from heat.

3. With fork, beat egg yolks until well blended. Stir in a little of cheese sauce. Slowly stir this mixture back into rest of cheese sauce.

4. With electric mixer or hand beater, beat egg whites until stiff but not dry. Slowly pour in cheese sauce, folding until no large areas of egg white remain.

5. Pour mixture into *ungreased* 2-qt. casserole up to within ¼" of top. (Bake any extra mixture in small *ungreased* casserole.)

6. To form crown, with teaspoon, make shallow path in soufflé mixture about 1" in from edge of casserole all the way around. Bake, uncovered, 1¼ hr.; *don't open oven while soufflé is baking.*

7. Serve at once, as is or with Quick Mushroom Sauce (see p. 528). Sautéed tomato halves and crisp bacon are nice accompaniments. Makes 6 servings.

BAKED EGGS IN CHEESE SAUCE

3 tablesp. butter or	tard
margarine	1½ cups milk
3 tablesp. flour	1 cup grated process
Speck pepper	Cheddar cheese
¾ teasp. salt	(¼ lb.)
1 teasp. prepared mus-	6 eggs

1. Melt butter in double boiler; stir in flour, pepper, salt, mustard, then milk. Cook, stirring, until smooth and thickened.

2. Add cheese; stir until melted. Start heating oven to 325°F.

3. Cover bottom of greased 10" x 6" x 2" baking dish with half of sauce. Carefully break eggs, one by one, into cup; then slide into sauce, side by side; cover with rest of sauce.

4. Bake, uncovered, until eggs are as well done as family likes them — about 20 to 25 min. Serve from dish or on toast. Makes 6 servings of 1 egg apiece.

CHEESE-AND-ONION CASSEROLE

1 cup minced onions	⅛ teasp. pepper
¼ cup shortening or	½ teasp. dry mustard
salad oil	7 day-old white-bread
2 cups grated process	slices
sharp Cheddar	2 tablesp. butter or
cheese (½ lb.)	margarine
½ teasp. salt	2 cups milk

1. Start heating oven to 350°F. Sauté onions in fat till golden. Add cheese, salt, pepper, mustard; cook, stirring, until cheese is melted; remove from heat.

2. Spread bread slices with butter. In 1½-qt. casserole, alternate layers of bread and cheese. Pour on milk. Bake, uncovered, 1 hr. Makes 4 servings.

SWISS PIE

1 qt. toasted ½″ bread squares	Swiss cheese (½ lb.)
2 tomatoes, sliced	2 eggs
Salt	½ teasp. paprika
Pepper	½ teasp. dry mustard
2 cups grated natural	1½ cups milk

1. Start heating oven to 350°F. Place bread squares in 9″ pie plate; top with tomato slices; sprinkle with salt, pepper, cheese.
2. With fork, mix eggs with ¾ teasp. salt, paprika, mustard, ⅛ teasp. pepper, and milk; pour over cheese. Bake 40 min., or until puffy and brown. Makes 4 servings.

WAFFLE DEVILS

8 bread slices	cheese
1 2¼-oz. can deviled ham	Melted butter or margarine
1 3-oz.pkg. cream	

1. Preheat waffle iron as manufacturer directs. Spread half of bread slices with deviled ham, the rest with cream cheese. Put together sandwich-fashion, then brush with butter.
2. Toast in waffle iron until golden brown. Makes 4 servings.

SUSAN'S VERY SPECIAL BREADS

Hot breads, whether quick or yeast, are fun to make, especially with Susan's step-by-step, easy-to-follow recipes. Before you start one of her yeast breads, read Yeast Breads, p. 499.

APRICOT-WALNUT BREAD

2¼ cups packaged biscuit mix	baking powder
1 cup uncooked rolled oats	½ cup snipped dried apricots
¾ cup granulated sugar	1 cup broken walnut meats
¼ teasp. salt	1 egg, well beaten
1 teasp. double-acting	1¼ cups milk

1. Start heating oven to 350°F. Grease, then flour, 9″ x 5″ x 3″ loaf pan.
2. In large bowl stir biscuit mix with rolled oats, sugar, salt, baking powder; stir in apricots and nuts till well coated.
3. Into well-beaten egg, blend milk with hand beater. Quickly stir into biscuit-mix mixture, then, with spoon, beat it hard 30 sec.
4. Turn batter into loaf pan and bake 1 hr., or till cake tester, inserted in center, comes out clean.
5. Cool in pan 10 min.; then remove from pan to rack to finish cooling. Let mellow overnight, wrapped in saran or foil, before serving.

WONDERFUL CHEESE BREAD

1½ cups warm water	2 eggs, beaten with fork
2 pkg. active dry, or 1 cake, yeast	2 cups grated process sharp cheese
2 tablesp. sugar	¼ cup caraway seeds
2¼ teasp. salt	Melted butter or margarine
6¼ to 6½ cups sifted all-purpose flour	

1. *Early in the day:* In large bowl, onto warm water, sprinkle yeast. Stir in sugar and salt until dissolved. Add 2 cups flour; beat well with spoon.
2. Now add eggs, cheese, and caraway seeds; beat well. Beat in 4 more cups flour to make a soft dough, using hands if necessary to work it in.
3. Turn dough onto lightly floured surface; cover with inverted bowl; let rest 10 min. Now, into dough, knead enough more of remaining flour, a small amount at a time, to produce a smooth, elastic dough with small blisters under its surface; this takes about 10 min.
4. In lightly greased large bowl, place ball of dough; turn it once to grease its surface and so keep crust from forming as dough rises. Cover with towel; let rise in warm place (80°F. to 85°F.) till doubled — about 1½ hr.
5. Now punch down dough by gently pressing fist into its center; let rise again till almost doubled. Punch down; turn onto lightly floured surface.
6. Cover dough with bowl; let rest 10 min. Meanwhile, grease two 9″ x 5″ x 3″ bread pans.
7. Now, with sharp knife, divide dough into four equal parts. With palms of hands, roll each part on board into a roll 12″ long.

8. Twist two of rolls together like a rope so they are entwined; seal ends carefully; lay in bread pan against one side. Repeat with 2 other rolls, then lay in second bread pan.

9. Now cover loaves with towel, then let rise till almost doubled — 30 to 45 min. Then start heating oven to 350°F.

10. When loaves have doubled, brush tops lightly with melted butter. Bake 35 min., or until each loaf sounds hollow when tapped with finger.

11. Now, carefully remove loaves from pans; brush tops with more butter; cool on side on wire rack, away from draft.

12. Serve, sliced, for dinner, toasted for breakfast, or for sandwiches. Or freezer-wrap in foil; then freeze for later use. Makes 2 loaves.

CORN CRISPS

1 cup yellow corn meal	3 tablesp. melted shortening or salad oil
½ cup sifted all-purpose flour	⅓ cup milk
½ teasp. salt	Melted butter or margarine
¼ teasp. baking soda	

Make a week or two ahead, or early on the day, as follows:

1. Start heating oven to 350°F. Sift corn meal with flour, salt, soda; stir in shortening, milk. On lightly floured surface, knead dough 6 to 8 times, or until it just holds together.

2. Break off a nickel-size piece; with stockinet-covered rolling pin, roll into a paper-thin, 5″ circle, with ragged edges. Lay on ungreased cookie sheet. Repeat until all dough is rolled out. Then bake 10 to 15 min., or until golden; cool on wire racks until served. Or, if for later on (up to 2 weeks), store, covered, in dry place at room temperature.

3. Just before serving, brush each Corn Crisp with melted butter or margarine; sprinkle with salt. Delightful with any chicken dish including curries, chowders, and main dish salads. Makes 20 to 24.

To Vary: Sprinkle celery, poppy, or sesame seeds or curry or chili powder on Crisps after they're baked and buttered. Or lightly sprinkle with shredded Parmesan cheese just before baking.

LEMON BUBBLE LOAF

1 cup granulated sugar	½ cup warm water
¼ teasp. mace	3 pkg. active dry, or cakes, yeast
Grated rind 2 lemons	2 eggs, well beaten
1 cup milk	5¾ to 6¼ cups sifted all-purpose flour
1 teasp. salt	2 tablesp. melted butter or margarine
¼ cup butter or margarine	

1. *Early in the day:* In a small bowl, combine ½ cup sugar, mace, lemon rind; set aside.

2. In small saucepan, scald milk until tiny bubbles appear around its edges. Then stir in ½ cup sugar, salt, ¼ cup butter or margarine; cool till lukewarm.

3. In very large bowl, onto warm water, sprinkle yeast; stir until dissolved. Then stir in milk mixture, eggs, and 3 cups flour, and beat all till smooth.

4. Into dough, stir 2½ cups more flour, or enough to make a soft dough that just cleans sides of bowl. Sprinkle a board with half of remaining flour, turn dough onto it, then knead until smooth and elastic, with small blisters under its surface.

5. Place dough in large greased bowl, turning it to grease all sides. Cover with towel, and let rise in warm place (80°F. to 85°F.) about 45 min., or till doubled.

6. Into center of dough, poke 2 fingers about 1″ deep. If they leave an indentation, punch dough down.

7. Now turn dough onto floured surface, cover it with bowl, and let it rest 10 min. Grease angel-*loaf* pan 15½″ x 4½″ x 4½″.

8. Now cut dough in half; cut each half into 16 equal pieces. Shape each piece into a ball, tucking any ends under.

9. Place 16 balls in a layer in loaf pan, brush with half of melted butter, sprinkle with half of lemon-mace mixture. Shape remaining 16 pieces into balls, arrange as second layer, brush and sprinkle as before.

10. Cover loaf with towel, then let rise in warm place 45 min., or till doubled. Start heating oven to 350°F.

11. Bake loaf 35 min., or till done. It should sound hollow when tapped with finger. Cool in pan 5 min., then turn it out, on wire racks, to finish cooling.

REFRIGERATOR ROLLS

2 cups hot potato water, drained from boiled potatoes	1 egg, beaten
½ cup granulated sugar	7 cups sifted all-purpose flour
1½ teasp. salt	½ cup cooled, melted shortening
2 pkg. active dry, or cakes, yeast	Melted butter or margarine

1. Cook 4 pared potatoes in 2½ cups hot water until just tender — about 15 min.; drain, reserving water. (Refrigerate potatoes for later use.)

2. In large bowl, combine sugar, salt, potato water; stir until sugar dissolves.

3. Cool mixture till just warm; onto it, sprinkle yeast; stir until dissolved. Stir in beaten egg.

4. With spoon, beat in 3½ cups flour until batter is very elastic and almost smooth. Then beat in melted shortening until well blended.

5. Gradually add 3½ cups more flour, working it in with the hands, if necessary, until dough is no longer sticky. Turn dough onto lightly floured surface; let rest, covered, 10 min.

6. With floured hands, knead dough 8 to 10 min., or until smooth and elastic. Then put it back in greased clean bowl. Cover with clean towel; let rise in warm place (80°F. to 85°F.) until doubled in bulk and very light to touch — about 1½ to 2 hr.

7. Punch down dough; turn it over, with rounded side up; brush with melted butter or margarine. Cover bowl tightly with wax paper and damp towel; store in refrigerator. (You may keep dough 2 to 3 days in refrigerator. Occasionally redampen towel and punch down dough.)

8. To use, remove dough from refrigerator. From it, cut off amount needed. Form into long rolls, about 1″ thick, then cut into 1″ pieces. Shape each piece into ball; then place 3 balls in each greased muffin-pan cup. Brush rolls with melted butter or margarine. Cover with clean towel; let rise in warm place until doubled in bulk. Start heating oven to 425°F.

9. Bake rolls 15 to 18 min., or until golden brown. Remove from pans; brush with melted butter or margarine. Serve at once. Makes 4 doz.

HOT CROSS BUNS

¾ cup scalded milk	About 3½ to 4 cups sifted all-purpose flour
½ cup shortening	
⅓ cup granulated sugar	Salad oil
1 teasp. salt	1 egg white, slightly beaten
¼ cup warm water	
1 pkg. active dry, or cake, yeast	1 cup confectioners' sugar
1 egg, beaten	2 tablesp. hot water
¾ cup currants	½ teasp. vanilla extract
½ teasp. mace	

1. In large bowl, combine milk, shortening, granulated sugar, salt; cool till lukewarm.

2. In small bowl, onto warm water, sprinkle yeast; stir until dissolved. Add to milk mixture, with egg, currants, mace, and as much flour as can be stirred into dough — about 3½ cups.

3. Place in greased clean bowl. Brush top with salad oil. Cover with clean towel; let rise in warm place (80°F. to 85°F.) until doubled in bulk — about 2 hr.

4. Turn onto lightly floured surface; knead 1 min.; shape into 18 2″ balls. In each of 2 greased 8″ x 8″ x 2″ pans, arrange 9 balls, about 1″ apart.

5. With greased scissors, snip *deep* cross in each bun. Brush with egg white. Cover with towel; let rise in warm place until doubled in bulk.

6. Start heating oven to 425°F. Bake buns 25 min., or until done. Cool on wire rack; fill in the cross on each bun with combined confectioners' sugar, hot water, and vanilla extract. Makes 1½ doz.

To Vary: With egg and milk, in buns, add 3 tablesp. finely snipped preserved orange or lemon peel and 3 tablesp. citron.

BLUEBERRY MUFFINS

1 cup fresh blueberries	baking powder
Granulated sugar	1 teasp. salt
2 cups sifted all-purpose flour	1 egg
	1 cup milk
3 teasp. double-acting	6 tablesp. melted shortening

1. Wash and drain berries; pat dry on paper towels; sweeten to taste with 2 or 3 tablesp. sugar; set aside. (Or use 1 cup frozen blueberries; don't sweeten.)

2. Start heating oven to 425°F. Grease 14 2½″ muffin-pan cups well. Into mixing bowl, sift flour, baking powder, salt, 2 tablesp. sugar.
3. Beat egg till frothy; add milk and shortening; mix well. Make small well in center of flour mixture; pour in milk mixture all at once. Stir quickly and lightly — *don't beat* — *until just mixed, but still lumpy.* Quickly stir in berries.
4. Quickly fill muffin cups two-thirds full with batter; wipe off any spilled drops. (If batter does not fill all cups, fill empty ones with water to keep grease from burning.) Sprinkle tops of muffins with 4 teasp. granulated sugar. Bake 25 min., or until wire cake tester, inserted in center of a muffin, comes out clean. Then run spatula around each muffin to loosen it; lift out into napkin-lined basket and serve piping hot. Makes about 14.
P.S. If muffins are done before rest of meal, loosen, then tip slightly in pans and keep warm right in pans so they won't steam and soften.

✤ FOR 2: Use 1 egg; halve rest of ingredients.

SOME GREAT SALADS

For Susan's salads to be a success, the greens must be crisp and perky. So be sure to read Care of Salad Greens, p. 445.

SKILLET POTATO SALAD

2 lb. potatoes (6)	1 teasp. prepared mustard
6 bacon slices	
¼ cup bacon fat	2 celery stalks, sliced
1½ tablesp. flour	1 small head romaine
1 cup water	1 cucumber, thinly
⅓ cup vinegar	sliced, or 2 cups
1¾ teasp. salt	cooked green beans
⅛ teasp. pepper	or peas
1 tablesp. sugar	2 small onions, sliced
	6 red radishes, sliced

1. Boil unpared potatoes *just* until tender. Meanwhile, in cold 10″ skillet, over low heat, fry bacon until crisp, pouring fat into measuring cup as bacon cooks. Remove skillet from heat; drain bacon on paper towels; crumble slices.
2. Return ¼ cup bacon fat to skillet; stir in flour, then water, until smooth; add vinegar, salt, pepper, sugar, mustard. Cook over low heat, stirring, until thickened; remove from heat.
3. When potatoes are *just* tender, drain; peel; slice. Put skillet back over low heat; add layer of potatoes, then layer each of celery, romaine in bite-size pieces, cucumber, and onions, repeating till all are used. Toss gently. Top with radishes and bacon bits. Nice with cold sliced meats and rye bread. Makes 6 servings.
SKILLET LUNCHEON SALAD: Brown 6 franks, sliced on angle, in bacon fat before stirring in flour, water, etc., in step 2.

CRACKER CRISP SALAD

Crisp salad greens (iceberg, Boston, or Bibb lettuce; romaine; etc.)	1 tablesp. wine vinegar
	¼ teasp. Worcestershire
2 to 4 tomatoes, peeled	1 1-lb. can salmon; or 1 6½- or 7-oz. can tuna, drained; or
1 clove garlic	
¾ teasp. salt	1 can boned chicken (1 cup)
½ cup mayonnaise or cooked salad dressing	
	6 to 8 radishes, sliced
	1 cup packaged small cheese crackers

1. *Just before suppertime:* Tear crisp cold salad greens into bite-size pieces (about 1 qt. in all) right in salad bowl. Now slice peeled tomatoes, vertically, with stem ends down. (This way they lose less juice, salad doesn't get watery.) Cut half of slices into chunks; then add them to greens.
2. With fork, mash garlic with salt until garlic disintegrates. Combine with mayonnaise, vinegar, Worcestershire; set aside.
3. Break salmon into large chunks over greens; also scatter on radish slices and cheese crackers. Pour on dressing; toss to coat well. Garnish with remaining tomato slices. Makes 4 generous servings.

COLESLAW QUINTET

COLESLAW: Gently toss 4 cups finely shredded green or Chinese cabbage with 1 tablesp. minced onion, ⅓ cup diced celery, ⅓ cup slivered green peppers or raw green beans, ⅓ cup grated carrot, and ¼ cup sliced radishes. Toss with Coleslaw Dressing, below, hot Cooked Salad Dressing, p. 472, or Tarragon-Sour-Cream Dressing, p. 470. Makes 4 servings.

To Vary: Substitute ½ cup diced tomatoes for carrot and radishes.

OLIVE COLESLAW: Toss 4 cups finely shredded green or Chinese cabbage with ¾ teasp. celery seeds, ½ cup sliced stuffed olives, 1 tablesp. minced onion. Toss with Coleslaw Dressing, below; ½ cup hot Cooked Salad Dressing, p. 472. You may add 5 coarsely grated franks.

CHOPPED COLESLAW: Toss 3 cups chopped green cabbage and ¼ cup chopped green pepper with 1 teasp. salt, ¼ teasp. pepper, ½ teasp. dry mustard, 1 teasp. celery salt, 2 tablesp. sugar, 1 tablesp. chopped pimento, 1 teasp. grated onion, 3 tablesp. salad oil, and ⅓ cup vinegar. Garnish with sliced olives or tomatoes. Makes 4 servings.

WALDORF COLESLAW: Toss 4 cups shredded green or Chinese cabbage with ½ cup diced unpared red apple, ¼ cup broken nut meats, and ½ cup light or dark raisins or grapes, or diced oranges, pineapple, or peaches. Toss with Coleslaw Dressing, below.

CALICO COLESLAW: Place 5 cups shredded cabbage in bowl with ¼ cup each minced green pepper and shredded carrot. Combine 1 teasp. salt, ¼ teasp. pepper, ½ teasp. each dry mustard and grated onion, 2 tablesp. each sugar and salad oil, and ⅓ cup vinegar. Pour over cabbage; toss until well mixed.

BOWL STYLE: Slice off top half or third of green cabbage head; with knife, carefully scoop out center of core end, leaving "bowl" intact. Use cutout cabbage and top to make any coleslaw above; heap in "bowl."

COLESLAW DRESSING

½ cup mayonnaise or cooked salad dressing	Dash paprika
	½ teasp. sugar
¾ teasp. salt	1 tablesp. vinegar or lemon juice
Speck pepper	1 tablesp. milk

Blend all ingredients; refrigerate. Especially nice on cabbage salad. Makes ½ cup.

RAW RELISHES

Try serving raw relishes on a tray or serving dish right along with the meat course, so no separate salad is necessary. For those who crave it, have a tiny pitcher of French dressing in the center of the tray.

Radishes: Wash crisp radishes; then remove all but tuft of leaves. With sharp knife, cut off roots.

ROSES: Cut 4 thin slices from sides of each radish, all equidistant; next cut thin slice, not quite to stem, behind each white spot. Refrigerate, on ice, until red-rimmed petals open. Pat dry on towels.

FANS: Cut each radish crosswise into thin slices, from top, not quite down to stem end. Refrigerate on ice. Pat dry on towels.

Carrots:

CURLS: With vegetable parer, shave lengthwise strips from pared long straight carrots. Curl each strip around forefinger; then place on ice, tucking them in tightly. Let stand 1 hr. Pat dry on towels.

FANS: With very sharp thin knife, cut pared, chilled young carrots into ¼"-thick lengthwise slices. Cut each slice in half crosswise. Then make lengthwise cuts ¼" apart, almost to end of each slice. Refrigerate on ice.

Celery:

HEARTS: Break off heavy outer stalks, then cut tops from bunch of celery (Pascal, the all-green kind, is nice). Wash; pare root; halve bunch lengthwise through root. Cut each half lengthwise into 2 or 3 pieces, then make 3 or 4 gashes along outside stalk of each. Refrigerate on ice. Pat dry on towel before serving.

CURLS: Cut each large tender stalk of celery into 3" pieces; slit each piece, almost to end, into narrow, parallel strips. Or slit both ends almost to center. Refrigerate on ice until ends curl. Pat dry on towel.

Cauliflowerets: Remove outside stalks from well-chilled cauliflower. Wash and break head into small flowerets. Serve raw.

Cucumber Slices: Pare cucumber; then score by running sharp-tined fork down length of cucumber from end to end. Cut crosswise into very thin slices; refrigerate on ice cubes; pat dry on towel. Sprinkle with snipped parsley.

Or pat finely snipped parsley or chives into grooves of a scored, pared cucumber. Refrigerate. Then slice. Or slice unpared cucumbers thinly.

Beet, Cucumber, Carrot, Turnip Sticks: Cut each washed, pared, chilled raw vegetable lengthwise into 1/8" slices; cut each slice into thin sticks. (If carrot or cucumber is very long, first cut it in half.) If desired, string ripe pitted olives on sticks.

Scallions (spring or green onions): Wash; cut off all but 2" of green tops. Cut off roots; remove loose skin. Wrap in damp cloth; refrigerate. Use green tops in soup.

Stuffed Raw Mushrooms: Wash 1 doz. medium mushrooms (about 1/4 lb.); dry; remove stems. Mix 1/2 3-oz. pkg. soft cream cheese, 1 teasp. Worcestershire, 2 tablesp. minced onion or chives. Use to fill mushroom caps.

Relish Nibblers: Arrange assortment of raw relishes on tray, with one of dunks, p. 155, in bowl in center of tray. Serve as first course in living room; let guests dip relishes into dunk.

OLD-FASHIONED LETTUCE BOWL

2 medium heads Boston lettuce	1 teasp. sugar
1/2 cup light cream	1/4 teasp. salt
1/4 cup vinegar	3 or 4 scallions

1. Wash, then refrigerate heads of lettuce, as soon as they come from grocer's.
2. Make this dressing right in measuring cup: To light cream in cup, add vinegar, sugar, and salt; refrigerate.
3. At mealtime, with kitchen scissors, break lettuce into bite-size pieces, right in salad bowl. Snip scallions over lettuce. Refrigerate till needed.
4. *Just before serving:* Toss salad with dressing. Makes 4 servings.

SPECIAL-OCCASION DISHES

Gourmet and foreign dishes are not so difficult to prepare if you carefully follow Susan's directions. Here is her very special collection for company.

SHRIMP CREOLE

1 1/2 seeded green peppers, chopped	1/2 teasp. dried rosemary
3 or 4 cloves garlic, minced	1/2 teasp. paprika
3 large onions, chopped	6 dashes Tabasco
6 tablesp. salad oil	2 1-lb.-13-oz. cans tomatoes (about 6 cups)
4 cups hot seasoned cooked rice	3 lb. raw shrimp, shelled, deveined
1 tablesp. salt	1 cup snipped parsley
1/8 teasp. pepper	

1. Into automatic skillet (or large regular skillet), put green pepper, garlic, and onion; add salad oil. Sauté vegetables at 375°F. (medium heat) until tender.
2. Meanwhile, start cooking rice as label directs.
3. To tender vegetables, add salt, pepper, rosemary, paprika, Tabasco, and tomatoes. Cook all at 225°F. (medium-low heat) 15 min., stirring occasionally. Now add shrimp and cook just until shrimp turn pink. Then turn automatic skillet to 150°F.
4. Add parsley to rice. Arrange rice in ring around Shrimp Creole either in skillet or serving dish. Makes 8 to 10 servings.

♣ FOR 4: Halve all ingredients.

FILLETS THERMIDOR

3 lb. fish fillets (list, p. 299)	Cheddar cheese
2 1/4 cups milk	1/2 cup butter or margarine
1 1/2 teasp. salt	1/2 cup flour
1/8 teasp. pepper	1/2 cup lemon juice or sherry
1/2 lb. process sharp	

1. Start heating oven to 350°F. Roll up each fillet (split lengthwise if 8" or longer); stand on end in shallow 2-qt. casserole.
2. Pour milk over fish; sprinkle with salt, pepper. Bake, uncovered, about 30 min., or until easily flaked with fork *but still moist.* (Thick fillets may take 40 min.) Meanwhile, coarsely grate cheese.
3. When fish is done, remove from oven; turn oven up to Broil. Spoon some of milk from fish into large measuring cup, to avoid spilling, then carefully pour in rest of milk. Melt butter in double boiler; stir in flour; then slowly stir in milk drained from fish.
4. Cook, stirring, until thickened. Add cheese;

stir until melted. Add lemon juice. Pour over baked fillets; sprinkle with paprika, if desired. Brown quickly under broiler.

♣ FOR 4: Use 1½ lb. fish. Reduce milk to 1½ cups, salt to 1 teasp. Use speck pepper, ¼ lb. cheese, 3 tablesp. each butter, flour, and sherry or lemon juice. Bake in 10″ x 6″ x 2″ baking dish.

WITH SHRIMP OR LOBSTER SAUCE: To cheese sauce add 1 lb. cooked, cleaned shrimp, or 2½ cups cooked lobster chunks.

To Vary: Sprinkle fillets with dried tarragon or marjoram before rolling.

CHAFING-DISH SEA FOOD NEWBURG

2 qt. water	6 tablesp. butter or
2 teasp. salt	margarine
1 tablesp. shrimp	2 tablesp. flour
spice	⅛ teasp. nutmeg
1 lb. sea scallops	Dash paprika
1 lb. deveined,	1 teasp. salt
shelled, raw shrimp	3 tablesp. sherry
6 round buns	2 cups light cream
Melted butter or mar-	3 egg yolks, slightly
garine	beaten

1. *Half an hour before supper:* Bring water to boil with 2 teasp. salt and shrimp spice, tied in cheesecloth bag.
2. Cut scallops in half; drop into boiling water. When water boils again, add shrimp. Cook all, covered, 3 min., then drain and set sea food aside.
3. Now start heating oven to 400°F. Make mock patty shells this way: With fork, scrape out center of top of round buns, then place them on ungreased cookie sheet.
4. Brush buns with melted butter or margarine, then bake them about 10 min., or till toasty. Keep warm while cooking Newburg in chafing dish as follows.
5. Heat water in hot-water pan of chafing dish until it simmers. Melt butter or margarine in chafing dish. Stir in flour, nutmeg, paprika, and 1 teasp. salt until smooth.
6. Stir in sherry, then sea food. Cook mixture until sea food is heated through.
7. Combine cream and egg yolks; slowly pour into chafing dish, stirring constantly. Continue stirring gently until sauce becomes thickened and smooth.
8. Spoon into "patty shells." Serve with green

beans mixed with peas, also celery and carrot sticks. Makes 6 servings.

P.S. This superb dish may be made in a double boiler, if more convenient.

EGGS BENEDICT

Easy Hollandaise,	4 slices cooked or
p. 531	boiled ham
2 English muffins	4 eggs
Butter or margarine	Water cress

1. Make Easy Hollandaise.
2. Preheat broiler 10 min., or as manufacturer directs. With fork, deeply prick each muffin midway all around side, then gently pull halves apart. Spread muffins with butter or margarine; place on cookie sheet (or broiler pan), with ham alongside. Broil till muffin halves are toasted, ham is curled. Then, on platter, place a ham slice on each muffin half.
3. Now fill buttered skillet with enough water to cover eggs by 1″. Bring to boil; then lower heat so water just simmers.
4. Break egg into cup; lower cup close to surface of water; quickly slip egg into water. Repeat, placing 4 eggs side by side.
5. Cover skillet; while keeping water hot, not simmering, cook eggs until whites are solid, yolks of desired firmness — 3 to 5 min.
6. Now slip slotted spoon under each egg, lift out of water, tilt slightly against side of skillet to drain well, then set on one of ham-topped muffins. Repeat till all eggs are removed.
7. Now spoon on Easy Hollandaise; garnish with cress and serve. Makes 4 servings.

P.S. Eggs may be prepared in egg poacher if preferred.

BLANQUETTE DE VEAU

2 lb. boned veal	Butter or margarine
shoulder	15 small white onions
4 whole cloves	(1 lb.)
1 small onion	½ lb. small fresh
1 qt. boiling water	mushrooms, washed
5 medium carrots,	¼ cup all-purpose
scraped, quartered	flour
1 bay leaf	2 egg yolks
⅛ teasp. dried thyme	2 tablesp. lemon
2 sprigs parsley	juice
½ cup thinly sliced	Hot fluffy rice or
celery	mashed potatoes
4 peppercorns	Snipped dill or pars-
1 tablesp. salt	ley

1. *About 2½ hr. before serving:* Remove membrane and fat from veal, then cut it into 1¼″ pieces. Simmer, in deep covered saucepan, with clove-studded onion, boiling water, carrots, bay leaf, thyme, parsley, celery, peppercorns, salt, for 1 hr., or until tender. Drain stock from veal, reserving 3½ cups stock. Discard onion, bay leaf, peppercorns, and parsley. (Veal may be cooked day before, refrigerated, then reheated over very low heat.)

2. *Thirty minutes before veal is done:* Melt ¼ cup butter in large heavy skillet; add white onions, and simmer, tightly covered, over low heat, 30 min., or until tender. Add to drained, cooked veal.

3. In same skillet, uncovered, cook mushrooms in ½ cup veal stock 15 min. Add veal and onions.

4. Next, in same deep saucepan in which veal cooked, melt 2 tablesp. butter, then stir in flour till smooth. Next, slowly stir in 3 cups reserved stock and cook, over medium heat, stirring, till thickened and boiling.

5. In bowl, with wire whip, beat egg yolks slightly with lemon juice, then slowly stir in some of hot sauce, and slowly stir this back into rest of hot sauce in pot.

6. Now add hot sauce to veal in skillet. Heat it, but do not let it boil.

7. To serve, arrange ring of fluffy rice or mashed potatoes around veal, then sprinkle on dill. Makes 6 servings.

NOTE: May be made day before, refrigerated, then reheated over very low heat.

CHICKEN TETRAZZINI

1 4½-lb. roaster, cut up	rooms, sliced
3 cups hot water	1 tablesp. lemon juice
Salt	2 tablesp. flour
1 teasp. onion salt	Paprika
½ teasp. celery salt	¼ teasp. pepper
½ lb. spaghettini	⅛ teasp. nutmeg
6 tablesp. butter or margarine	1 cup heavy cream
½ lb. fresh mush-	⅔ cup grated Parmesan cheese

1. *Day before:* In deep kettle, place chicken, water, 2 teasp. salt, onion salt, celery salt. Simmer, covered, until chicken is fork-tender, 1 to 1¼ hr. (As chicken cooks, add water if needed.)

2. Remove bird to bowl (reserve broth); when cool enough to handle, remove meat from bones in big pieces; cut breast into thirds; refrigerate chicken meat, in covered bowl, at once.

3. Set aside 2½ cups chicken broth. To rest of broth in kettle, add 3 qt. water, 2 tablesp. salt; bring to boil, then slowly add spaghettini (so water won't stop boiling) and cook 6 min., or until tender, stirring occasionally.

4. Drain; place spaghettini in a 12″ x 8″ x 2″ baking dish.

5. Meanwhile, in medium skillet, heat 3 tablesp. butter or margarine. Add mushrooms; sprinkle with lemon juice and ½ teasp. salt. Sauté mushrooms until soft, but *not* brown, stirring occasionally; toss them and their butter with cooked spaghettini; then refrigerate all, covered.

6. In saucepan, melt 3 tablesp. butter or margarine; then remove pan from heat and stir in flour, ¼ teasp. paprika, 1½ teasp. salt, pepper, nutmeg. Slowly stir in the 2½ cups reserved broth (¼ cup sherry may replace ½ cup of this broth). Cook sauce, stirring, until thickened; add cream. Then pour sauce over chicken in bowl; refrigerate all, covered.

7. *Next day, 1 hr. before serving:* Start heating oven to 400°F. With fork, stir up chicken and sauce, then pour as much of sauce as possible over spaghettini, while tossing to mix well. Place rest of chicken mixture in center of spaghettini. Sprinkle all with Parmesan, more paprika. Bake 25 min., or until hot. Makes 8 servings.

SUKIYAKI

½ cup soy sauce	1 or 2 canned bamboo shoots
¾ cup canned chicken broth	About ⅓ can bean curd (optional)
3 tablesp. sugar	1 cup canned shirataki (optional)
About ½ head Chinese cabbage	1 lb. very thinly sliced beef tenderloin or sirloin
About ½ lb. fresh spinach	2″ square suet or 2 tablesp. salad oil
12 scallions	
1 large onion	
2 large mushrooms	

About 1 hr. before serving:

1. In pitcher combine soy sauce, broth, and sugar; set aside.

2. Next, slice enough Chinese cabbage in ½" diagonal slices to make 3 cups. Then, snip enough spinach to make 3 cups, and slice scallions in 2" lengths. Cut onion in half lengthwise, then into ¼" slices. Slice mushrooms and bamboo shoots. Cut bean curd into 8 small cubes.

3. On a platter or tray, arrange all vegetables, shirataki, and the meat.

4. Heat suet in skillet set over hibachi, or in electric skillet. Into it, with long fork, push from tray all but meat and spinach. Then pour on soy-sauce mixture; cook over high heat 8 min.

5. Next push spinach and meat onto vegetables; simmer all 2 min., then push them down into sauce, and cook all 3 min.

Serve with rice and hot green tea. Makes 6 servings.

LASAGNA

¾ lb. chuck, ground
¼ lb. boned pork shoulder, ground
4 eggs, unbeaten
About 1 cup grated Romano or Parmesan cheese
¾ cup packaged dried bread crumbs
7 tablesp. snipped parsley
Salt
1 lb. sweet or hot Italian sausages
2 cloves garlic

1 6-oz. can tomato paste (⅔ cup)
3 1-lb.-13-oz. cans Italian-style tomatoes (10 cups)
½ teasp. fennel seeds
1 lb. lasagna noodles
1 teasp. dried basil
3 lb. ricotta or cottage cheese
½ to 1 teasp. freshly ground pepper
1 lb. Mozzarella or natural Swiss cheese, thinly sliced

Day before:

1. Mix chuck, pork, 2 eggs, 2 tablesp. grated Romano cheese, crumbs, 1 tablesp. snipped parsley, 1 teasp. salt. Divide mixture in half. Shape half into 10 large meat balls, rest into tiny balls — about 4 doz.

2. In Dutch oven, brown sausages with 1 clove garlic until some fat collects. Add meat balls; brown. Remove sausages and meat balls.

3. To fat remaining in Dutch oven, add tomato paste; cook over low heat a few min. Add tomatoes, 1 tablesp. salt, fennel seeds; simmer, uncovered, stirring frequently, about 1 hr., or until very thick. Add sausages, meat balls, 2½ cups water; cook slowly, uncovered, about 2 hr.

4. Remove sausages and large meat balls. Cool; refrigerate all.

About 2 hr. before serving:

1. Cook lasagna noodles, as label directs, until they seem tender — and not hard in center. (Taste a strand now and then to be sure and not overcook them.) Quickly drain noodles and hang them over side of colander for easier handling.

2. Meanwhile, heat sauce over low heat until it bubbles; add 2 tablesp. snipped parsley, 1 minced clove garlic, basil. Remove 1 cup of sauce, add it to large meat balls and sausages, then set aside.

3. Blend well ricotta, 2 eggs, ¼ cup snipped parsley, 1 tablesp. salt, pepper.

4. Start heating oven to 400°F. In shallow open pan, 14" x 10" x 2", spread one fourth of sauce. Lay about a third of lasagna noodles, one at a time, over sauce in pan, till bottom is entirely covered with noodles. Spread half of ricotta mixture over noodle layer. Sprinkle this with about ⅓ cup grated Romano cheese; dot with ⅓ lb. Mozzarella, in thin slices. Repeat layers of sauce, noodles, ricotta mixture, and cheeses, then add another one fourth of sauce and remaining noodles. Sprinkle top layer of noodles with remaining grated cheese, spread rest of sauce over entire surface, and dot with remaining Mozzarella slices.

5. Bake lasagna 1 hr., then remove from oven and let it stand on top of range 15 to 30 min. so it will cut easily. Meanwhile, slowly reheat reserved sausages and large meat balls in sauce.

6. When serving lasagna, pass sausages and meat balls in sauce. Nice with a large tossed green salad with anchovies and pimento, plus fresh fruit or sherbet for dessert. A wonderful repast for 10 to 12 hungry people.

CREAMED CHICKEN DE LUXE

⅓ cup butter or margarine
⅔ cup sliced fresh mushrooms
5 tablesp. flour
½ teasp. salt
Dash pepper

1⅓ cups chicken broth, canned if desired
½ cup light cream
2 cups cut-up chunks of cooked or canned chicken or turkey

1. In double-boiler top, over direct heat, melt

butter; add mushrooms; sauté 5 min. Stir in flour, salt, pepper, till smooth.

2. Place over boiling water; slowly stir in broth, cream; cook, stirring, until thickened. Add chicken; heat well.

3. Serve on, with, or in:

Toast
Waffles
Baking-powder biscuits
Split hot corn bread
Mashed potatoes
Buttered noodles, with croutons, almonds, or poppy seeds added
Fluffy rice, tossed with snipped parsley or chutney
Baked potatoes
Broiled pineapple slices
Chow-mein noodles
Toasted, split English muffins
Pancakes
Deviled-ham pin wheels
Scrambled eggs or omelet
Cooked broccoli or asparagus
Patty shells
Avocado halves
Corn crisps

CREAMED CHICKEN AND HAM: Substitute cut-up, cooked ham for part of chicken.

CHICKEN A LA KING: Increase mushrooms to ¼ lb. Add 1 cut-up pimento and sherry to taste.

PARTY SANDWICH LOAF

Fillings (see right)
½ 5-oz. jar sharp-cheese spread
2 tablesp. hot water
3 3-oz. pkg. soft cream cheese
¼ lb. Danish blue cheese
⅓ to ½ cup light cream
Day-old loaf unsliced bread
6 thin tomato slices
Radish slices
Snipped parsley

1. *Night before, if convenient:* Prepare 3 of fillings; *refrigerate at once.*

2. *In morning:* Blend sharp-cheese spread with hot water. For Cream-Cheese Frosting: Blend cream cheese and blue cheese with enough cream to spread easily.

3. Then, with sharp knife, trim all crusts from bread. Lay loaf on side and slice lengthwise into 5 even slices, about ½" thick. (You may use ruler as guide to keep slicing straight.)

4. Spread bottom bread slice with sharp-cheese spread. Spread second bread slice with half of Chicken Salad; top with tomato slices, trimming them so they cover salad evenly; top with rest of Chicken Salad. Place on cheese-spread slice.

5. Spread third bread slice with Egg Salad; place on Chicken Salad layer. Avoid pressing layers together too firmly, lest fillings ooze.

6. Spread fourth slice with Ham Salad; place on Egg Salad layer. Top loaf with last bread slice, with rounded side up; gently shape loaf with hands so all sides are even. Remove any oozing bits.

7. With spatula, "frost" top and sides, with Cream-Cheese Frosting, in step 2.

8. Refrigerate loaf several hr., or till easy to cut.

9. To serve, top loaf with sliced radishes; sprinkle with snipped parsley. With sharp knife, cut into 10 1" slices. Cake server makes serving easy. Makes 10 servings.

Fillings (choose any 3 of these):

HAM SALAD: Mix ½ cup ground cooked or canned ham or chopped canned ham or luncheon meat with 2 tablesp. minced green pepper, 1 teasp. prepared mustard, 2 tablesp. mayonnaise, 1 tablesp. minced onion. Refrigerate.

CHICKEN SALAD: Mix ½ cup ground or finely chopped cooked or canned boned chicken or turkey, ¼ cup minced celery, 2 tablesp. pickle relish, ½ teasp. salt, dash pepper, 2 tablesp. mayonnaise. Add pinch of curry if desired. Refrigerate.

TUNA, SALMON, OR CRAB SALAD: Use flaked fresh or canned fish or shellfish in Chicken Salad above; refrigerate.

EGG SALAD: Mix 2 finely chopped hard-cooked eggs, 2 tablesp. minced ripe olives, ½ teasp. salt, dash pepper, ½ to ¾ teasp. prepared mustard, 2 tablesp. mayonnaise; refrigerate.

CANNED DEVILED HAM AND THIN TOMATO SLICES

PURPLE-PLUM DUCKLINGS

2 5- to 6-lb. ducklings, quartered
Onion salt
Garlic salt
4 oranges, halved crosswise
¼ cup butter or margarine
1 medium onion, chopped
1 17-oz. can purple plums
1 6-oz. can frozen lemonade, unreconstituted
⅓ cup chili sauce
¼ cup soy sauce
1 teasp. Worcestershire
1 teasp. ginger
2 teasp. prepared mustard
2 drops Tabasco

1. Sprinkle duck quarters with onion and garlic salts; set each, on an orange half, on a

trivet in a roasting pan, then roast them at 350°F. for 1½ hr.

2. While ducklings roast, melt butter in large skillet, add onion, and cook until tender. Set aside.

3. Empty the can of plums, juice and all, into a food mill or strainer set over a bowl. Pit plums and purée them. Add purée to onion and blend in frozen lemonade, chili sauce, soy sauce, Worcestershire, ginger, mustard, and Tabasco, and simmer all 15 min.

4. After quarters have roasted 1½ hr., remove them, oranges, and trivet from roasting pan. Drain off fat.

5. Arrange ducklings and oranges, side by side, in pan. Brush them with plum sauce, and return them to oven for 15 min. Then pour more sauce over them; return to oven. Continue roasting. Pour more sauce over them every 10 min., until quarters are tender, oranges and ducklings glazed.

6. Arrange duckling quarters and orange halves on a large heated platter, and pass rest of sauce. Makes 4 generous servings of 2 quarters each.

FOR A SWEET TOOTH

Young marrieds and oldtimers alike will find Susan's fabulous collection of cakes, pies, cookies, and desserts a great success. The crowning glory to any meal.

CHRISTMAS PIE

8″ or 9″ Brazil-Nut Crust, p. 594
1 env. unflavored gelatine
½ cup granulated sugar
⅛ teasp. salt
3 egg yolks
1¾ cups milk, scalded
½ cup thinly sliced glacéed cherries
2 tablesp. white rum
3 egg whites
¼ cup shelled Brazil nuts
Boiling water
¾ to 1 cup heavy cream

Day before or early in day:

1. Bake pie crust, then cool.

2. Make custard filling: In double boiler, combine gelatine, ¼ cup sugar, and salt. Stir in egg yolks *well;* then *slowly* stir in scalded milk. Cook over simmering water, stirring

constantly, until mixture coats metal spoon. Remove from heat.

3. Cool custard filling; refrigerate till some of it mounds when dropped from spoon. (Or chill in bowl of ice water, stirring constantly.) Beat smooth with hand beater; add cherries and rum.

4. Beat egg whites till in soft peaks; gradually add ¼ cup sugar, while beating till stiff. Fold into filling.

5. Pour all but 1 cup of filling into nut crust; refrigerate pie and reserved filling. As soon as reserved filling mounds when dropped from spoon, heap on center of pie; refrigerate till serving time (allow about 4 hr. to chill it firm enough to cut).

6. Soak Brazil nuts in boiling water ½ hr. Then, with sharp paring knife, shave the nut meats to sprinkle over pie.

At serving time: Whip cream; sweeten, if desired; spoon around edge of pie. Garnish pie with shaved Brazil nuts.

CROWNING-GLORY ORANGE SOUFFLE

Salad oil or soft butter
3 env. unflavored gelatine
¾ cup cold water
8 eggs, at room temperature
1¼ cups granulated sugar
½ cup finely grated orange rind
3 tablesp. finely grated lemon rind
1 teasp. salt
¾ cup orange juice
¼ cup lemon juice
2 cups heavy cream
3 medium oranges, sectioned
¼ cup currant jelly
Few drops liquid red food color

1. Start making soufflé about 5 hr. before dinner. With cellophane tape, fasten 30″ x 6″ band of foil around top outside of a 1½-qt. soufflé dish so foil stands about 4″ above rim; tape inside and outside seams of foil, then brush inside of it with salad oil or soft butter.

2. In small bowl, sprinkle 2 env. gelatine onto ½ cup cold water to soften, then stir it, set over or in saucepan of hot water, till gelatine is dissolved.

3. Separate eggs, placing yolks in double-boiler top and whites in large bowl. To yolks, add ½ cup sugar, rinds, salt, and juices; beat until fluffy with hand beater. Then cook mixture, over simmering water, stirring constantly, till thickened. Stir in dissolved gelatine.

4. Cool this custard, over ice, stirring constantly, till it *just begins to mound.*

5. Now beat egg whites until frothy; then gradually add ¾ cup sugar, while beating till whites hold soft peaks. Now whip cream and pile it on egg whites. Then fold in custard till no large areas of white remain.

6. Spoon all carefully into soufflé dish and refrigerate for 3 hr., or till set.

7. Meanwhile, fix this garnish: Dry orange sections on paper towels. In saucepan, melt currant jelly. Then soften 1 env. gelatine in ¼ cup cold water; stir it over hot water till dissolved. To jelly, add 1 tablesp. of gelatine mixture, along with enough red food color to make jelly glow. When jelly mixture cools a bit, dip each orange section in it, then drain them on a rack.

8. To serve soufflé, carefully remove foil. Then garnish top of soufflé with orange sections. Makes 10 to 12 servings.

CREAM PUFFS AND ECLAIRS

½ cup butter or mar-	1 cup sifted all-
garine	purpose flour
1 cup boiling water	4 eggs, unbeaten
½ teasp. salt	

1. Start heating oven to 400°F. In medium saucepan heat butter with boiling water, over high heat, stirring occasionally, until butter is melted. Then turn heat low, add salt and flour, *both at once*, and stir vigorously, over low heat, until mixture leaves sides of pan in a smooth compact ball.

2. Immediately remove from heat, then quickly add eggs, one at a time, beating with spoon until smooth after each addition. After last egg has been added, beat until mixture has satinlike sheen.

3. Drop mixture by tablespoonfuls, 3″ apart, on greased cookie sheet, shaping each into a mound that points up in center.

4. Bake 50 min. — without peeking. Cream Puffs should be puffed high and golden. Remove with spatula to wire rack to cool.

5. *To serve:* Split Cream Puffs almost all the way around. Or slice off top of each. Fill with Cream-Puff Filling, p. 642; Chocolate-Cream Filling, p. 642; sugared strawberries; ice cream; or sweetened whipped cream, flavored with almond, vanilla, or rum extract. Set tops back on. Top with confectioners' sugar, half recipe for Bittersweet Frosting, p. 644, and nuts; hot Butterscotch Sauce, p. 534; crushed, sweetened berries; or sliced peaches. Makes 8 puffs.

TO DO AHEAD: Make Cream Puffs one day. Next day, reheat in 325°F. oven 5 min.; cool; split; fill.

FROZEN CREAM PUFFS: Make Cream Puffs. Fill with ice cream; freezer-wrap; freeze; will keep 3 or 4 weeks. Slightly thaw in refrigerator before serving.

PETITE: Drop cream-puff mixture by rounded teaspoonfuls onto lightly greased cookie sheet. Bake at 400°F. about 30 min. Cool. Fill and serve as above, 2 per person for dessert. Or fill with cream cheese for cocktail hour.

CHOCOLATE ECLAIRS: Start heating oven to 400°F. Make cream-puff mixture, above. Drop rounded tablespoonfuls, about 2″ apart, in rows 6″ apart, onto ungreased baking sheet. Now, working carefully with small spatula, spread each ball of dough into 4″ x 1″ rectangle, rounding sides and piling dough on top. Bake 40 min., or until golden. When done, cool on rack.

To serve: Make lengthwise slit in side of each; fill with Cream-Puff Filling, p. 642, or whipped cream; top with half recipe for Bittersweet Frosting, p. 644, or Thin Chocolate Glaze, p. 650.

CRANBERRY CHEESECAKE

1 cup packaged	flour
cornflake crumbs	½ cup heavy cream
Granulated sugar	1 tablesp. lemon
½ teasp. cinnamon	juice
3 tablesp. melted but-	1 tablesp. vanilla ex-
ter or margarine	tract
4 8-oz. pkg. creamed	2 cups whole fresh
cottage cheese	cranberries
4 eggs	1½ teasp. unflavored
¼ cup all-purpose	gelatine

Day before:

1. Combine cornflake crumbs, ¼ cup granulated sugar, cinnamon, and melted butter. Press mixture over bottom of 9″ spring-form pan firmly.

2. Start heating oven to 350°F. Next, with spoon, press cottage cheese through a fine sieve into large bowl. Then, with electric

mixer at high speed, beat in the eggs, one at a time, beating well after each addition.

3. Next, thoroughly beat in the flour and 1 cup granulated sugar. Then beat in the cream, lemon juice, and vanilla and continue beating until very well blended. Pour cheese mixture into crumb-lined pan. Bake 50 min., then turn off the oven heat; leave cake in the oven 30 min. longer. (It may develop cracks while cooling.) Then remove cake from oven to a wire rack to finish cooling. Refrigerate overnight.

About 6 hr. before serving:

1. In a saucepan combine cranberries, ¾ cup water, and 1 cup sugar; cook 5 min., or until cranberry skins pop, stirring occasionally. Meanwhile, soften gelatine in 2 tablesp. water, then stir into the hot cranberries until dissolved. Refrigerate mixture until it just begins to thicken.

2. Now gently loosen cheesecake from sides of pan with a spatula, then carefully remove the sides of the pan. Loosen the cheesecake from the bottom of the spring-form pan; slowly slide it onto serving plate. Gently pour cranberry mixture onto cheesecake, spreading over top of cake. Refrigerate until topping is set — about 3 hr. Serve in wedges, with a cracked walnut in the shell as a go-along. Makes 16 servings.

NAPOLEONS

4½ cups sifted all-purpose flour	1 cup confectioners' sugar
1 lb. butter, chilled	¼ cup semisweet-chocolate pieces
Water	
1 tablesp. vinegar	1 teasp. white corn syrup
Custard Filling, p. 127	

Several days before serving:

1. In large bowl put flour and ½ lb. butter, in small pieces (refrigerate rest of butter). With pastry blender, cut in butter, till mixture is like corn meal.

2. Mix 1 cup cold water with vinegar, then pour over flour mixture. With fork, mix well; shape into ball, wrap. Refrigerate ½ hr.

3. On well-floured surface, with stockinet-covered rolling pin, roll this pastry dough into a rectangle ¼" thick.

4. Then, starting at narrow end of dough, dot

two thirds of it with remaining chilled ½ lb. butter. Now fold unbuttered third over center third, then fold last third on top, making 3 layers. Next, fold opposite ends so they completely overlap each other, making equal thirds and a block shape with straight sides. Wrap in foil, refrigerate ½ hr.

5. Now reroll dough and repeat folding, wrapping, and refrigerating three more times. Then refrigerate dough overnight or for several days.

Early on the day:

1. Remove dough from refrigerator; let rest ½ hr.; then divide dough into 6 *equal* parts.

2. Start heating oven to 425°F. On very well floured surface, as above, roll one of the sixths of dough into rectangle about 14" x 12". Fold in half, then lift to a large ungreased cookie sheet; unfold. Prick top generously with a fork. Bake 10 min., or until a rich golden brown. Carefully remove to flat surface and cool completely.

Repeat rolling, etc., with remaining 5 portions of dough, baking 1 sheet at a time and making 6 14" x 12" pastry rectangles in all.

3. Then make up Custard Filling, p. 127.

4. Freezer-wrap and freeze 3 baked pastry rectangles for use on a later day.

A few hr. before serving:

1. Lay remaining 3 pastry rectangles out in a row. Then, for icing, in small bowl, stir confectioners' sugar with about 1½ tablesp. water till smooth.

2. Over *warm* water, melt chocolate with corn syrup and stir in 1 teasp. water for glaze. Place in wax-paper cone with small opening.

3. Generously frost top of 1 pastry rectangle, using all of white icing; then with chocolate glaze, make crosswise lines, 1" apart, from one side to the other. Then *quickly*, while icing is wet, lightly draw tip of knife lengthwise through icing and chocolate crosslines, drawing lines 1" apart, at opposite ends of rectangle to form a zigzag design. Set decorated pastry rectangle aside.

4. Now place 1 of the 2 remaining pastry rectangles on a cookie sheet; over pastry spread one half of Custard Filling; cover with second pastry rectangle, then spread with rest of Custard Filling. Top with decorated pastry rectangle; refrigerate at least 1 hr.

5. Now, with *very sharp knife*, trim off un-

even ends, making 4 straight sides. Next, with same *sharp* knife, along long side, cut it in thirds crosswise. Then along narrow side, make 5 lengthwise cuts, each about 1½" apart, making 18 Napoleons in all. Place on serving dish and refrigerate until served.

CUSTARD FILLING:

1. Cook 2 pkg. vanilla pudding and pie-filling mix as label directs, using 3 cups milk. Pour into large bowl; cover with wax paper, resting directly on warm pudding; refrigerate till completely chilled.
2. Sprinkle 1 env. unflavored gelatine on 3 tablesp. water to soften; stir over hot water until completely dissolved; cool slightly.
3. Now whip 2 cups heavy cream with 1 teasp. vanilla extract until just starting to mound; gradually add cooled gelatine while continuing to beat cream stiff. Beat chilled pudding mixture until blended. Into it fold whipped-cream mixture; refrigerate. Makes enough filling for 18 Napoleons.

FRESH APPLE PIE

Flaky Pastry for Two-Crust Pie, pp. 584–586, or 1 pkg. piecrust mix	½ teasp. grated lemon rind
⅔ to ¾ cup granulated sugar (or half granulated and half brown sugar)	1 to 2 teasp. lemon juice
	¼ teasp. nutmeg
	½ teasp. cinnamon
1 to 2 tablesp. flour (if fruit is very juicy)	6 to 7 cups thinly sliced, pared, cored cooking apples (2 lb.)*
⅛ teasp. salt	1 tablesp. butter or margarine

1. Use half of pastry to make 9" bottom crust as in Making a Two-Crust Pie, pp. 584–586; refrigerate. Start heating oven to 425°F.
2. Combine sugar with flour, salt, rind, lemon juice, nutmeg, and cinnamon (amount of sugar depends on tartness of apples).
3. Place half of apples in pastry-lined pie plate, with sharp edges facing inward; sprinkle with half of sugar mixture.
4. Top with rest of apples, heaping them in center, then with rest of sugar mixture. Dot with butter.
5. Trim bottom pastry even with rim of pie plate, using scissors or knife. Moisten edge of pastry with water.

6. Roll out rest of pastry, then fit and seal as top crust on apples, following steps 1–4, in If Two-Crust Pie, p. 584.
7. Bake 40 to 50 min., or until filling is tender and crust nicely browned. Especially nice warm.
Use firm, tart, juicy cooking apples as listed on p. 543.

To Vary: To sugar mixture, add ½ cup chopped nuts or raisins. Or before adjusting top crust, pour ⅔ cup heavy cream, slightly whipped, over apples. Or when pie is done, pour 3 tablesp. brandy through slits in crust.

SLIPPED CUSTARD PIE

Baked 9" Pie Shell, p. 585	½ teasp. salt
4 eggs, slightly beaten	1 teasp. vanilla extract
½ cup granulated sugar	2 cups milk
	½ teasp. nutmeg

1. Make, bake, cool, 9" pie shell as directed.
2. Start heating oven to 350°F. Combine eggs, sugar, salt, vanilla, milk; beat well.
3. Butter a second 9" pie plate; set in shallow baking pan. Pour egg mixture into pie plate; sprinkle with nutmeg.
4. Set in oven; pour enough hot water into baking pan to come halfway up side of pie plate. Bake 35 min., or till silver knife, inserted in center, comes out clean.
5. *Cool well on rack at room temperature.*
6. When baked pie shell and custard are cool, tilt custard a bit. With small spatula, gently pull custard away from side of pie plate; then, holding plate level with both hands, shake gently. Now, holding plate, tilted, over baked pie shell, with far edge of custard just above and close to far edge of shell, shake gently; as custard slips out, quickly pull plate back toward you till all custard rests in shell.
7. Let pie settle a few min.; then serve at once as is. Or top it with fruit or berries and whipped cream; toasted coconut; or drizzling of maple-blended syrup and nuts. Makes 1 9" pie.

CHOCOLATE-CRESTED CUSTARD PIE: Melt 1 sq. unsweetened chocolate over very low heat. Stir in 2 tablesp. granulated sugar and 2 tablesp. hot water, a little at a time. Spread over custard in pie shell.

COCONUT CUSTARD PIE: Just before or after baking, sprinkle custard with ½ cup flaked coconut.

LATTICE TOPPED: Melt ⅓ cup semisweet-chocolate pieces with 1 teasp. shortening. Dip metal or wooden skewer into melted-chocolate mixture, then draw it across top of cooled baked pie in crisscross manner, without marring custard, dipping skewer into chocolate as needed. Let settle a few min.; then serve at once.

FUDGE-NUT PIE

Flaky Pastry, pp. 584–586, or 1 pkg. pie-crust mix	3 eggs, unbeaten
	¼ teasp. salt
	½ cup milk
2 sq. unsweetened chocolate	¼ cup corn or maple-blended syrup
½ cup light-brown sugar, packed	1 cup finely chopped walnuts
¼ cup butter or margarine	1 teasp. vanilla extract
¾ cup granulated sugar	¼ cup broken walnut meats

1. Roll half of pastry into circle with diameter slightly larger than top of 9″ pie plate; then invert pie plate on pastry and with point of sharp knife trace around edge of plate. Now pull excess pastry away from plate, and lift off plate. Fit circle of pastry into bottom and part way up sides of pie plate.
2. Roll out other half of pastry, then, with floured 2″ cutter, cut it into about 20 rounds. Place a round on inside of pie plate so it overlaps bottom pastry and comes up a bit above rim of pie plate. Moisten one edge of this round with water, then overlap it slightly with another pastry round, pressing it into place. Repeat this all around pie plate, forming petals. Refrigerate this pie shell.
3. Start heating oven to 350°F. In double boiler, over hot, *not boiling*, water, melt chocolate. Remove double-boiler top from water, then, into chocolate, stir brown sugar and butter. With electric mixer at high speed, or with spoon, beat until blended; add granulated sugar and beat again.
4. Then, to chocolate mixture, add eggs, one at a time, beating well after each addition. Now add salt, then combined milk and syrup; beat until foamy.

5. Replace double-boiler top over hot, *not boiling*, water and cook pie filling 5 min., while stirring. Remove from hot water, stir in finely chopped walnuts and vanilla. Pour into chilled, unbaked pie shell.
6. Bake pie at 350°F. 55 min. Then open oven, pull out rack part way, and scatter broken walnuts over pie. Bake 5 min. longer. Serve warm, topped with ice cream.
P.S. If preferred, make pie day before, then refrigerate; to serve it, warm up at 350°F. about 15 min.

Or make, bake; then freeze wrapped pie a week or so ahead; for serving, heat unwrapped frozen pie at 350°F. about 20 min.

HEAVENLY PIE

1½ cups granulated sugar	4 egg yolks
¼ teasp. cream of tartar	3 tablesp. lemon juice
	1 tablesp. grated lemon rind
4 egg whites	⅛ teasp. salt
3 tablesp. flaked coconut (optional)	1 pt. heavy cream
	Strawberries

1. *A day ahead:* Make pie as follows: Start heating oven to 275°F. Sift 1 cup sugar with cream of tartar. Beat egg whites with hand beater or electric mixer, at medium speed, till they stand in stiff, not dry, peaks. Then slowly add sugar mixture, while beating until very stiff and glossy.
2. Spread this meringue over bottom and up sides, just to rim, of well-greased 9″ pie plate, making bottom ¼″ thick, sides 1″ thick. Sprinkle rim with 2 tablesp. coconut. Bake 1 hr.; meringue shell should be light brown, crisp. (Toast remaining coconut while meringue bakes.) Then cool shell.
3. Meanwhile, beat egg yolks slightly in double-boiler top, then stir in ½ cup sugar, lemon juice and rind, salt. Cook these, while stirring, over boiling water, till thickened — about 8 to 10 min.; cool.
4. Whip 1 cup cream; fold into cooled lemon mixture. Pour into center of cooled meringue shell, making sure all the little pockets are filled as you go along. Smooth top.
5. Refrigerate pie at least 12 hr. — preferably 24 hr. Then serve it, topped with 1 cup heavy cream, whipped, then sprinkled with toasted coconut and garnished with berries.

LEMON PARFAIT PIE

Baked 8″ Pie Shell,
p. 585
1 3-oz. pkg. lemon-
flavor gelatin
1¼ cups hot water

1 teasp. grated lemon
rind
3 tablesp. lemon
juice
1 pt. vanilla ice
cream

1. Make and bake 8″ pie shell. Then, in 2-qt. saucepan, dissolve gelatin in hot water; add lemon rind and juice.
2. Add ice cream by spoonfuls, stirring until melted. Refrigerate until thickened but not set — 25 to 30 min.
3. Turn into shell. Refrigerate until firm — 25 to 35 min.

LIME-PINEAPPLE: Make and bake 9″ pie shell. Substitute lime-flavor gelatin for lemon. Drain juice from a 1-lb.-4-oz. can crushed pineapple. Add enough water to juice to make 1¼ cups; heat and use to dissolve gelatin as above. Omit lemon rind and juice. At end of step 2, fold in 1 cup of crushed pineapple (reserve rest for garnish).

STRAWBERRY CHEESE PIE

1 cup sifted all-
purpose flour
¼ cup granulated
sugar
1 teasp. grated lemon
rind
½ cup butter or mar-
garine, cut into
pieces
1 egg yolk
¼ teasp. vanilla ex-
tract
2½ 8-oz. pkg. soft
cream cheese (20
oz.)
1 cup granulated
sugar

1½ tablesp. flour
⅛ teasp. salt
¼ teasp. each grated
orange and lemon
rinds
3 eggs, unbeaten
1 egg white
2 tablesp. heavy
cream or evapo-
rated milk
¼ teasp. vanilla ex-
tract
1 qt. strawberries,
washed, hulled
¾ cup currant jelly,
melted

Day before or early in day:
1. In bowl, mix together 1 cup flour, ¼ cup sugar, and 1 teasp. grated lemon rind. Make well in center and drop in pieces of butter. Add egg yolk, then ¼ teasp. vanilla extract. Using fork, work butter into flour mixture until dough is soft and pliable. Then press dough into a ball.
2. With back of spoon, press two thirds of dough evenly over bottom of 10″ pie plate;

press rest around sides — not up on rim. Refrigerate this unbaked shell several hr. or overnight.
3. *Next morning:* Start heating oven to 400°F. Prick chilled shell all over with fork; bake 7 min., then cool.
4. Increase oven heat to 450°F. With spoon, or electric mixer at medium speed, beat cheese till fluffy. Slowly add combined 1 cup sugar, 1½ tablesp. flour, salt, orange and lemon rinds, beating until fluffy. Beat in eggs and egg white, one at a time, then cream and vanilla.
5. Pour most of filling into baked shell. To avoid spilling, set filled pie shell on oven rack and add rest of cheese mixture from a cup. Bake pie 7 min., or till crust is golden; then reduce oven heat to 200°F. and bake it 15 min. more (it will be puffy and set). Cool pie on wire rack away from drafts. (Don't worry, it will shrink, and may crack a little as it cools.)
6. Arrange well-drained strawberries over entire surface of cooled pie. Carefully spoon cooled, melted jelly over berries. Serve for lunch; or refrigerate till dinner. Makes 1 10″ pie.

STRAWBERRY TARTS

1 qt. strawberries,
washed, hulled
1 tablesp. lemon
juice
½ cup granulated
sugar
1 tablesp. cornstarch
2 tablesp. granulated
sugar

¼ teasp. cinnamon
1 pkg. piecrust mix
Light cream
1 8-oz. pkg. soft
cream cheese*
3 tablesp. milk
1 teasp. grated
lemon rind

1. In saucepan crush 1 cup strawberries with wooden spoon. Add lemon juice, ½ cup sugar, and cornstarch. Cook over low heat, stirring, until thickened and clear; set aside to cool.
2. For tart shells, add 2 tablesp. sugar and cinnamon to piecrust mix. Then prepare as label directs, substituting cream for water called for.
3. Start heating oven to 450°F. Roll pastry ⅛″ thick; cut out 6 5″ rounds. Over back of 3″ cup of muffin pan, fit a pastry round, making 6 pleats in it; repeat on alternate muffin cups. Then, with 4-tined fork, prick shells on

bottom. Bake all 5 min., or till golden; cool on wire rack.

4. Carefully fold remaining whole berries into cooled berry mixture till all are glazed.

5. Mix cream cheese with milk and lemon rind; spoon into cooled shells.

6. Now, for finishing flourish, use teaspoons to carefully lift each berry out of sauce and heap on cheese filling, dividing them equally among the 6 tart shells. Then drizzle any remaining strawberry syrup over them. Makes 6 servings.

*One pkg. vanilla pudding and pie-filling mix, made as label directs, may replace cheese as filling for tarts.

P.S. Tarts may be made any time of year by substituting well-drained, thawed frozen whole strawberries; drained canned or thawed frozen peaches or blueberries; or fresh or frozen raspberries for the fresh strawberries.

STRAWBERRY SHORTCAKE

2 cups sifted all-purpose flour	tional)
	½ cup shortening
3 teasp. double-acting baking powder	1 egg, beaten
	About ⅓ cup milk
¾ teasp. salt	Butter or margarine
3 to 5 tablesp. granulated sugar	4 cups sweetened sliced or crushed strawberries
1 teasp. grated lemon or orange rind (op-	1 cup heavy cream

1. Start heating oven to 450°F. Into mixing bowl, sift flour, baking powder, salt, sugar; add rind.

2. With pastry blender or 2 knives, scissor-fashion, cut shortening into flour mixture until like corn meal. Add beaten egg, then enough milk to make easily handled dough.

3. FOR LARGE SHORTCAKE: Roll or pat dough into ½"-thick round, to fit greased 9" layer pan. Bake 15 to 20 min., or until done.

FOR INDIVIDUAL SHORTCAKES: Roll or pat dough ½" thick; cut into 3" rounds. Place, 1" apart, on cookie sheet. Bake 12 to 15 min., or until done.

4. Split hot cake or cakes; butter well; fill with some of strawberries. Top with rest of berries, then with whipped cream or dessert topping. Or pass pour cream or commercial sour cream. Makes 6 to 8 servings.

To Do Ahead: Any time before meal, make

up dough to point of adding egg and milk; refrigerate. Just before serving, complete, and bake.

DROP BISCUIT SHORTCAKES: Increase milk in step 2 to about ½ cup. Drop dough into 6 to 8 3" mounds on greased cookie sheet. Bake 12 to 15 min., or until done.

PIN-WHEEL SHORTCAKES: Prepare dough as in steps 1 and 2 at left. Knead dough 1 min.; roll into 8" x 6" rectangle. Spread with 2 tablesp. soft butter or margarine; sprinkle with 1½ tablesp. sugar mixed with ¼ teasp. nutmeg. Roll up from long side, jelly-roll-fashion. Cut into 7 slices. Bake on greased cookie sheet, at 450°F., 12 to 15 min., or until done. Over each pin wheel, spoon strawberries and whipped cream. Makes 7 servings.

To Vary Fruit: Substitute one of these fruits for strawberries:

1. Half-and-half sweetened raspberries and strawberries or sliced bananas
2. Sweetened crushed raspberries or blackberries
3. Warm applesauce, topped with cinnamon-flavored whipped cream
4. Sweetened, sliced fresh, or thawed frozen or canned peach slices
5. Sliced bananas and drained canned fruit cocktail

LONG SHORTCAKE: Place dough on cookie sheet and pat it into an oval shape. Then roll it out into an oval 14" x 6". (It should just fit your serving plate.)

Next flute edge of shortcake in this way: Place index finger of left hand on inside edge of dough. Point it toward thumb and index finger of right hand, placed along outside edge of dough. Pinch dough around finger of left hand. Repeat this pinching all around the dough. Now sprinkle dough with 2 tablesp. sugar. Then bake at 450°F. 15 min., or till golden.

While shortcake bakes, peel and slice 1 qt. fresh peaches, wash 1 cup fresh raspberries. Sprinkle peaches with ¼ cup sugar, then refrigerate fruits.

When done, with help of 2 spatulas, remove hot shortcake to serving plate. Cut 2 tablesp. butter or margarine into small pieces, letting them drop onto hot cake.

Arrange peaches and scatter berries over

all. Along center of cake spoon firm or soft vanilla ice cream. (Or use whipped cream or dessert topping.) Serve in 6 to 8 crosswise slices.

Nice, also, topped with strawberries, orange and banana slices, or blackberries, brushed with red jelly.

BAKED CUSTARDS

4 eggs	or milk and cream
¼ cup granulated sugar	1 teasp. vanilla extract
¼ teasp. salt	Nutmeg or flaked coconut
2 to 2½ cups milk	

INDIVIDUALS:

1. Start heating oven to 300°F. Butter 5 or 6 custard cups. Into large bowl, break eggs; with electric mixer at medium speed, or hand beater, beat until fluffy.
2. Add sugar, salt; beat until *thick and lemon-colored*. Add milk, vanilla; beat again until thoroughly combined.
3. Pour mixture through fine strainer into custard cups, filling each to about ½" from top; top with nutmeg or coconut. Set custard cups in shallow baking pan; place on oven rack. Fill pan with hot water to ¾" from top of cups.
4. Bake about 1 hr. Near end of baking time insert silver knife in center of custard. When knife comes out clean, custards are done. Remove at once from oven, then lift at once out of water; let cool on wire rack. Refrigerate.
5. Serve right in custard cups. Or run spatula all around inside of each cup; place dessert plate, upside down, on top of each cup; then invert. Remove cup. Makes 5 or 6 servings.
6. If desired, top with one of these:
   a. Chocolate, caramel, or butterscotch sauce, maple syrup, or port wine.
   b. Sliced fresh, frozen, or canned fruit.
   c. Applesauce flavored with lemon rind.
   d. Grated chocolate or flaked coconut.
   e. A spoonful of jelly or jam.
   f. Plain or whipped cream, with a drop or two of almond extract.

LARGE: Turn custard mixture into buttered 1-qt. casserole. Place in baking pan; fill pan with hot water to ¾" from top of casserole. Bake at 300°F. 1¼ hr., or until knife, inserted in center, comes out clean. Remove

from oven, then from water. Cool on wire rack. Refrigerate until cold.

To serve, unmold. Or spoon into sherbet glasses. Makes 5 or 6 servings.

BAKED CARAMEL COCONUT: In skillet, over medium heat, melt ¼ cup granulated sugar, stirring constantly until it forms caramel-like syrup. Immediately pour into 6 buttered custard cups. Slowly pour custard mixture into cups; if desired, sprinkle with flaked coconut or chopped pecans; bake as directed for individual custards above. Refrigerate until cold; unmold. Caramel becomes sauce over custard.

BAKED CUSTARD SURPRISES: Just before serving individual custards in cups, lift spoonful of custard from center of each; drop in bit of jelly or chocolate sauce; replace custard. Top with whipped cream if desired.

BAKED MAPLE: Before pouring in custard mixture, place 1 tablesp. maple, maple-blended, or buttered syrup in each cup.

BAKED MARSHMALLOW: Before pouring in custard mixture, place a large marshmallow in bottom of each custard cup. Or cover bottom of large casserole with marshmallows.

CUSTARD BREAD PUDDING

1 qt. milk	½ teasp. salt
2 cups 2-day-old bread crumbs or ½" squares	¼ teasp. nutmeg
2 eggs	1 tablesp. vanilla extract; or 1 teasp. almond extract
¼ cup granulated sugar	2 to 4 tablesp. melted butter or margarine

1. Start heating oven to 350°F. Grease 1½-qt. casserole. In double boiler, heat milk until tiny bubbles appear around edges. Remove from heat; stir in bread crumbs; set aside.
2. Break eggs into casserole; beat slightly with fork. Stir in sugar, salt, then milk mixture, nutmeg, vanilla, butter.
3. Set casserole in baking pan; fill baking pan with warm water to come up 1" from top of casserole.
4. Bake, uncovered, 1 hr. 15 min., or until silver knife, inserted in center of pudding, comes out clean.
5. Serve warm or cold, with pour cream; whipped cream; Lemon Sauce, p. 538; Hard Sauce, p. 537; or sweetened crushed straw-

berries, flavored with almond extract. Or top with bits of jelly. Makes 6 to 8 servings.

♣ FOR 2 OR 3: Halve each ingredient; use 1-qt. casserole or 4 custard cups. Bake as directed 45 to 50 min., or until it tests done.

CAKE CRUMB: Substitute stale cake crumbs for bread crumbs.

CHOCOLATE NUT: In heated milk, melt 2 sq. unsweetened chocolate; with hand beater, beat until blended; add ½ cup chopped walnuts.

COCONUT: Before baking pudding, sprinkle top with ½ cup flaked coconut.

RAISIN OR DATE: With milk mixture, add ½ cup light or dark raisins, or snipped, pitted dates.

INDIVIDUAL: Use 8 greased custard cups; bake as directed 45 to 50 min., or until done.

QUEEN OF PUDDINGS: Use 2 eggs and 2 egg yolks. Use 6 to 8 greased custard cups; bake, in pan of warm water, at 350°F., 45 to 50 min., or until a silver knife, inserted in center, comes out clean. Remove from oven.

Beat 2 leftover egg whites until they form peaks when beater is raised; slowly add ¼ cup granulated sugar, beating till stiff. Heap on top of puddings, leaving depression in center of each. Bake in pan of warm water at 350°F. 12 to 15 min., or until golden. Serve warm or cold, with dab of currant jelly in center of each. Or spread jelly on puddings before topping with meringue. Makes 6 to 8 servings.

RICE CUSTARD PUDDING

½ cup uncooked regular rice	raisins
3 eggs	1½ teasp. grated lemon rind
⅓ cup granulated sugar	3½ cups milk
2 teasp. vanilla extract	1 teasp. nutmeg
½ cup light or dark	2 tablesp. butter or margarine

1. Start heating oven to 300°F. Cook rice tender, as package label directs.
2. Into 2-qt. casserole, break eggs; beat slightly with fork. Stir in sugar, vanilla, raisins, lemon rind.
3. Stir milk into rice; stir into egg mixture. Sprinkle with nutmeg; then dot with butter. Set casserole in baking pan; fill pan with hot water to 1″ from top of casserole.

4. Bake, uncovered, 1 hr. 25 min., stirring once after ½ hr. (To avoid breaking top, insert spoon at edge of pudding; draw gently back and forth along bottom of casserole.) Near end of baking time, insert silver knife in center of custard. If knife comes out clean, custard is done. Remove casserole from baking pan; cool.
5. Serve, slightly warm or cold, with pour cream; whipped cream; maple or maple-blended syrup; Hot Fudge Sauce, p. 537; or Butterscotch Sauce, p. 534. Makes 6 to 8 servings.

♣ FOR 2 OR 3: Use 3 tablesp. rice, 2 small eggs, 3 tablesp. sugar; halve rest of ingredients. Use 1-qt. casserole. Bake 55 min.

SNOW PUDDING
(Lemon Sponge)

2 teasp. unflavored gelatine	1 teasp. grated lemon or lime rind
¼ cup cold water	¼ cup lemon or lime juice
Granulated sugar	3 egg whites*
Pinch salt	
1 cup hot water	

1. In large bowl, sprinkle gelatine over cold water to soften. Add ½ cup sugar, salt, hot water; stir until gelatine dissolves. Add lemon rind and juice; stir until blended. Refrigerate, stirring often, until consistency of unbeaten egg white.
2. Then, with electric mixer at medium speed, or hand beater, beat egg whites until they form moist peaks when beater is raised. Then add ¼ cup sugar slowly, while beating until stiff. Add to gelatine mixture, beating until thoroughly combined.
3. Turn into 1-qt. mold; refrigerate until set, then unmold on serving dish. Or refrigerate, in bowl, until set; then pile in sherbets or nappy dishes.

Use 3 leftover egg yolks in making half recipe for Custard Sauce 1, p. 537. Serve over pudding, topped with sliced berries, peaches, bananas, etc., if desired. Or sprinkle with mace. Or drizzle on maple-blended or maple syrup. Makes 4 or 5 servings.

♣ FOR 2 OR 3: Use 2 egg whites; halve rest of ingredients, making as directed.

SNOWBALLS: Make Snow Pudding as above.

Spoon into 5 or 6 custard cups; refrigerate until set. Unmold in sherbets, or pile in serving dish. Spoon Custard Sauce over top; then drizzle on maple syrup. Makes 5 or 6 servings.

ORANGES IN THE CLOUDS: Make as on p. 132; in step 3, after pudding has refrigerated until set, spoon it into a serving bowl or sherbet glasses. Spoon some of Custard Sauce I, p. 537, over top (pass rest). Then tuck unpeeled orange slices, halved, here and there. Makes 5 or 6 servings.

EGGS A LA NEIGE

4 cups milk	tract
6 egg whites	6 egg yolks
1¼ cups granulated sugar	1½ tablesp. flour
Salt	2 pt. fresh strawberries
1½ cups heavy cream	1 sq. unsweetened chocolate
¾ teasp. vanilla ex-	

Day before, or early on day:

1. Scald milk in large skillet. (See Scald, p. 5.)
2. Meanwhile, beat egg whites till frothy, then gradually add ¾ cup sugar and ¼ teasp. salt, while beating stiff.
3. Now, onto hot milk, drop 3 large mounds of meringue, 1″ apart; cook them 5 min., turning once with slotted spoon; drain on paper towel. Repeat this step until all meringue is used, then refrigerate meringues.
4. In double boiler, scald cream with vanilla and 1½ cups of the milk used for the meringues.
5. Meanwhile, beat yolks till light, then beat in ½ cup sugar, pinch of salt, flour, and a little of hot cream-milk mixture. Stir this mixture into rest of hot cream-milk. Cook all, over hot, *not boiling*, water, while stirring, till sauce coats a metal spoon.
6. Let this custard sauce and meringues cool in refrigerator until 20 min. before dessert time. Then hull, wash, and slice strawberries into deep serving dish. Over them heap chilled meringues, then pour on custard.
7. Lastly, with vegetable parer, shave the chocolate over all. Makes 8 servings.

To Vary: You may substitute sliced peaches or bananas or any fruit of your choice for strawberries. Or serve Eggs à la Neige in individual nappy dishes; omit fruit.

SPONGECAKE

5 eggs, separated	2 tablesp. water
1 cup sifted granulated sugar	1 cup sifted cake flour
1½ teasp. grated lemon rind	¼ teasp. salt
4½ teasp. lemon juice	¼ teasp. cream of tartar

1. Take out eggs to warm up about ½ hr. before making cake.
2. Start heating oven to 350°F. In small bowl, with hand beater, or electric mixer at high speed, beat yolks until blended. Then gradually add ½ cup sugar, beating constantly.
3. Now combine lemon rind and juice with water, then add gradually to yolks, beating until fluffy and light.
4. Next, with rubber spatula or spoon, *gently* fold flour into yolks until they are completely blended.
5. Then, with hand beater, or mixer at high speed, in large bowl, beat egg whites with salt until foamy. Add cream of tartar, then continue beating until whites form moist peaks when beater is raised.
6. Now beat in ½ cup sugar, 2 tablesp. at a time.
7. Turn egg-yolk mixture onto beaten whites. Then with rubber spatula *gently* fold yolks into whites until so thoroughly blended that there are no streaks of yolks or whites.
8. Then pour mixture into ungreased tube pan, 9″ across and 3½″ high, turning pan slowly as you pour. Next, to remove large air bubbles, cut through batter with small spatula, in shape of square, lifting spatula out of batter and inserting it again at each corner of square.
9. Bake cake 40 to 45 min. Test for doneness as in step 10, p. 620. Remove it from oven and cool, then remove pan as in steps 6 and 7, p. 630.
10. Serve in wedges as is, or topped with fresh or frozen strawberries. Or split into 2 or 3 layers and fill with whipped cream and sliced peaches or strawberries.

SPONGECAKE LAYERS: Bake spongecake batter in 2 ungreased 9″ layer pans, 1½″ deep, at 350°F. for 25 min., or until done.

SPONGE TEACAKES: Bake in ungreased pan, 13″ x 9″ x 2″, at 350°F. for 25 to 30 min., or until done; when cool, cut into diamonds or oblongs, then sprinkle with confectioners' sugar.

SPONGE CUPCAKES: Bake in 2½″ paper cups, set in cupcake pans, and filled half full, at 350°F. 12 to 15 min., or until cake tester, inserted in center, comes out clean. Cool, then serve in or out of paper cups.

BOSTON CREAM PIE: Bake 2 Spongecake Layers as on p. 133. When cool, fill with Luscious Cream Filling, p. 642; frost top with Thin Chocolate Coating, p. 650.

WASHINGTON PIE: Bake 2 Spongecake Layers as on p. 133. When cool, fill with jelly. Sift confectioner's sugar over the top.

ANGEL-FOOD CAKE

1¼ cups egg whites (10 to 12 eggs)	1¼ teasp. cream of tartar
1 cup plus 2 tablesp. sifted cake flour	1 teasp. vanilla extract
1½ cup sifted granulated sugar	¼ teasp. almond extract
¼ teasp. salt	

1. Set out egg whites about 1 hr. ahead.
2. When ready to make cake, start heating oven to 375°F. Sift flour with ½ cup sugar 4 times.
3. In large bowl, combine egg whites, salt, cream of tartar, extracts. With electric mixer at high speed (or with hand beater or flat wire whip), beat egg whites until stiff enough to hold soft, moist peaks.
4. With mixer at same speed, beat in 1 cup sugar, sprinkling ¼ cup at a time over egg whites. Beat until sugar is just blended. (To beat by hand, beat 25 strokes or turns, after each addition.)
5. Stop mixer. Sift in flour mixture by fourths, folding in each addition with 15 complete fold-over strokes of spoon, rubber spatula, or wire whip and turning bowl often. After all flour has been folded in, give batter 10 to 20 extra strokes.
6. Gently push batter into *ungreased* 4″-deep 10″ tube pan. With spatula, cut through batter once without lifting spatula out of batter.
7. Bake 30 to 35 min., or until cake tester, inserted in center, comes out clean. Cool, then remove as in steps 6 and 7, p. 630. Serve as on p. 630.

MACAROON: After sifting flour with sugar, add ⅓ cup finely snipped coconut; toss with fork. Omit vanilla; increase almond extract to 1¼ teasp.

ORANGE: After sifting flour with sugar, add 3 tablesp. grated orange rind; toss with fork. Substitute 1 teasp. orange extract for vanilla and almond extracts.

YELLOW LAYER CAKE

2 eggs	sugar
1 cup milk	3 teasp. double-acting baking powder
½ cup soft shortening*	1 teasp. salt
2½ cups sifted cake flour	1 teasp. vanilla extract
1½ cups granulated	

1. *An hour ahead:* Set out eggs, milk, and shortening to come to room temperature. Line 2 8″ layer pans, 1¼″ deep, with wax paper; grease paper. Or use floured greased pans.
2. Now start heating oven to 375°F. Into large bowl, sift flour, sugar, baking powder, and salt. Drop in shortening, then pour in ⅔ cup milk and vanilla.
3. Beat with electric mixer at medium speed for 2 min. Or beat with spoon in 300 sweeping round-the-bowl strokes, or 2 min. by clock, rotating bowl and scraping it often.
4. Now add ⅓ cup milk and the eggs, unbeaten, and beat with mixer at medium speed 2 min. or with spoon 300 strokes — 2 min.
5. Pour batter into 2 layer pans, dividing equally. Bake at 375°F. 25 to 30 min., or until they spring back when touched lightly in center.
6. Cool layers in pans on wire racks 10 to 15 min. Then, with spatula, loosen each cake around sides, place rack on top, invert cake on it, and lift off pan. Remove wax paper, then turn cakes right side up to cool.
7. Fill layers with apricot jam, then frost with Seven-Minute Frosting, p. 646.
Use any shortening that comes in a 1-lb. or 3-lb. can.

To Vary: Bake in a greased, floured pan, 14″ x 10″ x 2″, at 375°F. 30 min., or, until done; cool, then sprinkle with confectioners' sugar and cut into diamonds. So nice at dessert time.

WALNUT CAKE
(have shortening, eggs, and milk at room temperature)

3 cups sifted cake flour	4 medium eggs, un-beaten
2 teasp. double-acting baking powder	¾ cup milk
1¾ cups granulated sugar	2 teasp. vanilla extract
1½ teasp. salt	1 cup *very finely chopped* walnuts
1 cup soft shortening*	

1. Start heating oven to 375°F. Grease 9″ tube pan, 3½″ deep, then line bottom with wax paper.
2. Into large bowl sift flour, baking powder, sugar, salt. Drop in shortening, 2 eggs; pour in milk, vanilla.
3. With electric mixer at medium speed, beat 2 min., scraping bowl and beaters as needed (or beat 300 brisk, round-the-bowl strokes with spoon). Add 2 eggs; repeat, beating as before. Fold in nuts.
4. Turn batter into pan. Bake 1 hr., or until cake tester, inserted in center, comes out clean.
5. Now set pan on wire rack; cool 10 to 15 min.; then loosen cake with spatula, remove, and cool.
6. Serve unfrosted. Or boil 2 tablesp. white corn syrup with 2 tablesp. butter or margarine 3 min., *no longer*. Decorate cake with a few walnut halves and pieces of candied citron or pineapple, then drizzle with this glaze.

Use any shortening that comes in a 1-lb. or 3-lb. can.

To Vary: Substitute very finely chopped Brazil nuts or pecans for walnuts. Or substitute 1 teasp. almond extract and 1 teasp. orange extract for vanilla.

This cake freezes well.

THREE-LAYER FUDGE CAKE

2 cups sifted cake flour	½ cup soft shortening*
2 cups granulated sugar	3 sq. unsweetened chocolate, melted
1 teasp. salt	1¼ cups milk
1½ teasp. baking soda	1 teasp. vanilla extract
¾ teasp. double-acting baking powder	3 medium eggs, un-beaten

1. Start heating oven to 350°F. Grease, then line with wax paper, bottoms of 3 8″ layer pans, 1¼″ deep.
2. Into large bowl, sift flour, sugar, salt, soda, and baking powder. Drop in shortening; pour in chocolate, ¾ cup milk, vanilla.
3. With electric mixer at medium speed, beat 2 min., scraping bowl and beaters as needed (or beat 300 brisk, full, round-the-bowl strokes with spoon). Add ½ cup milk, eggs; repeat beating as before.
4. Turn into pans. Bake 35 to 40 min., or until cake tester, inserted in center, comes out clean.
5. Now set pans on wire racks; cool 10 to 15 min.; then loosen cakes with spatula, remove and cool.

Use any shortening that comes in a 1-lb. or 3-lb. can.

FROSTINGS: Fill and frost with Seven-Minute Frosting, p. 646, or double recipe for Mocha Butter Cream, p. 645.

TWO-LAYER FUDGE CAKE: Bake in 2 1½″-deep 9″ layer pans at 350°F. 35 to 40 min., or until done. Fill and frost with Chocolate Fluff, p. 649.

CHOCOLATE ROLL

4 eggs	1 teasp. vanilla extract
½ cup sifted cake flour	2 tablesp. granulated sugar
½ teasp. double-acting baking powder	¼ teasp. baking soda
¼ teasp. salt	3 tablesp. cold water
2 sq. unsweetened chocolate	Confectioners' sugar
¾ cup sifted granulated sugar	1 cup heavy cream
	¼ teasp. almond extract

1. Set out eggs about 1 hr. ahead.
2. When ready to make cake, start heating oven to 375°F. Grease 15″ x 10″ x 1″ jelly-roll pan (or 17½″ x 11½″ x 2¼″ open roasting pan), then line bottom of pan with wax paper. Sift flour, baking powder, and salt onto piece of wax paper. Melt chocolate in double boiler over hot, *not boiling*, water.
3. Break eggs into large bowl; sift ¾ cup sugar over them; with electric mixer at high speed (or with hand beater), beat until *very thick and light*.
4. With rubber spatula or spoon, fold flour mixture and vanilla, all at once, into egg mixture. To melted chocolate, add 2 tablesp.

sugar, soda, cold water; stir until thick and light; quickly fold into batter.

5. Turn into pan. Bake 15 to 20 min., or just until cake springs back when gently touched with finger. (If cake is baked in roasting pan, it may take a little longer.)

6. While cake bakes, place clean dish towel on flat surface; over it, sift thick layer of confectioners' sugar. When cake is done, with spatula, loosen it from sides of pan, invert onto towel. Lift off pan; carefully peel off paper; with very sharp knife, cut crisp edges from cake, to make rolling easier. Cool exactly 5 min.

7. Now fold hem of towel over edge of cake. Then roll up cake very gently from narrow end, rolling towel up in it (this prevents cake's sticking). Gently lift rolled cake onto wire rack to finish cooling — about 1 hr. (If cake is warm, whipped-cream filling will melt.)

8. *Just before serving:* Carefully unroll cake so it will be on towel. Quickly spread cake with almond-flavored whipped cream to within 1″ of edges. Start rolling up cake from narrow end by folding edge of cake over, then tucking it under; continue rolling cake, lifting towel higher and higher with one hand as you guide roll with other hand. Finish with open end of cake on underside. Cut into crosswise slices.

Serve slices plain; or top with vanilla or coffee ice cream. For a holiday touch garnish with maraschino cherries with stems, dipped, first in hot corn syrup, then in chopped nuts. Makes 8 to 10 servings.

FRUIT CAKELETS

4 cups sifted all-purpose flour	1 15-oz. pkg. white raisins
3 teasp. double-acting baking powder	1½ cups canned slivered toasted almonds
1 teasp. salt	
½ teasp. ground nutmeg	1 7-oz. pkg. fine grated coconut
½ lb. diced preserved citron	1½ cups butter or margarine
½ lb. diced preserved orange peel	1½ cups granulated sugar
½ lb. diced preserved pineapple	1 cup canned pineapple juice
½ lb. whole candied cherries	10 egg whites

1. Buy about 100 petal-edged pink, green, gold, silver, and blue foil nut cups,* in which to bake Fruit Cakelets.

2. Place nut cups either in cupcake-pan cups or on cookie sheets.

3. Sift flour with baking powder, salt, nutmeg.

4. In large 4½-qt. bowl or pan, mix citron, orange peel, pineapple, cherries, raisins, almonds, with the coconut; then add flour mixture and stir to coat fruits well.

5. In another 4½-qt. bowl, work butter or margarine with spoon or mixer till creamy; then gradually beat in sugar till light and fluffy.

6. Stir in floured fruit mixture alternately with pineapple juice, starting and ending with fruit mixture.

7. Start heating oven to 325°F. Beat egg whites stiff; then carefully fold them into batter till no egg-white flecks remain.

8. Put a rounded measuring tablespoonful of batter in each foil cup, pushing and leveling it with a small spatula. Bake cakelets 40 min., or till done, then cool them on cake rack; repeat bakings until all batter is used.

9. When all cakelets are cool, wrap and then refrigerate them until needed. Makes about 100.

10. For a party arrange fruits, nuts, and some of the cakelets on a tiered epergne. Cut 12 multicolored taper candles to proper height and, with a bit of melted wax, fasten each candle to edge of epergne, spacing them evenly.

May be purchased from Maid of Scandinavia Co., 3245 Raleigh Ave., Minneapolis, Minnesota.

FLUFFY FROSTING

1¼ cups granulated sugar	Pinch salt
⅛ teasp. cream of tartar	3 egg whites
6 tablesp. water	1 teasp. vanilla extract

1. In small saucepan, combine sugar, cream of tartar, water, salt; stir over low heat until sugar dissolves. Cook, *without stirring*, to 260°F. on candy thermometer, or until a little mixture dropped in cold water forms hard ball.

2. Set syrup aside. Using electric mixer at

high speed (if you must use hand beater, ask a friend to help), beat egg whites until they form moist peaks when beater is raised.

3. Now add syrup gradually, while beating. When all syrup has been added, add vanilla; continue beating until mixture forms stiff peaks when beater is raised and is thick enough to spread. (Fills and frosts 2 8″ or 9″ layers.)

To Vary: Sprinkle chopped nuts or shaved unsweetened chocolate in a border around top edge of cake.

DOUBLE CHOCOLATE-WALNUT DROPS

1½ cups sifted all-purpose flour	1 egg, unbeaten
1 teasp. double-acting baking powder	2 tablesp. milk
¾ teasp. salt	1 teasp. vanilla extract
¾ cup soft shortening	½ cup semisweet-chocolate pieces
¾ cup granulated sugar	¾ cup chopped walnuts
1 sq. unsweetened chocolate, melted	Walnut halves

1. Start heating oven to 350°F. Sift flour, baking powder, salt.
2. In large bowl, with electric mixer at medium speed, or with spoon, mix shortening with sugar, then with melted chocolate and egg, until light and fluffy.
3. At low speed, mix in milk, then flour mixture; add vanilla, chocolate pieces, chopped walnuts.
4. On greased cookie sheet, drop by heaping teaspoonfuls, 1″ apart; press walnut half into top of some. Bake 15 to 18 min. Cool on cake rack. Makes about 4 doz.

TOFFEE BARS

½ cup soft butter or margarine	½ cup sifted all-purpose flour
¼ cup granulated sugar	½ cup uncooked rolled oats
¼ cup brown sugar, packed	1 6-oz. pkg. semisweet-chocolate pieces (1 cup)
¼ teasp. salt	¼ cup flaked coconut
1 teasp. vanilla extract	¼ cup chopped walnuts
1 egg, unbeaten	

1. Start heating oven to 350°F. Grease well 11″ x 7″ x 1½″ baking pan.

2. Mix butter, sugars, salt, vanilla, and egg until very *light and fluffy.*
3. Mix in flour and rolled oats; then blend well. Spread in pan.
4. Bake 30 min., or until done. Cool 10 min.
5. Meanwhile, melt chocolate over hot, *not boiling,* water; stir until smooth; spread over baked layer; sprinkle half with coconut, rest with nuts. Cool in pan. Cut into 24 bars. Delicious with cold milk.

To Vary: Double all ingredients. Make as above. Bake in 2 greased 11″ x 7″ x 1½″ baking pans as above. Makes 48 bars.

BROWNIES

¾ cup sifted cake flour	tract
½ teasp. double-acting baking powder	2 to 2½ sq. unsweetened chocolate, melted
¾ teasp. salt	1 cup chopped walnuts, almonds, pecans, Brazil nuts, pistachio nuts, or peanuts
1 cup granulated sugar	
½ cup soft shortening	
2 eggs, unbeaten	
1 teasp. vanilla extract	

1. Start heating oven to 350°F. Grease well 8″ x 8″ x 2″ pan. Sift flour, baking powder, salt.
2. Gradually add sugar to shortening, mixing until *very light and fluffy.* Add eggs, vanilla, mix till smooth. Mix in chocolate, then flour mixture and nuts. (If desired, save half of nuts to sprinkle on top of batter before baking.)
3. Turn into pan. Bake 30 to 35 min., or until done. Cool slightly; cut into 16 squares or bars; sprinkle with confectioners' sugar if desired. Store right in pan.

FUDGIES: Change flour to ½ cup sifted all-purpose flour; baking powder and salt to ⅛ teasp. of each. Use butter as shortening. Bake at 325°F. 30 to 35 min.

FRUIT: For part or all of nuts, substitute snipped raisins, pitted dates, or dates and nuts.

FROSTED: Frost with Peppermint Butter Cream, p. 645. When frosting is firm, drizzle on 1 sq. unsweetened chocolate melted with 1 tablesp. margarine. Or frost with Quick-As-A-Wink Frosting, p. 645.

COCONUT: Substitute flaked coconut for all or half of nuts. Some may be sprinkled on top of batter.

PEANUT: Substitute ¼ cup peanut butter for ¼ cup shortening.

DOUBLE DECKER: Omit chocolate, nuts. Remove one fourth of batter to small bowl; to it, add ⅓ cup flaked coconut and ½ teasp. almond extract. To rest of batter, add 1½ sq. melted unsweetened chocolate; pour into pan. Spread with coconut batter. Bake.

MOCHA: Add 1 tablesp. instant coffee to chocolate.

CHOCOLATE-ORANGE: Add 1 tablesp. grated orange rind to batter. Frost with Orange Butter Cream, p. 645; top with more nuts.

REFRIGERATOR COOKIES

1½ cups sifted all-purpose flour
½ teasp. baking soda
¾ teasp. salt
½ cup soft shortening
1 cup granulated sugar; or ½ cup each granulated sugar and brown sugar, packed
1 egg, unbeaten
2 or 3 teasp. vanilla extract, or ½ teasp. almond extract
½ cup coarsely chopped nuts (optional)

1. Sift flour, soda, salt. Mix shortening with sugar, egg, and vanilla until *very light and fluffy*. Gradually mix in flour mixture and nuts.
2. Turn dough onto large piece of wax paper or foil. Shape into roll 1½″ in diameter; then wrap in wax paper, foil, or saran. Refrigerate several hr., overnight, or for a week, if desired.
3. When you want cookies, start heating oven to 375°F. With sharp thin knife, dipped into hot water, then wiped dry, slice off from roll as many ⅛″- to ¼″-thick slices as you need. (Return rest of roll, wrapped, to refrigerator to bake later.)
4. Place on ungreased cookie sheet. Bake 10 min., or until done. Cool on wire rack; store in tightly covered container. Makes about 5 doz.

CHOCOLATE: Add 3 sq. melted unsweetened chocolate to egg mixture before adding flour. Decrease vanilla to 1 teasp.

ORANGE: Add 1 tablesp. grated orange rind to egg mixture; substitute orange juice for vanilla.

DATE: Add ½ cup chopped, pitted dates to flour mixture.

SPICE-NUT: Sift ½ teasp. cinnamon and ¼ teasp. nutmeg with flour mixture.

COCONUT: Increase shortening to ¾ cup. Use granulated-brown sugar combination. Add 2 cups flaked coconut.

To Vary: Double ingredients. Make as above, but shape into roll 2″ in diameter; makes about 65. Or 2 rolls 1½″ in diameter; makes about 122.

GOOD BEGINNINGS

The appetizer course, prelude to good things to come, should whet, not dull, the appetite — not too many and not too much. And today's busy hostess-cook will often find it easier to serve this traditional at-table first course in the living room, from a tray. For that allows her a few moments in which to chat with her guests before being excused to put dinner on the table.

Before using these recipes, refer to How To Use Our Recipes, p. 3. Always use standard measuring cups and measuring spoons; measure level.

FRUIT BEGINNINGS

FINGER FRUITS

When it's fruit first in the living room, finger fruits are ideal.

Choose one or more of the following for a fruit hors-d'oeuvre platter. They can pinch-hit for the first or salad course at the table, too.

Serve them alone or with crackers to nibble on.

1. Pineapple chunks on toothpicks. Guests dip them into mace-sprinkled sour cream or deviled-ham-and-cheese spread.
2. Apple or pear wedges (dipped into lemon juice) topped with sharp-cheese spread or a mixture of Roquefort and cream cheese.
3. Pineapple chunks topped with Camembert cheese.
4. Pear wedges (dipped into lemon juice), to dunk into cream cheese whipped up with orange juice until fluffy.
5. Banana spears (dipped into lemon juice) rolled in finely chopped nuts.
6. Prunes stuffed with crunchy peanut butter.
7. Avocado cubes with toothpicks (dipped into lemon juice or Spicy Dunk Sauce, p. 530). Guests dunk them in grated process Cheddar cheese.

FRUIT CUPS

Fruit cups are ideal for your at-table service. For fun, serve them in sherbet glasses whose

139

rims are frosted as on p. 682. Or heap the fruit in avocado quarters or halves, or in orange or grapefruit shells. Or, for a frosty touch, top the fruit with a small ball of sherbet — cranberry, pineapple, orange, lime, lemon, or raspberry.

Garnish the cups with fresh mint, strawberries, raspberries, fresh or maraschino cherries, or lemon or lime wedges. Or substitute grenadine or crème de menthe for some of the fruit syrup. Try these fruit-cup go-togethers. They should suggest others.

1. Any fresh, canned, or thawed frozen fruit, alone or combined with a sprinkling of lemon or lime juice. Or top with chilled ginger ale, ginger ale frozen to mush, grenadine, crème de menthe, or wine. Or top with small amount of one of frozen juice concentrates, thawed just enough to spoon out of can.
2. Orange sections, seedless grapes, just-thawed frozen strawberries, sprinkling of lemon or lime juice.
3. Pineapple chunks, apple slices, cubes of mint jelly.
4. Pear chunks, apricot quarters, sliced bananas, canned whole-cranberry sauce, grated lemon rind.
5. Canned cling-peach slices and pineapple tidbits, sliced celery, chopped nuts.
6. Slice a frozen-juice pop over any fruit-cup combination.
7. Drained canned fruit cocktail, chopped apple, ginger ale, grated orange rind.

ITALIAN PROSCIUTTO WITH MELON
(Prosciutto Con Melon)

Cut chilled cantaloupe or honeydew melon in half; remove seeds; pare off rind. Slice each half into thin wedges. Arrange one or more melon wedges on each dessert plate; top with paper-thin slices of prosciutto (Italian-style ham). Or place prosciutto at the side of melon. Eat with fork and knife.

GRAPEFRUIT STARTER
Prepare Chilled Grapefruit Halves, p. 548, or any of its variations. Or tuck thin avocado slices between grapefruit sections, pin-wheel-fashion; sprinkle with French dressing.

MELON BALLS IN GRAPEFRUIT JUICE

½ small watermelon; or 2 honeydew or casaba melons — 2 cups grapefruit juice / Mint sprigs

If using honeydew or casaba melons, cut them in halves; remove seeds. From melon meat, scoop out balls, using a fruit-ball cutter or ½ teasp. of round-measuring-spoon set. Fill 6 sherbet glasses two thirds full with melon balls and add ⅓ cup grapefruit juice to each. Chill; garnish with mint. Makes 6 servings.
MELON-BALL-LEMON-ICE COCKTAIL: Top melon balls or cubes in each sherbet glass with small spoonful of lemon, raspberry, or mint ice.

GRAPEFRUIT-AND-AVOCADO COCKTAIL

24 fresh or canned grapefruit sections / ¼ cup French dressing — 1 ripe avocado / ¼ cup French dressing / Parsley

Combine grapefruit sections with ¼ cup French dressing. Pare avocado; halve; remove pit; cut into crosswise slices ¼" thick. Pour ¼ cup French dressing over slices. Arrange 4 grapefruit segments and 4 avocado slices in each of 6 sherbet glasses; garnish with parsley. Makes 6 servings.
ORANGE-AVOCADO COCKTAIL: Substitute orange sections, or part orange and part grapefruit sections, for grapefruit.

AVOCADO COCKTAIL

1 large ripe avocado / ¼ cup chili sauce / 1 teasp. horse-radish / ½ teasp. Worcestershire — 1 tablesp. lemon juice / 1 tablesp. mayonnaise / ¼ teasp. salt

Chill avocado. Blend remaining ingredients; refrigerate. Just before serving, pare avocado and cut into cubes or wedge-shaped pieces. Arrange in 3 or 4 sherbet glasses; top with sauce. Makes 3 or 4 servings.

JUICE COCKTAILS

Juice cocktails are a happy choice, whether for living-room or at-table service.

Living-Room Style: Arrange filled glasses on a tray along with small cocktail napkins and small plates to place under glasses, if desired. Pass simple hors d'oeuvres if you wish.

At-Table Style: For a separate first course, place each filled glass on small plate (on service plate if desired). Or, simpler still, place each filled glass to right of water glass, to be sipped during main course.

FRUIT JUICES

LIME-PINEAPPLE: Float small ball of lime ice on pineapple juice.

CRANBERRY-PINEAPPLE: Combine two thirds cranberry-juice cocktail with one third pineapple juice. Or float small ball of cranberry sherbet on pineapple juice.

SPARKLERS: Reconstitute frozen juice concentrates (orange, grapefruit, grape, pineapple, lemonade, limeade, etc.) with chilled ginger ale instead of water. Serve at once, garnished with twist of lemon peel.

Or combine equal parts of canned fruit juice (apple, whole-fruit nectar, cranberry-juice cocktail, etc.) and chilled ginger ale.

FRUIT COMBOS: Combine reconstituted frozen fruit juices such as these: pineapple and limeade; lemonade and orange; grape and lemonade; orange and grapefruit; orange and pineapple.

HOT SPICED PINEAPPLE JUICE

Simmer 1 1-lb.-4-oz. can pineapple juice with 2″ stick cinnamon 10 min. Add 2 tablesp. granulated sugar and 2 tablesp. lemon juice. Remove cinnamon. Serve hot. Makes 2½ cups.

PINEAPPLE-LEMON FOAM COCKTAIL

1 1-lb.-4-oz. can pineapple juice	½ cup water
⅔ cup lemon juice	2 egg whites
⅓ cup granulated sugar	1 cup finely crushed ice

Combine all ingredients in jar or shaker. Cover; shake until frothy. Pour into cocktail glasses. Makes 6 servings.

FRUIT WITH FRUIT JUICE

Arrange several pieces of fruit in each fruit-juice glass; then add juice to fill. Have a few toothpicks ready, too, for those who wish to spear their fruit. Try any of these:

1. Ginger ale over seedless grapes
2. Grape juice over grapefruit sections
3. Cranberry-juice cocktail over canned apricot chunks
4. Lemonade or limeade (use frozen concentrate) over orange sections and pineapple chunks
5. Orange juice over pineapple chunks and diced fresh pears or banana slices
6. Cider over apple slices or canned pineapple tidbits
7. Pineapple juice over frozen strawberries (cut frozen block into cubes)
8. Cranberry-juice cocktail over orange sections, canned sliced peaches, or pineapple chunks

TOMATO COCKTAILS

FROSTED TOMATOES

1 small white onion	3 tablesp. mayonnaise
4 large ripe tomatoes, peeled	1 tablesp. snipped parsley
1¼ teasp. salt	½ teasp. curry powder
Speck pepper	

In wooden bowl, finely chop onion and tomatoes. Add salt, pepper. Turn into special ice-cube tray, p. 610; freeze until ice crystals start to form.

Meanwhile, combine mayonnaise, parsley, and curry. Arrange frosty tomato mixture in chilled soup cups; top each with mound of curry mayonnaise. Makes 3 or 4 servings.

TOMATO JUICE

TOMATO-SAUERKRAUT: Combine equal parts of canned tomato juice and sauerkraut juice; add Worcestershire to taste.

TOMATO-CLAM: Combine equal parts of canned tomato juice or vegetable-juice cocktail and clam juice; season with minced onion, salt, pepper.

PEPPY TOMATO: To each cup of canned tomato juice, add lemon juice, pinch of dried basil, and celery salt to taste. Or add some grated cucumber and onion, plus a dash of Tabasco and Worcestershire.

HOT TOMATO: Heat 1 1-lb.-4-oz. can tomato juice with 1 bouillon cube. Serve hot.

VEGETABLE-JUICE COCKTAIL: Canned vegetable-juice cocktail is skillfully seasoned and is very refreshing just as it comes from the can.

OLD-FASHIONED TOMATO COCKTAIL

Drain juice from 1 1-lb.-13-oz. can solid-pack tomatoes (3½ cups). Season tomatoes with salt, pepper, bit of onion salt, celery seeds, snipped parsley, etc., as desired. Chill well. Serve in sherbet glasses, with lemon wedges. Makes 4 servings.

P.S. Don't forget those delicious canned stewed tomatoes, either. They are so refreshing served nice and cold as a first course.

SEA-FOOD COCKTAILS

At-Table Style: Chilled cooked, cleaned shrimp; chunks of fresh or canned lobster; fresh, drained canned, or thawed frozen King-crab meat; canned tuna, etc., plus a zippy cocktail sauce, are traditionally served in lettuce-lined sherbet glasses. However, you might like one of these ways better:

1. Place sea food that has been dipped into sauce in hollowed-out small tomatoes. Set on beds of water cress on small plates.
2. Or heap sea food in green-pepper rings set on plates; spoon on sauce.
3. Or arrange sea food on small plates; place lettuce cup or romaine leaf filled with sauce in center.

Living-Room Style: Just arrange the sea food on a tray or platter, with the sauce in a custard cup, scooped-out tomato, grapefruit shell, scallop or lobster-tail shell, half an avocado shell, or seeded green-pepper half. Garnish with something green. Place toothpicks nearby, for dunking and finger eating.

SHRIMP, CRAB, OR LOBSTER COCKTAILS

SHRIMP: Allow about 6 cooked, cleaned shrimp per serving. Serve with Tangy Cocktail Sauce, p. 143.

CURRIED SHRIMP: Allow about 6 cooked, cleaned shrimp, or 3 shrimp and 3 canned or frozen pineapple chunks, per serving. Serve with Curry Cocktail Sauce, p. 143.

CRUNCHY CRAB AND SHRIMP: Allow about 2 tablesp. fresh, drained canned, or thawed frozen King-crab meat chunks; 4 cooked, cleaned shrimp; and 2 tablesp. minced celery per serving. Serve with Superb Cocktail Sauce, p. 143.

CRAB: Allow about ¼ or ⅓ cup flaked fresh or drained canned or thawed frozen King-crab meat per serving. Serve with Tangy Cocktail Sauce, p. 143.

LOBSTER: Allow about ¼ to ⅓ cup cooked or canned lobster meat, in chunks, per serving. Serve with Easy Cocktail Sauce, p. 143.

FRUITED SEA FOOD: Allow about ¼ to ⅓ cup fresh, drained canned, or thawed frozen King-crab meat chunks, or 4 cooked cleaned shrimp, and 3 or 4 grapefruit sections per serving. Serve with either Tangy or Easy Cocktail Sauce, p. 143.

CRAB-STUFFED AVOCADOS

½ cup mayonnaise or cooked salad dressing	Dash Tabasco
	2 ripe avocados
	Salt
½ cup minced celery	Crisp salad greens
¼ cup minced pimento	1½ cups cooked or drained canned or thawed frozen King-crab meat, chilled
Lemon juice	
⅛ teasp. Worcestershire	

Combine mayonnaise, celery, pimento, 2 teasp. lemon juice, Worcestershire, Tabasco. Halve avocados lengthwise; remove pits; peel; sprinkle with lemon juice and salt. Arrange each avocado half on a bed of crisp greens; fill with some of crab meat, then top with mayonnaise mixture. Makes 4 servings.

MARINATED CRAB MEAT

⅓ cup salad oil	2 cups thinly sliced celery
⅓ cup dry white wine	
¼ teasp. Tabasco	1 lb. flaked fresh or drained canned or thawed frozen King-crab meat; cooked, cut-up scallops; or any flaked white fish
¼ teasp. salt	
¼ teasp. dried thyme	
½ cup mayonnaise or cooked salad dressing	
	Salad greens

In bowl, combine salad oil, wine, Tabasco, salt, thyme, mayonnaise. Toss with celery and crab meat; refrigerate ½ hr. Serve on salad greens. Makes 6 servings.

OTHER SEA-FOOD COCKTAILS

TUNA: Allow about ¼ to ⅓ cup canned tuna, in chunks, per serving. Serve with any of Cocktail Sauces, at right.

CLAMS, OYSTERS, OR SCALLOPS: Allow 6 shucked raw littleneck or cherry-stone clams or raw oysters, or 6 small cooked scallops, per serving. Serve with Tangy Cocktail Sauce, at right.

To Cook Scallops: Place scallops in saucepan. Add 1 cup boiling salted water for each 1 cup scallops. Boil, covered, 8 to 10 min. Drain; refrigerate until well chilled; then use in scallop cocktail.

CALIFORNIA COCKTAIL

2 grapefruit	King-crab meat; or
1 cup cooked or	½ cup of each
canned lobster meat	3 tablesp. orange juice
or drained canned	¼ cup catchup
or thawed frozen	¼ cup mayonnaise

Halve grapefruit; remove pulp; cut fruit into small pieces. With scissors, snip out membrane, then notch edges of grapefruit shells. Snip lobster or crab meat into bite-size pieces. (Toss lobster and crab together if using both.) Blend orange juice, catchup, mayonnaise; mix with sea food and grapefruit; use to fill shells. Makes 4 servings.

OYSTERS OR CLAMS ON THE HALF SHELL

Allow 6 to 8 oysters or clams per serving. Have shells opened at market. Serve each oyster or clam on deeper half of shell; arrange on bed of crushed ice, tucking sprigs of water cress or parsley between shells if desired. In center of each plate, place small glass or lettuce cup filled with some Tangy Cocktail Sauce, below; add lemon wedge.

If desired, pass horse-radish, Tabasco, or Worcestershire, as well as tiny oyster crackers.

COCKTAIL SAUCES

TANGY: Combine ⅔ cup catchup, 3 tablesp. chili sauce, 2 tablesp. horse-radish, 3 tablesp. lemon juice, dash cayenne pepper, dash Tabasco. If desired, add minced onion or celery, grated cucumber, or pickle relish. Refrigerate. Makes 6 to 8 servings.

SUPERB: Combine 1 cup catchup, ½ cup Worcestershire, ½ cup grated Parmesan cheese, 1 tablesp. butter or margarine, 1 minced small onion, ⅛ teasp. pepper, and ¼ cup water. Bring to boil; turn heat very low, and simmer 30 min. Refrigerate until 2 hr. before serving. Makes 6 to 8 servings.

CURRY: Combine 1 cup mayonnaise, ½ teasp. curry powder, 1 tablesp. minced onion, 1 tablesp. lemon juice, and 2 tablesp. chutney. Refrigerate. Makes 6 to 8 servings.

EASY: Combine ¼ cup mayonnaise, ½ cup chili sauce or catchup, 2 tablesp. prepared mustard, 1 tablesp. Worcestershire, 1 tablesp. horse-radish, and ½ teasp. monosodium glutamate. Refrigerate. Makes 6 to 8 servings.

LEMON COCKTAIL: Combine ⅔ cup mayonnaise, 2 teasp. horse-radish, 2 teasp. snipped chives, 2 teasp. prepared mustard, 2 to 4 tablesp. lemon juice. Makes ⅔ cup.

P.S. Also see Cucumber, Louis, and Red Sauces, pp. 529–530.

DIPS, DUNKS, & NIBBLERS

Whether you call them canapés, hors d'oeuvres, nibblers, or snacks, you'll be serving these tantalizing little party foods that look irresistible and taste even better, not only as a dinner prelude, but as round-the-clock party fare. Probably you'll set them out on the coffee table so guests can help themselves. Guests love making their own, which leaves you, the hostess, free to enjoy your guests or to tend to last-minute details in the kitchen, and generally guarantees the success of your entertaining.

Three tips to remember: Plenty of one or two kinds of nibbler is more appealing than an overwhelming variety. These tasty tidbits should be paired with a drink of some kind for greatest enjoyment. And don't forget to check your grocer's shelves for newcomers in the nibbler family.

Before using these recipes, refer to How To Use Our Recipes, p. 3. Always use standard measuring cups and measuring spoons, and measure level.

DO-AHEAD NIBBLERS—HOT

HOT BAKED-HAM MIDGETS

Bake and glaze a whole or half ham, or a cooked smoked boneless shoulder butt. (Or roast a chicken or turkey.) Arrange on platter, garnished with cress. Set on small side table, with carving fork and knife. Nearby, place napkin-lined basket of thin slices of French, salty rye, raisin, or whole-wheat bread, or tiny hot biscuits. Set out bowls of pickle relish, prepared mustard, horse-radish, catchup, barbecue sauce, etc. Cut tidbits of hot ham same size as bread slices. Guests make their own!

TOASTED-CHEESE SQUARES

12 1" cubes day-old bread (from un-sliced loaf)	margarine
¼ cup soft butter or	¼ lb. natural Ched-dar cheese, grated (1 cup)

Early in day: Butter bread cubes on all sides but one. Roll cubes in cheese; arrange, un-buttered side down, on cake rack; refrigerate.

Just before serving: Set rack on cookie sheet; broil squares about 2 min., or until cheese melts and browns. Serve at once. Makes 1 doz.

BACON BITES

Early in day: With toothpicks, secure halved bacon slices around any of the following. Re-frigerate.

Pineapple chunks	Cooked shrimp
Stuffed olives	Raw oysters
Canned-peach chunks	Watermelon pickle
Pitted prunes	Luncheon-meat cubes
Sautéed chicken livers	Frank chunks
Pickle chunks	Vienna sausages
Brazil nuts	Canned mushrooms or
Pickled onions	water chestnuts
Raw scallops	Splits, p. 154

At serving time: Broil bacon bites till bacon is crisp; serve hot.

EMMY'S PATE TURNOVERS

1¼ cups sifted all-purpose flour	½ teasp. curry pow-der
¼ teasp. salt	½ teasp. prepared mustard
½ cup butter or mar-garine	¼ teasp. pepper
2 tablesp. light cream	Dash paprika
4 bacon strips	2 tablesp. snipped parsley
3 chicken livers	¾ teasp. salt
½ teasp. salt	1 egg, beaten
1 hard-cooked egg	

One or two weeks ahead, if desired:

1. Into medium bowl, sift flour with ¼ teasp. salt. With pastry blender or two knives, used scissors-fashion, cut in butter until it's like coarse corn meal.

2. Add cream, mix until just blended; refrig-erate.

3. Meanwhile, in skillet, cook bacon till crisp; remove bacon; pour off and reserve bacon fat. In 2 tablesp. bacon fat, in same skillet, sauté chicken livers till golden; add ½ teasp. salt;

simmer 5 min.; then drain and chop. Shell, then chop, hard-cooked egg.

4. In bowl, combine chicken livers, bacon, egg, curry, mustard, pepper, paprika, parsley, ¾ teasp. salt, 2 teasp. bacon fat. Mix well; refrigerate.

5. On lightly floured surface, roll out refrig-erated dough ⅛" thick; with 2¾" cookie cutter, cut out rounds; repeat with trimmings, making 25 rounds in all. Then, on half of each round, place a heaping half teaspoonful of chicken-liver mixture.

6. Brush edge of each round with beaten egg. Then fold over, making semicircle; press the edges together with a fork.

7. Arrange turnovers, side by side, on foil-covered cardboards or cookie sheets. Freeze until firm; then freezer-wrap and freeze.

To serve: About 1 hr. before serving, start heating oven to 425°F. Take desired number of turnovers from freezer. Unwrap; arrange on ungreased cookie sheet.

Brush with beaten egg. Bake 20 to 25 min., or until golden-brown. Serve warm. Makes 25.

HASH MOUNDS

Several hr. ahead: Lightly spread 9 slices of white bread with prepared mustard. Cut each slice into 4 squares. Top each square with pickle slice. Shape 1 1-lb. can corned-beef hash into small balls; place 1 ball atop each pickle slice. Refrigerate.

To serve: Broil mounds until bread is toasted and hash balls are golden and heated through. Makes 36.

CURRIED TUNA TOASTIES

2 6½- to 7-oz. cans tuna (2 cups)	2 regular loaves fresh unsliced white bread
1 cup mayonnaise	
1 teasp. instant minced onion	Soft butter or margarine
1 teasp. curry powder	Paprika

Day before:

1. In bowl, combine tuna, mayonnaise, onion, and curry powder until creamy.

2. Next, with sharp knife, carefully trim all crust from each loaf of bread. Lay each loaf on its side; then, starting at the bottom, slice off 5 ½" slices lengthwise. Lightly spread the 10 slices with butter.

3. Spread each slice with 2 rounded tablesp. tuna mixture; sprinkle with paprika.

4. Next, starting at the narrow end, roll up each slice; then wrap it tightly in wax paper. Refrigerate until needed next day.

Just before serving: Cut each roll crosswise into 6 or 7 slices. Lay on cookie sheet; toast under broiler, turning once. Serve hot. Makes 5 doz.

DO-AHEAD NIBBLERS—COLD

SPICED-PINEAPPLE PICKUPS

1 1-lb.-13-oz. can pine-apple chunks	Dash salt
¾ cup vinegar	6 to 8 whole cloves
1¼ cups granulated sugar	1 4″ piece stick cinnamon

A day or two ahead: Drain syrup from pineapple. To ¾ cup syrup, add vinegar, sugar, salt, cloves, and cinnamon. Heat 10 min. Add pineapple; bring to boil. Refrigerate.

To serve: Drain pineapple. Serve, ice-cold, with toothpicks.

NIPPY CARROT NIBBLERS

1 lb. carrots	1½ teasp. salt
3 tablesp. salad oil	½ teasp. dry mustard
3 cloves garlic, minced	1 tablesp. whole pickling spices
1 tablesp. coarsely chopped onion	⅛ teasp. pepper
¼ cup vinegar	1 onion, thinly sliced

Day before, or several days ahead:

1. Cut pared whole carrots into lengthwise slices ¼″ thick. Then cut into strips 3″ long and ⅜″ wide.

2. In salad oil, in skillet, sauté garlic and chopped onion till almost tender — about 5 min. Stir in vinegar, salt, mustard, pickling spices tied in cheesecloth, pepper, and carrots. Simmer, covered, 5 min.; carrots should be very crunchy and crisp. Remove cheesecloth. Transfer carrot mixture to shallow dish; top with layer of thinly sliced onions; cover, then refrigerate till needed, basting occasionally.

Serve cold as an appetizer, along with shrimp, cherry tomatoes, crisp celery, and bunches of green grapes. Makes about 8 to 12 servings.

NOTE: The marinade, as made in step 2, is heavenly on cooked shrimp, too.

SHRIMP RELISH

1½ lb. large fresh shrimp, cooked and cleaned	⅔ cup salad oil
	⅓ cup vinegar
	1 clove garlic, minced
1 cup minced onion	1½ teasp. salt
1 cup snipped parsley	Speck pepper

Few hrs. ahead:

1. In large bowl, combine shrimp, onion, and parsley. In small bowl, mix salad oil, vinegar, garlic, salt, and pepper; beat well. Pour over shrimp.

2. Refrigerate shrimp 1 hr., or until served.

At serving time: Heap shrimp in serving dish, with a few on rim. Guests spear their own with picks. Makes about 30.

DEVILED-HAM-CHIVE BALLS

3 2¼-oz. cans deviled ham	shire
	Speck pepper
¼ cup coarsely crushed pretzels	3 3-oz. pkg. cream cheese
½ teasp. Worcester-	Snipped chives

Early in day or day before: Blend deviled ham with pretzels, Worcestershire, and pepper. Form into 25 balls, using a rounded half teaspoonful for each. Arrange on cookie sheet, then freeze for 30 min.

Meanwhile, work cream cheese with fork until soft. Roll each firm ham ball, first in 1 tablesp. cream cheese or enough to cover it, then in snipped chives. Refrigerate until served. Serve on picks. Makes 25.

BLUE CHEESE-WALNUT BALLS

2 5-oz. jars pasteurized blue-cheese spread	¾ cup chopped walnuts

Early on the day, if desired: Shape cheese into 18 balls. Roll in chopped walnuts; refrigerate till served. Makes 18.

ROQUEFORT OLIVES

Dry well-drained large stuffed olives on paper towels; roll in Roquefort-cheese spread, using knife to coat well, then in chopped walnuts mixed with a bit of salt; shape into balls. Refrigerate.

CURRIED RIPE OLIVES

To favorite Italian dressing, add curry powder to taste. Pour over drained ripe olives. Refrigerate for several hours, then drain and serve as snacks.

BAKED LIVER PATE

2 cups water	3 packaged zwiebacks
Salt	2 eggs, beaten
1 lb. beef-liver slices	2 tablesp. cornstarch
½ lb. lean pork, finely ground	½ teasp. pepper
	2½ cups milk
1 medium onion	Bay leaves

Make pâté several days ahead:

1. Bring water to a boil, add 1 teasp. salt and liver, then simmer, uncovered, about 6 to 8 min.; drain. Start heating oven to 325°F.
2. Meanwhile, put finely ground pork through fine blade of food grinder, with onion and zwiebacks.
3. Now grind drained, cooked liver in same way, then add to pork-onion mixture. Pass this mixture through fine blade of food grinder three times more.
4. Next, with fork, beat eggs with cornstarch, pepper, and 1½ teasp. salt, until smooth. Then, gradually, while stirring, add milk, which has been brought to a boil. Pour slowly into liver-pork mixture while blending smooth.
5. Pour at once into a pretty casserole or a 9" x 5" x 3" loaf pan (1-qt. capacity); pour extra into smaller ovenproof dishes. Now arrange bay leaves on top of casserole of pâté. Set in shallow roasting pan containing water ½" deep. Bake, uncovered, 1½ hr., or until a silver knife, inserted in center, comes out clean. Let pâté cool, then refrigerate, covered, until needed.
6. Serve pâté, unmolded, on serving platter, with crisp crackers, rye crisp, or toast on which to spread it.

SUPER STUFFED CELERY

1. Fill crisp celery stalks, 2" to 3" long, with any of fillings below; refrigerate.
2. Or stuff long, wide celery stalks; chill well. Then cut into bite-size pieces and serve.
3. Or stuff crisp large stalks; put together in pairs, with fillings touching; roll tightly in wax paper; chill well. Cut into ½" slices and serve.

Fillings:

OLIVE-NUT: Into 1 3-oz. pkg. soft cream cheese, stir 4 chopped stuffed olives; 10 minced, blanched almonds; 1 tablesp. mayonnaise.

HAM AND CHEESE: Mash 2 tablesp. blue cheese with 1 3-oz. pkg. soft cream cheese, 1 2¼-oz. can deviled ham, some minced green pepper.

SHARP PINEAPPLE: Mix 1 3-oz. pkg. soft cream cheese with ¼ cup drained canned crushed pineapple and 1 teasp. horse-radish.

RED AND WHITE: Mix 1 cup cottage cheese with 1 tablesp. minced onion, 5 radishes, minced, ½ teasp. salt, ⅛ teasp. pepper.

POTPOURRI CHEESE

1 12-oz. can or bottle beer	½ teasp. salt
	1 teasp. dry mustard
1½ lb. natural Cheddar cheese, grated (6 cups)	2 tablesp. soft butter or margarine
¼ lb. Danish blue cheese, crumbled	1 teasp. Worcestershire
	⅛ teasp. Tabasco

Open beer; let stand. Mix cheeses, salt, mustard; blend in butter, Worcestershire, Tabasco. Add beer gradually, beating with electric mixer until creamy.

Refrigerate mixture in covered jars. Or use to fill small covered pottery jars for gifts. Keeps several weeks. Makes 5 cups.

MEAT ROLL-UPS OR TRIANGLES

THE MEAT: Use thin slices of salami, bologna, boiled ham, or canned chopped ham or luncheon meat.

THE FILLING: Use soft cream cheese seasoned with one or more of these: grated onion, Worcestershire, prepared mustard, horse-radish. Or use one of the many delicious cheese spreads now on the grocer's shelves.

To Assemble: Spread some cheese filling on

each meat slice. Roll up each tightly; chill well; then serve as is, or cut into bite-size pieces.

Or stack 5 spread salami or bologna slices; top with an unspread slice; wrap in wax paper; chill well; then cut each stack into 8 pie-shaped wedges or triangles.

CORNUCOPIAS

For each cornucopia, roll ½ thin slice bologna or salami around 1 stuffed olive or pickled onion, making cornucopia shape; secure with toothpick.

Or roll salami or bologna into cornucopia; then, into center, insert thin sliver of raw carrot or celery, securing with toothpick. Or fill with dab of cream cheese seasoned with horseradish. Or fill with any spread in Spread-Your-Owns, p. 153. Refrigerate.

PICKLED MUSHROOMS

2 6-oz. cans broiled mushroom crowns	¾ cup dark-brown sugar, packed
½ cup liquid drained from mushrooms	2 teasp. whole pickling spices
1 cup vinegar	

Two days ahead: Drain mushrooms, reserving ½ cup liquid. Combine liquid with vinegar, sugar, pickling spices; simmer 5 min. Pour over mushrooms. Refrigerate 2 days.
To serve: Drain mushrooms; then arrange, a pick in each. Makes about 40.

CONVERSATION PIECES

They look like production numbers and are often less work for the hostess.

MAN-PLEASERS

Thinly sliced roast turkey	Thin half slices cooked ham
Cream cheese	Potato salad
Capers	Butter or margarine
Thin half slices roast beef	Salty-rye slices
Coleslaw	Chives

1. Spread turkey slices with cream cheese

mixed with capers and enough caper juice to make spreadable; roll up each.
2. Top roast-beef slices with coleslaw; roll up. Top ham slices with potato salad; roll up.
3. Arrange meats along one side of a long serving board; cover; refrigerate.
4. *At serving time:* Cut each meat roll into 2 pieces without lifting from board. Butter slices of salty rye; sprinkle with snipped chives; arrange in row beside meat.
5. With a pick, guest lifts a meat roll onto each bread slice.

CHABLIS-CHEESE DIP

2 4-oz. pkg. Liederkranz cheese	¼ teasp. celery salt
	¼ teasp. garlic salt
2 8-oz. pkg. soft cream cheese	¼ cup chablis

About 1 week ahead:
1. In large bowl, with mixer at medium speed, beat Liederkranz cheese until smooth. Beat in cream cheese, celery and garlic salts. While beating, gradually add chablis, blending well — about 3 min.
2. Spoon cheese mixture into 1 large or several smaller, *very clean,* containers. Refrigerate, tightly covered, for a week or so, so flavors can blend and ripen before serving with crisp crackers, raw vegetables, or the like. Makes about 3½ cups. Nice to give as gifts in dainty tea or demitasse cups.

COMPANY GOUDA

1 10-oz. Gouda cheese	1 teasp. bottled thick meat sauce
2 tablesp. butter	
1 cup crumbled Roquefort cheese	1 teasp. Worcestershire
1 cup grated process Cheddar cheese	1 teasp. prepared mustard
Dash Tabasco	Beer and sherry

Early in the day, or day before if desired:
1. With sharp knife, cut very thin slice from top of Gouda; make scalloped edge around top. Scoop out enough cheese to leave ½″ shell; then grate 1 cup of this cheese.
2. In bowl, with mixer at low speed, cream butter. Beat in grated Gouda, Roquefort, and Cheddar, then Tabasco, meat sauce, Worcestershire, and mustard.
3. Now beat in 3 tablesp. beer, then 3 tablesp. sherry or enough to make of dip consistency.

Heap hollowed Gouda with some of dip; refrigerate all.

One hour before serving: Let Gouda and extra dip soften at room temperature. Then center Gouda on serving dish with crisp crackers or chips; refill as needed.

EVER-READY CHEESE LOG

½ lb. process sharp
  Cheddar cheese,
  grated
1 to 2 tablesp. minced
  onion
3 tablesp. minced
  green pepper
3 stuffed olives,
  chopped

2 tablesp. chopped
  pickle
1 tablesp. chopped
  pimento
1 hard-cooked egg,
  chopped
½ cup finely crushed
  saltines
¼ cup mayonnaise
½ teasp. salt

Combine cheese with rest of ingredients; form into long roll; wrap in wax paper. Refrigerate till firm. Serve on tray, surrounded by crackers and olives. Guests slice log as they eat.

HOLIDAY CHEESE-BALL TRIO

RED CHEESE BALL

½ lb. natural Ched-
  dar cheese, finely
  grated
1 3-oz. pkg. soft cream
  cheese
3 tablesp. sherry
¼ cup coarsely
  chopped pitted

ripe olives
½ teasp. Worcester-
  shire
Dash each onion, gar-
  lic, and celery salts
½ cup coarsely
  snipped dried beef

Several days ahead, if desired, or day before:
1. In large bowl, with mixer at medium speed, thoroughly combine cheeses, sherry, ripe olives, Worcestershire, and salts.
2. Now shape mixture into a ball; wrap in foil; then refrigerate until needed.

About 30 min. before serving: Remove foil from cheese ball. Reshape into ball with hands; then roll it in the dried beef until it's completely coated. Makes about 3" ball.

GREEN CHEESE BALL

¼-lb. wedge natural
  blue cheese, cut
  from wheel
1 tablesp. minced
  celery
2 or 3 scallions, tops
  and all, finely

snipped
2 tablesp. commer-
  cial sour cream
3 5-oz. jars blue-
  cheese spread
1 cup coarsely
  snipped parsley

Several days ahead, if desired, or day before:
1. In large bowl, with mixer at medium speed, mix crumbled blue cheese, celery, scallions, sour cream, and blue-cheese spread till fluffy.
2. Refrigerate mixture overnight. Then shape into ball; wrap in foil; refrigerate.

About 30 min. before serving: Remove foil from cheese ball. Reshape into ball with hands; then roll it in parsley until it's completely coated. Makes about 4½" ball.

GOURMET CHEESE BALL

3 8-oz. pkg. soft
  cream cheese
1 cup drained pre-
  served ginger,

coarsely snipped
¾ cup canned diced,
  roasted, buttered
  almonds

Several days ahead, if desired, or day before:
1. In large bowl, with mixer at medium speed, beat cheese and ginger till thoroughly combined.
2. Then shape into ball; wrap in foil; refrigerate.

About 30 min. before serving: Remove foil from cheese ball. Reshape into ball with hands; then roll it in almonds until it's completely coated. Makes about 4½" ball.

NOTE: Arrange this cheese trio side by side, in a row on a serving dish. They're especially tasty when spread on crackers, avocado chunks, tomato wedges, etc.

BEEF-LIVER PATE MOLD

1 lb. beef liver, sliced
⅔ cup cut-up chicken
  fat
½ lb. onions, coarsely

cut
4 hard-cooked eggs
1½ teasp. salt
Dash pepper

Day before, or early on the day:
1. Cut out veins and cut skin from liver.
2. Broil liver until medium, not well done.
3. Place cut-up chicken fat in skillet with onions; stir occasionally to prevent scorching. Cook until fat is melted and onions are lightly browned. Remove and reserve onions. Pour off liquid chicken fat into measuring cup. Place liver in same skillet and pan-fry till well done. Cool slightly.
4. In food grinder with fine blade, or in chopping bowl, grind, or chop fine, liver, hard-cooked eggs, and onions.
5. Place liver mixture in bowl. Add salt, pep-

per, and about ¼ cup liquid chicken fat, and/or salad oil — a tablesp. at a time — blending with mixer at medium speed.

6. Shape into a ball or bell, or use to fill simple, well-oiled mold; refrigerate.

At serving time: Serve pâté on salad greens, garnished with green-pepper rings, radish roses, and parsley. Especially good spread for rye bread. Makes 3 cups.

LOBSTER WITH GREEN-GODDESS DRESSING

4 large frozen rock-lobster tails	Green-Goddess Dressing, p. 470

Day before:

1. Cook lobster tails as on p. 321.
2. Make Green-Goddess Dressing; refrigerate.
3. When lobster tails are cool, carefully remove meat from shells; refrigerate shells and meat.

At serving time: Arrange shells on serving tray. Cut lobster meat into bite-size chunks; heap them in three shells. Fill fourth shell with dressing. Guests spear lobster bites and dip into dressing. Makes 36 servings.

PATE DE MAISON

1 4½-oz. can liver pâté	¼ teasp. salt
1½ tablesp. soft butter or margarine	Snipped parsley
	Crisp salty crackers or pumpernickel fingers
1 tablesp. whisky	

In small bowl, mash pâté; blend with butter, whisky, and salt until smooth. Chill well. Serve in bowl, sprinkled with parsley and surrounded by crisp salty crackers or pumpernickel fingers.

KING-SIZE STEAK BITS

Powdered seasoned instant meat tenderizer	½ cup butter or margarine, melted
1 3¾-lb. round steak (2" thick)	1 tablesp. dry mustard
	½ teasp. garlic salt
1 cup red wine or beer	1 teasp. Worcestershire
1 clove garlic, crushed	Dash pepper
	Few drops Tabasco

About 2 hr. before serving:

1. Apply meat tenderizer to steak as label directs. Then marinate steak in 1 cup red wine,

with garlic, in refrigerator, about 1 hr., turning once.

2. Meanwhile, in pan, mix butter, mustard, garlic salt, Worcestershire, 2 tablesp. marinade, pepper, Tabasco.

3. Broil steak, 3" to 4" from heat, 18 to 20 min., or till medium rare, turning once. Heat butter sauce.

4. Cut steak into bite-size strips, heap in chafing dish or casserole, pour on sauce, and serve at once, with picks. Or serve sauce in bowl, each guest dunking his own.

5. Serve with warmed cocktail-rye bread, snappy cheese to heap in crisp celery, mince turnovers, and milk, coffee, or tea. Makes 12 to 16 tidbit servings.

SHORT-ORDER NIBBLERS— HOT

FRENCH-FRY DUNK

Prepare frozen French fries as label directs, sprinkling with Parmesan cheese while they heat, or omit Parmesan. Provide bowl of catchup or chili sauce for dunking.

MUSHROOM TAPAS

Lightly sauté fresh or canned mushroom caps in butter or olive oil, cooking only until mushrooms are a delicate brown — about 2 min. Then sprinkle them with garlic salt and snipped parsley. Serve with a toothpick in each, so guests can help themselves.

BAKED-BEAN BITES

Season baked beans with catchup; spread on pieces of brown bread. Top each with a Cheddar-cheese slice, then with an onion slice. Broil until bubbly, then halve or quarter and serve.

ZIPPY EGG NIBBLERS

6 tablesp. soft butter or margarine	mustard
	1 teasp. sesame seeds
¾ cup minced onions or scallions	6 hard-cooked eggs, chopped
3 tablesp. snipped parsley	20" loaf French bread, split in half lengthwise
3 tablesp. prepared	

Preheat broiler 10 min., or as manufacturer

directs. Combine butter, onions, parsley, mustard, sesame seeds, and eggs. Spread on cut surfaces of French bread; broil, 6″ to 8″ from broiler heat, until *just* hot, but not really browned. Cut into diagonal slices for serving.

TANGY FRANK SPREAD

1½ cups grated sharp Cheddar cheese	shire
6 tablesp. green pickle relish	1½ cups diced frank-furters
3 tablesp. chili sauce	Dash Tabasco
¼ teasp. Worcester-	20″ loaf French bread
	Prepared mustard

Preheat broiler 10 min., or as manufacturer directs. Combine cheese, pickle relish, chili sauce, Worcestershire, frankfurters, and Tabasco. Split French bread in half lengthwise; spread cut surfaces with mustard; top with frankfurter mixture. Broil, 4″ from broiler heat, until hot and lightly browned. Cut into diagonal slices for serving. Makes 40 servings.

MINIATURE PIZZA PIES

Before guests arrive: Slice large French rolls into circles about ½″ thick. Place on cookie sheet. Spread lightly with soft butter or margarine. Dot with flakes of canned tuna, cubes of natural sharp Cheddar cheese, bits of cooked ham. Add dash of catchup; sprinkle with crumbled orégano, then generously with grated Parmesan cheese. Refrigerate.
A few min. before serving: Broil slowly until bubbly and hot.

APPETIZER CRESCENTS

Separate 1 can refrigerated crescent dinner rolls into 8 triangles; cut each triangle into 3 small triangles. Top with one of fillings below. Roll up into crescent shapes. Bake at 375°F. 10 to 12 min., or until golden-brown. Makes 24 appetizers.

SHRIMP: Place 1 cooked shrimp in center of each small triangle. Top with chili sauce.

DEVILED HAM: Spread each small triangle with deviled ham, then with a little prepared mustard.

SAUSAGE: Center a Vienna sausage on each

small triangle, then top with prepared mustard.

HAM: Center ham strip on each small triangle.

SIX-IN-ONE COCKTAIL HASH

½ cup butter or margarine	2 cups packaged bite-size shredded rice
1 tablesp. Worcestershire	2 cups packaged bite-size shredded wheat
¼ teasp. celery salt	2 cups packaged bite-size toasted corn cereal
¼ teasp. seasoned salt	
¼ teasp. cayenne	
¼ teasp. onion salt	1 cup very thin pretzel sticks
¼ teasp. garlic salt	½ cup slivered almonds
1 cup packaged toasted oat cereal	

Make several weeks ahead, if desired:
1. Start heating oven to 250°F. In shallow roasting pan, melt butter; stir in Worcestershire, seasonings, cereals, pretzels, and almonds, then toss all together well.
2. Bake about 1 hr., or until well heated, stirring occasionally.
3. Serve warm, or cool well, then store in covered container until needed. Makes 2 qts.

COCKTAIL HASH: Start heating oven to 300°F. Combine ¼ cup melted butter or margarine with ½ teasp. Tabasco; spread 3 cups bite-size shredded-wheat or -rice biscuits or doughnut-shaped oat cereal and 1 cup salted peanuts in shallow baking pan. Sprinkle with ¼ teasp. salt and the butter mixture. Bake 20 min., stirring occasionally. Makes about 4 cups.

NUT NIBBLERS

BRAZIL-NUT CHIPS: Start heating oven to 350°F. Cover 1½ cups shelled Brazil nuts with cold water; simmer 2 to 3 min.; drain. Cut into thin lengthwise slices; spread in shallow pan; dot with 2 tablesp. butter or margarine; sprinkle with 1 teasp. salt. Bake, stirring occasionally, 15 min., or until toasted.

GARLIC CHIPS: After dotting Brazil-Nut Chips, above, with butter, sprinkle with ½ teasp. each celery and garlic salts, and ½ teasp. paprika. Bake as directed.

HOT PEANUTS: Open can of salted peanuts; heat in 350°F. oven. Toss with raisins if desired. Or heat unshelled peanuts.

ROASTED WALNUTS: Start heating oven to 350°F. Spread cracked unshelled walnuts in large shallow pan. Bake 30 min. Serve hot; guests do the shelling.

SKILLET-TOASTED NUTS: In 2 tablesp. butter or margarine in skillet, sauté 1 cup shelled walnuts, almonds, or pecans until crunchy — 5 min. Drain on paper; sprinkle with salt or seasoned salt, plus a little curry or chili powder if desired.

DEVILED ALMONDS: In 2 tablesp. salad or olive oil in skillet, sauté 2 cups blanched almonds, stirring 5 min., or until crunchy. Drain on paper. Add 1 teasp. salt, ⅛ teasp. chili powder, ⅛ teasp. cayenne; toss.

PEPPERY NUTS: In 2 tablesp. hot butter or margarine in skillet, sauté 1 lb. pecan or walnut halves until hot and buttery. Add 2 teasp. Worcestershire, a few dashes Tabasco, ½ teasp. salt, ⅛ teasp. pepper. Place in shallow baking pan, and bake at 325°F. 20 min. Serve warm or cold. Makes about 4 cups.

GARLIC-FLAVORED POTATO CHIPS OR PEANUTS: Halve 2 cloves garlic; insert toothpick into each garlic half. In tightly covered container, place 1 qt. potato chips or ½ lb. salted peanuts, then garlic. Let stand several hr., occasionally shaking and turning container. Remove garlic before serving.

POPCORN TRICKS

GARLICKY: In skillet, heat packaged popcorn with butter or margarine and sliced clove garlic. Remove garlic before serving.

CHEESE, HOME STYLE: In skillet, heat packaged popcorn with butter or margarine; then toss with grated Parmesan or Cheddar cheese.

SEASONED POPCORN: Pop a big bowlful of popcorn; sprinkle with seasoned salt.

FROM CHAFING DISH OR SKILLET

Have everything ready on a tray. Then make dish right in front of your guests.

LIBBY'S SWISS FONDUE

½ lb. natural Swiss cheese, grated (2 cups)	¼ teasp. salt
	Speck pepper
1½ teasp. flour	Sprinkling of nutmeg
1 clove garlic (optional)	2 tablesp. kirsch or cognac (optional)
¾ cup Chablis or sauterne	French bread, cut into bite-size chunks

Toss cheese with flour. Rub skillet or blazer of chafing dish with garlic; pour in wine; heat over low heat till almost boiling. Add cheese; stir until melted. Add salt, pepper, nutmeg, kirsch. When Fondue is bubbly, it's ready.

To serve: Do not remove Fondue from heat. Let each person spear a bread chunk with fork or toothpick, then dunk it into Fondue, stirring. (If Fondue becomes too thick, you may add a little heated wine.) Makes 6 to 8 nibbler servings or 3 or 4 main dish servings. P.S. A delicious cheese Fondue now comes packaged, all ready to melt in the chafing dish.

CHAFING-DISH MEAT BALLS

1½ lb. chuck, ground	2 cups canned tomato juice
½ cup finely sifted dried bread crumbs	2 tablesp. flour
1 teasp. salt	¾ cup bottled barbecue sauce
¼ teasp. pepper	¼ cup water
1 egg, slightly beaten	1 1-lb.-4½-oz. can pineapple chunks, drained
½ cup milk	
¼ cup shortening	

Early in day:

1. In bowl, with two-tined fork, toss together chuck, bread crumbs, salt, pepper, egg, and milk until well blended.

2. Shape into ½" to ¾" balls. Place in shallow pan (ours was 12" x 8" x 2") with shortening; refrigerate.

3. In saucepan, combine tomato juice and flour until smooth. Add barbecue sauce and water and blend well. Set aside.

About 1½ hr. before party:

1. Start heating oven to 350°F.; bake meat balls 30 min.

2. Now drain excess fat from browned meat balls, then pour on tomato sauce. Bake 45 min. longer.

3. Then, to serve, spoon meat balls and sauce into chafing dish, electric skillet, or attractive

serving dish, with pineapple chunks here and there. Makes about 48 meat balls.

CRAB-MEAT RABBIT

3 tablesp. butter or margarine	3 cups milk
½ cup all-purpose flour	About ½ lb. natural sharp cheese, grated (2 cups)
½ teasp. salt	2 8-oz. pkg. frozen
⅛ teasp. prepared mustard	King-crab meat, thawed, well
Dash cayenne pepper	drained, in chunks
¾ teasp. Worcester-shire	Crisp crackers or toast

1. In chafing dish or double boiler, over simmering water, melt butter or margarine. Gradually stir in flour, salt, mustard, cayenne, Worcestershire, then milk. Cook, while stirring, until thickened and smooth.
2. Add cheese; cook, stirring occasionally, until melted. Gently fold in crab-meat chunks; heat, stirring occasionally, until hot.
3. Guests dunk crisp crackers or Melba toast into crab-meat mixture. Makes 8 servings.

SPICY APPETIZER FRANKS

1 pkg. spaghetti-sauce mix	1½ cups water
	2 tablesp. salad oil
1 8-oz. can tomato sauce	1 to 2 lb. franks

Early in day: Prepare spaghetti-sauce mix with tomato sauce, water, salad oil, as label directs. Cut franks into 1" pieces. Refrigerate both.

At serving time: Heat franks in sauce in chafing dish or skillet. Provide toothpicks so guests can spear their own. Nice with chunks of French bread. Makes enough for 8 to 16 people, allowing 1 frank per person. (Serve leftovers over spaghetti next day.)

NOTE: Equally good with brown-and-serve sausages or canned Vienna sausages.

SHORT-ORDER NIBBLERS— COLD

All these nibblers may be made up on short notice. Or if there's time, you may fix most of them ahead and refrigerate them until guests arrive.

SPREAD-YOUR-OWNS

Fill bowl, several small bowls, small mold, hollowed-out fresh pineapple or green-pepper half, or avocado or lobster shell with your choice of spreads that follow. Arrange on attractive tray or chop plate; surround with one or more of these foundations:

BREAD: rounds, squares, triangles, or fingers of white, pumpernickel, salty-rye, whole-wheat, French, cheese, nut, or raisin bread.

CRISP CRACKERS: round scalloped, cheese, shredded wheat, and oyster crackers, saltines, plain and seasoned rye wafers, and a host of newcomers!

OTHERS: Melba toast, bread sticks, toast strips, tiny baking-powder biscuits, etc.

EVER-READIES

Ask your grocer about those fine dip mixes — onion, garlic-olive, blue cheese, etc. — that come in envelopes all ready for you to stir quickly into cream or cottage cheese or sour cream and serve as a dip or spread.

Or look in the dairy section for the "buy-and-serve" kind that comes in foil, plastic, or other cups — sour-cream dips, Neufchâtel-cheese spreads, as well as dill pickle, onion, bacon, horse-radish, clam, and other cheese dips — all ready to take home and serve.

SHRIMP ROUNDS

With 1½" biscuit cutter, cut rounds from thin bread slices. Mix equal parts of bottled tartar sauce and bottled cocktail sauce (if too "hot," add mayonnaise to taste); spread on bread. Split cooked, cleaned shrimp in halves lengthwise; top each bread round with split shrimp half. (You may prepare and refrigerate makings early, then put them together at last minute.)

DEVILED HAM A LA CREME

About ½ hr. before serving: Line bottom and side of a shallow serving plate (size of 9" pie plate) with 4 4½-oz. cans deviled ham. Heap center with mixture of 1½ cups commercial sour cream, ¼ teasp. seasoned salt, 1 teasp. powdered dill. Top with ½ cup seeded green grapes. Guests help themselves to crisp crackers, then top with ham, then sour-cream-grape mixture.

HAM D'OEUVRES

8 thin slices cooked ham	or margarine
¼ cup softened butter	8 long bread sticks
	Seedless grapes

Spread ham slices lightly with butter. Wrap middle section of each bread stick with buttered ham slice. Place grapes in center of breadbasket. Stand Ham d'Oeuvres around them. Makes 8 servings.

HAM-GRAPE PICKUPS

12 round scalloped crackers	About ¼ cup commercial sour cream
1 2¼-oz. can deviled ham	6 halved, pitted green grapes

Spread each cracker with deviled ham. Top with small mound of sour cream. Press grape half, rounded side up, into cream on each. Makes 12.

QUICKIES

ORANGE-CHIVE CHEESE: Mix chive cream cheese with a few orange-section bits. Serve with whole-wheat crackers.

SAUCY: Place 1, 2, or more 3-oz. pkg. cream cheese, one atop the other, in a serving dish. Pour on 2 or 3 tablesp. bottled steak sauce. Let guests spread their own assorted crisp crackers.

CHILI SAUCE: Place bowl of chili sauce in center of tray; surround with chunks of sharp natural Cheddar and Swiss cheese on toothpicks.

CAMEMBERT: Set out very soft Camembert, squares of rye or pumpernickel, small bowl of dill-pickle or crisp-bacon bits. Guests spread their own.

TOASTIES: Let guests spread hot buttered toast strips with mashed Roquefort cheese, then with catchup or chili sauce.

ROLL OF SMOKY CHEESE: Form into balls, then roll in chopped walnuts.

CRISP ROUND CRACKERS: Top each cracker with 1 slice Swiss-cheese roll, a little prepared mustard, then 1 slice canned or regular frank.

HALVED TOMATO SLICES: Top with cottage cheese, then sprinkle with seasoned salt and coarsely crushed corn crisps.

RED RADISHES: Split lengthwise; put back together with Gorgonzola.

CORNED-BEEF HASH: Heat; season to taste with pickle relish, mustard, horse-radish, or lemon juice. Serve in bowl, with crisp crackers and catchup on the side.

DEVILED HAM OR TONGUE: Use as is. Or mix with pickle relish, horse-radish, grated onion or scallions, cheese, sour cream, or chopped hard-cooked eggs, etc. Guests spread mixture on bread fingers or crisp crackers. Have Tabasco nearby.

SPLITS: Split franks (canned or regular) or Vienna sausage. Spread with pimento- or smoky-cheese spread, or cream cheese mixed with blue cheese or minced ripe olives. Put franks back together. Cut into 1" pieces.

CHUNKS: On toothpicks, serve cubes of liverwurst or salami, or canned luncheon meat, spiced ham, chopped ham, or corned beef (or cheese). Use French dressing, other tangy sauce, chili sauce, or catchup for dunking.

HOLIDAY COTTAGE CHEESE: In center of a large serving dish heap some red caviar, with a ring of small-curd cottage cheese around it, and Melba rounds around both of them. Refrigerate. Just before serving, sprinkle caviar generously with minced onion, sprinkle cottage cheese with snipped chives and parsley. Guests top Melba rounds, first with cottage cheese, then with caviar.

ONION TOASTIES: Combine minced onion with an equal amount of mayonnaise; season with paprika, salt, pepper, Worcestershire. Spread over entire surface of each crisp cracker. Broil till bubbly.

CAESAR MUSHROOMS: Drain juice from canned whole mushrooms, or green, ripe, or stuffed olives. Pour in bottled Caesar dressing to cover. Refrigerate 2 hr. or so. Drain (you can re-use dressing). Serve on toothpicks.

CHUTNEY: Spread shredded-wheat wafers with chutney.

PEANUT-BUTTER TOASTIES: Top each cracker with a thin onion slice, dab of peanut butter, then dab of catchup. Toast under broiler.

CUBE CRUNCHIES: Cut 1 peeled, pitted avocado into cubes. Roll cubes first in lemon juice, next in French dressing if desired, then in crushed potato chips. Serve on toothpicks.

SARDINES: Serve with buttered rye-bread fingers. Place a few lemon or lime wedges nearby to squeeze over sardines; or set out tiny bowl of hot chili sauce or catchup.

FIX-YOUR-OWNS

Arrange one or more of the following dippers or foundations around bowl of dunk or spread; guests fix their own, with the help of picks nearby.

Pretty to hold the dunk or spread: a goblet, an unpared avocado, cucumber, green-pepper, tomato, pineapple, or melon half, hollowed-out.

Dippers:

Tomato wedges	Chinese-cabbage chunks
Pineapple sticks	Cucumber strips
Radishes	Carrot or celery sticks
Green-pepper strips	or fans
Scallions	Apple chunks, dipped
Crisp endive leaves	into lemon juice
Raw cauliflower buds	

Foundations:

Cucumber slices	Fresh apple or pear
Celery chunks, 1" long	slices, dipped in
Carrot slices	lemon juice

Combinations:

Mandarin oranges (canned), around bowl of chive cream cheese

Melon balls, or apple wedges dipped in lemon juice, around bowl of blue-cheese dip

Tomato chunks around bowl of Roquefort or cream-cheese dip

Canned hearts of palm, sliced, around bowl of hot cocktail sauce

Belgian endive leaves, stuffed with seasoned cottage cheese, to dip in Italian dressing

Bite-size tuna chunks around bowl of cranberry sauce

King-crab-meat chunks (canned or frozen), around bowl of mayonnaise with grated cucumber, lemon juice, prepared mustard, and garlic salt added

Lobster-tail chunks, surrounding lobster shell filled with curry mayonnaise

SHRIMP DIPS

Arrange chilled, cooked, cleaned shrimp (whole, or split if shrimp are plump) on plate or tray. In center, place bowl of Spicy Dunk Sauce, p. 530, or mayonnaise with prepared mustard, horse-radish, chili sauce, catchup, chives, or curry powder added. Have tiny bowl of toothpicks handy.

SHRIMP-AVOCADO: With toothpick secure a cube of avocado in center of each cooked, cleaned shrimp. Serve with bowl of sauce for dunking, as above.

DIPS AND DUNKS

HERB CHEESE: Combine 1 cup cottage cheese with ½ teasp. grated onion, 3 tablesp. milk, dash pepper, ½ teasp. each dried sage and celery salt, and 1 tablesp. lemon juice.

RAINBOW CHEESE: Combine cottage cheese with one or more of these: snipped chives or scallions, sliced or diced radishes, grated carrot, minced green pepper, raisins.

ANCHOVY-CELERY DIP: Mince 2 cloves garlic. Drain oil from 1 2-oz. can flat anchovy fillets, reserving 2 teasp. oil. Mash anchovies with garlic till smooth. Stir in 2 teasp. vinegar, then reserved 2 teasp. oil. Serve in small bowl on plate; surround with raw celery sticks, radishes, or scallions that have been slit several times. Guests dunk vegetables in sauce. Makes 4 servings.

LUSTY ITALIAN DIP: Several hours ahead, or day before, in bowl, combine: 1 pt. commercial sour cream (or use one 8-oz. pkg. cream cheese, stirred smooth with ½ cup milk), 1 1½-oz. pkg. spaghetti-sauce mix, 1 tablesp. instant minced onion. Refrigerate until served. Makes about 2 cups.

WEST COAST: Combine 1 8-oz. pkg. cream cheese, 1 tablesp. garlic-cheese salad-dressing mix, ¼ cup milk, ¼ teasp. seasoned salt. Serve with potato chips.

EDAM BOWL: With knife, remove small cone from center top of baby Edam or Gouda. Leaving rind intact, carefully scoop out chunks of cheese. Fill Edam shell with mayonnaise mixed with French dressing, half and half. Insert toothpicks in cheese chunks; arrange around Edam.

TOMATO CURRY: To 1 3-oz. pkg. cream cheese, add ¼ teasp. Worcestershire, dash Tabasco, ¼ teasp. onion salt, ½ teasp. curry powder; thin with about 2 tablesp. milk. Let guests spread mixture on tomato wedges.

CHEESY EGG DUNK

1 6-oz. pkg. soft chive
  cream cheese
2 tablesp. mayonnaise
1 teasp. prepared mus-
  tard
½ teasp. Worcester-

shire
¼ teasp. salt
⅛ teasp. pepper
2 hard-cooked eggs,
  chopped
3 tablesp. milk

Combine all ingredients. Makes 1 cup.

TUNA-CREAM DIP

2 3-oz. pkg. cream
  cheese
¼ teasp. Tabasco
3 tablesp. mayonnaise

1 6½- or 7-oz. can
  tuna
1 tablesp. lemon juice

Early in day, if desired: In bowl, combine cream cheese and rest of ingredients. Refrigerate until served. Makes about 1½ cups.

DEVILED-HAM DIP PIQUANT

1 8-oz. pkg. cream
  cheese
¼ teasp. Tabasco
¼ cup mayonnaise
2 tablesp. prepared
  mustard

2 4½-oz. cans deviled
  ham
1 teasp. minced onion
2 tablesp. chopped
  stuffed olives

Early in day, if desired: Combine cream cheese, Tabasco, mayonnaise. Then stir in mustard, deviled ham, onion, and olives. Refrigerate until serving time. Makes about 2¼ cups.

CREAMY GARLIC-CHEESE DIP

1 8-oz. pkg. soft cream
  cheese
¼ cup milk
1 tablesp. garlic,
  cheese-garlic, or

onion salad-dress-
  ing mix
1 tablesp. grated Par-
  mesan cheese

Place cream cheese in small bowl; add milk, salad-dressing mix, and Parmesan cheese. Beat until smooth and blended. Serve with small crackers or crisp vegetable sticks. Makes about 1⅔ cups.

CREAMY AVOCADO DIP

2 ripe medium avo-
  cados, peeled, pitted
1 cup commercial
  sour cream

½ teasp. monosodium
  glutamate
½ teasp. salt
2 tablesp. horse-radish
1 small onion, grated

With wooden spoon or electric mixer, or in electric blender, mash avocados to smooth pulp. Add rest of ingredients; beat well.

Serve as a dunk for bread sticks, crisp crackers, etc. Nice, too, as dunk for shrimp or chunks of lobster meat. To preserve color, refrigerate any leftovers, covered. Makes 2 to 2½ cups.

CRAB DIP

1 6½-oz. can King-
  crab meat
⅔ cup commercial
  sour cream
2 teasp. horse-radish

½ teasp. pepper
2 tablesp. Italian
  dressing
Pumpernickel

Day before, or early on the day: Drain crab meat well. Add it to sour cream with horse-radish, pepper, and Italian dressing; toss. Refrigerate.

To serve: Place Crab Dip in small bowl surrounded by tiny squares of pumpernickel. Guests spread their own. Makes about 2 cups.

PARTY DIP

1 pkg. cream-of-
  leek soup mix

1 cup commercial sour
  cream
½ cup cottage cheese

In small bowl, stir together soup mix, sour cream, and cheese. Cover; refrigerate at least 2 hr. before serving. Makes about 1½ cups.

CALICO RELISH DIP

½ cup commercial
  sour cream
¼ cup salad dressing
1 teasp. sugar
½ teasp. salt
2 tablesp. minced
  scallions
2 tablesp. minced rad-
  ishes

2 tablesp. minced cu-
  cumber, drained
2 tablesp. minced
  green pepper
½ clove garlic,
  minced
Raw cauliflowerets
Raw carrot strips
Celery fans
Cucumber sticks

Combine sour cream with salad dressing, sugar, salt, scallions, radishes, cucumber, green pepper, and garlic. Refrigerate.

Serve, in a small bowl, surrounded by cauliflowerets, carrot strips, celery fans, and cucumber sticks, to be used as dippers. Use any leftover dip as dressing in potato salad. Makes about 1 cup.

SLIMMERS

These are special nibblers for the weight watchers.

ENDIVE FINGERS: Fill with cottage cheese seasoned with garlic salt. Sprinkle with chopped ripe olives.

CUCUMBER SLICES: Top with Neufchâtel-and-pimento spread.

BOLOGNA SLICES: Spread with cottage cheese mixed with horse-radish. Roll up; fasten with toothpicks.

CELERY STALKS: Fill with cottage cheese seasoned with onion salt. Sprinkle with poppy seeds.

STUFFED OLIVES: Split; put back together with Neufchâtel.

RAW CARROT SLICES: Top with cottage cheese moistened with pineapple juice. Insert plumes of water cress.

THIN BOLOGNA SLICES: Spread with Neufchâtel mixed with bit of dried thyme. Roll up half of slices, roll up each of these in 1 remaining slice. Refrigerate. To serve, slice ¼″ thick.

DILL-PICKLE SLICES: Top with cottage cheese mixed with garlic powder.

HALVED ORANGE SLICES: Top with dab of Neufchâtel mixed with snipped chives.

HAM ROLLS: Roll thin slices of boiled ham around cooked asparagus spears or apple, melon, celery, cucumber, or chicken fingers.

FILLED MUSHROOMS: Wash 1 doz. medium mushrooms (about ¼ lb.); dry; remove stems. Mix ¼ cup cottage cheese with 1 tablesp. deviled ham and seasoned salt to taste. Use to stuff mushroom caps. Add chopped stems to the next day's vegetable or gravy.

RADISH HALVES: Split radishes lengthwise; top each radish half with cottage cheese or deviled ham.

STICK-AND-PICKS

Pretty to hold the kabobs: Shiny purple eggplant, green avocado, pineapple, French artichoke, red, red apple, or grapefruit, set on a few pine twigs.

HOT KABOBS: On toothpicks, string pineapple chunks or pickled onions and one of the following. Then broil, till done.

Ham cubes	Scallops
Cooked, cleaned shrimp	Franks, in 1″ pieces
Halved chicken livers	

COLD KABOBS: On toothpicks or carrot or celery sticks, string 2 or more of these:

Melon balls	Luncheon-meat cubes
Apple chunks	Chicken chunks
Orange chunks	Cooked, cleaned shrimp
Pineapple chunks	Radishes
Celery chunks	Ham cubes
Cherry tomatoes	Canned mushrooms

FRUITS: Serve bowl of pineapple chunks, cherries on stems, unhulled strawberries, etc., with toothpicks.

MORE KABOB COMBINATIONS

Pineapple chunk, rolled in flaked coconut, then cooked-ham chunk

Tomato wedge between two sautéed mushroom caps stuffed with Danish blue cheese

Avocado chunk (dipped in lemon juice), tongue chunk, and pitted ripe olive

Cooked, deveined shrimp and avocado chunk, dipped in lemon juice

Tuna chunk and pineapple chunk

Apple wedge, wrapped in thin salami slice, and cocktail onion

Two raw mushroom caps, stuffed with blue cheese, with a ham chunk between them

Assorted cheese balls (cream cheese plus curry, Cheddar plus prepared mustard, blue cheese plus cottage cheese and wine), rolled in snipped dried beef, then stuck in grapefruit with picks

String 1 pineapple chunk or onion with 1 cube Cheddar on toothpick

On each long thin pretzel stick, string 1 gherkin with 1 cube Cheddar

Cover cubes of natural or process sharp Cheddar cheese with wine such as Burgundy. Let stand in refrigerator 24 hr. or longer. To serve, drain and spear each cube with toothpick; arrange around crackers.

SOUPS AND CHOWDERS

Whether from scratch, off the pantry shelf, or out of the freezer, soup may be the bright beginning of a good dinner. Take your choice from a clear broth to a hearty chowder. Select the kind of soup that balances the other foods on your menu. Or make it the meal's mainstay, served alone or teamed with a salad and/or sandwich, plus dessert.

The recipes that follow give you soups packed with flavor, and good-for-you eating. Just be sure to serve the hot ones *hot*, the cold ones *cold*. Better be prepared for encores too!

Before using these recipes, refer to How To Use Our Recipes, p. 3. Always use standard measuring cups and measuring spoons; measure level.

With a Can of Soup

Keep a supply of cook-saving canned condensed soups on your pantry shelf or frozen soups in your freezer. They can mean good

eating at the turn of a can opener, gracious hospitality in a hurry. They may be served singly or in combination. To help you plan balanced meals, choose soups with the following basic food groups as a guide.

1. **MILK SOUPS** (prepared with milk): Cheddar-cheese soup, cream-of-asparagus, cream-of-celery, cream-of-chicken, cream-of-mushroom, cream-of-pea, and cream-of-vegetable. In the frozen group are: Clam chowder (New England Style), cream-of-potato, cream-of-shrimp, and oyster stew.

2. **MEAT, SEA-FOOD, AND LEGUME SOUPS:** Bean with bacon, beef, beef broth, black-bean, chicken-vegetable, chili-beef, consommé, green-pea, pepper-pot, Scotch broth, split-pea, split-pea with ham, vegetable-bean, vegetable-beef, etc. In the frozen group are: Cream-of-shrimp, green-pea with ham, oyster stew, old-fashioned vegetable with beef, etc.

3. **VEGETABLE SOUPS:** Chicken-vegetable, clam chowder (Manhattan style), cream-of-asparagus, cream-of-vegetable, green-pea, minestrone,

Scotch broth, tomato, tomato-rice, vegetable, vegetable-bean, vegetable-beef, vegetarian-vegetable, frozen cream-of-potato soup, etc.

4. CEREAL SOUPS: Beef-noodle, chicken-gumbo, chicken-noodle, chicken-rice, Scotch broth, tomato-rice, turkey-noodle, minestrone, etc.

With a Soup Mix

With packaged soup mixes such as chicken-rice, cream-style chicken, chicken-noodle, country-style potato, beef-flavor noodle with vegetables, onion, tomato, green-pea, tomato-vegetable soup with noodles, alphabet-vegetable, etc., that steaming bowl of soup for lunch or supper is ready in no time. Just try them and see how delicious they are.

Be sure to try, too, those splendid new Swiss soup mixes. Onion, cream-of-mushroom, chicken-noodle, smoky-green-pea, garden-vegetable, beef-noodle, and cream-of-leek soup mix are among the flavors and all are delightful.

Still another new-comer to the soup mix family comes in special, hermetically sealed cans that protect its flavor — two cans to a carton. The present choice includes onion, cream-of-mushroom, noodle, beef-noodle, and chicken-noodle soup mix. The latter soup contains diced chicken meat which has been freeze-dried for fuller flavor.

Bouillon Cubes and Granules

Beef, vegetable, and chicken bouillon, in cubes or instant granule form, make for speedy and refreshing hot or cold bouillon, as well as ingredient use in soups, gravies, etc. So it's wise to keep some on hand.

A Bit of Herb

Adding a pinch of dried or snipped fresh herb to canned or frozen soups or soup mixes, while they heat, makes new soups from old favorites. We find fresh or dried rosemary, tarragon, basil, thyme, and dill all special favorites.

A Bit of Garnish

For that finishing touch, top your soup with one of these:

Snipped chives	Grated cheese
Slivered almonds	Crumbled blue cheese
Croutons, p. 8	Snipped water cress
Crisp ready-to-eat cereal	Sliced stuffed olives
	Thin lemon slices
Whipped cream plus horse-radish	Salted whipped cream
	Sour cream and nutmeg
Snipped parsley	
Fresh herbs	Paper-thin carrot or radish slices
Popcorn	
Browned onion rings	Thin celery rings
Frank slices	Crumbled potato chips
Crisp bacon bits	Diced fresh tomato

Serve Them Simply

These days, many hot soups can be sipped in the living room from cups or mugs with crisp crackers or a Nibbler, p. 144.

Or if you prefer to serve them at-table style, don't forget those attractive pottery bowls and individual casseroles which can make a meal-in-a-dish soup an occasion.

Go-Alongs

With your soup, serve something crisp and perhaps salty: Packaged crisp crackers, corn chips, pretzels, potato chips, Melba toast, buttered toast strips, etc. Or try one of our easy Nibblers, p. 144.

IN NO TIME AT ALL

BURGER SOUP

½ lb. chuck, ground	1 10½-oz. can condensed minestrone, undiluted
¾ teasp. salt	
Dash pepper	
2 tablesp. butter or margarine	1 soup-can water
	½ teasp. dried marjoram

Lightly combine chuck, salt, and pepper; shape into balls the size of walnuts. In butter in saucepan, sauté balls just till browned on outside. Stir in soup, water, and marjoram. Heat. Serve for dinner with Italian bread sticks, tossed green salad, frozen apple pie, and coffee. Makes 2 servings. Double recipe for 4 servings.

OYSTER-STEW SPECIAL

In a saucepan, combine 1 can frozen oyster stew with 1 soup-can milk; heat. When frozen stew has melted, stir in 2 oz. process cheese spread, cut into pieces; heat gently until cheese melts and stew comes to boil. Serve at once. Makes 2 servings. Double recipe for 4 servings.

DEVILED CORN CHOWDER

¼ cup butter or margarine	1 soup-can water
1 medium onion, sliced	1 1-lb. can cream-style corn
2 10½-oz. cans cream-of-chicken soup, undiluted	1 12-oz. can vacuum-packed whole-kernel corn
2 2¼-oz. cans deviled ham	Dash nutmeg
	½ teasp. paprika
	Melba-toast rounds

In butter in saucepan, sauté onion 5 min. Stir in soup and 1 can deviled ham; then stir in water, cream-style corn, whole-kernel corn, nutmeg, and paprika. Heat over medium heat until soup boils. To serve, float Melba-toast rounds, liberally spread with deviled ham, on top of soup. Makes 4 servings.

CREAMY POTATO SOUP

6 slices bacon	chicken soup, undiluted
1 cup chopped onions	2 soup-cans milk
2 cups cubed potatoes	1 teasp. salt
1 cup water	2 tablesp. snipped parsley
2 10½-oz. cans condensed cream-of-	

In saucepan, cook bacon until crisp; set bacon aside. Pour off all but 3 tablesp. drippings from saucepan; add onions; brown a bit. Add potatoes and water. Cook, covered, about 15 min., or until potatoes are tender. Blend in chicken soup, milk, and salt; heat, but do not boil. To serve, garnish with crisp bacon slices and parsley. Makes 4 servings.

ONION SOUP, FRENCH-MARKET STYLE

Heat 1 10½-oz. can condensed onion soup, undiluted, with 1 soup-can water. Pour into 3 individual casseroles. Cover soup with layer of French bread, sliced ¼″ thick; top with ¼ lb. sliced Muenster cheese, another layer of bread slices, then ¼ lb. sliced Muenster. Bake at 475°F., uncovered, 15 min., or till bubbling. Eat with fork and spoon, along with anchovy-filled celery sticks, tossed green salad, fresh pears and peaches, and coffee or wine. Makes 3 servings.

SWISS HOT POT

2 tablesp. salad oil	vegetable soup mix
1 lb. trimmed pork, cubed	½ small head cabbage, cut into wedges
2 cups water	
1 pkg. Swiss garden-	

In large, deep skillet, heat salad oil. Add pork and brown on all sides. Stir in water and soup mix. Cover; simmer until meat is tender, about 1 hr. Push meat toward center of skillet. Arrange cabbage wedges, cut side down, around meat. Cover; cook until cabbage is tender, 15 to 20 min. Makes 4 servings.

SUMMER SOUP SUPREME

1. Heat a can of frozen cream-of-potato soup, using water or milk as label directs. Serve hot, topped with generous sprinklings of crisp bacon squares and snipped chives.
2. Or heat, whip, and refrigerate as label directs for Vichyssoise; serve cold, garnished with bacon and chives.
3. Or add some grated raw carrot, before heating.

SWISS POTATO SOUP

Put 1 unopened can frozen cream-of-potato soup in warm water for 2 to 3 min.; empty into saucepan. Add 1 cup light cream, ¾ cup milk, ⅛ teasp. each of nutmeg and pepper, and ¼ cup grated Swiss cheese; heat, stirring occasionally. Garnish with cress. Serve with deviled ham on Melba toast, followed by cantaloupe halves filled with ice cream and blueberries. Makes 4 servings.

TOMATO-CHEESE SOUP

In saucepan, combine, then heat slowly, while stirring, 1 10½-oz. can condensed tomato soup, undiluted; 1 soup-can milk; 1 cup grated sharp Cheddar cheese, or 1 8-oz. jar pasteurized process cheese spread (cheese sauce), and ¼ teasp. each onion salt and pepper. Then stir in 3 tablesp. sherry, if desired. Sip along with broiled hamburgers, green-bean salad, and hot corn toasties. Top off with sugared raspberries over ice cream. Makes 3 or 4 servings.

SOUP ITALIAN

In Dutch oven, combine 2 10½-oz. cans condensed vegetable soup, undiluted; 1 soup-can water; 3 1-lb.-4-oz. cans kidney beans, drained; 4 franks, sliced on angle; and ¼ lb. salami slices, cut into sixths. Heat.

Serve for lunch or supper with romaine-salad bowl, then cheesecake and fresh strawberries or pineapple chunks. Makes 8 servings.

HOT OR COLD VICHYSSOISE

1 can frozen cream-of-potato soup
½ 10½-oz. can condensed cream-of-chicken soup, undiluted
1 cup light cream
½ cup heavy cream
Snipped chives

In electric blender, combine soups and creams. Mix well until combined and smooth; refrigerate until well chilled. Just before serving, mix again in blender.

Serve in cream-soup cups or bowls; sprinkle with chives. Makes 4 servings.

P.S. On a chilly day, this Vichyssoise is nice mixed again in blender, then heated while stirred.

CREAM MONGOLE WITH SHERRY

1 10½-oz. can condensed tomato soup, undiluted
1 10½-oz. can condensed green-pea soup, undiluted
¾ cup water
1 teasp. sugar
1 cup light cream*
2 teasp. Worcestershire
5 tablesp. sherry

Combine soups and water; heat over very low heat, stirring until smooth. Slowly stir in sugar, cream, and Worcestershire. Remove from heat; slowly add sherry. Makes 5 or 6 servings.

*Half and half cream and milk may be used.

MEXICAN BEAN SOUP

In saucepan, combine 1 10½-oz. can condensed black-bean soup, undiluted; 1 1-lb.-4-oz. can chili con carne without beans; 1¾ cups water; and ½ teasp. onion salt. Heat.

Serve, topped with diced fresh tomatoes, for supper, along with guacamole or sliced avocado on lettuce, saltines, chilled baked custard, and coffee. Makes 5 hearty servings.

CHICKEN CORN SOUP

2 10½-oz. cans condensed chicken-with-rice soup, undiluted
2 soup-cans milk
2 1-lb.-1-oz. cans
cream-style corn
¼ cup snipped parsley
½ teasp. salt
Generous pinch dried tarragon

In large saucepan, combine soup, milk, corn, parsley, salt, and tarragon. Cook until heated thoroughly. Makes 8 servings.

CHICKEN-PEPPER-POT

2 tablesp. butter or margarine
1 onion, thinly sliced
1 10½-oz. can condensed pepper-pot soup, undiluted
1 soup-can water
1⅓ cups cooked or canned chicken, in large pieces
¼ teasp. curry powder

In butter, in saucepan, sauté onion just until golden. Stir in soup, water, chicken, and curry. Heat.

Serve with tossed green salad and crispy rye wafers, followed by lemon-chiffon pie in a crumb crust for dinner. Makes 5 servings.

CURRY-CHICKEN SOUP

1 10½-oz. can condensed cream-of-chicken soup, undiluted
1 soup-can milk
1 cup light cream
2 teasp. curry powder
¼ teasp. onion salt
1 apple, pared
1 tablesp. lemon juice

In saucepan, combine soup, milk, light cream, curry powder, and onion salt; heat. Meanwhile, grate apple; toss with lemon juice. Add to soup, heat, and pour into mugs.

Serve for a company lunch with chicken-and-cress sandwiches, followed by Dutch plum cake and iced tea. Makes 4 servings.

DOWN-EAST CORN CHOWDER

1 can frozen cream-of-potato soup	1 cup cooked, canned, or thawed frozen whole-kernel corn, drained
1 cup light cream	
1 cup milk	
⅛ teasp. pepper	

Put unopened can of soup in warm water for 2 or 3 min.; empty into saucepan. Add cream, milk, pepper, and corn. Stirring occasionally, heat slowly to boiling point.

Serve in bowlfuls, with tuna salad in toasted buns, blackberry gelatin with sugared blackberries, and iced coffee or tea. Makes 2 or 3 hearty servings.

OLD-WORLD MUSHROOM SOUP

¼ cup butter or margarine	densed cream-of-mushroom soup, undiluted
¼ lb. fresh mushrooms, sliced	1 teasp. ground dill
1 10½-oz. can con-	1 soup-can water

In saucepan, melt butter; in it sauté mushrooms 5 min. Add soup and dill; gradually stir in water; heat.

Serve bowlfuls with hamburgers or franks in toasted buns, then fresh watermelon wedges, sprinkled with sherry. Makes 4 servings.

TOMATO SIP

2 10½-oz. cans condensed beef bouillon, undiluted	⅛ teasp. dried basil
	½ teasp. salt
2½ cups canned tomato juice	½ teasp. sugar
	¼ teasp. monosodium glutamate
2 lemon slices	2 tablesp. sherry
6 whole cloves	

In large saucepan, combine bouillon, tomato juice, lemon, cloves, basil; simmer 5 min.; strain. Stir in salt, sugar, monosodium glutamate, and sherry.

Serve hot in mugs or cups, each guest helping himself to one or more of the tasty garnishes on p. 159. Makes 6 servings.

SAUSAGE MINESTRONE

¼ lb. sausages	1 soup-can water
1 10½-oz. can condensed minestrone, undiluted	1 tablesp. snipped parsley

In saucepan, sauté sausages until done; drain off fat; with tip of spoon, cut sausages into 1″ pieces. Add minestrone, water; heat; sprinkle with parsley.

Serve in bowls for lunch with ripe olives, celery and tomato wedges, rye bread and butter, and baked apples with custard sauce. Makes 4 servings.

CAN-OPENER MINESTRONE

1 10½-oz. can condensed vegetable soup, undiluted	2 1-lb. cans kidney beans (drain 1 can)
	1 clove garlic, minced
1 10½-oz. can condensed chicken-noodle soup, undiluted	⅓ cup snipped parsley
	Lots of grated Parmesan cheese
1 soup-can water	

Combine vegetable soup, chicken-noodle soup, water, kidney beans, garlic, and parsley. Heat until very hot. Ladle into soup bowls; pass bowlful of Parmesan cheese. Makes 4 servings.

CURRY-POTATO SOUP

1 can frozen cream-of-potato soup	⅛ teasp. pepper
	¼ teasp. curry powder
1 cup light cream	
½ cup milk	

Let unopened potato soup stand in warm water for 2 or 3 min.; empty contents into saucepan. Add cream, milk, pepper, and curry powder; heat, stirring occasionally.

Serve in mugs to sip along with ham-and-Swiss-cheese sandwiches, seedless grapes in grape juice, and walnut cookies — a nice luncheon. Makes 2 or 3 servings.

CHILLED CURRY-AVOCADO SOUP

1 tablesp. butter or margarine	1 pkg. chicken-noodle soup mix
¼ teasp. curry powder	1 avocado, peeled
	½ cup milk
2 cups water	1 cup light cream

In saucepan, melt butter; stir in curry powder; cook over low heat 3 min. Stir in water, soup mix; bring to boil; simmer, covered, 7 min. Into electric blender pour just enough hot soup to conceal blades. Cover; start blender; uncover, and gradually add rest of soup. Blend till smooth. Add half of avocado; blend ½ min. Pour soup into bowl; stir in milk, cream; slice in remaining avocado; refrigerate.

Serve — indoors or out — as an introduction to broiled chicken, corn on the cob, grilled tomatoes, lettuce sandwiches, butter-pecan ice cream. Makes 6 servings.

BOUILLON-ON-THE-ROCKS

In each low 9-oz. glass, place 2 or 3 ice cubes. Over cubes, pour undiluted canned condensed bouillon, stirring well. Garnish with a twist of lemon slice or sprig of mint. One can of bouillon fills 3 glasses.

PANTRY-SHELF CORN CHOWDER

1 tablesp. butter or margarine	½ teasp. salt
2 12-oz. cans vacuum-packed whole-kernel corn	½ teasp. seasoned salt
	⅛ teasp. celery salt
	¼ teasp. Worcestershire
1 can frozen condensed potato soup	2 tablesp. snipped parsley
2 soup-cans milk	Nutmeg
½ cup light cream	Crisp bacon bits

1. In butter in saucepan, simmer corn 5 min. Add frozen soup, milk, cream, salts, Worcestershire.
2. Over medium heat, bring to boil, stirring until soup is melted and heated through. Remove from heat; add parsley, a little nutmeg; top with bacon. Serve at once. Makes 6 servings.

MINTED GREEN-PEA SOUP

Put 1 unopened can frozen green-pea-with-ham soup in warm water for 2 or 3 min.; empty into saucepan. Add ½ soup-can milk and ½ soup-can water. Stirring occasionally, heat slowly to boiling point. Add 1 tablesp. snipped fresh mint. Serve topped with mint sprigs.

Sip from cups for dinner, along with sliced savory chicken, rice, crisp rolls, and pickled peaches. For dessert, try orange sherbet in melon wedges. Makes 5 or 6 demitasse-cup servings.

BLACK-BEAN SOUP WITH HERBS

In saucepan, heat 1 10½-oz. can condensed black-bean soup, undiluted; 1 soup-can water; ¼ teasp. each dried rosemary, pepper; and ½ teasp. Worcestershire. Top with diced fresh tomatoes.

Serve on a hot or cold day with tongue sandwiches on rye, dill pickles, coffee ice cream with grated chocolate. Makes 4 servings.

WHITE-AND-GOLD SOUP

Prepare and heat 3 cans frozen condensed potato soup as label directs. Add 3 cups shredded raw carrots, and continue heating 5 to 8 min. Makes 8 servings.

OF YOUR OWN MAKING

Many of these are hearty soups. A big steaming bowlful can make a wonderful meal-in-a-dish. A cupful can be a good beginning to lunch or dinner.

SWEDISH CABBAGE SOUP

1 tablesp. whole allspice	1 cup sliced, pared carrots
2 lamb shanks (3 lb.)	¼ cup snipped parsley
2 beef-bouillon cubes	½ cup sliced celery
½ teasp. pepper	2 qt. medium shredded cabbage (8 cups)
2 tablesp. salt	
2 qt. water	
1 cup chopped leeks or onions	2 cups pared, diced potatoes
½ cup diced, pared parsnips	

Day before: Tie allspice in cheesecloth; place in kettle with shanks, bouillon cubes, pepper, salt, water. Simmer, covered, 2 hr. Refrigerate overnight.

About ½ hr. before dinner: Skim most of fat from top of soup. Remove meat from bones; cube. Bring broth to boil; remove allspice; add leeks, parsnips, carrots, parsley, celery. Simmer, covered, 10 min. Add cabbage, potatoes, meat; cook, covered, 20 min. Makes 6 hearty servings.

CORN-AND-FRANKFURTER CHOWDER

¼ cup butter or margarine	1⅔ cups evaporated milk, undiluted
¾ cup chopped onion	1 16-oz. can whole-kernel or cream-style corn
¾ cup coarsely cut celery	
¼ teasp. salt	4 frankfurters, sliced crosswise
½ cup water	

In large saucepan, melt butter. Add onion and celery, then cook until onion is tender, but not brown. Add salt, water, evaporated milk, corn, and frankfurters. Heat to serving temperature. Makes 4 servings.

SWISS CREAM-OF-POTATO SOUP

4 medium potatoes, pared	½ teasp. nutmeg
2 bacon slices, diced	Dash cayenne pepper
¼ cup minced onion	¼ teasp. dry mustard
2 tablesp. butter or margarine	1 teasp. Worcestershire
1 tablesp. snipped parsley	3 cups milk
2 teasp. salt	½ cup grated natural Swiss or process Cheddar cheese

Cook potatoes till tender; drain. Meanwhile, sauté bacon and onion over low heat, stirring, until brown and tender. Mash potatoes; add bacon, onion, butter, parsley, salt, nutmeg, cayenne, mustard, Worcestershire. Stir in milk. Heat over low heat, stirring. Sprinkle with cheese. Serve at once. Makes 4 servings.

CREAM-OF-MUSHROOM SOUP

¼ lb. whole fresh mushrooms; or 1⅛ cups minced mushroom stems	2 chicken-bouillon cubes
	2 cups boiling water
1 tablesp. butter or margarine	1 tablesp. butter or margarine
1 tablesp. minced onion	3 tablesp. flour
	2 cups milk
	1 teasp. salt
¼ teasp. celery seeds	⅛ teasp. pepper

Wash whole mushrooms; chop fine. Add 1 tablesp. butter, onion, celery seeds; simmer, covered, 5 min. Add bouillon cubes, boiling water; simmer, uncovered, 10 min.

In double-boiler top over direct heat, melt 1 tablesp. butter. Add flour; stir till smooth. Add milk, salt, pepper. Cook over boiling water, stirring, till thickened. Add mushroom mixture; heat. Makes 6 servings.

SOUP FROM LEFTOVER BONES

Bones left over from poultry, roast, steak, etc.	1 stalk celery, sliced
	2 sprigs parsley
	1 bay leaf
Any leftover stuffing (optional)	3 whole black peppers
2 qt. cold water	2 teasp. salt
1 carrot, pared, sliced	⅛ teasp. pepper
1 onion, sliced	

In large kettle, combine all ingredients; simmer, covered, 2 hr. Strain; season to taste. If made in advance, cool quickly as on p. 173; refrigerate. Reheat to serve. Makes 1½ qt.

To Vary: To completed soup, add canned tomatoes, or 1 or 2 cut-up fresh tomatoes; any diced leftover meat; some cooked rice; some curry; dried or fresh herbs; frozen mixed vegetables, etc. Simmer, covered, 10 to 15 min.

DAD'S MEAL-IN-A-SOUP

2 lb. shin beef plus split large soupbone	½ 10-oz. pkg. frozen lima beans
4 qt. water	½ 10-oz. pkg. frozen peas
1 tablesp. salt	
½ medium cabbage, sliced	1 12-oz. can vacuum-packed whole-kernel corn
2 onions, chopped	
6 carrots, pared, cut into 3″ pieces	1 potato, pared, cubed
	2 tablesp. snipped parsley
2 stalks celery, coarsely cut up	¾ cup catchup
¼ medium green pepper, cut up	½ teasp. ground cloves
1 1-lb.-13-oz. can tomatoes (3½ cups)	1 teasp. sugar
	1 teasp. salt
½ 9-oz. pkg. frozen cut green beans	¼ teasp. pepper
	4 whole ears corn

Day before: In large kettle, place meat and bone, water, and salt. Bring to boil; skim. Add cabbage, onions, carrots, celery, green pepper, and tomatoes. Cook, covered, 30 min. Add rest of ingredients except ears of corn; simmer, covered, 3½ hr. Taste for seasoning. Remove meat and bone from soup. Cut up meat; return to soup. Cool; refrigerate.
To serve: Skim any fat from soup. Over medium heat, bring soup to boil. Break ears of corn into 2″ pieces; add to soup; simmer, covered, 5 min., or until tender. Makes 12 servings. (Serve any leftovers another day.)
To freeze soup: Remove ears of corn after soup has cooled; then freeze soup as on p. 709.

DELMARVA CHICKEN SPECIAL

1 3-lb. stewing chicken	¾ cup packaged pre-cooked rice
2½ qt. cold water	2 eggs
1 tablesp. salt	¼ cup lemon juice
½ teasp. monosodium glutamate	½ lemon, sliced
2 tablesp. butter or margarine	2 tablesp. snipped parsley

Day before or early in day: In large kettle, place chicken, water, salt, monosodium glutamate, and butter; simmer, covered, about 1½ hr., or until chicken is tender. Remove chicken from soup. Cut meat from bones in serving-size pieces; return to soup. Cool; then refrigerate.

To serve: Bring chicken mixture to boil; add rice; simmer 5 min., or until rice is tender; remove from heat. Beat eggs well; slowly stir in lemon juice; then gradually stir in about 2 cups broth (without chicken); now stir this mixture into rest of soup. Garnish with thin lemon slices, parsley. Makes 8 servings. (Refrigerate leftovers for lunch another day.)

KNIFE-AND-FORK VEGETABLE SOUP

2 tablesp. salad oil	2 outer stalks celery, cut into 1″ pieces
1 large, or 2 small, fairly lean, meaty short ribs, cut into 2″ squares (about 2 lb.)	4 carrots, pared, cut into 1″ pieces
	4 zucchini, trimmed and cut into ½″ pieces
2 cloves garlic, minced	1 ear corn, broken into 4 pieces; or ½ cup cooked or canned whole-kernel corn
2½ teasp. salt	
1 large onion, coarsely chopped (about 1 cup)	
2 qt. hot water	Pepper and salt
2 bouillon cubes	

Early in day: Heat salad oil in Dutch oven, or large kettle; add meat and brown on all sides — about 15 min.

Sprinkle garlic with 1 teasp. salt; mash well with side of knife; add with onion to meat. Cook, stirring, 2 to 3 min. Add hot water, bouillon cubes; simmer, covered, 1½ hr., or till meat is just tender.

Add 1½ teasp. salt, celery, carrots. Cook, covered, 15 min. Then add zucchini; simmer, covered, 10 min. Lastly, add corn; simmer,

covered, 5 min. longer. Season to taste. Refrigerate till needed.

To serve: Reheat soup; ladle into soup plates, with big piece of meat and some of each vegetable in each serving. Serve with knife, fork, and soup spoon. Makes 6 to 8 large servings.

BARNEGAT CHICKEN CHOWDER

1 6-lb. roasting chicken	pared, diced
	About ¼ lb. salt pork, in small strips
1 tablesp. salt	¼ teasp. pepper
1 bay leaf	1 teasp. salt
4 medium onions, sliced	8 cups milk
4 medium potatoes,	

Place chicken in deep kettle; cover halfway with hot water. Add 1 tablesp. salt, bay leaf, and half of onions; simmer, covered, 2 hr., or until tender. Remove chicken; cool quickly as on p. 261; remove skin; cut meat into large cubes; refrigerate. Remove bay leaf from broth; add potatoes; simmer, covered, 15 min.

In small skillet, sauté salt pork till crisp; add remaining onions; sauté 2 to 3 min. Add to broth, with chicken, pepper, 1 teasp. salt, and milk. Heat. Makes 8 to 10 generous servings.

PENNSYLVANIA DUTCH CHICKEN-CORN CHOWDER

2 3- to 4-lb. stewing chickens	1¼ teasp. nutmeg
	10 ears fresh corn
3 qt. cold water	1 egg
3 medium onions, minced	½ cup milk
	1 cup sifted all-purpose flour
1 cup chopped celery	
2½ tablesp. salt	2 hard-cooked eggs
¼ teasp. pepper	Snipped parsley

Early in day, or day before, if desired:
1. In Dutch oven, place chickens, cut into eighths, water, onions, celery, salt, pepper, and nutmeg. Cover; simmer 2 to 2½ hr., or until chickens are fork-tender; add water if needed.
2. Remove chickens from broth; refrigerate separately till fat solidifies on broth. With knife, split corn kernels, cutting lengthwise on ears; cut off kernels; refrigerate.

About 45 min. before serving:
1. Remove fat from chicken broth. If necessary, add water to broth to make 10 cups; add

corn; cover, and simmer until corn is tender.
2. Meanwhile, remove chicken meat from bones; cut it into 1½″ chunks. Make this batter for rivels (tiny dumplings found in Pennsylvania Dutch soups): In small bowl, beat 1 egg till light in color; add milk; then beat in flour until mixture is smooth.
3. Now add chicken to broth mixture. Bring to simmer; then let batter fall into it from large serving spoon, making each drop, or rivel, the size of a cherry pit by using a knife to stop the flow of batter. Simmer 2 to 3 min., or until rivels are cooked. (Or cook 4 oz. fine noodles in simmering broth as label directs.)
4. Stir in chopped hard-cooked eggs; top with parsley. Makes 10 to 12 main dish servings.

FRENCH SPRING SOUP
(Potage Printanier)

3 tablesp. butter or margarine	¼ cup uncooked regular rice
3 leeks, snipped	12 stalks fresh or frozen asparagus, cut into 1″ pieces
1 small onion, minced	
3 potatoes, pared, thinly sliced	½ lb. raw spinach leaves, snipped rather fine
1 carrot, pared, thinly sliced	
Salt	Dash pepper
2 qt. water	1 cup heavy cream

1. In hot butter in kettle, slowly sauté leeks and onion until tender. Add potatoes, carrot, 1½ teasp. salt, water. Cover; bring to boil; simmer 15 min.
2. Stir in rice, asparagus; cover; simmer 25 min.
3. Add spinach; cover; simmer 5 min. Stir in 4 teasp. salt, pepper, cream. Serve with a meat or egg sandwich. Makes 8 lunch-size servings.

GERMAN LENTIL SOUP
(Linsensuppe)

1 1-lb. pkg. lentils	2½ to 3 teasp. salt
¼ lb. bacon, diced	½ teasp. pepper
2 medium onions, sliced	½ teasp. dried thyme
	2 bay leaves
2 medium carrots, diced	1 large potato, pared
2 qt. water	1 ham bone (left from cooked shank)
1 cup sliced celery	2 tablesp. lemon juice

Night before: Wash lentils. Soak overnight in cold water to cover.

Early next day:
1. Drain lentils. Then, in Dutch oven, sauté diced bacon until golden. Now add sliced onions and diced carrots, and sauté until onions are golden.
2. Next, add lentils, water, sliced celery, salt, pepper, thyme, and bay leaves.
3. Now, with medium grater, grate pared potato into lentil mixture; add ham bone.
4. Simmer, covered, 3 hr., when lentils should be nice and tender. Remove bay leaves.
5. Now remove ham bone; cut all bits of meat from it, and return meat to soup.

To serve at once, add lemon juice. Or refrigerate soup till next day; then add lemon-juice, reheat, and serve. Makes 9½ cups, a luscious, hearty soup.

OLD-COUNTRY BORSCH

6 cups water	cut into wedges
1 lb. beef brisket, cut into 6 pieces	1 bay leaf
	1 tablesp. salt
2 onions, sliced	2 beets, coarsely grated (about 1 cup)
2 stalks celery, cut into 1″ lengths	
4 medium beets, pared, sliced (about 2 cups)	1 6-oz. can tomato paste (⅔ cup)
	2 tablesp. vinegar
4 carrots, pared, thinly sliced (1½ cups)	1 tablesp. sugar
	2 teasp. salt
	½ pt. commercial sour cream
1 small head cabbage,	

Day before or early in day: In large kettle, place water, beef, onions, celery, sliced beets, carrots, cabbage, bay leaf, 1 tablesp. salt; simmer, covered, about 2 hr. Add grated beets and rest of ingredients except sour cream. Simmer, covered, 15 to 20 min. Cool; refrigerate. *To serve:* Skim any fat from soup. Bring soup to boil over medium heat; lower heat; simmer, covered, 10 min. Serve topped with sour cream. Makes 4 to 6 servings.

NOTE: Leftovers may be frozen. Cool, then pack in straight-sided jars or containers. See To Freeze Soup, p. 709.

OLD-FASHIONED SPLIT-PEA SOUP

In kettle, place ham bone (such as that left over from cooked shank), 3 qt. water, 2 cups split green peas, 2 teasp. salt, ¼ teasp. pepper, 1 medium onion, sliced. Simmer, covered, over low heat 2½ to 3 hr.

Remove bone from soup; cut off any bits of ham; add to soup, along with 1½ cups slivered, cooked ham if you have it. Heat. Makes 8 generous servings.

DANDY BEAN CHOWDER

¾ cup diced, pared carrots	1½ teasp. salt
2 tablesp. butter or margarine	⅛ teasp. pepper
2 tablesp. minced onion	1 cup milk
2 tablesp. minced green pepper	1 1-lb. can baked beans in tomato sauce
2 tablesp. flour	3 franks, grated (1 cup)

Cook carrots in 1″ boiling salted water, covered, till tender; drain, reserving liquid and carrots. In hot butter in saucepan, sauté onion and green pepper until golden. Add flour, salt, pepper.

To carrot liquid, add enough water to make 1 cup; combine with milk; stir into flour mixture. Heat until thickened, stirring constantly. Add carrots, beans, franks. Heat well. Makes 4 servings.

BOSTON CLAM CHOWDER

3 doz. shucked raw soft-shell clams, with strained liquid	2 tablesp. flour
2 cups cold water	¼ teasp. celery salt
¼ lb. salt pork, diced; or 2 tablesp. butter or margarine	¼ teasp. pepper
2 medium onions, sliced	Salt
	3 cups diced, pared potatoes
	3 cups scalded milk
	1 tablesp. butter or margarine

1. Snip off necks of clams; cut necks fine with scissors; leave soft parts whole.
2. In saucepan, place clams (necks and soft parts) with liquid. Add water; bring to boil. Drain, reserving liquid and clams.
3. In large kettle, sauté salt pork until golden. Add onions; cook until tender.
4. Into onions, stir flour, celery salt, pepper, clam liquid, 2 teasp. salt, potatoes.
5. Cook, covered, 8 min., or until potatoes are

tender. Add milk, clams, 1½ teasp. salt, butter.
6. Ladle into big soup bowls, or into mugs if you're serving out of doors. Makes 8 servings.

GINNY'S SKILLET CORN CHOWDER

6 bacon slices	1½ cups milk
1 medium onion, thinly sliced	1 teasp. salt
1 1-lb. can cream-style white corn	⅛ teasp. pepper
	2 tablesp. snipped parsley

In large skillet, sauté bacon until crisp; remove; drain; break into large pieces. Pour off most of bacon drippings; then in remaining drippings, sauté onion until golden. Add corn, milk, salt, and pepper. Heat.

Just before serving: Top with bacon and parsley. Makes 2 main dish servings. Double recipe for 4 servings.

MANHATTAN CLAM CHOWDER

3 bacon slices, diced	1 1-lb.-13-oz. can tomatoes (3½ cups)
Dried thyme	1½ cups diced, pared carrots
1 cup sliced onions	
3 cups cubed, pared potatoes	3 cups clam liquid
½ cup diced celery	2 doz. shucked raw hard-shell clams
5 cups hot water	1 tablesp. snipped parsley
2 teasp. salt	
⅛ teasp. pepper	

1. In deep kettle, sauté bacon until crisp. Stir in 1 teasp. thyme and onions; cook, stirring occasionally, until tender.
2. Add potatoes, celery, water, salt, pepper. Simmer, covered, 5 min.
3. Add tomatoes, carrots, clam liquid (if you do not have 3 cups, add water to make up difference). Simmer, uncovered, over very low heat 1 hr.
4. Meanwhile, pick over clams to remove any shells. Cut clams into small pieces. Add to soup mixture, with parsley, ½ teasp. thyme.
5. Simmer, uncovered, 10 min. Add salt to taste. Makes 6 servings.

To Do Ahead: Make night before; refrigerate; heat next day.

FISHERMAN'S CHOWDER

1½ lb. fresh or thawed frozen haddock, cod, or flounder fillets	Salt
	Pepper
	3 cups boiling water
	1 qt. milk, scalded
12 medium white onions	1 cup evaporated milk
Butter or margarine	1 ripe tomato
4 or 5 potatoes, thinly sliced, pared	Assorted crisp crackers

About 1 hr. before dinnertime:

1. Skin and bone fish; cut each fillet into 2 or 3 pieces.
2. In 4-qt. Dutch oven, sauté whole onions with ¼ cup butter until golden; then cook, uncovered, 10 min.
3. Add potatoes, 4 teasp. salt, ½ teasp. pepper, and boiling water; stir well to blend seasonings.
4. Arrange fish fillets on top; cover; simmer 15 to 20 min., or until vegetables are fork-tender. Add milk, evaporated milk, 3 tablesp. butter; heat, don't boil.
5. Slice tomato thinly; sprinkle with salt, pepper; float on chowder. Serve with crisp crackers. Makes 4 servings.

BOUILLABAISSE, BUFFET STYLE

2 cups olive oil	4 whole fish, boned and cleaned (bonito, mackerel, bluefish, or sea bass)
3 large onions, cubed	
2 large green peppers, cubed	
3 large carrots, pared, cubed	About 5 cups water
	2 tablesp. salt
50 small hard-shell clams, scrubbed	½ to 1 teasp. pepper
	1″ slices French bread
1 lb. unshelled large raw shrimp	Melted butter or margarine
3 live lobsters, split	Garlic salt or minced garlic

1. In very large kettle (at least 3½ gal. capacity), heat olive oil. Add onions, green peppers, carrots; brown lightly.
2. In same kettle, arrange fish in this order: clams; then shrimp; then lobster; and lastly, on top of all, whole fish.
3. Add water (enough to half fill kettle), salt, pepper. Cover kettle tightly; bring mixture to boil; reduce heat and cook 15 to 20 min., or until clams open, lobsters are pink and tender,

and the whole fish is easily flaked with a fork.

4. While fish cooks, toast bread in 425°F. oven; brush with combined butter and garlic salt. When all is done, carefully arrange each kind of shellfish and fish on a separate heated platter.
5. Place 1 or 2 slices toasted bread in each soup dish. After stirring broth well, pour some over bread in each dish; arrange dishes on table, along with platters of fish.
6. Each person helps himself to different kinds of fish, placing them in soup bowl. Makes 8 to 10 servings.

GOURMET STYLE: Substitute dry white wine for 1 cup water. Add ½ teasp. each dried thyme and sage.

MINESTRONE

1 lb. shin beef with bone	2 cups finely shredded cabbage
5 qt. cold water	1½ cups diced, pared carrots
3 tablesp. salt	
1 cup dried red kidney beans	1 1-lb.-13-oz. can tomatoes (3½ cups)
2 tablesp. salad or olive oil	1½ cups broken-up spaghetti
2 cloves garlic	1 cup thinly sliced zucchini or small yellow squash
1 medium onion, minced	
½ cup snipped parsley	1 10-oz. pkg. frozen peas
½ lb. chuck, ground	Grated Parmesan or Romano cheese
¼ teasp. pepper	
1 cup diced celery	

Day before: In large kettle, place shin beef with bone, water, salt, beans. Bring to boil; skim. Cover; simmer 3 hr. In oil, sauté garlic, onion, parsley, chuck, and pepper until onion is tender; discard garlic. Remove bone from soup; cut off meat. Add meat to soup, along with onion mixture, celery, cabbage, carrots, tomatoes. Simmer, covered, 20 min., or until vegetables are tender. Refrigerate.

About 30 min. before serving: Skim fat from soup. Bring soup slowly to boil; add spaghetti, zucchini, peas; cook, covered, about 10 min. Add salt and pepper to taste.

Serve from soup tureen, large casserole, or mixing bowl, letting guests top soup with cheese. Makes 8 servings.

TUNA-CORN CHOWDER

2 6½- or 7-oz. cans tuna (2 cups)	3 cups water
4 medium onions, sliced	1 qt. milk
5 medium potatoes, pared, sliced	1 10-oz. pkg. frozen whole-kernel corn, thawed
3½ teasp. salt	2 tablesp. butter or margarine
⅛ teasp. pepper	Fresh dill sprigs

Into Dutch oven or large kettle, drain oil from tuna. In oil, sauté onions till golden, stirring often. Add potatoes, salt, pepper, water; cook, covered, 15 min., or until tender. Add milk, corn, and tuna in large pieces. Heat. Float butter and dill on top. Makes 6 to 8 servings.

TURKEY-CORN CHOWDER

¼ cup butter or margarine	2 12-oz. cans vacuum-packed whole-kernel corn
4 medium onions, sliced	¼ teasp. dried thyme
5 medium potatoes, pared, sliced	1 cup light cream
2 stalks celery, sliced	1 1-lb. can cream-style corn
4 teasp. salt	1½ teasp. paprika
½ teasp. pepper	3 cups cut-up roast turkey or chicken
2 cups water	2 tablesp. butter or margarine
1 chicken-bouillon cube	Parsley
5 cups milk	

In ¼ cup butter, in large kettle, sauté onions till golden, stirring often. Add potatoes, celery, salt, pepper, water, bouillon cube. Cook, covered, 15 min., or until vegetables are tender. Add milk and rest of ingredients except 2 tablesp. butter and parsley. Heat; dot with butter; snip parsley over top. Makes 8 to 10 servings.

OYSTER STEW

2 doz. shucked raw oysters with liquid	1 teasp. celery salt
¼ cup butter or margarine	¾ teasp. salt
1 tablesp. Worcestershire	⅛ teasp. pepper
	¼ teasp. paprika
	1 qt. milk

Carefully pick over oysters to remove bits of shell. In deep skillet or kettle, heat butter until sizzling. Add oysters with liquid, Worcestershire, celery salt, salt, pepper, paprika. Heat until edges of oysters curl *slightly*; add milk. Heat quickly, *but do not boil*.

Serve in bowls, topped with paprika and lumps of butter. Pass oyster crackers if desired. Makes 4 servings.

DE LUXE: Use part milk and part cream.

CLAM: Substitute 2 doz. shucked raw soft-shell clams with liquid for oysters.

LOBSTER: Substitute 1 to 1½ cups cooked lobster meat for oysters with liquid.

SCALLOP STEW

½ to ¾ lb. sea scallops	1 teasp. monosodium glutamate
2 tablesp. butter or margarine	1 teasp. salt
2 cups milk	Dash pepper
1½ teasp. Worcestershire	2 oz. process cheese spread, cut into pieces

1. Slice scallops in half, across the grain.

2. In hot butter in large skillet, sauté scallops till golden — 5 to 7 min. Add milk, Worcestershire, monosodium glutamate, salt, and pepper.

3. Simmer scallops until milk is bubbly. Add cheese; stir until melted. Serve topped with oyster crackers or snipped scallions. Makes 2 servings.

CREME VICHYSSOISE

4 leeks; or 1½ cups minced onions	1 cup light or heavy cream
3 cups sliced, pared potatoes	1 cup milk
3 cups boiling water	1 teasp. salt
4 chicken-bouillon cubes	¼ teasp. pepper
3 tablesp. butter or margarine	2 tablesp. snipped chives or water cress
	¼ teasp. paprika

Cut into fine pieces leeks and 3″ of their green tops. Cook with potatoes in boiling water, covered, until very tender — about 40 min. Press, without draining, through fine sieve into double boiler.

Add bouillon cubes, butter, cream, milk, salt, pepper; mix well. Reheat.

Serve hot or very cold, topped with chives or water cress, and paprika. Makes 6 servings.

To Vary: Add ¼ teasp. curry powder.

BLENDER VICHYSSOISE

1 cup coarsely diced raw potatoes	1 cup raw green peas
¼ cup snipped scallions	⅛ teasp. celery salt
	⅛ teasp. curry powder
1½ cups chicken broth	1 cup heavy cream
	Snipped parsley

Day before: Cook potatoes with scallions, chicken broth, and peas, covered, 10 min., or until vegetables are barely tender. Place undrained vegetables in glass container of electric blender; add celery salt, curry powder. Cover; blend until smooth — 30 sec. Remove; stir in cream. Refrigerate.

Serve cold, sprinkled with snipped parsley. Makes 4 servings.

CALICO CHEESE SOUP

½ clove garlic	2 cups scalded milk
¼ cup salad oil	2 cups canned chicken broth
½ cup finely chopped carrots	½ lb. process Cheddar cheese, shredded
½ cup finely chopped celery	2 cups small fresh bread cubes
¼ cup butter or margarine	¼ cup grated Parmesan cheese
2 tablesp. minced onion	
3 tablesp. flour	

Day before: Add garlic to oil; let stand overnight at room temperature; then remove garlic clove and set garlic-flavored oil aside.

About 1 hr. before serving: In boiling salted water to cover, cook carrots and celery, covered, until just tender-crisp; drain.

Meanwhile, in butter, in double-boiler top, over low heat, sauté onion until tender. Place double-boiler top over boiling water; then blend in flour, milk, broth; stir until slightly thickened. Stir in cheese until melted. Add carrot mixture and cook 10 min.

While soup cooks, toast bread cubes under broiler until golden; toss with Parmesan cheese and reserved garlic-flavored oil.

Serve soup, piping hot, with croutons floating on top. Makes 4 to 6 servings.

HEARTY OXJOINT-VEGETABLE SOUP

2½ lb. oxjoints, cut into 2″ lengths	1 1-lb.-13-oz. can tomatoes
½ cup flour	1½ qt. cold water
1 teasp. seasoned salt	12 3″ bias celery slices
3 tablesp. fat or salad oil	½ cup diced celery
½ cup minced onion	12 raw yellow turnip sticks, 3″ long
1 tablesp. salt	½ cup diced raw yellow turnips
⅛ teasp. black pepper	12 3″ bias raw carrot slices
3 bay leaves	½ cup diced raw carrots
4 or 5 parsley sprigs	Few drops Tabasco

Day before:

1. Singe oxjoints, if necessary; wipe with a damp cloth; then cut off all excess fat.
2. In small bowl, combine flour and seasoned salt; dredge each piece of oxjoint.
3. In large Dutch oven, heat fat. In it brown oxjoint pieces well, a few at a time; then brown onion.
4. Return all oxjoint pieces to Dutch oven; now add salt, pepper, bay leaves, parsley, tomatoes, and water. Cover; simmer 2 hr., or till fork-tender.
5. Cool; then refrigerate overnight.

About 1 hr. before serving:

1. Skim fat from surface of soup. Bring soup to boil; add vegetables; then simmer, covered, 45 min., or until large pieces of vegetables are fork-tender.
2. Now add Tabasco. Serve soup from tureen in bowls. Makes 8 servings.

THE STORY OF MEATS

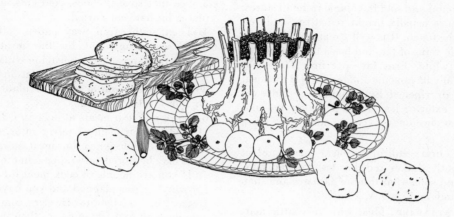

The old American custom of serving lots of meat is a fine one. Few foods are a richer source of important food values, with fine flavor and good appetite satisfaction at the same time. These things are true of any meat if it's properly prepared, regardless of cut and grade — or whether it's cut to order, prepackaged fresh, quick-frozen, cured, "cured and smoked," or canned. Use the recipes that follow and you can be sure of delectable meat and still make every meat penny count.

Busy day dinners need be no problem if you make use of some of the speedy meat dishes included on these pages. Many of the most delectable meat dishes make use of less expensive meat cuts.

Before using these recipes, see How To Use Our Recipes, p. 3. Always use standard measuring cups and measuring spoons; measure level.

To Buy Meat

It takes an expert to judge the quality of meat just by looking at its color, the fat, and the bone. So, for most of us, it's safer to rely on a meat packer's brand or a Federal grade, to be sure of getting the quality we pay for.

First Check for Wholesomeness. All meat shipped in interstate commerce is Federally inspected. The round purple U.S. Inspected and Passed stamp on a cut of meat guarantees that the meat came from an animal judged wholesome by a Federal inspector and that the plant where it was processed passed sanitary regulations (Fig. 1). The stamp's purple dye is not harmful and need not be cut off the meat before cooking; usually, however, for the sake of appearance, you'll want to trim it off.

Then Look for the Packer's Brand Name. Several well-known meat packers stamp or burn their own brands on better-quality beef, veal, lamb, and cured meats (Fig. 1). Fresh pork is seldom branded because there is less variation in the tenderness of this meat. Once you find the brand you like, stick to it.

The packer's brand on packaged and canned meats (bacon, ham, sausage, franks, etc.) indicates the quality too.

Or Look for a Federal Grade. Some beef, veal, and lamb cuts carry a U.S.D.A. grade stamp to indicate quality. This shield-shaped

171

stamp runs like a purple ribbon along the entire length of the carcass (Fig. 1).

Take beef as one example. The U.S.D.A. grades of beef are:

U.S.D.A. PRIME: Highest grade. The supply is relatively limited.

U.S.D.A. CHOICE: Highest grade of beef commonly found and sold in volume in retail stores. The lean is usually bright red, firm, and velvety to the touch. It is well streaked (marbled) with little veins of fat, and has a thick, white or creamy white, firm fat covering. The meat is especially flavorsome and tender. (If the meat is aged or ripened by hanging in cold storage, the exterior lean turns a darker red and the meat becomes even juicier and more tender).

U.S.D.A. GOOD: Still of excellent quality. Meat is a slightly darker red, has less fat and marbling, and somewhat thinner fat covering than that found in U.S.D.A. Choice.

U.S.D.A. STANDARD: Meat with very little marbling. These meats are better for braising (pot roast, Swiss steaks, etc.) and cooking in liquid (stews). See Instant Meat Tenderizer, p. 101.

U.S.D.A. COMMERCIAL AND U.S.D.A. UTILITY: These are lower grades, with a thin or very thin fat covering. These meats are lower priced and are usually better for braising (pot roast, Swiss steaks, etc.) and cooking in liquid (stews), than for roasting. See Instant Meat Tenderizer, p. 101.

Tendered Beef

Recently a new method of tendering beef has been developed which, through the introduction of a food enzyme (papain) into the circulatory system of the beef animal, assures tenderness throughout all the beef roasts and steaks when cooked.

With this process, beef cuts such as top and bottom round, rump, blade, chuck, etc., which we usually think of as less tender and in need of pot roasting or braising, can now be broiled, grilled, rotisseried, or oven roasted if desired. You can identify this beef by a foil name tag, reading "Swift's ProTen Tendered Beef." Prepare as label directs.

To Store Meat

FRESH MEATS:

1. If meat is wrapped in market paper, unwrap. Separate different kinds of meat.
2. Do not wash meat; it keeps better if surface is not damp.
3. See that steaks, chops, cold cuts, and large pieces lie flat, not curled.
4. Then, with saran, wax paper, foil, or the inner wrapping used by the meat dealer, *loosely* rewrap each kind, leaving ends open.
5. Keep prepackaged fresh meat in original wrapper, but loosen to allow circulation of air. Or follow label directions.
6. Store all fresh meats at once in coldest part of food compartment of refrigerator, or in the compartment designed for meat storage. The meat may be stored, unwrapped, in the latter.
7. If you are unable to cook meat for the meal for which it was planned and you have a home freezer or refrigerator-freezer combination, freezer-wrap and freeze meat; then use within recommended storage time, p. 701.

If you have no freezer, only the frozen-food compartment of a conventional refrigerator, you can keep freezer-wrapped meat in it for 1 or 2 weeks.
8. If you lack freezing facilities, refer to the storage time guide on p. 173 for the maximum time meat may be kept in the food compartment of the refrigerator *for maximum flavor and eating pleasure*. However, this chart is only a general guide; many factors influence the length of time a meat can be kept satisfactorily. So use the meat you buy *as promptly as possible*; or freeze it as in step 7, above.

CURED AND SMOKED MEATS: Today's prepackaged ham, bacon, and sausage should be refrigerated at once in their original wrappers. When removing some of the meat from the refrigerator, return the unused portion to the refrigerator at once, to retain freshness and maximum flavor.

CANNED FULL-SIZE HAMS: These must be refrigerated as label very prominently directs.

CANNED SMALL 1½-LB. HAM PIECES: These may be stored on pantry shelf.

OTHER CANNED MEATS: If they're not labeled "Keep in Refrigerator," they may be kept on pantry shelf.

STORAGE TIME GUIDE FOR MEATS
(kept in cold refrigerator at 36°F. to 40°F.)

MEAT (loosely covered)	STORAGE LIMIT FOR MAXIMUM QUALITY
Uncooked Meats	
BEEF	
Corned beef	7 days
Hamburger	2 days
Pot roast	5 to 6 days
Short ribs	2 days
Standing rib roast	5 to 8 days
Standing and rolled rump and sirloin tip	5 to 6 days
Steak	3 to 5 days
Stew meat	2 days
Tenderloin	3 to 5 days
PORK (*fresh*)	
Chops	3 days
Pork sausage	2 to 3 days
Roast	5 to 6 days
Spareribs	3 days
Knuckles or hocks	3 days
HAM, BACON (*cured pork*)	
Bacon	6 to 7 days
Half ham	7 days
Whole ham	1 to 2 weeks
Sliced ham	3 days
Picnic	1 to 2 weeks
LAMB	
Chops	3 days
Roast	5 days
Shank	2 days
Stew meat	2 days

MEAT (loosely covered)	STORAGE LIMIT FOR MAXIMUM QUALITY
VEAL	
Chops and steak	4 days
Roast	5 to 6 days
Stew meat	2 days
VARIETY MEATS	
Brains	1 day
Heart	2 days
Kidney	1 day
Liver, sliced	2 days
Sweetbreads, cooked	2 days
Tongue, fresh	2 days
Tongue, smoked	7 days
Cooked Meats	
FRANKS	4 to 5 days
HAM OR PICNIC	7 days
MEAT COOKED AT HOME	4 days
SLICED READY-COOKED MEATS	
Dry sausage	1 to 2 weeks
Liver sausage	2 to 3 days
Luncheon meat	3 days
Meat loaves	3 to 4 days
Semidry sausage	7 to 8 days
UNSLICED READY-COOKED MEAT	
Bologna	4 to 6 days
Dry and semidry sausage	2 to 3 weeks
Liver sausage	4 to 6 days
Meat loaves	4 to 6 days

FROZEN MEATS: These must be kept frozen at 0°F. or lower until ready to use.

COOKED MEATS: Don't make the mistake of letting hot cooked, roasted, or leftover cooked meats stand until cold before refrigerating them. This is a risky practice, which only invites food poisoning.

Either refrigerate the meat at once (this does not impair its flavor, despite old wives' tales), or cool meat quickly, then refrigerate at once. To hasten cooling of meat in broth, lift meat from broth to wire rack to cool; then cool kettle of broth in cold water in sink, changing water and stirring broth often. At end of ½ hr., no longer, refrigerate meat and broth at once.

In any case, *never* let cooked meat stand out of the refrigerator longer than 2 hr. And plan to use it up within 4 days.

LET'S HAVE BEEF

When you buy beef, look for the Federal U.S. Inspected and Passed stamp; then check for the packer's brand name or U.S.D.A. grade stamp, described in To Buy Meat, p. 171. Top-quality beef is bright red, with white, firm fat; in lower grades, the red deepens and the fat takes on a yellowish cast.

In the following pages, we suggest and describe favorite uses for many of the retail cuts of beef. Our diagram of the beef animal, under Popular Cuts of Meat, will help you to identify these cuts better.

RIB ROASTS OF BEEF

Roasting ribs of beef at a low temperature gives a tender, juicy, flavorful oven roast. There's little work involved, no spattering of fat, and a minimum amount of shrinkage.

To Buy and Store Rib Roasts

Rib oven roasts are among the finest, most tender, and highest-priced cuts of beef.

Select a Cut: There are usually 7 ribs in the rib section of beef from which the meat dealer cuts the 3 rib roasts below:

FIRST-RIB ROAST: This is the choicest and most tender rib roast. It comes from the short loin end of the rib section; the "rib eye" of solid, tender meat predominates. In a few markets, it is known as eleventh-and-twelfth rib roast.

CENTER-RIB ROAST: This roast, cut from the center of the rib section, is often priced lower than the first-rib roast and higher than the sixth-and-seventh rib roast. The "rib eye" of solid tender meat is somewhat less predominant in this cut than in the first-rib roast.

SIXTH-AND-SEVENTH RIB ROAST: This roast, cut from the chuck (shoulder) end of the rib sec-

tion, is likely to be the least tender and lowest priced of the 3 rib roasts. Its "rib eye" of solid, tender meat is the smallest of the 3 rib roasts.

Choose a Style: You can buy the rib roasts, left, in any of the 4 styles below:

STANDING 10″ RIB ROAST (Fig. 5) has 10″-long ribs, with backbone and small bones still on. A 2-rib standing rib roast weighs about 7 lb. If desired, the meatman can cut about 3″, or 1½ lb., from the rib ends to cook as short ribs or use in soup.

STANDING 7″ RIB ROAST (Fig. 5) has only 7″ ribs, because 3″ of the short ribs, plus backbone and small bones, have been cut off. A 2-rib standing rib roast weighs about 5 lb.

ROLLED RIB ROAST (Fig. 3) looked like the standing rib roast in Fig. 5 before it was boned, rolled, and tied, with the boned short ribs wrapped around the roast. It weighs about 6 lb.

RIB EYE ROAST (DELMONICO) (Fig. 6) is a boneless roast which is the large muscle from a rib roast.

Amount To Buy:

STANDING RIB ROAST: Buy at least a 2-rib roast. Allow ½ to ¾ lb. bone-in roast per serving. Plan on leftovers. For easier carving, ask meatman to saw across ribs close to backbone so it can be removed easily after roasting.

ROLLED RIB ROAST: Buy at least a 4-lb. roast. Allow ¼ lb. boned roast per serving. Plan on leftovers.

RIB EYE: Buy at least a 4-lb. roast. Allow ½ to ¾ lb. per serving.

Be sure to have the meat dealer mark the weight of the oven-ready roast on the bill to guide you in computing the roasting time.

To Store: Store as in To Store Meat, p. 172.

Other Roasts of Beef

STANDING OR ROLLED RUMP (Fig. 4): A high quality prime or choice rump may be oven roasted. It is a triangular piece of beef, sold either bone-in or boneless. It is juicy and tender, with a moderate amount of fat. Follow directions for Roast Beef, p. 175.

SIRLOIN TIP (Fig. 7): If of top quality, these roasts may be oven roasted. Follow directions for Roast Beef, p. 175.

Amount To Buy: For standing rump allow ¾ to 1 lb. per serving. For boneless rump or sirloin tip allow ½ to ¾ lb. per serving.

To Store: Store as in To Store Meat, p. 172.

ROAST BEEF

1. Check roasting timetable, p. 176, to see about how long roasting will take. Plan so roast is done about 20 min. before serving; it will slice more easily, and you will have time to make gravy, if desired.
2. Start heating oven to 325°F.
3. Do not wash roast. If necessary, wipe with damp cloth or paper towel.
4. If it's a standing rib roast, stand it on rib bones in shallow open pan. If it's a rolled rib roast, place on rack, with fat side up. Roasts should never be covered; a cover holds in the steam and the meat acquires a steam-cooked, not true roast, flavor.
5. Never flour the roast; never add water. If desired, season with salt, pepper, and mono-sodium glutamate, or seasoned salt. But actually the salt will not penetrate the roast more than ¼".
6. *Caution:* Roasts vary so in size, shape, amount of lean, bone, and fat, etc., that a roasting timetable can only be approximate at best. So use a roast-meat thermometer if you want to be sure that every roast is done just right. Such a thermometer indicates the interior temperature of the meat, and you can count on it to indicate when the roast is done to your liking. Remember the smaller the diameter of a rib roast the shorter the cooking time (a shorter rib roast takes longer time).
7. Insert roast-meat thermometer carefully. To determine how deep meat thermometer should be inserted, place it against cut side of roast, with its point at center of roast. Note part of thermometer that is just even with top of roast. Make a hole for thermometer with skewer; then insert thermometer into center of roast up to that point. *Make sure* pointed end of thermometer does not rest on bone, fat, or gristle.
8. Roast meat, using timetable, p. 176, as an approximate guide. Don't baste or turn. Let the roast-meat thermometer be your guide as to when the roast is rare, medium, or well done; but be sure to read the thermometer in the oven. For easier carving, and more attractive servings, it is desirable to allow a cooked roast to "set" 20 to 30 min. Meat continues to cook upon removal from oven. So, to permit roast to "set," it should be removed from the oven when the thermometer registers 5° to 10° lower than desired doneness.

9. Sometimes during roasting, the meat thermometer moves out of its original position. Before removing roast from oven, you can check this by gently pressing top of thermometer; if it drops in temperature, you know the tip was not in the center of the roast. If this happens, continue to roast meat until right temperature is reached.
10. When roast is done, remove to large heated platter, with broader cut surface resting on platter; keep warm while making Velvety Meat Gravy, p. 177, from drippings in pan.

To serve: From roast, remove skewers, if any, but not string. If space permits, place one of vegetables around meat (don't crowd; let carver have plenty of room!). If it's a standing rib roast, set before host, with rib bones to his left and smaller rib ends pointing toward him, as on p. 293.

Pass gravy, Worcestershire, Horse-radish Sauce I or II, p. 532, bottled thick meat sauce, or Tabasco. Pan-roasted Sweet Potatoes, p. 410, are especially nice with rib roast.

If you're serving your rib roast cold, don't slice it hot. Refrigerate until serving time; then slice.

To Carve Rib Roast: See p. 293.

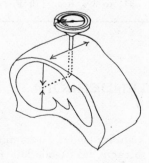

CORRECT PLACEMENT OF ROAST-MEAT THERMOMETER

TIMETABLE FOR ROASTING BEEF

Beef refrigerated till roasted at 325°F. Use shallow open pan. Add no water. Do not baste.

OVEN-READY WEIGHT	APPROXIMATE ROASTING TIME	MEAT THERMOMETER READING

STANDING RIB ROAST

*4 lb. *(6" from tip of rib to backbone)*

	1¾ hr.	140°F. *(rare)*
	2¼ hr.	160°F. *(medium)*
	3 hr.	170°F. *(well done)*

*6 lb. *(6" from tip of rib to backbone)*

	3¼ hr.	140°F. *(rare)*
	3¾ hr.	160°F. *(medium)*
	4¼ hr.	170°F. *(well done)*

*8 lb. *(6" from tip of rib to backbone)*

	3½ hr.	140°F. *(rare)*
	4½ hr.	160°F. *(medium)*
	5 hr.	170°F. *(well done)*

SIRLOIN TIP

4 lb.	2¼ hr.	140°F. *(rare)*
	2¾ hr.	160°F. *(medium)*
	3¼ hr.	170°F. *(well done)*

ROLLED RUMP

4 lb.	2½ to 3 hr.	140°F. *(rare)*
	3 to 3½ hr.	160°F. *(medium)*
	3¼ to 3¾ hr.	170°F. *(well done)*

ROLLED RIB ROAST

**4 lb. *(4½" to 5" width)*

	2¾ hr.	140°F. *(rare)*
	3¼ hr.	160°F. *(medium)*
	3½ hr.	170°F. *(well done)*

**6 lb. *(5½" to 6½" width)*

	3½ hr.	140°F. *(rare)*
	4¼ hr.	160°F. *(medium)*
	4¾ hr.	170°F. *(well done)*

RIB EYE***

4 lb.	1¼ to 1⅓ hr.	140°F. *(rare)*
	1⅓ to 1½ hr.	160°F. *(medium)*
	1½ to 1⅔ hr.	170°F. *(well done)*

STANDING RUMP

4 lb.	2½ hr.	140°F. *(rare)*
	3 hr.	160°F. *(medium)*
	3¼ hr.	170°F. *(well done)*

*   One cut longer than 6" will take less time.
**   If thinner, these take less time.
***Roast at 350°F. oven temperature.
For larger roasts, see p. 721.

BEEF TENDERLOIN
(filet of beef)

Because it's always tender, cooks quickly, and is so easy to carve, beef tenderloin (Fig. 12), the long muscle that lies along the backbone and inside the loin, is excellent company fare.

To Buy Beef Tenderloin

For roasting, order a lower-quality grade of beef tenderloin so it will have less fat covering and, therefore, will brown well. Trim away most of fat from a top-quality tenderloin, as it prevents that luscious browning.

Amount To Buy: A whole beef tenderloin,

stripped of fat and connective tissue, weighs about 4 to 6 lb. and makes 8 to 12 1"-thick servings. A half tenderloin (2 to 3 lb.) makes 4 to 6 1"-thick servings.

To Store: Store as in To Store Meat, p. 172.

ROAST BEEF TENDERLOIN

1. Start heating oven to 450°F. Remove surface fat and connective tissue from tenderloin. If desired, rub well all over with garlic. Or make several gashes in top surface of tenderloin; then insert piece of garlic in each gash (remove before serving).
2. Place tenderloin on rack in shallow open pan, tucking narrow end under to make roast uniformly thick. Brush with salad oil or bacon fat. Insert roast-meat thermometer into center of thickest part.
3. *Roast 4- to 6-lb. whole tenderloin* (with fat and tissue removed) about 45 to 60 min., or to 140°F. on roast-meat thermometer.
   Roast 2- to 3-lb. half tenderloin (with fat and tissue removed) about 45 to 50 min., or to 140°F. on meat thermometer. Meat should be crusty brown outside, pink to red inside.
4. When done, place tenderloin on heated platter. Keep warm while making Velvety Meat Gravy, below, from drippings in pan. To gravy, add ¼ lb. sautéed mushrooms and a little sherry. Pour some gravy over tenderloin; pass rest.
   Or pass Quick Mushroom Sauce, p. 528, or Horse-radish Sauce I or II, p. 532, or Bordelaise Sauce, p. 531. Fried onions are nice with tenderloin too.

VELVETY MEAT GRAVY

¼ cup fat drippings from roast	¼ cup flour
	Bottled sauce for gravy
2 cups warm water (or cooking liquid from vegetables)	Salt
	Pepper

1. When roast is done, keep warm on heated platter. Pour clear fat from roasting pan into bowl, leaving brown bits in pan. Measure ¼ cup of this clear fat; pour into skillet or saucepan.
2. *Pour 1 cup warm water into roasting pan; scrape and stir until all flavorful brown bits are loosened, heating mixture if necessary.
3. In skillet over medium heat, heat fat. Gradually add flour, stirring with broad spatula or spoon, until smooth and light brown. Then, stirring and scraping constantly, slowly add brown liquid in roasting pan plus 1 cup warm water.
4. Bring mixture in skillet to boiling point over medium heat; cook, stirring well, until as thick as heavy cream. Add enough bottled sauce for gravy to get the rich color you want. Season to taste, as on p. 5. If, in spite of all your care, gravy has lumps, strain.
5. If gravy must stand before serving, you may have to stir in a little water to bring it back to its right consistency. Makes about 2 cups.
If you're making gravy for meat cooked in a skillet, omit steps 1 and 2; in step 3 use ¼ cup fat, and 2 cups warm water as liquid.

To Vary: Add 2 tablesp. minced chutney; ½ cup canned cranberry sauce, beaten smooth with fork; a few herbs; 2 tablesp. light cream, or a little sherry or Burgundy.

IN-A-PINCH GRAVY: If roast has no fat drippings, substitute butter or margarine. Use diluted canned condensed bouillon, or 2 beef-bouillon cubes dissolved in 2 cups water, as liquid; or use water plus meat-extract paste.

PANTRY-SHELF GRAVY: Use canned beef or mushroom gravy; they're delicious. Or use one of the sauce mixes, p. 102. Or dilute canned condensed cream-of-mushroom soup with canned condensed consommé or bouillon. Add minced onion or chives to either if you wish. Nice for meat dishes.

ALL-AMERICAN STEAKS TO BROIL

To Buy and Store

Because you want the most tender, top-quality steaks for broiling, ask for a packer's top brand or grade of beef (see To Buy Meat, p. 171). Choose one of steaks below, cut 1" to 2" thick.

Select a Cut:
FILET MIGNON (Fig. 12): This boneless, very tender little steak is cut from the beef tender-

loin. It is an expensive steak. A 1″-thick steak weighs 4 to 6 oz. Serve 1 thick, or 2 thin, steaks per person.

PORTERHOUSE STEAK (Fig. 14) (also called T-bone by some meatmen): This steak, from the large end of the short loin, has a T-shaped bone and the largest portion of tenderloin. A 1½″-thick steak may weigh about 3 lb. and make 3 or 4 servings.

T-BONE STEAK: This steak, from the center section of the short loin, looks like a porterhouse but is smaller. It has a T-shaped bone and some tenderloin. A 1½″-thick steak may weigh about 1½ to 2 lb. and make 2 or 3 servings.

CLUB STEAK (Fig. 15): This triangular steak, from the rib end of the short loin, is the smallest in the short loin, and has no tenderloin. A 1″-thick steak may weigh about ½ to ¾ lb. and make 1 or 2 servings.

BONELESS LOIN STEAK (HOTEL STYLE) (Fig. 13): This is a most desirable boneless loin steak with no tenderloin. However, it is not widely available in retail markets. A 1″-thick steak weighs 8 to 10 oz. and makes 1 serving.

SIRLOIN STEAK: A sirloin steak (full cut) is a nice buy for a family meal and is less expensive than the steaks above.

A steak from the round end of the sirloin section is the largest and is sometimes called a wedge bone (Fig. 17). The steaks get smaller as they near the short loin end; the smallest is sometimes called a pinbone (Fig. 16). A 1½″-thick sirloin steak, full cut, may weigh 3 to 4½ lb. and make 4 or 5 generous servings.

RIB STEAK (Fig. 18) (sometimes called club): Sliced from the rib section, the best rib steaks are those from the loin end. A 1″-thick steak may weigh 12 to 14 oz. and makes 1 generous serving.

DELMONICO STEAK: A steak cut from the rib eye roast.

Amount To Buy: For each serving, order about ⅓ to ½ lb. of boned steak, or ⅓ to ¾ lb. bone-in steak.

To Store: Store as in To Store Meat, p. 172.

BROILED STEAK

1. Set oven regulator for broiling. If you have no oven regulator, turn broiler on full. Preheat broiler 10 min., or as manufacturer directs. Line broiler pan, under rack, with foil, with corners turned under, to catch drippings and save dishwashing.
2. Trim surplus fat from steak. If it's a very lean steak, like beef tenderloin, brush with salad oil.
3. With scissors or sharp knife, slash edge of fat at 2″ intervals, to keep steak from curling during broiling. If desired, rub steak with cut clove garlic; or spread lightly with prepared mustard or bottled sauce for gravy.
4. Rub broiler rack with a bit of fat trimmed from steak. Place steak on rack. Then place broiler pan so top of steak, if it's a thin one, is about 2″ from heat. Or if steak is thick, place 3″ to 5″ from heat. Or place as manufacturer or recipe directs.
5. Broil steak on one side, using timetable on p. 179 as an approximate guide. Season as on p. 5. Turn (use tongs to avoid piercing meat); broil second side almost same length of time.
6. *Test for Doneness:* Cut slit in meat near bone; note if color inside is of desired rareness. Season.
7. *Caution:* Because steaks vary so in size, shape, amount of bone and fat, etc., a broiling timetable can only be approximate at best. If you prefer steak rarer or more well done, decrease or increase broiling time accordingly. Remember, too, that steak may continue to cook after you remove it from broiler.

To serve: Serve steak at once on heated platter, topped with one of Seasoning Touches, below. Or pass Help-Yourself Tray, p. 179. Or surround steak with vegetables such as sautéed or French fried onions, mashed potatoes, or any of the wonderful vegetables in Vegetables That Say "More," p. 389. Leave room for carver to work!

Seasoning Touches After Broiling:

SIMPLE: Worcestershire, bottled thick meat sauce, Tabasco, chili sauce, or barbecue sauce.

BUTTERY: Dab of butter or margarine. Or melted butter plus prepared mustard.

ZESTY CHEESE: A little mashed Roquefort or Danish blue cheese, some butter or margarine, and a few drops of Worcestershire.

MUSHROOM: Lots of sautéed mushrooms.

SCALLION BUTTER: Sliced scallions or snipped parsley in melted butter or margarine, with Worcestershire if you like.

LEMON: Squeeze or two of lemon or lime juice.
SMOKY: Bit of powdered or liquid smoke.
WINE BUTTER: Half-and-half Burgundy and melted butter or margarine.

Help-Yourself Tray: Serve small bowls and pitchers filled with butter or margarine creamed with lemon juice, snipped chives, Danish blue or Roquefort cheese, bottled thick meat sauce and barbecue sauce, etc.

BROILED STEAK TIMETABLE
(refrigerated until broiled in preheated broiler)

THICKNESS	APPROXIMATE MIN. PER SIDE

FILET MIGNON, DELMONICO, PORTERHOUSE, T-BONE, CLUB, RIB, PINBONE SIRLOIN

1″	5 min. *(rare)*
	6 min. *(medium)*
	7 to 8 min. *(well done)*
1½″	9 min. *(rare)*
	10 min. *(medium)*
	12 to 13 min. *(well done)*
2″	16 min. *(rare)*
	18 min. *(medium)*
	20 to 21 min. *(well done)*

WEDGE-BONE AND OTHER LARGE SIRLOINS

1″	10 min. *(rare)*
	12 min. *(medium)*
	14 min. *(well done)*
1½″	12 min. *(rare)*
	14 min. *(medium)*
	16 min. *(well done)*

PLANKED BROILED STEAK

Use a special hardwood plank about 15″ x 10″, available in housewares departments.

Cook 2 vegetables such as hot mashed potatoes, hot buttered peas, green beans, Brussels sprouts, slivered carrots, cauliflower. Broil steak (usually a T-bone) as on p. 178.

Meanwhile, heat plank in 400°F. oven. Arrange 2 hot buttered vegetables around edge of heated plank; place broiled steak in center.

Spread steak with butter or Lemon Butter, p. 533; sprinkle with salt, pepper, and snipped parsley. Serve. (Plank may be set on platter or tray, or into special holder.)

PLANK-STYLE CHUCK: Use 2½ lb. chuck roast, 1″ thick. Rub both sides liberally with ½ cup lemon juice; sprinkle with salt, pepper, garlic salt. Broil, 12″ from heat (or with broiler heat turned low), about 25 min. on one side, and 15 min. on the other side, or until a nice brown and medium rare. Arrange on heated plank, see left. Surround with hot mashed potatoes; run under broiler to brown. Meanwhile, combine ¼ cup melted butter or margarine with 1 tablesp. each of lemon juice and snipped parsley and dash of cayenne; serve over thinly sliced chuck. Makes 6 to 8 servings.

FILET OF BEEF BEARNAISE

2 center cut slices filet mignon, 1½″ thick	garine
Melted butter or mar-	Béarnaise Sauce, p. 529

Preheat broiler, with broiler pan and rack in place. Brush both sides of beef with melted butter; broil, 3″ from heat, about 6 min. on each side, or until medium rare, brushing with butter. Serve with bowl of Béarnaise Sauce. Makes 2 servings.

DOUBLE-THICK RARE STEAK

1 porterhouse steak, 3″ thick	1 teasp. Worcestershire
1 clove garlic, cut	1 tablesp. prepared mustard
½ cup crumbled Danish blue cheese	1 tablesp. lemon juice
¼ cup soft butter or margarine	1 teasp. salt
	½ teasp. freshly ground pepper

Preheat broiler and rack 10 min., or as manufacturer directs. Then rub steak with garlic. Broil steak, 5″ below heat, 20 to 25 min. on first side, or until browned. Meanwhile, cream together blue cheese, butter, Worcestershire, mustard, lemon juice, salt, and pepper. Then turn steak and broil on other side 20 to 25 min. Now cut steak near bone and check rareness. Broil longer if necessary. Spread cheese mixture on steak and broil 5 min. longer, or until topping is golden brown.

Serve at once on hot platter. Makes 6 to 8 servings.

MIXED GRILL

A mixed grill is a combination of meat, fish, or poultry with vegetables and maybe a fruit or two, broiled and served together. You'll find it a quick, easy, dish-saving main course. Check page references for broiling time.

1. *Choose 1 or 2 of these to broil:* Steak, p. 179; hamburgers, p. 190; franks, p. 245; ham, p. 215; bacon, p. 217; kidneys, p. 241; lamb chops, p. 223; liver, p. 235; fish, p. 303; sweetbreads, p. 238; lobster, p. 320; chicken, p. 263.

2. *Choose a vegetable or two, or a fruit, to broil:* Mushrooms, p. 406; sweet potatoes, p. 410; tomatoes, p. 417; apple rings, p. 438; fresh peaches, p. 438; canned peaches, pears, or pineapple, p. 438; bananas, p. 438.

3. Preheat broiler 10 min., or as manufacturer directs. Grease broiler rack; then start broiling the food that takes the longest; add rest of food so that all will be done at same time, ready to be arranged and served on heated platter.

PAN-BROILED STEAK

T-BONE, CLUB, SIRLOIN, OR RIB STEAK: Order steak cut ½″ to ¾″ thick. Rub skillet with just enough fat to keep meat from sticking; heat skillet. Rub steak with cut clove garlic if desired; place in skillet (do not add water or cover). Brown one side; turn; brown other side. Reduce heat; cook about 10 min. on each side, or until of desired doneness, turning steak to cook it evenly. Season as on p. 5.

Serve hot, with butter or margarine; Lemon Butter, p. 533; bottled thick meat sauce; barbecue sauce; or Tabasco.

MINUTE OR CUBE STEAKS: Minute steaks are thin steaks, ¼″ to ½″ thick, cut from the short loin or rib section.

Cube steaks are little, thin, not-so-tender steaks, such as round or chuck, that have been scored, "cubed," or "Frenched" by a special machine to cut the fibers and make the meat more tender.

Pan-broil either minute or cube steaks as above, cooking 2 to 3 min. on each side, or until done as you prefer them.

Season as on p. 5, and serve as above. Or to drippings left in skillet, add 2 tablesp. water for each steak. Heat, stirring, until rich in color. Pour over steaks. Nice between toasted, split rolls or toast slices, with or without thin sweet-onion slices.

CUBE STEAKS WITH HASTY-TASTY SAUCE

Buy 4 small cube steaks (about 1 lb.); see Minute or Cube Steaks, left. Sprinkle with 1 teasp. salt, ⅛ teasp. pepper, 3 tablesp. flour. In 3 tablesp. hot fat in skillet, brown steaks quickly on both sides. Remove.

To fat left in skillet, add 1 teasp. dry mustard; 1 teasp. Worcestershire; 3 tablesp. chili sauce or catchup; 2 tablesp. lemon juice. Heat till boiling, stirring. Spoon over steaks. Serve at once. Makes 4 servings.

MINUTE STEAKS AU POIVRE

4 cube steaks	margarine
Coarsely ground black pepper	2 tablesp. cognac
	¼ cup white wine
2 buttered split English muffins	½ teasp. salt
	2 tablesp. snipped parsley
4 tablesp. butter or	

1. Sprinkle steaks with pepper. Start toasting muffins.

2. In 3 tablesp. hot butter in skillet, quickly sear steaks on each side; then add cognac; light with match. When blaze burns out, blend in wine, 1 tablesp. butter, salt.

3. Arrange steaks at once on English muffins; spoon on sauce; sprinkle with parsley. Makes 4 servings.

Serve for luncheon or supper with zucchini and corn, Caesar salad, frozen raspberry sundae, and coffee.

MORE STEAK SPECIALS

BEEF STROGANOFF

3 tablesp. flour	1 10½-oz. can condensed chicken soup, undiluted
1½ teasp. salt	
¼ teasp. pepper	
1 lb. beef tenderloin, ¼″ thick	1 lb. sliced mushrooms
1 clove garlic, cut	1 cup commercial sour cream
¼ cup butter or margarine	Snipped parsley, chives, or dill
½ cup minced onions	
¼ cup water	

Combine flour, salt, pepper. Trim fat from

meat. Rub both sides of meat with garlic. With rim of saucer, pound flour mixture into both sides of meat. Cut meat into 1½″ x 1″ strips.

In hot butter, in Dutch oven or deep skillet, brown meat strips, turning them often. Add onions; sauté till golden. Add water; stir to dissolve brown bits in bottom of Dutch oven. Add soup, mushrooms; cook, uncovered, over low heat, stirring occasionally, until mixture is thick and meat is fork-tender — about 20 min.

Just before serving, stir in sour cream; heat, but do not boil. Sprinkle with parsley. Serve with hot fluffy rice or wild rice, boiled noodles, or mashed potatoes. Makes 4 to 6 servings.

BEEFSTEAK, PIZZA STYLE
(Bistecca alla Pizzaiola)

2 lb. sirloin or chuck steak, 1″ to 1¼″ thick	1 garlic clove, minced
1 1-lb. can whole tomatoes, undrained	1 tablesp. minced onion
½ teasp. dried orégano	¼ teasp. salt
1 teasp. snipped parsley	Dash pepper
	2 tablesp. olive or salad oil
	4 slices Mozzarella cheese

1. Start heating oven to 350°F. Arrange steak in 10″ x 6″ x 2″ baking dish. Mash tomatoes with spoon; spread evenly over steak. Sprinkle with orégano, parsley, garlic, onion, salt, pepper, oil. Bake, uncovered, 1¼ hr.
2. Top steak with cheese; bake ½ hr., or until tender. Makes 6 servings.

STEAKS TO BRAISE

Browning, then long slow simmering with a little water (braising), develops tenderness in less-tender beef steaks just as it does in pot roasts. See Instant Meat Tenderizer, p. 101.

To Buy and Store

Select a Cut:
ROUND STEAK (Fig. 10): This popular, oval-shaped steak with its small, round bone is usually sold as one cut; but sometimes it is cut into top round and bottom round.

Top Round is the more tender part of round steak. (If it's of top quality it may even be pan-broiled.) A good layer of fat, and streaks of fat in the lean, indicate better-quality meat. A 1″-thick steak weighs 2 to 3 lb.

Bottom Round is the less tender part of round steak. It's usually cut ½″ thick, though it may be cut thicker for Swiss steak. It may also be cut into smaller steaks, or cubed. A ½″-thick steak weighs about 12 oz.

RUMP STEAK: This steak, from a rump pot roast, p. 183, is usually boned. A ½″-thick steak weighs 5 to 6 oz.

FLANK STEAK: See Flank Steak, p. 182.

SIRLOIN-TIP STEAK: This steak, from a sirloin-tip roast, is lean and boneless. A ½″-thick steak weighs 5 to 6 oz.

CHUCK STEAK: This steak is cut from a chuck pot roast, p. 183, and may have a round bone or a blade bone or be boneless. A ½″-thick steak weighs 8 to 12 oz.

Amount to Buy: Allow ¼ to ⅓ lb. boned steak per serving.

To Store: Store as in To Store Meat, p. 172.

BRAISED STEAK

Season one of steaks to braise above, as on p. 5; dip into flour to coat lightly. In 1 or 2 tablesp. hot fat or meat drippings, in skillet, brown steak *well* on both sides, turning with tongs — about 15 to 20 min.

Then add ½ to 1 cup water, tomato juice, or seasoned diluted vinegar, the amount depending on size of steak. Cook slowly, on top of range, or in 350°F. oven, covered, until steak is fork-tender — 45 min. to 2 or 3 hr., depending on thickness of steak. Replenish water if necessary. When done, remove steak to heated platter.

Serve with gravy from pan. Or make more gravy by adding water and beef-bouillon cube (or canned bouillon) to gravy in pan. Thicken as on p. 6; season if needed. Nice with boiled or mashed potatoes and colorful vegetables.

To Vary: With water, add sliced onion or celery, diced fresh or canned tomatoes, chili sauce, chili powder, or horse-radish. Or during last half hour of cooking, add a few sliced carrots, potatoes, turnips, etc.

SWISS STEAK

1½ lb. round or rump steak, 1½″ thick	3 large onions, thinly sliced
2 tablesp. flour	1 stalk celery, diced
1 teasp. salt	1 clove garlic, minced
⅛ teasp. pepper	1 tablesp. bottled thick meat sauce
2 tablesp. salad oil or fat	¼ cup light or dark raisins (optional)
1½ cups canned tomatoes	

1. Trim excess fat from meat. Combine flour, salt, pepper. Lay meat on board; sprinkle with half of flour mixture; with rim of saucer, pound in mixture. Turn meat; repeat until all flour is used.

2. In hot oil in heavy skillet or Dutch oven over medium heat, brown meat *well* on both sides — about 15 to 20 min.

3. Add rest of ingredients. Stir well. Simmer, covered, about 2 to 2½ hr., or until meat is fork-tender. Skim off fat if necessary.

Serve on heated platter, with sauce over and around meat. Nice with mashed potatoes, boiled noodles, or hot fluffy rice, etc. Makes 4 servings.

To Vary: Substitute canned tomato sauce or vegetable-juice cocktail for tomatoes; thicken sauce if desired; season to taste.

Or substitute 1½ cups boiling water, 2 tablesp. catchup, and ½ teasp. prepared mustard for tomatoes; thicken sauce if desired.

Or during last half hour of cooking, add diced carrots or celery, or canned peas or corn.
P.S. Swiss steak is nice reheated next day.

FLANK STEAK

This thin, boneless, less-tender steak from the beef flank (Fig. 11) is about 12″ to 14″ long, 4″ to 6″ wide, and 1″ thick; it weighs 1 to 2 lb.

Top-quality flank steak has a good portion of fat and is fine for London Broil, below. Braise leaner, low-quality flank steak as in Braised Steak, p. 181. See Instant Meat Tenderizer, p. 101.

LONDON BROIL

Order a 2- to 2½-lb. aged, top-quality flank steak; it *must* be tender. Have excess fat and membrane trimmed, and surface scored on both sides.

Preheat broiler 10 min., or as manufacturer directs. Arrange scored flank steak on greased broiler rack. If desired, rub with cut clove garlic. Brush with salad oil.

Place steak 1½″ to 2″ below heat; broil just 5 min. on each side. Then place on heated platter. Season as on p. 5; top with butter or margarine. Cut, diagonally across grain, into *very thin slices*. Pass mushroom sauce. Nice, too, for hot grilled beef sandwiches.

BLUE-CHEESE TOPPED: Refrigerate flank steak 8 to 24 hr. in mixture of 1 cup salad oil, 2 tablesp. vinegar, 1 mashed clove garlic, turning steak 2 or 3 times. Remove from oil; then broil as above. During last few minutes, spread with some blue-cheese spread.

CAPER-BUTTERED STEAK SANDWICHES: Melt ½ cup butter or margarine; add 4 teasp. vinegar, 2 tablesp. capers, and 2 tablesp. snipped parsley. Remove crust from 15 thin bread slices; toast on both sides; halve toast. For each serving spoon some of the caper-butter sauce over 5 or 6 toast halves. Top with slices of broiled flank steak. Makes 5 or 6 servings.

ITALIAN-STYLE FLANK STEAK

1 2-lb. flank steak	2 beef-bouillon cubes; or 2 teasp. meat-extract paste
2 tablesp. salad or olive oil	
1 clove garlic	1 cup water
1 small lemon, thinly sliced	1 tablesp. butter or margarine
4 whole cloves	1 tablesp. flour

Order steak scored at ¼″ intervals, ⅛″ deep, on both sides. Cut into 2 pieces so it fits into Dutch oven. In hot oil, in Dutch oven, sauté steak till golden-brown on both sides; add garlic.

Arrange lemon slices between and on top of steak pieces. Add cloves and bouillon cubes, dissolved in water. Simmer, covered, about 2 hr., or until fork-tender. Remove steak and lemon slices to platter. Drain off pan juices — about 1 cup. Melt butter in Dutch oven; stir in flour till smooth. Slowly stir in pan juices. Simmer, stirring, till thickened; serve with steak. Nice with buttered broad noodles. Makes 6 servings.

Fisherman's Chowder, p. 168

BRAISED, STUFFED FLANK STEAK

1 1½-lb. flank steak	1 tablesp. fat or salad
2 cups fresh bread	oil
crumbs	1 cup hot water
¼ cup minced onion	½ teasp. whole black
1 tablesp. snipped	peppers
parsley	1 teasp. garlic wine
½ teasp. salt	vinegar (optional)
⅛ teasp. pepper	1 cup hot water
½ teasp. celery salt	1 beef-bouillon cube
½ teasp. dried sage	¼ cup flour
1 tablesp. butter or	6 tablesp. cold water
margarine	

Have meatman score one side of steak in diamond pattern. Combine crumbs, onion, parsley, salt, pepper, celery salt, sage; arrange on unscored side of steak, patting it till it nearly reaches edges. Dot with butter. Roll up, jelly-roll-fashion; secure with skewers or string.

In hot fat in Dutch oven, brown steak *well* on both sides — about 15 to 20 min. Add 1 cup hot water, whole peppers; sprinkle with vinegar. Simmer, covered, 2 hr., or until fork-tender. Remove peppers; arrange steak on heated platter; remove skewers.

Into liquid in Dutch oven, stir 1 cup hot water and bouillon cube, then flour mixed with cold water to form smooth paste. Cook until thickened. Season if needed. Makes 6 servings.

GINGER BEEF

2 onions	grain, into thin
3 cloves garlic	slices or 2″ x ½″
1½ teasp. turmeric	strips
¼ teasp. dried chili	3 tablesp. peanut or
peppers (optional)	salad oil
5 teasp. powdered gin-	1 1-lb.-3-oz. can to-
ger (or 2″ piece	matoes
fresh ginger,	1 10½-oz. can con-
chopped)	densed onion soup,
1½ teasp. salt	undiluted
1¼ lb. flank steak, cut	4 to 6 cups hot cooked
diagonally across	rice
	Pickled watermelon

1. In chopping bowl, combine onions, garlic, turmeric, chili peppers, ginger, and salt; chop fine.
2. Add flank steak slices or strips and toss together. To season, let stand in refrigerator from 15 min. to 3 hr., depending upon your schedule.
3. Then, in Dutch oven, heat oil. Add flank steak and onion mixture; brown lightly. Add

tomatoes; then cook, uncovered, over high heat, 10 min.
4. Add soup; cover and simmer 1 hr., if steak is sliced, or 1½ to 2 hr. if it's in strips, or until steak is tender.
5. *To serve:* Measure hot rice into oval vegetable dish; place cookie sheet on top of it; press down well. Then remove cookie sheet and unmold rice in center of oval platter. Over rice, spoon a few pieces of the steak, then spoon rest of mixture around it. Garnish at either end with pickled watermelon. Makes 4 or 5 servings.

POT ROASTS OF BEEF

Browning, then long, slow simmering with a little water (braising), with or without vegetables, turns less tender cuts of beef into fork-tender pot roasts of wonderful flavor. See Instant Meat Tenderizer, p. 101.

To Buy and Store

You don't need to buy top-quality beef, but a piece with a good fat covering and streaks of fat through the lean will be juicier than a lean cut. Here are 5 fine cuts to choose from:

Select a Cut:

BONED RUMP POT ROAST (Fig. 4): An excellent meaty pot roast cut from the hip. (If bone is left in, roast is too difficult to carve.) Weighs 4 to 5 lb.

SIRLOIN-TIP POT ROAST (Fig 7): A good meaty pot roast from side of the round; it may lack fat covering. Have it boned, rolled, and tied. Weighs 4 to 8 lb.

ARM (CHUCK) POT ROAST (Fig. 8): A fine meaty pot roast from the chuck, with small round bone. A ½″-thick piece weighs 3 to 4 lb.

THREE-IN-ONE ARM (CHUCK) POT ROAST:
1. From its round end, cut off a boneless piece to cube for stew.
2. Cut a piece from the center for a small one-meal pot roast.
3. Split remaining piece to make two attractive Swiss steaks to braise.

BLADE (CHUCK) POT ROAST (Fig. 9): A moderate-priced pot roast from the chuck. Has section of blade bone, and 2 or 3 smaller bones. A 1½″-thick piece weighs 3 to 4 lb. May be boned and sold as boned pot roast.

Amount to Buy: Allow ⅓ lb. bone-in pot roast per serving, ¼ lb. boned roast per serving. Plan on leftovers.

To Store: Store as in To Store Meat, p. 172.

POT ROAST

3 tablesp. fat or salad oil	¼ teasp. pepper
	1 tablesp. water
4- to 5-lb. boned rump pot roast*	1 small onion, sliced
2 teasp. salt	Pinch dill seeds

1. In hot fat in Dutch oven or heavy kettle over medium heat, brown meat *well* on all sides, turning it as it browns. Pour off fat drippings, season with salt and pepper. This may take 15 to 20 min.
2. Add water, onion, dill seeds. Cover tightly; simmer, *don't boil,* over low heat, turning occasionally to cook it evenly throughout, about 4 to 4½ hr.,* or until fork-tender. If needed, add a few tablespoonfuls of hot water during cooking.
3. When meat is done, remove it to heated platter; keep warm.
4. Make gravy as follows: Skim fat from broth in Dutch oven. To broth, add water to make 2 or 3 cups liquid. Heat; thicken as on p. 6; season if needed.

To serve: Let host carve pot roast; or serve it sliced. Pass gravy in bowl. Mashed or boiled potatoes; Potato Pancakes, p. 414; or Poppy or Caraway Noodles, p. 378, are especially nice with pot roast. Pass Worcestershire, horseradish, prepared mustard, Tabasco, or chili sauce. Serves a family of 4 for 2 meals.

*If you use a 3-lb. bone-in pot roast, 2″ thick, simmer about 2½ to 3 hr. If you use a 5-lb. bone-in pot roast, 3″ thick, simmer about 3½ to 4 hr.

OVEN STYLE: Use Dutch oven. Increase water to 1 cup. Bake, covered, at 350°F., adding water, if needed, to keep about ½″ liquid in Dutch oven.

WITH CHILI SAUCE: About 45 min. before pot roast is done, add 3 sliced medium onions, 1¼ cups chili sauce, and ½ cup chopped dill pickles. Don't thicken broth in kettle; just skim off fat; thin broth with a little water if it seems too thick. Season.

CURRY: Add 3½ teasp. curry powder and ½ teasp. sugar with salt and pepper in step 1.

WITH VEGETABLES: About 50 min. before meat is done, add 2 cups white onions, 8 pared small carrots, and 6 to 8 pared small potatoes. Sprinkle with 1 teasp. salt; cook, covered, until vegetables are tender-crisp. Or substitute 1 lb. green beans for onions, adding them ½ hr. before vegetables are done. Serve vegetables around pot roast.

SPICY: About 45 min. before meat is done, add 1 minced clove garlic; 1 sliced, pared carrot; a few sprigs parsley; 8 whole black peppers; ¼ teasp. ginger; 1 bay leaf; 3 whole cloves; ⅛ teasp. allspice; ¼ cup vinegar. Simmer, covered, 45 min., or until tender. Remove meat; strain liquid; make gravy.

WITH WINE: After browning meat in step 1, add 1 minced clove garlic, pinch dried thyme, 1 bay leaf, ¼ cup red wine. When making gravy, substitute ½ cup red wine for ½ cup water.

To Use Leftover Pot Roast: See p. 252.

SAUERBRATEN

1½ cups vinegar	3½ teasp. salt
½ cup red wine	4 lb. boned rump or chuck pot roast
1 cup water	2 tablesp. flour
2 tablesp. sugar	Speck pepper
1 teasp. whole black peppers	¼ cup fat
4 bay leaves	⅓ cup gingersnap crumbs
4 onions, sliced	½ cup commercial sour cream*
18 whole cloves	Salt and pepper
1½ teasp. mustard seeds	

Two to four days before serving: In large bowl, make this marinade: Combine vinegar, wine, water, sugar, ½ teasp. whole peppers, bay leaves, 3 onions, 12 cloves, 1 teasp. mustard seeds, and 2 teasp. salt. Set meat in marinade; refrigerate, covered, 2 to 4 days, turning meat each day. (If you like a sour sauerbraten, let meat stand 4 days.)

On the day: Remove meat, reserving marinade; dry meat *well* on paper towels. Combine flour, 1½ teasp. salt, speck pepper; use to coat meat on all sides. In hot fat in Dutch oven, brown meat well on all sides — about 15 to 20 min. Add ¾ cup reserved marinade, 1 sliced onion, ½ teasp. mustard seeds, 6 cloves, ½ teasp. whole peppers. Simmer, covered, about 3½ to 4 hr., or until meat is fork-tender, adding ¼ cup marinade if needed.

Remove meat to hot platter, slicing it first if desired; keep warm. Strain drippings from Dutch oven into glass measuring cup; let stand 2 min. to settle. Pour off all except bottom ⅓ cup drippings; return these to Dutch oven. Stir in crumbs. Slowly stir in 2 cups strained, reserved marinade (add water if necessary). Cook, stirring, until thickened.

Stir in sour cream; heat, *but do not boil.* Season if necessary. Spoon some gravy over meat; pass rest. Makes 8 to 10 servings.
Or use ½ 3-oz. pkg. cream cheese, beaten smooth with ⅓ cup milk.

MOTHER'S POT ROAST WITH VEGETABLES

5- to 6-lb. boned rump pot roast	⅛ teasp. orégano
⅓ cup all-purpose flour	3 tablesp. wine vinegar
2 tablesp. fat	1 medium onion, sliced
Monosodium glutamate	2 cups small whole white onions
2 teasp. salt	8 small carrots, pared
⅛ teasp. pepper	3 tablesp. flour
Pinch celery seeds	½ cup water

1. On wax paper, roll beef in ⅓ cup flour to coat all sides. In hot fat, in Dutch oven, over medium heat, brown beef well on all sides, turning it as it browns and sprinkling well with monosodium glutamate and salt and pepper. This may take 15 to 20 min.
2. Add celery seeds, orégano, vinegar, 1 sliced onion. Cover tightly; simmer over low heat, turning occasionally, about 3½ hr.
3. Now add 2 cups small onions and carrots, tucking them into gravy around beef. Cover; simmer 1 hr., or until beef is fork-tender and vegetables are done. Remove beef and vegetables to heated platter; keep warm.
4. If desired, pass gravy made as follows: Skim fat from broth in Dutch oven. To broth, add enough water to make 2½ cups liquid. In small bowl, combine 3 tablesp. flour with ½ cup water; stir into liquid. Cook until thickened. Season to taste. Makes 8 to 10 servings.

BEEF A LA MODE

4 lb. round, larded with strips of pork fat	¼ teasp. dried thyme
1 cup red wine	2 celery tops, finely cut up
Water	3 cloves garlic, cut in half
Salt	¼ cup brandy or water
Whole black peppers	4 bouillon cubes
1 to 2 tablesp. fat	1½ to 2 lb. veal bones
2 cups strained marinating liquid	3 large carrots, pared
2 onions, sliced	1 tablesp. butter or margarine
1 carrot, pared, diced	12 small white onions
2 bay leaves	

In advance: Place beef in bowl. Add wine, 1 cup water, 1 teasp. salt, and ½ teasp. peppers. Cover; store in refrigerator 8 to 12 hr., turning once.
About 4 hr. before serving: Remove beef from marinade. Pat dry. In large Dutch oven, or deep kettle, sauté beef in fat until brown on all sides. Add marinade, 2 sliced onions, 1 carrot, bay leaves, thyme, ¼ teasp. salt, ¼ teasp. whole black peppers, celery tops, garlic, 1¾ cups water, brandy, and bouillon cubes; tuck bones around meat. Cover tightly; simmer slowly for 4 hr., or until a fork pierces beef easily. Meanwhile, cut 3 pared carrots in 1" diagonal pieces. Then, in butter, in covered skillet, sauté them with 12 onions, turning frequently, till brown — about 15 min. Remove tender meat from Dutch oven; discard bones; strain juices into bowl; let stand until fat rises; pour off fat. Place meat in Dutch oven with strained juices, carrots, and onions. Cook, covered, 15 min., or until vegetables are tender,
To serve: Arrange meat in center of large heated platter; ring with vegetables; pass gravy, seasoned if needed. Makes 6 servings with leftovers. See Beef à la Mode in Aspic, p. 253.

BEEF SHORT RIBS

To Buy Beef Short Ribs

Beef short ribs (Fig. 2) are like baby pot roasts. They are cut off the ends of standing rib roasts, then into 2" squares. Each square is streaked with lean meat and fat, and has a piece of rib bone on one side; each piece weighs 4 to 6 oz.

Amount to Buy: Allow 1 or 2 pieces per serving.

To Store: Store as in To Store Meat, p. 172.

BARBECUED SHORT RIBS I

Order 3 lb. short ribs, cut into 2″ squares. Brush with 1 tablesp. bottled sauce for gravy. Brown well in 2 tablesp. fat in Dutch oven; remove.

In same fat, sauté 1 clove garlic, minced, with ½ cup each minced onions and celery, 2 min. Stir in 2 tablesp. cornstarch, 1 8-oz. can tomato sauce, ½ cup water, 1 teasp. salt, ⅛ teasp. each pepper and ground allspice, 1 tablesp. each prepared mustard and vinegar; then add meat. Simmer, covered, 1½ to 2 hr., or until fork-tender. Makes 4 servings.

BARBECUED SHORT RIBS II

3 lb. short ribs, cut into 3″ pieces	1 tablesp. brown sugar
1½ to 2 teasp. salt	1 tablesp. Worcestershire
½ cup minced onions	1 teasp. paprika
½ cup catchup	1 teasp. dry or prepared mustard
½ cup water	
¼ cup wine vinegar	

In pressure cooker, brown ribs on all sides, sprinkling with salt. Drain off most of fat. Combine onions with rest of ingredients; pour over meat. Cook at 15 lb. pressure 25 to 30 min., or as manufacturer directs. Reduce pressure immediately. Makes 4 servings.

OUTDOORS: See Barbecued Short Ribs, p. 734.

SWEDISH BRAISED SHORT RIBS

1 tablesp. butter or margarine	2 teasp. sugar
3 lb. short ribs (cut into 4 serving pieces)	½ teasp. whole allspice
	2 bay leaves
	1 cup hot water
1 medium onion, sliced	¼ cup cold water
1 teasp. salt	1 tablesp. flour
¼ teasp. white pepper	2 tablesp. heavy cream

Heat Dutch oven until very hot; add butter, then meat. Cook over high heat until meat is very well browned on all sides. Add onion; with fork, push down into fat around meat; cook a minute or so, or until browned. Now add salt, pepper, 1 teasp. sugar, allspice, bay leaves, hot water. Simmer, covered, 1½ to 2 hr., or until fork-tender.

Remove meat to heated platter and keep hot. Skim about ¼ cup fat from liquid in Dutch oven. Stir cold water into flour; slowly add, stirring, to liquid; cook until thickened. Stir in cream and 1 teasp. sugar; bring to boil once; pour over meat; serve at once.

Especially nice with buttered carrots, green beans, and dill potatoes (make parsley potatoes, adding snipped fresh dill instead of parsley). Makes 4 servings.

BEEF STEWS, CURRIES, MEAT PIES, ETC.

A little care in cooking, and a dash of ingenuity in the sauce or seasoning, will bring out any thrifty meat's flavor and succulent tenderness. See Instant Meat Tenderizer, p. 101.

If you would win a reputation as a cook, serve one of our recipes below.

To Buy and Store Beef for Stews, etc.

Select a Cut: You may be able to buy "stew beef" in 1″ to 2″ pieces of boned meat, cut from less-tender, but flavorful, cuts of beef. But be sure the beef is bright red, with white fat.

Or you may prefer to buy a piece of beef you can identify, such as one of those below, and cut it up yourself.

CHUCK: This cut from the shoulder makes a fine stew. Costs more than some other cuts.

BOTTOM ROUND: This less-tender part of the round is boneless, lean, and fine-flavored.

NECK MEAT: This may be sold as boned or bone-in stew meat. It needs long cooking to become tender.

SHANK MEAT: This lean, flavorful meat has considerable connective tissue. It requires long cooking for tenderness. Some cuts may contain too much bone for a good stew.

FLANK, PLATE, FRESH BRISKET: Order these low-priced cuts, boned. Avoid pieces that are too fatty.

Amount to Buy: Allow 1 lb. boned beef for 4 to 6 servings.

To Store: Store as in To Store Meat, p. 172.

OVEN BEEF STEW

2 lb. boned chuck or bottom round, in 2″ cubes
¼ cup flour
3 tablesp. salad oil
1 teasp. monosodium glutamate
1 teasp. salt
3 tablesp. prepared mustard
2½ cups tomato juice or water
12 small white onions
12 pared small carrots, quartered lengthwise
1 10-oz. pkg. frozen whole-kernel corn, thawed just enough to separate

Start heating oven to 350°F. Sprinkle meat with flour. Reserve leftover flour. In hot oil, in skillet, brown meat well on all sides — 15 to 20 min. Remove meat to 3-qt. casserole.

Into oil, stir monosodium glutamate, salt, mustard, and any remaining flour. Slowly add tomato juice, stirring constantly; then pour over meat. Bake, covered, 1 hr. Add onions and carrots. Bake, covered, 45 min. Add corn. Bake, covered, 15 min., or until vegetables are tender. Before serving, stir stew with fork to bring meat chunks to top. Makes 6 servings.

To Vary: Add 12 pared small potatoes with carrots; substitute peas for corn.

LAMB STEW: For beef, substitute 2 lb. boned lamb shoulder, with as much fat trimmed off as possible. Increase flour to 5 tablesp. Before stirring stew to serve it, spoon off any fat that may have risen to surface during cooking.

VEAL STEW: Substitute 2 lb. boned veal shoulder for beef, 1 to 1½ cups white wine for 1 to 1½ cups tomato juice, ½ lb. mushrooms for corn. Use 5 tablesp. flour.

BEEF CURRY DELICIOUS

1 tablesp. flour
1⅛ teasp. salt
⅛ teasp. pepper
1 lb. round, cut into ¾″ cubes
¼ cup fat or salad oil
2 cups sliced onions
½ clove garlic, minced
1 teasp. curry powder
1 beef-bouillon cube
1 cup boiling water
½ cup tomato juice

Combine flour, salt, pepper; roll meat in flour mixture. In 2 tablesp. hot fat, in skillet or Dutch oven, brown meat well on all sides. Add rest of fat, onions, garlic; sauté until light brown. Sprinkle with curry powder; add bouillon cube, water.

Simmer, covered, 1¼ hr., or till meat is fork-tender. Add tomato juice; reheat.

Serve on hot fluffy rice, or with mashed or boiled potatoes. Pass Curry Accompaniments, p. 330. Makes 4 servings.

To Do Ahead: Day before or early in day, prepare and cook curry till tender as at left. Refrigerate. At serving time, add tomato juice; reheat; serve as above.

LAMB CURRY OR VEAL CURRY: For beef, substitute boned lamb or veal shoulder or breast.

DANISH GOULASH

1 lb. round, ¼″ thick
3 tablesp. salad oil
Speck pepper
¾ cup very thinly sliced onions
2 teasp. salt
2½ cups cold water
1 tablesp. brown sugar
3 small bay leaves
3 tablesp. flour
5 tablesp. cold water

Cut meat into ¼″ cubes; brown well in hot oil with pepper. Add onions; stir until light brown. Add salt, 2½ cups water, sugar, bay leaves. Simmer, covered, 1¼ hr., or until fork-tender. Remove bay leaves. Then stir in flour mixed with 5 tablesp. water till smooth. Cook until smooth and thickened.

Serve over boiled noodles or rice or Mashed Potatoes à la Phyfe, p. 412. Makes 4 servings.

STEW A LA MODE
(Porkolt à la Gundel)

1 lb. beef tenderloin, ½″ thick
3 tablesp. flour
2 teasp. salt
½ teasp. dried marjoram
¼ teasp. pepper
¼ teasp. monosodium glutamate
½ lb. calf liver, ½″ thick
¼ cup butter or margarine
3 medium onions, thinly sliced
¾ cup water
½ cup Burgundy wine
1 9-oz. pkg. frozen cut green beans
1 10-oz. pkg. frozen green peas

About 45 min. before serving:
1. Trim fat from tenderloin. Combine flour, salt, marjoram, pepper, monosodium glutamate. With rim of saucer, pound this flour mixture into both sides of beef; use rest of flour mixture to coat liver. Then cut both pieces of meat into strips 2″ x 1″.
2. In hot butter, in large skillet, sauté onions until golden, remove and reserve.
3. In same butter, brown tenderloin and liver strips, turning them often. Add onions, water,

wine. Simmer, uncovered, over low heat, stirring occasionally, until mixture is slightly thickened and meat is fork-tender, about 15 min.

4. Meanwhile, cook beans and peas 1 min. less than package labels direct; drain. Just before serving, gently stir them into stew. Serve with hot buttered noodles and crisp salad. Makes 4 to 6 servings.

HUNGARIAN GOULASH

3 tablesp. butter or margarine	1½ lb. boned chuck, rump, or round, cut into 1″ cubes
3 cups thinly sliced onions	4½ teasp. paprika
2¼ teasp. salt	About 3 cups water
1½ teasp. paprika	

In hot butter in Dutch oven or deep kettle, sauté onions with salt until golden. Stir in well 1½ teasp. paprika, meat; simmer, covered, 1 hr. Add 4½ teasp. paprika and enough water to just cover meat. Simmer, covered, 1 hr., or until meat is fork-tender, adding more water toward end of cooking time if you want extra gravy.

Serve with boiled noodles; Poppy or Caraway Noodles, p. 378; mashed potatoes; or hot fluffy rice. Makes 4 or 5 servings.

To Vary: During last half hour of cooking, add 4 quartered, pared medium potatoes, with a little water if needed. Omit noodles, etc.

BEEF BIRDS WITH OLIVE GRAVY

1 lb. round steak, ½″ thick	cooked rice
1 teasp. salt	¼ cup minced onion
¼ teasp. garlic salt	¼ cup thinly sliced celery
¼ teasp. celery salt	½ cup all-purpose flour
¼ teasp. pepper	1 teasp. paprika
2 bouillon cubes; or 2 teasp. meat-extract paste	5 tablesp. fat or salad oil
2 cups hot water	⅓ cup chopped ripe olives
2 cups fresh bread crumbs; or 1 cup	

Early in day: With edge of heavy plate, pound both sides of meat. Cut meat into 3″ squares; sprinkle with ½ teasp. salt, garlic and celery salts, and pepper; pound again. Dissolve bouillon cubes in hot water. Mix bread or rice with onion and celery; add just enough bouillon to moisten slightly. Place about 2 tablesp. stuffing on each meat square; roll up; tie or skewer; refrigerate rolls, bouillon also.

About 1¾ hr. before dinner: Combine flour, ½ teasp. salt, paprika; use to coat stuffed meat rolls. Brown rolls in hot fat in Dutch oven or electric combination fryer-casserole; add bouillon. Cook slowly, covered, about 1½ hr., or until meat is very tender. (Add more water, if needed, so there will be about 1 cup thickened gravy left.) Last 5 min., stir in olives. Serve birds with gravy. Makes 4 servings.

CANTON SKILLET BEEF

¼ cup salad oil or fat	1 tablesp. Worcestershire
1 cup sliced onions	1 tablesp. soy sauce
2 green peppers, cut in strips	1 teasp. vinegar
1 lb. chuck, cut in 1″ chunks	1½ teasp. salt
1 1-lb.-4-oz. can apple slices, with ¼ cup their liquid	¼ teasp. pepper
	½ teasp. monosodium glutamate
1 cup water	Raisin Rice, p. 371

1. *About 2 hr. before supper:* In hot oil in large skillet, sauté onions and green peppers until tender. Add chuck; cook until it loses its red color.

2. Stir in apples, water, Worcestershire, soy sauce, vinegar, salt, pepper, monosodium glutamate; stirring occasionally, simmer, covered, 1½ hr., or until meat is tender.

3. *To serve:* Arrange meat mixture and rice in twin serving dishes. Nice for supper with big tossed salad and cheese biscuits. Makes 4 servings.

BOILED BEEF WITH HORSE-RADISH SAUCE

3 qt. boiling water	2 teasp. salt
1 bay leaf	4 lb. fresh beef brisket
6 whole cloves	Horse-radish Sauce I or II, p. 532; or Caper Butter Sauce, p. 527
2 cloves garlic	
1 small onion	
2 stalks celery	
2 tablesp. vinegar	
2 tablesp. sugar	

In large kettle or Dutch oven, combine all ingredients except meat and sauce; simmer, covered, 30 min. Add meat; simmer, covered, 3½ to 4 hr., or until fork-tender, replenishing water if needed. When meat is done, remove; slice; arrange on heated platter. Pass sauce. Serve with boiled new potatoes. Makes 6 servings, with leftovers.

BOEUF BOURGUIGNON I

5 lb. chuck, trimmed of all fat, in 2″ cubes
All-purpose flour
Butter or margarine
¼ teasp. pepper
¼ cup cognac
1 2¼-oz. bottle meat-extract paste
½ lb. sliced bacon, diced
4 garlic cloves, minced
2 carrots, coarsely chopped

2 leeks, coarsely chopped
2 cups coarsely chopped onions
Snipped parsley
2 bay leaves
1 teasp. dried thyme
1½ cups Burgundy
1 cup sweet sherry
2 lb. small white onions
Sugar
2 lb. fresh mushrooms
2 teasp. lemon juice

Day before:

1. Roll beef cubes in ⅓ cup flour. In ¼ cup hot butter in Dutch oven, brown meat *very well* on all sides; sprinkle with pepper; pour on cognac; then ignite with a match. When flame dies out, stir in meat-extract paste.

2. Start heating oven to 350°F. To beef, add bacon, garlic, carrots, leeks, chopped onions, 1 tablesp. snipped parsley, bay leaves, thyme, 1 cup Burgundy, sherry. Bake, covered, 2 to 2½ hr., or till beef is fork-tender.

3. When meat is fork-tender, remove from Dutch oven. Then put all vegetables and liquid through a coarse strainer or food mill, mashing vegetables as you strain. Return strained liquid and meat to Dutch oven; refrigerate.

About 45 min. before serving:

1. Start reheating meat mixture in Dutch oven over low heat on top of range. Now, in 2 tablesp. hot butter in skillet, brown whole onions well on all sides; add 1 teasp. sugar, ½ cup Burgundy; cook, covered, 15 to 20 min., or till onions are tender, adding ¼ cup water if needed; add to meat, with liquid and 1 tablesp. sugar.

2. In 2 tablesp. butter in skillet, sauté half of mushroom caps till golden on one side; sprinkle with 1 teasp. lemon juice; turn to brown other side; add to meat mixture. Repeat, sautéing rest of mushrooms; keep warm, uncovered.

To serve: Pour meat mixture from Dutch oven into 3-qt. casserole or serving dish; garnish with remaining mushroom caps and snipped parsley. Makes 12 servings.

HAMBURGER
(ground beef)

To Buy

Ready-ground Hamburger: Buy freshly ground beef. It usually comes in varying proportions of fat and is often so identified; all is ground twice.

REGULAR GROUND BEEF contains from 20 to 25 per cent fat and is likely to be the lowest in price.

GROUND CHUCK contains from 10 to 20 per cent fat and is intermediate in price.

GROUND ROUND OR LEAN GROUND BEEF contains less than 10 per cent fat.

Ground-to-Order Beef: Buy boned chuck or boneless meat for stew, then have it ground. If you buy round, be sure to have 2 oz. suet ground with each 1 lb. round. When any of our recipes call for 1 lb. chuck (or any other meat), ground, we mean for you to buy 1 lb. boned meat, then have it ground.

Number of Grindings: Hamburger becomes more compact the more grindings it gets. This is fine for meat loaves, meat balls, etc. But if you are ordering hamburger for extra-nice, juicy, tender patties, ask meatman to grind meat coarsely — and only once.

Amount to Buy: A pound of hamburger makes 4 good servings. When other ingredients such as rice, spaghetti, or vegetables are added, it may make 5 servings. A meat loaf made with 2 lb. hamburger as the base will probably serve 4 persons for 2 meals.

To Store:

TO USE SAME OR NEXT DAY: Wrap loosely in wax paper, with ends open; refrigerate at once. Be sure to use within 2 days.

TO USE WITHIN A WEEK: Shape into patties; stack between squares of wax paper; wrap tightly in 2 thicknesses of wax paper or foil.

Store in frozen-food compartment or special ice-cube tray, p. 610, of conventional refrigerator. Be sure to use within 7 days.

IF YOU HAVE A HOME FREEZER OR REFRIGERATOR-FREEZER COMBINATION: Wrap patties in freezer-wrapping material; store at 0°F. in freezer. Use within 2 or 3 months.

OUR BEST-EVER HAMBURGERS

1 lb. chuck, ground once	2 tablesp. minced onion
1 teasp. salt	¼ teasp. monosodium glutamate
¼ teasp. pepper	

Toss meat lightly with salt, pepper, onion, monosodium glutamate. (Some cooks prefer to shape unseasoned chuck into patties, then to sprinkle seasonings onto both sides of patties before cooking. This eliminates too much handling.)

With help of kitchen fork, and using as little pressure as possible, divide meat; gently shape and flatten *loosely* into 4 thick patties, 3½″ x ¾″, or 8 thin patties, 3″ x ¼″. Cook in one of these 3 ways:

SKILLET-COOKED: Heat 2 tablesp. fat or salad oil in skillet or on griddle. Cook patties until done as your family likes.

If patties are *thick*, we allow about 4 to 8 min. over medium heat, turning once.

If patties are *thin*, we allow about 2 to 6 min., turning once. Don't flatten or "spank" patties with spatula — it presses out juices.

PAN-BROILED: Heat heavy skillet or griddle till sizzling hot. If you're afraid meat will stick, rub skillet *lightly* with fat or salad oil; or sprinkle with salt. Brown patties on both sides; then cook over medium heat for about same time periods as in Skillet-Cooked.

OVEN-BROILED: Preheat broiler 10 min., or as manufacturer directs. Arrange thick patties on cold broiler rack. (If you can, line broiler pan under grid with foil, with corners turned under, to catch drippings and save dish-washing.)

Broil patties about 3″ from heat, turning once, until done as your family likes. We allow about 8 to 12 min., turning once.

After turning patties, you may top them with one of the following; then complete broiling.

1. Cheese slice, a little prepared mustard
2. Catchup or chili, soy, or barbecue sauce
3. Grated sharp cheese or ¼ cup crumbled Danish blue cheese, mashed with ¼ cup soft butter or margarine, ½ teasp. dry mustard, 1 teasp. salt, 2 teasp. Worcestershire

QUICK: Well-known brands of frozen hamburgers or flaked, shaped "beef steaks" come as 2-oz. or 3-oz. packaged patties. Cook as label directs; vary as above. Especially nice for outdoor cooking.

DANISH BURGERS

¼ lb. Danish blue cheese	Few drops Worcestershire
⅓ cup butter or margarine	6 Best-Ever Hamburger patties, at left
1½ tablesp. prepared mustard	6 split hamburger buns
Bit of grated garlic or garlic salt	

Preheat broiler 10 min., or as manufacturer directs. Meanwhile, in small bowl, blend cheese with butter, mustard, garlic, and Worcestershire until almost smooth; set aside. In skillet, sauté hamburger patties until done. In broiler, toast cut side of split hamburger buns. Quickly spread buns with cheese mixture. Place hamburger between 2 bun halves. Makes 6 servings.

HAMBURGER SPREAD-ONS

Cook Our Best-Ever Hamburgers, left, your favorite way. Whisk them to heated platter; spread with one of these wonderful butter spreads, made while patties cook.

To 2 tablesp. melted butter or margarine, add one of these:

2 tablesp. minced stuffed or ripe olives
2 tablesp. catchup, prepared mustard, or capers
2 tablesp. crumbled Danish blue cheese or grated sharp cheese. Add chili sauce if you wish
2 tablesp. snipped chives, scallions, or onions
2 tablesp. chili sauce, 1 teasp. prepared mustard, pinch chili powder
¼ teasp. salt, pinch dried thyme
1 tablesp. horse-radish, pinch garlic salt
2 tablesp. chopped dill pickle or pickle relish, plus a little minced onion or garlic
2 tablesp. prepared mustard, snipped parsley
Soy or barbecue sauce, or French dressing
¼ cup canned crushed pineapple or applesauce, or apple jelly, plus pinch nutmeg

1 teasp. snipped parsley, 1 teasp. minced onion,
  bit of Worcestershire, salt
3 tablesp. lemon or orange juice, pinch nutmeg

HAMBURGER GO-BETWEENS

Shape Our Best-Ever Hamburger mixture, see
p. 190, into 8 thin patties. Place one of fillings
below on half of patties; top with remaining
patties. Press edges together; cook these sur-
prise-filled hamburgers till of desired doneness.

BLUE CHEESE: Combine ¼ cup crumbled
Danish blue cheese, 2 tablesp. mayonnaise, 1
tablesp. Worcestershire, ½ teasp. dry mustard,
2 teasp. prepared hamburger relish (optional).

CHILI-CHEESE: Mix 1 cup grated process Cheddar cheese, 1 tablesp. Worcestershire, ¼ cup
chili sauce.

CHILI-ONION: Use sautéed onions, chili sauce.

RELISH: Top thin onion slices with prepared
mustard, then with pickle relish or chili sauce.

STUFFING: Mix 2 tablesp. melted butter or margarine with 1¼ cups fine fresh bread crumbs;
½ teasp. dried thyme; a little minced onion;
1 teasp. lemon juice.

TOMATO-CHEESE: Top thin tomato slices with
onion salt, then with grated Cheddar cheese.

HAMBURGER SPOON-ONS

While Our Best-Ever Hamburgers, p. 190, cook,
make one of these quick sauces to top, or serve
with them:

Avery Butter, p. 527	Sautéed Mushrooms,
Chive Cheese, p. 527	p. 406
Curry, p. 527	Curry-Sautéed Onions,
Mustard, p. 532	p. 408
Onion, p. 528	Sour Cream, p. 528
Quick Mushroom,	Tomato-Horse-radish,
p. 528	p. 528

HAMBURGER TOSS-INS

Vary Our Best-Ever Hamburger mixture, see
p. 190, in one of these ways:

BACON-WRAPPED: Wrap thick patties in bacon
slices, securing each with toothpicks; broil.

BEAN BURGERS: Use ¾ lb. chuck, ground. Toss
in 1 cup mashed, drained canned kidney beans.
Skillet-cook patties in bacon fat.

BOHEMIAN BURGERS: Increase minced onion to
3 tablesp. Toss in 3 tablesp. minced dill pickle;
½ cup minced pickled beets; and 1 cup finely
chopped, cooked potatoes. Skillet-cook patties.

CHEESEBURGERS: Toss in ¼ lb. grated process
Cheddar cheese (1 cup); add ¼ cup water.

CHIP BURGERS: Toss in 1 cup crushed potato
chips.

DEVILED BURGERS: Increase minced onion to 3
tablesp. Add 1½ teasp. prepared mustard, ¼
cup catchup or chili sauce, 2 teasp. horse-
radish, 1½ teasp. Worcestershire.

EXTRA-JUICY: Add ¼ cup evaporated milk, undiluted, or water.

JUMBO BURGERS: Increase onion to ¼ cup.
Add 1¾ cups fresh bread crumbs, 1 beaten egg,
¼ cup milk.

HERB BURGERS: Add ¼ teasp. each dried marjoram and thyme. Increase onion to ¼ cup;
add ¼ cup minced celery, 1 teasp. snipped
parsley, ½ teasp. garlic salt. After cooking, top
with 2 tablesp. melted butter or margarine,
mixed with 3 tablesp. lemon or orange juice,
pinch nutmeg.

MOREBURGERS: Add 1 cup wheat flakes, cracker
crumbs, or cooked rice; or ½ cup uncooked
rolled oats. Also add ½ cup milk or tomato
juice, plus a little prepared mustard, horse-
radish, or catchup.

MUSHROOM BURGERS: Add ½ cup chopped
mushrooms.

NUT BURGERS: Toss in ½ cup chopped walnuts.

HAMBURGER MIXED GRILL

See Mixed Grill, p. 180. Try these combinations:
1. Hamburgers; tomato halves; mushroom
caps; French-bread slices, topped with grated
cheese and sprinkling of orégano.
2. Hamburgers; scored, cooked potato halves;
canned peach or pear halves, or pineapple
chunks or slices.
3. Hamburgers, bacon, banana halves, franks.

BIG BURGER

Cook 4 sliced medium onions in boiling salted
water to cover 3 to 4 min. Shape Our Best-
Ever Hamburger mixture, p. 190, into 1 large
patty, 6½" x ¾". Spread patty with 2 tablesp.

soft butter or margarine; place, with butter side down, in hot skillet. Brown; turn. Drain onions; put in skillet around patty; sprinkle both with ¼ cup soy sauce and ⅛ teasp. pepper. Stir onions with fork. Cook till medium rare — about 6 min. Makes 4 servings.

BARBECUED HAMBURGERS

Shape Our Best-Ever Hamburger mixture, see p. 190, into 4 large patties. In 1 tablesp. hot fat or salad oil in skillet, brown patties on both sides.

Combine 1 cup catchup, 1 sliced onion, ¼ cup vinegar, 1 tablesp. sugar, ½ teasp. dry mustard. Pour over patties; simmer, covered, 20 min. Makes 4 servings.

HAMBURGERS CUM LAUDE

1½ lb. chuck, ground	2¼ cups chicken
1 egg	broth
2 teasp. prepared mustard	3 tablesp. Burgundy wine
1½ teasp. salt	2 tablesp. flour
3 tablesp. butter or margarine	2 tablesp. bottled meat sauce
Speck pepper	½ cup catchup
3 tablesp. Worcestershire	2 tablesp. snipped parsley

About 1 hr. before serving:

1. Combine chuck with egg, 1 teasp. mustard, salt, 1 tablesp. butter, pepper, 1 tablesp. Worcestershire, ¼ cup chicken broth, and wine. Set aside.
2. In a saucepan, melt 2 tablesp. butter; stir in flour till brown. Blend in 2 cups chicken broth, 1 teasp. mustard, 2 tablesp. Worcestershire, bottled meat sauce, and catchup. Simmer together, stirring, until thickened.
3. Using a 6-oz. teacup (¾ cup) as a mold, shape meat mixture into 4 cup-shaped burgers.

Just before serving:

1. Preheat broiler 10 min., or as manufacturer directs.
2. Broil burgers to medium doneness, allowing 8 min. on rounded side, then 6 min. on flat side.
3. Meanwhile, heat catchup sauce; pass, with snipped parsley as garnish. Makes 4 servings.

POTATO BURGERS

½ lb. chuck, ground	1 teasp. salt
1 cup grated raw potatoes	3 tablesp. fat or salad oil
2 tablesp. minced onion	½ teasp. dry mustard
⅛ teasp. pepper	1 tablesp. snipped parsley

Mix meat, potatoes, onion, pepper, salt. Shape into 8 patties. In hot fat in skillet, sauté patties until crisp and brown; then remove from skillet; keep warm. Add mustard and parsley to drippings in skillet; heat; pour over patties. Makes 4 servings.

BURGUNDY MEAT BALLS

¾ lb. chuck, ground	¾ cup light cream
¾ cup packaged dried bread crumbs or finely crushed corn chips	Salt
	¼ cup fat or salad oil
	3 tablesp. flour
	2 cups water
1 small onion, minced	1 cup Burgundy wine
¾ teasp. cornstarch	2 beef-bouillon cubes
Dash allspice	⅛ teasp. pepper
1 egg, beaten	

Combine meat, crumbs, onion, cornstarch, allspice, egg, cream, ¾ teasp. salt; shape into 30 to 32 small balls. Into hot fat in skillet, drop balls, a few at a time; brown well on all sides. Transfer balls to warm plate.

Blend flour with remaining fat in skillet; stir in water, wine, bouillon cubes, ½ teasp. salt, pepper. Cook, stirring, until smooth. Then arrange meat balls in sauce; simmer, covered, 30 min.

Serve on hot mashed potatoes, fluffy rice, or buttered noodles. Makes 6 servings.

To Do Ahead: Prepare, then refrigerate the entire dish a day ahead. To serve, reheat. Or shape balls ahead; refrigerate. About ¾ hr. before serving, start cooking.

E. I.'S SWEDISH MEAT BALLS

4 tablesp. butter or margarine	¼ teasp. nutmeg
⅓ cup minced onion	1 lb. chuck, ground
1 egg	¼ lb. shoulder pork, ground
½ cup milk	3 tablesp. flour
½ cup fresh bread crumbs	1 teasp. sugar
2½ teasp. salt	⅛ teasp. pepper
2 teasp. sugar	1 cup water
½ teasp. allspice	¾ cup light cream

In 2 tablesp. hot butter in large skillet, sauté onion until golden. Meanwhile, in large mixing bowl, beat egg; add milk, crumbs. Let stand 5 min. Add 1¼ teasp. salt, 2 teasp. sugar, all-spice, nutmeg, meats, onion. Blend well with fork. In same skillet, heat 2 tablesp. butter. Using 2 teaspoons, shape meat mixture into small balls, about ½″ to ¾″ in diameter. Drop some balls into skillet; brown well on all sides; remove to warm casserole; repeat until all meat balls are browned.

Into fat left in skillet, stir flour, 1 teasp. sugar, 1¼ teasp. salt, pepper; slowly add water, cream; stir until thickened. If desired, return meat balls to gravy; heat well. Or serve meat balls in covered casserole; pass gravy. Makes 6 servings.

To Do Ahead: Make day ahead; refrigerate. Reheat just before serving.

MEAT-BALL STEW EN CASSEROLE

2 lb. potatoes, pared, quartered	shire
	⅔ cup milk
1½ lb. small white onions	⅓ cup salad oil
	1½ lb. small mush-
1 bunch small carrots, halved lengthwise	rooms
	1 10½-oz. can con-
1 10-oz. pkg. thawed frozen peas	densed cream-of-mushroom soup,
2 lb. chuck, ground	undiluted
1 egg	¾ teasp. nutmeg
1 cup day-old bread crumbs	¾ teasp. bottled sauce for gravy
¾ teasp. dried mar-joram	¾ teasp. onion salt or monosodium
2½ teasp. salt	glutamate
¾ teasp. Worcester-	Milk

In large saucepan, place potatoes in layer, then onions, then carrots. Cook in 1″ boiling salted water, covered, 20 min., or until barely tender-crisp; top with peas; cover; turn off heat.

Meanwhile, with fork, lightly mix meat with egg, crumbs, marjoram, salt, Worcestershire, milk. Drop by teaspoonfuls into hot oil in skil-let; brown quickly on both sides; remove. In same skillet, sauté mushrooms until tender; re-move. Then, in skillet, heat soup with nutmeg, bottled sauce for gravy, onion salt.

Start heating oven to 400°F. Arrange drained peas, carrots, onions, mushrooms, and meat balls in 3-qt. casserole. Near edge of cas-serole, pour in sauce. Mash and season potatoes

as on p. 412; arrange in mounds around edge; brush with milk. Bake uncovered 35 min., or till browned and bubbly. Makes 8 servings.

MEAT BALLS STROGANOFF

1½ lb. chuck, ground	½ lb. mushrooms, sliced
¾ cup milk	
¾ cup packaged dried bread crumbs	¾ teasp. paprika
	2 tablesp. flour
Salt	1 can condensed beef
Pepper	bouillon, undiluted
3 tablesp. snipped parsley	½ teasp. Worcester-shire
¼ cup butter or mar-garine	½ cup commercial sour cream
¾ cup minced onions	Hot fluffy cooked rice
	Snipped fresh dill

1. With fork, combine chuck, milk, bread crumbs, 1½ teasp. salt, ¼ teasp. pepper, and parsley. Shape into 1¼″ balls; sauté in 2 tablesp. hot butter or margarine, in skillet, un-til browned; remove and reserve.
2. Add 2 tablesp. more butter or margarine to skillet, then sauté onions and mushrooms with paprika until tender, about 5 min.
3. Sprinkle flour over mushroom mixture; stir. Then, while stirring, slowly add beef bouillon, ¾ teasp. salt, ⅛ teasp. pepper. Return meat balls to sauce; cover, simmer 10 min.
4. Just before serving, stir in Worcestershire, sour cream; heat. Serve with hot cooked rice, sprinkled with dill. Makes 6 to 8 servings.

HAMBURGER STROGANOFF

¼ cup butter or mar-garine	1 10½-oz. can con-densed cream-of-chicken soup, un-diluted
½ cup minced onion	
1 lb. chuck, ground	
1 clove garlic, minced	1 cup commercial
2 tablesp. flour	sour cream
2 teasp. salt	6 hard rectangular
¼ teasp. monosodium glutamate	bakers' or baked brown-and-serve
¼ teasp. pepper	club rolls, hollowed
¼ teasp. paprika	out
1 lb. mushrooms, sliced	Snipped parsley, chives, or fresh dill

In hot butter in skillet, sauté onions till golden. Stir in meat, garlic, flour, salt, monosodium glutamate, pepper, paprika, mushrooms; sauté

5 min. Add soup; simmer, uncovered, 10 min. Stir in sour cream. Serve in rolls or on hot mashed potatoes, fluffy rice, buttered noodles, or toast; sprinkle with parsley. Makes 4 to 6 servings.

BEANS AND BURGERS

1½ lb. chuck, ground	¼ teasp. pepper
1 small onion, minced	¼ cup packaged dried
1 tablesp. bottled	bread crumbs
thick meat sauce	2 tablesp. salad oil
1 tablesp. snipped	1 8-oz. can tomato
parsley	sauce
½ teasp. dried	⅓ cup catchup
orégano	½ cup commercial
½ teasp. dried rose-	sour cream
mary	1 1-lb. can red kid-
Dash paprika	ney beans, drained,
Salt	rinsed, then drained

1. *About 30 min. before serving:* In large bowl, thoroughly mix chuck, onion, meat sauce, parsley, orégano, rosemary, paprika, 1½ teasp. salt, and pepper.
2. Shape meat mixture into 10 or 12 meat balls; roll in bread crumbs; then, in hot oil in large skillet, sauté till browned on all sides.
3. Meanwhile stir together tomato sauce, catchup, sour cream, and ¾ teasp. salt; add, with kidney beans, to browned meat balls in skillet; stir gently. Simmer over low heat, uncovered, 10 min., or until meat is done.
4. Serve right from skillet, with toasted French bread and a tossed raw vegetable salad with cheese dressing. Makes 5 to 6 servings.

CHILI CON CARNE

2 tablesp. fat or salad	1½ tablesp. chili
oil	powder
½ cup thinly sliced	2 tablesp. cold water
onions	¼ teasp. salt
2 tablesp. diced green	1 teasp. sugar
pepper	1½ small cloves gar-
½ lb. round, rump,	lic, minced
or chuck, ground	2 cups cooked or
½ cup boiling water	canned kidney
1 cup canned tomatoes	beans, undrained

In hot fat in skillet, cook onions and green pepper until tender. Add meat; cook, uncovered, until meat starts to sizzle and brown. Add boiling water, tomatoes, chili powder mixed with cold water till smooth, salt, sugar, garlic. Simmer, covered, 1 hr. Uncover; simmer ½

hr. Add a little hot water if mixture thickens too much. Add beans; heat.

Serve in soup bowls, with rolls or crackers and a salad. Or serve over hot or toasted split corn bread, buttered spaghetti, or fried mush.

To Vary: If you prefer a slightly thinner chili con carne, stir in about ¼ cup hot water just before serving. Or replace canned tomatoes with 1⅓ cups diced fresh tomatoes.

CREOLE STUFFED GREEN PEPPERS

4 large green peppers	½ cup light cream or
1 cup boiling water	evaporated milk,
Salt	undiluted
1 lb. chuck, ground	1 1-lb.-4-oz. can to-
½ cup minced onion	matoes (2½ cups)
½ cup minced celery	1 tablesp. sugar
¼ cup minced green	¼ teasp. cinnamon
pepper (optional)	6 whole cloves
1 egg, unbeaten	1 tablesp. flour
	¼ cup cold water

Wash 4 green peppers; cut thin slice from stem end of each; remove seeds. Boil peppers in boiling water with 1¼ teasp. salt, tightly covered, 5 min.

Meanwhile, combine meat, ¼ cup onion, celery, 1 teasp. salt, ¼ cup minced green pepper, egg, cream. Drain boiled peppers; stuff with meat mixture. Place in 8" x 8" x 2" baking dish.

Start heating oven to 350°F. In saucepan, combine tomatoes, ¼ cup onion, ½ teasp. salt, sugar, cinnamon, cloves; simmer, uncovered, 10 min.; then strain, reserving liquid. Stir flour and cold water till smooth; add to strained liquid; cook, stirring, until slightly thickened; pour over peppers. Bake 45 to 50 min. Makes 4 servings.

STUFFED CABBAGE

Large head cabbage	2 8-oz. cans tomato
1 lb. chuck, ground	sauce
½ cup uncooked reg-	2 1-lb.-13-oz. cans to-
ular or processed	matoes (7 cups)
white rice	Juice of 2 lemons
1 small onion, grated	1 teasp. salt
2 eggs	¼ teasp. pepper
1 teasp. salt	½ to 1 cup brown
¼ teasp. pepper	sugar, packed
1 large onion, sliced	

Remove 12 large leaves from cabbage. Trim off thick part of each leaf. Let boiling water stand on leaves a few minutes, so they become easy to roll.

Combine meat, rice, grated onion, eggs, 1 teasp. salt, ¼ teasp. pepper. Place mound of meat mixture in cup part of each leaf. Loosely fold over sides of each leaf; roll up.

Start heating oven to 375°F. In bottom of Dutch oven, place a few of remaining cabbage leaves. Arrange layers of stuffed cabbage, with seam sides down, and sliced onion in Dutch oven. Pour on tomato sauce, tomatoes, lemon juice. Add 1 teasp. salt, ¼ teasp. pepper. Bring to boil on top of range. Sprinkle with sugar to taste. Bake, covered, 1 hr.; uncover; bake 2 hr. Makes 8 servings.

HINGHAM GOULASH

1 8-oz. pkg. flat ¼″ noodles
6 bacon slices, in small pieces
1 large onion, chopped
1 lb. ground chuck
1 3-oz. bottle stuffed olives, sliced
1½ 10½-oz. cans condensed tomato soup, undiluted
½ can water
1 10½-oz. can condensed consommé, undiluted
½ teasp. salt
⅛ teasp. pepper
½ teasp. sugar
1½ teasp. bottled thick meat sauce
½ teasp. dried orégano
½ teasp. dried thyme
1 cup grated Cheddar cheese

About 2¼ hr. before serving:

1. Start heating oven to 300°F. Cook noodles as label directs; drain. Meanwhile, in skillet, cook bacon until crisp; remove.

2. In bacon drippings, brown onion, then add chuck and quickly brown it. Stir in olives, undiluted tomato soup, water, consommé, salt, pepper, sugar, meat sauce, orégano, and thyme, then heat.

3. Arrange noodles in buttered 2½-qt. casserole. Pour on sauce, top with bacon, toss well, then sprinkle cheese over all. Bake, covered, 1 hr., then uncovered, ½ hr. Then remove from oven and let stand 15 min. before serving.

Serve it buffet style, with tossed mixed vegetable salad, garlic bread, raspberry-sherbet-and-vanilla-ice-cream balls, ginger cookies, and coffee. Makes 6 servings.

DO-AHEAD SPAGHETTI

½ cup melted butter or margarine
1½ lb. chuck, ground
1 cup chopped onions
1½ cups chopped celery
1 tablesp. butter or margarine
1 teasp. seasoned salt
1 teasp. sugar
½ teasp. monosodium glutamate
1 6-oz. can tomato paste
2 cups tomato juice
1 3- or 4-oz. can mushrooms, sliced
½ cup dry sherry
1 8-oz. pkg. spaghetti
Grated Parmesan cheese

About 2½ hr. before supper: In ½ cup melted butter, in Dutch oven or heavy skillet, sauté chuck, over low heat, until brown. Meanwhile, in another skillet, sauté onions and celery in 1 tablesp. butter until onion is golden; combine with meat. Add seasoned salt, sugar, monosodium glutamate, tomato paste, and tomato juice. Cover and simmer over low heat 1½ hr., stirring often. Then add mushrooms and sherry; simmer ½ hr. longer.

About 15 min. before serving: Cook spaghetti as label directs; drain. Place on heated platter; pour on meat sauce; top with cheese. Makes 4 to 6 servings.

To freeze: Make sauce several days ahead, cool, freezer-wrap, and freeze. See p. 708.

MAZETTI

¾ cup finely chopped celery
¼ cup melted butter or margarine
1 cup minced onion
¾ cup minced green pepper
1 lb. chuck, ground
1 lb. pork, ground
1½ teasp. salt
½ teasp. pepper
1½ 8-oz. pkg. wide noodles
¼ cup butter or margarine
1 3- or 4-oz. can sliced mushrooms, undrained
2 10½-oz. cans condensed tomato soup, undiluted
Grated Parmesan cheese

Day before or early in the day:

1. In saucepan, in water to cover, cook celery until tender; drain; reserve.

2. In large skillet, in ¼ cup butter, sauté onion, green pepper 5 min.; stir in chuck, pork, salt, pepper; cook, uncovered, until meat loses its red color.

3. Cook noodles as package label directs; drain; rinse. Turn into 3-qt. casserole; toss with

¼ cup butter; stir in meat mixture, celery, mushrooms, tomato soup; mix well. Sprinkle with Parmesan; cover; refrigerate.

One hour before serving: Start heating oven to 400°F. Bake casserole, uncovered, 1 hr. 15 min., or until hot in center. Makes 12 servings.

EGGPLANT PARMIGIANO AMERICANO

1½ lb. chuck, ground
1 teasp. onion salt
¼ teasp. pepper
2 tablesp. salad oil
1 medium eggplant
⅓ cup flour
½ teasp. salt
⅛ teasp. pepper
¼ cup salad oil

2 8-oz. cans tomato sauce
¼ lb. process sharp Cheddar cheese, grated (1 cup)
¼ teasp. dried orégano
Snipped parsley

Start heating oven to 350°F. With fork, combine ground chuck, onion salt, and ¼ teasp. pepper; lightly form into 8 patties. In 2 tablesp. hot salad oil in skillet, sauté patties till brown on both sides but rare inside; remove. Wash eggplant; cut into 8 ½"-thick slices. Sprinkle with mixture of flour, salt, and ⅛ teasp. pepper. In ¼ cup hot salad oil in skillet, sauté eggplant slices until golden on both sides. In greased 12" x 8" x 2" baking dish, arrange half of eggplant slices with half of meat patties. Spread with 1 can tomato sauce; then sprinkle on half of cheese and orégano. Repeat. Bake, uncovered, 30 min., or until cheese is bubbly. Top with snipped parsley. Makes 4 servings.

SPOON BREAD TAMALE BAKE

¼ cup olive oil
1½ lb. chuck, ground
1 cup chopped onions
1 clove garlic, minced
½ cup chopped green peppers
1 1-lb.-4-oz. can tomatoes (2½ cups)
1 12-oz. can vacuum-packed whole-kernel corn
Salt
1½ tablesp. chili powder

¼ teasp. pepper
1 cup corn meal
1 cup water
1 cup pitted ripe olives
1½ cups milk
2 tablesp. butter or margarine
¼ lb. process Cheddar cheese, grated (1 cup)
2 eggs, slightly beaten

Start heating oven to 375°F. In hot oil, in skillet, brown meat; add onions, garlic, green pep-

pers; cook, stirring, until onions are golden. Stir in tomatoes, corn, 1 tablesp. salt, chili powder, pepper; simmer 5 min. Stir in ½ cup corn meal, mixed with water; simmer, covered, 10 min. Add olives; turn into 3-qt. casserole.

Now heat milk with 1 teasp. salt and butter. Slowly stir in ½ cup corn meal; cook, stirring, until thickened. Remove from heat. Stir in cheese, eggs; pour over meat mixture. Bake, uncovered, 30 to 40 min. Makes 6 to 8 servings.

To Do Ahead: Make casserole dish early in day; refrigerate. At mealtime, bake at 375°F. 1 hr. 10 min., or until bubbling hot.

SUPERB SKILLET BURGER LOAF

1 egg, beaten
¾ lb. chuck, ground
¾ teasp. salt
¼ cup minced onion

3 packaged process Cheddar-cheese slices
¼ teasp. pepper

About 25 min. before supper: Mix egg, meat, salt, onion. Grease 8" skillet with metal handle; lightly pat half of meat over bottom of skillet. Arrange cheese slices on top of meat; cover with rest of meat, patting smooth. Sprinkle with pepper. Cut into 4 pie-shaped wedges. Cook on top of range, over fairly high heat, until well-browned on bottom. Turn; brown on other side; or slide the skillet under broiler until top of meat is nicely browned. Makes 4 servings.

HAMBURGER POT ROAST

1½ lb. chuck, ground once
2 tablesp. snipped parsley
Salt
½ teasp. onion salt
1 teasp. caraway seeds
3 tablesp. evaporated milk, undiluted

¼ cup all-purpose flour
1 teasp. paprika
3 tablesp. butter or margarine
¼ cup Burgundy wine
1 large onion, sliced
2 bay leaves

1. Lightly combine chuck, parsley, 1 teasp. salt, onion salt, caraway seeds, milk. Shape into loaf, 2½" thick.
2. Combine flour, ½ teasp. salt, paprika; use to coat meat loaf.
3. In hot butter in large skillet, gently brown meat loaf, turning once. Add wine, onion, bay leaves. Simmer, covered, 30 min., or until done.

4. Carefully lift loaf to heated platter; top with onion slices from pan juice. Remove bay leaves; serve juice as is. Or for extra deliciousness, stir in 2 teasp. sugar, ½ cup light cream, ⅓ cup Burgundy wine, ¼ teasp. salt; heat gently; pass separately. Makes 6 servings.

HAMBURGER CRUNCH

1 8-oz. pkg. spaghetti	1 soup-can water
2 large onions, minced	1 3- or 4-oz. can sliced or chopped mushrooms, drained
2 tablesp. salad oil	
2 lb. chuck, ground once	
	1 cup cut-up natural Cheddar cheese
2 teasp. salt	
½ teasp. pepper	1 teasp. sugar
½ teasp. monosodium glutamate	2 tablesp. Worcestershire
1 10½-oz. can condensed tomato soup, undiluted	1 7-oz. can salted mixed nuts, coarsely chopped

Cook spaghetti as label directs, until barely tender; drain. In large Dutch oven, sauté onions in oil until golden. Add meat; brown until it is crumbly. Add salt, pepper, monosodium glutamate. Stir in soup, water, mushrooms, ⅔ cup cheese, sugar, Worcestershire, and then spaghetti. Cover and simmer 20 min.

Start heating oven to 350°F. Turn spaghetti-beef mixture into 2½-qt. greased casserole. Push nuts down into mixture; sprinkle with ⅓ cup cut-up cheese. Bake 30 min. Makes 8 to 10 servings.

♣ FOR 4: Use half an 8-oz. pkg. spaghetti; half can of nuts. Prepare meat sauce as directed; freeze half of it to serve heated over cooked rice or noodles another day. Add spaghetti to half of sauce; simmer and bake as directed.

CORNED BEEF

To Buy and Store

Today meat packers are packaging a branded extra-fine-quality brisket of corned beef which has a special mild cure and is truly delicious. Rump and plate are also used in making corned beef.

Look for corned beef with about a fourth as much fat as lean.

With one method of corning, the corned beef retains its red color after cooking. With the other method, only sugar and salt are used and the corned beef, when cooked, has a grayish brown color; this type is popular in New England.

Amount to Buy: A 4-lb. piece of corned beef makes about 8 servings.

To Store: Store as in To Store Meat, p. 172.

MUSTARD-GLAZED CORNED BEEF

Buy corned-beef brisket in transparent-plastic casing. Cook as directed in Susan's Corned Beef and Cabbage, p. 108. Dot with cloves; spread on 1 tablesp. prepared mustard mixed with ¾ cup brown sugar; broil till bubbly.

BEEF-BACON SLICES

Now you can enjoy a beef product that looks very much like packaged sliced bacon but has a wonderful flavor all its own. The meat, which has been sugar-cured and smoked, comes sliced and wrapped in cellophane. It may be pan-fried or broiled, and cooks in the same time as bacon.

To cook, just follow label directions; cook until crisp but not brittle. Serve with fried or scrambled eggs, waffles, pancakes, etc. Nice, too, in sandwiches.

OXTAILS

Though oxtails (the tails of cattle) have much bone, they also have a good share of sweet, rich-flavored meat. They need long, slow simmering.

To Buy and Store

FRESH OXJOINTS are disjointed sections of oxtail about 1½″ to 2″ long.

FROZEN OXJOINTS, packaged by well-known packers, are excellent. Cook as label directs.

Amount to Buy: Allow about 1 to 1½ lb. oxjoints for 2 servings.

To Store: Keep fresh oxjoints, loosely wrapped, in refrigerator; use within 24 hr. Keep frozen oxjoints frozen until time to use.

BRAISED OXJOINTS

2 lb. oxjoints, cut into 2″ lengths	1 tablesp. vinegar
3 tablesp. fat or salad oil	½ teasp. minced garlic
1 cup minced onions	2 teasp. salt
2 cups hot water	⅛ teasp. pepper
	1 tablesp. sugar

Preheat broiler 10 min., or as manufacturer directs. Broil oxjoints about 10 min., turning them frequently, until browned on all sides. Meanwhile, in hot fat in Dutch oven, sauté onions until tender. Add meat and rest of ingredients; simmer, covered, 3 to 4 hr., or until meat is tender, adding more boiling water if necessary.

Remove meat to heated platter; keep warm. Thicken gravy as on p. 6. Pour over or serve with meat.

Serve with buttered noodles or mashed potatoes. Makes 4 servings.

OXJOINT RAGOUT

½ cup all-purpose flour	6 cups water
4 teasp. salt	2 cups sliced, pared carrots
¼ teasp. pepper	1 cup sliced celery
3 oxjoints, cut into 2″ lengths	½ lb. small mushrooms
¼ cup fat	¼ teasp. paprika
1 bay leaf	4 cups oxjoint liquid
4 whole black peppers	¼ lb. medium noodles (2 cups)
3 large onions, sliced	

In paper bag or bowl, combine ¼ cup flour, 2 teasp. salt, ⅛ teasp. pepper. Toss oxjoints with flour mixture; then sauté in hot fat in Dutch oven or kettle till browned on all sides. Add bay leaf, black peppers, onions, water; simmer slowly, covered, till very tender — 3 to 4 hr. Remove meat from bones. (For best flavor, do this day before; refrigerate meat and liquid until used.)

Make sauce: With spoon, skim all fat from oxjoint liquid. In 2 tablesp. of this fat in skillet, sauté carrots and celery 5 min. Halve mushrooms; sauté with carrots and celery 1 min.

Sprinkle with combined 2 teasp. salt, ⅛ teasp. pepper, paprika, ¼ cup flour; toss well. Slowly stir in oxjoint liquid; simmer, covered, ½ hr., or until vegetables are done.

Meanwhile, cook noodles as label directs; drain. Add oxjoint meat to sauce; heat. Add salt and pepper to taste.

Serve on noodles. Makes 4 to 6 man-size servings.

P.S. Instead of plain noodles, use fine noodles, tossed with poppy or caraway seeds; mashed potatoes; cubed, boiled potatoes; or fluffy rice.

CURRIED: Before tossing oxjoints with flour, add 1 teasp. curry powder.

BURGUNDY: Substitute ⅓ cup Burgundy wine or sherry for ⅓ cup water.

ITALIAN STYLE: Add 1 clove garlic, minced, with onions.

WITH HERBS: Add ½ teasp. dried thyme with bay leaf and whole black peppers. Before serving, sprinkle generously with snipped parsley.

LET'S HAVE FRESH PORK

Pork, with its consistent tenderness and superb flavor, and more lean than ever before, is indeed good eating. And, contrary to popular opinion, it is equally available in summer and in winter.

Because there is little difference in its tenderness, pork does not carry a packer's brand name or Federal grade stamp. However, be sure to look for the round purple U.S. Inspected and Passed stamp. See To Buy Meat, p. 171.

The lean of quality pork should be firm and tender, with a pinkish cast and some marbling. The fat on the outside should be firm and snowy white.

In the following pages, we suggest and describe favorite uses for many of the retail cuts of pork. Our diagram of the pork animal, under Popular Cuts of Meat, will help you to identify these cuts better.

The All-Important Rule

Always Serve Fresh Pork Well Done. All fresh pork must be thoroughly cooked. When

POPULAR CUTS OF MEAT

*You'll find all you need to know about these cuts of meat
under each meat section in this chapter.*

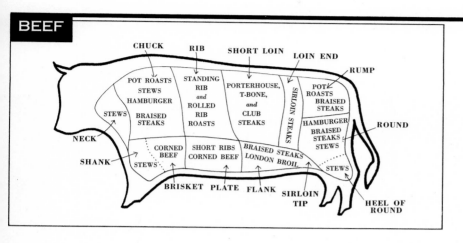

BEEF

CHUCK · RIB · SHORT LOIN · LOIN END · RUMP

POT ROASTS / STEWS / HAMBURGER / BRAISED STEAKS

STANDING RIB *and* ROLLED RIB ROASTS

PORTERHOUSE, T-BONE, *and* CLUB STEAKS

SIRLOIN STEAKS

POT ROASTS / BRAISED STEAKS

HAMBURGER / BRAISED STEAKS / STEWS

ROUND

STEWS

NECK

SHANK

STEWS

CORNED BEEF

SHORT RIBS CORNED BEEF

BRAISED STEAKS LONDON BROIL

STEWS

HEEL OF ROUND

BRISKET · PLATE · FLANK · SIRLOIN TIP

1 · GOVERNMENT SEALS

USDA CHOICE

2 · SHORT RIBS

3 · ROLLED RIB ROAST   4 · BONED ROLLED RUMP

5 · STANDING 10" AND 7" RIB ROASTS   6 · RIB EYE ROAST

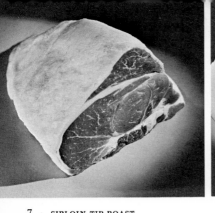

7 · SIRLOIN TIP ROAST   8 · CHUCK *(arm or round bone)*   9 · CHUCK *(blade bone)*

10 · ROUND STEAK   11 · FLANK STEAK   12 · TENDERLOIN *(with filet mignon)*

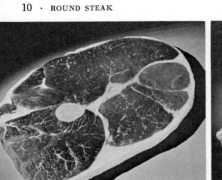

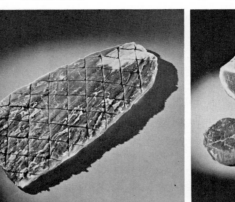

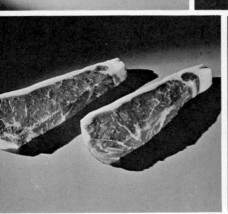

13 · LOIN STEAKS *(hotel style)*   14 · PORTERHOUSE STEAK   15 · CLUB STEAK

16 · SIRLOIN STEAK *(pinbone)*   17 · SIRLOIN STEAK *(wedge bone)*   18 · RIB STEAK

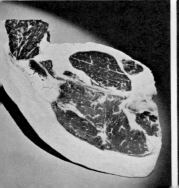

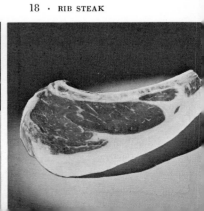

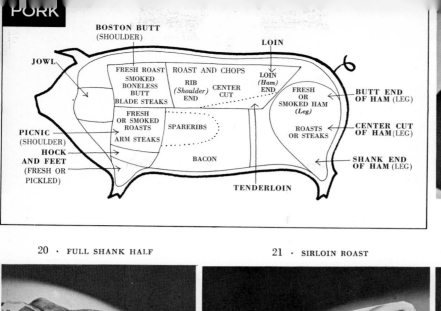

PORK

BOSTON BUTT
(SHOULDER)

JOWL

LOIN

FRESH ROAST | ROAST AND CHOPS
SMOKED
BONELESS | RIB | LOIN
BUTT | (Shoulder) | CENTER | (Ham)
BLADE STEAKS | END | CUT | END

FRESH
OR
SMOKED HAM
(Leg)

BUTT END
OF HAM (LEG)

FRESH
OR SMOKED
ROASTS | SPARERIBS

ARM STEAKS

ROASTS
OR STEAKS

CENTER CUT
OF HAM (LEG)

PICNIC
(SHOULDER)

HOCK
AND FEET
(FRESH OR
PICKLED)

BACON

SHANK END
OF HAM (LEG)

TENDERLOIN

19 · FULL BUTT HALF

20 · FULL SHANK HALF   21 · SIRLOIN ROAST   22 · CENTER-CUT ROAST

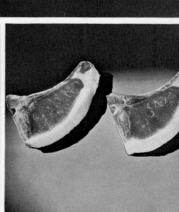

23 · BLADE LOIN ROAST   24 · PORK SPARERIBS   25 · RIB CHOPS

26 · BLADE STEAK (shoulder)   27 · LOIN CHOPS   28 · ARM STEAK (shoulder)

VEAL

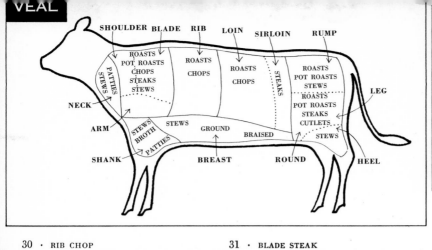

SHOULDER BLADE RIB LOIN SIRLOIN RUMP

PATTIES STEWS — ROASTS POT ROASTS CHOPS STEAKS STEWS — ROASTS CHOPS — ROASTS CHOPS — STEAKS — ROASTS POT ROASTS STEWS

ROASTS POT ROASTS STEAKS CUTLETS

NECK

LEG

ARM

STEWS BROTH — STEWS — GROUND — BRAISED — STEWS

PATTIES

SHANK — BREAST — ROUND — HEEL

29 · LOIN CHOP

30 · RIB CHOP

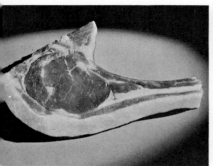

31 · BLADE STEAK

32 · ARM STEAK

LAMB

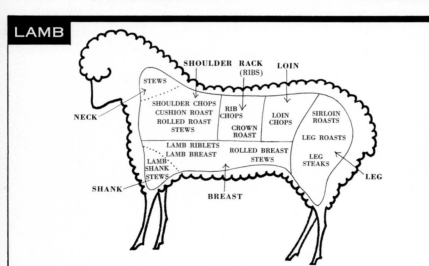

SHOULDER RACK (RIBS) LOIN

STEWS

SHOULDER CHOPS CUSHION ROAST ROLLED ROAST STEWS

RIB CHOPS

LOIN CHOPS

SIRLOIN ROASTS

LEG ROASTS

NECK

CROWN ROAST

LAMB RIBLETS LAMB BREAST — ROLLED BREAST STEWS

LEG STEAKS

LAMB SHANK STEWS

LEG

SHANK — BREAST

33 · LOIN CHOPS OF TODAY AND TOMORROW

34 · SHORT LEG (round) ROAST (sirloin chops cut off)

35 · RIB CHOP

36 · SHOULDER ARM OR ROUND BONE CHOP (left) SHOULDER BLADE BONE CHOP (right)

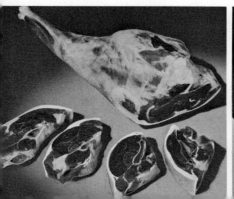

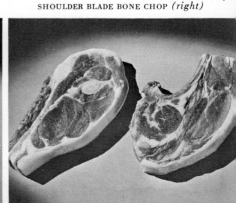

pork reaches the well-done stage, all the pink color disappears, the meat itself becomes gray, and the meat juice is clear.

FRESH-PORK ROASTS

To Buy and Store

Select a Cut:

LOIN ROASTS: A loin of pork extends from the shoulder to the fresh ham. A loin weighing 10 to 14 lb. may be cut into chops, cut into the 3 loin roasts below, or cut to order.

For easy carving, have meatman free backbone from rib of pork roast by sawing close and parallel to backbone.

Sirloin Roast (Fig. 21): Contains tenderloin and some bone, and is difficult to carve. Weighs 3 to 4 lb.

Center-cut Roast (Fig. 22): The center cut of the loin; this section is usually cut into center-cut chops, both rib and loin. Weighs 4 to 7 lb.

Blade Loin Roast (Fig. 23): May contain a section of blade bone, also rib bones. It is the most economical part of the loin. May be cut into chops. Weighs 3 to 5 lb.

SHOULDER ROASTS: A pork shoulder is cut into the following pieces:

Boston-Butt (Shoulder) Roast weighs 3 to 8 lb. It may be sold boned or with bone in.

Picnic (Shoulder) Roast weighs 4 to 10 lb. It may be sold with bone in, or boned, rolled, and tied.

Cushion Shoulder Roast is a boned, but not rolled, picnic shoulder. It weighs 3 to 8 lb.

LEG (FRESH HAM): This cut is a fine choice for a large family, because it has a high percentage of lean meat to bone. It may also be boned, rolled, and tied. Can weigh 5 lb. and up.

CROWN ROAST: This is a party roast, made from the center-cut rib sections from two or more loins. It is shaped and tied to form a circle, with the ends of the rib bones pointing up. The rib ends are usually Frenched, *i.e.*, the meat is cut from the ends of the bones. Be sure backbone has been completely removed to make carving easier.

Do not fill center with ground meat — this increases roasting time. Cover rib ends with bread squares, pieces of bacon, salt pork, or foil during roasting.

Amount to Buy: Buy at least a 3-lb. roast. Allow 2 or 3 servings per lb. bone-in pork roast, 3 or 4 servings boned roast. If you're buying a crown roast, allow 2 ribs per serving.

Be sure to have meatman note on the bill the weight of the oven-ready roast to guide you in computing the roasting time.

To Store: Store as in To Store Meat, p. 172.

ROAST PORK

1. Check roasting timetable, p. 200, to see about how long roasting will take. Plan so pork is done 20 min. before serving; it will slice more easily, and you will have time to make gravy.
2. Start heating oven to 325°F. Do not wash roast. Place pork, with fat side up, on rack in shallow open pan.
3. If desired, rub surface of pork lightly with:
   Seasoned salt and pepper; or salt, pepper, and monosodium glutamate
   Or dried sage, thyme, or rosemary
   Or mixture of 1 tablesp. salt, 1 tablesp. paprika, and 1 teasp. dry mustard
   Or cut clove garlic
4. Insert roast-meat thermometer through fat surface into center of roast. Don't let it touch bone. If you're roasting a crown roast, insert thermometer into center of meaty part of one chop. Don't add water; don't cover.
5. Roast pork to 185°F. on roast-meat thermometer, using timetable, p. 200, as an approximate guide. Pork must be *well done* with no tinge of pink. Don't baste or turn pork during roasting.
6. *Caution:* Roasts vary so in size, shape, amount of bone and fat, etc., that a roasting timetable can be only approximate at best. So rely on a roast-meat thermometer if you want to be sure.
7. When pork is done, remove to heated platter; keep warm while making Velvety Meat Gravy, p. 177, from drippings in pan.

To serve: Serve with Baked Apples, p. 544; Saucepan Applesauce, p. 544; Speedy Whole-Cranberry Sauce, p. 440; Fried Apple Rings, p. 436; Sautéed Pineapple, p. 436; Sautéed

Bananas, p. 436; pickled peaches; currant jelly; or canned cranberry sauce.

If it's a crown roast, serve as in Crown Roast of Lamb, p. 220. Or place on heated platter or chop plate; alternate mounds of mashed potatoes and baked small apples or Rosy Cinnamon Apples, p. 434, around base.

To Carve a Loin of Pork: See p. 295.

To Use Leftover Roast Pork: See p. 252 and Soup from Leftover Bones, p. 164.

TIMETABLE FOR ROASTING FRESH PORK

Pork refrigerated till roasted at 325°F. Use shallow open pan. Add no water. Do not baste.

OVEN-READY WEIGHT (lb.)	APPROXIMATE ROASTING TIME (hr.)	MEAT-THERMOMETER READING (well done)
LOIN		
2 to 3	1½ to 2	185°F.
5 to 7	3 to 4	185°F.
BOSTON BUTT (SHOULDER)		
4	3½	185°F.
BONE-IN FRESH PICNIC (SHOULDER)		
5	3⅓	185°F.
ROLLED, BONED FRESH PICNIC (SHOULDER)		
4	3⅔	185°F.
CUSHION SHOULDER		
5	4	185°F.
LEG (FRESH HAM)		
5	4½	185°F.
CROWN ROAST (NO FILLING IN CENTER)		
6 to 7	3½ to 4	185°F.

HOLIDAY CROWN ROAST OF PORK

Crown roast of pork (2 half-loin crowns of 13 ribs each)	Apricot preserves, melted
Seasoned salt	1 cup fresh or frozen whole cranberries
Ground sage	1 12½-oz. jar preserved kumquats
Twice recipe for Cranberry Apple, or Cranberry and Mixed Fruit Stuffing, p. 341	Water cress or parsley

In ordering crown roast of pork above, you will have 24 to 26 ribs, or 2 ribs per serving for 12 or 13 guests.

About 6 hr. before serving:

1. In large shallow open roasting pan, without a rack, place crown roast of pork with its rib ends up. Lightly sprinkle with some seasoned salt and ground sage.

2. Make Cranberry Apple Stuffing or Cranberry and Mixed Fruit Stuffing, reserving some of apple slices from stuffing to garnish the top of it.

3. Start heating oven to 325°F. Mound stuffing in the center of crown, with apple slices around the top edge inside of the ribs. With foil, loosely cover stuffing and also tightly cover rib ends.

4. Insert roast-meat thermometer between two ribs into center of meat (*don't touch bone or stuffing*). Roast pork about 3 hr., then remove all foil, brush apple slices with melted apricot preserves, and roast about 40 min. longer, or until roast-meat thermometer reads 180°F.

5. Then remove roast from oven, brush all meat surfaces and bone with melted apricot preserves, and return to oven for about 30 min. longer, or until meat thermometer reaches 185°F. (well done).

6. Meanwhile, with needle and thread, string the cranberries; also slit the narrower end of each preserved kumquat so it will slip over the end of one of the ribs.

7. When the crown roast of pork is done, remove it from the oven. Then, with the help of 2 large spatulas or pancake turners, carefully lift it to a heated serving platter.

Just before serving:

1. Drape or loop string of cranberry "jewels" in and out around ribs of crown. Place kumquats on alternate ends of ribs. (If desired, garnish with additional kumquats — one or

two 12½-oz. jars — at base of crown) ; add sprigs of water cress or parsley.

2. In serving roast, carve from top down between ribs, allowing 2 ribs per serving. Spoon some stuffing onto each plate, too. Makes about 13 servings.

♣ FOR 9 TO 10 GUESTS: Order crown roast of pork, 18 to 20 ribs. Proceed as on p. 200, making once the recipe for stuffing. Reduce roasting time to 3 hr. and 20 min. in step 4; to 20 min. in step 5.

SWEET-PUNGENT PORK LOIN

3 large cloves garlic, crushed	2 cloves garlic, each cut into 6 slivers
6 tablesp. soy sauce	18 whole cloves
½ cup catchup	2 cups apricot preserves
¼ cup lemon juice	
½ teasp. pepper	6 spiced crab apples
1 12-rib pork loin roast (6 to 6½ lb.)	

Day before:

1. In bowl, combine crushed garlic cloves, soy sauce, catchup, lemon juice, and pepper. Then make 2″ slash between every two rib bones on pork loin roast.

2. Make 12 small gashes along meaty side of roast below rib bones; insert sliver of garlic in each. Stud the surface with whole cloves.

3. Now place pork roast, with meat side down, in 13″ x 9″ x 2″ baking dish; pour soy-sauce marinade over it; cover with foil; refrigerate until 3 hr. before serving.

On the day, 3 hr. before serving:

1. Start heating oven to 325°F. Lift pork from marinade. Place, with rib bones up, in shallow roasting pan; baste with soy-sauce marinade. Wrap tips of rib bones with a strip of foil.

2. Insert meat thermometer into thick part of roast, away from fat or bone. Roast about 2 hr., or until thermometer reaches 170°F.; then remove from oven.

3. Meanwhile, heat apricot preserves till melted. Brush ½ cup over meaty side of pork, keeping rest to pass as sauce. Then continue roasting pork 20 to 30 min., or till thermometer reads 185°F. Use the thermometer reading as final guide.

4. Now place roast on large platter, and remove foil. Then, between every two bone tips, anchor a spiced crab apple, securing it with a toothpick if necessary. Arrange rest of apricot preserves in bowl to be passed at table. Makes 12 servings.

PORK-CHOP ROAST

2- to 2½-lb center-cut pork loin, cut into 4 uniform chops	Salt Pepper

Start heating oven to 350°F. Trim off part of fat from chops. Sprinkle all surfaces of chops generously with salt and pepper. Then put chops together in original shape; tie snugly with white cord. Stand chops on flat, bony side in shallow open pan.

Insert roast-meat thermometer into edge of one of chops; don't let it touch bone or fat. Roast 2-lb. loin 1½ hr., 2½-lb. loin 1¾ hr., or to 185°F. on roast-meat thermometer. After first hour, spoon off fat as it accumulates in pan; save for gravy.

When meat is done, remove to heated platter. Remove cord, and it's ready to serve without carving! Now make Velvety Meat Gravy, p. 177, from drippings. Makes 4 servings.

ITALIAN PORK-AND-RICE CASSEROLE

2 tablesp. salad oil	1 3-lb. center-cut pork loin, cut from bone into ¼″ slices
2 medium onions, sliced	
1 clove garlic	¾ teasp. salt
1 10¾-oz. can beef gravy	¼ teasp. pepper
	2 tablesp. salad oil
3 8-oz. cans tomato sauce	2 cups uncooked regular or processed white rice
1 3- or 4-oz. can whole mushrooms, undrained	3 or 4 onions, sliced
	3 green peppers, cut into eighths
2 tablesp. snipped parsley	½ teasp. salt

Day before: In 2 tablesp. hot oil in skillet, sauté 2 onions and garlic until golden; discard garlic. Add gravy, tomato sauce, mushrooms, parsley. Simmer, uncovered, 1 hr.

Meanwhile, sprinkle meat with ¾ teasp. salt, pepper; sauté in 2 tablesp. hot oil in another skillet until well browned on both sides. Remove meat.

To drippings in skillet, add a little mushroom sauce; stir till brown bits dissolve; add to rest of sauce. In 3-qt. casserole, arrange half of meat slices; top with rice combined with half of sauce. Add half of 3 or 4 sliced onions, rest of meat. Cover with rest of onions, then with peppers. Sprinkle with ½ teasp. salt. Pour on rest of sauce. Refrigerate.

About 1¾ hr. before serving: Start heating oven to 350°F. Bake casserole, covered, 1½ hr., or until hot. Makes 8 servings.

CALIFORNIA CHOP SUEY

½ lb. boned lean pork shoulder, cut into thin strips	1 cup celery, cut lengthwise into thin strips, then into 1″ lengths
½ teasp. salt	1 1-lb.-4-oz. can mixed Chinese vegetables or bean sprouts, drained
⅛ teasp. pepper	
2 tablesp. salad or olive oil	
¼ cup coarsely chopped onion	2 teasp. cornstarch
1½ cups hot water	1 teasp. sugar
2 bouillon cubes; or 2 teasp. meat-extract paste	3 tablesp. warm water
	1 tablesp. soy sauce
	Canned chow-mein noodles

Early in day: Sprinkle meat with salt, pepper. In hot oil in large skillet, cook meat about 10 min.; do not brown. Add onion; cook 5 min. Add hot water, bouillon cubes; simmer, covered, 15 to 20 min., or until meat is fork-tender. Refrigerate.

About 20 min. before dinner: To meat mixture, add celery; bring to boil, covered; cook 5 min. Add Chinese vegetables; mix lightly; heat till boiling. Combine cornstarch, sugar, warm water, soy sauce; stir into hot mixture; cook 1 or 2 min., or until slightly thickened. Taste; season if necessary.

Serve on heated chow-mein noodles, shoestring potatoes, or hot rice. Makes 4 servings.

SPICY MEAT BALLS EN BROCHETTE

¾ lb. boned pork shoulder, ground	1 1-lb.-4-oz. can pineapple chunks, drained
1 12-oz. can luncheon meat, ground	½ cup brown sugar, packed
1 cup fresh bread crumbs	½ teasp. dry mustard
1 egg, beaten	¼ cup vinegar
¼ cup milk	¼ cup water

Start heating oven to 350°F. Combine meats, crumbs, egg, milk; shape into 18 small balls. On each 8″ skewer, place 3 meat balls, alternating each ball with 2 pineapple chunks; place skewers in a shallow open pan about 13½″ x 10″ x 2″.

Combine brown sugar, mustard, vinegar, water; stir until sugar dissolves. Pour over meat balls, along with any leftover pineapple chunks. Bake 1 hr., basting frequently.

Serve on skewers with baked pineapple chunks. Makes 6 servings.

To Do Ahead: Early in day, shape balls; refrigerate. About 1 hr. 10 min. before serving, start baking.

TRANSYLVANIA GOULASH
(Székely Gulyás)

2 lb. boneless pork or veal shoulder	1 tablesp. salt
6 medium onions, chopped	1½ 10½-oz. cans condensed beef bouillon, undiluted
¼ cup snipped fresh dill or 1 teasp. ground dill seed	4 teasp. paprika
	1 1-lb.-11-oz. can sauerkraut, drained
1 clove garlic, minced	2 pt. commercial sour cream
1 teasp. caraway seeds	

One day or several days ahead:

1. Trim fat from meat; cut meat into 3″ pieces.

2. In Dutch oven or heavy kettle, combine meat, onions, dill, garlic, caraway seeds, salt, and bouillon. Bring to boil; simmer goulash, covered, 1 hr.

3. Then dissolve paprika in 1 cup hot broth from goulash; add to goulash along with sauerkraut.

4. Simmer, covered, 1 hr. longer, or until meat is tender. Stir in sour cream; refrigerate, covered.

To serve: Reheat goulash over very low heat, uncovered, stirring occasionally, about 40 min., or until heated through. Serve with parsley-buttered potatoes and, if desired, with more sour cream and dill. Makes 6 servings.

PORK CHOPS AND STEAKS

Pork chops are favorites when braised to rich-brown, tender, juicy perfection. Broiling is not always as satisfactory. Unless broiled at a moderate temperature, they may become hard and dry by the time they are well done in the center.

To Buy and Store

Select a Cut:

LOIN PORK CHOPS:

Rib Chop (Fig. 25) usually has 1 rib; may be boneless. A 1"-thick chop weighs 4 to 5 oz.

Loin Chop (Fig. 27) is the most popular pork chop because it has tenderloin. A 1"-thick chop weighs 5 to 6 oz.

Boned Loin Chop is a special loin chop, with bones removed.

Blade Loin Chop (also called first cut) is cut from shoulder end of loin. A ½"-thick chop weighs 4 to 6 oz.

Sirloin Chop is cut from ham end of loin and contains tenderloin. A ½"-thick chop weighs 4 to 6 oz.

SHOULDER STEAKS:

Blade Steak (Fig. 26) contains only small piece of blade bone. A ⅓"-thick chop weighs 5 to 7 oz.

Arm Steak (Fig. 28) has small round bone and is a thrifty buy. A ⅓"-thick chop weighs 5 to 6 oz.

Leg Steaks are cut from the fresh leg (ham), and have only a small round bone. They are sometimes called pork cutlets.

Amount to Buy: Allow ½ to ¾ lb. bone-in chops per serving, ⅓ to ½ lb. boned chops per serving. One-inch thick chops take longer to cook, but make a finer appearance than thin chops.

To Store: Store as in To Store Meat, p. 172.

BRAISED PORK CHOPS OR STEAKS

Pork chops and steaks are usually braised, but pork chops are also popular for outdoor cooking over coals. They should be cooked well done.

1. Choose loin or shoulder pork chops or pork steaks that are 1" thick*; when done, they're more attractive than thinner ones. Allow 1 per person. Trim a bit of fat from chops or steaks. Lightly sprinkle both sides of chops with salt and pepper or monosodium glutamate; rub with cut clove garlic if desired.

2. In skillet over low heat, heat a piece of fat; then remove. Brown chops slowly in melted fat till rich golden brown on both sides — 15 to 20 min. (Spoon off excess fat as it accumulates.)

3. Add ⅓ to ½ cup boiling water; canned tomatoes; commercial sour cream; or pineapple, orange, or tomato juice. (The thinner the chops or the smaller the skillet, the less liquid is needed.) Also add a little minced onion.

4. Cover skillet. Simmer chops or steaks slowly about 45 to 60 min.,* or until fork-tender and *well done*, turning them several times during cooking. Season to taste. Remove to heated platter. Keep warm while making Velvety Meat Gravy, p. 177, from drippings in skillet.

If you're braising ½" loin or shoulder pork chops, braise 30 min. after browning.

WITH GLAZED APPLES: After browning chops or steaks, add 2 tablesp. minced onion and ½ cup tomato juice. Serve with Glazed Apple Quarters, p. 436.

WITH APPLE: Serve chops or steaks with Fried Apple Rings, p. 436, or with applesauce.

BREADED: Before browning chops or steaks, dip into flour or beaten egg, then into packaged dried bread crumbs.

BARBECUED: Use ⅓ to ½ cup barbecue sauce instead of boiling water.

WITH HERBS: Mix each ¼ cup flour with ¼ teasp. dried marjoram, sage, or thyme. Sprinkle over chops or steaks before browning.

WITH PINEAPPLE: Use ¼ to ⅓ cup syrup from canned sliced pineapple instead of boiling water. Serve chops or steaks with Sautéed Pineapple, p. 436.

PORK-CHOP-LIMA SUPPER

4 loin pork chops, ¾" thick	1 10½-oz. can condensed cream-of-mushroom soup, undiluted
Salt	
Pepper	
3 cups drained cooked or canned dried limas	½ cup milk
2 onions, thinly sliced	1 teasp. caraway seeds (optional)

1. Sprinkle chops on both sides with salt and pepper. In a little fat in skillet, brown chops well on both sides. Pour off fat. Top chops with limas and onion slices.

2. Mix cream-of-mushroom soup with milk; pour over chops. Sprinkle with caraway seeds.

3. Cover skillet; simmer pork chops 45 min., or until done.

Nice with buttered spinach (frozen or fresh) with lemon or lime wedges, canned stewed tomatoes, rye bread, sliced bananas with flaked coconut, and tea or coffee. Makes 4 servings.

✣ FOR 2: Halve all ingredients except soup.

BROWNED RICE-AND-PORK CASSEROLE

4 loin pork chops, ¾" thick	¼ cup water
Seasoned salt	1 teasp. salt
½ cup uncooked regular or processed white rice	Dash pepper
	4 medium onions
1 10¾-oz. can beef gravy (1¼ cups)	2 large carrots, cut on angle into 1" slices

About 1½ hr. before dinner: Start heating oven to 350°F. Trim bit of fat from chops and heat in skillet. Sprinkle chops well with seasoned salt; then brown well on both sides in hot skillet; remove to 2-qt. casserole. Add rice to drippings in skillet, and cook, stirring, until browned; stir in gravy, water, salt, pepper. Arrange onions and carrots on top of chops; pour on gravy mixture. Bake, uncovered, 1 hr., or until chops and vegetables are tender. Makes 4 servings.

BAKED PORK CHOPS WITH MIXED BEANS

4 loin pork chops or shoulder steaks, ½" thick	½ teasp. dry mustard
	1 1-lb.-4-oz. can kidney beans, drained
Salt and pepper	1 1-lb.-4-oz. can green limas, drained
¼ cup minced onion	
1 clove garlic, minced	¼ cup catchup
1 teasp. brown sugar	2 tablesp. vinegar

Start heating oven to 350°F. Trim a bit of fat from chops; in skillet over low heat, heat piece of fat; then remove. Brown chops slowly in melted fat till rich golden brown on both sides — 15 to 20 min. (Spoon off excess fat as it accumulates.) Sprinkle chops with salt, pepper; set aside.

In drippings in skillet, sauté onion and garlic 5 min., or until tender. Stir in brown sugar, mustard, beans, catchup, vinegar; mix well; season if necessary. Pour into 2-qt. casserole. Arrange chops over beans. Bake, cov-

ered, 45 min., or until chops are fork-tender. Makes 4 servings.

PORK CHOPS ITALIANO

4 shoulder pork chops, about 1" thick	½ clove garlic, sliced (optional)
Seasoned salt	2 large green peppers, cut in ¾" strips
Pepper	2 8-oz. cans tomato sauce
½ lb. small fresh mushrooms (optional)	½ bay leaf
	1 tablesp. lemon juice
1 tablesp. salad oil	⅛ teasp. dried sage
1 medium onion, chopped	

About 1¾ hr. before serving:

1. Trim pork chops of all excess fat; sprinkle with seasoned salt and pepper. In large skillet, sauté chops till well browned, draining fat as it collects; place chops in a large roasting pan or 2½-qt. casserole.
2. Arrange mushrooms (if large, halve) around chops. Start heating oven to 375°F.
3. In a clean, large skillet, in salad oil, sauté onions, garlic, and green peppers until golden; add tomato sauce, 1 teasp. seasoned salt, ⅛ teasp. pepper, bay leaf, lemon juice, and sage; simmer, covered, until vegetables are almost fork-tender. Pour sauce over chops and mushrooms, covering all.
4. Bake, covered, until pork chops are done — about 1 hr.
5. When chops are done, uncover and rearrange them, mushrooms, and pepper strips, skimming off fat if necessary. Makes 4 servings.

PORK TENDERLOIN

To Buy and Store

Pork tenderloin is a 9"- to 12"-long, tapering, tender piece of lean meat that lies along the backbone, inside the loin. It weighs ¾ to 1½ lb. It's sold whole, thickly sliced, or flattened into fillets and is the most tender and one of the most popular pork cuts.

Frozen pork-tenderloin patties, packaged by well-known meat packers, are excellent; cook as label directs.

Amount to Buy: Allow 2 or 3 servings per lb.

To Store: Store as in To Store Meat, p. 172. Keep frozen tenderloin patties frozen until time to use.

BAKED, STUFFED PORK TENDERLOIN

3 pork tenderloins (¾ lb. each)	½ recipe Buttery Bread Stuffing, p. 340
Salt	
Clove garlic, cut (optional)	

Start heating oven to 350°F. Split each tenderloin lengthwise almost all the way through. Lay flat; sprinkle with salt; rub with garlic. Spread half of each tenderloin with stuffing. Fold halves together; tie with string. Set on rack in shallow open pan. Bake 1¼ hr., or until tender; remove string. Makes 6 servings.

BREADED PORK TENDERLOIN

3 pork tenderloins (¾ lb. each)	1 egg, slightly beaten
Clove garlic, cut (optional)	2 tablesp. water
Seasoned Flour, p. 9	Packaged dried bread crumbs
	¼ cup fat or salad oil

Cut meat into 2″-thick slices. Rub lightly with garlic. Dip into Seasoned Flour, then into egg mixed with water, then into crumbs. In hot fat in skillet, cook meat until golden brown on all sides; then cook over low heat, covered, 30 min., or until tender.

Serve with Italian Tomato Sauce, p. 530. Makes 6 servings.

PIGS' KNUCKLES OR HOCKS

To Buy and Store

Pigs' knuckles are the lower part of the picnic shoulder or the leg of pork and may be purchased as fresh, or as cured and smoked.

Amount to Buy: Allow 1 lb. per serving.

To Store: Store as in To Store Meat, p. 172. Use fresh pork knuckles in 2 to 3 days; cured and smoked knuckles in 1 to 2 weeks.

PIGS' KNUCKLES WITH CABBAGE

4 pigs' knuckles	1 clove garlic, minced
1 tablesp. salt	1 medium head green cabbage, cut into 2″-wide wedges
1 cup celery tops	
1 bay leaf	
8 to 10 whole black peppers	2 teasp. salt

Wash knuckles; place in Dutch oven; cover with boiling water. Add 1 tablesp. salt, celery tops, bay leaf, black peppers, garlic. Simmer, covered, 2 hr., or until tender. Then add cabbage, 2 teasp. salt; cook, covered, 10 min., or until cabbage is tender. Lift cabbage and meat to heated platter. Makes 4 servings.

WITH LIMA BEANS: Omit cabbage. Soak 2 cups large California dried limas in 1 qt. cold water overnight. In morning, drain, reserving liquid. Add liquid to pigs' knuckles in Dutch oven; add enough boiling water to cover. Add 1 tablesp. salt, celery tops, bay leaf, black peppers, garlic. Simmer, covered, 2 hr., or until knuckles are tender. Add lima beans, 2 teasp. salt; cook, covered, 40 min., or until beans are tender. Makes 4 servings.

SPARERIBS

Spareribs are the ribs and breast bone which have been removed from a fresh side of pork. See Fig. 24.

To Buy and Store

Most spareribs are fresh pork and are pink in color. Ribs are also sold as pickled or cured and smoked. Sometimes in the South, cured ribs, grayish in color, are sold; before you use them, these must be soaked in water to remove excess salt. So know what you are buying.

There are 2 sheets, or sides, of spareribs to each pork animal. Top-quality ones have a good portion of meat between the rib bones and a thin covering over the bones. They weigh 1½ to 3 lb. Ask meatman to chop through ribs at large end.

Amount to Buy: Allow about ¾ to 1 lb. spareribs per serving.

To Store: Store as in To Store Meat, p. 172.

BARBECUED SPARERIBS I

2 lb. spareribs
½ cup light molasses
½ cup catchup
½ cup chopped
  onions
1 clove garlic, minced
3 whole cloves
4 diced narrow strips
  of orange rind
Juice of ½ orange
1 tablesp. vinegar
1 tablesp. salad oil

½ teasp. prepared
  mustard
¼ teasp. salt
¼ teasp. pepper
1 tablesp. bottled
  thick meat sauce
½ teasp. Worcester-
  shire
¼ teasp. Tabasco
1 tablesp. butter or
  margarine

Start heating oven to 325°F. Place spareribs in shallow open pan; cover with foil; roast ½ hr. Pour off fat; roast ½ hr. longer.

Meanwhile, make sauce: Combine molasses and rest of ingredients; boil 5 min. Pour off excess fat from ribs; cover ribs with sauce. Increase oven heat to 400°F. Roast spareribs, uncovered, basting often, 45 min., or until they are fork-tender, very brown, and glazed.

To serve: With scissors, cut spareribs into pieces. Makes 2 or 3 servings.

BARBECUED SPARERIBS II

3 tablesp. honey
⅓ cup soy sauce
3 tablesp. grenadine
1 tablesp. salt
⅓ cup bourbon or
  rye

2 tablesp. granulated
  sugar
½ teasp. black pep-
  per
4 to 5 lb. spareribs
  (2 racks)

In large bowl, stir together honey, soy sauce, grenadine, salt, bourbon, sugar, and pepper. Marinate spareribs in this mixture 2 or 3 hr.

Preheat broiler as manufacturer directs. Broil ribs 5″ from heat, turning and basting often, until meat becomes a deep-brown color. Makes 6 to 8 servings.

For Outdoor Grilling: These spareribs are great, grilled over hot coals. Barbecue them slowly, turning frequently and basting often.

SPARERIBS AND SAUERKRAUT

2 to 4 tablesp. fat or
  salad oil
3 lb. spareribs
2 large onions, sliced
¼ teasp. salt
⅛ teasp. pepper
½ cup boiling water

1 1-lb.-13-oz. can
  sauerkraut
¼ to ½ teasp. cara-
  way seeds
1 cooking apple,
  pared, cored,
  grated

In hot fat (amount depends on fat on meat) in Dutch oven, sauté spareribs until brown on all sides. Add onions; sauté until tender. Sprinkle with salt, pepper. Add water; simmer, covered, 1 hr. Move spareribs to one side of Dutch oven; place sauerkraut, caraway seeds, and apple on other side; cook, covered, 20 to 30 min. Season to taste.

To serve: Lift sauerkraut from liquid; arrange on one end of platter. With scissors, cut spareribs into pieces; place on other end of platter. Makes 3 or 4 servings.

PINEAPPLE-SPARERIB BARBECUE

3 lb. spareribs
Salt
2 tablesp. butter or
  margarine
¼ cup chopped onion
¼ cup chopped celery
¼ cup chopped green
  pepper

1 tablesp. cornstarch
1 1-lb.-4-oz. can pine-
  apple chunks
¼ cup wine vinegar
1 tablesp. soy sauce
Dash pepper

Start heating oven to 450°F. Lightly sprinkle spareribs with salt; place in shallow open pan. Roast ½ hr., pour off fat. Reduce oven heat to 350°F.

Meanwhile, in hot butter in saucepan, cook onion, celery, and green peppers 5 min. Stir in cornstarch, 1 cup syrup drained from pineapple chunks; cook, stirring, till transparent. Add vinegar, soy sauce, pepper, pineapple chunks; pour over ribs. Bake uncovered, basting occasionally, 1 hr., or till fork-tender.

To serve: With scissors, cut spareribs into pieces. Makes 3 to 4 servings.

PURE FRESH-PORK SAUSAGE

To Buy and Store

Fresh, preseasoned, pure pork sausage comes as links, patties, or sausage meat in rolls and packages.

Because of great differences in the quality and flavor of pork sausage, your safest guide is to buy a trusted brand. Be sure, too, that the sausage has been kept refrigerated at market and has a fresh pink color.

Amount to Buy: Allow 1 lb. sausage links, patties, or meat for 4 servings.

To Store: Store at once as in To Store Meat, p. 172.

TO COOK FRESH-PORK SAUSAGE

Pork sausage must be cooked well done, or till it loses all its pink color and is nicely browned. But it should not be dry.

PAN-FRIED SAUSAGE PATTIES: Shape packaged meat into ½″-thick patties. Cook slowly over low heat, turning occasionally, 12 to 15 min., or until meat is brown outside and gray inside, with no trace of pink. Pour off fat as it collects (refrigerate fat; use as in Leftover Bacon Fat, p. 217).

PAN-FRIED SAUSAGE LINKS: Place links in cold skillet with ¼ cup water. Simmer, covered, 5 min. (Don't boil, don't prick with fork.) Drain off water; then pan-fry slowly, turning with tongs, until evenly browned and crisp — 8 to 10 min.

BAKED SAUSAGE LINKS: This is a nice way to cook a pound of sausage at a time. Arrange links in shallow baking pan (don't pile). Bake at 400°F., turning with tongs, until evenly browned — 20 to 30 min.

To serve: Serve sausage with eggs cooked your favorite way. Or serve on canned pineapple slices, sautéed in sausage fat. Or serve with applesauce, chili sauce, or Fried Apple Rings, p. 436.

SAUSAGE CASSEROLE DE LUXE

8 pork sausage links
1 1-lb.-2-oz. can sweet potatoes, drained
3 medium apples, pared
1 tablesp. flour
½ teasp. salt
1 tablesp. brown sugar
¼ cup canned pineapple juice
¼ cup water

About 1 hr. before serving:
1. Start heating oven to 375°F. In large skillet, lightly brown sausage links.
2. Into a 2-qt. casserole slice potatoes and apples.
3. In small bowl blend flour, salt, brown sugar, pineapple juice, and water; pour over potatoes and apples; top with sausage. Bake 45 min., or until apples are tender.

Serve with green-bean-and-cabbage slaw, then sherbet glasses of prunes, sauced with vanilla pudding. Makes 4 servings.

TWELVE O'CLOCK LENTIL SAUSAGES

1 cup dried lentils
1 qt. cold water
⅔ cup minced onions
1 tablesp. snipped parsley
½ clove garlic, minced
3 tablesp. minced celery
2 teasp. salt
⅛ teasp. pepper
1 tablesp. fat or salad oil
1 tablesp. flour
½ lb. fresh pork-sausage links
2 medium tomatoes, sliced, peeled
Seasoned salt

Day before: Wash and pick over lentils; soak overnight in cold water.

The day: Drain lentils, reserving liquid; heat 2 cups liquid. Add lentils, onions, parsley, garlic, celery, salt, pepper; simmer, covered, 12 to 15 min., or until nearly tender.

Drain lentil mixture; measure liquid. Place lentil mixture in greased 10″ x 6″ x 2″ baking dish. Melt fat in saucepan; stir in flour; add 1¼ cups lentil liquid; cook until thickened; pour over lentils.

Start heating oven to 350°F. Pan-fry sausage links as at left. Sprinkle tomato slices with seasoned salt. Place sausages and tomatoes on top of lentils. Bake 20 min. Makes 4 to 5 servings.

BROWN 'N' SERVE PORK SAUSAGE

To Buy, Store, and Heat

Good news! You can now buy packaged, fully cooked sausage links, or patties, with a fine fresh-pork-sausage flavor, that need only to be browned.

Amount to Buy: Allow ½ lb. fully cooked brown 'n' serve sausage for 4 to 5 servings.

To Store: Keep refrigerated. Use within 10 days.

To Cook: Because brown 'n' serve sausages are fully cooked, they need only a quick 3 min. browning and heating in a skillet or broiler —

and there will be almost no drippings — a real time-saver. So they are excellent in mixed grills and quick-grilled sandwiches as well as fine for breakfast. Try them, too, in casserole and combination dishes, and in poultry stuffings.

HERB-STUFFED PEPPERS WITH SAUSAGES

2 large green peppers	1 celery top, snipped
1 large onion, minced	½ teasp. salt
¼ cup butter or margarine	⅛ teasp. pepper
	1 egg, beaten
4 slices white bread, crumbed	2 8-oz. cans tomato sauce
½ teasp. dried marjoram	1 pkg. brown 'n' serve sausages
½ teasp. dried thyme	

1. Start heating oven to 400°F.
2. Meanwhile, halve peppers lengthwise; remove seeds; in boiling, salted water, cook, covered, 5 min. Sauté onion in butter until tender. To onion, add bread, marjoram, thyme, celery, salt, pepper, egg; toss to blend.
3. In 10″ x 6″ x 2″ baking dish, place tomato sauce; set pepper halves in it; heap bread mixture in peppers. Place sausages in pie plate. Bake both 20 min. To serve, arrange sausage around peppers.

Serve with antipasto (celery, olives, anchovies, coleslaw), corn with mushrooms, crisp rye wafers, cheesecake topped with crushed pineapple, and coffee with twist of lemon. Makes 4 servings.

SMOKED COUNTRY AND POLISH SAUSAGE

To Buy, Store, and Cook

These 2 types of smoked link sausage come 4″ to 5″ long, or as large rings of 1 lb. or more. (Polish sausage contains garlic.) Top-quality ones are branded.

Amount to Buy: Allow about 1 lb. sausage for 6 servings.

To Store: Keep refrigerated. Use within 6 days.

To Cook: Simmer sausages in water to cover about 20 min.; drain; serve. Or simmer about

10 min.; drain; then in skillet, brown slowly on all sides.

SAUCY LINKS, POLENTA STYLE

1 cup yellow corn meal	2 tablesp. butter or margarine
8 packaged smoked sausage links	1 onion, chopped
	1 8-oz. can tomato sauce

Cook corn meal into a mush as package directs; spoon into 2-qt. casserole. Arrange sausage links on top. Start heating oven to 350°F. In butter, in skillet, sauté onion until golden; add tomato sauce; pour over sausages. Bake 30 min. Makes 4 servings.

LET'S HAVE CURED PORK

Never before has cured pork been available in such a variety of types and sizes.

HAMS AND PICNICS

Today well-known meat packers proudly brand and clearly identify each style of ham and smoked picnic on the wrapper, tag, and often the meat itself. These markings, together with the information on the wrapper, can guide you in buying just the style you want. The purple U.S. Inspected and Passed stamp on the meat itself assures its wholesomeness. If the wrapper is missing, use the buying guides below.

To Buy Hams and Picnics

If you have ample time in which to bake a ham or smoked picnic, you will probably choose one of the uncooked, or cook-before-eating, styles.

If time is precious, however, consider a ham or smoked picnic labeled "fully cooked." Or buy a trusted canned brand. Don't be misled by such terms as "tenderized," "tendered," etc. These are advertising slogans and must never be construed to mean that the ham is cooked.

Uncooked (Cook-before-Eating) Hams and Picnics:

WHOLE HAM: Today's fine, wrapped, mild-cured ham (8 to 24 lb.), labeled "cook before eating," has a mild, rich flavor and extra tenderness. It needs no soaking or parboiling and cooks in less time than the old-fashioned kind.

THREE-IN-ONE HAM: Instead of baking a whole ham, you may wish to have the meatman cut a whole ham (8 to 24 lb.) into a shank end, center cut, and butt end. Then you can bake the shank and butt ends and broil, pan-broil, or bake the center slices.

HALF A HAM: If half a ham (4 to 12 lb.) seems the best buy for you, ask for a *full butt half* (Fig. 19), or *full shank half* (Fig. 20). If you want sliceable meat, don't buy an end piece of ham; the end piece is what's left *after* the center slices have been sold.

FULL SHANK HALF OF HAM: This is a real economy buy, and if you cut it in two as follows you can get a choice boneless piece, which you can slice and then pan-fry, broil, or bake. The bone-in piece that's left can be simmered (allow about 25 min. per lb.).

To Cut Shank in Two: Place shank, with cut side down, on board. Then, starting at top and hugging bone closely with sharp knife, cut shank lengthwise into 2 pieces — one meaty, the other with the bone.

SKINLESS, SHANKLESS HAM: This uncooked (cook-before-eating) ham has had the bony shank end, tough skin, and excess fat removed. The meaty, round roast that is left comes wrapped and branded with detailed baking directions on the label. It carves easily and beautifully into big horseshoe slices, starting right at the end of the ham. It comes in sizes from 6 lb. on up; or you can buy a half ham or center slices.

ROLLED, BONED WHOLE HAM: Here you have the advantage of easily carved, handsome slices and little waste. Completely boned and rolled, this ham (6 to 14 lb.) comes tied or wrapped in transparent casing. You can buy the whole ham, a piece, or slices by the pound, all ready to cook.

By the way, that casing on a boned ham is removed more easily before cooking than after. Just slit the casing lengthwise with the tip of a knife; then slip it off.

SMOKED PICNIC (SHOULDER): This is the lower half of the pork shoulder containing the arm bone. It weighs 4 to 10 lbs. It not only looks like ham, but has a true ham flavor when baked and glazed.

SMITHFIELD OR TENNESSEE STYLE HAM: This ham (9 to 16 lb.) has had a long cure, or cure and smoke, and so needs special handling. Follow label directions or Old-fashioned Country-Cured Hams, p. 212.

Cooked Hams and Picnics:

FULLY COOKED HAM: This wrapped, cooked ham comes with bone in (8 to 22 lb.) or rolled and boned (11 to 12 lb.). You can buy it whole, by the piece, or in slices. It may be served as is, or baked, pan-fried, or broiled. Check wrapper information carefully.

FULLY COOKED, SKINLESS, SHANKLESS HAM: This skinless, shankless ham, which is described at left, also comes fully cooked. Serve ham cold just as it comes from the wrapper; or you may serve it hot, following the heating directions on the label.

COOKED SMOKED PICNIC (SHOULDER): This wrapped, bone-in, cooked picnic (3 to 9 lb.) comes all ready to serve sliced cold, quickly heated, or glazed.

COOKED SMITHFIELD STYLE HAM: This cooked bone-in ham (8 to 12 lb.), with its distinctive flavor, is sold at specialty shops only.

BOILED HAM: This is cooked, boned ham, which is sold sliced.

PROSCIUTTO (ITALIAN STYLE HAM): This lean whole ham (12 to 20 lb.) has been pressed and aged in spices to achieve a concentrated, rich, mellow flavor. It is ready to serve, without further cooking, and should be sliced paper-thin.

CANNED BONED HAMS AND PICNICS: See p. 248.

AMOUNT OF HAM OR PICNIC TO BUY PER SERVING

Uncooked, bone-in	½ to ¾ lb.
Uncooked, boned	⅓ lb.
Cooked, bone-in	⅓ lb.
Cooked, boned	⅛ to ¼ lb.

To Store Hams and Picnics

Uncooked Ham or Smoked Picnic: Today's mild-cure meats must be handled like any fresh meat. Refrigerate an uncooked whole ham or picnic at once. See To Store, p. 172.

Home-cooked or Fully Cooked Ham or Smoked Picnic: Don't hold cooked ham or picnic longer than 7 days in refrigerator.

Don't Freeze Uncooked Mild-Cure Hams or Smoked Picnics Longer Than 1 Month. The fat of salted meat tends to become rancid when frozen. You may freeze leftover cooked-ham pieces, removed from bone, up to 4 to 6 weeks.

Smithfield or Tennessee Style Ham: Because of their heavy cure, these may be stored, uncooked, in a cool place for several months. Store cooked ones in refrigerator.

BAKED HAM

1. Check wrapper directions on an uncooked (cook-before-eating) ham and follow them to the letter. However, if the ham has no directions, check baking timetable that follows at right to decide about how long baking will take. Plan so that ham is done 20 min. before serving; this gives it time to firm up, and it will slice more easily. And don't forget to allow yourself 15 to 20 min. to skin and score the ham.

2. Start heating oven to 325°F. Place whole ham, with fat side up, or half ham, with cut side down, on rack in shallow open pan.

3. Insert roast-meat thermometer through fat side into center of thickest part of ham; don't let it touch bone. Don't add water; don't cover. Then bake, using timetable at right as an approximate guide.

4. *Caution:* Hams vary so in size, shape, amount of bone and fat, etc., that a baking timetable can only be approximate at best. So rely on a roast-meat thermometer if you want to be sure.

5. About ½ hr. before ham is done, remove from oven. Spoon drippings from pan into small dish; save for pan-frying, etc. Cut away any rind left on ham.

6. Then quickly score ham as follows: With sharp knife, make diagonal cuts, ⅛″ deep and about ¾″ apart, across entire fat surface of ham. Repeat, at an angle, to make squares or diamonds. Then stud top of ham, in pattern, with whole cloves.

7. Drizzle on molasses or honey, or maple, maple-blended, or buttered syrup. Then pat on brown sugar. Or substitute one of Glazes, p. 211.

TIMETABLE FOR BAKING UNCOOKED (COOK-BEFORE-EATING) SMOKED HAMS, PICNICS, AND BONELESS SHOULDER BUTTS

Refrigerated till baked at 325°F. Use shallow open pan. Add no water. Do not baste.

WEIGHT (*lb.*)	*APPROX-IMATE TOTAL BAKING TIME (hr.)	†MEAT THERMOMETER READING
BONE-IN WHOLE HAM		
8 to 10	3½	160°F.
10 to 12	3½ to 4	160°F.
12 to 15	4 to 4½	160°F.
15 to 18	4½ to 5	160°F.
18 to 22	5 to 6	160°F.
BONE-IN FULL BUTT OR SHANK HALF HAM		
5 to 8	3¼ to 3½	160°F.
BONED WHOLE HAM		
8 to 11	2½ to 3¼	160°F.
11 to 14	3¼ to 4	160°F.
BONED HALF HAM		
5 to 8	2½ to 3½	160°F.
BONE-IN SMOKED PICNIC		
4 to 6	2½ to 3	170°F.
6 to 8	3 to 4	170°F.
8 to 10	4 to 4½	170°F.
SMOKED BONELESS SHOULDER BUTT		
2	2	170°F.
3	3	170°F.

*Glaze, p. 211, may be applied ½ hr. before baking time is up. Or complete baking at 325°F.; then put on glaze and brown at 450°F.

†Indicates internal temperature at end of total baking period. Thermometer may be removed to glaze ham.

8. Return ham to 325°F. oven for ½ hr., or until nicely glazed (internal temperature will be 160°F.).

9. Or complete baking at 325°F. as timetable directs. Then score, stud, glaze, and bake at 450°F. until brown.

To Carve Baked Ham: See p. 296.

BAKED SMOKED PICNIC: Follow wrapper directions; or bake as on p. 210, using timetable as an approximate guide for baking time.

To Use Leftover Ham or Smoked Picnic: See p. 252, and Old-Fashioned Split-Pea Soup, p. 166.

GLAZES FOR BAKED HAM AND PICNICS

Spread baked ham, scored as in step 6, p. 210, with one of glazes below. Complete as in steps 8 and 9, above, adding rest of glaze in 2 or 3 applications (about every 10 min.) during rest of baking. Don't baste ham with glaze that has run down into drippings; it dulls luster of glaze.

HONEY-ORANGE: Mix ½ cup honey or corn syrup with 1 cup brown sugar and ½ cup orange juice.

MARMALADE: Mix 1 cup honey with ½ cup orange marmalade and dash Tabasco.

JELLY: With fork, stir ½ teasp. dry mustard and 1 to 4 tablesp. horse-radish into 1 cup red jelly.

APRICOT-PINEAPPLE: Combine 1 cup brown sugar, ½ cup canned whole fruit apricot nectar, ½ cup pineapple juice. Cook until thickened.

CRANBERRY: Mix ½ cup white corn syrup with 1 cup canned whole or jellied cranberry sauce. **P.S.** Halve above recipes to glaze a baked half ham or smoked picnic, a baked or simmered smoked boneless shoulder butt, or 2 cans luncheon meat or chopped ham.

TO HEAT FULLY COOKED HAMS AND PICNICS

Check wrapper directions on a fully cooked ham (whole or half) or smoked picnic, and follow them to the letter.

However, if the ham or picnic has no directions, place it on a rack in shallow open pan. Heat, using timetable, right, as an approxi-

TIMETABLE FOR HEATING FULLY COOKED HAMS AND PICNICS

Refrigerated till heated at 325°F. Use shallow open pan. Add no water. Do not baste.

WEIGHT (lb.)	*APPROXIMATE TOTAL HEATING TIME (hr.)	†MEAT THERMOMETER READING
BONE-IN WHOLE HAM		
8 to 10	2¼ to 2½	130°F.
10 to 12	2½ to 3	130°F.
12 to 15	3 to 3½	130°F.
15 to 18	3½ to 4	130°F.
18 to 22	4 to 4¾	130°F.
BONE-IN-FULL BUTT OR SHANK-HALF HAM		
5 to 8	1¾ to 2	130°F.
BONED WHOLE HAM		
10 to 12	2½ to 2¾	130°F.
12 to 14	2¾ to 3	130°F.
BONED HALF HAM		
5 to 8	1½ to 2¼	130°F.
BONE-IN SMOKED PICNIC		
4 to 6	1¾ to 2¼	130°F.
6 to 8	2¼ to 2¾	130°F.
8 to 10	2¾ to 3¼	130°F.

*Glaze, left, may be applied ½ hr. before heating time is up. Or complete heating at 325°F.; then put on glaze and brown at 450°F.

†Indicates internal temperature at end of total heating period. Thermometer may be removed to glaze meat.

mate guide; score as in step 6, p. 210; glaze as on p. 211; then bake at 450°F. until golden.

PARTY TOPPINGS FOR BAKED HAMS AND PICNICS

Bake or heat a whole or half ham or smoked picnic for complete time period in timetables, p. 210 or p. 211. Score as in step 6, p. 210. Then glaze and decorate as below.

STUDDED: Spread scored ham or picnic with some of Jelly Glaze, p. 211. Bake at 450°F. about 15 min., basting with more glaze. Set pecan or walnut halves, drained canned pineapple chunks, or orange cubes, in center of diamonds. Brush with more glaze; bake about 5 min.

ALMONDETTE: Spread scored ham or picnic with some of Honey-Orange Glaze, p. 211. Bake at 450°F. about 15 min., basting with more glaze. On meat, arrange sliced, slivered almonds and maraschino-cherry dots, placing 2 almonds together, fan-fashion, with cherry at base. Brush lightly with more glaze. Bake about 5 min.

PEACH: *Day Before:* Combine syrup from a 1-lb.-13-oz. can cling-peach slices with ¼ cup vinegar; ½ cup brown sugar, packed; 1 teasp. whole cloves; 1 stick cinnamon. Simmer 10 min. Add peaches; bring to boil. Refrigerate. When baking ham or picnic, use 1 cup of this syrup, mixed with 1 teasp. cornstarch, to baste it. Garnish top of baked ham or picnic with peach slices; or arrange slices in groups around meat.

OLD-FASHIONED COUNTRY-CURED HAMS

Virginia, Smithfield, and Tennessee style hams, with their special cure and firm texture, need presoaking and boiling. Unwrap ham; soak 24 to 30 hr. in cold water to cover; drain. Then place ham in large pot or old-fashioned wash boiler (cut off tip end of ham if necessary). Cover with water; simmer, covered, until tender (allow about 25 to 30 min. per lb.), or until large bone in heavy end of ham becomes loose and protrudes. Remove ham; remove skin. If desired, score fat as in step 6, p. 210. Top with one of Glazes for Baked Hams and Picnics, p. 211. Bake at 450°F. 15 min. Serve hot or cold, sliced paper-thin.

SMOKED BONELESS SHOULDER BUTT

To Buy and Store

National meat packers are now marketing packaged cured, smoked boneless shoulder butts with the packer's name on the label. These have a delightfully mild, sweet cure and taste, and can be used like ham.

Amount to Buy: Smoked boneless butt weighs from 1 to 4 lb. The 2-lb. size is a fine buy for a small family.

To Store: Refrigerate as in To Store Hams and Picnics, p. 209.

BAKED SMOKED BONELESS SHOULDER BUTT

Follow wrapper directions; or use timetable, p. 210, as an approximate guide for roasting time.

SIMMERED SMOKED BONELESS SHOULDER BUTT

Place 2- to 2½-lb. smoked boneless shoulder butt in deep kettle; add boiling water to cover. Simmer, covered, allowing about 50 min. per lb., or until fork-tender. Drain.

Serve hot or cold, as is. Or serve with barbecue sauce; Horse-radish Sauce I or II, p. 532; Mustard Sauce, p. 532; Curried Pineapple Sauce, p. 528; or Savory Jelly Sauce, p. 528. Makes 4 servings, plus leftovers (use leftovers as suggested for ham on pp. 252–258).

SAVORY: To boiling water in which smoked butt cooks, add 1 clove garlic, 6 whole cloves, 1 bay leaf, 4 whole black peppers. (Or omit peppers and add 1 teasp. celery seeds, ½ cup vinegar.)

GLAZED: Place hot simmered butt in shallow baking pan. Spoon on ½ recipe for one of Glazes for Baked Hams and Picnics, p. 211. Bake at 450°F. 15 min.

GOLDEN: Place hot simmered butt in shallow baking pan. Cover with honey, brown sugar, or marmalade. Bake at 400°F. about 15 min.

PAN-FRIED: Cut cold simmered butt into ¼″ slices; pan-fry until brown on both sides.

SMOKED HAM WITH BASIL RICE: Make Basil Rice, p. 370. Serve on platter, topped with sliced, cooked boneless shoulder butt. Makes 4 servings.

SMOKED BUTT, SOUTHERN STYLE

1 2- to 2½-lb. smoked boneless shoulder butt	¼ cup vinegar
	1 teasp. dry mustard
¼ cup butter or margarine	2 1-lb.-1-oz. cans kidney beans, drained
½ cup minced onion	1 1-lb. can green lima beans, drained
1 clove garlic, minced	½ cup catchup
2 teasp. brown sugar	Salt and pepper

About 3 hr. before serving: Cook butt as in Simmered Smoked Boneless Butt, p. 212.

About 15 min. before butt is done:

1. Start heating oven to 350°F. In butter, in skillet, sauté onion and garlic about 5 min., or until tender.
2. Add sugar, vinegar, mustard, drained kidney and lima beans, and catchup; mix well. Taste, then add salt and pepper if needed.
3. Pour bean mixture into 2-qt. casserole. Over beans arrange slices of butt, cut ¾″ thick. Bake, covered, about 15 min.; then, uncovered, 15 min. longer. Makes 6 servings.

SLICE OF HAM OR PICNIC

BAKED HAM OR PICNIC SLICE

UNCOOKED (COOK-BEFORE-EATING) HAM OR SMOKED PICNIC SLICE:

1. Use ham or smoked picnic slice, 1½″ to 2″ thick. Start heating oven to 325°F.
2. With scissors or knife, snip fat edge of slice in several places to keep it from curling; stud with whole cloves.
3. Place slice in 2- or 3-qt. baking dish. Then, if desired:

   a. Cover with ¼ recipe for one of Glazes for Baked Hams and Picnics, p. 211.

   b. Or spread with a little prepared mustard; then top with 2 tablesp. crushed cornflakes (optional).

   c. Or sprinkle with 2 tablesp. brown sugar mixed with ⅛ teasp. ground cloves or a little mustard. Then top with drained canned apricots, peach halves, or pineapple slices if desired.

4. Bake 1½″-thick ham or picnic slice about 1 to 1¼ hr.; 2″-thick slice, 1¾ to 2 hr., or until fork-tender, covered. Uncover last 15 to 20 min. to brown.

FULLY COOKED HAM OR SMOKED PICNIC SLICE: Prepare slice, 1½″ to 2″ thick (or thinner), as at left. Bake in baking dish, uncovered, at 325°F. 30 to 40 min., or until well browned.

HAM A LA STUFFING

3 tablesp. melted butter or margarine	Speck pepper
	⅛ teasp. poultry seasoning
¼ cup minced onion	
3 tablesp. minced celery	¼ cup cooked or canned whole-kernel corn
2 cups day-old bread crumbs	
	1 slice fully cooked ham, 1″ thick (about 1¼ lb.)
1 tablesp. minced green pepper	
⅛ teasp. salt	

Start heating oven to 350°F. In hot butter in large skillet, sauté onion until tender. Add celery, crumbs, green pepper, salt, pepper, poultry seasoning, corn. Heat well, stirring. Place ham in baking dish; top with stuffing. Bake uncovered 30 min. Makes 4 to 6 servings.

PINEAPPLE-STUFFED HAM: For stuffing, decrease bread crumbs to 1½ cups; substitute ¾ cup drained canned crushed pineapple for corn. Bake as above. Makes 4 to 6 servings.

SCALLOPED HAM, POTATOES, AND CARROTS

1 thin center slice uncooked (cook-before-eating) ham (¾ lb.)	1 cup milk
	3 cups thinly sliced, pared potatoes
2¼ teasp. flour	1 cup thinly sliced, pared carrots
1 10½-oz. can condensed cream-of-mushroom soup, undiluted	¼ cup minced onion
	¾ teasp. salt
	¼ teasp. pepper

Start heating oven to 325°F. In skillet, brown ham lightly on both sides; remove; cut into serving pieces. Stir flour into drippings left in skillet. Add soup, then slowly stir in milk. Heat, stirring, until boiling.

In 2-qt. casserole, arrange layers of ham, potatoes, carrots, and onions until all are used, sprinkling vegetables with combined salt and pepper. Pour on soup mixture. Bake, covered, 1 hr. Uncover; bake 15 min., or until potatoes and carrots are tender. Makes 3 or 4 servings.

PARTY STYLE: Double each ingredient. Use a 4-qt. casserole; bake, covered, 1 hr.; uncover, and bake ½ hr. until potatoes and carrots are tender. (Or bake in two 2-qt. casseroles as above.) Makes 8 servings.

FRIEDA'S HAM AND ENDIVES AU GRATIN

6 to 8 Belgian en-dives, roots trimmed	Dash cayenne pepper
½ cup butter or mar-garine	2 cups milk
⅓ cup lemon juice	¾ cup grated sharp Cheddar cheese
Salt	6 to 8 thin slices boiled ham
¼ cup all-purpose flour	Paprika

1. In large skillet, arrange endives in ¼ cup melted butter, lemon juice, 2 tablesp. water; sprinkle with ¼ teasp. salt. Simmer, covered, 30 min. (Add a little water if needed.)
2. Meanwhile, start heating oven to 450°F. In saucepan, melt ¼ cup butter; remove from heat. Stir in flour, cayenne, milk; bring to boil, stirring; reduce heat; add ½ cup cheese. Simmer over low heat until thickened and cheese is melted.
3. Drain tender endives; wrap each with a ham slice, leaving ends uncovered. Arrange in baking dish; cover with sauce; top with ¼ cup grated cheese, sprinkle of paprika. Bake 15 min. Makes 3 to 4 servings.

MUSHROOM-BAKED HAM

1 teasp. dry mustard	or fat
½ teasp. ground ginger	3 tablesp. butter or margarine
½ cup dry white wine	1 small onion, minced
1 2-lb. slice fully cooked ham, 1½" to 2" thick	¼ cup all-purpose flour
	1 cup milk
2 tablesp. salad oil	1 3- or 4-oz. can sliced mushrooms

1. Blend mustard, ginger, and wine; pour over ham slice in shallow dish; refrigerate at least 1 hr., turning occasionally.
2. *About 40 min. before dinner:* Start heating oven to 425°F. Drain ham slice well, reserving marinade. In hot oil, in large skillet with metal handle, sauté ham until brown on both sides; then remove from skillet and set aside; pour all fat from skillet.
3. In hot butter in same skillet, sauté onion just until soft.
4. Remove skillet from heat; blend in flour; then very slowly stir in milk and liquid from mushrooms. Return to heat, and cook slowly until smooth and thickened, stirring constantly; stir in mushrooms and marinade.
5. Arrange ham slice in sauce in skillet; bake 20 min., or until heated through and bubbly.

Nice with buttered green limas and peas, tossed salad with pickle-relish dressing, and rye bread. Makes 4 to 6 servings.

CRANBERRY-GLAZED HAM ROLLS

1 cup uncooked regular or processed white rice; or 2 cups packaged pre-cooked rice	½ teasp. salt
	¼ teasp. pepper
	2 cans whole-cranberry sauce
½ cup butter or margarine	½ cup brown sugar, packed
½ cup minced onion	¼ cup lemon juice
½ cup sliced celery	16 thin slices cooked ham

1. *Day before:* Cook rice as label directs. Meanwhile, in skillet, melt butter; in it sauté onions and celery until tender; add salt, pepper; refrigerate along with rice.
2. *Make sauce:* In medium saucepan, combine cranberry sauce, brown sugar, and lemon juice; refrigerate.
3. *The day:* At least 50 min. before serving, combine rice with celery mixture. Then, on each ham slice, place 1 spoonful of rice mixture; roll up; place, seam side down, in jelly-roll pan or roasting pan; refrigerate.
4. *About 30 min. before serving:* Start heating oven to 350°F. Meanwhile, heat cranberry sauce; then place a tablespoonful over each ham roll, using about one-third of sauce.
5. *About 20 min. before serving:* Place ham rolls in oven and bake 20 min., or until well heated through.
6. Arrange 2 ham rolls on each of 6 heated dinner plates (there will be 4 ham rolls left for seconds). Spoon a little more sauce over each ham roll; pass rest. Makes 6 servings.

Lamb Shanks with Parsley Pockets, p. 224

BROILED HAM OR PICNIC SLICE

1. Use uncooked or fully cooked ham, or smoked picnic slice, ½″ to 1½″ thick. (See timetable, below.)
2. With scissors or knife, snip fat edge of slice in several places to keep it from curling.
3. Preheat broiler 10 min., or as directed.
4. Arrange slice on broiler rack, with top of meat about 3″ below heat. Broil, using timetable, below, for approximate min. per side.
5. After broiling one side of slice, you may turn it and spread lightly with one of these:

1 tablesp. prepared mustard plus ¼ cup brown sugar
¼ cup tart jelly plus 1 tablesp. horse-radish
Orange, peach, or apricot marmalade; or honey
Melted butter or margarine, mixed with sliced scallions
½ cup brown sugar heated with 2 tablesp. prepared mustard, ¼ cup vinegar, and ½ cup canned pineapple juice

6. Or prepare any Broiled Fruit, p. 438; arrange on broiler pan in time to finish broiling with ham.
7. Or arrange halved, cooked white or sweet potatoes, mushroom caps, tomato halves, or cooked onions brushed with melted butter or margarine, on broiler pan in time to finish broiling with ham.

TIMETABLE FOR BROILING HAM OR PICNIC SLICE

Refrigerated till broiled in preheated broiler

THICKNESS OF SLICE	APPROXIMATE MINUTES PER SIDE
UNCOOKED (COOK-BEFORE-EATING) HAM OR SMOKED PICNIC	
1½″	10 to 15 min.
1″	9 min.
¾″	7 min.
½″	4 min.
FULLY COOKED HAM OR SMOKED PICNIC	
1″	5 min.
¾″	3 min.
½″	3 to 5 min. (don't turn)

PAN-BROILED HAM OR PICNIC SLICES

1. Use ham or smoked picnic slices ¼″ to ¾″ thick. (See timetable, below.)
2. Trim piece of fat from edge of slice; rub over heated skillet. With scissors or knife, snip fat edge of slices in several places to keep from curling.
3. Place slices in skillet. Pan-broil slowly, using timetable, below, as an approximate guide. When slices are done, they should be nicely browned on both sides.
4. Just before slices are done, sprinkle lightly with granulated or brown sugar. Also, on top and around ham, place canned pineapple slices or chunks, cling-peach halves, or apricot halves, if desired.
5. Or after pan-broiling, remove slices to heated platter. To fat in pan, add 3 tablesp. vinegar, 1½ teasp. prepared mustard, ½ teasp. sugar, ⅛ teasp. paprika, 1 tablesp. currant jelly. Stir well; heat; pour over slices.

Or pass one of these sauces: Quick Mustard, p. 528; Savory Jelly, p. 528; Horse-radish Sauce I or II, p. 532; Currant-Mint, p. 527; Curried Pineapple, p. 528.

TIMETABLE FOR PAN-BROILING HAM OR PICNIC SLICES

THICKNESS OF SLICES	APPROXIMATE MINUTES PER SIDE
UNCOOKED (COOK-BEFORE-EATING) HAM OR SMOKED PICNIC	
¾″	6 min.
½″	4 to 5 min.
¼″	2 to 3 min.
FULLY COOKED HAM OR SMOKED PICNIC	
¾″	3 min.
½″	2 min.
¼″	1½ min.

HAM A LA SWISS

About 15 min. before serving: For each serving, place 2 Swiss-cheese slices between two ¼″-thick cooked-ham slices. In 1 tablesp. hot butter in skillet, sauté "sandwich" 5 min. on each side, or till ham is golden and cheese begins to melt. Serve with canned whole or jellied cranberry sauce.

A Man's Barbecued Chicken, p. 271

GROUND HAM

CRANBERRY-HAM LOAF

2 eggs	ground
¾ cup milk	1 lb. boned pork
1 teasp. salt	shoulder, ground
⅛ teasp. pepper	1 cup canned whole-
1 cup fresh bread	cranberry sauce
crumbs	¼ teasp. ground
1 lb. uncooked (cook-	cloves
before-eating) ham,	

Start heating oven to 400°F. With fork, slightly beat eggs; add milk, salt, pepper, crumbs; let stand a few minutes. Add ham, pork; combine well.

In shallow baking dish, shape meat into oval loaf. Mash cranberry sauce with cloves; spread on top of loaf. Bake 1 hr.

To serve: With 2 broad spatulas, lift onto heated platter. Makes 8 servings.

APPLE STUFFED HAM LOAF: Omit cranberry sauce and cloves. Make this apple stuffing: Sauté 1 minced small onion in ¼ cup butter or margarine until tender. Add 1 diced, pared, cored large cooking apple; 3 cups ½″ fresh bread squares; ½ cup dark or light raisins, rinsed in hot water; 1 teasp. salt; ⅛ teasp. pepper; ¼ teasp. dried sage; 1 tablesp. sugar.

Press half of meat mixture into 10″ x 5″ x 3″ loaf pan; pack stuffing on top, then rest of meat. Bake at 400°F. 1 hr. Place platter on top of loaf; then turn loaf out, upside down.

TWO-DAY CARAMEL HAM LOAF

3 cups fine fresh	¾ lb. uncooked
bread crumbs	(cook-before-
2 cups milk	eating) ham,
2 eggs	ground; or 1 can
½ teasp. salt	luncheon meat,
¼ cup nonfat dry	coarsely grated
milk	1 cup brown sugar,
½ teasp. dry mustard	packed
1½ lb. round beef,	2 teasp. whole cloves
ground	

Start heating oven to 350°F. Soak crumbs in 2 cups milk 5 min. With fork, beat eggs; add salt, nonfat dry milk, mustard, meats. Toss; then, with 2-tined fork, stir in crumb mixture, tossing well. Sprinkle bottoms of 2 9″ x 5″ x 3″ loaf pans with ½ cup brown sugar and 1 teasp. whole cloves; then firmly pack meat into pans.

(Or sprinkle bottom of shallow pan with ½ cup brown sugar and 1 teasp. whole cloves; place meat on top; shape into 2 flat loaves.) Sprinkle top of loaves with remaining sugar and cloves. Bake 1 hr. Remove from pans.

Serve 1 loaf hot, with drippings. Refrigerate other loaf for next day. Each loaf makes 4 servings.

ONE-LOAF STYLE: Sprinkle bottom of greased 10″ x 5″ x 3″ loaf pan with ½ cup brown sugar, packed, and 1 teasp. whole cloves. Firmly pack meat mixture into pan. Top with remaining sugar and cloves. Bake at 350°F. 1 hr. 15 min. Makes 8 servings.

BACON

To Buy and Store

Different brands of bacon vary in quality, flavor, uniformity, and size of slices, and in proportion of lean to fat. Once you know the brand you like, stick to it to be sure you get exactly what you pay for.

PACKAGED SLICED BACON: Sliced bacon comes in ½- and 1-lb. packages. Some is packaged in jars.

SLAB BACON: Slab bacon comes in pieces with the rind on. Slice it as you need it, using a sharp knife. Or have the meatman slice it to your order.

Amount to Buy: Buy only enough bacon for 1 week, as it begins to lose its fine flavor if it's held longer. There are about 8 to 10 slices in ½ lb. Allow about 2 slices per serving.

To Store: Keep bacon in refrigerator, well wrapped and away from strong-flavored foods. See To Store, p. 172. Remove bacon from protective wrapping only when ready to use it; remove only as much as you plan to cook. Don't freeze bacon. The fat may become rancid within a month.

To Cook Bacon

PAN-FRIED BACON: In large cold skillet or on griddle, over low heat, place overlapping slices of bacon, just as they come from the package. While they heat, separate them with 2 forks so that they lie flat. Cook slowly over low heat, turning with 2 forks or tongs, until crisp but not brittle, spooning off fat as it accumulates.

Allow 5 to 8 min. cooking time. Don't let fat smoke, or bacon flavor will be affected. Remove each slice as it browns; drain on paper towels or brown paper; keep hot.

BROILED BACON: Preheat broiler 10 min., or as manufacturer directs. Separate bacon slices carefully, to avoid tearing; place on broiler rack. Place 3″ from heat; broil 3 to 4 min. per side, or until crisp but not brittle, turning only once. Don't let bacon burn.

BAKED BACON (ideal for cooking a large quantity of bacon): Start heating oven to 400°F. Separate bacon slices. Place, with fat edge of each slice overlapping lean of next slice, on a rack in shallow pan. Bake 12 to 15 min., or until crisp but not brittle. No turning or draining is needed; bacon browns evenly.

BACON CURLS: Slowly pan-fry or broil bacon slices until light brown but still limp. Insert tip of fork in end of each slice; turn fork to wrap bacon around it. Carefully slip bacon curl off fork; finish frying. Makes attractive garnish for omelets, chops, vegetables, cheese soufflé, etc.

LEFTOVER BACON: Use leftover crisp bacon bits in vegetable salads, cream soups, creamed vegetables, eggs, or sandwiches.

LEFTOVER BACON FAT: Refrigerate in covered jar. Plan to use within 2 weeks. Nice for seasoning green beans, green limas, greens, macaroni, scalloped potatoes, etc. Nice, too, for making sauces and soups, for frying eggs, potatoes, meats, etc.

BACON CHOP SUEY

1 cup uncooked regular or processed white rice	1½ tablesp. cornstarch
½ lb. sliced bacon	1 teasp. salt
1 cup sliced onions	⅛ teasp. pepper
1½ cups sliced celery	1½ teasp. soy sauce
1 cup sliced mushrooms	2 cups shredded cabbage
2 cups water	1 cup sliced green peppers

Cook rice as label directs; keep hot. Fry half of bacon until crisp but not brittle; remove bacon. In bacon fat, brown onions, celery, mushrooms. Blend water with cornstarch; stir into onions; simmer, covered, 10 min. Add salt, pepper, soy sauce, cabbage, green peppers, and crisp bacon, in pieces. Cook covered, until just tender. Meanwhile, fry rest of bacon.

To serve: Make ring of cooked rice on platter; pour suey in center; garnish with bacon slices, halved. Makes 4 servings.

YANKEE PORK-AND-BEAN PIE

10 bacon slices	¼ cup maple-blended syrup
2 tablesp. bacon fat	1 teasp. salt
1 cup chopped onions	2 teasp. dry mustard
½ cup chopped green peppers	Dash paprika
2 1-lb. cans pork and beans with tomato sauce	1 10-oz. pkg. cornbread mix

Start heating oven to 425°F. In skillet, sauté bacon till light golden; drain on paper towels. Discard all but 2 tablesp. bacon fat; in it sauté onions and green pepper over low heat till tender. In 1½-qt. shallow baking dish, combine beans, syrup, salt, mustard, and paprika with onion-green pepper mixture. Prepare cornbread mix as label directs; arrange it, by heaping tablespoonfuls, around top edge of bean mixture. Bake 20 min., or till golden brown. Garnish with bacon strips. Makes 4 servings.

CANADIAN-STYLE BACON

To Buy and Store

Canadian-style bacon is a cured, smoked boneless strip of pork loin, much leaner than bacon. It comes by the pound in a casing, or sliced, prepackaged, and branded by well-known meat packers. Most of it today is ready to eat, but be sure to check on this when you are buying. Cook as wrapper directs, or by any of the methods on p. 218.

Amount to Buy: Buy by the pound, in one piece, to simmer or bake. Or buy, sliced, to pan-fry or broil. Allow about 2 to 4 oz., or 2 to 4 thin slices, per serving.

To Store: Refrigerate as in To Store Hams and Picnics, p. 209.

To Cook Canadian-Style Bacon

PAN-FRIED: In skillet, pan-fry ⅛″- to ¼″-thick slices of Canadian-style bacon very slowly as in Pan-Fried Bacon, p. 216, allowing about 5 min. on each side.

BROILED: Broil ¼″-thick slices of Canadian-style bacon about 3″ from heat as in Broiled Bacon, p. 217, allowing about 5 min. for each side.

BAKED CANADIAN-STYLE BACON

Start heating oven to 325°F. Slip off casing from a piece of Canadian-style bacon while holding bacon under cold running water. Place bacon, with fat side up, on rack in shallow open pan; insert roast-meat thermometer into center of bacon. Bake to 170°F. on roast-meat thermometer, or approximately as follows:

2-lb. piece: about 1½ hr.
4-lb. piece: about 2 hr. 20 min.
6-lb. piece: about 3 hr.

Then stud surface of bacon with whole cloves; spread with brown sugar, orange or peach marmalade, canned crushed pineapple, or jelly. Bake at 400°F. 15 min., or until browned. Serve sliced, hot or cold.

GOLDEN-TOPPED BAKED BEANS

2 1-lb. cans baked beans in tomato sauce	style bacon slices, ¼″ thick
1 tablesp. minced onion	4 ¼″-thick halved orange slices
1 teasp. prepared mustard	¼ cup brown sugar, packed
1 teasp. horse-radish	1 tablesp. butter or margarine
Prepared mustard	Whole cloves
8 uncooked Canadian-	

Start heating oven to 400°F. In deep fluted 9″ pie plate or shallow casserole (5-cup capacity), combine beans, onion, 1 teasp. mustard, horse-radish. Spread bit of mustard on each Canadian-style bacon slice; arrange with orange slices, pin-wheel fashion, on top of beans. Sprinkle all with brown sugar; dot with butter; stud meat with cloves. Bake 25 min. Makes 4 servings.

PINEAPPLE-STYLE BAKED BEANS: Make as above, substituting 4 halved, well-drained canned pineapple slices for oranges. Substitute 12-oz. can luncheon meat, cut into 6 slices, for Canadian-style bacon.

LET'S HAVE LAMB

Lamb is on the market the year round, but the supply in some areas may vary. The many different cuts add pleasing variety to family and company meals.

The lean of quality lamb should be pinkish to deep red in color, firm and fine-textured, with an even covering of clear, white brittle fat and a moderate amount of marbling in the lean.

Your guides to buying quality lamb are the round purple U.S. Inspected and Passed stamp for wholesomeness, plus the packer's trusty brand name, or Federal grade stamps.

On the following pages, we suggest and describe favorite uses for many of the retail cuts of lamb. Our diagram of the lamb animal, under Popular Cuts of Meat, will help you to identify these cuts better.

LAMB ROASTS

To Buy and Store

Select a Cut:

FULL LEG OF LAMB: This roast, containing sirloin and short leg, weighs 6 to 10 lb. It's a good buy for a large family as it has little waste. It may be cut into 2 roasts, the Sirloin Roast and Short Leg (Round) Roast, or into Sirloin Chops and Short Leg (Round) Roast. See Two-In-One Roast, below:

Sirloin Roast is the broad upper end of a full leg of lamb. When cut off, it makes a good, but difficult to carve, small roast of 2 to 2½ lb.; or it may be cut into chops (Fig. 34).

Short Leg (Round) Roast (Fig. 34) is the full leg of lamb *after* the sirloin roast or chops have been cut off; it weighs 5 to 6 lb. If the meat has been trimmed from the end of the leg bone, it is called "French Style."

Sometimes the shank bone is removed, and the meat is folded and skewered to the thicker part of the leg. This compact roast fits nicely into a small pan for roasting. It is called an "American Leg."

HALF LEG OF LAMB: When a full leg of lamb is cut in half, either half of the leg — shank end or sirloin end — is a good buy for 2 or 3 persons. It can weigh 3 to 5 lb.

ROLLED, BONED LEG: This is the full leg with bone removed; meat is rolled and tied. Roast weighs 3 to 6 lb.

TWO-IN-ONE ROAST: Buy a full leg of lamb. Have meatman cut off 3 or 4 steaks, 3/4″ to 1″ thick, from sirloin end, to broil, p. 223, or pan-broil, p. 224, or store in freezer for later use. Roast rest of leg.

CUSHION SHOULDER ROAST: This square, flat roast from the lamb shoulder resembles a pillow. Bones are removed to form a pocket for stuffing. After stuffing, the open sides should be sewed or skewered. It weighs 2½ to 4 lb.

ROLLED, BONED SHOULDER ROAST: For this cut, the shoulder of lamb is boned, rolled, and tied. It weighs 2½ to 4 lb., is tender, juicy, easy to carve.

CROWN ROAST: This makes a nice company dish. A crown of lamb usually contains 14 ribs tied in a circle, and weighs about 2½ to 4 lb. Larger crowns may contain any desired number of ribs. The meat is trimmed from the end of the rib bones, French style. Be sure the backbone is cut off; otherwise, crown will be difficult to carve.

Amount to Buy: Allow ½ to 3/4 lb. bone-in lamb roast per serving, 1/4 to ½ lb. boned lamb roast per serving. Allow 2 or 3 ribs per serving if it's a crown roast.

Be sure to have the meatman note on the bill the weight of the oven-ready roast, to guide you in computing the roasting time.

To Store: Store as in To Store Meat, p. 172.

ROAST LAMB

1. Use one of leg cuts, or a rolled shoulder of lamb.
2. Check roasting timetable, p. 220, to see about how long roasting will take. Plan so lamb is done 20 min. before serving; it will slice more easily, and you will have time to make gravy.
3. Start heating oven to 325°F.
4. Do not remove the "fell," the thin paper-like covering on the lamb. The leg of lamb will hold its shape better during cooking.
5. Sprinkle lamb with salt and pepper. Or add one of the following seasonings:
CHILI-MUSTARD: Omit salt and pepper. Rub lamb with cut clove garlic; sprinkle with 1½ teasp. salt, ½ teasp. pepper, ½ teasp. dry mustard, 1/4 teasp. chili powder, and 1 tablesp. caraway seeds. Add a little chili sauce to gravy.
GARLIC: Rub lamb with cut clove garlic; or tuck small pieces of garlic in small gashes in surface of meat.
HERBS: Rub lamb with 1 teasp. dried marjoram, rosemary, or thyme.
MARINADE: To 1 cup French dressing, add 2 sliced small onions, 2 cut cloves garlic, ½ teasp. dried thyme. Pour over lamb in deep dish. Refrigerate 6 hr. or longer, turning once. Drain; then roast.
MINT OR PARSLEY: Make a few gashes in top of roast. Insert a few leaves or some snipped mint or parsley.
SPICE: Rub 2 teasp. curry powder or ground ginger into lamb.
6. Place roast, with fat side up, on rack in shallow open pan.
7. Insert roast-meat thermometer through fat side into center of roast. Don't let it touch bone. Don't add water; don't cover.
8. Roast lamb to 175°F. on roast-meat thermometer for medium-done meat; to 180°F. for well-done meat; use timetable, p. 220, as an approximate guide. Don't baste or turn lamb during roasting.
9. *Caution:* Roasts vary so in size, shape, amount of bone and fat, etc., that a roasting timetable can only be approximate at best. So rely on a roast-meat thermometer if you want to be sure.
10. If desired, glaze roast as follows: Omit seasonings in step 5. About 20 min. before lamb is done, spread with this mixture: Combine 2 tablesp. each currant jelly and brown sugar, 1 tablesp. vinegar, and 1/4 teasp. ground cloves.
11. When lamb is done, remove to heated platter. Keep warm while making Velvety Meat Gravy, p. 177, from drippings in pan.

To serve: Serve hot roast lamb with gravy or Currant-Mint Sauce, p. 527; barbecue sauce; or mint or currant jelly.

Or garnish with Broiled Fresh Peach Halves, p. 438; Broiled Pear Halves, p. 438; or sprigs of fresh herbs, water cress, or parsley.

Or spread hot roast lamb with mint jelly. Or garnish roast with canned pear or peach halves set on orange or canned pineapple slices, then filled or topped with mint jelly.

To Carve a Leg of Lamb: See p. 294.

To Use Leftover Roast Lamb: See Soup from Leftover Bones, p. 164.

COLD ROAST LAMB DE LUXE: Roast lamb day before; refrigerate, unsliced, until served; then slice. Lamb will have nice color, will slice easily.

PARSLEYED LAMB ROAST: Wash large bunch of parsley; remove thicker stalks. With small sharp paring knife, make 1"-deep slashes or pockets at an angle in meaty part of 6- to 6½-lb. leg of lamb. Stuff pockets with parsley. Rub ½ teasp. pepper, 1 teasp. salt over lamb. Roast as below. Brush with ½ cup Lemon-Parsley Sauce, p. 534. Serve rest of sauce, heated.

TIMETABLE FOR ROASTING LAMB

Lamb refrigerated till roasted at 325°F. Use shallow open pan. Add no water. Do not baste.

OVEN-READY WEIGHT (lb.)	APPROXIMATE ROASTING TIME (hr.)	MEAT-THERMOMETER READING
SIRLOIN ROAST		
2 to 3	2 to 3	180°F. *(well done)*
FULL, SHORT, OR HALF LEG		
4 to 6	2½ to 3	175°F. *(medium)*
	3½ to 4	180°F. *(well done)*
8	4	175°F. *(medium)*
	4½	180°F. *(well done)*
ROLLED, BONED LEG		
3 to 5	2¼ to 3¾	180°F. *(well done)*
5 to 6	3¾ to 4½	180°F. *(well done)*
CUSHION SHOULDER		
4	2½	180°F. *(well done)*
ROLLED, BONED SHOULDER		
3	2¾	180°F. *(well done)*
5	3¼	180°F. *(well done)*
CROWN ROAST (NO FILLING IN CENTER)		
4	3	180°F. *(well done)*
5	3¾	180°F. *(well done)*

CUSHION SHOULDER OF LAMB

1. Check roasting timetable, left, to see how long to roast meat. Start heating oven to 325°F.
2. Fasten 3 sides of roast together with skewers. Season inside of pocket with salt or monosodium glutamate, allowing 1 teasp. per 1 lb. meat. Fill pocket with about 2 cups any moist bread stuffing, packing loosely. Close opening with skewers, or sew.
3. Place roast, fat side up, on rack in shallow open pan. Don't add water; don't cover. Roast as in roasting timetable, left. Complete as in step 11, p. 219. Serve as in To Serve, under Roast Lamb, p. 219.

CROWN ROAST OF LAMB

1. Check roasting timetable, left, to see about how long roasting will take. Start heating oven to 325°F.
2. Do not leave ground meat in center of crown — this increases roasting time.
3. Cover rib ends with bread squares, pieces of bacon, salt pork, or foil.
4. Sprinkle crown with salt and pepper; place with rib bones up, on rack in shallow open pan. Don't add water; don't cover. Insert roast-meat thermometer into meaty part of one of ribs.
5. Roast as in roasting timetable at left.
6. When crown roast is done, remove covering on ends of bones. Remove roast to heated platter. Keep warm while making Velvety Meat Gravy, p. 177, from drippings in pan.

To serve: Serve as is. Or fill center with mashed white or sweet potatoes, buttered peas or onions, mashed squash, buttered cauliflower, sautéed mushrooms, or Spanish Rice, p. 372. Garnish with Broiled Peaches or Pears, p. 438.

ROAST LAMB SPECIALS

LAMB STEW

2 lb. boned lamb shoulder	2 teasp. celery seeds
3 tablesp. fat	8 medium carrots, pared
¼ cup minced onion	1 doz. small white onions, halved
2 or 3 cloves garlic, minced	2 teasp. Worcestershire
¼ cup flour	2 tablesp. snipped parsley
Salt	
Speck pepper	

1. Remove excess fat, skin, and gristle from lamb. Cut meat into 2″ cubes.

2. In hot fat, in Dutch oven or deep kettle, sauté minced onion and garlic until golden and tender; remove; set aside.

3. Meanwhile, combine flour, 1 teasp. salt, pepper; use to coat lamb lightly. Save leftover flour.

4. In hot fat left in Dutch oven, brown lamb *well* on all sides. Then add leftover flour, 2 teasp. salt, browned onion and garlic, 3 cups boiling water, celery seeds.

5. Simmer gently, covered, 1½ hr., or until lamb is fork-tender. Remove any excess fat on surface.

6. Add carrots, cut lengthwise into quarters, and onions; continue to simmer, covered, until tender — about 20 to 30 min. Stir in Worcestershire; sprinkle with parsley.

Serve piping hot, as is or with Dumplings for Stew, p. 478; Golden Noodles, p. 378; or ring of Mashed Potatoes, p. 412. Or add 2 or 3 quartered, pared potatoes in step 6. Makes 4 to 6 servings.

♣ FOR 2: Make and serve as directed. Place heated leftovers in greased 1-qt. casserole; top with ½ recipe Hot Baking-Powder Biscuits, p. 475. Bake at 450°F. 20 to 25 min., or until biscuits are done.

PIQUANT LAMB STEW: To gravy, add a few capers or chopped pickle.

IRISH STEW: Omit browning of lamb in step 4. If desired, substitute 1 cup white wine for 1 cup water.

LAMB PIE: Pour Lamb Stew into 2-qt. casserole. Top with Mashed Potatoes, p. 412; Hot Baking-Powder Biscuits, p. 475, cut with doughnut cutter; or any Flaky Pastry, pp. 584–586, with gashes cut in it. Bake at 450°F. 20 to 25 min., or until golden and done. Makes 4 servings.

POT ROAST OF LAMB SHOULDER

3 tablesp. fat	⅛ teasp. pepper
3- to 4-lb. rolled, boned lamb shoulder	1 clove garlic, minced
	½ teasp. celery seeds
1 medium onion, sliced	½ cup water
	1 tablesp. flour
1 teasp. salt	1½ tablesp. water

In hot fat, in Dutch oven, brown lamb well on all sides — 15 to 20 min. Add onion, salt, pepper, garlic, celery seeds, ½ cup water; simmer, covered, 2 hr.,* or until fork-tender. Remove meat.

Pour off juices and fat left in Dutch oven; measure. Add enough water to make 1 cup liquid; return to Dutch oven. Mix flour and 1½ tablesp. water to form smooth paste; stir into liquid; simmer, stirring, until smooth and thickened. Add bit of chili sauce or canned tomato sauce, if desired. Serve with lamb. Serves a family of 4 for 2 meals.

If you use a 2- to 3-lb. lamb shoulder, allow 1½ to 2 hr., or until fork-tender. If you use a 4- to 5-lb. shoulder, allow 2¼ to 2½ hr.

HERB: Add pinch dried basil, thyme, or marjoram to other seasonings.

WITH VEGETABLES: About 30 min. before lamb is done, add 8 pared small carrots, 2 cups small white onions, and 8 scraped small new potatoes. Sprinkle with 1 teasp. salt; simmer, covered, 30 min., or until tender, adding a little boiling water, if needed. Remove meat to heated platter; place vegetables around it. Make gravy as above.

TOMATO: Substitute tomato juice for ½ cup water.

SUREN'S SHISH KABOB

1 5- to 7-lb. boned leg of lamb	ground black pepper
1 clove garlic, minced (optional)	½ teasp. orégano
	1¼ teasp. salt
3 medium onions, chopped	¼ teasp. dried thyme
	6 whole green peppers
2 tablesp. olive oil	
⅓ cup sherry or cooking sherry	6 not-too-ripe tomatoes
½ to ¾ teasp. freshly	Melted butter or margarine

Night before: Cut lamb into 1½″ chunks; trim off gristle and most of fat. Put into large bowl, with marinade of garlic, onions, oil, sherry, pepper, orégano, salt, thyme. Toss well. Refrigerate 24 hr.

Shortly before serving: Start preheating broiler 10 min., or as manufacturer directs. String peppers, tomatoes, and lamb on separate 6″ skewers. Brush vegetables with butter.

Broil all, 2″ to 3″ from heat, till tender, turning to cook evenly. Meanwhile, pour marinade from bowl into Dutch oven or kettle; heat. Slip tender peppers and tomatoes into Dutch oven; cut into quarters; cover. Add lamb when tender. Serve with Pilaf, p. 373. Makes 5 servings.

KITCHEN KABOBS: You'll find kabobs to grill outdoors on p. 734. If you want to kitchen-broil them, preheat broiler 10 min., or as manufacturer directs. Use 6″ skewers; broil kabobs 2″ to 3″ from heat, turning with broad spatula.

CURRIED LAMB STEW WITH POPPY-SEED NOODLES

4 tablesp. butter or margarine	¼ cup chutney
2 cups chopped onions	1 green apple, peeled and finely chopped
3 lb. lean leg of lamb, cut into cubes	2½ tablesp. corn-starch
2 bay leaves, crushed	⅓ cup cold water
1 clove garlic, minced	½ cup light cream
2 tablesp. curry powder	1 8-oz. pkg. medium noodles
¼ teasp. dried thyme	12 small white onions, peeled
1 tablesp. salt	1 10-oz. pkg. frozen Fordhook limas, thawed
4 cups canned condensed beef broth, undiluted	1 1-lb. can whole carrots, drained
2 tablesp. canned tomato sauce	¾ lb. fresh mushrooms, sliced
2 tablesp. flaked coconut	2 tablesp. poppy seeds

Day before, if desired:

1. In Dutch oven, melt 2 tablesp. butter; add chopped onions, and cook until golden.
2. Stir in lamb, bay leaves, garlic, curry powder, and thyme; sprinkle with salt. Add broth and tomato sauce.
3. Bring mixture to boil. Cover; simmer slowly about 1½ hr., or till lamb is fork-tender.
4. Add coconut, chutney, and green apple; continue cooking, covered, 15 min.
5. Blend cornstarch with cold water. Stir into lamb mixture; continue cooking, while stirring, till thickened. Cool; refrigerate.

One half hour before serving:

1. Stir cream into stew in Dutch oven; then reheat until simmering.
2. Meanwhile, start cooking noodles as label directs.
3. Add white onions to simmering stew; cook, covered, 20 min.
4. Now add limas, carrots, and mushrooms. Continue cooking 5 min.
5. Add poppy seeds and 2 tablesp. butter to drained cooked noodles; serve with stew. Makes 10 servings.

To freeze: When stew is cool, turn into freezer containers; cover; freeze. About 45 min. before serving, place frozen stew in Dutch oven. Heat over low heat till simmering. Then stir in cream, and proceed with steps 2 through 5 under "½ hr. before serving" (left).

LAMB CHOPS OR STEAKS

The fat covering of lamb chops may carry a packer's brand name or Federal grade stamp to indicate quality. A good covering of firm white fat and streaks of fat in the pinkish to deep-red lean signify quality lamb chops or steaks.

To Buy and Store

Select a Cut:

LOIN CHOP (Fig. 33) is a meaty chop with T-shaped bone, and is the most desirable and usually highest-priced chop. (Dotted line shows loin chop of tomorrow.) A 1″-thick chop weighs 4 to 6 oz.

RIB CHOP (Fig. 35) is smaller than a loin chop. It contains rib bone and an "eye" of tender meat. A 1″-thick chop weighs 3 to 4 oz.

DOUBLE-RIB CHOP has 2 rib bones and tender meat. About 2″ thick, it weighs 5 to 7 oz. Allow 1 chop per person.

FRENCH CHOP has the meat removed from the end of the rib bone; a paper frill is used to cover the bone end.

SIRLOIN CHOP (Fig. 34) is a good-sized and meaty chop cut from sirloin section of leg. A 1″-thick chop weighs about 4 to 8 oz.

ENGLISH CHOP is cut from unsplit loin, is 2″ thick, and weighs 7 to 12 oz. Usually, the bone is removed and the flank ends are wrapped around a lamb kidney, when it is called English Kidney Chop. (You may cook kidney separately; serve it on top of broiled chop.)

SHOULDER (ARM OR ROUND BONE) CHOP (Fig. 36, on left) with small round bone, and SHOULDER (BLADE BONE) CHOP (Fig. 36, on right) with blade bone, are larger than rib or loin chop and lower-priced. A ¾″-inch chop weighs 5 to 8 oz.

LEG STEAK is cut from across the large leg of lamb, is meaty, and most of the steaks contain a small round bone. A ½"-thick steak weighs 5 to 8 oz.

LAMB RIBLETS are 1"-thick strips of breast meat; the lean is streaked with fat and attached to a rib bone. Usually 4" to 6" long.

MUTTON CHOPS (see p. 225) include rib and T-bone chops. They are larger than lamb chops. A 1"-thick chop weighs 6 to 12 oz.

Amount to Buy: Have chops and steaks that are to be broiled cut 1" to 2" thick. Thinner chops, ½" to ¾" thick, may be pan-broiled or braised. Allow ⅓ to ¾ lb. per serving.

To Store: Store as in To Store Meat, p. 172.

BROILED LAMB CHOPS AND STEAKS

1. Set oven regulator for Broil. If you have no oven regulator, turn broiler heat on full. Preheat broiler 10 min., or as manufacturer directs. Then, if you can, line broiler pan under rack with foil, with corners turned under, to catch drippings and save dishwashing.

If your family is small and you want to broil only enough for 2, there are available small aluminum broiling pans with rack, which save washing the larger broiler pan.

2. Remove the thin "fell" covering on fat of meat. With scissors or knife, slash fat edge at 1" intervals on a slant so meat won't curl.

3. If desired, rub meat with cut clove garlic. Arrange meat on rack; place in broiler oven so top of meat is about 3" from heat. Or place as manufacturer directs.

4. Broil meat on one side, using the timetable, right, as an approximate guide. Season as on p. 5. Turn with tongs; broil second side almost same length of time.

5. *Test for Doneness:* Make slit in meat near bone; note if color inside is of desired rareness. If meat is not quite done, continue broiling. When done, season.

6. *Caution:* Because meats vary so in size, shape, amount of bone and fat, etc., a broiling timetable can only be approximate at best. If you prefer your meat rarer or more well done, decrease or increase broiling time given accordingly. Remember, too, that meat may continue to cook after you remove it from broiler.

To serve: Serve chops or steak piping hot, with butter; Lemon Butter, p. 533; barbecue sauce; Currant-Mint Sauce, p. 527 or Quick Mushroom Sauce, p. 528. Or place meat around

TIMETABLE FOR BROILING LAMB CHOPS AND STEAKS

THICKNESS	APPROXIMATE MIN. PER SIDE
LOIN OR RIB CHOPS	
1"	6 min. *(medium)*
	7 min. *(well done)*
1½"	9 min. *(medium)*
	11 min. *(well done)*
DOUBLE RIB CHOPS	
2"	12 min. *(medium)*
	15 min. *(well done)*
SIRLOIN CHOPS	
1"	6 min. *(medium)*
	7 min. *(well done)*
ENGLISH CHOPS	
2"	12 to 15 min. *(medium)*
SHOULDER (ARM OR BLADE BONE) CHOPS	
1"	8 min. *(well done)*
LEG STEAKS	
1"	8 min. *(well done)*
LAMB RIBLETS	
1"	10 min. *(well done)*
MUTTON CHOPS	
1"	10 min. *(well done)*

mound of mashed potatoes; sprinkle with snipped parsley.

MIXED GRILL: See p. 180.

LAMB CHOPS WITH MINTED GRAPEFRUIT: While lamb chops broil, drain syrup from a 1-lb. can grapefruit sections. In skillet, melt ½ cup mint jelly; arrange grapefruit sections in it and heat, turning once. Then group sections, as garnish, down center of lamb-chop platter.

PAN-BROILED LAMB CHOPS AND STEAKS

1. Buy loin, sirloin, rib, or shoulder chops, or leg steaks, cut about ½" to ¾" thick.
2. If desired, rub meat with cut clove garlic or piece of lemon rind. Trim piece of fat from meat. Heat skillet over low heat; rub the piece of fat over surface of skillet; then remove.
3. Arrange meat in skillet. Cook over moderate heat until well browned, turning with tongs; pour off excess fat. Continue cooking, turning occasionally, until of desired doneness.
4. *Test for Doneness:* Make slit along bone, and note whether inside color is as rare, medium, or well done as desired.
To serve: Season as on p. 5. Then serve hot, with butter; Lemon Butter, p. 533; or Avery Butter Sauce, p. 527. Or garnish with parsley or mint. Nice with creamed potatoes.

Or make this flavorful pan gravy: To drippings in pan, add 1 tablesp. water for each chop. Simmer until hot, stirring well with fork to mix in all rich drippings; season; pour over chops.

CURRIED LAMB CHOPS WITH SHELL MACARONI: Cook 4 cups shell macaroni as label directs; arrange on heated platter; top with 6 pan-broiled shoulder or loin lamb chops, ¾" thick. Pour fat from skillet; in skillet, heat 2 10½-oz. cans condensed cream-of-mushroom soup, undiluted, with ⅔ cup milk and 2 tablesp. curry powder. Pour over macaroni and chops; serve at once. Makes 6 servings.

LAMB CHOPS HARBERT

4 lean loin lamb chops, 2" thick	¼ lb. Roquefort or Danish blue cheese
1 clove garlic, cut	Few drops Tabasco
Salt	1 teasp. Worcestershire
Pepper	
Monosodium glutamate	½ can condensed consommé, undiluted

Start heating oven to 350°F. Rub each chop with cut clove of garlic; sprinkle with salt, pepper, and monosodium glutamate. In small bowl, with fork, mix cheese, Tabasco, and Worcestershire. Coat chops with cheese mixture; stand them, on bone ends, in 10" x 6" x 2" baking dish; pour in soup. Bake 1 hr. 15 min., or until chops are well done, basting occasionally with consommé in dish. Makes 2 to 4 servings.

SPECIAL LAMB STEAKS

Dip 4 1"-thick leg steaks into one of mixtures below; let stand in refrigerator at least 3 hr., preferably overnight. Then broil, 3" from heat, till brown on one side — about 8 min.; turn and broil same time on other side. Makes 4 servings.

SOY SPECIAL: Combine 1 or 2 mashed cloves garlic, ⅓ cup salad oil, 3 tablesp. soy sauce, 2 tablesp. catchup, 1 tablesp. vinegar, ¼ teasp. black pepper.

BARBECUE: Combine 2 tablesp. Worcestershire, 1 tablesp. vinegar, 1 tablesp. bottled thick meat sauce, 1 tablesp. sugar, ¼ cup catchup, dash Tabasco.

LAMB SHANKS

Lamb shanks, which are cut from the foreleg of the lamb, yield a generous portion of lean meat. One lamb shank, weighing 1 to 2 lb., makes 1 generous serving.
To store: Store as in To Store Meat, p. 172.

LAMB SHANKS WITH PARSLEY POCKETS

6 1-lb. lamb shanks	¼ cup butter or margarine
1 bunch parsley	½ teasp. salt
3 teasp. unseasoned instant meat tenderizer	12 whole carrots, pared
1 6-oz. can frozen orange juice concentrate, unreconstituted	1 large green cabbage, in 6 wedges
¼ cup lemon juice	½ cup minced celery
	¼ cup snipped fresh mint

About 2½ hr. ahead:
1. With small, sharp paring knife, make 3 slashes or pockets, each about 1" deep and at an angle, in meaty part of each shank. Then stuff pockets with parsley.
2. Sprinkle ½ teasp. meat tenderizer over all surfaces of each shank. Pierce generously with fork; leave at room temperature 45 min.
3. Meanwhile, in small saucepan, combine orange juice concentrate, lemon juice, butter, and salt. Heat sauce until butter melts, then simmer 5 min.
4. Start heating oven to 325°F.
5. Place shanks on rack in large roasting pan;

brush with some of orange sauce. Roast, basting several times, 1 to 1½ hr., or till roast-meat thermometer registers 175°F. to 180°F.

6. *About 45 min. after meat starts roasting:* Begin cooking whole carrots 20 to 40 min., or till tender-crisp. Then cook cabbage wedges 8 to 12 min.

7. To rest of orange sauce add celery and simmer 5 min. Stir in mint.

8. On heated platter arrange shanks, with cabbage wedges and carrots as garnish. Put mint-orange sauce in bowl to be passed. Makes 6 servings.

Nice with: Crisp crackers, then baked custards with a "jam surprise" inside. (With spoon, lift up top of each custard; drop in jam, then replace top.)

INDIVIDUAL LAMB-SHANK ROASTS

4 lamb shanks, well trimmed of fat	2 tablesp. grated lemon rind
1 clove garlic, quartered	2 bay leaves
¼ cup flour	4 whole black peppers
2 teasp. salt	4 medium sweet potatoes, halved, pared
1 teasp. paprika	
2 tablesp. salad oil	1 9-oz. pkg. frozen cut green beans, thawed just enough to separate
½ cup lemon juice	

Start heating oven to 350°F. Make slit in each lamb shank; insert piece of garlic in each slit. Combine flour, salt, paprika; use to coat shanks.

In hot oil, in skillet, brown shanks well on all sides — 15 to 20 min.; place in 3-qt. casserole. Add lemon juice to skillet; stir to loosen brown bits; pour over shanks. Add lemon rind, bay leaves, whole peppers.

Bake, covered, 1 hr. Add potatoes, beans; bake, covered, 45 min. to 1 hr., or until fork-tender. Makes 4 servings.

BREAST OF LAMB

Lamb breast is a flat piece of meat that weighs about 2 lb., is 1" to 2" thick and quite fatty. It can be boned and rolled for a pot roast, or stuffed, then braised. Or it can be cut into riblets and broiled as on p. 223, or simmered in a sauce.

LAMB WITH LENTILS

3½ lb. lamb breast, cut into 2 rib pieces	Water
3 large onions, sliced	1 cup dried lentils
2 cloves garlic, minced	½ cup packaged precooked rice
1½ cups celery in ¾" pieces	3 large carrots, sliced ¼" thick
1 tablesp. salt	½ cup coarsely snipped parsley
¼ teasp. pepper	
¼ teasp. dried orégano	

About 2½ hr. before serving:

1. In Dutch oven, in a little fat if necessary, brown lamb well.

2. Drain all fat from lamb. To lamb add onions, garlic, celery, salt, pepper, orégano, and 1 cup water. Cook, covered, 1 hr. 15 min.

3. Rinse lentils in cold water; arrange with rice and carrot slices around lamb. Add 2 cups water; cook, covered, 1 hr., or until all are tender.

4. Arrange on platter; sprinkle with parsley. Makes 4 servings.

The green vegetables can be either kale, broccoli, or spinach, served with crusty rolls. The strawberry gelatin for dessert is topped with soft vanilla ice cream.

LET'S HAVE MUTTON

Mutton, the flesh of sheep over 1 year of age, while usually considerably cheaper than lamb, is not widely sold in this country. Its flesh varies in color from dark pink to dark red. The fat has a deeper, creamier color than that of lamb and is somewhat flaky. It has a stronger flavor than lamb.

Mutton chops can be broiled like lamb chops; see timetable, p. 223.

Mutton roasts can be roasted just as lamb is roasted. However, such cuts as the leg and shoulder may be braised as a pot roast.

POT ROAST OF MUTTON

Make several slits in shoulder or leg roast of mutton; insert garlic slivers. In kettle or Dutch oven, brown meat well on all sides. Slip trivet under meat. Add 1 cup water and 1 tablesp. vinegar; or use 1 cup tomato juice and ½ teasp. curry powder. Simmer, covered, allowing about 45 min. per lb., or until meat is fork-tender, adding more water, if needed.

Serve hot or cold, with tomato or mustard sauce.

LET'S HAVE VEAL

Veal is young beef 4 to 14 weeks of age. It has a delicately flavored, grayish-pink flesh, which resembles chicken in flavor. It is more abundant in late winter and spring. The rest of the year, most of the veal sold is *calf*, which is an animal 14 weeks to 1 year of age with a deeper-pink flesh. Veal has very little exterior fat and what it has is firm and creamy white. It has no marbling.

Your guides to buying quality veal are the round purple U.S. Inspected and Passed stamp for wholesomeness, plus the packer's trusty brand name or Federal grade stamps (they're the same as for beef). See To Buy Meat, p. 171.

Since it has so little fat, veal is at its best roasted, braised, or cooked in liquid to the well-done stage.

On the following pages, we suggest and describe favorite uses for many of the retail cuts of veal. Our diagram of the veal animal, under Popular Cuts of Meat, will help you to identify these cuts better.

VEAL ROASTS

To Buy and Store

Select a Cut:

LOIN OR RIB ROAST: Loin (T-bone) and rib veal roasts are fine buys. Usually, however, these sections are cut into chops.

LEG ROAST: This fine meaty roast has only a small round bone; its cut surface resembles a round steak. It may be cut as a 4-lb., 6-lb., or larger roast (the center cut is especially choice). It is often cut into steaks and cutlets.

RUMP ROAST: This wedge-shaped piece of meat from the upper part of the leg is nice boned, rolled, then roasted or braised. It weighs 3 to 5 lb., and is fine for a small family.

SHOULDER ROAST: This roast is best when boned and rolled, to make carving easier. It may be roasted or braised. It weighs 7 to 8 lb. Or a smaller roast may be cut from it.

Amount to Buy: Buy at least a 3- to 4-lb. roast. Allow 1/2 to 3/4 lb. bone-in veal per serving; 1/3 to 1/2 lb. boned veal per serving.

Be sure to have the meatman note on the bill the weight of the oven-ready roast to guide you in computing the roasting time.

To Store: Store as in To Store Meat, p. 172.

ROAST VEAL

1. Check roasting timetable, p. 227, to see about how long roasting will take. Plan so that roast is done 20 min. before serving; it will slice more easily and you will have time to make gravy.
2. Start heating oven to 325°F.
3. If desired, rub cut surface of veal roast with cut clove garlic.

Or make several slits in roast and insert slivers of garlic or a little dried marjoram.

Or brush roast with soy sauce or barbecue sauce.

Or rub roast with dried thyme or crumbled bay leaf.
4. If roast has little fat covering, lay several thin strips of salt pork or fat bacon on top. Sprinkle with salt and pepper, if desired.
5. Place roast, with fat side up, on a rack in shallow open pan. Don't add water; don't cover.
6. Insert roast-meat thermometer into center of roast. *Don't let it touch bone.*
7. Roast veal to 180°F. on roast-meat thermometer, using timetable, p. 227, as an approximate guide. Don't baste; don't turn roast.
8. *Caution:* Roasts vary so in size, shape, amount of bone and fat, etc., that a roasting timetable can only be approximate at best. So rely on a roast-meat thermometer if you want to be sure.
9. When veal is done, remove to heated platter. Keep warm while making Velvety Meat Gravy, p. 177, from drippings in pan. Add sautéed mushrooms to gravy if desired.

To serve: Serve with gravy; Quick Mushroom Sauce, p. 528; or tomato sauce. Nice with canned whole-cranberry sauce; one of Fresh Cranberry Relishes, p. 440; Glazed Pineapple Chunks, p. 436; or Sautéed Bananas, p. 436.

To Use Leftover Roast Veal: See p. 252.

TIMETABLE FOR ROASTING VEAL

Veal refrigerated till roasted at 325°F. Use shallow open pan. Add no water. Do not baste.

OVEN-READY WEIGHT	APPROXIMATE ROASTING TIME	MEAT-THERMOMETER READING *(well done)*
LOIN OR RIB ROAST		
5 lb.	3⅓ hr.	180°F.
LEG ROAST (BONE IN)		
3 lb.	2 hr.	180°F.
6 lb.	3⅓ hr.	180°F.
8 lb.	4 hr.	180°F.
RUMP ROAST		
4 lb.	2⅔ hr.	180°F.
ROLLED, BONED SHOULDER ROAST		
3 lb.	2 hr.	180°F.
4 lb.	2⅔ hr.	180°F.
5 lb.	3 hr.	180°F.

ITALIAN VEAL WITH TUNA SAUCE
(Vitello Tonnato)

2 tablesp. butter or margarine	½ cup water
2 celery stalks, diced	1 6½- or 7-oz. can tuna
¼ cup minced onion	6 anchovy fillets
1 clove garlic, minced	2 small sour pickles, minced
1 bay leaf	1 tablesp. capers
2 lb. rolled boned leg of veal	¼ cup olive or salad oil
2 bouillon cubes	

1. *About 2 days ahead:* In hot butter, in Dutch oven, sauté celery, onion, garlic, and bay leaf until vegetables are golden. Add veal; brown on all sides — about 10 min.
2. Add bouillon cubes and water. Simmer, covered, about 1 hr. 15 min., or until veal is tender. Remove veal. Drain off and reserve liquid.
3. With fork, very finely mash vegetables left in Dutch oven. Add tuna, anchovies, pickles, and capers, a little at a time, continuing to mash with fork.
4. Stir in oil and reserved liquid. Place veal in bowl; pour sauce over veal; refrigerate 1 or 2 days.

5. *To serve:* Thinly slice veal; arrange on platter; spoon a little sauce over each slice. Makes 24 slices to be used as an antipasto or main dish.

POT ROAST OF VEAL

Rolled, boned veal rump, shoulder, and round roasts are good for pot roasts. Use at least a 3- to 4-lb. piece or cut.

Season meat; roll in flour. In 2 tablesp. hot fat or salad oil, in kettle or Dutch oven, brown meat *thoroughly* — about 15 to 20 min. Place rack under meat. Add about 1 cup water or tomato juice, plus ½ teasp. salt for each 1 lb. meat. If desired, also add 1 clove garlic, 1 bay leaf, 1 teasp. celery salt, or ½ teasp. dried thyme.

Cover; simmer slowly over low heat or in 350°F. oven, allowing about 40 min. per lb., or until meat is fork-tender. (Or for approximate total simmering time period, after browning, follow roasting timetable, at left.)

About 45 min. before meat is done: If desired, cover pared potatoes and carrots, and onions, with boiling water; bring to boil; drain. Then place around meat 30 min. before it is done. Add extra salt to season vegetables.

When meat is done, remove meat and tender vegetables to hot platter. Measure broth, adding water if needed; thicken it as on p. 6. Serve with veal.

LOUISIANA POTTED VEAL

½ cup all-purpose flour	2 tablesp. shortening or salad oil
1 teasp. seasoned salt	1 cup water
⅛ teasp. pepper	1 cup tomato juice
6 lb. rolled boned veal shoulder	1 bay leaf

1. Combine flour, seasoned salt, and pepper; use to coat veal thoroughly. Reserve any leftover flour mixture.
2. In 2 tablesp. hot shortening, in Dutch oven, brown veal well on all sides — about 15 to 20 min. Add water, tomato juice, bay leaf; simmer, covered, about 3 hr., or until veal is fork-tender.
3. Remove bay leaf; then lift veal to heated platter. Skim fat from liquid in Dutch oven and place fat in small bowl. To fat, add reserved flour; blend well; stir into liquid in Dutch

oven; then cook, stirring constantly, until thickened. Strain, if desired; pass gravy separately. Makes 10 servings.

BAYOU STYLE: Coat and brown veal as in steps 1 and 2, p. 227, adding ½ teasp. dried sage to flour mixture. Next add 2 tablesp. water; simmer, covered, 2 hr., adding more water, if necessary. Then add 1 1-lb. can tomatoes, 1 teasp. monosodium glutamate; simmer, covered, 1 hr., or until veal is fork-tender. Remove veal and make gravy as in step 3, p. 227.

VEAL POT ROAST, SMITANE

3 tablesp. butter or margarine	1 pkg. onion-soup mix
6 lb. boned veal rump roast	¼ cup finely snipped fresh dill; or 2 teasp. dill seeds
1 pt. commercial sour cream	1 teasp. salt
	¼ teasp. pepper

1. In hot butter, in Dutch oven, brown veal well on all sides.
2. Combine sour cream and onion-soup mix; spread over top and sides of roast. Add dill, salt, pepper. Simmer, covered, 2½ to 3 hr., or until veal is fork-tender.
3. Remove veal to heated platter. Pass gravy separately. Makes 8 to 10 servings.

VEAL SCALOPPINE

2½ lb. boned veal shoulder	1 1-lb.-4-oz. can tomatoes, strained; or 1¾ cups canned tomato juice
½ cup flour	
½ teasp. salt	
⅛ teasp. pepper	1 teasp. sugar
½ cup salad oil or fat	1½ teasp. salt
½ cup minced onions	⅛ teasp. pepper
¾ cup canned whole or sliced fresh mushrooms	Hot fluffy rice

Start heating oven to 350°F. Cut veal into 1¼" cubes; roll lightly in flour combined with ½ teasp. salt, ⅛ teasp. pepper. In hot salad oil, in skillet, sauté onions until tender; remove onions to greased 2-qt. casserole.

Sauté veal in oil left in skillet until brown on all sides. Place veal in casserole, along with mushrooms, tomatoes, sugar, 1½ teasp. salt, ⅛ teasp. pepper. Bake, covered, 1½ hr., or until fork-tender.

Serve with rice. Makes 5 or 6 servings.

♣ **FOR 2:** Use 1 3- or 4-oz. can whole mushrooms, drained; 1 cup canned tomato juice. Halve rest of ingredients. Bake 1¼ hr.

VEAL PAPRIKA

2 tablesp. bacon fat or shortening	1 medium onion, thinly sliced
2 lb. boned veal shoulder, cut into 1" cubes	1 teasp. salt
	¼ teasp. pepper
1 teasp. monosodium glutamate	2 teasp. paprika
	1⅓ cups uncooked regular or processed white rice*
2 teasp. meat-extract paste; or 2 beef-bouillon cubes	1 3- or 4-oz. can sliced mushrooms
3½ cups boiling water	1 pt. commercial sour cream

To hot bacon fat, in large skillet or Dutch oven, add veal. Sprinkle with monosodium glutamate; sauté till browned on both sides. Dissolve meat paste in boiling water; add to veal, along with onion, salt, pepper, paprika. Simmer, covered, 45 min. Add rice, mushrooms with liquid; stir well; simmer, covered, 25 min., or until rice is done. Stir in sour cream. Add salt if needed. Makes 8 servings.

To use packaged precooked rice, use 2¼ cups rice, 2½ cups boiling water; reduce simmering time with veal and mushrooms to 5 min.

CURRIED VEAL PAPRIKA

½ cup butter or margarine	2½ cups commercial sour cream
4 lb. boned veal shoulder, in 1½" cubes	⅔ cup all-purpose flour
	⅔ cup cold water
2 teasp. salt	1 cup snipped parsley
1 tablesp. sugar	1 8-oz. pkg. broad noodles
4 teasp. curry powder	
1¼ teasp. pepper	¼ cup toasted slivered almonds
¼ teasp. paprika	
1 10½-oz. can condensed beef broth, undiluted	½ tablesp. poppy seeds

About 2 hr. before dinner:

1. In hot butter, in Dutch oven, brown one-third of veal cubes well; remove to plate. Repeat twice more; then combine in Dutch oven.
2. Sprinkle veal with salt, sugar, curry, pepper, paprika; add broth, sour cream; stir in flour, blended smooth with water, and parsley. Simmer, covered, 1 hr., or till veal is tender, stirring occasionally. Cook noodles as label directs; drain.

About 30 min. before dinner: Start heating oven to 350°F. Arrange noodles in ring around edge of shallow baking dish. Spoon veal into center; top with almonds, poppy seeds. Cover with foil; bake 15 min. Makes 8 servings.

VEAL STEW

Make Lamb Stew, p. 220, substituting 2 lb. boned veal shoulder for lamb.

BREAST OF VEAL

This flat cut, which weighs about 3 lb., comes boned or bone-in and is fine for stews or for braising. It can be stuffed before braising.

POTTED STUFFED VEAL

3 lb. boned veal breast, in one piece	2 cups fine fresh bread crumbs
½ lb. smoked ham, ground twice; or 2 4½-oz. cans deviled ham	½ teasp. salt
	Speck pepper
	½ cup snipped parsley
¼ cup butter or margarine	2 teasp. dried sage
¼ cup minced onion	3 tablesp. salad or olive oil
	1 cup water

1. Place breast of veal flat, with inside surface up; remove any excess fat; spread entire surface with ham.
2. In hot butter, in skillet, sauté onion until tender. Meanwhile, in large bowl, combine bread crumbs, salt, pepper, parsley, sage, sautéed onion; spread lightly on ham. Roll veal up, lengthwise, jelly-roll-fashion; tuck in ends; tie securely.
3. In hot salad oil, in Dutch oven, brown veal well on all sides — about 20 to 30 min. Add water; simmer, covered, 2 hr., or until veal is fork-tender. Remove veal to heated platter; let stand 20 min. before slicing. If desired, make cream gravy in medium saucepan; pass separately.
4. Or refrigerate fork-tender veal overnight; slice; serve cold. Makes 6 servings.

SAUSAGE-STUFFED VEAL POT ROAST: Over surface of veal breast, spread ¾ lb. fresh pure-pork sausage; roll up, jelly-roll-fashion; tuck in ends; tie securely. Brown as in step 3, above. Then add 1 teasp. dried rosemary; 1 10½-oz. can condensed tomato soup, undiluted; 1 onion, sliced; 1 clove garlic, minced; 2 tablesp. Wor-

cestershire. Simmer and serve as in steps 3 and 4, at left.

GREEN VEAL STUFFING: Mix 1½ cups fine fresh bread crumbs; 1 cup mashed cooked or canned peas; 1 egg, slightly beaten; 2 tablesp. melted butter or margarine; ½ teasp. salt; ⅛ teasp. pepper; 1 tablesp. snipped chives; ¼ teasp. dried rosemary. Use as alternate for stuffing in step 2, at left.

SWEET GOLD VEAL STUFFING: In a bowl, combine 1 cup finely chopped celery; 2 tablesp. snipped parsley; 1 small onion, grated; 1 cup finely snipped dried apricots; 2 cups fine fresh bread crumbs; 1 teasp. salt; ⅛ teasp. pepper. In hot skillet, melt 5 tablesp. butter or margarine; add apricot mixture; cook, stirring constantly, until thoroughly heated. Use as alternate for stuffing in step 2, at left.

VEAL CHOPS, STEAKS, AND CUTLETS

Veal chops, steaks, and cutlets should not be broiled. Braising is best and makes them the fork-tender, superbly flavored meat that everyone in the family enjoys.

To Buy and Store

Select a Cut:

RIB CHOP (Fig. 30) has rib bone and tender meat. You may shape it by wrapping the thin end around the thicker portion and securing it with a toothpick. A ½″-thick chop weighs about 4 oz.

LOIN CHOP (Fig. 29) has T-bone and very tender meat, and is the most desirable and most expensive veal chop. A large portion of the fat may be trimmed before cooking. A ¾″-thick chop weighs 6 to 8 oz.

BLADE STEAK (Fig. 31) has blade bone, is less tender and usually more economical than rib, loin, or leg cuts. It may be held in shape with toothpicks. A ½″-thick piece weighs 7 to 10 oz.

ARM STEAK (Fig. 32) is meaty, with round bone and little fat. It is less tender and usually more economical than rib, loin, or leg cuts. Leave it whole or cut into serving pieces before cooking. A ½″-thick steak weighs 7 to 8 oz.

LEG (ROUND) STEAK, cut from leg, resembles an arm steak but is larger. Leave whole or cut into serving-size pieces before cooking. A ½″-thick steak weighs 1 to 1½-lb.

CUTLETS are the same as leg or round steaks, cut about ¼″ to ½″ thick; sometimes they are flattened or "Frenched" by pounding. A ¼″-thick piece weighs 3 to 4 oz. Frozen veal steaks, plain or breaded, as packaged by well-known meat packers, are excellent; cook as label directs.

Amount to Buy: Allow ⅓ to ½ lb. bone-in veal per serving, ¼ to ⅓ lb. boned veal per serving.

To Store: Store as in To Store Meat, p. 172. Keep frozen veal frozen until ready to use.

BRAISED VEAL CHOPS, STEAKS, AND CUTLETS

1. Loin veal chops are usually cut about 1″ thick. Other veal chops and steaks are cut ½″ to ¾″ thick. Season veal as on p. 5.
2. Roll veal in flour, corn meal, or fine cracker crumbs to coat all sides. Or dip into 1 beaten egg mixed with 2 tablesp. milk, then into fine cracker or packaged dried bread crumbs.
3. In 2 to 4 tablesp. hot fat or bacon fat, in skillet, brown veal slowly until golden on both sides; do not burn.
4. Add ½ cup water, milk, or tomato or fruit juice. Simmer, covered, over low heat (or bake in 350°F. oven), turning once, until fork-tender as follows:

CHOPS, ½″ to ¾″ thick: about 45 min.

STEAKS OR CUTLETS, ½″ to ¾″ thick: about 1 hr.

CUTLETS (Frenched), ¼″ or less thick: about 25 min.

5. When veal is done, remove to heated platter. For gravy, to broth in pan, add enough milk to make desired amount of gravy. Thicken as on p. 6. Serve over veal.

To Vary:

1. Before coating veal, rub surface with cut clove garlic or hickory smoked salt; or brush with soy sauce; or let stand 15 min. in French dressing, seasoned with herbs or chili sauce.
2. Or instead of ½ cup water in step 4, above, add ½ cup sweet or sour cream; diluted canned cream-of-mushroom, celery, chicken, or tomato soup; cooked dried prunes or apricots with

syrup; or add ¼ cup tart jelly or marmalade, diluted with ¼ cup water.

3. Or to water, add one or more vegetables, such as sliced onion, diced celery, green beans, or peas.
4. Or if veal is baked in oven, top each piece with grated cheese, or with slice of bacon, onion, tomato, green pepper, or lemon.
5. Or sauté thinly sliced green-pepper and onion rings last few min. Stir in 1 10½-oz. can condensed cream-of-chicken soup, undiluted; ¼ cup white wine; pour over veal.

VEAL ROMAN STYLE
(Saltimbocca alla Romana)

1 lb. very thin cutlets, ¼″ thick	ham, or Canadian-style bacon
½ teasp. salt	3 tablesp. butter or margarine
¼ teasp. pepper	2 tablesp. water
½ teasp. dried sage	2 tablesp. butter or margarine
8 paper-thin slices prosciutto, cooked	

1. Have meatman flatten veal until 1/16″ to ⅛″ thick. Cut it into 8 pieces. Sprinkle both sides with salt, pepper, sage. On each piece of veal, lay 1 slice prosciutto; fasten with toothpicks.
2. In 3 tablesp. hot butter, in skillet, sauté meat, a few pieces at a time, about 2 min. on each side, or until golden. Remove to heated platter, with prosciutto side up; keep warm.
3. To fat left in pan, add water, stirring to loosen browned bits. Stir in 2 tablesp. butter just until melted; pour over veal. Makes 4 servings.

✤ **FOR 2:** Reduce butter to 2 tablesp. Halve rest of ingredients.

ITALIAN VEAL ROLLS

1½ lb. very thin veal cutlets (¼″ thick), from veal leg	ground pepper
	Flour
¾ cup finely snipped prosciutto	3 tablesp. butter or margarine
1 clove garlic, minced	1 cup dry white wine
2 tablesp. snipped parsley	2 cups chicken broth
¼ teasp. salt	¼ cup minced carrots
⅛ teasp. freshly	1 medium onion, minced
	¼ cup minced celery

1. Have meatman flatten veal until 1/16″ to ⅛″ thick; cut it into 5″ x 3″ pieces. In bowl, combine prosciutto, garlic, parsley, salt, pepper;

place about 2 teasp. in center of each veal piece. Roll up veal; secure with toothpicks.

2. Coat veal rolls with flour. In hot butter, in large skillet, sauté rolls until golden. (If necessary, remove rolls to heated platter as they brown.)

3. When all rolls are golden, return them to skillet. Add wine; simmer, uncovered, about 10 min. Add chicken broth; simmer, uncovered, 15 min.

4. Add carrot, onion, celery. Cook, uncovered, 20 min. Arrange veal rolls on heated platter; pour gravy over them. Serve with Polenta with Tomato Sauce, p. 347, and grated Parmesan cheese. Makes 4 servings.

✚ FOR 2: Halve ingredients; make as directed.

SWEDISH PARSLEY-STUFFED VEAL ROLLS

2 lb. thin veal cutlets	quartered
1½ teasp. salt	1 10½-oz. can con-
White pepper	densed beef bouil-
½ cup butter or mar-	lon, undiluted
garine	1 tablesp. all-purpose
1 cup snipped parsley	flour
2 medium carrots, cut	¾ cup light cream
into 1″ chunks	2 teasp. granulated
2 medium onions,	sugar

Early in day, or day before, if desired:

1. Have meatman flatten veal to ¼″ thickness. Cut into serving pieces; sprinkle both sides with salt and ½ teasp. pepper.

2. Melt ¼ cup butter; add parsley; spread some on each piece of veal; roll up, tie well with string; refrigerate.

About 1¾ hr. before serving:

1. In ¼ cup hot butter, in Dutch oven, sauté carrots, onions, and veal until meat is well browned.

2. Add water to bouillon to make 2 cups liquid; add to meat and vegetables; simmer, covered, 1 hr., or until meat is fork-tender.

3. Remove veal rolls; snip off string; then arrange on heated platter; keep warm.

4. *For gravy:* With fork, mash vegetables in liquid in Dutch oven. Into flour, gradually stir cream; then stir briskly into Dutch oven. Add ⅛ teasp. pepper and sugar; cook, stirring, just until heated. Strain; then serve with veal rolls. Nice with long thin asparagus spears in browned butter, cucumber relish, and Swedish crisp bread. Makes 6 servings.

VEAL ITALIAN WITH CARROTS

1½ lb. veal round	or marjoram
steak, ¼″ thick	¼ cup salad oil or fat
¼ cup flour	2 small cloves garlic
1½ teasp. salt	6 medium carrots,
¼ teasp. pepper	pared, halved
¼ teasp. dried thyme	1 cup dry white wine

Cut veal into 2″ pieces; roll in flour mixed with salt, pepper, thyme. In oil, with garlic, in skillet, brown meat. Discard garlic; add carrots, wine. Cover; simmer 30 min., or till meat is very tender. Makes 4 servings.

CUTLET OF VEAL A LA SUISSE

About 1½ lb. *thin*	1 cup sauterne or
veal cutlets (6)	Rhine wine
6 thin slices natural	1 cup leftover or
Swiss cheese	canned beef gravy
6 paper-thin slices	½ cup light cream
cooked ham	Dash salt
2 tablesp. flour	4 to 6 drops lemon
½ teasp. paprika	juice
⅓ cup butter or mar-	
garine	

Using edge of heavy saucer, pound cutlets well; halve each. On each of 6 cutlet halves, place ½ slice cheese; 1 slice ham, folded over; then another ½ slice cheese. Cover each with second cutlet half. Fasten securely with toothpicks. Coat lightly with flour mixed with paprika.

In hot butter, in skillet, brown cutlets on both sides. Add ½ cup wine; simmer, uncovered, until liquid is almost completely absorbed. Add remaining wine, gravy, cream; simmer, covered, 10 min., or until fork-tender. Just before serving, add salt, lemon juice; remove toothpicks. Makes 6 servings.

FRENCH VEAL CUTLETS

2 lb. veal cutlets	2 teasp. prepared mus-
1 tablesp. flour	tard
½ teasp. salt	1 bouillon cube
3 tablesp. fat or salad	1 cup boiling water
oil	1 cup commercial sour
1⅓ cups minced	cream
onions	¼ teasp. salt
2 tablesp. snipped	1 tablesp. flour
parsley	1½ tablesp. cold
1 teasp. paprika	water

Have meatman flatten veal ¼″ thick. Cut into 5 or 6 pieces. Sprinkle with 1 tablesp. flour combined with ½ teasp. salt.

In 2 tablesp. hot fat, in skillet, sauté onions until tender; remove. Add 1 tablesp. fat to skillet; brown veal until golden on both sides. Add onions, parsley, paprika, mustard, and bouillon cube dissolved in boiling water. Simmer, covered, over low heat 45 min., or until veal is very tender.

Remove veal to heated platter. To liquid in skillet, add sour cream; heat thoroughly. Stir in combined ¼ teasp. salt, 1 tablesp. flour, cold water. Cook, stirring, until thickened; pour over veal. Makes 5 or 6 servings.

SCALOPPINE OF VEAL MARSALA

1 lb. *thin* veal cutlets	thinly sliced
⅓ cup grated Parmesan cheese	Dash cayenne pepper
	¼ bouillon cube or
¼ cup butter or margarine	1 teasp. meat-extract paste
1 clove garlic	¼ cup hot water
4 or 5 mushrooms,	¼ cup Marsala wine

Have meatman flatten veal ¼″ thick. Cut into 2″ pieces; coat *well* with Parmesan.

In some of hot butter, in skillet, over medium heat, sauté garlic and veal, a few pieces at a time, until golden brown on both sides. Add rest of butter as needed and set veal pieces aside as they brown. Discard garlic.

In same butter sauté mushrooms 5 min., remove, and set aside. To butter, in skillet, add cayenne, bouillon cube, hot water; stir until brown bits clinging to pan dissolve. Add veal, mushrooms. Cook 1 min. over high heat. Add wine. Serve at once. Makes 3 or 4 servings.

BAKED: Start heating oven to 400°F. After sautéing meat and mushrooms, remove to 1½-qt. casserole. In skillet, combine rest of ingredients except wine; stir until brown bits clinging to pan dissolve; pour over meat. Bake, covered, 15 min. Add wine; bake, covered, 5 min.

THIN VEAL FORESTIER

1½ lb. *thin* veal cutlets	½ lb. mushrooms, thinly sliced
Clove garlic, cut	½ teasp. salt
Flour	Dash pepper
¼ cup butter or margarine	⅓ cup dry vermouth
	1 teasp. lemon juice
	Snipped parsley

Have meatman flatten veal ¼″ thick. Cut into 2″ pieces. Rub both sides of each piece with garlic; sprinkle with flour. In hot butter, in

skillet, sauté veal, several pieces at a time, until golden brown on both sides. Heap mushrooms on top of all pieces in skillet. Sprinkle with salt, pepper, vermouth.

Cook, covered, over low heat 20 min., or until veal is fork-tender, checking occasionally to make sure it's moist and adding 1 tablesp. or so of water, if necessary.

To serve: Sprinkle with lemon juice and parsley. Makes 6 servings.

WIENER SCHNITZEL

6 boneless anchovies	cut into 6 pieces,
6 thin lemon slices	then pounded ⅛″
Bottled capers	thick
Sweet-dill-pickle strips	2 eggs, beaten
Fresh horse-radish (optional)	¾ cup packaged dried bread crumbs
¼ cup flour	½ cup butter or margarine
1 teasp. salt	3 tablesp. lemon juice
½ teasp. pepper	3 tablesp. snipped parsley
1½ lb. veal cutlet,	

1. Roll each anchovy into circle with hollow center; set on lemon slice; fill center with capers. Thinly slice dill-pickle strips. With knife, shred a little horse-radish. Refrigerate all.

2. Mix flour, salt, pepper. Dip veal in it, then in eggs, then in crumbs.

3. Slowly heat large skillet; in it, melt half of butter. In hot butter, brown veal quickly on all sides, a few pieces at a time. Over low heat, cook veal slowly about 15 min., or until tender; remove veal to heated platter.

4. In same skillet, brown remaining butter; stir in lemon juice and parsley; pour over veal. Top each piece with lemon slice, pickle on one side of lemon, horse-radish on other. Makes 4 to 6 servings.

BOHEMIAN VEAL

2 tablesp. flour	mustard
¼ teasp. salt	¼ teasp. Worcestershire
⅛ teasp. pepper	
1 lb. arm or round veal steak, ½″ thick, cut into serving pieces	¼ teasp. dill seed
	1 tablesp. catchup
	2 tablesp. slivered blanched almonds
2 tablesp. salad oil	½ cup water
¼ teasp. garlic salt	½ cup dry white wine
¼ teasp. paprika	½ cup commercial sour cream
¼ teasp. prepared	

1. Mix flour, salt, and pepper; use to coat veal well. In hot salad oil, in skillet, brown veal on both sides.

2. Meanwhile, combine garlic salt, paprika, mustard, Worcestershire, dill seed, catchup, 1 tablesp. almonds, water, and wine; pour over veal; cover. Simmer, turning meat occasionally, until tender — about 50 min.

3. Remove veal to platter; keep warm. Into drippings, in skillet, stir sour cream; heat, but not not boil; pour over meat; sprinkle with 1 tablesp. almonds. Serve for dinner with herb-buttered broccoli, hot noodles, tossed fruit salad, French-bread chunks, and chocolate ice-cream balls, sprinkled with instant coffee. Makes 2 generous servings.

VEAL DE LANUX

About 1¼ lb. very thin veal cutlets	1 3- to 4-oz. can sliced mushrooms, drained
¼ cup butter or margarine	3 tablesp. Marsala wine or dry sherry
¾ cup heavy cream	Hot cooked rice

About 20 min. before serving:

1. Have meatman flatten veal to 1/16″ to 1/8″ thickness. Melt butter in large skillet; in it, over high heat, quickly sauté cutlets till well browned, and butter is browned, not burned. Remove cutlets to heated platter.

2. Into brown butter, stir cream, while scraping bottom of skillet vigorously with wooden spoon.

3. Over medium heat, stir in drained mushrooms, then wine. Immediately pour over veal cutlets. Arrange hot rice around it, or serve separately. Makes 4 servings.

VEAL PARMIGIANO

1 lb. *thin* veal cutlets	¼ teasp. dried thyme
3 tablesp. olive or salad oil	1 egg
3 cloves garlic, finely minced	¼ cup packaged dried bread crumbs
1 onion, minced	½ cup grated Parmesan cheese
1 1-lb.-4-oz. can tomatoes (2½ cups)	3 tablesp. olive or salad oil
1¼ teasp. salt	½ lb. Mozzarella or Muenster cheese
¼ teasp. pepper	
1 8-oz. can tomato sauce	

Ask meatman to cut veal into 8 pieces of about 4½″ x 2″ size.

In 3 tablesp. hot olive oil, in saucepan, sauté garlic and onion until golden. Add tomatoes, salt, pepper; break up tomatoes with spoon; simmer, uncovered, 10 min. Add tomato sauce, thyme; simmer, uncovered, 20 min.

Beat egg well with fork. Combine crumbs, ¼ cup Parmesan cheese. Dip each veal piece into egg, then into crumbs; sauté 3 pieces in 1 tablesp. hot olive oil in skillet, turning once, until golden brown on both sides. Repeat until all are done. Set slices, side by side, in baking dish 12″ x 8″ x 2″.

Start heating oven to 350°F. Thinly slice Mozzarella. Pour two thirds of tomato mixture over veal, straining it, if desired. Arrange Mozzarella on top; spoon on rest of tomato mixture. Sprinkle with ¼ cup Parmesan. Bake, uncovered, 30 min. Makes 4 generous servings.

VEAL INVERNESS ON GREEN RICE

1 or 2 cloves garlic, mashed (optional)	chops, ¾″ thick
⅓ cup salad oil	1 cup uncooked regular or processed white rice; or 2 cups packaged precooked rice
3 tablesp. soy sauce	
2 tablesp. catchup	
1 tablesp. vinegar	
¼ teasp. black pepper	2 tablesp. salad oil
2 lb. veal steak, ¼″ thick; or 4 veal loin	Snipped parsley

Night before: For marinade, in shallow pan, combine garlic, ⅓ cup salad oil, soy sauce, catchup, vinegar, pepper. Cut veal steak into serving pieces. Place in marinade; turn to coat well. Refrigerate.

About 35 min. before serving: Start cooking rice. In 2 tablesp. hot salad oil, in skillet, sauté veal over medium heat, about 15 min. on each side, or until nicely browned and fork-tender.

Serve on hot seasoned rice, tossed with a little snipped parsley. Makes 4 servings.

COLD STUFFED VEAL-ROLL SLICES

1 qt. fresh bread crumbs	6 tablesp. butter or margarine
¾ teasp. salt	3 tablesp. minced onion
2 teasp. dried sage	
2 tablesp. chopped celery	1 1¼ lb. veal cutlet, ¼″ thick
2 teasp. snipped parsley	Seasoned Flour, p. 9
Speck pepper	1 cup hot water

Day before: Combine crumbs, salt, sage, celery, parsley, pepper. In ¼ cup hot butter in skillet, cook onion until tender; add crumb mixture; heat. Spread crumb mixture on veal; then roll up veal tightly and tie with string.

Start heating oven to 350°F. Roll veal in Seasoned Flour; then sauté in 2 tablesp. butter until golden on all sides. Place in 1½-qt. casserole. Add water. Bake, covered, 1 hr., or until fork-tender. Refrigerate.

To serve: Arrange veal roll, sliced, on platter, with mold of currant or grape jelly. Makes 6 servings.

SWISS VEAL WITH LIMAS

¼ cup flour	2 medium onions,
1 teasp. salt	sliced
⅛ teasp. pepper	½ medium green pep-
½ teasp. monosodium	per, slivered
glutamate	1 cup tomato juice
2 lb. veal steak, 1″	1 10-oz. pkg. frozen
thick	green limas, par-
2 tablesp. salad oil	tially thawed
	1 teasp. salt

Early in day: Mix flour, 1 teasp. salt, pepper, monosodium glutamate; with edge of heavy saucer, pound mixture into veal. In hot salad oil, in skillet, sauté veal until well browned on both sides; remove to 10″ x 6″ x 2″ baking dish. In same skillet, place onions, green pepper; stir, coating with drippings; stir in tomato juice; then pour this mixture over veal. Refrigerate.

About 1¾ hr. before serving: Start heating oven to 350°F. Cover top of baking dish containing veal with foil. Bake 40 min. Uncover; place limas around veal; sprinkle with 1 teasp. salt. Bake, covered, 45 min., or until veal is fork-tender. Makes 4 servings.

VEAL SHANKS

Veal shank contains four shank bones with meat attached. Veal shank crosscuts are made by cutting across the shank to form pieces of any desired thickness.

LINDA'S BRAISED VEAL SHANKS
(Osso Buco alla Linda)

6 2½″ veal shank	1 peeled tomato,
crosscuts	chopped
Salt and pepper	2 chicken- or beef-
½ cup butter or mar-	bouillon cubes
garine	2 cups hot water
1 medium onion,	¼ cup dry white wine
minced	1 teasp. dried rose-
1 pared carrot, diced	mary
1 celery stalk, diced	½ teasp. salt
1 clove garlic, minced	⅛ teasp. pepper
2 tablesp. flour	1 tablesp. snipped
	parsley

1. Sprinkle veal with salt, pepper. In ¼ cup hot butter, in Dutch oven, brown veal, removing pieces as they brown.

2. Add onion, carrot, celery, and garlic to Dutch oven. Sauté, stirring occasionally, until tender — about 5 min.

3. Return meat to Dutch oven. Add combined ¼ cup butter and flour, tomato, bouillon cubes dissolved in water, wine, rosemary, salt, pepper; stir well. Simmer, covered, 2 hr., or until meat is tender.

4. Just before serving, stir in snipped parsley. Makes 6 servings.

✤ FOR 3: Halve ingredients; make as directed.

LET'S HAVE VARIETY MEATS

Liver, kidney, tripe, heart, brains, sweetbreads, tongue — these are the variety meats, the edible parts of animal meat that are not classified as flesh.

LIVER

Liver — veal, calf, lamb, beef, or pork — is our richest food source of iron, so necessary to prevent nutritional anemia. It is especially rich in vitamin A, iron, copper, and B-vitamins.

To Buy and Store

Veal, calf, lamb, beef, and pork liver are usually sold sliced and labeled to indicate the kind of liver. All have about the same nutritional value. Veal, calf, lamb, and *young* beef liver may be pan-fried. Pork and most beef liver are best when braised.

Select One of These:

VEAL LIVER, the most popular and highest-priced liver, comes from milk-fed animals. Slightly more tender than calf liver, it is mild in flavor and light-colored. It is often called calf liver.

CALF LIVER comes from animals fed on milk and grass and is not so light-colored as veal liver. Mild in flavor and tender, it tastes like veal liver. Pan-fry it.

LAMB LIVER is also mild-flavored, tender liver. Broil or pan-fry it.

BEEF LIVER is tender to less tender, more pronounced in flavor and lower priced. Pan-fry or braise it.

PORK LIVER is less tender, more pronounced in flavor, and usually the lowest priced. Braise it.

FROZEN SLICED LIVER, packaged by well-known meat packers, is excellent. Cook as label directs.

Amount to Buy: Allow about 1 lb. liver for 4 servings.

To Store: Keep fresh liver, loosely wrapped, in coldest part of refrigerator. Use within 24 hr., if possible. Keep frozen liver frozen until time to use. See To Store Meat, p. 172.

BROILED LIVER

Preheat broiler 10 min., or as manufacturer directs. Place veal, calf, or lamb liver, cut ½″ thick, on broiler rack or in shallow baking pan. Brush with melted butter or margarine. Broil, about 3″ or 4″ from heat, turning once, until delicate pink or well done inside — about 4 to 8 min. in all. You may broil bacon at same time. Or serve as in one of variations of Susan's Pan-Fried Liver and Bacon, p. 108.

VENETIAN LIVER
(Fegato alla Veneziana)

1. In ½ cup hot butter or margarine, in skillet, sauté 1 sliced onion until golden.
2. Meantime, cut 1 lb. calf or beef liver, sliced very thin, into 3″ x ½″ strips. Add to onion;

sauté just until all red color disappears, tossing with spatula.
3. Cover skillet; heat 1 min. Uncover; heat 1 min. longer. Sprinkle with salt and pepper. Makes 4 servings.

♣ FOR 2: Halve ingredients; make as directed.

LIVER AND ONIONS AU FROMAGE

3 tablesp. flour	3 tablesp. butter or
½ teasp. salt	margarine
¼ teasp. garlic salt	⅓ cup grated process
⅛ teasp. pepper	Cheddar cheese
1 lb. beef liver slices,	⅓ cup snipped scal-
½″ thick	lions or minced
	onions

About 45 min. before serving:

1. In small bowl, combine flour, salt, garlic salt, and pepper with spoon. Use to sprinkle on both sides of liver slices.
2. Melt butter in skillet over medium heat; in it, sauté liver slices slowly until golden brown on both sides.
3. Now sprinkle liver slices with cheese and scallions. When cheese is slightly melted, remove liver to a heated platter and serve immediately. Makes 4 servings.

NOTE: Bacon lovers will enjoy substituting bacon drippings for the butter. Sauté onions, if desired.

Serve with baked white or sweet potatoes, cut wax and green beans, your favorite hot rolls, and raspberry-lemon gelatin dessert served with cream or dessert topping.

FRICASSEE OF LIVER FRANCOISE

1⅓ cups packaged	mushroom soup,
precooked rice, or	undiluted
1 cup uncooked reg-	3 tablesp. milk
ular rice	1 3- or 4-oz. can
5 tablesp. butter or	chopped mushrooms
margarine	Dash pepper
1 medium onion,	1 4-oz. can pimentos,
sliced	drained, quartered
½ lb. calf liver	¼ teasp. dried thyme
1 10½-oz. can con-	Snipped parsley
densed cream-of-	

1. *About 15 min. before dinner:* Start cooking rice as label directs.
2. In 3 tablesp. butter, in skillet, sauté onion until almost tender. Add liver, cut into strips 3″ x ½″; sauté with onion about 5 min.; add

soup, milk, 3 tablesp. liquid from mushrooms, pepper; heat, stirring; add pimentos.

3. Lightly sauté drained mushrooms in 2 tablesp. butter; toss with hot rice and thyme. Onto heated platter, spoon rice in ring; fill with fricassee of liver. Sprinkle all with parsley.

Serve with buttered broccoli, Boston-lettuce salad bowl with sliced radishes, toasted English muffins topped with caraway seeds, apple crisp, cheese, and instant coffee. Makes 4 servings.

BRAISED BEEF OR PORK LIVER

Slice beef or pork liver ½" thick. Sprinkle with Seasoned Flour, p. 9. In 1 or 2 tablesp. hot bacon or other fat in skillet, brown liver on both sides. Add ⅓ cup water or tomato juice; simmer, covered, 30 min., or until fork-tender.

LIVER POT ROAST IMPERIAL

1 2½- to 3-lb. calf liver, unsliced	¼ teasp. pepper
3 salt-pork slices, ¼" thick	1 cup canned bouillon or consommé, undiluted
¼ cup brandy	1 large onion, sliced
¼ cup snipped parsley	6 bacon slices, diced
⅓ cup olive or salad oil	12 small whole white onions
2 bay leaves	½ cup white wine
2 tablesp. lemon juice	2 to 3 teasp. sugar
½ cup butter or margarine	½ cup light cream
1 teasp. salt	2 egg yolks, well beaten

1. In large bowl, place liver, salt-pork slices, brandy, parsley, oil, bay leaves, lemon juice. Refrigerate 15 min.; turn liver; refrigerate 15 min. longer. Drain liver; reserve salt pork and liquid (marinade).

2. In hot butter, in Dutch oven, brown liver well on all sides, using wooden spoons to turn it. Add salt, pepper, ½ cup bouillon, marinade; on top of liver, place salt-pork and onion slices. Simmer, covered, 1 hr., basting occasionally and turning once or twice (replace salt pork on top of liver each time).

3. Meanwhile, in hot skillet, cook bacon until crisp and golden; reserve. Pour off all but 2 tablesp. bacon fat; in same skillet, brown whole onions; add ½ cup bouillon; simmer, covered, about 20 min., or until onions are tender. Remove liver, onions, to heated platter.

4. Into combined pan juices, stir wine, sugar, cream; heat slowly. Carefully stir in egg yolks; cook until thickened; strain.

5. Slice liver; sprinkle with reserved bacon bits. Nice with French fries. Pass sauce separately. Makes 6 to 8 servings.

BARBECUED BEEF LIVER

1 lb. beef liver, in ¼" slices	1 teasp. sugar
Salt and pepper	⅛ teasp. pepper
2 tablesp. butter or margarine	1 teasp. prepared mustard
1 cup sliced onions	⅛ teasp. chili powder
1 tablesp. vinegar	1 tablesp. water
1 tablesp. Worcestershire	¼ cup catchup

Start heating oven to 325°F. Cut liver slices in half, crosswise. Place half of slices, side by side, in covered, shallow baking dish; sprinkle lightly with salt, pepper. In butter, in small skillet, sauté onion; arrange half on liver. Mix vinegar with next seven ingredients; spoon 4 teasp. sauce over onion. Top with rest of liver, then onion; cover. Bake 25 min.; pour on rest of sauce. Bake, uncovered, 10 min. Makes 4 servings.

LIVER CREOLE

1 6-oz. can tomato paste	1 teasp. dried basil
1 tomato-paste can of water	Dash cayenne pepper
1 small onion, sliced	About 2 tablesp. sugar
2 tablesp. prepared mustard	1 lb. beef liver, thinly sliced
About 1½ teasp. salt	1⅓ cups packaged precooked rice
¼ teasp. pepper	1 tablesp. butter or margarine

1. In small saucepan, over medium heat, combine tomato paste and water. Add onion, mustard, salt, pepper, basil, cayenne, and sugar. Simmer, covered, stirring occasionally, 30 min.

2. Meanwhile, slice liver in julienne strips. Also, cook rice as label directs.

3. In skillet, over medium heat, melt butter; in it, sauté liver till lightly browned.

4. Spoon rice onto heated platter. Arrange liver strips over it; then top with sauce. Makes 4 servings.

LIVER 'N' NOODLES

¼ cup salad oil	1 cup boiling water
2 onions, sliced	1 10-oz. pkg. frozen
½ green pepper, cut	peas
into strips	1½ teasp. salt
1 lb. calf or beef liver,	¼ teasp. pepper
cut into ½" strips	4 oz. medium noodles

In hot oil, in large skillet, sauté onions, green pepper, and liver 5 min., or until tender. Stir in boiling water, frozen peas, salt, pepper, and uncooked noodles. Cook, covered, stirring occasionally to keep mixture from sticking, 10 min., or until noodles are tender. Makes 4 to 6 servings.

HEART

To Buy and Store

Heart is a good buy as it has very little waste. There are 4 kinds of fresh heart. Veal heart is the most delicate in flavor, and the most tender.

Select One of These:

BEEF HEART weighs 3 to 3½ lb. and makes 8 to 10 servings.

VEAL HEART weighs about ¾ lb. and makes 2 or 3 servings.

PORK HEART weighs about ½ lb. and makes 2 servings.

LAMB HEART weighs about ¼ lb. and makes 1 serving.

FROZEN LAMB HEARTS, packed by well-known meat packers, are excellent. Cook as label directs.

To Store: Wrap fresh hearts loosely; refrigerate; use within 24 hr., if possible. Keep frozen hearts frozen until time to use. See To Store Meat, p. 172.

SIMMERED HEART

Trim off coarse fibers at top and inside of heart. Wash well; drain. Cover with water; add 1 teasp. salt, pinch dried thyme, and 1 onion, sliced. Simmer veal or lamb heart, covered, about 2 hr., beef or pork heart about 3 hr., or until fork-tender.

Nice ground, chopped, or cut up as meat in a hash, meat pie, or casserole. Or you may serve veal or lamb heart, sliced, hot or cold.

BRAISED HEARTS

Trim 2 pork, or 4 lamb, hearts as in Simmered Heart, left. Quarter pork hearts; or halve lamb hearts. Coat with Seasoned Flour, p. 9. In 3 tablesp. hot fat or salad oil, in skillet, brown hearts well with 2 onions, thinly sliced. Add 2 teasp. salt, ½ cup water. Simmer, covered, over low heat, 2 to 2½ hr., or until fork-tender, adding water if necessary. Nice with Spanish or tomato sauce. Makes 4 servings.

BRAISED, STUFFED VEAL OR LAMB HEARTS

3 veal hearts	1 clove garlic; or
Buttery Bread Stuff-	¼ cup sliced
in, p. 340	onion
Seasoned Flour, p. 9	Salt
¼ cup fat or bacon	⅛ teasp. pepper
drippings	

Trim off coarse fibers at top and inside of hearts. Wash well; drain. Fill cavities with stuffing; close openings with skewers; tie. (Any leftover stuffing is nice toasted lightly in a little hot butter or margarine in skillet.) Roll in Seasoned Flour; brown hearts well in hot fat in Dutch oven or deep kettle. Add enough boiling water, or part water and part tomato juice, to come halfway up hearts; add garlic, 1 teasp. salt per qt. water, and pepper. Simmer, covered, adding water, if necessary, until fork-tender — 2 to 2½ hr.

Serve hot, sliced, with gravy made by thickening broth, as on p. 6. Or slice; serve cold. Makes about 6 servings.

SWEETBREADS

To Buy and Store

This delicate, tender meat is the thymus gland of a calf, young beef, or lamb. Each animal has two kinds of sweetbreads: heart sweetbreads, which are rounded, and throat or neck sweetbreads, which are elongated.

Select One of These:

VEAL SWEETBREADS are the most popular and highest priced. Like lamb sweetbreads, they are white and tender.

BEEF SWEETBREADS are usually only neck sweetbreads. They are reddish in color, and are inclined to be tough when pressed with fingers. **FROZEN SWEETBREADS** packaged by well-known meat packers are excellent. Cook as label directs.

Amount to Buy: 1 lb. sweetbreads makes about 4 servings.

To Store: Use fresh sweetbreads as soon as they're purchased. Or precook, below, then refrigerate; use within 24 hr. Keep frozen sweetbreads frozen until time to use. See To Store Meat, p. 172.

TO PRECOOK SWEETBREADS

Precook sweetbreads this way before using them: Simmer sweetbreads 20 min. in water to cover. Add 1 teasp. salt and 1 tablesp. lemon juice or vinegar for each qt. of water used. The acid helps to keep the sweetbreads white and firm. Then, holding sweetbreads under cold running water, slip off membrane with fingers. With knife, cut out dark veins and thick connective tissue. Cut very thick sweetbreads in halves, lengthwise. Use at once, or refrigerate.

BROILED SWEETBREADS

Preheat broiler 10 min., or as manufacturer directs. Precook the sweetbreads, as above; then split. Brush with melted fat or salad oil; sprinkle with salt and pepper; then broil about 3" from heat until golden brown — about 4 to 6 min. on each side. Spread with soft butter or margarine, or Lemon Butter, p. 533. Sprinkle with slivered almonds; or serve with canned pineapple chunks.

PAN-FRIED SWEETBREADS

Precook the sweetbreads as above; then split. Dip into packaged dried bread crumbs, then into 1 beaten egg, then again into crumbs. In hot butter or margarine, in skillet, pan-fry until delicate brown on both sides.

Serve with tomato sauce, fried ham or bacon, or lemon quarters.

CREAMED SWEETBREADS

Precook 1 lb. sweetbreads, as above. Meanwhile, make 2 cups Béchamel Sauce, p. 533, or Medium White Sauce, p. 533, using 3 tablesp. flour instead of ¼ cup. Break precooked sweetbreads into pieces; combine with sauce; heat.

Serve on toast or in Toast Cups, p. 497. Makes 4 servings.

To Vary: To sauce, add 2 teasp. white wine, sherry, or lemon juice, with a little snipped parsley.

Or add 1 cup cooked peas or cut-up asparagus.

Or add ⅓ cup slivered, toasted, blanched almonds.

Or substitute equal amounts of diced, cooked chicken and sweetbreads, or sautéed sliced mushrooms and sweetbreads, for sweetbreads.

SWEETBREADS EN BROCHETTE

½ lb. veal sweetbreads	½ teasp. salt
	⅛ teasp. pepper
12 small mushrooms	6 bacon slices, halved
3 tablesp. lemon juice	¼ cup melted butter
1 teasp. Worcestershire	or margarine
	Snipped parsley

1. *Day before:* Precook the sweetbreads, as at left. Cut sweetbreads into 12 chunks; refrigerate, covered.
2. Meanwhile, remove stems from mushrooms. Place mushroom caps in bowl; combine lemon juice, Worcestershire, salt, and pepper; pour over mushroom caps; refrigerate, tossing occasionally.
3. *About 30 min. before dinner:* Preheat broiler 10 min., or as manufacturer directs. Roll up each bacon slice. On each of 3 10" skewers, string sweetbread chunks, mushroom caps, then bacon rolls; in shallow, open pan, arrange, side by side; brush with some of butter. Broil, 6" from heat, often turning and brushing with butter, 15 to 20 min., or until sweetbreads are golden and mushrooms done. Pour on remaining butter; sprinkle with parsley. Makes 2 servings.

BRAINS

To Buy and Store

Brains are a very delicate, tender meat.

Select One of These:
VEAL BRAINS: These are the most popular, and highest priced. They weigh ½ lb. each.
BEEF BRAINS: These weigh about ¾ lb. each.

LAMB AND PORK BRAINS: These weigh ¼ lb. each.

FROZEN BRAINS packaged by well-known packers are excellent. Cook as label directs.

Amount to Buy: Allow about 1 lb. brains for 4 servings.

To Store: Use brains as soon as they're purchased. Or precook, as below; refrigerate; then use within 24 hr. If brains are frozen, keep frozen until ready to use.

TO PRECOOK BRAINS

Wash brains and precook as in Sweetbreads, p. 238; drain. Remove membrane with tip of paring knife.

To serve: Reheat in Quick Mushroom Sauce, p. 528; Drawn Butter Sauce, p. 533; or Lemon Butter, p. 533. Or cut up and substitute for part of chicken in Susan's Creamed Chicken De Luxe, p. 122.

BROILED BRAINS: Precook brains as in Sweetbreads, p. 238. Then brush well with melted butter or margarine and broil 10 to 15 min., or until lightly browned, turning occasionally. Serve with lemon wedges; Quick Tartar Sauce, p. 530; Broiled Bacon, p. 217; Broiled Tomatoes, p. 417; or Beet and Horse-radish Relish, p. 439.

SAUTEED BRAINS: Precook brains as in Sweetbreads, p. 238. Then dip into beaten egg, then into packaged dried bread crumbs or corn meal. Sauté in hot fat in skillet until brown on all sides. Serve as above.

TONGUE

Uncooked tongues may be bought fresh, smoked, corned, or pickled. There are also ready-to-eat whole tongues, as well as canned whole, or sliced. Tongue provides a variety of tasty main dishes.

To Buy and Store

Uncooked Tongues:

BEEF TONGUE: A beef tongue weighs 2 to 5 lb. and comes fresh, smoked, or cured. Smoked beef tongue often comes in a transparent wrapping and carries a packer's brand name.

VEAL TONGUE: Veal tongue weighs ½ to 2 lb. and comes fresh.

LAMB TONGUE: Lamb tongue weighs 3 to 4 oz. and comes fresh or pickled.

Cooked and Canned Tongues:

READY-TO-EAT SMOKED BEEF TONGUE: This fully-cooked, whole smoked tongue comes packed in a vacuum package. It has been completely skinned and boned, and is all ready to slice and serve cold, or to heat as label directs. It comes in sizes weighing 1½ to 2½ lb.

You can also buy cooked trimmed beef tongues in cans and jars.

LAMB TONGUE: Comes in jars.

PORK TONGUE: Weighs ½ to 1¼ lb. and usually comes in cans or jars as "lunch tongue."

Amount to Buy: Allow 1 lb. for 4 or 5 servings.

To Store: Refrigerate fresh tongue, loosely wrapped; use within 24 hr. if possible.

Refrigerate smoked tongue and pickled tongue, covered; see To Store Meats, p. 172.

COOKED TONGUE
(fresh, smoked, cured, or pickled)

1. Wash tongue. (If tongue is highly cured, soak 2 hr. in cold water to cover; then drain before cooking.) Place in large deep kettle or Dutch oven; cover with cold water. (To fresh tongue, also add 1½ teasp. salt.)

2. Then add either of these groups of seasonings, if desired:

   A. 1 bay leaf, 2 or 3 whole cloves, 1 large onion, sliced, and 1 tablesp. grated orange or lemon rind

   B. Or 2 cloves garlic, 2 stalks celery, 1 onion, sliced, 1 carrot, pared, 1 teasp. whole black peppers

3. Simmer tongue, covered, until fork-tender, allowing about 3 to 4 hr. for a beef tongue, 1 to 1½ hr. for veal, lamb, or pork tongue. Remove from water; cool, only slightly, in cold water, then remove skin immediately.

4. To remove skin, slit skin on underside from thick end to tip; then, with paring knife, loosen skin all around thick end. Turn tongue, top side up, with tip toward you. Grasp skin at thick end; pull off like glove, all in one piece. (With pork tongue, it may be necessary to slice

off most of skin.) Trim off bone and gristle at thick end.

Serve tongue, hot or cold, with Horse-radish Sauce I or II, p. 532; barbecue sauce; Quick Tartar Sauce, p. 530; Mustard Sauce, p. 532; or California Raisin Sauce, p. 533. Or serve with horse-radish, prepared mustard, chili sauce, pickle relish, pickled beets, or cranberry sauce.

TONGUE DINNER: About 45 min. before tongue is done, add 5 pared small white potatoes. Simmer, covered, 10 min. Add 10 small white onions. Simmer, covered, 5 min. Place ½ medium cabbage, quartered, with most of core removed, on top of tongue. Cook, covered, until vegetables are tender. Serve with Horse-radish Sauce I or II, p. 532, horse-radish, or mustard pickle.

WITH PICKLE SAUCE: Make 1 cup Drawn Butter Sauce, p. 533, using 1 cup tongue liquid for water and browning butter slightly before adding flour. Add 2 tablesp. minced sweet pickle, ¼ cup pickle juice. Serve over or with sliced, cooked tongue.

CRANBERRY-RAISIN TONGUE

1 3½- to 4-lb. smoked beef tongue	2 tablesp. minced onion
⅓ cup tongue broth	1 16-oz. can whole-cranberry sauce
3 tablesp. butter or margarine	⅓ cup dark or light raisins

Cook tongue as on p. 239; reserve ⅓ cup broth. When tongue is cooked, make sauce: In saucepan, over medium heat, melt butter; add onion and sauté until golden. Now add cranberry sauce and tongue broth. Stir until smooth; then add raisins. Simmer 5 to 8 min.

Serve tongue, sliced, hot or cold, with sauce. Makes 10 to 12 servings.

TRIPE

To Buy and Store

Tripe is the inner lining of the stomach of beef. There are 3 kinds of tripe: honeycomb, pocket, and plain (or smooth); honeycomb tripe is considered the greatest delicacy. All 3 come fresh, pickled, or canned.

FRESH TRIPE is cooked before you buy it, but needs more cooking.

PICKLED TRIPE is usually thoroughly cooked, but should be soaked before using.

CANNED TRIPE is ready to heat and serve.

Amount to Buy: Allow about 1 lb. for 4 or 5 servings.

To Store: Keep in refrigerator. Use fresh tripe within 24 hr.

COOKED FRESH TRIPE

Cover fresh tripe with water; add 1 tablesp. salt. Simmer, covered, 1½ hr., or until fork-tender. Drain; dry between paper towels; then cut into serving pieces. Serve with tomato sauce.

SAUTEED TRIPE

Cook fresh tripe as above; then cut into serving pieces. Dip pieces into 1 beaten egg, mixed with 2 tablesp. water, then into packaged dried bread crumbs. In small amount of hot fat, in skillet, sauté tripe until golden brown on both sides.

Serve with lemon wedges, hot canned tomato sauce, or Mustard Sauce, p. 532.

BROILED TRIPE

Preheat broiler 10 min., or as manufacturer directs. Use fresh tripe, cooked as above. Cut into serving pieces. Brush with melted butter or margarine. Broil about 3″ from heat 5 min. Turn; brush with butter; broil 5 min., or until golden brown. Brush with melted butter; sprinkle with salt, pepper, and paprika, or seasoned salt; then serve.

KIDNEYS

The delicacy and flavor of kidneys are highly prized by epicures; veal, lamb, and beef kidneys are special favorites.

To Buy and Store

Select One of These:

VEAL KIDNEYS weigh 8 to 12 oz. each and are so tender that they need very little cooking. They are usually broiled or sautéed.

LAMB KIDNEYS weigh 2 oz. each, are very tender, and are delightful broiled or sautéed.

BEEF KIDNEYS weigh about 1¼ lb. each and need thorough braising or simmering.

Amount to Buy: 1 veal or lamb kidney makes 1 serving; 1 beef kidney makes 4 servings.

To Store: Keep, loosely wrapped, in refrigerator. Use within 24 hr.

MAC'S SAUTEED KIDNEYS

Remove any outer membrane from lamb or veal kidneys. Then split kidneys in halves, lengthwise; or slice ¼″ to ½″ thick. With scissors remove fat and white veins; wash; dry between paper towels.

Rub skillet lightly with cut clove garlic; then melt ¼ cup butter or bacon fat in skillet. Sauté kidneys in butter, turning them frequently, 10 to 15 min., or until tender. Season with a little lemon juice or sherry. Sprinkle with parsley. Serve as is or on toast.

P.S. Before adding kidneys, you may sauté ¼ cup sliced onion in butter till tender. Omit garlic. A few caraway seeds may be added.

BROILED KIDNEYS ON TOAST

Preheat broiler 10 min., or as manufacturer directs. Remove any outer membrane from lamb or veal kidneys. Cut in halves, lengthwise; then, with scissors, remove fat and white veins; wash; dry between paper towels.

Brush kidneys with melted butter or margarine, salad oil, or French dressing; sprinkle with salt and pepper. Broil 3″ from heat about 5 to 7 min. on each side, or until well browned.

Serve on buttered toast, with melted butter or margarine to which a little salt, pepper, cayenne, and lemon juice have been added.

KIDNEYS EN BROCHETTE: Arrange split kidneys and squares of bacon alternately on skewers; place on greased broiler rack; broil as above. Or wrap kidneys in bacon slices; then broil.

MUSHROOM-AND-KIDNEY SAUTE

3 tablesp. butter or margarine	4½ teasp. flour
½ green pepper, minced	½ lb. mushrooms, sliced
2 medium onions, minced	1¼ teasp. salt
4 veal kidneys	Speck pepper
	2 tablesp. water
	2 tablesp. sherry

In skillet, in butter, sauté green pepper and onion until tender. Meanwhile, cut membranes from kidneys; cube kidneys; sprinkle with flour; add kidneys and mushrooms to onions; sprinkle with salt and pepper. When kidneys are lightly browned, simmer them, uncovered, for 10 min. Add water; cook till thickened; add sherry. Serve kidneys on fluffy rice. Makes 6 servings.

BEEF-KIDNEY STEW

1 beef kidney	⅛ teasp. pepper
6 cups boiling water	⅛ teasp. paprika
¼ cup all-purpose flour	3 tablesp. butter or margarine
6 tablesp. cold water	1 hard-cooked egg, chopped
1½ teasp. salt	

Remove any outer membrane from kidney. Split kidney in half, lengthwise; with scissors, remove fat and white veins. Cut into ¼″-thick crosswise slices, then into pieces. Cover with cold water; press meat to squeeze out blood; drain; repeat. Now let meat soak 2 hr. in cold water; then drain.

Add boiling water to kidney; simmer, uncovered, 1 hr. Cover; simmer ½ hr., or until kidney is tender and broth is reduced to 3 cups.

Mix flour and cold water to a smooth paste; add to stew gradually, stirring constantly; simmer until thickened. Add salt and rest of ingredients; heat. Makes 4 servings.

Serve as is, on toast, or with mashed or hashed brown potatoes. A grand dish for Sunday breakfast or supper.

P.S. This dish tastes even better if kidney is simmered and refrigerated day before, then thickened and seasoned just before serving. If desired, add 2 tablesp. minced onion before simmering kidney; or add sherry to taste or a few cooked peas just before serving.

To Freeze Meats

See How To Freeze Meats, p. 703, for freezing and cooking directions.

FROZEN FARM-RAISED DOMESTIC RABBIT MEAT

For all those who cherish the luscious flavor of domestic all-white rabbit meat, it is good news that it is now nationally available in packaged frozen form — one or one half of a 2- to 3-lb. tender, young rabbit, cut up, to each package.

Fried, broiled, barbecued, or roasted, it's a real treat, especially when prepared by one of the twenty or more recipes which the packer provides.

LET'S HAVE READY-COOKED MEATS

To Buy and Store

Delicious ready-cooked meats are a boon to menu planners — but not just for sandwiches, for they may be baked, sautéed, or served as hot or cold main dishes. For short-order occasions, they're a blessing, too!

Select a Meat:

BOLOGNA has a mild, pleasing flavor. There are dozens of varieties, including veal, beef, and ham bologna. Most common kinds are large bologna and ring bologna. Buy by the piece, or sliced.

CERVELAT (SUMMER SAUSAGE) is a combination of beef and pork, mildly spiced, then smoked or dried. It has no garlic. Buy by the piece, or thinly sliced.

COOKED HAMS AND PICNICS: See p. 209.

LIVER CHEESE (LIVER LOAF) is fine for those who want sandwich-shaped slices of liver sausage. It's generally firm, made in a loaf shape, and covered with fresh white pork fat to keep it moist. Use hot or cold.

LIVER SAUSAGE (LIVERWURST) varies from soft, light-pink braunschweiger (smoked) to darker, firmer sausage. Delicately spiced and seasoned, the smoked varieties are most popular. Liver sausage is particularly rich in iron and vitamins A and B, and is best bought by the piece, as all types discolor when sliced.

LUNCHEON LOAF comes in a square, round, or loaf shape. It has a hamlike flavor. Serve cold, sautéed, or baked.

MEAT LOAF is a combination of the same meats and seasonings that are used in homemade meat loaf. Buy it sliced for sandwiches and cold plates, or as a whole or half loaf to bake as a main dish.

SALAMI comes in these 2 varieties:

Hard: This is a firm, smoked or unsmoked sausage with a snappy, garlicky flavor. Nice to eat as a nibbler, in sandwiches or salads, or to add, diced or chopped, to scalloped potatoes, spaghetti sauce, etc. Buy by the piece, or thinly sliced.

Cooked: This is made and seasoned like hard salami but is softer (semidry). It's preferred for sandwiches because it's less chewy.

SOUSE (HEADCHEESE) consists of cooked, jellied pork products in a round sausage shape, or as loaves.

SPECIALTY LOAVES include meat, with cubes of cheese throughout; pickle-and-pimento loaves; pepper loaves of many varieties, etc.

THURINGER CERVELAT is a medium-dry sausage with a distinctive tangy flavor.

FULLY COOKED TONGUE: See p. 239.

JELLIED TONGUE is cured whole beef, pork, or veal tongue, with gelatine added. Or it is chopped or cubed, jellied tongue.

Amount to Buy: For a cold-meat platter, allow about 2 to 3 oz. meat per serving. For salads and sandwiches, allow 1 to 2 oz. per serving.

To Store: Make sure meat slices lie flat; keep prepackaged meats in wrapper. Wrap sliced meat in wax paper, saran, or foil. Refrigerate.

To enjoy the fine flavor, use unsliced dry or semidry sausage within 2 to 3 weeks. For others, check Storage Time Guide, p. 173.

To Serve Ready-Cooked Meats

Serve Them Cold:

1. Use in cold platter combinations, with or without home-cooked or canned meats and assorted cheese slices or balls.

For platter, choose meats that give a variety of flavors, colors, shapes, textures.

Arrange meats in an orderly design. Cut larger slices in two (sometimes from corner to corner). Fold some to make cones; roll others around cooked asparagus stalks, green beans seasoned with French dressing, or pieces of cheese.

Garnish platter in center, at ends, or down sides with pickled fruits, etc. See the Elegant Extras, p. 442.

2. Serve in sandwiches.

3. Add to one of Chef's Salad Bowls, p. 457.

4. Serve as nibbler; see p. 144.

Serve Them Hot:

1. Add meat, cut up, to scalloped potatoes, macaroni with cheese, Spanish rice, etc.

2. Use snipped cervelat or salami as meat in Italian spaghetti. See Salametti, p. 379.

3. Slice, then sauté, liver sausage, bologna, or luncheon loaf until hot; serve with creamed or scalloped vegetables.

4. Use as meat in stuffed peppers, stuffed tomatoes, etc.

5. Slice, quickly broil or sauté, and serve with broiled or sautéed tomatoes, sweet potatoes, or peach halves. Or serve with potato salad.

6. Sauté or broil, to fill buttered toasted split buns. Serve with coleslaw.

7. Heat in barbecue sauce; serve on buttered toasted split rolls.

8. Pan-fry with thinly sliced onions.

9. Simmer a ½- to 1-lb. piece of cervelat in hot water to cover, about 8 min.; serve as hot meat at dinner.

10. Sauté bologna slices until they curl up into cup shapes. Fill "cups" with hot baked beans or hot potato salad.

11. Place slices of canned luncheon meat in pie plate; cover with seasoned, mashed sweet potatoes. Sprinkle with brown sugar. Bake at 350°F. about 30 min., or till steaming hot in center.

RICE-BOLOGNA HALF SHELLS

1⅓ cups packaged precooked rice	1 tablesp. butter or margarine
1½ cups water	1 tablesp. fat
½ cup catchup	8 slices bologna, about ¼″ thick
2 teasp. Worcestershire	
1 tablesp. vinegar	4 packaged process Cheddar-cheese slices
½ teasp. sugar	

In saucepan, place rice, water, catchup, Worcestershire, vinegar, sugar; stir just till rice is moistened. Bring to boil, uncovered, over high heat, fluffing rice gently once or twice with fork. Cover; remove from heat. Let stand 5 min. Add butter. Meanwhile, preheat broiler 10 min. or as manufacturer directs. In hot fat, in skillet, sauté bologna on one side until cup-shaped; turn; brown on other side. Spoon rice into bologna cups. Top each with ½ slice cheese; broil until cheese is bubbly. Makes 4 servings.

BARBECUED BOLOGNA CROWN

¼ cup butter or margarine	1 teasp. celery salt
½ cup minced onions	½ teasp. dry mustard
1 cup chili sauce	1 1-lb. loaf Vienna bread
¼ cup vinegar	12 slices bologna, ¼″ thick
2 tablesp. Worcestershire	½ cup grated process Cheddar cheese
4 teasp. brown sugar	

Start heating oven to 400°F. In butter, in skillet, sauté onions until tender. Stir in chili sauce, vinegar, Worcestershire, sugar, celery salt, mustard; cook over low heat about 5 min., or until thickened. Meanwhile, cut bread crosswise into 13 slices, not quite through to bottom crust; place on foil. Turn loaf on its side; into each cut, insert 1 tablesp. chili-sauce mixture, then 1 slice bologna, folded. (Loaf will bend into crown shape.) Spread 3 or 4 tablesp. chili-sauce mixture over top of loaf; sprinkle with grated cheese. Wrap loaf in foil. Bake 15 min. To serve, snip slices apart with scissors. Pass rest of sauce. Makes 6 servings of 2 slices each.

LIVERWURST AU GOURMET

1 cup uncooked regular or processed white rice	½ cup snipped parsley
1½ lb. liverwurst, unsliced	2 drops Tabasco
	1 medium onion, grated
½ cup very soft butter or margarine	1 tablesp. Worcestershire
	2 tablesp. sherry

Preheat broiler 10 min., or as manufacturer directs. Cook rice as label directs. Meanwhile, cut liverwurst on angle into 8 slices; place in shallow pan. In small bowl, combine butter with parsley, Tabasco, onion, Worcestershire, and sherry. Spread on liverwurst. Broil, 3″ from heat, about 6 min., or until browned. Arrange bed of rice on heated platter; top with meat; spoon on pan juices. Makes 4 servings.

CROUSTADIN

½ lb. bacon slices	1 tablesp. butter or margarine
1 lb. liverwurst (6 slices, about ½″ thick)	6 French bread slices, ½″ thick
Flour	Lemon wedges
	Snipped parsley

1. *About 30 min. before serving:* In skillet, fry

bacon till crisp — about 8 min. Remove bacon; drain off all but 3 tablesp. drippings.

2. Sprinkle both sides of liverwurst with flour; sauté in drippings till brown; remove from skillet; drain off drippings.

3. In skillet, heat butter till brown; in it, lightly toast bread on both sides; top each with a liverwurst slice, then with bacon slices. Squeeze on lemon juice; sprinkle with parsley.

Serve with limas and carrots, tossed pineapple salad, baked custards topped with chocolate sauce, nut cookies, and coffee. Makes 4 to 6 servings.

LENTIL CASSOULET

2 cups dried lentils	¼ teasp. dried thyme
Salt	1 tablesp. vinegar
½ lb. soft salami	1 1-lb. can cooked
1 large onion, minced	dried limas
¼ cup butter or margarine	1 large tomato, slivered
Pepper	

1. *One hour and a half ahead:* Simmer lentils in 3 qt. water with 1 tablesp. salt, uncovered, 45 min.; drain.

2. *About 45 min. ahead:* Start heating oven to 350°F. Cut salami into strips 1″ x ½″ x ¼″. Sauté onion in butter until tender; into onion, stir lentils, 1 teasp. salt, ⅛ teasp. pepper, thyme, vinegar, limas (plus ⅓ cup of their liquid).

3. In 2-qt. casserole, arrange ⅓ of lentils; cover with ⅓ of salami, then ⅓ of tomato, sprinkled with salt. Repeat, making 2 more layers of lentils, salami, and tomato. Bake, covered, 30 min. Serve with apple-and-grape salad, hard rolls, vanilla ice cream with melted jelly, spritz cookies, and coffee. Makes 6 servings.

BAVARIAN SUPPER

1 1-lb.-13-oz. can sauerkraut	¼ lb. thinly sliced hard salami
¼ cup butter or margarine	4 Knockwursts
¼ cup heavy cream	1 cup packaged biscuit mix
1 tablesp. instant minced onion	1 teasp. dry mustard
1 teasp. juniper berries (optional)	2 tablesp. melted butter or margarine
	Snipped parsley

1. *About 30 min. before dinner:* Open sauerkraut; drain lightly; place in skillet; dot with ¼ cup butter; pour on cream; sprinkle with onion and juniper berries; heat. Meanwhile, tuck halved salami slices in kraut; lay Knockwursts on top. Heat, covered, until bubbling.

2. Prepare biscuit mix for dumplings as label directs. Arrange mixture, in 6 spoonfuls, on bubbling kraut. Cook, covered, 10 min.; then cook, uncovered, 10 min., or until done.

3. Meanwhile, thoroughly blend mustard with 2 tablesp. melted butter. As soon as dumplings are done, serve skillet supper, topped with mustard butter and snipped parsley.

Serve with chilled tomato juice, cheese-stuffed celery, heated salty rye, baked pears with ice cream, and tea. Makes 4 servings.

FRANKFURTERS
(hot dogs or franks)

Today's hot dog is one of America's finest meats. It's a combination of tender, lean, juicy meats and aromatic spices and seasonings, which are encased, then smoked over hickory or other hardwood.

If simply served, these hot dogs or franks are as fine for children as for grownups. They supply the same high-quality protein and meat values as roasts, chops, and steaks and are a very thrifty buy.

To Buy and Store

You can't tell a good hot dog just by looking at it! A well-known brand name is your best guide, a packaged hot dog your best buy. Every frank in the cellophane-wrapped packages is full of tender, lean beef and juicy pork — and sometimes tasty veal. Some are all-beef. They have no waste.

Some franks are sold by the link or portion of a pound. If they've been government-inspected, several franks out of each 5-lb. carton carry a little band giving the packer's name and exact ingredients. Ask to see this label.

There are also franks containing some wheat or soy flour; the label usually declares such additions.

Choose a Style (skinless or natural casing): There are all-meat franks, all-beef franks, and kosher franks.

Choose a Pack: Franks come in ½-lb. and 1-lb. cellophane packages, 2- or 3-lb. cartons with cellophane windows, as well as in cans and jars — some with a sack of barbecue or relish sauce inside.

Choose a Size: Regular franks average 9 to 10 per lb.; dinner franks (larger) 5 per lb.; cocktail franks (smaller) 26 to 28 per lb.

Amount to Buy: Allow 1 or 2 regular-size franks per serving for lunch; 2 or 3 for dinner.

To Store: Keep in original cellophane package in coldest part of refrigerator. Wrap bulk franks loosely in wax paper. Use within 3 or 4 days.

To Freeze: You may freeze very fresh franks in their original package a week or so in the home freezer. If you plan to freeze them up to a month, wrap in freezer-wrapping material.

To Serve Franks

Serve Them Cold: Franks are cooked, so use them right from the package — whole or cut up, in salads, sandwiches, etc.

Serve Them Hot:

SIMMERED: Heat franks in water just below boiling point 5 to 8 min. (Do not boil or pierce skins; franks will split.) Remove from water with tongs.

BROILED: Preheat broiler 10 min., or as manufacturer directs. Brush or rub each frank with melted butter or margarine, or salad oil. Broil about 2″ to 3″ from heat, allowing about 4 min. on each side.

Or cut franks lengthwise, not quite through; arrange with cut sides up, on broiler rack. Place cheese strip and ½ bacon slice on each frank. Broil.

PAN-BROILED: In 1 tablesp. hot fat, in skillet, sauté whole franks, turning them occasionally until just brown. If franks are split, sauté cut side first, then skin side.

FRANKS FOR DINNER

FRANKS ITALIAN

1 medium eggplant	2 8-oz. cans tomato
⅓ cup flour	sauce
½ teasp. salt	¼ lb. process sharp
⅛ teasp. pepper	Cheddar cheese,
⅓ cup salad oil	grated (1 cup)
8 franks	Snipped parsley

Start heating oven to 350°F. Wash eggplant; cut into 8 ½″-thick slices. Coat with mixture of flour, salt, pepper. In hot salad oil, in skillet, sauté eggplant slices until golden on both sides. In greased 12″ x 8″ x 2″ baking dish, place 4 eggplant slices, side by side. On top of each, place 1 frank, halved lengthwise. Spread with 1 can tomato sauce; then sprinkle with half of cheese. Repeat layers. Bake 30 min., or until cheese is bubbly. Top with parsley. Makes 4 servings.

HAMBURGER: Substitute 8 sautéed thin hamburger patties for franks. Add ¼ teasp. orégano to cheese.

HARVEST TWOSOME

3 medium zucchini, sliced ½″ thick	⅛ teasp. pepper
4 franks, sliced	¼ lb. process Cheddar cheese, grated (1 cup)
1 tomato, cut into wedges	2 tablesp. butter or margarine
½ teasp. salt	

Start heating oven to 350°F. Cook zucchini in 1″ boiling salted water, covered, 5 to 7 min., or until tender-crisp. In greased 8″ or 9″ pie plate, arrange zucchini, then franks; tuck in tomato wedges; then sprinkle with salt, pepper, and cheese. Lastly, dot with butter. Cover with second pie plate or foil. Bake 20 min. Makes 2 servings.

HOT BARBECUED FRANKS

2 tablesp. fat	1 tablesp. Worcestershire
⅓ cup minced onions	
¾ teasp. paprika	3 tablesp. catchup
¼ teasp. pepper	2 tablesp. vinegar
2 teasp. sugar	8 franks
¾ teasp. dry mustard	

Start heating oven to 350°F. In fat, in skillet, sauté onions until tender. Add paprika, pepper, sugar, mustard, Worcestershire, catchup, and vinegar. Slit franks lengthwise; arrange in baking dish; pour sauce into slits. Bake 20 min., basting often. Makes 4 servings.

BARBECUED FRANKS — THREE STYLES

¾ cup catchup	1 teasp. sugar
1 tablesp. Worcestershire	Dash Tabasco
1 teasp. chili powder	1 cup water
½ teasp. salt	8 to 12 franks

Start heating oven to 350°F. In saucepan, combine all ingredients except franks; bring to boil; reduce heat and simmer 15 to 20 min. Place franks in casserole; pour on sauce. Bake, uncovered, 30 min., turning occasionally.

Serve in toasted split buns, on hot fluffy rice, buttered noodles, or creamy mashed potatoes; or with baked or boiled potatoes. Makes 4 to 6 servings.

SKILLET-BARBECUED: Make sauce in skillet; bring to boil; add franks; simmer 15 to 20 min. **PICNIC-STYLE:** Let sauce simmer 15 to 20 min. Put broiled, pan-broiled, or outdoor-grilled franks in split frank buns; spoon on sauce. **SAVORY BARBECUE SAUCE:** Before combining sauce ingredients in saucepan, sauté 1 minced medium onion in 2 tablesp. butter or margarine; add rest of sauce ingredients.

BARBECUE-BUFFET STEW

⅓ cup salad oil	3 cups drained canned whole-kernel hominy
2 medium onions, sliced	
1 small clove garlic, minced	1 tablesp. chili powder
1 doz. franks, sliced ½″ thick	2 teasp. salt or celery salt
1½ cups pitted ripe olives	1¾ cups tomato juice
2 cups drained canned or cooked kidney beans	1½ cups grated process Cheddar cheese
	Buttered French bread slices

Early in day: In hot salad oil, in skillet, sauté onions and garlic until golden. Add franks; sauté 5 min. Meanwhile, cut ¾ cup ripe olives into large pieces, leaving remaining olives whole; add to franks, along with beans, hominy, chili, salt, tomato juice; heat till boiling. Blend in cheese. Turn into 12″ x 8″ x 2″ baking dish. Refrigerate.

About 50 min. before dinner: Start heating oven to 400°F. Cover casserole mixture with bread. Bake 40 min. Makes 8 to 10 servings. P.S. If you make this stew just before dinner, bake 20 min.

FRANK CURRY BAKE

¼ lb. wide noodles (2 cups)	powder
1 cup commercial sour cream	½ teasp. salt
	⅛ teasp. pepper
¾ to 1 teasp. curry	5 franks
	Celery or poppy seeds

Start heating oven to 400°F. Cook noodles as label directs; drain. Add sour cream, curry,

salt, pepper; toss lightly. Turn mixture into 10″ x 6″ x 2″ baking dish. Arrange franks on top; sprinkle lightly with celery seeds. Bake 15 min., or until heated through. Makes 2 or 3 servings.

FRANKFURTERS GARNI

1 lb. frankfurters	gravy
4 tablesp. butter or margarine	2 tablesp. instant minced onion
1 15½-oz. can small whole boiled onions, drained	1 tablesp. granulated sugar
	2 tablesp. sherry
¾ lb. mushrooms	¼ teasp. dried thyme
1 10¾-oz. can beef	2 bay leaves

About 20 to 25 min. before serving:
1. Cut each frankfurter on diagonal into 4 pieces; sauté in 2 tablesp. butter or margarine in Dutch oven until brown, turning occasionally. Add drained whole onions; sauté them till brown, then remove both cut-up frankfurters and browned whole onions to serving dish.
2. In same Dutch oven, in 2 tablesp. butter or margarine, sauté mushrooms (if large, halve them) until just tender. Then add beef gravy, instant minced onion, sugar, sherry, dried thyme, and the bay leaves. Return frankfurters and boiled onions to Dutch oven and heat all. Makes 4 servings.

BARBECUED FRANK KABOBS

1 cup chili sauce	½ teasp. salt
1 tablesp. brown sugar	1 tablesp. snipped parsley
3 tablesp. vinegar	2 tablesp. butter or margarine
3 drops Tabasco	
1 small onion, sliced	3 bacon slices
1½ cups boiling water	6 franks, quartered crosswise
1⅓ cups packaged precooked rice	

Preheat broiler 10 min., or as manufacturer directs. In saucepan, combine chili sauce, sugar, vinegar, Tabasco, onion; simmer 5 min. To boiling water in another saucepan, add rice, salt, parsley; cook as rice label directs. Stir in butter.

Cut each bacon slice into 6 pieces. On each of 4 skewers, arrange frank pieces alternately with bacon. Broil till light brown, turning. Spread with half of sauce. Broil 5 min.; turn; spread with remaining sauce. Broil 5 min.

Serve kabobs atop rice. Makes 4 servings.

TWENTY-MINUTE BOILED DINNER

1 head cabbage cut into 6 wedges	2 tablesp. flour
1 lb. franks	1½ cups milk or liq- uefied nonfat dry milk
1 qt. boiling water	
1 teasp. salt	1 teasp. salt
2 tablesp. butter or margarine	2 to 3 tablesp. pre- pared mustard

In Dutch oven or large kettle, place cabbage wedges; top with franks. Add boiling water, 1 teasp. salt. Boil, covered, 10 min., or until cabbage is tender-crisp.

Meanwhile, make mustard sauce as follows: In saucepan, melt butter. Add flour; stir till smooth. Remove from heat. Add milk, stirring constantly. Then add 1 teasp. salt, mustard. Stir over low heat until thickened.

Remove cabbage wedges and franks to heated platter. Spoon on some of sauce; pass rest. Makes 6 servings.

BARBECUED FRANKS AND BEANS

2 tablesp. butter or margarine	1 tablesp. vinegar
1 medium onion, sliced	1 teasp. Worcester- shire
1 tablesp. flour	½ teasp. sugar
½ cup canned tomato sauce	½ teasp. chili powder
	½ teasp. salt
½ cup canned con- densed beef bouil- lon, undiluted	1 cup drained canned red kidney beans
	½ lb. franks, cut di- agonally into chunks

About 15 min. before serving: In large skillet, melt butter; add onion and sauté until tender.

Meanwhile, blend flour with tomato sauce, bouillon, vinegar, Worcestershire, sugar, chili powder, and salt; quickly stir into onion, in skillet.

Add kidney beans and franks; simmer, cov- ered, just until heated through. Makes 2 hale and hearty servings.

FRANKS AND SAUERKRAUT

PEASANT STYLE: Start heating oven to 350°F. In 2-qt. casserole, mix 1 undrained 1-lb. can sauerkraut with 1 undrained 1-lb.-4-oz. can peas, ½ teasp. salt, and ⅛ to ¼ teasp. pepper. Arrange 1 lb. franks on top. Bake, covered, 15 min.; uncover; bake 15 min. longer. Makes 4 servings.

BARBECUE FASHION: Just make up Barbecued Franks, p. 245, placing 1-lb.-13-oz. can sauer- kraut, drained, in casserole, before adding franks and sauce.

MOTHER'S BEST: In saucepan, heat 1 undrained 1-lb.-13-oz. can sauerkraut with 1 teasp. cara- way seeds. Make Mustard Sauce, p. 532. Top sauerkraut with heated, broiled, or pan-broiled franks; pour sauce over all.

TOP-HATTER FRANKS

2 tablesp. butter or margarine	mustard
	1 10½-oz. can con- densed bean-and- bacon soup, undiluted
1 medium onion, minced	
1 green pepper, sliced	
½ cup minced celery	1 soup-can milk or diluted evaporated milk
1 lb. franks, sliced ½″ thick	
2 tablesp. prepared	1 pkg. corn-muffin mix

Start heating oven to 350°F. In hot butter, in skillet, sauté onion, green pepper, and celery until tender. Stir in franks, mustard, soup, milk. Turn into 12″ x 8″ x 2″ baking dish. Prepare muffin mix as label directs; pour over frank mixture. Bake 35 min., or until corn-muffin mix is done. Makes 8 servings.

MAMMY'S WAY: Substitute the following corn- bread batter for corn-muffin mix: Into mixing bowl, sift 1 cup corn meal, ¼ cup sifted all- purpose flour, 2 tablesp. sugar, ½ teasp. salt, 1½ teasp. double-acting baking powder. Add 2 tablesp. salad oil, 1 egg, ½ cup milk. With hand beater, beat until smooth — about 1 min. Pour over frank mixture; then bake as above.

HOT DIGGETY DOGS

1 lb. franks	sommé, undiluted
3 tablesp. salad oil or fat	2 1-lb. cans kidney beans, drained
1 teasp. monosodium glutamate	1 1-lb. can kidney beans, undrained
2 onions, thinly sliced	¼ cup vinegar
	3 tablesp. brown sugar
2 tablesp. flour	2 teasp. Worcester- shire
1 8-oz. can tomato sauce	1 teasp. chili powder
½ cup canned con-	1½ teasp. salt

1. *About 30 min. before supper:* Quarter franks diagonally; in hot salad oil, in 10″ skillet, sauté them with ½ teasp. monosodium glutamate until brown; remove franks and set aside.

2. In same skillet, sauté onions until slightly tender; stir in flour, then tomato sauce and consommé; cook, stirring, until mixture thickens.

3. Add beans, vinegar, brown sugar, Worcestershire, chili powder, ½ teasp. monosodium glutamate, and salt. Bring to boil; cover; simmer gently 10 min.

4. Add franks; cover; simmer 5 min. longer. Serve with hot corn-bread squares and green salad. Makes 6 servings.

LET'S HAVE CANNED MEATS

The time-saving virtues of reliable brands of canned meat make them a staple must in many homes. But other features should place them high on your list of menu aids, too.

There's a kind and flavor of canned meat to suit every taste.

Canned meats meet budget needs because they are so reasonably priced. And since they are precooked, their preparation involves no trimming, shrinkage, or kitchen waste.

They team up with other foods and flavors.

Some canned meats, such as luncheon meat, corned beef, chopped ham, tongue, franks, dried beef, Vienna sausage, etc., are ready to open and eat. Or they may be heated or used in combination dishes.

Other canned meats, such as corned-beef hash, beef or chicken stew, chili con carne, tamales, etc., need brief heating before serving.

To Buy Canned Meats

CANNED HAM: There are 1½-lb. cans containing a solid, boneless piece of ham. There are also canned full-size boned whole hams of 6¾ to 12 lb., as well as smoked picnics of 4½ to 8 lb.

CANNED MEAT LOAVES: These handy 12-oz. cans contain all chopped ham, cured-pork luncheon meat, or cured-pork-and-beef loaf. There are also smaller cans of beef loaf and veal loaf.

CANNED CORNED BEEF, TONGUE, FRANKS, ETC.: You can buy:

1. A solid pack of delicately cured corned beef or corned-beef brisket.

2. Small luncheon tongues; larger beef tongues.

3. Franks (some with sack of sauce inside); Vienna sausage (little sausages with open ends); pork sausage.

4. Beef in natural juices; roast beef; beef patties; sandwich steaks and gravy; tripe; etc.

5. Fully cooked cured, smoked back ribs with barbecue sauce; heat as directed.

CANNED MEAT COMBINATIONS: Choose from:

1. Corned-beef hash.

2. Beef, lamb, or chicken stew, with fine flavor.

3. Chili con carne (with or without beans) or tamales.

4. Spaghetti with meat or meat balls, spaghetti sauce with meat, etc. See p. 102.

5. Chop suey or chow mein, to serve over rice or chow-mein noodles. See p. 102.

6. Ham à la king, chicken à la king, etc.

CANNED MEAT SPREADS: These tasty meat spreads include deviled ham (2¼- and 4½-oz. sizes), potted meat, or deviled luncheon meat (3-oz. size); liver, chicken, or ham *pâté*, etc.

CANNED MEATS FOR BABIES AND JUNIORS: These are nice to add to sandwich fillings, creamed dishes, casseroles, cocktail dips, etc.

To Store Canned Meats

Read can label for storage directions.

CANNED HAM AND SMOKED PICNICS must be refrigerated at all times, unless the label indicates that refrigeration is not necessary.

Other canned meats may be kept in a cool dry place.

UNOPENED CANNED HAMS may be frozen for about 3 months.

Once canned meats are opened, treat them like cooked meat: Cover; refrigerate; use within 1 or 2 days.

To Serve Canned Meats

Serve Them Hot: Open can; turn out contents. Heat slowly just until hot enough to serve; don't overcook or stir; shape and texture of meat may be harmed.

Or serve as below, as in To Serve Ready-Cooked Meats, p. 242, or as in the Last of the Meat, p. 252.

Never try to heat any canned food in the unopened can; the can may explode.

LUNCHEON MEAT OR CHOPPED HAM OR BEEF: Broil or sauté slices. Or shred, coarsely grate, or cut up; then use as ham in macaroni, potato, or other casseroles. Or use in creamed eggs, chef's salad, etc.

CORNED BEEF: Slice; then sauté in butter. Or add to casserole dishes. Or heat with cabbage, as in Skillet-Boiled Dinner, p. 250.

CORNED-BEEF HASH: Bake in casserole at 350°F. Or sauté in butter or margarine until brown. Or slice; then sauté, broil, or bake until brown on both sides. Or heat, and use as sandwich or toast spread. Serve with Mustard Sauce, p. 532; Zippy Cheese Sauce, p. 530; chili sauce; chutney; etc.

CHILI CON CARNE: Heat; serve with crackers, or in ring of hot fluffy rice or macaroni.

PORK SAUSAGE: Sauté or broil. Serve with scalloped potatoes, scrambled eggs, etc.

VIENNA SAUSAGE: Sauté or broil; then serve as nibblers to dunk into hot chili sauce, or barbecue sauce, etc. Or serve with eggs, cut up in salads, etc.

TAMALES: Heat, remove wrappers; serve as is, or spoon chili over them. Serve them over scrambled eggs, top with cheese.

SPAGHETTI WITH MEAT, RAVIOLI WITH MEAT SAUCE, ETC.: Heat; top with cheese.

BEEF STEW: Heat with a little red wine or pinch of dried thyme. Or add sautéed mushrooms or sautéed, sliced onion while heating. Serve over biscuit or corn-bread squares.

CANNED BEANS AND FRANKS IN TOMATO SAUCE OR BEANS AND GROUND BEEF IN BARBECUE SAUCE: Heat them as label directs; spoon them over hot toasted buttered English muffins, hot buttered biscuits (from mix), crisp crackers, or potato chips. Nice with hot-dog relish.

Serve Them Cold: Refrigerate unopened cans of meat or meat loaf 1 to 2 hr. To remove from can, open both ends completely; push meat out; slice.

Use in cold-meat platters, in sandwiches, cut up in tossed salads, or as nibblers — see To Serve Ready-Cooked Meats, p. 242.

CANNED HAMS AND PICNICS

Serve canned ham or smoked picnic sliced as it comes from the can, as in To Serve Ready-Cooked Meats, p. 242.

Or heat as label directs. Or remove from can to wire rack in shallow pan. Heat in 325°F. oven as follows:

Piece of Ham: about 10 to 12 min. per lb.
6¾-lb. Ham: about 20 min. per lb.
10- to 12-lb. Ham: about 15 min. per lb.
4½- to 8-lb. Picnic: about 10 to 15 min. per lb.

Glaze, p. 211, may be applied ½ hr. before heating time is up. Or heat; then glaze at 450°F. until brown.

CANNED LUNCHEON MEAT

Start heating oven to 350°F. Place 2 cans luncheon meat or 2 cans chopped ham together to form 1 long loaf in baking dish; score as in step 6, p. 210. Bake, uncovered, 30 min.

Serve with barbecue sauce; Savory Jelly Sauce, p. 528; Horse-radish Sauce I or II, p. 532; Mustard Sauce, p. 532; California Raisin Sauce, p. 533. Makes 8 servings.

SPICY BAKED: After scoring luncheon meat or chopped ham, spread with mixture of ¼ cup brown sugar, packed; 1 tablesp. vinegar; 1 teasp. prepared mustard; 2 teasp. flour. Bake at 375°F. about 30 min.

CLOVE MIDGET: Stud scored luncheon meat or chopped ham with whole cloves. Spread with ½ recipe Marmalade Glaze or another glaze, p. 211. Bake as in Spicy Baked, above, basting often.

STUFFED: Cut 2 luncheon-meat or chopped-ham loaves lengthwise in half; place in 8″ x 8″ x 2″ pan. Into 2 cups mashed potatoes, stir ¼ cup minced onion and 2 tablesp. snipped parsley. Spread over meat; sprinkle with paprika. Bake as above.

PEACH DINNER LOAF: Start heating oven to 375°F. Drain 1 1-lb.-13-oz. can peach slices, reserving syrup. Slice loaf of luncheon meat crosswise into 4 sections, almost, but not quite, through. Arrange peaches between and around meat slices in shallow pan. Blend 2 tablesp. brown sugar with ¼ cup peach syrup; spoon over loaf. Stud with cloves. Bake 35 min. Makes 4 servings.

GRETCHEN'S CASSEROLE

1 1-lb. or 1-lb.-4-oz. can sauerkraut	2 tablesp. butter or margarine
1 1-lb.-4-oz. can apple slices	2 12-oz. cans luncheon meat
1/3 cup brown sugar, packed	1/4 cup brown sugar, packed
2 tablesp. vinegar	2 teasp. prepared mustard
1/4 cup minced onion	

Start heating oven to 400°F. In 2-qt. casserole, combine sauerkraut and apples, undrained, with 1/3 cup brown sugar, vinegar, onion; dot with butter. Slice meat into 8 to 12 slices; arrange on top of sauerkraut mixture. Combine 1/4 cup brown sugar with mustard; spread on meat. Bake, uncovered, 30 to 40 min., or until meat is glazed and sauerkraut is heated through. Makes 4 to 6 servings.

♣ FOR 2: Use 1¼ cups canned sauerkraut, 1¼ cups canned apple slices, 2½ tablesp. brown sugar, 1 tablesp. vinegar, 2 tablesp. minced onion, 1 tablesp. butter or margarine, 1 can luncheon meat, 2 tablesp. brown sugar, 1 teasp. prepared mustard. Bake in 1-qt. casserole.

APPLE-SWEET-POTATO CASSEROLE

1 1-lb. or 1-lb.-4-oz. can sliced apples	1 12-oz. can luncheon meat, cut into 4 slices
1 1-lb.-7-oz. can vacuum-packed sweet potatoes	1/4 cup brown sugar, packed
	1/2 teasp. cinnamon

Start heating oven to 400°F. In greased 2-qt. casserole, arrange alternate layers of apples and sweet potatoes, cutting large potatoes in half, lengthwise. Arrange slices of luncheon meat on top. Sprinkle with brown sugar and cinnamon. Bake, uncovered, 25 min. Makes 4 servings.

BEST-EVER BAKED BEANS

2 onions, minced	2 1-lb. cans baked beans in tomato sauce
Butter or margarine	
2 2¼-oz. cans deviled ham	4 tomato slices

Sauté onions in a little butter until tender; add with deviled ham to beans. Turn into 2-qt. covered casserole; top with tomato slices; bake at 400°F. 35 min. Makes 4 servings.

SKILLET-BOILED DINNER

8 small new potatoes, scraped	quartered
	1/4 cup melted butter or margarine
3 medium carrots, pared, halved crosswise	1/3 cup snipped parsley
1 teasp. salt	1/3 cup mayonnaise
1 1½-lb. head cabbage, quartered	1 tablesp. prepared mustard
1/4 teasp. salt	1 tablesp. drained horse-radish
1 12-oz. can corned beef, chilled, then	

In large skillet, chicken fryer, or Dutch oven, place 1/2″ water; heat. Add potatoes, carrots, 1 teasp. salt; cook, covered, 10 min. Push potatoes and carrots to side of skillet; place cabbage wedges in bottom of skillet; sprinkle with 1/4 teasp. salt. Cook, covered, 10 to 15 min., or until almost tender. Top with corned beef. Cook, covered, 5 min.; drain. Pour melted butter or margarine over all. Sprinkle with parsley.

Serve with mustard sauce made by combining mayonnaise, mustard, and horse-radish. Makes 4 servings.

EAST-WEST CHILI BAKE

2 1-lb. cans pork and beans with tomato sauce	1 15½-oz. can tamales in chili gravy
	1 cup grated process Cheddar cheese
1 15-oz. can chili con carne, without beans	1/2 cup minced onion

About 40 min. before dinner:
1. Start heating oven to 425°F. Spread pork and beans in 12″ x 8″ x 2″ baking dish, or 3-qt. shallow casserole. With fork, break up the chili con carne and sprinkle on top.
2. Arrange tamales lengthwise down center; sprinkle them with cheese.
3. Bake 30 min., or until hot and bubbly.
4. Just before serving, sprinkle some minced onion between every two tamales. Makes 4 or 5 servings.

TAMALE PIE

2 cups white corn meal	2 cans chili con carne, without beans
1 teasp. salt	Grated sharp cheese
5 cups hot water	

In top of double boiler, combine corn meal and salt; add hot water, stirring. Cook mixture, covered, stirring occasionally, 30 min., till fairly stiff.

Start heating oven to 350°F. In saucepan, heat chili. Line bottom and sides of 2-qt. casserole with ⅔ of corn-meal mush. Pour in chili. Dot with rest of mush. Bake for 30 min. Cheese may be sprinkled on top of pie when served. Makes 8 servings.

CORN-AND-CHILI CASSEROLE

1 15-oz. can chili con carne, without beans	1½ to 2 cups medium day-old bread crumbs
1 1-lb. can cream-style corn	1¼ teasp. salt
2 eggs, separated	Dash pepper
¾ cup canned tomato juice	¼ teasp. orégano
	1 teasp. Worcestershire

1. Start heating oven to 375°F. Oil 2-qt. casserole.
2. In bowl, combine chili, corn, egg yolks, tomato juice, crumbs, salt, pepper, orégano, Worcestershire. Fold into stiffly beaten egg whites. Turn into casserole.
3. Bake, uncovered, 45 min., or till set. Makes 6 servings.

SKILLET HASH

Remove ends from 2 1-lb. cans corned-beef hash; remove hash. Slice each into 3 slices; sauté in 3 tablesp. butter or margarine, in skillet, until brown, turning once. Add 1 16- or 17-oz. can peas, drained; heat. Top each hash slice with 2 teasp. hot-dog or hamburger relish. Serve from skillet. Makes 6 servings.

FRESH CABBAGE GARNI

2 tablesp. butter, margarine, or salad oil	cabbage, coarsely shredded
Black pepper	¼ cup butter or margarine
1 tablesp. prepared mustard	¼ cup water
1½ tablesp. flour	2 tablesp. salad oil
Salt	2 15-oz. cans corned-beef hash
1 cup milk	2 teasp. lemon juice
1 small head green	

About 30 min. before serving:
1. In double boiler, melt 2 tablesp. butter or margarine; stir in dash pepper, prepared mustard, flour, and ½ teasp. salt. Slowly stir in milk; cook, stirring, until smooth and thick-

ened — about 5 min.; keep warm until needed.
2. Now cook shredded cabbage in large skillet or Dutch oven with ¼ cup butter or margarine, 1 teasp. salt, ¼ teasp. pepper, and the water, covered, for about 10 min., or until tender-crisp, tossing well with fork occasionally.
3. Meanwhile cook hash-balls as follows: Heat salad oil in 10″ skillet. As each spoonful of hash is removed from one of the cans, form it into 1″ ball and then drop it into oil; sauté until brown on both sides, using a spoon to turn and remove them. Repeat with other can of hash.
4. Now spoon cabbage onto center of a heated platter; heap hash-balls on top in center. Stir lemon juice into mustard sauce; then spoon it over the hash-balls.

Serve with canned stewed tomatoes, pumpernickel bread and butter, and applesauce-topped spice cake. Makes 6 servings.

ONION-CRESTED HASH CASSEROLE

3 tablesp. salad oil	⅓ cup milk
4 cups sliced onions	½ teasp. curry powder
2 1-lb. cans corned-beef hash	½ cup soft day-old bread crumbs
½ teasp. Worcestershire	½ cup grated Cheddar cheese
½ teasp. salt	
⅛ teasp. pepper	

About 45 min. before serving:
1. Start heating oven to 400°F. In salad oil, in skillet, sauté onions until tender-crisp and golden.
2. Arrange hash in 10″ x 6″ x 2″ baking dish; add Worcestershire, salt, and pepper, and toss with fork until mixed. Then spread out hash to fill dish, without packing; pour on milk.
3. Add curry to onions; toss well, then arrange over top of hash. Now toss bread crumbs with cheese; sprinkle over onions. Bake 20 to 30 min., or until heated through. Makes 6 servings.

Serve with buttered peas, mixed-up lettuce, carrot, and spinach salad, rye bread, and nutmeg-topped canned apricots.

DRIED BEEF

To Buy and Store

National packers supply dried beef in packages or glass jars. When fresh, the meat is bright red with no brown spots and is moist, not brittle.

To Store: Keep packaged dried beef in refrigerator, tightly wrapped; use within 6 to 7 days. Store unopened jars on a cool shelf; plan to use within 4 to 6 weeks.

To Prepare: Tear dried beef into medium shreds. If dried beef seems too salty, pour boiling water over it; let stand 1 min.; then drain. Or use beef right from package or jar, if you prefer a full flavor.

CREAMED DRIED BEEF

¼ lb. dried beef	evaporated milk
¼ cup butter or mar-	plus 1 cup water
garine	1 teasp. bottled thick
3 tablesp. flour	meat sauce (op-
2 cups milk or 1 cup	tional)

Tear dried beef into medium pieces; then prepare as in To Prepare, above.

In double-boiler top, over direct heat, melt butter. Add dried beef; cook until edges curl. Stir in flour. Place over boiling water. Add milk slowly, stirring. Cook, stirring, until smooth and thickened. Add meat sauce.

Serve on toast, small baked potatoes, waffles, fluffy white rice, or split hot baking-powder biscuits. Or serve over Baked or Broiled Tomatoes, p. 417, or over hot whole hard-cooked eggs on toast. Makes 4 servings.

To Vary: If desired, simmer ¼ cup minced onion and 2 tablesp. minced green pepper in butter. Or add 1 chopped hard-cooked egg to sauce.

WITH MUSHROOMS: Add ¼ lb. sautéed, sliced fresh mushrooms to sauce.

CURRIED: Add ¼ to ½ teasp. curry powder to sauce.

LAST OF THE MEAT

Refrigerate Leftover Meat at Once. Leftover cooked roasts, meats, etc., should be loosely covered and refrigerated *at once* (see p. 173). Plan to use them up within a day or two, while they're at their best.

Leftover gravy should also be refrigerated at once, and used within 2 days.

Or Freeze Leftover Meat: You may freezer-wrap and freeze unsliced portions of leftover roast (trimmed of excess fat); sliced leftover roast, meat loaf, etc.; leftover stew; scaloppine, etc. (see p. 708). Don't keep them in the freezer longer than 1 to 3 months.

If the Meat Can Be Sliced

With roast beef, pork, lamb, or veal — or with pot roast, meat loaf, ham, smoked picnic, corned beef, tongue, etc. — there are likely to be leftovers for 1 or 2 more meals. If the meat is sliceable, serve it in one of these ways:

Serve It Cold:

1. On cold-meat platters. Add garnishes, as in The Gay Garnish, p. 441. Or top each slice with coleslaw, then roll up.

2. With hot or cold sauce. Try:
   Currant-Mint, p. 527; Savory Jelly, p. 528; Horse-radish I or II, p. 532; California Raisin, p. 533; Dilly, p. 530; Barbecue Sauce, p. 528; whole-cranberry (your own or canned).

3. Stretched with one of these:
   Cheese slices, one or several varieties.
   Cottage-cheese mounds, in lettuce cups.
   Deviled Eggs, p. 364.
   Other home-cooked, canned, or ready-cooked meats.
   Salad — coleslaw; molded fruit or vegetable salad; marinated tomato slices; a main-dish salad such as egg, potato, chicken.
   Susan's Raw Relishes, p. 118.

4. On hot-and-cold platter. Arrange cold meat slices around one of these:
   A casserole — Cheese Soufflé for 4, p. 366; Elena's Macaroni Bake, p. 382; Spanish Rice, p. 372, etc.
   Fruit — broiled canned fruits, sautéed bananas, fried apple rings, etc.
   Omelet or scrambled eggs.
   Vegetables — your choice of hot cooked vegetables; cooked broccoli with cheese sauce; cheese-topped, broiled tomatoes, etc.

Serve It Hot:

1. With gravy. Reheat roast lamb, veal, or pork slices, in gravy. Serve roast beef cold, with hot gravy.

2. With sauce. Reheat meat in one of these sauces; or pass sauce separately.

Bert's Superb Barbecue, p. 531; Curry, p. 527; Italian Tomato, p. 530; Mustard, p. 532; Onion, p. 528; Quick Mushroom, p. 528; Zippy Cheese Sauce, p. 530.

3. In hot sandwiches. See Lunch and Supper Sandwiches, p. 516. Or try one of these:

Add a few sliced mushrooms to gravy or sauce in Hot and Cold Meat Sandwiches, p. 518.

Reheat meat slices in Bert's Superb Barbecue Sauce, p. 531; serve on toasted buns.

If the Meat Is in Small Pieces

When only tag ends remain of a roast, pot roast, steak, ham, etc., cut them up and try them in one of these:

TONGUE-SPAGHETTI: Add slivered tongue or cut-up meat loaf to canned spaghetti in tomato sauce with cheese. Or add to your favorite spaghetti sauce during last 10 min. of heating.

CHEF'S SALAD BOWLS: See p. 457.

SALADS PLUS: Add to salads such as kidney bean, potato, egg, etc.

FRITTERS: Add to batter for corn fritters.

SAVORY OMELET: Use as filling for French Omelet, p. 361.

SOUPS: Top cream soups with slivers of cooked meat.

STEW ENCORE: Stew usually tastes even better the second day. It can be given a new look with the addition of a different cooked vegetable — corn, peas, tomatoes, mushrooms, okra, etc.

VEGETABLES: Add strips of meat to hot cooked, buttered or creamed vegetables.

P.S. Cold veal tastes much like chicken in salads and sandwiches.

If the Meat Is In Bits

1. Use ground, chopped, or bits of meat in: Wonderful Hash, right; sandwich fillings (see Make It Meat or Poultry, p. 521); stuffed peppers; omelet filling.
2. Use bones and bits in: Soup from Leftover Bones, p. 164; Old-fashioned Split-Pea Soup, p. 166.

BEEF A LA MODE IN ASPIC

Thinly slice leftover Beef à la Mode, p. 185; fix in layers in 10″ x 6″ x 2″ dish or deep platter, sprinkling each layer lightly with salt and pepper. Top with 6 or 8 slices leftover cooked carrots. Skim fat off leftover pan gravy; strain over meat. Chill. Slice ½″ to ¾″ thick. Serve, right from dish, with mustard or horse-radish sauce.

CHILEAN MEAT PIE
(Pastel de Choclo)

1 medium onion
2 cups cut-up leftover pot roast of beef or lamb
10 stuffed or pitted ripe olives
2 hard-cooked eggs
1 teasp. orégano
Salt
⅛ teasp. cayenne pepper
¼ cup canned condensed bouillon or consommé, undiluted
1 1-lb.-4-oz. can cream-style corn
2 eggs, well beaten
⅛ teasp. pepper

1. In food grinder, finely grind onion, meat, olives, hard-cooked eggs.
2. Start heating oven to 375°F. Combine meat, orégano, ½ teasp. salt, cayenne, bouillon. To corn, add eggs, ¼ teasp. salt, ⅛ teasp. pepper; mix well.
3. With meat mixture, line bottom and sides, up to rim, of well-greased 9″ pie plate, patting mixture in place; top with corn mixture. Bake 45 min. Then increase oven heat to 400°F. and bake 15 min. Remove from oven; cool 10 min.; then cut into 6 wedges. Makes 6 servings.

WONDERFUL HASH

2 cups chopped, cooked roast beef, lamb, veal, ham, or pork*
3 cups chopped, cold, cooked potatoes
½ cup minced onions
1 teasp. salt
¼ teasp. pepper
¼ cup nonfat dry milk (optional)
⅓ cup milk, or evaporated milk, undiluted
2 tablesp. salad oil

Coarsely chop meat and potatoes, separately, in chopping bowl; combine. Then stir in onions, salt, pepper, dry milk, milk. Heat salad oil in large skillet; spread hash evenly in bottom of skillet; cook over low heat 30 to 40 min., or until underside is brown and crusty. Do not stir, but occasionally lift edge of hash to check browning. Run spatula around edge of hash to loosen; fold one half onto other half; remove hash to platter.

Serve with chili sauce, piccalilli, or horse-radish. Or else serve with Easy Poached Eggs, p. 358; Broiled Tomatoes, p. 417; or canned tomato sauce. Makes 4 servings.

Or use cooked or canned corned beef, tongue, or luncheon meat.

To Vary: To hash mixture, add snipped parsley, green pepper, horse-radish, or pickle relish. Or reduce potatoes to 2 cups; then add 1 cup chopped, cooked beets or carrots. Or substitute tomato juice for milk. Or add 1 to 2 tablesp. chutney and a little curry powder.

CORNED-BEEF HASH AND TOMATO BAKE: Use corned beef as meat. Instead of cooking in skillet, turn into greased 1½-qt. casserole or shallow dish. Press tomato halves into top of mixture; spread each half with a little prepared mustard; sprinkle with salt, pepper, minced onion, Worcestershire, a few fresh bread crumbs, and bits of butter. Bake at 375° F., uncovered, 30 to 35 min., or until brown.

FRENCH STUFFED CABBAGE
(Chou Farci)

1 medium head green cabbage	1 cup cooked rice
1 tablesp. butter or margarine	½ teasp. salt
	Dash pepper
¼ cup minced onion	1 clove garlic, minced
¼ lb. pork-sausage meat	1 egg, beaten
	1 carrot, pared and sliced
1 cup chopped cooked lamb or beef	1 onion, thinly sliced
2 tablesp. fresh bread crumbs	2 bacon slices
	2 cups canned tomatoes

1. In kettle, in boiling salted water to cover, simmer whole cabbage 5 min. Plunge into cold water; drain well.
2. Meanwhile start heating oven to 400°F. Also, prepare this stuffing: In hot butter, in small skillet, sauté minced onion until tender. Toss with meats, crumbs, rice, salt, pepper, garlic; mix in egg.
3. In 3-qt. casserole, spread carrot and onion slices; on them, arrange 2 lengths of string (to be used for tying cabbage), then drained cabbage, stem end down. With knife, cut out 3″ round center of cabbage to about 2″ from bottom. Press stuffing into cavity.
4. Top cabbage with bacon; with string, tie head together firmly, pulling up leaves over stuffing. Around it, pour tomatoes. Cover casserole; bake 1½ hr. Cut string. Serve in casserole, cut into wedges. Makes 6 main-dish servings.

CRANBERRY-BEEF PATTIES

1½ cups chopped, cooked pot roast	1 teasp. Worcestershire
1½ cups diced, cooked potatoes	1 teasp. salt
1½ cups diced, cooked beets	⅛ teasp. pepper
	¼ cup all-purpose flour
1 onion, chopped	2 tablesp. butter or margarine
⅓ cup packaged dried bread crumbs	½ can whole-cranberry sauce
½ cup milk	
1 egg, slightly beaten	

Mix together pot roast, potatoes, beets, onion, bread crumbs, milk, egg, Worcestershire, salt, pepper. Form into 8 patties. Dip lightly into flour. Sauté in hot butter, in skillet, until browned on both sides and heated through. Add cranberry sauce; heat until melted. To serve, spoon sauce on top of patties. Makes 8 servings.

TANGY COLD BEEF-AND-ONION PLATTER

¾ teasp. salt	1 tablesp. salad or olive oil
Pinch seasoned salt	
1 teasp. dry mustard	8 thin slices cooked or canned corned beef or tongue
1 teasp. brown sugar	
1 teasp. mixed whole pickling spices	2 onions, thinly sliced
3 tablesp. wine vinegar	Shredded lettuce
	Tomatoes, quartered

At your convenience: Make marinade by mixing well salt, seasoned salt, mustard, sugar, spices, vinegar, oil. Arrange meat slices in shallow open pan; top with onion slices; pour marinade over both. Refrigerate.

At serving time: Arrange meat and onions on bed of shredded lettuce on platter. Garnish with tomato quarters. Makes 4 servings.

MEAT AND NOODLES, BOHEMIAN STYLE

3 tablesp. butter	2 teasp. salt
2 medium onions, sliced	⅛ teasp. pepper
1 cup diagonally-sliced celery	6 tablesp. grated Parmesan cheese
2½ cups cut-up pot roast of beef, lamb, veal, or chicken	1 teasp. monosodium glutamate
	1½ cups evaporated milk, undiluted
1 8-oz. pkg. medium noodles	2 tablesp. snipped parsley

1. In hot butter, in large skillet, sauté onions and celery until just limp; push to one side; add meat. Heat slowly.

2. Meanwhile, cook noodles as label directs; drain. Combine with salt, pepper, Parmesan cheese, monosodium glutamate, milk. Add to meat mixture.

3. Heat, stirring occasionally, about 5 min., or until hot. Serve topped with parsley. Makes 6 servings.

SHEPHERD'S PIE

½ recipe for Mashed Potatoes, p. 412	6 small onions, cooked, drained
2 cups cut-up, cooked roast beef, lamb, veal, or pork	1 cup cooked quartered carrots, drained
1 tablesp. flour	1 cup cooked or canned peas, drained
2 tablesp. fat or salad oil	
Leftover gravy	1 egg, beaten

Grease 1½-qt. casserole. Prepare mashed potatoes. Start heating oven to 425°F.

In bowl, lightly roll meat in flour until coated. In hot fat, in skillet, brown meat lightly on all sides. Add 2½ cups leftover gravy (or as much gravy as you have on hand, adding enough hot water to make 2½ cups in all; season to taste; thicken if necessary). Add onions, carrots, peas. Heat; then pour into casserole.

Fold egg into potatoes; arrange in ring on top of meat. Bake until gravy bubbles and potato ring is light golden brown — about 10 to 15 min. Makes 4 servings.

AU GRATIN VEAL WITH OLIVES

2 cups diced, leftover pot roast of veal	1 tablesp. butter or margarine
1 cup quartered stuffed olives	1 tablesp. flour
½ cup canned sliced mushrooms	½ teasp. salt
¼ cup canned condensed bouillon or consommé, undiluted	⅛ teasp. pepper
	½ teasp. ground nutmeg
1 10-oz. pkg. frozen green peas, partly thawed	¼ teasp. ground ginger
	3 to 4 tablesp. grated Parmesan cheese
	1½ cups milk
	Toast points

1. In large skillet, combine veal, olives, mushrooms, bouillon, peas; simmer, covered, 10 min.
2. Meanwhile, melt butter in saucepan; then stir in flour, salt, pepper, nutmeg, ginger, cheese. Cook over low heat, stirring constantly, and slowly adding milk, until slightly thickened.

Pour over veal mixture; cook, stirring, until thickened — about 5 min. Serve over toast points. Makes 4 servings.

LAMB BARBECUE

1 tablesp. butter or margarine	1 teasp. Worcestershire
1 small onion, sliced	1 cup cut-up cooked roast lamb
1 to 2 tablesp. vinegar	1½ cups uncooked medium noodles
2 teasp. brown sugar	
½ cup catchup	Melted butter or margarine
¼ cup water	

In hot butter, in small saucepan, sauté onion until lightly browned. Add vinegar, brown sugar, catchup, water, Worcestershire; simmer, covered, 15 min. Add lamb; simmer until heated.

Meanwhile, cook noodles as label directs. When tender, drain and toss with melted butter. Serve lamb and sauce over noodles. Makes 2 servings.

SWEET-SOUR ROAST PORK

3 tablesp. butter or margarine	1 cup canned crushed pineapple, undrained
¼ cup green pepper, cut into strips	2 tablesp. vinegar
¼ cup coarsely chopped onion	1 tablesp. soy sauce
1 tablesp. cornstarch	4 ½"-thick slices cooked roast pork

Preheat broiler 10 min., or as manufacturer directs. In hot butter, in skillet, sauté green pepper and onion about 5 min.; stir in cornstarch, then pineapple. Heat, stirring, until thickened. Add vinegar, soy sauce. Pour over pork in shallow open pan. Broil about 4½" below heat about 5 min. Makes 4 servings.

LAMB CURRY

4 cups hot cooked rice, p. 370	1 teasp. curry powder
2 tablesp. butter or margarine	Salt
¾ cup sliced onions	2 cups lamb gravy, diluted with water; or 2 chicken- or beef-bouillon cubes, dissolved in 2 cups hot water
1 cup diced celery	
1 clove garlic, minced	
1½ cups cut-up, cooked roast lamb	Snipped parsley

Cook rice. Meanwhile, in hot butter, in skillet, sauté onions, celery, and garlic until lightly browned. Add lamb, curry powder, salt to taste, gravy. Simmer, covered, 30 min. If necessary, thicken, as on p. 6.

To serve: Arrange hot rice in ring on platter. Sprinkle with parsley. Turn lamb curry into center. Pass choice of Curry Accompaniments, p. 330, if desired. Makes 4 servings.

VEAL CURRY: Make as on p. 255, substituting cut-up, cooked roast veal for lamb.

HAM-TOMATO CHEESE PIE

1 baked 9″ pie shell	⅛ teasp. pepper
1 cup ground cooked ham or canned luncheon meat	¼ cup mayonnaise or salad dressing
2 medium tomatoes	1 8-oz. pkg. process Cheddar cheese, grated
1 tablesp. instant minced onion	8 tomato wedges (optional)
½ teasp. orégano	Parsley sprigs
½ to 1 teasp. salt	

About 45 min. before dinner:

1. Start heating oven to 350°F. Line pie shell, baked earlier in the day, with ground ham; cover with tomatoes, sliced. Sprinkle with onion, orégano, salt, pepper. Bake 20 min.
2. Meanwhile, combine mayonnaise with grated cheese. Spread over ham-tomato filling; then bake pie 5 to 10 min. longer, or until cheese melts.
3. Just before serving, garnish pie with tomato wedges and parsley sprigs, if desired.

Serve with your favorite green vegetable and a crisp romaine salad. Dessert is blackberry gelatin dessert with whipped topping. Makes 8 servings.

HAM-AND-MUSHROOM PUFF

3 tablesp. butter or margarine	4 eggs, separated
3 tablesp. flour	1⅓ cups finely crushed saltines
1 teasp. prepared mustard	1 teasp. instant minced onion
¼ teasp. salt	2 cups ground cooked ham
2 drops Tabasco	¼ lb. fresh mushrooms, thinly sliced
2 cups milk	
1 8-oz. pkg. process Cheddar cheese, grated	2 tablesp. shredded Parmesan cheese

About 2½ hr. before serving:

1. With cellophane tape or string, fasten a folded band of foil about 6″ wide and 30″ long, around outside of a 1½-qt. soufflé dish or round casserole, so that it stands about 3″ above rim. Lightly grease inside surface of wax paper only (not dish).
2. In double boiler, melt butter. Stir in flour, mustard, salt, Tabasco; gradually stir in milk; cook, stirring, until smooth and slightly thickened. Add grated cheese, stirring until cheese is melted and sauce is smooth; remove from heat. Start heating oven to 325°F.
3. With fork, beat yolks until blended. Stir in a little cheese sauce. Slowly stir this back into rest of sauce.
4. In large bowl, place saltines, onion, and ham; then pour in cheese sauce and blend well.
5. Beat egg whites until stiff but not dry; then gently fold into cheese-ham mixture, folding until no large areas of egg white remain.
6. Pour one third of this mixture into prepared dish; top with half of mushrooms; repeat, ending with remaining third of cheese-ham-egg mixture. Top with Parmesan.
7. Bake, uncovered, 1½ hr.; don't open oven while puff is baking. Serve at once. Makes 6 servings.

Serve with crisp French fries, tossed tomato salad, canned pineapple chunks, gingersnaps, and tea.

CALIFORNIA HAM SUPREME

2 tablesp. butter or margarine	1½ tablesp. prepared mustard
¼ cup minced green pepper	½ teasp. Worcestershire
2 tablesp. minced onion	¼ teasp. salt
3 tablesp. flour	⅛ teasp. pepper
1 cup boiling water	1 tablesp. lemon juice
1⅔ cups evaporated milk, undiluted	6 slices white bread, with crusts removed
1½ cups diced, cooked or canned ham or canned luncheon meat	Melted butter or margarine
	1 slivered, peeled avocado

Start heating oven to 500°F. In saucepan, melt 2 tablesp. butter; add green pepper, onion; cook, stirring occasionally, until tender. Gradually stir in flour, then boiling water; cook, stirring, until thickened. Stir in milk; cook until slightly thickened. Add ham, mustard, Worcestershire, salt, pepper, lemon juice; keep warm.

Meanwhile, press each bread slice into muffin-pan cup; brush with melted butter. Toast in

500°F. oven until light brown. Remove from pans.

Fold avocado into ham mixture; use to fill toast cups. Makes 6 servings.

DEVILED TONGUE MOLD

2 env. unflavored gelatine	1 tablesp. prepared mustard
1 cup cold water	¼ cup chopped sour pickle
1¼ cups boiling water	
¼ cup mayonnaise	2 cups chopped, cooked or canned tongue
2 tablesp. horse-radish	
1 teasp. salt	
¼ teasp. pepper	2 hard-cooked eggs, chopped

Sprinkle gelatine on cold water, to soften; add boiling water; stir until dissolved; cool. Beat in mayonnaise, horse-radish, salt, pepper, mustard. Refrigerate until slightly thickened. Fold in rest of ingredients. Pour into 9″ x 5″ x 3″ loaf pan. Refrigerate until firm. Unmold; slice. Makes 8 servings.

DEVILED HAM MOLD: Substitute cooked or canned ham or canned luncheon meat for tongue.

THIRTY-MINUTE GLAZED HAM PATTIES

4 cups medium-ground, cooked ham*	Dash pepper
	⅛ teasp. dried thyme
	¼ cup minced onion
⅓ cup fine cracker crumbs	⅓ cup brown sugar, packed
1 egg, beaten	1 tablesp. vinegar
⅔ cup evaporated milk, undiluted	½ teasp. dry mustard
	1½ tablesp. flour

Start heating oven to 350°F. Combine ham, crumbs, egg, milk, pepper, thyme, onion; pack into 6 greased 3″ muffin-pan cups. Bake 20 min. Meanwhile, in saucepan, blend brown sugar, vinegar, mustard, flour; boil 1 min., stirring occasionally. Spoon over hot baked patties; broil 2 min. Makes 6 patties.

Or use canned ham, chopped ham, luncheon meat, or corned beef.

SWISS HAM AND EGGS

½ lb. natural-Swiss-cheese slices	¼ teasp. salt
	⅛ teasp. pepper
4 to 6 pieces of cooked ham	Dash paprika
	4 to 6 buttered toast slices
¾ cup heavy cream	
4 to 6 eggs	

Start heating oven to 425°F. Line well-buttered, 9″-deep, fluted pie plate or shallow baking dish with overlapping cheese slices. Top with half of ham. Pour half of cream over ham. Carefully break eggs into pie plate. Sprinkle with salt, pepper. Arrange rest of ham around eggs. Pour rest of cream over all. Sprinkle with paprika. Bake 15 to 20 min., or until eggs are of desired doneness. Serve at once on buttered toast slices. Makes 4 to 6 servings.

LENTEN VERSION: Omit ham; increase cream to 1 cup. Make and bake as above. Makes 6 brunch servings.

HAM-CHICKEN SUPREME

3 tablesp. flour	1½ cups diced cooked chicken
½ teasp. salt	
⅛ teasp. pepper	4 thin slices boiled or baked ham
1¼ cups liquefied nonfat dry milk or skim milk	2 English muffins, halved
3 tablesp. sherry	Snipped parsley

Sprinkle flour, salt, and pepper onto milk in saucepan. Beat with rotary beater until blended. Cook over medium heat, stirring until thickened. Add sherry and chicken, and continue cooking about 5 min. In skillet, heat ham slices; arrange each on a toasted English-muffin half; top with creamed chicken. Garnish with snipped parsley. Serve with a large tossed salad or a green, leafy vegetable. Makes 4 servings.

DINNER CROQUETTES

1 cup Thick White Sauce, p. 533	or canned lemon juice
1 teasp. snipped parsley	Salt
	Speck pepper
1 teasp. minced onion	Pinch dried sage (optional)
2 cups ground, cooked roast lamb, veal, beef, ham, chicken, or turkey*	1 egg
	1 tablesp. water
	Packaged dried bread crumbs
½ teasp. fresh, frozen,	Fat or salad oil

1. Combine white sauce, parsley, onion, meat, lemon juice; mix well. Add salt and pepper if needed, plus sage. Refrigerate until well chilled—several hr. or overnight.

2. Divide chilled mixture into 8 portions. (Mixture is soft to handle but will make delightfully tender croquettes.) Spoon out each portion; shape into cylinder, cone, or ball.

3. With fork, beat egg and water just till blended. Put bread crumbs on piece of wax paper.

4. Roll croquettes first in crumbs, then in egg, then again in crumbs, making sure all surfaces are well coated. Refrigerate again.

5. Deep-fry as on p. 6, or shallow-fry as on p. 7, at 390°F. on deep-fat-frying thermometer. Fry, turning occasionally, 2 min., or until golden.

6. When croquettes are done, remove with slotted spoon; drain on paper towels. If necessary, keep warm in 300°F. oven.

Serve alone, or with canned tomato sauce; Quick Mushroom Sauce, p. 528; or Horseradish Sauce I or II, p. 532. Makes 8.

*Or use canned ham, chicken, turkey, or luncheon meat.

♣ FOR TWO: Use 1 egg; halve rest of ingredients.

Skillet: If preferred, form croquette mixture into patties; brown on both sides in a little hot salad oil in skillet.

SAVORY HAM AND CAULIFLOWER

1 medium head cauliflower	2 cups cut-up, cooked ham
1 10½-oz. can condensed cream-of-chicken soup, undiluted	⅛ teasp. dried savory
	¼ lb. process sharp Cheddar cheese, grated (1 cup)
¼ cup milk	

Break cauliflower into flowerets; cook till tender-crisp, as on p. 423; drain.

Start heating oven to 350°F. Combine soup and milk in 10″ x 6″ x 2″ baking dish. Fold in cauliflowerets, ham, savory, ½ cup cheese. Sprinkle top with ½ cup cheese. Bake 30 min. Makes 4 servings.

USING THE LAST DELICIOUS BITS
(cooked or canned ham, chopped ham, tongue, corned beef, or luncheon meat)

MEAT SCRAMBLE: In small amount of butter or margarine, in skillet, brown bits of meat; pour in scrambled-egg mixture. Scramble as usual.

PICKLE BUNS: In hot butter, in skillet, lightly brown thin pieces of cooked meat; place between buttered toasted split hamburger buns. Top with pickle relish or chutney.

CREAMED POTATOES PLUS: Fold slivered, cooked meat into creamed potatoes (bake extra potatoes night before). Sprinkle with snipped chives.

SAVORY BEANS: In small amount of fat or salad oil, in skillet, sauté slivers of cooked meat with a little minced onion, green pepper, and celery until golden. Add canned baked beans; heat.

SPAGHETTI ROLL-UPS: On each thin slice of cooked (or boiled) ham, arrange some canned spaghetti in tomato sauce with cheese. Sprinkle well with grated Parmesan cheese. Roll up lengthwise; fasten with toothpick. Broil slowly 10 to 15 min., or until golden brown and hot, brushing occasionally with melted butter or margarine.

CLUB SPECIAL: Top toasted, split corn-bread squares with thin pieces of cooked ham or tongue, then with hot chicken à la king. (You may use frozen chicken à la king or creamed chicken, adding sherry to taste.) Sprinkle with sliced ripe olives or slivered toasted almonds.

LUNCHEON PANCAKES: Prepare batter for pancakes as pancake-mix label directs. Add ½ cup each of slivered cooked ham and drained cooked whole-kernel corn. Bake as usual. Serve with hot maple-blended syrup, or buttered syrup.

POULTRY

Time was when turkey appeared on the table only at holidaytime and fried chicken was a summer-only treat. These days, however, production and marketing methods make it possible to serve fine poultry of all kinds at all seasons of the year.

Like meat, poultry is a rich source of important food values. It is lower in calories and equal to or higher than meats in protein content. So, serve it often, for good health and good eating.

Before using these recipes, refer to How To Use Our Recipes, p. 3. Always use standard measuring cups and measuring spoons; measure level.

CHICKEN

Guide to Buying

You will want to select just the right bird for the dish you plan to prepare. In most markets, you'll find chicken available in the following styles:

Ready-to-Cook Chicken: These meaty, tender, top-quality birds come either fresh, ice-chilled, with a tag identifying the brand, or quick-frozen in a branded package. They have been fully drawn, pinfeathered, cleaned inside and out — are all ready for the oven or pan.

You can buy them whole, with the cleaned giblets and neck wrapped separately, in the body. Or you can buy them cut up — split in halves, quartered, or disjointed and cut up for frying.

Ready-to-cook birds have another plus. Their tag, wrapper, or package is your buying guide. It carries the packer's name, the bird's weight, the price, as well as the U.S. inspection mark, or U.S. grade and inspection mark denoting a high quality, wholesome bird. The wrapper of quick-frozen chicken also carries cooking directions.

Selected Chicken Parts: For small families and those preferring only light or dark meat or a special part, chicken is now being marketed fresh by the piece — breasts, drumsticks, thighs (or legs), wings, etc. Chicken parts also come packaged frozen — as chicken breasts, drumsticks, thighs (or legs), wings, etc. These parts are usually broiler-fryers, but similar stewing chicken parts are available in some markets.

259

AMOUNTS OF CHICKEN TO BUY PER SERVING*

For Sautéing or Frying	¾ to 1 lb.
For Roasting	¾ to 1 lb.
For Stewing	¾ to 1 lb.†
For Broiling	¼ to ½ bird
Rock-Cornish Hen	1 bird per serving (1 to 1¼ lb.)

Per serving, not per person. Some persons take more than 1 serving.

†*Buy smaller amount if serving chicken with rice, macaroni, or biscuits.*

Kinds of Chicken

Five kinds of chicken are available; they differ in size, tenderness, age.

ROCK-CORNISH HENS, the smallest, youngest members of the chicken family, are at their peak when 6 weeks old. They average 16 oz. to 1¼ lb., never more than 2 lb. ready-to-cook weight. The bird is a cross between a Cornish chicken and another breed of chicken. The word "hen" does not imply female. This is usually a one-per-serving bird which may be roasted, barbecued, or "rotisseried" whole. Cut in half it may be broiled, fried, or baked. The larger size will serve two.

BROILER-FRYER CHICKENS are small tender birds, usually 9 weeks old, of 1½ to 4 lb. ready-to-cook weight. A 2- to 2½-lb. bird should make 4 servings. If it is cut up, you may sauté, oven-fry, bake, or broil it. Roast, simmer, barbecue, or "rotisserie" whole birds.

ROASTING CHICKENS are a little older and larger than the broiler-fryer and of 3½ to 6 lb. ready-to-cook weight. Roast, barbecue, or "rotisserie" these sweet, tender-meated birds; or, if for a crowd, cut them up, to fry or oven-fry.

HEN, STEWING CHICKEN, OR FOWL is a mature, less tender 2½- to 5-lb. hen, with more fat than other kinds of chicken. Heavier, meatier birds, weighing 5 to 8 lb., are called bro-hens; they come from flocks used to produce broiler-fryer chickens. Bro-hens may take less time to cook than other stewing chickens of the same size. They are excellent for soup and do well in dishes calling for leisurely stewing. They provide ample tender meat for dishes made with chicken such as chicken fricassees, stew, chicken pie or à la king or creamed dishes.

CAPONS are young desexed male chickens of 6 to 8 lb. ready-to-cook weight. They have exceptional tenderness and flavor and a large amount of white meat. They are usually roasted.

Guide to Storing

If Quick-Frozen, Ready-to-Cook Chicken: Put bird in freezer as quickly as possible. Keep frozen until time to thaw for cooking. Stored at 0°F. or less, for maximum quality, frozen chicken may be held for several months, if properly wrapped.

Completely thaw bird before cooking, following label directions. Or leave bird, in original wrapper, in food compartment of refrigerator 12 to 24 hr. Or, for quicker thawing, place chicken, in its original wrapper, in pan, under running cold water, for ½ to 1 hr., depending upon size of bird. Once thawed, remove giblets and neck from body, then cook bird at once exactly as if fresh.

If It's Fresh, Ice-Chilled, Ready-to-Cook Chicken: Buy only from a market that keeps birds refrigerated. Once home, quickly remove wrapper. Remove giblets and neck from body. Then wrap bird loosely, with ends open, in wax paper, foil, or saran. Store in coldest part of food compartment of refrigerator. Use whole bird within 24 hr. Clean and cook giblets as on p. 261.

To Freeze Chicken: See To Freeze Poultry, p. 704.

To Care for Cooked Chicken

If Roasted Chicken: For safety's sake, always put leftover roast chicken in the refrigerator *at once.* But first remove stuffing from body and neck cavities. Also, if most of bird has been carved, remove rest of meat from bones, so you can make broth from bones to use in leftover-chicken dishes. (Broth will have fuller flavor made now than if you wait until carcass is bare.) Immediately refrigerate meat, stuffing, and gravy in separate containers.

When reheating stuffing or gravy, heat only as much as is needed, leaving rest in refrigerator. Both uncooked and cooked stuffings and gravies spoil quickly if kept warm very long.

For maximum flavor enjoyment plan to use up stuffing within 2 days, gravy within 3 days; heat both *thoroughly* to serve. Use up cooked chicken within 3 days.

If Simmered Chicken: If you have simmered a chicken to use later, as on p. 277, cool it quickly this way: Set kettle of chicken and broth in cold water in sink, changing water and stirring broth often. At the end of ½ hr. (no longer), put both bird and broth in refrigerator at once. Use within 3 days.

The Giblets

To Clean: Giblets include the heart, gizzard, and liver of poultry; with a ready-to-cook, whole bird, the neck is often included too. Wash all fresh giblets *thoroughly*; refrigerate at once. Cook within 12 hr. after buying. You can also buy packaged quick-frozen livers, hearts, and gizzards.

To Cook: In saucepan, place heart, gizzard, liver, neck, and salt. Add 1 celery stalk, 2 peppercorns, tip of bay leaf, 1 small onion, sliced, and water to cover. Simmer, covered, until easily pierced with fork — about ½ hr. if giblets are from a young bird; about 1 hr. if they're from an older chicken; about 2 to 3 hr. if they're from a turkey. Remove cooked liver after first 10 to 20 min. of cooking, depending upon size of liver.

To Use: Use cooked giblets, coarsely chopped, in Chicken Gravy, p. 262, sandwich fillings, stuffings, or as the meat in Italian spaghetti, rice dishes, etc.

Use giblet broth as part of liquid in gravy or to moisten stuffing.

Ready-to-Serve Canned Chicken Items

What a convenience chicken is in handy cans, all ready to eat or heat. You can choose whole chicken, boneless fricassee, fricassee with vegetables or dumplings, boned chicken, chicken à la king, noodle-chicken dinner, chicken spread, chicken gravy, etc. And there's luscious canned cream-of-chicken, chicken noodle, chicken gumbo, chicken with rice, Swiss chicken noodle soup, chicken vegetable soup, chicken broth, and others.

Ready-to-Serve Frozen Chicken Items

Don't wait for company to try quick-frozen packaged chicken à la king, individual chicken pies, chicken chow mein, creamed chicken, or fried chicken dinner, fried chicken with whipped potatoes, chicken noodle dinner, etc. Use as label directs.

ROAST CHICKEN
(Broiler-Fryer, Capon, Roaster, Cornish Hen)

To Buy: Buy ready-to-cook roasting chicken, capon, broiler-fryer, or Rock-Cornish hen, allowing ¾ to 1 lb. ready-to-cook weight per serving. (See Kinds of Chicken, p. 260.)

To Prepare Chicken for Oven:
1. Compute roasting time, using ready-to-cook weight of bird. If chicken is of a national brand, follow roasting directions on wrapper or package. Otherwise follow the timetable on p. 262. Plan to have bird done 20–30 min. before serving. This will give you time to make gravy and remove trussing cords, if any. Bird will be easier to carve too.
2. Choose roasting pan. It should be an open, shallow pan (2″ to 3″ deep) with a wire rack.
3. Clean and cook giblets as at left; then refrigerate with broth until needed.
4. For safety's sake, never make stuffing or stuff bird the day before. However, you may prepare stuffing ingredients the day before, refrigerating such perishables as chopped giblets, giblet broth, celery, etc. See Stuffings for Chicken, Duckling, or Pheasant, p. 340, and What You Shoud Know About Stuffings, p. 337.
5. *Just before roasting bird,* rub neck and body cavities lightly with salt, pepper, and monosodium glutamate. Make stuffing, if any.
6. Then, if bird is to be stuffed: Stuff neck cavity lightly (stuffing expands during cooking). Pull neck skin to back, over stuffing;

fold ends of skin under neatly; secure to back with skewer. Now turn bird, breast side up, on flat table surface. Lift each wing up and out, forcing tip back until it rests flat against neck skin — akimbo style. (Eliminates need for skewers; gives bird platform to rest on in roasting pan and on serving platter.) Next stuff body cavity loosely. Then tie drumsticks to tail or push them under band of skin, if present.

7. If you prefer to bake stuffing separately, fasten neck skin of bird to back, shape wings akimbo style, and fix drumsticks as in step 6, p. 261. Then pile stuffing lightly in a foil-lined or greased casserole or loaf pan, or in a foil package. Bake, uncovered, with bird during last hour of roasting.

8. Brush bird with soft butter, margarine, or salad oil.

To Roast Chicken:

1. Start heating oven, as in Timetable, right, or as chicken label directs. Place bird, breast side up, on wire rack in *shallow open pan.* If desired, make a loose covering of foil over the bird.

2. Roast bird, as label directs, or use Timetable at right as approximate guide. *Remember,* chickens vary in type, so you may have to increase or decrease indicated time.

3. *Test For Doneness:* About 25 min. before bird is supposed to be done, start testing it for doneness. Grasp end of drumstick. If it moves up and down and twists easily out of thigh joint, and if fleshy part of drumstick feels very soft when pressed with fingers (protect fingers with paper towel), bird is done.

4. When bird is done, remove skewers and string if any; place bird on heated platter.

To Serve: Garnish chicken with a few sprigs of parsley, mint, or water cress; slices of orange or canned jellied cranberry sauce; pickled or canned pear, peach, or apricot halves.

To Make Gravy: See Chicken Gravy, right.

To Carve: See p. 297.

If There Are Leftovers: See To Care for Cooked Chicken, p. 260; Last of the Bird, p. 288; and Soup from Leftover Bones, p. 164.

APPROXIMATE TIMETABLE FOR ROASTING POULTRY
(Broiler-Fryer, Roaster, Cornish Hen, Capon)

Use shallow open pan. Don't baste or turn.

NAME	READY-TO-COOK WEIGHT (LB.)	OVEN TEMPERATURE	*APPROX. TIME (HR.) IF UNSTUFFED	IF STUFFED
Broiler-Fryer†	1½ to 2	400°F.	¾ to 1	1 to 1½
"	2 to 2½	400°F.	1 to 1½	1½ to 1¾
"	2½ to 3	400°F.	1½ to 2	2 to 2¼
"	3 to 4	400°F.	2 to 2½	2½ to 3
Roaster	3½ to 6	375°F.	3 to 3½	3½ to 4
Cornish Hen	1 to 2	400°F. to 450°F.	1	1 to 1¼
Capon	6 to 8	350°F.	3 to 3½	3½ to 4½

*Since time periods are only approximate, be sure to test chicken for doneness as at left.
†If preferred, you may roast all broiler-fryers over 1½ lb. in weight at 350°F. for about 30 min. per lb. If a 1½ lb. bird, allow 40 to 45 min. per lb. Omit wire rack.

CHICKEN GRAVY

1. Remove chicken from roasting pan to heated platter; keep warm. Pour drippings from pan into cup.

2. For 2 cups gravy, return 3 tablesp. drippings to pan. Place over low heat. Blend in 3 tablesp. flour while stirring. Add a pinch of nutmeg, paprika, or curry.

3. Have ready 2 cups giblet or chicken broth, water, milk, or vegetable liquid (you may use part thin cream or evaporated milk). Pour 1 cup of it into roasting pan, scraping and stirring until brown bits are loosened. Add rest of liquid; then stir until velvety smooth and piping hot.

4. If desired, add a little bottled sauce for gravy, p. 8, to add color. Season with monosodium glutamate, salt, and pepper. Makes 2 cups. To step up flavor, you may use one of the following:

Chopped cooked giblets
Lemon juice
Grated lemon rind
Worcestershire

Prepared mustard
Seasoned salt or pepper
Few whole cloves
Tabasco

Few bottled capers
Minced chives or
  celery
Minced chutney
Canned whole-cran-
  berry sauce

Sautéed fresh, or
  drained canned
  mushrooms
Sherry to taste
1/3 cup commercial
  sour cream
Catchup

ROAST ROCK-CORNISH HENS

6 frozen Rock-Corn-
  ish hens, each about
  1¼ lb.
¾ cup butter or mar-
  garine
¾ cup dry white wine

3 tablesp. dried tar-
  ragon
6 cloves garlic, peeled
Salt and pepper
Garlic salt
1 bunch water cress

Day before: Let Cornish hens thaw overnight in refrigerator; save giblets to serve another day.

Early on the day: Make basting sauce: In saucepan, melt butter; add wine, 1 tablesp. dried tarragon. In each Cornish hen, place 1 clove garlic, 1 teasp. dried tarragon, ¼ teasp. salt, ⅛ teasp. pepper. Sprinkle outside liberally with garlic salt; refrigerate.

About 1 hr. before serving: Start heating oven to 400°F. to 450°F. In large shallow open pan, without rack, roast Cornish hens 1 hr., or until well browned and drumstick twists easily out of thigh joint, basting several times with basting sauce.

Then arrange birds on bed of water cress on serving platter; pour drippings from the roasting pan over them. Makes 6 servings.

CORNISH HENS ON COMPANY RICE: When hens are done, arrange on bed of Company Wild Rice, p. 376.

Wonderful Broiler-Fryers

With all-purpose broiler-fryers, you can prepare dishes that range from delicious, simple, low-calorie ones, to the most exotic from all parts of the world.

BROILED CHICKEN

To Buy: You may broil any tender, small chicken, but 1½- to 2½-lb. broiler-fryers are especially nice. Have each bird halved, quartered, or cut into serving pieces. Allow ¼ to ½ a bird per serving.

To Store: See Guide to Storing, p. 260.

To Broil:

1. Preheat broiler 10 min., or as manufacturer directs. Remove rack from broiler pan, line pan with foil for easier cleaning, then arrange chicken, skin side down, in pan.

2. Sprinkle chicken with salt or seasoned salt and paprika or monosodium glutamate. Brush with melted butter or margarine, or salad oil. Sprinkle lightly with paprika.

3. Place pan in broiler so surface of chicken is 7″ to 9″ from heat and chicken can broil slowly. (The distance depends on the type of broiler.) If it is impossible to place broiler pan this low in your range, lower heat (if oven is thermostatically controlled, turn temperature control to about 350°F.).

4. Broil chicken 30 min. on one side; turn; brush with melted butter, then broil 15 to 30 min., or until fork-tender, nicely browned, and crisp — 45 to 60 min. in all.

Test for Doneness: Drumsticks and wing joints should move easily, and thickest part of chicken should yield easily to pressure from fork.

5. If you wish, brush whole mushrooms or uncooked chicken livers and cooked hearts, gizzards, and necks with butter. (See To Cook Giblets, p. 261.) Broil with chicken last 15 min.

6. Serve chicken, skin side up, with pan juices, Bert's Superb Barbecue Sauce, p. 531, or bottled barbecue sauce. Nice with baked white or sweet potatoes or waffles. Also hot canned cling peaches.

Special Touches: Choose any of these:

BARBECUE: Twenty to thirty minutes before broiling is completed, brush chicken with one of barbecue sauces, pp. 528, 531, 532, or bottled barbecue sauce, instead of melted butter.

HERB: To melted butter for brushing chicken, add one of these: minced garlic or onion, snipped chives or parsley, sliced scallions, white wine, or pinch of dried thyme, rosemary, tarragon, or poultry seasoning.

DELMARVA: Before broiling chicken as above, rub well with cut lemon. Then, after brushing with melted butter, lightly sprinkle with granulated sugar.

MUSHROOM: Heat, then pass canned mushroom gravy, or Swiss cream-of-mushroom soup mix as gravy, or mushroom gravy mix; see p. 102.

PIQUANT: To ¼ cup melted butter for brushing chicken, add 3 tablesp. lemon juice, ¼ teasp. Tabasco, ½ teasp. paprika.

UNDER COVER: For each chicken, mix ¼ cup snipped parsley, 1 tablesp. snipped chives, bit of fresh or dried tarragon, 3 tablesp. soft butter or margarine, and ¼ teasp. salt. With tip of paring knife, loosen skin on breast of chicken. Then, with small spatula, spread flesh, under skin, with butter mixture. While broiling chicken, p. 263, brush skin often with salad oil.

ANNE'S GLAZE: Sprinkle 2 2½- to 3-lb. broiler-fryers with 2 teasp. salt; then brush with mixture of 2 tablesp. crab-apple jelly, mashed; ¼ cup white wine; and ½ cup melted butter or margarine. While broiling, p. 263, baste with rest of jelly mixture. Serve with pan juices.

SAVORY: About 10 min. before split broiler-fryers are done broiling, p. 263, sprinkle each with ¾ teasp. celery seeds, 1 teasp. curry powder, and 1 small onion, sliced. Lay 2 strips of bacon on each chicken; then continue broiling until done, basting with pan drippings and turning bacon as needed.

SKILLET-FRIED CHICKEN

To Buy: Buy 2- to 3-lb. broiler-fryers. Have them halved, quartered, or cut up. Or buy chicken parts. Allow ¾ to 1 lb. chicken per serving.

To Store: See Guide to Storing, p. 260.

To Coat: Coat chicken in one of these ways:

SEASONED FLOUR: For every 2 lb. chicken, in paper bag combine ½ cup flour, 1 teasp. salt, ⅛ teasp. pepper. Drop in chicken, 2 or 3 pieces at a time; shake until coated. (If there's time, let dry on wire rack ½ hr. before frying.) Save leftover flour for gravy.

CORN MEAL AND FLOUR: Substitute ¼ cup corn meal and ¼ cup flour for each ½ cup flour in Seasoned Flour, above.

EGG AND SEASONED FLOUR: For every 2 lb. chicken, blend 1 beaten egg, 2 teasp. water, 1½ teasp. salt. Dip chicken into egg mixture; then coat with Seasoned Flour, above. Save leftover flour for gravy.

To Fry:

1. In chicken fryer or large skillet, place ½″ of your favorite shortening or salad oil. Heat until a drop of water in shortening sizzles.
2. First brown meaty pieces of chicken, uncovered, turning with tongs or 2 spoons so chicken will brown lightly, evenly. (Don't use a fork; it pierces skin, causes loss of juices.)
3. As first pieces of chicken brown, slip in less meaty pieces; or use second skillet. Browning may take 15 to 20 min.
4. When all chicken has browned, reduce heat and cook, tightly covered, turning chicken to continue even browning, until meatiest pieces are fork-tender — 20 to 40 min., depending on size and thickness of pieces. (If cover doesn't fit tightly or chicken pieces are large, add 1 to 2 tablesp. water, uncovering last 10 min. to recrisp skin.)

To test for doneness, cut into thickest part of drumstick, or test with fork. Chicken should cut easily, be fork-tender, and show no pink at bone.

5. Uncooked liver and cooked heart, gizzard, and neck (see To Cook Giblets, p. 261) may be rolled in flour and added last 15 min.

To Serve: Serve chicken hot or cold. Or after removing to heated platter, make Cream Gravy, below. Pour over chicken, or serve separately. Or serve with your favorite barbecue sauce.

Nice with Corn Fritters, Northern Style, p. 400; Fluffy Hot Rice, p. 370; Candied Sweet Potatoes, p. 410; or hot waffles. Pass fresh or canned cranberry sauce, of course.

CREAM GRAVY

1. After chicken is skillet-fried, pour drippings from skillet. Return ¼ cup drippings to skillet; add 3 to 4 tablesp. flour (left over from coating chicken, plus more flour if needed). Stir over low heat, loosening brown bits from skillet, till smooth.
2. After browning flour slightly, stir in 2½ cups milk (or 1 cup milk and 1½ cups light cream; or 1 cup chicken broth and 1½ cups light cream; or 1½ cups chicken broth and 1 cup evaporated milk, undiluted).
3. Cook, stirring, until thickened. Season, adding a little bottled sauce for gravy and 1 tablesp. snipped parsley, or sherry to taste.

(If gravy gets too thick, stir in a little water.) Serve with chicken.

FRIED CHICKEN SUPERB

1 2½- to 3-lb. broiler-fryer, quartered or cut up	½ cup packaged dried bread crumbs
Seasoned Flour, p. 264	½ cup grated Parmesan cheese
1 egg, beaten	½ cup butter or margarine
2 tablesp. water	

Coat chicken with Seasoned Flour; dip into combined egg and water; then roll in combined bread crumbs and cheese. In hot butter, in large skillet or chicken fryer, sauté chicken, uncovered, until golden on all sides. Then lower heat; cook, uncovered, turning occasionally, 20 to 40 min., or till fork-tender and brown. Makes 4 servings.

CRUNCHY STYLE: For bread crumbs and cheese, substitute 1 cup crushed corn flakes combined with ½ cup flour.

CURRY STYLE: Omit cheese. To crumbs, add ½ teasp. curry powder and 1 teasp. poultry seasoning.

FRIED CHICKEN CURRY

1 2½- to 3-lb. broiler-fryer, quartered or cut up	rooms
	⅓ cup minced onion
¼ cup salad oil	1 cup diced, pared, cored cooking apples
1 cup raw regular or processed white rice; or 1⅓ cups packaged precooked rice	3 tablesp. flour
	2 teasp. salt
	1½ teasp. curry powder
¼ cup butter or margarine	¾ cup light cream
¾ lb. sliced mush-	¼ cup snipped parsley

Simmer backbone, neck, wing tips, and giblets of chicken in 2 cups cold water, covered, about ½ hr., or until tender; strain; reserve broth. Meanwhile, in hot oil in skillet, sauté chicken until golden on all sides. Reduce heat; cook slowly, covered, turning occasionally, 20 to 40 min., or until fork-tender.

Meanwhile, cook rice as label directs; drain; keep hot. Melt butter in saucepan; add mushrooms, onion, apples; sauté until mush-

rooms and onion are tender. Stir in flour, salt, curry, then cream, and ¾ cup reserved broth. Heat, stirring, until thickened.

Now toss parsley with rice; arrange in center of heated platter. Surround with chicken; pour curry sauce over chicken. Pass Curry Accompaniments, p. 330, if desired. Makes 4 servings.

CHICKEN TROPICAL

1 3-lb. broiler-fryer, cut up	1 teasp. ground nutmeg
Seasoned Flour, p. 264	1 teasp. dried basil
½ cup shortening	12 small new potatoes
1 teasp. salt	1 1-lb.-13-oz. can cling-peach slices, drained
1 cup orange juice	
2 tablesp. brown sugar	Parsley
2 tablesp. vinegar	

Lightly coat chicken with Seasoned Flour. In hot shortening, in chicken fryer or large skillet, sauté chicken until golden on all sides. Sprinkle with 1 teasp. salt. Combine orange juice, brown sugar, vinegar, nutmeg, and basil; pour over chicken. Place well-scrubbed new potatoes between and around chicken pieces. Cook, covered, over medium heat, 25 min., or until chicken and potatoes are tender. Then add peaches; heat, covered, 5 min. Serve at once, garnished with parsley. Makes 4 to 6 servings.

OVEN-EASY CHICKEN

1 2½- to 3-lb. broiler-fryer, cut up	p. 264
Seasoned Flour,	¼ cup butter or margarine

Start heating oven to 425°F. Coat chicken with Seasoned Flour. In shallow open pan in oven, melt butter. Remove pan from oven; in it, arrange chicken in single layer, skin side down. Bake, uncovered, 30 min.; turn; bake 15 min., or until brown and fork-tender. Serve with Cream Gravy, if desired. Makes 3 or 4 servings.

WITH BISCUITS: Prepare and bake chicken 30 min. as above; then turn. Meanwhile, make up biscuit dough, using 2 cups packaged biscuit mix, as label directs; roll dough ½" thick; cut out biscuits. Place biscuits in single layer, alongside chicken in single layer, in pan. Bake

15 min., or until biscuits are lightly browned and chicken is tender.

MARYLAND: Coat chicken with Seasoned Flour; dip into 1 egg, beaten with ¼ cup milk, then into 1 cup packaged dried bread crumbs. Bake and serve as above.

SICILIAN CHICKEN AND ZITI: Buy 2 2-lb. broiler-fryers. Coat with Seasoned Flour as above. Increase butter or margarine to ½ cup, then bake chickens as directed. Meanwhile, cook ¾ lb. packaged ziti (2″ tube-style macaroni) as label directs; drain. In skillet, in ¼ cup butter, sauté 1 clove garlic, minced, until golden; add ½ cup snipped parsley, ¼ teasp. pepper, ½ teasp. salt; remove from heat. Add ¼ cup drippings from chicken pan, cooked ziti; toss. Arrange chicken and ziti on platter. Makes 6 to 8 servings.

FRIED CHICKEN IMPERIAL

4 whole chicken breasts, halved and skinned	onion
	2 cups heavy cream
Seasoned Flour, p. 264	¼ cup sherry
½ lb. butter or margarine	1 teasp. salt
	⅛ teasp. pepper
1½ lb. small mushrooms (or large ones, halved)	1½ tablesp. flour
	¼ cup water
	Diced canned pimento
1 tablesp. minced	Parsley sprigs

Start heating oven to 400°F. Coat chicken breasts with Seasoned Flour. In ¼ lb. hot butter, in large skillet, sauté chicken, a few halves at a time, until golden on all sides. Then, in shallow open roasting pan, arrange breasts, bone side up; sprinkle each with 1 tablesp. drippings from skillet. Bake, uncovered, 5 min.; turn; brush with drippings; bake 10 to 15 min., or till meat is tender.

Meanwhile, in same large skillet, melt ¼ lb. butter; in it, cook mushrooms, uncovered, over high heat 10 min.; then stir in onion, cream, sherry, salt, and pepper. Simmer 5 min.; then stir in flour combined with water; cook, stirring, until thickened and smooth.

Arrange cooked chicken on heated platter with mushroom sauce in center. Top mushrooms with pimento; garnish with parsley. Nice served with tender carrots, topped with lemon slices, fluffy mashed potatoes, fruit salad, and hot biscuits. For dessert an ice-cream parfait. Makes 6 to 8 servings.

CHICKEN 'N' BISCUIT SKILLET DINNER

¾ cup flour	1 broiler-fryer, cut up
2 teasp. salt	½ cup shortening
¼ teasp. pepper	1 can refrigerated biscuits
¾ teasp. poultry seasoning	

Combine flour, salt, and pepper; add poultry seasoning. Into this flour mixture dip chicken until coated on all sides.

Melt shortening in large skillet. Add chicken, then brown on both sides over medium heat. Cover and sauté until tender — 45 to 60 min., turning occasionally. Remove chicken to one end of heated platter and keep warm. Pour all but 2 tablesp. fat from skillet.

Arrange biscuits in skillet, cover, then cook over low heat, 3 to 4 min., or until golden brown on bottom. Gently turn them, cover, and cook about 3 min. more. (If desired, make gravy after biscuits are done.) Serve biscuits at other end of platter of fried chicken. Makes 4 to 5 servings.

SAUTEED (BRAISED) CHICKEN

To Buy: Buy cut-up or quartered small broiler-fryer. Or buy chicken parts. Allow ¾ to 1 lb. chicken per serving.

To Store: See Guide to Storing, p. 260.

To Cook:

1. Dust cut-up chicken lightly with flour if desired. In large skillet or chicken fryer, heat 3 to 4 tablesp. butter, margarine, salad oil, or bacon fat until bubbling. In it, brown chicken, uncovered, quickly but well on all sides, turning with tongs. (If you're cooking 2 chickens, use 2 skillets, one for meaty and one for less meaty pieces.)

2. When chicken is nicely browned, turn heat low. Then add ½ cup liquid (water, bouillon, tomato juice, or red or white wine) and any of these seasonings:

Dried or fresh basil, thyme, or rosemary	Sliced and lightly floured mushrooms
Minced celery	Minced onion, chives, shallots, or garlic
Curry powder	
Garlic, celery, or onion salt	Minced pimento
	Salt and pepper
Minced green pepper	Seasoned salt
Monosodium glutamate	

3. Now cover skillet. Let chicken cook slowly,

turning it occasionally to cook evenly, 25 to 30 min., or until fork-tender. For crisp-crusted chicken, uncover last 10 min. Just before removing chicken to platter, sprinkle with snipped parsley and paprika.

4. Now arrange chicken on heated platter; pour pan juices over all.

Superb Variations: After chicken has cooked, covered 15 min., as in step 3, p. 266, you may add one of these:

> Slivered, blanched almonds
> Pinch dried or fresh chervil or dill
> Sliced green, ripe, or stuffed olives
> Cut-up canned peaches, pears, or pineapple
> 2 or 3 chopped, peeled tomatoes

Or, after removing tender chicken, into juices stir ½ cup heavy or commercial sour cream, ¼ cup white wine, dash lemon juice, or a little grated lemon rind.

Or sprinkle chicken with chopped crisp bacon.

CHICKEN MARENGO

1 2½- to 3-lb. broiler-fryer, cut up	¼ lb. sliced mushrooms
½ teasp. salt	2 cloves garlic, minced
⅛ teasp. pepper	½ cup water
¼ cup flour	¼ cup sherry
¼ cup salad oil	4 tomatoes, quartered, or 1 cup drained canned tomatoes
12 small white onions	1 teasp. salt
¼ cup butter or margarine	

Lightly coat chicken with combined ½ teasp. salt, pepper, flour. In hot oil in skillet, sauté chicken until golden on all sides. Then cook slowly, covered, about 30 min., or until fork-tender. Meanwhile, boil onions till nearly tender — about 12 min.; drain.

In hot butter in another skillet, cook onions with mushrooms and garlic, covered, 15 min., stirring often. Stir in 2 tablesp. flour (use up any flour left over from coating chicken), water, sherry, tomatoes, 1 teasp. salt. Heat, stirring, until smooth and thickened. Cook, covered, 10 min.; taste; add more seasonings if needed.

Now remove chicken to heated platter; pour sauce over it. Makes 4 servings.

♣ FOR 2: Use 1 1½-lb. broiler-fryer and same amount of other ingredients.

GEORGIA COUNTRY CAPTAIN

½ cup salad oil	1 green pepper, coarsely chopped
2 cloves garlic, halved	1 1-lb.-13-oz. can tomatoes (3½ cups)
2 medium onions, thinly sliced	1 cup raw regular or processed rice
½ cup all-purpose flour	¼ cup currants
Salt	2 tablesp. butter or margarine
¼ teasp. pepper	⅓ cup blanched almonds
1 3½-lb. broiler-fryer, cut up	Snipped parsley
1 tablesp. curry powder	
½ cup chopped celery	

In hot salad oil, in large skillet, over medium heat, sauté garlic and onions until tender but not brown; remove them from oil.

Meanwhile, combine flour, 1 teasp. salt, and pepper in paper bag. In the bag, coat the chicken pieces one at a time. In hot salad oil, in two batches if necessary, fry chicken until golden, turning once. Now add garlic and onions, 2 teasp. salt, curry powder, celery, green pepper, and tomatoes. Cover; simmer 45 min., or until chicken is tender.

Meanwhile, cook rice as label directs; add currants; toss lightly. Also, in melted butter, in small skillet, over medium heat, brown the blanched almonds.

When chicken is done, arrange it at one end of heated platter, rice at other end. Remove garlic from sauce; spoon some of sauce over chicken; pass rest. Sprinkle all with almonds and snipped parsley. Makes 4 servings.

CHICKEN WITH SHERRY SAUCE

2 1¾- to 2-lb. broiler-fryers, quartered	1 cup canned chicken broth
2 teasp. salt	1 clove garlic, minced
½ teasp. pepper	2 celery stalks, chopped
1 3- or 4-oz. can button mushrooms	½ cup snipped parsley
6 tablesp. butter or margarine	3 tablesp. flour
¾ cup minced onion	½ cup heavy cream
1 cup dry white wine	1 tablesp. sherry
	1 tablesp. brandy

Sprinkle chickens with salt and pepper. Drain mushrooms; reserve juice.

In Dutch oven, in ¼ cup butter, sauté onion

with chicken, covered, 10 min., turning once. Add wine, broth, mushroom juice, garlic, celery, and parsley. Cover; simmer 45 min., or till chicken is tender.

Remove chicken to heated platter or chafing dish; keep warm. Blend 1 tablesp. butter with flour; stir into gravy left in Dutch oven; simmer till thickened; add cream, sherry, and brandy; boil 3 min. Strain through fine sieve; pour over chicken. Meanwhile, in small skillet, in 1 tablesp. butter, sauté drained mushrooms 5 min. Use to garnish chicken. Makes 6 servings.

EASY CHICKEN SAUTE

¼ cup butter or margarine	1 3- or 4-oz. can mushrooms
Small broiler-fryer, quartered	Canned shoestring potatoes
Seasoned salt	

In butter, in skillet, quickly brown chicken quarters. Sprinkle with seasoned salt and drained mushrooms. Cook over low heat, covered, until tender — 25 to 35 min. Garnish with potatoes which have been tossed with pan juices. Makes 4 servings.

CHICKEN AND SCAMPI

1 3½-lb. broiler-fryer, cut up	3 tablesp. snipped parsley
1 tablesp. salt	½ cup port wine
½ teasp. pepper	1 8-oz. can tomato sauce
¼ cup butter or margarine	1 teasp. dried basil
3 small onions, finely chopped	1 lb. shelled, deveined shrimp
1 clove garlic, minced	Snipped parsley

Rub chicken well with salt and pepper. In hot butter or margarine, in large skillet, sauté chicken until golden on all sides.

Now add onions, garlic, 3 tablesp. snipped parsley, wine, tomato sauce, and basil; simmer, covered, about 30 min., or until chicken is tender.

Now push chicken pieces to one side of skillet; turn up heat so tomato mixture boils, add shrimp; then cook, uncovered, 3 to 4 min., or until just pink and tender.

Pile golden chicken pieces in serving dish; top with pink shrimp. If necessary, skim all fat from surface of sauce; then pour sauce over chicken and scampi. Sprinkle on a little snipped parsley. Makes 6 servings.

TENNESSEE BRUNSWICK STEW

4 cups water	½ pkg. frozen okra
1¼ lb. chuck, in 1″ cubes	1 16- to 17-oz. can cream-style corn
½ broiler-fryer (1½ lb.)	1 1-lb.-4-oz. can tomatoes (2½ cups)
2 teasp. salt	1 tablesp. sugar
2 medium potatoes, pared	3 teasp. salt
2 medium onions, peeled	½ teasp. pepper
	Pinch cayenne pepper
½ cup raw regular rice	½ teasp. celery seeds

Early in day: In Dutch oven, combine water, chuck, chicken, and 2 teasp. salt; simmer, covered, 1 hr., or till chuck and chicken are tender. Remove chuck and chicken from broth. Skin and bone chicken; cut chicken meat into small pieces. Set aside 1 cup chicken broth (use rest when desired). Refrigerate all.

About 1¼ hr. before serving: Boil potatoes and onions, covered, about 20 min., or until partially cooked; drain.

In Dutch oven, combine 1 cup chicken broth, chicken, chuck, rice, okra, corn, tomatoes, sugar, 3 teasp. salt, peppers, and celery seeds. Add diced potatoes and chopped onions. Simmer, covered, ¾ hr. Serve at once (or refrigerate; then reheat next day). Makes 6 to 8 servings.

CHICKEN DELLA ROBBIA

6 tablesp. butter or margarine	glutamate
2 2½- to 3-lb. broiler-fryers, cut up	½ teasp. ground cloves
2 medium onions, sliced	½ teasp. allspice
½ lb. mushrooms, sliced	½ teasp. ginger
1 cup dark or light raisins	¼ cup brown sugar
4 teasp. salt	1 cup walnut halves
¼ cup lemon juice	4 teasp. cornstarch
2 teasp. monosodium	2 cups seedless grapes
	2 cups orange sections
	12 maraschino cherries

In butter, in Dutch oven, sauté chickens golden. Add onions, mushrooms, raisins, 1¼ cups water, salt, lemon juice, monosodium glutamate, cloves, allspice, ginger, and brown sugar. Simmer, covered, turning occasionally, 40 min., or till tender; add walnuts.

Push chicken to one side of Dutch oven. Blend cornstarch with ½ cup water; stir into chicken liquid; heat till smooth and thickened. Add grapes, orange sections, and washed cherries; heat 2 min. Serve at once on platter or in chafing dish.

Delightful for a dinner party, with fluffy rice, peas, romaine salad, brown 'n' serve brioches, floating island bedecked with grated chocolate, tea or coffee. Makes 8 servings.

CALIFORNIA CHICKEN FRICASSEE

1 3- to 3½-lb. broiler-fryer, cut into eighths
3 cups water
Salt
1 carrot, pared
1 onion, sliced
1 celery stalk, sliced
6 whole black peppers
6 whole allspice
3 tablesp. butter or margarine
¼ cup flour
1 egg yolk, slightly beaten
½ cup light cream
1 tablesp. lemon juice
1 teasp. sugar
¼ teasp. pepper
1 lemon, sliced
Snipped parsley

In covered large kettle, simmer cut-up chicken in water, with 1 tablesp. salt, carrot, sliced onion, sliced celery, whole black peppers, and allspice — about 40 min., or until tender. Arrange chicken on heated large platter; keep warm.

Strain broth. In double boiler, melt butter; stir in flour until smooth, then 2 cups strained chicken broth. While stirring, cook sauce over boiling water until thickened. Combine egg yolk, cream, and lemon juice; add to sauce, stirring constantly; cook 1 min. Season with 1 teasp. salt, sugar, and pepper.

Pour some of sauce over chicken; garnish with lemon slices and 2 tablesp. snipped parsley. Pass rest of sauce, sprinkled with snipped parsley. Makes 4 to 6 servings.

CHICKEN IN WINE

¼ cup butter or margarine
1 3-lb. broiler-fryer, cut up
1 medium onion, sliced
1 clove garlic, minced
2 tablesp. flour
½ teasp. salt
¼ teasp. pepper
1 chicken-bouillon cube
1 cup hot water
10 small new potatoes
¼ cup red wine
Snipped parsley

In hot butter, in chicken fryer or Dutch oven, sauté chicken until golden brown on all sides. (As some of chicken browns, add more pieces, a few at a time, heaping those that are done at side of pan.) Then add onion, garlic. Meanwhile, combine flour, salt, pepper; slowly stir in bouillon cube, dissolved in hot water; pour over browned chicken. Add well-scrubbed potatoes. Cook over low heat, covered, 30 min., or until chicken and potatoes are tender. Then stir in red wine.

Serve at once, garnished with snipped parsley. Makes 4 servings.

CHICKEN CACCIATORE

6 tablesp. fat or salad oil
2 2½- to 3-lb. broiler-fryers, cut up
1 cup minced onions
¾ cup minced green peppers
4 cloves garlic, minced
1 1-lb.-13-oz. can tomatoes (3½ cups)
1 8-oz. can tomato sauce
½ cup Chianti wine
3¾ teasp. salt
½ teasp. pepper
½ teasp. allspice
2 bay leaves
½ teasp. dried leaf thyme
Dash cayenne pepper

In hot fat in large skillet, sauté chicken until golden on all sides. Add onions, green peppers, garlic; brown lightly. Add tomatoes, tomato sauce, wine, salt, pepper, allspice, bay leaves, thyme, cayenne pepper. Simmer, uncovered, 30 to 40 min., or until chicken is fork-tender.

Now arrange chicken on heated platter; pour sauce over all. Pass French bread. Makes 8 servings.

✤ FOR 2: Use 1 1½-lb. broiler-fryer. Halve rest of ingredients.

CHICKEN CHASSEUR

1 2- to 2½-lb. broiler-fryer, cut up
Seasoned Flour, p. 264
¼ teasp. dried thyme
3 tablesp. butter or margarine
4 scallions or small onions, chopped
¼ lb. mushrooms,
chopped
1 teasp. sugar
1 teasp. salt
2 tablesp. lemon juice
⅓ cup apple juice
2 tomatoes, diced
2 tablesp. snipped parsley
2 tablesp. snipped chives

Coat chicken with Seasoned Flour to which thyme has been added. In hot butter in large skillet, sauté chicken until golden on all sides. Add scallions, mushrooms, sugar, salt, lemon juice, apple juice, tomatoes. Cook slowly, covered, 30 to 40 min., or until chicken is fork-tender. Sprinkle with parsley and chives. Makes 3 or 4 servings.

POULET A LA CREME JOUBINE

¼ cup butter or margarine	sliced (about 2 cups)
1 2½- to 3-lb. broiler-fryer, cut up	2 tablesp. white wine
Salt	2 sprigs parsley
Pepper	1 stalk celery
1 lb. onions, thinly	1 tablesp. brandy
	½ cup heavy cream

Heat butter in Dutch oven. Generously sprinkle chicken with salt, pepper; sauté in hot butter until golden on all sides, removing pieces when done. Place onions in Dutch oven; add wine, then chicken, parsley, celery, brandy. Cook slowly, covered, 30 to 40 min., or until fork-tender.

Remove chicken to heated serving dish; keep hot. Discard parsley and celery. Bring onion mixture to boil. With back of spoon, break up onions into as little pieces as possible. Slowly add cream, stirring constantly; cook until of desired thickness. Taste; season if necessary; pour over chicken. Garnish with more parsley. Makes 4 servings.

HUNGARIAN-STYLE FRICASSEE CHICKEN
(Becsinsält Chirke)

1 2- to 2½-lb. broiler-fryer	1 10-oz. pkg. frozen peas
3 tablesp. butter or margarine	2 or 3 pared carrots, cut into ½″ pieces
2 medium onions, minced	2 stalks celery, in ¼″ to ½″ slices
2 tablesp. snipped parsley	1 cup hot water
2 teasp. salt	2 tablesp. cold water
¼ teasp. pepper	2 tablesp. flour
½ teasp. sugar	Boiled noodles (¼ lb. uncooked), or cooked rice (1 cup uncooked regular)
1 or 2 cloves garlic, minced	
1 lb. shelled fresh or	

Have chicken cut into smaller pieces than usual, with legs and thighs halved, breasts quartered; avoid pieces of splintered bone.

Melt butter in chicken fryer, Dutch oven, or deep skillet; add onions and cook about 5 min., or until tender. Add parsley, chicken, salt, pepper, sugar, and garlic. Cover and cook over low heat, turning chicken often, until partially tender — about 15 to 20 min. Add peas, carrots, celery, and hot water; cook, covered, until vegetables are tender — about 25 min. Meanwhile, add cold water to flour and mix until smooth. When vegetables are done, stir a little of hot chicken broth into flour mixture; then stir into rest of broth in skillet. Cook a couple of minutes, stirring, until thickened. Serve with noodles. Makes 4 servings.

BAKED BROILERS SAUTERNE

2 2-lb. broiler-fryers, halved	2 tablesp. snipped scallions
¾ cup sauterne or other white wine	¼ cup melted butter or margarine
2 tablesp. snipped parsley	Salt and pepper
	Paprika

Early in day: Let chickens stand in sauterne in refrigerator 3 to 4 hr.

About 1 hr. before serving: Start heating oven to 450°F. Pour wine from chickens; to wine, add parsley, scallions, butter. Sprinkle chickens with salt, pepper, paprika; place, skin sides down, in shallow open pan. Pour on wine mixture. Bake, uncovered, 25 min., basting frequently. Turn skin sides up; bake 20 min., or until fork-tender and brown. Makes 4 to 6 servings.

SESAME POLYNESIAN CHICKEN

¼ cup butter or margarine	apple chunks, drained
1 broiler-fryer, cut up	1 7-oz. pkg. frozen shrimp
½ cup flour	1 10½-oz. can condensed tomato soup, undiluted
2 teasp. salt	
¼ teasp. pepper	
1 small green pepper, thinly sliced	¼ cup chili sauce
1 small onion, thinly sliced	¼ cup canned pineapple syrup or water
⅓ cup sliced stuffed olives	1 can refrigerated sesame dinner rolls
1 13½-oz. can pine-	

1. Start heating oven to 375°F. In baking pan, 13″ x 9″ x 2″, melt butter. Roll chicken in mixture of flour, salt, and pepper, then place, skin side down, in pan. Bake 30 min.

2. Turn chicken pieces, then top with green pepper and onion rings, olives and pineapple chunks. Rinse shrimp in cold water until ice coating is removed; add to chicken. Combine tomato soup, chili sauce, and pineapple syrup; pour over chicken. Cover pan with foil. Bake 30 min.

3. Now cut each sesame roll into 4 pieces, making tiny sesame squares; arrange on top of chicken. Bake, uncovered, 15 min., or until rolls are golden brown. Serve hot. Makes 4 to 6 servings.

WAISTLINE BARBECUED CHICKEN

2 tablesp. salad oil or fat	4 medium onions, sliced
2 3-lb. broiler-fryers, quartered	3 tablesp. Worcestershire
3 cups canned tomato juice	½ cup catchup
½ cup vinegar	4 teasp. prepared mustard
1 tablesp. sugar	1 teasp. pepper
	2 teasp. salt

Start heating oven to 350°F. In hot salad oil, in skillet, brown chicken well on all sides. Remove to shallow baking pan.

In saucepan, combine tomato juice, vinegar, sugar, onions, Worcestershire, catchup, mustard, pepper, salt; heat; pour over chicken. Bake chicken, uncovered, 1 hr., or until tender, basting every 10 min. with sauce. (If sauce is thick, stir in a little water.) Makes 8 servings.

COQ AU VIN

½ cup diced salt pork	rooms
2 tablesp. butter or margarine	3 shallots; or ½ cup sliced scallions
1 3½- lb. broiler-fryer, quartered	1 clove garlic, minced
1¼ teasp. salt	2 tablesp. flour
⅛ teasp. pepper	1½ to 2 cups red wine
½ lb. small white onions	3 parsley sprigs
½ lb. small mush-	½ bay leaf
	⅛ teasp. dried thyme
	Snipped parsley

In Dutch oven, cook salt pork in boiling salted water to cover 5 min.; drain off water. To pork add butter; sauté pork until browned; remove; reserve. Sauté chicken in Dutch oven until golden on all sides; sprinkle with salt, pepper. Add onions, mushrooms. Simmer, cov-

ered, 15 min., or until onions are partly tender and golden. Start heating oven to 400°F.

Pour off all but 2 tablesp. fat from Dutch oven; add shallots, garlic; simmer 1 min. or so. Stir in flour, then wine; cook, stirring, until thickened. Sprinkle with parsley sprigs, bay leaf, thyme, diced pork.

Bake chicken, covered, 45 to 60 min., or until fork-tender. Sprinkle with snipped parsley. Serve with gravy spooned over it. Makes 4 servings.

INDOOR CHICKEN CLAMBAKE

1 cup raw regular rice	Salt
1¾ cups water	Pepper
1 teasp. salt	2 doz. littleneck clams in shell
⅛ teasp. saffron, crushed	½ lb. hot Italian sausages
2 3½-lb. broiler-fryers, cut up	

Preheat broiler 10 min., or as manufacturer directs. Meanwhile, in covered saucepan, simmer rice, in water, with salt, 5 min.; stir in saffron. Spread rice, undrained, in bottom of 14″ x 9″ x 2¼″ roasting pan.

Sprinkle chickens with salt and pepper; arrange in shallow pan. Broil, 7″ to 9″ from heat, 15 min. on each side. (If you can't place broiler pan this low in range, turn temperature control to about 350°F.) Meanwhile, scrub clams. Then cut sausages into 1″ pieces.

Reset oven control to 325°F. Top rice with chicken; tuck in clams here and there; scatter sausage pieces over all. Cover pan with foil; bake 1 hr. Uncover; bake 10 min.

Serve with crusty bread, salad, dessert. Makes 6 servings.

A MAN'S BARBECUED CHICKEN

2 teasp. salt	¾ cup cider vinegar
¼ teasp. pepper	1 teasp. sugar
1½ cups canned tomato juice	3 cloves garlic, minced
¼ teasp. cayenne pepper	3 tablesp. butter, margarine, or salad oil
¼ teasp. dry mustard	2 2½- to 3-lb. broiler-fryers, quartered
1 bay leaf	3 medium onions, thinly sliced
4½ teasp. Worcestershire	

Early in day or day before: Make barbecue

sauce by combining, in saucepan, salt, pepper, tomato juice, cayenne, mustard, bay leaf, Worcestershire, vinegar, sugar, garlic, butter. Simmer, uncovered, 10 min. Refrigerate.

About 1 hr. and 30 min. before serving: Start heating oven to 425°F. Arrange chickens, skin sides down, in single layer in shallow open pan. Sprinkle lightly with some salt and pepper. Arrange onions on chicken, tucking a few slices under wings, legs. Pour on barbecue sauce. Bake, uncovered, basting often, ½ hr.; turn; bake, basting often, 45 min., or until fork can be inserted easily into legs. Makes 4 to 6 servings.

♣ FOR 2: Use 1 1½-lb. broiler-fryer and same amount of sauce.

OCEANIA CHICKEN

1 2½- to 3-lb. broiler-fryer, cut up	½ teasp. nutmeg
⅔ cup all-purpose flour	¼ cup butter or margarine
1 teasp. salt	1 1-lb.-4-oz. can sliced pineapple
½ teasp. celery salt	½ cup soy sauce
½ teasp. garlic salt	2 tablesp. sugar

Wipe chicken, pat dry. Start heating oven to 350°F. Mix flour, salt, celery salt, garlic salt, and nutmeg in paper bag, if desired. Use to coat pieces of chicken on all sides.

In hot butter, in large skillet, brown chicken on all sides. Place chicken pieces in 2½-qt. casserole.

Combine syrup from canned pineapple with soy sauce and sugar. Pour over chicken. Cover casserole, then bake chicken about 1 to 1½ hr., or until it is tender, basting several times.

Meanwhile, sauté pineapple slices in butter left in chicken skillet (add more butter if needed), until golden on both sides. Fifteen minutes before chicken is done, top it with pineapple. Makes 4 to 6 servings.

Chicken Parts for Particular People

Most of the recipes tend to be glamorous, all are scrumptious.

OVEN-FRIED DRUMSTICKS

24 chicken drumsticks	1 teasp. curry powder
½ cup flour	3 teasp. poultry seasoning
2¾ teasp. salt	
½ teasp. pepper	½ cup butter or margarine
2 teasp. paprika	

Start heating oven to 450°F. Push skin of each chicken leg up over broad cut end. In heavy brown paper bag, combine flour, salt, pepper, paprika, curry, and poultry seasoning. From double thickness of regular foil or single thickness of heavy-duty foil, fashion two pans each 13″ x 9″ x 1″. Lay each pan on cookie sheet; place ¼ cup butter in each. Set in oven to melt butter.

Place about three chicken legs at a time in bag with flour mixture. Shake to coat legs well, remove, and arrange in one of pans. Repeat till 12 coated chicken legs are in each pan.

Bake two pans of chicken, uncovered, on two racks in oven for 30 min. Then turn legs, reverse position of pans, and bake chicken 15 min. longer, or until fork-tender and golden brown.

Serve hot or cold. Makes 8 to 10 servings.

CHICKEN HICKMANO

½ cup butter or margarine	1 teasp. dried orégano
¼ cup olive oil	1 teasp. salt
4 cloves garlic, minced	1 teasp. pepper
3 medium onions, minced	8 to 10 whole boned chicken breasts
2 pared carrots, grated	⅓ cup flour
¼ cup snipped parsley	1 teasp. salt
1 1-lb.-13-oz. can Italian tomatoes (3½ cups)	¼ teasp. pepper
	¼ cup butter or margarine
4 6-oz. cans tomato paste (2⅔ cups)	¼ cup olive oil
	1 lb. Mozzarella cheese
	Grated Parmesan cheese

In Dutch oven, heat ½ cup butter and ¼ cup oil. Add garlic, onions, carrots, parsley; sauté until tender. Add tomatoes, tomato paste; simmer, uncovered, ½ hr. Add orégano, 1 teasp. salt, 1 teasp. pepper; simmer ½ hr. longer.

Meanwhile, start heating oven to 350°F. Coat chicken with combined flour, 1 teasp. salt, ¼ teasp. pepper. In skillet, heat ¼ cup butter and ¼ cup olive oil. Add chicken;

sauté slowly until golden on all sides and quite tender. Place 1 chicken piece in each of 8 to 10 individual casseroles; or divide pieces between 2 shallow baking dishes. Top each with several slices Mozzarella cheese. Bake, uncovered, 15 min., or until cheese is melted. Spoon generous helpings of hot sauce over chicken. Serve at once. Pass Parmesan cheese. Makes 8 to 10 servings.

CHICKEN SOUR AND SWEET
(Kai Priao Wan)

1½ chicken breasts	2 tablesp. shortening
5 chicken livers	½ cup canned con-
2 large carrots, pared	densed chicken
1 large cucumber,	broth, undiluted
pared	1 tablesp. flour
3 small tomatoes,	2 tablesp. sugar
peeled	¼ cup soy sauce
1 large onion	¼ cup vinegar
3 cloves garlic,	Hot fluffy rice
crushed	Chow-mein noodles

Thinly slice chicken breasts, quarter livers, slice carrots ⅛″ thick. Split cucumber lengthwise, then slice it crosswise ⅛″ thick. Cut tomatoes into eighths and onion into ¼″ wedges.

In large skillet sauté garlic in shortening till golden. Add chicken, livers, and carrots. Cook over medium heat, while stirring, 5 min. Add cucumber, tomatoes, onion, and broth. Cover; simmer 5 min.

Combine flour, sugar, soy sauce, and vinegar. Pour over chicken and vegetables in skillet, while stirring; cook till thickened.

Serve in heated large bowl with hot fluffy rice and chow-mein noodles. Makes 6 servings.

BREAST OF CHICKEN PERIGOURDINE

8 whole chicken	8 large mushrooms,
breasts	sliced
1 13¼-oz. can chicken	⅓ cup all-purpose
broth	flour
2 canned truffles,	¼ teasp. salt
cut up	½ cup water
3 tablesp. dry sherry	2 tablesp. light cream
Butter or margarine	Easy Hollandaise
	Sauce, p. 531

Let meatman bone chicken breasts, reserving bones. Simmer chicken bones in chicken broth, covered, about 1 hr.; discard bones. Let truffles stand in sherry 1 hr.

In small amount of hot butter in large, metal-handled skillet, gently brown chicken breasts on both sides, adding more butter as needed; remove. In more butter in same skillet, sauté sliced mushrooms until golden; remove. In about ¼ cup drippings in skillet, stir flour, ¼ teasp. salt, water, 1 cup broth (add water, if necessary, to make 1 cup), light cream. Cook, stirring, over medium heat till thickened and smooth. Place chicken breasts in sauce; simmer gently, covered, about 20 min., or until chicken is tender. Add truffles, with sherry, and drained, sautéed mushrooms.

Meanwhile, preheat broiler 10 min., or as manufacturer directs. Make Easy Hollandaise Sauce, spread over chicken. Run under broiler a few minutes to brown. Makes 8 servings.

CHICKEN KIEV

½ cup butter or mar-	⅛ teasp. pepper
garine	1 egg, slightly beaten
1 clove garlic, crushed	1 tablesp. water
2 teasp. snipped	4 ½-lb. chicken
chives	breasts, boned
2 teasp. snipped pars-	Shortening or salad
ley	oil
½ teasp. salt	¼ cup all-purpose
½ teasp. crumbled	flour
rosemary	

In small bowl, combine butter, garlic, chives, parsley, salt, rosemary, and pepper; blend well. Lay on sheet of wax paper; fold paper over top; then pat into ¾″-thick roll. Wrap in the wax paper; freeze or refrigerate till *very hard*.

In bowl, blend egg and water well. Then, with rolling pin, pound each chicken breast to ¼″ thickness. Now cut hard roll of butter mixture into four equal pieces; lay one piece on chicken breast, and roll it up in the chicken; secure with skewer or string. Repeat.

In Dutch oven, heat 1½″ shortening or salad oil to 370°F. on deep-fat-frying thermometer, or until square of day-old bread browns in 60 sec. Meanwhile, dip chicken rolls in flour, then in egg mixture, then in flour. Now, with tongs, lower two chicken rolls into hot fat; fry about 15 min., turning occasionally; then drain on paper towels. Repeat. Remove skewers or string; serve hot. Makes 4 servings.

NOTE: If preferred, coated chicken rolls may be pan-fried. Melt ¼ cup butter or margarine in a skillet; brown chicken rolls on all sides; cover, and cook 12 min.; then uncover, and cook 5 min., or until crisp, turning once.

CHICKEN LIVERS WITH RICE

¼ cup butter or margarine	Seasoned Flour, p. 264
3 tablesp. minced onion	1 10½-oz. can condensed cream-of-chicken soup, undiluted
1⅓ cups packaged precooked rice	½ cup milk
½ lb. fresh or thawed frozen chicken livers, cut into 1″ pieces	1 tablesp. snipped parsley
	Pinch dried basil

Start heating oven to 375°F. In 1 tablesp. hot butter in saucepan, sauté onion until tender. Add onion to rice; cook as label directs. Meanwhile, lightly roll chicken livers in Seasoned Flour; sauté in remaining 3 tablesp. butter in skillet until browned on all sides.

In 1½-qt. casserole, combine livers, rice, soup, milk, parsley, basil. Bake, uncovered, 30 min. Makes 5 or 6 servings.

SPANISH CHICKEN, RICE, AND SHELLFISH

(Paella Valenciana)

⅓ cup salad oil	2 cups raw regular rice
2 whole chicken breasts, split	1 16- to 17-oz. can tomatoes (2 cups)
4 chicken legs	3 chorizos (Spanish sausages)*
1 cup chopped onion	
1 clove garlic, minced	1½ lb. shelled, deveined shrimp
2 14-oz. cans chicken broth (4 cups)	12 littleneck clams or mussels
1 teasp. white pepper	1 10-oz. pkg. frozen peas
3½ teasp. salt	
¾ teasp. dried tarragon	1 7-oz. can artichoke hearts
½ teasp. paprika	
1 teasp. saffron	

In salad oil in Dutch oven, sauté chicken pieces until golden brown on all sides; remove and set aside. In same oil, sauté onion and garlic till golden. Then add chicken broth, pepper, salt, tarragon, paprika, and saffron; bring to boil. Now add rice; cook, covered, over medium heat till about half of liquid has been absorbed. Next add tomatoes, sliced chorizos, shrimp, and chicken, and simmer, covered, for about 30 min., or until rice is almost dry.

Meanwhile, steam clams or mussels in a little water until their shells pop open — about 10 min. Also cook peas as label directs. Add peas and artichoke hearts to rice mixture and toss.

Serve, heaped in a 3-qt. casserole or large serving bowl, with the clams as a garnish. Makes 8 servings.

If unavailable, substitute pepperoni sausage, and add, sliced, toward end of 30 min. cooking time.

CHICKEN CHOP SUEY—CHICAGO

1 lb. boned chicken breasts	peas or peas and carrots
¼ cup salad oil	2 tablesp. cornstarch
1 teasp. salt	1 tablesp. soy sauce
½ cup chicken broth	⅓ cup cold water
1 6-oz. can sliced broiled mushrooms	½ cup canned toasted slivered almonds
2 cups diagonally sliced celery	¼ cup sliced scallions
1 10-oz. pkg. frozen	4 cups hot fluffy rice
	Soy sauce

Remove skin from chicken breasts; then cut chicken meat into ½″ chunks. Next, in large skillet, heat salad oil. Add salt, then chicken chunks, and sauté, stirring frequently with a fork, until lightly browned. Add broth and undrained mushrooms. Now add sliced celery and unthawed peas. Cover with tight-fitting cover; simmer till vegetables are tender-crisp — about 10 min.

Meanwhile, blend together cornstarch, 1 tablesp. soy sauce, and cold water. Stir gently into liquid in skillet, and cook, stirring constantly, until the liquid thickens and chicken mixture is very hot. Arrange at once on heated platter; sprinkle top with slivered almonds and scallions. Serve with hot rice. Pass soy sauce. Makes 4 servings.

CALIFORNIA'S CHICKEN CHOW MEIN: Place a ring of hot fluffy rice on a large platter; surround with ring of crisp chow-mein noodles; spoon piping hot chop suey into center of ring.

CHICKEN LIVER SAUTE

1 lb. fresh or thawed frozen chicken livers	¼ cup flour
	2 cups hot water
	1 teasp. salt
¼ cup butter or margarine	Sherry to taste; or 2 teasp. bottled thick meat sauce
1 small onion, minced	

Halve livers. In hot butter, in skillet over low heat, sauté livers with onion about 5 min., turning often. Remove livers. Into butter, stir flour; then gradually stir in water; cook, stirring, until thickened. Add salt, sherry, livers.

Serve on toast; toasted, split English muffins; or pancakes. Or serve with omelet. Makes 6 servings.

MUSHROOM: Sauté a few sliced mushrooms with livers.

CURRIED: Substitute curry to taste for sherry.

WAYSIDE CHICKEN

2 tablesp. butter or margarine	vegetable soup, undiluted
2 1-lb. pkg. frozen chicken breasts, thawed	⅓ cup milk
	2 tablesp. snipped parsley
1 10¾-oz. can condensed cream-of-	½ clove garlic, minced
	Tabasco

In butter, in skillet, brown chicken breasts. Add soup, milk, parsley, garlic, and few drops Tabasco. Cook, covered, over low heat 45 min., or until tender, stirring often. Makes 4 servings.

The Great Roaster

Its sweet tender meat goes well in dishes other than just Roast Chicken.

CHICKEN SANTA FE

¼ cup salad oil	2 1-lb.-1-oz. cans kidney beans, drained
1 4- to 5-lb. roasting chicken, cut up	1 12-oz. can whole-kernel corn
2 onions, sliced	
2 cups water	1 1-lb. can Blue Lake cut green beans
5 teasp. salt	
½ to 1 teasp. pepper	1 16- to 17-oz. can tomatoes
½ teasp. dried whole-leaf sage	
8 oz. elbow macaroni	4 dashes Tabasco

In hot salad oil in 7-qt. Dutch oven or kettle, brown chicken well. Add sliced onions and sauté until golden. Then add water, salt, pepper, and sage. Cook, covered, about 1¼ hr., or until the chicken is fork-tender.

Meanwhile, cook and drain elbow macaroni, as label directs.

When chicken is tender, add kidney beans, corn, green beans, tomatoes, macaroni, then Tabasco; heat.

Serve in rimmed soup plates if you have them, with warmed French bread and tossed endive salad. Then, for dessert, Concord grapes and hot brewed coffee. Makes 8 servings.

CHICKEN CORN SQUARES

1 1-lb.-4-oz. can cream-style corn	¼ teasp. pepper
	½ cup minced onions
2 cups canned tomato juice	½ green pepper, minced
1 cup grated process Cheddar cheese (¼ lb.)	3 eggs, beaten
	1 cup undiluted evaporated milk
1 cup yellow corn meal	Twice recipe Susan's Creamed Chicken de Luxe, p. 122
1 teasp. salt	

Day before: Mix corn, tomato juice, grated cheese, corn meal, salt, pepper, onions, green pepper. Refrigerate.

About 1½ hr. before serving: Start heating oven to 300°F. To corn mixture, add eggs, milk. Pour into well-greased 13" x 9" x 2" baking pan; set in pan of hot water. Bake 1¼ hr., or till firm, and silver knife inserted in center comes out clean. Loosen edges with pancake turner. Cut into squares. Remove with turner.

Serve, topped with creamed chicken. Makes 12 servings.

CHICKEN-SPAGHETTI PLATTER

¼ cup fat or salad oil	pepper
	1 teasp. paprika
1 3-lb. roasting chicken, cut up	¼ cup chopped pimento
1 veal knuckle	12 oz. thin spaghetti
2 teasp. salt	1 cup slivered ripe olives
¼ teasp. pepper	
¼ cup minced onion	1½ cups grated process Cheddar cheese
¼ cup minced green	

In hot fat in skillet, brown chicken well on all sides. Remove to deep kettle. Add knuckle, just enough boiling water to cover chicken, salt, pepper. Simmer, covered, 1 to 1¼ hr., or until very tender. Then remove meat from chicken and veal bones; cut into strips or cubes.

Skim fat from broth; measure broth; add enough water to make 2 qt. In skillet in which chicken browned, cook onion, green pepper, paprika, until light brown. Add to broth, with pimento and cut-up chicken; heat till boiling. Add spaghetti; cook, uncovered, 15 to 20 min., or until spaghetti is tender; do not drain. Add olives, 1 cup cheese. Heat well.

Serve on large, deep platter or serving dish; top with rest of cheese. Makes 8 to 10 servings.

CHICKEN WITH HERBS EN CASSEROLE

1 4-lb. roasting chicken, cut up	3 cups milk
2 tablesp. bacon fat	2½ teasp. salt
Butter or margarine	⅛ teasp. pepper
6 tablesp. flour	¾ teasp. dried thyme
	¾ teasp. dried sage

Wash, then dry pieces of chicken. Trim off excess fat. In bacon fat, in heavy skillet, cook chicken pieces, a few at a time, turning now and then, till golden. Then lay, side by side, in 12″ x 8″ x 2″ baking dish or 2-qt. casserole. Start heating oven to 325°F.

Measure fat left in skillet and add enough melted butter to make ½ cup. Pour back into skillet; add flour; blend till smooth. Then stir in milk, salt, pepper, thyme, and sage; cook till smooth and thickened. Pour this sauce over chicken. Bake, uncovered, about 1 hr., or until fork-tender. Makes 6 servings.

ARROZ CON POLLO

1 4-lb. roasting chicken, cut up	2 cups uncooked regular or processed white rice
½ cup flour	
½ cup shortening	1 tablesp. salt
1 large onion, minced	¼ teasp. pepper
1 1-lb.-4-oz. can tomatoes (2½ cups)	2 bouillon cubes
2 small cans pimentos, cut up	½ lb. fresh pork sausage links
1 small jar stuffed olives	1 10-oz. pkg. frozen peas

In paper bag, shake chicken with flour until coated. In hot shortening in Dutch oven, sauté

chicken, a few pieces at a time, until golden on all sides; set chicken aside.

In same fat in Dutch oven, sauté onion until golden. Drain tomatoes, adding enough water to tomato liquid to make 2¼ cups. To onions, add tomato liquid; tomatoes; pimentos and their liquid; olives and their liquid; rice; salt; pepper; bouillon cubes; and sausages, cut into ½″ pieces. Place chicken on top. Simmer, covered, 30 min., lifting rice occasionally with fork to avoid sticking. Then uncover and add thawed peas. If there is any liquid left in pan, cook mixture, uncovered, 10 min. (If mixture seems dry, cook covered; it should be moist, not soggy.) Makes 8 generous servings.

STUFFED CHICKEN POT ROAST

6 day-old bread slices, cubed	1 teasp. monosodium glutamate
¼ cup finely diced celery	3 tablesp. butter or margarine
¼ cup minced onion	¼ cup water
½ teasp. salt	8 small new potatoes, scrubbed
⅛ teasp. pepper	8 small whole white onions
½ teasp. poultry seasoning	
¼ cup butter or margarine	1 10-oz. pkg. frozen mixed vegetables, thawed just enough to separate
2 tablesp. hot water	
1 3½- to 4-lb. roasting chicken	¾ cup water
2 teasp. salt	1 teasp. salt

In large bowl, combine bread cubes, celery, onion, salt, pepper, poultry seasoning, ¼ cup butter, 2 tablesp. hot water; use to stuff body cavity of chicken. Combine 2 teasp. salt, monosodium glutamate; use to rub into skin of chicken.

In 3 tablesp. hot butter in Dutch oven, brown chicken well on all sides — 20 to 25 min. Add ¼ cup water; simmer, covered, 1 to 1½ hr., or until nearly tender, adding more water if necessary. Add potatoes, onions, mixed vegetables, ¾ cup water, 1 teasp. salt; cook, covered, 30 min., or until vegetables are tender. Remove chicken to heated platter; arrange vegetables around chicken. Makes 6 servings.

More than a Stewing Chicken

This bird does well in soups and dishes calling for leisurely cooking.

SIMMERED CHICKEN
(nice for cold sliced chicken, salad, etc.)

To Buy: Buy 1 4½-lb. stewing chicken or bro-hen, cut up. (See Kinds of Chicken, p. 260.)

To Store: See Guide to Storing, p. 260.

To Simmer:

1. To chicken, add 3 cups hot water, 1 clove-studded onion, 3 celery tops, 1 tablesp. salt, 1 bay leaf, 1 carrot. Cook by either method below.

IN PRESSURE COOKER: Place chicken, water, and seasonings in pressure cooker. Cook at 15 lb. pressure 25 to 35 min., or as manufacturer directs; reduce pressure slowly.

OR IN DEEP KETTLE OR DUTCH OVEN: Simmer chicken in water with seasonings, covered, about 1½ to 2 hr., or until fork-tender. Peek now and then, adding more water if needed.

2. Cool chicken and broth quickly as in To Care for Cooked Chicken, p. 260. If meat is to be used later in salads, sandwiches, creamed chicken, etc., remove it from bones in as large pieces as possible; wrap. Refrigerate meat and broth (strained if desired) at once.

Yield: A 4½-lb. stewing chicken yields about 3 cups firmly packed, coarsely diced, cooked chicken for salads, creamed chicken, etc.

CHEESY CHICKEN CASSEROLE

1 4 lb. stewing chicken or bro-hen, or 6 chicken breasts	2 8-oz. pkg. cream cheese
	1 teasp. salt
2 10-oz. pkg. frozen broccoli	¾ to 1 teasp. garlic salt
2 cups milk	1½ cups shredded Parmesan cheese

Early on the day:
1. Gently simmer whole chicken as directed in Simmered Chicken above, or simmer chicken breasts in seasoned boiling water to just cover, until tender. Then remove chicken or breasts; let cool, then remove skin. Slice thinly, cover with wax paper; refrigerate.

About 1 hr. before serving:
1. Start heating oven to 350°F. Lightly grease a 2-qt. oblong casserole. Cook broccoli as label directs. Then cut each broccoli spear into bite-size pieces and arrange in bottom of casserole.

2. In double boiler, over hot *not boiling* water, blend milk, cream cheese, salt, and garlic salt until smooth and hot. Stir in ¾ cup shredded Parmesan until smooth.

3. Pour 1 cup of this cream-cheese sauce over broccoli, then top with all the sliced chicken, in one layer. Cover chicken with rest of cream-cheese sauce. Sprinkle ¼ cup shredded cheese on top. Bake 25 to 30 min., or until piping hot; remove; let stand 5 to 10 min.

4. Serve with rest of shredded cheese. Makes 6 to 8 servings.

MOM'S CHICKEN STEW

1. Prepare Simmered Chicken, left, browning pieces first if desired. (Substitute canned tomato sauce or tomato juice, or white wine, for 1 cup water if you wish.)

2. Arrange hot cooked chicken in serving dish; keep warm. Skim fat from strained broth. Measure broth, adding milk if needed to make desired amount of gravy; return to cooker or kettle. For each cup broth, blend 1½ tablesp. flour and 3 tablesp. water, milk, or cream to form smooth paste; gradually stir into broth.

3. Simmer, stirring, until smooth and thickened. Season, adding 1 teasp. curry powder, pinch dried tarragon, or some slivered green pepper and tiny whole canned mushrooms if desired.

4. Pour gravy over chicken. Around edges, tuck Hot Baking-Powder Biscuits, p. 475 (add a little grated carrot to biscuit flour mixture if desired). Makes 4 to 6 servings.

CHICKEN STEW WITH DUMPLINGS: When broth for Mom's Chicken Stew is thickened, return chicken to it; bring to boil; turn heat low.

Make Dumplings for Stew, p. 478, drop on top of chicken pieces in boiling stew; cook as recipe directs. When dumplings are done, arrange on rim of platter, with stew in center. Or carry stew to table in Dutch oven.

CHICKEN FRICASSEE

1. Buy a 4½- to 5-lb. stewing chicken or bro-hen, cut up. Coat chicken pieces, giblets, and neck with Seasoned Flour, p. 264.

2. In thin layer of hot fat or salad oil in skillet or Dutch oven, brown chicken pieces slowly, turning them with tongs as they brown. Remove chicken; drain off fat.

3. Return chicken to skillet. Add 1 cup water (or a substitute, below) and one or more added extras, below.

Substitutes for 1 Cup Water: Canned tomatoes or tomato juice, wine, or diluted canned condensed cream-of-celery, -mushroom, -chicken, or -tomato soup.

Added Extras: Chopped shallots, onions, or scallions; a few whole cloves or celery tops; a little lemon juice; or dash nutmeg, curry powder, or dried thyme or rosemary.

4. Simmer chicken, covered, over low heat until largest, meatiest pieces are fork-tender — about 1½ to 2 hr. Peek now and then, adding more water or liquid as needed.

5. When fricassee is done, taste; add more seasonings if necessary; serve.

Or if you prefer a thickened gravy, remove chicken from skillet when done; set aside. Skim fat from surface of broth as on p. 7. Measure broth, adding milk if needed to make desired amount of gravy; return to skillet.

For each cup of broth, blend 1½ tablesp. flour with 3 tablesp. water, milk, or cream until smooth. Gradually stir into broth; then simmer, stirring, until smooth and thickened. Replace chicken in gravy; season well. Makes 6 servings.

6. Serve chicken fricassee on, with, or in ring of:

Buttered noodles, with poppy seeds and snipped parsley added
Fluffy rice, with toasted, slivered almonds
Canned chow-mein noodles
Baked white or sweet potatoes
Fluffy mashed potatoes
Toast points, hot waffles, or dumplings
Parsley new potatoes or potato pancakes
Toasted, split English or corn muffins
Toasted, split corn-bread squares
Thick slices French bread, sautéed until golden in butter or margarine
Hot buttered split biscuits

WHITE CHICKEN FRICASSEE: Omit flouring and browning in steps 1 and 2.

SALLY'S BATTER CHICKEN

1 4-lb. stewing chicken or bro-hen, cut up	1 teasp. salt
	¼ cup undiluted evaporated milk
3 cups chicken gravy	1 cup shortening
3 egg whites	2 tablesp. butter or margarine
3 egg yolks	
3 tablesp. flour	

Day before: Cook chicken as in Simmered Chicken, p. 277. Remove meat from bones in large serving-size pieces. Refrigerate meat and broth.

About ½ hr. before serving: Make 3 cups gravy from chicken broth as in step 5 of Chicken Fricassee, left; keep hot. Beat egg whites till stiff; with same beater, beat egg yolks with flour, salt, milk; fold in whites. In large skillet, heat shortening with butter. Dip chicken meat into fluffy batter. Sauté in hot fat about 5 min., or until brown on both sides.

Serve at once with spoon bread or mashed potatoes and chicken gravy. Makes 6 servings.

DIFFERENT CHICKEN CURRY

1 4- to 5-lb. stewing chicken or bro-hen, cut up*	powder
	½ teasp. salt
	½ teasp. allspice
1½ cups raw regular or processed white rice; or 2⅔ cups packaged precooked rice	½ teasp. mace
	½ teasp. ginger
	Speck cayenne pepper
	¼ cup flour
¼ cup butter or margarine	1½ cups chicken broth
2 to 3 teasp. curry	1 cup heavy cream
	½ cup applesauce

Day before: Cook chicken as in Simmered Chicken, p. 277. Cut meat from bones; refrigerate meat and broth.

About 30 min. before serving: In double boiler, heat cut-up chicken. Meanwhile, cook rice as label directs; keep hot. In saucepan, melt butter; stir in curry, salt, allspice, mace, ginger, cayenne, flour. Add broth, cream; cook, stirring, until smooth and thickened. Add applesauce; cook about 5 min. Taste; add more seasonings if needed; mix with chicken. Heat 20 to 25 min.

Serve with hot fluffy rice. Pass Curry Accompaniments, p. 330, if desired. Makes 8 servings.

Or use 4 to 5 cups cooked or canned chicken or turkey and canned chicken broth.

Shrimp Casserole Harpin, p. 327

HERB-DUMPLING CHICKEN PIE

1 4½- to 6-lb. stew-
ing chicken or bro-
hen, cut in pieces
1 whole carrot
¾ lb. small white
onions
1 celery stalk
1 whole clove
1 whole black pepper
Salt
2 cups diagonally
sliced, pared carrots
All-purpose flour
1 teasp. paprika
1 10½-oz. can con-
densed cream-of-
chicken soup, un-
diluted
1 10-oz. pkg. frozen

peas, or 1 16- or
17-oz. can peas,
drained
4 teasp. double-acting
baking powder
1 teasp. poultry sea-
soning
1 teasp. celery seeds
2 teasp. poppy seeds
1 teasp. instant
minced onion
¼ cup salad oil
½ cup evaporated
milk, diluted with
½ cup water
¼ cup melted butter
or margarine
1¾ cups fresh bread
crumbs

Early on the day or day before: In large Dutch oven, place chicken; cover it with hot water, then add whole carrot, 1 onion, celery stalk, clove, pepper, 2 teasp. salt. Cover; simmer 1½ hr., or till fork-tender.

Remove chicken, vegetables from broth. Remove chicken meat from bones in large pieces. Measure broth, adding water if needed, to make 3 cups. Refrigerate meat, broth.

One hour and 15 min. before serving: In covered Dutch oven, in the 3 cups chicken broth, simmer rest of whole onions and sliced carrots 12 to 15 min., or till tender-crisp.

Combine ¼ cup flour and paprika. Stir in enough chicken broth to make a smooth paste, then stir into rest of broth and vegetables. Cook until smooth and thickened, stirring constantly. Stir in cream-of-chicken soup till blended. To thickened broth add chicken meat and peas. Heat until very hot and bubbly, stirring occasionally.

Start heating oven to 425°F. Meanwhile, sift together into bowl 2 cups sifted all-purpose flour, baking powder, ½ teasp. salt, poultry seasoning, celery and poppy seeds. Add instant onion, oil, milk; stir until just moistened. Mix butter with crumbs. Transfer hot, bubbly chicken mixture to 3-qt. casserole, or leave in Dutch oven. Drop rounded tablespoonfuls of herb-dumpling dough in crumb mixture; roll to coat well with crumbs. Arrange in circle around outer edge of chicken mixture.

Bake 25 to 30 min., or till dumplings are done. Serve with chilled canned fruit cocktail plus lemon juice, over split bananas. Makes 6 to 8 servings.

BOER CHICKEN PIE

2 3-lb. stewing
chickens, quartered
Salt
1 teasp. whole all-
spice
1 teasp. peppercorns
3 bay leaves
3 medium carrots,
halved
3 celery stalks, halved
3 medium onions,
quartered
About 10 parsley
sprigs

¼ lb. cooked ham,
sliced, then quar-
tered
4 hard-cooked eggs,
sliced
¼ cup butter or mar-
garine
¼ cup flour
⅓ cup sherry
2 tablesp. lemon juice
¼ teasp. mace
¼ teasp. pepper
2 egg yolks
1 pkg. piecrust mix
1 egg, beaten

Early in the day, or day before:
1. In a large kettle, bring chickens to a boil in 1 qt. water with 1 tablesp. salt, allspice, peppercorns, and bay leaves. Add carrots, celery, onions, and parsley; simmer, covered, ½ hr., or until vegetables are tender-crisp.
2. Remove vegetables and chicken from kettle; strain broth. Slice carrots and celery diagonally ½" thick. Carefully cut chicken from bones in chunks, removing skin. In 12" x 8" x 2" baking dish, arrange chicken, vegetables, ham, and hard-cooked eggs.
3. In saucepan, melt butter or margarine; stir in flour, then gradually add 2 cups chicken broth, sherry, lemon juice, mace, 1 teasp. salt, and pepper. Cook, while stirring, until thickened.
4. Beat egg yolks, then slowly stir into sauce; heat, while stirring, until thickened, *but do not boil.* Pour over chicken. Prepare piecrust mix as label directs, then roll into 14" x 10" rectangle. Fold in half crosswise; unfold, as top crust, over chicken. Turn overhang under; press firmly to edge of dish, then make scalloped edge.
5. In center of top crust, with knife, cut out a rectangle 7" x 3". At each corner of rectangle, make a ½" diagonal slit, then turn its piecrust edges up to form a scalloped edge. With remaining dough and small cookie cutter, cut out small designs; arrange over top of piecrust; then refrigerate.

Curried Four-Fruit Bake, p. 437

About 45 min. before serving: Start heating oven to 425°F. Brush pie with beaten egg. Bake 30 min., or until golden and hot. Makes 8 servings.

♣ FOR A FOURSOME: Make half the recipe, using a 10″ x 6″ x 2″ baking dish.

Fix-and-Serve Chicken

Add your own little touch to any of the all-ready-to-use canned or frozen chicken dishes in the market today.

CHICKEN A LA KING SURPRISE

1 pkg. frozen chicken à la king	4 bread slices Sharp cheese spread

Heat chicken à la king as label directs. Meanwhile, toast bread; spread with cheese. Arrange on heated platter; top with chicken. Makes 4 servings.

CHICKEN BISCUIT PIE

2 tablesp. fat or salad oil	undiluted
4 onions, thinly sliced	½ cup milk
1 tablesp. minced green pepper	1 cup cooked chicken in large pieces
1 10½-oz. can condensed cream-of-mushroom soup,	½ cup cooked vegetables
	1 can refrigerated biscuits

Start heating oven to 425°F. In hot fat, sauté onions and green pepper until tender. Add soup, milk, chicken, and vegetables. Turn into 9″ pie plate. Top with biscuits; bake about 15 min., or until they are done. Makes 4 servings.

TURKEY

To Buy Turkeys

In most markets today, you'll find turkey in the following styles:

Ready-to-Cook Turkeys:
These tender top-quality birds come either fresh ice-chilled, with a tag identifying the brand, or quick-frozen, in a branded package. They have been fully drawn, pinfeathered, cleaned inside and out, with giblets and neck wrapped separately in the body. They are all ready for oven or pan.

Many of today's turkeys also have a band of skin near the tail under which you can tuck the legs, thus eliminating the need for trussing or lacing after stuffing.

These birds have another plus: Their tag, wrapper, or package is your buying guide. It carries the packer's name (a guide to quality), the bird's weight and price, as well as the U.S. Department of Agriculture's inspection mark, denoting a wholesome bird. The wrapper of quick-frozen turkey also carries cooking directions; *follow them closely.*

As for sizes, fresh ice-chilled and quick-frozen birds weigh as follows:

SMALL TURKEYS   4 to 9 lb.
MEDIUM TO LARGE TURKEYS   10 to 24 lb.

When buying ready-to-cook turkeys under 12 lb., allow ¾ to 1 lb. *per serving.* When buying birds of 12 lb. and over, allow ½ to ¾ lb. *per serving.* Or follow chart below:

SERVINGS FROM TURKEYS

READY-TO-COOK TURKEY (POUNDS)	NUMBER OF SERVINGS
6 to 8	6 to 10
8 to 12	10 to 20
12 to 16	20 to 32
16 to 20	32 to 40
20 to 24	40 to 50

Frozen Stuffed Turkeys:
These frozen birds come already stuffed, in weights of about 6 to 16 lb. They're a help if you're pressed for preparation time. But be sure to follow label directions *exactly.*

A roast-meat thermometer is a must with these birds. When done, the meat in the center of the inside thigh muscle or the thickest part of the breast muscle must register about 185°F.; the stuffing must register 165°F. at the same time.

Remember, too, that these frozen, pre-stuffed birds are an exception to the thaw-before-roasting rule. They're roasted frozen and, unless roasted covered, will take considerably more time than is normally required; so, if you're having a large turkey, plan your dinner hour with this in mind.

Fresh or Frozen Turkey Parts:
You can now buy fresh turkeys cut up into breasts, drumsticks, etc. Also there are packaged frozen turkey parts such as whole breasts

(4 to 10 lb.) and legs including drumsticks and thighs (2½ to 3 lb.).

Frozen Boned Rolled Turkey Roasts:

These come frozen and since they are boned are especially convenient to slice after roasting. Handle as label directs.

Smoked Turkey:

Some come ready to eat; some require further cooking. So check label and follow its directions for handling. For maximum flavor enjoyment, plan to use any refrigerated leftovers within 10 to 14 days. Serve as label directs.

To Store Turkeys

If Fresh, Ice-Chilled, Ready-to-Cook Turkeys: Remove giblets and neck from body. Refrigerate bird, loosely wrapped, in original wrapper, wax paper, or aluminum foil; plan to roast within 2 days. Clean giblets; cook as at right.

If Quick-Frozen, Ready-to-Cook Turkeys: Get these birds into your freezer as quickly as possible. Keep them frozen until time to thaw for cooking. Stored at 0°F. or lower, these frozen turkeys may be held several months. Once thawed, they should be cooked within one day.

If Frozen Stuffed Turkeys: Be sure to follow label directions *exactly.* Remember too that these birds are always roasted in their frozen state — never thawed.

To Thaw Frozen Unstuffed Turkeys

All frozen unstuffed turkeys should be thawed slowly and *never* at room temperature or in warm water. In thawing, follow label directions, or thaw by one or a combination of these methods.

1. Place bird, still in its original body wrap, under running cold water. Allow 2 to 6 hours for thawing.
2. Leave bird in its original body wrap. Place on tray in refrigerator. Allow 1 to 3 days for thawing.

Prompt cooking of a fresh or thawed turkey is preferable. A thawed, ready-to-cook or a fresh turkey can be kept for 2 to 3 days in a refrigerator at 38°F. or less; wrap bird loosely in foil or saran for refrigerator storage. *Don't* refreeze poultry.

ROAST TURKEY

Preliminaries: See To Prepare Chicken for Oven, p. 261, and Stuffings for Turkey or Goose, p. 338.

To Prepare Turkey for Oven: Follow To Prepare Chicken for Oven, p. 261. Season turkey generously inside and out with monosodium glutamate. Add ½ teasp. monosodium glutamate to stuffing for birds from 6 to 8 lb., or 1 teasp. monosodium glutamate to stuffing for larger birds.

To Roast:

1. Plan to have turkey done 20 to 30 min. ahead of serving time, so you'll have time to make gravy, arrange bird on platter, etc.
2. Start heating oven to 325°F. Place turkey, breast side up, on rack in *shallow open pan.* Brush skin with fat. *Do not add any water.*
3. Insert roast-meat thermometer so that bulb is in center of inside thigh muscle or thickest part of breast meat. Be sure bulb does not touch bone. *It is essential* that you use a roast-meat thermometer if you want to be sure your turkey is done as you like it.
4. If desired, make a loose covering of foil over bird. Also, you may wrap a piece of foil around end of each leg bone to prevent drying.
5. Roast bird as directed on wrapper or package. Or use timetable below. Remember, however, that turkeys vary in type, so roasting time periods are *only approximate* and you may have to increase or decrease indicated time.
6. When turkey is about two-thirds done according to timetable, cut band of skin between drumsticks; this helps shorten cooking time.

TIMETABLE
FOR ROASTING TURKEY
(In 325°F. Oven)

READY-TO-COOK WEIGHT	APPROX. ROASTING TIME* FOR STUFFED TURKEY
6 to 8 lb.	2 to 2½ hr.
8 to 12 lb.	2½ to 3 hr.
12 to 16 lb.	3 to 3¾ hr.
16 to 20 lb.	3¾ to 4½ hr.
20 to 24 lb.	4½ to 5½ hr.

Time will be slightly less for unstuffed turkeys. Difference in individual birds may necessitate increasing or decreasing cooking time slightly.

7. *Test for Doneness:* Start testing bird about 25 min. before it is supposed to be done. Move drumstick up and down; if it moves easily and fleshy part of drumstick feels very soft when pressed with fingers (protect fingers with paper towel), bird is done.

Roast-meat thermometer should read 180°F. to 190°F., or about 185°F., depending upon your taste. If stuffing is used, it should register 165°F. at the same time.

8. When bird is done, remove skewers and string, if any; place bird on warm platter. To garnish, see To Serve Roast Chicken, p. 262.

To Make Gravy: See Chicken Gravy, p. 262.

To Carve: See p. 297.

Caution: For safety's sake, always roast the bird completely done in one continuous period. Never partially roast a large turkey one day, then leave it out of refrigerator overnight, and complete the roasting the next day.

If There Are Leftovers: See To Care for Cooked Chicken, p. 260; Last of the Bird, p. 288; Soup from Leftover Bones, p. 164.

Small meal-size units of leftover roast turkey may be frozen and held up to 1 month before serving.

Never try to freeze an uncooked turkey which you have stuffed. Never freeze a home-stuffed turkey which you have roasted; the *stuffing must always be removed first.*

FOIL-COOKED TURKEY

A foil-wrapped turkey cooks in less time than when uncovered. Here's how:

1. To prepare bird, with or without stuffing, follow To Prepare Chicken for Oven, p. 261.
2. Lay trussed bird on its back in middle of a large piece of heavy-duty aluminum foil. (For birds over 18 lb. use two 18″ widths, double-folded together.)
3. Brush bird all over with soft shortening, butter, or margarine.
4. Place small folds of foil over the ends of legs, tail, and wing tips, to prevent puncturing outer wrapping. Bring long ends of foil up over the breast of turkey and overlap 3″ to 4″. Close two other open ends by folding foil up 3″ to 4″, so drippings won't run out — large birds may have 3 pt. of drippings. Don't seal airtight.

5. Place bird in shallow open roasting pan, not on a rack. Roast as in chart below.

TIMETABLE FOR FOIL-COOKED TURKEY
(In 450°F. Oven)

READY-TO-COOK WEIGHT	APPROX. COOKING TIME STUFFED OR UNSTUFFED
7 to 9 lb.	2¼ to 2½ hr.
10 to 13 lb.	2¾ to 3 hr.
14 to 17 lb.	3 to 3¼ hr.
18 to 21 lb.	3¼ to 3½ hr.
22 to 24 lb.	3½ to 3¾ hr.

6. *Browning:* About thirty minutes before bird is expected to be done, open foil and check tenderness of bird. Meat should be soft to the touch and thigh joint should move easily. Fold foil back, pan-fashion. At this point insert roast-meat thermometer so the bulb is in the thickest part of the breast meat; be sure bulb does not touch bone; it will register 180°F. to 190°F., depending upon doneness you prefer. Now spoon juices over bird; then return it to oven to brown to desired degree.

7. When bird is done, remove any skewers or string; then lift turkey onto a heated platter.

8. Ladle drippings from foil into saucepan and skim off fat. (If they are not brown, place a small amount in a pie plate and return to oven for about 10 min., or till brown.) Add this to gravy for additional color after making as in Chicken Gravy, p. 262.

ROTISSERIED TURKEY

Turkeys of any size may be cooked on a rotisserie. Some rotisseries may be limited to a certain maximum weight bird, so it is wise to check manufacturer's weight suggestions before buying a turkey for rotisserie cooking.

For operation of rotisserie, follow manufacturer's directions.

Rub body cavity lightly with salt, if desired. Push drumsticks under band of skin at tail, if present, or tie drumsticks securely to tail. Fasten neck skin to back with skewer. Flatten wings over breast, then tie cord around breast to hold wings securely.

Insert spit rod through center of bird from

tail end toward front. Insert skewers firmly in place in bird and screw tightly. Test the balance. *Bird must balance on spit so it will rotate smoothly throughout the cooking period.* Place spit in rotisserie. Brush turkey with melted butter or margarine. Barbecue sauce may be used, if desired, the last 30 to 45 min. of cooking. Follow manufacturer's directions for rotisserie temperature setting and roast until done.

TIMETABLE FOR ROTISSERIED TURKEY

READY-TO-COOK WEIGHT	INTERIOR TEMPERATURE	GUIDE TO TOTAL COOKING TIME
4 to 6 lb.	185°F.	1½ to 2 hr.
6 to 8 lb.	185°F.	2 to 2½ hr.
8 to 10 lb.	185°F.	2½ to 3 hr.
10 to 12 lb.	185°F.	3 to 3½ hr.

TURKEY BARBECUE

Young turkeys take to the outdoors beautifully. Try them the next time you have a barbecue, using above directions.

ROAST BONELESS TURKEY ROLL

To Prepare:
1. Thaw frozen roll in refrigerator, allowing 1 to 2 days. Then remove wrapper, leaving on string.
2. Rinse roll with cold water; drain; pat dry. Season with salt and pepper, if not preseasoned.

To Roast:
1. Start heating oven to 350°F. Plan on allowing roast to stand 20 to 30 min. out of the oven before carving to allow absorption of juices and easier slicing. Insert roast-meat thermometer in center of roll.
2. Place roll on rack in shallow baking pan. Brush with melted butter or margarine.
3. Roast as label directs. Or use timetable at right. Baste or brush it occasionally with pan drippings or more melted butter or margarine.
4. If roll becomes too brown during roasting, cover loosely with tent of foil.
5. *Test for doneness:* Roast-meat thermometer should read 170°F. to 175°F.

TIMETABLE FOR ROASTING TURKEY ROLL
(At 350°F.)

READY-TO-COOK WEIGHT	APPROX. ROASTING TIME*
3 to 5 lb.	2 to 2½ hr.
5 to 7 lb.	2½ to 3¼ hr.
7 to 9 lb.	3¼ to 4 hr.

*Shorten roasting time about ½ hr. if rotisserie cooking.
*Lengthen roasting time ½ hr. if you are cooking the roll from the frozen state.
*Roast-meat thermometer should register 170°F. to 175°F.

To Make Gravy: See Chicken Gravy, p. 262.

To Carve: Remove string; with sharp knife slice thinly at an angle across roast.

To Rotisserie: Prepare roll as for roasting. Insert spit rod through center of length of turkey roll. Insert skewers firmly in roast. Be sure roll is balanced on spit. Place spit in rotisserie. Follow manufacturer's directions for rotisserie temperature setting and roast until done, or to 170°F. to 175°F. on meat thermometer, which has been inserted in center of roll (don't let it touch spit).

BROILED TURKEY

Split a 4- to 6-lb. turkey in half lengthwise. Follow range directions for using broiler. Turkeys over 6 lb. in weight are not suitable for broiling.
1. Fold wing tips onto back (cut side).
2. Place turkey, skin side down, in broiler pan (do not use the rack). Turkey should fill the pan, one layer deep, without crowding or leaving any pan area exposed.
3. Brush well with melted fat or salad oil. Season each half with 1 teaspoon salt, ½ teaspoon sugar; sprinkle with pepper.
4. Place pan in broiler about 9 inches from heat, regulating the distance or the heat so that surface of turkey *just begins* to brown after 20 min. of cooking. Broil slowly until nicely browned, about 40 min.
5. Turn skin side up. Baste with pan drippings and additional fat if necessary. Continue broiling until turkey is brown, crisp, and well done, 40 to 50 min. Baste with pan drippings

or fat several times during broiling to brown and cook evenly. Total cooking time: 1¼ to 1½ hr.

6. *To test doneness:* The drumstick twists easily in the thigh joint and breast meat near shoulder joint is fork-tender.

7. Divide halves into quarters for serving. Serve on warmed platter.

FRIED TURKEY

Select a whole 4- to 9-lb. turkey, cut up to yield 2 drumsticks, 2 thighs, 4 breast pieces, 2 wings, 3 back pieces, neck, giblets. Or, select by-the-piece for choice of favorite parts. Only the small turkey, in the 4- to 9-lb. range, can be successfully pan- or oven-fried.

Pan-Frying:

1. For each 5 pounds of cut-up turkey blend together ¾ cup flour, 1 teaspoon paprika, 4 teaspoons salt, and ½ teaspoon pepper in a bag. Shake turkey, 2 or 3 pieces at a time, in flour mixture in bag to coat evenly. Save any leftover mixture for gravy.

2. Heat ½ inch of fat or salad oil in a heavy skillet until a drop of water just sizzles.

3. Start browning meaty pieces first, slipping less meaty pieces in between as turkey browns.

4. Turn as necessary with kitchen tongs or two spoons to brown and cook evenly.

5. When pieces are *lightly* and *evenly* browned, about 20 min., reduce heat; add two tablespoons water; cover tightly.

6. Cook slowly until thickest pieces are fork-tender, 45 to 60 min. Turn pieces 2 or 3 times to assure even cooking and browning. Uncover pan the last 10 min. of frying to re-crisp skin. Total cooking time: 1 to 1¼ hr.

Oven Frying:

1. Coat turkey with seasoned flour. (See Pan-Frying, above.) Meanwhile, melt 1 cup butter or margarine (for each 5 pounds of turkey) in a shallow baking pan at 350°F.

2. Place coated pieces in pan, turn to coat both sides with the butter or margarine, then leave skin side down. Turkey should fill pan, one layer deep, without crowding or leaving any pan area exposed.

3. Bake at 350°F. 45 min. Turn turkey skin side up and bake until fork-tender, about 45 min. Total cooking time: about 1½ hr.

TURKEY FRICASSEE

Buy cut-up 4- to 9-lb. turkey, or young turkey parts. Coat, then cook, as in Chicken Fricassee, p. 277.

POT ROAST OF TURKEY

¼ cup butter or margarine	Neck, gizzard, heart of turkey
1 6-lb. turkey	⅓ cup all-purpose flour
Salt and pepper	
2 chicken bouillon cubes	1 teasp. salt
1 cup boiling water	1 pt. commercial sour cream
2 tablesp. paprika	

In hot butter in Dutch oven, brown turkey well on all sides, sprinkling with salt and pepper — about 20 to 30 min. Place turkey on trivet in Dutch oven. Dissolve bouillon cubes in boiling water; add paprika; add to turkey, along with neck, gizzard, heart. Simmer, covered, 2 to 2½ hr., or until fork-tender, turning occasionally. Remove turkey to heated platter; keep warm.

Chop heart and gizzard fine; discard neck. Measure liquid in Dutch oven; add water to make 2 cups. In small bowl, make paste of flour, 1 teasp. salt, and some liquid. Stir paste into rest of hot liquid in Dutch oven. Cook, stirring, until thickened. Add sour cream, heart, gizzard; heat, but do not boil.

Nice served on bed of cooked rice, garnished with sautéed mushrooms and snipped parsley. Makes 8 servings.

POT ROAST OF CHICKEN: You may substitute 1 4-lb. roasting chicken for turkey. Simmer chicken about 1 to 1½ hr. Makes 6 servings.

SMOKED TURKEY

There are two kinds of smoked turkey in the retail market. Some requires additional cooking before serving. Some comes ready to eat. Let the label tell the story. Refrigerate smoked turkey as soon as received and prepare as label directs. Don't plan to keep leftovers more than 10 to 14 days.

For Dinner: Serve cold, thinly sliced. Or reheat on rack, in covered roasting pan, with 1 to 2 cups water, at 325°F., allowing about 5 to 10 min. per lb.

For Buffets, Suppers, Parties: Serve, sliced

and cold, like any roast turkey. Or slice thin; pass in hot buttered biscuits. Or alternate slices of roast chicken and smoked turkey on platter.

As Nibblers: Serve slices with punch. Or spread buttered bread fingers with cream cheese; top with smoked-turkey slices; sprinkle with pepper.

Or grind ½ cup each of white and dark smoked turkey meat; add mayonnaise and pepper to taste; use for tiny sandwiches.

Or spread thin slices of smoked turkey with cream cheese; roll up; tuck cress in one end.

As Brunch Treat: Thinly slice smoked turkey; sauté slightly in butter; accompany with scrambled or fried eggs, hot biscuits, and coffee.

In Creamed Dishes, etc.: Use in any dish that calls for cooked turkey or chicken — but omit salt and go easy on other seasonings.

DUCKLING

To Buy

Ready-to-Cook Duckling: Packaged Long Island and other specially raised, brand-name ducklings come to market frozen whole with giblets and neck, as well as in parts; or you can buy them fresh, ice-chilled.

Allow at least ¾ to 1 lb. duckling per serving. A 4- to 5-lb. bird makes 4 servings.

To Store

Quick-Frozen, Ready-to-Cook Duckling: Keep frozen, as in Guide to Storing Chicken, p. 260, until time to thaw for cooking as label directs. To thaw, place bird, in its original wrapper, *without* puncturing wrapper, in refrigerator, then allow 1 to 1½ days for thawing. Use promptly after thawing.

Fresh, Ice-Chilled, Ready-to-Cook Duckling: Wrap loosely in wax paper, aluminum foil, or saran; then refrigerate until roasting time. Use within 2 days.

To Cut Up for Cooking: Thaw frozen bird. Then, with heavy scissors, halve each duckling lengthwise, first along backbone, then along breastbone on other side; then cut 2 halves crosswise, just above thigh, making 4 pieces. Next, if desired, cut away extra skin and fat.

ROAST DUCKLING

1. Start heating oven to 325°F. With sharp knife score skin of entire duckling at 1″ intervals for a more crisp skin. Rub body cavity of thawed bird lightly with salt, monosodium glutamate, and any other seasonings (pepper, dried thyme, etc.) if desired.
2. If stuffing bird, use one of these: quartered, cored unpared cooking apples; halved onions; celery stalks. Or see Stuffings for Chicken, Duckling, or Pheasant, p. 340. With skewer, fasten neck skin over back. Close body opening, then loop cord around leg ends, bring together and tie.
3. Place duckling, breast side up, in shallow open pan on rack that is level with, or higher than top of pan. Do not add water; do not cover; do not baste.
4. Roast at 325°F. until thick portion of leg feels soft when pressed and legs can be easily moved up and down. A 4- to 5-lb. unstuffed duckling requires 2½ to 3 hr. Increase roasting time about ½ hr. if a stuffed bird. Duckling is well done when drumstick meat is soft when pressed between fingers.
5. About ½ hr. before duckling is done, brush with mixture of 2 tablesp. honey and 1 teasp. bottled sauce for gravy; or ½ cup orange marmalade; or ½ cup currant jelly. Increase oven heat to 400°F. and finish cooking. Duckling will have a beautiful glaze. Makes 4 servings.

To Serve: We do not recommend carving a duck as you do a chicken or turkey. Rather, with poultry scissors and sharp knife, cut duckling into quarters, as directed in "To Cut Up For Cooking," either at table by host or in the kitchen before serving. Serve with gravy made from drippings, as in Chicken Gravy, p. 262.

If There Are Leftovers: See To Care for Cooked Chicken, p. 260, and Last of the Bird, p. 288.

ROAST DUCKLING WITH PINEAPPLE

1 4- to 5-lb. duckling, quartered
1 teasp. salt
⅛ teasp. pepper
2 tablesp. butter or margarine
1 1-lb.-4½-oz. can pineapple slices
½ cup white wine
1 tablesp. wine vinegar

Start heating oven to 325°F. Rub duckling quarters with salt, pepper. In shallow open pan, on rack, place quarters, skin down. (Do not add water; do not cover; do not baste.) Roast 30 min.; turn pieces; roast 2 to 2½ hr. longer, or until thickest portions of legs feel soft when pressed. Place on heated platter; keep hot.

In hot butter, in skillet, sauté pineapple slices (reserve juice) until golden; arrange on and around duckling. Into same skillet pour pineapple juice; stir until browned bits are loosened; cook, stirring occasionally, until almost caramelized. Stir in wine and vinegar and bring just to boiling. Serve duckling, passing sauce. Makes 4 servings.

ROAST DUCKLING WITH ORANGE GLAZE

1 4- to 5-lb. duckling
1 teasp. caraway seeds
1 qt. day-old bread crumbs
¼ cup minced onion
¼ cup minced green
pepper
½ cup minced celery
1 teasp. salt
⅛ teasp. pepper
1 tablesp. crushed sage

Start heating oven to 325°F. Sprinkle cavity of duckling with caraway seeds. Combine rest of ingredients; use to stuff bird. Fasten neck skin to back; close body opening and tie leg ends as in Roast Duckling, p. 285. Then roast as in Roast Duckling, at 325°F. 2½ to 3 hr., or until tender.

To serve: With kitchen scissors and sharp knife, halve duckling lengthwise, then crosswise. Arrange with stuffing on large platter. Pour some of Orange Glaze, below, over duckling; pass rest. Makes 4 servings.

ORANGE GLAZE: In saucepan, combine ⅓ cup brown sugar, packed; ⅓ cup granulated sugar, and 1 tablesp. cornstarch. Add 1 tablesp. grated orange rind, 1 cup orange juice, and ¼ teasp. salt; stir over low heat until sugars dissolve. Simmer until transparent and thickened — about 3 min. Makes 1½ cups.

CANETON MONTMORENCY

1 4- to 5-lb. duckling, quartered
Duckling giblets and neck
1 16- to 17-oz. can pitted, dark sweet cherries, drained
¾ cup port wine
1 cup raw wild rice
¼ cup butter or margarine
¼ cup minced onion
3 tablesp. flour
1 tablesp. meat-extract paste
3 tablesp. currant jelly

Start heating oven to 325°F. Wash and dry duckling; remove any pinfeathers. In shallow, open roasting pan, on a rack, roast duckling, skin side up, 2½ to 3 hr., or until tender.

Make duckling broth by simmering giblets (omitting liver) and neck with 2 cups water, covered, about 1½ hr. Also let cherries stand in ¼ cup port wine.

About 1 hr. before serving, wash rice well in 3 changes of cold water. Then add slowly to 4 cups boiling water. Boil, covered, stirring occasionally with fork, about 45 min., or till rice is tender and water is absorbed. Add 2 tablesp. butter. Keep warm.

When done, remove duckling from roasting pan to serving platter. Pour drippings from pan; in pan, melt 2 tablesp. butter, stirring to dissolve browned bits in pan. Add onion; cook, stirring, until tender; remove from heat. Stir in flour, meat-extract paste, currant jelly, 1½ cups strained duckling broth, ½ cup wine. Cook, stirring, over medium heat until thickened. Add cherries in wine.

Serve duckling on wild rice, with sauce poured over. Makes 4 servings.

BROILED DUCKLING

Quarter duckling; remove neck, backbone, and wing tips. With sharp knife score skin, over duckling quarters, at intervals of 1", to give a more crisp skin; arrange on rack in broiler pan. Broil as in Broiled Chicken, p. 263, until fork-tender, omitting brushing with melted butter. About 3 min. before bird is done, brush with mixture of 2 tablesp. honey, 1 teasp. bottled sauce for gravy, and 1 teasp. Worcestershire. Makes 4 servings.

GOOSE

Geese come packaged quick-frozen, and ready-to-cook. Market sizes vary from 4 to 14 lb.

Amounts to Buy: Allow about 1 to 1½ lb. ready-to-cook goose per serving.

ROAST GOOSE

Prepare for roasting as in Roast Chicken. Do not brush surface of goose with fat or oil.

If you prefer goose unstuffed, just rub cavity of bird with salt, pepper, and split clove garlic; sprinkle with 2 teasp. caraway seeds. Quartered apples, peeled onions, or celery stalks may be placed in cavity, then discarded after roasting. If you like stuffed goose, see Stuffings For Turkey or Goose, p. 338.

TIMETABLE FOR ROASTING UNSTUFFED GOOSE
(At 325°F.)

READY-TO-COOK WEIGHT	APPROX. ROASTING TIME*
4 to 6 lb.	2¾ to 3 hr.
6 to 8 lb.	3 to 3½ hr.
8 to 10 lb.	3½ to 3¾ hr.
10 to 12 lb.	3¾ to 4¼ hr.
12 to 14 lb.	4 to 4¾ hr.

For stuffed goose add 30 min. to roasting time if 4- to 8-lb. birds; about 20 min. for all birds over 8 lb.

GUINEA HEN

Guinea hens have a gamey flavor and are tenderer, but drier, than chicken. They average about 1½ to 2¼ lb. each after cleaning. The choice meat is on the breast; it is white, thick, tender. One hen makes 2 or 3 servings.

ROAST GUINEA HEN

1 1½- to 2-lb. cleaned guinea hen	1 medium onion
2 tablesp. butter or margarine	1 carrot, pared
	1 stalk celery, cut up
⅛ teasp. pepper	4 salt-pork or bacon strips
1 teasp. salt	

Start heating oven to 350°F. Rub body cavity of guinea hen with butter, pepper, salt. Place onion, carrot, and celery in cavity. Close body opening with skewers; lace with twine; with ends of twine, tie legs to tail.

Place bird, breast side down, on rack in shallow open pan. Place pork strips across back. Bake, uncovered, 45 min. Turn bird; place pork strips across breast. Bake 45 min. longer, or until tender. Serve with or without gravy (see Chicken Gravy, p. 262). Makes 2 or 3 servings.

SQUAB

Squabs are very young pigeons, averaging about 1 lb. apiece. Allow 1 squab per person.

ROAST SQUAB

4 1-lb. cleaned squabs	½ teasp. pepper
½ cup butter or margarine	⅛ teasp. nutmeg
	½ teasp. celery salt
½ lb. mushrooms, minced	Dash cayenne pepper
2 teasp. minced onion	4 cups fresh bread crumbs
½ cup melted butter or margarine	½ cup melted butter or margarine
2 teasp. snipped chives	½ teasp. salt
2 tablesp. snipped parsley	1 cup water
	¼ teasp. dried sage
2 teasp. salt	¼ teasp. dried savory
	¼ teasp. dried thyme

Start heating oven to 500°F. Wash and dry squabs. In ½ cup hot butter in skillet, sauté mushrooms and onion until tender; add ½ cup melted butter, chives, parsley, 2 teasp. salt, pepper, nutmeg, celery salt, cayenne, crumbs; mix. Use mixture to stuff squabs; close openings with poultry pins; lace with white twine.

Place, breast sides up, on rack in shallow open pan; top with ½ cup melted butter, ½ teasp. salt, water, sage, savory, thyme. Bake, uncovered, at 500°F. 15 min., then at 400°F. 30 min., basting every 10 min. with drippings. Makes 4 servings.

SAUTEED SQUAB

Season cleaned, split squabs with salt and pepper. In hot butter or margarine in skillet, sauté squabs until golden brown on both sides and very well done — about 20 to 30 min.

BROILED SQUAB

Wash, dry, and split cleaned squabs. Season with salt and pepper. Broil as in Broiled

Chicken, p. 263, until *well done* — 30 to 45 min.

LAST OF THE BIRD

Never throw out leftover chicken or turkey. Even the bones are good for a soup! In fact, why not plan on a big enough bird so that you will have planned leftovers for such dishes as these?

TURKEY-OLIVE CURRY

2 tablesp. butter or margarine	1 chicken-bouillon cube
½ cup sliced onions	1½ cups milk
1 cup diced celery	1 cup pitted ripe olives
2½ tablesp. flour	1 cup diced, cooked turkey or chicken
½ teasp. salt	
¼ teasp. curry powder	1 3-oz. can chow-mein noodles

In hot butter in skillet, sauté onions and celery until tender. Remove a few onion rings; set aside for garnish. To skillet, add flour, salt, curry powder, and crumbled bouillon cube; cook until bubbling. Slowly stir in milk; cook over medium heat, stirring occasionally, until thickened. Add three fourths of olives, all of turkey; heat. Top with onion rings, rest of olives. Serve over noodles. Makes 4 servings.

WILD-RICE-AND-TURKEY CASSEROLE

1½ cups wild rice	mushroom soup, undiluted
4 cups boiling water	
1 teasp. salt	1 teasp. Worcestershire
1 lb. bulk pork sausage	12 slices roast turkey or chicken
1 3- or 4-oz. can whole mushrooms, undrained	1½ cups day-old bread crumbs
2 10½-oz. cans condensed cream-of-	¼ cup melted butter or margarine

Early in day: Wash rice; simmer in boiling water with salt, covered, for 30 to 40 min., or until tender and water is absorbed.

Meanwhile, in skillet, cook sausage over medium heat till browned, stirring and breaking it into bits and draining off fat as it accumulates. Stir in mushrooms, soup, and Worcestershire; lightly stir this mixture into drained cooked wild rice. Into well-greased 12″ x 8″ x 2″ baking dish, spoon half of rice

mixture; arrange turkey slices, in layer, on top; then spoon on rest of rice mixture. Refrigerate. *At dinnertime:* Start heating oven to 375°F. Mix crumbs with butter; sprinkle over rice in 1″ border around edge of casserole. Bake about 30 min., or until hot and golden. Makes 8 servings.

FOR FOURSOME: Make ½ recipe; bake in a 10″ x 6″ x 2″ baking dish.

BROCCOLI WITH SOUR CREAM ON TURKEY

1 bunch broccoli	¼ teasp. lime juice
1½ cups commercial sour cream	1 teasp. salt
2 teasp. prepared mustard	4 large slices cold roast turkey breast
	Paprika

Prepare and cook broccoli as on p. 421. Meanwhile, combine sour cream, mustard, lime juice, and salt. Arrange turkey slices on platter; top each slice with 3 pieces broccoli; spoon sauce on top; sprinkle with paprika. Makes 4 servings.

TURKEY CASHEW CASSEROLE

1 cup cut-up, cooked or canned turkey or chicken	¼ lb. cashew nuts, salted or unsalted, coarsely chopped
1 10½-oz. can condensed cream-of-mushroom soup, undiluted	Dash pepper
	Salt
1½ cups coarsely cut celery	30 crisp round scalloped crackers, coarsely crumbled (about 2 cups crumbs)
1 tablesp. minced onion	

Start heating oven to 325°F. Mix turkey, soup, celery, onion, nuts, pepper. Taste; add salt if unsalted nuts are being used. In 1½-qt. casserole, place layers of turkey mixture and crumbs, ending with crumbs. Bake, uncovered, 40 min. Makes 4 servings.

LUSCIOUS TURKEY HASH

2 cups cut-up, cooked turkey or chicken	1 medium onion
	¼ cup diced pimento
4 medium potatoes, pared	1 teasp. salt
	⅛ teasp. pepper
½ seeded green pepper	3 tablesp. butter or margarine

Put turkey, potatoes, green pepper, and onion

through food grinder, using medium blade. Mix in pimento, salt, pepper. In large skillet, melt butter. Pour in hash mixture; cook over low heat, covered, 15 min., or until potatoes are cooked and hash is browned on bottom. Uncover; let stand 1 min. to dry out a bit. Then loosen edge with spatula; turn one half onto other half; turn onto serving platter. Serve with chili sauce. Makes 4 servings.

DELMONICO TURKEY SANDWICHES

3 tablesp. butter or margarine	grated (2 cups)
3 tablesp. flour	4 toast slices
¾ teasp. salt	8 medium slices cooked or canned turkey or chicken
¼ teasp. prepared mustard	Dash paprika
Dash cayenne pepper	4 crisp bacon slices
2 cups milk	2 medium tomatoes, sliced
½ lb. process sharp Cheddar cheese,	

Start heating oven to 450°F. In saucepan over low heat, melt butter. Gradually add flour, salt, mustard, cayenne, then milk. Cook, stirring, until thickened. Remove from heat. Stir in cheese until melted. In 10" x 6" x 2" baking dish arrange toast; top with turkey; pour cheese sauce over turkey. Sprinkle with paprika. Bake 10 min. Garnish with bacon and tomato slices. Makes 4 servings.

TURKEY PASTY

¼ cup grated Parmesan cheese	cooked turkey or chicken
1 pkg. piecrust mix	1½ teasp. caraway seeds
6 tablesp. butter or margarine	½ teasp. salt
½ cup minced onions	¼ lb. fresh mushrooms
½ cup coarsely cut celery	1 cup cheese sauce in jar, or turkey gravy
½ cup chopped pecans	¼ cup sliced pimentos (optional)
3 cups* coarsely cut,	

Add cheese to piecrust mix. Make pastry as label directs. Form into ball; wrap in wax paper; refrigerate.

Start heating oven to 425°F. Meanwhile, in ¼ cup hot butter in skillet, sauté onions, celery, and pecans until golden. Add turkey, caraway seeds, salt. Cool slightly.

On floured surface, roll pastry to make 13"

square. Transfer to large greased cookie sheet. Place turkey filling on pastry, covering half, from corner to corner. Turn opposite corner over to cover, making triangle. Seal edges, using tines of fork. Bake 25 to 30 min., or until browned. Meanwhile, in 2 tablesp. hot butter, sauté whole mushrooms until tender. To hot cheese sauce, add pimento. Serve Pasty garnished with cheese sauce and mushrooms. Makes 8 servings.

If you have only 1½ cups cooked turkey, make ½ recipe for 4 servings.

TURKEY DRESSING STRATA

1 10½-oz. can condensed cream-of-mushroom soup, undiluted	turkey or chicken
	1½ cups leftover turkey or chicken stuffing
¾ cup milk	1 teasp. grated Parmesan cheese
3 cups cubed cooked	

Start heating oven to 375°F. In saucepan, heat soup with milk; add turkey.

In 1½-qt. casserole, arrange stuffing and turkey mixture in layers, having turkey on top. Sprinkle with cheese. Bake 30 min. Makes 6 servings.

FLORENTINE TURKEY

1 10-oz. pkg. frozen chopped spinach	¼ cup grated Parmesan cheese
Butter or margarine	½ cup light cream
3 tablesp. flour	2 cups cooked turkey or chicken, in chunks
1 teasp. monosodium glutamate	
1 teasp. salt	¼ cup packaged dried bread crumbs
Dash cayenne pepper	Butter or margarine
1½ cups milk	

Early in the day: Cook spinach as label directs; drain well, then arrange in 1½-qt. casserole.

In saucepan, melt 2 tablesp. butter. Stir in flour, monosodium glutamate, salt, and cayenne. Gradually stir in milk; then cook, stirring constantly, until it thickens and comes to a boil. Now add cheese and cream. Stir, over low heat, until cheese melts; then add turkey, and pour over spinach. Sprinkle casserole with bread crumbs, then refrigerate.

About 30 min. before serving: Start heating oven to 350°F. Dot casserole with butter. Bake 15 min., then set under broiler to lightly brown top. Makes 4 servings.

SWEET-POTATO CHICKEN PIE

2 1-lb.-2-oz. cans yams or sweet potatoes
½ teasp. nutmeg
¼ teasp. allspice
¼ teasp. salt
2 tablesp. melted butter or margarine
1 tablesp. sherry (optional)
2 tablesp. butter or margarine
1 medium onion, minced

2 3- or 4-oz. cans sliced mushrooms, undrained
½ cup quartered large stuffed olives
1 10½-oz. can condensed cream-of-mushroom soup, undiluted
Dash pepper
2 cups cut-up cooked or canned chicken or turkey

1. In bowl place drained yams and mash well. Then beat in nutmeg, allspice, salt, 2 tablesp. melted butter, and sherry.
2. Use this potato mixture to line a 9″ pie plate, building up the edges about ½″ high. Start heating oven to 350°F.
3. In skillet, in 2 tablesp. hot butter or margarine, sauté minced onion till tender. Add mushrooms, with their liquid, olives, soup, pepper, and chicken; heat, stirring occasionally.
4. Pour mixture into prepared crust. Bake 30 min. Makes 4 servings.

CHICKEN 'N' HAM PIE

1 cup sifted all-purpose flour
1 teasp. double-acting baking powder
½ teasp. salt
1 cup unseasoned mashed sweet potatoes
⅓ cup melted shortening
1 egg, beaten
1 10½-oz. can condensed cream-of-chicken soup, un-

diluted
¼ cup milk
1 cup diced cooked ham
1 cup diced cooked chicken or turkey
⅛ teasp. pepper
⅛ teasp. ground cloves
2 teasp. dried parsley flakes
1 cup cooked or canned peas

Into bowl sift flour, baking powder, and salt. Add sweet potatoes, melted shortening, and egg; blend well. Refrigerate several hours.

Then start heating oven to 425°F. Heat soup with milk; add ham, chicken, pepper, cloves, and parsley. Into 9″ pie plate turn half of chicken mixture. Scatter peas on top; top with rest of chicken mixture. On very well-floured board, gently roll out sweet-potato mixture into 10″ circle. Lift onto pie plate over chicken mixture. Flute edge; make slits in top crust. Bake 25 to 30 min. Serve at once.

CREAMED CHICKEN, CHINESE STYLE

3 tablesp. cornstarch
2 cups milk
2 cups diced, cooked or canned chicken or turkey
1 10½-oz. can condensed cream-of-mushroom soup, undiluted
1 3- or 4-oz. can chopped mushrooms, undrained

1 8-oz. can water chestnuts, drained, sliced
⅛ teasp. each salt, pepper, dried marjoram, and monosodium glutamate
½ teasp. paprika
1 tablesp. sherry
2 3-oz. or 1 6-oz. can chow-mein noodles

In saucepan, mix cornstarch with some of milk to form smooth paste; add rest of ingredients except noodles. Cook over low heat till hot. *To serve:* Arrange noodles on large platter; spoon on chicken. Makes 6 servings.

CHICKEN A LA QUEEN

2 tablesp. butter or margarine
¼ cup slivered, blanched almonds
¼ cup butter or margarine
2 tablesp. flour
Speck pepper
1½ teasp. salt
Dash paprika
2 cups light cream

1 egg yolk, beaten
2 cups cut-up, cooked or canned chicken or turkey
1 1-lb.-4-oz. can pineapple tidbits, drained
Toast slices, canned chow-mein noodles, or mashed sweet potatoes

In 2 tablesp. hot butter in skillet, sauté almonds until light golden; set aside. Then, in double boiler, melt ¼ cup butter; add flour, pepper, salt, paprika, stirring, until blended and smooth. Slowly stir in cream. Then stir small amount of sauce into egg yolk; return yolk mixture to remaining sauce, continuing to stir until smooth and thickened. Add chicken, pineapple. Pour over toast, chow-mein noodles, or mashed sweet potatoes; top with sautéed almonds. Makes 6 servings.

HALF-AND-HALF: Substitute cut-up, cooked ham for 1 cup chicken. If desired, substitute chopped walnuts or pecans for slivered almonds.

CHICKEN CRUNCH

¾ cup raw regular or processed white rice; or 1⅓ cups packaged precooked rice
2 tablesp. butter or margarine
1 medium onion, sliced
1 medium green pepper, cut into strips
1¼ cups chicken broth*
3 cups sliced celery

1 tablesp. soy sauce
2 cups cut-up, cooked or canned chicken or turkey
1 3- or 4-oz. can mushrooms, drained
2 tablesp. cornstarch
3 tablesp. liquid drained from mushrooms
½ cup coarsely broken walnuts or almonds

Cook rice as label directs; keep hot. Meanwhile, in hot butter in skillet, sauté onion until tender; stir in green pepper, chicken broth, celery, soy sauce. Simmer, covered, 10 min. Add chicken, mushrooms. Mix cornstarch with mushroom liquid; stir into chicken mixture; bring to boil. Add walnuts.

Serve on rice. Makes 6 servings.

You may use canned broth.

CRUNCHY CREAMED TURKEY

2 tablesp. butter or margarine
¼ cup chopped green pepper
1 onion, thinly sliced
1 10½-oz. can condensed cream-of-chicken soup, undiluted
½ cup milk

½ teasp. seasoned salt
¼ cup coarsely cut cashew nuts
2 cups cut-up cooked turkey or chicken
1 cup cooked carrot slices
Savory Noodles, below

In butter, in saucepan or large skillet, sauté green pepper and onion until tender. Stir in soup, milk, seasoned salt; then add nuts, turkey, and carrots; heat thoroughly. Serve in ring of Savory Noodles; sprinkle with parsley. Makes 4 servings.

SAVORY NOODLES: Cook 1 8-oz. pkg. wide noodles as label directs; drain. Into a large bowl, measure 1 teasp. salt, ½ teasp. nutmeg, ¼ teasp. pepper, 2 tablesp. butter or margarine, 2 tablesp. grated Parmesan cheese; add noodles, and toss gently with a fork. Makes 4 servings.

OVEN-BAKED CHICKEN HASH

2 cups diced, cooked potatoes
2 cups diced, cooked or canned chicken or turkey
1 cup heavy cream; or ¼ cup melted

butter or margarine plus ¾ cup milk
2½ teasp. onion salt; or 2 teasp. salt plus 1 tablesp. grated onion
¼ teasp. pepper

Start heating oven to 375°F. In 10″ x 6″ x 2″ baking dish, combine all ingredients. Bake 20 min., or until bubbling hot.

Serve this moist, creamy hash with corn sticks. Makes 4 servings.

ADAMS CASSEROLE

6 cups crumbled corn bread
½ teasp. poultry seasoning
1 teasp. celery seeds
⅛ teasp. pepper
¾ teasp. salt
¼ cup minced onion
3 tablesp. snipped parsley
½ cup melted butter or margarine

5 cups cooked or canned chicken or turkey, in small or large pieces
¼ cup butter or margarine
¼ cup flour
1½ teasp. salt
2 cups chicken broth
2 eggs, well beaten
1 qt. milk

Start heating oven to 375°F. In large bowl, combine corn bread, poultry seasoning, celery seeds, pepper, ¾ teasp. salt, onion, parsley, ½ cup melted butter. Toss together with a fork. Spread in layer, in 13″ x 9″ x 2″ baking dish. Arrange chicken evenly over top.

In large skillet, melt ¼ cup butter; stir in flour and 1½ teasp. salt until smooth. Stir in broth; heat. Then combine eggs and milk; add to sauce; cook until slightly thickened, stirring. Pour this sauce over chicken, and bake 45 min. Makes 8 to 10 servings.

COMPANY CHICKEN ODETTE

Crêpes, p. 578
¼ cup butter or margarine
2 cups finely cut-up cooked chicken or turkey
½ teasp. salt
¼ teasp. pepper
¼ cup all-purpose flour
1 cup chicken broth

1 cup light cream
1 bay leaf, crumbled
½ teasp. celery salt
1 tablesp. sherry
Easy Hollandaise Sauce, p. 531
¼ cup light cream
½ cup heavy cream, whipped
2 tablesp. grated Parmesan cheese

Early in day, or day before, if desired:
1. Make twelve 6" crêpes; cool on paper towels.
2. In hot butter in large skillet, sauté chicken, stirring, just until hot — about 3 min. Stir in salt, pepper, flour, then broth, 1 cup light cream, bay leaf, celery salt, sherry; simmer 5 min., or until thickened. Remove from heat.
3. Down one side of each crêpe, spoon some of chicken mixture; roll up crêpe. Arrange, seam side down, in ungreased 12" x 8" x 2" baking dish; refrigerate, covered. Also cover and refrigerate leftover creamed-chicken mixture.

One half hour before serving:
1. Start heating oven to 350°F.
2. Make Easy Hollandaise Sauce.
3. Meanwhile, in medium saucepan, reheat leftover creamed-chicken mixture. Uncover and bake crêpes 10 min. so they're heated through; then remove from oven.
4. Preheat broiler 10 min. or as manufacturer directs.
5. Into leftover chicken mixture, stir ¼ cup light cream, Easy Hollandaise Sauce, then whipped cream. Spoon mixture over heated crêpes; sprinkle with cheese. Broil about 2 min., or until golden. Makes 4 to 6 servings.

WHEN HE CARVES

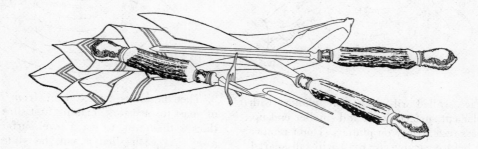

IF IT'S A STANDING RIB ROAST

1. It will be much easier for host to carve a standing rib roast if you have the meatman cut backbone from the ribs when you buy the roast. Place roast on platter, with broader cut surface down; set it before host, with rib side to his left and ends of ribs pointing toward him, as shown in Fig. 1. Be sure knife is razor sharp.

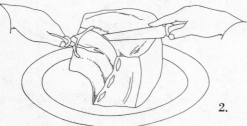
2.

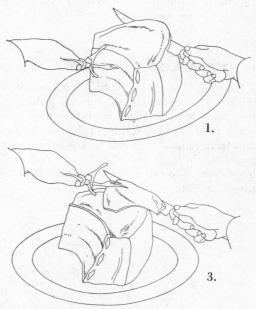
1.

3.

2. To carve the roast, the host inserts carving fork securely, with guard up, between two top ribs, as shown. Then, starting at right outside edge, at broadest point, he slices across face of roast toward rib side, as shown in Fig. 1, making slices about ¼" thick.

3. When knife blade meets rib bone, he loosens slice by cutting along full length of rib bone with point of knife, as shown in Fig. 2. As each slice is cut, he slides knife blade under it, steadies it with fork, and lifts it to platter, as shown in Fig. 3.

IF IT'S TONGUE

Place trimmed, skinned tongue, p. 239, before host, with tip to his right. With fork inserted at top, at his left, host starts slicing thin part, straight down, at whichever angle produces the largest slices. He keeps slices parallel, as shown at right.

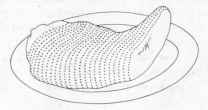

IF IT'S A ROLLED RIB ROAST

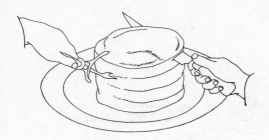

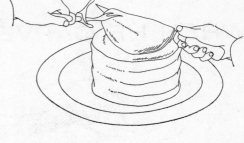

1. Place rolled rib roast on platter with broader cut surface down and smaller end up, so roast rests firmly on platter. (Don't remove cords before carving, or roast will fall apart.) Host inserts carving fork securely, with guard up, into left side of roast, about 1″ or 2″ below top, as shown above.

2. Then he slices across grain, from far side of roast toward fork, making first slice a little thicker than rest, to get a level surface right away. As each slice is cut, he slides knife blade under it, steadies it with fork, and lifts it to platter, as shown above. He re-inserts fork lower in meat for each slice, severing each cord as it is reached.

IF IT'S A LEG OF LAMB

1. On one side of the lamb's leg bone is a thick meaty section; on the other is a thinner, less meaty section. Place leg before host with shank to his right and thinner, less meaty section facing him. He inserts fork securely, with guard up, in large end of leg and cuts 2 or 3 lengthwise slices from thin side near him, as shown at right.

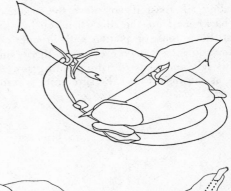

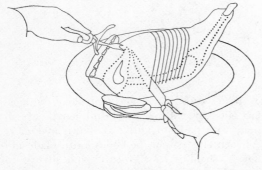

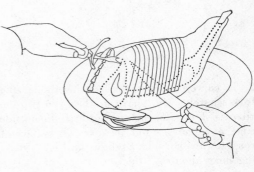

2. Now he turns leg of lamb so it rests firmly on cut surface. This puts the thick meaty section in an upright position, with the shank end pointing up. Then, with fork in large end of roast, host starts slicing from right end of roast, close to shank end. He cuts straight down to leg bone, as shown above.

3. He continues to cut parallel slices (as many as are needed) down to leg bone, keeping slices about 1/4″ thick, as shown above. Then, with fork still in place, he runs carving knife under slices, parallel to and along leg bone. This releases all slices at one time. Now lamb is ready to serve.

IF IT'S A PORTERHOUSE STEAK

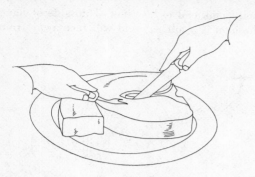

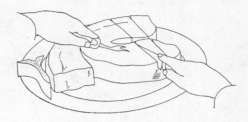

1. Set steak before host, with tapered end at left, as shown above. With point of knife, he cuts around bone closely, freeing it from meat; he lifts bone to side of platter.

2. Then, with knife at right angles to platter, he slices across full width of steak, making slices 1″ wide, as shown above. He cuts across width of tapered end in same way.

IF IT'S A LOIN OF PORK

To make carving easy, have meatman saw across base of ribs of loin of pork, close and parallel to backbone, to loosen backbone.

1. As soon as loin is roasted, place it, with rib side up, on cutting board. Then remove backbone: With fork astride rib bones, run blade of knife along backbone, close and parallel to it, as shown at right. Once this preparation is done, carving the roast will be much easier.

2. Now place roast on platter, with rib ends up, and cut surface, from which backbone has just been removed, facing down. Set platter before host, with rib side facing toward him and meaty side facing those at table, as at left. Now host can use ribs as slicing guide.

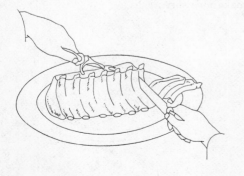

3. Host inserts fork securely in top of roast. He starts cutting at right end of loin, carving vertical slices and progressing toward left end as he slices, as shown at left. For first slice, he keeps blade close to left side of first rib. Next slice will probably be thin, boneless. Then he will get either boneless slice or one with rib.

IF IT'S A WHOLE HAM

Place whole ham before host, with scored side up and shank end to his right. Thin side of ham, from which first slices are made, will face host if the ham is a left leg, and will face away from him if ham is a right leg.

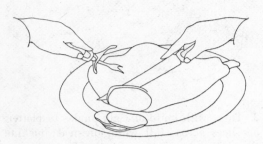

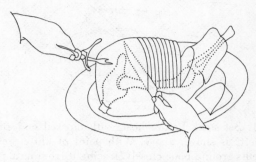

1. Ham shown here is a left leg of ham, with thin side nearer host. Host inserts carving fork securely in heavy part of ham, to the left, and cuts 2 or 3 thin oval slices, parallel to length of ham, from nearer side, as shown above.

2. Then he turns ham upright so it rests on cut surface. Next, about 6″ in from shank end, he makes a straight cut to leg bone, as for slicing. He makes another cut at an angle to this, close to shank end, and removes this wedge of meat, as shown above. Now ham is easy to carve into slices.

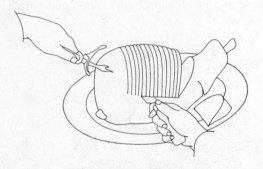

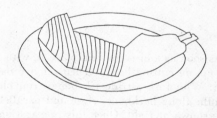

3. With carving fork steadying ham, host cuts thin slices (as many as are needed) down to leg bone. Then he runs carving knife along leg bone, at right angles to slices, releasing all slices at one time, as shown above.

4. If more servings are required, host turns ham back to its original position on platter, with scored-fat side up. He then carves at right angles to bone, as shown above. Though these slices are not so large as cushion slices, they make nice servings.

IF IT'S A SHANK END OF HAM:
First, host removes meaty cushion in 1 piece: Starting at meat's face, he cuts close to leg bone, straight along to shank end. Then he lays cushion flat side down, and slices it thinly. Next he severs joint between shank and leg bones, cuts out leg bone, then slices boned piece like cushion, as shown at right.

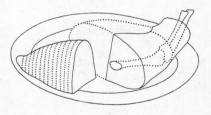

IF IT'S A CHICKEN OR TURKEY

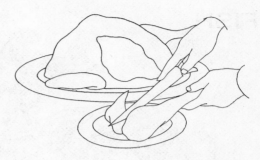

1. Place roast bird before host, with legs to right. Starting at side facing him, host cuts leg from body, bending it back with left hand, as shown above.

2. Next he lifts leg to side plate nearby. While holding leg with left hand, he severs thighbone from drumstick, just over round bone, as shown above.

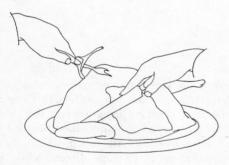

3. He slices all meat from leg. With fork close to the breastbone, he cuts down sharply where wing joins body, severing wing completely, as shown above.

4. Now starting just above joint from which wing was removed, he cuts thin slices of white meat, working upward, always cutting parallel to breastbone, as shown above.

5. After breast has been sliced, it's easy to reach stuffing, as shown at left. For second servings, host turns platter and carves other side of bird. And he doesn't forget that choice bit of dark meat, the oyster, in a cavity near the tail.

FISH

Today there are such delicious quick-frozen fish, as well as fresh and canned fish, that families everywhere can enjoy a superb fish dinner any day of the week. Better still there's no more disagreeable cleaning for Mother to do.

Before using these recipes, refer to How To Use Our Recipes, p. 3. Always use standard measuring cups and measuring spoons; and measure level.

TODAY'S FROZEN FISH

FROZEN FILLETS AND STEAKS: For these, halibut, flounder, ocean perch, pike, cod, sole, whiting, catfish, etc., are so quickly frozen in fillet or steak form that their fresh flavor and fine food value are retained. All you do is thaw each package in the refrigerator an hour or two, or just until fish can be separated. Then you broil, fry, or bake it until easily flaked with a fork, *but still moist,* as label directs.

FROZEN BREADED FISH PORTIONS (also called fillets, cutlets, steaks, burgers, etc.): These are equal-sized portions of uncooked fish which have been dipped in batter, then breaded before quick-freezing. All you do is fry, broil, or bake them as package directs, while still frozen.

FROZEN HEAT-AND-EAT STICKS: For these, the cleaned fish is cut into sticks, breaded, fried until crisp and brown, or left uncooked, then quick-frozen. All you do is complete them as package label directs, before serving.

TODAY'S FRESH FISH

You're blessed if you have at hand a good source of fresh fish. Try them in these forms:
STEAKS: These are cut crosswise from such fish as halibut, swordfish, salmon, and cod, and are about 3/4″ to 1″ thick.
FILLETS: These are sides or parts of fish, cut lengthwise and boned, with all or most of the skin removed.

DRESSED WHOLE: Look for fish with red gills, scales that adhere closely to the body, bright, bulging eyes, firm flesh, and fresh, sweet odor. *To Store:* Wrap in wax paper, saran, or foil and refrigerate in coldest section. Plan to use the same day if possible.

AMOUNT OF FROZEN OR FRESH FISH TO BUY

FOR 2 SERVINGS	CUT OF FISH	FOR 4 SERVINGS
About ¾ lb.	Fillets	About 1½ lb.
About 1 lb.	Steaks	About 2 lb.
About 1½ lb.	Whole	About 3 lb.

Baked With Ease

EASY BAKED FILLETS OR STEAKS

1. Buy packaged quick-frozen or fresh fish fillets or steaks, some of which are listed below. (See Amount to Buy, above.) If frozen, thaw if and as label directs.

FISH FILLETS		FISH STEAKS	
Cod	Ocean Perch	Cod	Pollock
Flounder	Sole	Haddock	Salmon
Haddock	Whiting	Halibut	Swordfish

2. If necessary cut fish into serving portions. Then season both sides with salt (or seasoned, onion, celery, or garlic salt), monosodium glutamate, and pepper.
3. Make a Butter Baste by mixing ¼ cup melted butter or margarine with 2 tablesp. lemon juice, 1 teasp. minced onion, and a little Tabasco. Into this mixture dip each piece of fish.
4. Then arrange fish in greased baking dish, lined with foil if desired, or on a broil-and-serve platter. (Placing fish on bed of celery leaves or mixture of chopped celery, parsley, and onion, helps prevent sticking and adds flavor.)
5. Start heating oven to 350°F. Pour any left-over Butter Baste over fish. Then, bake, uncovered, 25 to 30 min., or until easily flaked with a fork, *but still moist.*
6. Sprinkle fish with paprika, then serve at once from broil-and-serve platter or on a warm platter.
P.S. For sauces to pass with fish, see Just for Fish Sauces, p. 529. See Relishes and Garnishes, p. 433.

BAKED STUFFED FILLETS OR STEAKS

1. Buy 2 fish fillets or steaks, about 1 lb. each, then season both sides as in step 2 of Easy Baked Fillets or Steaks, at left.
2. Place one fillet or steak in a well-greased baking pan. Spread packaged stuffing or one of Fish Stuffings, p. 341, over top; then cover with other fillet or steak, fastening together with toothpicks.
3. Start heating oven to 350°F. Brush top of fish with ¼ cup melted butter or margarine, then lay 3 bacon slices over all.
4. Bake, uncovered, 30 to 40 min., or until fish flakes easily, *but is still moist.* Remove toothpicks. Makes 4 to 6 servings.
P.S. Well-seasoned tomato slices, sprinkled with minced onion, may replace stuffing.

SUPERB FISH ROLLS

2 tablesp. butter or margarine	minced
3 shallots, minced, or ¼ cup minced onion	2 tablesp. canned tomato purée
2 cloves garlic, minced	Salt
	Pepper
¼ lb. shrimp, sliced, cleaned, cooked	3 large fish fillets (about 2 lbs.)
1 tablesp. snipped chives	1 cup hot water
	¼ cup white wine
2 tablesp. fresh bread crumbs	1 tablesp. lemon juice
	Special Sauce, p. 300
1 large mushroom,	Grated Parmesan cheese
	Sprigs of water cress

1. Start heating oven to 400°F. In small skillet, heat butter or margarine. Add shallots and garlic and sauté 2 min.
2. Now add and sauté the shrimp 1 min.
3. Next add chives, bread crumbs, minced mushroom, tomato purée, ¼ teasp. salt, and a dash of pepper.
4. Now lay fish fillets on a flat surface; sprinkle lightly with salt and pepper. Spread shrimp mixture over them.
5. Roll up each fillet; place in shallow baking dish.
6. Combine hot water, wine, and lemon juice; pour over fish rolls.
7. Bake fish rolls, uncovered, 30 min., or until fish flakes easily with fork, *but is still moist.* While rolls bake, make Special Sauce, p. 300.

8. To serve, lift fish rolls from liquid onto platter; spoon on sauce; then sprinkle with Parmesan.

9. Lastly, garnish platter with sprigs of water cress. Makes 6 servings.

SPECIAL SAUCE: In double boiler melt 2 tablesp. butter or margarine; stir in 1 tablesp. flour, 1 cup milk; cook, stirring, until smooth and thickened. Now add: ¼ cup white wine, 1 tablesp. soy sauce, ½ teasp. salt, dash pepper. Cook a few minutes. Then stir in 3 egg yolks, slightly beaten. Now cook, stirring, until sauce is thickened.

BAKED STUFFED WHOLE FISH

1. Order a dressed 2- to 3-lb. whole fish with backbone removed, if desired. Choose from among these:

Bluefish	Lake Trout	Shad
Catfish	Mackerel	Spanish Mackerel
Cod	Mullet	Whitefish
Haddock	Red Snapper	Yellow Pike
Hake	Sea Trout	

2. Make 3 or 4 gashes in back of fish to keep it from bursting. Fill gashes with raw bacon, or bits of butter.

3. Make one of Fish Stuffings, p. 341. Season fish inside and out with salt, pepper, monosodium glutamate. Fill pocket with stuffing, then close opening with toothpicks, placed vertically across opening.

4. Set fish in oiled baking dish, then brush with salad oil. Bake, uncovered, at 400°F., allowing 12 min. per lb., or until easily flaked with fork, *but still moist.*

5. Serve, right from baking dish, or on warm platter, garnished as on p. 441. Or pass one of Just for Fish Sauces, p. 529. Makes 4 to 6 servings.

FLOUNDER FLORENTINE

1 10-oz. pkg. frozen chopped spinach	½ cup evaporated milk, undiluted
Salt	1 cup shredded Cheddar cheese
Pepper	
1 tablesp. butter or margarine	¼ teasp. Worcestershire
1 12-oz. pkg. frozen flounder fillets, thawed	½ teasp. dry mustard
	Dash nutmeg

1. Start heating oven to 375°F.

2. Cook spinach as label directs; season with salt, pepper, and butter. Arrange in greased 10″ x 6″ x 2″ baking dish. Arrange fillets on spinach.

3. Mix milk with remaining ingredients; pour over fillets.

4. Bake 25 min., or till fish flakes easily with fork. If desired, sprinkle with paprika. Makes 3 servings.

BAKED SOLE IN WHITE WINE
(Sült Hal Fehérborban)

½ lb. mushrooms	Paprika
4 cold cooked medium potatoes, thinly sliced	⅔ cup white wine
	1 cup commercial sour cream
2 tablesp. butter or margarine	2 lb. fresh fillets of sole
1½ teasp. salt	Snipped parsley or chives
½ teasp. pepper	

About 1½ hr. before serving:

1. Start heating oven to 375°F.

2. Wash mushrooms; trim off ends; then slice lengthwise.

3. In buttered 12″ x 8″ x 2″ baking dish, arrange potatoes; top with mushrooms; dot with butter; sprinkle with half of salt and pepper and ½ teasp. paprika; pour wine over all. Spread with half of sour cream.

4. Arrange pieces of fish over all; sprinkle with rest of salt and pepper and ½ teasp. paprika; top with rest of sour cream.

5. Bake 30 to 40 min., or until fish is done; sprinkle with paprika and parsley; serve. Makes 6 to 8 servings.

SPICED BAKED BASS

¼ teasp. salt	½ cup melted butter or margarine
⅛ teasp. pepper	
1 clove garlic, minced	3 tablesp. soy sauce
Lemon slices	3 tablesp. lime juice
2 lb. boned striped bass	¼ teasp. crushed (not ground) red pepper

Day before: Wrap salt, pepper, garlic in one piece of foil; lemon in another. Refrigerate. *About 45 min. before serving:* Start heating oven to 400°F. Meanwhile, place striped bass, cut side up, in 13″ x 9″ x 2″ baking dish; rub salt mixture into bass. Combine butter, soy sauce, lime juice, red pepper; pour over bass. *About 30 min. before serving:* Bake bass, basting occasionally with soy sauce mixture, till fish flakes easily with a fork and is *still moist.* Cut fish into squares; arrange on heated platter; pour sauce over it. Garnish with lemon. Makes 4 to 6 servings.

CHEESE-BAKED HADDOCK

¾ lb. thawed frozen or fresh haddock or cod	½ teasp. salt
	⅛ teasp. pepper
	¼ teasp. dry mustard
2 tablesp. butter or margarine	1 cup milk
	⅛ lb. sliced process Cheddar cheese
2 tablesp. flour	

Start heating oven to 350°F. Place fish in greased 10″ x 6″ x 2″ baking dish. Melt butter in saucepan; stir in flour, salt, pepper, mustard; add milk gradually; cook, stirring, till thickened. Add cheese; stir till melted; pour over fish. Bake, uncovered, 25 to 30 min., or till fish flakes easily with fork, *but is still moist.* Makes 2 servings.

FILET DE SOLE MARGUERY

2 tablesp. butter	shelled, deveined
¼ lb. small mush-rooms, halved	6 fillets of sole or flounder
Salt	1 doz. shucked raw oysters
2 teasp. lemon juice	
6 thin onion slices	½ cup butter or mar-garine (¼ lb.)
4 parsley sprigs	
10 whole black pep-pers	Chablis
	5 egg yolks
Pinch dried thyme	⅛ teasp. pepper
1 bay leaf	Canned truffles (op-tional)
1 whole clove	
1 cup water	2 tablesp. whipped heavy cream
1 doz. raw shrimp,	

1. Start heating oven to 325°F. Meanwhile, in 2 tablesp. butter in skillet, sauté mushrooms till golden, sprinkling with ¼ teasp. salt and lemon juice. Remove mushrooms from skillet; set aside.
2. In same skillet, combine onion slices, parsley, ½ teasp. salt, black peppers, thyme, bay leaf, clove, and water. Bring to boil; then add shrimp, and cook, covered, until shrimp are done — about 3 min.; remove shrimp from liquid; reserve both.
3. Meanwhile, lay 3 fillets, side by side, in 14″ x 9″ x 2″ oval baking dish; sprinkle with ¼ teasp. salt; top with 3 more fillets. Arrange oysters around fillets. Strain shrimp broth over all; cover with foil. Bake 15 to 20 min.,

or until fillets are easily flaked with fork. Remove from oven; turn broiler to Broil.
4. Remove oysters from fillets; set aside. Drain broth from fillets into skillet; simmer till reduced to ¼ cup; add ½ cup butter and ¼ cup Chablis; heat slowly till butter is just melted.
5. Meanwhile, in double boiler, stir together egg yolks, 2 tablesp. Chablis, ⅛ teasp. salt, and pepper; then slowly stir in butter-wine mixture.
6. Cook butter-wine mixture over hot, *not boiling,* water (make sure water does *not* touch bottom of top), *stirring constantly,* till like thin custard; remove from heat and from double boiler *immediately.*
7. Again drain fillets well, discarding liquid. Pour wine sauce over and around fillets, then circle with mushrooms, shrimp, and oysters, then top with a few slices truffles if desired.
8. For golden highlights on sauce, top it with about 6 small mounds of whipped cream; then gently stir into sauce with back of spoon.
9. Run under broiler till *just* lightly browned. Serve at once. Nice with buttered potato balls, topped with snipped parsley. Makes 6 servings.

FRESH TUNA OR SWORDFISH PROVENCAL

1¾- to 2-lb. slice fresh tuna or sword-fish, 2″ thick	½ cup white wine
	½ teasp. lemon juice
Seasoned salt	1 stalk celery, 3 sprigs parsley, and 1 bay leaf, tied together
Pepper	
¼ cup salad oil	
2 tablesp. minced onion	Pinch dried thyme
	1 tablesp. soft but-ter or margarine
4 tomatoes, peeled, chopped (or 1 cup canned)	1½ teasp. flour
	1 tablesp. bottled capers
2 cloves garlic, minced	1 tablesp. snipped parsley

Start heating oven to 400°F. Sprinkle fish with seasoned salt and pepper; brown on both sides in hot oil in skillet. Remove to a 9″ x 9″ x 2″ baking dish; add onion, next 6 ingredients. Bake, uncovered, 25 min., or till easily flaked with fork, *but still moist.*

Remove fish to heated platter; discard celery, parsley, bay leaf. Pour sauce into skillet; heat. Add butter blended with flour; heat, stirring; pour over fish. Top with capers, parsley. Makes 4 or 5 servings.

FISH STICKS AND CHIPS IBERIA

1 pkg. frozen fish sticks	onion salt
1 9-oz. pkg. frozen French fries	1 tablesp. catchup
	¼ teasp. Tabasco
½ cup mayonnaise	1 tablesp. vinegar
¼ teasp. dry mustard	4 or 5 medium stuffed
Generous sprinkling of garlic salt and	olives, minced
	1 gherkin, minced
	Snipped parsley

Bake fish sticks and French fries at 425°F. until hot. For sauce, combine rest of ingredients, using a little parsley. On platter arrange fish sticks, French fries, bowl of sauce (sprinkle sauce with more parsley). If desired, garnish with lemon slices dipped into paprika. Makes 3 or 4 servings.

LEON'S BAKED STRIPED-BASS FILLETS

2 lb. striped-bass or other fish fillets (list, p. 299)	3 tablesp. butter or margarine
Seasoned salt	2 tomatoes, peeled, sliced, seasoned
Pepper	½ sliced green pepper
1 large onion, thinly sliced	2 teasp. Worcestershire
1 cup white wine	

Day before, or early in the day: Sprinkle fish with seasoned salt and pepper. Place in shallow baking dish; cover with onion slices; pour on wine. Cover; refrigerate.
About 45 min. before serving: Start heating oven to 375°F. Melt butter in large shallow baking pan; lift fish and onion from wine to pan. Top with tomatoes, green pepper. Bake, uncovered, 35 min., or until easily flaked with fork, *but still moist*, basting often with leftover wine mixed with Worcestershire. Makes 5 or 6 servings.

CRISP-COATED FISH FILLETS

1 cup fine cornflake crumbs	1½ lb. haddock, flounder, or sole fillets
1 teasp. monosodium glutamate	½ cup evaporated milk
1 teasp. salt	
⅛ teasp. pepper	

Start heating oven to 375°F. Combine cornflake crumbs, monosodium glutamate, salt, pepper. Dip fish fillets, first into evaporated milk, then in crumb mixture, turning them to coat both sides. Arrange fillets in foil-lined, shallow baking pan. Bake about 20 min., or until easily flaked with fork, *but still moist*. Makes 4 servings.

SO-EASY SALMON THERMIDOR

4 salmon steaks (about 1¼ lb.)	undiluted
	2 tablesp. sherry
½ cup milk	2 hard-cooked eggs, sliced
¼ teasp. salt	
⅛ teasp. pepper	½ cup grated Swiss cheese
1 10½-oz. can condensed cream-of-mushroom soup,	Paprika

About 40 min. before dinner: Start heating oven to 350°F. Place salmon in shallow baking dish; pour on milk; sprinkle with salt, pepper. Bake 30 min., or until salmon flakes, *but is still moist*, when tested with fork.

Meanwhile, in saucepan, stir soup till smooth; add sherry; heat till boiling. When salmon is done, arrange sliced eggs around fish; pour on sauce. Sprinkle with cheese, paprika. Place low under broiler until bubbling hot — about 5 min. Makes 4 servings.

CURRIED HADDOCK FILLETS

2 to 2½ lb. haddock fillets	1 teasp. salt
	Dash pepper
1 cup sliced celery	1 teasp. curry powder
1 cup sliced onions	¾ cup top milk or light cream
3 tablesp. butter or margarine	

Start heating oven to 350°F. Place fillets in greased 12" x 8" x 2" baking dish. Sauté celery and onions in butter 5 min. Stir in salt, pepper, curry; stir in milk gradually. Heat; pour over fish. Bake 30 min., or until easily flaked with fork, *but still moist*. Makes 5 servings.

SEA-FOOD FILLETS

1½ lb. flounder fillets	shrimp soup
¾ teasp. salt	1 cup grated sharp cheese
Dash pepper	
¾ cup milk	3 tablesp. sherry
1 can frozen cream-of-	Paprika

Start heating oven to 350°F. Roll up each of fillets. Stand them up in 10" x 6" x 2" baking dish; sprinkle with salt, pepper. Over fish pour milk. Bake, uncovered, 30 min.; then remove from oven, drain off milk and reserve. Thaw shrimp soup as label directs, mix with reserved milk; heat, stirring, until hot and smooth. Add ¾ cup grated cheese; stir until melted; add sherry. Pour over fish; top with ¼ cup grated cheese, dash of paprika. Brown under broiler. Makes 4 servings.

TOMATOED FILLETS SURPRISE

4 thawed frozen or fresh haddock fillets (about 1¼ lb.)	4 slices process sharp cheese (about ¼ lb.)
Salt and pepper	1 8-oz. can tomato sauce
4 teasp. minced onion	⅔ cup fresh bread crumbs
¼ teasp. dried tarragon	1 tablesp. butter or margarine

1. Start heating oven to 375°F. Wipe fillets with dampened paper towel. Sprinkle lightly with salt, pepper, onion, and tarragon.
2. Place a slice of cheese at end of each fillet; roll up each and fasten with toothpick. Place in 10" x 6" x 2" baking dish; pour tomato sauce over all; sprinkle with crumbs, dot with butter.
3. Bake 30 min., or until easily flaked with fork, moist, and brown. Makes 4 servings.

♣ FOR 2: Halve each ingredient, using ½ cup canned tomato sauce; make and bake as directed, in 8" pie plate.

Broiled to a Turn

EASY BROILED FISH
(*no sticking or breaking; no pan to clean*)

Choose fish:

Order frozen or fresh fish fillets or steaks, or whole fresh fish, with lists below as guides. If frozen, thaw if and as label directs. (See Amounts to Buy, p. 299.)

FILLETS

Bass	Haddock	Pollock
Bluefish	Hake	Red Snapper
Carp	Lingcod	Sole
Catfish	Mackerel	Spanish Mackerel
Cod	Ocean Perch	Whiting
Flounder	Pike	

STEAKS

Bass	Haddock	Red Snapper
Cod	Halibut	Salmon
Fresh Tuna	Muskellunge	Swordfish

DRESSED WHOLE

Bass	Mullet	Smelts
Bluefish	Pike	Spanish Mackerel
Butterfish	Porgy	Trout
Carp	Red Snapper	Whitefish
Catfish	Sea Trout	Whiting
Flounder	Shad	Yellow Pike
Mackerel		

Prepare fish:
1. Preheat broiler 10 min., or as directed.
2. Lay a sheet of heavy-duty foil, a little larger than the fish would cover, over the broiler pan rack; or lay it on a shallow pan like a cookie sheet or jelly-roll pan. If necessary turn up edges all around to hold in juices.
3. Brush area on foil where fish will rest with melted shortening or salad oil. Arrange fish right on foil. Brush with melted butter or margarine or salad oil, then sprinkle with seasoned salt, lemon juice, and perhaps a little dried basil. Or use Butter Baste, p. 299; or bottled Italian salad dressing.

Broil fish:
1. Broil fish, using timetable below as guide, to a crisp brown deliciousness, or until easily flaked with a fork, *but still moist.* If turned, repeat brushing and seasoning on second side.

FILLETS (¼" to 1" thick): Broil 2" from heat, for 6 to 10 min. (don't turn).

STEAKS (½" to 1½" thick): Broil 2" from heat, for 6 to 16 min. (turn once).

DRESSED WHOLE: Broil 3" from heat, if thin; 6" from heat, if thick. Allow 5 min. on one side, then 5 to 8 min. on other.

2. For the last few minutes of broiling, you may arrange tomato halves, halved mushrooms, cooked sweet potatoes, or seedless grapes, brushed and seasoned, around fish.

Serve fish:
1. When fish is broiled, slip foil and all onto warm serving platter (avoid breaking fish); flute foil around edge to form decorative border; garnish fish liberally with parsley or water cress. No platter or pan to wash! Or, if preferred, arrange fish on warm platter.
2. If you own a broil-and-serve platter, use it for both broiling and serving. Or use one of the disposable foil broiler pans which come in small and large sizes.

BARBECUED BROILER TREAT

3 tablesp. salad oil	thawed
1 teasp. dry mustard	3 large fresh mush-
1 teasp. Worcester-	rooms
shire	Salt
½ teasp. salt	Pepper
⅛ teasp. pepper	2 small zucchini
¼ cup catchup	(trim ends; then
1 teasp. lemon juice	halve lengthwise)
1 small onion, thinly	Melted butter or
sliced	margarine
1 tablesp. diced celery	Grated Parmesan
¼ cup water	cheese
1 1-lb. pkg. frozen	Paprika
haddock, just	

Preheat broiler as manufacturer directs. For barbecue sauce, in small saucepan, combine salad oil, dry mustard, Worcestershire, salt, pepper, catchup, lemon juice, onion slices, celery, and water; simmer 5 min.

Meanwhile, cut block of thawed fish into thirds and place on rack of broiler pan. Wash mushrooms; remove and chop stems; mix stems with a little salt and pepper; use to fill cavities of mushroom caps; place on broiler rack beside fish. Place zucchini, with cut sides up, beside mushrooms; draw tines of fork across cut surfaces. Brush mushrooms and zucchini liberally with melted butter. Sprinkle zucchini with salt and pepper, then generously with Parmesan cheese, and lastly with paprika. Spoon barbecue sauce over fish.

Broil all, 2″ to 3″ from heat, basting mushrooms now and then with melted butter, 6 to 10 min., or until fish is easily flaked by fork and zucchini are tender. To serve, arrange on individual plates. Or place broiler rack on board; serve at table. Makes 3 servings.

BROILED FILLETS AU GRATIN

2 10-oz. pkg. frozen,	margarine
or 3 lb. fresh, broc-	2 teasp. lemon juice
coli	½ cup milk
1½ lb. cod or had-	½ lb. process Ched-
dock fillets	dar cheese, grated
2 tablesp. butter or	(2 cups)

Preheat broiler 10 min., or as manufacturer directs. Cook broccoli until just tender. Place fillets, side by side, in greased shallow baking pan (if very thin and small, place two together, sandwich-style). Dot with butter; sprinkle with lemon juice. Broil, 2″ below heat,

without turning, 8 to 10 min., or until easily flaked with fork, *but still moist.*

Meanwhile, in double boiler, heat milk with cheese until a smooth sauce. Transfer fish to 12″ x 8″ x 2″ baking dish; arrange broccoli over fish; pour sauce over all. Broil low in broiler until golden. Makes 6 servings.

A LA FLORENTINE: For broccoli, substitute 2 10-oz. pkg. frozen chopped spinach; cook; then add ¼ cup minced onion, sautéed till tender in 2 tablesp. butter or margarine.

SUMMER STYLE: For broccoli, substitute 2 10-oz. pkg. frozen, or 2½ lb. fresh, asparagus, cooked.

BROILED HERB SALMON STEAKS

Order 2 fresh salmon steaks, ¾″ thick. About 50 min. before serving, in shallow dish, combine 1 clove garlic, minced, ¼ cup salad oil, 3 tablesp. lemon juice, ½ teasp. each dried thyme and salt. Let fish stand in this marinade 30 min., in refrigerator, turning occasionally.

Preheat broiler 10 min., or as manufacturer directs. Broil salmon, 2″ from heat, about 3 min. on each side, or until easily flaked with fork. Makes 4 servings.

P.S. To cook outdoors, grill marinated fish in folding wire broiler, close to hot coals, as above.

MIXED FISH GRILL

Be smart! Broil the whole main course — fish, vegetable, and garnish — at the same time. Turn to Mixed Grill, p. 180, for suggestions.

Golden Fried Fish

SAUTEED OR PAN-FRIED FISH

The family's going to love your pan-fried fish if you'll just remember three things:

1. To cook it last, when the rest of dinner is almost ready.

2. Not to overcook it — 2 or 3 min. on each side is usually enough.

3. To serve it immediately, while it's still crisp, juicy, and hot.

And now for the few easy how to's which you will want to follow in sautéing it.

Choose one of these fish:

Order frozen or fresh fish fillets or steaks,

or dressed small whole fish from list below. (See Amount to Buy, p. 299.) Thaw if and as label directs.

FILLETS OR STEAKS

Cod	Ocean Perch	Shad (and/or
Flounder	Pickerel	Shad roe)
Haddock	Pollock	Sole
Halibut	Red Snapper	Swordfish
		Tuna

DRESSED SMALL FISH

Bass	Pike	Sunfish
Butterfish	Pompano	Trout
Lake Herring	Porgy	Whitefish
Mackerel	Sand Dab	Whiting
Perch	Smelts	

Prepare fish this way:

1. Dip fish into one of these: milk, evaporated milk, cold water, French dressing, or an egg, beaten with 2 tablesp. water or white wine.
2. Now sprinkle fish well with seasoned salt, some monosodium glutamate, or salt, then with pepper, seasoned pepper, or paprika.
3. Then coat each piece with one or a blend of two of these:

Flour	Crushed corn or wheat
Corn meal	cereal flakes
Pancake mix	Packaged dried bread
Biscuit mix	or cracker crumbs
Ready-mixed bread-	
ing	

Sauté fish as follows:

1. In a large skillet, or 2 skillets, if you're sautéing a large amount of fish, heat enough shortening, salad oil, butter, margarine, or bacon fat to just cover bottom; *never let fat smoke.*
2. Arrange fish in skillet; quickly sauté over moderate heat till a crisp golden on underside — about 2 or 3 min.
3. Then, with broad spatula, carefully turn fish and quickly brown other side — about 2 or 3 min. *Don't let fish get dry* — it should be easily flaked with fork, *but still moist.*
4. Drain fish on paper toweling; arrange at once on heated platter.

Serve fish in one of these ways:

1. Topped with snipped parsley, mint, or chives; or a sprinkle of fresh or dried basil, rosemary, dill, or tarragon. Or garnished with lemon or lime wedges.

2. Or serve with one of Just for Fish Sauces, p. 529.
3. Or top with 1/4 cup melted butter or margarine plus a little Tabasco, Worcestershire, prepared mustard, horse-radish, or catchup; or plus chopped stuffed or ripe olives, capers, or snipped chives.
4. Or in skillet melt 1/4 cup butter or margarine; in it toast 1/4 cup slivered almonds until golden. Then add 1/4 cup white wine and a pinch of dried tarragon. Heat and pour over fish.

GOLDEN FISH FILLETS WITH ONIONS

Butter or margarine	6 fillets of sole or
1 large onion, sliced	flounder (about
1/4 cup all-purpose	2 lb.)
flour	1/4 cup lemon juice
1 teasp. salt	1/2 teasp. Worcester-
1/4 teasp. pepper	shire
1/4 teasp. paprika	Water cress
	Lemon wedges

About 45 min. before serving:

1. In 2 tablesp. butter or margarine, in large skillet, sauté onion till tender; remove to platter; keep warm.
2. Meanwhile, combine flour with salt, pepper, paprika. In it lay sole or flounder fillets, halved crosswise; turn until coated.
3. In 1/4 cup butter or margarine in same skillet, over medium heat, sauté 6 fish fillet halves till golden, turning once; remove to heated large platter. Repeat with remaining 6 fish fillet halves.
4. To butter mixture left in skillet, add lemon juice, Worcestershire; bring to boil, while stirring; pour over fish. Top with sautéed onion; garnish with water cress and lemon wedges. Nice with parsleyed new potatoes. Makes 6 servings.

PARMESAN FISH FILLETS

6 tablesp. grated Par-	3 tablesp. butter or
mesan cheese	margarine
3 tablesp. flour	2 tablesp. snipped
1 to 1 1/2 lb. fish fillets	parsley

1. In shallow dish, combine cheese with flour. Dip fish into mixture, coating it on all sides.
2. In hot butter, in skillet, sauté fish over moderate heat until golden on both sides and easily flaked with fork — about 4 to 6 min. altogether.

3. Remove fish to warm platter; pour fat from skillet over fish; sprinkle with parsley. Nice with lemon wedges. Makes 4 servings.

♣ FOR 2: Make half recipe, but use 2 tablesp. butter.

SAUTEED KIPPERED HERRING

Use 1 smoked kippered herring for each serving. Soak herring in boiling water to cover 10 min.; drain; dry. In a little hot salad oil in skillet, sauté herring about 5 min., turning once.

Serve with Lemon Butter Sauce, p. 533.

MARGARET'S FRIED FISH
(Pesce Fritto alla Margherita)

¼ cup olive or salad oil	2 8-oz. cans tomato sauce
¼ cup butter or margarine	1 teasp. dried orégano
1½ lb. fillets of sole or flounder	2 tablesp. snipped parsley

1. In hot oil and butter in large skillet, slowly sauté fish about 5 min. on each side; remove to platter.
2. Into fat left in skillet, stir tomato sauce, orégano, parsley, till blended. Return fish to sauce. Simmer, uncovered, 10 min., occasionally basting with sauce. Nice over hot cooked spaghetti or mashed potatoes. Makes 4 servings.

♣ FOR 2: Halve recipe, making as above.

SHALLOW-FRIED FISH

Shallow-frying is so named in contrast to deep-frying. It produces the same crisp crust, but you use a deep skillet instead of a deep kettle and so it's easier.

1. Sprinkle cut-up fish fillets or steaks, or dressed small fish, as listed in Sautéed Fish, p. 304, with salt. Dip them into 1 egg, beaten with 2 tablesp. cold water, then into packaged dried bread crumbs or corn meal.
2. In deep skillet or saucepan, heat 1″ to 1½″ salad oil or shortening (not butter or margarine) to 370°F. on deep-fat thermometer, or till hot enough to brown a 1″ bread square in 1 min. (See Shallow-Frying, p. 7.)
3. With broad spatula or pancake turner, lower pieces of fish, one by one, into hot fat — as many pieces as will not crowd pan.

4. Fry quickly until golden on underside — about 2 to 4 min.; then turn carefully and brown similarly on second side.
5. When easily flaked with fork, *but still moist*, lift out carefully with broad spatula onto paper toweling to drain.
6. Serve at once, piping hot, with sprinkle of snipped parsley and paprika, and garnish of lemon wedges. Or pass tartar sauce. Always nice with mashed potatoes and coleslaw or a leafy green vegetable.

OVEN-FRIED FISH

It's hard to believe — but it's true. With this method there's no pot watching, no turning, and no odor. Try it.

1. Choose fillets, steaks, or dressed small fish as listed in Sautéed Fish, p. 305.
2. Mix ¼ cup milk or evaporated milk, and 2 teasp. salt with a bit of dried thyme, tarragon, dill, or rosemary, or minced onion or garlic or Tabasco in shallow dish.
3. In second dish, combine ½ cup packaged dried bread crumbs or crushed corn or wheat flakes with ½ teasp. paprika and a little dry mustard, grated cheese, chili powder, or snipped parsley.
4. Start heating oven to 500°F. Now, with one hand, dip each piece of fish into milk, then with other hand roll it in crumbs, arranging, side by side, in greased shallow baking dish, lined with foil, if desired.
5. Drizzle a little salad oil or melted butter or margarine onto fish. Then bake 12 to 15 min., or until golden and easily flaked with a fork — *but still moist*.
6. Serve on heated platter "as is" or with one of Just for Fish Sauces, p. 529.

Perfect Poached Fish

Connoisseurs extol the delicate flavor of fish cooked this way. And any homemaker can do it!

Three Points to Remember:

Poach your fish in a large skillet, in which you can also serve it. This removes the main hazard of the fillets breaking when moved from pan to platter.

Secondly, use a circle of wax paper with a

small hole in the center as a cover. Then you can cook the fillets without drowning them in liquid.

Thirdly, choose a soft fish like flounder, Boston sole, ocean perch, haddock, or cod, if you can poach and serve in the same skillet. Halibut, bass, English sole, and pompano are firm enough to poach in a skillet and then transfer to a platter, if you prefer.

FILLETS OF FISH VERONIQUE
(poached fish with grapes)

Poach fish as in Fillets of Fish Dugléré, right, omitting tomatoes, parsley; increase wine to ½ cup. Complete as in Skillet Style, right, adding 2 cups fresh seedless grapes after sauce has thickened. Or if Platter Style, right, place grapes around fish; fold 2 tablesp. cream, whipped, into sauce just before pouring over fish.

POACHED FISH, U.S.A.
(nice for fish fillets or steaks, 1" thick)

To Buy: Use same varieties of fish fillets or steak as for Easy Broiled Fish, p. 303.

To Poach: Place fillets or steaks in skillet with enough boiling water to just barely cover. Season water with snipped parsley, minced celery or onion, a little garlic, white wine, or a few whole black peppers. Simmer, covered, until fish is easily flaked with a fork, *but still moist* — 10 min. or less.

To serve: Remove fish to heated platter; sprinkle with salt; serve at once, with one of Just for Fish Sauces, p. 529.

POACHED SHAD ROE

Cover shad roe with boiling water to which you have added 3 tablesp. lemon juice, ½ teasp. salt, and, if desired, a little pickling spice. Simmer about 15 min., or until white and firm. Drain, cover with cold water, cool, and drain again. Remove membrane or not, as desired.

STEAMED FISH, NEW ENGLAND STYLE
(nice for large chunks of fish like salmon)

Use deep saucepan, Dutch oven, or pressure cooker with greased rack in bottom. Fill with 1½" to 2" water, adding snipped parsley, minced celery, or onion, a little garlic or white

wine, or a few whole black peppers. When water boils, place chunk of fish (you may wrap it in cheesecloth) on rack; cover tightly. (If using pressure cooker, use cover without pressure gauge.) Steam about 1 min. per ounce, or until easily flaked with fork, *but still moist,* turning once if fish is very thick.

To serve, lift fish to warm platter; sprinkle with salt; serve with one of Just for Fish Sauces, p. 529. Or chill; serve with Quick Tartar Sauce, p. 530. Or flake for salads, sandwiches, etc.

FILLETS OF FISH DUGLERE
(superb poached fish with tomato)

1½ lb. thawed frozen or fresh fish fillets*	(optional) ¾ cup well-drained canned tomatoes
1 teasp. salt	Snipped parsley
⅛ teasp. pepper	¼ cup white wine;
1 clove garlic (optional)	or ¼ cup water plus ½ teasp. lemon
1 tablesp. butter or margarine	juice
1 medium onion, minced	¼ cup light cream 1 tablesp. soft butter or margarine
2 shallots, minced	1 teasp. flour

To Poach:

1. Set out large skillet (about 10") with cover. Tear or cut circle of wax paper to fit skillet; tear small hole in center; set aside. Sprinkle fish with salt and pepper. Stick toothpick in garlic.
2. Melt 1 tablesp. butter in skillet; add onion, shallots, garlic; top with fish, then tomatoes, then 1 tablesp. snipped parsley; pour in wine. Place paper circle on fish.
3. Bring to boil; cover; cook over high heat 5 to 10 min, or until easily flaked with fork *but still moist.* Remove cover, paper, garlic.
4. Complete as in Skillet or Platter Style, following. Makes 4 servings.

SKILLET STYLE: Pour cream around fish. Mix 1 tablesp. butter with flour; stir into cream; move skillet in circular motion to combine and thicken sauce. Spoon some sauce onto fish; sprinkle with parsley. Serve from skillet.

PLATTER STYLE: Gently remove fish, with tomatoes on top, to broil-and-serve platter or shallow casserole. Then, into skillet, pour cream mixed with 1 egg yolk, then butter-flour mixture. Cook over medium heat, stirring, till thickened; taste; add seasoning if needed. Pour sauce over fish; then, if desired, broil until just golden.

See list under Perfect Poached Fish, p. 307.

OUR BEST CREAMED FISH

2 cups flaked canned or cooked tuna, salmon, cod, halibut, finnan haddie, etc.	2 cups milk
	2 eggs, beaten
	½ teasp. salt (omit with finnan haddie)
¼ cup butter or margarine	⅛ teasp. pepper
¼ cup flour	2 tablesp. chopped green pepper

Flake fish. In saucepan, melt butter; stir in flour. Add milk; cook slowly, stirring, until thickened. Add fish; heat. Add eggs; heat quickly, stirring; then add rest of ingredients.

Serve Over:

1. Hot fluffy rice tossed with grated carrot and snipped parsley
2. Buttered noodles, plus a little grated cheese; garlic, celery, or onion salt; dried thyme; or few poppy seeds
3. Hot toast, cut into rounds, squares, triangles, or fingers and brushed lightly with melted butter or margarine. Sprinkle with a little curry powder; garlic, onion, or celery salt; or dried herb. Or spread lightly with prepared mustard, horse-radish, or catchup
4. Heated crackers, sprinkled with grated cheese if desired
5. Cooked frozen or canned mixed vegetables, or leftover cooked vegetables
6. Mashed or baked potatoes

CREAMED SHRIMP, CRAB, LOBSTER, OR SCALLOPS: For fish, substitute 2 cups cut-up, cleaned, cooked or canned shrimp; flaked, cooked or canned crab or lobster meat, well drained; or cooked scallops; or a mixture of these.

PANTRY SHELF SPECIALS

Canned Tuna

Canned tuna, America's most popular canned sea food, not only offers a delicious meal at minimum cost and time, but is an excellent source of the same fine protein you find in meats, eggs, cheese, and poultry.

Kinds Canned:

Albacore, prized for its white meat; Yellowfin, largest in size and abundance; Skipjack, the smallest, but second only to Yellowfin in the canned pack; and Bluefin, a favorite of sportsmen.

Styles of Packs:

SOLID PACK — in which free flakes shall not exceed 18 per cent. Ideal for cold plates, etc.

CHUNKS — pieces, not less than 50 per cent of which, by weight, are retained in a ½" mesh screen. Fine for salads and other dishes where small pieces are desirable.

FLAKES — pieces, more than 50 per cent of the weight of which will pass through a ½" mesh screen.

GRATED — particles, not a paste, which pass through a ½" mesh screen. Excellent for sandwich fillings, canapés, etc.

Can Sizes:

Tuna is packed in 3¼- to 3½-oz., 6½- to 7-oz., 9¼-oz., and 12½- to 13-oz. cans. The 6½- to 7-oz. size can represents most of the pack.

Liquid They're Packed In:

Most domestic tuna is packed in such vegetable oils as corn, cottonseed, or soy oil. Some also comes in vegetable broth. Dietetic tuna, with its low salt content, is packed in distilled water, with no salt added.

TUNA TETRAZZINI

½ 8-oz. pkg. spaghettini	1 8-oz. pkg. process Cheddar cheese, grated
3 tablesp. bottled garlic spread	½ teasp. seasoned salt
¼ cup all-purpose flour	¼ teasp. pepper
1 cup milk	2 6½- or 7-oz. cans tuna, drained
¼ cup sherry	2 tablesp. grated Parmesan cheese
2 3- or 4-oz. cans button mushrooms	

About 1 hr. before serving:

1. Cook spaghettini as directed on package; drain and set aside.
2. In double boiler, over boiling water, melt garlic spread; stir in flour. Then add milk, a little at a time; sherry; and ½ cup liquid drained from mushrooms. Cook this sauce till thickened, while stirring.
3. Start heating oven to 350°F. To sauce, add

cheese, seasoned salt, pepper; stir till cheese is melted; then stir in spaghettini, tuna, and mushrooms. Pour into 1½-qt. shallow baking dish; sprinkle with Parmesan cheese. Bake 20 min., or till light golden. Makes 6 servings.

TUNA-CORN SAUTE

About 15 min. before serving: In 2 tablesp. butter or margarine, sauté 1 green pepper, finely minced, until tender-crisp. Then add 2 12-oz. cans whole-kernel corn, drained; ½ cup heavy cream; 1 teasp. salt; and ¼ teasp. pepper. Next, add 2 6½- or 7-oz. cans tuna, drained, in large chunks, and heat. Sprinkle with paprika. Serve as is, or heap on toast or on heated frozen potato patties. Makes 6 servings.

TUNA-CASHEW CASSEROLE

1 3-oz. jar chow-mein noodles	tuna (1 cup)
1 10½-oz. can condensed cream-of-mushroom soup, undiluted	¼ lb. cashew nuts, salted or unsalted
	1 cup finely diced celery
¼ cup water	¼ cup minced onion
1 6½- or 7-oz. can	Dash pepper
	Salt

Start heating oven to 325°F. Set aside ½ cup chow-mein noodles. In 1½-qt. casserole, combine rest of noodles with soup, water, tuna, nuts, celery, onion, pepper. Taste; add salt if nuts were unsalted. Sprinkle reserved noodles over top. Bake, uncovered, 40 min. Makes 5 servings.

TOPSY-TURVY TUNA-LEMON PIE

1 lemon, sliced, unpeeled	½ teasp. dry mustard
1 6½- or 7-oz. can tuna (1 cup)	2 tablesp. lemon juice
	⅓ cup catchup
2 tablesp. minced onion	1 egg, well beaten
1 tablesp. minced green pepper	About ¼ lb. sliced process Cheddar cheese
¼ cup fresh bread crumbs	6 tablesp. milk
	1 cup packaged biscuit mix

Start heating oven to 400°F. Grease 8″ round shallow casserole. Arrange lemon slices in bottom of dish. Mix tuna, onion, green pepper, crumbs, mustard, lemon juice, catchup, egg; spread over lemon slices. Top with cheese slices. With fork, stir milk into biscuit mix to make soft dough. Spread dough over cheese layer.

Bake, uncovered, 15 to 20 min., or until light brown. Loosen edges; quickly invert onto serving dish; cut into wedges.

Serve hot, as is or with Thin White Sauce, p. 533. Makes 6 to 8 servings.

TUNA-STUFFED ACORN SQUASH

2 medium acorn squash	1 teasp. salt
Butter or margarine	¼ teasp. pepper
¼ cup minced onion	¼ teasp. dried thyme
¼ cup minced celery	Packaged dried bread crumbs
1 6½- or 7-oz can tuna, drained	Paprika

About 1 hr. before serving:
1. Start heating oven to 400°F.
2. Cut washed squash in half lengthwise; remove seeds.
3. Spread 1 tablesp. butter or margarine on all cut surfaces of squash halves; place, cut side down, in shallow baking dish. Bake 30 to 40 min., or until very tender. Remove from oven; scoop cooked squash from shells.
4. Mash squash, then combine with onion, celery, 1 tablesp. melted butter or margarine, tuna, salt, pepper, and thyme; mix well.
5. Pile tuna-squash mixture lightly in shells. Sprinkle lightly with bread crumbs and 2 tablesp. melted butter; dust with paprika.
6. Return to oven and bake 10 min. Makes 4 servings.

CURRY OF THE SEAS

5 tablesp. butter or margarine	1 can chicken broth, undiluted
½ cup minced onion	2 cups milk
¼ cup minced green pepper	4 6½- or 7-oz. cans tuna, drained
⅓ cup flour	2 cups cooked or canned shrimp, drained
1 tablesp. curry powder	
¼ teasp. salt	3 cups hot cooked rice
¼ teasp. ground ginger	

1. In hot butter, in blazer of chafing dish, over direct heat, sauté onion and green pepper until golden. Stir in flour, curry powder, salt, ginger.

2. Gradually stir in broth and milk; cook, stirring, until thickened. Add tuna in large chunks, then shrimp; mix gently. Heat.

3. Serve with rice and such curry accompaniments as chutney, shredded fresh or flaked coconut, salted peanuts, drained canned pineapple chunks, raisins if desired. Makes 8 servings.

SHERRY TUNA

2 6½- or 7-oz. cans tuna, well drained (2 cups)	⅛ teasp. pepper
½ teasp. coarsely grated lemon rind	1 tablesp. butter or margarine
1 tablesp. lemon juice	2 teasp. flour
⅓ cup sherry or dry sauterne	1 tablesp. snipped parsley
	½ cup ripe olives, drained

About 30 min. before serving: In saucepan, gently heat together tuna, lemon rind, lemon juice, sherry, pepper.

Meanwhile, in small saucepan, melt butter; stir in flour; cook till bubbling hot and lightly browned. Drain hot liquid from tuna into measuring cup; add more sherry, if necessary, to make ½ cup; add to flour mixture; cook, stirring, until smooth and thickened.

Turn hot tuna into serving or chafing dish; pour sauce over tuna. Sprinkle with parsley; garnish with olives. Makes 4 servings.

PANTRY TUNA SCALLOP

1 4½- or 5⅓-oz. pkg. scalloped potatoes with seasonings	2 6½- or 7-oz. cans tuna
1 cup thinly sliced onions	½ cup mayonnaise or cooked salad dressing
3 tablesp. butter or margarine	½ cup grated process Cheddar cheese
3 tablesp. flour	½ teasp. Tabasco
½ teasp. salt	1 teasp. prepared mustard
⅛ teasp. pepper	Paprika
1¼ cups milk	

About 1 hr. before serving:

1. In 2-qt. casserole, prepare potatoes for baking as label directs, adding the onions. Then bake at indicated oven temperature about 15 to 25 min., or until completely hot; remove from oven; stir with fork.

2. Meanwhile, in saucepan, over low heat, melt butter; stir in flour, salt, and pepper un-

til well blended. Stir in milk gradually; cook, while stirring, until thickened and smooth; fold in drained tuna.

3. Pour tuna mixture over potatoes. Spread with combined mayonnaise, cheese, Tabasco, and mustard.

4. Return to oven. Bake, uncovered, 10 to 15 min. longer, or until hot and bubbly. *Let cool 10 min.;* sprinkle with paprika; serve. Makes 4 to 6 delicious servings.

BAKED TUNA SANDWICHES

1 can refrigerated biscuits	sharp Cheddar cheese
1 6½- or 7-oz. can tuna (1 cup)	3 tablesp. mayonnaise
½ cup diced natural	1 tablesp. melted butter or margarine

Pat each biscuit into thin 3½" x 4" oval. Arrange half of biscuits on greased cookie sheet. Mix tuna, cheese, mayonnaise. Spread on biscuits on cookie sheet. Top with remaining biscuits, pressing edges together. Brush tops with melted butter. Start heating oven to 425°F. Let biscuits stand 15 to 20 min. Then bake about 15 to 20 min., or until browned. Perfect for Sunday-night supper, with marinated tomatoes and cucumbers. Makes 5 servings.

TUNA CORN-BREAD PIE

12 thin lemon slices	1 10½-oz. can condensed cream-of-mushroom soup, undiluted
1 6½- or 7-oz. can tuna	
½ cup fresh bread crumbs	1 pkg. corn-muffin or corn-bread mix
2 tablesp. minced onion	Snipped parsley
2 eggs, beaten	

About 45 min. before serving:

1. Arrange lemon slices on bottom of lightly greased 10" pie plate.

2. Drain, then flake, tuna; blend well with bread crumbs, onion, eggs, and soup. Spoon into pie plate over lemon slices.

3. Start heating oven to 400°F. Prepare corn-muffin mix as label directs, then spoon gently over tuna mixture until level with inner edge of pie-plate rim (turn any excess into a custard cup). Bake 30 min., or until golden. Let cool 10 min.

4. Now, with spatula, loosen sides of pie. Invert serving dish on top of pie, then invert

Roast-Beef Hearty Party Salad, p. 459

both, unmolding pie, bottom side up. Sprinkle with snipped parsley. Makes 4 or 5 servings.

CREAMED TUNA SUPREME

2 6½- or 7-oz. cans tuna, flaked	undiluted
2 tablesp. cut-up canned pimento	¾ cup milk
	6 eggs, separated
2 10½ oz. cans condensed cream-of-mushroom soup,	⅛ teasp. salt
	1 tablesp. heavy cream
	⅛ teasp. pepper

Start heating oven to 400°F. Fold tuna and pimento into combined soup and milk. Pour into a greased 12″ x 8″ x 2″ baking dish. Bake until bubbling hot — about 12 min. Meanwhile, beat egg whites with salt until they peak when beater is withdrawn. Beat egg yolks well, until light and fluffy; beat in cream, pepper. Fold whites into yolks, then pour this omeletlike mixture over hot tuna. Return to 400°F. oven for 15 min., or until firm when tested with cake tester. *Serve at once* in baking dish. Makes 6 to 8 servings.

♣ FOR 2: Halve ingredients; make as directed in 10″ x 6″ x 2″ dish.

TUNA SUPPER CASSEROLE

1 10-oz. pkg. frozen spinach; or 1 lb. fresh spinach, washed	3 tablesp. butter or margarine
	1 tablesp. minced onion
1 6½- or 7-oz. can solid-pack tuna (1 cup)	2 tablesp. flour
	½ teasp. salt
	⅛ teasp. pepper
1 3- or 4-oz. can sliced mushrooms	1 bay leaf, crushed
	1 egg, slightly beaten
2 tablesp. lemon juice	

Start heating oven to 350°F. If using frozen spinach, cook as package directs; if fresh, cook in ½″ boiling water 6 to 10 min., or until tender-crisp. Drain spinach well; season. Drain excess oil from tuna. Drain mushrooms; to mushroom liquid, add lemon juice, then enough water to make 1 cup liquid. In small saucepan, melt 2 tablesp. butter; blend in minced onion, flour, salt, pepper, and bay leaf; then blend in mushroom liquid. Cook, stirring, until thick and smooth. Beat sauce into egg; then add mushrooms. Arrange spinach in 1½-qt. casserole; top with tuna in big chunks; then top with sauce. Dot with 1 tablesp. butter. Bake 30 min. Makes 4 servings.

TUNA PARTY PILAF

2 6½- or 7-oz. cans tuna	½ cup sliced Brazil nuts
1 cup sliced celery	1 teasp. salt
⅓ cup minced onion	½ teasp. monosodium glutamate
1 large green pepper	
3 cups cooked rice	¼ teasp. pepper
⅓ cup diced canned pimento	1 teasp. dried rosemary
1 3- or 4-oz. can sliced mushrooms	1 teasp. dried marjoram

About 15 min. before serving:

1. Drain oil from tuna into skillet; heat. Add celery, onion, green pepper in slivers; cook about 3 min., or till tender-crisp.
2. Add tuna, rice, pimento, mushrooms with liquid, Brazil nuts, salt, monosodium glutamate, pepper, rosemary, and marjoram. Heat to serving temperature, then serve. Makes 4 to 6 servings.

QUICK CURRIED TUNA

1 10½-oz. can condensed cream-of-mushroom soup, undiluted	1 teasp. curry powder
	1 6½- or 7-oz. can tuna, coarsely flaked
⅓ cup milk	4 buttered toast slices

Into soup, in a saucepan, stir milk and curry powder. Add tuna; heat. Serve on buttered toast or hot rice. Makes 4 servings.

SKILLET TUNA CASSEROLE

1 10½-oz. can condensed tomato soup, undiluted	¼ teasp. dried marjoram
	2 6½- or 7-oz. cans tuna, drained and flaked
¾ cup water	
½ cup packaged pre-cooked rice	
¼ cup instant minced onion	4 packaged process Cheddar-cheese slices
⅓ cup chopped green peppers	⅓ cup ripe olives, quartered
¼ teasp. salt	

1. In medium skillet, heat tomato soup with water to boiling.
2. Stir in rice, onion, green peppers, salt, and marjoram. Remove skillet from heat; cover and let stand 5 min.
3. Remove cover; fold in tuna. Top with cheese slices, cut into thin strips, and olive

pieces. Cover; heat gently until cheese melts. Nice with green beans with mushrooms. Makes 4 or 5 servings.

CRUNCHY TUNA-RICE CONES

Butter or margarine	Lemon juice
2 tablesp. all-purpose flour	Granulated or brown sugar
½ cup milk	2 egg whites, slightly beaten
2 egg yolks, slightly beaten	1¼ cups crushed cornflakes
¼ cup grated process Cheddar cheese	Salad oil or fat
2 cups cooked rice	2 10-oz. pkg. frozen broccoli*
1 6½- or 7-oz. can tuna, drained, flaked	1 10½-oz. can condensed cream-of-mushroom soup, undiluted
1 teasp. salt	
5 canned pineapple slices, drained	Paprika (optional)

Day before or early on the day:

1. In saucepan, over low heat, melt 2 tablesp. butter. Stir in flour till blended, then milk. Cook till a thickened, smooth sauce; pour into large bowl.
2. Into sauce, stir egg yolks, cheese, rice, tuna, salt; refrigerate.

About 1 hr. before serving:

1. Place pineapple slices on cookie sheet; sprinkle with lemon juice; brush with some melted butter; sprinkle with sugar.
2. Shape tuna mixture into 5 cones. Dip each in egg whites, then roll in cornflakes till coated.
3. In large deep skillet, heat 1½″ salad oil to 350°F. on deep-fat thermometer. Preheat broiler as directed.
4. Fry cones, all at one time, in hot oil till golden brown; drain on paper towels; keep warm.
5. Meanwhile, cook broccoli as label directs. Also broil pineapple slices, 3″ to 4″ from heat, 8 min., or till golden brown. Heat mushroom soup.
6. On warm large platter, arrange border of pineapple slices, then top each with a cone, spoon on some of mushroom soup, sprinkle with paprika. Then arrange broccoli in center. Pass remaining mushroom soup. Makes 4 to 5 servings.

Another vegetable may be substituted.

COMPANY TUNA-RICE CONES: Double ingredients above, then proceed as directed, making 10 cones and frying 4 or 5 of them at a time. Makes 8 to 10 servings.

SCALLOPED POTATOES AND TUNA

Add two layers of canned tuna to your scalloped potatoes; lay four overlapping tomato slices on top. Then bake as usual.

Canned Salmon

Canned salmon, another pantry shelf favorite, comes in three can sizes: 1 lb., 7¾ oz., and 3¾ oz.

Always check the can label for the variety best suited to your needs, using guide below:

1. *For salads, canapés, or open-face sandwiches* in which a rich salmon color and large firm flakes are important, choose:

Sockeye	Blueback	Coho
Red	Medium Red	Silver

2. *For closed sandwiches or creamed salmon dishes* choose Chinook or King Salmon. Both of these range in color from deep salmon to light pink and are a good buy.

3. *For delicate soups or bisques* Pink Salmon is especially suitable in both color and flake.

4. *For croquettes, fish cakes, casseroles, and other dishes* where color is not important, try Chum or Keta. They're light pink and have large, coarse flakes.

CHEESE-SALMON BAKE

2 tablesp. butter or margarine	noodles (2 cups)
2 tablesp. flour	½ lb. process sharp Cheddar cheese, grated
1 cup milk	
1 1-lb. can salmon, drained and flaked	1 teasp. salt
½ 8-oz. pkg. medium	⅛ teasp. pepper

1. Start heating oven to 375°F. Grease a 1-qt. casserole.
2. In saucepan, melt butter; add flour, stirring until blended, smooth. Slowly add milk, stirring constantly to avoid lumps. Cook, stirring, until smooth and thickened.
3. To salmon, add uncooked noodles, cheese, salt, pepper, and sauce; combine thoroughly. Pour into casserole. Bake 30 min., or until set. Makes 4 servings.

TUCKER SALMON PIE

2 1-lb. cans red sal-
mon
2 cups milk
4 eggs, slightly beaten
1 cup fresh bread
crumbs

1 teasp. grated onion
½ teasp. salt
2 tablesp. snipped
parsley
2 teasp. lemon juice

1. *About 1¼ hr. before dinner:* Start heating oven to 375°F. Grease well 10″ x 5″ x 3″
loaf pan.
2. Drain salmon; to salmon liquid, add
enough milk to make 2 cups liquid. Flake
salmon. Add liquid, rest of ingredients; mix
lightly.
3. Turn into loaf pan. Bake in loaf pan 1 hr.
5 min.; serve sliced. Makes 8 servings.

For 4 servings: Halve all ingredients, making
as above. Bake in 8″ pie plate 45 min. Serve
in 4 wedges.

QUICK SALMON PLATTER

1 1-lb. can salmon
(2 cups)
2 tablesp. butter or
margarine
2 tablesp. flour
¼ teasp. dry mustard
⅛ teasp. salt

⅛ teasp. Tabasco
1 cup milk
½ cup grated process
Cheddar cheese
Hot cooked, seasoned
broccoli, green
beans, or asparagus

Heat salmon gently in its own liquid. Meanwhile, melt butter; add flour, mustard, salt,
Tabasco; stir until smooth. Add milk; cook,
stirring, until mixture thickens and comes to
boil. Remove from heat. Add cheese; stir until melted. Arrange salmon, in large pieces,
on hot platter, with broccoli around it. Serve
with sauce. Makes 4 servings.

SALMON LOAF, WEST-COAST STYLE

1 1-lb. can salmon
(2 cups)
¾ cup fresh bread
crumbs
1 egg, slightly beaten
¾ cup milk
2 tablesp. minced
onion

Salt
⅛ teasp. pepper
2 tablesp. melted but-
ter or margarine
3 tablesp. lemon juice
¼ cup melted butter
or margarine
¼ cup lemon juice

Start heating oven to 350°F. To drained salmon, add bread crumbs, egg, milk, onion,
½ teasp. salt, pepper, 2 tablesp. butter, 3
tablesp. lemon juice; toss with fork. Turn into
greased 9″ x 5″ x 3″ loaf pan. Bake 40 to

55 min., or until done. Meanwhile, for sauce,
combine ¼ cup melted butter, ¼ cup lemon
juice, ⅛ teasp. salt.
To serve: Pour sauce over salmon in pan. Or
serve loaf and sauce separately. Makes 4 servings.

SALMON SCALLOP DIVAN

1 10-oz. pkg. frozen
broccoli, thawed
just enough to sep-
arate
3 tablesp. butter or
margarine
3 tablesp. flour
½ teasp. salt
⅛ teasp. pepper
2 cups liquefied non-
fat dry milk
1 1-lb.-4-oz. can to-

matoes, drained
½ cup grated process
sharp Cheddar
cheese
1½ cups day-old
bread crumbs
1 1-lb. can Chum sal-
mon, in large
chunks
2 hard-cooked eggs,
sliced lengthwise

Start heating oven to 375°F. Place broccoli in
2-qt. casserole; cover; then put in oven to bake
while preparing rest of dish — about 10 min.
In saucepan, melt butter; blend in flour, salt,
and pepper, then milk. Cook, stirring, until
thickened and smooth; remove from heat.
Carefully fold in tomatoes, cheese, and bread
crumbs. Remove casserole from oven; arrange
salmon over broccoli; then pour on tomato
mixture. Arrange egg slices on top, pressing
them down into sauce. Bake 25 min. Makes 4
servings.

SALMON LOAF SUPREME

2 cups fresh bread
crumbs
½ cup milk
2 eggs, well beaten
½ teasp. salt
¼ teasp. Tabasco
¼ teasp. monosodium
glutamate

¼ teasp. poultry
seasoning
1 1-lb. can red sal-
mon, drained
Speedy Pickled
Peaches, p. 433
Creamy Pea and Scal-
lion Sauce, p. 314

About 1 hr. before serving:
1. Start heating oven to 375°F. In large
bowl, with fork, combine bread crumbs, milk,
eggs, salt, Tabasco, monosodium glutamate,
and poultry seasoning, until mixed.
2. Add chunks of salmon; with fork, mix well.
Lightly turn into greased 9″ x 5″ x 3″ loaf pan;
smooth off the top.
3. Bake 45 min., or until firm in center. Turn
out, place right side up, on heated platter.

4. Serve, sliced, with peaches as the garnish, and Creamy Pea and Scallion Sauce over each slice. Makes 4 servings.

CREAMY PEA AND SCALLION SAUCE: In saucepan, over low heat, melt 2 tablesp. butter or margarine; stir in 2 tablesp. flour, speck pepper, and ½ teasp. salt until blended and smooth. Slowly add 2 cups milk, stirring constantly to avoid lumps. Cook, stirring, until smooth and thickened; then stir in 2 cups hot, drained cooked or canned peas and ⅓ cup snipped scallions or minced onions. Serve hot, as sauce, over Salmon Loaf Supreme. Makes 2 cups.

Other Canned Fish Favorites

Canned sardines, those little fish of the sea which we enjoy as hors d'oeuvres and in sandwiches and other hearties, come from Maine, where they are packed in vegetable oil, mustard sauce, or tomato sauce, in 3¾- or 4-oz. cans. Pacific sardines, which are larger than Maine sardines, are packed, for the most part, in tomato sauce in 1-lb. cans. From Norway and Portugal come tiny sardines (Bristling or Sprat) neatly packed in oil.

Browse through your grocer's shelves, too, for canned tomato herring, gefilte fish balls or patties, halibut, oysters, sauries, smoked clams and oysters — the list is endless!

SHELLFISH

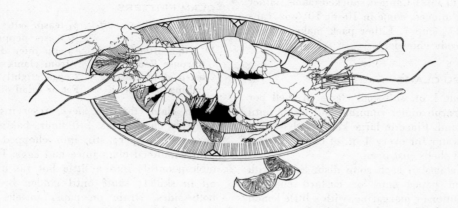

Thanks to improved transportation and freezing methods most varieties of shellfish, as with fish, are available and reasonable everywhere today.

To keep your shellfish at the best from market to table, don't overlook these important pointers.

If Raw Fresh: Plan to use raw fresh shellfish within a day or two after you buy it. If not using it promptly, refrigerate at once, either wrapped in saran or foil, or in a tightly covered dish; keep there till used. (If shellfish needs cleaning, dip into cold salted water, then wipe with a damp cloth.)

If Cooked Fresh: You'll want to refrigerate and then use cooked fresh shellfish as soon after buying as possible. It's highly perishable and deteriorates quickly if not refrigerated.

If Frozen: Whether frozen raw or cooked shellfish, store in your freezer as soon after purchase as possible. When time to use, transfer in original package to refrigerator to thaw or not, as recipe or label directs.

If Canned: Store in a cool dry place. Once can has been opened, refrigerate, covered, and use promptly.

When It's Clams

Kinds You'll Meet In Market:

SOFT-SHELL CLAMS: These are very popular for steaming, Boston Clam Chowder, p. 167, fried clams, clam fritters, clam broth, etc.

There are two sizes, the smaller ones being known as "steamers," the larger ones as "in shells."

If your recipe calls for shucked clams, order them by the pint or quart. If you're serving them in the shell, buy them by the dozen, peck, quart, or pound. Always make sure the shells are tightly closed but for the protruding neck and that they close quickly when touched. Reject all broken ones.

HARD-SHELL CLAMS: These are called "quahogs" in New England, "clams" in much of the East, and "round clams" or "littlenecks" in the South.

There are three sizes, dealers calling the large ones "chowder-clams," medium ones "cherry stones," and smaller ones "littlenecks." They're purchased shucked, or in the shell, as in Soft-Shell Clams above.

Large-size hard-shells are popular in Manhattan Clam Chowder, p. 167, and for broth.

Medium and smaller ones are famous in Clam Cocktail, p. 143, or as Clams on Half Shell, p. 143.

PACIFIC-COAST CLAMS: These include the butter, littleneck, razor, and 1½-lb. pismos up to giant 6-lb. geoducks.

CANNED CLAMS: Canned shucked clams, either whole or minced, come in 10- or 10½-oz. cans (about 1¼ cups). Either pack makes a delicious speedy chowder.

STEAMED CLAMS

Use about 1 qt. soft-shell clams in shell per person. Scrub under running cold water until free of sand. Place in large kettle with ½ cup boiling water for every 4 qt. of clams. Cover; steam till shells *just* open.

Heap clams in each soup dish. Serve with individual paper cups or custard cups of melted butter or margarine, with a little lemon juice added. Strain hot broth from kettle through fine cheesecloth; serve in cups, with thin lemon slice floating on top of each. Guests shell each clam, dip into broth, then into butter. Provide paper napkins or bibs.

CLAMS OR OYSTERS ON HALF SHELL*

Arrange about 6 clams or oysters on half shells on each plate, with tiny bowl of chili sauce or cocktail sauce in center. Set on service plate, then place, before dinner is announced.

Or arrange several dozen clams or oysters on half shell (about 6 per person) on large tray, with bowl of cocktail sauce in center; serve as first course in living room. Guests spear clams with picks or oyster forks, then dip them into sauce.

*See To Open Oysters in the Shell, p. 323.

FRIED CLAMS

Beat 1 egg with 2 tablesp. water. Drain 1 qt. shucked raw soft-shell clams, removing bits of shell; dip each into egg, then into packaged dried bread crumbs, corn meal, or fine cracker crumbs.

Fry in 1½" fat or salad oil at 365°F. on deep-fat-frying thermometer, until nicely browned on all sides (see Shallow-Frying, p. 7). Drain on paper towels.

Serve with Quick Tartar Sauce, p. 530, chili sauce, or chutney. Makes 4 servings.

Nice, too, heaped on toast and served with lemon wedges, or tartar or chili sauce in lettuce cups.

CLAM FRITTERS

1 pt. shucked raw soft-shell clams	¾ teasp. salt
	⅛ teasp. pepper
1⅓ cups sifted all-purpose flour	½ cup juice drained from clams
2 teasp. double-acting baking powder	2 eggs, slightly beaten
	Fat or salad oil

Drain clams through sieve, reserving juice. Coarsely chop clams. Sift flour, baking powder, salt, pepper; stir into chopped clams, with combined clam juice and eggs. Drop by tablespoonfuls into a little hot fat or salad oil in skillet; sauté until golden brown on both sides. Drain on paper towels. Makes about 2 doz.

LUNCHEON CLAMBAKE

4 eggs	clams, with liquid
2 cups milk	¼ cup minced onion
2½ cups soda-cracker crumbs (about 20 large or 30 small crackers)	2 tablesp. minced green pepper
	½ teasp. salt
	½ teasp. Worcestershire
⅓ cup melted butter or margarine	Pepper to taste
2 10½-oz. cans minced	

Early in day: In mixing bowl, beat eggs well. Add milk, cracker crumbs; let stand 20 min. Add butter, rest of ingredients. Taste; add more salt if needed (crackers and clams vary somewhat in saltiness). Pour into a greased 8" x 8" x 2" or 9" x 9" x 2" pan; refrigerate. *One hour before lunch:* Bake mixture at 350°F. about 1 hr. Cut into squares.

Serve as is. Or top each serving with spoonful of Anchovy Sauce, p. 533. Or garnish with crisp bacon. Makes 9 servings.

When It's Crab

Kinds You'll Meet In Market:

FRESH BLUE CRABS: These are the most familiar kind in Eastern markets and come from the Atlantic and the Gulf of Mexico. In both hard-shell and soft-shell states, and alive or cooked, they may be sold in the shell individually, by the dozen, or by the pound.

Soft-shell blue crabs are also marketed frozen.

FRESH HARD-SHELL CRABS: These are available throughout the year, but are more plentiful in the summer. They should be alive and usually weigh from 1/4 to 1 lb.

FRESH SOFT-SHELL CRABS: When a hard-shell crab sheds its shell and the new one has not yet hardened, it is called soft-shell crab. It is a great delicacy, available in the spring and summer. Each weighs 1/7 to 1/3 lb.

Frozen soft-shell crabs are available the year round.

FRESH ROCK CRABS: Most abundant off the New England coast, this crab is said to have more meat than blue crabs and the same flavorsome meat. Each weighs about 1/3 lb., and the meat is brownish-white.

FRESH DUNGENESS OR PACIFIC CRABS: This crab weighs from 1¾ to 3½ lb. and is usually sold by the pound. The meat is pinkish-white.

COOKED FRESH CRAB MEAT: From both the Atlantic and Pacific coasts and the Gulf of Mexico, this meat of the crab comes, by the pound, in pry-open cans — about three cups per pound — in ice, under refrigeration. The meat is graded, the top grade being lump white meat, also known as "special" or backfin lump.

FROZEN ALASKA KING-CRAB MEAT: From the icy waters of Alaska, King crabs supply the large, luscious crab meat chunks for salads, casseroles, etc., that you find, frozen, in each 6-oz. package.

Completely drain the thawed frozen crab meat before using. This liquid may replace an equal amount of the liquid called for in the recipe. Remove any membrane.

CANNED JAPANESE KING-CRAB MEAT: Only the claws of the giant North Pacific King crabs supply the tasty pink and white crab meat chunks you find in each 6½-oz. can. All you do is remove any membrane and *completely* drain the crab meat before using.

FROZEN ALASKA KING-CRAB LEGS: Split leg sections of King crabs, in the shell, and cut into serving portions, come frozen in 12-oz. packages. Nice for broiling, barbecuing, etc.

HARD-SHELL CRABS

To Boil: Order live hard-shell crabs; 6 crabs yield about 1 cup meat.

1. Pick up crabs with tongs or by back feelers; place in colander in sink full of cold water. Plunge colander in and out of water until crabs seem clean; drain.

2. Plunge crabs, head first, into enough rapidly boiling water to cover completely. (Let water return to boiling before adding each crab.) Add 1 tablesp. salt per 1 qt. water, 1 onion, sliced, 1 bay leaf, 1 tablesp. vinegar. Cover; boil 15 to 20 min., or until red.

3. Drain; plunge into cold water. Drain; allow to cool on tray.

To Remove Meat: When crabs are cool, scrub shells under running water. Twist off claws and legs close to body; with nutcracker or hammer crack all over. With pointed knife, pick out meat.

Lay each crab on its back shell. Slip knife under point of segment ("apron") that folds under body from rear; lift up, bend backward; break off. Take crab in both hands, with thumbs at tail; pull upper and lower shells apart. Discard top shell.

Hold crab under running water until loose matter is washed away. Break body in half, down center. With scissors, cut off membranous covering along edges. With nutpick, remove meat between sections, keeping meat whole if possible. Remove any cartilage.

SOFT-SHELL CRABS

To Buy: Order cleaned soft-shell crabs, allowing 2 per person. Or if you must clean them:

1. With scissors, remove head of each crab, cutting across crab ½" behind eyes.

2. Back of soft-shell crab tapers to a point at each side. Lay crab on its back shell; then take one of these points between thumb and forefinger of left hand; pull shell back halfway. Scrape off lungs or spongy substance thus exposed. Do same on other side.

3. Remove segment ("apron") that folds under body from rear and spongy substance under it. Wash crabs under running cold water.

To Boil: Plunge cleaned soft-shell crabs into boiling water to cover, adding 1 teasp. salt per 1 qt. water. Cover; boil 15 min.; drain. Serve, hot or cold, on platter with mayonnaise and lemon wedges, or with Quick Tartar Sauce, p. 530.

To Broil: Combine ¼ cup melted butter or margarine; 1 tablesp. lemon juice; pinch salt; speck pepper; dash cayenne pepper. Roll 6 cleaned soft-shell crabs in this mixture, then in flour. Broil under medium heat 8 to 10 min., turning once and basting with rest of butter mixture. Serve on toast with Quick Tartar Sauce, p. 530, and lemon wedges. Makes 3 servings.

SAUTEED SOFT-SHELL CRABS

Sprinkle 8 cleaned soft-shell crabs with salt, pepper. In ½ cup butter or margarine, in skillet, sauté crabs, a few at a time, 3 min. on each side, or until just golden. Keep warm while sautéing rest of crabs.

Then, to butter left in skillet, add 1 tablesp. snipped parsley, 1 teasp. lemon juice, and dash of Worcestershire. Pour over crabs. Or serve crabs on or between toast slices, with Quick Tartar Sauce, p. 530. Makes 4 servings.

ALMONDINE: Add ¼ cup slivered, blanched almonds to butter before sautéing crabs.

CRAB MEAT A LA NOME

2⅔ cups cooked fresh, or thawed frozen or canned King-crab meat, drained	⅛ teasp. pepper
	6 slices bread
	4 tablesp. melted butter or margarine
1 egg yolk, beaten	½ cup fresh bread
½ cup heavy cream	crumbs
½ teasp. salt	Parsley

Start heating oven to 400°F. Combine crab meat with egg yolk, cream, salt, pepper. Brush bread slices on one side with 3 tablesp. melted butter, then sauté on buttered side in skillet until golden; or arrange, after buttering, in greased baking pan, unbuttered side up. Heap crab-meat mixture on top of bread; sprinkle with bread crumbs combined with 1 tablesp. melted butter. Bake 10 min., then garnish with parsley and serve. Makes 6 servings.

♣ FOR 2: Use 1 egg yolk; halve rest of ingredients; make as directed.

SOUTHERN CRAB CAKES

3 cups cooked fresh, or thawed frozen or canned King-crab meat, drained	1 tablesp. mayonnaise
	2 teasp. snipped parsley
1½ teasp. salt	Flour
1 teasp. dry mustard	1 egg, slightly beaten
½ teasp. pepper	2 tablesp. water
1 egg yolk	Packaged dried bread crumbs
2 teasp. Worcestershire	Butter or margarine

Mix crab meat, salt, mustard, pepper, egg yolk, Worcestershire, mayonnaise, parsley; press firmly into 8 small cakes. Refrigerate until well chilled.

Just before serving, dip cakes in flour, then into egg combined with water, then into crumbs. In skillet melt a little butter; in it, over high heat, sauté cakes rapidly until a delicate brown. Nice served with potato salad, coleslaw, or French fries. Or serve on hot toasted rolls for lunch or supper. Makes 4 servings.

CRAB MEAT MARYLAND

¼ cup butter or margarine	Dash Tabasco
3 tablesp. flour	2 tablesp. sherry
2 cups milk	1 egg, beaten
2 tablesp. minced onion	1 teasp. salt
½ teasp. celery salt	Speck pepper
⅛ teasp. grated orange rind	3 cups flaked fresh or thawed frozen or canned King-crab meat, drained
1 tablesp. snipped parsley	½ cup fresh bread crumbs
1 tablesp. minced green pepper	1 tablesp. melted butter or margarine
1 pimento, minced	

Start heating oven to 350°F. In double boiler, melt ¼ cup butter; stir in flour, milk; cook, stirring, until thickened. Add onion, celery salt, rind, parsley, green pepper, pimento, Tabasco. Remove from heat; add sherry. Stir some of sauce slowly into egg; stir egg mixture into rest of sauce. Add salt, pepper, crab meat; turn into greased 1½-qt. casserole. Sprinkle with crumbs mixed with 1 tablesp. butter. Bake, uncovered, 15 to 20 min., or until brown. Makes 6 servings.

♣ FOR 2: Halve ingredients; use 1-qt. casserole.

To Vary: Toss bread crumbs with ½ cup grated process sharp Cheddar cheese; then sprinkle around top edge of casserole. Bake at 350°F. 10 min. Then arrange 3 half tomato slices down center of casserole and bake 5 min. longer, or until golden.

BUFFET STYLE: Double recipe, increasing flour to 1 cup, and topping crab-meat mixture with ¾ cup fresh bread crumbs tossed with ¾ cup grated cheese. Bake in 3-qt. casserole, set in pan half filled with boiling water, for 20 min., or until crumbs are brown. Makes 12 servings.

CRAB NEWBURG: See p. 322.

CRAB AND CORN A LA CREME

¼ cup butter or margarine	½ teasp. dry mustard
2 cans Mexican-style corn, drained	1½ teasp. grated lemon rind
2 6½-oz. cans King-crab meat, drained	1 teasp. Worcestershire
¾ teasp. salt	1 cup heavy cream
⅛ teasp. pepper	6 bread slices
⅛ teasp. paprika	Snipped parsley

1. In blazer of chafing dish, or in a saucepan over direct heat, melt butter; stir in corn, crab meat, salt, pepper, paprika, mustard, lemon rind, Worcestershire, cream. Cook, stirring, until hot.
2. Meanwhile, toast bread; cut into triangles. On it, serve corn mixture, sprinkled with parsley. Makes 6 servings.

When It's Live Lobster

To Buy: Live Northern or Maine lobsters, so named, come from East Coast waters and are available the year around. Peak production in Maine is in the early fall, often carrying through into December.

The live lobster shell varies from a bluish-green, with touches of red, to a brownish color; during cooking, it turns bright red. Most of its meat is in the two large claws and tail section. The most desirable live lobsters weigh 1 to 2 lb. each, the 1 pounders being called "chicken lobsters." The female, preferred by many, is recognized by the softness of its two uppermost appendages.

When buying live lobsters to cook at home, check their tails to be sure they're alive. The tail of a live lobster should curl under the body when the lobster is picked up — a sign of freshness. If its tail is limp and extended out straight, the lobster is probably dead. Since you have no way of knowing how long ago this happened, don't use it.

Always refrigerate live lobsters until ready to cook. But never place them in water or in fresh-water ice — they'll smother.

To Buy Cooked Live Lobster: When buying a cooked live lobster, make sure its tail curls toward body and springs back into place after being straightened. Refrigerate cooked meat as soon as possible.

Live lobsters may be shipped directly to your home. The Public Relations Office of the Department of Sea and Shore Fisheries, Augusta, Maine, will provide you with the latest information on these shipments. Cook the lobsters as soon as possible after arrival, following label directions closely.

BOILED LIVE LOBSTER

To Prepare:
1. Allow 1 small, or ½ large, lobster per person. Grasp each live lobster by body, with claws away from you (so it can't nip you); or use tongs.
2. Plunge lobster, head first, into rapidly boiling salted water — 3 tablesp. salt to 3 qt. water. (You may also add a few whole black peppers, onion slice, bay leaf, celery tops, parsley sprig, some lemon juice or slices.)
3. Cover; boil 12 to 15 min. after water comes back to boil.

To Serve Hot in Shell:
1. When lobster is done, remove from water; place on back shell. With sharp knife or kitchen scissors, slit center of thin undershell from head to tail.
2. Spread open; remove dark vein and small sac about 2″ long just below head. Leave in the delicious green liver (tomalley), if any. Or remove it; season well; serve in lettuce cups. Crack large claws.
3. Serve hot, with cut side up, garnished with lemon wedges and parsley. Serve small side dishes of melted butter (if lobster contains

any red roe, or "coral," it may be sprinkled on butter). Furnish nutcrackers and finger bowls. Nice with French fries.

To Serve Cold in Shell:

When lobsters are done, refrigerate. To serve, split and serve, p. 319, substituting mayonnaise, horse-radish, or tartar sauce for butter.

To Remove Lobster Meat for Salads, etc.:

1. Place boiled lobster on back shell. Twist off claws close to body.
2. With sharp knife or scissors, slit center of thin undershell from head to tail. Spread open with left hand; then insert fingers of right hand under tail meat and force it out in one piece.
3. Place tail meat on table, with striped side down. Run sharp knife down center to expose dark vein; remove and discard.
4. In female lobsters you may find red roe, or "coral." Remove; crumble, as garnish, over mayonnaise, lobster salad, etc.

Green liver is also a delicacy; see To Serve Hot in Shell, step 2, p. 319.

5. Cut tail shell from body shell. Hold body shell in left hand; with first two fingers and thumb of right hand, draw out body, leaving in shell the small sac about 2″ long just below head. Discard sac and spongy, grayish lungs covering sides of body.
6. Break body into several pieces and, with nutcracker or fork, pick out flesh around cartilage. Tweezers are also good for this job.
7. Crack large claws with hammer or nutcracker; remove meat. Use small claws as garnish.
8. Body and tail shells, if not broken, may be washed, dried, and fitted together. Use to hold lobster salad or Lobster Thermidor with Pilaf, at right.

BROILED LIVE LOBSTER

To Prepare: Allow 1 small, or ½ large, lobster per person. Order lobster split lengthwise and cleaned, with large claws cracked. Or do it yourself this way (be sure to cook same day):

1. Lay lobster on back shell on board. Where tail and body come together, insert point of knife through to back shell. (Or place in cold water in kettle over low heat until lobster reddens.) With heavy mallet or hammer, crack large part of each large claw.
2. Then cut down through center of thin undershell from head to tail, just to back shell, which should be left intact.
3. Spread lobster open as wide as possible. Discard dark vein down center, also small sac about 2″ long just below head. Leave in green liver and "coral." Crack large claws.

To Broil:

1. Preheat broiler 10 min., or as manufacturer directs. Place lobster, with meat side up, on broiler rack, 3″ from heat. Brush with melted butter or margarine, or melted butter mixed with green liver.
2. Sprinkle with salt, pepper, snipped parsley, and bit of garlic (optional).
3. Broil 15 to 20 min., depending on size of lobster and desired doneness, brushing with butter now and then. If broiling several lobsters, cut off large claws; arrange around sides of broiler pan, with body sections in center.

To Serve: Serve hot as in Boiled Live Lobster, p. 319.

BROILED STUFFED LOBSTER: Prepare lobster as at left. Combine 5 tablesp. fresh bread crumbs, 2 tablesp. snipped parsley, ¼ teasp. salt, 2 tablesp. melted butter or margarine, speck pepper, pinch dried herb, and a little grated onion. Broil lobster 10 min. as in step 3 above; then sprinkle with crumbs and broil 5 min., or until golden.

LOBSTER THERMIDOR WITH PILAF

4 2-lb. live lobsters	1 teasp. salt
Raisin Pilaf, p. 373	3 tablesp. sherry
6 tablesp. butter or	1½ cups light cream
margarine	¼ cup grated Cheddar cheese
3 tablesp. flour	
⅛ teasp. nutmeg	Lemon wedges
Dash paprika	Parsley

Early in day, or day before:

1. Grasp each lobster by body, claws away from you.
2. Then plunge it, head first, into boiling salted water — 3 tablesp. salt to 3 qt. water.
3. Cover; boil 12 to 15 min. Then remove from water.
4. Cut heads (with large claws) from tails.

Reserve one head as garnish. Remove meat, in large chunks, from tails and remaining heads (3 cups in all). Refrigerate lobster meat, empty tail shells, and reserved head.

One hour before serving:

1. Prepare, then start baking pilaf.
2. Then, in double-boiler top, melt butter. Stir in flour, nutmeg, paprika, salt, sherry, and cream, mixing well. Add lobster meat; cook over hot water, stirring, till just thickened.
3. Arrange tail shells on broiler rack; then fill with lobster mixture, and sprinkle with cheese.
4. When pilaf is finished baking, turn oven heat up to Broil, and then lightly brown Lobster Thermidor.
5. Spoon pilaf in layer onto heated platter. Arrange tails, in a row, on pilaf at one end, with reserved head at other end; garnish with lemon wedges and parsley. Makes 4 servings.

NOTE: Rock-lobster tails may replace live lobsters.

When It's Rock-Lobster Tails

To Buy: All rock-lobster tails come quick-frozen and have the country of origin clearly marked on the package. Especially desirable are those rock-lobster tails fished in the icy waters of the Benguela current, which comes up from the Antarctic along the coast of South Africa. These are labeled South African and have a rough-looking reddish-brown shell. Cold-water tails from Australia and New Zealand are also available.

Frozen rock-lobster tails also come from the warm waters of the Caribbean and other warm-water areas in the world. The warm-water rock lobsters have smooth, spotted, light-colored shells.

The meat in rock lobsters lies in the tail section and is tender, white, and delicious. Frozen South African rock-lobster tails are sold in 9-oz. and 1½-lb. cartons. Each tail in the cartons weighs about 3 to 4 oz.; larger sizes can be bought in tray packs in supermarkets or "loose" in fish markets. Rock-lobster meat also comes canned.

Amounts to Buy: In rock-lobster dishes, 4 oz. of rock-lobster meat is an ample portion.

When served broiled, allow 2 4-oz. tails per person.

To Boil: Drop solidly frozen rock-lobster tails into boiling salted water to cover (1 teasp. salt per 1 qt. water). When water reboils, simmer 3 min. longer than ounce weight of tails — for example 7 min. for 4-oz. tails.

When done, drain lobster tails; then, with scissors, cut away thin underside membrane. Serve hot or cold as in Boiled Live Lobster, p. 319.

To Remove Meat for Salads, Hors d'Oeuvres, etc.: Boil rock-lobster tails as above, drain, drench with cold water, drain again. Cut away underside membrane. Grasp tail meat between thumb and fingers and gently pull it away from shell in one piece. Chill; use whole, or slice, dice, or cut into chunks.

To Parboil for Newburgs, Curries, etc.: Drop solidly frozen rock-lobster tails into boiling salted water to cover. When water reboils, boil 1 min.; then immediately drain, drench with cold water, and drain again. Cut away underside membrane and remove meat from shells. Cut up as required for recipe. This rock-lobster meat will not be thoroughly done, but it will finish cooking in the sauce.

To Broil: Thaw tails by letting stand at room temperature; cut away underside membrane. Grasp tail in both hands and bend backwards toward shell side to crack and prevent curling. Or insert skewers. Preheat broiler 10 min., or as manufacturer directs. Place tails shell side up, 5″ below heat. Broil 2 min.; turn and spread flesh side with butter; broil 3 min., or until opaque. Serve in shell with melted butter.

ROCK-LOBSTER RICE

8 5-oz. frozen rock-lobster tails	Dash pepper
2 cups cooked rice	2 dashes angostura bitters
¼ cup butter or margarine	¼ cup sherry
2 tablesp. flour	Paprika
1 cup light cream	Lime wedges
¾ teasp. salt	Preserved guava shells (optional)

1. Boil lobster tails as label directs. Remove meat from shells; cut into 1½″ chunks; reserve with shells; preheat broiler for 10 min., or as manufacturer directs.

2. Line lobster shells with a thin layer of rice. Put rest of rice into large bowl; add lobster meat, reserving some especially choice pieces for topping.

3. In small saucepan, over medium heat, melt butter. Stir in flour, cream, salt, pepper, and angostura. Cook, stirring, until thickened; then stir in sherry.

4. Pour sauce over rice and lobster; toss lightly. Pile in rice-lined shells; top with reserved lobster pieces.

5. Broil about 4″ from heat for 4 min., or until nicely browned. Sprinkle with paprika.

6. Put on serving platter. Garnish with lime wedges, which guests squeeze over lobster; also guava shells, if desired. Makes 4 servings.

LOBSTER-CORN SAUTE

3 tablesp. butter or margarine	in chunks
½ green pepper, cut into strips	1½ cups cooked fresh, frozen, or canned whole-kernel corn
1 cup sliced fresh mushrooms	½ teasp. onion salt
3 cups cooked rock-lobster-tail meat,	⅛ teasp. pepper
	¼ cup light cream

1. *Just before serving:* Melt butter in medium skillet. Add green pepper and mushrooms; cook until tender-crisp — about 5 min.

2. Add lobster meat, corn, onion salt, pepper, and cream.

3. Heat; then serve as lunch or supper main dish. Makes 4 servings.

BARBECUED ROCK-LOBSTER TAILS

6 frozen rock-lobster tails	Caper-Butter Sauce or Creamy Catchup Sauce, below
Seasoned salt	

1. Prepare solidly frozen lobster tails as in To Broil, p. 321. Sprinkle each tail with seasoned salt, then broil as directed.

2. Meanwhile, make either Caper-Butter Sauce or Creamy Catchup Sauce.

3. When lobster tails are done, top with sauce and serve. Makes 6 servings.

CAPER-BUTTER SAUCE: In saucepan melt ¼ lb. butter or margarine. Add ¼ cup snipped parsley; 2 tablesp. capers, chopped; 1 teasp. lemon juice; ½ teasp. salt; speck pepper. Serve at once.

CREAMY CATCHUP SAUCE: In small bowl combine ½ cup commercial sour cream, ¾ cup catchup, ¾ teasp. seasoned salt, ¼ teasp. prepared mustard; blend well. Refrigerate until served.

LOBSTER NEWBURG

6 tablesp. butter or margarine	Dash paprika
2 tablesp. flour	1 teasp. salt
3 cups cut-up, cooked or canned lobster meat	3 tablesp. sherry
	3 egg yolks
⅛ teasp. nutmeg	2 cups light cream
	Toast points

In double-boiler top, over low heat, melt butter; stir in flour, lobster, nutmeg, paprika, salt, sherry. Beat yolks slightly; add cream; mix well. Slowly stir yolks into lobster; cook over hot water, stirring, till just thickened.

Serve at once on toast, in patty shells, or in Croustades, p. 497. Or place in individual baking dishes; top with buttered fresh bread crumbs; brown under broiler. Makes 6 servings.

CRAB, SHRIMP, OR OYSTER NEWBURG: For lobster, substitute 2 cups flaked fresh or thawed frozen or canned King-crab meat, drained; cleaned, cooked or canned shrimp; or raw oysters in their liquid, heated until edges *just* curl, then drained.

LOBSTER, OLD-FRENCH STYLE

2 tablesp. butter or margarine	1 teasp. meat-extract paste, or 1 beef-bouillon cube
4 small white onions	1 cup water
Meat from 1 thawed frozen rock-lobster tail or 1 medium live lobster	4 small mushrooms
	1 small tomato, chopped, peeled
1 tablesp. minced onion	1 sprig parsley, snipped
⅛ teasp. salt	¼ clove garlic, minced
1 black peppercorn, crushed	¼ teasp. dried thyme
	1 bay leaf
3 tablesp. Burgundy wine	Few drops thick meat sauce
1 teasp. canned tomato paste (optional)	½ recipe Orange Rice, p. 372
1 tablesp. flour	

In small covered saucepan, place 1 tablesp. butter and onions. Simmer till tender — about

15 min. Meanwhile, in skillet, melt 1 tablesp. butter; add lobster meat, cut into 1″ chunks, minced onion, and salt. Simmer, covered, 2 min.; add peppercorn, wine, and tomato paste; simmer, covered, till wine is almost absorbed. Sprinkle on flour; stir in meat-extract paste, dissolved in water. Simmer, stirring, until just thickened.

Deeply gash edges of mushrooms at 1/8″ intervals to give fluted "French" effect. Add to small whole onions, simmering in butter; cook 2 min. Then add to thickened lobster mixture with tomato, parsley, garlic, thyme, bay leaf, and meat sauce. Continue to simmer 3 min. Serve on Orange Rice. Makes 2 servings.

JANE'S COMPANY LOBSTER

3 cups cut-up, cooked or canned lobster meat	1/4 teasp. dry mustard
	3/4 teasp. salt
	Speck pepper
3 tablesp. lemon juice	2 cups milk
1/2 teasp. mace	1/2 lb. process Ched-
1/4 lb. elbow maca- roni (1 cup)	dar cheese, grated (2 cups)
4 teasp. minced onion	1/4 cup sherry
2 tablesp. butter or margarine	1/3 cup crushed crisp round scalloped
1 tablesp. flour	crackers

Start heating oven to 400°F. Sprinkle lobster with lemon juice, mace. Cook macaroni as label directs; drain. In double boiler, combine onion, butter, flour, mustard, salt, pepper; stir in milk. Cook, stirring, until smooth. Add 1½ cups cheese; stir until melted. Add lobster, sherry. Arrange macaroni in 12″ x 8″ x 2″ baking dish; pour on lobster mixture; sprinkle with rest of cheese, then with crackers. Bake, uncovered, 20 min., then remove from oven and let stand in warm place 5 min. before serving. Makes 4 to 6 servings.

LOBSTER TAILS A LA BARBER

8 4- to 5-oz. frozen rock-lobster tails	Salt to taste
1/4 cup butter or mar- garine	2 cups fresh bread crumbs
1/4 cup sherry	1/4 cup melted butter or margarine
2 tablesp. flour	1/4 cup snipped chives
1 teasp. paprika	1/4 teasp. salt
3/4 cup light cream	1/8 teasp. pepper

Boil frozen lobster tails as on p. 321; remove meat, keeping shells intact. Cut meat into chunks. Refrigerate all.

About 15 min. before serving: In saucepan, heat lobster meat with 1/4 cup butter and sherry 3 min. Stir in flour, paprika, cream, salt; cook, stirring, until thickened. Use to stuff lobster shells; top with crumbs mixed with 1/4 cup melted butter, chives, salt, pepper. Broil 2 or 3 min., or until brown. Makes 6 to 8 servings.

When It's Frozen Langostinos

These are the frozen bite-size tails of tiny Chilean lobsters, somewhat resembling shrimp. They are cooked, shelled, then sold frozen in rose-pink blocks of 6 and 12 oz. May be used in place of cooked shrimp, lobster, or crab.

When It's Oysters

RAW SHUCKED OYSTERS: Eastern oysters come extra large, large, medium, small, and very small. Western Olympia oysters come small. Pacific oysters are larger than Eastern oysters.

Any and all of these fresh varieties are sold raw, shucked by the dozen, or in 1/2-pint, 1-pint, and 1-quart containers. They should be a natural gray in color, plump, with clear liquor, and free from shell particles.

OYSTERS IN THE SHELL: All varieties of Eastern, Western, and Pacific oysters are sold in the shell by the dozen.

OYSTERS ON THE HALF SHELL: These are prepared to order, to be served as are Clams on Half Shell, p. 316.

To Open Oysters in the Shell: Scrub shells well; rinse in cold water. Insert point of sharp thin knife into hinged end of oyster; push blade between shells until muscle at center is cut and valves begin to separate. Run knife around shell; separate valves; loosen oyster from shell.

To Remove Bits of Shell: Put shucked oysters in sieve to drain; pick over oysters, taking each between finger tips, to remove bits of shell.

BROILER-FRIED OYSTERS

¾ cup packaged dried bread crumbs
½ teasp. dry mustard
Dash cayenne pepper
¼ teasp. paprika
½ teasp. salt

2 doz. shucked raw oysters, drained
¼ cup melted butter or margarine
Lemon wedges

Preheat broiler 10 min., or as manufacturer directs. Combine crumbs, mustard, pepper, paprika, salt. Remove any bits of shell from oysters. Drain oysters; roll in crumb mixture; place, in single layer, in greased baking pan. Sprinkle with half of melted butter. Broil quickly till golden brown. Turn; sprinkle with rest of melted butter. Broil quickly till golden brown. Serve with lemon wedges. Makes 4 servings.

SKILLET-FRIED OYSTERS

3 tablesp. butter or margarine
3 tablesp. shortening
2 doz. shucked large raw oysters, drained
Finely crushed crisp round scalloped

crackers
¾ to 1 teasp. salt
¼ teasp. pepper
Snipped parsley or paprika
Lemon wedges

Melt butter and shortening in skillet. Roll oysters in cracker crumbs; sauté in butter mixture until golden brown, turning once and sprinkling with salt and pepper.

Serve as is or on buttered toast. Sprinkle with snipped parsley or paprika; garnish with lemon wedges. Makes 4 servings.

CORN-SCALLOPED OYSTERS

¼ cup butter or margarine
¼ cup light cream
½ teasp. salt
⅛ teasp. pepper
½ teasp. Worcestershire
2 tablesp. snipped parsley

1¼ cups coarsely broken saltines
½ cup grated process Cheddar cheese
2 doz. shucked oysters, drained (1 qt.)*
1 12-oz. can whole-kernel corn, drained

1. Start heating oven to 400°F. In small saucepan, combine butter, cream, salt, pepper, Worcestershire, parsley; heat just long enough to melt butter.
2. Meanwhile, in greased 10" x 6" x 2" baking dish, arrange half of saltines.

3. Over crackers, sprinkle cheese; on top, arrange oysters and corn. Pour butter mixture over all; then sprinkle with remaining cracker crumbs.
4. Bake 20 to 25 min. Serve immediately. Makes 4 to 5 servings.
*With fingers, pick over oysters, to remove bits of shell.

FRIED OYSTERS

Prepare and serve as in Fried Clams, p. 316, substituting drained, shucked large raw oysters for clams.

OYSTER CLUB SANDWICHES: Use fried oysters, with lettuce, thin tomato slices, and crisp bacon, as filling for hot-buttered-toast sandwiches.

When It's Scallops

Scallops, one of the tastiest gifts of the sea, come in two varieties in this country — sea scallops and bay scallops. Allow about 1 lb. of scallops for 3 or 4 servings.

SEA SCALLOPS: These are harvested in deep waters off the New England coast and are available the year round in fresh and frozen form. Their meat is sweet, nutlike, and firm and there's no waste to pay for. They're larger than bay scallops — 1" to 1½" across.

BAY SCALLOPS: These tiny luscious scallops — ½" to ¾" across — come from tidal inlets and bays and are not distributed as widely or in the volume that sea scallops are.

FROZEN FRENCH-FRIED SCALLOPS: They're wonderful — breaded and French-fried, or breaded, uncooked. All you do is heat them as label directs.

CURRIED SCALLOPS IN RICE RING

1 cup flaked coconut
3 tablesp. butter or margarine
3 medium onions, chopped
1 clove garlic, minced
1 tablesp. curry powder
1 green pepper,

chopped
2 teasp. salt
4 whole cloves
1 cinnamon stick
1½ lb. sea scallops, split in halves into disks
1 tablesp. cornstarch
Ring of hot fluffy rice

1. In saucepan, bring coconut and 2 cups
About 1 hr. before serving:

water to boil. Remove from heat; cover; let stand 30 min.; drain, reserving coconut liquid.

2. In melted butter, in large skillet, sauté onions and garlic till golden; stir in curry, pepper, coconut liquid, salt, cloves, cinnamon. Simmer, stirring occasionally, 10 min.

3. Next add scallops, then cornstarch stirred smooth in a little cold water; simmer, while stirring, about 5 min. Remove cinnamon stick.

4. Arrange scallops in rice ring on heated platter. Makes 6 servings.

SCALLOPS BAKED IN SHELLS
(Coquilles Saint-Jacques)

¾ cup water	minced
¼ cup sauterne	1 teasp. snipped
½ teasp. salt	parsley
Few grains cayenne	1 egg yolk, well
1 pt. sea scallops	beaten
2 tablesp. butter or	¾ cup buttered tiny
margarine	fresh bread crumbs
1 small onion, minced	2 tablesp. grated Par-
2 tablesp. flour	mesan cheese
½ clove garlic,	

1. Start heating oven to 425°F. In skillet, combine water, sauterne, salt, cayenne; in it, simmer scallops 5 min.; drain, reserve liquid. Coarsely chop scallops (or try snipping them with kitchen shears).

2. In hot butter in same skillet, sauté onion until tender; stir in flour well; stir in reserved liquid and cook until thickened. Add garlic and parsley; then, stirring constantly, cook 5 min.

3. Now, gradually stir some of sauce into beaten egg yolk; then, into remaining sauce, slowly stir egg-yolk mixture. Add scallops; heat gently.

4. Into 5 buttered 6″ pie plates or into scallop shells, spoon scallop mixture. Top with crumbs and cheese; bake until brown — about 5 min. Makes 5 servings.

GOLDEN SCALLOPS

In large skillet, heat 2 tablesp. butter or margarine, ½ teasp. salt, ⅛ teasp. pepper, and ¼ teasp. paprika till bubbling hot. Add 2 tablesp. minced onion or 1 clove garlic, slivered. Using 1 lb. bay scallops (1 pt.) in all, drop in enough scallops to cover bottom of skillet (don't crowd). Sauté over high heat, tossing

occasionally, 5 to 7 min., or until golden; remove to heated platter. Repeat. Sprinkle scallops with snipped parsley.

Serve with lemon wedges. Or top with sautéed, sliced mushrooms or crumbled crisp bacon. Makes 3 or 4 servings.

SCALLOP SAUTE

Dip 1 lb. sea scallops first into milk, then into Seasoned Flour, p. 9. In hot melted butter or margarine in skillet over low heat, sauté scallops, a few at a time, until just cooked but juicy — about 8 min.

Serve, sprinkled with melted butter or margarine combined with snipped parsley or chives; garnish with lemon wedges. Makes 3 or 4 servings.

SCALLOP BROIL

Preheat broiler 10 min., or as manufacturer directs. Arrange 1 lb. sea scallops in 1 layer in shallow pan; sprinkle with garlic salt, pepper, paprika. Broil about 4 min., turning often and sprinkling with ¼ cup melted butter or margarine mixed with 1 tablesp. lemon juice. Sprinkle *lightly* with packaged dried bread crumbs; broil 1 min. longer. Makes 3 or 4 servings.

CHINA SCALLOPS

1½ lb. fresh or	1¼ teasp. salt
thawed frozen sea	¼ cup catchup
scallops	1 cup milk
1 medium cucumber	2 teasp. cornstarch
¼ cup butter or mar-	2 tablesp. dry sherry
garine	6 cups hot fluffy white
1 4-oz. can pimentos,	rice
diced	

1. Slice scallops crosswise into ¼″-thick disks, Pare cucumber; cut lengthwise into 16 strips, then crosswise into fourths.

2. In butter in skillet, cook scallops till golden — about 3 min. Add cucumber, pimentos, salt; cover; simmer 3 min. Add catchup and ½ cup milk.

3. Blend cornstarch with remaining ½ cup milk. Add to scallop mixture; stir over medium heat until thickened and boiling. Stir in sherry.

4. Serve on hot fluffy rice. Makes 6 servings.

SAUTEED SCALLOPS WITH SCALLIONS

1 lb. bay scallops
  (1 pt.)
½ cup packaged
  dried bread crumbs
¼ teasp. paprika
6 tablesp. butter or

margarine
⅓ cup finely sliced
  scallions or minced
  onion
½ teasp. salt
⅛ teasp. pepper

Roll scallops in combined crumbs and paprika. In skillet, heat butter with scallions, salt, pepper; add scallops and sauté over high heat until scallops are golden on all sides. Makes 3 or 4 servings.

SEA FOOD SUPREME

½ lb. raw scallops
  (1 cup)
¼ cup butter or mar-
  garine
3½ tablesp. flour
¼ teasp. salt
Speck pepper
½ cup cream or top
  milk
½ cup milk
1 teasp. paprika
½ teasp. Worcester-
  shire, or sherry to

taste
Dash cayenne pepper
1 cup cleaned canned
  or cooked fresh
  shrimp
1 doz. raw oysters,
  drained (about 1
  pt.)
1 cup cooked fresh
  crab meat, or
  canned or thawed
  frozen King-crab
  meat, drained

Cook scallops in 1 cup boiling, salted water, covered, 10 min.; drain. Melt butter in double boiler. Add flour, salt, pepper; blend well. Slowly add cream and milk, stirring; cook over boiling water until thickened, stirring occasionally. Blend in paprika, Worcestershire, and cayenne pepper; cover, then cook 10 min. over medium heat. Add scallops and shrimp; cook 15 min. Add oysters and crab meat; cook 10 min., stirring occasionally. Makes 6 servings.

SCALLOPS VINAIGRETTE

1. In salted water to cover, in medium saucepan, simmer ½ lb. fresh or thawed frozen sea scallops, sliced, for 5 min.; drain; cool.
2. Then combine scallops; 2 cooked medium potatoes, peeled and thinly sliced; 2 tablesp. minced onion; and 2 tablesp. snipped parsley.
3. Mix together 2 tablesp. vinegar, 2 tablesp. salad oil, ¾ teasp. salt, and ⅛ teasp. pepper. Pour over scallop mixture and toss lightly.
4. Refrigerate till serving time. Garnish with snipped dill or chives. Makes 2 main dish servings. For 4 servings, double recipe.

When It's Shrimp

Kinds You'll Meet In Market:

FRESH RAW SHRIMP IN SHELL: Some are shipped to market between layers of ice. Many more are frozen before shipping and then thawed by the dealer before he sells them. They are neither cleaned nor shelled.

FRESH COOKED SHRIMP: In some markets you will find freshly cooked shrimp — usually by the pound — which have been shelled and deveined. Make sure they've been kept refrigerated or packed in ice.

PACKAGED FROZEN SHRIMP: These come to market in these several packs:
  a. Raw, in the shell
  b. Raw, in shells, but deveined
  c. Raw, shelled and deveined
  d. Cooked, in shells
  e. Cooked, shelled and deveined

PACKAGED FROZEN BREADED SHRIMP: These come either "round" or fantail (sometimes called "butterflied") in these packs:
  1. Cleaned and breaded, but uncooked
  2. Cleaned, breaded and cooked — all ready to heat as label directs

Amounts to Buy: One pound of frozen or fresh uncooked shrimp, after cooking and shelling, yields 1⅓ to 1⅔ cups (or ½ lb.) or 2 or 3 servings.

CANNED SHRIMP: These come deveined or non-deveined in 4½- and 5-oz. cans (1 cup), either "wet pack" (in brine) or "dry pack" (in a vacuum without liquid). Always drain them, then rinse under tap water before using.

How to Prepare and Cook Raw Shrimp:

TO SHELL SHRIMP:* Raw shrimp may be shelled either before or after boiling. We prefer to shell them raw, for then, after cooking, they seem plumper. To shell, hold tail end of shrimp in left hand; slip thumb of right hand under shell between feelers, and lift off several segments of shell. Then, holding firmly to tail, pull out shrimp from rest of shell and tail.

TO DEVEIN SHRIMP:* The black vein in shrimp is harmless, but removing it, before or after cooking, makes the shrimp more attractive. To devein, with sharp knife, cut about ⅛" deep
Special devices for shelling and deveining shrimp are now available.

along outside curve of shrimp; then lift out black vein, washing shrimp under water.

TO COOK SHRIMP: Shell and devein shrimp before cooking. Then drop shrimp into boiling salted water to cover, using 1 tablesp. salt per 1 qt. water (if desired, also add 1 sliced small onion, a few parsley sprigs, 4 whole black peppers). Simmer, covered, 2 to 5 min.— never longer—or until pink and tender. Drain, then refrigerate.

SHRIMP CASSEROLE HARPIN

2½ lb. large raw shrimp, shelled, deveined	pepper
	¼ cup minced onion
	1 teasp. salt
1 tablesp. lemon juice	⅛ teasp. pepper
3 tablesp. salad oil	⅛ teasp. mace
¾ cup uncooked regular or processed white rice, or 1 cup packaged precooked rice	Dash cayenne pepper
	1 10½-oz. can condensed tomato soup, undiluted
	1 cup heavy cream
2 tablesp. butter or margarine	½ cup sherry
	¾ cup slivered blanched almonds
¼ cup minced green	

Early in the day: Cook shrimp in boiling salted water for 5 min.; drain. Place in 2-qt. casserole; sprinkle with lemon juice and salad oil. Meanwhile, cook rice as label directs; drain. Refrigerate all.

About 1 hr. and 10 min. before serving:
1. Start heating oven to 350°F. Set aside about 8 shapely shrimp for garnish.
2. In butter in skillet, sauté green pepper and onion for 5 min. Add, with rice, salt, pepper, mace, cayenne pepper, soup, cream, sherry, and ½ cup almonds, to shrimp in casserole. Toss well.
3. Bake, uncovered, 35 min. Then top with 8 reserved shrimp and ¼ cup almonds. Bake 20 min. longer, or till mixture is bubbly and shrimp are slightly browned. Makes 6 to 8 servings.

SHRIMP CASSEROLE HARPIN, BUFFET STYLE: Make three times above recipe, using 5-qt. casserole and topping with about 1 doz. shrimp and ¼ cup almonds. Bake as directed, increasing second baking to 35 min. (With 2 2½-qt. casseroles, divide same mixture between them; top each with about 8 shrimp and ¼ cup almonds; bake as directed.) Makes 18 to 24 servings.

GARLIC-BROILED SHRIMP

2 lb. large raw shrimp	2 tablesp. snipped parsley
2 teasp. salt	
1 to 2 teasp. minced garlic	½ cup butter or margarine

Night before: With scissors, split shrimp shells; remove or not as you wish. Devein shrimp; arrange in one tight layer in shallow pan; cover pan with foil; refrigerate.

About 25 min. before serving: Sprinkle shrimp with salt, garlic, parsley; top with bits of butter. Broil 4″ from heat 6 to 7 min.; turn; broil 6 to 7 min. Sprinkle with more parsley. Makes 4 servings.

✤ FOR 2: Make as above, halving ingredients.

SHRIMP, SAILOR STYLE
(Scampi alla Marinara)

5 tablesp. olive or salad oil	¼ teasp. pepper
	1 teasp. dried orégano
2 garlic cloves, minced	⅔ cup canned tomato paste
1 1-lb.-13-oz. can Italian tomatoes, undrained	½ teasp. garlic salt
	2 lb. cooked, shelled, deveined shrimp
2 tablesp. snipped parsley	Grated Parmesan cheese
½ teasp. dried basil	Hot cooked spaghetti or rice (optional)
2½ teasp. salt	

1. In hot oil, in skillet, brown garlic. Add tomatoes, parsley, basil, salt, pepper. Simmer, uncovered, ½ hr.
2. Stir in orégano, tomato paste. Cook, uncovered, 15 min.
3. Stir in garlic salt, shrimp. Heat. Serve, topped with grated cheese, over spaghetti or rice if desired. Makes 4 servings.

✤ FOR 2: Make as above, halve ingredients. ents, but using 1 16- or 17-oz. can of tomatoes.

HOT SPICY SHRIMP

Spicy Sauce, p. 530	2 tablesp. salt
1 lb. raw, unshelled shrimp	1 tablesp. pickling spice
1 qt. boiling water	

Two or three days ahead: Make Spicy Sauce; refrigerate.

About ½ hr. before serving: Wash shrimp. Put in kettle with boiling water, salt, and pickling spice. Simmer, covered, 5 min. Remove from heat; let stand 20 min. in liquid. Then strain, saving broth.

In center of 2 dinner plates, place small dishes of Spicy Sauce; arrange hot shrimp around them. Each person shells shrimp and dunks into sauce. Serve with piping hot cups of the shrimp broth. Accompany with a hearty green salad and a crusty bread. Makes 2 servings as a main dish.

HOT SPICY SHRIMP HORS D'OEUVRES: Prepare Hot Spicy Shrimp, p. 327. In center of 6 salad plates, place small paper cups or small dishes of Spicy Sauce. Arrange shrimp around sauce. Garnish with parsley. Serve as first course, dunking shrimp in sauce. Makes 6 servings.

JOSIE'S LEMON SCAMPI

2 lb. thawed frozen or fresh jumbo raw shrimp	Juice 1 medium lemon
¼ cup butter or margarine	¼ cup melted butter or margarine
2 cloves garlic, minced	½ teasp. salt
	⅛ teasp. pepper
	Snipped parsley

Early in day: Peel shrimp; leave tail shells on; devein. Refrigerate.

Half hour before serving:
1. Preheat broiler 10 min., or as manufacturer directs.
2. Melt ¼ cup butter in small skillet over medium heat. Add garlic, lemon juice; simmer, stirring often, 3 min.
3. Meanwhile, arrange shrimp on heatproof platter or broiler pan.
4. Blend ¼ cup melted butter with garlic butter; pour over shrimp. Sprinkle with salt and pepper. Broil about 4″ from heat, turning once, 5 to 7 min.
5. Sprinkle with parsley; serve at once with pan juices. Makes about 5 main dish servings or 38 nibblers.

BARBECUED SHRIMP

Night before or early in day if desired: Peel 1 lb. raw shrimp, leaving on tail shells; devein shrimp; refrigerate.

About 40 min. before serving: Combine ½ cup catchup or chili sauce, 1 tablesp. Worcestershire, 1 teasp. dry mustard, 3 dashes Ta-basco. Add shrimp; toss well; refrigerate 30 min. Meanwhile, preheat broiler 10 min., or as manufacturer directs. Drain shrimp, reserving sauce; broil 5 min. on each side, brushing often with sauce. Serve, garnished with parsley. Makes 2 or 3 servings.

SHRIMP-RICE PARMESAN

¼ cup salad oil	1 small onion, minced
⅔ cup packaged precooked rice	1 cup coarsely grated, pared carrots
1 cup water	1 lb. thawed frozen or fresh large raw shrimp, shelled and deveined
1 1-lb.-4-oz. can tomatoes (2½ cups)	
2½ teasp. salt	
⅛ teasp. pepper	Grated Parmesan cheese
1 teasp. Worcestershire	

About 1 hr. and 15 min. before serving:
1. In hot oil, in skillet, over medium heat, cook rice, stirring constantly, until golden.
2. Add water, tomatoes, salt, pepper, Worcestershire, onion, carrots. Cook, covered, till carrots are tender.
3. Add shrimp; cook 5 min., or until shrimp are tender. Serve, passing cheese. Makes 4 servings.

SHRIMPALAYA CASSEROLE

¼ lb. elbow macaroni (2 cups)	½ lb. cubed, cooked ham or canned luncheon meat (about 1¼ cups)
2 strips bacon, diced	
½ cup minced onions	
½ cup minced green peppers	1 cup cooked, cleaned shrimp
½ clove garlic, minced	½ cup day-old bread crumbs
1 1-lb.-4-oz. can tomatoes (2½ cups)	2 tablesp. grated Parmesan cheese
1 teasp. salt	2 tablesp. melted butter or margarine

Early in day: Cook macaroni as label directs; drain. Meanwhile, in skillet, sauté bacon till quite crisp. Add onions, green peppers, and garlic; sauté till tender. Add tomatoes and salt; heat. Add macaroni, ham, and shrimp; pour into 1½-qt. casserole. Refrigerate.

To serve: Combine bread crumbs, cheese, and butter; sprinkle on top of mixture in casserole. Bake at 350°F. about 1 hr., or until hot and bubbly. (If made and baked at one time, bake 30 min.) Makes 4 servings.

CREAMED SHRIMP ON CRISP RICE

1 can frozen cream-of-shrimp soup
¾ cup milk, or light or heavy cream
¼ teasp. onion salt (optional)
Dash pepper
½ lb. cooked, deveined, shelled shrimp
¼ cup melted butter or margarine
4 cups ready-to-eat tiny crisp rice-cereal squares
Chives, parsley, or dill

In saucepan or double boiler, heat soup with milk, onion salt, pepper. Meanwhile, split shrimp down back almost all the way through; add to soup; heat. Melt butter in large saucepan; add rice cereal; toss to coat. Place rice cereal on platter, with shrimp in center; snip chives over top. Makes 4 to 6 servings.

FRIED SHRIMP
(Ju Har-Kow)

1 egg, beaten
2 tablesp. flour
½ teasp. salt
Dash pepper
1 lb. deveined, shelled large raw shrimp
½ cup salad oil
⅔ cup minced onions
1 tablesp. cornstarch
1 teasp. soy sauce
¾ cup canned chicken consommé

For batter, combine egg, flour, salt, pepper. Add shrimp; stir to coat well. Heat oil in skillet until very hot. Using fork, lift shrimp, one by one, from batter; drop into oil; sauté until golden — 5 to 7 min. Drain on paper towels. Remove to heated platter.

For sauce, sauté onions in 2 tablesp. oil left in skillet; add combined cornstarch, soy sauce, consommé. Cook, stirring, *just* until thickened. Pour over shrimp. Serve with hot fluffy rice. Makes 4 servings as appetizer.

SWEET PUNGENT: To sauce, add 2 tablesp. each vinegar and sugar, 1 8-oz. can pineapple tidbits, and 1 seeded medium green pepper, sliced.

BUTTERFLY SHRIMP

Shell, then devein raw shrimp, leaving tails on. Split along back curve, cutting deep, almost to inner edge; open; then press flat with bottom of measuring cup. Prepare batter for Fried Shrimp, above; add shrimp; stir to coat well. Lift out, one by one, with fork. Fry as in Shallow-Frying, p. 7, at 365°F. on deep-fat-frying thermometer, until golden. Serve with bowl of soy sauce or chutney for dunking.

SHRIMP BROIL

Shell, then devein, 2 lb. raw shrimp; arrange, in layer, in shallow pan or pie pan. Sprinkle well with seasoned salt, monosodium glutamate, then with 3 tablesp. melted butter or margarine mixed with 2 to 3 tablesp. lemon juice. Broil until shrimp turn pink — about 5 min. Serve as is or on toast. Makes 4 to 6 servings.

IN BACON CURLS: Sprinkle shrimp with seasoned salt, pepper, lemon juice. Wrap each in ½ bacon slice; secure with wooden toothpick. Broil, turning once, about 6 min., or until bacon is crisp.

ELLEN'S SHRIMP GUMBO

¼ cup butter or margarine
2 tablesp. flour
2 cloves garlic, minced
2 onions, sliced
½ green pepper, thinly sliced
1 1-lb.-4-oz. can tomatoes (2½ cups)
1 1-lb.-4-oz. can okra, drained; or 1 pkg. frozen whole okra
1 6-oz. can tomato paste
3 beef-bouillon cubes; or 1 tablesp. meat-extract paste
4 teasp. Worcestershire
⅛ teasp. ground cloves
½ teasp. chili powder
Pinch dried basil
1 bay leaf
1½ tablesp. salt
¼ teasp. pepper
3 cups water
1½ lb. deveined, shelled raw shrimp
3 cups hot cooked rice
¼ cup snipped parsley

Early in day: In Dutch oven or heavy kettle, melt butter. Stir in flour, then cook over low heat until brown. Add garlic, onions, green pepper; cook slowly until tender. Add tomatoes and rest of ingredients except shrimp, rice, parsley. Simmer, uncovered, 45 min. Cool; refrigerate.

To serve: Heat tomato mixture over medium heat till just boiling; add shrimp; simmer, covered, about 5 min., or until shrimp are pink and tender. Combine rice with parsley. Serve gumbo in shallow plates; add "island" of parsleyed rice at side of each plate. Makes 8 servings.

CHARLESTON SHRIMP SAUTE

Shell, then devein, 2 lb. raw shrimp. In 2 tablesp. butter or margarine in skillet, sauté shrimp with 3 scallions, sliced, 1½ teasp. salt, and ⅛ teasp. pepper, tossing to cook all sides, till opaque — 3 to 5 min. Add 2 tablesp. sherry or a little lemon juice, then snipped parsley. Makes 4 to 6 servings.

INDIAN SHRIMP CURRY

1 to 1½ cups un-cooked regular or processed white rice; or 1½ to 2 cups packaged pre-cooked rice	6 tablesp. flour
	2½ teasp. curry powder
	1¼ teasp. salt
	1½ teasp. sugar
	¼ teasp. ground ginger
1 chicken-bouillon cube	
1 cup boiling water	2 cups milk
5 tablesp. butter or margarine	3 lb. cooked, shelled, deveined shrimp (4 cups)
½ cup minced onions	1 teasp. lemon juice

Cook rice as label directs; keep hot. Dissolve bouillon cube in water. In double-boiler top, over direct heat, melt butter. Add onions; simmer till tender. Stir in flour, curry, salt, sugar, ginger. Gradually stir in bouillon, milk. Cook over boiling water, stirring, until thickened. Add shrimp, lemon juice; heat.

Serve ring of hot rice on heated platter, with curry in center. Serve with some of Curry Accompaniments, below. Makes 6 to 8 servings.

CURRY ACCOMPANIMENTS: A curry dish is at its best served with one or more of these accompaniments, arranged in separate bowls:

Chutney	Crisp bacon bits
Tomato wedges	Currant jelly
Raisins	Chopped, hard-cooked eggs
Salted almonds	
Salted peanuts	Sweet or sour pickles
Snipped parsley	Flaked coconut
Sautéed onion rings	Sliced avocado
Pineapple chunks	Grated orange rind

LOBSTER, CRAB, OR SCALLOP CURRY: For shrimp, substitute 4 cups flaked, cooked or canned lobster meat, cooked or drained canned or thawed frozen King-crab meat, or cooked scallops.

SHRIMP CREOLE

¼ cup butter or margarine	⅛ teasp. dried rosemary (optional)
1 large onion, chopped	⅛ teasp. paprika
½ cup minced green peppers	2 cups cooked or canned tomatoes
1 clove garlic, minced	1 lb. cooked, shelled, deveined shrimp (1⅓ cups)
1 teasp. salt	
Dash pepper	2 to 3 cups hot cooked rice

Melt butter in saucepan. Add onion, green peppers, garlic; sauté 10 min., or until tender. Add salt, pepper, rosemary, paprika, tomatoes. Bring to boil; reduce heat and simmer 15 min. Add shrimp; heat thoroughly. Serve on hot fluffy rice. Makes 4 servings.

To Vary: If you like a "hot" Shrimp Creole, add 1¼ teasp. chili powder and 2 dashes Tabasco with tomatoes.

SUPER SKILLET SHRIMP

2 cloves garlic, chopped fine	½ cup dry white wine
¼ cup salad oil	½ teasp. dried orégano
¼ cup butter or margarine	½ cup grated Parmesan cheese
3 cups cooked, deveined, shelled shrimp (2½ lb. raw)	4 teasp. snipped parsley
	½ cup fresh bread crumbs
½ teasp. salt	
⅛ teasp. pepper	About 3 cups hot fluffy rice
1 tablesp. flour	

Day before: Let garlic stand in oil, at room temperature, overnight; then remove garlic.

About 45 min. before serving:
1. Start heating oven to 350°F.
2. In butter or margarine, in large skillet, heat shrimp; add salt, pepper. Spoon, without butter, into 1½-qt. casserole or 4 individual casseroles.
3. Mix flour with a little wine; stir into butter in skillet. Simmer to a light golden; stir in orégano, rest of wine, garlic oil; pour over shrimp.
4. Combine Parmesan, parsley, crumbs; sprinkle over shrimp. Bake 30 min., or until light brown. Serve on hot rice. Makes 4 servings.

When It's Mussels

Mussels, a neglected yet delicious shellfish, have one advantage — they are in season when oysters are out of season. They can be had the year round, but are at their best in the winter.

To Buy: Mussels should be bought alive. If the shells gape and do not stay closed when squeezed shut, the mussels are either dead or weak and should not be used. Keep them covered with a wet cloth, in a cool dark place, until used.

To Prepare: Mussel shells should be washed *very well* before cooking. The little tuft of black hair (the byssus) is easily removed after cooking. Cook the mussels just as you would oysters or clams. Sometimes you'll find little sandcrabs inside the mussels; discard these.

Amounts to Buy: One half peck of mussels, steamed, makes 5 servings.

FRENCH MUSSELS

3 qt. mussels (3 lb.)	2 tablesp. butter or
½ teasp. minced	margarine
onion or 1 minced,	Salt
peeled clove garlic	Pepper
½ cup dry white wine	Cayenne pepper
3 teasp. snipped parsley	

Wash and scrape mussels well in cold water, changing water *several times* to remove all sand. Place in large kettle. Add onion, wine, 1½ teasp. snipped parsley, and 1 tablesp. butter. Sprinkle with salt, pepper, and cayenne. Cover; boil until mussels open — about 8 to 10 min. Pour off stock carefully without disturbing sediment. Boil down stock to 2 cups. Discard half of shell to which meat is not attached. Arrange rest, open side up, in deep soup dishes. To hot stock, add 1 tablesp. butter and seasonings to taste. Pour over mussels. Sprinkle with 1½ teasp. snipped parsley. Makes 3 servings.

GAME

Count yourself fortunate if there's a hunter in your family. Don't expect game to taste like other meat. It has a unique flavor. If you can roast a leg of lamb or chicken or make beef stew, you can just as easily roast venison or wild duck or make a *civet*, or game stew.

Proper Care of Game in the Field

Urge the hunters in your family to handle their take correctly and promptly.

BIRDS: Eviscerate them promptly and cool them. Too often the birds are thrown into the automobile trunk for the long drive home. With no chance for body heat to escape, the meat deteriorates.

SMALL GAME (rabbits, squirrels, etc.): Dress game promptly. Transport it in open air to keep it cool.

VENISON: Bleed it promptly and thoroughly. Dress it carefully, removing offal and wiping body cavity well. Use a dry cloth or dry leaves rather than water, as wet meat spoils quickly. Cool quickly. Don't carry it home on the hot radiator of the car. The roof is better, especially if the evening is cool.

To Store Game

Wrap game loosely to allow air circulation. Refrigerate in the meat compartment at least 2 or 3 days before cooking. Game improves with a little aging.

Store cooked game in a covered container in refrigerator. Use within 4 days.

To Freeze Game

GAME: Skin or pluck it, draw it, and cool it overnight. Have the game thoroughly clean and dry. Wrap in moisture-vapor-proof material. Store at 0°F. or lower.

VENISON: Since there is so much meat to freeze at one time, try to take deer to local meatman or freezer locker to be cut, wrapped, and frozen. Freeze venison at below 0°F., store at 0°F. For 15¢ you may send for: Extension Bulletin 800, "Venison," Bulletin Clerk, Oregon State College, Corvallis, Oregon.

ROAST PHEASANT

Use a young pheasant—one whose spur at back of foot is pliable and has rounded end.

Start heating oven to 450°F. Heat shallow open pan in oven. Finish cleaning bird; with string, tie legs and wings close to body. Sprinkle with salt, pepper. Completely cover breast with slices of fat salt pork or bacon; tie in place with string. Place bird on its side in heated pan; pour 1/4 cup salad oil over all.

Roast bird, uncovered, 15 min., basting often. Turn onto other side; roast 15 min. Then turn bird onto its back and roast 10 to 15 min., basting often. (Bird is done when juice, which runs out when bird is lifted and held tail down, is clear and without pink tinge.)

Remove bird from pan; cut away string. Pour off fat from pan. Add about ¾ cup water to pan; simmer, stirring to loosen brown bits that cling to pan, until liquid is reduced to about ½ cup. Season with salt, pepper; quickly stir in 1 tablesp. butter or margarine; remove gravy from heat as soon as butter is melted.

Slice meat from pheasant; serve on toast spread with Rouennaise, p. 336. Top with gravy.

Especially nice with cabbage, braised celery, wild rice, or tart jelly. One pheasant makes 2 to 4 servings.

NOTE: If you roast several birds in one pan, increase oven heat to 500°F. and increase water for gravy accordingly.

BRAISED PHEASANT WITH CABBAGE

¼-lb. piece fat salt pork	1 faggot, p. 8
1 pheasant (an older one)	2 cups hot water
2 slices fat salt pork	1 medium head cabbage (savoy preferred)
1 teasp. salt	1 carrot, pared
⅛ teasp. pepper	1 Knockwurst or frankfurter
1 onion, studded with cloves	1 cup hot water

Simmer salt-pork piece in water to cover a few min. Finish cleaning bird; cut into quarters. In Dutch oven, brown salt-pork slices; set aside. In Dutch oven, brown quartered bird. Then add salt, pepper, onion, faggot, simmered salt-pork piece, browned salt-pork slices, 2 cups hot water. Simmer, covered, 40 min.

Meanwhile, separate cabbage leaves; put into kettle with water to cover; simmer 5 min. Drain; dip into cold water; drain. To pheasant, add cabbage, carrot, Knockwurst, 1 cup hot water. Cook, covered, 45 to 60 min., or until meat is tender and leg separates from body.
To serve: Remove cabbage; drain thoroughly; place on heated platter with pheasant quarters. Remove and slice salt-pork piece. Surround pheasant with carrot, onion, Knockwurst, salt pork. Makes 4 servings.

BRAISED PARTRIDGE WITH CABBAGE: Substitute 2 whole partridge for pheasant. To serve: Split each partridge in half, allowing ½ bird per serving.

SALMI OF PHEASANT

1 pheasant (an older one)	⅔ cup red or white wine
2 tablesp. salad oil	1 cup canned tomatoes
1 medium onion, chopped	½ teasp. salt
1 shallot, chopped (optional)	3 whole black peppers
1 clove garlic, mashed	1 faggot, p. 8
4½ teasp. flour	12 mushrooms
	3 tablesp. butter or margarine

Day before: Roast a cleaned pheasant as on p. 332; refrigerate.
Next day: Cut breasts and legs from roast pheasant; cut up carcass; set aside. For sauce, in saucepan, heat salad oil; add onion; cook until golden. Add shallot, garlic, flour; cook 2 min. Stir in wine; cook, stirring, until thickened. Add tomatoes, salt, peppers, faggot, cut-up carcass, pheasant legs. Simmer, covered, 1 hr.

Remove legs; remove and discard skin; slice meat from bone. Slice breast meat. Place leg and breast meat in skillet; strain sauce over them; heat over low heat until meat is hot. Meanwhile, sauté mushrooms in butter 5 min.
To serve: Top pheasant and sauce with mushrooms. If desired, garnish with toast spread with Rouennaise, p. 336. Makes 2 or 3 servings.

SALMI OF PARTRIDGE: Substitute 2 cleaned partridge for pheasant. To roast, see Roast Partridge, below, then Roast Pheasant, p. 332.

ROAST PARTRIDGE

Use young partridge—one with breastbone that breaks easily when bent and leg bone that is plump and round near foot.

Finish cleaning bird; with string, tie legs and wings close to body. Roast, uncovered, as in Roast Pheasant, p. 332.

Serve it on toast spread with Rouennaise, p. 336. Serve with sauerkraut or cabbage. One small partridge makes 1 serving; split large bird to make 2 servings.

ROAST GUINEA HEN

Finish cleaning small young guinea hen; with string, tie legs and wings close to body. Roast, uncovered, as in Roast Pheasant, p. 332. One hen makes 2 to 4 servings.

NOTE: If bird is old, cook as in Chicken Fricassee, p. 277, and serve with sauerkraut.

ROAST WILD DUCK

Start heating oven to 475°F. Heat shallow open pan in oven. Finish cleaning wild duck; with string, tie legs and wings close to body. Place in heated pan. For very rare bird, roast, uncovered, 12 to 15 min.; for medium rare, 20 to 25 min. Remove from oven; let stand at least 5 min.

Make Sauce au Sang, p. 336, up to adding juices from roast duck. Sauté 3 bread slices in butter or margarine till golden on both sides.

Cut breast meat from duck and slice if desired. Also remove legs; if too rare, broil a short time; slice off meat. Now add juices from duck to Sauce au Sang.

Arrange breast and leg meat on 2 sautéed bread slices; pour on sauce; garnish with third bread slice, cut into triangles.

Serve with turnips, peas, or wild rice and cranberry or currant jelly. Makes 2 servings.

WILD DUCK, TEXAS STYLE

1 cup diced celery	2 2- to 2½-lb.
1 cup minced onions	wild ducks
1 cup seeded raisins	6 bacon slices
1 cup coarsely	1 cup catchup
chopped pecans	½ cup chili sauce
1 qt. fresh bread	¼ cup Worcester-
crumbs (4 cups)	shire
1½ teasp. salt	Water cress or parsley
2 eggs, beaten	Thin orange slices
½ cup scalded milk	Currant jelly

Start heating oven to 500°F. Combine celery, onions, raisins, pecans, crumbs, salt; add eggs; mix well. Stir in milk. Finish cleaning ducks; weigh; compute roasting time, allowing 60 min. per lb. (use weight of heavier bird). Stuff neck and body cavities with bread mixture; close opening as in Roast Chicken, 6, p. 261. Place 3 bacon slices across breast of each duck. Place ducks on wire rack in shallow open pan.

Roast ducks, uncovered, at 500°F. 15 min.; then reduce heat to 350°F. for remaining time. About ½ hr. before removing ducks from oven, mix catchup, chili sauce, Worcestershire; pour over ducks. Complete roasting.

To serve: Arrange ducks on heated platter. Garnish with water cress and orange slices topped with jelly. For spicy sauce, use sauce in pan, skimming off fat; if necessary, thicken as on p. 6; pass. Makes 4 to 6 servings.

ROAST QUAIL

Start heating oven to 450°F. Heat shallow open pan in oven. Finish cleaning quail; wrap in grape leaves if available. Cover with slices of fat salt pork; tie in place with string. Place quail with breast side up, in heated pan; spread with a little butter or margarine. Roast, uncovered, basting often, 15 to 20 min., depending on degree of rareness desired. When quail is roasted, remove from pan; remove leaves; place under broiler a few minutes to brown.

Meanwhile, add about ½ cup water to pan; simmer, stirring to loosen all browned bits that cling to pan. If desired, add 1 tablesp. dry sherry, ¼ cup seedless grapes. Taste; add salt if needed.

Serve bird on toast spread with Rouennaise, p. 336. Top with some of gravy; pass rest. Serve with potato chips, cranberry or currant jelly, or Bread Sauce, p. 336. Allow 1 bird per serving.

BROILED QUAIL

Preheat broiler, with broiler pan in place, 10 min., or as manufacturer directs. Finish cleaning quail; split. Sprinkle with salt; spread with soft butter or margarine. Place, with skin sides up, on heated broiler pan. Broil 5 min. Turn; broil 6 to 7 min. Remove to heated platter. Make Quick Cream Sauce for Game, p. 336.

Serve birds on toast spread with Rouennaise, p. 336; top with sauce. Allow 1 bird per serving.

ROAST WOODCOCK

Start heating oven to 475°F. Heat shallow open pan in oven. Finish cleaning bird; wrap in slices of fat salt pork; tie in place with string. Spread with a little butter or margarine. Place in heated pan. Roast, uncovered, 8 to 15 min., depending on rareness desired. Remove bird; keep warm.

Add about ½ cup water to pan; simmer till liquid is reduced to about half. Add 1 tablesp. butter or margarine; heat until just melted. (For de luxe taste, add a few dry juniper berries—you can buy them at a drugstore.) Taste gravy; add salt if needed.

Serve bird on toast, with gravy. Allow 1 bird per serving.

ROAST GROUSE: Roast cleaned grouse as above, allowing 10 to 20 min., depending on rareness desired. Make gravy as above. Serve with Bread Sauce, p. 336, dried bread crumbs sautéed in butter or margarine, gravy, and currant jelly. Allow 1 bird per serving.

CIVET OF VENISON

3 lb. venison shoulder, neck, or other less tender part	2 tablesp. brown sugar
Raw Marinade, right	½ lb. mushrooms (quartered if large)
½ cup salad oil	
1 cup diced fat salt pork	2 tablesp. flour
12 to 15 small onions	1 clove garlic, mashed
2 carrots, pared, sliced	⅔ cup red wine
	1 faggot, p. 8
	Snipped parsley

Remove skin, tough sinews, and bones from meat; cut into pieces as for stew. Cover with Raw Marinade; refrigerate 24 hr. or longer.

To Cook: Remove meat from marinade; strain marinade; reserve. Dry meat with paper towels. In hot oil in skillet, brown salt pork; set pork aside. To skillet, add onions; when onions are partially brown, add carrots; sprinkle with brown sugar; cook until vegetables are brown; set aside.

Sauté mushrooms in same skillet until brown all over; set aside. Then brown meat (don't crowd skillet); remove to large saucepan. Sprinkle meat with flour; cook until flour browns. Add garlic, wine, faggot, reserved marinade, and just enough water to cover meat; simmer 1 hr., or until quite tender. Add salt pork, onions, carrots, mushrooms; cook 40 min. Remove faggot; taste stew; season to taste. Serve sprinkled with parsley. Makes 8 servings.

ROAST VENISON

Cover 5- to 7-lb. leg of venison with Cooked Marinade, right; then refrigerate at least 24 hr. or longer if convenient.

To roast: Start heating oven to 450°F. Heat shallow open pan in oven. Remove venison from marinade; remove skin and tough sinews. Sprinkle venison with salt; cover with slices of fat salt pork. Place in heated pan; add enough salad oil to cover bottom of pan. Roast, uncovered, basting with salad oil, allowing about 15 min. per lb. for medium-rare meat. Or roast 45 to 60 min. for very rare meat.

Serve with Quick Poivrade Sauce, p. 336, or Quick Cream Sauce for Game, p. 336, wild rice, and currant jelly. Makes 6 to 8 servings.

GRENADIN OF VENISON

Cut 1½″-thick slices from loin of venison. (They will look like filet mignon.) Cover with Raw Marinade, below; store in refrigerator 2 days or longer.

To cook: Remove venison from marinade; drain well; dry thoroughly with paper towels. Strain marinade; reserve. Cover bottom of skillet with salad oil; heat till very hot. Cook slices of venison 8 to 10 min. on each side. (If you have several slices, use 2 skillets, to insure browned, sautéed surface.)

Serve with Quick Poivrade Sauce, p. 336, or Quick Cream Sauce for Game, p. 336.

RAW MARINADE

2 medium onions, thinly sliced	¼ teasp. dried thyme
1 carrot, pared, thinly sliced	2 bay leaves
2 shallots, minced (optional)	12 whole black peppers
2 stalks celery	2 whole cloves
1 clove garlic	2 cups red or white wine
1 teasp. salt	½ cup salad oil

Mix all ingredients; pour over venison or any furred game as recipe directs. Refrigerate 24 hr. or longer before cooking. Makes enough to cover 2 to 3 lb. meat.

COOKED MARINADE

1 qt. water	1 teasp. dried thyme
1½ cups vinegar	
2 onions, chopped	4 sprigs parsley
1 carrot, pared, diced	12 whole black peppers
1 clove garlic	1 tablesp. salt

Put all ingredients in saucepan; bring to boil; simmer, covered, 1 hr. Cool. Pour over venison or any furred game as recipe directs. Refrigerate 24 hr. or longer before cooking. Makes enough to cover 5- to 7-lb. venison roast.

For uses of Frozen Farm-Raised Domestic Rabbit Meat, see p. 241.

GAME SAUCES

QUICK SAUCE FOR FURRED GAME

2 teasp. minced onion or shallots	1⅓ cups strained Raw Marinade, p. 335
2 tablesp. butter or margarine	2 teasp. currant jelly
2 tablesp. flour	Salt
⅔ cup red wine	

After removing cooked venison or other furred game from pan, pour off fat. Stir in onion, butter, flour; cook about 2 min. Add wine; mix well. Slowly stir in marinade; cook, stirring constantly, until thickened. Add jelly. Taste; add salt if needed. Pour over venison—chops, *grenadin*, or sliced roast. Makes 1½ cups.

QUICK CREAM SAUCE FOR GAME

2 teasp. minced onion or shallots	Marinade, p. 335, or 1 teasp. lemon juice
2 tablesp. butter or margarine	1½ cups heavy cream
2 teasp. flour	2 teasp. currant jelly
½ cup strained Raw	Salt

After removing roast venison or other furred game from pan, pour off fat. Stir in onion, butter, flour; cook about 2 min. Add marinade if available. Slowly add cream; cook, stirring, until blended and thickened. (Now add lemon juice if used instead of marinade.) Add jelly. Taste; add salt if needed. Pour over venison. Makes 1¾ cups.

BREAD SAUCE

1 medium onion	1 cup fresh bread crumbs
2 whole cloves	
2 cups milk	1 tablesp. butter or margarine
Dash cayenne pepper	
¼ teasp. salt	

Stud onion with cloves. Place in saucepan with milk, cayenne, salt. Bring to boil; simmer about 5 min.; strain. Add bread crumbs; stir in butter. Use with grouse or other game birds. Makes 2 cups.

SAUCE AU SANG

¼ cup red wine	1 tablesp. butter or margarine
5 whole black peppers	½ teasp. flour
1 small bay leaf	Juices collected when roast duck is done
¼ teasp. dried thyme	
1 medium onion, minced; or 2 shallots, minced	Salt
	Pepper

In saucepan over low heat, cook wine, peppers, bay leaf, thyme, and onion until reduced to 2 tablesp. Blend butter with flour; stir into wine mixture until melted and mixed; strain through fine sieve. Briskly stir all juices from carved duck into sauce. (Do not boil or sauce will curdle.) Taste; add salt and pepper if needed. Pour over duck. Makes enough for 1 duck.

ROUENNAISE

2 tablesp. diced fat salt pork	1 bay leaf
1 cup chicken or duck livers	1 teasp. salt
	⅛ teasp. pepper
Pinch dried thyme	1 to 2 tablesp. sherry or brandy

Fry salt pork in skillet until very crisp. Add livers, thyme, bay leaf, salt, pepper. Cook over high heat 3 to 4 min.; stir in sherry. Place in wooden bowl; pound with mallet until soft. Rub through sieve to make paste. To use, spread on toast, served with game. Makes about ½ cup.

QUICK POIVRADE SAUCE FOR VENISON

2 tablesp. fat and pan drippings	Raw Marinade, p. 335
1 teasp. minced onion or shallot	2 cups red wine
1 tablesp. flour	Salt
3 tablesp. vinegar or ½ cup strained	Pepper
	2 tablesp. currant jelly

After removing cooked venison from pan, pour off all fat and drippings. Return 2 tablesp. fat and drippings to pan; add onion or shallot. (If onion is used, brown slightly; if shallot, do not brown.) Add flour; blend well. Add vinegar and wine; cook, stirring, until reduced to half. Taste; add salt and pepper if needed. Stir in currant jelly. Pour over venison—chops, *grenadin*, or sliced roast. Makes 1½ cups.

STUFFINGS

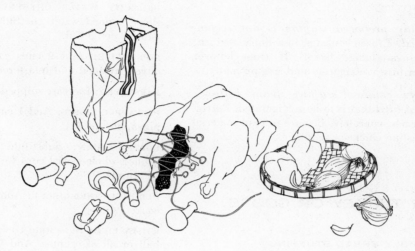

There's something about a stuffed turkey, chicken, fish, or roast that makes any meal a feast. Choose one of our stuffings that will compliment the flavor, preserve the shape, and make the servings bigger and better.

Before using these recipes, refer to How To Use Our Recipes, .p. 3. Always use standard measuring cups and measuring spoons; measure level.

What You Should Know About Stuffings

For crumbs, use bread 2 or 3 days old. If you're starting with sliced bread, stack several slices; cut off crusts; cut bread into strips, then into ½″ squares.

If you're starting with an unsliced loaf, cut it in two; fork out inside of loaf, leaving crust. With fork or finger tips, pick bread pieces apart to make fine and even crumbs.

Allow about 1 cup stuffing per 1 lb. of bird. Any extra stuffing can be baked in a greased casserole or loaf pan, or wrapped in foil, then baked during last half hour of roasting bird.

This is true, too, if you're roasting your bird in foil.

Are two stuffings popular at your house? Make both if you're roasting a large bird; use one to stuff neck, other to fill body cavity.

Packaged ready-to-use stuffings are so easy to use and are excellently seasoned. Just follow directions on package.

Wait to make stuffing for bird until just before roasting it. You may prepare stuffing ingredients the day before, refrigerating such perishables as liquid, celery, etc. But *never* make stuffing until *just before roasting bird.*

Stuffing the turkey a day ahead is a risk in the home kitchen and is not advised. Too much opportunity is afforded for the development of dangerous toxins (due to bacterial growth) which are not destroyed during roasting.

Don't "pack" stuffing too tightly. It absorbs juices and expands during roasting.

Partially cooking either the turkey and stuffing together, or each separately, on

337

the day before is a risk. The roasting process, once started, should be completed without interruption.

Never freeze cooked stuffed poultry. Always remove the stuffing, then wrap the poultry before freezing.

Freezing prepared stuffing is not recommended. Frozen stuffings lose fluffy texture; seasonings change flavor. If from leftover roasted bird, refrigerate and use promptly.

Always remove stuffing from leftover roasted bird that is to be refrigerated. Refrigerate each separately. Be sure to read material on roasting chickens, p. 261.

FOR TURKEY OR GOOSE

CRUMBLY BREAD STUFFING

1⅛ cups butter, margarine, or salad oil	¼ cup diced celery
¾ cup minced onions	1½ teasp. poultry seasoning
4½ qt. day-old bread crumbs or ½″ squares (18 cups), lightly packed	½ cup snipped parsley (optional)
	¼ teasp. pepper
	2¼ teasp. salt

In hot butter in deep kettle, sauté onions till tender. Combine rest of ingredients; add to onions; heat well without browning, stirring frequently.

Loosely stuffs neck and body cavity of a 10-lb. turkey.

FOR SMALL TURKEY: To stuff neck and body cavity of turkey of 4 to 5 lb. weight, use Buttery Bread, p. 340, or Buttery Celery Stuffing, p. 340.

MUSHROOM: Sauté ½ lb. sliced mushrooms and 6 tablesp. minced green pepper (optional) with onions in butter, covered. Or add two 3- or 4-oz. cans sliced mushrooms, drained.

TOASTED NUT: Add 1 cup canned slivered toasted almonds, or chopped walnuts.

ORANGE-HERB: Omit poultry seasoning. Add 1 tablesp. grated orange rind and a pinch of dried rosemary.

SLIVERED HAM: Add 1 to 2 cups finely slivered cooked ham.

GREEN PEPPER: Omit parsley. Add ½ to 1 cup minced green pepper, sautéed in a little butter or margarine till tender, but not brown.

CRUNCHY WATER CHESTNUT: Add 2 cups sliced canned water chestnuts; their crunchiness is delightful.

RIPE OLIVE: Add 2 cups canned pitted ripe olives, drained and quartered.

PARSLEYED: Increase snipped parsley to ¾ cup.

PINEAPPLE TIDBIT: Add 1 cup drained canned pineapple tidbits.

GOLDEN CORN: Substitute 2 cups drained canned whole-kernel corn for an equal amount of crumbs.

OLD-FASHIONED GIBLET: Add coarsely chopped cooked giblets.

RAISIN RICE: Substitute cooked white rice for half or all of crumbs. Add ½ cup raisins.

APPLE: Make up half basic stuffing. Add 5 cups chopped apples and a few raisins.

STUFFED OLIVE: Add 1 cup sliced stuffed or green olives.

SAUSAGE: Add ½ lb. cooked sausage links, sliced.

POTATO: Substitute unseasoned mashed white or sweet potatoes (the instant mashed white kind is so easy) for half of bread crumbs.

OYSTER: Add 1 pt. oysters, drained, cut up.

MOIST BREAD STUFFING

1½ cups boiling water	2 tablesp. snipped parsley
½ to ¾ cup butter, margarine, or salad oil	2 tablesp. diced celery
½ cup minced onions	3 qt. day-old bread crumbs or ½″ squares (12 cups), lightly packed
¼ teasp. pepper	
1 teasp. poultry seasoning	2 tablesp. dry or prepared mustard
1½ teasp. salt	

In large kettle, combine water, butter, onions; simmer 5 min. Add rest of ingredients; mix well.

Stuffs body cavity of 8-lb. turkey.

MUSHROOM-RICE STUFFING

½ cup butter or mar-
garine
2⅔ cups packaged
precooked rice
½ cup chopped
onions
1 lb. mushrooms,
chopped
2 cups diced celery
½ cup snipped cel-
ery leaves

1 tablesp. salt
⅛ teasp. pepper
½ teasp. dried mar-
joram
⅛ teasp. dried sage
⅛ teasp. dried thyme
2½ cups water
⅔ cup chopped pe-
cans

In large saucepan, melt butter; add rest of
ingredients except water, pecans; sauté, stirring, until onions are golden. Mix in water.
Bring to boil over high heat; simmer 2 min.,
gently fluffing rice once or twice with fork.
Remove from heat; add pecans.

Lightly stuffs body cavity of 6- to 7-lb. turkey.

SAUSAGE STUFFING

1 lb. pork sausage
meat
1 cup diced celery
1 cup minced onions
2 qt. day-old bread

crumbs or ½"
squares (8 cups),
lightly packed
2 tablesp. snipped
parsley

In skillet, over medium heat, cook sausage
meat, celery, and onions together about 10 min.,
or until sausage is cooked. Add crumbs, parsley.

Stuffs body cavity of 8-lb. turkey.

CHESTNUT STUFFING

½ lb. chestnuts (1 cup
boiled)
1 tablesp. butter, mar-
garine, or salad oil
½ lb. pork sausage
meat
¼ cup minced onion
½ cup hot water

1 teasp. dried sage
1½ teasp. salt
⅛ teasp. pepper
2 cups toasted bread
crumbs, lightly
packed
2 tablesp. sherry

Wash chestnuts; make long slit on both sides
of each shell. Bake at 500°F. 15 min. Shell
and skin nuts; then boil in salted water to cover,
covered, 20 min. Drain; chop medium fine.

In butter in skillet, sauté sausage meat and
onion about 10 min., or until sausage is cooked,
onion is tender. Combine hot water, sage, salt,
pepper, crumbs, sherry. Then add chestnuts,
sausage mixture.

Stuffs neck cavity of 8-lb. turkey. Fill body
cavity with any other desired stuffing.

CORN STUFFING

3 cups diced celery
2 cups boiling water
⅔ cup minced onions
½ to 1 cup butter,
margarine, or salad
oil
1 teasp. dried sage
2 qt. day-old bread

crumbs or ½"
squares (8 cups),
lightly packed
2¼ teasp. salt
¾ teasp. pepper
3 12-oz. cans vacuum-
packed whole-
kernel corn

Cook celery in boiling water, covered, 15 to
20 min., or until tender; drain. Sauté onions
in butter until transparent; add, with celery,
to rest of ingredients in large bowl.

Stuffs neck and body cavity of 7-lb. turkey.

SAGE-AND-ONION STUFFING

12 medium onions
1 to 2 tablesp. dried
sage
1 teasp. poultry sea-
soning
2 to 3 teasp. salt

¼ to ½ teasp. pepper
2 qt. day-old bread
crumbs or ½"
squares (8 cups),
lightly packed

Boil onions till tender-crisp; drain; chop fine.
Add rest of ingredients; mix well.

Stuffs neck and body cavity of 10-lb. goose.

DOWN-SOUTH STUFFING

½ cup butter or mar-
garine
¾ cup minced onions
½ cup minced green
peppers
½ cup minced celery
1 chicken-bouillon
cube
5 cups day-old white-
bread crumbs
5 cups crumbled corn

bread (made with-
out sugar)
½ lb. fresh pork-
sausage links, cut up
¼ teasp. salt
⅛ teasp. pepper
½ teasp. poultry sea-
soning
2 eggs, beaten
¾ cup chopped pe-
cans

In hot butter in skillet, sauté onions, green
peppers, celery until tender. Dissolve bouillon
cube in about ⅔ cup hot water; sprinkle over
white- and corn-bread crumbs. Add sautéed
vegetables. In same skillet, sauté sausages until
browned. To crumb mixture, add salt, pepper,
poultry seasoning, eggs, pecans, then sausages
and drippings; toss.

Divide one third of stuffing between crop
and tail end of 10-lb. turkey (this helps to
plump bird). In 8" x 8" x 2" pan, place rest

of stuffing. Refrigerate; then bake, uncovered, with turkey at 325°F. last 45 min.

TASTY NOTE: Baste bird with ¼ cup butter or margarine heated with ¾ cup red wine; use liquid left in pan to make gravy; serve over bird and stuffing.

FOR CHICKEN, DUCKLING, OR PHEASANT

SAVORY RICE STUFFING

¼ cup butter or margarine	1 teasp. salt
¾ cup minced onions	¼ teasp. pepper
1½ cups diced celery	¼ teasp. dried sage
1⅓ cups cooked rice	¼ teasp. dried thyme

In skillet, melt butter. Add onions, celery; sauté till tender—about 3 min. Add rice, rest of ingredients; toss.

Stuffs neck and body cavity of 4-lb bird.

APRICOT: With rice, add 1 cup snipped dried apricots. Omit sage.

RICE-AND-OLIVE: Use only 1 cup diced celery, ¼ teasp. salt. With rice, add 1 cup chopped stuffed olives. (Double recipe to stuff dressed 6- to 8-lb. fish.)

BUTTERY BREAD STUFFING

1½ qt. day-old bread crumbs or ½″ squares (6 cups), lightly packed	1 teasp. celery seeds
	⅛ teasp. pepper
	¾ teasp. salt
½ teasp. poultry seasoning; or ½ teasp. dried thyme, marjoram, or sage	½ cup butter, margarine, or salad oil
	¼ cup minced onion
	3 tablesp. snipped parsley

Combine bread crumbs, poultry seasoning, celery seeds, pepper, salt. In large skillet, melt butter. Add onion; simmer until tender but not browned. Add crumb mixture, parsley; heat well without browning, stirring often.

Stuffs neck and body cavity of 4-lb. bird.

MOIST GIBLET: Add, with crumb mixture, ½ cup giblet water, milk, or cream and coarsely chopped, cooked giblets.

MUSHROOM: Sauté ¼ lb. mushrooms, sliced, with onion in butter, covered.

CORN: Increase onion to ½ cup, salt to 1 teasp., pepper to ¼ teasp. Add, with crumb mixture, 1 12-oz. can vacuum-packed whole-kernel corn, drained.

FRUIT: Reduce bread crumbs to 3 cups. Add, with crumb mixture, 1 cup cut-up, drained, cooked dried apricots or pitted prunes.

CORN BREAD: Substitute corn-bread crumbs for bread crumbs. Bacon fat may replace part of butter; or add 4 diced crisp bacon slices.

BUTTERY CELERY STUFFING

1½ cups finely diced celery	½ teasp. poultry seasoning
⅔ cup boiling water	1 teasp. salt
7 cups day-old bread crumbs or ½″ squares, lightly packed	¼ teasp. pepper
	¼ cup minced onion
	⅓ to ½ cup butter, margarine, or salad oil

Simmer celery in boiling water, covered, 15 to 20 min., or until tender. Drain, reserving ⅓ cup liquid. In large bowl, combine bread crumbs with poultry seasoning, salt, pepper.

Slowly cook onion in butter till tender but not brown. Add, with celery and celery liquid, to crumbs.

Stuffs neck and body cavity of 5-lb. bird.

OYSTER: Add, to crumbs, ½ cup chopped, drained, shucked raw oysters. Substitute oyster liquid for celery liquid.

BAKED STUFFING BALLS

2 qt. day-old ½″ bread squares (8 cups), firmly packed	½ cup snipped parsley (optional)
	1 cup minced celery
1 teasp. poultry seasoning	½ cup butter or margarine
1½ teasp. salt	½ cup water
½ teasp. pepper	2 beef-bouillon cubes
2 tablesp. minced onion	2 egg whites

Early in day: Toss bread squares with poultry seasoning, salt, pepper, onion, parsley, celery. Heat butter with water and bouillon cubes, stirring; toss well with crumbs. Beat egg whites until just foamy; mix with crumbs. Lightly press handful of mixture into ball; if it doesn't hold its shape, add a little more water.

Shape mixture into balls a little larger than golf-ball size—about ½ cup mixture per ball.

Place on greased baking sheet; refrigerate till needed.

About 1 hr. before serving: Bake at 325°F. 1 hr., or till crisp and lightly browned. Nice with hot or cold chicken, turkey, ham, or pork. Makes 8.

TINA'S WILD-RICE STUFFING

¼ cup bacon fat, butter, or margarine	1 cup seedless grapes
2 medium onions, minced	¼ cup sherry
	2 cups cooked wild rice
½ cup minced celery	1 teasp. salt

In hot bacon fat in skillet, sauté onions until tender; add rest of ingredients.

Stuffs body cavity of 4- to 5-lb. bird, or 4 1- to 1½-lb. birds.

FOR CROWN ROAST PORK

CRANBERRY-APPLE STUFFING

¼ cup butter or margarine	½ teasp. poultry seasoning
1 onion, chopped	⅛ teasp. pepper
1½ cups chopped celery	1 cup fresh cranberries, chopped
4 cups day-old bread cubes	2 cups sliced, pared apples
1 teasp. salt	

In small skillet melt butter; in it cook onion until brown. In large bowl combine celery, bread cubes, salt, poultry seasoning, pepper, and cooked onions. Toss in cranberries and apples (reserve some slices for garnish, if desired). Use to stuff an 18- to 20-rib crown roast of pork. Double recipe for 24- to 26-rib crown roast.

CRANBERRY AND MIXED FRUIT STUFFING

2 cups fresh cranberries	2½ cups small day-old bread cubes
1 cup water	1 medium onion, sliced
¾ cup granulated sugar	½ teasp. allspice
1 12-oz. pkg. dried mixed fruit, cut into small pieces	½ teasp. salt
	1 1-lb.-6-oz. can sliced apples, drained

In medium saucepan, combine cranberries, water, and sugar; cook, stirring occasionally, until berries pop. Stir in mixed fruit; cook about 5 min. Stir in bread cubes, onion, allspice, salt, and apple slices (reserve some slices for garnish, if desired). Use to stuff an 18- to 20-rib crown roast of pork. For 24- to 26-rib crown roast, make twice the recipe, but use only 1 pkg. dried fruit and 1 can apples.

FOR FISH

CAPTAIN'S STUFFING

1 cup minced celery	lightly packed
½ cup water	3 tablesp. minced onion
6 tablesp. butter or margarine	1 to 1½ teasp. dried sage
1 qt. day-old bread crumbs or ½″ squares (4 cups),	¾ teasp. salt
	½ teasp. pepper

Cook celery, water, and butter until butter is melted; pour over rest of ingredients combined.

Stuffs dressed 3-lb. shad, with backbone removed. Or halve recipe to stuff dressed 3-lb. fish or to fill pairs of 1½- to 2-lb. fillets.

MUSHROOM: Add ½ lb. mushrooms, chopped.
CUCUMBER: Add ½ cup coarsely chopped cucumber.

RICE-AND-OLIVE STUFFING: See p. 340

MUSHROOM-CRACKER STUFFING

¼ cup butter or margarine	1 tablesp. snipped parsley
¼ cup minced celery	2 cups coarsely crushed crackers
¼ cup minced onion	
¼ to ½ lb. mushrooms, sliced; or	¼ teasp. poultry seasoning
1 3- or 4-oz. can mushrooms, drained	½ teasp. salt (unless crackers are salty)

In hot butter in large skillet, cook celery and onion till golden. Add mushrooms; cook 3 min. Add parsley, rest of ingredients.

Stuffs 4- to 6-lb. dressed salmon or salmon shoulder. Or halve recipe to stuff dressed 2- to 3-lb. fish, or to fill pairs of 1½- to 2-lb. fillets.

CHEESE STUFFING

½ cup sliced onions
¼ cup butter or mar-
  garine
¾ teasp. salt
Dash pepper

1½ cups fresh bread
  crumbs
⅓ cup grated proc-
  ess Cheddar cheese

Sauté onions in butter till tender. Toss with salt, pepper, bread crumbs, cheese.

Use to top 2-lb. cod or haddock fillets or to fill pairs of 1- to 1½-lb. fillets.

GARDEN STUFFING

1 small clove garlic
1 teasp. salt
⅓ cup minced scal-
  lions
½ cup chopped green
  peppers

½ cup chopped
  celery
2 tomatoes, peeled,
  coarsely chopped
3 tablesp. snipped
  parsley

With 4-tined fork, mash garlic with salt in bottom of bowl; add rest of ingredients.

Stuffs and tops dressed 6- to 7-lb. fish.

CHEESE

Because it is so adaptable, and because there's a type for every taste, cheese is the good cook's stand-by for dishes from soup to dessert. Since all varieties are easily digested, it's good for oldsters and youngsters alike.

Many of the cheese recipes that follow are especially suitable for luncheon or supper main dishes. Check the Index for other appearances of cheese throughout the book.

Before using these recipes, refer to How To Use Our Recipes, p. 3. Always use standard measuring cups and measuring spoons; measure level.

Its Place in Our Meals

You get your money's worth when you buy a whole-milk cheese like Cheddar. It has the same kind of protein as meat—high quality. In fact, 3 oz. Cheddar (as well as most other varieties of cheese) provides as much or more protein as the same amount of meat. Cheese gives you extra dividends too, for it has plenty of calcium and vitamin A, and there's no waste.

If you're counting your calories cottage cheese is for you! Although it's simply bursting with food value, ⅓ cup (about what you'd use in a salad) will set you back only 75 calories (85 calories if it's creamed).

KINDS TO BUY

Natural Cheeses

All natural cheeses begin with fluid milk.

Bulk natural cheese comes in huge wheels, bricks, blocks, etc., from which the grocer slices off what you want.

Prewrapped natural cheese is cut and packaged, either at the factory or by your grocer, in oblongs, wedges, discs, triangles, slices, etc.

Types of natural cheeses:
VERY HARD, such as Parmesan, Romano, Sbrinz, sapsago.
HARD, such as Cheddar, Swiss, Provolone, caciocavallo.
SEMIHARD, (SEMISOFT), such as brick, Muenster, Edam, Gouda; or Oka (or Port du Salut or Trappist); or Roquefort, Danish blue, bleu, Gorgonzola, Stilton (blue-mold cheeses).
SOFT, RIPENED, such as Bel Paese, Brie, Camembert, Limburger, Liederkranz.
SOFT, UNRIPENED, such as cottage, cream, Ricotta.

Process Cheeses

PROCESS CHEESES are natural cheeses, melted, pasteurized, then blended with an emulsifier

343

agent. Heating halts the ripening, so their flavor and texture are always uniform. Process cheese has no rind or waste and melts smoothly without ever getting stringy during cooking. It comes in several tasty flavors—in slices, in ½ lb. or economy 2 lb. loaves, etc.

PROCESS CHEESE FOODS spread, melt, and cook more easily than process cheese, because they contain extra moisture and less fat. They come in ½ lb., 1 lb., and 2 lb. loaves; in rolls, etc.

Care after Opening Cheeses

If It's Process Cheese, Cheese Food, or a Cheese Spread: Open packaged kind with care, so that unused cheese can be carefully rewrapped in original wrapping and refrigerated. If wrapper is not usable again, wrap cheese tightly in foil, saran, plastic bags, etc.

If It's a Loaf Process Cheese, do not remove all of wrapper. Simply cut off what cheese you need; then cover exposed surface with foil.

If It's a Jar Spread, refrigerate, with lid tightly in place, after using.

If It's Packaged Prepared Cheese Dips: Use up dips, such as cottage cheese, cream cheese, or sour cream, promptly after opening.

If It's Natural Cheese: To store small pieces, wrap tightly in foil, saran, etc.; refrigerate.

To store a large piece over a long period, cover cut surfaces with a coating of melted paraffin; then wrap tightly in foil; refrigerate. Or, if it's to be used daily, wrap in a clean kitchen towel, dampened with a vinegar solution of 1 teasp. vinegar to 1 qt. water.

To store ends of cheese, grate; refrigerate in covered jar; use in casseroles, etc.

To store cheese with a very strong aroma, like Limburger, etc., use a covered container; plan to use within a week after refrigerating.

Mold on natural cheeses is not harmful to the cheese. Cut or scrape off the mold; then use cheese beneath.

If It's Cottage or Cream Cheese (soft cheeses): Refrigerate, tightly covered, and plan to use promptly after purchase.

To Freeze Cheese: Research indicates that, in general, cheeses do not freeze without damage to texture and consistency.

To Grate Cheese with Ease

If cheese is soft, like process cheese, use a coarse grater, which insures long flakes of grated cheese. Many times you can merely slice or dice a soft cheese and add it to sauce.

If cheese is very dry, use a fine grater.

Cheese as a Garnish

From the first to the last of the meal, a little cheese can enhance many everyday dishes.

CHEESE CROUTONS: Cut cheese into small cubes; drop into bowls or cups of soup just before serving.

CHEESE POPCORN: Mix equal parts of grated cheese and melted butter or margarine; pour over freshly popped corn.

EASY STUFFED TOMATOES: Marinate cheese cubes in French dressing; use to stuff seasoned hollowed-out tomatoes; serve on lettuce as salad.

CHEESE-SALAD CURLS: Run vegetable parer down side of ½ lb. piece of packaged process cheese. Roll up each thin shaving. Use as garnish for fruit or tossed green salad.

CHEESE SCRAMBLE: Just before scrambled eggs are done, sprinkle with grated cheese.

CRUNCHY CHEESE TOPPING: After tossing fresh bread crumbs with melted butter or margarine, toss with some grated cheese (Parmesan or process Cheddar). Use to top main-dish casseroles or scalloped vegetables. Or just sprinkle over hot seasoned vegetables before serving.

CHEESE PICKUPS FOR VEGETABLES: Stir a little grated cheese into canned or stewed tomatoes.

Top creamed onions with grated cheese, tossed with chopped nuts.

Stir a little grated cheese into creamed potatoes—just enough to give a subtle flavor.

REAL CHEESE APPLE PIE: Before adjusting top crust, place a few slices of process sharp cheese on top of apples.

CHEESE AS THE MAIN DISH

CHILI RABBIT

1 can chili con carne	undiluted
½ cup light cream	1 lb. process sharp
½ cup canned con-	cheese slices
densed consommé,	Corn crisps

In blazer of chafing dish, over direct heat, to chili con carne, add light cream, consommé, and cheese. Cook, stirring occasionally, until cheese melts and is blended into mixture. Serve over corn crisps. Makes 6 servings.

MIDNIGHT RABBIT

½ lb. process Cheddar or sharp cheese	2 teasp. minced onion
1 8-oz. can tomato sauce	Several drops Tabasco

Into chafing dish or double boiler, slice cheese. When melted and saucelike, stir in tomato sauce, onion, and Tabasco; heat through. Serve over chunks of canned tuna, toasted English muffins, hot fluffy rice, potato chips, or crisp crackers. Makes 3 or 4 servings.

OLD-TIME WELSH RABBIT

3 tablesp. butter or margarine	¾ teasp. Worcestershire
½ cup flour	3 cups milk
½ teasp. salt	½ lb. sharp natural Cheddar cheese, grated (2 cups)
⅛ teasp. dry mustard	Crisp crackers or toast
Dash cayenne pepper	

In double boiler, melt butter. Stir in flour, salt, mustard, cayenne, Worcestershire, then milk; cook, stirring, until thickened and smooth. Add cheese; cook, stirring occasionally, until melted.

Serve over crisp crackers. Makes 6 servings.

WELSH RABBIT WITH BEER

1 tablesp. butter or margarine	1 tablesp. dry mustard
1 lb. process Cheddar cheese, grated (4 cups)	½ teasp. Worcestershire
	¼ teasp. salt
¾ cup light beer	1 egg, unbeaten
Dash cayenne pepper	Crackers or toast

Melt butter in double boiler. Slowly stir in cheese. As cheese melts, stir all but 1 tablesp. beer into it, a little at a time, over a period of about ½ hr. Combine cayenne, mustard, Worcestershire, salt with 1 tablesp. beer. Add egg; stir smooth quickly with spoon. Add to cheese mixture. As soon as well mixed, serve at once over crackers or toast. Makes 4 or 5 servings—a nice company dish.

NOTE: You can buy delicious Welsh Rabbit in jars or cans.

SUPERB SWISS-CHEESE PIE
(Quiche Lorraine)

1 9" unbaked pie shell, well chilled	Pinch nutmeg
1 tablesp. soft butter or margarine	Pinch sugar
	Pinch cayenne pepper
12 bacon slices*	⅛ teasp. pepper
4 eggs	¼ lb. natural Swiss cheese, grated (1 cup)
2 cups heavy cream	
¾ teasp. salt	

Start heating oven to 425°F. Rub butter over surface of unbaked pie shell. Fry bacon until crisp; crumble into small pieces. Combine eggs, cream, salt, nutmeg, sugar, cayenne, pepper; with hand beater, beat just long enough to mix thoroughly.

Sprinkle pie shell with bacon and cheese; pour in cream mixture. Bake at 425°F. 15 min. Reduce oven heat to 300°F.; bake 40 min., or until silver knife inserted in center comes out clean.

Serve at once, cut into wedges, as luncheon or dinner main dish. Makes 6 to 8 servings.

*If you prefer, save 6 bacon slices as garnish. Fry them until done but not too crisp. Immediately roll up each slice; arrange, seam side down, in bed of parsley around pie plate.

NIBBLER LORRAINE: Substitute 11" unbaked pie shell, well chilled, for 9" unbaked pie shell. Serve as first course, cut into about 20 wedges.

QUICHE LOUISIANE: Omit bacon. Substitute 1 cup split, cooked, deveined, shelled shrimp tossed with 2 tablesp. chili sauce and dash Tabasco.

QUICHE MANHATTAN: Omit bacon. Substitute 1 cup finely cut-up cooked ham, tongue, or Canadian bacon; or 2 tablesp. snipped anchovy fillets.

SWITZERLAND CHEESE-AND-ONION PIE

1 9" unbaked pie shell	1 tablesp. flour
2 large onions, thinly sliced (about 1 cup)	3 eggs
	1 cup milk or light cream
2 tablesp. butter or margarine	½ teasp. salt
½ lb. natural Swiss cheese, grated	⅛ teasp. pepper

Start heating oven to 400°F. In small skillet, sauté onions in butter until tender; turn into pastry-lined pie plate. Toss grated cheese with flour; sprinkle over onions. Beat eggs well;

stir in milk, salt, pepper; pour over cheese. Bake 20 min. Now reduce oven heat to 300°F. and bake 25 min. longer, or until knife inserted in center comes out clean.

Serve hot, cut into wedges, for lunch or supper. Or serve, cut into smaller wedges, as an evening snack. Makes 6 to 8 servings.

HAM 'N' CHEESE PIE

1 9″ unbaked pie shell	boiled ham
2 4-oz. pkg. shredded, sharp Cheddar cheese, or 1 8-oz. pkg. process sharp Cheddar cheese, grated	¼ cup all-purpose flour
	1 teasp. seasoned salt
	¼ teasp. caraway seeds
	1 cup milk
2 medium onions, cut into rings	3 eggs
2 thin slices	Few sprigs fresh or dried dill or parsley

About 1½ hr. before serving:
1. Start heating oven to 350°F. Over bottom of pie shell, evenly spread 1 pkg. shredded cheese; over it spread half of onion rings. Cover onion rings with second package of shredded cheese.
2. Cut the 2 ham slices into 1½″ squares. Over the top layer of shredded cheese, overlap these ham squares alternately with rest of onion rings in circle around top edge of pie.
3. Now, in small bowl, mix flour, seasoned salt, and caraway seeds; gradually add milk and eggs, while beating smooth with wire whip or hand beater. Pour over cheese-onion mixture. Bake 55 to 65 min., or until egg mixture is firm and a light brown.
4. Decorate edge of pie with small sprigs of fresh dill; or sprinkle pie with a little dried dill. Serve at once as dinner main dish. Makes 6 servings.

CHEESE AND TUNA SOUFFLE

1⅓ cups evaporated milk	½ teasp. monosodium glutamate
4 tablesp. flour	½ lb. process sharp Cheddar cheese
½ teasp. salt	
¼ teasp. dry mustard	4 eggs, separated
¼ teasp. Tabasco	¾ cup flaked canned tuna

1. Start heating oven to 300°F. Into top of double boiler pour evaporated milk. Add flour, salt, mustard, Tabasco, and monosodium glutamate; beat with hand beater until smooth.

Place over boiling water and beat until slightly thickened, about 5 min.
2. Slice cheese into milk mixture, then blend occasionally with hand beater until thickened and cheese has melted—about 10 min. Beat until smooth. Remove from heat.
3. Add egg yolks, one at a time, beating after each addition. (Now wash beater thoroughly; any trace of fat will prevent egg whites from whipping.) Fold in tuna. In ungreased 2-qt. casserole beat egg whites until very stiff, but not dry; gradually fold in cheese mixture. Bake 1 hr. Serve immediately. Makes 4 servings.

Variation: Finely chopped cooked chicken may replace tuna. Or, for a Cheese Soufflé, omit tuna.

CHICKEN-CHEESE FONDUE

4 egg whites	cheese
4 egg yolks	1 10½-oz. can condensed cream-of-chicken soup, undiluted
2 cups small fresh bread cubes	
1 cup grated process sharp Cheddar	

Start heating oven to 325°F. Grease 1½-qt. casserole. In medium bowl, with mixer or hand beater, beat egg whites until stiff but not dry. Next, with same beater, beat yolks until thick and lemon-colored; add bread cubes, cheese, and soup; mix well. Fold gently into stiffly beaten egg whites; then turn into casserole. Bake 1 hr., or until silver knife, inserted in center, comes out clean. Serve at once. Makes 6 dinner-size servings.

MUSHROOM-CHEESE SOUFFLE

2 eggs, separated	1 cup cottage cheese
2 tablesp. milk	2 tablesp. minced onion
3 tablesp. flour	
½ teasp. salt	1 3- or 4-oz. can sliced mushrooms, drained
Dash pepper	

Start heating oven to 300°F. With hand beater, beat egg yolks till light and foamy. Stir milk gradually into flour; add to egg yolks; beat well. Add salt, pepper, and cheese; beat till blended. Gently fold in onion, mushrooms, and egg whites, stiffly beaten. Turn into greased 1-qt. casserole. Bake about 50 min., or until golden brown on top. Makes 2 servings.
NOTE: Or bake in 2 greased 2-cup casseroles at 300°F. for 45 min.

POLENTA WITH TOMATO SAUCE

¾ cup corn meal	½ cup salad oil
2 cups milk or water	2 cloves garlic
1 egg, unbeaten	½ cup minced onions
1 cup grated Parmesan cheese	1 6-oz. can tomato paste
2½ teasp. salt	1 1-lb.-4-oz. can tomatoes (2½ cups)
Pepper	

Place corn meal in saucepan; gradually stir in milk. Cook over *very low heat*, stirring constantly, until mixture thickens and comes to boil. Boil 3 min., stirring often; remove from heat. Stir in egg; beat well. Add ½ cup grated cheese, 1½ teasp. salt, ⅛ teasp. pepper, ¼ cup salad oil. Turn into 9″ x 5″ x 3″ loaf pan. Refrigerate overnight, or until firm.

Start heating oven to 400°F. Cut corn-meal mixture into 8 squares; put in 10″ x 6″ x 2″ baking dish. In ¼ cup hot salad oil in skillet, sauté garlic 3 min.; remove from heat; discard garlic. Stir in onions, tomato paste, tomatoes, 1 teasp. salt, and ¼ teasp. pepper; pour around squares. Sprinkle with ½ cup grated cheese. Bake, uncovered, ½ hr.; let stand 5 to 10 min. before serving. A nice luncheon dish. Makes 6 servings.

GNOCCHI

3 cups cold water	More grated Parmesan cheese
Salt	⅓ cup melted butter or margarine
1 cup white or yellow corn meal	3 tomatoes
⅔ cup grated Parmesan cheese	2 pkg. brown-and-serve sausages or
2 teasp. dry mustard	12 Canadian-bacon slices
1 egg, slightly beaten	
Pepper	

Day before or early in day:

1. In saucepan, bring water and 2 teasp. salt to boil.
2. Gradually shake in corn meal, stirring constantly to prevent lumping; continue cooking, stirring, until corn meal is thickened and mixture comes away from sides of pan. Cook, covered, over low heat, 10 min. longer.
3. Stir in ⅔ cup grated cheese, mustard, egg, ¼ teasp. salt, ⅛ teasp. pepper; turn *gnocchi* into lightly greased 10″ x 6″ x 2″ flat baking dish; spread evenly; refrigerate.

About 15 min. before serving:

1. Start preheating broiler oven 10 min. or as manufacturer directs.
2. Cut *gnocchi* into rounds or squares; arrange in center of skillet with metal handle or on a broil-and-serve platter; top with ½ cup grated cheese, then melted butter.
3. Cut each tomato into 6 wedges; arrange at end of skillet; sprinkle with salt, pepper, and more grated cheese.
4. Broil about 10 min. or until top is golden and browned. Meanwhile, on same broiler, broil sausages until browned; serve in skillet with *gnocchi* as main dish. Makes 6 servings.

GNOCCHI U.S.A.

¼ cup butter or margarine	½ cup shredded Parmesan cheese
1 1-lb.-13-oz. can hominy	1 teasp. salt
	¼ teasp. pepper

In skillet, melt butter or margarine; add *well-drained* hominy, and heat. Then toss with Parmesan cheese, salt, and pepper. Most tasty with chicken, veal, pork, or franks. Makes 4 servings.

CHEESE STRATA

12 day-old bread slices	milk plus 1¼ cups water
½ lb. process Cheddar cheese, thinly sliced	½ teasp. prepared mustard
4 eggs	1 tablesp. minced onion
2½ cups milk or 1¼ cups evaporated	1 teasp. salt
	⅛ teasp. pepper

Remove crusts* from bread. Arrange 6 bread slices in greased 12″ x 8″ x 2″ baking dish; cover with cheese slices, then with rest of bread. Beat eggs; blend in milk and rest of ingredients; pour over bread. Refrigerate for 1 hr. Bake, uncovered, at 325°F. about 50 min., or until puffy and brown. *Serve at once.* Makes 6 servings.

*Use bread crusts to make Dried Bread Crumbs, p. 8.

♣ FOR 2: Halve ingredients; use 10″ x 6″ x 2″ baking dish.

CHEESE PUDDING: Omit mustard and onion. Serve with jelly.

CORN-CHEESE BAKE: Spread 1½ cups cooked, frozen, or canned whole-kernel corn on top of cheese. Bake 1 hr.

L.B.'S BAKED SANDWICHES: Blend ½ lb. process pimento cheese, grated, with 1 cup sliced ripe olives, 1 4½-oz. can deviled ham, ¼ cup minced onion, ½ cup minced celery, 2 tablesp. catchup, 1 teasp. salt, and ¼ cup mayonnaise.

Spread this cheese mixture over 6 bread slices in baking dish, as in Cheese Strata; cover with remaining bread slices. Pour on egg and milk mixture. Refrigerate 1 hr., then bake at 325°F. 45 min. To serve, cut around each sandwich and lift to heated platter.

NAN'S FRENCH FONDUE

1½ long loaves French bread	thick
½ cup butter or margarine	4 eggs, well beaten
	5 cups hot milk
½ cup sharp prepared mustard	1½ teasp. Worcestershire
1½ lb. sharp natural or process Cheddar cheese, sliced ¼″	1 teasp. salt
	⅛ teasp. cayenne
	¼ teasp. paprika

1. *Day before:* Slice French bread into ½″ slices; spread generously with butter, mustard.
2. In 4-qt. casserole, alternate layers of bread and cheese slices to fill casserole.
3. Combine eggs, milk, Worcestershire, salt, and cayenne. Pour over bread and cheese layers. Sprinkle top with paprika. Refrigerate, covered, until next day.
4. *About 1¾ hr. before serving:* Start heating oven to 350°F. Bake fondue, uncovered, 1½ hr. Makes 8 servings.

♣ FOR 4: Use ¾ of a long loaf of French bread. Reduce milk to 2 cups; rest of ingredients to half. Bake in 2-qt. casserole for 1 hr.

CHEESE AS DESSERT

One of the easiest desserts or evening refreshments to serve—and such a favorite with everyone, especially men—is cheese, with or without crackers and with or without fruit.

Just remember, *cheese is at its best at room temperature.* So remove it from the refrigerator at least 1 hr. ahead (cottage and cream cheese are exceptions).

Five Ways to Serve It

1. On tray, arrange 1 or 2 choice cheeses, crackers, and bowl of fruit. Tuck in green leaves here and there. Set dessert plate and fruit knife before each person.
2. Or arrange a fruit or fruits on each dessert plate, with a fruit knife if needed. Pass tray of assorted cheeses and crackers.
3. Or make fruit your centerpiece. At dessert time, pass tray of assorted cheeses and cheese spreads.
4. Or group cheese, crackers, and 1 or 2 kinds of jam or jelly on tray. Pass at table, or serve in living room.
5. Or serve cheese, crackers, and one of sippers below:

Hot coffee

Well-chilled juice (cranberry, prune, apricot nectar, orange, pineapple, grapefruit, tomato, etc.)

Sweet wine, such as port, muscatel, etc.; or champagne or sauterne

SURE TO PLEASE FRUIT AND CHEESE COMBINATIONS

1. Danish blue cheese, spread on thin apple slices that have been dipped into lemon juice. Put together sandwich-fashion. Pass salted nuts or hot crackers
2. Danish blue or Roquefort cheese, with juicy fresh pears (whole or sectioned)
3. Danish blue, Roquefort, or cream cheese, with preserved or fresh kumquats
4. Camembert, with tart plums and cracked, roasted walnuts
5. Camembert, with apple rings (dipped into citrus-fruit juice) placed around wedges of cored pears (also dipped into juice) that have been arranged petal-fashion
6. Camembert or Chantelle, with crisp red and yellow apples and crisp crackers
7. Cheese spreads in jars (a choice), with unpared crisp apples cut part way through into quarters, then arranged with peeled whole oranges (sections separated) and small bunches of grapes
8. Edam in center, with wedges of Roquefort, cream cheese, and some Cheddar cheese too. Pass fruits and crackers separately
9. Liederkranz or other soft ripened cheese, with Tokay grapes
10. Roquefort-cheese spread, sandwiched between halves of cored ripe juicy pears
11. Swiss-cheese slices and/or cream cheese, with sectioned oranges and tangerines
12. Take zesty red-coated Chantelle wedge and slice of mild smoky Provolone. Add a bunch of green grapes, a pear, or an apple. Add a few stubby bread sticks or crunchy crackers
13. Cut off a wedge of soft, creamy, robust Port du Salut. Add a quartered apple to spread with cheese, plus a few common crackers, split, then toasted

14. Let a wedge of piquant Brie stand out till very soft. Serve with a big juicy pear or a crisp cold apple, thin slices of party rye or half slices of pumpernickel

15. Cut a wedge of lordly blue-veined English Stilton. Add half an all-yellow banana, sliced, skin and all. Add crisp shredded-wheat crackers. Serve with steaming coffee

16. Stand an individual wedge of process Gruyère alongside a few dried figs and preserved kumquats. Pass crisp crackers.

ISLAND FRUIT AND CHEESE

To pass at the table or grace your buffet. Cut green crown and thin slice of fruit from top of *small pineapple*. Now insert point of long knife between skin and meat; cut down vertically almost to base of pineapple; then cut all the way round. Next, with knife blade, 1/4″ from base, and parallel to bottom, cut across almost to other side, without detaching bottom. Insert fingers where cut was made, and push cylinder of pineapple up and out.

Halve pineapple cylinder lengthwise; cut each half into wedge-shape sticks, removing core. Cut green crown lengthwise into thirds; with toothpicks, attach each to side of pineapple. Fill center of pineapple with sticks, tucking them in part way.

Next, set pineapple on one end of a rectangular tray. Group *two other fruits*, such as grape bunches and peaches, around pineapple. Use remaining tray space for *Roquefort, cut into diamond shapes*; *Cheddar cheese, cut into wedges*; and *a variety of crisp crackers*.

"DEVONSHIRE" CREAM

1 3-oz. pkg. cream cheese, softened	sugar
	Pinch salt
1 tablesp. granulated	1 cup heavy cream

Mash cheese with sugar and salt; stir smooth; stir in cream. Whip stiff with hand beater or electric mixer. Makes 2 cups. Serve a dab in center of each dessert plate; surround it with whole strawberries and place a few Melba rounds on plate.

Guests eat berries with the "Devonshire" Cream. If any cream is left, they scoop it up with Melbas and sprinkle with cinnamon sugar.

PURPLE PLUMS WITH "DEVONSHIRE" CREAM: In center of each nappy dish, place mound of "Devonshire" Cream. Spoon on 3 or 4 canned purple plums with some of their juice.

HEART OF CREAM CHEESE WITH FRUIT
(borrowed from our French friends)

1 8-oz. pkg. soft cream cheese	tioners' sugar
	1/4 teasp. almond extract
1 cup heavy cream, whipped	Big strawberries, unhulled
2 tablesp. confec-	

Line a heart-shape layer-cake pan (5 cup capacity), or six heart-shape individual molds, with wax paper extended well above edges. In small bowl, with mixer, beat cream cheese until fluffy; fold in whipped cream, sugar, and extract; pack into pan or molds. Refrigerate about 3 hr.

At dessert time, invert, then unmold large heart on shallow serving plate. (Unmold individual hearts on dessert plates.) Remove wax paper; then outline heart with strawberries or orange sections or other favorite small fruit. Guests dip fruit into cheese mixture. (Or, if individual molds, top with thawed frozen raspberries or strawberries or canned cranberry sauce.) Makes 6 servings.

FRUIT-AND-CHEESE BOMBE
(much loved in the old country)

2 env. unflavored gelatine	cheese
1/2 cup cold water	1 4-oz. pkg. Camembert cheese
1/2 cup boiling water	4 egg yolks, unbeaten
1 cup blue cheese	2 cups heavy cream, whipped
2/3 cup grated Swiss	

Butter a 1 1/2-qt. plain or fancy mold; then refrigerate till needed. Meanwhile, sprinkle gelatine over cold water to soften; add boiling water and stir till dissolved.

In small bowl, with mixer at high speed, beat blue cheese with Swiss cheese and Camembert till very creamy. Add egg yolks, then beat till well blended. Now mix in dissolved gelatine; beat well. Press through a fine sieve. Fold in whipped cream; let stand for 5 min., or till like unbeaten egg white. Turn into chilled mold; refrigerate until well set — about 3 1/2 hr.

At serving time, loosen edges of cheese bombe with spatula. Quickly dip mold in and out of hot water, and unmold on a tray or large serving plate. Garnish with one of these fruits: apple or pear wedges dipped in lemon juice, grapes, orange sections, or strawberries. Tuck cracked walnuts here and there. Guests choose favorite fruits to enjoy with a wedge of the bombe and French bread or crackers. Makes 12 dessert servings.

CHEESE DICTIONARY

Varieties so marked are made in U.S.A. and are normally available

NATURAL CHEESES

KIND, ORIGIN, SHAPE	DESCRIPTION	USES
*BEL PAESE Circular cake	*Surface:* Slate gray *Interior:* Light yellow. Soft to solid consistency *Flavor:* Mild	Dessert—with fruit or crackers
*BLUE (*blue-vein cheese*) Wheels Portions	Danish blue cheese, imported from Denmark, is a creamy white cheese with blue-green veins, made from cows' milk. Blue cheese is also made in U.S.A. *Flavor:* Has delightful tang, poignant aroma.	Dessert—with crackers or fruit Salads—popular in tossed ones Salad dressings Appetizers—as a spread
*BRICK Rectangular Slices, sticks	*Surface:* Yellowish brown *Interior:* White to light cream. Pliable body and somewhat open texture *Flavor:* Mild to pronounced	Sandwiches—especially for lunch or lunch box With cold cuts—use sliced, to round out meat platters
*CACIOCAVALLO (*originally from Italy*) Made in a number of unusual shapes, often in pairs	*Surface:* Light brown and paraffined *Interior:* Rather hard, dry. Very solid body and texture *Flavor:* Somewhat salty, smoky	As table cheese when fresh For grating and cooking when fully cured
*CAMEMBERT (*originally from France*) Portion servings	*Surface:* Thin, whitish crust *Interior:* Soft, creamy, yellowish. Before serving, soften at room temperature until almost fluid. Eat crust *Flavor:* Luscious flavor all its own	Dessert or salad—the universal favorite with crackers or such fruits as pears, apples, etc.
*CHANTELLE (*trade-mark name*) Wheel shape	*Surface:* Red-coated *Interior:* Cream to light orange. Semihard. Rather open texture *Flavor:* Mild to pronounced, depending on age	With cold meats As dessert or party refreshment—with crackers or fruit, etc.

Cheese / Form	Description	Uses
*CHEDDAR Circular cake or cylindrical Rectangular blocks or bars Sticks, wedges, slices, shredded	*Surface:* Waxed yellow-brown block or bar *Interior:* Light cream to orange Close texture. Few, if any, irregular small openings *Flavor:* Mild when fresh; sharp and pleasing when cured or aged	Sandwiches—a favorite filling With pies and cobblers Salads—adds heartiness to tossed salads In salad dressings In dishes such as soufflés, casseroles, etc.
*COTTAGE Bulk or packages	Made from skim milk, coagulated by pure lactic-acid bacteria culture. Some have cream added. White *Flavor:* Pleasing, slightly acid. Other flavors: chive, pineapple, fruit salad, vegetable salad	Salads—adds heartiness to fruit and vegetable ones. Season with chives, pickle relish, diced tomatoes, etc. Sandwiches
*CREAM Packages, loaf, bars, in glasses, plastic dishes, etc.	Made from a mixture of cream and milk with minimum fat content of 33 per cent. Comes with chives, relish, pimento, dates, bacon, pineapple, etc., added. Also comes whipped. White. Smooth *Flavor:* Delicate, slightly acid	Sandwiches Salads—adds heartiness to fruit and vegetable ones Salad dressings Dessert—with crackers and jelly
*EDAM *(originally from Holland)* Round ball	*Surface:* Red-coated *Interior:* Body and texture usually somewhat grainy *Flavor:* Mild. Slightly salty when fresh, pronounced when cured	Dessert—popular in wedges, with fruit or salad Appetizer or nibbler. To serve, cut off top; hollow out center; dice; refill.
*GORGONZOLA Cylindrical	Blue-mold cheese made from cows' milk *Surface:* Clay color *Interior:* Blue streaks produced by mold spores *Flavor:* Rich, piquant, when fully cured	Salads and salad dressings—add cheese crumbled Dessert—with fruit, salad, or crackers
*GOUDA *(originally from Holland)* Ellipsoid	Made from partly skimmed milk *Surface:* Usually red *Interior:* If imported, solid; often contains small round holes. If domestic (baby Gouda), softer, closer body *Flavor:* Often slightly acid	Same as Edam
*GRUYERE *(originally from Switzerland)* Cylindrical—weighs 55 to 110 lb. Sold in pie-shaped individual portions, foil wrapped	Made from whole cows' milk *Surface:* Grayish-brown *Interior:* Light yellow, semihard, with small holes throughout *Flavor:* Similar to but slightly sharper than Swiss	Dessert or nibbler—with crackers or fruit

NATURAL CHEESES (continued)

KIND, ORIGIN, SHAPE	DESCRIPTION	USES
*LIEDERKRANZ (trade-mark name) Rectangular packages	Surface: Russet Interior: Creamy yellow, soft Flavor and odor: Robust	Appetizer—on crackers, toast, etc. With salad, crackers Dessert—with crackers, fruit
*LIMBURGER (originally from Belgium) Cubical; rectangular; in jars	Surface: Grayish brown Interior and flavor: When fresh, is white, odorless, and tasteless. As curing progresses, odor, flavor, and color develop	Sandwiches—especially good with rye, pumpernickel, or other dark breads; or on crackers Nice appetizer
*MOZZARELLA (originally from Italy) Irregularly spherical in shape	Made from cows' milk. Semisoft. Light cream colored Flavor: Mild	Especially enjoyed in main dishes such as eggplant or veal parmigiano, pizza, etc., because of elastic quality of melted cheese
*MUENSTER (originally from Germany) Cylindrical Slices, sticks	Surface: Yellowish tan Interior: White when fresh. Turns light cream when fully cured Flavor: Mild to pronounced	Sandwiches—good with rye or pumpernickel bread Appetizers or nibblers—nice with scallions, carrot or cucumber sticks, radishes, etc.
*MYSOST (Gjetost or primost) Cubical; rectangular	Made from whey. White to brown Flavor and odor: Sweet flavor, distinct odor	Serve thin slices on bread or crackers, at lunch, supper, etc.
*NEUFCHATEL (originally from France) 2- or 3-lb. loaves	A cream-cheese-type product with lower fat content than cream cheese—20 per cent minimum. White. Soft Flavor: Mild	Sandwiches or salads Nibblers or light refreshments—good on crackers
OKA (Port du Salut) (made in Canada) Circular cakes, 1 and 5 lb.	Made from cows' milk Surface: Russet Interior: Creamy yellow. Semisoft Flavor: Robust	Dessert—an excellent choice. Especially good with port wine

KIND. ORIGIN. SHAPE	DESCRIPTION	USES
*PARMESAN (Reggiano) Cylindrical Grated, shredded	Surface: Black or very dark green Interior: Light yellow, with green tinge. Very hard Flavor: Mild unless cheese is old	Grated—serve with Italian spaghetti; on soups such as onion and minestrone, in all kinds of cookery
*PROVOLONE (originally from Italy) Pear, ball, or sausage shape, tied with rope Slices	Includes such styles as Provolette, Provoloni, Salami, etc.	Dessert or nibbler—with crackers
*RICOTTA (originally from Italy)	Made from whey, with whole or skim milk added. Soft texture Flavor: Mild	Popularly used in ravioli, lasagna, etc.
ROQUEFORT (made in France) Cylinders, 4½ to 6 lb. Portions	Made from sheep's milk Surface: Yellowish-brown rind Interior: White, with blue-green mold. Semisoft Flavor: Spicy	Dessert—superb with pears or other fruit, crackers, nuts, etc. Salad dressings—crumble into French dressing; or blend with mayonnaise Appetizers, nibblers—blend with cream or cream cheese to make spread, filling for stuffed celery, etc.
*SWISS—DOMESTIC (originally from Switzerland) Wheels or blocks Slices, portions	Surface: Grayish brown Interior: White or slightly glossy cream color. Round, shiny holes throughout Flavor: Mild, nut sweet to robust. Also with sapsago, caraway	Sandwiches Sliced—with cold meats Salads—adds heartiness to fruit or vegetable ones In dishes such as Swiss-cheese pies, fondue

NOTE: Natural cheeses such as Cheddar, Swiss, brick, etc., may now be purchased in factory-wrapped packages in a variety of sizes—also conveniently sliced. Look for them in refrigerated display case.

The flavor of all natural cheeses, except cream and cottage cheeses, is enhanced if the cheese stands at room temperature a while before serving. (Cut into servings if needed.)

CHEESE DICTIONARY (continued)

*Varieties so marked are made in U.S.A. and are normally available

PROCESS CHEESES

KIND. ORIGIN. SHAPE	DESCRIPTION	USES
*PACKAGED PROCESS CHEESE (¼ to 5-lb. packages)	Made by mixing 2 or more "wheels" of same variety of cheese, or 2 or more varieties (except cream or Neufchâtel cheese), into a homogeneous mass, with aid of heat and with (or without) water, salt, harmless coloring, and emulsifying agent. Must be heated to pasteurizing temperature during manufacturing, and labeled "process cheese" *Flavors:* Cheddar, white Cheddar, pimento, Swiss, brick, Limburger, sharp, caraway, Gruyère, etc.	Cookery—because it melts easily; it's excellent for all cheese cookery Sandwiches—process cheeses slice well
*PACKAGED PROCESS-CHEESE SLICES (6 oz. and 12 oz. packages)	The same cheese as packaged process cheese, but sold in sliced form. Packaged for easy separation *Flavors:* Cheddar (mild and sharp), Swiss, Gruyère, caraway, pimento, etc.	Sandwiches Any dish calling for process cheese
*GRUYERE Portion servings and slices in 6 oz. packages	This light-yellow process cheese is hard and has no holes. Its flavor is similar to, but slightly sharper than, Swiss cheese	Portions: For dessert or as nibbler—with crackers or fruit Slices: For sandwiches, rabbits, cheeseburgers, and to top casseroles
*PROCESS-CHEESE SPREADS Jars and packages Loaf, as dips, etc.	These flavored process-cheese spreads and blends have a soft spreading consistency *Flavors:* pineapple, pimento, blue, relish, olive-pimento, Swiss, Cheddar, sharp, Limburger, smoked, bacon, clam, onion, dill pickle, etc.	Sandwiches Salads Nibblers Sauces, etc.

KIND, ORIGIN, SHAPE	DESCRIPTION	USES
*PROCESS-CHEESE FOODS (or cheese-food compounds) Packages Loaf, slices, links, etc.	*Flavor:* Deliciously mild to sharp process-cheese foods are made of Cheddar cheese with milk solids added. Pimento, bacon, smoke, garlic may be added to links	Sauces Sandwich spreads—they melt smoothly and evenly To slice as nibblers
*PROCESS GRATED CHEESE In canisters or glass jars	Two types: Cheddar. Also Italian including Parmesan and Parmesan Romano	Cheddar—for au gratin dishes, soups, etc. Italian—for sprinkling on salads, etc.
*PROCESS SMOKED CHEESE	A process-cheese food that is hickory-smoked or has smoke-flavored solids added	Appetizer or nibbler—delicious served thinly sliced or cubed Also nice on soups, casseroles, veal dishes, etc.
*TRIPLE-USE CHEESE SPREAD OR SAUCE In jars or glasses	A pasteurized process-cheese spread. Can be spread, spooned, or heated	Sauce—delicious on vegetables, meats, etc. Spread—tasty on bread, crackers, etc.

EGGS—PLAIN AND FANCY

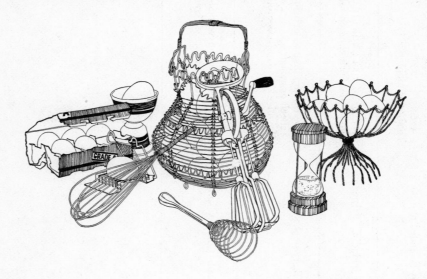

Eggs, the American breakfast mainstay, are equally qualified for luncheon, supper, and snacks. A "friendly" food, they go with everything and combine tastefully with other foods. The sensitive egg responds to care and gentle, respectful handling. Too often it is the victim of thoughtless cruelty in handling and in cooking. "Do right by the egg, and it does more than right by you."

Before using these recipes, refer to How To Use Our Recipes, p. 3. Always use standard measuring cups and measuring spoons; measure level.

To Be a Smart Egg Shopper

Be a Choosy Buyer: If possible, buy from a dealer who keeps eggs in refrigerated display cases. Heat lowers egg quality rapidly. For example, eggs left 4 days in a warm store or kitchen (70°F. to 80°F.) lose as much freshness as those kept several weeks in a refrigerator. And come higher midsummer temperatures, such losses occur even more rapidly.

Buy Only Graded, Cartoned, Refrigerated Eggs: The carton should carry a label with a trusted brand name or trade-mark or the letters "U.S." Egg grades are established by the U.S. Department of Agriculture. (Check with your county or state agriculture department to see if your state has an established program.) Such eggs have been graded for quality and size. *If they have been properly stored,* their label is a reliable buying guide.

Nearby Eggs: By all means, take advantage of locally produced eggs. But be sure the "egg man" handles them properly and guarantees their quality (freshness).

Note Quality Grades: With eggs, "fresh" implies high quality. In some states the term "fresh" may legally identify Grade AA and A eggs, but may not signify B and C grade eggs. Grade A eggs are most commonly available.

Age alone does not determine the quality, or "freshness" and grade, as much as the conditions under which the eggs have been kept. To protect and hold the original fine quality that

Madam Hen normally puts into each egg, they should be kept covered and cold.

GRADE AA OR GRADE A eggs are top quality, with a large amount of firm white and a well-rounded, high-standing yolk. While good for all uses, their high quality and freshness are most appreciated for poaching, frying, or cooking in the shell.

GRADE B AND GRADE C eggs have thinner whites and the yolks tend to flatten out. But many families find it pays to buy these lower-grade, lower-priced eggs for making omelets and salad dressings, scrambling, thickening sauces, baking, and combining with such other foods as tomatoes, cheese, onions, etc. They offer the same food value as top-grade eggs.

As For Color: Shell color does not indicate food value or quality of contents, yet it influences egg prices in some localities. There is absolutely no reason for paying a higher price for a particular shell color. Often you can save money by buying brown eggs where white ones are in greater demand and vice versa.

While shell color is determined chiefly by the breed of hen, yolk color is influenced by the feed. Modern management and scientific feeds have pretty much standardized yolk color—to a middle-of-the-road yellow.

Note Size and Weight Classes: Egg size and quality are not related. And don't let your eye deceive you. A round-shaped egg, though appearing smaller, may actually weigh more than a larger-appearing long oval egg.

"Large" (2 oz. each or 24 oz. to the doz.) eggs make up the bulk of the market supply. Some retail markets handle only "large" eggs.

The established legal weight classes are by 3-ounce gradations, as indicated in the table below:

EGG SIZE	MINIMUM NET WEIGHT PER DOZEN
Jumbo	30 oz., or 1 lb. 14 oz.
Extra Large	27 oz., or 1 lb. 11 oz.
Large	24 oz., or 1 lb. 8 oz.
Medium	21 oz., or 1 lb. 5 oz.
Small	18 oz., or 1 lb. 2 oz.
Peewee	15 oz.

Since eggs do not roll off Nature's production line in absolute uniformity or exact sizes to conform with the weight table, slight tolerances are permitted within the dozen.

Sizes and Seasons and Prices: Prices have steadied and seasonal market supplies of eggs have leveled off as modern poultry management has modified the seasonal fluctuations in egg production. When different-size eggs of like quality are offered at retail counters, consumers often find a price advantage in selecting the size most plentiful in market at the time.

There's a Size for Every Need: Large eggs are preferred for use at breakfast and for main dishes at luncheon and dinner. Medium and small eggs are excellent for out-of-hand eating (such as hard-cooked eggs for lunch boxes, picnics, and deviled eggs). Most standard recipes are based on the use of large and medium eggs.

For Babies: Strained egg yolks have now joined the huge family of canned foods for babies.

To Be a Smart Egg User

To Keep Eggs: Eggs lose quality rapidly if left in a warm kitchen. So get them into your refrigerator quickly, making sure each rests with broad end up. Don't keep them long—use them. Remove only as many eggs as you are going to use at one time.

To Separate Eggs: Remove eggs from refrigerator about 45 min. before using, since the separation of yolks from whites is quicker and better if eggs are first brought to room temperature. Break shell with sharp tap at center—with knife blade or on edge of bowl. Press thumb tips into crack; pull shell apart, retaining yolk in one half, letting white pour out of other half. Rock yolk from one half of shell to other half, so remaining white pours off.

If Any Yolk Gets Into White: Egg whites will not beat up to full volume if there's even a speck of yolk or fat in them. So if a yolk should break when you separate eggs, you'll find it easy to remove every trace of it with egg shell or paper towel. And use egg shell to remove any bits of egg shell.

When Beating Eggs: Eggs beat up faster—to larger volume—when brought to room temperature before beating.

When combining beaten eggs with a hot mixture, stir hot mixture slowly into eggs. Otherwise, flecks of cooked egg may appear in mixture.

Leftover Yolks and Whites: If yolks are not to be used immediately, cover with cold water in a covered jar and refrigerate. Use within 2 or 3 days, drained. Or hard-cook the yolks to use in salads, sandwiches, and scalloped dishes, or as garnish.

Refrigerate leftover egg whites in tightly covered container and use within 10 days.

To Freeze Eggs: When eggs are plentiful, or if you've bought more than you can use, it may be economical for you to freeze them, p. 705.

When Soft- or Hard-Cooking Eggs: Choose a stainless-steel, enamel, or top-range glass utensil, to avoid that annoying discoloration on the inside of the saucepan.

To Ease Dishwashing: Rinse "eggy" utensils and dishes promptly with cold water. Hot water tends to cook the egg and causes it to stick to the utensil or dish. After a scrambled-egg session, use a woven-plastic scouring ball to rid the skillet or double boiler of that inevitable film of cooked egg.

A Plus for Eggs: Every egg that's called for in a recipe, or used as garnish, adds extra goodness. An egg is a sealed container of important nutrients. The protein in egg is of the highest quality; it supplies all of the amino acids needed for building and repairing body tissues. They make a substantial contribution of vitamins A and D and contain small amounts of B-complex vitamins and essential minerals.

A Basic Rule for Good Egg Cookery: Use gentle low to moderate cooking heat.

FOR BREAKFAST OR BRUNCH

FRIED EGGS, SUNNY SIDE UP

1. In skillet over low heat, heat butter or margarine (1 tablesp. per 2 eggs) till hot enough to make drop of water sizzle.
2. Break egg into cup; lower cup close to fat; slide egg into skillet. Repeat, arranging eggs side by side. Lower heat.
3. Gently cook eggs over low heat, spooning hot fat over them, 3 to 4 min., or until of desired firmness. (Instead of basting, you may cover skillet.) Sprinkle with salt (seasoned salt is wonderful!) and pepper.
4. Remove eggs with pancake turner, tilting them against side of skillet to drain well.

Serve alone or with crisp bacon, sausage, or ham. Season at table if necessary. Pass catchup or Tabasco.

FRIED EGGS, OVER: Fry eggs as in steps 1, 2, and 3, left. Then, with broad spatula, turn carefully so yolks do not break; fry to desired firmness. Pass catchup or Tabasco.

BACON OR HAM AND EGGS: Pan-fry bacon as on p. 216, or pan-broil ham, p. 215; keep hot. Drain all but 2 tablesp. fat from skillet; use to fry eggs as above. Serve eggs circled with bacon or ham. Sautéed bananas, canned pineapple slices, or peach or apricot halves go well with them, too.

SAUCE FOR HAM AND EGGS: Pour off most of ham fat left in skillet. Pour in 2 tablesp. bottled thick meat sauce. Stir in ¼ cup heavy cream, ¼ teasp. paprika. Pour over ham.

EASY POACHED EGGS

In Skillet:

1. Butter skillet. Fill with enough water to cover eggs 1″. Bring to boil; then lower heat so water is *just at* simmering point.
2. Break egg into cup; lower cup close to surface of water; quickly slip egg into water. Repeat, placing eggs side by side.
3. Cover skillet; keep water hot, not simmering. Cook eggs until whites are solid, yolks of desired firmness—3 to 5 min.
4. When eggs are done, slip slotted spoon or pancake turner under each; lift out of water; tilt slightly against side of skillet to drain. Sprinkle with monosodium glutamate.

In Egg Poacher: Today you can buy egg poachers for 1, 2, or more eggs. These do the poaching easily, perfectly; see label directions.

Serve on:

Hot buttered toast or toasted English muffin	Toasted split corn bread
Toast, topped with baked-ham slices or deviled ham	Hot asparagus on toast
	Split hot franks on toast
Hot seasoned spinach	Sautéed corned-beef-hash slices

Top with:

Black Butter, p. 533	Cheese Sauce, p. 533
Hot chili sauce	Shrimp Sauce, p. 533
Quick Mushroom Sauce, p. 528	Easy Hollandaise, p. 531
Catchup	

Chili-Poached: For each egg, melt 1 tablesp. butter or margarine in small skillet; add 2 tablesp. catchup. Heat well; then carefully slide in eggs. Cover; cook over low heat until of desired doneness. Serve on toast.

COUNTRY POACHED EGGS

1 tablesp. butter or margarine	flakes, or cracker crumbs
¾ to 1 cup light cream	4 slices hot buttered toast
4 eggs	Seasoned salt
2 tablesp. crushed corn or wheat	Pepper
	Paprika

In skillet, melt butter; add cream; heat till bubbling. Break eggs, one by one, into cup; slip, side by side, into skillet. Cook over low heat until whites are firm around edges. Sprinkle with cornflakes; cover; cook until eggs are of desired doneness.

Arrange eggs, with cream from skillet, on toast. Sprinkle with seasoned salt, pepper, paprika. Makes 2 to 4 servings.

BENEDICT-STYLE POACHED EGGS

2 tablesp. butter or margarine	⅓ cup milk
½ cup minced onions	6 eggs
1 10½-oz. can condensed cream-of-mushroom or -chicken soup, undiluted	3 English muffins, split
	6 thin slices cooked ham

In butter in skillet, cook onions till tender; blend in soup and milk; heat till boiling; then lower heat. Carefully break eggs, one by one, into saucer; then slide into sauce, side by side. Cook, covered, about 10 min., or until eggs are of desired doneness. Meanwhile, toast and butter muffins.

To serve: Top each muffin half with ham slice, then with egg and some of sauce. Makes 6 servings.

SHIRRED (BAKED) EGGS

Start heating oven to 325°F. Butter individual shallow baking dishes. Pour 1 tablesp. light cream into each dish if you wish. Carefully break 1 or 2 eggs into each dish. Sprinkle with monosodium glutamate, salt, pepper, paprika;

dot with butter or margarine. Bake, uncovered, 12 to 18 min., or until of desired doneness.

Serve from baking dishes, garnished with snipped chives, parsley, or water cress.

To Vary:
1. First circle strip of partially cooked bacon around inside edge of each dish.
2. Or line bottom of each baking dish with buttered crumbs; top with slice of cheese, then with eggs. Top with grated cheese. Proceed as above.
3. Or line each baking dish with ¼ cup minced, cooked ham or corned-beef hash.
4. Pass catchup or Tabasco.

SCRAMBLED EGGS

6 eggs	Pinch mixed dried herbs (optional)
½ teasp. salt	2 tablesp. butter, margarine, or salad oil
⅛ teasp. pepper	
6 tablesp. milk or light cream	

In Skillet:
1. Break eggs, one at a time, into cup, then turn each into mixing bowl. Add salt, pepper, milk, herbs. With fork, mix thoroughly if uniform yellow is preferred; mix slightly if streaks of white and yellow are desired.
2. In 9″ skillet, melt butter, tilting skillet so bottom and sides are well covered. When hot enough to make drop of water sizzle, pour in egg mixture; reduce heat.
3. Cook slowly, gently lifting from bottom and sides with spoon as mixture sets, so liquid can flow to bottom. *Avoid constant stirring.*
4. Cook until set *but still moist and slightly underdone.* Remember, the heat in skillet, after skillet is removed from range, completes cooking. Makes 3 or 4 servings.

In Double Boiler: Melt butter in double boiler; tilt top so butter covers its bottom, sides; pour in egg mixture. Cook as in steps 3 and 4, above.

BEST-EVER: Substitute ⅔ cup evaporated milk, undiluted, for milk; reduce butter to 1 tablesp.

To serve: Serve promptly, as is or:
With catchup or Tabasco
On toast, spread with deviled ham or anchovy paste, topped with a little minced raw onion
With sausages, ham, or bacon
On toast, topped with chicken à la king or creamed chicken

In Toast Cups, p. 497, or on split, toasted buns or muffins

✤ **FOR 2**: Make in 8″ skillet, using 4 eggs, ¼ teasp. salt, speck pepper, ⅓ cup milk or light cream, 1½ tablesp. butter or margarine, pinch herbs.

ADDITIONS: When eggs are partly cooked, you may add snipped parsley or chives; minced cooked ham, liver, or tongue; rinsed, shredded dried beef; sautéed mushrooms; grated cheese; cream cheese in pieces; crab-meat chunks; seasoned avocado slices; or slivers of seasoned fresh tomato.

TOP SPRINKLES: Sprinkle with grated cheese, or snipped chives, parsley, or fresh tarragon.

CHILI-SAUCE STYLE: As eggs start to set, step 3, p. 359, quickly stir in 1 tablesp. melted butter or margarine blended with ¼ cup chili sauce and 1 teasp. minced onion.

SPANISH: Substitute canned stewed tomatoes for milk.

CHEESY SCRAMBLE: To scrambled-egg mixture, add 1 6-oz. (or 2 3-oz.) pkg. crumbled chive cream cheese; cook as directed.

QUICKIE SCRAMBLE: Stir well 1 10½-oz. can condensed cream-of-celery soup, undiluted; add 8 eggs, ¼ teasp. pepper; beat until just blended. Scramble in saucepan as in steps 2, 3, and 4, Scrambled Eggs, p. 359.

VEGETABLE SCRAMBLE: Sauté ½ green pepper, sliced, in butter in skillet. Set aside. To scrambled-egg mixture, add ¾ teasp. onion salt (omit salt), pepper; pour into skillet; add ½ cup grated process Cheddar cheese, ¼ cup cooked vegetables. Cook as on p. 359. Top with ¼ cup hot canned tomatoes and green pepper.

BREAKFAST-IN-THE-SKILLET

6 bacon slices	chives
2 tomatoes, peeled, diced	1 tablesp. snipped parsley
½ cup grated process Cheddar cheese	¼ teasp. pepper
6 eggs, beaten	1 tablesp. Worcestershire
1 tablesp. snipped	¼ teasp. salt

In large skillet, cook bacon until crisp, then drain on paper towel. To bacon fat, add tomatoes; sauté 3 min.; then with wooden spoon, blend in grated cheese.

Pour eggs into skillet. Cook mixture over low heat, lifting it occasionally from bottom of skillet with pancake turner, until eggs are set but still very soft. Break bacon into small pieces; add to eggs along with chives, parsley, pepper, Worcestershire, salt; toss lightly. Makes 2 generous servings.

LEE'S SPANISH CHILI WITH EGGS

2 tablesp. fat or salad oil	sauce
½ cup minced onions	1¼ teasp. salt
1 clove garlic, minced	1 teasp. sugar
½ lb. chuck, ground	1 teasp. chili powder
1 8-oz. can tomato	6 eggs
	¼ cup milk

In hot fat in skillet, sauté onions and garlic until tender. Push to one side; then brown beef. Add tomato sauce, ¾ teasp. salt, sugar, chili. Heat, stirring, till boiling.

Make Scrambled Eggs as on p. 359, using eggs, milk, and ½ teasp. salt. Arrange in center of hot platter with hot chili around them. Keep warm. Makes 4 servings.

RABBIT SCRAMBLE

1 tablesp. butter or margarine	evaporated milk
	½ teasp. salt
¼ lb. sharp natural Cheddar cheese, grated (1 cup)	Dash pepper
	3 tablesp. catchup
	2 teasp. Worcestershire
4 eggs	
¼ cup undiluted	Toast

In double boiler, melt butter; add cheese, stirring occasionally, until melted. With fork, beat eggs, milk, salt, and pepper just until blended; stir into cheese. Cook, lifting mixture from bottom and sides with spoon, until partially scrambled. Add catchup, Worcestershire. Cook until set *but still moist.*

Serve on toast. Makes 3 or 4 servings.

BUFFET SCRAMBLED EGGS

1 loaf unsliced white bread	2 6-oz. pkg. chive cream cheese, crumbled
Melted butter or margarine	¼ cup butter or margarine
1 doz. eggs	6 slices bologna, halved
1 teasp. salt	
⅛ to ¼ teasp. pepper	
⅔ cup milk	

For giant toast cups, cut loaf of bread in half horizontally; slice piece off rounded top half so it will rest flat. Remove most of bread from inside of each half, leaving 2 shells about ½″ thick; gash sides of each shell for easier serving. Brush shells with melted butter; set aside.

Into medium bowl, break eggs; add salt, pepper, milk, and cream cheese; with fork, beat just enough to blend. In 10″ skillet, melt ¼ cup butter, tilting so bottom and sides are well covered. When hot enough to make drop of water sizzle, pour in egg mixture.

Cook eggs over low heat, as in steps 3 and 4 in Scrambled Eggs, p. 359.

While eggs are cooking, toast bread cups in broiler until golden. Sauté bologna in bit of butter or margarine until lightly browned. Then line one side of each toast cup with bologna; spoon scrambled eggs into center. Makes 6 to 8 servings.

MUSHROOM SCRAMBLE: Increase milk to 1 cup (or use light cream). Substitute 2 cups sautéed fresh mushrooms for chive cream cheese.

CHEESE SCRAMBLE: Increase milk to 1 cup (or use light cream). Substitute ⅔ cup grated process sharp Cheddar cheese for chive cream cheese; add bit of minced onion or parsley.

BACON SCRAMBLE: Increase milk to 1 cup (or use light cream). Substitute 8 crisp bacon slices, crumbled, for chive cream cheese; or substitute ½ cup minced cooked ham or tongue.

CURRIED EGGS WITH CORN

4 tablesp. butter	6 eggs
½ cup corn, cut from cob, or frozen whole-kernel corn	¼ cup water
	¾ teasp. salt
	2 tablesp. cream
¼ teasp. curry powder	(optional)

In 2 tablesp. butter, in small skillet, lightly sauté corn. In chafing dish or another skillet, melt 2 tablesp. butter with curry. Beat together eggs, water, and salt; stir into curry butter. Cook slowly, scraping sides with spatula as eggs set. When eggs begin to cook, fold in corn; then add cream to keep mixture soft.

Serve with hot buttered rolls and tart currant or grape jelly. Makes 4 servings.

SOFT-COOKED EGGS

1. Have unshelled eggs at room temperature; place in saucepan; add enough cold water to cover tops by at least 1″. Cover; rapidly bring to boil.

2. Remove from heat, or, if cooking more than 4 eggs, turn heat very low. Let stand, covered, as below:

Very soft-cooked eggs	2 min.
Medium soft-cooked eggs	3 to 3½ min.
Firm soft-cooked eggs	about 4 min.

3. Promptly cool eggs in cold water a few seconds to prevent further cooking and to make them easy to handle.

Serve immediately in shells, big end up, in egg cups, each person cracking and removing shell at big end.

Or remove from shells as follows: Hold egg over heated saucer or egg cup. Hit sharply at center with cutting edge of knife. Insert thumbs in crack. Pull shell apart. With spoon, scoop egg from both shell halves; sprinkle with salt and pepper; dot with butter or margarine.

HARD-COOKED EGGS

1. Follow steps 1 and 2 of Soft-Cooked Eggs, left, but let eggs stand, covered, 15 min.
2. Cool promptly and thoroughly in cold water—this makes shells easier to remove and prevents dark surface on yolks.
3. To remove shells, tap entire surface of each egg to crackle it. Roll egg between hands to loosen shell, then peel, starting at large end. Dipping egg into bowl of cold water will help ease off shell.

To Hard-Cook Leftover Egg Yolks: Put egg yolks in strainer; lower into simmering water to cover; simmer until firm—about 6 min.; remove. Sieve or mince, then use in or over salads, sauces, vegetables, etc.

FRENCH OMELET

1 to 1½ tablesp. butter or margarine	1 tablesp. cold water
	1 teasp. salt
8 eggs	Speck pepper

1. In 10″ skillet, over low heat, melt butter; tilt skillet back and forth to grease well. With electric mixer or blender, or hand beater, beat eggs with water, salt, and pepper just until blended.
2. Pour eggs into skillet over low heat. As mixture sets at edge, with fork, draw this portion toward center so that uncooked portions flow to bottom. Tilt skillet as necessary to hasten flow of uncooked eggs to bottom. Shake skillet to keep omelet sliding freely. Keep mixture as level as possible. When eggs are set and surface

is still moist, increase heat to brown bottom quickly.

3. With spatula, loosen edge of omelet all around. Tilt skillet. With help of spatula, carefully roll up omelet from skillet handle toward opposite side; or fold in half.

4. Hold skillet with one hand, heated platter with other hand, so that bottom edge of skillet rests on edge of platter. Slowly tip the two together until omelet rolls out onto platter. Pass catchup or Tabasco. Makes 4 servings.

✙ FOR 2: Make in 8″ skillet as on p. 361, using 1½ tablesp. butter or margarine, 4 eggs, ¼ cup water, ½ teasp. salt, ⅛ teasp. pepper. If using a filling, divide in half.

INDIVIDUAL OMELETS: Make each omelet in 8″ skillet, using 1½ tablesp. butter or margarine, 2 eggs, 2 tablesp. water, ¼ teasp. salt, pinch pepper. Nice with French fries and catchup.

CHRISTMAS OMELET: In a little butter, in 10″ skillet, sauté some minced green pepper and slivered pimento. Then add omelet mixture, p. 361, and make as directed.

BACON, CHEESE, OR MUSHROOM OMELET: When eggs are set in step 2, p. 361, arrange 6 crumbled crisp bacon slices, ⅓ cup grated process Cheddar cheese, or 1 cup sautéed sliced mushrooms over half of omelet opposite skillet handle. Continue as in steps 3 and 4.

CHICKEN CURRY OMELET: Sauté 1 tablesp. minced onion in 2 tablesp. butter until tender; add 1 cup cut-up, cooked or canned chicken; heat. Add ¼ teasp. curry powder, ½ teasp. salt. Use as filling for French Omelet, p. 361; when set as in step 2, continue as in steps 3 and 4.

HAM OMELET: Omit salt. Before cooking, fold into egg mixture ½ cup deviled ham or minced cooked ham mixed with ½ teasp. prepared mustard and ½ teasp. minced onion.

OMELET COEUR A LA CREME: Combine half a 3-oz. pkg. of soft cream cheese with ½ cup creamed cottage cheese, 1 teasp. grated orange rind, 2 teasp. sugar.

Prepare French Omelet, p. 361. In step 3, just before folding, cover half of omelet, away from handle, with cheese mixture. With skillet tilted at 45° angle, fold uncovered half of omelet over cheese. Remove as in step 4. Sprinkle omelet with confectioners' sugar; then spoon on some of 1 pkg. of frozen strawberries, thawed; garnish with fresh berries if desired. Pass rest of frozen berries. Makes 4 servings as delicious guest luncheon main dish or dessert.

FRENCH OMELET FILLINGS

At end of step 2, French Omelet, p. 361, you may arrange one of fillings below over that half of omelet which is opposite skillet handle. Then proceed with steps 3 and 4.

Or fold one of fillings below into omelet mixture in step 1 before making as directed.

1. 1 cup sautéed mushrooms plus a little sherry
2. 1 cup diced tomatoes plus seasoned salt and pepper to taste
3. Favorite jelly or marmalade (in omelet, omit pepper; reduce salt to 1 teasp.; add 1 tablesp. sugar)
4. ¼ teasp. dried thyme or mixed herbs and 1 teasp. snipped parsley and chives
5. Strawberries or raspberries, sugared and warmed a little
6. Snipped fresh tarragon and parsley or scallions, or sautéed minced leeks
7. ½ to 1 cup hot chopped, cooked chicken or lamb, plus pinch curry and onion salt

PUFFY OMELET

6 eggs, separated	⅛ teasp. pepper
6 tablesp. water	2 tablesp. fat or salad
1 teasp. salt	oil

1. Start heating oven to 325°F. In large bowl, with electric mixer or hand beater, beat egg whites with water and salt until whites are stiff and shiny but still moist, and peaks form when beater is raised.

2. With same beater, beat well yolks and pepper until thick and lemon-colored. Lightly but *completely*, fold yolk mixture into whites.

3. Heat fat in 10″ skillet (choose one with handle that will withstand oven heat) until just hot enough to make drop of water sizzle; tip skillet to grease bottom and side. Pour in omelet mixture.

4. Cook over low heat about 5 min., or until omelet is puffy and golden on underside when gently lifted at edge with spatula.

5. Then bake omelet in same skillet about 12 to 15 min., or till surface feels dry and center springs back when pressed lightly with finger tips.

6. Now quickly run spatula around inside of skillet to loosen omelet. With 2 forks, tear gently into pie-shaped wedges. Invert wedges onto serving platter, with brown side up.

7. Or, with spatula, cut down through center of omelet, *only part-way through,* at right angles to handle. Tip handle up and, with aid of spatula, fold upper half over lower half. Hold skillet with left hand so bottom edge rests on heated platter held with right hand. Slowly tip skillet and platter together until omelet rolls out onto platter. Pass catchup or Tabasco. Makes 4 servings.

♣ FOR 2: Halve ingredients; use small 8″ skillet.

To Vary: See French Omelet, p. 361.

FRENCH OMELET, COUNTRY STYLE

2 tablesp. butter or margarine	½ teasp. salt
¼ cup diced bacon	¼ teasp. seasoned salt
2 medium potatoes, finely diced	Dash onion salt
4 eggs	1 teasp. snipped parsley

1. In 8″ skillet, in 1 tablesp. butter, cook bacon until brown. Add potatoes; sauté until potatoes are tender and golden.

2. In bowl, with fork, beat eggs with seasonings, parsley. Stir in potato mixture.

3. Meanwhile, in same skillet, heat remaining butter. Pour in egg mixture. As eggs set at edges, with spatula, draw this portion toward center so that uncooked portions flow to bottom.

4. When omelet starts to brown on bottom, divide it in half with knife; with wide spatula, turn each half over to brown other side. Then, with spatula, lift each half to a luncheon plate. Serve at once. Makes 2 hearty servings.

THE BEST CREAMED EGGS

6 eggs	1 teasp. Worcestershire (optional)
3 tablesp. butter or margarine	2 cups milk
1 tablesp. minced onion (optional)	1 tablesp. snipped parsley
3 tablesp. flour	Pinch mixed dried herbs (optional)
½ teasp. salt	
Speck pepper	

1. Hard-cook eggs as on p. 361; then shell.

2. In double-boiler top over direct heat, melt butter. Add onion; simmer till tender; remove from heat. Stir in flour, salt, pepper, Worcestershire.

3. Slowly stir in milk. Cook over boiling water, stirring, until thickened. Add parsley, herbs. Cut eggs into slices, halves, or quarters; fold into sauce; heat.

Serve in one of following ways. Makes 6 breakfast or 4 luncheon servings.

On toast, topped with crisp bacon
On toast, spread with deviled ham
On hot cooked asparagus or rice
In Toast Cups, p. 497

WITH CHEESE: After adding milk, add ¼ to ½ cup grated process Cheddar cheese.

WITH HAM: On toast or toasted corn bread, arrange thin slices of cooked ham, luncheon meat, crisp bacon, or tongue; or spread bread with deviled ham. Top with creamed eggs.

A LA KING: Before adding eggs, to sauce add 1 cup sautéed, sliced fresh mushrooms; ½ cup cooked or canned peas; and 1 pimento, cut into strips.

WITH TOMATOES: Sauté or broil 1″-thick tomato slices. Arrange 1 or 2 of these tomato slices on each slice of buttered toast; top with creamed eggs.

CREAMED DEVILED EGGS: Substitute Deviled Eggs, p. 364, for hard-cooked eggs; add ½ cup grated cheese to sauce.

FOR LUNCH

EGG-AND-BACON SAVORY

6 slices bacon	3 tablesp. all-purpose flour
½ cup sliced fresh or drained canned mushrooms	2 cups milk
1 tablesp. minced onion	¾ teasp. salt
2 tablesp. chopped green pepper	⅛ teasp. pepper
	6 sliced, shelled hard-cooked eggs
	1 1-lb. can chow-mein noodles

In large skillet, pan-fry bacon slices until crisp, then set aside. In ¼ cup bacon drippings, sauté mushrooms, onion, green pepper, until onion is tender; now blend in flour, then milk. Cook, while stirring, until smooth and thickened; then add salt, pepper, eggs, and 4 bacon slices, crumbled.

Serve over a mound of chow-mein noodles on heated platter; garnish with 2 bacon slices, crumbled. Makes 4 luncheon-size servings.

CURRIED EGGS AND MUSHROOMS

1 tablesp. butter or margarine	2 tablesp. slivered toasted almonds
1/4 lb. fresh mushrooms, sliced	2 shelled hard-cooked eggs, sliced
1/2 cup canned condensed cream-of-celery soup, undiluted	4 toasted English-muffin halves, buttered
1/4 cup milk	1 tablesp. snipped parsley
1/2 teasp. curry powder	

1. In hot butter, in small skillet, sauté mushrooms 3 min.
2. Meanwhile, mix soup, milk, and curry powder; pour over mushrooms.
3. Add almonds and eggs; stir gently just until heated.
4. Serve over English muffins, sprinkled with parsley. Makes 2 servings.

DEVILED EGGS

6 shelled hard-cooked eggs	1/4 teasp. prepared mustard
1/4 cup melted butter or mayonnaise	1 teasp. minced onion
1/4 teasp. salt	1/4 teasp. curry powder (optional)
Speck pepper	

1. Cut shelled eggs into lengthwise halves. With teaspoon, carefully remove yolks to small bowl; set whites aside.
2. Mash yolks until very fine and crumbly; blend in butter, rest of ingredients.
3. Generously refill hollows in whites with yolk mixture, slightly rounding each. If desired, garnish with strips of pimento, ripe or green olives, parsley, water cress, or capers. Makes 12 halves.

Serve as hors d'oeuvres; as salad on salad greens; as garnish for chicken, meat, fish, or vegetable salad; or on cold-meat platter.

CHEESE STYLE: Mash yolks with mayonnaise; add dash each of salt, pepper, and Worcestershire; 1 tablesp. each minced onion and celery; 1/4 teasp. prepared mustard; 1/3 cup grated process Cheddar cheese. Use to refill whites as above.

CHICKEN CURRY: Mash yolks with mayonnaise, salt, pepper; add 1/2 cup minced, cooked or canned chicken, 1 tablesp. minced celery, and 1 teasp. curry powder. Use to refill whites as at left.

CRAB OR SHRIMP: Mash yolks with mayonnaise; add 1 teasp. lemon juice; 1 1/2 teasp. onion salt; 2 crumbled crisp bacon slices; dash Tabasco; 1/2 cup flaked fresh or drained canned or frozen King-crab meat, or cleaned cooked or canned shrimp. Use to refill whites, left.

DE LUXE: Mash yolks with mayonnaise, salt, pepper; add 1 tablesp. grated onion, 1 teasp. minced celery, and 1 tablesp. anchovy paste or 6 small mashed sardines. Use to refill whites as at left.

NORDIC: Mash yolks with melted butter or margarine; salt; pepper; prepared mustard; 1 minced onion; add 1/3 cup flaked tuna, cut-up cleaned cooked or canned shrimp, or fresh or drained canned or thawed frozen King-crab meat. Use to refill whites as at left.

PICNIC: When stuffing eggs, level off filling. Put eggs together in pairs; wrap in wax paper; twist ends of paper.

DOUBLE-DEVILED EGGS: Cut 12 shelled hard-cooked eggs in half lengthwise. To mashed yolks, add favorite seasonings, together with 2/3 cup grated sharp cheese. Use generously to refill whites, slightly rounding each. Put halves back together; wrap in saran; refrigerate until needed. Makes 12.

DEVILED EGGS AND BACON MORNAY

18 eggs	Paprika
3/4 cup salad dressing, mayonnaise, or soft butter	1/4 cup butter or margarine
Salt	1/4 cup flour
Pepper	3 cups milk
Prepared mustard	1/2 lb. process sharp Cheddar cheese, grated (2 cups)
1 tablesp. minced green onion or minced onion	24 slices Canadian bacon

Day before, if desired:
1. Hard-cook eggs; cool; shell.
2. Cut small slice from one end of each shelled egg so egg stands upright. Now cut a deep cross in the other end; then, while holding egg, carefully trim, with small paring knife, each of four sections formed by the cross, to resemble petal.
3. Carefully scoop out the yolk of each egg, keeping white petals intact. (It may be neces-

sary to trim a small amount of white from underside of each petal.) Refrigerate all.

Morning of brunch:

1. Mash egg yolks till fine and crumbly; blend in salad dressing, ¾ teasp. salt, dash pepper, ¾ teasp. prepared mustard, and green onion.
2. Spoon this mixture into center of each petal-shaped egg white, forming peak (or use pastry bag with no. 22 tube to fill each).
3. Sprinkle eggs with paprika; refrigerate.

Just before serving:

1. In electric skillet at 200°F. to 220°F., make a white sauce, using ¼ cup butter, flour, 1 teasp. salt, dash pepper and paprika, and milk.
2. Turn skillet to Warm; then blend 2 teasp. prepared mustard and grated cheese into sauce till smooth.
3. Set stuffed eggs upright in cheese sauce in skillet; cover skillet, leaving temperature control set at Warm.
4. Meanwhile, cook bacon in another skillet until done; drain; tuck between eggs. Makes 8 to 10 servings.

BAKED EGG SANDWICHES DE LUXE

4 hamburger buns	⅓ cup grated natural
4 tomato slices, ¼″	sharp Cheddar
thick	cheese
Salt and pepper	¼ cup light cream
4 eggs	3 tablesp. snipped
	scallions

Start heating oven to 375°F. Cut thin slice from top of each bun; with fork, remove most of crumbs, leaving shell about ½″ thick. Arrange shells in shallow baking pan. In bottom of each shell, place tomato slice; sprinkle with salt and pepper; carefully break egg over tomato. Sprinkle with salt and pepper, then with cheese, cream, scallions. Bake, uncovered, 20 to 30 min., or until eggs are of desired doneness. Makes 4 servings.

EGGS MORNAY

2 tablesp. butter or	shire
margarine	1½ teasp. prepared
2 tablesp. flour	mustard
½ teasp. salt	2 cups milk
Dash pepper	¼ cup pasteurized
½ teasp. paprika	process cheese
Dash Tabasco	spread
⅛ teasp. Worcester-	6 eggs

Start heating oven to 400°F. In saucepan, melt butter; stir in flour, salt, pepper, paprika, Tabasco, Worcestershire, mustard, then milk. Cook, stirring, until thickened. Stir in cheese spread until smooth. Pour thin layer of sauce into 3 well-greased individual baking dishes. Slip 2 eggs into each. Add rest of sauce, leaving yolks partially uncovered. Bake 15 to 20 min., or until eggs are of desired doneness. Makes 3 servings.

CORN SOUFFLE

¼ cup milk	Dash pepper
½ cup grated natural	1 12-oz. can vacuum-
sharp Cheddar	packed whole-kernel
cheese	corn, drained
½ cup mayonnaise	2 tablesp. snipped
¼ cup all-purpose	parsley
flour	4 egg whites
¼ teasp. onion salt	

1. Start heating oven to 325°F. Oil 1-qt. casserole. In small saucepan, heat milk with cheese until cheese melts.
2. In small bowl with spoon, mix mayonnaise, flour, onion salt, pepper; slowly stir in milk mixture; blend well. Stir in corn, parsley.
3. In large bowl, with electric mixer or hand beater, beat egg whites until stiff.
4. With spoon, gently fold corn mixture into egg whites until blended. Pour into casserole.
5. Bake, uncovered, 50 min., or until silver knife inserted into center comes out clean.

Serve at once, as vegetable. Or if used as main dish, serve with heated cheese sauce (it comes in jars; or use canned Cheddar cheese soup or a cheese-sauce mix, p. 102). Makes 4 servings.

STUFFED EGGS DE LUXE

4 shelled hard-cooked	½ teasp. dried rose-
eggs	mary
2 tablesp. soft Danish	2 tablesp. mayon-
blue cheese	naise or cooked
1 teasp. prepared mus-	salad dressing
tard	Salt and pepper to
1 teasp. snipped	taste
chives	Paprika

1. Split eggs lengthwise; remove yolks.
2. Combine yolks with cheese, mustard, chives, rosemary, mayonnaise, salt and pepper; mix until fluffy; use to fill egg whites. Top each with a little paprika. Makes 8.

MAN-STYLE BAKED EGGS

3 tablesp. butter or margarine	2 tablesp. packaged dried bread crumbs
2 medium onions, thinly sliced	4 packaged process sharp Cheddar-cheese slices
Salt and pepper	
4 eggs	

Start heating oven to 350°F. In butter in skillet, cook onions about 5 min., or until just tender. Arrange in 8″ pie plate; sprinkle with salt, pepper. Carefully break eggs over onions; sprinkle lightly with salt and pepper, then with crumbs; top with cheese slices. Bake, uncovered, 10 min., or until eggs are of desired firmness. Makes 4 servings.

VAL'S PEPPER AND EGGS

6 medium green peppers	1 tablesp. canned tomato sauce
½ cup olive or salad oil	1 teasp. salt
	4 eggs, beaten

Seed, then cut peppers into ½″ strips. In hot oil, in skillet, sauté peppers until tender — about 10 min. Pour oil from skillet. To peppers, add tomato sauce, salt, and eggs. Stir over medium heat until eggs are just delicately "set." Makes 4 servings.

SALAMI AND EGGS

8 slices salami	¼ teasp. salt
3 eggs, beaten	

In large skillet, arrange salami. Cook over medium heat about 5 min., or until salami begins to curl; turn slices. Pour eggs, combined with salt, over salami. Cook just until eggs are set. Fold one half over other; turn onto serving plate.

Serve with catchup and buttered toast or toasted English muffins. Makes 2 servings.

CHEESE SOUFFLE FOR FOUR

1 cup milk; or ½ cup evaporated milk plus ½ cup water	¼ cup flour
	½ teasp. salt
4 eggs	Speck cayenne pepper
3 tablesp. butter or margarine	¼ lb. process sharp Cheddar cheese

1. Start heating oven to 300°F. In saucepan, heat, but do not scald, milk. Separate eggs, putting whites in large bowl, yolks in smaller one.

2. In double boiler, melt butter. Stir in flour, then heated milk, salt, cayenne; cook, stirring, until smooth and thickened. Thinly slice cheese right into sauce. Stir until cheese melts completely and sauce is velvety smooth; remove from heat.

3. With fork, beat egg yolks until well blended. Stir in a little of cheese sauce. Slowly stir this mixture back into rest of cheese sauce.

4. With electric mixer or hand beater, beat egg whites until stiff but not dry. Slowly pour in cheese sauce, folding until no large areas of egg white remain.

5. Pour mixture into *ungreased* 1½-qt. casserole till ¼″ from top. (Bake any extra mixture in small *ungreased* casserole.)

6. To form crown, with teaspoon, make shallow path in soufflé mixture about 1″ in from edge of casserole all the way around. Bake, uncovered, 1¼ hr.; *don't open oven while soufflé is baking. Serve at once.* Makes 4 servings.

BACON: With egg whites, fold in ½ cup crumbled crisp bacon.

HAM AND CHEESE: With egg whites, fold in ½ cup ground cooked ham.

GARDEN: Before pouring in soufflé, place the following in bottom of 1½-qt. casserole: 1 cup cooked frozen or canned mixed vegetables or any favorite vegetable.

SWISS CHEESE: Substitute 1½ cups grated natural Swiss cheese (6 oz.) for process Cheddar cheese.

TO KEYNOTE DINNER

EGG PIZZA

⅔ cup milk	⅔ cup well-drained canned tomatoes
2 cups packaged biscuit mix	1½ tablesp. minced onion
1 tablesp. salad or olive oil	½ teasp. salt
7 shelled hard-cooked eggs	¼ teasp. dried orégano
Salt	¼ teasp. dried thyme
Pepper	½ lb. Mozzarella cheese, grated
1 6-oz. can tomato paste	

1. Start heating oven to 450°F. Add milk to biscuit mix; stir with fork till a soft dough.

Roll around on surface, lightly dusted with biscuit mix; then knead gently 8 to 10 times.
2. On ungreased cookie sheet, pat out dough into 12″ circle, ¼″ thick. Pinch up edge of dough to make ½″-high rim; then brush all dough, but rim, with oil. Now slice eggs (reserve 8 center slices for garnish). Coarsely cut up rest of eggs; sprinkle over dough. Sprinkle lightly with salt and pepper.
3. In bowl, combine tomato paste, tomatoes, onion, salt, orégano, and thyme. Spread over eggs; top with cheese. Bake 20 min., or till biscuit dough is brown and cheese is bubbly.

Serve at once, cut into wedges, with an egg slice on top of each wedge. Makes 8 servings.
NOTE: If desired, a few cut-up anchovies may be sprinkled over cheese before baking.

CURRIED EGGS

2 tablesp. butter or margarine	¼ teasp. pepper
2 tablesp. minced onion	2 teasp. grated orange rind
2 tablesp. flour	¼ cup orange juice
1 teasp. curry powder	6 shelled hard-cooked eggs, quartered
2 cups milk	3 cups hot fluffy rice
1 teasp. salt	Parsley

In butter in skillet, sauté onion until tender. Stir in flour, curry powder, until bubbly. Then stir in milk. Cook, stirring, until thickened. Add salt, pepper, orange rind, and juice. Add eggs. Heat, stirring gently to avoid breaking eggs. Spoon over hot rice, garnish with parsley.

Serve with choice of these accompaniments: pickle relish, chopped peanuts, flaked coconut, chutney, pickled onions, crumbled crisp bacon. Makes 4 to 6 servings.

SPICY EGGS 'N' HAM

3 tablesp. butter or margarine	Dash Tabasco
3 tablesp. flour	6 shelled hard-cooked eggs, sliced
1 teasp. dry mustard	2 cups diced, cooked ham
¾ teasp. salt	½ cup cut-up ripe olives
⅛ teasp. pepper	¾ cup diced process sharp Cheddar cheese
1½ cups milk	
1 teasp. horse-radish	
1 tablesp. Worcestershire	
1 tablesp. chili sauce	

Start heating oven to 400°F. In saucepan, melt butter; stir in flour, mustard, salt, pepper, then milk; cook, stirring, until thickened. Stir in horse-radish, Worcestershire, chili sauce, and Tabasco. In 1½-qt. casserole, arrange layers of eggs, ham, olives, cheese, sauce. Bake 25 to 30 min. Makes 4 or 5 servings.

CHINESE EGGS FOO YOUNG

Sauce:

2 teasp. soy sauce	1 teasp. vinegar
1 teasp. cornstarch	¾ teasp. salt
1 teasp. sugar	½ cup cold water

Egg Mixture:

1 cup drained canned bean sprouts	coarsely cut up (or chopped leftover roast pork)
⅔ cup thinly sliced onions	6 eggs
1 cup cleaned, cooked or canned shrimp,	2 tablesp. bacon fat or salad oil

About 50 min. before supper: Make this sauce: In saucepan, combine soy sauce, cornstarch, sugar, vinegar, salt; stir in water; cook over low heat until thickened.

Combine bean sprouts with onions and shrimp. Then, with fork, beat eggs; add bean-sprout mixture. In hot fat in skillet, fry, as pancakes, about ¼ cup mixture at a time, turning once. Fold pancake over; keep hot until all mixture is cooked. Arrange on hot platter; cover with heated sauce.

Nice with canned chow-mein noodles or hot fluffy rice. Makes 3 or 4 servings.

EGGS DIVAN

Deviled Eggs:

6 hard-cooked eggs	½ teasp. salt
1 2¼-oz. can deviled ham	½ teasp. dry mustard
¼ teasp. Worcestershire	Dash pepper
½ teasp. grated onion	1 to 2 tablesp. light cream or milk

Broccoli and Sauce:

1 pkg. frozen broccoli	Dash pepper
1½ tablesp. butter or margarine	¾ cup milk
1½ tablesp. flour	½ cup grated process sharp Cheddar cheese
⅛ teasp. dry mustard	
½ teasp. salt	

Prepare Deviled Eggs as follows: Cut ¼″ slice from one end of each shelled egg; carefully remove yolk. Mash yolks and end slices; add ham, Worcestershire, onion, salt, mustard, pepper, light cream. Mix well; then use to fill egg whites.

Cook broccoli as label directs. Start heating oven to 400°F. In saucepan, make this sauce: Melt butter; stir in flour, mustard, salt, pepper, then milk; cook until thickened. Add cheese; stir until smooth.

Arrange broccoli in 10″ x 6″ x 2″ baking dish. Stand eggs, with stuffed ends up, between and on broccoli pieces. Pour sauce over all. Bake, uncovered, 40 min., or until bubbly. Makes 4 or 5 servings.

VEGETABLE-CHEESE BAKE

4 eggs, separated	cooked vegetables
1 cup milk	1 small onion, minced
3 slices white bread, crusts removed	2 tablesp. minced green pepper or snipped parsley
¾ teasp. salt	1 10½-oz. can con-
½ teasp. dry mustard	densed tomato soup,
¼ teasp. monosodium glutamate	undiluted
⅛ teasp. pepper	2 tablesp. butter or margarine
1 cup cottage cheese	
2 cups finely chopped,	

Day before: In mixing bowl, beat egg yolks with fork. Add milk, bread, salt, mustard, monosodium glutamate, and pepper. Let bread soften; break up with fork; add cottage cheese, cooked vegetables, onion, green pepper. Refrigerate.

About 1 hr. before serving: Start heating oven to 350°F. Beat egg whites till stiff; fold into cheese mixture. Pour into a well-greased 10″ x 6″ x 2″ or 8″ x 8″ x 2″ baking dish. Bake 45 min., or till firm. Cut into squares. For sauce, heat soup with butter.

Serve with hot sauce. Makes 4 servings.

BAKED EGGS AU GRATIN

2 cups fresh bread crumbs	1 cup grated process Cheddar cheese
8 eggs	¼ cup butter or mar-
1 teasp. salt	garine
½ teasp. pepper	1 cup milk
2 teasp. prepared mustard	

Start heating oven to 325°F. Grease 4 individual baking dishes. Over bottom of each, sprinkle ¼ cup fresh bread crumbs; then slip 2 eggs into each. Sprinkle each with ¼ teasp. salt and ⅛ teasp. pepper; top each with ½ teasp. mustard and ¼ cup cheese. Melt the butter; toss with remaining 1 cup bread crumbs; use to top all the eggs. Then into each baking dish, pour ¼ cup milk. Bake 20 to 30 min., or until of desired doneness. Makes 4 dinner-size servings.

SWISS STYLE: Start heating oven to 425°F. Line well-buttered, deep, fluted 9″ pie plate with ½ lb. overlapping, natural Swiss-cheese slices. Pour in 1 cup heavy cream. Slip in 6 eggs, side by side; sprinkle with ¼ teasp. salt, ⅛ teasp. pepper, dash paprika. Bake 10 to 15 min., or until eggs are done as you like them. Serve on toast.

ZESTY BAKED EGGS: Substitute process Cheddar-cheese slices for Swiss cheese in Swiss Style, above. Add ½ teasp. Worcestershire to cream.

RICE

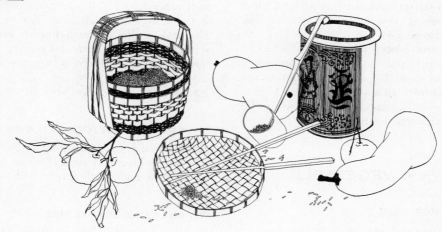

Because of today's scientific milling, rice is an ideal time-saver. It no longer needs to be washed or rinsed before cooking — you lose valuable vitamins and minerals if you do this. There's no more draining to do after the rice is cooked — it's all absorbed in the cooking. And the preparation time is less — only about 15 min. for regular rice, 25 min. for processed and brown, and 5 min. for packaged precooked. Most folks with food allergies enjoy rice in their diets.

Before using these recipes, refer to How To Use Our Recipes, p. 3. Always use standard measuring cups and measuring spoons, measure level.

The Rice Family

Here are the varieties of packaged white and brown rice you are likely to find on your grocer's shelf:

REGULAR WHITE RICE, packaged in long-, medium-, and short-grain types, has the entire outer coating of bran removed. It may be polished or unpolished. Some brands are enriched by partial restoration of vitamins and minerals lost in milling. Check the label.

Long-grain rice is especially nice to serve instead of potatoes or in a main dish, because it is plump and flaky when cooked.

Medium- or short-grain rice is popular for rice pudding, croquettes, molded rings, and other dishes in which creaminess is desired.

PROCESSED (ALSO KNOWN AS PARBOILED OR CONVERTED) WHITE RICE is a packaged long-grain white rice that has been processed to retain a large percentage of the natural vitamins and minerals present in the bran of the whole grain.

PACKAGED PRECOOKED ENRICHED WHITE RICE (QUICK) is made of long-grain white rice. It's completely cooked, then dehydrated and dried. You get fluffy white rice in a jiffy — without washing, rinsing, draining, or steaming.

REGULAR BROWN RICE is the whole unpolished grain of rice, with just the outer husk removed. So it retains all of its natural vitamins and minerals. It has a nutty flavor and is excellent as stuffing for game, as a vegetable, in main dishes, etc. Cook as label directs.

How Much Rice to Cook

REGULAR WHITE RICE swells to about 3 times its original measure — 1 cup uncooked rice making about 3 cups cooked.

PROCESSED WHITE RICE swells to about 4 times its measure — 1 cup uncooked rice making about 4 cups cooked.

PACKAGED PRECOOKED WHITE RICE doubles its volume in preparation — 1⅓ cups precooked rice making about 2⅔ cups after preparation.

REGULAR BROWN RICE swells to about 4 times its measure — 1 cup uncooked brown rice yielding approximately 4 cups cooked.

RICE AS A VEGETABLE

FLUFFY HOT RICE

If Regular White Rice

1 cup uncooked rice	2 cups boiling
1 teasp. salt	water

1. In tightly covered saucepan combine ingredients.
2. Bring to a boil and stir once or twice. Then lower heat to simmer and cook rice, covered, about 14 min., *without removing lid or stirring,* or until liquid is absorbed and rice tender. Turn into serving dish and fluff with fork. Makes 3 cups rice or 4 servings.
P.S. Or cook as package label directs.

If Processed White Rice

1 cup uncooked rice	2½ cups boiling
1 teasp. salt	water

1. In tightly covered saucepan combine rice, salt, water.
2. Cook, over low heat, 20 to 25 min., or until rice feels tender between fingers and all the water is absorbed. Turn into serving dish and fluff up with fork. Makes 4 cups rice or 5 servings.
P.S. Or cook as package label directs.

If Packaged Precooked Rice

Follow label directions as to proportions of rice, water, salt, and butter; also as to preparation. The cooking time is brief.

If Regular Brown Rice

1 cup uncooked rice	2½ cups boiling
1 teasp. salt	water

1. In tightly covered saucepan combine rice, salt, water.
2. Cook, over low heat, 25 to 35 min., or until rice feels tender between fingers and all the water is absorbed. Turn into serving dish and fluff up with fork. Makes 4 cups rice or 5 servings.
P.S. Or cook as package label directs.

TO REFRIGERATE COOKED RICE

Cooked rice keeps beautifully in the refrigerator for as long as a week. Be sure to store it covered, so grains will not dry out.

TO FREEZE COOKED RICE

Cooked rice can be frozen alone, or in combination, with any food that will freeze. In fact, if placed in a suitable container and freezer-wrapped, cooked rice may be frozen for as long as 6 to 8 months. To thaw it, unwrap, then thaw at room temperature for about 3 to 4 hours. Reheat as below, if desired.

TO REHEAT COOKED RICE

When reheating cooked rice, place enough water in a saucepan to cover the bottom — about 1 tablesp. per cup of cooked rice. Add cooked rice; cover; then simmer over low heat until as hot and fluffy as when freshly cooked — about 8 to 10 min. Or add the same amount of water, and heat, covered, in a 300°F. to 350°F. oven for 15 min.

SAVORY RICE

Cook the rice as directed in Fluffy Hot Rice, at left. Then add one of these:

ALMOND: Slivered, toasted almonds.
APPLE-CURRY: Sauté an apple, cut into small chunks, in 3 tablesp. butter or margarine with ¼ teasp. curry powder, till tender. Fold into hot seasoned fluffy rice.
BASIL: In ¼ cup hot butter or margarine, sauté 2 tablesp. minced onion till golden. Add 1½ tablesp. wine vinegar, ½ teasp. salt, ½

teasp. sugar, 1 teasp. dried basil. Add to 3 cups hot cooked rice.

BUTTERED: 1 tablesp. butter or margarine.

CARROT-PARSLEY: Grated raw carrot, plus snipped parsley.

CHEESE: Little grated cheese.

CURRIED-PINEAPPLE: In 2 tablesp. butter or margarine and ½ teasp. curry powder in a skillet, heat one 13- to 14-oz. can pineapple tidbits, drained, for 5 min. Fold into 3 cups hot seasoned fluffy rice.

MUSHROOM: Sautéed mushroom slices.

OLIVE: Few sliced stuffed or ripe olives.

ONION: ¼ cup minced onion, sautéed tender in 2 tablesp. butter or margarine.

PARSLEY: Little snipped parsley or pimento.

PEAS AND SCALLIONS: Toss with some hot seasoned peas. Top with snipped scallions, then heated canned cheese sauce or soup.

POPPY SEED: Add 1 tablesp. poppy seeds for each cup cooked rice.

RAISIN-CURRY: Few raisins and generous sprinkle of curry. Especially nice with lamb, veal, or chicken dishes.

SCALLION: Sliced scallions, sautéed in a little butter till tender-crisp.

SPINACH: ½ cup chopped, cooked spinach, ¼ cup sautéed onions, and ½ cup grated Cheddar cheese. Season to taste.

TOMATO: A diced slice or two of tomato.

VEGETABLE: Toss with hot whole-kernel corn or mixed vegetables and a few cocktail onions.

COMPANY RICE

Vary liquid in which Regular White Rice cooks, p. 370, as below:

CHERRY: Substitute ½ cup maraschino cherry juice for equal amount of water.

CHICKEN: Substitute fresh or canned chicken broth for water. Sprinkle with paprika before serving.

CONSOMME: Substitute diluted canned condensed consommé for water.

ORANGE OR APPLE: Substitute ½ cup orange, apple, or tangerine juice for ½ cup water.

VEGETABLE: Substitute 1 cup canned vegetable juice cocktail or tomato juice for 1 cup water.

RAISIN RICE

Add ¼ cup raisins to Fluffy Hot Rice, p. 370, before cooking.

HERB RICE

In cooking rice as label or Fluffy Hot Rice, p. 370, directs, add one of these to water:

Omit salt; add onion soup mix or one of salad dressing mixes to taste.

About ⅛ teasp. dried thyme, orégano, sage, rosemary, basil, or savory.

About ½ teasp. celery seeds or dried dill.

Seasoned salt instead of salt.

About ¾ teasp. dried marjoram.

About 2 teasp. poppy seeds.

1 small bay leaf.

When done, add butter if desired. Especially nice with creamed tuna, beef stew, a vegetable plate, chicken, or almost any meat.

P.S. There's a packaged Herb Rice which has packet of herbs in with rice. Or you can buy herb seasoning in a jar to add yourself.

GOLDEN RICE

In saucepan, melt 2 tablesp. butter. Add 1⅓ cups packaged precooked rice; then sauté until golden brown, stirring constantly. Stir in ½ teasp. salt; then *slowly* add 1⅓ cups water. Bring to boil quickly; cover; then remove from heat. Let stand 5 min. Makes 4 servings, as vegetable, or topped with creamed chicken, fish, or meat.

SAVORY: Sauté 1 cup thinly sliced celery and 3 tablesp. each minced onion and green pepper with rice. Serve, sprinkled with snipped parsley.

RICE RING

Prepare enough rice as in Fluffy Hot Rice, p. 370, to make 4 cups cooked. When done, stir in 2 tablesp. butter or margarine. Gently pack it into buttered 1-qt. ring mold, let stand about 1 min. or so, then invert on heated platter and lift off mold.

Serve ring, sprinkled with snipped parsley and filled with any creamed mixture. Makes 4 generous servings.

NOTE: To keep rice ring hot 5 to 10 min. before unmolding, set mold in pan containing a little hot water; simmer on top of range.

CURRIED RICE

It comes packaged, with the packet of curry powder in with the rice. Or you can buy a jar of curry and season your rice yourself.

SAFFRON RICE

2 tablesp. butter or margarine	broth or 2 chicken-bouillon cubes
½ medium onion, minced	1⅓ cups packaged precooked rice*
½ teasp. dried saffron	2 tablesp. butter or margarine
2 cups canned chicken	

1. In 2 tablesp. butter in skillet, sauté onion until golden. Mix saffron with 1 tablesp. chicken broth; set aside.
2. In saucepan, bring remaining broth to boil. Add rice, onion; mix until all rice is moistened. Cover; remove from heat; let stand 5 min.
3. With fork, lightly mix in saffron and 2 tablesp. butter. Nice with broiled chicken or sea-food curry. Makes 4 servings.

Or use 1 cup uncooked regular or processed white rice. Combine with 2⅔ cups chicken broth; simmer, covered, 20 min.; add sautéed onion, saffron, butter.

P.S. There's a packaged Saffron Rice which has a packet of saffron in with the rice. Or buy saffron powder in a jar and add to the rice yourself.

OVEN DINNER RICE

If Regular or Processed Rice

1 cup uncooked regular or processed white rice	2 tablesp. butter or margarine
	2 cups boiling water*
	1 teasp. salt

Start heating oven to 350°F. In greased 1½-qt. casserole, combine all ingredients. Bake, covered, 30 min., or until rice feels tender between fingers and all water is absorbed. Uncover at once.

To serve: Fluff up rice with 2-tined fork. Makes 4 servings.

For processed rice, use 2¼ cups water.

PILAF: Before combining butter with rice, sauté 1 medium onion, minced, in butter until golden. Dilute 1 can condensed consommé with ⅔ cup water; bring to boil; substitute for boiling water. Omit salt. Bake as above, or at 400°F. 25 min. For a special touch, sprinkle with pine nuts or slivered almonds.

RISOTTO STYLE: Sprinkle Pilaf with grated Parmesan cheese.

CURRIED: First brown the white rice lightly in 2 tablesp. salad oil. Omit butter. Add 1½ teasp. curry powder, 1 medium onion, minced. Bake as at left, or at 400°F. 30 min.

If Packaged Precooked Rice

1⅓ cups packaged precooked rice	1 teasp. butter or margarine
½ teasp. salt	1⅓ cups boiling water*

Start heating oven to 425°F. In 8″ x 8″ x 2″ pan place rice, salt, butter. Add water. Cover with foil. Bake 5 min. Before serving, mix lightly with fork. Makes 4 servings.

Hot tap water may be used instead of boiling water. Cover and bake at 450°F. 10 to 15 min., or until water is absorbed.

ORANGE RICE

If Regular or Processed Rice

¼ cup butter or margarine	orange rind
⅔ cup diced celery with leaves	1 cup orange juice
	1 teasp. salt
2 tablesp. minced onion	⅛ teasp. dried thyme (optional)
1½ cups water	1 cup uncooked regular or processed white rice
2 tablesp. grated	

In hot butter, in saucepan, cook celery and onion until tender but not brown. Add water, orange rind, juice, salt, thyme. Bring to boil; slowly add rice. Cook, covered, over low heat 25 min., or until tender.

Delicious served with ham, duckling, chicken, etc. Makes 6 servings.

If Packaged Precooked Rice

Use 1½ cups packaged precooked rice. Prepare as above. After adding rice to liquid, cover, remove from heat. Let stand 5 min. Makes 4 servings.

SPANISH RICE

If Regular or Processed Rice

½ cup uncooked regular or processed white rice	1 1-lb.-4-oz. can tomatoes (2½ cups)
2 tablesp. butter or margarine	3 tablesp. minced green pepper
1 cup sliced onions	2 whole cloves
1⅛ teasp. salt	1 small bay leaf
	2 teasp. sugar

Cook rice as label directs; drain. In hot butter, in skillet, cook onions until golden and tender. Add salt, tomatoes, green pepper, cloves, bay leaf, sugar. Simmer, uncovered, 15 min.; remove bay leaf, cloves. Add rice; mix well; turn into greased 1-qt. casserole. Bake, uncovered, at 375°F. 30 min. Makes 4 servings.

P.S. If desired, top with packaged cheese slices before baking.

✦ FOR 2: Halve ingredients; use 3 custard cups.

If Packaged Precooked Rice

¼ cup salad oil or fat	2 8-oz. cans tomato
1⅓ cups packaged precooked rice	sauce
	1 teasp. salt
½ cup thinly sliced onions	¼ teasp. monosodium glutamate
⅓ cup diced green pepper	Dash pepper
1¾ cups hot water	1 teasp. prepared mustard (optional)

In hot salad oil in skillet, quickly brown rice with onions and green pepper; add water, tomato sauce, salt, monosodium glutamate, pepper, mustard. Bring to boil; simmer, covered, 5 min. Makes 4 servings.

PACKAGED PRECOOKED SPANISH RICE MIX: One comes all ready to quickly fix-and-serve—you just add tomatoes.

PACKAGED PROCESSED SPANISH RICE MIX is processed rice with tomatoes, seasonings, and rice—all in one package.

CANNED SPANISH RICE just needs to be heated in skillet or double boiler. Nice topped with grated sharp cheese or crumbled crisp bacon.

SPANISH RICE SEASONING MIX comes in envelopes or a jar—all ready for you to add to the boiling water in which you are cooking your rice.

PILAF ORIENTAL

½ cup butter or margarine	mato juice
	1 13¾-oz. can chicken broth (1¾ cups)
2 cups uncooked regular or processed white rice	½ teasp. salt
	Snipped parsley
1 1-pt.-2-oz. can to-	

One hour before serving:

1. Start heating oven to 375°F. In butter, in Dutch oven, sauté rice until it is brown and almost all of butter is absorbed, stirring fre-

quently to prevent rice from scorching.
2. Then, while stirring, slowly add tomato juice, chicken broth, and salt. Pour into a 2½-qt. casserole.
3. Bake, covered, 45 min., or until rice is tender. Uncover immediately, fluff up with a fork, sprinkle with parsley, and serve. Makes 8 servings.

GARDEN PILAF

¾ cup butter or margarine	½ teasp. pepper
	3 teasp. salt
½ cup almonds, blanched	2 teasp. dried rosemary, crushed
10 cups hot cooked rice	2 medium tomatoes
	Seasoned salt
½ cup instant minced onion	2 cups hot cooked or canned peas

In Dutch oven, in butter, sauté almonds till golden. Add hot rice, onion, pepper, salt, and rosemary; toss. Cut each tomato into eighths; sprinkle with seasoned salt; add to rice with hot peas; toss. Makes 12 servings.

VEGETABLE: Make as above, omitting tomatoes and peas. Add hot sautéed sliced mushrooms (1 lb.) and hot Blue Lake green beans, drained, (1 lb. can) to rice just before serving.

RAISIN PILAF

Start heating oven to 375°F. Grease 1½-qt. casserole. In saucepan, melt ¼ cup butter or margarine; in it, sauté 1 small onion, sliced; ¼ cup slivered almonds; ¼ cup raisins till golden. Add 1 cup uncooked regular or processed white rice; mix well. Add 2 cups hot canned clear chicken broth. Place in casserole; cover. Bake 30 min., or till all liquid is absorbed. Makes 4 servings.

VENETIAN RICE AND PEAS

4 bacon slices, diced	ular white rice
3 tablesp. butter or margarine	2 cups canned chicken broth
1 small onion, minced	1 teasp. salt
1 10-oz. pkg. frozen peas	Dash pepper
¾ cup uncooked reg-	¼ cup shredded Parmesan cheese

In heavy skillet, sauté diced bacon until crisp. Remove bacon; pour off fat. In butter, in same skillet, cook onion with peas, 5 min., stirring frequently. Then add rice and cook until well coated with butter. Now stir in broth, salt, pepper. Simmer, covered, stirring occasionally, about 20 min., or until rice absorbs all liquid and is tender. Toss with cheese and crisp bacon. Makes 3 or 4 servings.

BUFFET RICE

At your next buffet, give guests a choice of these three rices, handsomely arranged on an impressive tray or platter.

Begin it thus: For 9 to 12 servings, cook ⅔ cup wild rice as label directs. Also cook enough of your favorite Fluffy Hot Rice, p. 370, to make 10 cups, cooked. Have both rices ready and hot at the same time. Then, to the measured cooked rice, add these special touches:

For Avocado Rice: Toss 4 cups Fluffy Hot Rice with ⅛ teasp. pepper and ¾ teasp. each of salt and dried tarragon. Serve topped with slices of avocado, which were previously dipped in lemon juice.

For Bacon-Pepper Rice: Sauté ½ lb. diced bacon with ½ cup coarsely chopped green pepper till bacon is crisp. Add 4 cups Fluffy Hot Rice; toss.

For Almond Wild Rice: Toss the cooked wild rice with 2 cups hot Fluffy Hot Rice and ½ cup blanched whole almonds.

GAY GARNISH: Heap the Avocado Rice, Bacon-Pepper Rice, and Almond Wild Rice, side by side, on a spacious platter or tray. Between the piles, garnish with sliced tomatoes that have been sprinkled with seasoned salt or bottled Italian dressing, and with Curried Peach Halves, p. 437.

RICE AS A MAIN DISH

GREEN-AND-GOLD CASSEROLE

2 cups milk	½ clove garlic, minced
2 cups grated Cheddar cheese	2 eggs, slightly beaten
2 cups cooked rice	1 10½-oz. can condensed cream-of-mushroom soup, undiluted
1 cup snipped parsley	

Start heating oven to 350°F. Heat milk with cheese until cheese partially melts. Add cooked rice, parsley, garlic, eggs, soup; mix well. Pour into 2-qt. casserole.

Place casserole in large baking pan; set on oven rack. Fill pan half full of hot water. Bake, uncovered, 1 hr. 20 min., or until mixture is browned and set. Makes 6 servings.

HAITIAN RICE AND MUSHROOMS

½ lb. fresh mushrooms	scallions
2½ cups hot water	1½ teasp. salt
1 tablesp. salad oil	¼ teasp. dried thyme
½ lb. lean pork, diced	1 clove garlic, minced
2 oz. lean salt pork, diced	1 green pepper, halved, seeded
1 tablesp. snipped	1 cup uncooked regular white rice
	3 frankfurters

Cut up mushrooms into bowl, then pour on hot water. In skillet, heat salad oil; add diced pork and salt pork; sprinkle with scallions, salt, thyme, and garlic. Cook, stirring often, until pork and salt pork are nicely browned. With one hand, squeeze mushrooms in water to make water dark-colored. Add mushrooms and their liquid to skillet; bring to boil. Then add green pepper and rice. Cover and cook over low heat, stirring occasionally with fork, 15 min., or until liquid is absorbed. Slice franks; add to rice mixture; cook, uncovered, 1 min., or until franks are hot. Serve at once. Makes 4 to 6 servings.

SAVORY RICE AND CHEESE

¾ cup uncooked regular or processed white rice	2 tablesp. minced onion
2 tablesp. fat or salad oil	1¼ teasp. salt
	¼ teasp. pepper
½ cup diced celery	½ lb. process sharp Cheddar cheese, grated (2 cups)
¼ cup minced green pepper	⅔ cup milk

Cook rice as on p. 370. Start heating oven to 425°F. In hot fat, in skillet, sauté celery, pepper, and onion until tender-crisp; stir in salt, pepper.

In greased 1½-qt. casserole, arrange layers of rice, sautéed vegetables, and cheese, ending with cheese. Pour on milk. Bake, uncovered, 35 min., or until golden brown. Makes 4 servings.

✦ FOR 2: Halve ingredients; use 1-qt. casserole.

ITALIAN RICE WITH EGGPLANT
(Risotto con Melanzane)

Olive or salad oil	1 cup water
1 large eggplant, pared, thinly sliced	1 teasp. salt
	¼ teasp. pepper
1 tablesp. butter or margarine	4 cups chicken broth
	1½ cups uncooked regular white rice
1 thin slice salt pork, diced	¼ cup butter or margarine
1 medium onion, minced	¼ lb. Mozzarella cheese, thinly sliced
1 6-oz. can tomato paste	¼ cup grated Parmesan cheese
2 8-oz. cans tomato sauce	1 teasp. dried basil

1. In a little hot oil in Dutch oven, sauté eggplant slices on both sides until golden; remove eggplant.
2. In same Dutch oven, heat 1 tablesp. each of oil and butter. In it, sauté salt pork and onion until salt pork is crisp.
3. Add tomato paste, tomato sauce, water, salt, pepper; simmer, covered, 40 min.
4. Add chicken broth and rice. Bring to boil; then simmer, covered, 45 min., stirring occasionally. Stir in ¼ cup butter.
5. Start heating oven to 400°F. In greased 3-qt. casserole, arrange half of rice, half of eggplant, then half of Mozzarella; repeat.
6. Top with Parmesan and basil. Bake, uncovered, 25 min. Makes 6 servings.

WILD RICE

Wild rice is not rice at all, but the seed of a shallow water grass. The grains are long, spindly, and grayish, and when cooked as the label directs, are especially nice with game, poultry, etc. Wild rice is more expensive than white rice.

P.S. You can also buy a packaged mix of long-grain white rice and wild rice, complete with seasonings.

BOILED WILD RICE

¾ cup uncooked wild rice	2 teasp. butter or margarine
3 cups boiling water	Dash pepper
1 teasp. salt	

Wash rice well. To boiling water and salt, add rice very slowly so that water keeps boiling. Simmer, covered, stirring occasionally with fork, 30 to 45 min., or until rice is tender and all water is absorbed. Add butter, pepper. Nice with game or poultry. Makes 2¼ cups, or 3 servings.

WILD RICE BAKED IN CONSOMME

1 cup uncooked wild rice	½ lb. mushrooms, sliced
1 10½-oz. can condensed consommé, undiluted	1 tablesp. butter or margarine

Wash rice well. Place in greased 1½-qt. casserole; add consommé. Let stand 3 hr. Bake, covered, at 350°F. 45 min., adding a little water if rice becomes too dry. Meanwhile, sauté mushrooms in butter about 5 min., or until tender; stir into rice. Then let dry out a little, uncovered, in 300°F. oven. Should be moist, with all liquid absorbed. Especially nice with poultry or game. Makes 4 servings.

WILD AND FLUFFY WHITE RICE

1 cup uncooked wild rice	ular white rice, or
1 cup uncooked reg-	1¾ cups packaged precooked rice

Cook both kinds of rice as labels direct. Then toss cooked rices together and season as in Savory Rice, p. 370. Makes 8 servings.

EPICUREAN WILD RICE

⅓ cup butter or margarine	1 10½-oz. can condensed consommé, undiluted
½ cup snipped parsley	1½ cups boiling water
½ cup chopped green scallions, tops and all	1 teasp. salt
	½ teasp. dried marjoram
1 cup diagonally sliced celery	½ cup sherry
1¼ cups wild rice	

1. In Dutch oven or heavy skillet with tight-fitting cover, melt butter; add parsley, scallions, and celery; sauté until soft but not browned.
2. Then add rice, consommé, water, salt, and marjoram. Cook, covered, over low heat, for about 45 min., stirring lightly with fork now and then and adding a little hot water if mixture becomes dry and starts to stick.

3. When rice is tender and all liquid has been absorbed, stir in sherry. Cook, uncovered, about 5 min., or until sherry is absorbed, stirring occasionally.

Makes a wonderful accompaniment for baked Rock-Cornish hens or sautéed chicken. Makes 6 servings.

POLYNESIAN RICE MINGLE

1 cup uncooked wild rice	4 chicken-bouillon cubes
1 cup uncooked regular white rice	4 cups boiling water
3 tablesp. minced onion	½ cup Macadamia nuts, coarsely chopped (optional)
3 tablesp. soy sauce	¼ cup snipped parsley (optional)

About 1 hr. before serving:

1. Start heating oven to 350°F. In 2-qt. casserole, combine wild rice, regular white rice, minced onion, and soy sauce.
2. Now dissolve chicken-bouillon cubes in boiling water, then stir bouillon into rice-and-soy mixture in casserole.
3. Cover casserole, then bake rice 45 min. Just before serving, sprinkle it with Macadamia nuts and parsley. Makes 4 to 6 servings.

COMPANY WILD RICE

½ cup uncooked wild rice	½ 10½-oz. can condensed cream-of-mushroom soup, undiluted
1½ cups boiling water	
½ teasp. salt	½ cup heavy cream
1 tablesp. butter or margarine	⅛ teasp. dried marjoram
2 tablesp. minced onion	Dash dried basil
1 tablesp. minced green pepper	Dash dried tarragon
½ 3- or 4-oz. can sliced mushrooms, drained	¼ teasp. curry powder
	¼ teasp. salt
	⅛ teasp. pepper

1. Wash rice well in three or four changes of cold water. Then, to boiling water in saucepan, add ½ teasp. salt; stir in rice. Simmer, covered, 30 min., or until rice is tender and water is absorbed.
2. While rice cooks, in 1 tablesp. hot butter in another saucepan, sauté onion, green pepper, and drained canned mushrooms 5 min. Stir in cream-of-mushroom soup, cream, marjoram, basil, tarragon, curry, ¼ teasp. salt, and ⅛ teasp. pepper; heat 10 min.
3. Then add cooked wild rice to this mixture, and heat, stirring occasionally. Nice with Roast Rock-Cornish Hens, p. 263. Makes 2 servings.

THE MACARONI FAMILY

Members of the macaroni family are no mere "starchy fillers." Since, with even small additions of meat, fish, cheese, eggs, or milk, their cereal proteins are given a big "lift," they are a fine prop for a shaky budget. They make pleasant substitutes for potatoes, too. And since they have a long life on the pantry shelf, they can always be available.

Fortunately for all of us, the macaroni family of macaroni, spaghetti, and egg noodles comes in a fascinating number of shapes and sizes. Among the most popular are:

MACARONIS — of tubular shape in long, elbow, shell, manicotti, tufoli, rigatoni, mostaccioli, ditali, ziti, other styles, and lasagna.

SPAGHETTIS — of solid rodlike shape, in varying widths including spaghetti, linguine, elbow spaghetti, and fusilli.

EGG NOODLES — ribbonlike lengths in fine, medium, and broad styles, as well as in bows, bow ties, rings, alphabets, etc.

Best quality macaroni and spaghetti are made from a mixture of semolina (from durum wheat) and water.

Egg noodles are made from durum flour, water, and at least 5.5 per cent egg solids, as required by law.

Furthermore, most manufacturers are enriching their macaroni products with vitamins B_1, and B_2, niacin, and iron, the label indicating this enrichment.

Before using these recipes, refer to How To Use Our Recipes, p. 3. Always use standard measuring cups and measuring spoons; measure level.

When You Cook Macaroni, Spaghetti, or Noodles

Eight ounces of packaged macaroni makes about 4 to 5 cups, cooked. Eight ounces of packaged spaghetti or noodles makes about 3 to 4 cups, cooked. Either yields enough for 4 to 6 servings.

Never overcook macaroni, spaghetti, or noodles. Use package label directions, but remember that the actual number of cooking minutes will depend upon how well done you like your macaroni — "al dente," which is just tender, or more well done. So test the degree of doneness by biting a piece. If it's firm all the way through and not hard in the center, it's just ready to drain and serve.

Don't rinse macaroni products unless they are to be chilled and used in a salad; then use cold water. Serve them, seasoned with salt and pepper, then with 3 to 4 tablesp. butter or margarine. Or try the variations which follow.

To Serve as a Vegetable
(after cooking as on p. 377)

CRUNCHY: Sprinkle hot seasoned macaroni, spaghetti, or noodles with a few fresh bread crumbs, browned in butter or margarine.

CHEESY MACARONI: After draining hot cooked macaroni, stir in ⅔ cup milk, ½ teasp. prepared mustard, and 1½ cups grated process Cheddar cheese. Heat slightly; season if needed.

PIMENTO CHEESE: Into drained hot cooked spaghetti, stir 2 to 4 tablesp. butter or margarine and 1 6-oz. pkg. crumbled pimento-cheese spread. Heat till cheese melts.

GOLDEN NOODLES: After draining hot cooked noodles, heat 2 tablesp. butter or margarine in skillet. Add noodles, ½ teasp. salt, ⅛ teasp. paprika, ⅛ teasp. pepper, ⅓ cup grated Parmesan cheese. Sauté over medium heat, stirring occasionally, till slightly browned.

ONIONY: Simmer a little minced onion and green pepper in 3 or 4 tablesp. butter or margarine till tender, then add to drained hot cooked macaroni, spaghetti, or noodles.

POPPY OR CARAWAY NOODLES: After draining hot cooked noodles, stir in 3 or 4 tablesp. butter or margarine, 2 to 2½ teasp. poppy or caraway seeds, salt and pepper to taste. (For crunchy effect, first sauté ⅓ cup chopped, blanched almonds in butter until light brown; add, after seasoning.)

SPAGHETTI PARMESAN: After draining hot cooked spaghetti, stir in ¼ cup minced onion, ¾ teasp. dried savory (optional), 2 tablesp. butter or margarine, and ½ cup grated Parmesan cheese.

WHITE SPAGHETTI: After draining cooked spaghetti blend in ⅔ cup hot canned chicken broth and 5 tablesp. melted butter or margarine. Arrange in serving dish and sprinkle generously with grated Parmesan.

SAVORY NOODLES: After draining hot cooked noodles, add a little nutmeg, butter, pepper, grated Parmesan cheese, and salt if needed.

Other Macaroni Dress-Ups

To vary hot, seasoned cooked macaroni, spaghetti, or noodles try one of suggestions below. Reheat, if necessary, in skillet.

For A Vegetable Add:

Sautéed mushrooms	Cooked or canned peas
Fresh tomato chunks	
Tender green beans	Tabasco
Canned or cooked frozen mixed vegetables	Curry powder
	Lemon juice
	Prepared mustard
Tender-crisp spinach	Barbecue sauce
Shredded raw carrots	Stuffed olives
Chopped dill pickles	

For A Main Dish Add:

Chunks of canned tuna	Leftover meat loaf in chunks
Cut-up canned Vienna sausages	Cubes of table-ready meats plus some pickle
Cut-up cooked or canned shrimp	Sautéed hamburger plus chili sauce
Shredded dried beef, chicken, or turkey	Slivers of frankfurters
Diced cooked ham	

For Crisp Go-Alongs Try:

Crusty French bread	Coleslaw
Hard rolls	Rye crisps
Radishes, celery sticks, or carrot strips	Crisp crackers
	Bread sticks
Raw vegetable salad	

For Crisp Toppings Try:

Crisp cornflakes	Potato chips
Corn chips	

French-Fried Noodles: These crisp canned French-fried noodles are at their best topped with creamed sea food, chicken or turkey, hard-cooked eggs, or vegetables.

NOODLE RING

1. Cook 8 oz. noodles as label directs. Into drained, hot cooked noodles stir 2 to 4 tablesp. butter or margarine. Pack into well-buttered 6 cup (1½-qt.) ring mold.
2. Set mold in a shallower pan of hot water; then bake at 375°F. 20 min.
3. To unmold, lift mold from hot water; invert heated serving platter over top of ring mold. Turn both mold and platter over simul-

taneously, holding them securely. Noodle ring should slip out intact; then lift off mold.

4. Fill ring with chicken, shellfish, or eggs in sauce or gravy, or with mixed vegetables, or a favorite green vegetable.

SPAGHETTI WITH SAUCES

SALAMETTI

3 tablesp. salad oil
1 cup chopped onions
1 tablesp. flour
½ lb. salami, slivered
2 cups canned tomato juice
2 tablesp. Worcestershire
¼ teasp. pepper

2 tablesp. snipped parsley
1 6-oz. can sliced mushrooms, drained
¼ cup chopped green pepper
16 oz. spaghetti
Grated Parmesan cheese

In hot oil in large skillet, sauté onions until golden. Stir in flour, salami, tomato juice, Worcestershire, pepper. Simmer, uncovered, 25 min. Add parsley, mushrooms, green pepper; simmer 5 min. Meanwhile, cook spaghetti as label directs.

Serve sauce over spaghetti on platter or on individual plates; sprinkle with Parmesan cheese. Makes 4 servings.

TUNA SPAGHETTI

3 tablesp. salad oil
1 medium onion, minced
1 clove garlic, minced
1 3- or 4-oz. can mushrooms, undrained
1 1-lb.-4-oz. can tomatoes (2½ cups)

1 8-oz. can tomato sauce
1 bay leaf
1 6½- or 7-oz. can tuna (1 cup)
6 sliced or chopped green olives
16 oz. spaghetti
½ cup grated Parmesan cheese

In hot oil in skillet, sauté onion and garlic until golden. Add mushrooms, tomatoes, tomato sauce, bay leaf. Simmer, covered, about 1½ hours, or until thickened. Add tuna, olives; simmer 10 min.

Meanwhile, cook spaghetti as label directs. Pour sauce over spaghetti on platter; sprinkle with cheese. Makes about 6 servings.

FORTY-FIVE-MINUTE SPAGHETTI

¼ lb. bacon slices, cut into 1″ pieces
¾ cup sliced onions
½ lb. chuck, ground
1 teasp. salt
⅛ teasp. pepper
1 clove garlic, minced (optional)
1 teasp. Worcestershire

2 teasp. sugar
3 8-oz. cans tomato sauce
¼ cup sliced stuffed or ripe olives
8 oz. thin spaghetti
Grated Parmesan cheese

In large skillet, cook bacon until light brown, pouring off excess fat. Add onions, chuck; cook, stirring with fork, until brown. Add salt, pepper, garlic, Worcestershire, sugar, tomato sauce. Simmer, covered, 20 min. Add olives; simmer, covered, 15 min.

Meanwhile, cook spaghetti as label directs. Pour sauce over spaghetti on platter or on individual plates; sprinkle lightly with cheese. Makes 4 servings.

CHILI-SPAGHETTI

1 8-oz. pkg. spaghetti
½ cup margarine or shortening
1 lb. beef chuck, ground
3 medium onions, chopped
½ cup canned or cooked whole-kernel corn
1 10½-oz. can condensed tomato soup, undiluted

1 17-oz. can tomatoes
1 3- or 4-oz. can sliced or button mushrooms, undrained
1 4-oz. can pimentos, slivered
1 to 2 tablesp. chili powder
1 tablesp. salt
¼ teasp. pepper
1 teasp. sugar
Grated cheese (optional)

1. *About 2 hr. before serving:* Cook spaghetti as label directs, but reduce cooking time to 3 min. Drain, set aside.

2. In Dutch oven, over medium heat, melt margarine or shortening. In it, sauté chuck and onions until chuck loses red color. Add spaghetti, corn, tomato soup, tomatoes, mushrooms, pimentos, chili powder, salt, pepper, and sugar, mixing thoroughly.

3. Cook over very low heat, covered, stirring occasionally, 1 hr. Turn off heat and let stand 30 min. to develop flavors. Reheat if necessary.

4. Marvelous! Serve hot, passing grated cheese. Also serve garlic-buttered toast, tossed salad

with your special dressing, marshmallow-topped baked apples, and tea or coffee. Makes about 6 man-sized servings.

SPAGHETTI WITH ITALIAN MEAT SAUCE

¼ cup salad or olive oil	2½ teasp. salt
½ cup minced onions	½ teasp. pepper
1 lb. chuck, ground	¼ teasp. sugar
2 cloves garlic, minced	Tiny bit fresh or dried basil or thyme
2 3- or 4-oz. cans chopped mushrooms, undrained	1 cup Burgundy, claret, or other red wine
¼ cup snipped parsley	16 oz. spaghetti, or shell or elbow macaroni
1 8-oz. can tomato sauce	¼ lb. sharp Cheddar cheese, diced
1 1-lb.-4-oz. can tomatoes (2½ cups)	½ to 1 cup grated Parmesan cheese

In hot oil in skillet or kettle, simmer onions 5 min. Add chuck, garlic; cook, stirring, until meat loses red color. Add mushrooms, parsley, tomato sauce. Force tomatoes through sieve; add to sauce, with salt, pepper, sugar, basil. Simmer, covered, 1 hr. Add wine; simmer, covered, 1 hr.

About 20 min. before serving: Cook spaghetti as label directs. Add hot sauce and diced cheese; toss. Turn onto large platter; sprinkle generously with Parmesan cheese. Makes 6 to 8 generous servings.

To Do Ahead: Make sauce day before; refrigerate. Reheat while cooking spaghetti.

ITALIAN SPAGHETTI, CALIFORNIA STYLE

2 tablesp. bacon fat	drained
½ cup sliced onions	1½ teasp. salt
1 lb. chuck, ground	⅛ teasp. pepper
1 clove garlic, minced	1 teasp. dried sage
1 green pepper, minced	¼ teasp. dried thyme
1 1-lb.-13-oz. can tomatoes (3½ cups)	1 teasp. dried rosemary
2 8-oz. cans tomato sauce	1 bay leaf
	1 cup water
1 6-oz. can whole mushrooms, un-	2 tablesp. salad oil
	Meat Balls, at right
	16 oz. spaghetti

In bacon fat in large kettle, sauté onions un-

til tender. Add chuck; cook, stirring often, until meat loses red color. Add garlic, green pepper, tomatoes, sauce, mushrooms, seasonings, and water. Simmer, uncovered, stirring occasionally, 1½ hr., or until as thick as you like.

Meanwhile, in hot oil in skillet, brown Meat Balls quickly on all sides. About 20 min. before sauce is done, add Meat Balls to it. Also cook spaghetti as label directs.

To serve, pour sauce with Meat Balls over spaghetti on platter or individual plates. Makes 6 generous servings.

MEAT BALLS:

1 lb. chuck, ground	parsley
½ cup packaged dried bread crumbs	¼ cup grated Parmesan cheese
1 clove garlic, minced	1 egg
	½ teasp. salt
2 tablesp. snipped	⅛ teasp. pepper

Combine all ingredients; mix well. Shape into golf-ball-size balls. Use as directed in Italian Spaghetti, California Style. Or brown in salad oil in skillet, then add to favorite canned spaghetti sauce.

TAGLIARINI WITH CHICKEN LIVERS

½ cup dried mushrooms*	¼ teasp. dried marjoram
1 cup hot water	¼ teasp. dried rosemary
¼ cup olive oil	
1 10-oz. pkg. frozen chicken livers	¼ teasp. dried basil
½ cup minced onions	⅛ teasp. black pepper
½ cup minced celery	Dash cayenne pepper
1 tablesp. snipped parsley	1 clove garlic
	1 teasp. salt
1 8-oz. can tomato sauce	8 oz. fine egg noodles
½ 6-oz. can tomato paste (⅓ cup)	2 tablesp. butter or margarine
	1½ cups grated Parmesan cheese

Day before or early in day: Rinse dried mushrooms; add hot water; set aside. In hot oil in large skillet, brown chicken livers lightly; remove. To skillet, add onions, celery; sauté until golden. Add parsley, tomato sauce, tomato paste. Drain mushrooms, adding liquid to sauce in skillet. Finely chop mushrooms and chicken livers. Add to sauce, with marjoram, rosemary, basil, pepper, cayenne. Simmer, covered, 2 hr., stirring frequently. Mash garlic with salt; stir into sauce; cook 30 min. longer. Taste; add more seasonings if needed. Refrigerate until ready to use.

About 20 min. before serving: Start cooking noodles as label directs. Slowly reheat sauce. To drained noodles, add butter. Turn onto large platter; cover with sauce; sprinkle with 1/2 cup Parmesan. Pass rest of Parmesan. Makes 6 to 8 servings.

*Two 3- or 4-oz. cans chopped mushrooms, undrained, plus water to make 1 1/4 cups, may replace dried mushrooms and hot water.

GENOVESE GREEN SAUCE
(Pesto alla Genovese)

5 or 6 garlic cloves, minced	2 tablesp. finely chopped walnuts
1/4 cup snipped fresh basil; or 2 tablesp. dried basil	1/2 teasp. salt
	6 tablesp. olive or salad oil
1/4 cup grated Parmesan cheese	8 oz. noodles
	6 butter pats

1. In mortar (or small bowl) with pestle (or back of spoon), mix garlic, basil, cheese, walnuts, salt; pound mixture to smooth paste. Gradually add oil, working mixture to make smooth *pesto.*
2. Cook noodles as label directs. On each of 6 heated dinner plates, arrange mound of hot noodles; top with pat of butter, then with 1 tablesp. *pesto.* Just before eating, each person tosses noodles with *pesto.* Makes 6 servings.

ITALIAN WHITE CLAM SAUCE

8 oz. spaghetti	2 tablesp. snipped parsley
1/2 cup olive or salad oil	2 teasp. salt
1/2 cup butter or margarine	2 cups clam liquid
8 cloves garlic, minced	2 doz. shucked hard-shell clams

1. Cook spaghetti as label directs. Arrange on heated platter; keep hot.
2. Meanwhile, in hot oil and butter in skillet, sauté garlic till golden. Add parsley, salt, clam liquid. Simmer, uncovered, 10 min.
3. Add finely snipped clams; simmer 2 min. Pour over hot spaghetti. Makes 6 servings.

NANCY'S CURRIED SPAGHETTI

8 oz. spaghetti	2 tablesp. warm water
1 1/2 10 1/2-oz. cans condensed cream-of-chicken soup, undiluted	1 3- or 4-oz. can whole mushrooms, undrained
1 10 1/2-oz. can condensed cream-of-mushroom soup, undiluted	1 1/2 teasp. grated onion
	1/4 teasp. dried thyme
1/2 cup milk	1/8 teasp. dried basil
1/4 cup water	1/8 teasp. dried orégano
2 teasp. curry powder	1/4 cup grated Parmesan cheese

Cook spaghetti until barely tender as label directs; drain. Meanwhile, in saucepan, stir together soups, milk, 1/4 cup water; simmer, stirring, 10 min. Combine curry, 2 tablesp. water; add to soup mixture, along with mushrooms, onion, thyme, basil, and orégano. Simmer, stirring, 10 min. Arrange spaghetti in 2-qt. casserole; pour on soup mixture; toss lightly with fork; then sprinkle with cheese.

Serve at once. Or keep warm in 300°F. oven, covered, as long as 1 hr. Makes 9 or 10 servings.

DINNER-IN-A-DISH SPAGHETTI: When adding curry, add 2 cups cooked or canned turkey, tuna, chicken, or other meat except ham.

BUFFET STYLE: Double recipe. Use 3-qt. casserole. Makes 18 to 20 servings.

FOR LUNCHEON OR AS A VEGETABLE

SKILLET NOODLES AND PEAS

3 tablesp. salad oil	2 1/2 cups canned chicken broth
1/4 cup butter or margarine	1 cup light cream
8 oz. fine noodles	1 10-oz. pkg. frozen peas, slightly thawed
1/2 cup chopped onions	1 teasp. salt
1 clove garlic, minced	1/4 teasp. pepper

1. In large skillet, heat oil and butter; add noodles, onions, and garlic. Cook over me-

dium heat, stirring constantly, until noodles are golden.

2. Add broth, cream, and peas. Cook, covered, stirring occasionally, until noodles are tender — about 10 to 15 min. Then stir in salt and pepper; serve immediately. Makes 6 to 8 servings.

MACARONI SAUTE

1/3 cup fat or salad oil	1 clove garlic, minced (optional)
8 oz. elbow macaroni (2 cups)	3 cups canned tomato juice
1/2 cup minced onions	1 teasp. salt
1/2 cup minced green peppers	1/4 teasp. pepper
	2 tablesp. Worcestershire

In hot fat in skillet, sauté uncooked macaroni, onions, peppers, garlic about 10 min., or until macaroni turns yellow. Stir in tomato juice, salt, pepper, Worcestershire. Bring to boil over high heat; turn heat low and cook, covered, without stirring, 20 min. Nice with ham, bologna, brown 'n' serve sausages, canned luncheon meat, franks, etc. Makes 6 servings.

SKILLET MACARONI MEDLEY

4 oz. macaroni	2 onions, thinly sliced
1 10-oz. pkg. frozen mixed vegetables	2 8-oz. cans tomato sauce
1/4 cup butter or margarine	1/2 teasp. salt
	1/8 teasp. pepper

Cook macaroni as label directs. Cook mixed vegetables tender as label directs.

Meanwhile, in butter, sauté onions till tender; add tomato sauce, salt, and pepper. Simmer 5 min.; then, into mixture, fold the cooked macaroni and mixed vegetables, and heat. Makes 6 servings.

ELENA'S MACARONI BAKE

8 oz. macaroni, in 1 1/2" pieces, or elbow macaroni (about 2 cups)	1/4 cup butter or margarine
	3/4 teasp. salt
1/2 lb. process Cheddar cheese, diced	1/4 teasp. pepper
	1 cup commercial sour cream

1. Start heating oven to 350°F. Cook macaroni as label directs.

2. In 1 1/2-qt. casserole, place one third of macaroni and one third of cheese; dot with some of butter; sprinkle with some of salt and pepper; add one third of sour cream. Repeat till all ingredients are used, ending with sour cream. Bake, covered, 30 min. Makes 5 servings.

P.S. Nine tomato slices may be added to the layers if desired.

MARDI GRAS MACARONI AND CHEESE

6 oz. elbow macaroni (about 1 1/2 cups)	1/2 teasp. dry mustard
	1 1/2 teasp. Worcestershire
1 2/3 cups evaporated milk, undiluted	1/4 cup chopped pimento
1/2 teasp. salt	1/4 cup chopped green pepper
1/2 lb. process sharp Cheddar cheese, cubed	

Start heating oven to 350°F. Cook macaroni as label directs. Meanwhile, in saucepan over low heat, heat milk with salt to just below boiling. Add cheese; stir until thickened and smooth. Stir in mustard, Worcestershire. In greased 2-qt. casserole, combine macaroni, pimento, green pepper; pour on cheese sauce. Bake, uncovered, 25 to 30 min. Makes 4 servings.

♣ FOR 2: Halve ingredients; use 1-qt. casserole.

POLKA-DOT BAKED MACARONI

8 oz. elbow macaroni (2 cups)	6 oz. process sharp Cheddar cheese, grated (1 1/2 cups)
1/4 cup butter or margarine	1 10-oz. pkg. frozen peas and carrots, thawed
1/4 cup flour	
1 10 1/2-oz. can condensed cream-of-chicken soup, undiluted	1 tablesp. butter or margarine
	1/8 teasp. salt
1 cup milk	1 tablesp. water

Early in day: Cook macaroni as label directs. Meanwhile, in saucepan, melt 1/4 cup butter; stir in flour, then soup and milk; cook, stirring, until smooth and thickened. Combine macaroni, soup mixture, 3/4 cup cheese, and 1/2 pkg. peas and carrots. Turn into 2-qt. greased casserole; sprinkle rest of cheese on top. Place rest of vegetables in small casserole with 1 tablesp. butter, salt, and water. Refrigerate both.

About 40 min. before serving: Start heating oven to 400°F. Bake macaroni, uncovered, and vegetables, covered, 30 min., or until bubbling hot and golden. When done, spoon rest of carrots and peas around edge of macaroni to make colorful wreath. Makes 6 servings.

DINNER MAIN DISHES

DUTCH-OVEN DINNER

3 tablesp. fat or salad oil	1 3- or 4-oz. can sliced mushrooms, undrained
1 lb. chuck, ground	½ lb. medium noodles
1½ teasp. salt	
¼ teasp. black pepper	¼ lb. natural Cheddar cheese, grated (1 cup)
1 cup sliced onions	
1 green pepper, chopped	1 1-lb.-13-oz. can tomatoes (3½ cups)
1 12-oz. can vacuum-packed whole-kernel corn	Grated Parmesan cheese

In hot fat in Dutch oven, cook chuck, stirring, about 10 min. Stir in salt, next 5 ingredients. Top with uncooked noodles; sprinkle with 1 cup grated cheese; pour tomatoes over all. Simmer, covered, 1 hr. Serve with grated Parmesan. Makes 8 servings.

STREAMLINED LASAGNA

1 tablesp. salad oil or fat	matoes (2½ cups)
⅓ cup minced onion	1 8-oz. can tomato sauce
1 lb. chuck, ground	4 oz. lasagna (4 pieces)
1 clove garlic	¼ lb. natural ~~Swiss~~ MOZZARELLA cheese, thinly sliced
¾ teasp. salt	
¼ teasp. pepper	
¼ teasp. dried orégano	1½ cups ~~cottage~~ RICOTTA cheese
3 tablesp. snipped parsley	2 tablesp. snipped parsley
1 1-lb.-4-oz. can to-	

1. *Day before or early in day:* In hot oil in skillet, sauté onion until tender. Add chuck; cook until red color disappears. Slice garlic; mash with salt; add to meat, along with pep-

per, orégano, 3 tablesp. parsley, tomatoes, tomato sauce. Simmer, uncovered, 30 min. Refrigerate until ready to use.

2. *About 45 min. before serving:* Start heating oven to 350°F. Cook lasagna as label directs; drain; cover with cold water. In serving dish (ours was a copper skillet 12" long, 8" wide), arrange one third of meat sauce, then 2 pieces drained lasagna placed lengthwise (leave rest in water), half of Swiss cheese (reserve 1 slice), half of cottage cheese. Repeat, ending with remaining third of sauce and 1 Swiss-cheese slice, slivered. Bake 30 min. Just before serving, sprinkle with 2 tablesp. parsley. Makes 6 streamlined servings.

MACARONI LOAF WITH MEAT SAUCE

8 oz. elbow macaroni (2 cups)	Dash cayenne
	1 cup fresh bread crumbs
1 13-oz. can evaporated milk, undiluted (1⅔ cups)	¼ cup melted butter or margarine
½ lb. grated process Cheddar cheese (2 cups)	1 10½-oz. can condensed cream-of-chicken soup, undiluted
4 eggs, beaten	
¼ cup chopped canned pimentos	1 cup milk
¼ cup chopped green pepper	2 tablesp. instant minced onion
Salt	1 12-oz. can luncheon meat, coarsely chopped
⅛ teasp. paprika	

1. Start heating oven to 350°F. Cook macaroni as label directs.

2. In saucepan, heat evaporated milk about 2 min.; stir in cheese; cook over low heat, stirring constantly, until cheese melts.

3. In large bowl combine macaroni, cheese sauce, eggs, pimentos, green pepper, ¼ teasp. salt, paprika, cayenne, bread crumbs, and melted butter or margarine.

4. Grease 10" x 5" x 3" loaf pan well; turn macaroni mixture into it; bake 50 min., or until set.

5. Meanwhile, in saucepan, combine chicken soup with 1 cup milk; add onion and chopped luncheon meat; cook over low heat, stirring constantly, 10 min.

6. When done, remove macaroni loaf from oven and let stand 10 min.; then turn out onto heated platter. Serve it sliced and topped

with meat sauce, along with Swiss chard or zucchini, beet salad, spiced canned fruit cocktail, molasses cookies, and tea. Makes 6 servings.

WASHINGTON-SQUARE SPECIAL

4 oz. medium noodles
1 tablesp. butter or margarine
¼ cup canned slivered blanched almonds
1½ cups cooked or canned chicken, cut into large pieces; or 1½ cups diced, cooked veal

1 chicken-bouillon cube
½ cup hot water
¼ teasp. grated orange rind
¼ teasp. grated lemon rind
1 teasp. salt
¼ teasp. pepper
1 cup commercial sour cream
Snipped parsley

Cook noodles as label directs. In hot butter in skillet, brown almonds; set aside. To skillet, add chicken; heat gently. Dissolve bouillon cube in hot water. Add to chicken, along with grated rinds, salt, pepper, drained noodles; mix gently. Cook over medium heat about 10 min. Stir in sour cream. Heat quickly, but do not boil. Turn into serving dish. Sprinkle around edges with snipped parsley; heap browned almonds in center. Makes 4 servings.

MARTHA'S COMPANY CASSEROLE

8 oz. noodles
1 tablesp. butter or margarine
1 lb. chuck, ground
2 8-oz. cans tomato sauce
½ lb. cottage cheese (1 cup)
1 8-oz. pkg. soft

cream cheese
¼ cup commercial sour cream
⅓ cup snipped scallions
1 tablesp. minced green pepper
2 tablesp. melted butter or margarine

Start heating oven to 375°F. Cook noodles as label directs; drain. Meanwhile, in 1 tablesp. hot butter in skillet, sauté chuck until browned. Stir in tomato sauce. Remove from heat.

Combine cottage cheese, cream cheese, sour cream, scallions, green pepper. In 2-qt. casserole, spread half of noodles; cover with cheese mixture; then cover with rest of noodles. Pour on melted butter, then meat mixture. Bake, uncovered, 30 min. Makes 6 servings.

To Do Ahead: Make casserole early in day; refrigerate. To serve, bake at 375°F. 45 min., or until hot.

♣ FOR 2: Halve ingredients; use 1-qt. casserole.

BAKED ITALIAN HAM AND SPAGHETTI

¼ cup salad or olive oil
2 tablesp. minced onion
1 tablesp. minced green pepper
1 clove garlic, minced
¼ cup snipped parsley
2 teasp. mixed dried herbs (rosemary, marjoram, thyme)
2 cups cooked or canned ham or luncheon meat, diced

2 teasp. salt
¼ teasp. pepper
1 1-lb.-4-oz. can tomatoes (2½ cups)
1 3- or 4-oz. can sliced mushrooms, drained
1 cup liquid (mushroom liquid plus water to fill cup)
8 oz. spaghetti, broken into 2″ lengths
½ cup grated Parmesan or process Cheddar cheese

In hot oil in skillet, cook onion, green pepper, garlic, parsley, and herbs until brown. Add ham; brown. Add salt, pepper, tomatoes, mushrooms, and liquid. Simmer, covered, 20 min.

Start heating oven to 350°F. Cook spaghetti as label directs; add to ham mixture. Pour into 2-qt. casserole; sprinkle with cheese. Bake, covered, 40 min., or until bubbly. Makes 8 servings.

♣ FOR 4, OR 2 WITH LEFTOVERS: Halve all ingredients except mushrooms; use 1-qt. casserole.

SAVORY BAKED SPAGHETTI

3 tablesp. bacon fat or salad oil
2 medium onions, coarsely chopped
1 clove garlic (optional)
½ lb. chuck, ground
1½ teasp. salt
⅛ teasp. pepper

1 1-lb.-13-oz. can tomatoes (3½ cups)
1 teasp. chili powder
1 cup water
8 oz. spaghetti
¼ lb. process Cheddar cheese, grated (1 cup)

In fat in large skillet, slowly cook onions and garlic 5 min. Add chuck; cook, stirring occasionally, until meat loses red color. Stir in salt, pepper, tomatoes. Simmer, covered, 30 min.; discard garlic. Add chili, water.

Start heating oven to 325°F. Break half of uncooked spaghetti into greased 2-qt. casserole; pour on half of sauce; sprinkle with half of cheese. Break in rest of spaghetti; add rest of sauce and cheese. Bake, covered, 35 min. Uncover; bake 15 min. longer, or until brown. Makes 6 servings.

♣ FOR 2: Halve ingredients; use 1-qt. casserole.

QUADRETTINI SPINACH

¼ cup olive oil	1 tablesp. salt
⅓ cup minced onion	½ teasp. pepper
3 cloves garlic, crushed	4 oz. medium noodles
½ cup diced carrots	1 10-oz. pkg. frozen chopped spinach
3 celery stalks, diced	½ cup buttered fresh bread squares
1 lb. round, ground	
½ cup sherry	½ cup grated process Cheddar cheese
1 6-oz. can tomato paste (⅔ cup)	Grated Parmesan cheese
1 1-lb.-4-oz. can tomatoes (2½ cups)	

Day before or early in day: In hot oil in large skillet, sauté onion, garlic, carrots, and celery until lightly browned. Add round, and cook until red color disappears. Add sherry; simmer a few minutes. Add tomato paste, tomatoes, salt, pepper. Simmer, uncovered, 2 to 2½ hr. Season if necessary. Refrigerate.

About 45 min. before serving: Start heating oven to 350°F. Cook noodles as label directs. Cook spinach as label directs. Drain both very well; add to sauce. Turn into 1½-qt. casserole. Sprinkle with bread squares and ½ cup grated cheese. Bake, uncovered, 30 min., or until browned. Serve with Parmesan cheese. Makes 6 to 8 servings.

SPAGHETTI-SPARERIB SUPPER

1 1-lb.-4-oz. can tomato juice (2½ cups)	3 tablesp. vinegar
	1 tablesp. Worcestershire
2 tablesp. brown sugar	1 clove garlic, minced
1 teasp. salt	2 lb. spareribs
1 teasp. dry mustard	8 oz. spaghetti

Early in day: Start heating oven to 500°F.

For barbecue sauce, in saucepan, combine tomato juice, brown sugar, salt, mustard, vinegar, Worcestershire, garlic. Simmer, covered, 10 min.

Meanwhile, using kitchen shears, cut spareribs into serving-size pieces (2 or 3 ribs to each piece); place in shallow open pan. Bake 15 min., or until brown. Reduce oven temperature to 350°F. Bake ribs 45 min., basting every 15 min. with one fourth of barbecue sauce. Refrigerate ribs and rest of sauce.

About 45 min. before serving: Cook spaghetti as label directs. Start heating oven to 350°F. Place drained spaghetti in 1½-qt. casserole; mix with 1 cup sauce. Top with ribs; then pour remaining sauce over all. Bake, uncovered, about 30 min., or until ribs are tender. Makes 4 to 6 servings.

ELEVEN-LAYERED CASSEROLE

8 oz. elbow macaroni	¼ teasp. dried orégano
Butter or margarine	2 onions, thinly sliced
2 large tomatoes, sliced (optional)	1 13-oz. can evaporated milk, undiluted
2 cups grated process sharp Cheddar cheese	2 tablesp. grated Parmesan cheese
2 teasp. salt	
¼ teasp. pepper	

1. Cook macaroni as label directs.

2. Start heating oven to 350°F. Butter a 2-qt. casserole. Line sides of casserole with tomato slices, if desired.

3. Arrange half of macaroni in bottom of casserole; cover with 1 cup grated cheese.

4. Combine salt, pepper, orégano; sprinkle half of it over cheese.

5. Arrange half of onion slices on top; then pour in 1 cup evaporated milk. Add remaining macaroni, Cheddar cheese, salt mixture, onion slices, then evaporated milk.

6. Sprinkle with Parmesan cheese, then bake 30 min., or until sides bubble and top is slightly browned.

7. Serve this superb casserole with cooked frozen or canned mixed vegetables, curly-endive salad, warm baked pears, and tea. Makes 6 servings.

THOR'S COMPANY CASSEROLE

2 tablesp. salad oil	½ cup commercial
1 clove garlic	sour cream
1 lb. veal round (thin	¼ lb. Swiss cheese,
slice cut into 6	sliced
pieces)	2 tomatoes, sliced
Salt and pepper	½ cup dry white
2 3- or 4-oz. cans	wine
sliced mushrooms	½ cup grated Par-
4 oz. noodles	mesan cheese

Start heating oven to 400°F. In hot oil in skillet, brown garlic with veal, sprinkling veal with ½ teasp. salt, ⅛ teasp. pepper. Remove garlic. Add undrained mushrooms. Simmer, covered, 15 to 20 min. Meanwhile, cook noodles as label directs; drain; toss with sour cream.

In 1½-qt. casserole, place half of noodle mixture, half of veal and mushrooms, then half of Swiss cheese and tomato slices. Sprinkle with ½ teasp. salt, ⅛ teasp. pepper. Repeat. Into gravy in skillet, stir wine, Parmesan. Pour into casserole. Bake, uncovered, about 25 min. Makes 6 servings.

NOODLE STROGANOFF

¼ cup butter or mar-	3 tablesp. Burgundy
garine	or other red wine
¼ cup sliced scal-	1 10½-oz. can con-
lions or chopped	densed consommé,
onion	undiluted
1 clove garlic, minced	1 teasp. salt
½ lb. mushrooms,	¼ teasp. pepper
sliced; or 2 3- or	4 oz. medium noodles
4-oz. cans sliced	1 cup commercial
mushrooms, drained	sour cream
1 lb. chuck, ground	Snipped parsley
3 tablesp. lemon juice	

In hot butter in skillet, sauté scallions, garlic, and mushrooms until lightly browned. Add chuck; cook, stirring, until red color disappears. Stir in lemon juice, Burgundy, consommé, salt, pepper. Simmer, uncovered, 15 min. Stir in uncooked noodles. Cook, covered, 5 min., or until noodles are tender. Mix in sour cream; heat quickly but do not boil. Serve at once, sprinkled with parsley. Makes 6 servings.

ELENA'S MACARONI

¼ cup salad oil	1 8-oz. can tomato
1 lb. chuck, cut into	sauce
½" cubes	¾ cup catchup
1 cup chopped	¼ cup chili sauce
onions	¼ teasp. dried rose-
3 cloves garlic,	mary
minced	¼ teasp. dried thyme
½ cup chopped	12 oz. large sea-shell
celery	macaroni or elbow
⅓ cup snipped	macaroni
parsley	½ lb. Romano cheese,
1 1-lb.-4-oz. can to-	crumbled (1½
matoes (2½ cups)	cups)*

Day before or early in day: In hot oil in Dutch oven or large saucepan, brown chuck; add onions, garlic, celery, parsley. Cook about 5 min., or until golden. Add tomatoes, tomato sauce, catchup, chili sauce, rosemary, thyme. Simmer, covered, 2 hr. Refrigerate.

About 30 min. before serving: Heat sauce slowly. Cook macaroni as label directs. Place macaroni in kettle. Toss with hot sauce and crumbled Romano. Turn out onto large platter and serve at once. Makes 10 servings.

To crumble Romano cheese use a 4-tined fork to scrape cheese into small bits.

FIX-AND-SERVE MACARONI DISHES

Grocers' shelves and freezer cabinets are brimming with spaghetti and macaroni favorites that take only minutes to prepare for serving. Get acquainted with the host of macaroni main dishes, spaghetti sauces, etc., some of which are listed on p. 102. Learn to add your own special touch or use one of our recipes that follow.

Top Stove Specials

SAVORY SPAGHETTI: In skillet, sauté ½ to 1 lb. bulk pork sausage until nicely browned; pour off all but 1 tablesp. fat. Add 1 3- or 4-oz. can sliced mushrooms, drained; 1 medium onion, sliced; 1 clove garlic, minced;

½ teasp. salt; ⅛ teasp. pepper. Sauté until onion is tender. Add 2 cans spaghetti in tomato sauce with cheese; heat over low heat, covered, stirring occasionally. Makes 4 servings.

BEEF AND SPAGHETTI: In 1 tablesp. hot fat in skillet, sauté 1 small onion, minced, until tender; add ½ lb. chuck, ground. Cook, stirring occasionally, until meat loses red color. Add ½ teasp. salt or 1 teasp. garlic salt, and 1 can spaghetti in tomato sauce with cheese. Heat, uncovered, stirring often, till bubbling. Makes 4 servings.

CHICKEN-NOODLE BAKE: Cook ¼ lb. (2 cups) medium noodles as label directs. In 1 tablesp. hot butter or margarine in skillet, sauté 2 tablesp. minced green pepper until tender. Stir in 1 10½-oz. can condensed cream-of-chicken soup, undiluted, and 1 cup cooked or canned chicken, in large pieces. Add noodles. Cook over low heat, uncovered, 10 min. If desired, garnish with green-pepper rings and few chicken slices. Makes 4 servings.

SPAGHETTI CON CHILI: Into 1 can spaghetti and meat balls in tomato sauce, stir 1 teasp. chili powder. Heat. Makes 2 or 3 servings.

SPAGHETTI-STUFFED PEPPERS

6 medium green peppers	1 15½-oz. can spaghetti in tomato sauce with cheese
3 tablesp. fat or salad oil	3 cups diagonally sliced carrots
½ cup minced onions	½ teasp. salt
1 clove garlic, minced	⅓ cup water
1 12-oz. can luncheon meat	3 tablesp. butter or margarine
¼ teasp. dried basil	

Wash and dry green peppers, then cut thin slice from stem end of each, and remove seeds. In skillet, cook peppers in 2 cups boiling salted water, covered, 5 min.; then drain. Remove peppers. In same skillet, heat fat; add onions and garlic; sauté until tender but not brown. Grate luncheon meat on coarse grater; add to onions; sauté until lightly browned. Add basil and spaghetti; combine, using fork. Lightly fill (do not pack) peppers with spaghetti mixture. Arrange stuffed peppers along one side of skillet with sliced carrots along

other side. Sprinkle salt on carrots; then pour water into bottom of skillet. Simmer, covered, 20 min., or until carrots are tender. Spoon butter over carrots, and carry carrots and peppers, piping hot, to table, to be served right from skillet. Makes 6 servings.

PICNIC SPAGHETTI

To favorite spaghetti sauce (from scratch, mix, can, or packaged dinner), add chopped celery, chopped scallions, or pickle relish to taste. Toss some sauce with cooked spaghetti; carry to picnic in Dutch oven; reheat there, adding more hot sauce. Top with grated Swiss, Parmesan, or Cheddar. Pass rest of sauce.

Oven Macaroni Specials

BEEF-AND-CHILI BAKE: Start heating oven to 350°F. In 2 tablesp. hot fat or salad oil in skillet, sauté 1 lb. chuck, ground, till red color disappears; stir in 1 teasp. chili powder. Grate ½ lb. process sharp Cheddar cheese. Open 3 cans spaghetti in tomato sauce with cheese. Place 1 can spaghetti in 2-qt. casserole; top with one third of meat and one third of cheese. Repeat twice. Bake 45 min. Pass grated Parmesan cheese if desired. Makes 4 or 5 generous servings.

CHEESY SPAGHETTI OMELET: Mix 3 egg yolks, ¼ teasp. salt, and ⅛ teasp. pepper with 1 can spaghetti in tomato sauce with cheese. Beat 3 egg whites till stiff; fold into spaghetti mixture.

Start heating oven to 375°F. Heat 2 tablesp. butter or margarine in medium iron skillet; pour in spaghetti mixture. Cook over medium heat about 10 min., or until brown around edge when lifted with fork or spatula.

Sprinkle top with ¾ cup grated process sharp Cheddar cheese. Bake 10 to 12 min., or until cheese is melted and top is brown. To serve, cut into wedges. Makes 4 servings.

MACARONI-TUNA BAKE: Start heating oven to 375°F. In small saucepan, melt 2 tablesp. butter or margarine; toss with ½ cup fresh bread crumbs. In 1½-qt. casserole, combine 2 cans macaroni in cheese sauce with 1 6½- or 7-oz. can tuna (1 cup); top with crumbs. Bake 20 min. Makes 6 servings.

MACARONI-AND-BEAN CASSEROLE

1 15¼-oz. can macaroni in cheese sauce
¼ cup grated process Cheddar cheese
1 cup drained canned green beans (Blue Lake, etc.), seasoned to taste

Start heating oven to 375°F. In buttered 1-qt. casserole, place ½ can macaroni in cheese sauce; sprinkle with 2 tablesp. grated cheese; top with green beans. Cover with rest of macaroni in cheese sauce. Sprinkle with remaining grated cheese. Bake, uncovered, 15 to 20 min., or until hot and bubbling. Makes 4 servings.

✤ FOR 2: Use 1 7-oz. can macaroni in cheese sauce, 2 tablesp. grated cheese, and ½ cup green beans. Use 2-cup casserole.

SPAGHETTI AND MUSHROOM PARMESAN

2 tablesp. butter or margarine
½ lb. mushrooms, sliced
1 16-oz. can spaghetti in tomato
sauce with cheese
1 10¾-oz. can spaghetti sauce with meat
Grated Parmesan cheese

Start heating oven to 375°F. In hot butter in skillet, sauté mushrooms about 5 min. In greased 1-qt. casserole, combine cans of spaghetti and spaghetti sauce; cover with mushrooms; sprinkle with 3 tablesp. Parmesan. Bake, uncovered, 20 min. Let stand a few min. before serving. Serve with more Parmesan. Makes 4 servings.

VEGETABLES THAT SAY "MORE"

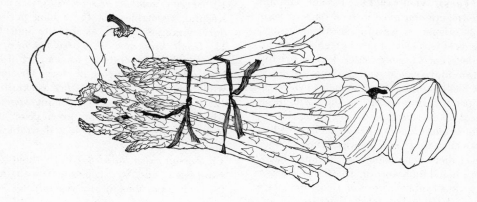

Want to hear more requests for "More, please!" when you serve vegetables? Then do as master chefs do:

1. Cook them gently, to retain vitamins and flavor and to produce delectable tender crispness.

2. Season them subtly; bring out, don't conceal, the wonderful vegetable flavor.

3. Add sauce or garnish carefully, choosing the finishing touch that provides the best possible combination of flavors in the most eye-catching way.

Before using these recipes, refer to How To Use Our Recipes, p. 3. Always use standard measuring cups and measuring spoons; measure level.

Shop Wisely

MARKET-FRESH VEGETABLES: These are available all year long but are the best buy when in their growing season in your locality. Keep these points in mind when buying:

1. Check on vegetable supplies in local markets through newspaper and radio reports.

2. Buy from a dealer who has a quick turnover and who keeps fresh vegetables under refrigeration or on crushed ice. They come to market at their peak of flavor and freshness, thanks to modern hydro-cooling at the farm (getting them cool through and through) and well-iced shipping conditions.

3. Buy only enough for 1 or 2 days' supply whenever possible; use promptly.

4. Go to market yourself whenever you can. In today's markets, vegetables are so attractively displayed you can quickly see daily specials and be reminded of vegetables that seldom appear on your menus.

5. More and more vegetables are coming to market washed and packaged. This means that they are not picked over by other shoppers.

FROZEN VEGETABLES: These are available all year long. They are always in season, so you always have a wide variety to choose from. The best of the crop is harvested at the peak of quality and rapidly frozen within a few hours; thus, nutritional losses are negligible. Keep these points in mind when buying:

1. Buy frozen vegetables from a grocer who keeps them in a freezer cabinet that maintains near 0°F. temperature. They should be frozen solid, not beginning to soften.

2. Watch for specials of the week — they'll be especially advantageous if you have freezer space available.

CANNED VEGETABLES: These offer a wonderful variety to choose from, too. To buy, see p. 88.

Store with Care

POTATOES, ONIONS, YELLOW TURNIPS: Store where cool air can circulate around them. Do not clean until ready to use. (Most potatoes are prewashed.) Keep cool and dry.

OTHER FRESH VEGETABLES: To cut vitamin losses, refrigerate *at once* in food bags or your vegetable crisper. If washing seems necessary, hold heads of lettuce and salad greens, stem end up, under faucet; rinse outer leaves briefly. Shake to remove excess water before storing.

GARDEN VEGETABLES: Pick home-grown vegetables just before cooking, so they will be at their peak of freshness and food value. Or refrigerate at once; then cook as soon as possible.

FROZEN VEGETABLES: Don't waste time — once you select them (take along an insulated bag), get them home and store in freezer at once.

CANNED VEGETABLES: Store in a cool dry place until used. If for salads, chill, then use.

LEFTOVER COOKED VEGETABLES: Store, covered, in refrigerator; plan to use next day.

Cook with Care

For specific instructions on buying, preparing, and cooking vegetables, see chart, p. 420. Check tips below for further help in serving attractive, wholesome vegetables.

1. *Cook only enough for one meal,* unless you have plans for using leftovers next day.
2. *When paring vegetables,* use a vegetable parer that makes thin parings.
3. *Scrub well,* but do not peel or pare tender carrots, new potatoes, summer squash, zucchini, or fresh mushrooms.
4. *Avoid presoaking;* it dissolves out precious vitamins and minerals.
5. *To cook leafy greens (except spinach),* use 1/4" boiling water; cover pot; cook 1 min., or until greens wilt and become compact. Then remove lid to let steam escape (about 1/2 min.), stir, cover, continue cooking. For spinach, see p. 430.
6. *Cook green vegetables (except zucchini)* in as little water as possible to prevent burning, 1/2" to 1", without the cover, for 5 min. after they boil. (Volatile substances which affect color and flavor escape.) Then cover for remainder of cooking. For zucchini, see p. 432.
7. *Cook all other vegetables* in tightly covered cooking utensil to shorten cooking time.

8. *Stir as little as possible.* Unnecessary stirring adds air to vegetables and increases the loss of vitamin C.
9. *Do not overcook.* Cook only until vegetables are just tender-crisp, no more. They'll taste better, look better, be better for you.
10. *Serve vegetables as soon as they're cooked.* Keeping vegetables hot for a long period reduces vitamins, as well as appetite appeal.
11. *Don't throw away that precious bit of cooking liquid.* Refrigerate it; use as part of liquid in sauces, soups, gravies, or stews. Or combine with tomato- or vegetable-juice cocktails.
12. *Avoid baking soda* in cooking vegetables. Although it helps bring out green color, it may make texture and flavor less desirable, may destroy vitamins.
13. *For an extra bit of flavor* (without adding sweetness), add 1/2 teasp. sugar with the salt for each 6 portions of any vegetables.

MARKET-FRESH OR GARDEN VEGETABLES

Here are several delectable ways to cook market-fresh or garden vegetables. Take your pick, depending on the vegetable, the amount of time you have, the meal you're serving.

In Covered Saucepan: Cook vegetable quickly in small amount of water — not more than 1". Check steps 5, 6, 7, and 8 under Cook with Care, left. Also see Vegetable Chart, p. 420.

In Pressure Cooker: Pour into pressure cooker amount of hot water that manufacturer directs, adding 1/4 teasp. salt, then vegetables; cover. Over high heat, bring to cooking pressure as manufacturer directs; then reduce heat to maintain same pressure throughout cooking.

Cook for time periods manufacturer directs. Or follow our Vegetable Chart, p. 420. These cooking times start after cooking pressure is reached and are for 15 lb. pressure only. At end of cooking time, reduce pressure immediately as manufacturer directs.

In Skillet: This method is especially nice for asparagus, shredded cabbage, kale, spinach, sliced young summer squash or zucchini, etc. Put prepared vegetable in large covered skillet, with a few tablespoonfuls of water, salt, and a little butter; cook, stirring once in a while, until just tender-crisp. Check Cook with Care, at left.

In Oven: Many vegetable combinations may be baked along with the main dish, at the same temperature. See list below, indicating temperature at which some of our favorite vegetable dishes bake. If baking times vary, plan to put each dish into oven so that both come out together.

AT 250°F.

Old-Fashioned Boston Baked Beans, p. 401

AT 300°F.

Kraut-Noodle Casserole, p. 415

AT 325°F.

Cheesy Swiss Chard, p. 406
Custard Corn Pudding, p. 400
Franconia, or Pan-Roasted, Potatoes, p. 411
Pan-Roasted Sweet Potatoes, p. 410
Savory Lima-Bean Pot, p. 401
Sweet-Potato Soufflé, p. 410

AT 350°F.

Baked Sweet Potatoes, p. 409
Buffet Cheese-Scalloped Carrots, p. 398
Casserole-Roasted Potatoes, p. 411
Eggplant Parmesan, p. 402
Endive au Four, p. 402
Gnocchi au Gratin, p. 412
Jamaican Yam Casserole, p. 410
John J. Limas, p. 404
Merle's Company Casserole, p. 419
Patty's Potato-Cabbage Casserole, p. 413
Rebaked Potatoes, p. 411
Southern Corn Pudding, p. 400
Stuffed Zucchini, p. 419
Baked Turnip Puff, p. 418

AT 375°F.

Baked Tomatoes, p. 417
Candied Sweet Potatoes, p. 410
Old-Time Scalloped Potatoes, p. 413
Savory Hubbard Squash, p. 416
Scalloped Tomatoes, p. 417
Stuffed-Pepper Twins, p. 404

AT 400°F.

Baked Acorn Squash, p. 415
Baked-Bean Casserole, p. 401
Baked Hubbard-Squash Squares, p. 416
Beans Très Bien, p. 403
Delmonico Potatoes, p. 412
Summer Squash en Casserole, p. 417

AT 425°F.

Apple-Acorn Squash, p. 416

AT 450°F.

Baked Potatoes, p. 411
Duchess or Plank-Border Potatoes, p. 412

FROZEN VEGETABLES

Saucepan-Cooked: Packaged frozen vegetables can be cooked quickly and easily. Just follow label directions. Be careful not to overcook; time carefully once water boils.

Quicker-Than-Ever to Cook: Do try some of the new, delectable, loose-frozen vegetable combinations, vegetables with sauces, vegetables with butter sauce, spinach soufflé, corn soufflé, potatoes au gratin, hashed in cream, etc., now in your grocer's freezer. They come all ready to heat — some in boilable film bags, some in foil pans to heat in the oven, some ready to turn into a pot for very brief cooking. Just follow label directions.

For Twosomes: A number of vegetables, including peas, cut green beans, cut corn, limas, etc., come loose-frozen. Just shake out the amount needed for two; freeze rest.

Fix-and-Serve Potatoes: There's quite a choice — French fries (crinkle cut or plain); potato patties, delicately flavored with onion; whipped or mashed potatoes; potato puffs and bite-size tiny-taters, delicious with meats or as nibblers; cottage fries and hash browns, so popular with men; and the whole potatoes, pared and ready to be pan-roasted around a roast, or creamed, or boiled. Just do as label directs.

Oven-Cooked: Another easy way to cook frozen vegetables is to bake them. When baking a casserole, meat loaf, etc., just bake regular-size box of frozen vegetables (for 3 or 4 servings), in a covered casserole, with 1 to 2 tablesp. butter or margarine and ¼ teasp. salt, right along with the meat, placing it in oven so it will be done at same time as main dish. Follow chart on p. 392.

CANNED VEGETABLES

To preserve the delicious flavor and food value in canned vegetables, treat them as follows:
PEAS, GREEN LIMAS, GREEN BEANS, CARROTS, ETC.: Drain liquid from can or jar into sauce-

TO OVEN-COOK FROZEN VEGETABLES

FROZEN VEGETABLE (regular-size package)	OVEN-COOKING TIME AT 350°F.*
Asparagus cuts	55 to 60 min.
Asparagus spears	55 to 60 min.
Broccoli, chopped	45 to 50 min.
Broccoli, spears	40 to 45 min.
Brussels sprouts	40 to 45 min.
Cauliflower	50 to 55 min.
Corn, whole kernel	45 to 50 min.
Green beans,	
cut	55 to 60 min.
French style	55 to 60 min.
Italian	55 to 60 min.
whole	55 to 60 min.
Green limas,	
baby†	55 to 60 min.
Fordhook‡	45 to 50 min.
Mixed vegetables	60 min.
Peas	45 to 50 min.
Peas and carrots	55 to 60 min.
Spinach	45 to 50 min.
Spinach, chopped	45 to 50 min.
Squash, cooked	45 min.
Succotash	55 to 60 min.
Wax beans, cut	60 min.

*If baking at 325°F., increase time about 10 min.
If baking at 375°F., decrease time about 10 min.
†Add ¼ cup water with butter and salt.
‡Add 2 tablesp. water with butter and salt.

pan. Boil it down till half or one third in volume; add vegetables; heat. Season with salt and pepper (or as at right), then with butter or margarine. (Blue Lake green beans are especially tasty.)

TOMATOES, CREAM-STYLE CORN, AND SQUASH: Heat contents of can; season; serve.

VEGETABLES TO USE COLD IN SALADS: Drain. Toss with, or arrange on, greens. (Use drained-off liquids in stews, soups, gravies, sauces, etc.)

CANNED MUSHROOMS: Canned mushrooms add glamour and flavor to a wide variety of other foods. They come whole, sliced, or chopped in their own pure mushroom broth, so use the broth as part of the liquid in the recipe, or save for soup or sauce. A 3- or 4-oz. can of mushrooms is equivalent to about ½ lb. of fresh mushrooms; a 6- or 8-oz. can, to about 1 lb. mushrooms.

THE INSTANT POTATO FAMILY

Instant potato products, now waiting for you on your grocer's shelves, are one of the wonders of our times. You'll find mashed, hashed brown, scalloped, au gratin, frying potatoes, potato pancakes, bakers in sour cream or cheese sauce, etc. New ones keep popping up. Such chores as paring, slicing, grating, and mashing have all been done for you. Try them with the suggestions under Serve with a Flair, below, or White Potatoes, p. 411, in mind.

Serve with a Flair

CUT THEM DIFFERENTLY

Dare to be different. Cut fresh vegetables on the bias, in slivers, or in slices. It means quicker cooking and handsomer, surer-to-please vegetables to take to the table.

SEASON TO TASTE

Use imagination when adding that lump of butter or margarine, that extra salt and pepper, to cooked vegetables. Try adding seasoned, garlic, or onion salt (omit regular salt), monosodium glutamate, seasoned pepper (omit regular pepper), a pinch of herbs, a dash of Tabasco, etc. See Shaker Seasonings, p. 99.

Under each vegetable in the following pages, you will find suggestions to start you on your way to new eating pleasures.

CRUMB STYLE

Sauté ½ to 1 cup fresh bread crumbs in 2 to 4 tablesp. butter or margarine until light brown. Add pinch of salt, speck each of pepper and paprika, 1 tablesp. lemon juice. If desired, add ½ cup grated cheese instead of lemon juice. Especially nice sprinkled over cooked cauliflower, asparagus, broccoli, or Brussels sprouts.

QUICK CREAM STYLE

Heat light cream. Season with salt, pepper, butter or margarine, and, if desired, some grated cheese. Or heat up a can of Cheddar cheese soup as label directs. Pour over any of these hot cooked vegetables:

Asparagus	Celery
Brussels sprouts	Whole-kernel corn
Cabbage	Green beans
Carrots	Green limas
Cauliflower	Peas

OLD-FASHIONED CREAMED

Use one, or a combination of two or more, cooked vegetables. Make Vegetable or Cheese Sauce, p. 533. (Allow about ½ cup sauce per 1 cup cooked vegetables.)

If creaming canned vegetables, boil down can liquid till one third in volume; use as part of milk.

Add hot sauce directly to vegetables; reheat. Or pour sauce over vegetable in serving dish and sprinkle with paprika. Three cups vegetables with 1½ cups sauce makes 4 servings.

SCALLOPED

For 4 servings, arrange 3 cups cooked vegetables and 1½ cups hot Vegetable or Cheese Sauce, p. 533, in alternate layers, in greased 1½-qt. casserole. Top with ⅓ cup buttered fresh bread crumbs (if desired, mix ¼ to ⅓ cup grated cheese with crumbs); sprinkle with paprika. Bake at 450°F. 5 to 10 min., or until vegetables are hot and crumbs brown.

DIFFERENT COMBINATIONS

Combine two or more vegetables after cooking. (Or combine before cooking if they cook in about the same time.) Then season and toss lightly. Try:

ASPARAGUS, cut up, with peas, green limas, or whole-kernel corn

GREEN LIMAS, with cauliflowerets, peas, slivered carrots, or sliced celery (cut on angle)

BRUSSELS SPROUTS, with peas, small onions, cauliflowerets, green beans, or sliced celery

CARROTS, with diced celery, sliced onions, green limas, peas, green beans, or cauliflowerets

CAULIFLOWER, with peas, green limas, or slivered carrots

WHOLE-KERNEL CORN, with peas, slivered carrots, green beans, or sliced zucchini

GREEN BEANS, with small whole onions, green limas, peas, whole-kernel corn, or sliced celery or carrots (cut on angle)

SMALL WHOLE ONIONS, with green limas, peas, slivered carrots, summer squash, green beans, or mushrooms

PARSNIPS, with peas or slivered carrots

PEAS, with diced white or yellow turnips, summer squash, whole-kernel corn, sliced celery, green beans, or mushrooms

SUMMER SQUASH, with peas, green limas, whole-kernel corn, green beans, or sliced zucchini

GLAMOROUS SERVING

Arrange 2 or 3 vegetables on one heated large chop plate or platter or in an attractive 3-qt. casserole or oversized vegetable dish — they'll stay hot longer and look handsome. And you'll have only one dish to wash.

BROCCOLI bunchlets down one side of platter; whole carrots down other

CAULIFLOWER HEAD in center of platter; slivered carrots and green beans, in groups, radiating from it

CAULIFLOWER HEAD in center of platter; green beans and onions around it

CAULIFLOWER HEAD, studded with almonds or topped with cheese sauce, in center of platter; green beans around it

CORN (MEXICAN STYLE), in center of heated casserole; green beans and small whole onions around it

MASHED POTATOES OR YELLOW TURNIPS in mound in center of chop plate; peas and onions around it

RICE IN CENTER OF PLATTER (place hot cooked rice in buttered 2-qt. casserole; unmold); peas and mushrooms around it

ACORN SQUASH, filled with peas and onions, down one side of platter; braised celery down other

MASHED TURNIPS OR SQUASH in ring (form with spoon); peas, with slivered almonds added, in center

ARTICHOKES—ITALIAN OR FRENCH

To Buy, to Prepare: See chart, p. 420.

To Cook: Stand artichokes upright (do not tip) in deep saucepan just big enough to hold them snugly. For each artichoke, add 1 tablesp. salad oil, small clove garlic, 1 thick lemon slice. Pour in 1" boiling salted water.

Boil artichokes, uncovered, 5 min.; cover, boil 30 to 35 min. for large, and 15 to 20 min. for small, or until a leaf can be easily pulled from stalk, or stem can be easily pierced with fork. (Add a little more boiling water if needed.) With 2 spoons, lift out artichokes; let drain upside down; cut off stubs of stems.

To serve: Arrange artichokes on salad plates, so waste leaves won't clutter dinner plates.

Serve with one of sauces below. If sauce is thick, serve in small lettuce cup on each salad plate; if thin, put in tiny bowl.

If serving ½ artichoke per person, place on dinner plate, with sauce poured over it.

Caper Butter, p. 527
Drawn Butter, p. 533
Easy Hollandaise, p. 531
Spur-of-the-Moment
Hollandaise, p. 530 (½ recipe)
Lemon Cocktail, p. 143
Louis, p. 530 (½ recipe)

Or, for sauce, melt ½ cup butter or margarine. Add 2 tablesp. each snipped parsley and lemon juice. Makes 4 servings.

Or, for still another sauce, sauté ¼ cup minced onion or 1 clove garlic, minced, in ½ cup butter or margarine. Makes 4 servings.

To eat: Pluck off leaves, one by one; dip base (light-colored end) of each into sauce; scrape off pulp at base with teeth; discard rest. When all outer leaves have been eaten, cut away fuzzy center, or "choke," with fork, knife; discard, exposing heart. Cut heart, or bottom, into chunks; dip into sauce; eat.

DILLED PEAS WITH ARTICHOKE HEARTS

1 15-oz. can artichoke hearts
Ground dill seeds
2 10-oz. pkg. frozen,
or 2 1-lb.-1-oz. cans, peas
½ teasp. salt
¼ cup butter or margarine, melted

Early on day or day before, if desired: Empty canned artichoke hearts, with liquid, into a small bowl; stir ½ teasp. ground dill seeds into

liquid. Refrigerate several hours or overnight, then drain.

About 15 min. before serving:

1. Cook frozen peas, or heat canned peas, as package or can label directs, adding ½ teasp. ground dill seeds.
2. When peas are done, pour their hot liquid over artichokes, let stand 1 min.
3. Now drain artichoke hearts. In heated serving dish, lightly toss them with hot peas, salt, ½ teasp. ground dill seeds, melted butter. Makes 8 to 10 servings.

ARTICHOKES ITALIAN

2 bacon slices, diced
1 medium onion, minced
1 6-oz. can tomato paste
½ cup white wine
1 teasp. dried orégano
1½ teasp. salt
¼ teasp. pepper
1 teasp. sugar (optional)
3 to 4 tablesp. hot butter or margarine
2 9-oz. pkg. frozen artichoke hearts, thawed
1 teasp. salt
Shredded Parmesan cheese

1. Preheat broiler 10 min., or as manufacturer directs. In small skillet, sauté bacon and onion till golden. Add tomato paste, wine, orégano, salt, pepper, sugar; simmer, uncovered, 10 min.
2. Meanwhile, in hot butter, in large skillet, lightly sauté artichokes; arrange in buttered 8" pie plate. Sprinkle with salt and 2 tablesp. shredded cheese; pour sauce in center; run under broiler till golden. Top with more cheese. Makes 6 servings.

JERUSALEM ARTICHOKES

To Buy, to Prepare, to Cook: See chart, p. 420.

To serve: Drain artichokes. Season with salt, pepper. Add Lemon Butter, p. 533, or butter or margarine and snipped parsley. Serve instead of potatoes.

ASPARAGUS

To Buy, to Prepare: See chart, p. 420.

To Cook: Spread stalks in 2 layers in 9" or 10" skillet. Sprinkle with 1½ teasp. salt. Pour on 1" boiling water. Boil, uncovered, 5 min.;

cover and cook 7 to 10 min. longer, or until lower parts of stalks, tested with fork, are just tender-crisp. With 2 forks or perforated pancake turner, lift out asparagus. Or drain; turn onto platter.

Or stand spears in lower part of double boiler, in boiling water to cover lower third of spears (tie into bundles with string if preferred). Invert top part of double boiler over lower, to cover loosely while cooking.

To serve: Sprinkle with salt, pepper. Melt ¼ cup butter or margarine, browning it slightly if desired. Pour over asparagus, as is or with one of following added:

Toasted, blanched almonds	Sautéed, sliced mushrooms
Crisp bacon bits	Prepared mustard or horse-radish
Bottled capers or celery seeds	Sprinkling of nutmeg
Grated cheese	Minced onion or garlic
Fresh or dried herbs	Snipped parsley, chives, or chervil
2 or 3 tablesp. lemon juice	Tarragon vinegar

Or spoon on one of these sauces:

Béarnaise, p. 529	Spur-of-the-Moment Hollandaise, p. 530
Drawn Butter, p. 533	Louis, p. 530
Chive Cheese, p. 527	Quick Mushroom, p. 528
Saucepan Cheese, p. 529	Sour Cream, p. 528
Dilly, p. 530	Thousand Island, p. 531
Easy, p. 531	Vinaigrette, p. 530
Easy Hollandaise, p. 531	

ASPARAGUS ON TOAST: Arrange hot cooked asparagus on buttered toast, toasted split buns, or Holland rusks. Pour on melted butter or margarine, a little asparagus liquid, or one of sauces, p. 530. Or place fried ham slice under asparagus. Or top asparagus with poached or creamed eggs.

MARINATED ASPARAGUS: Chill cooked asparagus. Top with French dressing and snipped parsley.

CHIVE ASPARAGUS: Slowly heat 1 3-oz. pkg. chive cream cheese while stirring until soft and creamy. Spoon over hot asparagus.

CHINESE ASPARAGUS: Wash 1½ lb. asparagus; remove, with knife, scales that hold sand and grit. Lay 1 or 2 asparagus stalks together on cutting board; with sharp knife, cut on very long, slanting diagonal to end of green length of stalk, making bias slices not more than ¼" thick and 1½" long.

Put 3 tablesp. butter or margarine and ¼ cup water in large skillet with tight cover; heat. Then add asparagus, about ½ teasp. salt, dash pepper. Cook, covered, over high heat 5 min., shaking skillet occasionally and checking once to see whether a bit more water is needed. Test asparagus with fork; if not tender-crisp, cook 1 min. more. Uncover at once; serve quickly. Makes 4 servings.

BEETS

To Buy, to Prepare, to Cook: See chart, p. 420.

To serve: Drain beets. If cooked whole, hold under running cold water; slip off skins, stems, and root end. (Leave beets whole; or slice or dice them.) Season with salt, pepper, and butter or margarine. Add a bit of lemon juice, sautéed onion, pinch of cloves or allspice, or a little commercial sour cream. Or add a little horse-radish and cream.

Or add grated orange rind, a sprinkle of snipped fresh dill or tarragon, caraway seeds, a little prepared mustard or dried thyme, or a dash of cloves or allspice.

Or mix sliced beets with one of sauces below, or serve beets whole; pass sauce in small bowl.

Avery Butter, p. 527	Easy Hollandaise, p. 531
Black Butter, p. 533	
Vinaigrette, p. 530	Sour Cream, p. 528

BUTTERY SHREDDED BEETS

6 pared medium beets	⅛ teasp. pepper
½ teasp. salt	2 tablesp. butter or
⅛ teasp. garlic salt	margarine

On medium grater, grate beets; arrange in skillet. Sprinkle with salt, garlic salt, pepper; dot with butter. Simmer, covered, 20 to 30 min., or until tender. Pass vinegar or lemon wedges at table. Makes 4 to 6 servings.

ZESTY BEETS

Into drained, heated contents of 1 8¾-oz. can whole beets, toss 1 tablesp. melted butter or margarine, 1 tablesp. horse-radish, ¼ teasp. prepared mustard, ⅛ teasp. seasoned salt. Makes 2 servings.

HARVARD BEETS

⅓ cup granulated sugar	2 tablesp. butter or margarine
½ teasp. salt	1 teasp. minced onion
1 tablesp. cornstarch	3 cups hot, diced or sliced, cooked or canned beets
½ cup vinegar	

In double boiler, blend sugar, salt, cornstarch; stir in vinegar; cook, stirring constantly, until smooth, thickened. Add butter, onion, beets; heat 20 min. Makes 5 servings.

BROCCOLI

To Buy, to Prepare, to Cook: See chart, p. 421.

To serve: With 2 forks or perforated pancake turner, lift out broccoli; drain; arrange on heated platter. Spoon on melted butter seasoned with salt, pepper, lemon juice.

Or spoon one of these sauces over upper part of hot cooked broccoli; pass rest.

Chive Cheese, p. 527	Horse-Radish I, p. 532
Egg, p. 533	Louis, p. 530
Easy Hollandaise, p. 531	Sour Cream, p. 528
Spur-of-the-Moment Hollandaise, p. 530	Thousand Island, p. 531
	Vinaigrette, p. 530

Also see Serve with a Flair, p. 392.

Or top hot cooked broccoli with grated raw carrot, poppy seeds, sautéed mushrooms, seasoned commercial sour cream, almonds, capers, Parmesan cheese, or cheese sauce.

Or sautéed minced onion or garlic, curry, tarragon, or marjoram does wonders, too.

BROCCOLI, CALIFORNIA STYLE

1½ lb. broccoli	1 or 2 dry hot peppers (optional)
¼ cup salad oil	
1 clove garlic	2 tablesp. water
⅓ cup minced onion	1 teasp. salt

Prepare broccoli. With knife, on chopping board, chop broccoli stalks and flowerets *very* coarsely.

In large skillet, heat salad oil. Add garlic, onion, peppers (long, tapering-pod cayenne peppers, found in mixed pickling spices). Simmer until onion is tender. Remove garlic and peppers; discard. Add broccoli, water, salt; cover; cook 12 to 15 min., or until just tender-crisp. Serve immediately. Makes 4 servings.

BRUSSELS SPROUTS

To Buy, to Prepare, to Cook: See chart, p. 421.

To serve: Drain sprouts. Season with salt, pepper, butter or margarine, then lemon juice, cream, Parmesan, curry, dab of prepared mustard, or tarragon vinegar.

Or sauté sliced mushrooms in butter; then add to sprouts.

Or add slivered almonds, thinly sliced onions or garlic, or seedless grapes. Or caraway seeds, nutmeg, or sage.

Or spoon one of these sauces over sprouts:

Drawn Butter, p. 533	Thousand Island, p. 531
Easy Hollandaise, p. 531	Vinaigrette, p. 530

Also see Serve with a Flair, p. 392.

BRUSSELS-SPROUT MEDLEY

Prepare 1 cup diced celery (or ½ lb. green beans, crosscut) and 1 lb. Brussels sprouts. Cook together as for Brussels Sprouts, p. 421. Drain. Season with salt, pepper, and butter or margarine. If desired, add a little cream or some grated process Cheddar cheese.

BRUSSELS SPROUTS ROYALE

2 10-oz. pkg. frozen Brussels sprouts	½ teasp. seasoned salt
1 5-oz. can water chestnuts	¼ cup snipped parsley
2 teasp. salt	¼ cup butter or margarine
1 teasp. sugar	

Halve larger sprouts. Drain chestnuts, reserving juice; dice chestnuts. Add enough water to chestnut juice to make 1 cup. Pour into saucepan; add salt, sugar, seasoned salt, and snipped parsley; bring to boil. Add Brussels sprouts; simmer, covered, 8 to 10 min., or till tender-crisp. Drain off liquid; toss in butter, chestnuts. Makes 6 servings.

CABBAGE
(green, savoy, Chinese, or red)

To Buy, to Prepare, to Cook: See chart, p. 421.

To Serve Shredded Green, Savoy, or Chinese

Cabbage: Drain cooked cabbage. Season with salt, pepper, and butter or margarine.

Or melt butter; then add to cabbage, along with one of these:

Diced crisp bacon	Prepared mustard, plus
Dried basil	a little lemon juice
Celery seeds	Minced onion
Grated cheese	Snipped parsley or
Chili sauce	chives
Hot cream	Curry powder and a
Lemon juice	little minced garlic

Or add lots of commercial sour cream, a dash of soy sauce, a little dried orégano, or a few seeds (caraway, dill, or poppy).

Also see Serve with a Flair, p. 392.

To Serve Wedges of Green or Savoy Cabbage: Drain cooked wedges. Season with salt, pepper; drizzle on melted butter or margarine.

Or spoon one of these sauces over wedges: Mustard, p. 532; Thousand Island, p. 531; Vinaigrette, p. 530.

To Serve Shredded Red Cabbage: Drain cooked red cabbage. Add salt, pepper; then drizzle on melted butter or margarine.

SKILLET CHINESE CABBAGE

7 tablesp. butter, margarine, or salad oil	6 tablesp. light cream
7 cups finely shredded Chinese cabbage (1 medium head)	½ teasp. salt Speck pepper

In skillet, melt butter. Add cabbage. Cook over medium heat, covered, 5 min. Stir in rest of ingredients. Cook, covered, 5 min., or until tender. Makes 4 servings.

SOUR-CREAM CABBAGE

3 tablesp. butter, margarine, or salad oil	⅓ cup commercial sour cream
½ clove garlic, minced	1 tablesp. lemon juice
8 cups finely shredded cabbage, firmly packed	1 tablesp. sugar 1 tablesp. salt ½ teasp. celery seeds
¼ cup boiling water	1 egg, beaten

In hot butter in large skillet, sauté garlic over low heat 5 min. Add cabbage, water. Simmer, covered, 8 to 15 min., or until tender. Add rest of ingredients combined; toss. Makes 4 or 5 servings.

♣ FOR 2: Use 1 egg; halve rest of ingredients.

QUICK-COOKED CABBAGE

Prepare 5 cups finely shredded cabbage. In 10" skillet, heat 2 tablesp. bacon fat; add shredded cabbage, ¾ to 1 teasp. salt, dash pepper. Toss several times — until cabbage is coated with bacon fat. Cook, covered, about 3 min. Makes 4 servings.

DUTCH HOT SLAW

6 cups shredded cabbage	½ teasp. salt
1 tablesp. butter or margarine	1½ tablesp. sugar ½ teasp. dry mustard
2 eggs	⅛ teasp. paprika ¼ cup water
¼ cup vinegar	¼ cup light cream

Cook cabbage as on p. 421. Drain; keep hot. Meanwhile, melt butter in double boiler; add eggs beaten with vinegar, salt, sugar, mustard, paprika, water. Cook, stirring, until thickened. Remove from heat. Add cream; beat smooth. Pour over cabbage. Makes 4 or 5 servings.

RED CABBAGE WITH APPLES

1 2½-lb. head red cabbage, shredded	¼ cup vinegar 1½ teasp. flour
¾ cup boiling water	¼ cup brown sugar, packed
3 large cooking apples, sliced, pared, cored	2 teasp. salt Speck pepper
3 tablesp. melted butter or margarine	

Put shredded cabbage in kettle. Add boiling water; cook, covered, 10 min. Add apples; cook 10 min., or until tender. Add rest of ingredients combined; heat. Makes 6 servings.

♣ FOR 2: Use 1-lb. head cabbage, 3 small apples; halve rest of ingredients.

PANNED CURRIED CABBAGE

2 tablesp. butter, margarine, or salad oil	1 teasp. curry powder
1 small clove garlic, minced	6 cups finely shredded cabbage 1 teasp. salt

In butter, in large skillet, sauté garlic 2 min. Stir in curry, cabbage, salt. Cook, covered, stirring occasionally, until tender — about 10 min. Makes 4 to 5 servings.

To Vary: Add 1 cup canned tomatoes just before cabbage is done. Season to taste.

CABBAGE SCRAMBLE

1 tablesp. butter or margarine	1 medium onion, thinly sliced
3 cups shredded green or Chinese cabbage	½ green pepper, cut into strips
1 cup thinly sliced celery	2 cups diced tomatoes
	1 teasp. salt
	⅛ teasp. pepper

In large skillet, heat butter. Add rest of ingredients. Cook, covered, 5 to 8 min., or until tender, stirring twice. Makes 4 servings.

CARROTS

To Buy, to Prepare, to Cook: See chart, p. 422. For savory touch, along with each 1 lb. carrots, cook 1 cup thinly sliced onions, ½ cup snipped scallions, or 1 cup diced celery.
To serve: Drain carrots. Season with salt or seasoned salt, pepper, butter or margarine, snipped parsley, or minced green pepper.

Or add ¼ teasp. dried tarragon, savory, or marjoram to each 1 lb. carrots.

Or, for fun, sprinkle on some chili powder, curry, poppy seeds, a little ginger, dried thyme, or nutmeg, or a good bit of grated cheese. Snipped mint, chervil, dill, or chives go beautifully in it, too.

Or add a little sweet or sour cream, some crisp bacon, a soupçon of white wine or cognac, or a good dash of dried orégano.

Or add 2 or 3 small sprigs, or a pinch, of rosemary. Or some whole-kernel corn.

Or mash or whip carrots with electric mixer; then season, adding pinch of nutmeg.

Also see Serve with a Flair, p. 392.

BUFFET CHEESE-SCALLOPED CARROTS

12 sliced, pared medium carrots	2 cups milk
¼ cup butter or margarine	⅛ teasp. pepper
1 small onion, minced	¼ teasp. celery salt
¼ cup flour	½ lb. packaged process sharp Cheddar-cheese slices
1 teasp. salt	3 cups buttered fresh bread crumbs
¼ teasp. dry mustard	

Start heating oven to 350°F. Cook carrots as on p. 422. Drain. Meanwhile, in butter in saucepan, gently cook onion 2 to 3 min. Stir in flour, salt, mustard, then milk; cook, stirring, until smooth. Add pepper, celery salt.

In 2-qt. casserole, arrange layer of carrots, then layer of cheese. Repeat until both are used, ending with carrots. Pour on sauce; top with crumbs. Bake, uncovered, 25 min., or till golden. Makes 8 servings.
To Do Ahead: Make early in day; refrigerate.
To serve: Bake, uncovered, at 350°F. 35 to 45 min., or until hot.

CARROTS VICHY

¼ cup butter or margarine	5 cups diagonally sliced carrots, ¼" thick
¾ cup boiling water	1 tablesp. lemon juice
2 teasp. salt	½ teasp. monosodium glutamate
¼ teasp. nutmeg	
⅛ teasp. pepper	¼ cup snipped parsley
1 tablesp. sugar	

Add butter to boiling water in saucepan. Add salt, nutmeg, pepper, sugar, and carrots. Simmer, covered, 8 to 10 min., or till tender-crisp. Stir in lemon juice, monosodium glutamate, and parsley. Makes 6 servings.

CAULIFLOWER

To Buy, to Prepare, to Cook: See chart, p. 423.
To serve: Drain cauliflower; season with salt, pepper, and butter or margarine.

Or add slivered dill pickles, chili powder, prepared mustard, sour cream plus chili sauce, or soy sauce.

Or cheese goes with it; so do slivered almonds, curry, mace, poppy seeds, ginger, or fresh or dried rosemary, basil, savory, dill, or tarragon.

Or pour one of these sauces over cauliflower in serving dish.

Saucepan Cheese, p. 529	Hollandaise, p. 530
Tomato Cheese, p. 530	Quick Mushroom, p. 528
Easy Hollandaise, p. 531	Thousand Island, p. 531
Spur-of-the-Moment	Vinaigrette, p. 530

Also see Serve with a Flair, p. 392.

CAULIFLOWER SUPREME

2 pkg. frozen cauli-flower	2 tablesp. flour
2 tablesp. butter or margarine	1 teasp. salt
	⅛ teasp. pepper
½ lb. mushrooms, thickly sliced	1 teasp. bottled thick meat sauce
	1 cup light cream

Cook cauliflower as label directs, until just tender-crisp. Meanwhile, in hot butter, in skillet, sauté mushrooms 10 min. Sprinkle with flour; add salt, pepper, meat sauce, cream. Cook, stirring occasionally, until smooth and thickened. When cauliflower is done, drain well. Serve topped with mushroom sauce. Makes 4 or 5 servings.

CHINESE CAULIFLOWER

Wash and remove lower stalks from small or medium *firm, crisp* head of cauliflower. With coarse shredder, shred entire head; or, with sharp knife, slice each floweret thinly. Place in skillet; sprinkle lightly with salt; add ⅓ cup hot water. Cook, covered, 5 to 7 min., or until slightly crisp; do not drain. Add 2 tablesp. each butter or margarine and heavy cream; heat, tossing with fork, 1 to 2 min. Serve at once, sprinkled with paprika or snipped chives or parsley. Makes 3 or 4 servings.

P.S. Some diced tomato, sautéed tender in a little butter, may be folded in.

CAULIFLOWER WITH GREEN GRAPES

1 large head cauli-flower	1 cup seeded green grapes
1½ cups boiling water	½ cup canned sliv-ered toasted almonds
1 tablesp. salt	
2 tablesp. butter or margarine	

Break off each floweret in cauliflower, then slice lengthwise, into slices ¼″ thick. In boiling water, with salt, in skillet, simmer cauliflower, covered, 5 min., or till tender. Fold in butter, grapes, and almonds. Makes 6 servings.

CELERIAC
(knob celery)

To Buy, to Prepare, to Cook: See chart, p. 423.

To serve: Season with salt, pepper, and butter or margarine.

Or reheat in thin cream.

Or mash, season, and add enough hot milk to beat until fluffy.

Or serve as salad: Pour a little French dressing over hot cooked celeriac at once so it won't discolor; refrigerate. Serve on salad greens.

CELERY

To Buy, to Prepare: See chart, p. 423. Use hearts and center stalks as relish or in salads. Use fresh leaves in soups, stews, salads, stuffings, sauces, etc.

To Cook: Cook outer stalks, slivered or diced, as on p. 423. Or use in soups.

To serve: Drain cooked celery. Season with salt, pepper, butter or margarine, and snipped parsley or paprika.

Or reheat in light cream.

Also see Serve with a Flair, p. 392.

BRAISED CELERY AND TOMATOES

2 tablesp. butter or margarine	⅛ teasp. pepper
	¼ teasp. onion salt
2 cups cleaned celery, cut into 1″ pieces	2 cups quartered, peeled tomatoes
¾ teasp. salt	

In saucepan or small skillet with tight cover, melt butter. Add celery, salt, pepper, onion salt. Simmer, covered, 10 min., or till tender-crisp. Add tomatoes; cook, covered, 5 min., or till celery is tender, tomatoes are hot. Makes 4 servings.

CORN

To Buy, to Prepare on Cob: See chart, p. 423.

To Cook: Cook at one time only enough ears of corn to serve everyone once. Drop into plenty of boiling salted water (1 teasp. salt per 1 qt. water). Boil, covered, until milk in corn is just set — about 5 to 6 min.

If boiling a few ears of corn, as for 2 servings, you may use a large covered skillet.

To serve on cob: With fork or tongs, remove corn from water to heated platter; cover with napkin (now start to cook second servings).

Serve at once, with butter or margarine; or with butter in which cut clove of garlic, snipped chives, or celery seeds have stood.

Or try chili, curry, garlic salt, seasoned salt, seasoned pepper, snipped chives, or peanut butter on it.

To serve "off the cob": With sharp knife, slice kernels from hot, boiled corn, being careful not to cut too close to cob.

Cut corn takes kindly to a bit of minced onion or green pepper or to slivers of toasted almonds or of tomato. Or try crisp-bacon bits, chopped or sliced stuffed olives, or light cream.

CORN FRITTERS, NORTHERN STYLE

3 egg yolks	¼ cup sifted all-
1⅔ cups cooked or	purpose flour
canned whole-kernel	3 egg whites, stiffly
corn	beaten
½ teasp. salt	6 tablesp. fat or salad
⅛ teasp. pepper	oil

Beat egg yolks until light; mix in corn, salt, pepper, flour. Fold in egg whites. Drop by tablespoonfuls into hot fat in skillet. Cook on both sides until brown and done.

Serve as vegetable, with chicken, meat, or fish. Or serve as main dish, with butter and syrup or crisp bacon. Makes 6 servings.

♣ FOR 2: Use 1 egg; halve rest of ingredients.
HICKORY CORN FRITTERS: Add 1 cup grated franks (about 3) with corn. Substitute seasoned salt for salt.

CORN FRITTERS, SOUTHERN STYLE

1 cup sifted all-	¼ cup milk
purpose flour	2 teasp. salad oil
1 teasp. double-acting	2½ cups cooked or
baking powder	canned whole-kernel
1 teasp. salt	corn
2 eggs	

Sift flour with baking powder, salt. Beat eggs; add milk, 2 teasp. salad oil. Stir in flour, then corn. Drop by tablespoonfuls into fat heated to 365°F. on deep-fat-frying thermometer as in Shallow-Frying, p. 7. Fry 3 to 5 min., turning once. Makes 5 to 6 servings.

SUCCOTASH

1½ cups hot cooked	beans, green limas,
or canned whole-	or shell beans
kernel corn	½ cup light cream
2 tablesp. butter or	Salt
margarine	Pepper or seasoned
1½ cups hot cooked	pepper
or canned green	

Combine all ingredients, adding salt and pepper to taste. Heat. Makes 6 servings.

CUSTARD CORN PUDDING

2 cups chopped,	1½ tablesp. melted
cooked or canned,	butter or margar-
whole-kernel corn	ine
2 eggs, slightly beaten	2 cups scalded milk
1 teasp. sugar	1¾ teasp. salt
	¼ teasp. pepper

Start heating oven to 325°F. Combine all ingredients; pour into greased 1½-qt. casserole. Set in pan of warm water. Bake, uncovered, 1 hr. 15 min. Makes 6 servings.

To Vary: Before baking pudding mixture, add ½ cup minced cooked ham or grated cheese, or 2 tablesp. minced onion.

♣ FOR 2: Halve ingredients; use 3 individual casseroles.

SOUTHERN CORN PUDDING

8 to 12 ears corn	1¼ cups light cream
1½ teasp. salt	

Start heating oven to 350°F. Husk corn. With sharp knife, split corn kernels, cutting lengthwise of ears. Then, with back of knife, scrape out kernels until you have 2 cups corn pulp. Combine with salt (or seasoned salt), cream; pour into greased 1½-qt. casserole. Bake, uncovered, 1 hr.

Serve hot, with butter. Makes 4 servings.

♣ FOR 2: Halve ingredients; use 1-qt. casserole. Bake at 350°F. 40 min.

CUCUMBERS

To Buy, to Prepare, to Cook: See chart, p. 423.

To serve: Drain cucumbers. Season with salt, pepper, and butter or margarine.

Or reheat in Vegetable Sauce, p. 533.

DRIED BEANS

To use dried beans, peas, and lentils in main dishes, see Dried Beans in Index.

NOTE: If beans are quick-cooking, follow label directions.

KIDNEY-BEAN SOPHISTICATE

2 tablesp. butter or margarine	¼ teasp. dried rosemary
½ cup minced onions	1 teasp. salt
1 1-lb.-4-oz. can kidney beans	¼ cup red wine

In butter, in skillet, sauté onions until tender. Add undrained beans, rosemary, salt, wine; simmer, uncovered, stirring occasionally, until enough liquid has evaporated to make mixture of desired consistency. Makes 4 servings.

OLD-FASHIONED BOSTON BAKED BEANS

1 lb. pea or navy beans	¼ cup molasses
Water	2 tablesp. sweet pickle juice; or
2 teasp. dry mustard	2 tablesp. vinegar, with speck ground cinnamon and cloves
Pepper	
1 tablesp. salt	
3 medium onions, quartered	¼-lb. piece salt pork
¼ cup brown sugar	

Pick over beans; wash. Cover with 3 cups water; soak 8 hr. or overnight; then add 2 cups water, mustard, ¼ teasp. pepper, and next 5 ingredients. Boil, covered, about 1 hr., or until skins of beans begin to wrinkle.

Start heating oven to 250°F. Cut salt pork at ½" intervals almost all the way through; place in 2-qt. bean pot; cover with hot beans and their liquid. Generously sprinkle with pepper. Bake 6 to 8 hr., covered, or until tender. When beans are two thirds baked, add about ¾ cup water, or enough to just cover. Uncover last ½ hr. Makes 4 to 6 servings.

Serve instead of potatoes, or with baked ham, franks, crisp bacon, etc. Or serve as breakfast, luncheon, or supper main dish, with brown bread, corn bread, etc.

As accompaniment, serve pickle relish, catchup, chili sauce, or mustard pickle, etc.

P.S. And if you are not already serving them, do try the canned beans and franks in tomato sauce, beans and ground beef in barbecue sauce, and barbecued beans, as well as that favorite — pork and beans with tomato sauce.

SAVORY LIMA-BEAN POT

4 cups large California dry limas, rinsed	½ cup catchup
4 teasp. salt	½ cup molasses
5 tablesp. butter or margarine	2 tablesp. vinegar
2 medium onions, sliced	½ teasp. Tabasco
1 green pepper, diced	2 teasp. dry mustard
	1 to 3 cups diced cooked ham

Place rinsed limas and salt in 2 qt. boiling water; simmer, covered, 2 hr., or until tender (add more boiling water if needed). Start heating oven to 325°F. In 2 tablesp. butter, sauté onions and green pepper until tender. Mix catchup with molasses, vinegar, Tabasco, mustard. When limas are tender, drain, reserving 1 cup liquid. Add this reserved liquid to catchup mixture.

In 3-qt. casserole or large bean pot, arrange, in layers, limas, onion-and-pepper mixture, ham; pour on catchup mixture. Dot with 3 tablesp. butter. Bake, uncovered, 1½ hr. Wonderful for a buffet. Makes 10 to 12 servings.

BOSTON STYLE: Substitute 4 cups dried pea beans, soaked overnight, for dry limas; simmer only 1 hr. Use 2¾ cups liquid drained from cooked beans instead of 1 cup. (When arranging layers, place beans on top.) Bake 2½ hr., or until beans are tender.

BAKED-BEAN CASSEROLE

2 tablesp. fat or salad oil	1 tablesp. prepared mustard
1 cup sliced onions	2 peeled tomatoes, sliced
2 1-lb. cans Boston-style baked beans	1 teasp. salt
1 2¼-oz. can deviled ham	2 teasp. brown sugar

Start heating oven to 400°F. In hot fat, in skillet, sauté onions until tender. Combine beans, ham, mustard; arrange half in 2-qt. casserole. Place half of onions and tomatoes over beans; sprinkle with half of salt and sugar. Repeat layers. Bake, covered, 30 min.; uncover; bake 5 min. Makes 4 servings.

EGGPLANT

To Buy, to Prepare: See chart, p. 424.

SAUTEED EGGPLANT

Pare large eggplant; cut into ¼″ crosswise slices. Sprinkle with salt, pepper, and a little flour. Or dip into beaten egg, then into cracker crumbs. In hot bacon fat or salad oil, in skillet, sauté eggplant till golden-brown on both sides — about 6 to 8 min.

Serve alone or with hot canned stewed tomatoes. Makes 6 servings.

EGGPLANT PARMESAN

1 large eggplant	½ cup grated Parmesan cheese
3 eggs, beaten	
1 cup packaged dried bread crumbs	2 teasp. dried orégano
	½ lb. Mozzarella cheese, sliced
¾ cup olive or salad oil	3 8-oz. cans tomato sauce

Start heating oven to 350°F. Pare eggplant if desired; cut into ¼″-thick slices. Dip each slice first into eggs, then into crumbs. Sauté in hot olive oil until golden-brown on both sides. Place layer of eggplant in 2-qt. casserole; sprinkle with some of Parmesan, orégano, and Mozzarella; then cover well with some of tomato sauce. Repeat until all eggplant is used, topping last layer of sauce with several slices of Mozzarella. Bake, uncovered, ½ hr., or until sauce is bubbly and cheese is melted. Makes 4 to 6 servings.

RATATOUILLE

3 tablesp. olive oil	1 unpared small eggplant, diced
2 medium onions, sliced	2 small zucchini, in ½″ slices
1 clove garlic, minced	1 bay leaf
2 peeled tomatoes, diced	3 bacon slices
1 seeded large green pepper, cut into ½″ strips	2 teasp. salt
	⅛ teasp. pepper

In hot oil, in Dutch oven, sauté onions with garlic until tender. Add tomatoes, green pepper, eggplant, zucchini, and bay leaf; sauté, over medium heat, stirring occasionally, 15 min.

Meanwhile fry bacon crisp. Crumble bacon; add to vegetables with salt and pepper. Cover; simmer 15 min.; uncover; simmer 10 min. Remove bay leaf. *Serve at once.* Makes 6 servings.

ENDIVE

To Buy, to Prepare: See chart, p. 424.

To Cook: There are three methods of cooking endive — boiling, stewing, and braising. Lemon may be added as a bleach.

To serve: Use as a vegetable, as an entrée, even in soup. Most popular uses are raw in salads or as a cocktail appetizer, and in sandwiches in place of lettuce.

ENDIVE AU FOUR

18 Belgian or French endives	¾ lb. natural Swiss cheese, coarsely grated
Salt	
¼ cup butter or margarine, cut in small pieces	Pepper
	½ cup light cream

Several hr. ahead: Wash endives. With tip of knife, remove small core from root end of each. Place endives in saucepan; add boiling water to cover and 1 teasp. salt. Cover, simmer 20 min. Drain well; refrigerate.

About 40 min. before serving: Start heating oven to 350°F. In greased 12″ x 8″ x 2″ baking dish, arrange half of endives. Top with half of butter and cheese. Sprinkle lightly with salt and pepper. Repeat a second layering. Pour cream over all. Bake 20 min., or until cheese is melted. Then turn temperature control of oven up to Broil; place endives under broiler for about 3 min., or until cheese is bubbling.

Nice with veal, chicken, or turkey, as a de luxe company vegetable. Makes 6 servings.

GREEN, WAX, OR SNAP BEANS

To Buy, to Prepare, to Cook: See chart, p. 424.

To serve: Drain beans, reserving liquid. Boil liquid down to a few tablespoonfuls; add to beans, with salt, pepper, butter or margarine.

Or add crisp bacon bits, lots of commercial sour cream, diced canned water chestnuts, sautéed scallions or mushrooms, snipped mint, caraway seeds, or slivered nuts.

Or add a pinch of herbs: orégano, rosemary, savory, or dill. Or try nutmeg, curry, French dressing, chili sauce, prepared mustard, or grated cheese; or canned tomato sauce or cream-of-mushroom soup.

Or spoon on, or toss drained beans with, one of these sauces:

Tomato-Cheese, p. 530	Thousand Island,
Quick Mushroom,	p. 531
p. 528	Vinaigrette, p. 530
Mustard, p. 532	

Also see Serve with a Flair, p. 392.

GREEN BEANS LYONNAISE

1¼ lb. green beans	1 teasp. tarragon vine-
4 bacon slices, diced	gar
¼ cup minced onion	Speck pepper
½ teasp. salt	

Prepare beans, French cut, then cook as on p. 424. Meanwhile, fry bacon crisp in skillet. Remove bacon bits; reserve. To bacon fat, add onion; sauté until tender. Add salt, vinegar, pepper, bacon bits; pour over drained beans. Toss with fork. Makes 4 servings.

BEANS TRES BIEN

2 9-oz. pkg. frozen French-style green beans	mushroom soup, undiluted
1 10½-oz. can con-densed cream-of-	1 3½-oz. can French-fried onions

Start heating oven to 400°F. Cook green beans 1 min. less than label directs. Then drain from them all but ½ cup liquid; turn beans into 1½-qt. casserole. Stir in soup and onions. Bake about 10 min., or until bubbly. Makes 4 servings.

GREEN BEANS DE LUXE

1 lb. green beans	chopped or sliced
2 tablesp. bacon fat, butter, or margarine	mushrooms* ½ teasp. salt
1 small onion, coarsely chopped	Pepper to taste ¼ cup light cream or
1 3- or 4-oz. can	undiluted evapo-rated milk

Prepare, then crosscut beans into 1″ lengths as on p. 424. Heat bacon fat in skillet. Add beans,

onion, mushrooms with their liquid, salt, pepper. Turn heat very low; cook, covered, 20 to 25 min. (If liquid cooks away so you can hear beans sizzle, add 1 or 2 tablesp. water.) When beans are barely tender, add cream; heat. Makes 4 servings.

If desired, substitute ¼ lb. sliced fresh mushrooms and ¼ cup water.

GREEN BEANS WITH HERB SAUCE

1 lb. green beans	¼ cup snipped pars-
¼ cup butter or mar-garine	ley ¼ teasp. dried rose-
¾ cup minced onions	mary
1 clove garlic, minced	¼ teasp. dried basil
¼ cup minced celery	¾ teasp. salt

Prepare beans, crosscut, then cook as on p. 424. Meanwhile, melt butter in saucepan. Add onions, garlic, celery; sauté 5 min. Add parsley, rosemary, basil, salt. Simmer, covered, 10 min. Toss well with drained beans. Makes 4 servings.

SWEET-SOUR GREEN BEANS

1 lb. green beans	3 tablesp. vinegar
2 tablesp. bacon fat	1 tablesp. soy sauce
1 cup boiling water	¼ cup cold water
½ teasp. salt	¼ cup sweet pickle
1 teasp. cornstarch	relish
3 tablesp. sugar	

Prepare, then crosscut beans into 1″ lengths as on p. 424. Place beans in large skillet or saucepan with tight cover; add bacon fat, boiling water, salt. Heat quickly, covered, until beans steam; then turn down heat and cook 15 to 20 min., or till tender-crisp. Do not drain. Mix cornstarch with sugar, vinegar, soy sauce, water, pickle relish; pour over beans; cook, stirring, until slightly thickened and clear. Makes 4 servings.

GREEN LIMAS

To Buy, to Prepare, to Cook: See chart, p. 425.

To serve: Drain limas. Season to taste with salt (try monosodium glutamate, too, or celery, garlic, onion, or seasoned salt), pepper, and butter or margarine.

Or sauté sliced mushrooms or minced onion in butter until tender; then add to limas.

Or add celery seeds, chili sauce, curry, dried basil or savory, or grated cheese.

Or add sautéed scallions or green pepper, some slivered fresh tomato, a little prepared mustard, or a few cocktail onions.

Or toss limas with one of these sauces:

Saucepan Cheese, p. 529
Tomato-Cheese, p. 530
Curry, p. 527

Quick Mushroom, p. 528
Italian Tomato, p. 528

Also see Serve with a Flair, p. 392.

GREEN LIMAS AND SCALLIONS

2 lb. green limas (about 2 cups, shelled)
2 tablesp. butter or margarine

6 snipped scallions
1 tablesp. flour
¼ teasp. paprika
½ teasp. salt
Speck pepper

Prepare, then cook, limas as on p. 425. Drain, reserving ½ cup liquid. In butter, in saucepan, simmer scallions 2 min. Stir in flour, then lima liquid; cook, stirring, until thickened. Add limas, paprika, salt, pepper; heat. Makes 4 to 6 servings.

LIMAS AND WATER CHESTNUTS

1 10-oz. pkg. frozen baby limas
½ cup sliced canned water chestnuts

¼ cup Italian dressing
1 teasp. dill seeds

Cook limas as label directs. Drain; combine with water chestnuts, dressing, and dill seeds; toss well. Refrigerate. Makes 4 or 5 servings.

JOHN J. LIMAS

1 10-oz. pkg. frozen Fordhook limas, cooked
½ cup crumbled Roquefort or Danish blue cheese

¼ cup undiluted canned condensed consommé
2 tablesp. fresh bread crumbs
Snipped parsley

Start heating oven to 350°F. In greased 1-qt. casserole, arrange beans and cheese in layers, ending with limas. Pour on consommé; top with bread crumbs. Bake 20 min.; sprinkle with parsley. Makes 2 man-size servings.

GREEN LIMAS A LA CREME

2 lb. green limas (about 2 cups, shelled)
½ teasp. minced onion
¼ cup grated process Cheddar cheese

1 tablesp. butter or margarine
¼ cup light cream
¼ cup milk
Salt
Pepper

Prepare, then cook, limas as on p. 425. Drain. Add onion, cheese, butter, cream, milk. With fork, toss lightly over low heat until cheese is melted. Season to taste. Makes 4 servings.

GREEN PEPPERS

To Buy, to Prepare: See chart, p. 425.

STUFFED-PEPPER TWINS

4 large green peppers, halved lengthwise
1½ cups cooked rice
¼ cup undiluted evaporated milk
¼ lb. sharp Cheddar cheese, grated (1 cup)
½ teasp. monosodium glutamate
Salt and pepper
2 medium tomatoes, peeled

4 teasp. butter or margarine
2 eggs
¼ cup light cream or milk
2 tablesp. melted butter or margarine
1½ cups cooked or canned corn (cream style or whole kernel)
1 cup coarsely crumbled crackers

Start heating oven to 375°F. Boil green peppers in boiling salted water 5 min.; drain.

For rice stuffing, mix rice, evaporated milk, cheese, monosodium glutamate, salt and pepper to taste. Cut tomatoes into thick slices; sprinkle with more salt and pepper; stand slice at one end, or at each end, of 4 pepper halves; then fill halves with rice stuffing; top each with 1 teasp. butter.

For corn stuffing, beat eggs with fork. Add light cream, melted butter, corn, crackers, ½ teasp. salt, speck pepper. Heap in remaining 4 pepper halves.

Arrange all stuffed-pepper halves in greased shallow baking dish. Bake, uncovered, about 30 min., or until corn stuffing is firm when tested with tip of knife. Add dash of paprika to corn stuffing. Serve 1 pepper half of each kind on each plate. Makes 4 servings.

ITALIAN-STYLE GREEN PEPPERS

4 large green peppers	2 cloves garlic, minced
3 tablesp. olive or salad oil	2 cups canned tomatoes
¼ cup boiling water	
1 teasp. salt	2 teasp. sugar
1 tablesp. olive or salad oil	1 teasp. salt
	⅛ teasp. pepper
1 medium onion, sliced	½ teasp. dried basil

Cut green peppers into 1½″ strips; then halve each strip crosswise. Heat 3 tablesp. olive oil in large skillet; add peppers; sauté 10 min., or until slightly browned. Add boiling water, 1 teasp. salt; simmer, covered, 20 min., or until tender.

Meanwhile, in 1 tablesp. olive oil in saucepan, sauté onion and garlic until golden. Add tomatoes, then sugar, salt, pepper, basil. Simmer, uncovered, 30 min., or until thickened. Put drained peppers in serving dish; pour on sauce. Makes 4 servings.

CREAMED GREEN PEPPERS

6 medium green peppers	2 tablesp. flour
	2 cups milk
2 tablesp. butter or margarine	1 teasp. salt
	¼ teasp. pepper

1. Lay green peppers directly on range burners over medium heat, and turn often until entire surface is charred.
2. Then, under running water, cut them open, remove seeds, and, with sharp knife, scrape off all charred skin.
3. Cut flesh into slivers with scissors, then combine with butter in saucepan. When butter is melted, add flour; stir smooth. Stir in milk, salt, pepper. Simmer, stirring often, until thickened and peppers are tender — about 15 min. Thin with milk, if necessary. Makes 5 or 6 servings.

GREENS

Beet tops	Mustard greens
Collards	Spinach
Dandelion greens	Swiss chard (young)
Kale	Turnip greens, etc.

To Buy, to Prepare, to Cook: See chart, pp. 425–426.

To serve: Drain cooked greens well several times. If desired, slash through them with scissors or 2 knives. Add salt, pepper, and butter or margarine. If desired, sauté a little minced onion in butter or margarine before adding to greens.

Or, after seasoning, toss one of following with, or sprinkle over, greens: crumbled crisp bacon, chopped cooked beets, chili sauce, chopped hard-cooked egg, French dressing, horse-radish, lemon juice, nutmeg, fresh or dried rosemary, flavored vinegar.

Or spark the greens with slivered almonds, poppy or sesame seeds, wine, cayenne, or a shake of Tabasco.

PANNED SPINACH

2 lb. spinach	1 teasp. salt
1 tablesp. bacon fat, butter, or margarine	⅛ teasp. pepper
	½ cup milk
1 clove garlic, minced	1 teasp. lemon juice
	1 tablesp. flour

Prepare spinach as on p. 430. Meanwhile, heat bacon fat in kettle. Add garlic; sauté till tender. Add spinach, salt, pepper. Cook, covered, over medium heat, stirring occasionally, until tender — about 5 min. Slowly add milk and lemon juice to flour, stirring till smooth; pour over spinach. Cook, tossing with fork, until sauce is smooth and thickened. Makes 4 servings.

VINAIGRETTE SPINACH

2½ lb. spinach	2 tablesp. lemon juice or vinegar
6 tablesp. butter or margarine	¾ teasp. salt
1 teasp. minced onion	⅛ teasp. pepper
½ teasp. prepared mustard	2 hard-cooked eggs, chopped

Prepare and cook spinach as on p. 430. Drain well; chop. In 1 tablesp. butter, sauté onion till tender. Add rest of ingredients except spinach; heat. Pour over spinach; toss. Makes 4 servings.

MATURED SWISS CHARD

To Buy: Matured Swiss chard usually comes tied in bunches and has large, ribbed leaves and broad, cream-colored stalks.

To Cook Stalks: Cut stalks from 2 lb. large Swiss-chard leaves; wash both well. Cut stalks into 2″ pieces; cook in 1″ boiling water with 1 teasp. salt, covered, 15 min., or until tender. Drain; add 2 tablesp. butter or margarine, speck pepper, and salt if necessary. Or make Old-Fashioned Creamed Vegetables, p. 393.

To Cook Leaves: While stalks cook, cook washed leaves in ½″ boiling water with ¾ teasp. salt, covered, 10 min., or until tender. Drain; add 2 tablesp. butter or margarine, speck pepper, and salt if necessary.

To serve: Place cooked leaves in center of serving dish, with stalks around them. Or toss together. Pass lemon wedges. Makes 4 servings.

CHEESY SWISS CHARD

2 lb. matured Swiss chard	2 tablesp. flour
	½ cup milk
2 teasp. salt	¼ lb. diced process
2 tablesp. butter or margarine	Cheddar cheese

Start heating oven to 325°F. Cut stalks from washed chard into 1″ pieces; cook in ½″ boiling water with salt, covered, 5 min. Then add torn leaves; cover; cook 5 min. Drain well, using saucer to press out liquid.

Meanwhile, melt butter in saucepan; stir in flour, then milk; cook, stirring, over medium heat until thickened. Add cheese; toss with chard. Turn into 1½-qt. casserole. Bake, uncovered, 45 min. Makes 4 servings.

♣ FOR 2: Halve ingredients; use 2-cup casserole.

KOHLRABI

To Buy, to Prepare, to Cook: See chart, p. 426.

To serve: Drain kohlrabi. Season with salt, pepper, butter or margarine, few drops lemon juice or little snipped parsley or chives. Also see Serve with a Flair, p. 392.

MUSHROOMS

To Buy, to Prepare: See chart, p. 426.

Remember, too, the wonderful canned mushrooms; they come broiled — whole, sliced, or chopped — or plain — as slices, buttons, or stems and pieces.

To serve: Fresh or canned mushrooms are even more marvelous with minced onion, lemon juice, or a bit of sherry in the butter. And they combine beautifully with almost any other vegetables.

BROILED MUSHROOMS

Allow 3 or 4 fresh mushrooms per person. Wash mushrooms well; remove stems and reserve for Cream-of-Mushroom Soup, p. 164. In shallow baking pan, place mushroom caps, with rounded sides down; in each upturned cavity, place ½ teasp. butter or margarine. Sprinkle lightly with salt, pepper, dash of nutmeg, a little lemon juice; brush with melted butter. Broil 5 to 8 min. Also see Mixed Grill, p. 180.

Serve with steaks, chicken, etc., or on vegetable plate. Or serve on toast with bacon.

CREAMED MUSHROOMS

1 lb. mushrooms	1 teasp. salt
2 tablesp. butter or margarine	⅛ teasp. pepper
	1 teasp. lemon juice
2 tablesp. minced onion	¾ teasp. celery salt
	1½ cups milk
2 tablesp. flour	3 tablesp. sherry

Slice or halve washed mushrooms (caps and stems) lengthwise. In butter, in large skillet, over low heat, sauté onion until tender; add mushrooms. Sauté over medium heat, covered, stirring occasionally, 8 to 10 min. Stir in flour, salt, pepper, lemon juice, celery salt, then milk. Cook over low heat, stirring, until thickened. Add sherry.

Serve as is or on toast. Or serve as main dish, on toast, topped with Baked Tomatoes, p. 417, or with bacon. Makes 4 servings.

SAUTEED MUSHROOMS

1 lb. mushrooms	1 teasp. lemon juice
¼ cup butter or margarine	½ teasp. salt or seasoned salt
2 tablesp. minced onion	⅛ teasp. pepper

Cut washed whole mushrooms into thick slices. Meanwhile, in butter, in large skillet over low heat, sauté onion until tender. Add mushrooms.

Sauté over medium heat, covered, stirring occasionally, 10 min. Turn off heat; let stand, covered, 4 to 5 min., to absorb juice in pan. Sprinkle with lemon juice, salt, pepper; toss. Serve as is, or on toast, with steaks, chops, chicken, vegetable dinner, etc. Makes 4 servings.

P.S. If you prefer to leave mushrooms whole, sauté as above 12 min.

MUSHROOMS IN CREAM: Omit lemon juice. Stir in 2 tablesp. sherry, then 1/3 cup light cream.

STUFFED MUSHROOMS

1 lb. medium mushrooms	1 teasp. Worcestershire
Butter or margarine	1/2 teasp. salt
1/4 cup finely minced onion	Speck pepper
1/4 cup finely minced celery	Monosodium glutamate

Wash mushrooms; drain. Remove stems; chop fine. In large skillet, heat 1/4 cup butter; add onion, celery, mushroom stems. Simmer until celery is tender. Stir in Worcestershire, salt, pepper, a little monosodium glutamate. Brush mushroom caps with melted butter; then fill with onion mixture. Arrange caps, with stuffed sides up, in same skillet. Simmer 5 min., or until lightly browned (cover first 2 or 3 min.). Serve with steak, chops, chicken, etc. Makes 4 servings.

POLISH MUSHROOMS WITH SOUR CREAM
(Grzyby w Smietanie)

6 tablesp. butter or margarine	1 1/2 cups commercial sour cream
1 large onion, chopped	1 1/4 lb. mushrooms, sliced
2 tablesp. flour	3/4 teasp. salt
2 tablesp. milk	1/4 teasp. pepper
	1/4 teasp. paprika

In melted butter, in large skillet, sauté onion till golden. Sprinkle with flour; add milk and 3/4 cup sour cream; while stirring, bring just to a simmer. Then add sliced mushrooms, salt, pepper, and paprika. Simmer, covered, 5 min., stirring occasionally. Stir in remaining sour cream; heat thoroughly, while stirring constantly. Serve at once. Makes 6 servings.

OKRA

To Buy, to Prepare, to Cook: See chart, p. 427.
To serve: Drain cooked okra. Add salt, pepper, and butter or margarine. Also add a little lemon juice, herb vinegar, French dressing, chili sauce, or commercial sour cream.

Or first sauté snipped scallions or finely minced onion in butter; then add to okra.

Or serve one of these sauces in small dishes. Dip okra into sauce.

Drawn Butter, p. 533	Thousand Island, p. 531
Easy Hollandaise, p. 531	Vinaigrette, p. 530

OKRA MEDLEY

1 1/2 cups sliced summer squash	1 1/4 teasp. salt
1 1/2 cups okra, cut into 1/2" slices	1 bunch scallions
	Speck pepper
1 cup thinly slivered, pared carrots	3 tablesp. butter or margarine

If squash is large, cut in half lengthwise; then slice. Cook squash, okra, and carrots with salt in 1" boiling water, covered, about 7 min. Meanwhile, cut scallions (green tops and all) into 1" pieces. Add to okra; cook 3 to 5 min., or until all vegetables are just tender-crisp. Season with pepper, butter, and more salt if needed. Makes 4 servings.

ONIONS

To Buy, to Prepare, to Cook: See chart, p. 427. Or use canned onions—they're good!
To serve: Drain cooked onions. Season with salt, pepper, and butter or margarine. Try small ones, whole, in sweet or sour cream! Or make it big ones, sliced and sautéed, with pepper.

Or add a little sherry, chili, or curry.

Or try the flavor surprise of cloves, almonds, peanuts, snipped parsley, mint, caraway seeds, soy sauce, or nutmeg.

Or cream onions as in Old-Fashioned Creamed Vegetables, p. 393, adding sherry, nutmeg, or curry powder to taste.

Or toss onions with one of these sauces:

Saucepan Cheese, p. 529	Quick Mushroom, p. 528
Curry, p. 527	Thousand Island, p. 531
	Tomato-Cheese, p. 530

Also see Serve with a Flair, p. 392.

GLAZED ONIONS

Prepare and cook 1½ lb. onions till almost tender, as on p. 427. Drain. In large skillet, over low heat, blend 2 tablesp. butter or margarine, 6 tablesp. granulated sugar, 2 teasp. water. Add onions; cook until golden and glazed, turning often. Makes 4 servings.

BERMUDA ONIONS PIQUANT

4 Bermuda onions	3 tablesp. butter or
½ cup onion liquid	margarine
2 cups grated process	1 teasp. Worcester-
Cheddar cheese	shire
(½ lb.)	Speck pepper

Prepare onions, slice ¼″ thick, and cook as on p. 427. Drain; to ½ cup onion liquid, add cheese, butter, Worcestershire, pepper. Stir gently over low heat till cheese is melted. Pour over onions.

Serve as is or on toast. Makes 6 servings.

To Vary: Use 18 small onions.

FRENCH-FRIED ONIONS

3 large onions	⅓ cup flour
⅓ cup milk	¼ teasp. salt

Peel onions; slice ¼″ thick; separate into rings. Dip into milk, then into combined flour and salt. Fry until light brown, a few rings at a time, as in Shallow-Frying, p. 7, at 380°F. on deep-fat-frying thermometer. Drain on paper towels; sprinkle with salt.

Serve hot, with steak, liver and bacon, etc. Makes 4 servings.

SKILLET ONIONS

3 tablesp. butter or	onions, peeled
margarine	½ cup water
2 lb. small white	Paprika

Heat butter or margarine in a 10″ skillet; in it, brown small white onions on all sides. Then add water; cover, and simmer 25 to 30 min., or until fork-tender. Arrange on meat platter; sprinkle with paprika. Makes 4 servings.

CURRY SAUTEED ONIONS

12 medium onions	1 teasp. salt
¼ cup butter or mar-	1 teasp. curry powder
garine	2 teasp. lemon juice

Peel, then slice onions ¼″ thick. In hot butter, in large skillet, sauté them slowly, turning often, 25 to 30 min., or until tender and golden. Sprinkle with salt, curry, and lemon juice. Or add Tabasco or soy sauce to taste.

Serve with chops, steak, hamburgers, liver, etc. Makes 6 servings.

ONIONS PARMESAN

2 lb. medium onions	⅛ teasp. pepper
Butter or margarine	½ teasp. seasoned salt
½ cup shredded Par-	¼ teasp. Worcester-
mesan cheese	shire
2 tablesp. flour	1 cup light cream
2 teasp. salt	Paprika

1. Cut peeled, washed onions into rings ¼″ thick.
2. In lightly buttered 10″ electric (or regular) skillet, place half of onions in rows. Top with half of cheese, then rest of onions, then cheese.

Mix flour, salt, pepper, seasoned salt, Worcestershire, and light cream until smooth; pour over onions. Cook, covered, at 275°F., 40 to 50 min., or until tender-crisp. (If in regular skillet, simmer over low heat same time.) Dust with paprika. Makes 6 servings.

PARSNIPS

To Buy, to Prepare, to Cook: See chart, p. 428.
To serve: Drain cooked parsnips. Season with salt, pepper, butter or margarine, and snipped parsley or paprika.

Or mash well; then season, adding a little hot milk or cream; beat until fluffy.

Or sauté cooked parsnips in a little hot fat in skillet until golden brown on all sides, sprinkling with salt and pepper.

Or spoon one of these sauces over parsnips:

Béchamel, p. 533	Easy Hollandaise,
Drawn Butter, p. 533	p. 531

PARSNIP PATTIES

4 cups thinly sliced,	1 egg, beaten
pared, cored pars-	½ cup coarse fresh
nips	bread crumbs
⅓ cup sliced onions	Speck pepper
1¾ teasp. salt	Packaged dried bread
1¼ cups boiling water	crumbs
¼ cup snipped pars-	2 tablesp. fat
ley	

Cook parsnips with onions and salt in boiling water, covered, 15 min., or until tender. Drain; mash. Add parsley, egg, fresh bread crumbs, pepper. Chill well. Form into 8 patties. Roll in packaged crumbs. In hot fat in skillet, sauté patties on both sides until brown. Makes 8 servings.

PEAS

To Buy, to Prepare, to Cook: See chart, p. 428. For variety, add one of the following before cooking peas:

2 or 3 lettuce leaves
Pinch dried marjoram or savory
Fresh mint sprigs
Sliced or minced onions
Snipped scallions

To serve: Drain cooked peas, reserving liquid. Boil liquid down to a few tablespoonfuls; add to peas, with salt, pepper, butter or margarine. If desired, add a little cream and snipped fresh mint.

Or sauté sliced mushrooms in butter or margarine before adding to peas.

Or dress up peas with a sprinkle of snipped scallions, chives, parsley, or mint; diced canned water chestnuts; a few cocktail onions; or grated cheese.

Or add excitement with wine, commercial sour cream, mayonnaise, curry, or slivered almonds.

Or spoon one of these sauces over peas:

Saucepan Cheese, p. 529
Quick Mushroom, p. 528
Sour Cream, p. 528

Also see Serve with a Flair, p. 392.

PEAS AND SCALLIONS

2 tablesp. butter or margarine
12 to 14 scallions snipped into 1" pieces
2 teasp. flour
½ teasp. salt
1 teasp. sugar
⅛ teasp. pepper
¼ teasp. nutmeg
¾ cup liquid drained from peas
2 cups drained hot cooked or canned peas

In hot butter over medium heat, sauté scallions 3 min. Stir in flour, salt, sugar, pepper, nutmeg;

then add pea liquid. Cook, stirring, until thickened. Add peas. Makes 4 servings.

PEAS CONTINENTAL

2 tablesp. butter or margarine
1 cup sliced fresh or canned mushrooms
¼ cup minced onion
¼ teasp. salt
Speck pepper
¼ teasp. nutmeg
⅛ teasp. dried marjoram
2 tablesp. sherry (optional)
2 cups drained hot cooked or canned peas

In hot butter, in skillet, sauté mushrooms and onion about 5 min., or until tender. Add salt, pepper, nutmeg, marjoram, sherry, then peas. Makes 4 servings.

BLACK-EYED PEAS

Have you tried frozen black-eyed peas? Look for them in your local market — they're delicious. Cooking directions are on the label.

SWEET POTATOES AND YAMS

Sweet potatoes and yams may be used interchangeably in recipes.

To Buy, to Prepare: See chart, p. 428.

BAKED SWEET POTATOES

Start heating oven to 350°F. Scrub and dry 4 unpared medium or large sweet potatoes of same size. Rub each with a little salad oil. Arrange on small baking sheet or oven rack. Bake 45 to 50 min., or till tender when tested with fork.

To serve: Remove potatoes from oven at once; with fork, prick to let out steam. Immediately cut 1½" cross in top of each. Then, holding potato with clean towel, press from bottom until tender interior partially bursts through cross. Break up lightly with fork. Top with butter or margarine, salt or seasoned salt, and paprika. Serve at once, to avoid sogginess. Makes 4 servings.

For Oven Meals: If oven is set for another dish at a temperature other than 350°F., bake sweet potatoes along with it till tender.

STUFFED BAKED SWEET POTATOES: Bake sweet

potatoes. Immediately cut slice from top of each. With spoon, scoop out potatoes (do not break skins); mash well. Beat in enough hot milk to make potatoes creamy. Add butter or margarine; season to taste. Pile back into shells.

BOILED SWEET POTATOES

Prepare and cook unpared sweet potatoes as on p. 428. Drain. Hold each potato on fork; peel off skin. Serve whole, with butter or margarine; sprinkle with paprika or snipped parsley.

MASHED SWEET POTATOES: Peel hot cooked sweet potatoes; mash well. Add hot milk or cream; beat with potato masher until creamy. Add salt, pepper, and butter or margarine to taste. If desired, also add a few tablespoonfuls of drained canned crushed pineapple or chopped pecans, or dash of nutmeg or cinnamon. Or add two spoonfuls of orange juice, or a spoonful of sherry. Or sprinkle sautéed walnuts on top.

BROILED SWEET POTATOES

Peel cooked sweet potatoes; halve lengthwise. Brush with melted butter or margarine; sprinkle with salt, pepper, and a little sugar if desired. Broil, without turning, 8 min., or till golden brown.

Or slice peeled, cooked sweet potatoes lengthwise in halves or thirds; arrange in baking pan. Pour on combined melted butter or margarine and brown sugar, allowing 1/4 cup butter and 1/2 cup brown sugar for every 4 medium potatoes. Broil as above.

CANDIED SWEET POTATOES

6 medium sweet potatoes	1/2 cup dark corn syrup
1/4 cup butter or margarine	2 tablesp. water
	1/4 cup brown sugar, packed

Cook unpared scrubbed sweet potatoes in boiling water 15 min. Cool; peel; halve lengthwise.

In skillet,* place butter, corn syrup, water, brown sugar. Arrange potatoes on top, with cut sides down. Cook over very low heat, uncovered, basting occasionally, about 1 hr., or until potatoes are tender and well glazed. Makes 6 servings.

*Or use shallow baking dish. Then bake, un-covered, basting occasionally, at 375°F. 1 hr., or until well glazed.

QUICK-CANDIED SWEET POTATOES

In large skillet, simmer together for 5 min. 3/4 cup brown sugar, packed, 1/2 cup water, 1/2 teasp. salt, 2 tablesp. butter or margarine, dash cinnamon. Add 1 1-lb.-2-oz. can sweet potatoes. Turn heat low; cook, uncovered, turning occasionally, 15 to 20 min., or until potatoes are well glazed. Or place potatoes in greased shallow baking pan; add syrup. Bake, uncovered, turning now and then, at 400°F. 20 to 25 min. Makes 5 or 6 servings.

PAN-ROASTED SWEET POTATOES

Substitute sweet potatoes for white potatoes in Franconia, or Pan-Roasted, Potatoes, p. 411.

FRIED SWEET POTATOES

Make Susan's Hashed Brown Potatoes, p. 111, using cold cooked sweet potatoes cut into 1/4" cubes and stirring cubes often so they will brown on all sides.

JAMAICAN YAM CASSEROLE

1 1-lb. can yams, drained	1/8 teasp. pepper
1/2 medium banana, thickly sliced	2 tablesp. coarsely chopped pecans
1/4 cup orange juice	2 tablesp. toasted flaked coconut
1/2 teasp. salt	

Start heating oven to 350°F. In a buttered 1-qt. casserole, arrange yams, banana. Pour juice over all. Sprinkle with salt, pepper. Top with pecans and coconut. Bake, covered, 30 min. Makes 2 servings.

SWEET-POTATO SOUFFLE

2 cups mashed cooked sweet potatoes*	1/4 teasp. ground cardamom
3/4 cup hot milk	1 tablesp. grated orange rind
3 tablesp. butter or margarine	2 egg yolks
1/4 teasp. salt	2 egg whites
1/4 teasp. allspice	

Start heating oven to 325°F. Combine potatoes with milk, butter, salt, allspice, cardamom, and orange rind. Beat egg yolks well; add to potato mixture. Beat egg whites until stiff; carefully fold potato mixture into whites; turn into ungreased 1-qt. casserole. Bake, uncovered, 1½ hr. Makes 6 servings.

You may use canned ones.

WHITE POTATOES

To Buy, to Prepare: See chart, p. 429.

BAKED POTATOES

Start heating oven to 450°F. Wash, then dry, medium or large unpared potatoes of same size. Rub each with salad oil. Arrange on small baking sheet or oven rack. Bake 45 to 60 min., or till tender when tested with fork.

To serve: Remove potatoes from oven at once; with fork, prick to let out steam. Immediately cut 1½" cross in top of each. Then, holding potato with clean towel, press from bottom until snowy interior partially bursts through cross. Break up lightly with fork.

Top with salt, butter or margarine, and paprika. Or top with caraway, poppy, or sesame seeds; dried rosemary, snipped fresh mint, or dill; crumbled Danish blue cheese; or commercial sour cream and snipped chives. Serve at once to avoid sogginess.

For Oven Meals: If oven is set for another dish at temperature lower than 450°F., bake potatoes along with it until tender.

STUFFED BAKED POTATOES: Bake 7 unpared medium or large potatoes. Immediately cut slice from top of each. Scoop out potatoes (do not break skins); mash well. Beat in enough light cream to make potatoes fluffy. Add butter or margarine; season to taste. Pile into 6 shells; round slightly. Brush with melted butter or margarine; dust with paprika. Serve at once. Or lightly brown at 450°F. Makes 6 servings.

To Vary: Before piling mashed potatoes in shells, add 1 tablesp. grated cheese, or snipped chives or parsley, or minced onion.

CHEESE-STUFFED BAKED POTATOES: Prepare Stuffed Baked Potatoes, above, adding to mashed potatoes 2 to 4 tablesp. crumbled Danish blue cheese.

DEVILED BAKED POTATOES

Cut cross in each hot baked potato; press snowy-white interior through; top with deviled ham, then cheese sauce (from jar). Or use canned Cheddar-cheese soup as sauce.

REBAKED POTATOES

Start heating oven to 350°F. With fork, mash 1 minced clove garlic to pulp with ½ teasp. salt (or use garlic press); blend with 3 tablesp. soft butter or margarine, 2 tablesp. grated Parmesan cheese, ½ teasp. paprika, dash pepper. (Or substitute ½ cup cheese spread, sharp, Danish blue, or pimento, for this mixture.)

Slash 4 unpeeled, cold, baked medium potatoes into ½" slices almost all the way through. Spread garlic mixture between slices. Bake 20 min. Makes 4 servings.

CASSEROLE-ROASTED POTATOES

Start heating oven to 350°F. Wash and pare 4 medium potatoes; roll in 2 tablesp. melted butter or margarine, then in combined ¼ teasp. salt and ¼ cup packaged dried bread crumbs. Place in 2-qt. casserole. Bake, covered, 45 to 60 min., or until tender. Makes 4 servings.

✤ FOR 2: Halve ingredients; use 1-qt. casserole.

FRANCONIA, OR PAN-ROASTED, POTATOES

About 1¼ hr. before roast meat is done, boil 8 pared medium potatoes 10 min. Drain; arrange around roast in roasting pan. Bake 40 to 60 min., or until tender, turning occasionally and basting with fat in pan. Plan so roast and potatoes are done at same time. When roast is done, remove it to heated platter. If potatoes are not brown enough, place in pan under broiler; turn as they brown.

To serve: Sprinkle potatoes with paprika, snipped parsley, or dried thyme. Arrange around roast. Makes 8 servings.

To Vary: If no roast is available, after draining boiled potatoes, arrange in shallow pan, in 1 tablesp. butter or margarine for each potato. Bake at 400°F., turning often, 40 min., or until tender and brown.

BOILED MATURE POTATOES

Prepare, then cook potatoes, unpared or pared *very thinly.* Drain; then hold each potato on fork and peel if necessary. Return to saucepan;

heat, uncovered, over very low heat, shaking pan gently, 2 min., or until potatoes become mealy. Sprinkle with salt, pepper; pour on melted butter or margarine. If desired, to butter, add snipped parsley and a little lemon juice.

CREAMED POTATOES: After potatoes are drained and peeled, dice. Pour on hot Vegetable Sauce, p. 533. (Allow 1½ cups sauce per 3 to 3½ cups diced potatoes.) Sprinkle with snipped parsley or chives.

BOILED NEW POTATOES

Prepare, then cook, new potatoes as on p. 429 (leave skins on and scrape lightly; or pare off narrow strip from center of each). Drain. Season with salt, pepper; pour melted butter or margarine over all. Sprinkle with snipped parsley or paprika. Or add sautéed minced onion, or snipped chives, basil, or mint.

CREAMED NEW POTATOES: After draining cooked potatoes, heat in thin cream; season to taste. Or pour on one of the following sauces, then sprinkle with paprika or snipped parsley. Allow 1 cup sauce for every 8 hot small new potatoes.

Quick Mushroom,   Sour Cream, p. 528
    p. 528   Vegetable, p. 533

CREAMED NEW POTATOES AND PEAS: Toss hot peas with potatoes before adding sauce.

DELMONICO POTATOES: Turn Creamed New Potatoes made with Vegetable Sauce into greased casserole. Sprinkle with grated cheese, then with a few buttered fresh bread crumbs. Bake at 400°F. until brown.

NEW POTATOES WITH LEMON AND CHIVES: Peel 2 lb. hot cooked new potatoes. Toss with ¼ cup melted butter or margarine plus grated rind of 1 lemon, 2 tablesp. each of lemon juice and snipped chives. Sprinkle with salt, pepper, and dash nutmeg. Makes 6 servings.

MASHED POTATOES

9 medium potatoes   ¾ cup hot milk or
    (3¼ lb.)   diluted evaporated
6 tablesp. butter or   milk
    margarine   Speck pepper
                       Salt

Cook unpared potatoes as on p. 429. Drain; peel. Place over low heat 1 or 2 min. to dry out, shaking pan gently. With potato masher or electric mixer, mash potatoes thoroughly until no lumps remain. Beat with masher, mixer, or spoon, gradually adding enough combined butter and milk to make potatoes fluffy, creamy. Season to taste. Add sour cream or grated cheese if desired.

To serve: Heap potatoes at once in heated serving dish; top with lump of butter or margarine; sprinkle with paprika, a little nutmeg, mace, dried thyme, lemon juice, or snipped parsley, mint, water cress, or chives. Makes 6 servings.

To Keep Warm: If mashed potatoes cannot be served at once, cover them and set in pan of hot water over low heat.

DUCHESS OR PLANK-BORDER POTATOES: Mash potatoes, adding 2 beaten eggs and enough milk to make mixture smooth. Arrange, with spoon, in mounds, on greased cookie sheet. Brush with melted butter or margarine; brown under broiler or in 450°F. oven.

MASHED POTATOES A LA PHYFE: To Mashed Potatoes, add ½ minced clove garlic, sautéed 5 min. in 1 teasp. salad oil, with a sprinkle of paprika and ⅛ teasp. celery seeds. Serve with Danish Goulash, p. 187, etc.

MASHED-POTATO CAKES: Shape cold leftover mashed potatoes into flat cakes. With flour, dust on both sides; then sauté in butter, margarine, bacon fat, or salad oil till delicate brown on both sides.

SAVORY MASHED POTATOES: Just before serving, to mashed potatoes, add a few snipped mint or water cress leaves.

INSTANT MASHED POTATOES: Marvel of the pantry shelf! Add your own touch, or use them in any of our recipes that call for mashed potatoes, preparing as label directs. See The Instant Potato Family, p. 392.

GNOCCHI AU GRATIN

4 cups cold mashed   1 teasp. prepared mus-
    potatoes (2 to 2½   tard
    lb. potatoes)   5 2½-oz. jars shred-
1½ cups all-purpose   ded Parmesan
    flour   cheese
6 egg yolks   6 qt. hot water
2 teasp. salt   1 tablesp. salt
¼ teasp. pepper   ½ cup melted butter
                             or margarine

Start heating oven to 350°F. In large bowl, combine mashed potatoes, flour, egg yolks, 2 teasp. salt, pepper, mustard, and 4 jars of cheese.

Meanwhile, in a large kettle, bring the hot water to a slow boil; add 1 tablesp. salt. In large pastry bag, with large plain tube no. 8 in place, put some of potato mixture. Holding bag over simmering water, force contents through tube, snipping it into ¾" pieces of gnocchi with scissors. Cook gnocchi gently until they rise to surface, when they will be done. As gnocchi rise, remove at once with slotted spoon; drain well on paper towels; place in buttered 1½-qt. shallow casserole; keep warm in oven.

Repeat snipping, cooking, draining, and warming remaining dough until all is used up.

Remove casserole from oven; turn broiler to Broil; pour butter over gnocchi, and sprinkle with remaining jar of cheese. Broil till golden — about 5 min. Makes 12 servings.

PATTY'S POTATO-CABBAGE CASSEROLE

2 tablesp. butter or margarine
⅓ cup minced onion
1 10½-oz. can condensed cream-of-mushroom soup, undiluted
¾ cup milk
½ cup grated Cheddar cheese
1 teasp. salt
¼ teasp. pepper
Dash garlic salt
¼ teasp. dried marjoram or rosemary
2 large potatoes, cooked and sliced ¼" thick
2 qt. thinly sliced cabbage
1 cup fresh bread crumbs
2 tablesp. melted butter or margarine

1. Start heating oven to 350°F. Grease a 2-qt. casserole.
2. In 2 tablesp. butter, in skillet, sauté onion until tender. Add soup and milk, stirring until blended; gradually stir in cheese until thoroughly combined. Add salt, pepper, garlic salt, and marjoram.
3. In casserole, arrange half of potatoes, cabbage, and cheese sauce; repeat; top with crumbs, then 2 tablesp. melted butter.
4. Bake 25 to 30 min. Makes 6 servings.

COUNTRY (OR COTTAGE-FRIED) POTATOES

6 peeled, cold, cooked potatoes (boiled or baked)
3 tablesp. butter, margarine, or bacon fat
¾ teasp. salt
⅛ teasp. pepper

Slice or dice potatoes. Heat butter in skillet; add potatoes; sauté, without stirring, until golden on underside; turn; brown on other side. Sprinkle with salt and pepper. Makes 4 to 6 servings.

LYONNAISE: Sauté a little minced or thinly sliced onion with potatoes.

See Fix-and-Serve Potatoes, p. 391.

POTATOES IN CREAM

4 cups diced, cooked potatoes
½ teasp. salt
¼ cup butter or margarine
⅛ teasp. pepper
2 cups light cream
Snipped parsley

In large skillet, combine all ingredients except parsley; cook slowly until cream is slightly thickened and potatoes are hot. Sprinkle with parsley and a little grated cheese if desired. Makes 6 servings.

CRISPY NEW POTATOES

Fry 4 bacon slices till crisp but not dry; remove slices. To hot bacon fat, add sliced, washed, unpared new potatoes. Cook, covered, a few minutes, to steam. Uncover; season with salt and pepper; cook very slowly, stirring and turning frequently, until tender and flecked with crusty golden-brown bits — about 20 min. Crumble crisp bacon over top.

OLD-TIME SCALLOPED POTATOES

4 cups thinly sliced, pared potatoes
⅔ cup minced onions
2 tablesp. flour
1 teasp. salt
⅛ teasp. pepper
2 tablesp. butter or margarine
1½ cups scalded milk
Paprika

Start heating oven to 375°F. Arrange layer of potatoes in greased 2-qt. casserole. Cover with some of onions. Sprinkle with some of combined flour, salt, and pepper. Dot with some of butter. Repeat layers until all are used, ending with butter. Pour milk over all; sprinkle with paprika. Bake, covered, 45 min. Uncover; bake 15 min. longer, or until tender. Makes 4 servings.

✤ **FOR 2:** Halve ingredients; use 1-qt. casserole.
CURRIED: Add ½ teasp. curry powder to flour.
WITH HAM: Arrange 2 cups cooked ham strips in layers between potatoes and onions.

QUICK SCALLOPED POTATOES

In ½ cup boiling water in saucepan, cook 4 cups diced, pared potatoes, 1 cup minced onions, 2 teasp. salt, covered, 10 min. Uncover; simmer, stirring occasionally, until water is almost evaporated. Add ½ cup each light cream and grated cheese, plus speck pepper. Heat; add 2 tablesp. snipped parsley. Makes 5 or 6 servings.

P.S. Be sure to try the packaged scalloped-potato mix!

POTATOES PARMENTIERE
(buttery, skillet-toasted potatoes)

4 cups diced, pared potatoes	¼ cup butter or margarine
Salt	Pepper
½ cup shortening	Snipped parsley

1. Place potatoes in saucepan with 1" boiling water plus ½ teasp. salt for each cup water. Cover; bring to boil; boil 3 min.; drain.
2. In skillet, heat shortening; add potatoes. Sauté over medium heat until potatoes are golden-brown all over.
3. Remove potatoes from pan; pour off any shortening remaining in pan. Return potatoes to pan; add butter; heat slowly, tossing potatoes with spatula, until butter is melted. Season with salt and pepper; sprinkle with parsley. Nice with a roast or chicken. Makes 4 servings.

PARMESAN POTATO PATTIES

Shape cold leftover mashed potatoes into flat cakes. Dust on both sides with grated Parmesan cheese. Then sauté in butter, margarine, bacon fat, or salad oil till brown on both sides.

FRIED RAW POTATOES

¼ cup bacon fat or salad oil	4 cups sliced, pared potatoes, ¼" thick
1 cup sliced onions (optional)	1¼ teasp. salt
	⅛ teasp. pepper
	Snipped parsley

Heat bacon fat in skillet. Arrange onions and potatoes in layers in fat. Sprinkle with salt, pepper. Sauté, covered, over low heat 15 min. Then uncover; turn heat up slightly and sauté 10 min., or until brown and crispy on underside (do not stir). Sprinkle with parsley; then fold in half like omelet. Makes 3 or 4 servings.

To Vary: Use coarsely grated potatoes.

FRENCH FRIES
(two-step method)

Precooking: Several hours before serving, wash and pare 2 lb. potatoes. Cut into slices ⅜" thick, then into lengthwise strips ⅜" wide. Wash in cold water; dry well between towels. Fry as in Shallow-Frying, p. 7, or Deep-Frying, p. 6, at 370°F. on deep-fat-frying thermometer, 5 to 7 min., or until potatoes are tender but not brown. Drain on paper towels in baking pan. Cover with wax paper; set aside until just before mealtime.

Browning: Just before serving, fry potatoes at 390°F. until crisp and brown. Drain on paper towels; sprinkle with salt. Keep warm in 300°F. oven until all are browned. Serve at once. Makes 4 servings.

P.S. If you have an automatic electric deep fryer, p. 6, follow manufacturer's directions closely for excellent French-fried Potatoes.

SHOESTRING OR JULIENNE POTATOES: Cut potatoes into ¼" strips. Fry until tender.

QUICK OVEN FRENCH FRIES: You can buy excellent packaged frozen French fries, which need only heating in oven or broiler. Follow label directions. Also see Fix-and-Serve Potatoes, p. 391.

POTATO PANCAKES

5 tablesp. all-purpose flour	1 egg, unbeaten
	1 teasp. salt
1½ lb. pared potatoes	⅛ teasp. pepper
1 small onion, grated	Salad oil

To prevent darkening, plan to fry pancakes *as soon as mixture is made.* Measure flour into bowl. Over flour, grate potatoes on very fine grater; stir in rest of ingredients except oil.

Lightly grease medium skillet; place over medium heat. Drop potato mixture, by heaping tablespoonfuls, into hot skillet. Fry until crisp and golden-brown on underside; turn; brown other side, adding more oil as needed. Drain on paper towels.

Serve as vegetable with pot roast, short ribs, etc. Or serve with applesauce as luncheon or supper main dish. Makes about 16 pancakes.

♣ FOR 2: Omit egg; add 3 tablesp. milk. Divide each remaining ingredient by 3.

QUICK POTATO PANCAKES: Packaged potato-pancake mix is so good, so easy to use. Also see The Instant Potato Family, p. 392.

PUMPKIN

To Buy, to Prepare, to Cook: See chart, p. 429.

To Use: Drain pumpkin well; mash; drain again. For recipes, see Index.

SALSIFY
(oyster plant)

To Buy, to Prepare, to Cook: See chart, p. 429.

To serve: Drain salsify. Season with salt and pepper; then add butter or margarine. Or reheat in a little cream.

SAUERKRAUT

To Buy: Sauerkraut comes canned in 3 sizes; choose whichever you prefer.

To Cook: Turn can of sauerkraut, with all of its liquid, into a saucepan. Then heat it, covered, 30 min. or longer if desired. Drain. (Serve drained liquid, chilled, as juice cocktail.)

To hot sauerkraut, add butter or margarine, salt, and pepper to taste. Also add caraway or celery seeds. Or add a little minced onion, sautéed in butter till tender.

Nice with roast pork, pork chops, spareribs, pigs' knuckles, franks, goose, or duckling.

KRAUT-NOODLE CASSEROLE

4 oz. medium-wide noodles (2 cups)	kraut, drained (2½ cups)
2 tablesp. butter or margarine	Pepper
1 1-lb.-4-oz. can sauer-	¼ lb. packaged process Cheddar-cheese slices

Start heating oven to 300°F. Cook noodles as label directs until barely tender; drain. Add butter; toss until well mixed. Spread three fourths of sauerkraut in 1½-qt. casserole or 10" x 6" x 2" baking dish. Sprinkle with pepper. Top with noodles, cheese, rest of sauerkraut. Bake, covered, 1 hr. Makes 4 or 5 servings.

♣ FOR 2: Halve ingredients, using 1 1-lb. can sauerkraut. Leftovers may be reheated.

TOMATO SAUERKRAUT

½ cup sliced onions	1½ cups canned tomato juice
2 tablesp. butter or margarine	1 bay leaf
1 tablesp. flour	½ teasp. salt
4 cups drained canned sauerkraut	1 tablesp. honey

Cook onions in butter until tender. Add flour; cook until lightly browned. Add rest of ingredients except honey. Simmer, covered, 30 min. Remove bay leaf; stir in honey. Makes 3 or 4 servings.

ACORN SQUASH

To Buy, to Prepare, to Cook: See chart, p. 430.

To serve: Drain squash halves well. With fork, mash squash in shells a little; season to taste with salt, pepper or seasoned pepper, and butter or margarine. Serve in shells.

STUFFED ACORN SQUASH

Prepare and cook 3 halved acorn squash as on p. 430. Sauté 6 tablesp. minced onion in ¼ cup butter or margarine until tender but not brown. When squash are done, remove from kettle; do not break shells.

With spoon, carefully scoop squash from shells. Reserve 4 shells. To squash, add sautéed onion, 1½ teasp. salt, ¼ teasp. pepper, 2 tablesp. light cream; beat well with fork. Lightly pile mixture into shells; sprinkle with paprika. Broil 10 min., or until a delicate brown. Makes 4 servings.

BAKED ACORN SQUASH

Start heating oven to 400°F. Prepare 2 medium acorn squash as on p. 430. Brush cut surface of each half with melted butter or margarine;

then sprinkle each with ¼ teasp. salt or seasoned salt. Arrange, with cut sides down, in baking pan. Bake 30 min.

Turn squash, with cut sides up; brush with combined ¼ cup melted butter or margarine and ¼ cup corn syrup. Bake until tender, brushing often with syrup — about 30 min. Makes 4 servings.

To Vary: Omit corn syrup. About 10 min. before squash are done, sprinkle centers with thin, small pieces of sharp cheese. Or sprinkle grated Parmesan cheese, minced onion, a little brown sugar, honey, orange juice, or a dash of nutmeg in the center of each half.

WITH VEGETABLES: As soon as squash are baked, fill each half with ½ cup hot seasoned peas, onions, or Brussels sprouts.

APPLE-ACORN SQUASH

3 acorn squash
2 tablesp. melted but-
    ter or margarine
Salt

½ cup canned apple-
    sauce
2 tablesp. butter or
    margarine
¼ teasp. nutmeg

Start heating oven to 425°F. Cut washed squash in halves, lengthwise. Remove seeds; brush cut surface of each half with melted butter; sprinkle them with ½ teasp. salt. Arrange, cut side down, in shallow pan. Bake 30 min., or until tender.

Now scoop squash from shells; reserve 4 shells. Mash squash; add applesauce, butter, nutmeg, and 1 teasp. salt. Lightly heap mixture into shells. Bake 25 min., or until brown. Makes 4 servings.

HUBBARD SQUASH

To Buy, to Prepare, to Cook: See chart, p. 430.
To serve: Drain squash well; with spoon, scoop squash from shell. Mash well with potato masher; add salt, pepper, butter or margarine, and a little cream; beat well. Sprinkle with paprika, snipped parsley, grated cheese, ginger, or a little minced onion sautéed in butter.

HUBBARD SQUASH SAUTE

Remove seeds and stringy portion from 2- to 2½-lb. piece unpared Hubbard squash. Cut squash into 2″ cubes. Cook, covered, in ½″ boiling salted water until just tender — about 15 min. Drain well. In skillet, melt 3 tablesp. butter or margarine; add 1 tablesp. minced onion, 2 teasp. salt, and squash (with skin sides up). Cook over medium heat until squash is golden-brown. Serve with skin sides down. Makes 4 servings.

SAVORY HUBBARD SQUASH

2- to 2½-lb. piece
    Hubbard squash
1 medium onion,
    sliced
2 teasp. salt

⅛ teasp. pepper
¼ cup butter or mar-
    garine
1 8-oz. can tomato
    sauce

Start heating oven to 375°F. Remove seeds and stringy portion from squash; cut squash into 8 pieces; pare. Place in 2-qt. casserole; cover with onion slices. Sprinkle with salt, pepper; dot with butter; pour on tomato sauce. Bake, covered, 1 hr., or until tender. Makes 4 servings.

BAKED HUBBARD-SQUASH SQUARES

2½-lb. piece Hub-
    bard squash
3 tablesp. melted but-
    ter or margarine

1½ teasp. salt
¼ teasp. pepper

Start heating oven to 400°F. Scrub squash. With long sharp knife, cut squash into serving pieces about 4″ x 2″. With spoon, scrape out seeds and stringy portion. Brush with some of melted butter; sprinkle with some of salt and pepper.

Arrange squash pieces, side by side, with cut sides down, in greased baking pan. Bake, uncovered, 30 min. Turn cut sides up; brush with melted butter; sprinkle with rest of salt, pepper. Bake 30 min., or until tender, brushing often with melted butter. When squash is done, mash in each shell with fork. Makes 4 servings.

SUMMER SQUASH

To Buy, to Prepare, to Cook: See chart, p. 430.
To serve: Drain squash thoroughly. Season with salt, pepper, butter or margarine, and a little cream. Heat; sprinkle with snipped parsley, orégano, basil, nutmeg, chili sauce, or ba-

con. Or add sautéed minced onion and grated cheese. Or try chopped chives or scallions, or slivered tomatoes. Or add grated cheese, soy sauce, lots of pepper, some dill, or sour or sweet cream.

Or, before seasoning, mash thoroughly.

Also see Serve with a Flair, p. 392.

SUMMER SQUASH EN CASSEROLE

2 lb. summer squash	2 tablesp. butter or
1 teasp. salt	margarine
⅛ teasp. pepper	

Start heating oven to 400°F. Wash squash; cut into ½″ slices. Place in layers in greased 2-qt. casserole, sprinkling each layer with some of salt and pepper and dotting with some of butter, until all is used. Bake, covered, 1 hr., or until tender. Makes 4 servings.

SKILLET SQUASH AU GRATIN

¼ cup butter or margarine	Dash pepper
	¼ cup water; or
4 cups thinly sliced summer squash or zucchini	2 sliced, peeled tomatoes
	½ cup grated process Cheddar cheese
1 onion, sliced	
1 teasp. salt	Soy sauce (optional)

Melt butter in skillet. Add summer squash, onion, salt, pepper, water. Cook, covered, 10 to 15 min., or till squash is tender. Sprinkle with cheese, and soy sauce if desired. Makes 4 generous servings.

TOMATOES

To Buy: See chart, p. 431.

To Peel: Dip each tomato into boiling water for 1 min.; remove. Cut out stem end; with knife, pull off skin; refrigerate. Or hold tomato on fork over heat until skin wrinkles and splits; then pull off skin; refrigerate.

BAKED TOMATOES

3 medium tomatoes	1½ teasp. Worcestershire
¾ teasp. prepared mustard	Salt
1 tablesp. minced onion	3 tablesp. buttered fresh bread crumbs

Start heating oven to 375°F. Wash tomatoes; cut out stem ends; then halve crosswise. Arrange, with cut sides up, in baking pan. Spread with prepared mustard; top with minced onion, Worcestershire; sprinkle well with salt, then with crumbs. Bake, uncovered, 30 min.

Serve with meat, fish, or poultry, on vegetable plate, with omelets, etc. Makes 6 tomato halves.

BROILED TOMATOES: Prepare Baked Tomatoes; sprinkle with a little curry powder if desired. Broil, without turning, 15 min., or until nicely browned. Serve with meat, fish, on vegetable plate, with omelets, etc.

CHEESE TOMATOES WITH BACON: Arrange Baked or Broiled Tomatoes on toast; top with Zippy Cheese Sauce, p. 530, and crisp bacon. Nice luncheon dish.

SCALLOPED TOMATOES

3 tablesp. butter or margarine	Dash cayenne pepper
	1 1-lb.-13-oz. can tomatoes (3½ cups)
¼ cup minced onion	
2 cups fresh bread crumbs	¼ cup fresh bread crumbs
½ teasp. sugar	1 tablesp. melted butter or margarine
1 teasp. salt	
¼ teasp. pepper	

Start heating oven to 375°F. In 3 tablesp. butter, in small saucepan, sauté onion until tender. Add 2 cups bread crumbs, sugar, salt, pepper, cayenne. Arrange layer of tomatoes in greased 1½-qt. casserole. Top with layer of onion-bread mixture. Continue until all is used, ending with tomatoes on top. Combine ¼ cup bread crumbs with 1 tablesp. butter; sprinkle over tomatoes. Bake, uncovered, 45 min. Makes 5 or 6 servings.

✣ **FOR 2:** Halve ingredients; use 1-qt. casserole.

GRILLED TOMATOES AND MUSHROOM CAPS

6 to 8 small tomatoes	3 tablesp. minced onion
6 to 8 large mushrooms	Salt
2 tablesp. prepared mustard	Butter or margarine

Start heating broiler 10 min., or as manufacturer directs. Wash tomatoes; slice off stem ends. Wash mushrooms; remove stems (use another day). In shallow baking pan, arrange tomatoes; spread with mustard; sprinkle with minced onion and salt; dot with butter.

Around tomatoes, arrange mushroom caps, rounded side down; sprinkle with salt; dot with butter. Broil all, 4″ from heat, 12 to 15 min., or until nicely browned. Serve each tomato topped with a mushroom cap. Makes 6 to 8 servings.

SPEEDY STEWED TOMATOES

Stewed tomatoes now come canned — onions, green peppers, and celery have been added. Just heat and serve. Delicious!

CREAMY FRIED TOMATOES

6 large tomatoes	1½ cups milk
3 tablesp. flour	1½ teasp. sugar
Salt	¾ teasp. bottled thick
⅛ teasp. pepper	meat sauce
¼ cup butter or mar-	1½ teasp. prepared
garine	mustard

1. Cut out stem end of each tomato, then halve crosswise. Combine 1 tablesp. flour, ¾ teasp. salt, pepper; sprinkle over tomato halves. In butter, in skillet, sauté tomatoes until golden on both sides and just tender.
2. Arrange 10 halves on heated platter. To 2 tomato halves left in skillet, add 2 tablesp. flour, milk, ¾ teasp. salt, sugar, meat sauce, mustard. Cook until creamy. Pour over tomatoes. Serve for breakfast or lunch, as is, or on toast. Makes 5 servings.

SPEEDY: Prepare as in step 1, above. Then pour ⅓ to ½ cup undiluted evaporated milk or light cream over tomatoes. Cook, covered, 5 min., or until tomatoes are just heated through. Serve on toast rounds if desired, spooning rich cream gravy over tomatoes. Makes 4 servings.

WHITE TURNIPS

To Buy, to Prepare, to Cook: See chart, p. 431. Sometime, too, try cutting turnips, before cooking, with melon-ball scoop.

To serve: Drain turnips. Season with salt, pepper, and butter or margarine. Add a little lemon juice or light cream if desired. Garnish with snipped parsley or paprika.

Or, before seasoning, toss with hot peas. Or, before seasoning, mash well.

TOP-STOVE SCALLOPED TURNIPS

1 cup water	¼ cup diced green
1 cup milk	pepper
1 teasp. salt	1 tablesp. butter or
3 cups thinly sliced,	margarine
pared white turnips	¼ lb. process Ched-
2 cups sliced, pared	dar cheese, grated
carrots	(1 cup)
½ cup sliced onions	5 tablesp. finely crum-
¼ cup diced celery	bled saltines

Bring water and milk to boil; add salt, turnips, carrots, onions, celery, green pepper. Simmer, covered, about 20 min., or until tender. *Do not drain.* Add butter, cheese, saltines. Heat, covered, until cheese is melted. Makes 5 servings.

BAKED TURNIP PUFF

6 to 8 medium white	Dash pepper
turnips	2 teasp. sugar
2 tablesp. shortening	½ teasp. flour
or meat drippings	2 eggs, separated
1 teasp. salt	

Prepare, cube, then cook turnips as on p. 431. Start heating oven to 350°F. Drain turnips; mash well over low heat. Add shortening, salt, pepper, sugar, flour. Beat egg whites until stiff; set aside. With same beater, beat egg yolks until light; stir gradually into hot turnips. Fold in beaten whites. Pour into greased 1½-qt. casserole. Bake, uncovered, 30 to 35 min., or until puffy and lightly browned. Makes 6 servings.

YELLOW TURNIPS
(rutabagas)

To Buy, to Prepare, to Cook: See chart, p. 431.

To serve: Drain turnips. Season with salt, pepper, butter or margarine, then snipped parsley. Or, before seasoning, mash well.

SAVORY MASHED TURNIPS: To 3 cups hot, unseasoned, mashed yellow or white turnips, add 1 teasp. salt, ⅛ teasp. pepper, 2 tablesp. butter or margarine, ⅔ cup grated process Cheddar cheese, 1 tablesp. minced onion, and ½ teasp. bottled thick meat sauce. Mix well. Makes 4 servings.

MASHED TURNIPS WITH POTATOES: Combine 1½ cups hot, unseasoned, mashed yellow turnips with 3 cups hot mashed potatoes. Season with salt, pepper, and 6 tablesp. melted butter or margarine. Makes 4 to 6 servings.

ZUCCHINI

To Buy, to Prepare, to Cook: See chart, p. 432.

To serve: Drain zucchini well. Season with salt, pepper, butter or margarine, and a few chopped, sautéed almonds if desired. Or add minced onion, marjoram, basil, dill, light cream, a little Tabasco, or tomato slivers.

Or before seasoning, mash well. Drain again. Then season, adding a little soy sauce if desired.

STUFFED ZUCCHINI

1½ lb. small zucchini	2 tablesp. snipped
1½ cups fresh bread	parsley
crumbs	1¼ teasp. salt
¾ cup grated process	⅛ teasp. pepper
Cheddar cheese	2 eggs, beaten
¼ cup minced onion	2 tablesp. butter or
	margarine

Scrub zucchini well. Cut off ends; do not pare. Cook whole with 1 teasp. salt in 1″ boiling water, covered, about 5 to 7 min. Start heating oven to 350°F.

Cut squash in halves lengthwise. With tip of spoon, carefully remove squash from shells. Chop into small pieces; then combine with bread crumbs and rest of ingredients except butter and ¼ cup cheese. Pile mixture lightly into zucchini shells; dot with butter. Sprinkle with ¼ cup grated cheese. Arrange filled shells in large baking pan. Bake, uncovered, 30 min., or until brown on top. Makes 4 servings.

ZUCCHINI, ITALIAN STYLE

Scrub 2 lb. zucchini. Cut off ends; do not pare. Cut in halves lengthwise; cut crosswise into 3″-long pieces. In skillet, heat ¼ cup olive or salad oil. Add zucchini, with green sides up; sprinkle with 1½ cups sliced onions; lightly brown cut sides over low heat. Turn cut sides up; add 1½ teasp. salt, ¼ teasp. pepper, and 3 cups canned tomato juice. Cook, covered, over low heat 40 min., or until zucchini are tender and tomato juice forms thick sauce. Makes 4 servings.

ZUCCHINI, CHINESE STYLE

In skillet, heat ¼ cup bacon fat or salad oil. Add 1 lb. zucchini or summer squash, washed, unpared, thinly sliced; 1 small onion, thinly sliced; 1 clove garlic; and ¼ cup water (do not add salt); stir. Cook, covered, until zucchini is almost tender — 10 min. Discard garlic. Sprinkle 2 tablesp. soy sauce over zucchini. Cook, turning occasionally, 5 min., or till tender. Makes 4 servings.

MERLE'S COMPANY CASSEROLE

1 cup fresh bread	1 12-oz. can whole-
crumbs	kernel corn, drained
1 pimento, coarsely	3 tablesp. butter or
chopped	margarine
2 tablesp. snipped	3 tablesp. flour
parsley	1½ teasp. salt
3 small zucchini,	¼ teasp. pepper
thinly sliced	2 cups milk
1 large onion, sliced	1 egg yolk, well
	beaten

1. Start heating oven to 350°F. Line bottom of a 1½-qt. casserole with half of crumbs. Combine pimento and parsley.
2. Alternate layers of zucchini, onion, and corn until all are used. Top with pimento mixture.
3. In saucepan, melt 2 tablesp. butter; stir in flour, salt, pepper. Gradually add milk. Cook, stirring constantly, until thickened. Cool slightly.
4. Into sauce, stir egg yolk; pour over vegetables. Sprinkle on remaining crumbs; dot with 1 tablesp. butter. Bake 35 min., or until fork-tender. Makes 6 servings.

ZUCCHINI IN CREAM

6 small zucchini, cut	6 tablesp. grated
in ½″ slices	sharp Cheddar
⅔ cup commercial	cheese
sour cream	½ teasp. seasoned
1 tablesp. butter or	salt
margarine	3 tablesp. fresh bread
	crumbs

Start heating oven to 375°F. Simmer zucchini 10 min. in water to cover; drain; turn into 8″ pie plate. In small saucepan combine sour cream, butter, ¼ cup of the cheese, and salt. Heat, stirring, until blended. Pour over zucchini. Top with bread crumbs and 2 tablesp. grated cheese. Bake 10 min., or until crumbs are golden. Let stand 5 min., then serve. Makes 4 servings.

VEGETABLE CHART — BUYING, PREPARING, AND COOKING

Note: The following time periods are only approximate; exact cooking time varies with age of vegetables.

VEGETABLE	SEASON	AMOUNTS TO BUY	TO BUY, TO PREPARE	APPROXIMATE COOKING TIME
		*For 4**	*Wash all vegetables thoroughly before cooking, or as directed under each vegetable section.*	*Use ½"–1" boiling water with ½ teasp. salt per cup water, or as directed. Add vegetable; cover; boil as directed.*
				In a pressure cooker (see p. 390)
ARTICHOKES, Italian or French	Oct. through Jan.	Allow 1 per person—unless artichokes are large; then split lengthwise for 2.	Buy compact, tightly closed heads. Cut 1" off top, cutting straight across with sharp knife. Cut off stem about 1" from base, leaving stub. Pull off outside bottom leaves. With scissors, clip off any thorny tips on leaves.	6–10 min. Cook as on p. 394
ARTICHOKES, Jerusalem	Nov. through Jan.	1½ lb.	Buy artichokes free from blemishes. Scrub well. Pare thinly. Leave whole, dice, or slice.	15–35 min. Sliced: 8 min. Whole: 14 min.
ASPARAGUS	March through June	2 lb.	Buy straight, green, brittle stalks with close, compact tips. Break off each stalk as far down as it snaps easily. Remove scales with knife. Scrub with soft brush to remove sand. (Or scrub; then thinly pare length of stalk with vegetable parer.) Leave stalks whole, or cut Chinese style, p. 395.	Whole: see p. 394 Chinese: see p. 395 Whole: 2 min. (lay stalks crosswise) Cut-up: 1–2 min.
BEETS	All year	2 lb., topped	Buy smooth small or medium beets.	Use boiling salted water to cover.

	Season	Amount	Preparation	To cook	Time
BEETS, continued:			Leave whole; cut off tops, leaving 1" of stem and root end. Or for quick cooking, pare; then slice, dice, or sliver.	Whole, young: ½–1 hr. Old: 1–2 hr. Quick: 20–30 min.	10–12 min. 12–18 min. 5 min.
BROCCOLI	All year	2 lb.	Buy broccoli with tender, firm stalks and tightly closed green flowerets, with no yellow color evident. Cut off large leaves and bit of lower stalk. Wash well. If stalks are more than ½" in diameter, make lengthwise slits (about 4 or 6) almost to flowerets.	Lay in 9" or 10" skillet. Boil in 1" boiling salted water, uncovered, for 5 min.; then boil, covered, 5–10 min.	1½–2 min.
BRUSSELS SPROUTS	Sept. through Feb.	1 lb.	Buy green, fresh-looking sprouts. Avoid yellow spots or worm holes. Remove imperfect leaves; cut off bit of stem end.	Cook, uncovered, for 5 min. after they boil; then cover; boil 5–20 min.	2 min.
CABBAGE:	All year		Buy heads with fresh, crisp-looking leaves. Remove any wilted leaves; wash.		
Green and Savoy, shredded		1 lb.	To shred: Cut into quarters. Remove most of core. With sharp knife, thinly slice cut surface of each quarter into medium shreds. Or use shredder.	Cook, covered, 1 min., or until wilted. Then uncover; stir; cover; boil 4–7 min.	2 min.
Green and Savoy, in wedges		2 lb.	To quarter: Cut into wedges, then core each wedge, leaving just enough core to retain shape.	7–11 min.	4–6 min.
Chinese, shredded		1 medium head	To shred: Remove root end. With sharp knife, slice thinly into shreds.	3–4 min.	1–1½ min.

*For 2: Merely divide amounts for 4 in half. When buying a head of something, choose a smaller one.

VEGETABLE CHART — BUYING, PREPARING, AND COOKING (continued)

Note: The following time periods are only approximate; exact cooking time varies with age of vegetables.

VEGETABLE	SEASON	AMOUNTS TO BUY	TO BUY, TO PREPARE	APPROXIMATE COOKING TIME	In a pressure cooker (see p. 390)
		For 4*	*Wash all vegetables thoroughly before cooking, or as directed under each vegetable section.*	*Use ½"—1" boiling water with ½ teasp. salt per cup water, or as directed. Add vegetable; cover; boil as directed.*	
CABBAGE, continued: Red, shredded		1 lb.	*To shred:* See Green and Savoy.	14–24 min., adding 1–2 tablesp. lemon juice to water, to preserve color.	2 min.
CARROTS	All year	1 lb.	Buy bright, crisp carrots. Remove tops at once. Most come topped, washed, in 1-lb. film bags. Scrub. Scrape or pare thinly. Then leave whole. Or cut into halves or quarters. Or sliver, slice, or dice.		
			Whole carrots	20–40 min.	Whole: 5–6 min.
			Halved carrots	15–25 min.	
			Quartered carrots	12–20 min.	Sliced or slivered: 2–3 min.
			Thin slivers or strips of carrot	10–14 min.	
			Sliced large carrots	15–20 min.	
			Sliced small carrots	6–10 min.	
			(Use shorter time for tender-crisp carrots, longer time for well-done carrots.)	(A scant teasp. sugar gives 1 lb. of carrots a delicious sweetness.)	

	Season	Amount	Preparation	Cooking time
CAULIFLOWER	All year (peak in fall)	1 large head	Buy compact, crisp white head, as free from blemishes as possible, with fresh, green outer stalks.	20–30 min.
			Remove outer leaves and stalks; cut off any blemishes on flowerets. Wash well. Leave whole, removing as much of core as possible without altering shape.	
			Or break into flowerets.	8–15 min.
			Or thinly slice each floweret.	5–7 min. 2 min.
CELERIAC (variety of celery with root like turnip)	Sept. through May	1½ lb.	Buy firm, crisp roots. Cut away leaves and root fibers. Scrub well. Pare; then slice or dice.	25–27 min. 5 min.
CELERY	All year	Allow ½ to ¾ cup, diced, per serving.	Buy crisp stalks with fresh, green leaves. Pascal celery, with its green stalks, is especially tasty. Remove leaves; trim roots. Using soft brush, wash well. With knife, scrape off any discoloration. Dice or sliver outer stalks.	15–20 min. 3 min.
CORN ON THE COB	Some all year (peak May through Sept.)	Allow 1 or 2 ears per person.	Buy young corn that spurts milk when kernels are pressed. Refrigerate until ready to cook. Just before cooking, remove husks, all silk, and any blemishes or discoloration.	Boil in boiling water to cover 5–6 min. (see p. 399) 4–5 min.
CUCUMBER	All year	1 medium yields about 1½ cups, diced.	Buy firm cucumbers—not too plump or seedy. Cut off and discard ends down to where seeds begin. Pare. Then cut into thick slices, or dice.	15 min., or until tender

*For 2: Merely divide amounts for 4 in half. When buying a head of something, choose a smaller one.

VEGETABLE CHART — BUYING, PREPARING, AND COOKING (continued)

Note: The following time periods are only approximate; exact cooking time varies with age of vegetables.

VEGETABLE	SEASON	AMOUNTS TO BUY	TO BUY, TO PREPARE	APPROXIMATE COOKING TIME	
		For 4*	Wash all vegetables thoroughly before cooking, or as directed under each vegetable section.	Use ½"–1" boiling water with ½ teasp. salt per cup water, or as directed. Add vegetable; cover; boil as directed.	In a pressure cooker (see p. 390)
EGGPLANT	All year	1 medium (about 1½ lb.) makes 4 servings.	Buy well-shaped, purple, firm, shiny eggplant with no rust spots. Use soon after buying. Wash. Pare if necessary when ready to use. Eggplant discolors upon standing. Do not soak in salted water.	Cook as in recipes, p. 402	
ENDIVE (Belgian)	Sept. to May	1 lb. contains 4 to 6 endives, depending on size; allow 1 head per person.	Buy fresh-looking, well-bleached heads (4"–6" long). Keep wrapped to prevent light from turning endive green. Wash heads quickly in water; wipe dry with paper towel. Remove any bruised outer leaves. Cut off a small slice from the base of each stalk. Cut in half lengthwise.	See recipe, p. 402	
GREEN BEANS	All year	1 to 1½ lb.	Buy crisp, slender green pods that snap. Wash. Remove ends and string, if any. Then fix in one of these ways:	Boil, uncovered, 5 min. Then cover; boil as below:	
			SNAPPED: Snap or cut into 1" or 2" pieces.	10-25 min.	2-3 min.
			CROSSCUT: Cut crosswise into thin slanted slices.	5-15 min.	
			FRENCH CUT: Cut lengthwise into thin strips.	5-15 min.	1-2 min.
			1 lb. fresh green beans yields 3 cups cooked.		

	Season	Amount	Preparation	To Cook	Time
GREEN LIMAS	Some all year (peak July through Oct.)	2 to 3 lb.	Buy crisp, green, full pods. Snap open pods; remove beans. If necessary, cut off thin strip from inner edge of pod; push out beans. 1 lb. green limas makes 1¼ cups shelled.	Boil, uncovered, 5 min. Then cover; boil 15–25 min.	Small: 2 min. Large: 3–5 min.
GREEN PEPPERS	All year	4	Buy peppers that are thick-fleshed, crisp, and bright green. Buy wide, chunky ones for stuffing. Use hot and green peppers in relishes. Cut thin slice from stem end. Remove seeds and fibrous portion. Wash inside; then cut as recipe directs.	Cook as in recipes, pp. 404–405	
GREENS (except spinach)	All year	2 to 2½ lb.	Buy greens that have crisp, clean leaves with good color. Avoid seedy or woody stems. Discard ends, tough stems, and yellowed leaves. Wash 3 times in warm water, lifting greens out of water each time and shaking well so sand sinks to bottom.	Cook in ¼" boiling salted water, using ½ teasp. salt per 1 lb. greens. Cook, covered, 1 min. or until wilted. Uncover; stir; cover; boil as below. (If very young and tender use no water; greens will cook in water clinging to leaves after washing.)	
Beet tops	Nov. through July			5–15 min.	3 min.

*For 2: Merely divide amounts for 4 in half. When buying a head of something, choose a smaller one.

VEGETABLE CHART — BUYING, PREPARING, AND COOKING (continued)

Note: The following time periods are only approximate; exact cooking time varies with age of vegetables.

VEGETABLE	SEASON	AMOUNTS TO BUY	TO BUY. TO PREPARE	APPROXIMATE COOKING TIME	
		For 4*	*Wash all vegetables thoroughly before cooking, or as directed under each vegetable section.*	*Use ½"—1" boiling water with ½ teasp. salt per cup water, or as directed. Add vegetable; cover; boil as directed.*	*In a pressure cooker (see p. 390)*
GREENS, continued:					
Dandelion greens				10–20 min.	4 min.
Mustard greens				7–10 min.	
Swiss chard, young				3–10 min.	3–5 min.
Turnip greens				8–15 min.	
Kale or Collards	All year	2 to 2½ lb.	Buy fresh, crisp leaves or washed, bagged kind. Strip veins from leaves; discard. Wash rest of leaves in several changes of water, lifting leaves out of water each time.	10–15 min.	3½–5 min.
KOHLRABI	Some all year (peak June and July)	8 medium	Buy small or medium kohlrabi with fresh tops and rind that can be easily pierced with fingernail. Discard stems and leaves; wash. Pare thinly; then cut into slices, slivers, or quarters.	Boil, uncovered, 5 min. Then cover; boil 20–35 min.	5 min.
MUSHROOMS	All year	1 lb.	Buy firm, plump, cream-colored mushrooms with short stems. For safety's sake, buy only cultivated ones.	Cook as in recipes, pp. 406–407	Small: 3–4 min. Large: 7 min.

MUSHROOMS, continued:

Wash well, scrubbing if necessary with soft brush. Do not peel if fresh and tender. Cut thin slice off stem end; use rest. To slice whole, slice parallel to stem.

	Season	Amount	Preparation	Cooking time
OKRA	All year (peak June through Oct.)	1 lb.	Buy young, tender, crisp pods. Wash. Leave whole (do not cut off stems or tips). Or cut into ½" pieces.	Lay in 9" or 10" skillet with 1 teasp. salt and 1" boiling water. Boil, uncovered, 5 min. Then cover; boil 2–7 min. Whole: 3 min. Cut-up: 2 min.
ONIONS	Some varieties all year (peak Feb. through June)	1½ lb.	Buy clean, hard, well-shaped onions with brittle skins. Avoid any with developed stems. Cut slice from stem and root ends. Peel thinly, slipping off only first and second layers (do this under cold running water to prevent tears). Or slice onion; then pull off skin.	Small white: 22–35 min. Small white: 5–6 min. Yellow or white (2"): 28–30 min. 6–7 min. Sliced, ¼" thick: 10 min. 3–4 min.
Yellow or Red globe			Especially nice for seasonings.	
Small white				
Sweet Spanish	July through March		Excellent as whole cooked vegetable. Delicious French-fried or raw.	
Bermuda	Spring and early summer		Good raw or cooked.	

For 2: Merely divide amounts for 4 in half. When buying a head of something, choose a smaller one.

VEGETABLE CHART — BUYING, PREPARING, AND COOKING (continued)

Note: The following time periods are only approximate; exact cooking time varies with age of vegetables.

VEGETABLE	SEASON	AMOUNTS TO BUY	TO BUY, TO PREPARE	APPROXIMATE COOKING TIME
		For 4*	*Wash all vegetables thoroughly before cooking, or as directed under each vegetable section.*	*Use ½"—1" boiling water with ½ teasp. salt per cup water, or as directed. Add vegetable; cover; boil as directed.* In a pressure cooker (see p. 390)
PARSNIPS	All year (peak fall and winter)	1½ lb.	Buy smooth, firm, well-shaped small to medium parsnips. Soft or shriveled ones are apt to be pithy. Wash. Cut thin slice off top and bottom. Pare; halve; cut out center core. Cut into quarters or slices.	7–15 min. Diced: 2 min. Small whole: 8 min.
PEAS	All year	3 lb.	Buy well-filled fresh, green pods. Just before cooking, shell by pressing pods between thumbs to open; then remove peas. Discard any with shoots.	Add 1 teasp. sugar to water. Boil, uncovered, 5 min. Then cover; boil 3–20 min. Add a few pods for flavor. 1 min.
SWEET POTATOES or YAMS	All year	1½ to 2 lb.	Sweet potatoes have yellowish, fawn-colored skins and are mealy when cooked. Yams are really sweet potatoes with white to reddish skins, are moist when cooked, and have meat which is more orange in color. Buy smooth-skinned potatoes with bright appearance. Buy in small quantities; they're perishable. Scrub well.	Cook in jackets or skins 30–35 min. 8–10 min.

Vegetable	Season	Amount (for 4)	Preparation	Cooking time	Cooking time
WHITE POTATOES (mature or new)	Some variety all year	1½ to 2 lb.	Buy uniform, well-shaped potatoes; scrub with brush; remove blemishes and eyes. To save food value, cook in jackets or skins. Scrape or pare thinly if necessary.	Whole: 35–40 min. Cut-up: 20–25 min.	Whole: 10–20 min. Slices: 1½ min.
Long russets (Idaho baker)	All year		Russet skin, oval shape. Excellent for baking, frying. Noted for dryness, mealiness, fluffiness.		
Round whites (Maine or Eastern)	All year		Round white potato; good for boiling or potato salad.		
Round red (Florida new)	All year		Characteristic red skin. Good for boiling or salad.		
Long white (from Calif.)	Peak mid-April through Aug.		Smooth light-colored surface, long shape—good for boiling.		
PUMPKIN Small sugar or pie pumpkin, or Winter Luxury	Oct. (a few in Sept. and Nov.)	3 lb. raw yields 3 cups cooked and mashed.	Buy bright-colored, unblemished, firm pumpkins. Halve; remove seeds and stringy portion. Cut into small pieces; then pare.	25–30 min.	Leave on rind; cut into desired lengths; cook 15 min.
SALSIFY	Oct. and Nov.	1½ lb.	Buy firm, well-shaped medium roots. Scrub; then scrape or pare. Slice or sliver. Plunge into cold water containing a little vinegar to prevent discoloration.	15–20 min.	4–9 min.

*For 2: Merely divide amounts for 4 in half. When buying a head of something, choose a smaller one.

VEGETABLE CHART — BUYING, PREPARING, AND COOKING (continued)

Note: The following time periods are only approximate; exact cooking time varies with age of vegetables.

VEGETABLE	SEASON	AMOUNTS TO BUY	TO BUY, TO PREPARE	APPROXIMATE COOKING TIME	
		For 4*	*Wash all vegetables thoroughly before cooking, or as directed under each vegetable section.*		*In a pressure cooker (see p. 390)*
SPINACH	All year		See Greens. Comes washed, topped, sometimes in film bags.	6–10 min. After washing, add ½ teasp. salt per 1 lb. greens. Cook, covered, in water clinging to leaves.	1 min.
SQUASH Acorn	All year	2 large	Buy ridged, acorn-shaped squash that are green, firm, and oval or round. Scrub well. Cut in half lengthwise; remove seeds and stringy portion.	25 min.	10 min.
Butternut	All year	3 lb.	Scrub well. Cut into serving pieces; remove seeds and stringy portion.	12–15 min.	12–13 min.
Hubbard	Sept. through Feb.	2 to 3 lb.	Buy with hard, warted rind. Scrub well. Cut into serving pieces; remove seeds and stringy portion.	25–30 min.	
Summer Crookneck or yellow	All year	2 lb.	Buy squash with curved neck, deep-yellow color, and tender warted rind. Rind becomes rough and less tender as it matures.	15–20 min.	2–3 min.

Use ½"—1" boiling water with ½ teasp. salt per cup water, or as directed. Add vegetable; cover; boil as directed.

	Season	Amount	Preparation	Cooking Time
Cymling or pattypan Zucchini	All year	2 lb.	Scrub well. Cut slice from stem and blossom ends. (Do not pare or remove seeds if squash is young and tender.) Cut into pieces or thin slices. This type is flat, scalloped, and disk-shaped. Prepare as in summer squash. See Zucchini, p. 432.	2–3 min. 15–20 min.
TOMATOES	Some varieties all year	2 lb.	Buy large or small oval red and yellow tomatoes. Sometimes they are purchased green. Regardless of type, look for firm, plump, smooth tomatoes with good color and no blemishes.	Cook as in recipes, pp. 417–418
Vine ripened Carton			May be purchased at height of local season. 3 or 4 round tomatoes to a pkg., picked green, ripened under controlled atmosphere.	
Hothouse			Have green sepals left on (they should look fresh). Are picked ripe or nearly ripe, depending on how far they must travel.	
TURNIPS White	All year (peak in fall)	2 lb.	Buy white turnips with fresh green tops. Should be firm and heavy. Avoid those that are light-weight for size; they may be woody, pithy, strong in flavor. Scrub; pare thinly; then: Cut into ¼" slices, or into strips or ½" cubes.	5–6 min. 3–5 min. 9–12 min. 15–20 min.
Yellow, or rutabagas		2 lb.	Buy heavy, firm yellow turnips. Avoid light-weight ones; they may be woody, pithy, strong in flavor. Scrub well; pare thinly; then: Cut into 2" pieces. Cut into strips or ½" cubes.	15 min. 8–12 min. 35–40 min. 20–25 min.

*For 2: Merely divide amounts for 4 in half. When buying a head of something, choose a smaller one.

VEGETABLE CHART — BUYING, PREPARING, AND COOKING (continued)

Note: The following time periods are only approximate; exact cooking time varies with age of vegetables.

VEGETABLE	SEASON	AMOUNTS TO BUY	TO BUY, TO PREPARE	APPROXIMATE COOKING TIME	
		*For 4**	*Wash all vegetables thoroughly before cooking, or as directed under each vegetable section.*	Use ½"—1" boiling water with ½ teasp. salt per cup water, or as directed. Add vegetable; cover; boil as directed.	*In a pressure cooker (see p. 390)*
WAX BEANS	All year	1 to 1½ lb.	Same as Green Beans. Buy crisp, slender yellow pods that snap.	Snapped: 15–30 min. Crosscut: 10–20 min. French cut: 10–20 min.	2–3 min. 1–2 min.
ZUCCHINI, or Italian Squash	All year	2 lb.	Buy small and medium ones. Look like a cucumber, but are striped and likely to be longer, more irregular. Scrub well. Cut off dark spots and stem end, but do not pare. Cut into ¼" or ½" slices.	Cook in ¼" boiling water, uncovered, 5 min. Then cover; boil 5 min.	

*For 2: Merely divide amounts for 4 in half. When buying a head of something, choose a smaller one.

RELISHES AND GARNISHES

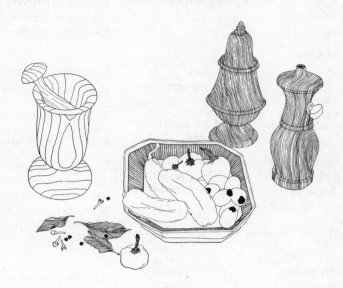

As the name implies, relishes add savor to eating, making many good things taste even better. They often can take the place of salad — so remember this on busy days.

Before using these recipes, refer to How To Use Our Recipes, p. 3. Always use standard measuring cups and measuring spoons; measure level.

RELISHES TO MAKE AND SERVE

SPEEDY PICKLED PEACHES

1 1-lb.-13-oz. can cling-peach halves, drained	peaches ½ cup vinegar 1 3″ stick cinnamon
Whole cloves 1 cup peach syrup, drained from	½ cup granulated sugar

Day or more ahead: Stud each peach half with 3 or 4 cloves. Simmer with peach syrup, vinegar, cinnamon, and sugar 3 or 4 min. Cool; refrigerate.

Serve with poultry, meat, or fish. Nice, too, as dessert, with vanilla ice cream. Makes 8 servings.

SPEEDY PICKLED PEARS: Substitute canned pears and pear syrup for peach halves and syrup.

QUICK SPICED PEARS: Turn can of pears, syrup and all, into saucepan; stud pears with a few cloves. To syrup, add 3″ cinnamon stick, strip of lemon peel. Simmer 5 min.; remove pears from syrup. Serve pears hot, with poultry, lamb, etc. Use syrup over cut-up fresh fruit.

JEWISH PICKLED BEETS

8 medium beets ½ cup water ½ cup lemon juice	2 tablesp. sugar ½ teasp. salt 2 teasp. horse-radish

Early in day, or several days ahead, cook beets as on p. 420; peel; slice. In saucepan, combine water, lemon juice, sugar, salt; bring to boil; stir in horse-radish. Pour over beets; refrigerate till needed. Makes 6 servings.

433

PICKLED PINEAPPLE BAKE

In pie plate, toss 1 1-lb.-4-oz. can pineapple chunks, drained, with 3 tablesp. brown sugar; 2 tablesp. vinegar. Dot with 2 tablesp. butter or margarine. Sprinkle with nutmeg. Bake at 350°F. 30 min. Serve warm with main course. Makes 6 servings.

PICKLED BEETS

½ teasp. dry mustard	½ clove garlic
1 tablesp. sugar	6 tablesp. vinegar
½ teasp. salt	¼ cup water
½ teasp. ground cloves	2 cups drained cooked or canned beets, sliced

Combine mustard, sugar, salt, cloves, garlic. Slowly stir in vinegar, water. When smooth, pour over beets. Refrigerate until well chilled. Remove garlic. Serve with meat or fish. Makes 6 servings.

P.S. Add pinch of fennel if desired.

PIMENTO PICKLES

4 medium dill pickles, sliced lengthwise ¼″ thick	cut into ¼″ strips
3 canned pimentos,	1 cup light-brown sugar, packed
	½ cup cider vinegar

A week or so ahead:

1. In a *very clean* 1-pint glass measuring cup, small old-fashioned bean pot, or jar, place half of pickles. Top them with half of the pimentos and half of the sugar; repeat.
2. Pour vinegar over all; cover, then refrigerate for at least a week to crisp them. Keep refrigerated while using. Makes about 1 pt.

SPICED JELLIED APRICOTS

1 1-lb.-13-oz. can apricot halves	12 cloves
¼ cup vinegar	1 stick cinnamon
½ cup granulated sugar	1 3-oz. pkg. orange-flavor gelatin

Day before: Into saucepan, drain syrup from apricots; add vinegar, sugar, cloves, cinnamon. Bring to boil. Add apricots; simmer 10 min. Remove apricots to 6 custard cups or individual molds. Strain syrup; add hot water to make 2 cups. Pour over gelatin; stir until

dissolved; pour over apricots. Refrigerate until set.

To serve: Unmold apricots onto relish tray. Nice with meat, poultry, fish, etc. Makes 6 servings.

JELLIED APRICOT SALAD: Unmold apricots onto water cress or curly chicory. Place spoonful of cottage cheese beside each mold.

ROSY CINNAMON APPLES

1 cup red cinnamon candies	pared, cored cooking apples
2⅔ cups boiling water	½ cup granulated sugar
8 small or medium	

In saucepan, dissolve candies in boiling water. Add apples. Simmer until tender, turning often. Remove apples to shallow dish. Add sugar to syrup; boil 3 min. Pour over apples, turning each apple to glaze it. Cool. Serve with meat. Makes 6 to 8 servings.

BARBECUED BAKED APPLES

Start heating oven to 350°F. Wash 4 cooking apples; cut in halves crosswise; remove cores. Place halves, with cut sides up, in shallow baking pan. On each half, put 1 tablesp. brown sugar and 1 tablesp. catchup; dot with butter or margarine. Pour ¼″ hot water around apples in pan; bake about 30 min. Serve hot, spooning liquid from pan over apples, as meat accompaniment. Makes 8 servings.

SPICED FRUIT COCKTAIL

1 1-lb.-13-oz. can fruit cocktail, drained	1⅓ cups granulated sugar
1 cup syrup drained from fruit cocktail	⅔ cup cider vinegar
	¼″ stick cinnamon
	1 teasp. whole cloves

Spread fruit cocktail in flat pan. In saucepan, combine syrup, sugar, and vinegar with cinnamon and cloves tied together in small piece of cheesecloth. Boil 5 min.; remove spice bag. Pour sauce over fruit cocktail (sauce will not be thick). Let stand in refrigerator at least 1 hr. or overnight. Drain syrup from fruit;

spoon fruit around meat loaf. Makes 8 servings.

For Special Occasions: Halve 4 small or medium oranges; scoop out orange pulp (save fruit for breakfast). Fill shells with Spiced Fruit Cocktail; arrange around meat loaf, roast, poultry, etc., with parsley sprigs between shells.

SPICED CRANBERRIES

2½ cups granulated sugar	Grated rind 1 lemon
½ cup water	2 tablesp. lemon juice
2 sticks whole cinnamon	4 cups fresh or frozen cranberries
1 teasp. whole cloves	

Early in day, or day before if desired:
1. In saucepan, combine all ingredients but cranberries. Simmer 5 min., stirring occasionally.
2. Now add cranberries and cook slowly until most of the skins pop open. Cool; then refrigerate until served. So nice as relish with meat, poultry, or fish. Makes 4 cups.

SPICED PRUNES

1 lb. large prunes	1 cup water
1 cup vinegar	1 teasp. ground cloves
1 cup granulated sugar	1 teasp. cinnamon

Week or so ahead: Rinse prunes; cover with cold water; boil 10 to 12 min.; drain. Combine vinegar, sugar, water, cloves, cinnamon; boil 1 min. Add prunes; bring to boil. Cool; refrigerate. Nice with poultry or roasts, or as garnish for fruit salads. Makes about 10 servings.

SPICED ORANGE SLICES

4 unpeeled medium oranges, cut into ⅜" slices	1 cup water
	⅓ cup white corn syrup
Whole cloves	¼ cup vinegar
1 cup granulated sugar	Pinch salt

Two days before serving:
1. Stud edge of each seeded orange slice with 3 or 4 cloves.
2. In saucepan, combine sugar, water, corn syrup, vinegar, salt. Simmer, uncovered, 5 min.

3. Now add orange slices and simmer 5 min. Cool; then refrigerate for at least two days. *At serving time:* Drain orange slices well. Arrange in serving dish, with a whole clove in center of each. Or use as garnish around duck, chicken, or turkey.

SPICED GRAPE CLUSTERS

1 cup water	cinnamon
1 cup granulated sugar	1 lb. Empress or Tokay grapes, in small bunches
1 cup vinegar	
12 whole allspice	Whole cloves
2 sticks whole	

Two days before serving:
1. In medium saucepan, combine water, sugar, vinegar, allspice, and cinnamon. Simmer, uncovered, 5 min.; then cool.
2. Prick each grape twice with a four-tined fork; then insert a whole clove in the end.
3. Add grapes to cooled syrup; refrigerate at least two days.
To serve: Drain grapes well on paper toweling; remove cloves if desired; then arrange in serving dish to serve with meat, fish, or poultry. Or use as a garnish around ham or poultry.

SPICED APRICOTS

1 1-lb. can whole, peeled apricots	10 whole cloves
	10 whole allspice
4 lemon slices	

Into saucepan drain syrup from apricots; add lemon slices, cloves, allspice; simmer 5 min. Add apricots; refrigerate.

At serving time, heat Spiced Apricots thoroughly. Makes 4 servings.

GINGERED PEACH NUGGETS

1 1-lb.-13-oz. can cling-peach halves	lemon rind
	2 tablesp. lemon juice
1 1½" piece dried ginger root	Whole cloves
1 teasp. grated	

Night before:
1. Into saucepan, drain syrup from peaches; add ginger root, lemon rind, and juice; simmer 5 min.

2. Into each peach half, stick 3 cloves; place in hot syrup and simmer 5 min.

3. From syrup, remove ginger root; then let peaches stand in syrup overnight at room temperature.

At serving time: Drain peaches; then use as a garnish for a platter of baked ham or turkey, fried chicken, chicken salad, or creamed chicken.

CINNAMON BRANDIED PEACHES

4 1-lb.-13-oz. cans cling-peach halves	Whole cinnamon sticks
	1½ cups brandy

Several days ahead:

1. Drain syrup from peaches into large saucepan. Place drained peaches in a 3-qt. bowl; cover, refrigerate.

2. To peach syrup add 1 cinnamon stick; boil down, over medium heat, till reduced to 3 cups — about 40 to 45 min. Remove from heat and pour into medium bowl, removing scum, if any. Stir in brandy; cool.

3. Into this mixture stir any syrup remaining in bottom of bowl of peaches, then pour, with additional cinnamon sticks if desired, over peaches. Cover; refrigerate. Makes 3 qt. Delicious with meat or poultry. Or serve over poundcake or ice cream.

SPICED MIXED OLIVES

½ 8½-oz. can ripe olives	1 teasp. mustard seeds
1 7¼-oz. jar stuffed olives	¼ teasp. dried thyme
2 cloves garlic, peeled, halved	¼ teasp. salt
2 bay leaves	Dash pepper

About a week or so ahead:

1. Drain liquid from ripe olives and discard it.

2. Drain liquid from stuffed olives and reserve it.

3. Arrange both kinds of olives in a *very clean* jar, coffee carafe, or china teapot.

4. To reserved stuffed-olive liquid, add garlic, bay leaves, mustard seeds, thyme, salt, and pepper; then use to fill jar, adding water to cover, if necessary. Refrigerate till needed and after opening. Makes 1 pt.

SAUTEED BANANAS

¼ cup butter or margarine	4 firm bananas*
	Salt

In large skillet, melt butter. Peel bananas; leave whole, or cut crosswise into halves. Sauté slowly in butter until easily pierced with fork, turning to brown bananas evenly. Sprinkle lightly with salt. Serve as vegetable, with meat, fish, poultry, etc. Makes 4 servings.

Use all-yellow or slightly green-tipped bananas.

SAUTEED FRESH PEACHES

Peel, pit, and quarter peaches. Sprinkle lightly with salt and flour; sauté in butter until tender. Serve with meat or fish.

SAUTEED PINEAPPLE

Dry canned pineapple slices on paper towels. Sauté in butter or margarine in skillet until golden brown, turning once. Serve with ham, sautéed or baked fish, or poultry.

GLAZED APPLE QUARTERS

In saucepan, or skillet, combine 2 teasp. grated orange rind, ½ cup orange juice, ½ cup granulated sugar. Arrange 4 quartered, cored unpared red cooking apples, with skin sides up, in mixture. Simmer, covered, over low heat 10 to 15 min., or until apples are tender but still hold their shape. Use as garnish for Braised Pork Chops, p. 203, or other pork dish. Cook down orange sauce until thickened; spoon over apples. Makes 4 servings.

GLAZED PINEAPPLE CHUNKS

In skillet, melt a little butter or margarine. Add drained canned pineapple chunks, then a generous dash of catchup; sprinkle lightly with brown sugar. Heat 5 min., or until glazed, tossing occasionally. Serve with meats, fish, etc.

FRIED APPLE RINGS

Select 3 large cooking apples. Wash; core; cut into ½″ to ¾″ slices. Sprinkle lightly with granulated or brown sugar. In a little hot butter or margarine in skillet, sauté apple slices until tender on both sides. Serve with pork, sausages, etc. Makes 18.

CRUSHED PINEAPPLE RELISH

1 1-lb.-4-oz. can crushed pineapple	2 tablesp. vinegar
3 tablesp. brown sugar, packed	1 tablesp. butter or margarine

Start heating oven to 350°F. Drain pineapple; in a pie plate toss it with brown sugar and vinegar; dot with butter. Bake 30 min. Serve warm with ham, pork, chicken, etc. Makes 6 servings.

PINEAPPLE TIDBIT RELISH

1 1-lb.-4-oz. can pineapple tidbits	powder
½ teasp. curry	2 cups flaked coconut

Drain pineapple tidbits; toss with curry and coconut; refrigerate. Serve with chicken, fish, pork chops, etc. Makes 6 to 8 servings.

SKILLET PINEAPPLE RELISH

2 tablesp. butter or margarine	2 tablesp. catchup
1 1-lb.-4-oz. can pineapple chunks	2 tablesp. brown sugar

In skillet, melt butter or margarine. Add drained pineapple chunks, catchup, and brown sugar. Heat 5 min., or until glazed, tossing often. Serve with lamb, turkey, shrimp, etc. Makes 6 servings.

CURRIED FOUR-FRUIT BAKE

⅓ cup butter or margarine	5 maraschino cherries (optional)
¾ cup brown sugar, packed	1 16-oz. can cling-peach or apricot halves
4 teasp. curry powder	
1 16-oz. can pear halves	1 1-lb.-4-oz. can pineapple slices or chunks

Start heating oven to 325°F. Melt butter; add sugar and curry. Drain and dry fruits; place in 1½-qt. casserole; add butter mixture. Bake 1 hr., uncovered.

Serve warm, from casserole, with ham, lamb, poultry, etc. Makes 12 servings.

To Do Ahead: Flavor will be even better if dish stands, covered, in refrigerator and is then reheated. It may be reheated several times, using a 350°F. oven for 30 min. Any leftover juice may be used as baster when baking ham slice; or serve it, thickened, as sauce over ham.

To Vary: For 4 fruits, substitute 1 1-lb.-13-oz. jar fruits for salad. Use ¼ cup butter, 1 tablesp. curry powder, and same amount of brown sugar. Bake in 1-qt. casserole.

CURRIED APRICOTS: In pie plate, arrange 1 16-oz. can apricot halves, drained. Combine 2 tablesp. melted butter or margarine; ¼ cup brown sugar, packed; and 1½ teasp. curry powder. Spoon mixture over fruit. Bake at 350°F. 30 min. Serve warm. Makes 6 servings.

CURRIED PEARS: In pie plate, arrange 1 16-oz. can or 1 1-lb.-1-oz. jar of pear slices, drained. Decrease butter and brown sugar to 1 tablesp. each. Add ¼ teasp. salt with curry powder. Complete as in Curried Apricots above. Bake at 325°F. 25 min.

FOR A CROWD: Make as in Curried Four-Fruit Bake above, using 2-qt. shallow baking dish, for 2 1-lb.-13-oz. cans cling-peach halves; 1 1-lb.-4-oz. can pineapple slices; 1 1-lb.-13-oz. can pear halves; 6 bottled maraschino cherries; ½ cup butter or margarine; 1 cup light-brown sugar, packed; 6 teasp. curry powder. Makes 20 servings.

CURRIED PEACH HALVES

1 1-lb. can cling-peach halves, drained	2 tablesp. brown sugar
2 tablesp. melted butter or margarine	¼ teasp. curry powder

In large skillet, arrange peach halves, with cut sides up. Brush with melted butter; sprinkle with brown sugar mixed with curry powder. Sauté for 8 to 10 min. Makes 6 servings.

HOT BANANA RELISH

⅓ cup butter or margarine	Salt
6 large bananas (slightly green-tipped or all yellow)	Lemon juice
	Chutney
	Lemon slices, halved

In large skillet, melt butter. Peel bananas; sauté slowly in butter, about 15 min., or till they're easily pierced with fork, turning now and then to brown evenly. Sprinkle lightly with salt and lemon juice.

Arrange on serving dish with mound of chutney at one end; top with lemon slices. Serve with favorite poultry, ham, pork, veal, etc. Makes 6 servings.

SPICY FRUIT MEDLEY

1 1-lb. can whole unpeeled apricots	2 whole cloves
1 1-lb. can cling-peach slices	¼ cup vinegar
	1 stick cinnamon
1 1-lb. can pear halves	½ teasp. salt
	¼ cup butter or margarine
1 1-lb.-4-oz. can pineapple spears	2 fresh limes, thinly sliced
½ cup brown sugar	

About 2 hr. before serving:

1. Open and then drain fruits, reserving syrup. Place drained fruits in 14″ x 10″ x 2″ roasting pan. Start heating oven to 350°F.
2. In saucepan, simmer 1½ cups reserved syrup from fruits with brown sugar, cloves, vinegar, cinnamon, and salt for 10 min. Strain over the fruits.
3. Dot the fruits with butter; bake 25 min. Then cool to lukewarm; add lime slices.
4. Serve warm in a bowl, to spoon over hot or cold sliced meat. Makes 7 or 8 servings.

MOLDED MANDARIN CRANBERRY RELISH

1 env. unflavored gelatine	1 16-oz. can whole-cranberry sauce
2 tablesp. sugar	½ cup finely diced celery
¼ teasp. salt	
1 11-oz. can mandarin oranges	¼ cup chopped walnuts or pecans
2 tablesp. lemon juice	Salad greens

Early in day or day before:

1. In saucepan, mix together gelatine, sugar, and salt. Drain mandarin oranges; stir syrup into gelatine mixture. Place over low heat; stir constantly until gelatine and sugar are dissolved, then remove from heat.
2. Add lemon juice, whole-cranberry sauce, diced celery, and chopped nuts.
3. In 9 individual ring molds, arrange orange sections. Spoon in cranberry mixture; refrigerate till firm.

4. Unmold relishes on individual beds of greens.
5. Serve as is or topped with mayonnaise thinned with fruit juice, along with chicken, ham, veal, etc. Makes 9.

BROILED FRUIT

CANNED PEACHES, PEARS, PINEAPPLE, OR APRICOTS: Preheat broiler 10 min., or as manufacturer directs. Place well-drained fruit on broiler rack or in broiler pan, lined with foil if desired. Sprinkle with a little lemon juice. Brush with melted butter or margarine or salad oil. Sprinkle with a little granulated or brown sugar, then with more lemon juice and pinch of ground cloves, cinnamon, or nutmeg. Broil 3″ to 4″ from heat 8 min., or until golden.

Serve as garnish for meat, fish, or poultry. Or top with vanilla ice cream for dessert.

FRESH PEACHES OR PEARS: Pare, halve, and pit or core fruits. Proceed as above. If you like, put ½ teasp. chili sauce or catchup in center of each peach or pear half; then broil. Or use canned cling-peach halves with chili sauce.

CRANBERRY-PEACH HALVES: Substitute cranberry jelly for chili sauce in broiled peaches above.

BANANAS: Peel firm, all-yellow or slightly green-tipped bananas. Proceed as above, broiling bananas about 5 min. on each side, or until brown and fork-tender.

BROILED APPLE RINGS

Wash and core large cooking apples; cut into ¼″ slices. Place on broiler rack; brush with melted butter or margarine mixed with lemon juice (1 teasp. lemon juice to each 1 tablesp. melted butter). Broil 4 to 5 min., or until slices begin to soften. Turn with broad spatula. Brush second side with butter and lemon juice; sprinkle with cinnamon and sugar. Broil 3 to 5 min., or until golden brown. Serve as garnish for meat or vegetable plate.

HOT FRUITED PEACHES

Preheat broiler 10 min., or as manufacturer directs. Meanwhile, drain 1 16-oz. can peach halves. In shallow baking pan, arrange peaches, with cut sides up; top each with 1 tablesp. prepared mincemeat; sprinkle each with 1 tablesp. grated sharp cheese. Broil till hot and bubbly. Makes 6 servings.

Or fill each drained canned peach half with 1 tablesp. drained canned crushed pineapple. Sprinkle each with 1 tablesp. grated sharp cheese; broil till hot and bubbly. Serve with hot or cold meat such as pork.

CRISP ONION RELISH

1 cup vinegar	fresh mint leaves
2 tablesp. confec-	2 cups thinly sliced
tioners' sugar	small onions
1½ cups chopped	

Day before: Combine vinegar, sugar, and mint; let stand 30 min.; add onions. Refrigerate until time to serve with favorite meat or fish. Makes 8 servings.

ONION-CELERY: Omit mint leaves; substitute 2 tablesp. celery seeds.

ONION-DILL: Omit mint leaves; substitute ½ cup snipped fresh dill.

SPEEDY CORN RELISH

2 cups drained canned or cooked frozen whole-kernel corn	pickle relish with liquid
¼ cup chopped green pepper	¼ teasp. celery seeds
½ medium onion, sliced thinly	½ teasp. salt
6 tablesp. sweet-	¼ teasp. dry mustard
	2 tablesp. vinegar
	2 tablesp. white corn syrup

1. In saucepan, combine corn, green pepper, onion, pickle relish, celery seeds, salt, mustard, vinegar, corn syrup; simmer 5 min.
2. Refrigerate, covered.
3. Serve cold, with a hot or cold roast, ham, franks, etc. Makes 1½ cups.

FRESH TOMATO RELISH

Several hours before serving: Chop 2 lb. tomatoes; 2 medium green peppers, seeded; 2 medium onions; drain slightly. Add 2 teasp. salt, 1 teasp. dry mustard, 1 teasp. celery seeds, ¼ cup vinegar, ¼ cup salad oil. Mix.

Refrigerate until served. Nice with ham, pork, eggs, chicken, shrimp, etc. Makes 1 qt.

MARINATED TOMATOES

Into shallow dish slice peeled ripe tomatoes. Cover lightly with thinly sliced scallions and green tops. Sprinkle with salt and, if desired, with bit of dried basil. Pour French dressing over all. Refrigerate. At serving time, drain tomatoes and serve with meat, fish, poultry, eggs, etc., in place of salad.

WITH OLIVES: Substitute whole ripe olives for scallions.

WITH AVOCADO: Substitute sliced avocados or cucumbers for scallions.

BEET AND HORSE-RADISH RELISH

1 1-lb.-4-oz. can beets	2 teasp. salt
1 tablesp. sugar	⅛ teasp. pepper
1 tablesp. minced onion	½ cup vinegar
	½ cup horse-radish

Drain beets; reserve liquid. Cut beets into small cubes; add sugar, onion, salt, pepper, vinegar, horse-radish. Add enough beet liquid to cover. Refrigerate overnight. Serve with meat or fish. Makes 6 servings.

PICKLED EGGPLANT ITALIAN
(Melanzane sott'Aceto)

1 large eggplant, unpared	½ teasp. dried basil or 2 teasp. fresh basil
2 cloves garlic	½ teasp. dried orégano or 2 teasp. snipped fresh orégano
1 teasp. salt	
½ cup wine vinegar	
½ teasp. freshly ground black pepper	¼ cup olive or salad oil

1. *About 12 or more hr. ahead:* Cut eggplant into large cubes. In 1″ boiling salted water in large saucepan, cook it about 10 min.; then drain thoroughly.
2. In large bowl, mash garlic with salt. Add eggplant, vinegar, pepper, basil, orégano. Refrigerate overnight or longer.
3. *Just before serving:* Stir in oil. Keeps a

week or longer, refrigerated. Makes about 8 servings as a first course.

FRESH CRANBERRY RELISHES

These delightfully crisp, crunchy cranberry relishes give a nice lift to breakfast, luncheon, or dinner. Start making them in October, when the new crop is so good. They keep well in the refrigerator.

CRAN-ORANGE: *Same day or several days before:* Put 1 lb. fresh cranberries (4 cups) and 2 oranges, seeded, quartered, unpeeled, through food grinder, using medium blade. Stir in 2 cups granulated sugar. Refrigerate several hr. or longer. Makes 2 pt.

CRAN-TANGERINE: *Same day or several days before:* Put 1 lb. fresh cranberries, plus pulp (seeds removed) and rind (membrane removed) of 3 tangerines, through food grinder, using medium blade. Add 2 cups granulated sugar. Refrigerate several hr. Makes 2 pt.

CRAN-PINEAPPLE: *Same day or several days before:* Put 1 lb. fresh cranberries and 1 lemon, seeded, quartered, unpeeled, through food grinder, using medium blade. Stir in 1 8-oz. can (1 cup) crushed pineapple and 2 cups granulated sugar. Refrigerate several hr. Makes 2 pt.

CRAN-APPLE: *Same day or several days before:* Put 1 lb. fresh cranberries (4 cups) and 2 cooking apples, cored and unpared, through food grinder, using medium blade. Quarter and remove seeds from 2 unpeeled oranges and 1 lemon; put through food grinder. Add to cranberries with 2½ cups granulated sugar; blend. Refrigerate several hr. Makes 3 pt.

SPEEDY WHOLE-CRANBERRY SAUCE

2 cups granulated sugar	1 lb. fresh cranberries (4 cups)
2 cups water	

In saucepan, combine sugar, water. Boil 3 to 5 min.; add cranberries. Bring to boil, uncovered. Cook, without stirring, until skins of berries pop open — about 5 min. Cool; refrigerate until served. Makes 1 qt.

QUICK: In saucepan, combine sugar, water, cranberries. Boil rapidly until skins of berries pop open — about 5 min. Cool; refrigerate until served. Makes 1¼ qt.

JELLIED CRANBERRY SAUCE

1 lb. fresh cranberries (4 cups)	2 cups granulated sugar
2 cups water	

Cook cranberries in water 5 to 10 min., or until all skins pop open. Strain through fine sieve to remove skins and seeds, pressing pulp through with juice; stir sugar into pulp. Boil about 3 min.; pour into mold; refrigerate until set; unmold. Or pour into bowl; refrigerate until set, then spoon into serving dish. Makes 1 qt.

CRANBERRY-CELERY RELISH

1 lb. cranberries, fresh or frozen	1 small or medium onion, chopped fine
½ cup thin, crosswise celery slices	1 cup granulated sugar

Several days ahead:
1. Grind cranberries, using coarse blade of food grinder.
2. Add celery, onion, and sugar and toss well together.
3. Store, covered, in refrigerator until needed, and while using. Makes about 3 cups.

Fix-and-Serve Cranberry Relishes

You'll find delicious jellied or whole-cranberry sauce, in large and small cans at your grocer's. Delightful as is, it can also be varied as below, to serve as a relish with chicken, turkey, ham, veal, pork, fish, etc.

NO-COOK CRANBERRY RELISHES

Day before: Into 1 1-lb. can whole-cranberry sauce, stir any of the following. Refrigerate until served. Makes about 2 cups.

CRANBERRY-GRAPE: 2 teasp. grated orange rind, ½ cup seedless grapes.

CRANBERRY-CHUTNEY: ½ cup light or dark raisins; ½ cup chopped, cored unpared cooking apples; ½ cup chopped celery; 1 teasp. ground ginger.

CRISP CRANBERRY: 2 grated, pared carrots; ½ cup diced celery; ½ teasp. mace or nutmeg; 1 teasp. lemon juice.

CRANBERRY-PEAR: 1 or 2 diced, cored pears; ½ seeded unpeeled lemon, put through food grinder; 1 teasp. ground ginger.

TANGY ORANGE-CRANBERRY: 2 tablesp. each grated orange rind, coarsely chopped walnuts, and pickle relish.

CRAN-APPLE-LEMON: 1 cored unpared large cooking apple and ¼ seeded unpeeled lemon, put through food grinder.

CRANBERRY BUTTER: ½ cup applesauce, ½ teasp. cinnamon. Extra nice if jellied cranberry sauce is used. Heat; then serve with lamb or pork roast or chops.

CRANBERRY GARDEN RELISH: Combine a 1-lb. can whole-cranberry sauce, well drained, with ¼ cup diced celery, ½ cup diced cucumber, ¼ cup diced green pepper, and 1 tablesp. lemon juice. Refrigerate several hours for flavors to blend. Wonderful with veal, pork, barbecued chicken, or turkey. Makes about 3 cups.

CRANBERRY MINT CHUNKS: Mash a 1-lb. can jellied cranberry sauce with fork. Add 1 cup canned-pineapple chunks, drained; ¼ teasp. peppermint extract. A treat with lamb.

GARLIC TOASTED COCONUT

1 cup flaked coconut	Italian salad
nut	dressing
2 teasp. bottled	

Start heating oven to 350°F. In shallow baking pan, toss coconut with dressing. Spread out in pan; bake 8 to 12 min., or until golden, stirring often. Serve in small bowls to accompany hot chicken or shrimp curry. Makes 1 cup.

TANGY MUSTARD COCONUT: Substitute 2 tablesp. prepared mustard for salad dressing. Use as a golden topping for hot broiled-ham slices.

CURRIED COCONUT: Substitute 1 teasp. curry powder for salad dressing. Try on your favorite cold meat or vegetable salad.

THE GAY GARNISH

Let your garnish provide color contrast. Make it pretty but not gaudy.

Choose the plate carefully. The dish, as well as the food, can be effective.

Always leave some plate showing. It provides a frame for the food.

Arrange food with imagination. Often the way you place food on the plate or platter is all the garnish that's needed.

Don't overgarnish, especially if you're serving buffet style or if someone is carving or dishing out the food.

Last but *not* least, use your imagination. Don't stick just to conventional garnishes.

Pretty Arrangements

It's so easy to add a bit of drama to your relish tray or dish when it's to serve instead of salad. Let these suggestions start you off.

GREEN AND WHITE: Make two rows, side by side — one of watermelon pickle, the other of celery hearts.

NIBBLER: Set bowl of mixed olives on small tray, carrot and dill-pickle sticks near bowl.

LAZY SUSAN: Set 4 or 5 small bowls of assorted relishes on tray, with flower in low bowl in center of tray.

PARSLEY BED: Top bed of parsley with carrot curls and green, ripe, and stuffed olives.

HELP YOURSELF: Place basket of salted nuts on one side of tray; radiate raw turnip chips, carrot sticks, green-pepper rings, and radish roses from basket on tray.

BLACK AND WHITE: Serve bowl of plump ripe olives, with fringed celery tucked here and there.

HOMEMADE: Roll pickled peaches in snipped celery leaves.

TAKE YOUR CHOICE: Place coleslaw in hollowed-out cabbage head on one end of tray, canned jellied-cranberry-sauce slices at other end.

IN PEWTER BOWL: Serve Spiced Grape Clusters, p. 435, and ripe and green olives.

RING-AROUND-A-ROSY BOWL: Pile olives or pickle slices in center of bowl; circle with carrot curls, then with cauliflowerets.

TRAY STYLE: In center of tray, set sherbet glass of homemade jelly; on one side, place celery curls; on other side, ripe olives.

YELLOW AND WHITE: In shallow glass bowl, place bed of carrot curls; top with celery fans.

TWO ROWS: Down one side of oblong dish, place overlapping slices of canned jellied cranberry sauce; down other side, pickles studded with almonds.

GRAPEFRUIT "BOWL": Use grapefruit shell as "bowl" for Cran-Orange Relish, p. 440.

CELERY 'N' FRUIT: Arrange a bowl of celery hearts, watermelon pickles, spiced crab apples.

ONE APIECE: Heap coleslaw, made with almonds, on cranberry-jelly slices.

TAKE YOUR PICK: Partner pickled pineapple chunks with ripe and green olives.

MARINATED DUO: Arrange marinated tomato and avocado slices with snipped parsley as garnish.

Elegant Extras

For the Holiday Bird or Beast:

A bit of holly

Tiny bunches of red and green grapes

Cranberry relish or whole-cranberry sauce in pear halves

Spiced crab apples, nestled in cress

Petite baked apples, each filled with sautéed sausage

Greens, topped with fruits, encircling platter

If It's Meat, Poultry, or Fish

Apricots* (studded with almonds)

Beet cups (with horse-radish)

Carrots (sticks or curls)

Celery (cheese-stuffed)

Celery (fans or sticks)

Chutney (in lettuce cups)

Currant jelly (spoonfuls)

Cucumber slices (fluted)

Dill sprigs or celery leaves

Green grapes (tiny bunches)

Green peppers (in rings)

Jellied cranberry sauce*

Kumquats (fresh or preserved: nest in cress)

Lemons, limes (halved lengthwise, then crosswise; dipped into snipped parsley or chives, or paprika)

Mushrooms (sautéed or broiled)

Ripe olives

Stuffed olives (in rows)

Onions (overlapping rings)

*Canned

Orange or lemon shells (filled with crushed pineapple)

Peaches* (pickled)

Pear halves* (filled with chili sauce or pickle relish)

Pickles* (dill, sour, sweet)

Pineapple chunks* (rolled in snipped mint)

Pineapple slices* (topped with coleslaw or whole or halved apricots*)

Mashed potatoes (nests, with peas)

Spinach (tender leaves)

Tomato slices (with pickle relish)

Tomatoes (tiny ones, filled with horse-radish)

Tomato wedges (dipped into snipped chives)

Turnips (thin slices, chilled on ice)

Water cress (perky sprigs)

Zucchini (cooked slices)

For Baked Ham, Broiled or Fried Chicken

Baked small apples (filled with brown-and-serve sausages)

Apricots, peaches, pears, or pineapple* (sautéed or broiled)

Banana halves (sautéed or broiled)

Bing cherries*

Corn fritters

Crab apples*

Jellied cranberry sauce*

Orange slices

Peaches* (pickled)

Pineapple chunks* (rolled in snipped mint)

Sweet-potato halves

Prunes (plain or stuffed)

For Chops, Steaks, or Hamburgers Plus

Danish blue cheese (crumbled)

Capers, bottled (just a few)

Chives (snipped)

Pickle relish

Banana halves (sautéed or broiled)

French fries

Onions (overlapping rings)

Peaches,* pears,* or apricots* (heated in syrup)

Peach halves* (topped with chili sauce)

For Oysters, Shrimp, Fish, or Scallops

Avocado balls

French fries

Pineapple slices* (sautéed)

*Canned

Potato chips or sticks

Tomato slices (with tartar sauce)

For Meat or Chicken Pie, Fricassee, or Stew

Danish blue cheese (crumbled)
Carrots (grated raw)
Capers, bottled (just a few)
Cheese (grated or shredded)
Chives (snipped)
Parsley (snipped)
Pimento* (diced or in strips)

For Tossed Green Salad

Sprinkling of pomegranate seeds or cranberries
Seedless green grapes and halved pitted red grapes
Avocado slices and bits of red cranberry jelly
Slivered almonds and small pitted ripe olives

For a Meat, Fish, or Fruit-Salad Platter

Pickled peaches or crab apples or small bunches of grapes
Spoonfuls of jellied cranberry sauce or grape jelly
Avocado slices or pineapple cubes, in snipped mint
Apricots* (studded with almonds)
Perky sprigs of water cress

For Potato, Macaroni, or Rice Salad

Dill (sprigs)
Celery leaves
Onion rings
Pickles (fans, chunks, or slices)
Tomato aspic in cubes
Tomato wedges (dipped into snipped chives)

Novel Hot Vegetable Partners

If acorn squash: peas, onions, or Brussels sprouts
If broccoli: sautéed mushrooms or slivered almonds
If Brussels sprouts: sautéed mushrooms, peas, seedless grapes, small onions, or cauliflowerets
If cauliflower: slivered tomato slices, sautéed mushrooms, cooked peas, or green beans
If Fordhook limas: slivered pimento
If green beans: green limas, onions, mushrooms, or cauliflowerets
Canned

If peas: tiny new potatoes or sautéed mushrooms
If sweet potatoes: walnuts, pineapple, or orange slices

For a Sweet Conclusion

Fresh strawberry with hull
Dessert topped (just before serving) with sugar cube dipped in lemon extract, then set aflame
Tiny bunch of red or green grapes
Wedge of red-skinned Gouda or Edam (for fruit pies)
Drift of flaked coconut (for chiffon-type pies)

If It's Soup: See a Bit of Garnish, p. 159.

If It's a Drink: See The Ice, p. 681, and Glamour Touches, p. 681.

If It's a Vegetable: See Serve With a Flair, p. 392.

If It's Ice Cream: See Sundae Toppings, p. 606.

Holiday Pretties

NEW YEAR'S

Flaked or fine grated coconut
Confectioners' sugar
Whipped cream or dessert topping (in drifts)
Silver *dragées*

ST. VALENTINE'S DAY, LINCOLN'S BIRTHDAY, WASHINGTON'S BIRTHDAY

Bing cherries*
Cinnamon candies (heart-shaped)
Jellied cranberry sauce* (cut into shapes)
Maraschino cherries (with stems)
Radishes (sliced, grated, or halved)

ST. PATRICK'S DAY

Coconut* (tinted green)
Crushed pineapple* (tinted green)
Melted mint jelly
Pickle relish*
Shamrocks (instead of cress or mint)
Canned

EASTER

Coconut* (tinted pink, green, or yellow)
Eggs (hard-cooked, chopped or quartered)
Strawberry, vanilla, or pistachio ice cream
    (scoopfuls)
Jelly beans
Fresh posies

FOURTH OF JULY

Celery fans (ends dipped into paprika)
Jellied cranberry sauce* (cut into stars)
Pimento* (strips)
Radishes (chopped or grated)
Strawberries and blueberries
Peppermint candies (striped)
Sugar (tinted red)
Watermelon balls

HALLOWEEN

Dried apricots and prunes
Cheese (pumpkin cutouts)
Canned

Chocolate (grated)
Blue grapes
Ripe olives
Orange slices

THANKSGIVING

Cheese pumpkins
Chrysanthemums (button)
Jellied cranberry sauce*
Salted nuts* and raisins
Peaches* (halves and slices)
Walnuts (in shell, cracked)

CHRISTMAS

Cinnamon drops
Currant and mint jelly
Red and green grapes (small bunches)
Holly sprigs
Preserved fruits
Snipped parsley and paprika

Canned

SALADS

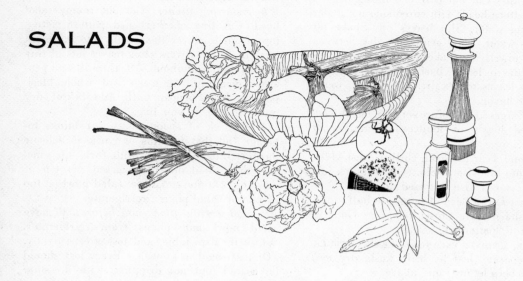

A salad can be as light as lettuce or hearty enough to be the whole meal. Remember, too, that a crisp salad is one of the most appealing ways of fitting necessary leafy green and yellow vegetables into the day's plan for good healthy eating. So try your hand with some of our recipes.

Before using these recipes, refer to How To Use Our Recipes, p. 3. Always use standard measuring cups and measuring spoons; measure level.

Salad Lore

SALAD GREENS: Iceberg and Boston lettuce are the salad greens used most often. Serve the following, too, when they are plentiful:

Beet greens, young	Escarole
Cabbage, green or red	Field salad
Celery, green tops	Kale
Chicory or American endive	Lettuce, Bibb or leaf
Chinese cabbage	Mustard greens
Dandelion greens, young	Nasturtium leaves
Endive, French or Belgian	Romaine
	Spinach, young raw
	Turnip greens
	Water cress (cress)

VITAMIN ROUNDUP: Don't discard the outer green leaves of lettuce, romaine, etc. Though they're not as tender as the inner leaves, they're especially rich in vitamins and minerals. So if they aren't bruised, wash them *very thoroughly*; dry; shred with scissors; use in salads, sandwiches, etc.

LETTUCE-CUPS: The family will be less likely to leave greens on the plate if you sprinkle them with dressing, or toss them in French dressing before arranging salad on top. Keep bed of greens small.

TOMATO TOUCH: Tomatoes are wonderful in tossed salad, but they tend to thin the dressing. So add at last minute. Also, cut them the French way — in vertical slices; they'll lose less juice.

Salad Greens—Their Care

To Store: Buy crisp, young salad greens. Remove bruised leaves, but keep heads whole. Rinse under running water; shake off excess water; then refrigerate in crisper.

To Prepare: Take out greens needed; prepare, p. 446; refrigerate if preparing ahead.

445

ICEBERG AND BOSTON LETTUCE:

For Cups: Cut out core. To loosen leaves, hold lettuce head, with cored side up, under running water. Slip leaves off. Shake off excess water. Then gently pat dry between paper towels; or shake dry in tea towel; or whirl dry in lettuce basket. Water left clinging to leaves makes dressing watery, weakens its flavor.

For Wedges: Just before serving, cut chilled, washed heads of lettuce in quarters or sixths.

To Tear: Tear or break chilled, washed lettuce into bite-size pieces. (Or for quick job, use scissors.) Use in tossed salads.

To Shred: Cut head of lettuce in half; then, with sharp knife, shred very fine. Good as base for "patterned" salads.

ROMAINE, ENDIVE, ESCAROLE, LEAF LETTUCE, ETC.: Separate, leaf by leaf; wash, dry *well* as for iceberg lettuce cups, above.

CHICORY, YOUNG SPINACH, ETC.: Wash in several changes of water; dry as in Greens, p. 425.

WATER CRESS, PARSLEY, MINT: Open up bunch; pick over; wash under running cold water. Drain well; store loosely — separate from other salad greens — with stem ends down, in covered jar in refrigerator.

THE GREAT GREEN SALAD

The most popular salad of all is the tossed green salad. It can be economical of time and dishes and couldn't be easier to make or more wonderful to eat — as an accompaniment or as a course by itself. Here's our favorite:

HELEN'S TOSSED GREEN SALAD

Greens: one, two, or more, above	1 tablesp. tarragon wine, wine, malt,
1 clove garlic	or other vinegar;
Salt	or lemon juice
Whole black peppers	¼ cup salad oil

Early in day: Wash and drain greens. (A nice combination is iceberg or Boston lettuce, escarole, endive, and water cress.) Tear leaves (no tough centers, please!) into bite-size pieces —

about 2 qt. Dry well; wrap in towel; refrigerate in vegetable crisper.

When starting dinner: Get out roomy salad bowl. Cut tiny checkerboard pattern across top of garlic clove; then, right into bowl, cut off 2 or 3 thin slivers (this makes lots of tiny garlic bits). Add about ½ teasp. salt and generous grinding (¼ teasp.) of whole black peppers from pepper mill. Add bit of dry mustard, too, if you like.

With back of spoon, mash seasonings together (all that remains of garlic is delicate flavor). Into seasonings, with fork, stir vinegar, then salad oil. Place greens on top of dressing, *but don't toss.* Set salad bowl on top of pile of salad plates; refrigerate.

At salad-serving time, not before: Remove salad bowl and plates from refrigerator. Whisk them to table, and toss greens lightly. (Or toss salad in kitchen.) Every leaf should be coated, but not dripping, with dressing. Serve at once. Makes 4 to 6 servings.

GREEN SALAD EXTRAS

Just before tossing Helen's Tossed Green Salad, add one or more of these for color:

Apples (sticks or wedges)
Artichoke bottoms (canned)
Avocado (slivers)
Bacon (crispy bits)
Cauliflowerets (raw)
Celery (sliced diagonally)
Cheese, any kind (crumbled, grated, or slivered)
Chicken, ham, luncheon meat, salami, turkey, tongue, or franks (in thin strips)
Chives or scallions (snipped)
Cucumber (chunks or slices)
Eggs (chopped, hard-cooked)
Grapefruit, orange, or tangerine sections
Grapes
Mushrooms (raw caps or slices)
Olives (stuffed, green, or ripe)
Pineapple (fresh, canned, or frozen: in tidbits or chunks)
Potato chips or corn chips (coarsely broken)
Radishes (sliced or grated)
Sweet onions (sliced paper-thin)
Tomatoes (tiny wedges)
Tuna, sardines, shrimp, salmon, crab meat, lobster
Vegetables (cold cooked)
Walnuts, pecans, or almonds

DRESSING EXTRAS

When mixing dressing for Helen's Tossed Green Salad, add one or more of these:

Anchovy (cut-up fillets or paste)
Bottled thick meat sauce (a few dashes)
Cheese (crumbled Danish blue, or grated sharp or Parmesan)
Chili sauce (a little)
Curry powder (a pinch)
Horse-radish (a little)
Monosodium glutamate (a pinch)
Onion, celery, seasoned, or garlic salt (a sprinkling)
Onions (minced)
Paprika (a pinch)
Parsley, chervil, or tarragon (fresh or dried)
Pickles (chopped)
Seeds—poppy, dill, celery, caraway, sesame, or fennel (a sprinkling)
Tabasco or Worcestershire (a few dashes)

Other Ways to Toss Green Salad

1. To table, take cruet of favorite ready-to-use salad dressing, p. 468, and bowl of greens. Shake dressing; drizzle over greens (about 1 tablesp. per serving); toss. Or do all this in kitchen.
2. Or, to table, take bowl of greens and tray of favorite salad-dressing ingredients, p. 471. Over greens, drizzle about 1 tablesp. salad oil per person; add seasonings; toss gently. Then sprinkle lightly with vinegar or lemon juice (about one fourth to one third as much as oil used); toss again. Or do all this in kitchen.

SUPERB VEGETABLE SALADS

These vegetable salads go well with the main course. Or they may be served as a separate course, alone or with oven-toasted, buttered crackers; one of our Favorite Quick Breads, p. 475, or Breads and Rolls You Buy, p. 491; pretzels; assorted crisp crackers; or thin wheat, rye, or shredded-wheat crackers.

THE TOSSED VEGETABLE SALAD

For 4 hungry people, toss about 1 qt. torn, chilled salad greens with 3 cupfuls of 2 or more vegetables listed below. Add enough French dressing or Half-and-Half Mayonnaise, p. 469, to coat greens but not leave pool in bowl — about ¼ to ⅓ cup.

Add one or more extras, below, if you wish.

RAW VEGETABLES:

Beets (coarsely grated)
Broccoli or cauliflower (tiny buds)
Carrots (thinly slivered or coarsely grated)
Cucumbers (slices or cubes)
Green pepper (rings or cubes)
Leeks or scallions (slices)
Mushrooms (slices or cubes)
Onions (thinly sliced)
Parsnips (coarsely grated)
Radishes (sliced or grated)
Tomatoes (small wedges or cubes)
Turnips (slivers)
Zucchini (thinly sliced or grated)

COOKED VEGETABLES (fresh, frozen, or canned):

Artichoke hearts	Lentils
Asparagus (cut up)	Limas
Beans, green	Mixed vegetables
Carrots	Peas
Corn	Sweet or white potatoes, etc.
Hearts of palm	

Or use leftover cooked vegetables. (It's better to serve them cold than to reheat them — reheating robs them of more vitamins.)

EXTRAS:

Anchovies (3 or 4 cut-up fillets)
Bacon bits (crumbled crisp slices)
Blue cheese, Danish (to taste)
Capers (1 or 2 tablesp.)
Cheese (grated or slivered)
Dill pickle (small one, diced)
Eggs (chopped, hard-cooked)
Lemon rind (grated)
Nuts (broken up)
Olives (ripe, green, or stuffed)
Pickle relish (1 or 2 tablesp.)
Sardines (cut up)

MAX'S SPINACH-BACON SALAD BOWL

6 (yes, 6) cloves garlic, quartered	8 bacon slices
¾ cup French dressing	1 lb. crisp young spinach, well washed (2 qt.)
3 eggs	

About 2 hr. ahead:
1. Add garlic to French dressing. Hard-cook

eggs; shell them. Fry bacon over low heat till crisp, pouring off drippings; drain bacon on paper towel. Refrigerate all.

2. In salad bowl, tear spinach into pieces; refrigerate.

At serving time: Chop eggs; crumble bacon; sprinkle both over spinach. Remove garlic from French dressing; then pour it over salad; toss; serve at once. Makes 6 servings.

✤ FOR 18: Make as on p. 447, using 18 (yes, 18) cloves garlic, quartered; 2¼ cups French dressing; 9 eggs; 24 bacon slices; 3 lb. (6 qt.) crisp young spinach, well washed.

HARRIET'S SPECIAL TOSSED SALAD

1 clove garlic, peeled, sliced	1 medium head lettuce, washed
1 teasp. salt	1 bunch water cress, washed
2 tablesp. lemon juice	
¼ teasp. sugar	½ very ripe avocado, cut in pieces
¼ teasp. pepper	
⅛ teasp. celery seed	¾ cup very tiny raw cauliflowerets
½ teasp. paprika	
¾ teasp. dry mustard	1 medium tomato, peeled, sliced
5 tablesp. salad oil	
1 clove garlic, peeled	½ cup sliced, toasted, blanched almonds

In advance, if desired: Make this salad dressing: In small bowl, with spoon, mash sliced garlic with salt. Add lemon juice, sugar, pepper, celery seed, paprika, and mustard. Blend well, then add salad oil. Pour into small jar with cover; shake to blend well; refrigerate.

To make salad: Rub salad bowl well with clove of garlic. Be sure greens are dry. Tear lettuce and water cress into salad bowl. Add well-chilled avocado, cauliflowerets, and tomato. Just before serving, toss salad with nuts and dressing. Makes 4 servings.

To Vary: Add raw carrot slices, hard-cooked-egg slices, toasted hazelnuts, or bits of cheese.

SPINACH SALAD A LA GRECQUE

6 cups (about ⅔ lb.) washed, well-dried spinach, in bite-size pieces	sliced
	½ teasp. salt
	⅛ teasp. pepper
	1 cup commercial sour cream
1 small Bermuda onion, sliced	
¼ cup diced celery	1 pkg. garlic-cheese salad-dressing mix
4 hard-cooked eggs,	3 tablesp. lemon juice

Early in day:

1. In large bowl, combine spinach, onion, celery, eggs, salt, pepper; toss well; refrigerate.

2. In separate bowl, combine and mix well sour cream, salad-dressing mix, lemon juice; refrigerate.

At serving time:

1. Thoroughly toss half of sour-cream mixture with spinach mixture.

2. Serve salad immediately right from bowl, or arranged on salad plates. Makes 4 to 6 servings.

P.S. Refrigerate rest of sour-cream mixture to use on other salads during the week.

HI'S CAESAR SALAD

1 clove garlic	½ cup salad oil
¼ cup salad oil	1 tablesp. Worcestershire
2 cups ¼" fresh bread squares	
	¾ teasp. salt
1 large head each romaine and iceberg lettuce (3 qt. bite-size pieces)	¼ teasp. freshly ground black pepper
	1 egg
¼ cup grated Parmesan cheese	¼ cup lemon juice
	8 anchovies, cut up (optional)
¼ cup crumbled Danish blue cheese	

Early in day: Quarter garlic; drop into ¼ cup oil; set aside. Toast bread squares in shallow pan at 300°F. 20 min., or until golden, tossing often with fork. Tear lettuce into bite-size pieces into salad bowl. Refrigerate all.

Just before serving: Sprinkle greens with cheeses; drizzle on ½ cup salad oil mixed with Worcestershire, salt, pepper. Toss gently until every leaf glistens. Break whole raw egg onto greens; pour lemon juice over all; toss until egg specks disappear.

Now pour the ¼ cup oil you set aside (remove garlic) over bread squares; toss; sprinkle over greens. Add anchovies. Toss salad; serve at once. Makes 4 or 5 servings.

P.S. You may add a generous handful of coarsely broken pretzels, instead of croutons.

ROMAINE OR ENDIVE SALAD

Arrange chilled romaine or endive on salad plates. Top with radish, cucumber, or celery slices; snipped chives; or grated cheese. Then drizzle on dressing (see French Dressing Plus, p. 469).

COLONEL'S LADY'S SALAD BOWL

Mixed greens: let-
tuce, curly endive,
romaine, few mus-
tard greens, Bibb
lettuce
1½ large cucumbers,
thinly sliced
1½ green peppers,
cut into long strips
9 scallions (tops and
all), snipped
3 stalks celery, sliced
diagonally
3 tablesp. sugar

3 tablesp. snipped
parsley
1 teasp. monosodium
glutamate
1½ teasp. garlic salt
1½ teasp. salt
¾ teasp. orégano
½ teasp. coarsely
ground black pep-
per
¾ cup salad oil
½ cup wine vinegar
Boiling water
1½ 10-oz. pkg. fro-
zen green peas

Early in the day:
1. Wash greens under running water; shake
off excess water; tear enough into bite-size
pieces to make 6 qt.; refrigerate.
2. Prepare, then wrap cucumbers, green peppers, scallions, and celery in foil; refrigerate.
3. On piece of wax paper, thoroughly mix
sugar, parsley, monosodium glutamate, garlic
salt, salt, orégano, and black pepper. Set aside.
4. Into small bowl, measure salad oil, then
vinegar; refrigerate.
Just before serving:
1. Pour boiling water, to cover, over frozen
peas; then drain at once.
2. Sprinkle orégano mixture over greens,
cucumber mixture, and peas in large salad
bowl. With fork, beat up oil and vinegar; then
pour over greens. Toss gently until all are well
coated; then serve. Makes 12 servings.

WILTED LETTUCE

1 head Boston let-
tuce, in bite-size
pieces
¼ cup thinly sliced
scallions; or 2
tablesp. minced
onion
1 tablesp. snipped
fresh herbs
5 bacon slices, diced

¼ cup bacon fat
¼ cup vinegar
1 teasp. dry mustard
⅛ teasp. garlic salt
1½ teasp. sugar
¼ teasp. salt
¼ teasp. pepper
2 hard-cooked eggs,
chopped

In salad bowl, combine lettuce, scallions,
herbs. Fry bacon over low heat until crisp,
pouring off fat as it cooks. Drain bacon; add
to salad bowl. Return ¼ cup bacon fat to
skillet; add vinegar and rest of ingredients

except eggs. Bring to boil, stirring; pour over
salad; toss. Sprinkle with eggs. Serve at once.
Makes 4 servings.

WILTED CHINESE CABBAGE: For lettuce, substitute 1 medium head Chinese cabbage, thinly
sliced.

HOT WINTER SALAD: For lettuce, substitute 2
cups young spinach, in bits; 1 grated, pared
raw white turnip; and 2 grated, pared carrots.

GREEN GODDESS SALAD

⅓ cup Green God-
dess Dressing,
p. 470
1 qt. mixed greens,
in bite-size pieces
1 cup cooked cleaned

shrimp, or fresh, or
canned or thawed
frozen King-crab
meat, flaked,
drained (optional)
2 tomatoes, quartered

Add dressing to greens and shrimp; toss. Garnish with quartered tomatoes. Makes 4 servings.

STUFFED LETTUCE

1 head iceberg let-
tuce
1 cup grated process
Cheddar cheese
¼ cup mayonnaise or
salad dressing
¼ teasp. curry pow-
der

½ cup thinly slivered
cooked ham slices
⅓ cup finely cut
celery
1 pimento, diced
¼ cup snipped pars-
ley
French dressing

Day before:
1. Wash, drain lettuce. With sharp knife, at
core end of head, cut a circle which is 1"
from the core all the way around. Then continue cutting straight down to within ½" of
the top of the head. Now, with fingers and
knife, hollow out this circle as evenly as possible, reserving these cut-out lettuce pieces for
later use.
2. In bowl, combine cheese with mayonnaise
and curry until smooth. Into it stir ham, celery, pimento, and parsley.
3. Use to stuff the hollowed-out lettuce, packing the filling in firmly; refrigerate until
served.
At serving time next day: With long sharp
knife, cut lettuce head into crosswise slices 1"
thick. Serve slices on salad plates; don't forget
to pass French dressing. Makes 4 servings.

VEGETABLE-STUFFED LETTUCE: Have 1 8-oz.

pkg. cream cheese at room temperature. Combine it with 1 tablesp. milk until smooth; then add few drops Tabasco, 1½ teasp. horseradish, ¼ cup diced pimentos, ¼ cup snipped parsley, and 1 cup canned or cooked peas. Use to stuff 1 head iceberg lettuce, hollowed out as on p. 449.

CRUNCHY STUFFED LETTUCE: Have 1 8-oz. pkg. cream cheese at room temperature. Combine it with ¼ cup mayonnaise or salad dressing; then stir in ½ cup finely grated carrots, ½ cup finely grated radishes, and ¼ cup snipped chives. Use to stuff 1 head iceberg lettuce, hollowed out as on p. 449.

FRUIT-STUFFED LETTUCE: Have 1 8-oz. pkg. cream cheese at room temperature. Combine it with 1 tablesp. lemon juice until smooth. Then add 2 canned pineapple slices, cut into ½" pieces; ½ unpared red apple, in thin slices, and ½ cup coarsely broken walnuts. Use to stuff 1 head iceberg lettuce, hollowed out as on p. 449.

FRENCH MIMOSA SALAD

1 head Boston lettuce	4 hard-cooked eggs
3 tablesp. snipped parsley	French or Italian dressing

Arrange washed, chilled lettuce leaves in bowl or on individual plates; sprinkle with parsley. Press egg whites, then yolks, through sieve over salad. Pass dressing. Makes 4 to 6 servings.

HEARTS-OF-PALM BUFFET SALAD

3 large heads iceberg lettuce, in bite-size pieces	and cut into ¼" slices
2 avocados, peeled, diced	¼ cup vinegar
3 14-oz. cans hearts of palm, drained	¾ cup salad oil
	1 teasp. salt
	¼ teasp. pepper

In salad bowl, toss lettuce, avocados, hearts of palm. In another bowl, mix vinegar, salad oil, salt, pepper; pour over greens; toss well. Makes 15 servings.

CRISP ARTICHOKE SALAD: Substitute 1 1-lb. can artichoke hearts, drained, for hearts of palm; omit avocado.

CUCUMBERS IN SOUR CREAM

Pare, then thinly slice, 3 cucumbers. Add 1½ teasp. salt, ⅛ teasp. pepper, 3 tablesp. minced chives or onion, 1 cup commercial sour cream, and 2 tablesp. lemon juice. Refrigerate until served. Makes 4 to 6 servings.

STUFFED TOMATOES—THREE STYLES

Cut ¼" slice from stem end of each chilled, peeled tomato. With teaspoon, scoop out pulp from tomato, leaving cup (save pulp for sauce, stewed tomatoes, etc.). Or cut each tomato into 5 or 6 sections almost to stem end; spread apart slightly.

Sprinkle inside of each tomato cup well with salt; then fill with one of fillings below. Serve on salad greens.

Our Best Chicken Salad, p. 460	Green Beans Parmesan, p. 451
Chunky Egg Salad, p. 458	Shrimp Salad, p. 458
	Crunchy Tuna Salad, p. 456

EASY STUFFED TOMATOES: Cut ¼" slice from stem end of each chilled, peeled tomato. Halve crosswise; season. Firmly pack one of salads below into custard cups; unmold onto each tomato half. Or place green-pepper ring on each tomato half; fill with salad.

Best-Ever Macaroni Salad, p. 453	Chunky Egg Salad, p. 458

FAN-TANS: Allow 1 chilled, peeled tomato per serving. Slice tomatoes vertically (French way) not quite through. Fill space between slices with Best-Ever Macaroni Salad, p. 453; drained Cucumbers in Sour Cream, above; or roll of chilled process-cheese food, sliced ⅛" thick. Top with favorite dressing.

TOMATOES WITH SEA-FOOD DRESSING

1 cup deveined cooked shrimp	Pepper
2 hard-cooked eggs, chopped	½ cup mayonnaise
1½ cups shredded raw carrots	2 tablesp. lemon juice
1 tablesp. minced onion	½ teasp. prepared mustard
Salt	Lettuce
	3 or 4 large ripe tomatoes, peeled and sliced

1. Combine shrimp with eggs, carrots, and onion; season with salt, pepper.

2. Blend mayonnaise, lemon juice, and mustard; toss with shrimp.

3. On lettuce, on individual plates, arrange sliced tomatoes; heap with dressing. Makes 4 to 6 servings.

GUACAMOLE

In chopping bowl, chop 1 small onion, 1 small dried red pepper (optional), 1 tomato, fine. Add 6 peeled avocados, 2½ teasp. salt, 2 teasp. lemon juice, 2 tablesp. mayonnaise, 1 teasp. salad oil, 4 drops Tabasco. Chop fine (don't mash). Serve in bowl or on greens. Makes 8 servings.

FLOATING SALAD

In bowl, arrange layers of thinly sliced onions, green-pepper rings, thick tomato slices, and, if desired, thinly sliced cucumber. Sprinkle layers lightly with salt and freshly ground black pepper (or seasoned pepper). Cover with flavored vinegar (wine, herb, garlic, etc.) diluted with equal quantity of cold water; refrigerate. Serve floating in vinegar.

THREE-BEAN SALAD

1 1-lb. can French-cut green beans	½ cup minced onion
1 1-lb. can yellow wax beans	½ cup salad oil
1 1-lb. can red kidney beans	½ cup cider vinegar
½ cup minced green pepper	¾ cup granulated sugar
	1 teasp. salt
	½ teasp. pepper

Day before, if desired: Drain beans; place in glass bowl. Add green pepper and onion. Mix oil and vinegar with sugar, salt, pepper. Pour over bean mixture; toss. Refrigerate, covered, until served. Makes 10 servings.

GREEN BEANS PARMESAN

2 lb. green beans	¼ teasp. pepper
1 small onion, minced	½ cup grated Parmesan cheese
½ cup salad oil	
¼ cup wine vinegar	2 tablesp. chopped anchovies (optional)
1 teasp. salt	

Cut beans on angle into 2″ pieces; cook until tender as on p. 424. Drain; cool; toss with rest of ingredients. Refrigerate. Makes 6 to 8 servings.

FROSTED GREEN-BEAN SALAD: Omit Parmesan. Serve bean mixture topped with spoonfuls of Chunky Egg Salad, p. 458.

LIMA SUPPER SALAD: Substitute 2 10-oz. pkg. or 1 large-size pkg. cooled, cooked frozen Fordhook limas for green beans. Omit Parmesan and anchovies. Just before serving, toss in 5 crumbled crisp bacon slices. Serve on greens.

CRUNCHY KIDNEY-BEAN SALAD

1 1-lb. can kidney beans	2 tablesp. snipped scallions
½ cup diced celery	¼ to ⅓ cup mayonnaise
⅓ cup diced sweet pickles	3 tablesp. chili sauce
½ cup sliced stuffed olives	½ teasp. salt
	Crisp lettuce leaves

Day before: Get beans and other ingredients into refrigerator to chill.

To serve: Drain kidney beans; rinse in cold water; drain well. Combine beans with rest of ingredients except lettuce; mix thoroughly. Turn into wooden salad bowl; arrange lettuce along one side of bowl. Makes 6 servings.

CURRY-VEGETABLE SALAD

1⅓ cups packaged precooked rice or 1 cup regular or processed white rice	Salt
	⅛ teasp. pepper
	½ teasp. dry mustard
¼ cup French dressing	½ cup diced celery
¾ cup mayonnaise	½ cup thinly sliced radishes
1 tablesp. minced onion	½ cup thinly sliced raw cauliflowerets
¾ teasp. curry powder	1 cup cooked or canned peas
	Lettuce

Day before:

1. Cook rice as label directs. Lightly toss in French dressing; cool; refrigerate.

2. In bowl, blend mayonnaise with onion, curry powder, salt, pepper, mustard; refrigerate.

3. Prepare celery, radishes, cauliflowerets, and peas; refrigerate.

About 1 hr. before serving: In bowl, toss rice, celery, radishes, cauliflowerets, peas with mayonnaise mixture; refrigerate. Serve in lettuce-lined salad bowl. Pass extra dressing of equal parts mayonnaise and French dressing. Makes 6 servings.

CURRIED RICE AND PEA SALAD

1⅓ cups packaged precooked rice	powder
1½ cups water	½ teasp. salt
½ teasp. salt	⅛ teasp. pepper
¼ cup French dressing	½ teasp. dry mustard
¾ cup mayonnaise	1 cup diced celery
1 tablesp. minced onion	1⅓ cups chilled, cooked frozen green peas
¾ teasp. curry	Lettuce

In saucepan, combine rice, water, ½ teasp. salt; cook as label directs. Lightly toss in French dressing; let cool to room temperature; refrigerate.

About 1 hr. before serving: In large bowl, mix mayonnaise, onion, curry, ½ teasp. salt, pepper, mustard. Add celery, peas, and rice; lightly toss. Refrigerate. Serve on lettuce. Nice with sliced ham. Makes 6 servings.

MARINATED-VEGETABLE MELANGE

2 14½-oz. cans chicken broth	size pkg. frozen Fordhook limas, partially thawed and broken into chunks
2 bay leaves	
Salt	
Pepper	
½ lb. small white onions	2 cups bias slices of fresh asparagus, ½″ thick
4 cups thin, diagonal raw carrot slices	¼ cup olive oil
2 9-oz. or 1 large-size pkg. frozen whole green beans, partially thawed and broken into chunks	½ cup lemon juice
	½ teasp. dry mustard
	½ teasp. brown sugar
	1 clove garlic, minced
2 10-oz. or 1 large-	Snipped parsley (optional)

Early in the day:

1. In undiluted chicken broth, with bay leaves, 4 teasp. salt, and ½ teasp. pepper, in covered kettle, cook onions and carrots 5 min.
2. Now, on top of onions and carrots, place beans, next limas, then asparagus; sprinkle with 1 teasp. salt. Cover; bring to boil; boil 8 to 10 min., or till vegetables are tender-crisp. Now drain, and refrigerate.

3. Combine olive oil, lemon juice, mustard, brown sugar, garlic, ½ teasp. salt, ¼ teasp. pepper; refrigerate.

At serving time: Strain dressing if desired; then toss well with mixed vegetables and parsley. Makes 12 servings.

TWIN VEGETABLE SALAD

3⅓ cups drained cold cooked or canned peas	2 tablesp. finely snipped parsley
3½ cups drained cold cooked or canned green beans, French-style	½ teasp. salt
	½ teasp. seasoned salt
	⅛ teasp. freshly ground pepper
¾ cup mayonnaise	2 teasp. sugar
2 teasp. lemon juice	

1. In large bowl, combine peas and French-style beans.
2. In small bowl, combine mayonnaise, lemon juice, parsley, salt, seasoned salt, pepper, and sugar; blend well. Pour over vegetables; toss well; refrigerate.

Just before serving: Remove salad from refrigerator. Arrange on platter, with cold sliced meat, if desired. Makes 6 to 8 servings.

MORE VEGETABLE SALAD SPECIALS

Serve these on salad greens, with your favorite or suggested dressing.

TOMATO DECKERS: Between 2 tomato slices, place one of these, sandwich-fashion:

Susan's Coleslaw, p. 117, or Cottage-Cheese Salad, p. 459

Soft cream cheese, mixed with mashed avocado, then seasoned

Danish blue cheese or chive-cheese spread

TOMATO CART WHEELS: Cut thin slice from stem end of each peeled tomato. With small spoon hollow out tomato, leaving ribs of tomato intact. Fill with smoky-, bacon-, or pimento-cheese spread. Refrigerate overnight. Slice thick; place 2 slices on each bed of greens.

BROCCOLI: Top hot broccoli with Tarragon Sour-Cream Dressing, p. 470.

DANDELION GREEN: Heap chopped, cooked dandelion greens and scallions on tomato slices; pass Blue-Cheese French Dressing, p. 469.

GREEN BEAN WITH RADISH: Toss chilled, cooked or canned green beans or limas with minced onion and sliced radishes.

ZUCCHINI: Sprinkle chilled, cooked zucchini halves or slices with minced, hard-cooked eggs, then with favorite French dressing.

OKRA: Chill cooked okra pods; top with French dressing with a little horse-radish added.

SUPER-STUFFED CELERY: Prepare as on p. 147. Serve cut into ½″ slices.

MUSHROOM: Cut raw mushrooms into thin vertical slices; let stand in French dressing about 1 hr. Drain before serving. (Re-use dressing.)

ASPARAGUS: Top hot asparagus with Puff Sour-Cream Dressing, p. 470.

SCALLION-TOMATOES: Cover sliced, peeled or unpeeled tomatoes with thin scallions and stuffed or green olive or avocado slices. Sprinkle with salt, bit of dried basil; pour French dressing over all. Refrigerate. Drain before serving. (Save dressing to use again.) Nice with meat or fish.

GREEN LIMA AND APPLE: Toss chilled, cooked green limas with coarsely chopped, unpared red apples and French dressing.

MANERO'S ROQUEFORT: To mixed greens, add diced tomatoes and minced green pepper. Toss with French dressing. Grate ¼ lb. Roquefort cheese over all.

FAVORITE POTATO SALADS

POTATO SALAD HARBERT

2 lb. new potatoes	9 tablesp. mayonnaise
½ cup thinly sliced Bermuda onions	1½ teasp. salt
1 8-oz. carton chive cottage cheese	Freshly ground pepper
	Cayenne pepper

Prepare the day before:
1. Boil potatoes in jackets until tender; drain; peel; slice (there should be 4 cups). Place about one third of the potatoes in salad bowl. Cover with one third of onion rings, one third of chive cottage cheese, and 3 tablesp. mayonnaise.
2. Sprinkle with ½ teasp. salt, freshly ground pepper, a little cayenne. Arrange 2 more layers.
3. Immediately cover salad, then refrigerate 12 to 24 hr. Just before serving, toss well.
4. Nice guest supper, with sliced ham and turkey, spiced peaches, ripe olives, and pretzels. For dessert — spongecake layers filled and topped with chocolate whipped cream; tea or coffee. Makes 8 servings.

MADISON AVENUE POTATO SALAD

3 tablesp. salad oil	sliced
1 tablesp. wine vinegar	1 cup thinly sliced celery
1½ teasp. salt	½ cup diced dill pickles
⅛ teasp. pepper	¼ cup diced pimento
2 cups diced warm cooked potatoes	1 teasp. grated onion
½ cup quartered ripe olives	1 tablesp. prepared mustard
2 hard-cooked eggs,	⅓ cup mayonnaise

Blend together oil, vinegar, salt, and pepper; pour over potatoes; toss lightly; refrigerate. *At serving time:* Add olives, eggs, celery, dill pickles, pimento, onion, mustard, and mayonnaise; toss. Makes 6 servings.

OLD-FASHIONED POTATO SALAD

4 cups diced, cooked potatoes	1 cup mayonnaise
1½ cups sliced celery	1 tablesp. vinegar
½ cup cut-up scallions	2 teasp. prepared mustard
¼ cup sliced radishes	½ teasp. celery seeds
2 tablesp. snipped parsley	1½ to 2 teasp. salt
	⅛ teasp. pepper
	Lettuce

Several hr. ahead: Combine all ingredients but lettuce; refrigerate. Serve on lettuce; garnish with tomato or hard-cooked-egg wedges, sliced olives, grated carrots, or pickles. Makes 6 servings.

INDIVIDUAL STYLE: Press potato salad into custard cups; refrigerate. Then turn each cupful onto thick, peeled tomato slice.

BEST-EVER MACARONI: Substitute 4 cups cooked elbow macaroni (½ lb. uncooked) for potatoes; increase vinegar to 2 tablesp. You may substitute 1 cup slivered process Cheddar cheese for ½ cup celery.

BEST-EVER RICE: Substitute 4 cups cold cooked rice for potatoes.

DE LUXE POTATO OR MACARONI: For ½ cup celery, substitute ½ cup sliced green olives, diced pared cucumber, or diced green pepper; or 4 chopped hard-cooked eggs. Add 1 lb. franks, in chunks, if desired.

POTATO SALAD WITH SAUERKRAUT DRESSING

5 cups sliced, cooked potatoes	⅓ cup canned sauerkraut juice
1½ tablesp. chopped onion	⅓ teasp. salt
¼ cup chopped pimento	⅓ cup liquefied nonfat dry milk or skim milk
⅓ cup snipped parsley	⅓ cup mayonnaise

1. Combine potatoes, onion, pimento, parsley; refrigerate.
2. In small bowl, combine sauerkraut juice, salt, milk, mayonnaise; with hand beater or electric mixer, beat until smooth and well blended; refrigerate.
3. At serving time, pour dressing over potato mixture; toss gently. Makes 8 streamlined servings.

GERMAN HOT POTATO SALAD
(Warmer Kartoffelsalat)

2 lb. small white potatoes	¼ to ⅓ cup vinegar
Salt	½ cup water
½ cup diced bacon	¼ cup minced onion
½ cup minced onion	2 tablesp. snipped parsley
1½ teasp. flour	1 teasp. celery seeds
4 teasp. sugar	½ cup sliced radishes
¼ teasp. pepper	Celery leaves

1. In 1" boiling water, in covered saucepan, cook potatoes, in jackets, with 1 teasp. salt until fork-tender — about 35 min. Then peel and cut into ¼" slices.
2. In small skillet, fry bacon until crisp. Add ½ cup minced onion and sauté until just tender, not brown.
3. Meanwhile, in bowl, mix flour, sugar, 1 tablesp. salt, and pepper. Stir in vinegar (amount depends on tartness desired) and water until smooth. Add to bacon; then simmer, stirring, until slightly thickened.
4. Pour this hot dressing over potatoes. Add

¼ cup minced onion, parsley, celery seeds, and radishes.
5. Serve lightly tossed and garnished with celery leaves. Makes 4 to 6 servings.

HOT BAKED-POTATO SALAD

8 baking potatoes	¼ teasp. pepper
Salad oil	6 tablesp. vinegar
8 bacon slices	4 teasp. sugar
½ cup minced onions	½ cup minced green peppers
2 teasp. salt	

About 1¼ hr. ahead: Start heating oven to 400°F. Rub potatoes with salad oil; bake 1 hr., or till done. Meanwhile, fry bacon till crisp; drain; crumble. Measure bacon fat (add salad oil to make ⅔ cup); return to skillet; add onions, salt, pepper, vinegar, sugar; heat.

Cut thin slice from top of each baked potato; scoop out centers; blend them with vinegar mixture, green peppers, bacon. Stuff back into potato shells. Makes 8 servings.

COLESLAW SALADS

SWEET-AND-SOUR COLESLAW

½ large head, or 1 medium head, green cabbage	2 tablesp. sugar
	⅓ cup vinegar
7 bacon slices	⅓ cup water
2 eggs	3 tablesp. bacon fat
1 teasp. salt	⅓ cup heavy cream

In advance: Finely shred 5 cups cabbage; wrap in foil; refrigerate.
About ½ hr. before serving:
1. Sauté bacon over low heat until crisp and brown. Drain, saving bacon fat; crumble or dice bacon and keep warm.
2. In double-boiler top, beat eggs, salt, sugar, vinegar, water until blended. Place over hot, *not boiling,* water. Add bacon fat, while stirring constantly with wire whip or rubber spatula until mixture thickens; do not boil. Cool until lukewarm; stir in cream; refrigerate.
3. Meanwhile, toss cabbage with bacon, reserving a few bits as garnish. Stir up dressing;

pour over cabbage; toss; sprinkle with bacon; serve at once. Makes 4 servings.

SOUR-CREAM SLAW

1 large head crisp green cabbage	1 cup commercial sour cream
Minced onion	½ teasp. sugar
⅔ cup diced celery	3 teasp. salt
⅔ cup slivered green pepper	2 tablesp. tarragon vinegar
⅔ cup coarsely grated carrots	Fresh or canned pineapple spears
½ cup sliced radishes	Large stuffed olives
	Large ripe olives

Early in the day, if desired:
1. Remove several shapely leaves from cabbage head and refrigerate; from rest prepare 8 cups finely shredded cabbage.
2. In large bowl, combine finely shredded cabbage, 2 tablesp. minced onion, diced celery, slivered green pepper, coarsely grated carrots, and sliced radishes; refrigerate.
3. In small bowl, combine commercial sour cream, 2 teasp. minced onion, sugar, salt, and vinegar; cover; refrigerate.
Just before serving:
1. Pour sour-cream dressing over cabbage mixture; toss lightly until cabbage is well coated with dressing.
2. Line a large salad bowl with cabbage leaves. Heap cabbage mixture in center; then garnish the top with pineapple spears and with stuffed and ripe olives. Makes 8 to 10 servings.

HUNGARIAN SWEET-SOUR RED CABBAGE
(Vörös Káposzta Saláta)

½ medium head red cabbage, finely shredded	½ cup water
1 tablesp. salt	¼ cup granulated sugar
½ cup vinegar	¼ teasp. pepper

Several hr. before serving:
1. In large bowl, sprinkle cabbage with salt; let stand ½ hr.
2. In saucepan, combine vinegar, water, sugar, pepper; bring to boil; pour over cabbage.
3. Refrigerate until serving time; drain. Good with pot roast or pork. Makes 4 servings.

SLAW SAVOY

Carefully hollow out a handsome head of savoy cabbage. Finely shred the center cabbage; then toss it with apple wedges, Swiss-cheese slivers, and mustard-mayonnaise. Present in the curly cabbage shell.

GREEN PEA SLAW

3 to 4 tablesp. mayonnaise	cabbage
3 tablesp. French dressing	1 8-oz. can peas, drained
3 cup finely shredded green or Chinese	1 1-lb. can pickled beets, chilled

1. *About 40 min. before dinner:* Stir mayonnaise with French dressing *until blended.* Toss with cabbage until well coated; toss in peas. Refrigerate.
2. To serve, arrange slaw down one side of platter, well-drained beets down other. Makes 2 servings.
✤ FOR A FOURSOME: Use 1 or 2 cans of beets and double rest of ingredients.

TOMATO COLESLAW

4 cups finely shredded cabbage	⅓ cup white vinegar
½ green pepper, chopped	2 tomatoes, quartered
1 tablesp. chopped pimento	1 teasp. salt
1 teasp. grated onion	¼ teasp. pepper
3 tablesp. salad oil	½ teasp. dry mustard
	1 teasp. celery salt
	2 tablesp. granulated sugar

Combine cabbage, green pepper, pimento, onion, salad oil, vinegar, and tomatoes. Refrigerate.
To serve, toss with salt, pepper, mustard, celery salt, and sugar. Makes 4 servings.

RADISH SLAW

5¼ cups coarsely grated cabbage	½ cup mayonnaise
⅓ cup chopped onion	1½ tablesp. light cream
½ cup chopped celery	1 tablesp. lemon juice
½ cup chopped green pepper	⅛ teasp. pepper
¾ cup sliced radishes	1½ teasp. sugar
	¾ teasp. salt

Early in the day, if desired:
1. In large bowl, combine cabbage, onion, celery, green pepper, and radishes.

2. In small bowl, combine mayonnaise, light cream, lemon juice, pepper, sugar, salt. Pour over cabbage; toss. Cover; then refrigerate till served. Makes 6 servings.

APPLE COLESLAW

4 cups shredded green cabbage	½ cup mayonnaise
½ cup diced unpared red apples	¾ teasp. salt
	Speck pepper
	Dash paprika
¼ cup broken walnut meats	½ teasp. sugar
	1 tablesp. vinegar
½ cup dark raisins	1 tablesp. milk

Toss cabbage with apples, nuts, and raisins; refrigerate.

In small bowl, combine mayonnaise, salt, pepper, paprika, sugar, vinegar, and milk; refrigerate. When ready to serve, pour dressing over cabbage; toss.

Serve in cabbage-leaf-lined salad bowl. Makes 6 servings.

CREAMY CELERY SLAW

1 teasp. salt	¼ cup commercial sour cream
1½ teasp. sugar	
⅛ teasp. pepper	2 cups celery, thinly sliced on diagonal
Dash paprika	
⅓ cup salad oil	1 pimento, slivered
2 tablesp. wine vinegar	

1. Combine salt, sugar, pepper, paprika, oil, and vinegar; with hand beater, beat well; then slowly beat in sour cream.
2. Pour this dressing over celery. Marinate in refrigerator about 3 hr.; then toss in pimento. Makes 3 servings.

CARAWAY COLESLAW: Substitute 2 cups finely shredded cabbage for celery. Omit pimento. Add ½ teasp. caraway seeds.

DUTCH CAULIFLOWER SLAW

1 small head crisp cauliflower	1½ teasp. salt
	1 teasp. sugar
4 bacon slices	¼ teasp. paprika
¼ cup salad oil	Lettuce
¼ cup vinegar	

Trim and core cauliflower; then slice it very thinly crosswise. Sauté bacon until crisp; remove; drain; crumble. To bacon drippings add salad oil, vinegar, salt, sugar, and paprika; pour over cauliflower; refrigerate 3 hr.; toss often.

Serve on lettuce with bacon garnish. Makes 8 servings.

SALADS THAT MAKE A MEAL

Hearty salads such as the ones that follow can be the main dish of a luncheon, supper, or hot-weather dinner. Make servings generous. With them, you may serve such hot breads as those in Favorite Quick Breads, p. 475, or Breads and Rolls You Buy, p. 491. Or serve with a sandwich.

CRUNCHY TUNA SALAD

¼ cup mayonnaise	½ cup sliced celery
2 tablesp. diced sweet pickle	½ cup chilled cooked or canned peas
1 tablesp. pickle juice	1 cup coarsely crushed corn or potato chips
1 cup canned tuna or salmon, or cut-up cooked or canned chicken or turkey	
	Salad greens

Toss mayonnaise with pickle, pickle juice, tuna, celery, peas. Add chips.

Serve at once on greens. Makes 4 servings.

CHEF SALAD, SKILLET STYLE

¼ cup salad oil or fat	6 hot hard-cooked eggs, shelled, quartered
1½ tablesp. flour	
1 teasp. salt	
1 teasp. garlic salt	2 celery stalks, sliced
1 teasp. onion salt	2 heads romaine, in bite-size pieces
⅛ teasp. pepper	
1 tablesp. sugar	1 cucumber, pared, thinly sliced, then halved
1 teasp. prepared mustard	
1 cup water	½ lb. natural Swiss-cheese slices, in strips ½″ wide
⅓ cup vinegar	
⅓ lb. soft salami, in ¼″ slices	
	2 tomatoes, sliced, halved
2 cups cooked or canned chicken, in ½″ strips	

1. In 11″ or 12″ skillet, heat salad oil; remove from heat; then stir in flour, salt, garlic and onion salts, pepper, sugar, mustard, water,

and vinegar until smooth. Cook over low heat, stirring, until thickened.

2. Now, in skillet, place salami, cut into strips, and chicken; heat. Then, on top, arrange layer each of eggs, celery, romaine, cucumber, Swiss cheese, and tomatoes, repeating until all are used.

3. Remove from heat; toss gently. Serve immediately for lunch with popovers, a mug of hot frozen potato soup, and brownie squares topped with chocolate ice cream. Makes 6 servings.

CHEF'S SALAD BOWLS

Make Helen's Tossed Green Salad, p. 446. After placing greens in salad bowl, top with one of the following chef combinations. Toss well just before serving. Makes 4 to 6 servings.

TONGUE AND CHEESE: Use 6 slivered slices canned tongue, corned beef, or luncheon meat; 1/4 lb. slivered Swiss cheese; 2 sliced, hard-cooked eggs; 1/2 cup sliced cucumbers; 2 coarsely grated carrots or 1/2 cup radish slices; and 1 medium onion, thinly sliced. Makes 4 servings. Sharp-Cream Mayonnaise, p. 469, may replace dressing.

SALAMI AND BOLOGNA: Use 1/4 lb. each slivered salami and bologna; 1/4 lb. coarsely grated process Cheddar cheese; and 1/2 cup tiny raw cauliflowerets or 2 chilled, peeled tomatoes, cut into strips.

CHICKEN AND HAM: Use 1/2 cup slivered, cooked or canned chicken or turkey; 1/2 cup cooked-ham strips; 2/3 cup slivered Swiss cheese; and 1 sliced hard-cooked egg or 1 cup cooked green limas.

HAM CLUB: Use 1 cup diced, peeled avocado; 1 cup diced tomatoes; 1 cup thinly sliced cucumbers; and 1 1/2 cups diced, cooked ham.

BRAZIL-NUT CRAB SALAD

2 6-oz. pkg. frozen King-crab meat, thawed and *well drained*	nuts
	1/4 cup chili sauce
1 cup sliced celery	2/3 cup mayonnaise
1 cup sliced Brazil	8 tablesp. lemon juice
	1/2 teasp. salt
	2 avocados

1. In medium bowl, combine crab meat, celery, and nuts.

2. In small bowl, mix chili sauce, mayonnaise,

2 tablesp. lemon juice, salt. Pour over crab; toss; refrigerate.

3. At serving time, skin, pit, and slice avocados; dip into 6 tablesp. lemon juice. Arrange crab salad on serving dish; garnish with avocados. Makes 6 servings.

LOBSTER-ARTICHOKE SALAD

4 cups cooked rock-lobster-tail meat, in chunks	3 tablesp. vinegar
	Salt
	1/4 teasp. white pepper
2 1/2 cups diced cooked potatoes	1 1/2 cups mayonnaise
2 cups quartered canned artichoke hearts	1 teasp. dried tarragon
	2 tablesp. chili sauce
1 cup minced dill pickle	1/2 teasp. dry mustard
1/4 cup white wine	2 teasp. chopped pitted ripe or green olives or truffles
6 tablesp. salad oil	

1. In large bowl, toss lobster meat, potatoes, artichokes, and pickle.

2. Combine wine, oil, vinegar, 1 teasp. salt, and pepper; pour over lobster mixture; refrigerate 1 hr. Then remove from refrigerator; drain off oil mixture.

3. Combine mayonnaise, tarragon, chili sauce, mustard, 1/2 teasp. salt. Pour over lobster; toss; refrigerate.

4. At serving time, garnish with ripe or green olives or truffles. Makes 6 servings.

CURRIED SEA-FOOD SALAD

1 6 1/2- or 7-oz. can tuna	1/2 cup chopped celery
1 cup deveined cooked or canned shrimp	1/2 cup cut-up ripe or stuffed olives
1/2 cup mayonnaise or cooked salad dressing	3 cups cold cooked rice
	2 or 3 tablesp. French dressing
2 tablesp. lemon juice	1/2 cup snipped parsley
1 teasp. curry powder	

Early in the day:

1. Drain tuna well.

2. In large bowl, combine tuna, in chunks, and shrimp (or use all tuna if you like). Cover with foil; then refrigerate till well chilled.

Just before serving:

1. In small bowl, blend mayonnaise, lemon juice, curry.
2. To tuna and shrimp mixture, add chopped celery and ¼ cup cut-up ripe olives; pour curried mayonnaise over all and toss.
3. Toss cold cooked rice with French dressing and snipped parsley. Spoon it onto serving platter; heap sea-food mixture on top. Sprinkle sea food with rest of cut-up ripe olives (¼ cup); serve. Makes 4 to 6 servings.

CURRIED CHICKEN SALAD: Make as on p. 457, substituting 2 cups cooked or canned chicken or turkey chunks for tuna and shrimp. Add ¼ cup chutney to mayonnaise.

CURRIED SHRIMP SALAD: Make as on p. 457, substituting shrimp for tuna and reducing rice to 2 cups.

CURRIED CRAB-MEAT SALAD: Make as on p. 457, substituting 2 cups *well-drained* canned or thawed frozen King-crab-meat chunks or cooked rock-lobster-meat chunks for tuna and shrimp.

SHRIMP SALAD

1⅛ lb. cooked, cleaned shrimp (1½ cups)	½ teasp. minced onion
1 cup sliced celery	½ cup mayonnaise
½ cup chopped walnuts (optional)	¼ cup French dressing
¼ cup sliced stuffed olives	Salt and lemon juice to taste
	Salad greens

Combine all ingredients but greens; refrigerate a short time. Serve on greens. Makes 4 servings.

Or serve with:

Tomato Aspic, p. 463, in 1¼-qt. ring mold (heap salad in center)

Pineapple slices (arrange salad between split slices)

Peach halves (fill fresh or canned halves with salad)

Jellied cranberry sauce (slice or spoon out as salad garnish)

Avocado halves (sprinkle with lemon juice, salt; fill with salad)

Tomato slices (arrange salad between slices)

Asparagus (heap salad on 3 or 4 cold cooked asparagus tips)

PINEAPPLE-SHRIMP: Use cooked, cleaned shrimp, split lengthwise. Substitute 1 cup fresh, frozen, or canned pineapple chunks for celery. Omit nuts.

LOBSTER OR CRAB MEAT: Substitute 1½ cups cooked or canned lobster or *well-drained* crab-meat chunks for shrimp.

TUNA: Substitute 2 6½- or 7-oz. cans drained tuna (2 cups) for shrimp.

SALMON: Substitute 1 1-lb. can salmon (2 cups), in chunks, for shrimp; substitute 2 shelled hard-cooked eggs, in large pieces, for nuts.

FIRST-COURSE SEA FOOD: Make salad servings small. Pass crisp crackers if you wish.

SHRIMP SALAD NEW ORLEANS

1 cup cold cooked rice	2 tablesp. French dressing
¾ lb. cooked, cleaned shrimp, cut up (1 cup)	1 tablesp. chopped stuffed olives
¾ teasp. salt	¾ cup diced raw cauliflower
1 tablesp. lemon juice	Speck pepper
¼ cup slivered green pepper	⅓ cup mayonnaise or cooked salad dressing
1 tablesp. minced scallions or onion	Lettuce

Toss together all ingredients but lettuce. Serve on lettuce. Makes 4 servings.

CHUNKY EGG SALAD

6 hard-cooked eggs	½ teasp. Worcestershire
1 cup sliced celery	Dash Tabasco
2 tablesp. minced green pepper	1 tablesp. vinegar
1 teasp. minced onion	1 teasp. salt
¼ cup mayonnaise	⅛ teasp. pepper
	Salad greens

Cut shelled eggs into big pieces; add rest of ingredients except greens; refrigerate. Serve on greens. Makes 6 servings.

BACON AND EGG: Add 3 crumbled crisp bacon slices or coarsely grated franks and 2 chopped stuffed olives. Serve on thick tomato slices.

KELLY'S BAKED BEAN AND EGG: Add 1 1-lb-4-oz. can Boston-style baked beans, drained. Reduce mayonnaise to 1 tablesp. Add 1 tablesp. chili sauce. Garnish with 4 sliced franks, sautéed in 1 tablesp. salad oil.

COAST STYLE: For 3 hard-cooked eggs, substitute 1 6½- or 7-oz. can tuna (1 cup) and 4 crumbled crisp bacon slices or 1 cup diced, cooked ham.

ZIPPY HOT EGG SALAD

6 hot hard-cooked eggs	1 tablesp. snipped parsley
¼ teasp. salt	¼ cup mayonnaise
⅛ teasp. pepper	2 tablesp. catchup or chili sauce
3 tablesp. snipped scallions	1 teasp. prepared mustard

Into warm bowl, slice shelled eggs. Toss with salt, pepper, scallions, parsley. Then toss with combined mayonnaise, catchup, mustard.

Serve on lettuce, on hot buttered, toasted, split rolls or toast. Makes 3 or 4 servings.

DIFFERENT EGG SALAD

1 1-lb.-4-oz. can baked beans	1 teasp. prepared mustard
4 hard-cooked eggs, coarsely chopped	¼ teasp. salt
½ cup minced onion	Dash pepper
1 tablesp. chili sauce	3 slices crumbled crisp bacon
1 tablesp. mayonnaise	3 tablesp. snipped parsley

Drain beans; add eggs and onions. Toss in combined chili sauce, mayonnaise, mustard, salt, and pepper. Serve in chilled salad bowl; sprinkle with bacon and parsley. Makes 4 servings.

COTTAGE-CHEESE SALAD

To ⅔ cup chilled cottage cheese, add one or more of these:

Celery or caraway seeds
Pickle relish or chili sauce
Minced dill pickle or horse-radish
Minced chives, scallions, or onion
Chopped celery, olives, or nuts
Cut-up radishes or tomatoes
Grated raw carrots
Mayonnaise or French dressing
Commercial sour cream or cream

Heap cottage-cheese mixture in a lettuce cup. Or heap in hollowed-out tomato (you may first spread inside of tomato with deviled ham). Or press into wet custard cup; invert onto greens. Top with French dressing. Makes 1 serving.

GREEN-GOLD PORK SALAD

2 cups diced cold roast pork	⅓ cup tiny white cocktail onions
1½ cups cooked peas	¼ cup mayonnaise or salad dressing
⅔ cup coarsely grated process Cheddar cheese	1 teasp. salt
	1 pimento, diced
	Lettuce

Combine pork with peas, cheese, cocktail onions, mayonnaise, salt, and pimento; toss; refrigerate. Serve on lettuce. Makes 6 servings.

ROAST-BEEF HEARTY PARTY SALAD

1 9-oz. pkg. frozen green beans, French-style	⅛ teasp. dried parsley flakes
1 10-oz. pkg. frozen lima beans	⅛ teasp. dried mint
½ lb. small white turnips	⅛ teasp. dried orégano
1 8¼-oz. can whole tiny carrots	½ cup Italian dressing
	3 lb. sirloin tip roast
	2-qt. salad or punch bowl

Day before, if desired, or early on the day:
1. Cook green beans and limas as labels direct, until just tender-crisp; drain. Prepare turnips (or small potatoes if you prefer), cutting them into quarters or sixths; cook until tender, then drain.
2. Toss together drained green beans, limas, turnips, and carrots. Sprinkle with parsley, mint, and orégano; pour on half of Italian dressing, then toss well. Cover with foil or saran and refrigerate.
3. In 325°F. oven, roast meat, on rack, to desired degree of doneness, using a roast-meat thermometer. When done, cool in pan; wrap well in foil and refrigerate until next day.
About 20 min. before serving:
1. Slice roast beef. Then use slightly overlapping slices to go around inside of bowl (preferably a glass one), placing them so they overhang about 1" at the top. Any extra roast-beef slices may be arranged on a platter and served "from the side."

2. Now heap marinated vegetables in bowl, piling them high in the center.

3. Serve, passing rest of Italian dressing in a pitcher.

Nice with a crisp bread and chilled radishes. For dessert we suggest grapes or other favorite fresh fruit and iced coffee.

♣ FOR 8 SERVINGS: Double all ingredients but sirloin tip roast; for it use 4-lb. roast.

OUR BEST CHICKEN SALAD
(or turkey)

4 to 5 cups cooked chicken or turkey chunks	¼ cup light cream
	⅔ cup mayonnaise or cooked salad dressing
2 teasp. grated onion	
1 cup celery, cut on angle	1 teasp. salt
	⅛ teasp. pepper
1 cup minced green peppers	2 tablesp. vinegar
	Salad greens

Combine chicken, onion, celery, peppers. Mix cream with mayonnaise, salt, pepper, vinegar; toss with chicken. Refrigerate till served.

To serve: Arrange salad on greens on chop plate. Makes 6 to 8 servings.

Circle with your choice of these if desired:

Asparagus tips	Seeded or seedless grapes
Avocado slices	
Cheese-stuffed celery	Ripe and stuffed olives
Spoonfuls of cranberry jelly	Pickled peaches
	Pineapple chunks
Sliced hard-cooked eggs	Spiced prunes

Or sprinkle with one of these:

Slivered almonds	Snipped parsley
Water cress or dill	Walnuts
Snipped mint	

EXOTIC CHICKEN: Add ⅔ cup slivered, toasted almonds or chopped pecans. Also add 2 cups halved, seeded green grapes or orange sections.

NEW CHICKEN: Omit celery, green peppers. Add 2 cups diced cucumbers, 1 cup drained canned pineapple tidbits. Top with ripe olives.

HAM AND CHICKEN: Substitute 2 cups cut-up cooked ham for 2 cups chicken. Add 1 to 2 cups fresh or drained canned pineapple chunks.

TOP HAT: Arrange chicken salad on canned pineapple slices.

WALDORF: Add 2 cups diced unpared red apples and ⅔ cup chopped walnuts or peanuts.

GLADYS': In 2 teasp. butter, sauté ½ cup broken walnuts with pinch salt 3 or 4 min., or until crisp. Cool. Add to chicken.

HAM, VEAL, OR LAMB: Halve ingredients, substituting 2 cups cut-up cooked ham, veal, or lamb for chicken. Makes 3 or 4 servings.

VIRGINIA CHICKEN-APPLE SALAD

5 cups cooked chicken chunks	⅓ cup salad dressing
	½ cup heavy cream, whipped
2 cups unpared, cubed apples	
	2 teasp. salt
Lemon juice	Bibb lettuce
2 cups sliced celery	Curly chicory
⅔ cup sliced stuffed olives	Unpared, cored apple rings, wedges
½ cup slivered almonds	

1. Combine chicken, cubed apples (dipped in and out of ½ cup lemon juice), celery, olives, almonds. Blend dressing, whipped cream, 2 tablesp. lemon juice, salt. Toss with chicken; refrigerate.

2. At serving time, heap salad on bed of lettuce and chicory. Dip apple rings and wedges in lemon juice, lay rings around salad, wedges on top. Tuck chicory in each ring and on top of salad. Makes 8 to 10 servings.

NEW ORLEANS STYLE: Garnish salad with olives, capers, and hard-cooked eggs.

TEXAS STYLE: Serve salad in balls, rolled in snipped parsley and nested in lettuce.

MAINE STYLE: Add chopped hard-cooked eggs and prepared mustard to taste.

GOURMET CHICKEN SALAD

½ cup mayonnaise	4 large thick pieces of cold cooked chicken or turkey
1 tablesp. lemon juice	
¼ teasp. salt	
⅛ teasp. pepper	Greens
2 tablesp. heavy cream	Tomato slices
	Cucumber slices
⅛ teasp. dried marjoram	Snipped parsley

Mix mayonnaise with lemon juice, salt, pepper, cream, and marjoram. Use to coat pieces of chicken.

Serve on greens, garnished with tomato and cucumber slices and snipped parsley. Makes 2 to 4 servings, depending on size of chicken pieces.

HOT BAKED CHICKEN SALAD

Start heating oven to 450°F. Toss 1½ cups cut-up, cooked (or 2 5-oz. cans) chicken or turkey with 1½ cups sliced celery, ½ cup chopped walnuts, ½ teasp. salt, dash pepper, 2 teasp. minced onion, 2 tablesp. lemon juice, ¾ cup mayonnaise. Heap in 4 individual baking dishes or 1 deep 9" pie plate. Sprinkle with 1 cup crushed potato chips. Bake 15 min., or until light brown. Makes 4 servings.

MANDARIN CHICKEN SALAD

2 or 3 cups cut-up cooked chicken
1 tablesp. minced onion
1 teasp. salt
2 tablesp. lemon juice
1 cup thinly sliced celery
1 cup seedless grapes
⅓ cup mayonnaise
or cooked salad dressing
1 11-oz. can Mandarin orange segments, drained, or 1 cup tangerine sections
½ cup toasted, slivered almonds
6 to 8 lettuce leaves
6 pitted ripe olives

1. In bowl, combine chicken, onion, salt, lemon juice, celery; refrigerate several hr., or until well chilled.
2. At serving time, toss chicken mixture lightly with grapes, mayonnaise, and all but a few orange segments and almonds.
3. Line salad bowl with lettuce leaves. Arrange chicken mixture on top; garnish with reserved orange segments and almonds, and ripe olives. Makes 6 servings.

DILLED TONGUE SALAD

1 9-oz. jar beef tongue, well chilled
3 hard-cooked eggs, chilled, coarsely chopped
2 scallions, snipped
1 large dill pickle, chopped
½ teasp. prepared mustard
1 tablesp. lemon juice
½ cup mayonnaise or salad dressing
¼ teasp. paprika
½ teasp. Worcestershire
Lettuce leaves
Fresh dill, snipped

1. *About 1 hr. before serving:* Cut tongue into ½" pieces, discarding fat and skin. In bowl, toss tongue with eggs, scallions, and pickle.
2. In small bowl, mix mustard and lemon juice; stir in mayonnaise, then paprika, Worcestershire; blend well. Toss with tongue mixture; refrigerate till well chilled.
3. To serve, arrange tongue salad in lettuce-lined bowl. Sprinkle with snipped dill. Makes 2 servings.

Serve with hot corn on the cob, bread sticks, and pear pie with Camembert-cheese wedges.

CHICKEN FRUIT BUFFET

Add 1 cup slivered, toasted almonds to Our Best Chicken Salad, p. 460. Arrange on half of large serving dish. On other half, arrange chilled honeydew-melon strips, grapefruit and orange sections, and balls made from chilled canned jellied cranberry sauce.

Or serve chicken salad in avocado or canned-peach halves. Makes 8 servings.

PEAS AND RICE PROVENCALE

5 cups hot cooked rice
2 tablesp. butter
2 tablesp. salad oil
1¼ cups chopped onion
1 clove garlic, crushed
1 cup large stuffed olives, sliced ¼" thick
½ cup chopped pi-
mentos
3½ cups drained canned or cooked peas
1 8-oz. can water chestnuts, sliced ⅛" thick
1½ teasp. seasoned salt
8 scallions
16 large salami slices

Early in the day:
1. To hot cooked rice, add butter; cool.
2. In salad oil, in skillet, sauté onion and garlic till tender; stir in olive slices.
3. In large bowl, combine rice, pimentos, peas, onion mixture, water chestnuts, and seasoned salt; toss well. Cover, refrigerate.
4. Clean scallions, leaving on 5" of green top. With small knife, starting at top of white part, split each green top leaf lengthwise 2 or 3 times to give fringed effect; refrigerate in pitcher of cold water.

Just before serving: Toss rice mixture well, heap in large serving bowl. Fold 1 salami slice around a scallion, leaving fringe free; then tuck into edge of salad. Repeat with rest of scallions — use to encircle salad. Pass remaining salami slices on small platter. Makes 8 servings.

MOLDED SALADS

It's so nice to have your salad prepared in advance, all ready to unmold and serve.

JEWEL-TONED HAM-SALAD MOLD

1 env. unflavored gelatine	2 tablesp. pickle relish
1/4 cup cold water	2 tablesp. mayonnaise
3/4 cup boiling water	2 1/4 cups shredded cabbage
2 teasp. minced onion	
1/2 teasp. salt	1 tablesp. diced pimento
1 teasp. horse-radish	
1/2 cup canned pineapple juice	1 1/2 cups ground, cooked ham
	Salad greens

1. *Early the day before:* Sprinkle gelatine over cold water in glass measuring cup to soften. Add boiling water; stir until dissolved. Refrigerate.
2. When gelatine is *slightly* thickened, add onion, salt, horse-radish, pineapple juice, pickle relish, mayonnaise.
3. Divide gelatine mixture in half. To one half, add cabbage, pimento; mix well; pour into 1-qt. mold. Refrigerate until set.
4. To other half of gelatine, add ham; mix thoroughly; spoon over cabbage mixture in mold. Refrigerate until needed.
5. *To serve:* Unmold and serve on salad greens with Cream-Cheese Dressing, p. 470.

FRUITED APRICOT MOLD

1 3-oz. pkg. orange-flavor gelatin	3 oranges, sectioned
1 env. unflavored gelatine	1 1-lb.-4 1/2-oz. can pineapple chunks
2 tablesp. sugar	1 1-lb.-1-oz. can spiced grapes, drained
3/4 cup water	Boston lettuce
1 12-oz. can apricot nectar	1 8-oz. pkg. cream cheese
2 tablesp. lemon juice	

Day before:
1. In saucepan, combine orange gelatin, unflavored gelatine, and sugar.

2. Stir in water and apricot nectar; heat over low heat, stirring, until the gelatins have been completely dissolved. Add lemon juice; refrigerate.
3. In bottom of 2-qt. ring mold, arrange oranges. Sprinkle with drained pineapple chunks (reserve syrup) and grapes. Pour on apricot-gelatin mixture; refrigerate overnight.
Fifteen minutes before serving:
1. Quickly dip mold in and out of hot water up to 1/2" of top. Invert serving dish on top; invert both; gently shake till salad slips out; lift off mold. Garnish with lettuce.
2. With mixer, beat cream cheese till soft; beat in enough pineapple syrup to make of dressing consistency. Serve over salad. Nice with deviled-ham fan-tans and milk shakes. Makes 6 servings.

MOLDED GRAPE SUPREME

1 env. unflavored gelatine	3 tablesp. lemon juice
1/4 cup cold water	3/4 cup halved seedless grapes
1 cup boiling water	
1/3 cup granulated sugar	2 medium bananas, diced
Dash salt	1/4 cup chopped walnuts
1 6-oz. can frozen grape-juice concentrate	Salad greens

Day before: Sprinkle gelatine over cold water to soften. Add boiling water, sugar, salt; stir until dissolved. Stir in grape juice, lemon juice. Refrigerate until partially thickened. Fold in fruits, nuts. Pour into 6 individual molds. Refrigerate until firm enough to unmold. Serve as dessert salad on greens, plain or with Half-and-Half Sour-Cream Dressing, p. 470. Make 6 servings.

COLESLAW SOUFFLE SALAD

1 cup hot water	2 cups finely chopped cabbage
1 3-oz. pkg. lemon-flavor gelatin	2 tablesp. minced green pepper
1/2 cup cold water	
2 tablesp. vinegar	1 tablesp. minced onion
1/2 cup mayonnaise	
1/4 teasp. salt	1/4 teasp. celery seeds
Dash pepper	Salad greens

Pour hot water over gelatin; stir until dissolved. Add water, vinegar, mayonnaise, salt,

pepper. With hand beater, beat until well blended. Pour into ice-cube tray, kept only for this purpose; quick-chill in freezing unit (without changing control) 15 to 20 min., or until firm about 1″ in from edges but soft in center. Turn into bowl; with hand beater, beat until fluffy. Fold in cabbage, pepper, onion, celery seeds. Pour into 1-qt. mold or 7 or 8 individual molds. Refrigerate until firm.
To serve: Unmold onto greens. Makes 7 or 8 servings.

CUCUMBER CREAM SALAD

1 3-oz. pkg. lemon-flavor gelatin	1 cup commercial sour cream
1 teasp. salt	Mayonnaise
1 cup hot water	1 cup drained finely chopped cucumbers
1 to 2 tablesp. vinegar	Salad greens
1 teasp. grated onion	

Early in day: Dissolve gelatin and salt in hot water. Add vinegar, onion. Refrigerate until syrupy, then beat in sour cream, 1/4 cup mayonnaise, and cucumbers. Pour into 6 individual molds. Refrigerate until firm. Unmold on salad greens; top with mayonnaise. Makes 6 servings.

OLIVE RELISH MOLD
(Perfection Salad)

2 env. unflavored gelatine	3/4 cup diced celery
1 cup cold water	1 1/2 cups shredded green or Chinese cabbage
1 1/2 cups boiling water	
1/3 cup granulated sugar	3/4 cup shredded, pared carrot
1 1/4 teasp. salt	1/4 cup chopped green pepper
1/4 cup vinegar	2 tablesp. diced pimento
1/4 cup lemon juice	
2/3 cup cut-up ripe olives	

Sprinkle gelatine over cold water to soften; add boiling water; stir until dissolved. Stir in sugar, salt, vinegar, lemon juice; cool. Add olives and rest of ingredients; mix well. Pour into 1 1/4-qt. mold or 8″ x 8″ x 2″ pan. Refrigerate until firm.
To serve: Unmold, or cut into squares; garnish with greens. Pass Half-and-Half Mayonnaise, p. 469. Makes 10 to 12 servings.
OLIVE-RELISH RING: Make in 1 1/4-qt. ring mold. Refrigerate until firm. Unmold. Fill with Tuna Salad, p. 458, or Shrimp Salad, p. 458.

♣ FOR 5 OR 6: Halve ingredients; use pan 8″ x 8″ x 2″.

TOMATO ASPIC
(Jellied Tomato Salad)

3 cups canned tomato juice	2/3 cup cold tomato juice
1 stalk celery	1/4 cup vinegar
1 small onion, sliced	About 1 1/2 cups chopped mixed raw vegetables or mixed cooked or canned vegetables (optional)
2 lemon slices	
1 small bay leaf	
1 teasp. salt	
1/8 teasp. pepper	
2 env. unflavored gelatine	Salad greens

Combine 3 cups tomato juice, celery, onion, lemon, bay leaf, salt, pepper. Simmer, uncovered, 10 min.; strain. Meanwhile, sprinkle gelatine over cold tomato juice and vinegar to soften; stir in hot mixture until dissolved. (If adding vegetables, refrigerate tomato mixture, stirring occasionally, till consistency of unbeaten egg white; fold in vegetables.) Pour into 7 individual molds. Refrigerate till firm.
To serve: Unmold onto greens; serve with Half-and-Half Mayonnaise, p. 469, or Creamy French Dressing, p. 471. Makes 7 servings.
TOMATO-CHEESE: When tomato mixture in each mold is partially set, drop in spoonful of cottage cheese or chive cottage cheese.
TOMATO RING: Pour tomato mixture into 1 1/4-qt. ring mold. When set, unmold; fill with tuna, shrimp, or chicken salad. Serve with Cucumber Mayonnaise, p. 469.
TWO-TONE: Pour half of tomato mixture into 7 individual molds; refrigerate till almost set. Refrigerate rest until consistency of unbeaten egg white; fold in 1 cup cottage cheese, 1 tablesp. snipped chives, 1 tablesp. diced celery; pour into same molds. Refrigerate till set.
HAM OR SEA-FOOD TOMATO ASPIC: Refrigerate tomato mixture till consistency of unbeaten egg white. Fold in 1/4 cup pickle relish and 1 cup slivered, cooked ham; 1 cup cooked, cleaned shrimp; or 1 cup canned tuna. Refrigerate in molds till firm.

TOMATO-OLIVE ASPIC: Place stuffed-olive slice (or hard-cooked-egg slice) in bottom of each individual mold; cover with small amount of Tomato Aspic mixture. Refrigerate till firm; fill with rest of aspic mixture. Refrigerate till firm.

PRESSED CHICKEN

2 4-lb. roasters, halved	¼ teasp. whole cloves
5 cups water	1 teasp. dried savory
1 beef-bouillon cube	10 parsley sprigs
1 tablesp. vinegar	1 clove garlic
1 carrot, pared and sliced	¾ cup minced onion
1 cup sliced celery	¼ teasp. whole black peppers
Green celery tops	1 tablesp. salt
1 leek, halved lengthwise (optional)	3 tablesp. snipped parsley
2 bay leaves	Lettuce
	Mayonnaise

Day before:
1. In kettle, place chickens and rest of ingredients except snipped parsley, lettuce, and mayonnaise. Cover; then simmer about 1½ hr., or until chickens are tender.
2. Remove chickens from broth; skim fat from broth.
3. Strain broth through fine sieve into saucepan. Boil down, uncovered, until only 2 cups remain. Meanwhile, remove chicken meat from bones and chop it very fine; refrigerate.
4. Add chicken to 2 cups concentrated broth. Simmer 10 min.; then stir in snipped parsley. Turn into 9″ x 9″ x 3″ loaf pan. Weigh down by placing another pan on top of mixture. Refrigerate overnight, or until firm.
At serving time: With a spatula, loosen chicken from pan. Unmold on bed of lettuce on serving platter; slice thin or thick. If desired, garnish with cranberry-jelly slices or dot with tart fruit jelly. Pass mayonnaise. Makes 8 servings.
EAST COAST PRESSED CHICKEN: Make as above, substituting 1 cup sherry for 1 cup water, omitting bouillon cube and vinegar, and leaving chicken in large pieces. In cutting, make slices ¾″ thick.

FIX-AND-SERVE MOLDED FRUIT SALADS

A variety of tasty molded fruit salads and salad desserts in plastic round containers are now available in the refrigerator section of many supermarkets. Unopened, they will keep up to three months in your refrigerator.

FRUIT SALADS

After a hearty main course, fruit salad makes a most welcome top-off. But it's equally delightful as a first or salad course. Serve any of these on greens, with suggested dressing.

PEAR WALDORF SALAD

2 cups diced, pared pears; or 1 cup each diced pears and unpared red apples.	1 cup thinly sliced celery
2 tablesp. lemon juice	½ cup broken walnuts or flaked coconut
1 teasp. sugar	Lettuce
½ cup mayonnaise	French dressing

Toss fruits with lemon juice, sugar, 1 tablesp. mayonnaise. Just before serving, add celery, walnuts, rest of mayonnaise; toss.
Serve on lettuce. Top with French dressing. Makes 4 servings.

To Vary: For pears, substitute fresh, frozen, or canned pineapple; banana cubes; or 1 cup orange sections and 1 cup grapes.
WALDORF SALAD: For pears, substitute 2 cups diced unpared red apples and ½ cup raisins.

HORSE-RADISH APPLE-PEAR SALAD

1½ cups finely sliced celery	toasted almonds
2 cups coarsely grated unpared pears	⅓ cup lemon juice
	¼ cup granulated sugar
2 cups coarsely grated unpared apples	¼ teasp. salt
	2 tablesp. drained horse-radish
½ cup slivered	¾ cup heavy cream

Early in the day or 2 hr. before serving: Toss celery, pears, apples, and almonds, with lemon juice, sugar, salt, and horse-radish; refrigerate.
Just before serving: Fold cream, whipped, into fruits. Nice with cold meat slices, folded over. Makes 4 or 5 servings.

LUSCIOUS FRUITED WALDORF SALAD

Carefully pare red eating apples so paring from each remains in one long piece. Arrange paring in ring on each salad plate. Fill with apple-celery-pineapple-grape salad. Top with chopped salted peanuts or chopped walnuts, Brazil nuts, pecans, almonds, or filberts.

THREE-FRUIT SALAD

1 8-oz. can pear halves	oranges
1 8¾-oz. can pineapple tidbits	1 cup unpared ¼″ apple cubes
1 11-oz. can Mandarin	½ cup seedless grapes
	½ cup dark raisins

Early in day: Cut pears in ¼″ cubes. In bowl, combine all the canned fruits and their syrups, plus apples and rest of ingredients; refrigerate.

Just before serving: Drain fruits well, reserving syrup for later use in a gelatin or other dessert. Makes 8 servings.

FRUIT-SALAD PLATES
(for lunch or supper)

MEDLEY: For each salad plate, select 3 or 4 fruits below. Arrange on crisp greens, with lettuce cup of Golden Cream-Cheese Dressing, p. 470, in center. At side, place dainty tongue sandwiches.

Peach or pear halves	Melon strips
Bing cherries	Banana chunks or frozen or canned pineapple chunks
Small bunches red or green grapes	
Grapefruit sections	Orange slices
Strawberries	

MELON RING: For each serving, place 2″-thick pared crosswise slice of seeded cantaloupe on crisp lettuce. Fill with raspberries or strawberries and seedless grapes. Top with favorite sherbet. At side, place buttered hot biscuits filled with thin ham slices.

WEST-COAST SPECIAL: For each serving, slice avocado onto nest of water cress; flank with finger sandwiches filled with chicken salad. Around these, arrange horseshoe of overlapping orange slices. Place cheese- and nut-stuffed celery in center. Pass Pineapple French Dressing, p. 469.

BIG FRUIT: For each serving, prepare 2 or 3 pared slender strips of cantaloupe or honeydew melon or both. On top and beside melon, arrange pitted Bing cherries, canned or frozen pineapple chunks, banana cubes, walnuts, water cress. At side, place dainty egg-salad sandwiches. Pass Lemon-Cream Mayonnaise, p. 470.

GOLDEN: For each serving, fill ½ seeded cantaloupe with canned or frozen pineapple chunks; top with chive cream cheese and water cress. Beside melon, place hot toasted corn muffins. Pass French dressing.

FRUIT CHEF SALAD: Tear 1 medium head iceberg lettuce or romaine into bite-size pieces. Toss with 1 cup cottage cheese; 1 cup fresh, canned, or frozen pineapple chunks; ¼ cup chopped walnuts; ¼ cup light or dark raisins; 3 sectioned oranges; 2 tablesp. French dressing. At side, place deviled-ham-and-egg sandwiches. Makes 4 servings.

FRUIT-CHEESE: Many other all-fruit salads can serve as a luncheon main dish if you couple them with such protein-rich cheeses as these:

Cottage-Cheese Salad mixture, p. 459 (on peach or pear halves, or orange or pineapple slices)
Camembert or Danish blue-cheese wedges
Sticks of natural or process Cheddar or Swiss cheese (about 4 or 5)
Slices of favorite cheese or spoonfuls of cheese spread

Or serve fruit salad with cheese and crackers, grilled cheese sandwiches, or one of hot Favorite Quick Breads, p. 475.

HEAVENLY FROZEN FRUIT SALAD

1 teasp. unflavored gelatine	¼ cup chopped nuts
2 tablesp. lemon juice	¼ cup quartered maraschino cherries
1 3-oz. pkg. soft cream cheese	1 1-lb.-4-oz. can crushed pineapple or 1 1-lb. can fruit cocktail, drained; or 1¾ cups mixed, sliced fresh fruit
¼ cup mayonnaise	
¼ teasp. salt	
2 tablesp. sugar	
½ cup heavy cream, whipped	

Turn temperature control of refrigerator to coldest setting. Sprinkle gelatine over lemon juice in glass measuring cup to soften. Stir over hot water until dissolved. Add to combined cheese, mayonnaise, salt, and sugar.

Fold in rest of ingredients. Pour into ice-cube tray kept just for this purpose; freeze just till firm. Then reset temperature control.

Serve, sliced, on greens. Makes 8 servings.

RAINBOW FRUIT BUFFET

A dramatic way to present a fruit salad. In bottom of large glass compote or snifter, or pretty glass bowl, arrange well-drained canned cling-peach halves from 2 1-lb.-13-oz. cans. Top with layer of sliced pared fresh pears tossed in orange juice; then a layer of large black grapes; next, chunks of watermelon; then seedless grapes; finally, orange sections, topped with more pared pear slices tossed in orange juice. As the top-off, use a large bunch of black grapes, snipped into serving-size bunches.

To serve, set compote on large glass plate, and surround it with crisp leaves of Bibb lettuce. Place a pretty bottle of French or Italian dressing nearby. Guests help themselves.

HONEYDEW SALAD SUPPER

2 honeydew melons	Few blueberries
2 cups cottage cheese	Oil-and-vinegar dress-
Few strawberries	ing

Several hr. ahead:

1. Cut a slice from top of each melon and reserve it; scoop out all seeds.
2. Place a generous spoonful of cottage cheese in each melon. Top with 2 or 3 strawberries, then more cheese, then a few blueberries; repeat until melons are filled.
3. Replace melon tops; secure with picks; refrigerate.

At serving time: Halve each melon lengthwise, arrange each half on a plate. Serve with dressing. Makes 4 servings.

P.S. If you don't have blueberries, substitute green grapes or blackberries; cantaloupe may replace honeydew.

FRUIT-AND-CHEESE SALAD

¼ cup Roquefort-	½ teasp. seasoned salt
cheese spread	1 cantaloupe
½ pt. commercial	½ lb. green grapes
sour cream	1 head iceberg lettuce

Early in day or several hr. before serving:

1. Blend Roquefort-cheese spread with sour cream and seasoned salt; then refrigerate.
2. Cut cantaloupe in half; remove seeds, pare off rind; cut its meat into bite-size chunks; refrigerate.
3. Wash and stem grapes (if not seedless, halve and remove seeds); refrigerate.
4. Cut lettuce into bite-size pieces — 1½ qt. in all. Turn into salad bowl; refrigerate until needed for tossing.

Just before serving: To lettuce add cantaloupe, grapes, and Roquefort dressing. Toss lightly to blend. Makes 6 servings. Serve with cold sliced turkey, crisp rolls, and chocolate sponge dessert.

MORE FRUIT SALADS

Serve any of these on greens, with suggested or your favorite dressing. Use as first course, with main course, or as dessert.

AUTUMN SALAD: Toss slivered unpared apples and pineapple with halved seeded grapes, cut-up celery, and walnuts. Arrange on canned jellied-cranberry-sauce slices if desired.

BANANA ROLL-INS: Roll banana chunks in minced salted peanuts.

FILLED AVOCADO: Halve, peel, and pit each avocado. Brush with lemon juice; sprinkle with salt. Set each avocado half on crisp greens; fill with one of combinations listed below; top with French dressing, to which curry powder, chutney, horse-radish, or Danish blue cheese has been added if desired.

Pineapple chunks and unpared apple cubes
Cut-up oranges
Cut-up grapefruit and cooked cleaned shrimp
Canned fruit cocktail with diced orange
Cottage cheese with bits of Roquefort cheese
Seedless or seeded grapes

MELON BOWL: Halve watermelon lengthwise, making one half larger than other. Cut red meat from both halves into chunks. Heap, with choice of added fruits, in larger half. Serve on large tray; pass French dressing.

ORANGE KABOBS: On skewers, string, alternately, orange and banana chunks, or orange slices and dates, or pear or apple slices. End each with grape or cherry. Dip into Lemon French Dressing, p. 471.

PEAR-ORANGE: Fill fresh or canned pear halves with cut-up oranges.

FROSTED HONEYDEW: Quarter honeydew melon; hollow out each quarter. Fill with berries, melon meat, and grapefruit or orange sections. Top with spoonfuls of favorite sherbet; tuck water cress or chicory along inside edge.

SUSIES: Arrange grapefruit or orange sections around cut-up nuts and dates.

STRAWBERRY: Toss strawberries with grapefruit or orange sections, grated orange rind, Manhattan French Dressing, p. 469.

GRAPE: Toss red, white, and blue grapes with Lorenzo French Dressing, p. 469.

FRUIT DESSERT SALADS

A fruit dessert salad is welcome at a dessert bridge, as an evening snack, with a hot bread or sandwich and a hot drink, or as a main dish accompaniment.

Whatever the occasion, try some of these.

TWENTY-FOUR-HOUR DESSERT SALAD

1 egg	tidbits
2 tablesp. lemon juice	1 cup diced oranges
2 tablesp. sugar	1 cup seedless grapes
Pinch salt	1 cup sliced bananas
½ cup heavy cream, whipped	8 maraschino cherries
12 large marshmallows, quartered	½ cup canned toasted, slivered almonds
1 cup drained canned pineapple	Salad greens

In double boiler, beat egg with fork; stir in lemon juice, sugar, salt. Cook over hot water, stirring 5 min., or until mixture thickens. Remove from heat; cool. Fold in cream, marshmallows, fruits. Refrigerate overnight. To serve, fold in almonds; arrange on greens. Makes 6 servings.

PINEAPPLE-SHELL SALAD: Spoon salad into hollowed-out pineapple shell.

FRUIT-AND-CHEESE DESSERT SALADS

These are nice served on crisp greens with suggested or your favorite dressing. Also serve as first course, or with main course.

CANTALOUPE CIRCLES: Fill each 1"-thick pared ring of seeded cantaloupe with cut-up water cress, tossed with Lemon French Dressing, p. 471. Serve with Camembert cheese at room temperature.

Or place each cantaloupe slice on lettuce; pass Roquefort French Dressing, p. 471.

ORANGE-NUT: Put 2 orange slices together with cream cheese; sprinkle with peanuts.

JUNE RING: Frost each pineapple slice with cottage cheese, cream cheese, or sour cream. Heap strawberries on top. Garnish with water cress. Pass Lorenzo French Dressing, p. 469.

PINEAPPLE-CHEESE: Mix cottage cheese with pineapple chunks; heap on lettuce; top with pineapple chunks and Chutney French Dressing, p. 469.

BANANA SPLIT: Toss cottage cheese with pineapple chunks; set big spoonful on each peeled banana, halved lengthwise. Top with currant jelly.

STUFFED PEACHES: Fill canned-peach halves with cream cheese or cottage cheese mixed with chopped celery and nuts.

PINEAPPLE-CHEESE RING: Top pineapple slices with chunks of Roquefort cheese. Pass Cranberry French Dressing, p. 469.

PINEAPPLE: Top pineapple slices with grated cheese, then with bit of tart jelly. Or top slices with flaked coconut or raspberries.

GRAPEFRUIT HALF SHELLS: Prepare grapefruit halves as on p. 548; tuck chickory around edges. Sprinkle with grated cheese, then with French dressing.

FROSTED FRUIT BOWLS: Fill soup bowls or individual casseroles with mixture of chilled cut-up oranges, 1 can fruit cocktail (juice and all), strawberries, and seedless grapes. Top each with mound of cottage cheese.

MELON RINGS: Place each 2"-thick pared ring of seeded cantaloupe on bed of lettuce. Fill with berries and seedless grapes. Top with sherbet. Garnish with sharp-cheese-and-nut balls.

CITRUS: To several orange or grapefruit sections, with or without bit of avocado, add French dressing or Roquefort French Dressing, p. 469.

SALAD DRESSINGS

The kind and the amount of salad dressing you use should compliment the taste and texture of your salad. Your salad will be a grand-slam success when teamed with the right dressing.

Before using these recipes, refer to How To Use Our Recipes, p. 3. Always use standard measuring cups and measuring spoons; measure level.

QUICK-AND-EASY DRESSINGS

Just take your pick below! Wise homemakers keep a variety of salad dressings—of national brands—on hand. They're delicious right from the refrigerated jar or bottle and so easy to vary to special tastes. Or make your own, using one of a variety of time-saving, tasty salad dressing mixes as the base.

BOTTLED FRENCH DRESSINGS: Today these are made of salad oil, vinegar, and seasonings, combined in a temporary emulsion by shaking or beating vigorously. They come creamy thick, or thin and clear, and are mildly seasoned or subtly flavored, in Italian, Russian, spicy, cheese, herb, and other styles. Always shake the bottle well before using, so ingredients will blend.

PACKAGED SALAD DRESSING MIXES: These offer an easy way to make a variety of French dressings with perfect flavor and proportions, simply by shaking up an envelope of the dry mix, first with vinegar and a little water, then with the salad oil, and then shaking again. You can choose from garlic, Italian, onion, blue cheese, Parmesan, creamy French, cheese garlic, old-fashioned French, etc.

MAYONNAISE: A combination of salad oil, vinegar, and seasonings, this dressing is held in stable emulsion by eggs. It is usually more bland than Cooked Salad Dressing and can be varied in so many delightful ways!

COOKED SALAD DRESSINGS: These have a white saucelike base, with seasonings, vinegar, sugar, and usually eggs added. They are a cross between old-fashioned boiled dressing and mayonnaise and keep indefinitely in the refrigerator. They, like mayonnaise, lend themselves to a number of tasty variations.

Other Uses for Quick-and-Easy Dressings

Today's salad dressings need not be limited to salad use either:

1. The bottled French dressing family, for example, is especially fine for marinating meats, chicken for frying, and sea food before cooking.

2. A spoonful or two adds zest and flavor to cooked vegetables. Steaks, chops, hamburgers, and chicken are all the tastier for being brushed with one of these dressings while being grilled or skilleted.

3. And next time you open a smoking hot baked potato give it a topping of cheese dressing.

4. Both the bottled dressings and salad dressing mixes, too, provide that something different in a dip, dunk, or spread when blended with cottage cheese, cream cheese, sour cream, or deviled ham.

FRENCH DRESSING PLUS

Into ½ cup bottled or homemade French dressing, stir one of the following. You'll have 23 exciting variations.

For Green or Vegetable Salads:

ANCHOVY: 2 teasp. finely cut anchovies

BOMBAY: ¼ teasp. curry powder, 1 chopped, hard-cooked egg, ½ teasp. minced onion

CHEESE AND PICKLE: 1 tablesp. each cottage cheese, pickle relish, and snipped parsley

CHIFFONADE: 2 teasp. each minced pimento and parsley, ½ chopped, hard-cooked egg

CURRY: ¼ teasp. curry powder

FLORENTINE: 1 tablesp. minced raw spinach

HERB: 2 teasp. snipped parsley, ½ teasp. minced fresh or dried tarragon or basil

MUSTARD: 1 tablesp. prepared mustard

PARMESAN:* 2 tablesp. grated Parmesan cheese

ROQUEFORT OR BLUE:* 1 to 2 tablesp. crumbled Roquefort or Danish blue cheese

VINAIGRETTE: 1 teasp. snipped chives, 1 chopped, hard-cooked egg

ZESTY: 1 tablesp. Worcestershire or bottled thick meat sauce

*Use on fruit too.

For Fruit Salads:

CHUTNEY:* 2 tablesp. cut-up chutney

CRANBERRY:* 2 tablesp. canned whole-cranberry sauce

CREAMY: 2 or 3 tablesp. heavy cream

CURRANT-NUT:* 1 tablesp. lemon or lime juice, ¼ cup currant jelly, ¼ cup chopped walnuts

HONEY: 1 tablesp. honey, 2 teasp. lemon juice, 1 teasp. grated lemon rind

LORENZO:* 2 teasp. chili sauce, 2 tablesp. snipped water cress, 2 tablesp. currant jelly

MANHATTAN: 1 teasp. angostura bitters

MINT:* 2 tablesp. snipped mint, 2 teasp. sugar

PINEAPPLE:* 3 tablesp. canned crushed pineapple

SUPERB: ¼ cup honey, ½ teasp. celery seeds

TWO FRUIT: 1 tablesp. lemon juice, ¼ teasp. grated orange rind, 2 tablesp. orange juice, 1 teasp. sugar, ¼ teasp. dry mustard

*Use on greens too.

MAYONNAISE PLUS

Into ½ cup bottled or homemade mayonnaise or cooked salad dressing, stir one of the following. Keep a choice on hand.

For Green or Vegetable Salads:

CELERY: ¼ cup minced celery, 1 tablesp. snipped chives

CHEESE: ¼ lb. process Cheddar cheese, grated (1 cup), 1 tablesp. vinegar, ½ minced clove garlic, ¼ teasp. salt, ½ teasp. Worcestershire

CUCUMBER: ½ cup minced cucumber, ¼ teasp. salt, ½ teasp. fresh or dried dill

HALF-AND-HALF: ½ cup French dressing

HERB: Few drops lemon juice, 1 teasp. each snipped parsley and chives (or minced onion)

HORSE-RADISH: 3 tablesp. horse-radish

MUSTARD: 1 tablesp. prepared mustard

ROQUEFORT OR BLUE: ½ cup French dressing, ¼ cup crumbled Roquefort or blue cheese

RUSSIAN: ½ cup French dressing, 1 green pepper, minced, 2 tablesp. chili sauce, 1 tablesp. minced onion

SHARP CREAM: 1 teasp. minced onion, 1 teasp. vinegar, ½ teasp. sugar, ½ cup light cream

THOUSAND ISLAND: 1 tablesp. chopped stuffed olives, 1 tablesp. chili sauce, 1 teasp. minced onion, 1 chopped hard-cooked egg, 1 tablesp.

minced green pepper, a little snipped parsley
TOMATO: 1 diced tomato, 2 chopped scallions, 1/4 teasp. salt, 2 tablesp. vinegar or lemon juice
TARRAGON: 1/2 teasp. diced tarragon, 2 teasp. snipped parsley

For Fruit Salads:

CHUTNEY:* 2 tablesp. cut-up chutney
CURRY:* 1/2 teasp. curry powder, 1/4 teasp. minced garlic
LEMON-CREAM: 3 tablesp. lemon juice (or pineapple or orange juice), 3 tablesp. confectioners' sugar, 3 tablesp. heavy cream, dash salt. Or omit cream; fold in 1/2 cup heavy cream, whipped
PARTY CREAM: 2 tablesp. currant jelly, beaten with fork, 1/4 cup heavy cream, whipped
RAISIN-NUT: 1 tablesp. snipped raisins, 2 tablesp. chopped nuts, 1/4 cup orange juice

*Use on greens too.

SOUR-CREAM DRESSINGS

Into 1/2 cup commercial sour cream, stir one of the following:

For Green or Vegetable Salads:

CELERY: 1/4 cup minced onion, 1 tablesp. vinegar, 1/2 to 1 teasp. celery seeds, 3/4 teasp. salt
CHIVE: 1 1/2 tablesp. snipped chives, 1 tablesp. vinegar, 1/4 teasp. salt
PIQUANT: 2 teasp. horse-radish, 1/4 teasp. salt, 1/2 teasp. sugar, 1/2 teasp. curry powder
PUFF: 1 tablesp. minced onion, 1 teasp. sugar, 1 tablesp. vinegar, 1/2 teasp. bottled capers, 1/4 teasp. paprika, 1/2 teasp. salt. Just before serving, fold in 1/2 cup croutons
TARRAGON: 1 tablesp. tarragon vinegar, 1 teasp. minced onion, 1/4 teasp. sugar, 1/4 teasp. salt
HALF-AND-HALF: 1/2 cup mayonnaise and seasonings to taste
CASA GRANDE: 1 minced scallion, 1 tablesp. mayonnaise, 1 tablesp. lemon juice, 1/4 cup blue cheese, salt and pepper to taste

For Fruit Salads:

FESTIVE: 1/4 cup beaten currant jelly, 1/8 teasp. salt
MINT: 1 tablesp. snipped mint, 1/2 teasp. sugar, 1/2 teasp. lemon juice, 1/4 teasp. salt

GREEN-GODDESS DRESSING

1 clove garlic, minced	wine vinegar
1/2 teasp. salt	3 tablesp. snipped chives
1/2 teasp. dry mustard	1/3 cup snipped parsley
1 teasp. Worcestershire	1 cup mayonnaise
2 tablesp. anchovy paste	1/2 cup commercial sour cream
3 tablesp. tarragon-	1/8 teasp. pepper

Early in day, or day before: Combine all ingredients; refrigerate, covered. Especially delicious on salad greens or sea food.

Or serve as a dunk for potato chips, cooked cleaned shrimp, or raw vegetables (cauliflowerets, carrot curls, radishes). Makes 1 3/4 cups.

CREAM-CHEESE DRESSINGS

To 1 3-oz. pkg. soft cream cheese, add one of the following; then whip smooth with fork.

For Fruit Salads Especially:

FRENCH: Thin with French dressing to sauce consistency
FRUITY: 1/4 cup orange juice, 4 teasp. lemon juice, 1/4 teasp. salt, 1 teasp. sugar, dash paprika
GOLDEN: 1/3 cup chopped walnuts, 1/4 cup mayonnaise, 1/3 cup orange juice, 2 tablesp. lemon juice, 1 tablesp. sugar, 1/4 teasp. salt
COCONUT: 1/4 cup milk or cream, dash salt. Add 3/4 cup flaked coconut just before serving

HORSE-RADISH-HERB DRESSING

1 1/2 tablesp. horse-radish	chives
1 cup commercial sour cream	1 tablesp. snipped fresh dill or 1 teasp. dried dill
1 tablesp. tarragon vinegar	1 tablesp. sugar
1 tablesp. snipped	3/4 teasp. salt
	1/4 teasp. paprika

1. Combine horse-radish, sour cream, and vinegar; mix until smooth.
2. Stir in chives, dill, sugar, salt, and paprika. Refrigerate, covered, at least 15 min.
3. Serve over tossed greens, sliced tomatoes or cucumbers, or fresh-fruit salad. Makes 1 cup.

COTTAGE-CHEESE DRESSINGS

To ½ cup cottage cheese, add one of the following:

For Fruit, Green, or Vegetable Salads:

CHIVE: 1 tablesp. lemon juice, 1 tablesp. salad oil, ½ teasp. salt, 2 teasp. snipped chives or minced onion

SAVORY THIN: 3 tablesp. lemon juice, ⅓ cup undiluted evaporated milk, ½ teasp. salt, 2 teasp. sugar, 1 tablesp. snipped chives or minced onion

SPICY CHEESE: ¼ cup mayonnaise, 1 teasp. prepared mustard, ½ teasp. lemon juice

DRESSING A LA DELICIOUS

1 8-oz. pkg. small-curd cottage cheese
2 oz. Danish blue cheese, crumbled
2 tablesp. grated onion
¼ teasp. Worcestershire
1 drop Tabasco
¼ cup commercial sour cream

In small bowl, combine cottage cheese with rest of ingredients. Beat, with electric mixer at high speed, till thoroughly blended; refrigerate. Makes about 1¼ cups.

IT'S FUN TO MAKE YOUR OWN SALAD DRESSINGS

Important Ingredients

Fine Salad Oil Is a Must. Choose one of the national brands described on p. 99, or a blend of these. Do not use mineral oil; it may rob the body of important vitamins.

Lemon or Lime Juice Gives a Nice Accent. Fresh, canned, or frozen, it not only adds the tartness you crave but vitamin C as well. Use interchangeably with vinegar.

Vinegar. Comes in a dozen or more exciting flavors, as described on p. 101.

Packaged Salad-Dressing Mixes. These mixes contain a just-right amount of seasonings, spices, etc., and save your having to measure out each. All you do is add salad oil, vinegar, and water. See p. 468.

FRENCH DRESSINGS

Choose one of dressings below, doubling or tripling recipe if you use it often.

Combine all ingredients in jar, bowl, or bottle. Shake or beat till blended; or mix in electric blender. Refrigerate, covered. Shake well before using. For variations, see French Dressing Plus, p. 469.

SIMPLE (makes 1 cup):

¾ teasp. salt
Speck pepper
Dash paprika
¼ teasp. sugar
¼ cup lemon juice, lime juice, or vinegar
¾ cup salad oil
1 clove garlic; or 1 tablesp. minced onion
½ teasp. caraway seeds (optional)

LEMON (makes 1⅔ cups):

1 cup salad oil
¼ to ⅓ cup granulated sugar
⅔ cup lemon juice
1½ teasp. salt
2 teasp. paprika
1 teasp. minced onion

CREAMY (makes 1¼ cups):

½ cup evaporated milk, undiluted
½ cup salad oil
¼ cup vinegar
½ teasp. sugar
½ teasp. dry mustard
½ teasp. salt
⅛ teasp. pepper
⅛ teasp. Worcestershire
⅛ teasp. Tabasco (optional)
1 egg white, unbeaten

FRUIT (makes ½ cup):

½ teasp. salt
1 teasp. sugar
Speck pepper
Dash paprika
⅓ cup salad oil
2 tablesp. vinegar
2 teasp. honey
2 teasp. lemon juice
¼ teasp. grated lemon rind

ROQUEFORT OR BLUE CHEESE (makes 1⅔ cups):

1 cup salad oil
1 teasp. sugar
1 teasp. salt
2 teasp. paprika
3 tablesp. lemon
juice or vinegar
3 oz. Roquefort or blue cheese
½ small onion, minced

WINE (makes about 1½ cups):

1 tablesp. sugar	¼ cup catchup
1 teasp. salt	¼ cup claret wine
½ teasp. dry mustard	¼ cup vinegar
1 teasp. Worcester-shire	¾ cup salad oil
	1 clove garlic, gashed

DE LUXE (makes about 1½ cups):

1¼ cups salad oil	3 tablesp. chili sauce
7 tablesp. vinegar or lemon juice	1 teasp. horse-radish
2¼ teasp. salt	1 teasp. prepared mustard
¼ teasp. pepper	2 cloves garlic, gashed
½ teasp. paprika	
1 teasp. sugar	

BIG THOUSAND ISLAND DRESSING

1 clove garlic, halved	½ cup coarsely cut-up stuffed olives
½ cup mayonnaise	
2 tablesp. light cream	1 hard-cooked egg, coarsely cut up
2 tablesp. chili sauce	½ teasp. salt
2 tablesp. chopped green pepper	½ teasp. paprika

Rub garlic well on inside of small bowl; discard. In bowl, blend mayonnaise with cream and chili sauce; add rest of ingredients; stir lightly. Refrigerate. Makes 1¼ cups.

MAYONNAISE

2 teasp. dry mustard	2 egg yolks
1 tablesp. lemon juice	1¾ cups salad oil
1 teasp. salt	2 tablesp. vinegar
1 teasp. sugar	1 tablesp. lemon juice
Dash cayenne pepper	

1. In cold bowl, with hand beater or electric mixer at medium speed, beat mustard with 1 tablesp. lemon juice, salt, sugar, cayenne.
2. Beat in egg yolks; then beat in oil, drop by drop, until ¼ cup has been added.
3. Continue beating in oil slowly; when mixture is thick, beat in vinegar and 1 tablesp. lemon juice alternately with oil until all are used.
4. Store, *covered, in least cold part of refrigerator.* (If too cold, mayonnaise may separate.) Makes 2 cups.

To Vary: See Mayonnaise Plus, p. 469.

SALAD DRESSING PAR EXCELLENCE

½ clove garlic	2 tablesp. wine vinegar
½ teasp. celery salt	
¼ teasp. freshly ground black pepper	1 teasp. catchup
	2 dashes Tabasco
	½ cup mayonnaise
½ teasp. salt	¼ cup heavy cream

In small bowl, with back of spoon (or use mortar and pestle), mash together garlic, celery salt, pepper, and salt. Add vinegar, catchup, Tabasco, mayonnaise, and cream; stir smooth. Refrigerate, covered, at least 2 hr. Makes ¾ cup.

FOR SHRIMP SALAD: Mash ½ teasp. dry mustard with garlic.

FOR CRAB SALAD: Add 2 tablesp. horse-radish with cream.

FOR TOSSED GREEN SALAD: Decrease salt to ¼ teasp. Add 2 tablesp. anchovy paste and ¼ cup snipped green-onion tops with cream.

COOKED SALAD DRESSING
(also called boiled salad dressing)

2 tablesp. sugar	1 egg
1 teasp. salt	¾ cup milk
1 teasp. prepared mustard	¼ cup vinegar
	1 tablesp. butter or margarine
1½ tablesp. flour	

In double boiler, thoroughly combine sugar, salt, mustard, flour, egg, and milk. Gradually stir in vinegar. Cook, over hot, *not boiling,* water 10 to 15 min., or until thickened. Remove from heat, stir in butter, cool, then refrigerate, covered, till needed. Makes about 1¼ cups.

FRUIT SALAD DRESSING

3 tablesp. granulated sugar	½ cup lemon juice
1 tablesp. flour	1 tablesp. butter, margarine, or salad oil
¼ teasp. dry mustard	
¼ teasp. salt	2 hard-cooked egg yolks, sieved
⅛ teasp. paprika	

In double boiler, combine sugar, flour, mustard, salt, paprika. Slowly stir in lemon juice. Cook over hot water, stirring, until slightly thickened. Stir in butter and sieved yolks. Refrigerate. Wonderful over fruits. Makes ½ cup.

RASPBERRY DRESSING

1 10½-oz. pkg. frozen raspberries, thawed	¼ teasp. salt
½ teasp. prepared mustard	2 tablesp. vinegar
	¼ cup salad oil

Press berries through strainer; set aside purée. Combine mustard, salt, and vinegar; gradually add oil, beating with hand beater until slightly thickened. Slowly add raspberries, beating constantly. Nice on cottage or cream cheese salad, or almost any fruit salad. Makes about 1 cup.

SEA-FOOD DRESSING

¼ cup mayonnaise or cooked salad dressing	3 small sweet pickles, minced
½ cup chili sauce	2 tablesp. snipped parsley
2 tablesp. snipped scallions	1 teasp. Worcestershire
2 tablesp. minced celery	1 teasp. horse-radish

Combine mayonnaise and chili sauce; then add rest of ingredients. Refrigerate. Nice on shrimp, tuna, or other fish salads. Makes ¾ cup.

TART AND TASTY FRUIT DRESSING

2 eggs	⅛ teasp. salt
¼ cup granulated sugar	½ cup heavy cream, whipped
¼ cup lemon juice	½ teasp. grated lemon rind
¼ cup pineapple or orange juice	

In double boiler, beat eggs. Stir in sugar, juices, salt; cook over hot, *not boiling,* water till thickened. Cool; fold in cream, rind. Makes 2 cups.

LOW-CALORIE DRESSINGS

Counting calories? Remember there are virtually no calories in salad greens, yet they supply essential vitamins and minerals. So enjoy them often.

For dressings use your favorite *sparingly.*

Or use one of the bottled low-calorie kind. These come in several flavors including Italian, French, and Cheese, and are both low in salad oil and skillfully seasoned with spices and herbs.

If you prefer to make your own low-calorie dressings try those which follow here.

LOW-CALORIE FRUIT-SALAD DRESSING

1 clove garlic, minced	¼ teasp. paprika
¼ cup vinegar	1 teasp. sugar
½ cup orange juice	½ teasp. salt
	⅛ teasp. pepper

Let garlic stand in vinegar 1 hr. Strain. Add rest of ingredients; shake or beat well. Refrigerate. Shake before using. Makes about 1 cup. (10 calories per tablespoon.)

LOW-CALORIE BUTTERMILK DRESSING

1½ teasp. sugar	pepper
1½ teasp. dry mustard	1 egg, slightly beaten
½ teasp. salt	½ cup buttermilk
⅛ teasp. paprika	1 tablesp. melted butter or margarine
1½ teasp. cornstarch	½ cup vinegar
⅛ teasp. onion salt	
Few grains cayenne	

In double boiler, mix sugar, mustard, salt, paprika, cornstarch, onion salt, cayenne. Add egg, buttermilk; stir until smooth. Cook over hot, *not boiling,* water until mixture begins to thicken. Add butter and vinegar, a little at a time; beat well. Refrigerate. Makes 1 cup. (15 calories per tablespoon.)

LOW-CALORIE TOMATO-JUICE DRESSING

½ cup canned tomato juice	1 teasp. salt
2 to 4 tablesp. salad oil	1 teasp. minced onion
2 tablesp. lemon juice	1½ teasp. bottled thick meat sauce
½ teasp. dry mustard	

Combine all ingredients. With hand beater or electric mixer, beat until well blended. Refrigerate. Makes about 1 cup. (25 calories per tablespoon.)

LOW-CALORIE FRENCH DRESSING

¾ cup water	1¼ teasp. prepared
2 teasp. cornstarch	mustard
¼ cup lemon juice	½ teasp. paprika
¾ teasp. salt	1 clove garlic
1½ teasp. sugar	½ teasp. Worcester-
2 tablesp. salad oil	shire
1 teasp. horse-radish	¼ cup catchup

Simmer water with cornstarch over low heat, stirring, until clear and thickened—about 5 min. Cool. Add lemon juice and rest of ingredients; with hand beater or electric mixer, beat until smooth and blended. Refrigerate. Shake before using. Makes about 1¼ cups. (20 calories per tablespoon.)

EGG: Add 1 finely chopped, hard-cooked egg. (25 calories per tablespoon.)

FRUIT: Substitute ¼ cup pineapple juice for ¼ cup water; omit sugar. Or add ¼ cup diced orange, peach, pear, apricot, grapefruit, etc. (25 calories per tablespoon.)

GARDEN: Add 2 tablesp. minced onion, 3 tablesp. minced cucumber, 2 tablesp. minced green pepper. (20 calories per tablespoon.)

YOGHURT DRESSING

1 cup yoghurt	¼ teasp. salt
2 tablesp. vinegar	¼ teasp. sugar
1 tablesp. minced	Speck pepper
onion	

Combine all ingredients; refrigerate. Makes 1⅛ cups. (About 10 calories per tablespoon.)

FAVORITE QUICK BREADS

Homemade quick breads give a wonderful lift to even the simplest meal. And they're easy to make, whether you work from scratch or use one of today's fine mixes or refrigerated biscuits or rolls.

Before using these recipes, refer to How To Use Our Recipes, p. 3. Always use standard measuring cups and measuring spoons; measure level. For milk called for, you may use regular, evaporated (diluted with an equal amount of water), or liquefied nonfat dry milk.

Serve with a Flair

Line a basket or plate with a pretty napkin or bun cozy. When hot bread is done, remove it, piping hot from the pans, and arrange on a napkin. Bring corners of napkin up and over bread, to keep it warm. Serve at once.

Some hot breads are pretty served right in the dish in which they were baked — they stay hot longer that way, too.

PERFECT HOT BISCUITS

HOT BAKING-POWDER BISCUITS

2 cups sifted all-purpose flour	6 to 7 tablesp. shortening
3 teasp. double-acting baking powder	About ⅔ to ¾ cup milk
1 teasp. salt	

1. Start heating oven to 450°F. Into bowl, sift flour, baking powder, salt. With pastry blender or 2 knives, used scissor-fashion, cut in shortening until mixture is like coarse corn meal.
2. Make well in center; pour in ½ cup milk. With fork, mix lightly, quickly. Add enough more milk to form dough, just moist enough to leave sides of bowl and cling to fork as ball. Turn onto lightly floured surface.
3. Knead 6 or 7 times, working *gently.*
4. Lightly roll dough out from center, lifting rolling pin as you near edges. Roll dough ½" to ¾" thick for high fluffy biscuits, ¼" thick for thin crusty ones.

475

5. With floured 2″ biscuit cutter, cut out biscuits, using straight, *not twisting*, motion and cutting biscuits close together. Between cuttings, dip cutter into flour.

6. With spatula, lift biscuits to ungreased cookie sheet. Place 1″ apart for crusty biscuits, nearly touching for soft-sided ones.

7. Lightly press dough trimmings together; roll and cut as before. With pastry brush, brush biscuit tops with milk, melted butter or margarine, or light cream. Bake 12 to 15 min., or until delicate brown. Serve *hot*. Makes about 19 2″ biscuits.

PIPING HOT: Bake biscuits in oven-glass pie plate or baking dish; rush them to table in same plate.

EXTRA RICH: Increase shortening to ½ cup.

SPEEDY: Roll biscuit dough into oblong; cut into squares, triangles, or diamonds; bake.

DROP: Increase milk to 1 cup. Drop biscuits 1″ apart onto greased cookie sheet; or fill greased muffin-pan cups two thirds full. Bake at 450°F. 12 to 15 min. Makes 12.

EASY STIR 'N' ROLL BISCUITS

2 cups sifted all-purpose flour	1 teasp. salt
	⅓ cup salad oil
3 teasp. double-acting baking powder	⅔ cup milk

Start heating oven to 475°F. Sift flour, baking powder, and salt into bowl. Measure oil, then milk, into one measuring cup (don't stir together). Pour, all at once, over flour mixture. With fork, mix to make soft dough that rounds up into ball.

Turn dough onto sheet of wax paper; knead lightly, without additional flour, 10 times, or until smooth. Between 2 sheets of wax paper, pat or roll dough ¼″ thick for thin, crusty "Southern" type biscuits, ½″ thick for "Northern" type. Then remove top sheet.

Cut with unfloured biscuit cutter. Bake on ungreased cookie sheet 10 to 12 min., or until golden brown. Makes 12 large biscuits, or 18 small ones.

BUTTERMILK BISCUITS: Make as above, reducing baking powder to 2 teasp., adding ¼ teasp. baking soda, and substituting buttermilk for the sweet milk.

SHORTCAKES: Sift 2 tablesp. granulated sugar with dry ingredients. If desired, add 1 egg to

oil in measuring cup; then pour in enough milk to make 1 cup liquid. Proceed as directed, cutting with 2½″ cutter. Bake as at left. Serve as in Susan's Strawberry Shortcake, p. 130. Makes 8.

HOT BISCUITS PLUS

Before adding liquid to Hot Baking-Powder Biscuits, p. 475, Easy Stir 'n' Roll Biscuits, at left, or 2 cups packaged biscuit mix, add one of these:

CHEESE: ¼ to ½ cup grated sharp Cheddar cheese; or ½ cup crumbled Danish blue cheese
CHIVES: ¼ cup snipped chives
CURRY: ¼ teasp. curry powder
HAM: ⅔ cup chopped cooked ham
HERB: ¼ teasp. dry mustard, ½ teasp. sage, 1¼ teasp. caraway seeds
ORANGE: Grated rind of 1 orange

CUT BISCUITS PLUS

Make Hot Baking-Powder Biscuit dough, p. 475, Easy Stir 'n' Roll Biscuit dough, left, or packaged biscuit-mix dough (2-cup recipe). Then choose:

ORANGE: Roll or pat dough ½″ thick; cut out biscuits. Place close together, or 1″ apart, on baking sheet. Rub halved sugar lumps on rind of 1 orange; dip quickly into orange juice; press ½ lump into top of each biscuit. Bake at 450°F. 12 to 15 min. Or dip halved sugar lumps into strong cold coffee before pressing into biscuits.

CHEESE TRIANGLES: Roll or pat dough into 8″ circle. Cut into 8 wedge-shaped pieces. Reassemble in circle on cookie sheet, leaving space between wedges. Mix 1 3-oz. pkg. pimento cream cheese, softened, with 1 tablesp. mayonnaise, 2 teasp. minced onion, and 1 tablesp. snipped parsley; spread on top of wedges. Bake at 450°F. 12 to 15 min.

DATE OR CHEESE: Roll or pat dough ¼″ thick. Cut out 2″ biscuits. Set pitted date or piece of cheese on each. Fold over; press edges together. Bake at 450°F. 12 to 15 min.

DROP BISCUITS PLUS

Make Hot Drop Baking-Powder Biscuit dough, p. 475, or drop-biscuit dough from packaged biscuit mix (2-cup recipe). Complete as below. Then bake at 450°F. 12 to 15 min.

BLUEBERRY: To dough, add 1 cup *well-drained*, washed fresh blueberries. Sprinkle biscuit tops with sugar. Bake.

HOT PIMENTO: Over hot water, melt 1 3-oz. pkg. pimento cream cheese with 2 tablesp. butter or margarine. Place spoonful on each drop biscuit on cookie sheet. Bake.

NUT-BUTTER: Mix ½ cup brown sugar, packed, with ¼ cup honey, 2 tablesp. butter or margarine, few chopped walnuts; place 1 tablesp. in each greased muffin-pan cup. Drop biscuit dough, by spoonfuls, on top. Bake.

TOPPED: Drop biscuit dough, by spoonfuls, into greased muffin-pan cups. Make slight impression in top of each biscuit. Top with one of the following combinations. Bake.

Honey, brushed on; then sprinkling of nutmeg

Drained canned crushed pineapple and sprinkling of brown sugar

Brown sugar mixed with butter or margarine, then with flaked coconut or chopped nuts

Grated orange or lemon rind with sugar

Melted butter or margarine, plus a little garlic salt or mixed herbs

About 1 teasp. raspberry jam

Pickle relish and dab of chili sauce or catchup

BISCUIT PIN WHEELS

Make Easy Stir 'n' Roll Biscuit dough, p. 476, Hot Baking-Powder Biscuit dough, p. 475, or packaged biscuit-mix dough (2-cup recipe). Roll into rectangle ¼" thick; then complete as below:

BUTTERSCOTCH: Spread dough with 2 tablesp. soft butter. Sprinkle with mixture of ¼ cup granulated sugar and 1 teasp. cinnamon, then raisins, if desired. Roll up from long side, jelly-roll-fashion. Cut into ½" to 1" slices; place, flat sides down, in greased muffin-pan cups. Bake at 425°F. about 15 min.

PARTY: Spread dough with soft cheese spread, deviled ham or tongue, or thick marmalade. Roll up from long side, jelly-roll-fashion; cut into ½"- to 1"-thick slices. Place, with flat sides down, in greased muffin-pan cups. Bake at 450°F. about 12 min., or until done.

PECAN: Make Butterscotch Pin Wheels, above. In bottom of each greased muffin-pan cup, put 1 teasp. melted butter or margarine, 1 teasp. brown sugar, 2 or 3 pecan halves. Top with pin wheels. Bake at 425°F. about 15 min.

BUTTER DIPS

⅓ cup butter or margarine	3½ teasp. double-acting baking powder
2¼ cups sifted all-purpose flour	1½ teasp. salt
1 tablesp. sugar	1 cup milk

Start heating oven to 450°F. Melt butter in oblong pan, 13" x 9" x 2", in oven. Sift together flour, sugar, baking powder, salt. Add milk; stir slowly with fork until dough just clings together — about 30 strokes. Turn onto well-floured board. Roll over to coat with flour. Knead lightly about 10 times. Roll out ½" thick into a rectangle 12" x 8".

With floured knife cut dough in half lengthwise, then crosswise into 16 strips. Dip each strip into melted butter, then lay, close together, in 2 rows in pan. Bake 15 to 20 min., or until golden. Serve hot. Makes 32.

CHEESE BUTTER DIPS: Add ½ cup grated sharp Cheddar cheese to flour mixture.

GARLIC BUTTER DIPS: Add ½ clove garlic, minced, to butter before melting.

CINNAMON BUTTER DIPS: Combine 2 tablesp. sugar and ½ teasp. cinnamon; sprinkle over Butter Dips before baking.

PACKAGED BISCUIT MIX

You'll love the wonderful rolled and drop biscuits, as well as breads, muffins, coffeecakes, etc., you can make so speedily from today's packaged biscuit mix. The recipes carried on the label are an inspiration.

TINY MARMALADE BISCUITS

1. Start heating oven to 425°F. Spread ½ cup orange marmalade mixed with 2 tablesp. soft margarine in 8" x 8" x 2" cake pan.
2. To 2 cups packaged biscuit mix add ⅔ cup milk. Stir with fork to soft dough. Beat vigorously 20 strokes, until stiff, slightly sticky.
3. Roll dough around on cloth-covered board, lightly dusted with packaged biscuit mix, to prevent sticking. Knead gently 8 to 10 times to smooth up dough; then roll into an 8" square and cut into 36 small squares.
4. Lift biscuits, with spatula, into pan (they

need not be separated). Bake 15 to 20 min. Invert pan on serving plate. Biscuits will break off into bite-size pieces. Serve warm, with coffee, at a salad luncheon or dinner.

TO REHEAT LEFTOVER BISCUITS

In Foil: Snugly wrap leftover baking-powder biscuits in foil. Bake at 375°F. about 20 min., or till heated. If served in foil wrappings (turn foil edges down to form basket), they'll keep hot to the last crumb.

In Covered Skillet: Put 2 tablesp. water in large skillet or electric skillet. Lay round trivet in bottom, with biscuits on it. Cover; leave over low heat 10 min., or till hot.

In Broiler: Split biscuits; butter. Then sprinkle with a little grated cheese, celery, poppy, or caraway seeds, or cinnamon and sugar. Or spread with cheese or garlic spread. Toast under broiler.

REFRIGERATED BISCUITS

These light, fluffy sweet-milk and buttermilk biscuits come in tubelike cans, all rolled out, cut, and ready to bake. The grocer keeps them in his dairy case — you should store them on one of your refrigerator shelves — not in the door. *Never* store them on pantry shelf or in freezer. On the end of each can is an expiration date; the dough should be used before this date for best volume and quality; the volume and quality will not be as good thereafter. Always bake *entire can* at one time, too.

They're delicious baked just as they come from the can, or varied as below.

PUFFS: In 8″ pie plate, arrange 10 refrigerated biscuits, overlapping slightly. With fork, beat 1 egg with 2 tablesp. light cream, 1/8 teasp. dry mustard, 1/4 teasp. salt, 1/2 cup grated process Cheddar or pimento cheese. Pour over biscuits. Bake at 450°F. 15 min.

QUICK COFFEECAKELETS: Dip refrigerated biscuits into melted butter; sprinkle with cinnamon and sugar. Bake at 425°F. 10 min., or until done.

FROSTIES: Combine 1 3-oz. pkg. pimento cream cheese, 1/2 teasp. cream, 1 tablesp. chopped pimento. Spread on 10 refrigerated biscuits. Bake at 425°F. 10 min., or until done.

UPSIDE-DOWN: In bottom of each of 10 muffin-pan cups, place some of one of mixtures below. Top each with refrigerated biscuit. Bake at 425°F. 15 to 18 min.; let stand in cups 1/2 min.; then invert pan onto wax paper. Cool 5 min.; then lift off pan.

Honey-Pecan: In each of 10 muffin cups, put 3 pecan halves, then some of 1/4 cup honey mixed with 1/2 teasp. cinnamon.

Butterscotch-Nut: In each of 10 muffin cups, place 1/2 teasp. melted butter or margarine and 1 teasp. corn syrup; stir; top with 3 pecans, flat side up.

Pineapple: In each of 10 muffin cups, place 1/2 teasp. melted butter or margarine and 1 teasp. brown sugar; stir; top with 2 teasp. drained canned crushed pineapple.

Orange: Simmer 1/2 cup granulated sugar with 1/4 cup orange juice, 1/4 cup butter or margarine, and 2 teasp. grated orange rind 5 min. Divide among 10 muffin cups.

COFFEE-ETTES: Use about 20 refrigerated biscuits. Dip each, first into 1/4 cup melted butter or margarine, then into 3/4 cup granulated sugar combined with 3/4 teasp. cinnamon, 1/3 cup chopped walnuts. Then arrange biscuits, overlapping, in greased 9″ layer-cake pan or on greased cookie sheet. Bake at 425°F. 20 to 25 min.

CHEESE TOP-UPS: Place 10 refrigerated biscuits close together in 9″ pie plate. Blend 1/4 lb. grated process sharp Cheddar cheese with 1/4 cup melted margarine; spread over biscuits. Bake at 450°F. 15 min.

CHEESE UPSIDE-DOWN: Place 2 tablesp. butter or margarine and 1/4 cup Danish blue- or pimento-cheese spread in 8″ pie plate. Set in 450°F. oven till partly melted; stir to blend. In mixture arrange about 10 biscuits, close together. Bake at 450°F. 15 min. Turn out of pan.

DUMPLINGS FOR STEW

2 cups sifted all-purpose flour	dried thyme or savory
3 teasp. double-acting baking powder	1/4 cup shortening
1 teasp. salt	1 cup milk; or 1/2 cup evaporated milk
1 teasp. snipped parsley; or 1/4 teasp.	plus 1/2 cup water

Sift flour, baking powder, salt; add parsley. With pastry blender or 2 knives, scissor-fashion, cut in shortening until like very coarse corn meal. With fork, lightly mix in milk to form soft dough (stir as little as possible). Drop dough, by tablespoonfuls, onto chicken pieces or vegetables in boiling stew. Simmer dumplings 10 min., *uncovered;* then cover and simmer 10 min.

Serve at table, right from Dutch oven if you like. Or with slotted spoon, remove from stew; arrange around edge of heated platter; place stew in center. Makes about 12.

NOTE: If stew provides only a little broth, stir in about ½ cup boiling water before adding dumplings.

✤ FOR 2: Halve ingredients.

CHIVE OR PARSLEY DUMPLINGS: Add ¼ cup snipped parsley or 3 tablesp. snipped chives to sifted flour mixture.

CHEESE DUMPLINGS: Add ¼ cup grated sharp cheese to sifted flour mixture.

SPEEDY: Use packaged biscuit mix to make dumplings, following label directions.

REFRIGERATED: Use a can of refrigerated biscuits, arranging them on top of stew. Simmer, covered, 15 to 20 min.

QUICK FRENCH BREAD

On ungreased cookie sheet, stand biscuits from 2 cans refrigerated biscuits on edge in one long roll, lightly pressing them together and shaping ends to form tapering loaf. Brush with beaten egg white; sprinkle with sesame seeds. Bake at 350°F. 30 to 40 min., or until deep golden. Then slice between biscuits almost to bottom crust and serve. Or spread a little garlic butter or spread between baked biscuits, pop into oven for a few minutes, then serve.

REFRIGERATED ROLLS

Refrigerated butter-flake, crescent, sesame, gem flake, and similar rolls come in tubelike cans, all ready to bake, like refrigerated biscuits. Baked as label directs, and piping hot from oven, they're luscious.

BUTTER-FLAKE ROLLS PLUS: Before baking, separate a few layers of each refrigerated butter-flake roll; sprinkle as in 1–4, right. Then put together again, bake as label directs.

1. Sprinkle with sesame or poppy seeds.
2. Sprinkle lightly with garlic or onion powder or garlic spread.
3. Sprinkle generously with grated Parmesan or Cheddar cheese.
4. See Fillings for Butter-flake Rolls, p. 495.

When it's refrigerated crescent rolls you're serving, try these:

CRESCENT SPECIALS: Unroll each roll in 1 can refrigerated crescent dinner rolls, making 8 triangles. Complete in one of ways below:

Jam Kolacky: Place 1 teasp. jam or preserves in center of each triangle, then fold the 3 points to center, overlapping them. Bake at 375°F. 10 to 15 min., or until golden brown. Sprinkle with a little sugar. Serve warm. Makes 8.

Cinnamon-Nut Crescents: Combine ¼ cup finely chopped nuts, 2 tablesp. brown sugar, 2 tablesp. granulated sugar, and ¼ teasp. cinnamon. Place 1 to 2 teasp. of this mixture near wide end of each triangle. Fold over and press edges together, then continue rolling as for crescents. Place on ungreased cookie sheet; curve into crescent shapes. Brush with melted butter, sprinkle with rest of sugar-nut mixture. Bake at 375°F. 10 to 13 min., or until golden brown. Serve hot. Makes 8.

Hot Dog Crescents: Partially split 8 franks, then insert a quarter slice of Cheddar cheese in each; lay one on each triangle; roll up as label directs. Set on greased cookie sheets, cheese side up. Bake at 375°F. 10 to 13 min., or until golden brown. Serve hot. Makes 8.

Ham Crescents: Fold 8 slices cooked ham in half; lay one on each triangle; spread lightly with prepared mustard. Roll up and bake at 375°F. 10 to 15 min., or until golden brown. Serve as is or with cheese sauce.

Cheese Crescents: Generously sprinkle each triangle with grated Parmesan cheese or shredded Cheddar. Roll up and bake as label directs. Serve hot. Makes 8.

GLAZED CRESCENTS: Bake refrigerated crescent rolls as label directs. Then spread tops with jelly, preserves, or 1 tablesp. honey mixed with 1 tablesp. soft butter or margarine; return to oven for 2 or 3 min., or until crescents are glazed. Serve hot. Makes 8.

TEA SCONES

2⅓ cups sifted cake flour	2 teasp. sugar
2½ teasp. double-acting baking powder	6 tablesp. shortening
	5 tablesp. milk or light cream
½ teasp. salt	2 eggs
	2 tablesp. sugar

Start heating oven to 450°F. Into bowl sift flour, baking powder, salt, and 2 teasp. sugar. With pastry blender or 2 knives, scissor-fashion, cut in shortening until like corn meal. Add milk. Separate 1 egg; reserve 1 tablesp. white; beat rest of egg with second egg; add to flour.

On lightly floured surface, roll dough ½" thick. Cut into 3" squares; cut each square into 2 triangles. Arrange on greased cookie sheet; brush with 1 tablesp. egg white, slightly beaten; sprinkle with 2 tablesp. sugar. Bake 10 to 15 min., or until done.

Serve hot, for luncheon, supper, or tea. Makes about 10.

BLUEBERRY: With eggs, add 1 cup well-drained, washed fresh blueberries. Makes about 18.

JAM: Increase flour to 2½ cups. Roll dough ¼" thick; cut into 2½" squares. Place 1 teasp. plum or other jam in center of each square; fold opposite corners toward center; with moistened finger tips, pinch together firmly. Makes about 12.

DAINTY TEA: Cut dough into 2" rounds.

TOASTED: Make and bake scones day before. On the day, split them; brush with melted butter or margarine; toast under broiler until golden brown.

SCOTLAND'S RAISIN SCONES: Add ½ cup light or dark raisins with milk. Serve, hot or cold, with butter or jam.

SCONE MIX: Yes, there's a packaged scone mix which makes melt-in-your-mouth scones. Wonderful with a favorite jelly.

MUFFINS

HOT MUFFINS

2 cups sifted all-purpose flour	2 tablesp. sugar
3 teasp. double-acting baking powder	1 egg
	1 cup milk
½ teasp. salt	¼ cup salad oil or melted shortening

1. Start heating oven to 425°F. Grease 14 2½" muffin-pan cups well. Into bowl, sift flour, baking powder, salt, sugar.
2. Beat egg till frothy; stir in milk and salad oil; mix well. Make small well in flour mixture; pour in milk mixture all at once. Stir quickly and lightly — *don't beat* — *until just mixed but still lumpy.*
3. Quickly fill muffin cups two thirds full; wipe off spilled drops of batter. (If batter does not fill all cups, fill empty ones with water to keep grease from burning.) Bake 25 min., or until cake tester, inserted in center of muffin, comes out clean.
4. To serve, run spatula around each muffin to loosen it; lift out onto heated dish. Makes about 14.

NOTE: If muffins are done before rest of meal, loosen; then tip slightly in pans; keep warm. Then they won't steam and soften.

SWEETER: Reduce flour to 1½ cups, baking powder to 2 teasp. Increase sugar to ½ cup.

♣ **FOR 2:** Use 1 egg; halve rest of ingredients.

WHOLE-WHEAT (GRAHAM): Decrease flour to ¾ cup; to it add 1 cup unsifted whole-wheat flour. Increase sugar to ¼ cup, baking powder to 4 teasp. Bake at 375°F. 35 min. Makes about 16.

APPLE: Make Sweeter Muffins, above, adding ½ teasp. cinnamon with flour. Add 1 cup grated raw apple (unpared) with shortening.

SURPRISE: Fill greased muffin cups half full of batter; drop scant teasp. of jelly on center top of each; add more batter to fill cups ⅔ full.

ORANGE: Increase sugar to ¼ cup. Reduce milk to ¾ cup. With milk, add ¼ cup orange juice, ¼ cup grated orange rind.

MUFFINS PLUS: You may like to bake half of muffins plain. To rest of batter, add one of following, bake; serve toasted next day.

Caraway: 1 tablesp. caraway seeds

Fruit: ½ cup light or dark raisins; or 1 cup cut-up pitted dates

Walnut: 1 cup finely chopped walnuts

To Reheat: Split, butter, then toast leftover muffins under broiler.

HOT MUFFINS—QUICK

Make and bake muffins, using one of packaged mixes such as plain, corn, orange, raisin bran, blueberry, or date muffin mix, or biscuit mix.

FILLED: Fill greased muffin-pan cups half full with plain muffin batter. Top with one of fillings below; then add more batter to fill each cup two thirds full. Bake as label directs.

Candied: Several bits of preserved orange or lemon rind, or citron

Fruitful: 1 drained, cooked dried apricot or pitted prune. Or 1 teasp. applesauce and a little cinnamon. Or 1 teasp. canned whole-cranberry sauce or *drained* crushed pineapple mixed with a little grated orange rind. Or 1 banana slice. Or a few blueberries, blackberries, or pitted canned Bing cherries. Or a few cut-up pitted dates or raisins

Jam-Dandy: ½″ cube of cream cheese and 1 teasp. raspberry, strawberry, or peach jam (extra nice for small muffins)

TIP-TOPPED: Turn muffin batter into about 14 2½″ muffin-pan cups; top with one of the following, then bake as label directs.

Flaked coconut or chopped nuts, as is, or mixed with brown sugar and butter

Sugar mixed with a little grated orange or lemon rind, or cinnamon

Honey, brushed on batter, then sprinkled with nutmeg or poppy seeds

Grated process Cheddar cheese; or caraway or poppy seeds (for corn or plain muffins)

Small dot of jelly

Tiny cube of cream cheese

BEST BRAN MUFFINS

1 cup sifted all-purpose flour	1 cup milk
½ teasp. salt	2 tablesp. soft short-ening
3 teasp. double-acting baking powder	¼ cup granulated sugar
1 cup packaged ready-to-eat bran	1 egg, beaten

Start heating oven to 400°F. Grease well about 12 2½″ muffin-pan cups. Sift flour, salt, baking powder. In medium bowl, soak bran in milk 5 min. Meanwhile, in small bowl, with spoon, beat shortening with sugar until light; add beaten egg; stir till smooth. Stir into bran. Add flour mixture, *stirring only until just mixed, no longer.* Fill muffin cups two thirds full. Bake 25 min., or until done. Makes about 12.

♣ **FOR 2:** Use 1 egg; halve rest of ingredients.

ORANGE GLAZED: Just before baking, sprinkle muffins with 2½ teasp. grated orange rind and ¼ cup granulated sugar, combined.

RAISIN-NUT: To flour mixture, add ½ cup chopped walnuts and ½ cup raisins.

SPICED APPLE MUFFINS

1 pkg. corn muffin mix	¼ teasp. cinnamon
1 apple, pared, cored	2 tablesp. sugar

Start heating oven to 400°F. Prepare mix as label directs. Cut apple into very thin wedges; roll each in mixture of cinnamon and sugar. Fill 6 greased muffin cups half full of batter; press narrow edge of 3 sugared apple wedges into top of each. Bake 15 min., or as mix label directs. Makes 6.

POPOVERS

OUR GIANT POPOVERS

6 eggs	2 cups sifted all-purpose flour
2 cups milk	1 teasp. salt
6 tablesp. melted butter or margarine	

About 1 hr. 20 min. before serving: Start heating oven to 375°F. Butter well 8 6-oz. pottery custard cups.* Arrange the custard cups in a jelly-roll pan or roasting pan.

With mixer at low speed, or with hand beater, beat eggs slightly; add milk and melted butter or margarine; beat until blended, then gradually beat in flour and salt. Pour batter into custard cups to within ¼ inch of top.

Bake popovers 60 min.; then remove them from oven. Quickly cut slit in side of each to let out steam; then return them to the oven for 10 to 15 min., or until their tops are very firm, crisp, deep brown. Then, so bottoms of the popovers won't steam and soften, promptly lift popovers out of custard cups with fingers onto a wire rack; or, if necessary, first loosen them with spatula.

Serve the popovers piping hot, with butter or margarine. Makes 8.

*Our custard cups are about 2⅜″ high, 2″ across bottom, 2½″ across top. They may be purchased from Ideal Restaurant Supply Company, 294 Bowery, New York City.

PECAN GIANT POPOVERS: Make as on p. 481. Just before baking sprinkle 1 tablesp. coarsely chopped pecans over batter in each cup (½ cup in all).

PARMESAN GIANT POPOVERS: Make as on p. 481, placing 1 tablesp. grated Parmesan cheese in each cup before pouring in batter. After baking 60 min., sprinkle top of each popover with 1 teasp. grated Parmesan, then slit and continue baking.

FAMILY POPOVERS

3 eggs	1 cup sifted all-
1 cup milk	purpose flour
3 tablesp. melted	½ teasp. salt
butter or margarine	

About 1 hr. before serving:

1. Start heating oven to 375°F. Butter well 9 3″ muffin-pan cups.
2. With mixer at low speed (or with hand beater) beat eggs slightly; beat in milk and melted butter or margarine; then gradually beat in flour and salt. Divide batter among the prepared muffin-pan cups.
3. Bake popovers 40 min.; then remove from oven. Quickly cut slit in side of each to let out steam; return to oven for 10 min., or until tops are very firm, crisp, brown.
4. Then, so bottoms won't steam and soften, promptly lift out each popover with fingers; or if necessary, first loosen gently with spatula. Serve, piping hot, with butter or margarine. Makes 9.

There's a fine popover mix on the market, too!

CORN BREADS

YANKEE-STYLE GOLDEN CORN BREAD

1¼ cups sifted all-	powder
purpose flour	1 teasp. salt
¾ cup yellow corn	1 egg
meal	⅔ cup milk
2 to 4 tablesp. gran-	⅓ cup melted butter,
ulated sugar	margarine, or fat,
4½ teasp. double-	or salad oil
acting baking	

1. Start heating oven to 425°F. Grease an 8″ x 8″ x 2″ pan. Into medium bowl, sift flour, corn meal, sugar, baking powder, salt.

2. In small bowl, beat egg well with fork; stir in milk, butter; pour, all at once, into flour mixture, stirring with fork until flour is *just moistened.* (Even if mixture is lumpy, do not stir any longer or holes or tunnels in corn bread will result.)
3. Quickly turn batter into greased pan; spread evenly with spatula.
4. Bake 25 to 30 min., or until done. Serve hot, cut into squares. Makes 9 servings.

✤ **FOR 2:** Use 1 egg; halve rest of ingredients; bake in 6″ pie plate or in muffin-pan cups.

To Do Ahead: Bake corn bread day before. Before mealtime, cut into squares. Split; butter; then quickly toast under broiler.

BACON: Add ⅓ cup crisp cooked bacon bits to batter.

BLUEBERRY CORN MUFFINS: To flour mixture, add 1 cup sugared fresh berries. Fill 16 greased muffin-pan cups two thirds full. Bake at 425°F. 25 to 30 min., or until done. Serve hot. Makes 16 2½″ muffins.

CORN-BREAD RING: Bake as above, using 8½″ (3-pt.) greased ring mold. Serve hot, cut into wedges. Or fill center with creamed ham, chicken, dried beef, oysters, etc.

CORN-BREAD SHORTCAKE: Split squares of hot corn bread. Fill, top, with chicken à la king, creamed ham and chicken, etc.

CORN MUFFINS: Fill about 12 well-greased 2½″ muffin-pan cups two thirds full. Bake as directed.

CORN STICKS: Melt ¼ cup shortening; use to grease corn-stick pans *very well.* Fill three fourths full with corn-bread batter. Bake as directed. Makes about 14.

LEFTOVER CORN BREAD OR MUFFINS: Split; toast as in Toasted Corn-Bread Cuts, p. 483.

SPEEDY CORN BREAD

You can buy excellent corn-muffin and corn-bread mixes — as good as they are quick. Just make as label directs. Or vary as below.

CHEESE-CORN STRIPS: Pour corn-muffin- or corn-bread-mix batter into 12″ x 8″ x 2″ greased pan. Sprinkle with 1 cup grated process Cheddar cheese and a few caraway seeds, if desired. Bake at 375°F. 25 min. When cool, cut in half, lengthwise; then cut into ¾″ crosswise strips.

CHILI-TOPPED CORN BREAD: After baking corn bread, serve squares topped with hot chili.

BACON-CHIVE CORN BREAD: Add 4 crumbled crisp bacon slices and 1 teasp. or so of snipped chives to batter.

DEVILED HAM CORN BREAD: Add a 2¼-oz. can deviled ham to corn-muffin- or corn-bread-mix batter. Serve hot, topped with creamed peas.

TOASTY GEMS: Split and toast corn muffins in the broiler. Serve with preserves.

TOASTED CORN-BREAD CUTS: Bake corn-muffin- or corn-bread-mix batter in 8″ x 8″ x 2″ greased pan at 375°F. 25 min. When cold, cut into squares; split squares. Spread with soft butter or margarine; sprinkle with poppy seeds, grated cheese, or dried thyme; or spread lightly with jelly. Broil till golden.

Or toast split squares in broiler; serve with cheese sauce; garnish with tomato slices.

SKILLET CUSTARD CORN BREAD

2 tablesp. butter or margarine	3 to 4 tablesp. granulated sugar
1⅓ cups yellow corn meal	1¼ teasp. salt
⅓ cup sifted all-purpose flour	1 cup milk
1 teasp. baking soda	2 eggs, unbeaten
	1 cup buttermilk
	1 cup milk

Start heating oven to 400°F. Heat butter in 9″ iron skillet or 9″ x 9″ x 2″ pan in oven.

Meanwhile, into bowl, sift corn meal, flour, soda, sugar, salt. Stir in 1 cup milk and eggs, then buttermilk. Pour into skillet; then pour 1 cup milk *over top* of corn mixture; *do not stir.* Bake 35 min.

Serve hot from skillet, cut into wedges, with lump of butter on each wedge. Corn bread will have layer of custard. Or serve with tart jelly or syrup. Eat with fork. Makes 6 servings.

MARJIE'S FLUFFY SPOON BREAD

1 qt. milk	2 tablesp. butter or margarine
1 cup corn meal (yellow or white)	4 eggs
1½ teasp. salt	

In double boiler, heat milk; gradually stir in corn meal mixed with salt; cook, stirring, until smooth and thick. Cover; cook until mushy. Meanwhile, start heating oven to 425°F. Remove the mush from heat; add butter. In bowl, beat eggs till well blended; slowly stir

into mush. Pour into well-greased 1½-qt. casserole. Bake, uncovered, 50 to 55 min.

Serve from casserole, spooning some onto each plate. Eat instead of bread, with lots of butter or margarine. Makes 4 or 5 servings.

STEAMED BOSTON BROWN BREAD

1 cup unsifted whole-wheat flour	1½ teasp. baking soda
1 cup unsifted rye flour	1½ teasp. salt
1 cup yellow corn meal	¾ cup molasses
	2 cups buttermilk

Grease and flour a 2-qt. mold. Combine flours, corn meal, soda, salt. Stir in molasses, buttermilk. Turn into mold, cover tightly. Place on trivet in deep kettle. Add enough boiling water to kettle to come half way up sides of mold; cover. Steam 3½ hr., or until done. Remove from mold to cake rack.

Serve hot, with baked beans, boiled tongue, franks, etc. Makes 1 loaf.

RAISIN: To flour mixture, add 1 cup seeded raisins.

TOASTED: Butter slices of leftover brown bread; toast under broiler.

SO QUICK: Canned brown bread is delectable. To heat it for serving, *remove bread from can;* heat, covered, in colander, over boiling water.

TEA AND NUT BREADS

DELICIOUS WALNUT-RAISIN BREAD

3 cups sifted all-purpose flour	1 cup raisins or chopped dates (optional)
1 cup granulated sugar	1 egg, beaten
1½ teasp. salt	1¼ cups milk
4 teasp. double-acting baking powder	2 tablesp. melted shortening or salad oil
1 cup chopped walnuts	

Start heating oven to 350°F., and grease 9″ x 5″ x 3″ loaf pan. Sift flour, sugar, salt, baking powder into bowl. Add walnuts and raisins. With fork beat egg with milk and shortening till blended. Stir into flour mixture; blend *thoroughly* with spoon; turn into pan. Bake 60 to 70 min., or until cake tester, inserted in center, comes out clean. Cool in pan 10 min.; remove. Serve next day.

ORANGE NUT BREAD: Decrease sugar to ½ cup; stir in ½ cup orange marmalade.

BISHOP'S BREAD

1½ cups sifted all-purpose flour	2 cups chopped walnuts
1½ teasp. double-acting baking powder	1 cup snipped, pitted dates
¼ teasp. salt	1 cup halved candied cherries
⅔ cup semisweet-chocolate pieces	3 eggs
	1 cup granulated sugar

1. Start heating oven to 325°F. Grease well a 10″ x 5″ x 3″ aluminum loaf pan; line bottom with heavy wax paper. Into bowl, sift flour, baking powder, salt; stir in chocolate, nuts, fruits.
2. In large bowl, with hand beater, beat eggs; with spoon, gradually beat in sugar.
3. Fold flour mixture into egg mixture. Pour into loaf pan. Bake 1½ hr., or until done. Cool in pan on wire rack. When cool remove from pan, wrap in foil, store. Serve, sliced, next day. Makes 1 loaf.

DATE-AND-NUT BREAD

¾ cup chopped walnuts	¾ cup boiling water
1 cup cut-up pitted dates	2 eggs
1½ teasp. baking soda	1 teasp. vanilla extract
½ teasp. salt	1 cup granulated sugar
3 tablesp. shortening	1½ cups sifted all-purpose flour

With fork, mix walnuts, dates, soda, salt. Add shortening, water; let stand 20 min. Start heating oven to 350°F. Grease 9″ x 5″ x 3″ loaf pan. With fork, beat eggs; beat in vanilla, sugar, flour. Mix in date mixture until just blended; turn into pan. Bake 1 hr. 5 min., or until cake tester, inserted in center, comes out clean. Cool in pan 10 min.; remove to wire rack to finish cooling. Then wrap in foil. Store overnight before slicing.

EXTRA-NICE QUICK WALNUT BREAD

Start heating oven to 350°F. Stir ¾ cup granulated sugar, 1 egg, and 1¼ cups milk with 3 cups packaged biscuit mix. Beat hard 30 sec. Stir in 1½ cups chopped walnuts. Bake in well-greased 9″ x 5″ x 3″ loaf pan about 50 min., or until cake tester, inserted in center, comes out clean. Cool on rack, then wrap in foil and store.

HOLIDAY WALNUT LOAF: Add ½ to ¾ cup glacé fruit mix with walnuts.

NUT-BREAD MIX: Let your young folks whip up this packaged nut-bread mix — they'll love it for their snacking!

CRANBERRY-WALNUT BREAD

2 cups sifted all-purpose flour	3 tablesp. white vinegar plus enough water to make ⅔ cup
1 teasp. baking soda	
1 teasp. salt	
¾ cup granulated sugar	¼ cup melted shortening
1 egg	1 cup halved or coarsely chopped raw cranberries
⅓ cup orange juice	
1 teasp. grated orange rind	1 cup chopped walnuts

Start heating oven to 350°F. Grease a 9″ x 5″ x 3″ loaf pan. In mixing bowl, sift flour, soda, salt, sugar. With fork, beat egg; stir in orange juice and rind, vinegar-water mixture, shortening. Add, all at once, to flour mixture; stir just until all flour is moistened. Add cranberries and walnuts; turn into pan. Bake 60 to 70 min., or until cake tester, inserted in center, comes out clean. Cool in pan 10 min.; remove. Cool overnight before slicing.

P.S. This bread freezes well too.

IRISH SODA BREAD

4 cups sifted all-purpose flour	¼ cup butter or margarine
¼ cup granulated sugar	2 cups light or dark raisins
1 teasp. salt	1⅓ cups buttermilk
1 teasp. double-acting baking powder	1 egg, unbeaten
	1 teasp. baking soda
2 tablesp. caraway seeds	1 egg yolk, or a little cream

Start heating oven to 375°F. Grease 2-qt. casserole. Into mixing bowl, sift flour, sugar, salt, baking powder; stir in caraway seeds. With pastry blender or 2 knives, scissor-fashion, cut in butter till like coarse corn meal; stir in raisins. Combine buttermilk, egg, soda; stir into flour mixture till just moistened.

Turn dough onto lightly floured surface; knead lightly till smooth; shape into ball. Place in casserole. With sharp knife, make 4″ cross, ¼″ deep, in top center. Brush with yolk, beaten with fork. Bake 1 hr. 10 min., or until done. Cool in pan 10 min.; remove. Cool before slicing.

FRUITED SODA BREAD: Along with raisins stir in ½ cup halved candied cherries and ¼ cup diced preserved orange peel.

QUICK IRISH SODA BREAD

6 tablesp. shortening	½ cup seedless raisins
2 cups packaged biscuit mix	1 tablesp. caraway seeds
1 tablesp. granulated sugar	¾ cup milk

Start heating oven to 375°F. With 2 knives or a pastry blender, cut shortening into biscuit mix until like coarse corn meal. Stir in sugar, raisins, caraway seeds; with a fork slowly stir in milk until blended. Turn into greased 9″ pie plate; spread smooth. Bake 30 min., or until a cake tester, inserted in center, comes out clean. Serve hot, in wedges, with apple butter or preserves. Makes 6 servings.

BANANA TEA BREAD

1¾ cups sifted all-purpose flour	⅓ cup soft shortening
2 teasp. double-acting baking powder	⅔ cup granulated sugar
¼ teasp. baking soda	2 eggs, unbeaten
½ teasp. salt	1 cup mashed ripe bananas (2 or 3)

Start heating oven to 350°F., and grease a 9″ x 5″ x 3″ loaf pan. Sift flour, baking powder, soda, salt. With electric mixer at medium speed (or with spoon), thoroughly mix shortening with sugar, then with eggs, until *very light and fluffy* — about 4 min. altogether. Then, at low speed, beat in flour mixture alternately with bananas just until smooth; turn into pan. Bake 1 hr., or until cake tester, inserted in center, comes out clean. Cool in pan 10 min.; remove. Cool overnight before slicing.

BANANA-APRICOT: To flour mixture, add 1 cup finely cut-up dried apricots. (If apricots are very dry, first soak in warm water until soft; drain; dry well.)

BANANA-DATE: To flour mixture, add ½ cup chopped, pitted dates.

BANANA-NUT: To flour mixture, add ½ cup coarsely chopped nuts.

BANANA-PRUNE: To flour mixture, add 1 cup finely cut dried prunes. (If prunes are very dry, first soak in warm water until soft; drain; dry well.)

BANANA-RAISIN: To flour mixture, add 1 cup light or dark raisins.

BANANA-BREAD MIX: Try it! It's ever so good.

COFFEECAKES

APPLE-CHIP BRUNCH CAKE

2 cups packaged biscuit mix	3 tablesp. salad oil or melted shortening
¾ cup granulated sugar	¾ cup milk
1 egg	1 cup finely chopped, pared apples

1. Start heating oven to 400°F., and grease a 9″ x 5″ x 3″ aluminum loaf pan. Combine biscuit mix with sugar.
2. In large bowl, with spoon, combine egg with salad oil and milk. Stir in biscuit-mix-and-sugar mixture. Beat ½ min. Fold in apples; turn into pan. Bake 35 to 40 min., or until done. Serve warm, sliced.

CLARA'S SPECIAL COFFEECAKE

½ cup granulated sugar	3 teasp. double-acting baking powder
1 teasp. cinnamon	
1 tablesp. cocoa	½ cup butter or margarine
½ cup chopped walnuts	1 cup granulated sugar
3 cups sifted all-purpose flour	3 eggs, unbeaten
1 teasp. baking soda	1¼ cups commercial sour cream

Start heating oven to 375°F. Grease 9″ tube pan. Make filling as follows: In small bowl, combine ½ cup sugar, cinnamon, cocoa, and walnuts; set aside. Sift flour with baking soda and baking powder.

In large bowl, with mixer at medium speed (or with wooden spoon), cream butter until light; gradually add 1 cup sugar, beating well.

Add eggs, one at a time, beating well after adding each. Blend in flour mixture alternately with sour cream. Into tube pan, turn half of batter, top with filling; spread remaining batter evenly over filling.

Bake 1 hr., or until done. Cool 10 min. in pan; then turn out of pan, and finish cooling on wire rack. Nice for morning, afternoon, or evening coffee.

To Freeze: Cool coffeecake; freezer-wrap in foil; then freeze. To serve, thaw, wrapped, several hr. at room temperature. Then heat at 400°F. 30 to 60 min., still wrapped.

SUPERB MARBLE COFFEECAKE

1¾ cups sifted cake flour	sour cream
1½ teasp. double-acting baking powder	1 teasp. vanilla extract
½ teasp. baking soda	¼ cup granulated sugar
½ cup shortening	2 teasp. cinnamon
¾ cup granulated sugar	½ cup light or dark raisins
2 eggs, unbeaten	½ cup chopped walnuts
½ pt. commercial	

1. Start heating oven to 350°F. Grease 9″ spring-form pan, with tube insert in place, or 9″ x 9″ x 2″ pan. Sift flour with baking powder and soda.
2. In large bowl, with mixer at medium speed, or with spoon, thoroughly mix shortening with ¾ cup sugar, then with eggs, until very light and fluffy. Then, with mixer at low speed, alternately beat in flour mixture with sour cream and extract.
3. Turn half of batter into pan. For topping, combine ¼ cup sugar with cinnamon, raisins, walnuts; sprinkle half over batter in pan. Top with rest of batter, then with rest of topping; press lightly with spoon.
4. Bake 45 min., or until done. Makes 9 to 12 servings.

PECAN RING PRONTO

2 tablesp. honey	½ cup finely chopped pecans
2 cans refrigerated biscuits	2 tablesp. honey

Start heating oven to 375°F. Meanwhile, into bottom of well-buttered 8″ ring mold, pour 2 tablesp. honey. Roll biscuits in chopped pecans;

place, slightly overlapping, in mold. Pour 2 tablesp. honey over top.

Bake about 30 min. Let stand 5 min.; turn out. Extra-special snack for the teen-age crowd to fix themselves.

SPICY ORANGE-PECAN BUNS

¼ cup granulated sugar	3 teasp. double-acting baking powder
3 tablesp. flour	1 teasp. salt
½ teasp. cinnamon	¼ cup shortening
½ teasp. nutmeg	½ cup chopped pecans
2 tablesp. butter or margarine	1 egg, slightly beaten
2 cups sifted all-purpose flour	½ cup orange juice
¼ cup granulated sugar	½ cup orange marmalade

Start heating oven to 375°F. For topping, combine ¼ cup sugar, 3 tablesp. flour, cinnamon, nutmeg; with pastry blender or 2 knives, used scissor-fashion, cut in butter until crumbly; set aside.

Into large bowl, sift 2 cups flour with ¼ cup sugar, baking powder, and salt. Cut in shortening until mixture looks like coarse meal; stir in pecans.

Mix egg, orange juice, marmalade; stir into flour mixture, just until mixture is moistened. Spoon into 12 2½″ paper-lined or greased muffin-pan cups; sprinkle with reserved topping. Bake 20 to 25 min. Makes 1 doz. Freeze, if desired, as in Clara's Special Coffeecake, p. 485.

QUICK BRAZIL-NUT COFFEECAKE

2 cups packaged biscuit mix	¾ cup milk
2 tablesp. granulated sugar	½ cup brown sugar, packed
1 cup finely cut-up dates	2 tablesp. flour
2 tablesp. grated orange rind	2 tablesp. salad oil or melted shortening
1 egg	½ cup chopped Brazil nuts

1. Start heating oven to 400°F., and grease an 8″ x 8″ x 2″ pan.
2. In large bowl, combine biscuit mix, granulated sugar, dates, orange rind. In small bowl, beat egg with milk; stir into biscuit-mix mixture until blended. Turn into pan.

3. Combine brown sugar, flour, salad oil, nuts; sprinkle over mixture in pan. Bake 25 min., or until done. Serve warm. Makes 12 servings.

EASY-DOES-IT APPLE CAKE

¼ cup granulated sugar	2 cans refrigerated biscuits
½ teasp. cinnamon	1 large red apple
¼ teasp. nutmeg	1 tablesp. butter or margarine

1. Start heating oven to 450°F. Meanwhile, mix sugar, cinnamon, and nutmeg. Roll each biscuit in sugar mixture; arrange in greased 9" layer-cake pan.
2. Core unpared apple; halve lengthwise; slice into 20 thin wedges. Put wedges between biscuits; dot with butter. Bake 20 to 25 min., or until browned. Wonderfully quick and easy for breakfast.

LAST MINUTE COFFEECAKES AND SWEET ROLLS

These are all so tasty, whether it's breakfast, morning coffee, picnic lunchbox, or evening treat you have in mind.

In a bag: Yes, one mix comes in a bag. All you do is mix it as label directs, then bake it in a special pan that's in package.

As a mix: Packaged apple-cinnamon, cinnamon-nut, cinnamon streusel coffeecake mix, etc. — they all make luscious coffeecakes.

Refrigerated: In tubelike cans, these refrigerated sweet rolls come all ready to bake; they include caramel nut, cinnamon, frosted orange, or raisin cinnamon, etc.

Frozen: Cinnamon-nut and pecan are two of these packaged frozen coffeecakes which come all ready for you to heat up and serve. And they're so delicious whether for a morning coffee, picnic lunchbox, or evening treat.

PANCAKE PLEASERS

Your Pancake Griddle

Greaseless griddles have a smooth, polished surface that helps keep batter from sticking.

Greasing is not necessary if medium or low heat is used and fat is added to batter.

Use low heat for all griddles. Heat griddle until drops of cold water dance in small beads on surface. Then pour on batter.

Electric griddles and skillets are ideal for pancakes, because the heat is controlled. They can be used at table too.

HOMEMADE PANCAKES

1¼ cups sifted all-purpose flour	¾ teasp. salt
2½ teasp. double-acting baking powder	1 egg
	1¼ cups milk*
2 tablesp. sugar	3 tablesp. melted butter, margarine, or fat, or salad oil

1. Set griddle over low heat to warm up. Into medium bowl or wide-mouthed pitcher, sift flour, baking powder, sugar, salt.
2. In small bowl, beat egg well; add milk, butter. Slowly stir into flour mixture, mixing *only until dry ingredients are wet*.
3. When griddle is hot enough to make a drop of cold water dance, *lightly* grease or not as manufacturer directs. Drop batter from pitcher or large spoon onto griddle, lightly spreading each cake with back of spoon into round about 4" in diameter. Don't crowd cakes or they will be difficult to turn. Cooking about 3 cakes at a time is usually safe.
4. Cook over low heat until rim of each cake is full of broken bubbles and underside is golden brown. With broad spatula or pancake turner, loosen and turn each cake; brown on other side. *Turn only once.*
5. When pancakes are done, remove to heated platter or plates, stacking 4 in each pile.

Serve at once with butter or margarine and maple, maple-blended, or buttered syrup, corn syrup, apple butter, marmalade, honey, molasses, shaved maple sugar, etc. Makes about 12 4" cakes.

*For thicker pancakes, use ¾ cup milk.

APPLE: Sift ¼ teasp. cinnamon with flour in step 1. To batter, add 1 cup finely chopped, pared, cored cooking apples.

BLUEBERRY: To batter, add ½ cup sweetened blueberries. Or before turning each pancake, sprinkle with 1 teasp. fresh or unthawed frozen blueberries.

CORN: Substitute ½ cup yellow or white corn meal for ½ cup flour.

SOUTHERN PANCAKES

½ cup sifted all-purpose flour	½ teasp. salt
3 teasp. double-acting baking powder	1 tablesp. sugar
	½ cup boiling water
	¼ cup milk
½ cup sifted water-ground corn meal	¼ cup melted shortening
	1 egg, well beaten

Sift flour with baking powder. Into bowl, sift corn meal, salt, sugar. Slowly stir in water; beat well. Stir in flour. Slowly stir in milk, shortening; fold in egg.

Drop batter, by tablespoonfuls, onto hot griddle; spread each, with back of spoon, into round. Cook until puffy, full of bubbles, and edges are cooked. Turn; cook other side.

Serve as in Homemade Pancakes, p. 487. Makes about 20 small thin cakes.

To Vary: Reduce flour to ¼ cup; with flour and baking powder, sift ¼ cup additional water-ground corn meal.

BUTTERMILK PANCAKES

1 cup sifted all-purpose flour	1 egg, separated
½ teasp. baking soda	1 cup buttermilk
¼ teasp. salt	1 tablesp. melted butter or margarine

Sift flour, soda, salt. In small bowl, with hand beater, beat egg white until it forms moist peaks; set aside. In medium bowl, using same beater (do not wash), beat egg yolk and buttermilk just till blended. Stir in flour mixture, then melted butter; stir till smooth. Fold in egg white. Drop by tablespoonfuls onto hot griddle. Cook until cakes are puffy, full of bubbles, and edges are cooked. Turn; cook other side. Serve as in Homemade Pancakes, p. 487. Makes about 10.

QUICK PANCAKES

Packaged mixes for plain, buttermilk, corn, and buckwheat pancakes or muffins, biscuits, corn muffins, and corn bread make wonderful pancakes in jig time. Make as label directs and vary pancakes or pancake batter in any of the delightful ways at right.

Vary the Batter:

APFEL PFANNKUCHEN: To batter, add about 1 cup grated, pared, cored tart apples, 1 tablesp. lemon juice, and 2 tablesp. sugar. Serve with sugar and cinnamon or syrup.

BANANA: For each pancake, place 3 or 4 banana slices on griddle. Pour pancake batter over banana slices. Bake till golden brown, turning only once. Serve with butter and confectioners' sugar.

BLUEBERRY: Before turning pancakes, sprinkle with a few unthawed frozen or fresh blueberries. Serve with honey stirred into soft butter or margarine.

CHEESE: To batter, add ½ cup grated sharp process cheese. Serve with creamed meats or vegetables, or with syrup.

CHOCOLATE CHIP: Before turning pancakes sprinkle them with a few semisweet-chocolate pieces. Serve with ice cream and chocolate syrup as dessert.

CORN: To batter, add ½ to 1 cup canned whole-kernel corn and ½ teasp. paprika. Serve with creamed dried beef or ham, or syrup.

FRANK: Before turning pancakes, dot with a few thin frankfurter slices. Serve with honey, stirred into soft butter or margarine, or with creamed vegetables.

NUTTY: To batter, add ¾ to 1 cup finely chopped walnuts. Or sprinkle nuts on stack of pancakes. Serve with syrup or ice cream.

PINEAPPLE: To batter, add ½ cup well-drained canned crushed pineapple and dash of ground cloves. Serve with fried ham, etc.

Vary the Pancakes:

CURRIED TUNA: Stir ⅓ cup milk and 1 teasp. curry powder into 1 10½-oz. can condensed cream-of-mushroom soup, undiluted. Add 1 6½- or 7-oz. can tuna; heat. Spoon over pancakes.

HAM-FILLED: Put spoonful of deviled ham between and on top of each stack of hot cakes. Serve with maple-blended or buttered syrup, or with brown sugar.

MEXICANA: Spoon heated canned chili con carne over each pancake, sprinkle with 1 tablesp. each minced onion and grated process Cheddar cheese. Roll up; sprinkle with more grated cheese. Serve 2 apiece.

PANCAKE SAUSAGE: Bake 8 pancakes. Place

one cooked sausage link on each pancake; roll up, serve with warm spicy applesauce.

PEACH: Top each stack of pancakes with canned sliced or halved peaches in syrup, to which bit of nutmeg has been added.

STRAWBERRY: Put pancakes together in stacks of 3, with butter or margarine and thawed frozen sliced strawberries as filling; top with butter, berries. (One 12-oz. pkg. frozen strawberries makes 4 servings.)

TROPICAL: Top each stack of pancakes with heated canned pineapple slice. Nice with sausages, etc.

DOUBLE-CORN PANCAKES

Start heating griddle. Prepare 1 pkg. corn muffin mix as label directs for pancakes; then add ½ cup canned or cooked whole-kernel corn. When griddle is hot, bake cakes until golden on one side; turn; bake until golden or done. Makes 16.

WAFFLE WONDERS

SPECIAL DAY WAFFLES

2 cups sifted all-purpose flour	1 teasp. salt
3 teasp. double-acting baking powder	2 cups buttermilk
	4 eggs, well beaten
1 teasp. baking soda	1 cup melted butter, margarine, or fat, or salad oil

Start heating waffle iron as manufacturer directs. Sift flour, baking powder, soda, salt. Combine buttermilk, eggs; add to flour mixture. With hand beater, or mixer at high speed, beat until smooth; stir in butter.

When waffle iron is ready to use, pour batter into center of lower half until it spreads about 1″ from edges. Bring cover down gently. Cook as manufacturer directs. *Do not raise cover during baking.*

When waffle is done, lift cover; loosen waffle with fork; serve at once. Reheat iron before pouring in next waffle. Makes 6 to 8.

EVERYDAY WAFFLES: Make as above, reducing eggs to 2 eggs and butter to 6 to 8 tablesp.

SWEET-MILK WAFFLES: Make as above, omitting soda. Increase baking powder to 4 teasp. Substitute sweet milk for buttermilk. Separate eggs; fold in whites, beaten stiff, at last.

SPEEDY WAFFLES

You can make luscious waffles from packaged pancake and waffle mix, or biscuit, muffin, or corn-muffin mix. Just follow label directions. Heat packaged frozen waffles as label directs. Then serve as:

Breakfast main dish, with favorite buttered syrup, maple-blended syrup, maple syrup, honey, apple butter, corn syrup, or molasses.

Accompaniment for sausages, bacon, creamed dried beef, creamed chicken, mushrooms, or fish, chicken curry, Welsh rabbit, etc.

Dessert, topped with fresh or frozen berries, fresh, frozen, or canned peach slices, ice cream, or a sauce such as chocolate, etc.

BERRY WAFFLES: Sprinkle 2 tablesp. fresh blueberries over batter as soon as it has been poured onto iron.

CHEESE WAFFLES: To batter, add ½ cup grated process Cheddar cheese. Serve topped with any creamed vegetable or creamed ham, etc.

CORN WAFFLES: To batter, add 1 cup drained canned whole-kernel corn. Nice with fried chicken, creamed chicken, or ham, etc.

CURRY WAFFLES: To batter, add ½ teasp. curry powder. Serve with creamed chicken or turkey.

NUT WAFFLES: Sprinkle 2 tablesp. coarsely chopped walnuts over batter as soon as poured onto iron.

COCONUT WAFFLES: To batter, add 1 cup fine grated coconut. Serve with fudge sauce.

DOUGHNUTS

OLD-FASHIONED DOUGHNUTS

3½ cups sifted all-purpose flour	1 teasp. salt
	2 eggs
2 teasp. double-acting baking powder	3 tablesp. soft shortening
1 teasp. baking soda	1 cup granulated sugar
½ teasp. cinnamon	¾ cup buttermilk
½ teasp. nutmeg	½ cup minced walnuts (optional)
½ teasp. mace	

Sift flour, baking powder, soda, cinnamon, nutmeg, mace, salt. In large bowl, with mixer at medium speed (or with spoon), beat eggs well; beat in shortening, sugar, then buttermilk. Add flour mixture, all at once; beat just until smooth. Quickly mix in nuts. Refrigerate 1 hr. or longer. On floured surface, roll dough ½" thick. With floured doughnut cutter, cut out doughnuts. Form dough trimmings into ball; roll; then cut.

To Fry: Fry doughnuts in 1½" fat or salad oil, heated to 370°F. on deep-fat-frying thermometer, or until square of day-old bread browns in 60 sec. (See Shallow-Frying, p. 7). Fry only as many doughnuts at one time as will float easily on fat. As soon as doughnuts rise to surface, turn with long-handled fork (don't pierce). Turn often thereafter until golden and done. Remove with fork; hold over fat 1 sec.; drain on paper towels. Or deep-fry as on p. 6.

Serve as is. Or dust with sugar, or sugar and cinnamon. Or shake, a few at a time, in sugar in paper bag. Makes about 2½ doz.

"HOLES": Use centers cut out from doughnuts; or using small biscuit cutter, cut all dough into "holes." Fry, sugar. Nice with fruit.

CHOCOLATE: Omit spices; increase sugar to 1¼ cups. After adding sugar, add 1½ sq. melted unsweetened chocolate and 1 teasp. vanilla extract.

DROPS: With rubber scraper, push heaping teaspoonfuls of dough into hot fat; fry, sugar.

FRENCH DOUGHNUTS

¼ cup granulated sugar	1 cup hot water
1 teasp. salt	1 cup sifted all-purpose flour
1 tablesp. grated orange rind	3 eggs
¼ cup shortening	Sugar Glaze, p. 649

In medium saucepan, place sugar, salt, orange rind, shortening. Add hot water; bring to boil. Add flour, all at once; stir until smooth. Cook, stirring, until mixture leaves sides of pan in ball, and spoon pressed into mixture leaves clear impression. Remove from heat; add eggs, one at a time, beating after each till smooth.

Cut 10 3" squares of aluminum foil or wax paper; grease each. Using cookie press and rosette tube, or teaspoon, form dough into 2½" rings, placing 1 ring on each square of foil. Let stand 15 min.

Heat fat to 370°F. as in Old-fashioned Doughnuts, To Fry, above. Then hold 1 ring of dough close to surface of fat; slip from foil into fat. Repeat. Fry as directed; drain on

paper towels. When cool, glaze tops with Sugar Glaze. Makes 10.

SO-EASY GOLDEN PUFFS

2 cups sifted all-purpose flour	1 teasp. salt
¼ cup granulated sugar	1 teasp. nutmeg or mace
3 teasp. double-acting baking powder	¼ cup salad oil
	¾ cup milk
	1 egg

Combine all ingredients. With fork, stir until well mixed. Fry teaspoonfuls of mixture at 375°F. until golden brown — about 3 min. — as in Old-fashioned Doughnuts, To Fry, left. Drain; then roll in cinnamon-sugar mixture; top with Sugar Glaze, p. 649. Makes 2½ doz.

JIFFY DOUGHNUTS

These refrigerated doughnuts come in the same type of can as do biscuits. Even the "holes" are good. In using, follow label directions. Serve them plain or frosted with thin chocolate frosting, marshmallow cream, or butter cream; then sprinkle with chopped walnuts, flaked coconut, or chocolate sprinkles.

JELLY DOUGHNUTS

Separate 1 can refrigerated doughnuts. Do not remove centers. Fry in hot oil as label directs. Then lift out the top of each center and fill with jelly. Replace center and sprinkle with powdered sugar. Makes 12.

HONEY RINGS

1 can refrigerated biscuits	¼ cup honey
3 tablesp. melted butter or margarine	⅓ cup sifted confectioners' sugar
	1 teasp. cinnamon

With ¾" round cutter, cut center hole from each biscuit. Let biscuits and holes stand 15 min. Then fry both as in Old-fashioned Doughnuts, To Fry, left. Brush each, while warm, with melted butter. Combine honey, confectioners' sugar, cinnamon; spread lightly on doughnuts and holes. Makes 10 rings, plus holes. Nicest warm.

DOUGHNUT PUFFS: Fry whole biscuits; dip warm in cinnamon sugar.

Also see Tasty Yeast Doughnuts, p. 512.

BREADS AND ROLLS YOU BUY

Today you can serve superb breads and rolls, even on short notice, for there's a delectable assortment to choose from — ready-to-eat or brown-and-serve — right at your baker's or supermarket. And you can make them distinctively yours by glamorizing them as suggested in the following pages.

Before using these recipes, refer to How To Use Our Recipes, p. 3. Always use standard measuring cups and measuring spoons; measure level.

When You Store Bread

First Choice: In Your Freezer. The best place to store packaged bread and rolls is in your freezer or the freezing compartment of your refrigerator. Wrapped securely in original wrapper or in moisture-vapor-proof material and stored in the freezer, bread will retain its moisture and flavor, remain free of mold, and keep its freshness for several weeks.

Second Choice: In Ventilated Breadbox. The next best place to store wrapped bread is in a clean, dry, ventilated breadbox at room temperature, away from such heat-producing

equipment as ranges, refrigerators, radiators, etc. Wrapped bread, stored in a breadbox, will stay acceptably fresh several days, but is more subject to mold than bread stored in refrigerator or home freezer.

Third Choice: In Refrigerator. The least desirable place to store wrapped bread is in the food compartment of the refrigerator. Here wrapped bread retains its moisture and is less subject to mold, but it stales more readily than in the breadbox.

Reheating Bread and Rolls

If Frozen: Thaw wrapped sliced bread or rolls at room temperature. Heat on cookie sheet, uncovered, at 325°F. about 2 min.; serve at once. Or if still frozen, reheat, foil-wrapped or in covered casserole, at 400°F. about 12 min.

In Aluminum Foil: Snugly wrap baked bread slices or rolls, except hard-crusted varieties, in aluminum foil. Bake at 350°F. about 8 min., or till heated. If they're served in foil wrappings (turn foil edges down to form basket), they'll keep hot to the last delicious crumb.

In Covered Skillet: Put 2 tablesp. water in large skillet. Place round trivet in bottom, with un-iced rolls on it. Cover; leave over low heat 8 min., or until rolls are hot. For Iced Sweet Rolls: Do not cover skillet. Place uncovered skillet over medium heat 5 min., or till rolls are hot.

In Covered Container: Heat bakers' dinner rolls or other un-iced rolls in covered foil pan or covered casserole in 325°F. oven 15 min.; or in 400°F. oven 10 min., or until rolls are hot. If using a bun warmer with plastic handles set it over medium heat on range for about 10 min. or until hot.

By Toasting: Split your rolls or muffins; spread them with butter or margarine; sprinkle with grated cheese, seasoned salt, poppy seeds, etc., if desired; broil until golden.

If frozen sliced bread, toast slices twice, un-thawed, right in electric toaster. Or if you're reheating a quantity of slices, broil until golden, turning.

COFFEECAKE: Reheat in aluminum foil, or covered skillet as above; serve cut into strips. Or split, brush with butter or margarine, then broil till golden.

Slicing Fresh Bread

Hold knife blade under very hot water until it is hot. A hot blade will cut the freshest bread into perfectly smooth slices.

TOASTED ROLLS IN LOAF

1. Buy loaf of unsliced bread (it's wise to place order a day ahead). Trim crusts from top and sides of loaf. (For rounded top, peel off top crust.)
2. Cut *almost* through to bottom crust of loaf in any of ways below:
SQUARES: Cut crosswise into 1½″ slices, then lengthwise through middle.
JUMBO SLICES: Cut crosswise into 1″ slices.
THINSIES: Cut crosswise into as thin slices as possible.
TIPSY SLICES: Cut crosswise into ¾″ slices, drawing knife on extreme slant down through bread.
DIAMONDS: Cut diagonally into 2″ crosswise slices. Then cut diagonally in opposite direction, to form diamonds.

3. Spread cut surfaces, top, and sides of loaf with one of mixtures below. Bake in shallow pan at 400°F. 18 min., or until golden. Snip apart to serve.
SAVORY CHEESE: Mix ½ cup soft butter or margarine, ¼ cup minced onion, 1 tablesp. each of prepared mustard and poppy seeds. Spread on all loaf surfaces. Then arrange halved or quartered Swiss-cheese slices between cuts; top loaf with 2 halved bacon slices.
BUTTER CRUST: Cream ½ cup soft butter or margarine with one of these:

Blue cheese and a little minced onion
Grated process sharp Cheddar cheese (2 to 3 cups)
Snipped parsley or chives, or grated onion (¼ cup)
Dried savory and thyme (½ teasp. each), plus some snipped parsley and garlic salt
Light-brown sugar and cinnamon

FLUFFY CHEESE: Cream ¼ cup soft butter or margarine with 1 cup grated process sharp Cheddar cheese. Beat in 2 egg yolks. Fold in 2 egg whites, beaten stiff.
HAM AND CHEESE: Mix 1 4½-oz. can deviled ham with 2 3-oz. pkg. soft cream cheese and 1 teasp. each lemon juice and horse-radish.
CREAM CHEESE: Mix 1 3-oz. pkg. soft cream cheese; 2 tablesp. milk; 1 cup grated process sharp Cheddar cheese; 1 tablesp. each snipped parsley, horse-radish, and pimento; 1 teasp. each grated onion and lemon juice; and ¼ teasp. salt. After spreading mixture on loaf, wrap loaf in aluminum foil, leaving top open.
CELERY: Mix ½ cup soft butter or margarine, ¼ teasp. salt, dash cayenne pepper, ¼ teasp. paprika, ½ teasp. celery seeds. Salad oil or vegetable shortening may replace butter; if so, double salt and paprika.

ONION-RYE ROLLS IN LOAF

1. Start heating oven to 425°F.
2. In top of oval loaf of unsliced rye bread make 11 evenly spaced crosswise cuts almost to bottom crust. Spread each cut surface with butter. Now insert a thin onion slice in every other slit; cover with foil; place on cookie sheet. Bake 15 min., or till hot. To serve, cut through slits that have no onion. Serve a "roll" to each. Makes 6.

FAN-TAN LOAF

In 10″ x 5″ x 3″ loaf pan, place day-old loaf of bakers' sliced bread, top side up. Fill, then top, as below. Bake at 425°F. 15 min., or until hot and toasty. If baking only part of a loaf, use inverted custard cup to prop slices up in loaf pan.

Serve in loaf form; or cut apart with scissors.

CHEESY: Between bread slices, spread soft butter or margarine mixed with a little prepared mustard; then spread with some grated cheese or cheese spread (or insert halved cheese slices). Spread top of loaf with a little mayonnaise or soft butter. Sprinkle with grated cheese, then with a little grated onion, snipped chives, or a few sliced scallions, tossed with melted butter.

RELISH: Between slices and over top of loaf, spread soft butter or margarine mixed with a little garlic salt and one of these: prepared mustard, horse-radish, snipped parsley, or blue cheese.

SAVORY: Between slices and over top of loaf, spread soft butter or margarine mixed with one of these: celery, garlic, seasoned or onion salt; dried thyme; curry or chili powder plus garlic salt. Sprinkle with celery or poppy seeds or paprika.

SAVORY FRENCH BREAD

Use yard-long or junior-size loaf of French bread. Slash into thin, thick, or diagonal slices, *almost* through to bottom crust. If desired, rub garlic very lightly over crust.

Spread cut surfaces with one or more of the spreads below; then, if you wish, sprinkle with grated Parmesan cheese. (If desired, wrap in aluminum foil, leaving foil partially open at top.) Bake at 375°F. 15 to 20 min.

BUTTERY SPREADS: Cream ½ cup soft butter or margarine with one of these:

¼ teasp. each paprika and seasoned salt
2 tablesp. each snipped chives or minced onion, plus snipped parsley
2 tablesp. anchovy paste or prepared mustard
½ cup crumbled Danish blue cheese, plus 2 tablesp. snipped chives
Generous pinch dried herbs such as marjoram, thyme, or savory
1 teasp. poppy, celery, or caraway seeds

Bit of minced or mashed garlic, or garlic salt, plus snipped parsley
2 cups grated process sharp Cheddar cheese
Generous dash of curry powder

CREAMY SPREADS: To ½ cup commercial sour cream add ¼ teasp. each salt and horse-radish, plus dash pepper. Then add one of these:

½ 6-oz. pkg. flavored cream cheese
½ teasp. celery or poppy seeds
½ teasp. garlic, celery, or onion salt
1 teasp. paprika or curry powder
Pinch herbs and a little prepared mustard

CHEESE SPREADS: Use one of these:

Soft chive cream cheese, with salt and milk to moisten
Smoky-, sharp-, or pimento-cheese spread
Soft cream cheese, seasoned with horse-radish and garlic salt, with milk to moisten
Any flavored process-cheese-food roll, cut into thin rings (tuck into slashes)
Grated cheese, mixed with snipped parsley, garlic salt, and a little lemon juice
Grated cheese, mixed with caraway seeds, onion salt, and mayonnaise to moisten

FRENCH ONION-CHEESE LOAF: Use one of Buttery Spreads, left. Before baking loaf, into each gash insert 1 thin cheese slice and 1 thin onion slice.

GARLIC BREAD: Use garlic butter above or garlic spread in jar. Sprinkle with orégano, then grated Parmesan cheese.

FRENCH HALF-AND-HALF

Split long loaf of French bread lengthwise in half. Slash each half into 1¼″ diagonal slices, *almost* through to bottom crust. Top each half with one of spreads for Savory French Bread, left. Bake at 375°F. 10 to 15 min., or until golden.

JUNIOR LOAVES
(from hard or soft rolls)

Use hard or soft white, wheat, French, or frankfurter rolls. Slash each, almost through to bottom crust, into 2 or 3 thick chunks. Spread with one of spreads in Savory French Bread, left. Bake at 425°F. 10 min.

TOASTED FRENCH BREAD WEDGES

Start heating oven to 425°F. Slice long loaf of French bread into wedge-shaped pieces. Spread with butter mixed with celery, garlic, seasoned or onion salt; grated Parmesan cheese, or celery, poppy, or caraway seeds. Reassemble loaf on cookie sheet. Bake 12 min.

RYE TOASTIES

Blend 2 tablesp. soft butter or margarine with 2 tablesp. grated Parmesan cheese. Spread on 2 doz. thin slices party rye bread. Toast, on cookie sheet, in 400°F. oven 10 min. Luscious as snack or with salad or soup.

GARLIC RYE TOASTIES: Substitute ¼ cup butter or margarine blended with a little minced garlic for cheese spread. Or use garlic spread that comes in jars.

WARM RYE BREAD FINGERS

| 1 round rye loaf | Soft butter or |
| | margarine |

Make rye bread and butter sandwiches; cut into fingers, 1″ wide; refrigerate, wrapped in foil, till 25 min. before serving. Start heating oven to 350°F. Heat rye fingers, foil-wrapped, 15 min.

TOASTY SWEET BREADS
(nice with tea, coffee, or cocoa)

RAISIN ROLLS IN LOAF: Cut loaf of unsliced raisin bread crosswise into 1½″ slices, *almost* through to bottom crust; then cut lengthwise through center *almost* to bottom. Brush cut surfaces and top with melted butter or margarine. Sprinkle with mixture of sugar and cinnamon. Bake at 375°F. 15 min., or until golden.

QUICK COFFEECAKE: From loaf of day-old unsliced white bread, trim crusts. Cut loaf lengthwise in half. Cut each half into 1½″ slices, *almost* through to bottom, to form squares.

Spread cut surfaces, top, and sides with soft butter or margarine, or salad oil. Then cover each half with one of mixtures below. Bake at 375°F. 15 to 20 min. To serve, break "rolls" apart.

Nutted: Mix ¼ cup brown sugar with 2 tablesp. chopped nuts.

Coconut: Spread with sweetened condensed milk, then with flaked coconut and chopped walnuts.

Honey: Mix 2 tablesp. each honey and brown sugar. After spreading on bread, top with 2 tablesp. chopped walnuts.

Rum-Raisin: Mix ¼ cup white corn syrup with 1 tablesp. rum. After spreading on bread, top with 2 tablesp. each raisins and chopped walnuts, then 1 tablesp. sugar and ¼ teasp. cinnamon.

Sugar and Spice: Mix sugar with cinnamon.

SLICETTES

To Bake: Use all white-, or half white- and half wheat-bread slices. Cut slices in half. Stand, with cut edges up, in loaf pan or shallow "box" made of folded aluminum foil.

Between slices and over top of "loaf," spread one of mixtures below. Bake at 450°F. 15 min., or until toasted.

CHEESY (with soup or salad): Mix grated cheese with mayonnaise. Or thin chive cream cheese with milk and use.

SAVORY (for dinner): Substitute mayonnaise for butter in Savory Fan-Tan Loaf, p. 493.

CRISPY (for lunch): Use soft butter or margarine, alone or mixed with one of these:

Celery, garlic or onion salt	Dried thyme or rosemary
Prepared mustard	Curry powder
Horse-radish	Snipped parsley

TEALETS (with hot drinks): Spread bread first with butter or margarine; then top with one of these:

Cinnamon-sugar	cranberry sauce
Brown sugar and coconut	Marmalade
Cream cheese and marmalade, or canned jellied	Honey and grated orange rind or cinnamon

To Broil:

PIZZA STYLE: Toast bread slices on one side in broiler. Turn; spread with butter or margarine; top with cheese spread, a little anchovy paste, then with chili sauce and a pinch of orégano. Broil till bubbly.

IMITATION ONION FOCACCIA: Slice scallions medium fine. Add equal parts of soft pimento cream cheese and butter or margarine. Season with seasoned salt. Spread on ½″ slices French bread. Broil until bubbly. Cut into strips.

EASY BREAD STICKS
(to serve with soup, salad, or main dish)

From Frankfurter or Hard Rolls: Quarter rolls lengthwise. Spread cut sides, or all sides, with soft butter or margarine or salad oil. Roll in one of these: snipped parsley or chives; finely chopped nuts; poppy, caraway, sesame, or celery seeds; grated Parmesan cheese; bit of dried rosemary or thyme. Or roll in cinnamon and sugar with or without chopped walnuts. Or try using garlic spread (in jar). Bake at 425°F. 5 to 10 min. Or broil till golden brown.

From Unsliced Bread: From loaf of day-old unsliced bread, trim crusts. Cut lengthwise into ¾″ slices; then cut each slice into 4″ x ¾″ strips. Brush on all sides, except bottom, with melted butter or margarine, or salad oil; or spread thinly with mayonnaise. Then roll in, spread, or sprinkle with one of the mixtures below. Bake on cookie sheet at 350°F. 20 min., or until golden. Or broil till golden brown.

Poppy, celery, sesame, dill, or caraway seeds
Finely chopped walnuts
Grated process pimento or sharp Cheddar cheese, mixed with celery seeds, snipped parsley, or minced garlic or onion
Finely chopped stuffed olives and nuts
Peanut butter, butter, and honey
Horse-radish and prepared mustard
Grated cheese and chopped cooked bacon

Rye or Whole-Wheat Bread Sticks: Leave crusts on bread; prepare as in From Unsliced Bread above.

From Sliced Bread: Trim crusts from bread slices; prepare as in From Unsliced Bread above.

PULLED BREAD

From loaf of day-old unsliced bread, peel crusts. Then, with 2 forks, pull off 1½″ slices. With fork, tear each slice into thirds. Bake on rack in shallow pan, turning often, at 350°F. 20 to 25 min., or until golden.

MELBA TOAST

MELBA: Cut day-old unsliced bread into ⅛″ slices. If you like, remove crusts; then cut bread slices diagonally into triangles. Bake at 325°F. 15 min., or until golden crisp and curled, turning once. Serve hot or cold, with soup, salad, or main course.

EASY MELBA: Your grocer carries delicious packaged Melba toast in white, rye, whole-wheat, sesame, etc., flavors. Check his shelves.

FILLED BUTTER-FLAKE ROLLS

Partly separate leaves of packaged butter-flake rolls. Spread *all* leaves with soft butter or margarine; then spread *a few* leaves with one of fillings below.

For toasted rolls, set filled rolls in muffin-pan cups; for soft rolls, wrap in aluminum foil. Bake at 425°F. 5 to 10 min.

Fillings:

Chili sauce or catchup, mixed with horse-radish
Marmalade or preserves, mixed with chopped nuts
Danish blue cheese or grated Parmesan, mixed with butter
Mayonnaise, mixed with garlic salt (omit butter)
Brown sugar and cinnamon or nuts, mixed with butter
Curry powder and snipped parsley, added to butter
Peanut butter, mixed with honey and a bit of grated orange rind
Cottage cheese, in half of each roll; strawberry or other jam in other half. Bake in foil
Deviled ham, alternated with grated cheese
Cheese spread, mixed with bit of prepared mustard, chili sauce, or sautéed mushroom slices
Chive cream cheese, or smoky- or pimento-cheese spread, thinned with milk
Canned tuna or mashed sardines, mixed with mayonnaise, chili sauce, and snipped parsley. Bake in foil
Sprinkle of sesame or poppy seeds
Sprinkle of garlic or onion powder
Omit butter; spread leaves of rolls with garlic spread (in jar)

MUSHROOM FAN-TANS: Combine 2 3- or 4-oz. cans sliced mushrooms, drained and coarsely chopped, with ½ cup soft butter or margarine. Open sections of 12 butter-flake rolls; spread sections and tops with mushroom-butter mixture. Wrap rolls, side by side, in foil. Bake at 375°F. 15 min., or until heated and crisp.

For uses of packaged biscuit and bread mixes, as well as refrigerated canned biscuits and rolls of all kinds, see pp. 477–479.

BROWN-AND-SERVE ROLLS

Packaged brown-and-serve rolls come completely "raised" and almost completely baked. The golden crust appears with the last-minute baking you give them.

Choose from: Parkerhouse, clover-leaf, bowknot, poppy-seed, sesame, crescent, club, and Vienna rolls, and French bread.

To Store: Refrigerate up to 2 weeks, or freezer-wrap and freeze up to 6 months.

To Bake: Rolls may be baked right from refrigerator or freezer. However, for best results, bring to room temperature before browning in oven as label directs.

BROWN-AND-SERVE STICKIES

In bottom of 9" x 5" x 3" loaf pan, spread one of mixtures below. Place 8 brown-and-serve soft rolls upside down, on mixture. Bake at 400°F. 25 min. Let stand 1 min.; invert pan; remove rolls.

NUT: Mix 3 tablesp. melted butter or margarine; 1/3 cup brown sugar, packed, and 3 tablesp. chopped nuts.

CARAMEL-ORANGE: Mix 1/4 cup granulated sugar, 1 teasp. grated orange rind, 1½ tablesp. orange juice, 1/4 teasp. mace, and 1 tablesp. melted butter or margarine.

GLAZE-TOPPED BROWN-AND-SERVES

In each greased muffin-pan cup, place one of mixtures below. Arrange brown-and-serve soft rolls, upside down, on mixture in cups. Bake at 400°F. 15 min. Let stand 1 min.; invert pan; remove. Serve at once.

COCONUT: For each muffin-pan cup mix 2 teasp. brown sugar, 1 teasp. flaked coconut, 1 teasp. melted butter or margarine, 1/2 teasp. water.

BUTTERSCOTCH: Boil 1/4 cup butter or margarine with 1/2 cup brown sugar, packed, and 1 tablesp. water for 8 to 10 min. Place 1 tablesp. of this syrup in each greased muffin-pan cup. Sprinkle with chopped nuts.

ORANGE: Mix 1/4 teasp. orange juice and a pinch of grated orange rind to place in each muffin-pan cup. (When rolls are baked, drizzle on icing made by mixing 1/2 cup confectioners' sugar with about 1 tablesp. orange juice.)

TOASTED ENGLISH MUFFINS
(plus variations)

For toasting, they're best pulled apart (not cut) as follows: With the tines of a dinner fork lightly puncture the edge of each muffin all the way around; then, with your fingers, gently pull the muffin apart, turning it slowly as you pull. The resulting hills and valleys on the surface of the split muffin make it toast (or broil), then "butter," to golden perfection.

To Vary: After spreading split muffins with butter, top with one of these; then toast under broiler.

Soft cream cheese, then bit of jelly
Caraway, celery, or poppy seeds
Grated cheese or crumbled Danish blue cheese
Cinnamon and sugar, then chopped nuts
Grated Parmesan cheese, then garlic salt
Soft sharp-cheese spread, then a little catchup, grated Parmesan cheese, snipped anchovies, garlic salt, and dried thyme

French Toasted: Dip split English muffin halves, one at a time, into French toast mixture, p. 497. Then sauté in hot shortening in skillet, first on split side, then on other side until golden, turning once. Serve with jelly, jam, honey, maple-blended or buttered syrup; or top with favorite creamed mixture.

TOAST

In Oven: Butter thinly sliced bread. Top with one of the following. Bake at 425°F. as directed.

Cream cheese, topped with marmalade, canned jellied cranberry sauce, or bits of blue cheese. Bake 8 min.
Snipped parsley or chives. Bake 5 min.

Broiler: Toast bread on one side in broiler. Then turn; butter; top with one of the following; finish toasting in broiler.

Prepared mustard and thin onion rings
Cheese spread, dots of anchovy paste, chili sauce or catchup, then orégano
Honey, then sprinkling of cinnamon
Honey, mixed with grated orange rind
Brown sugar, then chopped nuts or coconut
Garlic spread (in jar)

In Skillet: Melt butter or margarine in skillet. Sprinkle with paprika or celery, garlic, seasoned or onion salt. Sauté bread slices in this mixture till golden on both sides.

In Waffle Iron: Bake unbuttered bread slices in waffle iron till golden.

In Electric Toaster: Just pop bread into toaster. Today's toasters are better than ever.

CINNAMON TOAST

Mix 1 teasp. cinnamon with 3 tablesp. sugar. Or use packaged cinnamon-sugar mixture. Sprinkle generously over hot buttered toast. Serve hot, as is, or cut into strips or triangles.

Or toast bread on one side in broiler. Then turn; butter untoasted side; sprinkle with cinnamon-sugar mixture; broil until bubbly. Serve hot.

To Vary: For cinnamon mixture, substitute brown or maple sugar; honey; grated cheese; or a blend of 1 tablesp. orange juice, 1 tablesp. grated orange rind, and ½ cup granulated sugar.

CINNAMON-PUFF TOAST

From loaf of unsliced bread, cut 3 1"-thick slices. Remove crusts; cut each slice into 3 strips.

Quickly dip strips into ⅓ cup heavy cream. Brush with 2 tablesp. melted butter or margarine; then coat thickly on all sides with 1 tablesp. cinnamon mixed with 3 tablesp. sugar. Arrange on rack, set in shallow baking pan. Bake at 400°F. 20 min. Makes 9 toast fingers.

FRENCH TOAST

2 eggs	Butter, margarine, or
½ teasp. salt	bacon fat
1 tablesp. sugar	6 white- or whole-
¼ cup milk	wheat-bread slices

Break eggs into shallow dish; with fork, beat lightly; stir in salt, sugar, milk. Heat a little butter in skillet. *Quickly* dip bread slices, one at a time, into egg mixture; turn until just well coated. In hot butter, brown at once on both sides. Makes 6 servings.
Serve immediately with one of these:
Crisp bacon or fried ham
Buttered syrup, molasses, jelly, jam, marmalade, honey, maple-flavored syrup, or applesauce
Confectioners' sugar; sprinkling of lemon juice

FLUFFY: Separate eggs. Beat whites with salt and sugar until stiff. Beat yolks until thick and lemon-colored; add milk. Fold whites into yolks. Dip bread into mixture; brown as above.
DE LUXE: Substitute light or heavy cream for milk; add 2 teasp. sherry.
PETITE: Slice hard rolls or French bread ½" or ¾" thick. Dip and sauté as above. Or dip

slices into maple or maple-blended syrup; then sauté in butter or margarine till golden on both sides.
OVEN CINNAMON: Add 1 teasp. of cinnamon to egg mixture at left. Dip bread slices, then lay on well-greased cookie sheet. Bake at 500°F. 5 min. on each side. Serve with buttered syrup or maple-blended syrup.
FRENCH TOAST CUPS: Dip bread as for French Toast, left, then press each dipped bread slice in a buttered custard cup. Bake at 350°F. 20 min., or until golden. Remove, then spoon fluffy scrambled eggs or creamed dried beef into cups.
FROZEN FRENCH TOAST: Prepare as label directs. Sprinkle with cinnamon and sugar; or spoon on fresh or thawed frozen berries.

MOCK PATTY SHELLS

TOAST CUPS: Brush thinly sliced bread (crusts removed) with melted butter or margarine. Press each slice into 3" muffin-pan cup. Bake at 375°F. about 12 min., or until golden. Remove from cups. Use as patty shells to hold creamed mixture.
FRENCH TOAST CUPS: See above.
CROUSTADES OR TOAST CASES: Cut unsliced bread 2" thick; remove crusts. Cut into squares or oblongs; or with cutter, cut into rounds or hearts. Hollow out, leaving ⅜"-thick wall. Brush with melted butter or margarine. Bake at 375°F. about 12 to 15 min., or until golden. Use as patty shells to hold creamed mixture. Use leftover trimmings for bread crumbs.
CHEESE CROUSTADES: When Croustades, above, are partially toasted, brush with melted butter or margarine; then sprinkle with grated cheese.

FROZEN PATTY SHELLS

Delightful patty shells now come frozen. Bake them as label directs, sprinkling with grated Parmesan cheese last few minutes of baking time, if desired. Use to hold creamed mixtures, thawed frozen berries or mixed fruit, or ice cream topped with fruit.

HEART SHELLS

36 slices bread	⅓ cup melted short-
½ cup milk	ening

Start heating oven to 400°F. For each patty

shell use 3 slices bread. With a large heart cookie cutter, cut a heart from each bread slice. With a smaller heart cutter, cut centers from 24 of these hearts, leaving frames. Brush top side of each large heart and both sides of frames with milk. Stack 2 frames on each large heart base to form a heart patty shell. Brush top, side, and center of each patty shell with shortening. Place shells on a greased cookie sheet. Bake, along with the tiny heart cutouts, 10 min., or until crisp, golden. Serve filled with a favorite creamed food. Makes 12 heart shells.

BREAD PATTY SHELLS

18 slices bread
¼ cup milk
2 tablesp. melted shortening

Start heating oven to 400°F. Use 3 slices of bread for each patty shell. With a large cookie cutter cut each slice into a round. With smaller cookie cutter cut centers from 12 rounds to form circles. Brush the top side of the rounds and both sides of the circles with milk. Stack two circles on one round to form a patty shell. Brush top, side, and center of each patty shell with shortening. Place shells and centers on a greased cookie sheet. Bake 10 min., or until shells are crisp and lightly browned. Serve,

filled with a favorite creamed food, and topped with one of centers. Makes 6 bread patty shells. NOTE: Toast the leftover bread trimmings and use for bread crumbs.

COCONUT DESSERT SHELLS A LA MODE

18 slices bread
⅓ cup canned sweet-ened condensed milk
½ cup flaked coconut
or chopped walnuts
1 pint ice cream (any variety)
⅓ cup ice-cream sauce

Start heating oven to 400°F. Use three slices of bread for each dessert shell. With a large heart cookie cutter, cut a heart from each slice. With a smaller heart cutter, cut centers from twelve hearts, leaving frames. Brush the top side of the large heart bases and frames with condensed milk. Stack two frames on each large heart base to form a heart dessert shell. Brush sides with condensed milk. Press coconut against side, top, and inside surfaces of dessert shells. Place on a greased cookie sheet. Bake about 10 min., or until lightly browned. Cool. At serving time, place a scoop of ice cream in each shell and ladle sauce over all. Makes 6 dessert shells.

DELECTABLE YEAST BREADS

You've never worked with yeast before? Why not? It's so much easier nowadays, and your bakings are sure to charm your family.

Before you begin, be sure that utensils, work surfaces, and your hands are clean. This is a must for good yeast rolls, breads, and cakes. Remember, too, that yeast likes a cozy, warm, even temperature. And, of course, you'll use only the best ingredients.

Ingredients

ACTIVE DRY YEAST: This modern dry yeast, which comes in 1/4-oz. packages and in 4-oz. jars, stays fresh for several months on a cool, dry shelf and gives uniformly fine results if used before the expiration date on the package.

When dissolved in warm water, 1 pkg. active dry yeast works the same as a 3/5-oz. cake of compressed yeast; use it, as you would dissolved cake yeast, in any favorite recipe.

CAKE YEAST (COMPRESSED): Cake yeast is perishable and so must be kept in the refriger-

ator and for not longer than a week or two. It can be frozen for as long as six months, but when thawed, at room temperature, it should be used immediately. To determine whether it's usable, crumble it between your fingers; if it crumbles easily, even though the edges are slightly brown from drying, it is still good.

FLOUR: We use all-purpose wheat flour most often for bread making. See p. 92.

LIQUIDS TO DISSOLVE YEAST: Either milk or water is the liquid ordinarily used in yeast breads and cakes. The milk may be whole, diluted evaporated, or reliquefied nonfat dry milk.

Because yeast is a living plant, too much heat can kill its action, while not enough heat can slow it down.

DISSOLVING YEAST: For best results, sprinkle active dry, or crumble cake yeast, in warm water (105°F. to 115°F.), in a warm bowl. Let it settle for a few seconds, then stir to dissolve. To test temperature of liquid, drop a little on the inside of your wrist. It should feel comfortably warm but not hot.

ADDING OTHER LIQUIDS: Once the yeast is *dis-*

499

solved and ready to act, it must not come into contact with liquids that are warmer than luke-warm or its action may be killed. Test the milk mixture, if scalded, making sure it's cooled to lukewarm (90°F. to 95°F.) before adding dis-solved yeast. (A few drops on inside of wrist will feel neither warm nor cold.)

Beating Batters, Kneading Doughs

If Yeast Batter: After the first 1 or 2 cups of flour have been stirred into a batter bread mix-ture, beat it vigorously with a spoon or with an electric mixer. When it is beaten long enough, it tends to leave the sides of the bowl, follow the spoon or mixer beaters, and look shiny and smooth.

If Yeast Dough: After mixing up a bread dough as recipe directs, turn it onto lightly floured surface. A pastry board, canvas pastry cloth, or table top makes kneading easy — espe-cially if they're soft doughs, which make deli-cate breads. Measure out about ½ cup flour; use to sprinkle, little by little, on surface as you knead — the exact amount depending on the dough.

How to Knead: With floured hands, flatten dough very slightly by pressing it firmly; shape into round, flat ball. Now you are ready to knead as follows:
1. Pick up edge of dough at point farthest from you; fold over on top edge nearest you.
2. With heels of hands, press down, gently but firmly, pushing ball of dough away from you 3 or 4 times.
3. Now turn dough one quarter of the way around on board; repeat the folding, pushing, and turning until dough looks full and round-ed, smooth, satiny, and tightly stretched — about 8 to 10 min. Dough should no longer be sticky; if it has bits of fruit or nuts in it, the dough between the bits should be smooth.

Rising

If Yeast Batter: After beating, a bread bat-ter is ready to rise. With spatula, scrape it down from sides of bowl. Cover with wax paper and a clean towel — or a large pot cover, din-ner plate, or foil. Set bowl in a warm place (80°F. to 85°F.), free from drafts, until batter has doubled in bulk and looks moist and some-what rough, with small bubbles just under sur-face.

If Yeast Dough: Cover kneaded dough with one end of pastry cloth or paper towel while you wash out mixing bowl in which it was mixed. Grease bowl lightly. Place dough in bowl with its smooth top down; then turn dough over once, so its top is up. Now dough is all greased. Then cover it with a piece of wax paper and a clean towel and let rise, away from drafts, in a warm place (80°F. to 85°F.), until doubled in bulk.

If It's Hot Weather: Keep dough out of direct sunlight and away from extra heat of kitchen. You may have to place bowl of dough in a large pan of cool, not cold, water.

If It's Cold Weather: Warm bowl with hot water before putting in the dough. Then place bowl of dough in warm place — near range or radiator, *but never on top of either*. If the room is cold, you can place dough in an unheated oven, with a large pan of hot water on oven floor beneath it; or set it on the broiler rack, with hot water in broiler pan. Or set bowl of dough in a deep pan of water that is just barely warm, not hot, on your wrist.

Testing for Doubled in Bulk

Rich batters and doughs that contain large amounts of sugars, shortening, and eggs rise more slowly than less rich ones.
BATTER: When "doubled in bulk," bread bat-ter looks bubbly and moist, with a somewhat rough, rounded, and soft top. To test it, press lightly with little finger near edge of batter. If small dent remains, bread has risen enough.
DOUGH: To test bread dough for "doubled in bulk," press tip of 2 fingers, lightly and quickly, about ½ inch into top of dough. If dents re-main when fingers are withdrawn, dough is light enough to be called "doubled in bulk." If dents fill immediately, let dough rise about 15 min. longer and test again.

Punching Down

BATTER: When doubled in bulk, stir down bat-ter with a spoon to almost its original size.
DOUGH: When doubled in bulk, punch dough down by pushing fist into center of dough.

Then pull edges of dough to center and turn ball over so bottom is on top, with rounded sides up. If directed to do so, let dough rise again, then punch down again. Otherwise, turn it out onto a lightly floured surface.

Shaping Loaves

1. After punching down dough, form it into a smooth, round ball. Then, with sharp knife, cut into portions — one for each loaf desired; shape each into ball. Cover with towel and let "rest" on board 5 to 10 min. — so they will be easier to handle. Lightly grease desired number of 9″ x 5″ x 3″ loaf pans.
2. With fingers, flatten each ball of dough; then press flattened dough into oblong about 9″ x 7″ x 1″. Its width will be almost the length of the bread pan.
3. Fold each end of oblong to center, overlapping them slightly. Press each fold down firmly. (Working with both hands helps to shape loaf evenly.) Now pinch center overlap, then narrow ends, to seal dough into shape. Then place loaf, with sealed seam down, in greased loaf pan; brush with melted fat or salad oil. Repeat with other pieces of dough.
4. Cover loaves with clean towel. Set in warm place (80°F. to 85°F.); let rise until doubled in bulk, or until sides of dough have reached top of pan and center is well rounded above pan. At this stage dough will be puffy and light, and if pressed very gently with finger tip, slight indentation will remain.

Shaping Rolls

Make dough for Refrigerator Rolls De Luxe, p. 503; or Twinkling Rolls, p. 502. Or use packaged hot-roll mix.

Turn dough onto lightly floured surface. Shape as below; brush with melted butter or margarine; let rise; then bake as recipe directs.

CLOVERLEAF ROLLS: Form dough into long rolls, 1″ in diameter. Cut off 1″ pieces. Form each piece into smooth ball; dip into melted butter or margarine. Place 3 balls in each greased muffin-pan cup, with balls touching bottom of pan.

BREAD STICKS: Roll dough ½″ thick. Cut into 6″ x ½″ strips. Pinch each strip into pencil-like shape. Then, while still on board, place fingers on ends of each strip and gently roll strip back and forth, moving fingers to center, then out to ends again, to form evenly shaped 10″ x ⅜″ stick. Place sticks 1″ apart on greased cookie sheet.

CRESCENTS: Roll dough ¼″ thick. Cut into 9″ circles, using 9″ pie plate as guide. Cut each circle into 12 wedges. Brush with melted butter or margarine. Starting at wider edge, roll up each wedge. Place with center point down, 2″ apart, on greased cookie sheet. Curve ends to form crescents.

DINNER ROLLS: Shape pieces of dough into 2″ balls. With floured hands, roll each ball 4″ long, making ends taper. Place 1″ apart on greased cookie sheet. (Make finger or salad rolls smaller.)

VIENNA ROLLS: Make Dinner Rolls, above; brush with slightly beaten egg white mixed with 1 tablesp. water. Sprinkle with caraway seeds.

FAN-TANS: Roll dough into rectangle ⅛″ thick. Brush with melted butter or margarine. Cut into 1½″-wide strips. Stack 6 or 7 strips together. Cut into 1½″-wide pieces; place, with cut sides up, in greased muffin-pan cups.

OLD-FASHIONED PAN ROLLS: Cut off pieces of dough; shape into 2″ balls. Dip into melted butter or margarine. Place in greased 8″ layer pan, letting balls just touch each other.

PARKERHOUSE ROLLS: Roll dough ⅛″ thick. Cut into rounds with 2½″ floured cookie cutter. Crease each with dull edge of knife to one side of center. Brush lightly with melted butter or margarine. Fold larger side of each round over smaller, pressing edges together. Place rounds 1″ apart on greased cookie sheet.

Baking

Always bake bread batters and doughs in preheated oven. When baking 2 loaves or 2 pans of rolls, place on center shelf in oven with 2″ between pans to allow heat to circulate. For 4 loaves, stagger them on 2 shelves as follows: On upper shelf, place them at right front and left back; on lower shelf, place at left front and right back.

If breads brown too rapidly, cover with piece of heavy brown paper.

If desired, before baking loaves, brush with milk; or for every 4 loaves, mix 1 tablesp. egg yolk with ¼ cup water; brush on loaves — for a glazed crust.

Cooling and Crust Treatment

1. At end of baking time, remove bread or rolls from pans.
2. Then place, uncovered, on wire racks or across top edges of pans to cool, so air can circulate around them and preserve the bread's crispness.
3. Then grease or not as follows, depending on crust desired:

Crisp crust: Do not grease loaves again.

Soft tender crust: Brush loaves with soft shortening just after removing from oven.

Storing Yeast Breads

When thoroughly cool, wrap bread in wax paper, foil, or saran. Store in covered bread box or freeze. See When You Store Bread, p. 491.

LUSCIOUS ROLLS AND BUNS

TWINKLING ROLLS

¾ cup scalded milk	1 pkg. active dry, or
1 teasp. salt	cake, yeast
¼ cup soft shortening	¼ cup warm water
3 to 4 tablesp. granu-	3½ to 4 cups sifted
lated sugar	all-purpose flour
1 egg, slightly beaten	

In large bowl, cool scalded milk till lukewarm; stir in salt, shortening, sugar, egg. Sprinkle or crumble yeast into warm water in measuring cup; stir until dissolved. Stir into lukewarm milk mixture. Add half of flour; beat till smooth. Stir in rest of flour to form stiff dough; beat well.

Place dough in large, greased, clean bowl, turning dough to grease well. Cover with wax paper and clean towel; let rise in warm place (80°F. to 85°F.) until doubled in bulk. Turn out onto lightly floured surface; knead until smooth and elastic, adding flour if needed.

Cut into 18 equal pieces; form each into ball. Place 1 ball in each of 18 greased 2½" muffin-pan cups. Cover with towel; let rise in warm place until doubled in bulk. Bake at 425°F. 15 min., or until done. Makes 1½ doz.

BUTTERSCOTCH PECAN ROLLS: Make and raise dough, left. Meanwhile, boil ¾ cup water with 1 cup plus 2 tablesp. brown sugar, packed, 5 min. Place 1 tablesp. of this syrup in each of 18 greased 2½" muffin-pan cups. Put 4 pecan halves, with rounded sides down, on top of syrup in each cup.

Turn dough out onto lightly floured surface; cut into 18 equal pieces. Form each into ball; place 1 ball in each muffin-pan cup. Cover with towel; let rise in warm place until doubled in bulk. Bake at 425°F. 12 to 15 min. Invert pan at once. Remove rolls, turning pecan sides up. Makes 1½ doz.

CHEESE ROLLS: Add 1 cup grated process Cheddar cheese (¼ lb.) with first 2 cups flour.

WILLIAMSBURG BUNS: Decrease milk to ½ cup. Reduce flour to 2¼ cups, sifting it with ½ teasp. each nutmeg and mace. After first rising, beat well. Fill 12 greased 3" muffin-pan cups two thirds full. Cover with towel; let rise in warm place until it rounds slightly above tops of cups. Bake at 400°F. 15 min., or until done. (You may replace 2 tablesp. milk with 2 tablesp. sherry.) Makes 1 doz.

SUGAR-AND-SPICE BUNS: Make and bake Williamsburg Buns, above; then dip tops and sides *at once* into 6 tablesp. melted butter or margarine; then roll in combined ½ cup granulated sugar and 1 teasp. cinnamon.

WHOLE-WHEAT ROLLS: Substitute 1½ cups unsifted whole-wheat flour for 1½ cups sifted all-purpose flour.

LAST-MINUTE ROLLS

1¼ cups scalded milk	2 pkg. active dry, or
2½ tablesp. granu-	cakes, yeast
lated sugar	¼ cup warm water
1½ teasp. salt	3¼ cups sifted all-
¼ cup soft shortening	purpose flour

About 1½ hr. before dinner: Into scalded milk, in large bowl, stir sugar, salt, shortening; cool till lukewarm. Sprinkle or crumble yeast into warm water in measuring cup; stir until dissolved. Stir into lukewarm milk mixture. Add flour; stir until well blended — about 1 min.

Cover batter with wax paper and clean towel; let rise in warm place (80°F. to 85°F.) until doubled in bulk. Stir well; then beat vigorously

Our Giant Popovers, p. 481

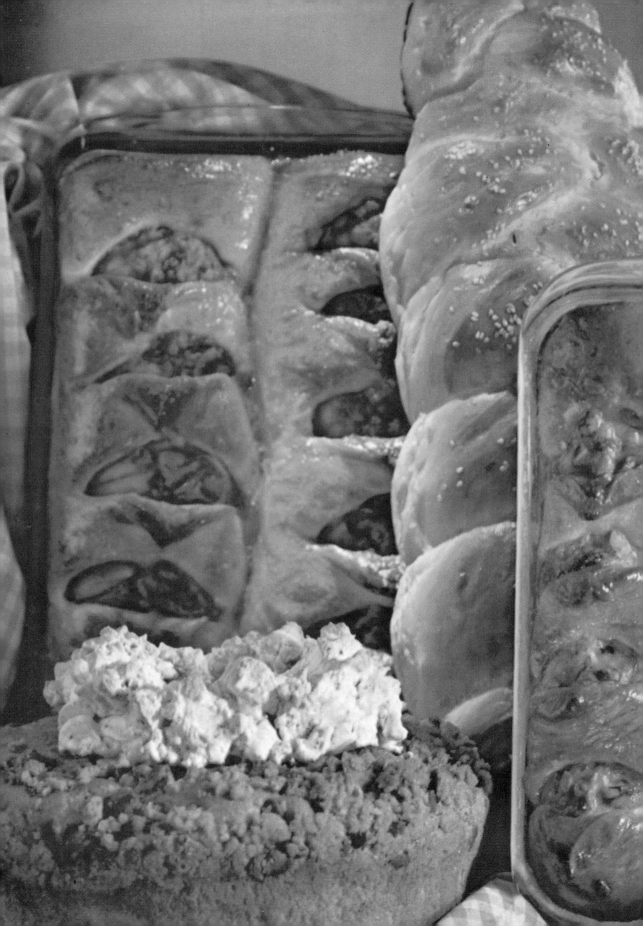

about ½ min. Fill greased 3″ muffin-pan cups about two thirds full. Bake at 400°F. about 25 min. Remove rolls from pans while hot. Makes 1 doz.

REFRIGERATOR ROLLS DE LUXE

1 pkg. active dry, or cake, yeast	1 cup unseasoned hot mashed potatoes
½ cup warm water	1 cup cold water
½ cup soft butter or margarine	1½ teasp. salt
½ cup soft shortening	About 6 to 6½ cups sifted all-purpose
¾ cup granulated sugar	flour

In large bowl, sprinkle or crumble yeast into warm water; stir until dissolved. Stir in butter, shortening, sugar, potatoes, then cold water, salt, and enough flour to make stiff dough. Place dough in greased large clean bowl. Turn to grease all sides. Then cover tightly with wax paper or foil and clean towel; refrigerate.

To use dough, cut off only as much as you need, returning rest to refrigerator, covered (dough keeps 2 or 3 days in refrigerator). Shape dough as in Shaping Rolls, p. 501. Brush lightly with melted butter or margarine. Cover with towel; let rise in warm place (80°F. to 85°F.) until doubled in bulk. Bake at 425°F. 20 to 25 min., or until done. Makes 3 doz.

In Sweden, on December 13th, the young daughters of the household bring coffee and saffron or cardamom buns to their parents.

SAFFRON LUCIA BUNS
(Lussekatt)

¾ cup milk	1 egg, beaten
½ teasp. saffron	3½ cups sifted all-purpose flour
1 pkg. active dry, or cake, yeast	
¼ cup warm water	¼ cup soft butter or margarine
¼ cup granulated sugar	Light or dark raisins
1 teasp. salt	Beaten egg

Make early on the day, or day before if desired:

1. In saucepan, combine milk and saffron; heat, while stirring, till saffron is completely dissolved; pour into large bowl; cool to luke-
2. Meanwhile, sprinkle or crumble yeast into warm.

warm water; stir till dissolved. Add to lukewarm milk with sugar, salt, 1 egg, 2 cups flour; beat with spoon till smooth. Cover with wax paper and clean towel; let stand in warm place (80°F. to 85°F.) 1 hr.
3. With spoon, beat in butter or margarine, then remaining flour, a little at a time, till smooth and elastic; add ¼ cup raisins; mix well. Cover; let rise in warm place (80°F. to 85°F.) until doubled in bulk — about 2 hr.
4. Turn dough onto lightly floured surface, knead 1 min., then make into one or several of shapes below.
5. Let rise in warm place until light — about 45 min. Meanwhile, start heating oven to 375°F. Bake buns 18 to 20 min., or till light golden; remove to rack. Makes 6 to 7.

LUCIA CATS: With palms of hands roll some of dough into pencil-shaped roll 15″ long, ½″ thick; cut in half. Lay two pieces, side by side, on greased cookie sheet; pinch together just in center. Then curl the ends outward; place a raisin in each curl. Repeat. Then brush cats with beaten egg, and let rise and bake as in step 5 above.

HALF LUCIA CATS: With palms of hands roll some of dough into pencil-shaped roll 8″ long, ½″ thick. Lay roll on greased cookie sheet; then shape into letter S; curl ends inward; place raisin in curl. Repeat. Then brush cats with beaten egg, and let rise and bake as in step 5 above.

CARDAMOM LUCIA BUNS: Omit saffron; add 1 tablesp. ground cardamom with flour in step 2.

FRENCH PETITS PAINS AU CHOCOLAT

1 pkg. active dry, or cake, yeast	4 eggs
¼ cup warm water	4½ cups sifted all-purpose flour
¾ cup scalded milk	Salad oil
½ cup shortening	Soft butter or margarine
½ cup granulated sugar	12 ⅞-oz. bars milk chocolate
¾ teasp. salt	

Start early in day:

1. Sprinkle or crumble yeast into warm water; stir until dissolved. In large bowl, combine milk, shortening, sugar, and salt; cool till lukewarm. Then stir in 3 beaten eggs.
2. With spoon, beat in 2 cups flour until batter is very elastic and almost smooth.

Chocolate-Flecked Coffeecake (lower left), p. 511
Braided Onion Bread (upper middle right), p. 506
Nut-Fruit Coffeecake (upper left), p. 510

3. Stir in yeast, then remaining 2½ cups flour. Brush top of dough with salad oil; cover with wax paper and clean towel; let rise in warm place (80°F. to 85°F.) until doubled in bulk.

4. Punch down dough by pressing gently into middle. Turn onto lightly floured surface; knead lightly 3 to 5 min.; then roll ¼″ thick.

5. With 3½″ floured biscuit cutter, cut dough into 24 circles. Pat each circle into a 4½″ oval; then spread with soft butter or margarine.

6. Place half of one chocolate bar, folded in half, in center of each oval. Pinch together lengthwise edges of each oval, enclosing chocolate bar. Place, seam side down, on ungreased cookie sheet.

7. Brush the rolls generously with 1 beaten egg. Let rise in warm place until doubled in bulk. Meanwhile, start heating oven to 400°F. When rolls have doubled, bake 15 min.

To serve:

Serve warm at your mid-morning coffee. Or, if for mid-afternoon or evening refreshment, reheat, wrapped in foil, in a 350°F. oven for about 15 min. Makes 2 doz.

NOTE: If you'd rather have the chocolate peek through the sides of the rolls, place pieces of chocolate ¼″ from lengthwise edge of ovals. Then fold far side of each oval over chocolate, and pinch front edges together.

You may substitute 1 heaping measuring teaspoonful of semisweet-chocolate pieces for bar chocolate in each roll.

BUNNY IN A BASKET

1 pkg. active dry, or cake, yeast	1 egg, well beaten
½ cup warm water	3 tablesp. orange juice
¾ cup milk, scalded	1½ tablesp. grated orange rind
6 tablesp. shortening	4¼ cups sifted all-purpose flour
½ cup granulated sugar	Salad oil
¾ teasp. salt	

Start day before:

1. Sprinkle or crumble yeast into warm water; stir until dissolved.

2. Into large bowl, pour scalded milk; add shortening, sugar, and salt. Cool to lukewarm. Add yeast mixture. Add egg, orange juice, and rind; mix well.

3. Gradually stir in flour; beat 4 min. Then brush top of dough with salad oil; cover; let

rise in warm place (80°F. to 85°F.) till doubled in bulk.

4. Then punch dough down; wrap it tightly in wax paper; refrigerate.

One and a half hours before serving:

1. On lightly floured surface, knead dough 8 to 10 min.; cut into 12 equal pieces.

2. With palms of hands, roll one of pieces into a 12½″ x ½″ rope. Cut 3½″ from rope, and set aside for bunny's head. Then, on ungreased cookie sheet, hold ½″ of one end of remaining rope upright (bunny's cottontail), while winding rest of rope twice around it in spiral and tucking other end under, to form his body.

3. With palm of hand, roll reserved 3½″ of rope into 1¼″ ball. Place at top of body for head. Midway, on both sides of head, make ⅜″ cut with scissors. Then, at top center of head, make a ½″ cut that divides upper half in two. Now pinch each of these halves into a tapered bunny's ear. Repeat for rest of bunnies.

4. Let bunnies rise until almost doubled in bulk. Meanwhile, start heating oven to 400°F. Bake them 10 to 12 min. Then, while they're still warm, brush with Orange Icing (below), if desired.

5. To serve, stand each bunny in tiny basket. Or tuck several in napkin-lined basket. Makes 12.

ORANGE ICING: Combine 1½ tablesp. orange juice, ¾ teasp. grated orange rind, ¾ cup sifted confectioners' sugar. Use to glaze warm bunnies.

BERT'S BRIOCHE

¼ cup scalded milk	sifted all-purpose flour
1 pkg. active dry, or cake, yeast	⅓ cup soft butter or margarine
¼ cup warm water	1 egg
¼ cup granulated sugar	2 egg yolks
¼ teasp. salt	½ teasp. lemon extract
2 cups plus 6 tablesp.	

Start afternoon before:

Cool milk till lukewarm. Sprinkle or crumble yeast into warm water; stir until dissolved. Add to lukewarm milk, with sugar, salt, 1 cup flour; with spoon, beat till smooth. Beat in butter, then egg and yolks, one at a time. Add 1 cup plus 6 tablesp. flour and extract; beat 5 min. Brush with salad oil. Cover with wax paper and clean towel; let rise in warm place (80°F.

to 85°F.) until doubled in bulk. Cover with wax paper and damp towel; refrigerate 12 hr. *Early next day:*

Turn dough onto lightly floured surface; form into 2″ balls. Place 1 ball in each of 18 to 20 3″ muffin-pan cups. Brush tops with salad oil. Cover with towel; let rise in warm place until doubled in bulk. Bake at 375°F. 15 min., or until done. Makes 18 to 20.

BRUNCH BRIOCHE: In morning, after dough has been refrigerated 12 hr., turn onto lightly floured surface. Roll into 14″ x 6″ x ½″ rectangle. Cut into 12 lengthwise strips, ½″ wide. Braid 3 strips together; cut into thirds; then pinch ends; repeat. Set on greased cookie sheet. Cover with towel; let rise in warm place until doubled in bulk. Bake at 375°F. 12 min., or until done. Remove; while brioche are warm, frost with Sugar Glaze, p. 649. Makes about 12.

BEAUTIFUL BREADS

WHOLE-WHEAT BREAD

¾ cup milk	2 pkg. active dry, or
3 tablesp. sugar	cakes, yeast
4 teasp. salt	4½ cups unsifted
⅓ cup margarine	whole-wheat flour
or butter	About 3¼ cups sifted
⅓ cup molasses	all-purpose flour
1½ cups warm water	

Scald milk; stir in sugar, salt, margarine or butter, and molasses; cool to lukewarm. Measure warm water into large warm bowl. Sprinkle or crumble in yeast; stir until dissolved. Stir in lukewarm milk mixture, 2 cups whole-wheat flour, and 2 cups all-purpose flour; beat until smooth. Add enough remaining flours to make soft dough. Turn out on lightly floured board and knead until smooth and elastic, about 8 to 10 min. Place in greased bowl, turning to grease top. Cover; let rise in warm place (80°F. to 85°F.), free from draft, until doubled in bulk, about 1 hr.

Punch down; divide in half; shape into loaves. Place in two greased 9″ x 5″ x 3″ bread pans. Cover; let rise in warm place, free from draft, until doubled in bulk, about 1 hr.

Bake at 400°F. about 25 to 30 min., or until done. Remove from pans and cool on wire racks. Makes 2 loaves.

WHITE BREAD

½ cup milk	1½ cups warm water
3 tablesp. sugar	1 pkg. active dry, or
2 teasp. salt	cake, yeast
3 tablesp. margarine	About 6¼ cups sifted
or butter	all-purpose flour

Scald milk; stir in sugar, salt, and margarine. Cool to lukewarm. Measure warm water into large bowl; sprinkle or crumble in yeast; stir until dissolved. Add lukewarm milk mixture and 3 cups flour; beat until smooth. Add enough additional flour to make a soft dough. Turn out onto lightly floured board. Knead until smooth and elastic, about 8 to 10 min. Form into smooth ball. Place in greased bowl, turning to grease top. Cover; let rise in warm place (80°F. to 85°F.), free from draft, until doubled in bulk, about 1 hr.

Punch down dough. Let rest 15 min. Then divide dough in half and shape each half into a loaf. Place each loaf in a greased 9″ x 5″ x 3″ bread pan. Cover; let rise in warm place, free from draft, until doubled in bulk, about 1 hr.

Then bake at 400°F. about 30 min., or until done. Makes 2 loaves.

PUMPERNICKEL RYE BREAD

2 pkg. active dry, or	2 tablesp. soft short-
cakes, yeast	ening
1½ cups warm water	⅓ cup molasses
2¾ cups unsifted rye	3¼ to 3¾ cups sifted
flour	all-purpose flour
1 tablesp. salt	Corn meal
1 tablesp. caraway	
seeds	

1. *Night before:* In large bowl, sprinkle yeast into warm water; stir till dissolved. Add rye flour; beat till smooth. Cover; let stand in warm place (80°F. to 85°F.) overnight.
2. *Next morning:* Mix in salt, caraway seeds, shortening, molasses, and half of all-purpose flour. Mix in more flour, a little at a time, until dough is quite stiff and cleans sides of bowl.
3. Turn dough onto lightly floured surface; knead about 5 min., or until smooth.
4. Place dough in greased bowl, turning to grease all sides. Cover; let rise in warm place about 1 hr., or until hole remains when finger is pressed deep into dough.
5. Punch down dough; divide in half. Round up each half into smooth ball; place at opposite

corners of corn-meal-sprinkled cookie sheet. Cover with wax paper; let rise in warm place 30 to 45 min., or until dent remains when finger is pressed gently into side of dough.

6. Brush tops of loaves with cold water. Bake at 375°F. 35 to 45 min., or until well browned and done. Cool on cake racks. Makes 2 loaves.

OLD-TIME SALLY LUNN

¼ cup scalded milk	2 cups sifted all-
6 tablesp. shortening	purpose flour
1 pkg. active dry, or	2 tablesp. sugar
cake, yeast	½ teasp. salt
¼ cup warm water	2 eggs

Combine milk, shortening; cool till lukewarm. Meanwhile, sprinkle or crumble yeast into warm water; stir until dissolved. In large bowl, combine flour, sugar, salt; make well in center; stir in yeast, then milk mixture. Let rise in warm place (80°F. to 85°F.) about 20 min.; stir in 1 egg, beaten; mix well. Cover with clean towel; let rise until doubled in bulk.

Turn dough onto lightly floured surface; knead lightly. Cut in half; mold each piece into round, flat loaf. Place loaves in 2 greased 8″ layer pans, pressing with knuckles to fit dough into pans. Cover with clean towel; let rise in warm place until doubled in bulk. Brush tops with beaten egg. Bake at 425°F. 15 to 20 min., or until done.

Serve hot, cut into wedges. Or next day, split; then toast wedges. Makes 2 loaves.

COLOSSAL CORN BREAD

1 pkg. active dry, or	3 cups sifted all-
cake, yeast	purpose flour
¼ cup warm water	2 eggs, well beaten
2 cups milk, scalded	1 cup yellow corn
⅓ cup granulated	meal
sugar	4 to 4½ cups sifted
⅓ cup shortening	all-purpose flour
1 tablesp. salt	

1. In measuring cup, sprinkle or crumble yeast into warm water; stir until dissolved.
2. In large mixing bowl, combine milk, sugar, shortening, and salt; cool to lukewarm; then stir in 3 cups flour until blended. Now add well-beaten eggs, yeast, and corn meal; then gradually stir in 4 cups flour.
3. On lightly floured board, using remaining flour, knead corn-bread dough 10 min., when it should be smooth and plastic.
4. Place corn-bread dough in large, greased bowl, turning it to grease all sides. Then cover it with wax paper and a clean towel, and let rise in a warm place (80°F. to 85°F.) about 1½ hr., or until it has doubled in bulk.
5. Turn dough onto floured surface and knead a minute or two; shape into one loaf; place, seam side down, in greased loaf pan 10″ x 5″ x 3″.
6. Let bread rise 20 min. in warm place. Then bake at 375°F. 35 to 45 min.; turn out, on side, on wire rack to cool. Serve, sliced, plain or with your favorite jelly or jam.

P.S. For the smaller family we suggest you make and bake Colossal Corn Bread, as directed. Then cut it in half crosswise, then freezer-wrap and freeze one half of it for later.

BRAIDED ONION BREAD

1 pkg. active dry, or	2 tablesp. granulated
cake, yeast	sugar
Warm water	2 teasp. salt
1 cup commercial sour	2 tablesp. soft butter
cream	or margarine
1 env. Swiss onion-	3 eggs
soup mix	6½ to 6¾ cups sifted
¼ teasp. baking soda	all-purpose flour
	Sesame seeds

Make ahead as follows:

1. Sprinkle or crumble yeast onto ¼ cup warm water to soften. In large bowl, combine sour cream, onion-soup mix, baking soda, sugar, salt, butter or margarine, 2 beaten eggs, and 1 cup warm water; stir in softened yeast until smooth.
2. Now gradually add enough all-purpose flour to form a stiff dough. Knead dough on a floured board until smooth — about 5 min. — then place in greased bowl and cover with towel. Let it rise in warm place (80°F. to 85°F.) until doubled in bulk.
3. Punch dough down; divide half of it into thirds. Roll each part into a strip about 15″ long. Braid the 3 strips together, sealing ends; repeat with remaining dough. Place braids on greased cookie sheet, side by side; let rise in warm place until light.
4. Meanwhile, start heating oven to 350°F. Brush braids with 1 beaten egg; sprinkle with

sesame seeds. Bake 40 to 45 min., or until golden and firm; then cool on wire racks, and serve.

5. Or freezer-wrap and freeze cooled onion braids. Then, to serve them, refrigerate fully wrapped frozen braids at least 5 hr., to thaw. Then heat, wrapped in foil, in 400°F. oven about 30 min.; unwrap, cut into slices, and serve. Makes 2 onion braids.

CASSEROLE RYE BATTER BREAD

1 cup milk	cakes, yeast
3 tablesp. sugar	Caraway seeds
1 tablesp. salt	3 cups sifted all-
1½ tablesp. short-	purpose flour
ening	1½ cups unsifted rye
1 cup warm water	flour
2 pkg. active dry, or	2 teasp. milk

Early in the day:

1. In saucepan scald 1 cup milk; then stir in sugar, salt, and shortening; cool to lukewarm. Turn into bowl.
2. Onto warm water, in small bowl, sprinkle yeast; stir until dissolved, then stir into lukewarm milk mixture along with 1 teasp. caraway seeds.
3. Now to milk mixture, all at once, add all-purpose and rye flours; stir until well blended.
4. Cover bowl; in warm place, free from drafts, let batter rise until doubled in bulk — about 50 min.
5. Then start heating oven to 400°F. Stir batter down, then stir vigorously about ½ min. Turn into well-greased 1½-qt. casserole. Brush top with 2 teasp. milk, then sprinkle with 1 teasp. caraway seeds. Bake about 50 min., or until done. Turn out, on side, on wire rack to cool. Makes 1 loaf.

ITALIAN BREAD STICKS

1 pkg. active dry	¼ cup soft shortening
yeast	1 egg, unbeaten
⅔ cup warm water	1 tablesp. water
1 teasp. salt	Sesame or poppy
1 tablesp. sugar	seeds
2 cups sifted all-	Soft butter
purpose flour	

1. In bowl, sprinkle yeast into ⅔ cup warm water; stir until dissolved. Add salt, sugar, 1 cup flour, shortening. Beat until smooth; mix in rest of flour.

2. Knead on floured, cloth-covered board until smooth — about 5 min. Place in large bowl; cover with wax paper and clean towel; let rise in warm place (80°F. to 85°F.) 1 hr., or until doubled in bulk.
3. Start heating oven to 375°F. Punch down dough, then cut it into 28 pieces; roll each into stick 8″ long. On greased cookie sheets, place 1″ apart. Beat egg with 1 tablesp. water; brush on sticks; sprinkle with seeds. Bake 18 min., or till golden. Serve with soft butter. Makes 28 sticks.

MINIATURE CINNAMON LOAVES

1 pkg. active dry, or	3½ to 3¾ cups sifted
cake, yeast	all-purpose flour
¼ cup warm water	1 egg, beaten
1 cup milk, scalded	½ cup granulated
¼ cup granulated	sugar
sugar	1 tablesp. cinnamon
¼ cup shortening	Milk
1 teasp. salt	Melted butter

Make week before, then freeze:*

1. Sprinkle or crumble yeast into warm water; stir until dissolved.
2. To milk, in bowl, add ¼ cup sugar, shortening, salt. Cool to lukewarm.
3. Then add 2 cups flour and beat well with rubber spatula or spoon.
4. Beat in dissolved yeast, egg, then enough more flour to make soft dough.
5. Turn out on lightly floured surface; cover with same bowl, and let stand 10 min.; now knead dough until smooth and elastic — about 8 to 10 min.
6. Place dough in same large bowl, lightly greased; turn once to grease top. Cover; let rise in warm place (80°F. to 85°F.) till doubled in bulk — about 1½ hr. Meanwhile, combine ½ cup sugar with cinnamon.
7. When dough is doubled in bulk, punch it down; then let rise again till doubled — about 45 min.
8. Punch down dough. Then divide it, with sharp knife, into three parts.
9. Roll each third into 10½″ x 4″ x ½″ rectangle; lightly brush each with milk; then sprinkle with 2 rounded tablesp. cinnamon-sugar mixture. Then, starting from 4″ side, carefully roll up each as for jelly roll; place in greased 5½″ x 3″ x 2¼″ loaf pan. Let rise till almost doubled in bulk — 30 to 40 min.

10. Meanwhile, start heating oven to 375°F. Just before baking, brush top of each loaf with melted butter; sprinkle with 2 teasp. cinnamon-sugar mixture.

11. Bake loaves 20 to 25 min., or till each sounds hollow when tapped with finger.

12. When done, remove at once from pans; lay on side on rack to cool (not in draft). Then wrap each loaf tightly in foil and freeze.

To serve: Let wrapped loaf or loaves thaw in refrigerator overnight. Then, 15 min. before serving, heat in 350°F. oven. For Easter touch, serve each loaf on a tiny breadboard with knife; slice each right at table. Makes 3 loaves, each serving two.

*May be made day before and heated next day, or made and served same day.

COFFEECAKES YOU'LL LIKE

SUPERB DANISH COFFEE TWIST

¾ cup scalded milk	1 cup melted shortening
¼ cup warm water	
2 pkg. active dry, or cakes, yeast	1 teasp. ground cardamom seeds
About 5 cups sifted all-purpose flour	1 cup seedless raisins
½ cup granulated sugar	1 cup cut-up citron
1½ teasp. salt	1 egg
3 eggs	½ cup confectioners' sugar
	½ cup chopped, blanched almonds

In medium bowl, cool milk till lukewarm. Into warm water, in measuring cup, sprinkle or crumble yeast; stir until dissolved. Stir into milk. Sift flour with granulated sugar, salt. Stir about 1 cup flour mixture into milk mixture. Beat in 1 egg. Stir in 1 cup flour; add 2 eggs, beating well after each addition. Add shortening and remaining 3 cups flour; stir till smooth. Mix in cardamom, raisins, citron.

Turn dough into large, greased bowl; knead several min., turning dough over and over in bowl. Cover with wax paper and clean towel; let rise in warm place (80°F. to 85°F.) until doubled in bulk. Punch down; turn out onto lightly floured surface; knead about 8 min.; divide in half. Roll each half into long sausage-like roll; twist each into pretzel shape. Place on greased cookie sheets. Flatten top of each twist slightly. Brush with beaten egg; sprinkle thickly with confectioners' sugar and chopped almonds. Let rise in warm place until doubled in bulk. Bake at 375°F. 25 to 30 min. Makes 2 twists.

HOLIDAY FRUIT LOAF

2 pkg. active dry, or cakes, yeast	1 cup quick-cooking rolled oats
¼ cup warm water	2 cups boiling water
1 teasp. granulated sugar	2 cups diced glacéed fruit (about ½ lb.)
¼ cup shortening	6 to 6½ cups sifted all-purpose flour
1 tablesp. salt	Melted butter (optional)
¼ cup light-brown sugar	

1. In small bowl, sprinkle or crumble yeast into warm water; add granulated sugar and stir until yeast is dissolved. Cover bowl with a towel and set aside.

2. Into large bowl, measure shortening, salt, brown sugar, rolled oats, and boiling water, stirring until shortening is dissolved; set aside until lukewarm. Meanwhile, finely chop, then lightly flour, glacéed fruit.

3. Then, with a rubber spatula, combine yeast with lukewarm rolled-oats mixture, cleaning bowl well. With a wooden spoon, stir in flour, one cup at a time, until a stiff dough is formed (about 6 cups); add glacéed fruits.

4. Turn dough onto a lightly floured board and knead 10 to 15 min., or until elastic and smooth. Then place in a large, greased bowl, turning it once to grease all sides. Cover with a towel, and let rise in a warm place (80°F. to 85°F.) until doubled in bulk — about 1¼ hr.

5. Now punch down dough; then cut off about one sixth of it and shape into a small loaf to fit a greased 6½" x 3" x 2¼" loaf pan. Shape remaining dough into one loaf and place in a greased 10" x 5" x 3" loaf pan. Cover both pans with a towel, then let dough rise until doubled, about 30 min. Start heating oven to 375°F.

6. When doubled, bake loaves 50 to 55 min., or until browned and done. Then, for a dark shiny crust, brush them with melted butter. Now turn loaves out on wire racks to cool. To keep your loaves fresh to the last slice, wrap in wax paper or foil.

For a terrific mother-daughter gift, put the large loaf on a giant breadboard and the smaller one on a miniature board. If it's Christmas time, tie each loaf with red ribbon and a bit of holly.

DANISH PASTRY

1 pkg. active dry, or cake, yeast	¼ teasp. mace
¼ cup warm water	3½ to 4 cups sifted all-purpose flour
⅓ cup granulated sugar	1 cup soft shortening
1 teasp. salt	Jam; or Cheese, Almond, or Prune Filling, below
¼ cup shortening	
1 cup scalded milk	1 egg
2 eggs	2 tablesp. sugar
¼ teasp. vanilla extract	⅓ cup chopped unblanched almonds or pecans or walnuts
½ teasp. lemon extract	

1. Sprinkle or crumble yeast into warm water; stir until dissolved. In large bowl, place ⅓ cup sugar, salt, ¼ cup shortening, milk; stir until blended. Cool till lukewarm; then beat in 2 eggs. Add yeast, extracts, mace, 3 cups flour; stir till smooth. Stir in enough more flour to make soft, easy-to-handle dough. Cover with wax paper and clean towel; let rise in warm place (80°F. to 85°F.) until doubled in bulk.
2. Meanwhile, let 1 cup shortening soften at room temperature. On lightly floured surface, roll dough into ¼"-thick square. Dot with half of shortening, leaving 2" border. Fold dough in half; press edges together. Dot with rest of shortening, leaving 2" border. Fold in half; seal edges. Roll dough into ⅓"-thick square; fold in half, then crosswise in half. Repeat rolling and folding 3 times. Place dough in greased bowl; cover with towel; let stand 20 min.
3. Now, on lightly floured surface, roll dough ⅓" thick. Cut into 3" squares; place spoonful of jam, or Cheese, Almond, or Prune Filling in center of each square. Fold 2 opposite corners to center; press to seal. Place on cookie sheet. Cover with towel; let rise in warm place (80°F. to 85°F.) until half double in size; brush with egg combined with 2 tablesp. sugar. Sprinkle with nuts. Bake at 475°F. 8 to 10 min., or until done. Makes 24. If desired, drizzle on Sugar Glaze, p. 649.

CHEESE FILLING: Combine 1 egg yolk, slightly beaten; 1 cup cottage cheese; ⅓ cup granulated sugar; ½ teasp. vanilla extract; 1 teasp. grated lemon rind.

ALMOND FILLING: Cream together ¼ cup butter or margarine, ¼ cup granulated sugar. Blend in 1 egg, ½ cup (¼ lb.) almond paste, ¾ teasp. almond extract.

PRUNE FILLING: Combine 1 jar or can (½ cup) baby-pack strained prunes, 2 tablesp. granulated sugar, 1 teasp. lemon juice, ¼ teasp. cinnamon. Simmer, stirring, until thick enough to mound when dropped from spoon.

CHRISTMAS STOLLEN

1 cup milk	1 cup slivered, blanched almonds
½ cup granulated sugar	Grated rind 1 lemon
½ teasp. salt	1 cup seedless raisins
1 pkg. active dry yeast	2 eggs, well beaten
¼ cup warm water	¾ cup soft butter or margarine
5 cups sifted all-purpose flour	¼ teasp. nutmeg
½ cup finely cut-up citron	¼ cup melted butter or margarine
½ cup finely cut-up candied cherries	½ teasp. cinnamon
	2 tablesp. sugar

In large saucepan, scald milk; add ½ cup sugar, salt; cool till lukewarm. Meanwhile, sprinkle yeast into warm water; stir until dissolved. Add to lukewarm milk, with 1 cup flour; with hand beater, beat to remove lumps. Cover with wax paper and clean towel; let rise in warm place (80°F. to 85°F.) until doubled in bulk — about 2 hr.

Now stir in citron, cherries, almonds, lemon rind, raisins, eggs, soft butter, nutmeg, then 3 cups flour. On lightly floured surface, knead 1 cup flour into dough until dough is smooth and elastic. Roll into large 18" x 12" oval, about ½" thick. Brush with some of melted butter; sprinkle with combined cinnamon and 2 tablesp. sugar.

Make lengthwise crease down center of dough; fold over. Remove to large, greased cookie sheet. Push into crescent shape; then, with palm of hand, press down along crease to shape. Brush with rest of melted butter. Cover with wax paper, then with clean towel; let rise in warm place until nearly doubled in bulk. Bake at 350°F. 45 to 50 min., or until golden. Cool; sift confectioners' sugar over top. Keeps well. Makes 1 large stollen.

P.S. If preferred, shape dough into 2 smaller stollens.

NUT-FRUIT COFFEECAKES

2 pkg. active dry, or cakes, yeast	6½ to 7 cups sifted all-purpose flour
½ cup warm water	1½ cups apricot preserves
½ cup granulated sugar	1 tablesp. lemon juice
½ cup melted butter or margarine	½ teasp. ground cardamom
2 teasp. salt	1 cup walnuts, chopped
1 cup scalded milk	Orange marmalade
2 eggs	Pecan-Raisin Filling (at right)
1 egg yolk	

Make ahead as follows:

1. Sprinkle or crumble yeast onto warm water to soften. In large bowl, combine sugar, melted butter, salt, and scalded milk; cool to lukewarm.
2. Into lukewarm milk, stir 1 unbeaten egg and egg yolk and softened yeast; gradually stir in enough flour to form stiff dough.
3. On floured board, knead dough until smooth — 5 min. Place in greased bowl, cover with towel, let rise in warm place (80°F. to 85°F.) until doubled in bulk — about 1¼ hr. Blend apricot preserves, lemon juice, cardamom. When dough has doubled, punch it down; divide a little more than half of it into 2 parts.
4. On floured board, roll 1 part into a 12″ square. Over it, spread ¾ cup apricot preserves; sprinkle with ½ cup walnuts. Roll up, jelly-roll-fashion. Repeat with other part, using rest of preserves and walnuts.
5. Place the rolls, side by side, in a greased 12″ x 8″ x 2″ baking dish; flatten lightly. With scissors, snip out 6 small V's down top of each, lifting each point up and back. Let rise, covered, in warm place until doubled in bulk.
6. Roll rest of dough into a rectangle 17″ x 8″. Over it, evenly spread 6 tablesp. orange marmalade, then Pecan-Raisin Filling. Starting with 8″ ends, roll up toward middle from both ends. Place in greased 10″ x 5″ x 3″ loaf pan. With scissors, snip out 4 small V's on each strip, down top of cake, lifting each point up and back. Then let rise, covered, in warm place, until doubled.
7. When both cakes have doubled, start heating oven to 350°F. Brush tops with 1 beaten egg; bake 35 to 40 min., or until golden and done. Cool on wire racks. Remove from baking dishes; serve, sliced.
8. Or freezer-wrap in foil and freeze. To thaw, place, still wrapped, in refrigerator, for at least 5 hr. To serve, bake, still wrapped, at 400°F. 30 to 40 min., or till hot; unwrap and slice. Makes 2 coffeecakes.

PECAN-RAISIN FILLING: Combine 1¼ cups pecans, finely ground, ½ teasp. cinnamon, ¼ cup granulated sugar, 1½ teasp. grated lemon rind, ½ cup seedless raisins, ½ cup light cream. Fills 1 coffeecake.

POTICA

2 pkg. active dry, or cakes, yeast	8 to 9 cups sifted all-purpose flour
½ cup warm water	1 lb. shelled walnuts
2 cups scalded milk	1 cup light cream
¾ cup granulated sugar	1½ cups granulated sugar
Salt	1 teasp. vanilla extract
¾ cup soft butter or margarine	¼ cup fresh bread crumbs
4 egg yolks	4 egg whites

Early in day:

1. In small bowl, sprinkle or crumble yeast into warm water; stir until dissolved. In large bowl, combine milk with ¾ cup sugar, 1 tablesp. salt, ½ cup soft butter. Cool till lukewarm. Stir in egg yolks, yeast mixture, then 2 cups flour; mix well. Stir in enough flour to make stiff dough.
2. On lightly floured surface, knead dough until smooth. Place in greased bowl, turning once to grease all sides. Cover with clean towel; let rise in warm place (80°F. to 85°F.) about 1 hr., or until dent remains when finger is pressed deep into side of dough.
3. While dough rises, grease 4 9″ x 5″ x 3″ loaf pans. Make filling: Put walnuts through fine blade of food chopper. In medium saucepan, heat cream to boiling point; remove from heat; stir in walnuts, then 1½ cups sugar, 1 teasp. salt, vanilla. In small saucepan, melt ¼ cup butter; stir in bread crumbs until lightly browned; add to walnut mixture. In bowl, beat egg whites till stiff; fold in walnut mixture.
4. When dough is raised, turn it onto lightly floured surface; divide into 4 parts; do not knead. Roll 1 piece into 16″ x 9″ rectangle; spread with one fourth of walnut filling. Roll up, jelly-roll-fashion, starting from short side. Pinch ends and side to seal. Place in one of loaf pans. Repeat with 3 other pieces of dough.
5. Let rise in warm place 1 hr. Meanwhile, start

heating oven to 350°F. Bake loaves 40 to 45 min., or until done. Makes 4 loaves. (For gift giving, make day ahead.)

CRUNCHY-TOP COFFEECAKE

2 pkg. active dry yeast	all-purpose flour
¼ cup warm water	½ cup granulated
¾ cup buttermilk	sugar
3 tablesp. granulated	2 tablesp. brown
sugar	sugar
1 teasp. salt	½ teasp. cinnamon
3 tablesp. soft short-	2 tablesp. melted but-
ening	ter or margarine
1 large egg, beaten	¼ cup chopped
2¾ to 3 cups sifted	walnuts

Early in day:

Sprinkle yeast into warm water; stir until dissolved. Heat buttermilk just till warm; pour into large mixing bowl with 3 tablesp. sugar, salt; blend; cool till lukewarm. Stir in yeast, then shortening, egg, half of flour; with spoon, beat until smooth. Add more flour until dough begins to clean sides of bowl.

Turn dough onto lightly floured surface. Knead lightly until smooth — about 30 sec. Cover with damp cloth; let rest 5 min. Place in lightly greased 9″ x 9″ x 2″ cake pan, or in 2 8″ layer pans; pat evenly into pans. Let rise in warm place (80°F. to 85°F.) until doubled in bulk — 30 to 40 min.

Mix ½ cup sugar, brown sugar, cinnamon, melted butter, walnuts. With fingers, make several dents in coffeecake; cover top with sugar mixture. Bake at 375°F. 35 to 45 min. Cool on rack.

If for an early breakfast: Day before, make dough as above; place in pans; sprinkle with topping; cover with wax paper or foil; refrigerate. Next morning, remove from refrigerator; bake as above.

SWISS LEMON-TWIST BREAD

¾ cup milk	¼ cup warm water
½ cup butter or mar-	4½ cups sifted all-
garine	purpose flour
⅓ cup granulated	2 eggs, beaten (re-
sugar	serve 1 tablesp.
½ teasp. salt	for later use)
1 pkg. active dry, or	Juice and grated rind
cake, yeast	½ lemon

Early in day:

1. In small saucepan, scald milk; stir in butter or margarine, sugar, and salt. Cool till lukewarm.
2. In small bowl, sprinkle or crumble yeast into warm water; stir until yeast is dissolved.
3. In large bowl, place flour; add milk mixture, dissolved yeast, eggs, and lemon juice and rind; mix well. On lightly floured surface, knead dough until smooth. Place in large greased bowl; cover with wax paper and clean towel. Let rise in warm place until doubled.
4. Then punch down dough, turn onto floured surface, divide in half. Roll each piece between hands into strip about 30″ long. Place one strip vertically and other horizontally, crossing in the middle. Now lift top end of vertical strip down to left side of its bottom end. Then lift left end of horizontal strip up and over lower two strips. Repeat this with right end of same strip. Alternate with top left and right strips in this manner until dough is used up; then pinch ends together securely. Place twist on greased large cookie sheet.
5. Brush twist all over with the reserved 1 tablesp. beaten egg. Let rise in warm place until about half double in size. Meanwhile, start heating oven to 325°F.
6. When half double in size, bake twist 10 min. at 325°F., then 30 to 35 min. at 350°F. When done, remove from cookie sheet with large spatula. Cool on rack.

P.S. Your twist will taste oven-fresh if you wrap it in foil and let it heat, low under the broiler, for about 10 to 15 min.

CHOCOLATE-FLECKED COFFEECAKE

¾ cup milk, scalded	*Topping*
1 stick margarine	½ cup sifted all-
(½ cup)	purpose flour
⅓ cup granulated	⅓ cup granulated
sugar	sugar
1 teasp. salt	½ cup walnuts,
¼ cup warm water	chopped
2 pkg. active dry, or	½ cup semisweet-
cakes, yeast	chocolate pieces
2 eggs	¼ cup margarine
3½ cups sifted all-	1½ teasp. cinnamon
purpose flour	
½ cup semisweet-	
chocolate pieces	

Make ahead as follows:

1. Grease well a 9″ angel-food tube pan. Into scalded milk, in small saucepan, stir 1 stick

margarine, 1/3 cup granulated sugar, and salt; cool to lukewarm.
2. Onto warm water, in large bowl, sprinkle yeast; stir until yeast is dissolved. Then, with electric mixer at low speed, beat in milk, eggs, and 2 1/2 cups sifted flour until smooth — about 1/2 min.
3. In small bowl, combine 1 cup flour with 1/2 cup semisweet-chocolate pieces; fold into yeast mixture; pour into tube pan.
4. In small bowl, combine all Topping ingredients until large crumbs are formed. Carefully spoon over top of yeast mixture in pan. Cover, let rise in warm place until doubled in bulk — about 1 hr.
5. Then bake at 400°F. 35 min., or until cake tester inserted in center comes out clean. Carefully turn out of pan at once; turn, topping side up; cool thoroughly on wire rack, then serve, sliced.
6. Or freezer-wrap and freeze cooled coffeecake. Then, to serve, remove it, wrapped, from freezer and let stand at room temperature at least 3 hr. Unwrap, then slice and serve. Makes 1 coffeecake.

P.S. If desired, make meringue from 2 egg whites and 1/4 cup granulated sugar; fold in 1/2 cup semisweet-chocolate pieces, finely chopped. Spread meringue on top center of baked coffeecake, then bake at 375°F. 12 min., or until golden. Serve in wedges.

TASTY YEAST DOUGHNUTS

EMILIE'S CHOCOLATE-FILLED DOUGHNUTS

1 pkg. active dry, or cake, yeast
1/3 cup warm water
3/4 cup butter or margarine
3/4 cup granulated sugar
3 egg yolks
1 egg
1/4 cup commercial sour cream
8 1/4 cups sifted all-purpose flour
1 teasp. salt
2 cups milk
3/4 cup semisweet-chocolate pieces
6 tablesp. light cream
3 egg whites
Granulated sugar

1. In small bowl, sprinkle or crumble yeast into warm water; stir until yeast is dissolved.
2. With electric mixer at medium speed (or with spoon), beat butter, while adding 3/4 cup sugar gradually, until light. With hand beater, beat egg yolks and egg until thick. Add to butter mixture, beating until light. Stir in yeast and sour cream.
3. Sift together flour and salt; with spoon, add alternately with milk to butter mixture. Beat well 5 min.
4. Scrape down bowl; cover with wax paper, then with clean towel; let rise in warm place (80°F. to 85°F.) until doubled in bulk.
5. Meanwhile, in saucepan, over low heat, melt chocolate with light cream, stirring until smooth. Cool.
6. When dough has raised, roll it 1/2″ thick on well-floured surface. Cut with floured 2″ cookie cutter. Brush edges of half of rounds with slightly beaten egg whites; then place 1/2 teasp. chocolate mixture in center of each. Top with rest of rounds; pinch edges together firmly. Arrange on floured cookie sheets; cover with clean towel; let rise in warm place till almost doubled and light to touch. Fry as in To Fry, below. Roll in sugar. Makes about 3 1/2 doz. Especially nice served warm.

To Fry: In deep saucepan, put enough fat or salad oil to come halfway up the side. Heat to 375°F. on deep-fat-frying thermometer. (Or use automatic deep fryer or fry pan as manufacturer directs.) Turning once, fry doughnuts, a few at a time, until golden brown and done. Lift out with slotted spoon or handle of wooden spoon; hold over fat a few seconds. Drain on crumpled paper towels.

FILLED BERLIN DOUGHNUTS
(Berliner Pfannkuchen)

1 pkg. active dry, or cake, yeast
1/4 cup warm water
1/4 cup butter or margarine
3/4 cup milk, scalded
1/4 cup granulated sugar
1 teasp. salt
2 eggs, unbeaten
3 3/4 cups sifted all-purpose flour
1 teasp. grated lemon rind
1 egg white, slightly beaten
Strawberry jam or applesauce
Granulated sugar

Early in day, or day before:
1. In small bowl, sprinkle or crumble yeast into warm water; stir until dissolved. Melt butter in milk; cool to lukewarm.

2. In large bowl, with mixer at medium speed (or with spoon), blend yeast with lukewarm milk, ¼ cup sugar, salt, and eggs. Add flour, a little at a time, and lemon rind; beat well. Cover with wax paper, then clean towel; let rise in warm place (80°F. to 85°F.) until doubled in bulk.

3. On lightly floured surface, knead dough a few times; then roll it ⅜" thick. Cut into rounds with floured 2¼" cookie cutter. Brush edges of half of rounds with egg white; then place 1 teasp. strawberry jam or applesauce in center of each.

4. Top with rest of rounds; firmly pinch edges together. Arrange on floured cookie sheets; cover with wax paper and clean towel; let rise in warm place till almost doubled and light to the touch.

5. Fry doughnuts as in To Fry, p. 512. Then roll each in granulated sugar.

6. Serve at once, with more strawberry jam or applesauce, if desired, for morning coffee or for dinner dessert with coffee. Or store doughnuts in a covered container, and serve next day for breakfast, a teen-age get-together, or an evening snack. Makes about 20.

TWO-WAY YEAST DOUGHNUTS

1½ cups milk	2 eggs, unbeaten
⅓ cup melted butter or margarine	2 pkg. active dry, or cakes, yeast
¼ cup granulated sugar	¼ cup warm water
2 teasp. salt	5 cups sifted all-purpose flour
2 teasp. nutmeg	Melted butter
½ teasp. cinnamon	Granulated sugar

1. In small saucepan, scald milk; then cool to lukewarm. Pour into large bowl; add ⅓ cup melted butter, ¼ cup sugar, salt, nutmeg, cinnamon, eggs. Mix till well blended.

2. Sprinkle or crumble yeast into warm water in a cup; stir until yeast is dissolved. Blend into milk mixture; then add flour gradually, mixing until dough is smooth (it will be *very* soft).

3. Shape dough into ball; place in greased bowl; turn to grease all sides. Cover with wax paper, then clean towel; let rise in warm place (80°F. to 85°F.) until doubled in bulk.

4. On well-floured surface, roll dough ½" thick. Cut with floured doughnut cutter; place,

1" apart, on floured cookie sheets; brush with butter. Let rise till doubled in bulk.

5. Fry as in To Fry, p. 512. Brush warm doughnuts with melted butter; then roll in granulated sugar (or cinnamon-sugar). Makes about 3½ doz., plus holes. Nicest served warm.

EASY-WAY MIX DOUGHNUTS: Follow directions on label of hot-roll mix, adding 2 tablesp. sugar, 1 tablesp. grated lemon rind, ½ teasp. cinnamon, and ½ teasp. nutmeg to yeast mixture. When dough has doubled, follow steps 4 and 5 in Two-Way Yeast Doughnuts. Makes 2 doz., plus holes.

CHOCOLATE DOUGHNUTS

1 cup milk	1 pkg. active dry, or cake, yeast
¾ cup granulated sugar	¼ cup warm water
⅔ cup cocoa	3 eggs, well beaten
1 teasp. salt	1 teasp. vanilla extract
⅓ cup butter or margarine	5 cups sifted all-purpose flour
	Granulated sugar

1. In medium saucepan, scald milk; mix in ¾ cup granulated sugar, cocoa, salt, and butter. Then cool this mixture to lukewarm.

2. Meanwhile, in large bowl, sprinkle or crumble yeast into warm water; stir until yeast is dissolved. Then add well-beaten eggs, vanilla extract, and lukewarm milk mixture, and mix until well blended.

3. Gradually add flour to milk mixture, beating until smooth.

4. Turn dough onto lightly floured surface; knead until smooth and satiny.

5. Roll dough about ½" thick; cut with floured doughnut cutter.

6. Then arrange on lightly floured board or cookie sheet; cover with clean towel; let rise in warm place (80°F. to 85°F.) until doubled.

7. Fry as in To Fry, p. 512. Roll warm doughnuts in sugar. Makes about 18, plus holes. Best served warm.

SUGAR TWISTS: Decreasing sugar to ⅓ cup, omitting cocoa, and increasing flour to 6 cups, make Chocolate Doughnuts as in steps 1 through 4. Roll kneaded dough into rectangle about 20" x 10". Cut dough into 5" x 1" strips; twist each strip several times. Complete doughnuts as in steps 6 and 7. Makes 40.

Also see Doughnuts, pp. 489–490.

ROLL MIX MAKES IT EASY

EMMY'S RAISIN RING

1 pkg. hot-roll mix	2 tablesp. cinnamon
½ teasp. salt	½ cup light or dark
¼-lb. stick soft butter	raisins
Salad oil	½ cup chopped wal-
¼ cup butter or mar-	nuts or almonds
garine	Beaten egg
¼ cup granulated or	1 tablesp. sugar
brown sugar	

1. Make up hot-roll mix as package insert directs for Richer Dough, adding ½ teasp. salt.
2. On lightly floured surface, roll dough into a 16" x 10" rectangle, with long side toward you.
3. Then, starting at your right, dot two thirds of dough surface with pieces of ¼ lb. soft butter. Fold unbuttered third of dough over center third; then fold remaining third on top.
4. Next, fold upper third of dough, then lower third, over center. Brush with oil. Cover with wax paper and clean towel; let rise in warm place (80°F. to 85°F.) until doubled in bulk — about 2 hr.
5. Meanwhile, in small bowl, blend well ¼ cup butter, ¼ cup sugar, and cinnamon.
6. When dough is doubled in bulk, roll it on lightly floured surface into 20" x 12" rectangle, long side toward you. Cut rectangle in half lengthwise; spread lengthwise center of each half with half of cinnamon-butter mixture. Then sprinkle each half with half of raisins, then with 2 tablesp. chopped walnuts. Now fold each upper third, then lower third, over center third.
7. Next, on greased 16" x 12" cookie sheet, twist filled strips together; then form into ring, pinching ends together. Brush with egg; sprinkle with ¼ cup chopped nuts, then 1 tablesp. sugar. Let rise until almost doubled in bulk — about 45 min.

8. Start heating oven to 400°F. When ring has risen, bake 20 to 25 min., or until done.
9. Serve on attractive tray with favorite fruits in center.

COFFEE COFFEECAKE

¼ cup warm water	½ cup milk, scalded,
1 pkg. hot-roll mix	cooled
¼ cup granulated	⅓ cup soft butter or
sugar	margarine
2 tablesp. very soft	½ cup brown sugar,
butter or margarine	packed
2 eggs, unbeaten	¾ cup coarsely
2 tablesp. instant	broken walnuts
coffee	Confectioners' sugar

1. In water, soften yeast from package of hot-roll mix.
2. In large bowl, with mixer at medium speed, combine granulated sugar and 2 tablesp. butter until light, fluffy; beat in eggs. Add coffee, milk, then yeast.
3. At low speed, mix in flour from package of hot-roll mix; beat 2 min. at medium speed. Cover with piece of wax paper and clean towel; let rise in warm place (80°F. to 85°F.) 1 hr., or until doubled in bulk.
4. Combine ⅓ cup butter with brown sugar and walnuts.
5. Grease 9" tube pan. With spoon, beat dough about 30 strokes. With fingers, spread one third of this stiff dough in tube pan; sprinkle with half of walnut mixture; top with another third of dough; sprinkle on remaining walnut mixture; then spread on last of dough.
6. Cover; let rise in warm place until doubled in bulk.
7. Start heating oven to 350°F. Bake coffee-cake 35 to 40 min., or until it tests done with cake tester. Cool; remove from pan; sprinkle with confectioners' sugar. Perfect for that mid-afternoon coffee break.

P.S. Other delicious bread recipes are on the Hot-Roll Mix label.

LET'S HAVE SANDWICHES

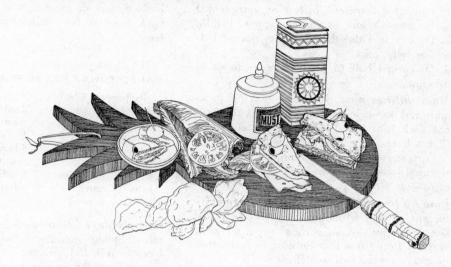

What wonderful variety there is in sandwiches! There are hearty sandwiches you can plan a meal around — knife-and-fork or finger style, hot or cold. There are good-traveler sandwiches, just right for the lunch box or picnic chest. And there are eye-catching party-time sandwiches that are as much fun to make as they are good to eat.

Here are recipes for our favorite sandwiches. When you make them, be sure to make enough. Remember, an invitation to "have another sandwich" is not often turned down. *Before using these recipes*, refer to How To Use Our Recipes, p. 3. Always use standard measuring cups and measuring spoons; measure level.

SANDWICH BREADS AND CRACKERS

Kind to Use:

For everyday sandwiches, fresh or day-old bread slices

For sandwich loaves, day-old unsliced bread

For roll-up, envelope, or pin-wheel sandwiches, very fresh unsliced or sliced bread (so bread won't break in rolling)

For cracker sandwiches, packaged crackers. Today they're crisper and more varied than ever. Some packages contain crackers wrapped in several packets, so you can open and use one packet at a time

Choose from:

BREADS:
Canned brown, date-nut, etc.
Caraway rye
Cheese
Cinnamon
Cracked wheat
French or Italian
Nut
Party rye
Pumpernickel
Raisin
Square sandwich
Swedish or plain rye
Enriched white
Whole-wheat

ROLLS, ETC.:
Biscuits
Brown 'n' serve rolls
Canned refrigerated rolls
Corn muffins
Crumpets
English muffins
Frankfurter rolls
Hamburger buns
Hard rolls
Rye rolls
Seeded rolls

CRACKERS:
Cheese crackers
Crisp round scalloped crackers
Rye wafers
Shredded-wheat wafers
Saltines
Many other varieties

515

PRODUCTION-LINE TECHNIQUES

Soften butter or margarine. For easy spreading, let butter or margarine soften at room temperature; or work it with spoon or electric mixer until spreadable.

If you must "stretch" butter or margarine:
1. Be sure it's soft, so you can spread it thin.
2. Or mix it with salad dressing, peanut butter, or jelly, etc.
3. Or spread half of bread slices with salad dressing.

Make fillings next. If you're making pack-and-carry sandwiches, choose fillings that will not soak into bread. Wrap separately items that wilt easily — lettuce, tomatoes.

For safety's sake, refrigerate all fillings until used — especially meat, fish, poultry, or eggs — at 40°F.

Line up bread slices. Use a good sharp knife for slicing and trimming bread. Place bread slices, two by two, in vertical rows, on work surface. Pair slices that lie next to each other in loaf, so edges will match.

Butter all slices to very edges, using a flexible spatula. This prevents the filling from soaking through the bread.

Place filling on slices in every other row, spreading from edge to edge. (Be generous, but not so lavish that filling oozes out.) Then close sandwiches.

Leave crusts on all but daintiest sandwiches; crusts help keep sandwiches fresh.

When wrapping sandwiches, set each, cut into halves or thirds, in center of square of wax paper, saran, or foil. Bring opposite sides of paper together, directly over center. Fold edges over and over until fold rests against sandwich. Dog-ear ends; tuck under.

A word of warning: Completed sandwiches are as perishable as the fillings alone. So, to avoid any possibility of food poisoning, refrigerate sandwiches at 40°F. as soon as made and right up to time of eating. Never cover them with a damp towel; use wax paper, saran, foil, or dry towel.

If sandwiches are for a picnic or lunch box, refrigerate them until just before packing. Plan to eat within 4 hr.

To freeze sandwiches ahead for parties, lunch boxes, picnics, etc., see p. 706.

LUNCH AND SUPPER SANDWICHES

Here's a choice selection of these wonderful broiled, baked, toasted, and untoasted sandwich hearties that make lunch or supper a feast.

BAKED TUNA-CHEESE BUNS

¼ lb. process Cheddar cheese, cubed	green pepper
3 hard-cooked eggs, chopped	2 tablesp. minced onion
2 tablesp. pickle relish	½ cup mayonnaise
1 6½- or 7-oz. can tuna (1 cup)	3 tablesp. chopped stuffed olives
1 tablesp. minced	6 split hamburger buns, buttered

Early in day: Combine all ingredients except buns. Spoon mixture between bun halves; wrap in foil. Refrigerate.

To serve: Bake wrapped buns at 400°F. 15 min. Serve hot. Makes 6.

To Vary: For tuna, substitute 1 cup cut-up cooked or canned chicken or turkey, sardines, ham, tongue, or flaked canned salmon.

STUFFED ROLLS

6 hard-cooked eggs, chopped	mustard
1 12-oz. can corned beef, chopped	Salt and pepper to taste
¼ cup sweet-pickle relish	12 frankfurter rolls; or 1½ doz. finger rolls
½ cup mayonnaise	Soft butter or margarine
2 teasp. prepared	

Early in day: Combine eggs, corned beef, pickle relish, mayonnaise, mustard, salt, pepper. Cut off tops of rolls; hollow out slightly. Lightly brush inside of each roll with soft butter. Fill with egg filling; replace top. Wrap in foil. Refrigerate.

Serve cold. Or bake wrapped rolls at 350°F. 10 to 15 min. and serve hot. Makes 12.

FRANK STYLE: Mix 3 frankfurters, minced; ¼ cup grated cheese; 1 hard-cooked egg, coarsely chopped. Use as filling for 4 hamburger rolls; wrap; bake as above. Makes 4.

CHILI-EGG BUNWICHES

3 hard-cooked eggs, chopped	2 tablesp. butter, margarine, or salad oil
3 tablesp. chopped green pepper	2 tablesp. chili sauce
1 tablesp. minced onion	⅛ teasp. salt
Bit of minced garlic	Dash pepper
1 tablesp. chopped pimento	2 tablesp. grated process Cheddar cheese
	6 frankfurter rolls

Day ahead: Mix all ingredients except rolls. With fork, scoop out center of each roll; fill with egg mixture. Wrap in foil. Refrigerate. *To serve:* Bake wrapped rolls at 400°F. 8 min. Serve hot. Makes 6.

CHICKEN-CHEESE SANDWICHES

2 tablesp. butter or margarine	dar cheese, grated (1 cup)
2 tablesp. flour	6 slices hot toast
½ teasp. salt	1 large avocado or tomato, peeled, sliced
¼ teasp. dry mustard	
1 cup milk	12 cooked chicken or turkey slices
¼ lb. process Ched-	Paprika

Melt butter. Stir in flour, salt, mustard, then milk; cook, stirring, until thickened. Add cheese; stir over very low heat until melted. Arrange toast in shallow pan; top with avocado, then chicken. Pour on sauce. Sprinkle with paprika. Broil until golden. Makes 6.

HOT-AND-COLD SANDWICH PLATES

4 hamburger buns, split	2 tablesp. mayonnaise
2 cups ground canned luncheon meat or cooked ham	2 cups potato salad
	4 canned cling peach halves
2 tablesp. prepared mustard	¼ cup brown sugar, packed
¼ green pepper, chopped	2 tablesp. butter or margarine
2 eggs, slightly beaten	Shredded lettuce

Several hr. ahead: Hollow out bun halves slightly. Mix crumbled bread with ground meat, mustard, green pepper, eggs, mayonnaise; refrigerate. Make potato salad; refrigerate. Wrap buns until ready to use. *About 20 min. before serving:* Preheat broiler 10 min. or as manufacturer directs. Place lower halves of buns on cookie sheet; heap meat filling in buns. Sprinkle peach halves with sugar; dot with butter; place on cookie sheet beside buns. Broil slowly, about 5 min. Meanwhile, fill top halves of buns with potato salad. Arrange hot-and-cold sandwich on each plate; garnish with peach half set in nest of shredded lettuce. Makes 4 servings.

CHEESEBURGER STACKS

1½ lb. chuck, ground	Fat or salad oil
2 tablesp. minced onion	6 tomato slices
	Seasoned salt
1½ teasp. salt	6 hamburger buns, split
⅛ teasp. pepper	
6 packaged process Cheddar-cheese slices	Soft butter or margarine

A few hr. ahead: Mix chuck with onion, salt, pepper. Shape into 12 thin patties, using about ¼ cup mixture for each patty. Put cheese slice between each 2 patties, pressing edges together to seal cheese inside. Refrigerate. *At lunchtime:* In small amount of hot fat in skillet, cook cheeseburgers to desired doneness. Meanwhile, sprinkle tomato slices with seasoned salt. Toast split buns; spread with butter or margarine. Insert cheeseburger and tomato slice between each split bun. Serve with tossed greens and pitcher of milk. Makes 6 servings.

CLUB SOUFFLE SANDWICHES

1 1-lb. can peas, drained	mushroom soup, undiluted
½ cup chopped celery	½ cup milk
¼ cup chopped scallions or onions	2 teasp. prepared mustard
6 bacon slices, diced and sautéed	2 eggs
⅔ cup canned condensed cream-of-	½ cup crumbled Danish blue cheese
	Butter or margarine
	8 white-bread slices

1. Start heating oven to 350°F. In bowl, combine peas, celery, scallions, bacon.
2. In another bowl, with hand beater, beat together soup, milk, mustard, eggs, cheese.
3. Grease an 8″ x 8″ x 2″ baking pan. Butter bread; then fit 4 slices, buttered side up, in pan; top with vegetable mixture, then remaining bread; pour soup mixture over all. Bake 40 min. Makes 4 servings.

SAVORY HAMBURGER BUNS

1 lb. chuck, ground	3 tablesp. catchup
2 tablesp. chopped onion	1½ tablesp. Worcestershire
¾ teasp. seasoned salt	¼ cup grated Parmesan cheese
⅛ teasp. pepper	
3 hamburger buns, split	¼ cup snipped parsley

Mix beef, onion, salt, pepper. Spread this meat mixture, about ¼″ thick, on each bun half. Mix catchup with Worcestershire; spread lightly over meat. Sprinkle with Parmesan and parsley. Broil to desired doneness. Serve 2 bun halves per person. Makes 3 servings.

DIVAN SANDWICHES

1 10-oz. pkg. frozen asparagus spears	Cheddar cheese, grated (1 cup)
1 tablesp. butter or margarine	4 buttered toast slices
2 tablesp. flour	4 large cooked turkey or chicken slices
1 cup milk	1 3- or 4-oz. can sliced mushrooms
¼ lb. process sharp	Snipped parsley

Cook asparagus as label directs; drain. In small saucepan, melt butter; stir in flour, then milk. Cook, stirring constantly, until thickened. Stir in cheese until melted. Place toast on cookie sheet. Top with asparagus spears, then with turkey slices and drained mushrooms; spoon on cheese sauce. Broil 3 to 5 min., or until golden. Sprinkle with parsley. Makes 4 servings.

ISLAND SANDWICHES

Soft butter or margarine	chicken slices
6 hamburger buns, split	¼ lb. process Cheddar cheese, grated (1 cup)
6 canned pineapple slices, drained	½ cup finely chopped pecans or walnuts
6 cooked or canned	

Start heating oven to 400°F. Butter buns. On cookie sheet, arrange each hamburger bun with pineapple on bottom half and chicken on top half. Sprinkle chicken with grated cheese. Bake 10 to 15 min., or until cheese and pineapple are nicely browned. Sprinkle pineapple with nuts. Serve with crisp celery hearts. Makes 6 servings.

HOT AND COLD MEAT SANDWICHES

Use hearty fillings of thinly sliced meat or poultry on, or between, hot buttered toast slices; buttered, toasted split buns; or buttered bread slices. Serve this way:

Roast Chicken, Turkey, or Duckling:
1. *Hot*, topped with hot giblet gravy, barbecue sauce, canned mushroom or chicken gravy, or soup from can or soup mix
2. *Cold*, with slices of Swiss cheese, salami, ham, tongue, or crisp bacon. Also canned cranberry sauce, dill pickles, or coleslaw

Roast Beef:
1. *Hot*, with bottled thick meat sauce, Worcestershire, hot gravy, or Quick Mushroom Sauce, p. 528
2. *Cold*, with pickle relish, chili sauce, barbecue sauce, horse-radish, or Tabasco

Roast Pork:
1. *Hot*, with hot applesauce, gravy, or barbecue sauce
2. *Cold*, with applesauce, dill pickle, horse-radish, or barbecue sauce

Roast Lamb:
1. *Hot*, with hot gravy (add sautéed, sliced mushrooms or cooked vegetables) or barbecue sauce
2. *Cold*, with mint jelly, curry mayonnaise, or barbecue sauce

Corned Beef:
1. *Hot*, with Mustard Sauce, p. 532, or dill pickle
2. *Cold*, with coleslaw, pickles, olives, or sauerkraut

Tongue:
1. *Hot*, with horse-radish sauce, or canned tomato sauce or soup, as gravy
2. *Cold*, with chili sauce or barbecue sauce

Baked or Canned Ham:
1. *Hot*, with horse-radish, mushroom gravy, or barbecue sauce
2. *Cold*, with prepared mustard, catchup, chili sauce, or canned cranberry sauce

Steak (or Cube Steaks):
1. *Hot*, alone or with thin sweet-onion slices or Steak Sauce, p. 528.
2. *Cold*, with Quick Mushroom Sauce, p. 528.

Bacon:
1. *Hot,* alone or with cheese or egg salad
2. *Cold,* with sliced, hard-cooked egg; sliced scallions; chopped stuffed olives; or chili sauce

BROILED OPEN-FACE SANDWICHES

Use buttered or toasted bread; or use buttered, toasted, split rolls, English muffins, or crumpets; or use buttered, split hot baking-powder biscuits.

On top of bread, arrange makings of any combination below, in order given. Then broil until bubbly and toasted.
1. Cheese and tomato slices (or chili sauce), semibroiled bacon slices
2. Chicken-Pecan, Tuna, or Egg Salad, p. 524; cheese slices
3. Cheese slices, prepared mustard or barbecue sauce
4. Creamed chicken or turkey, cheese slices. Serve with tomato slices and broiled bacon
5. Franks, split lengthwise, sharp-cheese slices, tomato slices
6. Deviled-ham spread, scrambled eggs (unsalted), grated cheese
7. Chicken or turkey slices, cheese sauce (bought in jar or can or homemade)
8. Turkey and tomato slices, semibroiled bacon slices, cheese slices
9. Chicken slices, cooked asparagus spears, cheese sauce

OTHER BROILED SANDWICHES

ONION-CHEESE: In 2 tablesp. butter or margarine, sauté 2 or 3 medium onions, thinly sliced, until tender and light brown. Add ½ teasp. salt, ⅛ teasp. pepper. Spread on 4 slices of hot toast; top with 4 packaged process Cheddar-cheese slices. Broil till cheese is melted. Makes 4.

SALAD BURGERS: Split hamburger buns. Spread half with cheese spread, rest with any of fillings in Susan's Party Sandwich Loaf, p. 123, doubling recipe if necessary. Then broil all till bubbly. Serve halves open-style; or top salad buns with cheese buns.

SALAD ROLLS: Hollow out frankfurter rolls. Fill with any of fillings in Susan's Party Sandwich Loaf, p. 123, doubling recipe if necessary. Top with grated cheese. Toast in broiler. Or split, toast, then butter rolls; top with salad, cheese; then broil.

FRANK BURGERS: Place heated franks in split frankfurter rolls. Spread with prepared mustard; top with cheese slices. Broil 3 min., or until cheese is melted. Spread pickle relish on cut edges of rolls.

AU GRATIN CORNED-BEEF HASH: In 1 tablesp. butter or margarine, sauté 2 teasp. minced onion till tender. Add 1½ cups canned corned-beef hash, 2 tablesp. catchup; heat well. Spread on 8 slices hot buttered toast. Sprinkle each with ¼ cup grated process Cheddar cheese. Broil till cheese is melted. Makes 8.

FRENCH-TOASTED SANDWICHES

Make up sandwiches with one of Fillings, below; refrigerate. For every 6 sandwiches, combine 3 beaten eggs, ½ cup milk, 1 teasp. sugar, ¼ teasp. salt. Dip each sandwich into this egg mixture.

Then, in ¼ cup hot butter, margarine, or salad oil, in skillet, brown each sandwich on both sides. Cut each sandwich in half. Serve on heated platter, with bowl of canned cranberry sauce, pickle relish, or pickled watermelon, pineapple, or peaches in center.

Fillings:
1. Thin ham and cheese slices
2. Chicken-Pecan, Tuna, Ham, or Egg Salad, p. 524 (double recipe if necessary)
3. Turkey or chicken slices
4. Sharp-cheese or cheese spread, prepared mustard
5. Corned-beef and Swiss-cheese slices
6. Cream cheese or deviled ham
7. Franks, split lengthwise and crosswise
8. Peanut butter and thin baked-ham slices

FRENCH-TOAST SANDWICHES

Slice a loaf of French bread diagonally, ¾" thick. Dip in egg-and-milk mixture as in French-Toasted Sandwiches, above; then brown on both sides in hot butter, in skillet, as directed. Spread half the slices with butter and marmalade; top with remaining slices. Serve with strips of boiled ham, browned in skillet, and halved slices of unpeeled orange.

OTHER SANDWICH HEARTIES

WESTERN: For each sandwich, to 1 beaten egg, add 1 tablesp. each minced onion and green pepper; 2 tablesp. each minced, cooked ham, milk; speck salt and pepper. Pour into greased 8″ skillet. Cook till set on both sides.

BACON-CHICKEN LIVER: Fry 3 bacon slices till crisp; remove from skillet. In bacon fat, sauté ½ lb. chicken livers and ¼ lb. mushrooms, chopped, till tender; chop fine, along with bacon. Add 1 tablesp. minced onion, ¾ teasp. salt, dash pepper. Fills 4 sandwiches.

GRILLED CHEESE SANDWICHES: Cover half of bread slices with cheese slices or cheese spread. Spread with prepared mustard, deviled ham, or barbecue sauce. Top with bread slices. Toast in broiler, skillet, or sandwich toaster.

HAMBURGERS: Use sautéed or broiled hamburgers with thin onion or tomato slices, or hot baked or chili beans, to fill bread-and-butter sandwiches. Nice, too, in toasted buns that have been spread with Danish blue cheese, cheese spread, barbecue sauce, chutney, pickle relish, catchup, or mustard.

TRICKS WITH DECKERS

Almost any combination that pleases your fancy may please your palate. Choose 2, 3, or more of the following fillings to put together with 3 bread slices (one or more kinds of bread, toasted or untoasted). Or if you're calorie conscious, choose only 2 bread slices, toasted, to make a junior club:

PICK YOUR BREAD
(fresh, not more than 1 day old)

Enriched white	Boston brown
Whole-wheat	Cheese
Cracked wheat	Cinnamon
Caraway rye	Orange
Swedish or plain rye	Banana
Pumpernickel	Nut
French or Italian	Date and nut
Raisin	

THE FILLING MAINSTAY

Sliced roast chicken or turkey	Hot or cold corned beef
Roast beef, lamb, or pork	Cold or canned tongue
	Hot Canadian-bacon slices
Baked ham or meat loaf	Sliced ready-cooked meats

Canned luncheon meat or chopped ham	Packaged process Cheddar- or Swiss-cheese slices
Canned deviled ham or tongue	Hard-cooked-egg slices
Crisp bacon slices	Sardines
Deviled luncheon meat	Tuna, crab, lobster, shrimp, ham, or tongue salad
Sautéed ground beef	
Ground sautéed liver	
Hot or cold split franks	Canned liver paté

FILLING GO-ALONGS

Butter or margarine	Apple butter
Mayonnaise or cooked salad dressing	Jams and jellies
Chili sauce	Preserves
Catchup	Honey
Mustard—any flavor	Peanut butter
Commercial sour cream	Cheese spreads (a host to choose from)
Anchovy paste	
Cottage cheese	Seasoned salt, mono-sodium glutamate
Relish—pickle, hot dog, hamburger, etc.	

GARNISHES

Thin cucumber, tomato, or onion slices	Stuffed celery
Green-pepper rings	Cauliflowerets
Lettuce, romaine, or water cress	Pickled beets
	Mushrooms
Sliced sweet and dill pickles	Pickled peaches or onions
Ripe and stuffed olives	Walnut, pecan, or peanut halves
Scallions	Raisins, dates, or figs
Radishes	Canned cranberry sauce
Carrot strips and curls	

JUNIOR CLUBS

Use any of the suggestions under Tricks With Deckers, left, omitting center toast slice. Or use one of these fillings:

CHICKEN: Combine 1 cup minced cooked or canned chicken; ½ cup minced celery; ¼ cup cooked salad dressing; ½ teasp. salt; ⅛ teasp. pepper; pinch monosodium glutamate; ¼ teasp. prepared mustard. Fills 4 sandwiches.

TUNA-CRANBERRY: In Chicken Junior Club, above, substitute flaked canned tuna for chicken. Top filling with thin canned jellied-cranberry slices.

CURRIED: In Chicken Junior Club, above, substitute flaked canned tuna, salmon, or King-crab meat for chicken. Or use chopped, cooked, cleaned shrimp; cooked ham or tongue; or hard-cooked eggs. Add curry to taste. Or add chopped, buttered, toasted walnuts.

SALAMI-BEAN: Snip ¼ lb. salami into bits. Add 1 1-lb. can baked beans with tomato sauce, 2 tablesp. chili sauce, 2 teasp. prepared mustard, a little minced onion. Mash with fork. Fills 6 sandwiches.

OPEN CLUBS

4 **English muffins,** split	¾ cup chopped ripe olives
¾ cup grated process Cheddar cheese	⅓ cup mayonnaise or cooked salad dressing
⅓ cup thinly sliced scallions or chopped onions	½ teasp. curry powder
	Tomato wedges

1. On cookie sheet, arrange split muffins; then toast in broiler.
2. In bowl, combine cheese, scallions, olives, mayonnaise, curry powder; use to top muffins; then run under broiler until cheese melts. Serve 2 to each person, garnished with tomato wedges. Makes 4 servings.

PICNIC CLUBS

½ cup mayonnaise or cooked salad dressing	slices
	8 thin baked-ham slices
2 tablesp. prepared mustard	Lettuce
16 pumpernickel	1 cup potato salad
	Toothpicks

1. Combine mayonnaise and mustard; spread on pumpernickel slices.
2. For each of 4 sandwiches, cover 1 bread slice with 2 ham slices; top with 1 bread slice, next with lettuce, then with third bread slice; on it, spread potato salad. Top all with 1 bread slice, spread side down.
3. Secure with picks; then cut diagonally in halves. Makes 4.

PACK-AND-CARRY SANDWICHES

Nine times out of ten the mainstay of a lunch box or picnic is sandwiches. So don't let yours be humdrum. Vary them from day to day with new fillings and new breads. It's an easy matter to keep hearty sandwiches on hand in the freezer. Be sure to read Production-Line Techniques, p. 516, and Freezing Chart, p. 709. Or you might like to pack fillings and bread, rolls, or crisp crackers separately so each person can make his own.

MAKE IT MEAT OR POULTRY

Add salad dressing, if desired, and seasonings to one of these meat combinations:
1. Sliced bologna, coleslaw
2. Chopped chicken or turkey, apple, and celery
3. Chopped chicken, walnuts, and olives
4. Sliced corned beef, chopped green pepper, horse-radish
5. Chopped franks, baked beans, catchup, minced onion
6. Ground ham or canned luncheon meat, Cheddar cheese, and dill pickle
7. Ground ham; drained, canned, crushed pineapple; a little brown sugar; powdered cloves
8. Chopped ham and pickle, cottage cheese
9. Chopped corned beef, minced onion and pickle
10. Chopped liver and crisp bacon, pickle relish
11. Sliced meat loaf, chopped green olives
12. Chopped roast pork, green pepper, celery
13. Sliced roast pork, apple butter
14. Sliced turkey or ham, canned cranberry jelly

MAKE IT CHEESE

Add mayonnaise, if desired, to one of these:
1. Grated cheese, shredded dried beef, chili sauce
2. Blue-cheese spread, chopped crisp bacon, chili sauce
3. Cheese and egg slices, chili sauce
4. Swiss-cheese slices, deviled ham, sweet pickle
5. Chopped dates or figs, chopped peanuts, cream cheese
6. Cream cheese, sliced radishes
7. Cottage cheese, chopped peanuts, peach jam
8. Sharp-cheese spread, sliced salami, prepared mustard

9. Swiss-cheese and tongue slices, pickle relish
10. Cream cheese; chopped, cooked, dried apricots and prunes
11. Cream cheese; chopped green pepper, olives, and celery
12. Cream cheese, peanut butter, orange juice, grated orange rind

MAKE IT EGG

Mix chopped, hard-cooked eggs with mayonnaise, desired seasonings, and one of these:
1. Chopped crisp bacon, snipped chives
2. Grated carrots, sliced ripe olives
3. Chopped celery, onion, and chicken
4. Chopped, cooked chicken giblets; catchup
5. Chopped corned beef or salami, mustard pickle
6. Sliced franks, chili sauce
7. Deviled ham, chopped pickle, prepared mustard
8. Chopped tongue, grated cheese, prepared mustard
9. Tuna or salmon, chopped celery, pickle relish

MAKE IT FISH

Add mayonnaise and seasonings to one of these:
1. Salmon, minced cucumber and onion
2. Cut-up shrimp, chopped green pepper and celery
3. Sardines, chopped celery, lemon juice
4. Tuna, chopped apple, lemon juice
5. Tuna, chopped celery and walnuts
6. Tuna, cottage cheese, pickle relish
7. Tuna; drained, canned, crushed pineapple; chopped celery

MAKE IT PEANUT BUTTER

Mix peanut butter with one of these:
1. Chopped crisp bacon and apple, a little cream
2. Chopped crisp bacon, catchup
3. Grated carrot, chopped raisins or celery
4. Minced ham, pickle relish
5. Chopped dates and figs, lemon juice
6. Deviled ham, chopped dill pickle, mayonnaise
7. Chopped nuts, honey

8. Applesauce, sliced dates
9. Cream cheese and apple butter or chopped, cooked, dried prunes
10. Marshmallow cream

PICKLED-BEEF SANDWICHES

Chop contents of one 12-oz. can corned beef. Mix with ¼ cup chopped sweet pickle and ¼ cup prepared mustard. Mix well, then use as filling for 8 sandwiches.

SANDWICH CREATIONS

Nice for easy entertaining, for lunch, Sunday supper, or evening refreshments. Most of them are prepared in advance.

HOT ITALIAN SALAD BOAT

1 1-lb. oblong loaf Italian bread	1½ cups diced celery
½ cup milk	⅓ cup diced stuffed olives
1 clove garlic	½ cup mayonnaise
¾ teasp. salt	About 2 tablesp.
1 raw egg	melted butter or
¼ teasp. pepper	margarine
½ teasp. mace	Bermuda onion
6 hard-cooked eggs	Green pepper

Start heating oven to 425°F. To prepare "boat," slice off top crust of bread in one piece; reserve for cover. With fingers, scoop out soft crumbs from inside of loaf. Set top crust back in position. Slice "boat" crosswise, almost to bottom crust, into 6 to 8 servings. Lift off top crust.

Measure 2 cups of the soft crumbs; place in bowl; add milk. Crush garlic with salt; place in small bowl; add raw egg, pepper, mace; with fork, beat just till mixed; add to crumbs. Coarsely chop hard-cooked eggs; add to crumbs, along with celery, olives, mayonnaise; mix well.

Fill "boat" with egg salad; then replace cover. Brush outside of "boat" with butter; wrap in foil. Bake 30 min. Unwrap "boat"; arrange on serving plank or tray; cut each slice through bottom crust; then garnish with thin slices of Bermuda onion and green pepper. Serve hot, to be eaten with fork and knife. Makes 6 to 8 servings.

HARLEQUIN SANDWICH LOAF

Ham-Horse-radish
  Filling, below
Parsley-Chive Fill-
  ing, below
Liverwurst-Mush-
  room Filling,
  below
Curry-Egg Filling,
  below

1 loaf day-old, un-
  sliced white bread,
  about 12″ long
Few thin pimento
  strips
Few thin green-pepper
  strips
Radish roses or plain
  radishes

Day before:

1. Make the 4 fillings; refrigerate.

2. With sharp knife, cut all crusts from bread. Then lay loaf on side and cut it lengthwise into 4 slices, each ½″ thick, using ruler as guide in keeping slices straight.

3. Set bottom bread slice on large sheet of foil; on bread slice, spread Ham-Horse-radish Filling in even layer; top with second bread slice. On it spread Parsley-Chive Filling; then spread this filling with the Liverwurst-Mushroom Filling and top this with the third bread slice.

4. On third bread slice spread Curry-Egg Filling. On it, lengthwise of loaf, alternate 5 rows of pimento and green-pepper strips. Top with fourth bread slice, then gently press and pat loaf into shape. Now wrap the sandwich loaf snugly in saran or foil, and refrigerate at once.

At serving time: Unwrap loaf, place on platter, garnish with radish roses. With sharp knife, cut crosswise into ¾″ slices. Makes 10 servings.

HAM-HORSE-RADISH FILLING: Mix 1½ cups ground cooked or canned ham with ⅓ cup chopped onions, ½ cup chili sauce, 1 tablesp. horse-radish, ¼ cup mayonnaise; then blend in ¼ cup soft butter or margarine.

PARSLEY-CHIVE FILLING: With spoon, work ¼ cup butter or margarine till light; stir in 1 teasp. prepared mustard, ¼ cup finely snipped parsley, and ¼ cup snipped chives.

LIVERWURST-MUSHROOM FILLING: With fork, work ¼ lb. liverwurst till smooth; then beat in ¼ cup soft butter or margarine, and one 3- or 4-oz. can chopped mushrooms, drained.

CURRY-EGG FILLING: Mix 4 hard-cooked eggs, chopped, with ½ teasp. curry powder, 1 teasp. seasoned salt, ⅛ teasp. pepper, and ¼ cup mayonnaise.

STUFFED ROLLS, FIRECRACKER STYLE

Crab-Meat Filling

1 6½-oz. can King-
  crab meat, drained,
  flaked
Dash lemon juice
¼ cup minced celery
¼ cup chopped
  cucumber
¾ teasp. salt
⅛ teasp. pepper
About ¼ cup mayon-
  naise

mustard
¼ to ½ cup mayon-
  naise

Chicken-and-Almond Filling

1 5-oz. can boned
  chicken
¼ cup canned
  roasted, diced
  almonds
¼ cup chopped
  stuffed olives
¼ teasp. curry pow-
  der
½ teasp. salt
¼ to ⅓ cup mayon-
  naise

Bologna-and-Egg Filling

¼ lb. bologna,
  coarsely grated
2 hard-cooked eggs,
  chopped
3 tablesp. pickle
  relish
1 teasp. salt
1 teasp. prepared

The Firecrackers

14 to 16 frank rolls
14 to 16 strips of
  pimento

Have all ingredients for sandwich fillings well chilled. With fork, mix together each filling, adding just enough mayonnaise to make it spreadable. To assemble firecrackers, fill each split roll with a filling; insert strip of pimento at one end, to form fuse. Makes 14 to 16 servings.

SMORGASBORD HELP-YOURSELF FILLINGS

Set out a tray of assorted breads, a platter of lettuce, tomato slices, etc., then several of the sandwich fillings below. Guests make their own sandwiches.

End of the Roast:

2 cups leftover roast
  veal or pork chunks
½ small onion
2 tablesp. melted but-
  ter or margarine

1 teasp. dry mustard
3 tablesp. mayonnaise
½ teasp. celery salt
Pinch cayenne pepper

Several hr. ahead: Put meat and onion through food grinder, using fine blade. Mix in remaining ingredients. Refrigerate. Makes 1⅓ cups.

Egg Salad:

6 hard-cooked eggs, chopped	2 teasp. prepared mustard
¼ cup finely chopped ripe olives	½ cup mayonnaise or cooked salad dressing
2 teasp. salt	
¼ teasp. pepper	

Several hr. ahead: Mix together all ingredients. Refrigerate. Makes 2 cups filling.

Chicken-Pecan:

2 cups minced cooked or canned chicken	⅓ cup mayonnaise or cooked salad dressing
½ cup minced celery	
1 cup finely chopped pecans	½ teasp. seasoned salt
	¼ teasp. pepper

Several hr. ahead: Mix together all ingredients. Refrigerate. Makes about 3½ cups filling.

Ham Salad:

½ cup ground cooked or canned ham, or chopped ham or luncheon meat	1 teasp. prepared mustard
	2 tablesp. mayonnaise
	1 tablesp. minced onion
2 tablesp. minced green pepper	

Several hr. ahead: Mix together all ingredients. Refrigerate. Makes about ¾ cup.

Tuna Salad:

2 6½- or 7-oz. cans tuna (2 cups)	cooked salad dressing
1 teasp. lemon juice	1 teasp. Worcestershire
2 tablesp. catchup	
⅓ cup mayonnaise or	

Several hr. ahead: Thoroughly mix all ingredients. Refrigerate. Makes 2 cups.

PETITE PARTY SANDWICHES

At a tea, bridge, shower, garden party, wedding, birthday — at any party, in fact — these dainty sandwiches star.

OPEN-FACE PRETTIES

Use single slice of bread; cut into fancy shape. Or use crisp round scalloped crackers. Spread with butter or margarine, then with any filling below; decorate gaily.

RED AND WHITE: Spread bread with jelly; sprinkle with flaked coconut.

CHEESE STRIPS: With cookie press, decorate bread strips with sharp- or blue-cheese spread. Top with poppy seeds or nuts.

OLIVE SCALLOPS: Halve stuffed olives lengthwise; slice crosswise. Place, with rounded sides down, along edge of bread round.

BORDERS: Spread bread with peanut butter or jelly; dip edges into chopped peanuts. Or spread with cheese spread; dip edges into snipped parsley or chives.

HALF-AND-HALF: Spread half of each bread round with jelly, rest of each round with deviled-ham or pineapple-cream-cheese spread.

ONE-TWO-THREE: Spread bread with favorite filling. Place 3 pecan or walnut halves, or stuffed-olive or radish slices, along center.

FRUIT 'N' CHEESE: Spread bread with seasoned cottage cheese. Set halved strawberries or blueberries, or canned cling-peach slices on top; sprinkle with nutmeg.

PARSLEY CRUSTS: Trim crusts from French-bread slices in oval pieces. Butter crusts; sprinkle with seasoned or onion salt and snipped parsley.

CUCUMBER-RADISH FLOWERS: Border edges of bread rounds with sliced radishes. Top each round with cucumber slice. Dot center with mayonnaise and snipped parsley.

TEA SANDWICHES

Fill dainty-shaped, buttered sandwiches with any of these:
1. Cheese spread, plus very thin tomato slices
2. Applesauce, plus nutmeg or peanut butter
3. Chicken salad, plus orange marmalade
4. Cream cheese, a bit of salad dressing, plus one of these:

Bacon bits, chutney	Minced maraschino cherries
Honey, raisins, nuts	
Snipped chives, canned crushed pineapple	Chopped salted peanuts
Sardines, lemon juice	Chopped, pitted dates; lemon juice
Snipped water cress, grated onion	Chopped almonds, lemon juice
Chopped watermelon pickle	Ground salami
	Minced nuts and stuffed olives

5. Chopped, hard-cooked egg, plus minced anchovy fillets; mayonnaise

6. Minced turkey or chicken, plus cream cheese, olive spread, peanut butter, or marmalade

7. Flaked canned tuna or salmon, plus mayonnaise, lemon juice, and minced onion or chives

8. Grated Parmesan cheese, plus mayonnaise

9. Liverwurst or canned liver pâté, plus dried thyme, snipped chives, mayonnaise

10. Banana mashed with lemon juice, mayonnaise, speck nutmeg

11. Avocado mashed with a little lemon juice or tarragon vinegar, salt, pepper, and a little chili powder or chili sauce

12. Peanut butter, plus deviled ham or ground corned beef, a little prepared mustard, horseradish, and mayonnaise

13. Your favorite bottled sandwich spread

MOSAICS

1. Cut 2 white and 2 whole-wheat-bread rounds. With small, round (or fancy-shaped) cutter, remove center of 1 white and 1 dark round. Insert small round of dark bread into hole in white ring, and small round of white bread into hole in dark ring. This makes 2 "mosaics."

2. Spread 2 plain rounds with one of fillings for Tea Sandwiches, p. 524. Cover white round with dark mosaic, dark round with white mosaic.

PIN WHEELS

1. Buy unsliced loaf of very fresh white bread. With long sharp knife, cut off all crusts except bottom one.

2. With crust side of loaf to left, cut into lengthwise slices, 1/8" to 1/4" thick. Run rolling pin over each slice, starting with narrow end (bread is less likely to crack).

3. Spread slices with soft butter or margarine to edges, then with any extra-smooth and creamy filling for Tea Sandwiches, p. 524. Then, if desired, place 3 stuffed olives or gherkins, 1 frank, or 2 Vienna sausages across short end.

4. Starting at end with stuffed olives, *tightly* roll up bread, being careful to keep sides in line.

5. Wrap rolls individually in wax paper, saran, or foil, twisting ends securely. Refrigerate several hours or overnight. (Or make ahead; wrap; freeze as on p. 709; thaw about 45 min.; slice.)

To serve: Cut chilled rolls into 1/4" to 1/2" slices. With broad spatula, lift onto serving plate. Or fix on trays; cover with wax paper, foil, saran, or dry towel; refrigerate until served.

P.S. Pin wheels are nice toasted.

ROLL-UPS

Trim crusts from thin fresh bread slices. Roll lightly with rolling pin. Spread each to edge with any one of tea-sandwich fillings, p. 524, that is extra smooth and creamy. Lay asparagus tip or stuffed celery stalk across one end; roll up.

Serve whole or cut into halves or thirds, with sprig of water cress, mint, or parsley tucked in one or both ends, if desired.

To toast: Place Roll-ups on cookie sheet; brush with melted butter or margarine or salad oil; broil till golden. Serve hot.

RIBBON SANDWICHES

1. Use fresh or day-old bread. For each stack, alternate 3 slices whole-wheat and 2 slices white bread, filling with any extra-smooth and creamy fillings for Tea Sandwiches, p. 524.

2. Firmly press together each stack of slices. Then, using sharp knife in sawing motion, slice off crusts from all sides of each stack.

3. Arrange stacks in shallow pan; cover with wax paper, saran, or foil. Refrigerate *at least* several hours. Then cut into 1/2" slices.

4. Cut each 1/2" slice into thirds, halves, or 2 or 3 triangles.

CHECKERBOARDS

1. Use fresh or day-old bread. For each stack, alternate 2 slices whole-wheat and 2 slices white bread, filling with one or more extra-smooth and creamy fillings for Tea Sandwiches, p. 524.

2. Firmly press each stack of slices together. Then, using sharp knife in sawing motion, slice off crusts from all sides of each stack. Wrap tightly in wax paper, saran, or foil; refrigerate several hours.

3. Now cut each stack into 6 ½" slices. Spread cut sides of slices with one of fillings for Tea Sandwiches, p. 524. Rebuild slices into stacks of 3 layers each, with outside white strips alternating with whole-wheat strips.

4. Wrap tightly in wax paper, saran, or foil. Refrigerate *at least* several hours. Then, with sharp knife, *immediately* cut into slices ¼" to ½" thick.

TO SAUCE THE DISH

The right sauce, well made, makes a wonderful dish even better. Choose your sauce with flavor and eye appeal in mind. Then follow recipe directions to the letter for a culinary work of art.

Before using these recipes, refer to How To Use Our Recipes, p. 3. Always use standard measuring cups and measuring spoons; measure level.

EXTRA-EASY MAIN COURSE SAUCES

For Meat, Poultry, Vegetables, Fish

JIFFY BARBECUE: Combine ½ cup catchup, 1 teasp. dry mustard, 3 dashes Tabasco, 1 tablesp. Worcestershire. Serve on franks, hamburgers, cube steaks, etc. Makes about ½ cup.

ONION BARBECUE: Sauté ½ cup minced onions in ¼ cup butter, margarine, or salad oil until tender. Add 1⅓ cups chili sauce, ⅓ cup bottled thick meat sauce. Serve on hamburgers, franks, cube steaks, chicken, etc. Makes about 2¼ cups.

AVERY BUTTER: Melt ¼ cup butter or margarine. Stir in 1 teasp. salt, 1 teasp. dry mustard, 1 teasp. paprika or snipped parsley, 2 teasp. water, 2 tablesp. lemon juice or orange juice, ¼ teasp. Tabasco. Especially nice on hamburgers or steak. Makes about ⅓ cup.

CAPER BUTTER: Melt ½ cup butter or margarine. Add 4 teasp. vinegar, 2 tablesp. bottled capers, 2 tablesp. snipped parsley. Nice with roast lamb or broiled steak, or on asparagus, cauliflower, fish, etc. Makes about ½ cup.

CHIVE CHEESE: Melt ½ pkg. chive cheese with 2 to 4 tablesp. milk. Nice on broccoli. Makes about ½ cup.

CURRANT-MINT: With fork, break up 1 cup currant jelly; mix in 2 tablesp. each grated orange rind and snipped mint leaves. Nice with roast lamb, ham, or chicken. Try also on broiled fish. Makes about 1 cup.

CURRY: In 2 tablesp. butter or margarine, sauté ¼ cup sliced mushrooms 5 min. Stir in 2 tablesp. flour, then 1 cup water, 1 beef-bouillon cube, ½ teasp. curry powder. Cook, stirring, till thickened. Nice on hamburgers or franks. Try also on broiled, baked, or fried fish. Makes about 1⅛ cups.

SAVORY JELLY: Combine ½ cup currant jelly or sieved canned whole-cranberry sauce, 1 tablesp. vinegar or sherry, ½ teasp. dry mustard, ⅛ teasp. each ground cloves and cinnamon. Cook over low heat, stirring, until jelly melts. Nice over baked, sautéed, or broiled ham. Makes about ½ cup.

QUICK MUSHROOM: Heat 1 10½-oz. can condensed cream-of-mushroom soup, undiluted, with 2 tablesp. butter or margarine and ⅓ cup milk or sherry. Add ½ cup drained canned mushrooms and ¼ cup grated cheese or pinch curry. Nice on hamburgers or lamb chops. Try also on chicken, fish, green beans, cauliflower, etc. Makes 1½ cups.

Or use canned mushroom gravy, or Swiss cream-of-mushroom-soup mix, as a sauce.

QUICK MUSTARD: Combine ½ cup vinegar, 1 tablesp. butter or margarine, 1 egg, slightly beaten, 1 tablesp. sugar, 2 tablesp. prepared mustard, 1 tablesp. paprika. Cook over low heat, stirring, until just thickened. Serve hot, with baked ham, tongue, etc. Makes about ½ cup.

P.S. Or try the delicious horse-radish mustard that comes in bottles.

ONION: Stir ½ cup water into 1 tablesp. cornstarch; add 2 tablesp. butter or margarine and 1 10½-oz. can condensed onion soup, undiluted. Heat until thickened.

Or increase water to 1½ cups and substitute ½ pkg. onion-soup mix for canned soup. Nice on hamburgers or cube steaks. Makes about 1½ cups.

CURRIED PINEAPPLE SAUCE: Simmer 1 9-oz. can crushed pineapple with 2 tablesp. butter or margarine and 1 teasp. curry powder, covered, 5 min. Serve with ham, chicken, or pork. Makes 1 cup.

SOUR CREAM: Stir 2 tablesp. flour into 2 tablesp. melted butter or margarine. Add ½ cup water, ½ cup commercial sour cream, 1 teasp. horse-radish, ¼ teasp. dried thyme, ¼ teasp. salt, ⅛ teasp. pepper. Heat. Good on hamburgers, broiled steak, or fried chicken. Try also on broccoli or asparagus. Makes about 1 cup.

STEAK SAUCE: Combine ½ cup melted butter or margarine, 1½ tablesp. catchup, 1½ teasp. Worcestershire, 1 teasp. dry mustard, and 2¼ teasp. lemon juice. Serve on broiled steak or chops. Makes about ⅔ cup.

TOMATO-HORSE-RADISH: Heat 1 10½-oz. can condensed tomato soup, undiluted, with 2 tablesp. butter or margarine, 2 tablesp. horseradish, 2 teasp. prepared mustard, pinch ground cloves, dash pepper. Use on hamburgers or pork or lamb chops. Try, too, on fried fish. Makes about 1¼ cups.

JUST AS IS: Canned tomato sauce, catchup, chili sauce, bottled thick meat sauce, tartar sauce, Worcestershire, or Tabasco. Or canned chicken, mushroom, or beef gravy.

MINT SAUCE

3 tablesp. white or cider vinegar	1 tablesp. lemon juice
⅔ cup water	1 tablesp. sugar
¼ cup dried mint	¼ teasp. salt

Several days ahead or early in day:

1. In saucepan, combine vinegar, ⅓ cup water, and 2 tablesp. mint; simmer 5 min.; strain.
2. Add remaining water and mint, lemon juice, sugar, and salt; bring to boil. Refrigerate.

At serving time: Reheat sauce over low heat. Serve on roast lamb or veal, lamb or veal chops, etc. Makes about ⅔ cup.

BARBECUE SAUCE

6 tablesp. minced onion	2 tablesp. brown sugar
3 tablesp. butter or margarine	2 teasp. prepared mustard
1 cup catchup	2 tablesp. Worcestershire
¼ cup vinegar	⅛ teasp. salt

In small saucepan, sauté onion in butter till tender, but not brown. Stir in catchup, vinegar, brown sugar, mustard, Worcestershire, and salt; simmer 10 min. Serve with Susan's Meat-Loaf Ring, p. 106.

P.S. Excellent barbecue sauce now comes in bottles, too.

BILLINGSLEY'S SORTILEGE SAUCE

¼ cup melted currant jelly
¼ cup bottled thick meat sauce
½ cup port wine
2 teasp. ground ginger
2 teasp. dry mustard
⅛ teasp. salt
Juice of 1 lemon

In small saucepan, combine jelly, meat sauce, and wine; bring to boil; simmer 5 min. Add ginger, mustard, salt; cook few minutes longer. Stir in lemon juice. Serve hot on roast lamb, veal, chicken, or turkey. Makes 1 cup.

MUSHROOM SAUCE

¼ cup butter or margarine
1 clove garlic
½ lb. mushrooms, sliced
3 tablesp. flour
2 cups water
½ teasp. salt
⅛ teasp. celery salt
⅛ teasp. pepper

In skillet, in butter, brown garlic; discard garlic. In same skillet, sauté mushrooms till golden; remove and set aside. Into remaining fat in skillet, stir flour; add water, salt, celery salt, pepper; cook, stirring, until thickened. Add mushrooms. Nice over meats. Makes 2¼ cups.

Just for Steak

MARCHAND-DE-VIN BUTTER

1 cup dry red wine
1 shallot, minced (or 1 teasp. minced onion)
⅛ teasp. freshly ground pepper
½ teasp. meat-extract paste
2 teasp. snipped parsley
¼ teasp. lemon juice
¾ cup soft butter or margarine

In small saucepan, simmer wine with shallot 20 min., or until reduced to ¼ cup. Stir in pepper, meat-extract paste, parsley, lemon juice. Cool; then blend well with butter. Use to top sizzling broiled steak. Makes 1 cup.

ANCHOVY BUTTER

½ cup soft butter or margarine
4 teasp. anchovy paste
¼ teasp. Worcestershire

Blend together all ingredients. Use to top sizzling broiled steak. Makes ½ cup.

SAUCY TOPPER I

2 tablesp. melted butter or margarine
1 tablesp. catchup
2 tablesp. soy sauce
1 tablesp. lemon juice
1 teasp. prepared mustard
Few grains pepper
2 teasp. snipped parsley

Blend butter with rest of ingredients. Spoon over sizzling steak.

SAUCY TOPPER II

½ teasp. Worcestershire
1 tablesp. prepared mustard
Few drops Tabasco
¼ cup butter or margarine

Blend Worcestershire with rest of ingredients. Spread over sizzling steak.

BEARNAISE SAUCE

1½ tablesp. tarragon vinegar
1½ tablesp. water
3 onion slices
2 egg yolks, slightly beaten
¼ teasp. salt
Dash paprika
2 tablesp. butter or margarine

In small saucepan, bring vinegar, water, onion slices to boiling. Discard onion. Into egg yolks, in top of double boiler, gradually stir vinegar mixture; add salt, paprika. Cook over hot water, stirring constantly, until mixture begins to thicken. Add butter, 1 tablesp. at a time, beating constantly until mixture is quite thick. Remove from water; cover; set aside. Spoon over steak.

Just for Fish

SAUCEPAN CHEESE: In ¼ cup butter or margarine, in saucepan, sauté ½ cup minced onions till tender-crisp — about 3 min. Add ½ cup undiluted evaporated milk, 2 dashes Tabasco, ½ lb. process sharp Cheddar cheese, sliced. Heat; stirring occasionally, till blended. Nice with baked or oven- or pan-fried fish. Makes 2 cups.
Also see Easy, p. 531.

CUCUMBER: Mix ¼ cup mayonnaise or commercial sour cream, ½ cup finely diced cucumbers, ¼ teasp. salt, ¼ teasp. celery seeds. Use for dunking cold cooked cleaned shrimp or lobster chunks. Or serve on sautéed scallops, etc. Makes ⅔ cup.

DILLY: Combine ½ cup mayonnaise, 1 tablesp. dried dill. Nice for dunking cold cooked cleaned shrimp or lobster chunks, etc. Makes ½ cup.

LOUIS: Mix 1 cup mayonnaise, ¼ cup French dressing, ¼ cup catchup or chili sauce, 1 teasp. each horse-radish and Worcestershire, and salt and pepper to taste. Serve on sea-food cocktails, broiled or fried fish, or in fish salads. Makes 1½ cups.

RED: Mix ¼ cup catchup, 2 tablesp. cooking sherry. Nice with broiled or fried fish, or on shellfish cocktails. Makes ⅓ cup.

QUICK TARTAR: Combine 1 cup mayonnaise and 1 to 2 tablesp. each minced pickle, parsley, bottled capers, onion, green or stuffed olives. Nice with hot or cold fish or shellfish. Makes 1¼ cups.
P.S. Don't forget you can buy fine bottled tartar sauce, too.

TOMATO-CHEESE: Heat 1 10½-oz. can condensed tomato soup, undiluted, with ¼ lb. process Cheddar cheese, grated (1 cup), and ¼ teasp. prepared mustard till cheese melts. Nice on baked or oven-fried fish. Makes about 1½ cups.

ITALIAN TOMATO: Sauté 2 tablesp. minced onion in 1 tablesp. butter or margarine until tender. Add 1 8-oz. can tomato sauce, 2 tablesp. grated Parmesan cheese; heat. Delicious on broiled or fried fish. Makes 1 cup.

SPICY DUNK SAUCE

½ cup chili sauce	1 tablesp. vinegar
¼ cup well-drained horse-radish	2 dashes Tabasco
1 teasp. Worcestershire	¼ teasp. bottled thick meat sauce
1 teasp. minced onion	1 teasp. celery seed
¼ teasp. garlic salt	2 tablesp. granulated sugar
½ teasp. salt	1 teasp. celery salt
⅛ teasp. pepper	

Combine ingredients. Keep in covered jar in refrigerator 2 or 3 days before using. Serve with Hot Spicy Shrimp, p. 327. Makes about ¾ cup.

Just for Vegetables

VINAIGRETTE SAUCE

3 tablesp. sweet-pickle relish	¾ teasp. sugar
2 tablesp. snipped parsley	1 teasp. salt
	6 tablesp. vinegar
	¾ cup salad oil

Combine all ingredients. Blend with hand beater or electric mixer. Serve on hot or chilled cooked asparagus or broccoli, on hot cooked greens or Brussels sprouts, etc. Makes about 1 cup.

SPUR-OF-THE-MOMENT HOLLANDAISE

Carefully heat 1 cup mayonnaise, stirring constantly. Then fold in ¼ cup heavy cream, whipped. Serve on hot asparagus, broccoli, etc. Makes about 1½ cups.

BLENDER HOLLANDAISE

1. In small saucepan, heat ½ cup butter or margarine till bubbling but not brown.
2. Into electric-blender container, put 3 egg yolks, 2 tablesp. lemon juice, ¼ to ½ teasp. salt, and pinch cayenne.
3. Cover container and turn motor on low speed. *Immediately* remove cover and pour in hot butter in steady stream. When all butter is added, turn off motor. Makes ¾ cup.
NOTE: Two whole eggs may replace 3 egg yolks.

CHEESE-SAUCE QUINTET

ZIPPY: In double boiler, place ⅓ cup milk, ½ lb. process cheese, sliced. Add dash of cayenne or Tabasco, or a little minced onion, sautéed till tender in a bit of butter. Heat, stirring, until blended and smooth. Serve on broccoli, cauliflower, asparagus, etc. Nice, too, on poached or baked fish. Makes 1⅓ cups.

ZESTY: Over low heat, blend 1 cup commercial sour cream with 1 cup shredded cheese, stirring constantly; stir in 2 tablesp. lemon juice, and salt, if needed. Makes about 2 cups.

THREE-MINUTE CHEESE SAUCE: Simmer 1⅔ cups undiluted evaporated milk with ½ teasp. salt, over low heat, to just below boiling — about 2 to 3 min. Add 2 cups grated process

Cheddar cheese, then stir over low heat until cheese melts.

EASY: One wonderful cheese sauce (pasteurized process-cheese spread) comes in jars, all ready to heat and spoon over hot vegetables, spread on sandwiches, etc. Canned Cheddar-cheese soup makes a deliciously quick and easy sauce, too.

SAUCE MIXES: See p. 102.

SWISS-CHEESE SAUCE

½ lb. process Swiss cheese, sliced
½ cup milk
¼ teasp. Worcestershire
3 drops Tabasco
2 tablesp. chopped pimento

In double boiler, heat cheese with milk until melted. Stir in Worcestershire, Tabasco, and pimento. If sauce seems too thick, thin as necessary with a little hot milk. Makes 4 servings.

MORE MAIN COURSE SAUCES

THOUSAND-ISLAND SAUCE

1½ tablesp. butter or margarine
3 tablesp. flour
¾ teasp. salt
⅛ teasp. pepper
¾ cup liquid from cooked vegetables
¾ cup evaporated milk, undiluted
¼ cup mayonnaise
¼ cup chili sauce

In saucepan, melt butter; blend in flour, salt, pepper. Slowly stir in vegetable liquid. Boil 2 min., stirring constantly. Add milk; heat thoroughly. Mix mayonnaise and chili sauce; stir into hot mixture. Thin with a little hot milk if desired. Superb on hot green beans, onions, cabbage, broccoli, fried fish, etc. Makes 2 cups.

EASY HOLLANDAISE

2 egg yolks
¼ teasp. salt
Dash cayenne pepper
½ cup melted butter or margarine
1 tablesp. lemon juice

1. With hand beater or electric mixer, beat egg yolks until thick and lemon-colored; add salt, cayenne.
2. Add ¼ cup melted butter, about 1 teasp. at a time, beating constantly.

3. Combine remaining ¼ cup melted butter with lemon juice. Slowly add, about 2 teasp. at a time, to yolk mixture, beating constantly.

Serve soon after making. Nice with broccoli, hot asparagus, broiled fish, poached or steamed salmon, etc. Makes ½ cup.

CURRY: With salt, add ¾ teasp. curry powder.
LEMON: To sauce, add 1 teasp. grated lemon rind.
MUSTARD: To sauce, add 1 teasp. prepared mustard.

BERT'S SUPERB BARBECUE SAUCE

¼ cup vinegar
½ cup water
2 tablesp. sugar
1 tablesp. prepared mustard
½ teasp. pepper
1½ teasp. salt
¼ teasp. cayenne pepper
1 thick lemon slice
1 onion, sliced
¼ cup butter or margarine
½ cup catchup
2 tablesp. Worcestershire
1½ teasp. liquid or powdered smoke (optional)

In saucepan, mix vinegar, water, sugar, mustard, pepper, salt, cayenne, lemon, onion, butter. Simmer, uncovered, 20 min. Add catchup, Worcestershire, smoke; bring to boil.

Serve hot, on spareribs, broiled chicken, short ribs, lamb chops, etc. Or use as baster when broiling chicken, roasting lamb or spareribs, braising short ribs, etc. Makes about 1¾ cups.

BORDELAISE SAUCE

2 tablesp. butter or margarine
1 shallot, minced
1 onion slice
2 carrot slices
Sprig parsley
6 whole black peppercorns
1 whole clove
½ bay leaf
2 tablesp. flour
1 10½-oz. can condensed bouillon, undiluted
¼ teasp. salt
⅛ teasp. pepper
¼ cup dry red wine
1 tablesp. snipped parsley

Day before:
1. In hot butter, in skillet, sauté shallot, onion, carrot, parsley sprig, peppercorns, clove, and bay leaf until onion is golden and tender.
2. Add flour; cook over low heat, stirring until flour is lightly browned.

3. Stir in bouillon; simmer, stirring, until thickened and smooth — about 10 min.; strain.
4. Add salt, pepper, red wine, and snipped parsley. Refrigerate.

About 15 min. before serving: Reheat sauce, covered, in double boiler (if sauce is too thick, thin with 1 or 2 tablesp. wine). Spoon some over roast tenderloin of beef or a steak; pass rest. Makes 8 to 10 servings.

LEMON BARBECUE SAUCE

1 cup butter or margarine	4 teasp. salt
1 clove garlic, minced	¼ teasp. pepper
4 teasp. flour	6 tablesp. lemon juice
⅔ cup water	¼ teasp. Tabasco
1 tablesp. sugar	½ teasp. dried thyme

In hot butter, in saucepan, sauté garlic a few min.; stir in flour, then rest of ingredients. Cook, stirring, until slightly thickened. Cool. Use as baster when broiling or grilling chicken, shrimp, scallops, etc. Makes about 2 cups.

POOR MAN'S TRUFFLE SAUCE

1 tablesp. butter or margarine	¾ cup sauterne or other white wine
1 onion, minced	1 beef-bouillon cube
1 tablesp. flour	½ cup ripe olives, cut from pits into pieces

About 15 min. before serving:
1. In hot butter, in skillet, sauté onion until golden; blend in flour; add sauterne, bouillon cube; bring to boil, stirring often.
2. When thickened and smooth, add olives. Serve over mound of hot, fluffy mashed potatoes, circled with pan-broiled lamb chops. Makes 6 servings.

MUSTARD SAUCE

2 tablesp. butter, margarine, or salad oil	1 tablesp. flour
Dash pepper	1 egg yolk, beaten
1 teasp. salt	¾ cup milk
1 tablesp. prepared mustard	1½ to 3 teasp. lemon juice

In double boiler, melt butter; stir in pepper, salt, mustard, flour, then combined yolk and milk. Cook, stirring, until smooth and thick-

ened, about 5 min. Remove from heat at once. Add lemon juice just before serving.

Serve on green beans, cauliflower, cabbage, etc. Try, too, on broiled, fried, or baked fish, hot baked ham, etc. Makes about ¾ cup.

To Vary: Make in saucepan. Omit egg yolk; increase milk to 1 cup. Add onion slice to milk if desired; remove onion before serving.

ONION MUSTARD: Simmer ¼ cup minced onion in butter, in double-boiler top over direct heat. Then complete over boiling water as at left.

P.S. Check your grocer's shelves for bottled mustard or mustard-horse-radish sauce.

CREAMY MUSTARD SAUCE

1 cup commercial sour cream	¼ teasp. salt
1 tablesp. prepared mustard	⅛ teasp. pepper
1 tablesp. minced onion	1 tablesp. chopped scallions (optional)

Combine sour cream, mustard, onion, salt, pepper. Heat over low heat. Sprinkle with scallions. Serve on grilled franks, hamburgers, tongue, luncheon meat, fish, etc. Makes about 1 cup.

HORSE-RADISH SAUCE I

½ cup day-old bread crumbs	¼ teasp. salt
½ cup light cream	Dash cayenne pepper or Tabasco
½ cup horse-radish	½ cup heavy cream

Combine crumbs, light cream, horse-radish, salt, cayenne; let stand until crumbs are soft. Shortly before serving, whip heavy cream till fairly stiff; fold in horse-radish mixture. Refrigerate.

Serve with broiled steak, tongue, roast beef, ham, corned beef, or poached, baked, or fried fish. Makes 2 cups.

HORSE-RADISH II: Into 2 tablesp. melted butter or margarine, in saucepan, stir 2 tablesp. flour. Stir in 1½ cups canned condensed chicken broth or beef broth, undiluted, a little at a time. Add 3 tablesp. lemon juice, ¾ teasp. salt (reduce to ½ teasp. if beef broth is being used), ⅛ teasp. pepper, 1 tablesp. sugar, and ¼ cup horse-radish. Simmer 2 or 3 min. Makes 1¾ cups.

P.S. Your family may enjoy bottled mustard-horse-radish sauce for table use.

CALIFORNIA RAISIN SAUCE

½ cup light or dark raisins	⅓ cup orange juice
½ cup water	¼ cup brown sugar, packed
⅓ cup port-wine or currant jelly	1 tablesp. cornstarch
½ teasp. grated orange rind	Dash salt
	Dash allspice

Rinse raisins. Add water, wine, orange rind, and juice; bring to boil. Blend sugar with cornstarch, salt, allspice; stir into orange mixture. Cook, stirring, until clear.

Serve hot, on broiled or baked ham, or on sliced tongue. Makes 1⅓ cups.

MEDIUM WHITE SAUCE
(Cream Sauce)

2 tablesp. butter or margarine	Dash paprika
2 tablesp. flour*	1 cup milk, or part milk and part light cream
Speck pepper	
½ teasp. salt	

1. In double boiler (or in saucepan over *low* heat), melt butter; add flour, pepper, salt, paprika; stir until blended smooth.
2. Slowly add milk, stirring constantly to avoid lumps.
3. Cook, stirring, until smooth and thickened. Makes 1 cup.
You may reduce flour to 1½ tablesp.

THIN: Reduce butter and flour to 1 tablesp. each.

THICK: Increase butter and flour to ¼ cup each.

ANCHOVY: Omit pepper, salt, paprika. To sauce, add ¾ to 1 teasp. anchovy paste, 2 tablesp. minced celery. Good on poached or steamed fish.

BECHAMEL: Substitute ½ cup chicken broth for ½ cup milk. Serve over fried chicken, etc.

CHEESE: To sauce, add ½ to 1 cup grated process or natural Cheddar cheese and ⅛ teasp. dry mustard. Heat, stirring until melted.

CURRY: To butter, add 2 teasp. curry powder, ¾ teasp. sugar, ⅛ teasp. ginger, ¼ cup minced onion. Just before serving, add 1 teasp. lemon juice. Delicious on fish, etc.

EGG: Increase butter to ¼ cup; decrease flour to 2 teasp. To sauce, add 2 teasp. prepared mustard and 2 sliced hard-cooked eggs. Nice on poached fish, etc.

NEWBURG: Just before serving sauce, add 1 cup cooked or canned lobster meat and 2 tablesp. cream mixed with 1 beaten egg yolk.

SHRIMP OR CRAB MEAT: To sauce, add 1 teasp. Worcestershire and ½ cup diced cleaned cooked or canned shrimp, or flaked fresh, drained canned, or thawed frozen King-crab meat. Serve with poached, broiled, or baked fish.

VEGETABLE: For part of milk, substitute liquid drained from cooked vegetables.

P.S. Also see Sauce Mixes, p. 102; Canned White Sauce, p. 102.

DRAWN-BUTTER SAUCE

¼ cup butter or margarine	½ teasp. salt
2 tablesp. flour	Dash paprika
Speck pepper	1 cup water
	1 teasp. lemon juice

In double boiler, melt butter. Stir in flour, pepper, salt, paprika, till smooth. Slowly stir in water. Cook until thickened. Just before serving, stir in lemon juice.

Nice on broiled or fried fish. Makes 1 cup.

PARSLEY: Add 2 tablesp. snipped parsley.

LEMON BUTTER
(Maitre-d'Hôtel Butter)

¼ cup soft butter or margarine	Dash cayenne pepper
1 tablesp. lemon juice	1 tablesp. snipped parsley
½ teasp. salt	

HOT: Melt butter; add rest of ingredients.

COLD: Work soft butter till creamy. Gradually stir in lemon juice, then rest of ingredients.

Serve with broiled or fried fish or hot shellfish. Try, too, on hot broccoli, spinach, cauliflower, etc. Makes about ½ cup.

MUSTARD: Stir in 2 tablesp. prepared mustard.

FINE HERB: Substitute 3 tablesp. white wine for lemon juice; stir in 2 tablesp. snipped chives, 1 teasp. dried or snipped fresh dill.

CAPER: Add 2 tablesp. bottled capers.

BLACK: Heat butter till frothy and brown; add rest of ingredients.

SUPREME: Make Hot Lemon Butter; cool; stir in ¼ cup heavy cream, whipped.

SOY: Add 1 tablesp. soy sauce.

CHILI: Add 1 tablesp. chili sauce plus a little prepared mustard and garlic salt.

LEMON-HERB: Increase butter to ½ cup. Omit lemon juice. Add 1 tablesp. grated lemon rind, ½ teasp. dried basil, 1 teasp. snipped parsley, ½ teasp. snipped chives. Makes ½ cup.

LEMON-PARSLEY SAUCE

½ cup butter or margarine	1 tablesp. sugar
¼ cup lemon juice	1 teasp. salt
½ cup orange juice	½ cup snipped parsley

In saucepan, melt butter; stir in juices, sugar, salt, and parsley; heat. Use half to brush on Parsleyed Lamb Roast, p. 220, while roasting. Reheat rest to pass. Makes 1¼ cups.

EXTRA-EASY DESSERT SAUCES

SIMPLICITY ORANGE: Stir ½ cup orange juice and ¼ cup granulated sugar till sugar dissolves. Nice on rice, tapioca, or bread pudding, etc. Makes about 4 servings.

SPICED CREAM: To heavy cream, add pinch nutmeg, cinnamon, or allspice. Serve in pitcher, to pour over fruit shortcakes or cobblers.

RED AND WHITE: Sprinkle canned whole-cranberry sauce with brown sugar mixed with cinnamon. Nice on vanilla pudding, baked custards.

NECTAR: Use canned whole-fruit apricot, peach, or pear nectar; sprinkle with flaked coconut. Wonderful on cake squares, ice cream.

MAPLE: Slowly stir ¼ cup hot maple-blended syrup into ½ cup heavy cream, whipped. Use on bread pudding, chocolate cake, etc. Makes 6 to 8 servings.

SUNDAE: Thaw frozen fruit juices, such as grape, pineapple, orange, etc., just enough to pour. Luscious on ice cream, sherbet, Bavarian cream, custards, bread pudding, etc.

CHOICE OF FLAVORS: Vanilla caramel, chocolate caramel, butterscotch, pineapple, and fruit toppings are only five of the fine dessert toppings you can buy — all ready to use. Check your grocer's shelves for others.

EASY CHOCOLATE SAUCE

In double boiler, heat 1 6-oz. pkg. semisweet-chocolate pieces (1 cup) with ½ to ¾ cup white corn syrup, stirring, until blended. Stir in ¼ cup light cream, 1 tablesp. butter or margarine, ¼ teasp. vanilla extract.

Serve warm, on chocolate or coffee ice cream. Makes 4 servings.

EASY CARAMEL SAUCE

In double boiler, place ½ lb. packaged vanilla caramels and ½ cup milk. Cook, stirring, until sauce is smooth. Serve hot, on vanilla or chocolate ice cream, cream puffs, etc. Makes 4 servings.

CHOCOLATE-PEPPERMINT SAUCE

In double boiler over hot, *not boiling*, water, melt 20 chocolate-covered peppermints with 2 tablesp. butter or margarine. Thin with light cream. Serve warm, on chocolate, coffee, or vanilla ice cream; white-cake squares, etc. Makes 4 to 6 servings.

CHOCOLATE-MARSHMALLOW SAUCE

In saucepan, combine ¼ lb. large marshmallows (16), ⅓ cup honey, ⅓ cup heavy cream, pinch salt, 1½ sq. unsweetened chocolate. Cook, stirring occasionally, till marshmallows are almost melted. Remove from heat; stir till entirely melted. Delicious on ice cream, cake squares, etc. Makes 10 servings.

SNOWY MARSHMALLOW: Omit chocolate.

MALLOW-MINT SAUCE

1 7-oz. jar marshmallow cream	¼ teasp. peppermint extract
1 tablesp. water	Few drops red or green food color

Combine marshmallow cream with rest of ingredients. Spoon over squares of warm chocolate or spice cake, brownies, or canned cling peaches. Makes about 1 cup.

MALLOW: Omit extract and food color. Serve over canned or thawed frozen fruit.

BUTTERSCOTCH SAUCE

Combine 1 cup brown sugar, packed; ¼ cup light cream; 2 tablesp. white corn syrup; 2

Caramel Apple Dumplings, p. 567

tablesp. butter or margarine. Bring to boil; cook, stirring, 3 to 4 min., or until thickened. Serve on butter-pecan or other ice cream, warm cake squares, etc. Makes 4 servings.

QUICK BUTTERSCOTCH SAUCE

¼ cup evaporated milk, undiluted	1 6-oz. pkg. butter-scotch pieces
¼ cup white corn syrup	2 tablesp. slivered crystallized ginger (optional)

In saucepan, bring evaporated milk and corn syrup to boil, over medium heat, stirring. Remove from heat; add butterscotch pieces; stir till melted. Add ginger. Serve warm or cold over ice cream, angel-cake squares, etc. Makes about 1½ cups.

BUTTER-CREAM SAUCE

In saucepan, combine 1 cup granulated sugar, ½ cup butter or margarine, ½ cup light cream, and 1 teasp. vanilla extract. Heat till boiling. Serve hot, on puddings, gingerbread, etc. Makes 6 to 8 servings.

QUICK RUM: Just before serving, stir in 2 to 3 tablesp. rum and a dash of nutmeg.

BING-CHERRY SAUCE

In skillet, melt ¾ cup currant jelly; add 1 1-lb.-13-oz. can pitted Bing cherries, drained. Heat slowly till boiling, stirring.

Serve, warm, on strawberry or vanilla ice cream, baked custards, etc. Makes 6 servings.

BRANDIED STRAWBERRIES

3 10-oz. pkg. frozen sliced strawberries, thawed	½ cup currant jelly Red food color ¼ cup brandy
1 tablesp. cornstarch	

1. Drain berries slightly; save ½ cup juice. Combine juice and cornstarch, stirring to dissolve lumps.
2. Melt jelly over low heat; add cornstarch mixture; cook, stirring, over low heat until thickened and clear. Tint with food color.
3. Add brandy and berries. Makes 2 cups. Nice over vanilla or pistachio ice-cream-topped Meringue Glacé, p. 578.

DATE-NUT SAUCE

Combine 1 8-oz. pkg. pitted dates, snipped; pinch salt; ½ cup water. Heat just till boiling. Remove from heat; stir in ½ cup each white corn syrup and chopped walnuts. Cool. Serve on coffee or vanilla ice cream. Makes 8 servings.

THREE SPEEDY CUSTARD SAUCES

1. Prepare 1 pkg. custard-dessert mix as label directs. Refrigerate; when cold, beat well. Makes 12 servings of 3 tablesp. each.
2. Or into 1 can strained custard pudding (baby pack), fold ⅓ cup heavy cream, whipped, and favorite extract to taste. Refrigerate. Nice on jellied desserts, cut-up fruit, coffee ice cream, etc. Makes 5 or 6 servings of 3 tablesp. each.
3. Or into ½ pkg. vanilla pudding (measure package contents; use half), in double boiler, gradually stir 1½ cups milk, or ¾ cup milk and ¾ cup cream. Cook, stirring, until smooth and thick enough to coat spoon. Refrigerate; add 1 teasp. almond or vanilla extract, or sherry to taste. Makes 9 or 10 servings of 3 tablesp. each.

WHIPPED CREAM

UNSWEETENED: With hand beater or electric mixer, beat chilled heavy cream until it *just* mounds. (Overbeating causes curdling. In hot weather, chill bowl and beater.)

SWEETENED: Allow 2 to 4 tablesp. granulated sugar to ½ pt. heavy cream (1 cup). Beat cream until it begins to thicken. Gradually add sugar, then ¼ teasp. vanilla or almond extract, or sherry to taste, beating until cream *just* holds shape.

BERRY: Fold drained, crushed, slightly sweetened berries into whipped cream.

CHOCOLATE: Place 2 tablesp. instant-cocoa mix, or 2 teasp. sugar and 2 tablesp. cocoa, in bowl; add 1 cup heavy cream. Beat until cream *just* mounds. Wonderful on angel-food cake.

COFFEE: Place 2 teasp. instant coffee in bowl; add 1 cup heavy cream. Beat until cream *just* mounds. Nice on any chocolate dessert.

MINT: Fold 2 tablesp. beaten mint jelly into

¼ cup heavy cream, whipped. Luscious on chocolate ice cream.

NOTE: In this book, when a recipe calls for "1 cup heavy cream, whipped," first measure 1 cup heavy cream, then whip. One cup heavy cream yields about 2 cups, whipped, or 16 servings of 2 tablesp. each.

For fewer calories, see Dessert Toppings on p. 92.

WHIPPED-MILK TOPPING

½ cup evaporated milk, undiluted	½ teasp. vanilla extract; or ¼ teasp.
1 tablesp. lemon juice	almond extract; or
½ cup confectioners' or granulated sugar	a little cinnamon or nutmeg

Chill milk in special ice-cube tray, p. 610, until soft crystals form throughout milk — about 15 to 20 min. Turn into bowl; whip until stiff enough to form peaks. Add lemon juice; whip just to blend well. Fold in sugar, vanilla. If topping is not to be used at once, refrigerate; it will hold up well 45 min. to 1 hr. Makes 1½ cups, whipped, or 6 servings of 4 tablesp. each.

ICE-CREAM SAUCES

With fork, stir 1 pt. vanilla ice cream until soft *but not runny*. Add sherry, almond or brandy extract, or bit of spice. Serve at once on warm fruit cobblers, brownies, angel cake, fruit gelatin, etc. Makes 6 to 8 servings.

COFFEE-RUM: Use coffee ice cream and 2 teasp. rum extract. Nice on warm fruitcake, bread pudding, baked apples, etc.

BRANDY-PECAN: Use butter-pecan ice cream, 1 tablesp. brandy extract. Luscious on warm baked apples or pears, broiled peaches, etc.

CHOCO-ALMOND: Use chocolate ice cream and ½ teasp. almond extract. So good on bread pudding.

FRUIT: Use vanilla ice cream and 2 tablesp. slightly thawed frozen orange, tangerine, or pineapple juice.

BERRY: Use vanilla ice cream and 2 tablesp. strawberry jam.

"FRESH" STRAWBERRY: Use 1 pt. vanilla ice cream; add 1 pkg. frozen strawberries, slightly thawed. Stir just enough to blend. Nice on

sponge or angel cake, Spanish cream, etc. Makes 8 to 10 servings.

P.S. A delicious variety of ice-cream sauces comes in jars, all ready to use.

OTHER DESSERT SAUCES

ICE-CREAM SAUCE

1 egg	or margarine
¼ cup granulated sugar	1 teasp. vanilla or brandy extract
Pinch salt	1 cup heavy cream,
⅓ cup melted butter	whipped

Beat egg until thick and light; beat in sugar and salt. Gradually beat in butter, extract. Fold in cream. Serve on warm chocolate- or white-cake squares. Makes about 12 servings.

BUTTER-CARAMEL SAUCE

¾ cup granulated sugar	¼ cup butter or margarine
⅛ teasp. salt	1 cup light cream
½ cup white corn syrup	½ teasp. vanilla extract

In saucepan, combine sugar, salt, syrup, butter, ½ cup cream. Cook slowly, stirring frequently, to 250°F. on candy thermometer, or until a little of mixture, in cold water, forms hard ball. Add ½ cup cream; cook to 216°F. on candy thermometer, or until a little of mixture forms thread when dropped from spoon. Remove from heat; add vanilla.

Serve warm, on chocolate ice cream, cream puffs, baked custard, warm cake squares, etc. Makes 4 servings.

RUM BUTTER: Add rum to taste.

HOT BRANDY SAUCE

½ cup soft butter or margarine	tioners' sugar
1 cup sifted confec-	1 egg, beaten
	2 to 3 tablesp. brandy

Day before:
1. With electric mixer at medium speed, beat butter until creamy; add sugar gradually, beating until light and fluffy.
2. Beat in egg; refrigerate.

About 15 min. before dessert time: Turn

sauce into double boiler; add brandy; heat, stirring occasionally, until hot. Serve at once over ice cream or fruitcake. Makes 8 servings.

HOT FUDGE SAUCE

2 sq. unsweetened chocolate	⅛ teasp. salt
½ cup water	1 teasp. vanilla extract
1½ cups corn syrup	

In saucepan over low heat, cook chocolate with water, stirring, 2 min., or until thick. Remove from heat; gradually add syrup, salt. Simmer 10 min., stirring often. Add vanilla. Serve hot or cold, on favorite ice cream. Or pour over warm cake squares, cream puffs, etc. Makes 10 servings.

CUSTARD SAUCE I
(3 eggs or 6 egg yolks)

2 cups milk; or 1 cup evaporated milk, undiluted, plus 1 cup water	3 to 4 tablesp. granulated sugar
	¼ teasp. salt
3 eggs; or 6 egg yolks	1 teasp. vanilla extract; or ½ teasp. almond extract

1. In double boiler, heat milk until tiny bubbles appear around edge.
2. In medium bowl, beat eggs or yolks slightly with fork; stir in sugar (amount depends on taste), salt. Add hot milk *slowly*, stirring constantly to avoid cooked-egg specks.
3. Return mixture to double boiler; cook over hot, *not boiling*, water, stirring constantly, until thick enough to coat spoon with thin film of custard.
4. Pour *at once* into cool bowl; cool; add vanilla. Cover; refrigerate until chilled. Serve over Snow Pudding Snowballs, p. 132, cut-up fruit, cake, coffee ice cream, fruit gelatin, etc. Makes 16 servings of 2 tablesp. each.

Important: If custard is not smooth when done, strain. If it curdles, set pan of custard in cold water and beat vigorously with hand beater. This restores smoothness, but custard may be a little thinner.

To Vary: To sauce, add ¼ cup flaked or fine grated coconut.

CUSTARD SAUCE II (2 EGG YOLKS): Make ½ recipe, using 2 egg yolks. If desired, add 2 teasp. grated orange rind. Makes 8 servings.

CUSTARD SAUCE DE LUXE: Substitute 1 cup heavy cream for 1 cup milk. Use 3 or 4 egg yolks. Add 1 tablesp. flour to sugar. Cook in double boiler until consistency of heavy cream. Substitute 3 tablesp. sherry for extract.

HOLIDAY CUSTARD SAUCE: Omit vanilla. Add sherry, rum, or brandy to taste. Nice on coffee ice cream, topped with grated chocolate.

EGGNOG SAUCE DE LUXE

⅔ cup light cream	Pinch salt
2 egg yolks	½ cup heavy cream
3 tablesp. confectioners' sugar	2 tablesp. rum

Early in day: In double boiler, scald light cream. Meanwhile, with hand beater, beat egg yolks well with sugar and pinch salt; slowly stir in scalded cream. Return to double boiler; cook, stirring, until mixture thickens slightly and coats spoon; refrigerate until cold.
To serve: Fold chilled egg-yolk mixture into heavy cream, whipped, along with rum. Delicious over coffee ice cream. Makes 1¾ cups.

HOLIDAY SAUCE

3 pkg. frozen sliced strawberries, thawed	Liquid red food color
	⅓ cup brandy
3 tablesp. cornstarch	1 tablesp. lemon juice

Press thawed berries through sieve; in saucepan, heat all but ¼ cup of this strawberry purée. In small bowl, combine cornstarch with reserved ¼ cup purée, stirring smooth; add to hot strawberry purée. Cook over low heat, stirring constantly, till thickened and clear. Add food color to make a bright red; add brandy and lemon juice; refrigerate. Makes 2⅔ cups.

HARD SAUCE

⅓ to ½ cup butter or margarine	sugar
1 cup confectioners'	½ teasp. vanilla or lemon extract

With spoon or electric mixer, beat butter with sugar till fluffy and creamy; beat in extract. Pile in pretty dish. Or make into balls and roll in grated orange rind. Refrigerate until firm. Serve on fruit cobblers, steamed puddings, bread pudding, etc. Makes 8 servings.

FLUFFY: Fold in ¼ cup heavy cream, whipped; refrigerate.

Or use 1/3 cup butter; blend with 2/3 cup confectioners' sugar; substitute 1 teasp. sherry for vanilla. Then beat 1 egg white until it forms peaks when beater is raised; gradually add 1/3 cup confectioners' sugar, beating; fold into sauce. Refrigerate.

ORANGE: Use 1/3 cup butter. For vanilla, substitute 2 teasp. orange juice, 1/2 teasp. orange extract, and 1 tablespoon grated orange rind.

STERLING SAUCE: Use 1/2 cup butter. Substitute brown sugar, packed, for confectioners' sugar. After blending butter with sugar, slowly add 1/4 cup light cream. Use 1 teasp. vanilla. Add rum to taste if desired.

VANILLA SAUCE

1/2 cup granulated sugar	1/4 cup butter or margarine
2 tablesp. cornstarch	2 teasp. vanilla extract
1/4 teasp. salt	
2 cups boiling water	Dash nutmeg or mace

In saucepan, combine sugar, cornstarch, salt; gradually stir in water. Boil, stirring constantly, 5 min., or until thickened. Add rest of ingredients.

Serve hot, on warm cake squares, Dutch Plum Cake, p. 566, etc. Makes 10 servings.

HOLIDAY: Omit vanilla, spices. Add brandy, rum, or sherry to taste.

LEMON: Use 1/2 cup granulated sugar, 1 tablesp. cornstarch, pinch salt, 1 cup boiling water, 2 tablesp. butter or margarine, 1 teasp. grated lemon rind, 3 tablesp. lemon juice. Make as above. Makes 5 servings.

ORANGE: Use 1/2 cup granulated sugar, 1 tablesp. cornstarch, dash each salt and cinnamon, 3/4 cup boiling water, 2 tablesp. butter or margarine, 1 teasp. grated orange rind, 1/4 cup orange juice, 1 tablesp. lemon juice. Combine sugar, cornstarch, salt, cinnamon; gradually stir in water; proceed as above. Makes 5 servings.

SUNSHINE FOAMY SAUCE

Beat 1 egg white with pinch of salt until foamy; slowly add 2 tablesp. brown sugar, beating until stiff. To 1 egg yolk, add 2 tablesp. brown sugar; beat until light-colored; fold into egg-white mixture. Fold in 1/4 cup heavy cream, whipped, and 1/2 teasp. vanilla extract.

Serve on warm gingerbread, or chocolate- or white-cake squares. Makes 6 servings.

ORANGE-FLUFF SAUCE

1/2 cup granulated sugar	orange-juice concentrate
Dash salt	2 egg yolks
1/2 cup thawed frozen-	1 cup heavy cream, whipped

Early in day: In saucepan, combine sugar, salt, orange juice. Cook over low heat, stirring until sugar dissolves. Beat egg yolks slightly; gradually beat in some of orange-juice mixture; return to rest of orange-juice mixture in saucepan. Cook, stirring, until slightly thickened. Cool to room temperature; fold in cream. Refrigerate until chilled. Makes 8 to 10 servings.

Serve over warm waffles (it's so easy to heat frozen ones in toaster). Nice, too, over devil's-food or spicecake squares.

MELBA SAUCE

1 pkg. frozen raspberries,* thawed	1 1/2 teasp. cornstarch
1/2 cup currant jelly	1 tablesp. cold water

In saucepan, mash raspberries. Add jelly; bring to boil. Add cornstarch mixed with water; cook, stirring, until clear. Strain if desired; cool. Serve on lemon sherbet or Peach Melba, p. 606. Makes 6 servings.

*Two cups fresh raspberries and 1/2 cup granulated sugar may replace frozen berries.

RUM SAUCE

3/4 cup heavy cream	sugar
3 egg yolks	1/8 teasp. salt
1 1/2 teasp. flour	3 tablesp. rum
3 tablesp. granulated	

Early in day: In double boiler, heat cream till tiny bubbles appear around edge. Beat yolks lightly with fork; stir in flour, sugar, salt. Gradually stir in cream; then cook over hot, *not boiling*, water, stirring constantly, till thick enough to coat spoon. Pour at once into small bowl; cover with wax-paper circle laid directly on surface. Refrigerate until serving time; then stir in rum. Delicious over Coffee Jelly, p. 574. Makes 6 servings.

WONDERFUL WAYS WITH FRUITS

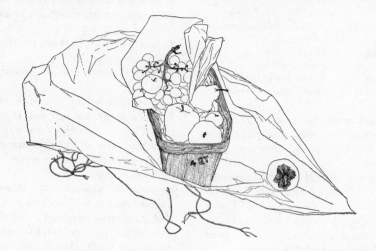

The popularity of fruits has zoomed, with more and more people becoming waistline conscious, and with better nutrition a national goal. Check the calorie charts to see what a bargain fruits are!

All fruits, fresh, frozen, canned, or dried, are important for their vitamins and minerals (the latter help maintain the alkaline reserve of the blood), their sugars, which help to satisfy appetite, and their bulk, which helps promote elimination. They are also important for the interest they add to meals.

Shop Wisely

MARKET FRESH FRUIT: It is possible to have fresh fruits from all growing areas in this country and from many parts of the world, thanks to modern methods, right at the farm, of packing fruits in protective boxes, hydrocooling them, and then sending them to market under refrigeration.

1. Check on fruit supplies in local markets through newspaper and radio reports.

2. When you shop, consider prepackaged fruit. It has not been handled or picked over as much as bulk fruit.

3. Don't buy more than you need for a few days.

4. Be sure to ripen fruit to your liking before storing it in the refrigerator.

5. The height of the local growing season is the best time to tuck some of your favorite fruits in the freezer, to can them, or to put them up as jams or jellies.

FROZEN FRUITS: Hurry them home and into your freezer. (Take along an insulated bag when you shop.) What delightful variety they add to your menus:

Blueberries	Sliced peaches
Grapefruit sections	Strawberries, sliced or
Melon balls	halved
Mixed fruit	Whole strawberries
Pineapple chunks	with syrup
Raspberries	Etc.
Rhubarb	

Most of these frozen fruits come sweetened and ready to eat or cook, as is or thawed. Check label for sweetening and thawing directions. Usually it's best to thaw them almost, but not completely; a few ice crystals should remain for these fruits to be at their best.

CANNED OR JAR FRUITS: Explore your grocer's shelves. Many real time-savers are waiting for you — for example:

Apples, sliced, baked, cinnamon rings, or applesauce
Apricots
Cherries, sweet or sour
Dried fruits — figs, prunes, fruit compote
Grapefruit sections
Mandarin orange sections

Cling-peach halves or slices
Pears
Pineapple — chunks, slices, tidbits, and crushed
Purple plums
Fruit cocktail
Fruits for salad
Many other varieties

Some fruits also come sweetened and thickened, ready to use as ice-cream toppings or pie fillings. These include apples, cherries, berries, pineapple, etc.

To serve: Just spoon chilled canned fruit into serving dishes as is, or sprinkled with nutmeg, grated lemon rind, etc. Or pour on heavy cream, dot of whipped cream or sour cream. Such fruits as cling peaches, apricots, and pears are wonderful served hot!

P.S. If you're counting calories, many canned fruits come artificially sweetened, or canned in fruit juice and/or water.

DESSERTS IN NO TIME

JUST FRUIT DESSERTS

CHERRIES ON STEMS: Arrange on green leaves on dessert plates. (Provide spoons for removing pits from mouth.)

CURRANTS: Wash; remove stems. Sprinkle currants with sugar; chill; then serve. Currants and raspberries are a wonderful team too.

FRESH FIGS: Wash; pare off outer skins. Serve whole, cut into halves, or sliced. Serve with cream. Or serve canned figs in syrup with a spoonful of commercial sour cream and a sprinkle of cinnamon on top.

GRAPES: Place small bunch of 2 or 3 kinds of grapes on each plate. (Provide spoons for removing pits from mouth.)

GRAPEFRUIT SECTIONS: Arrange drained canned or thawed frozen grapefruit sections, spoke-fashion, on glass plates with green grapes, strawberries, or melon balls in center.

KUMQUATS: Cut in halves; spread with cream cheese. Or serve whole, with mound of cream cheese for dunking. (Eat rind and pulp.) Nice hors d'oeuvre too.

MELONS: Cut into wedges; remove seeds; serve in one of these ways:

1. Serve with salt and lemon or lime wedges; or sprinkle with sherry. Nice too as breakfast fruit or first course.
2. Garnish with berries, cherries, mint sprigs, or grapes.
3. Sprinkle with a little ground ginger or nutmeg.
4. Top with lemon or raspberry sherbet.
5. On a large, rectangular tray, covered with lemon leaves, arrange 2 rows of melon wedges, sprinkled with nutmeg. Drape a cluster of red grapes over each melon wedge. Place a wedge of lime beside grapes.

ORANGE 'N' GRAPEFRUIT: Alternate layers of flaked coconut with mixed grapefruit, orange, and tangerine sections; sprinkle each layer with sugar; let stand 1 hr. before serving.

PEACHES: Wash; dry. Serve, unpeeled, in fruit bowl. Or serve, peeled and sliced, with pour cream or ice-cold custard sauce.

PEARS: Just before serving, cut into halves; then cut out cores. Serve with Danish blue-cheese wedges. Provide spoons.

PERSIMMONS: Wash; dry. Cut off stem ends; cut into halves crosswise. Provide spoon or fork.

PINEAPPLE OR MELON IN SHELLS: Quarter fresh pineapple lengthwise through green top. Or quarter honeydew melon; remove seeds. Run knife between shell and meat, loosening but not removing meat; cut meat into 1/4" to 1/2" crosswise slices. If desired, top with a few raspberries or flaked or toasted coconut. Or serve with lime wedges.

STRAWBERRIES: Wash berries; do not hull. Place mound of confectioners' sugar and whipped cream or cream cheese or sour cream on each plate. Circle with berries. To eat, dunk berries. Nice as breakfast fruit too.

TANGERINES: Cut tangerine peel into 6 sections; peel part way down. Spread sections apart, sunburst-fashion. Fill center with salted nuts or raisins.

WATERMELON: Cut into crosswise slices or wedge-shaped pieces. Or with tablespoon, scoop out medium-sized pieces; arrange 3 or 4 pieces, with rounded sides up, on each dessert plate; sprinkle with lime or lemon juice.

GAY FRUIT CENTERPIECES TO EAT

CHRISTMAS TREE: Buy a tiny Christmas tree. Set it in a tiny flowerpot, filled with wet sand. With narrow red satin ribbon, tie to its branches tiny bunches of grapes, small apples and pears, by their stems.

CROCK OF CHEESE: Tie a crock of very special homemade cheese spread with a huge Christmas bow, and set it in the center of a big board. Surround with fruits of the season; tuck in Christmas greens here and there. Nearby, set a basket of assorted crackers. Change color of bow when using any other time of year.

GRAPES ON PINE: Down the length of the table, place a row of pine branches. On them, group grapes — red, white, and green. Top the grapes with walnuts, Brazil nuts, pecans, almonds.

KNIFE BOX: In a Colonial knife box use diminutive fruits — lady apples; kumquats; grapes, cut in tiny bunchlets; strawberries; tangerines; etc., with pine cones placed here and there.

HEMLOCK-LINED BOWL: Line your biggest, most interesting bowl — of brass, glass, or wood — with sprays of hemlock. In it, arrange a hand of bananas, a bunch of green grapes, and a cluster of tangerines. If you wish, for holiday glitter, add a sparkling gold bow.

RING-AROUND-THE-CANDLE: Secure the biggest, fattest candle you can afford in the center of a nest of magnolia leaves; top leaves with fruits of the season.

AN ORANGE TREE: Fill a bowl with crushed chicken wire; then stick in it enough greens to cover it completely. Cut wooden sticks, 12" to 15" long; insert among the greens; then put an orange on the end of each. Set bowl on tray; place table raisins and salted nuts around base.

FROSTED FRUITS: Dip red apples, pears, lemons, oranges, and assorted grapes in egg white, beaten until frothy. Then dip them in granulated sugar. Keep on cake rack, over wax paper, until dry. Arrange in compote or silver bowl, or on cake stand, with laurel leaves tucked here and there.

NEW ENGLAND BASKET: Set a basket, preferably with handle, on its side. Arrange apples and cranberries so they appear to be tumbling out.

TABLE MIRROR: At one end of a rectangular mirror plateau, group grapes, apples, pears, and bananas in a high-low line, using a can to hold the grapes and leaves high. (Conceal can with heavier fruits at base.)

GREEN PLUS RED: Arrange soft-green pippin apples and red grapes on a board.

COMPOTE PERFECT: Set a compote in center of a large tray and a fresh pineapple in the compote. Arrange large bunches of green grapes and pears around pineapple. On the tray under the compote, arrange cheese and crackers, including a chunk of Swiss cheese, a wedge of Danish blue cheese, and Camembert.

STRAWBERRY BOUQUET: Set an apple in a goblet; insert toothpicks in apple about 1" apart. Stick unhulled strawberries on toothpicks. Use as both table centerpiece and help-yourself dessert. For a special dinner, slash center of paper doily; insert stem of goblet through slit; fasten doily to goblet with tape.

KUMQUAT BOUQUET: Substitute kumquats for strawberries in Strawberry Bouquet. Have cheese and crackers nearby.

FRESH FRUIT DRAMATICS

Look about your house for anything that might hold dessert fruits. Let your imagination run riot! For instance, select a:

French horn	Lazy Susan
Basket, on its side	Cake stand
Huge brandy snifter	Gigantic wooden chopping or salad bowl
Old-fashioned knife box	
	Brass tray
Punch bowl	Mirror plateau
Old brass coal scuttle	Brass log holder
Wicker cornucopia	

Go shopping, and select the prettiest fruits in the market, not forgetting more unusual ones, like kumquats, persimmons, pomegranates, fresh cranberries. Include in your market basket a few of the out-of-season items you may be lucky enough to chance upon — strawberries, grapes, cherries. Now look over the selection of extras — dates, nuts, table raisins, dried apricots and prunes, etc. Stop at the florist's, too, and pick up some choice pine, hemlock, etc.

Then, when you have an hour or so, assemble scissors, knife, clay, etc., and fashion the fruit centerpiece which is to double as your dessert!

PINEAPPLE TREE

Fresh or preserved kumquats	Diced roasted almonds
Pineapple cream-cheese spread	Ripe olives
Stuffed olives	Italian dressing
Cream cheese	Fresh pineapple, with handsome green top

Split each kumquat lengthwise, then fill with pineapple cream cheese. Split stuffed olives lengthwise; fill each with cream cheese blended with almonds. Marinate ripe olives in Italian dressing. Refrigerate all.
To serve: Set pineapple on attractive base. Cover it, porcupine-fashion, with kumquats and olives, arranged on picks. Guests help themselves.

FRUIT-CUP DESSERTS

Two or more fruits can taste newer than one. Top any of these fruit-cup combinations with sherbet and you'll have a de luxe dessert.
1. Banana chunks and thawed frozen strawberries, sprinkled with nuts
2. Grapefruit sections and pineapple chunks in grape juice
3. Diced oranges, snipped pitted dates, and sliced bananas
4. Sliced bananas in pink rhubarb sauce
5. Fresh, canned, or thawed frozen peach slices, topped with fresh or thawed frozen raspberries and slivered almonds
6. Fresh, canned, or thawed frozen pineapple chunks and seedless grapes in apricot nectar
7. Fresh, canned, or thawed frozen pineapple chunks tossed with strawberries
8. Canned cling-peach halves, filled with chopped nuts; peach syrup, flavored with almond extract, spooned over all
9. Canned fruit cocktail, sliced bananas, and unpared apple cubes
10. Melon cubes and seedless grapes, topped with slightly thawed orange-juice concentrate and fresh mint sprigs
11. Refrigerated fresh fruit sections (orange, grapefruit, and maraschino cherries) flavored with crème de menthe

OTHER QUICK FRUIT TOP-OFFS

SPLITS: Split each peeled banana lengthwise. Top each half with canned or frozen pineapple chunks, canned crushed pineapple, or whole or sliced strawberries. Pass whipped cream or dessert topping, with a little spice added.

Or put split bananas together with cream cheese thinned with milk; then top with thawed frozen, or fresh sliced strawberries.

FRUIT CREAM: Top sliced bananas or peaches, strawberries, or thawed frozen or canned pineapple chunks with spoonfuls of commercial sour cream. Sprinkle with brown sugar and cinnamon or nutmeg.

CHEESE BOWL: Top bowlful of cottage cheese with applesauce or fresh, canned, or thawed frozen peach slices or berries.

MINTED FRUIT: Top canned apricot, pear, or peach halves or pineapple slices with whipped cream into which a little mint jelly has been folded.

CHERRY-ORANGE MEDLEY: Serve hot canned Bing cherries over sliced oranges.

FROZEN FRUIT SAUTE: Sauté canned cling-peach halves or pineapple slices in butter or margarine till golden. Serve, topped with ice cream, then with some syrup from fruit, with a little sherry added.

MARMALADE FRUIT: To drained syrup from canned cling peaches, pears, or pineapple chunks, add spoonful of orange marmalade; heat. Pour over fruit. Serve warm, topped with whipped cream or dessert topping if desired.

FRUIT CREAM: Top canned peach or pear halves or pineapple slices with cream cheese, which has been whipped with a few fresh or thawed frozen raspberries.

BROILED FRUIT MEDLEY: Sprinkle canned pineapple slices and peach halves with brown sugar; dot with butter or margarine. Broil. Serve hot, topped with whipped cream or dessert topping.

FROZEN FRUIT FROST: Slice a block of frozen raspberries, peaches, or strawberries into ½" slices. Top each with whipped or commercial sour cream, or nuts.

Or, about 1 hr. before serving, cut 2 or 3 kinds of frozen fruit into squares. Arrange in sherbet glasses. Top with almond-flavored whipped cream, macaroon or other cookie crumbs, toasted coconut, or chopped nuts.

BERRY RICE: Into cold cooked rice, fold whipped cream or dessert topping, thawed frozen raspberries, and a little sugar.

COMPOTE DE LUXE: Heat 2 or 3 8-oz. cans of different fruits together. Flavor with lemon juice, vanilla extract, or nutmeg. Top with commercial sour cream and grated chocolate or slivered nuts.

TWO-TONE FRUITS: Serve fruit in a tasty juice. Try one of these:

Fresh strawberries in orange juice
Sliced bananas in cranberry-juice cocktail
Canned cling-peach halves or seedless grapes in grape juice
Canned or thawed frozen pineapple chunks in apricot nectar or orange juice; toss with seedless grapes
Grapefruit sections and pineapple chunks in grape juice

CANNED FRUIT PLUS: To drained canned fruit syrup, add a little almond, vanilla, or lemon extract; sherry; brandy; or lemon, lime, or orange juice. Pour over fruit. Top with whipped or frozen whipped cream.

FRUIT PARFAIT: Toss canned or thawed frozen pineapple chunks with slightly frozen orange-juice concentrate and grated orange rind. Serve in parfaits or dessert dishes.

FRUIT LAYERS: Layer orange sections and banana slices in sherbet glasses. Add a sprinkle of flaked coconut and a dash of sherry. Serve ice cold.

HOT APRICOTS: Heat canned apricots — juice and all — with piece of lemon peel. Serve as is; or top with whipped cream or vanilla ice cream.

QUICK CREME BRULEE

1 12-oz. pkg. frozen peaches, or 1 10-oz. pkg. frozen raspberries, thawed and drained	½ cup chilled commercial sour cream ¼ cup brown sugar, packed

In 6″ shallow baking dish, place fruit. Spread with sour cream. Sift brown sugar over sour cream. Broil 3″ from heat till sugar caramelizes — about 1 or 2 min. Serve at once. Makes 2 servings.

From Your Fruit Bowl

APPLES

To Buy: Fresh apples are on the market the year round, and are at their peak from October to March. Listed below are some of the commercial leaders. About 3 or 4 apples equal 1 lb.

VARIETY	COLOR	SEASON
For Cooking		
RHODE ISLAND GREENING	Green-yellow	Sept. to Mar.
ROME BEAUTY	Medium red	Nov. to May
For Eating		
DELICIOUS	Light red and striped with darker red	Oct. to May
For Cooking and Eating		
BALDWIN	Red, mottled with bright red	Nov. to May
GRAVENSTEIN	Mostly green with pale red stripes	July to Sept.
GRIMES GOLDEN	Yellow	Sept. to Jan.
JONATHAN	Deep red	Oct. to Feb.
MC INTOSH	Bright red	Sept. to May
NORTHERN SPY	Striped bright red over yellow	Oct. to May
WINESAP	Dark red	Jan. to June
YELLOW NEWTOWN	Greenish-yellow or yellow	Jan. to June

To Store: Keep apples in a cold, dry place. **THE CANNED KIND:** Canned applesauce comes in various degrees of sweetness. Canned apple slices and rings save you all the paring and slicing. Baked apples and cinnamon apple rings are ready with the turn of a can opener. *To serve:* See Fruit Cup Desserts, p. 542, Gay Fruit Centerpieces to Eat, p. 541.

SAUCEPAN APPLESAUCE

2 lb. unpared, cooking apples, cored, quartered (8)	About ½ cup granulated sugar or brown sugar,
½ cup water	packed

In saucepan, simmer apples with water, covered, 15 to 20 min., or until fork-tender. (Stir occasionally, adding water if necessary, to keep apples from scorching.) Put through food mill or coarse sieve. Stir in sugar (amount depends on desired sweetness) until dissolved. Adding a few drops of lemon juice or bit of butter will perk up the flavor.

Serve warm or cold, with cream, whipped cream, or dessert topping, custard sauce, ice cream, etc. Or use as breakfast fruit or meat accompaniment. Makes 6 servings.

To Vary: Pare and core apples before cooking. When cooked, beat smooth with spoon. Then add vanilla or almond extract or brandy to taste. Or stir in miniature marshmallows, or top with marshmallow cream. Sprinkle with a little nutmeg or cinnamon.

FRUITY: Before cooking, add 2 teasp. grated orange, lemon, or lime rind; or ½ cup canned crushed pineapple; or a bit of canned whole-cranberry sauce.

SPICED: Before cooking, add lemon juice to taste, plus ⅛ teasp. cinnamon or mace, or 8 whole cloves. To serve, remove cloves.

CINNAMON: Chill applesauce well. Just before serving, add a few tiny red cinnamon candies.

BAKED APPLES

6 medium red cooking apples	sugar
	1 cup water
¾ cup granulated	2 tablesp. sugar

1. Start heating oven to 350°F. Wash and core apples.
2. Starting at stem end, pare apples one third of way down. (This helps keep skins from bursting.) Arrange in shallow baking pan, with pared sides up.
3. Boil ¾ cup sugar with 1 cup water 10 min.

Pour over apples. (For color, cook a few parings with syrup; remove before using.)
4. Bake apples, ½ to 1 hr., or until easily pierced with fork, spooning syrup from pan over them frequently. (Time varies with apples.)
5. When apples are tender, remove from oven; sprinkle each with 1 teasp. sugar. Broil under low heat, basting often, till brown.

Serve cold or warm, as is or with pour cream, whipped cream, dessert topping, or ice cream. Or sprinkle with port or sherry. Also nice as breakfast fruit with cream. Makes 6.

To Vary: Before sprinkling sugar in step 5, place one of these in each baked apple:

Pitted, cooked prune	Currant jelly
Marshmallow	Orange marmalade
Cut-up pitted dates	A few raisins with
1 teasp. grated orange or lemon rind	chopped nuts
	Coconut mixed with
1 tablesp. prepared mincemeat	butter and brown sugar

CRANBERRY: Substitute 1 can whole-cranberry sauce for ¾ cup sugar. Combine sauce with water; pour over apples; bake as at left. Omit sprinkling with sugar and broiling. Nice as dessert.

SNOW PEAK: Top warm apples with a swirl of meringue, then a shower of coconut. Bake at 375°F. till toasted — about 15 min.

DANISH PORCUPINE APPLES
(Aeble Pindsvin)

3 large apples	2 tablesp. lemon juice
2½ cups water	½ cup slivered
¾ cup granulated sugar	toasted almonds
	Custard Sauce, p. 537

Pare apples; then, starting at blossom end, cut each in half; core. In large skillet, bring water, sugar, and lemon juice to boil. Add apples; simmer, covered, until tender. turning once.

Arrange apple halves, cut side down, on a deep serving platter. Boil syrup in which apples cooked until it's reduced to 2 cups.

Tuck some of slivered almonds into rounded side of each apple half, resembling porcupine. Pour on syrup; cool; refrigerate.

Serve with Custard Sauce. Makes 6 servings.

APPLE SNOW

To 1⅔ cups chilled, unsweetened applesauce, add dash nutmeg, pinch salt, 1 teasp. vanilla extract. Fold in 2 egg whites, beaten with ¼ cup granulated sugar till stiff.

Serve with cream, whipped cream or dessert topping, or custard sauce. Makes 5 or 6 servings.

PRUNE SNOW: Substitute 1¾ cups sieved, cooked prunes for applesauce; 2 tablesp. lemon juice, bit of grated lemon rind, and ⅛ teasp. cinnamon for vanilla. Reduce sugar to 3 tablesp.

APRICOTS

To Buy: Fresh apricots, in season from May through August, are at their peak in June and July. Look for orange-yellow, plump, juicy apricots. About 8 to 16, depending on their size, equal 1 lb.

To Store: Keep in refrigerator.

To Prepare: Peel like peaches, p. 552.

THE CANNED KIND: Most canned apricots are unpeeled halves; some are whole and a few are quartered. They may be packed in water, apricot juice, or syrup.

CINNAMON APRICOTS OR PEACHES

1 lb. apricots or peaches	1 teasp. cinnamon
⅓ cup granulated sugar	⅓ cup water
	¼ cup light cream

Bake night before: Start heating oven to 375°F. Halve, then pit unpeeled apricots or peeled peaches. Place in 1-qt. casserole. Combine sugar, cinnamon, water; pour over fruit. Bake, uncovered, basting occasionally, 30 to 40 min. Then pour on cream and bake 5 min.; refrigerate. Nice as dessert or for breakfast. Makes 4 servings.

BRANDIED APRICOTS

Drain syrup from 2 1-lb.-13-oz. cans whole unpeeled apricots into large saucepan. Boil it down till reduced to 1¾ cups — about 30 min.; then stir in ½ cup brandy and pour over apricots in large bowl. Let stand out at least 24 hr. before serving. Nice with or over poundcake wedges. Makes 12 to 16 servings.

AVOCADOS

To Buy, to Store: Avocados, a pear-shaped, dark-green fruit, are available all year long. The peak season for California avocados is February through April, for Florida avocados, September through November.

The avocado flesh when ripe is mellow and soft, yields readily to gentle pressure from palms of hands. If it's firm, you can hasten the softening by keeping the avocado in a warm room; then refrigerate it until used. Always be sure to soften a firm avocado before refrigerating it.

To Prepare: Just before using avocado, cut in half lengthwise. To open, hold between palms of hands and turn halves in opposite directions. Insert sharp paring knife into pit; lift out and discard it.

To serve: Tear glove-like skin from halves; then slice crosswise or lengthwise. Or halve avocado crosswise, turn halves, and pit as above; peel; then slice into rings. Or serve halves unpeeled.

To prevent darkening, dip avocado slices into lemon juice. Wrap any leftover avocado in wax paper or foil; store in refrigerator.

BANANAS

To Buy: Bananas are available the year round. Buy them by the hand or cluster at whatever stage of ripeness you find them in the store; they will finish ripening at home. About three bananas equal one pound.

To Store: Keep bananas at comfortable room temperature until they reach the desired stage of ripeness. When flecked with brown, they are at correct stage for infant feeding and ideal for mashing and blending into cakes, cookies, and breads.

When bananas have ripened to the stage you like best, they may be refrigerated, where they can be held for several days.

To Prepare: When slicing bananas, you may first run tines of fork down peeled surface to get fluted effect. Then slice crosswise or diagonally. To prevent darkening, dip banana slices into acid fruit juice, such as lemon or pineapple juice.

To serve: Slice them; sprinkle with red wine. Or serve, sliced, with orange slices and Custard Sauce, p. 537. Top with jelly or flaked coconut.

BAKED BANANAS

4 firm bananas*	ter or margarine
2 tablesp. melted but-	Salt

Start heating oven to 450°F. Peel bananas; place in well-greased baking dish. Brush well with butter; sprinkle lightly with salt. Bake 10 to 12 min., or till bananas are tender and easily pierced with fork. Serve hot, as vegetable, with ham, hamburgers, poultry, etc. Makes 4 servings.

*Use slightly green-tipped or all-yellow ones.
P.S. For a golden-brown tint, broil baked bananas about 1 min.

CRANBERRY: Pour 3/4 cup canned whole-cranberry sauce over bananas before baking. Serve with beef, ham, chicken, duckling, or turkey.

FOR DESSERT: Prepare Baked Bananas, above. Serve with cream, Lemon or Orange Sauce, p. 538, or Ice-cream Sauces, p. 536.

BANANA-COCONUT ROLLS

Start heating oven to 375°F. Halve 4 peeled firm bananas crosswise; place in a greased 10" x 6" x 2" pan. Brush with 2 tablesp. melted butter or margarine and 2 tablesp. lemon juice or lime juice; sprinkle with 1/2 cup flaked coconut. Bake 15 to 20 min., or until easily pierced with fork.

Serve warm, with cream. Makes 4 servings.

BANANAS ON THE HALF SHELL

Use unpeeled whole bananas or bananas halved crosswise. Remove top half of peel lengthwise, without removing fruit. Then cut fruit (not through peel) into 1/2" slices. Top with whipped cream; sprinkle with nutmeg.

BERRIES

To Buy: Fresh-berry time begins in April. The order of appearance is:
STRAWBERRIES: Peak season, April through July. Limited amounts available all year now, including mid-winter.
GOOSEBERRIES: June and July.
RASPBERRIES: June, July, August. Limited amounts in September, October, and November.
BLACKBERRIES: May through August; best in June, July, and August.
BLUEBERRIES: May to September; most plentiful in July.
LOGANBERRIES: April through September. Peak in June.

Choose berries that are ripe, well-colored, and free from off-color spots.

To Store: Pick over berries, removing spoiled ones; spread on tray; refrigerate, uncovered.

To Prepare: Just before using, wash as follows: Place berries in colander or sieve; gently run water over them. Drain well; hull. One quart yields about 3 1/2 cups.
THE CANNED KIND: They come in water or syrup, or as pie filling.
THE FROZEN KIND: Strawberries are frozen, sugared and sliced. Whole strawberries may or may not be sweetened. Raspberries are frozen, sweetened. Blueberries are usually unsweetened. There are mixed fruits, too. They are all excellent!

To serve: If tart, sprinkle with sugar; if bland, add lemon juice. Serve with cream, Custard Sauce, p. 537, or red or white wine. See Just Fruit Desserts, p. 540, Fruit-Cup Desserts, p. 542. Gay Fruit Centerpieces to Eat, p. 541, Other Quick Fruit Top-Offs, p. 542.

BERRY SPECIALS

HOT BERRY DESSERT: Heat a package of frozen blueberries with a dash of cinnamon and nutmeg. Serve hot, over French toast or in bakers' dessert shells.

RASPBERRY RIPPLE: Fold thawed frozen raspberries and whipped cream into cold, cooked rice.

RASPBERRY PEACHES: In saucepan, mix 1 to 2 tablesp. sugar and 1 teasp. cornstarch. Add 1 10-oz. pkg. frozen raspberries, thawed; 1 tablesp. lemon juice; 1/8 teasp. almond extract. Simmer 5 min.; cool. Add 1 1-lb. can cling-peach slices, drained. Serve as sauce over vanilla pudding or baked custard. Makes 4 to 6 servings.

FROSTED STRAWBERRIES: Top thawed frozen sliced strawberries with commercial sour cream, then a sprinkling of brown sugar.

QUICK BLUEBERRY LOAF

3 tablesp. butter or margarine	1/2 cup granulated sugar
4 bread slices	2 teasp lemon juice
1 pt. fresh, or 1 pkg. frozen, blueberries	1/4 cup water
	Dash allspice
	Whipped cream

At least 4 hr. before serving: Melt butter in saucepan. Remove crusts from bread; cube bread; add to butter and toss; transfer to bowl (3-cup capacity). In saucepan, heat together blueberries, sugar, lemon juice, water, and allspice, until berries are juicy but still plump and whole. Pour half of mixture over bread; toss lightly; pour remainder on top. Refrigerate 4 hr. or longer; unmold. Serve with whipped cream. Makes 4 servings.

TWO-BERRY AMBROSIA

1 10-oz. pkg. frozen raspberries	pitted Malaga grapes
1 10-oz. pkg. frozen strawberries	2 cups flaked coconut
1 lb. seedless grapes or 1/2 lb. halved,	1/2 to 1 pt. commercial sour cream
	Confectioners' sugar (optional)

When berries are just thawed, combine them. Then add grapes, coconut, sour cream, and sugar if mixture isn't sweet enough; toss together lightly.

Serve, buffet style, in a decorative bowl, topped with small blobs of sour cream and a sprinkling of coconut; or spoon it into sherbet glasses. Makes 10 servings.

CHERRIES

To Buy: Red, white, and black sweet cherries are available from May through August. They're delicious fresh or cooked.

Red sour cherries, in season from late June to mid-August, make fine cherry pies and preserves.

Cherries should be firm, shiny, plump, of fully ripe color, and free of spots.

To Store: Wash, drain; dry; refrigerate.

To Prepare: To pit, use a new wire paper clip, wire hairpin, metal end of pencil (eraser removed), or tip of vegetable parer.

THE CANNED KIND: Red tart cherries, cherry pie fillings, and light and dark sweet cherries all come canned.

To serve: See Just Fruit Desserts, p. 540, Gay Fruit Centerpieces to Eat, p. 541.

CHERRIES FLAMBE

In skillet or chafing dish, over direct heat, melt 3/4 cup currant jelly, stirring gently. Quickly drain 1 1-lb.-13-oz. can pitted Bing cherries; add cherries to jelly; heat slowly till simmering, stirring occasionally. Pour 1/2 cup brandy into center of cherries; heat undisturbed; then light with match. Quickly spoon flaming cherries over 8 servings (1 1/2 qt.) vanilla ice cream.

PEACH: Substitute 1 1-lb.-13-oz. can cling-peach halves for cherries. When peaches are heated, turn cut sides up; pour brandy into centers; don't stir. Light. Quickly spoon over 6 servings of ice cream.

CHERRIES JUBILEE: When adding Bing cherries to currant jelly, above, also add 1 qt. washed, hulled strawberries.

CRANBERRIES

To Buy: Fresh cranberries, available from September through March, are most plentiful from October through December. Choose berries that are firm, plump, fresh-appearing, and with high luster.

To Store: Refrigerate cranberries. Or freeze

as on p. 702; they keep well. Then use as you would fresh berries. Don't wait for berries to thaw.

To Prepare: Pick over; wash; drain; use. If frozen cranberries are to be ground don't thaw them.

THE CANNED KIND: Look for canned strained cranberry sauce (jelly) or whole berry sauce. *To serve:* See Gay Fruit Centerpieces to Eat, p. 541; Relishes and Garnishes, pp. 433–444.

CURRANTS

To Buy, to Store: July is the month for currants. Look for bright, plump currants; make sure they are not so ripe they fall off stems. Refrigerate on shallow tray.

Use white or red currants for eating, or in salads, fruit cups, or desserts. Use black currants for jelly or jam.

To Prepare: Wash; dry; serve in clusters, or with stems removed. *To serve:* See Just Fruit Desserts, p. 540.

FRESH FIGS

To Buy, to Store: Fresh figs, in season from June through November, are most plentiful in August, September, and October. They should be soft. Kadota figs should be greenish-yellow; Black Mission, purplish. Buy them slightly underripe; refrigerate until fully ripe, when they're ready to eat.

To Prepare: Wash; pare off outer skin. THE CANNED KIND: Canned fresh figs come whole and split, in water, juice, or syrup. *To serve:* See Just Fruit Desserts, p. 540. Or split figs, arrange on lettuce; top with cottage cheese, mixed nuts; pass French dressing.

GRAPEFRUIT

To Buy, to Store: Fresh Florida grapefruit are especially delicious from October through June. California and Arizona ship them the year round. They should be firm, well-shaped, heavy with juice, and thin-skinned. The color varies from pale yellow to reddish-brown. Rust spots and green tinges do not affect the inner quality.

Very often small grapefruit are sweeter and juicier than the large sizes. Small grapefruit can be easily reamed for fresh juice too. Store grapefruit in a cool place, preferably in refrigerator.

Grapefruit meat is white or pink, with or without seeds. Under U.S. Dept. of Agriculture rulings, any grapefruit containing fewer than 17 seeds is considered seedless.

GRAPEFRUIT SECTIONS: From chilled fresh grapefruit, cut off peel in strips, from top to bottom; or pare like an apple, cutting deep enough to remove white membrane. Now cut a slice from top and bottom of grapefruit. Go over fruit again, removing any remaining white membrane. Cut alongside of each dividing membrane, from outside down to core. Remove, section by section, over bowl, to catch juice from fruit.

THE CANNED KIND: These are packed as grapefruit sections (or segments), or, in combination, as orange and grapefruit sections.

THE FROZEN KIND: Frozen grapefruit sections are usually in cans, all ready to just thaw, open, and eat.

COMMERCIALLY CHILLED: Fresh grapefruit sections are available, packed in jars with orange sections and maraschino cherries, and labeled Fruit Sections. *To serve:* See Just Fruit Desserts, p. 540, and Fruit-Cup Desserts, p. 542.

CHILLED GRAPEFRUIT HALVES

1. Wash and dry chilled fresh grapefruit. Halve crosswise. Remove seeds with tip of sharp knife.* If desired, cut out core.
2. Then, with sharp knife, cut around each section to loosen flesh from membrane and skin (do not cut around outer edge of fruit). Remove remaining seeds.
3. If desired, sprinkle with a little sugar; then serve. Or refrigerate until served.

Serve as dessert or first course, topped with one of these:

Grape juice	Dash of bitters
Bottled grenadine	A red or green cherry

Diced oranges
Seeded grapes
Canned crushed pine-
apple
Crushed after-dinner
mints

Melon balls
Jelly cubes
Sherbet
Madeira wine
Sherry or crème de
menthe

If grapefruit contains many seeds, before freeing fruit from membrane, with scissors, cut around seeds, removing core and seeds all at once.

BROILED GRAPEFRUIT

Prepare fresh grapefruit as in Chilled Grapefruit Halves, p. 548. Sprinkle each half with 1 teasp. granulated sugar and 2 teasp. brown sugar. Brush with 1½ teasp. melted butter or margarine. Broil 10 min., or until golden. If desired, just before serving, pour on a little sherry or rum. Serve at once. Nice, too, as first course.

P.S. Brown sugar, honey, or maple-blended syrup may replace sugars. Sprinkle with ground cloves or nutmeg if desired.

BAKED: Instead of broiling grapefruit, bake at 450°F. 20 min.

SKILLET STYLE FOR 2: Melt 1 tablesp. butter or margarine in skillet; sprinkle lightly with brown sugar. Then, in this mixture, lightly brown 2 prepared grapefruit halves, with cut sides down. Serve syrup in skillet over fruit.

GRAPES

To Buy, to Store: June to April is the grape season. Choose firm, fresh-looking bunches, in which plump grapes cling to stems when gently shaken. Refrigerate.

To Prepare: Wash grapes; drain.

THE CANNED KIND: Packed as Thompson seedless in light, heavy, or extra heavy syrup. Some canned Muscat grapes are imported.

To serve: See Just Fruit Desserts, p. 540, Fruit-Cup Desserts, p. 542, Gay Fruit Centerpieces to Eat, p. 541.

GOURMET GRAPES: Combine ½ cup commercial sour cream with 2 tablesp. brown sugar; refrigerate at least 1 hr., or until well blended. Just before serving, toss with 1½ to 2 lb.

seedless grapes, stemmed, to coat grapes lightly. Makes 4 or 5 servings.

FROSTED GRAPES (OR CURRANTS): See Frosted Fruits, p. 541. Nice as garnish for baked ham, pie wedges, fruit salads, steamed puddings, etc.

KUMQUATS

To Buy, to Store: Kumquats are in season November through February. They are a small, orangelike fruit, resembling pecans in shape. Choose firm fruit, heavy for its size; refrigerate.

To Prepare: Wash; cut up or slice the kumquats for salads and fruit cups. Or use whole for preserved kumquats.

To serve: See Just Fruit Desserts, p. 540, Gay Fruit Centerpieces to Eat, p. 541.

LEMONS

To Buy, to Store: Big juicy fresh lemons, from California and Arizona, are in season the year round. You can keep some on hand in the refrigerator at all times.

To Prepare: A few drops of juice squeezed from a plump lemon wedge brings out the flavor of almost any meat, fish, poultry, vegetable, or salad. And since lemon contains virtually no sodium, it's a fine seasoning for low-sodium diets. Fine too as seasoning in low-calorie diets. For many other uses, see Index. For lemon juice, see Fresh Fruit Juices, p. 682.

LIMES

To Buy, to Store: Florida limes are most available between June and September; California limes, between October and December.

Look for limes that are green, not yellowish, and heavy for their size. Most of these will be Persians, which are the size and shape of lemons. The small round variety are Key limes. Refrigerate.

To Prepare: For the best flow of juice, cut limes lengthwise into wedges, or on the bias, which breaks more juice cells.

Serve in iced tea or squeeze over melon, ice cream, etc. For lime juice, see Fresh Fruit Juices, p. 682.

MANGOES

To Buy, to Store: Mangoes, in season from May through August, vary in size from a few ounces to 3 or 4 lb. Yellow or red in color, they have a soft, juicy, aromatic flesh. Wrap in wax paper; refrigerate.

To Prepare for Serving: With sharp knife, mark wide band in skin down one side. Peel skin back slightly; eat flesh with spoon, as dessert, putting skin back in place between bites. Or peel; slice; use in salads or fruit cups.

MELONS

To Buy: Melons must be fully ripe if you are to enjoy their wonderful flavor at its peak. Most ripe melons yield to pressure at the blossom end, and have a typical melon fragrance and yellowish tinge.

CANTALOUPES are in season from May into October; imported ones may come in earlier. They may be round, oval, or oblong, usually with over-all netted skins, and are light gray in color.

When ripe, they have a yellow ground color, distinct aroma, and smooth scar on the stem end. Blossom end yields to pressure.

CASABAS are in season from July into December. They are large, rough-skinned, roundish, sometimes considerably pointed and deeply ridged.

When fully ripe, their rind is golden yellow; the white flesh is very juicy and sweet. A melon weighs 4 to 10 lb.

CRENSHAWS are in season from June to November. They have a fairly smooth rind, mottled with gold and green. Their flesh is bright-

salmon color, thick, juicy. Melon weighs 4 to 8 lb.

HONEYBALLS are in season from May through August. They are like honeydews but are rounder and smaller, with a slightly netted skin.

HONEYDEWS are in season from January to November. The peak of their season is July through September. They are large, round or oval, averaging about 6 lb.; their smooth hard skin is without netting.

When vine-ripened, they are creamy or yellowish in color, showing softening at the blossom end, have smooth, well-rounded ridges next to stem, and are definitely fragrant. Their green flesh is exceptionally sweet.

PAPAYAS, in season all year, are melonlike in their superficial characteristics — thin, smooth skin; spherical to oblong shape; center cavity packed with seeds.

Papayas are ready to eat when the rind is yellow and the fruit feels soft. They taste and look (on the inside) like cantaloupe.

PERSIANS are in season from July into November. They look like large cantaloupes; are round, but have flat ends. They have a green rind with heavy netting.

When ripe, their rind has yellowish cast; flesh is pink, not as sweet as honeydew or honeyball but resembling cantaloupe in flavor. Melon may weigh as much as 10 lb.

SANTA CLAUS OR CHRISTMAS MELONS are winter melons; they look like small, oblong watermelons. They have a hard, thick, slightly netted green rind. Their light-yellow-to-green flesh is sweet. Signs of ripeness are light yellowing of rind, softness at blossom end.

To Store, to Prepare: Wash melon; dry; place in paper bag or wax paper; refrigerate. Just before serving, cut into halves, quarters, or wedges; scrape out seeds.

TO MAKE MELON BALLS: With fruit-ball cutter or the ½ teasp. in round measuring-spoon set, scoop out balls from edible portion of halved, seeded melon or watermelon wedge.

THE FROZEN KIND: These are packed as melon balls or in combination with other fruits as mixed fruits.

To serve: See Just Fruit Desserts, p. 540, and Fruit-Cup Desserts, p. 542.

MELON ARRAY: Serve honeydew, cantaloupe,

and watermelon wedges on tray. Tuck in sprigs of mint and lime wedges.

FRUITED MELON: Top melon quarters with canned fruit cocktail. Sprinkle with bit of grated orange rind; or pass pitcher of lime, lemon, or orange juice.

MELON CREAM: Fill melon halves or quarters with sherbet.

NECTARINES

To Buy: Nectarines, available in June, July, and August, are a kind of peach with a smooth skin like a plum; skin is greenish-white with a faint blush. Choose firm fruit, free from cuts and bruises.

To Store: Refrigerate.

To Use: Delicious to eat out of hand. Or use as you do fresh peaches.

ORANGES

To Buy: Oranges are available all year round. The two important varieties from California are Valencias, available May to November, and Navel Oranges, available November to May. Navel Oranges are not only easy to peel, but to section and eat out of hand. Valencias are rich in juice.

Florida ships Hamlins and Parson Browns (pale, thin-skinned, juice fruit), and Navel Oranges (large, thick, pebbly-skinned, for juice and fruit), from October to January. Pineapple Oranges (high in color with a smooth peel) are available from December through February and are known for their full-flavored juice. Then comes the Valencia season, from February through June.

Florida is growing increasing quantities of Temples, first cousins to tangerines; these peel easily and are available from December through February. Tangelos, a hybrid between tangerines and grapefruit, but similar in appearance and flavor to oranges, are available from November to March. The Murcott Honey Orange (high in color, with a rough peel) is available from February through June.

Toward the end of the orange season, the skin near the stem takes on a greenish tinge. This is not a sign of underripeness but is a peculiarity of citrus fruits.

All oranges must pass state maturity requirements before they can be shipped. To enhance the eye appeal of certain varieties, Florida oranges are sometimes colored with harmless color; such fruit is stamped "Color Added." Look for oranges that are firm and heavy for their size.

To Store: Keep oranges in a cool place, refrigerating those that will be used the next day for juice or salad. If space is available, and there are several persons in the family, it is economical to buy oranges by box or bag.

To serve: See Just Fruit Desserts, p. 540, Fruit-Cup Desserts, p. 542, Gay Fruit Centerpieces to Eat, p. 541.

ORANGE SECTIONS:

1. Peel or pare chilled fruit with knife, leaving some white membrane clinging to fruit if you wish. (This white membrane contains protopectin, minerals, and vitamins, valuable to health.)

2. Hold orange over bowl. With sawing motion, cut alongside of each dividing membrane, from outside down to core. Or cut halfway between each membrane instead of just alongside it. This way that white wall with its food value is a part of each orange wedge.

3. Loosen each section with knife; lift out. Remove seeds if any; drop section into bowl. Repeat. Squeeze juice from membranes over sections.

ORANGE CART WHEELS: For each serving, cut unpeeled or peeled orange into 3 or 4 crosswise slices. Arrange on dessert plates to eat out of hand for breakfast or dessert.

ORANGE TIDBITS: Stack cart wheels; then cut each slice into 4 bite-size wedges.

HURRY-UPS: Cut orange in half, starting at top and going almost to bottom peel. Cut each half into quarters; then cut through each quarter to make eighths. Pull each piece apart slightly until orange resembles open flower petals. Then eat "petals," watermelon style!

SUGARY ORANGES: Top cut-up oranges with brown sugar and flaked coconut.

DESSERT ORANGES: Cut unpeeled oranges into $1/4''$ crosswise slices; halve slices. Eat with fingers. Or heap soft cream cheese in center of plate; pile quartered orange slices around cheese. Let guests dip orange slices into cheese.

FOR FRESH ORANGE JUICE: See p. 682.

AMBROSIA

Slice 6 to 8 peeled oranges. In serving dish or sherbet glasses arrange orange slices in layers with confectioners' sugar and grated fresh, or flaked or fine grated coconut. Refrigerate until well chilled. Makes 6 to 8 servings.

To Vary: Arrange sliced bananas in layers with oranges. Or add some coarsely snipped dried figs and a bit of lime juice.

DE LUXE STYLE: Add 2 tablesp. grated orange rind to ½ cup heavy cream; chill. Whip cream until it forms soft mounds; stir in 3 tablesp. granulated sugar. Pass with Ambrosia.

AMBROSIA SHELLS: Buy the biggest oranges you can find. Cut a slice from top of each; then hollow them out. Fill with the traditional ambrosia mixture, or orange sections, canned crushed pineapple, and flaked coconut. Garnish each with a tiny bunch of grapes.

FRUIT-FILLED ORANGE SHELLS: Refill orange shells, made as in Ambrosia Shells, with orange sections tossed with halved strawberries and bias slices of banana. Serve, sprinkled with Lemon Sauce, p. 538. For some added crunch, mix canned slivered toasted almonds with the fruit.

SOUTHERN AMBROSIA: At serving time alternate layers of Custard Sauce De Luxe, p. 537, well-drained orange sections, and flaked canned or fresh coconut in one large dish or in individual dishes. Makes 6 to 8 servings.

MANDARIN ORANGES

Tiny, flavorful, whole segments of a special kind of orange, called Mandarin, are ready to use, just as they come from the can; all rind, membrane, and seeds are removed before the sections are vacuum-sealed in light syrup. Mandarin oranges can be used at any meal in a variety of tempting ways — salads, sauces, with cereals, desserts, fruit cups, casseroles, etc. Children — and adults too — love them right out of the can.

PEACHES

To Buy, to Store: Fresh peaches, in season from late May to mid-October, are at their best in July and August. They are white- or yellow-fleshed, either clingstone or freestone. Cling peaches are used for canning; freestones are fine for all uses.

Ripe peaches should be firm, but yield to gentle pressure, and should be free from brown spots. Flesh should be yellow or white, not green. (Ripen them at room temperature.) About 4 peaches equal 1 lb. Refrigerate.

To Prepare: If the freestone variety does not peel easily, let stand in boiling water to cover 1 to 2 min.; then plunge into cold water; peel; remove pits. Pare cling peaches.

THE CANNED KIND: Besides cling and freestone peaches (whole, in halves, quartered, sliced, or diced), peaches are also packed as pickled peaches, spiced peaches, and pie filling. Today's canned cling peaches are delicate and full-flavored and especially delightful served hot!

THE FROZEN KIND: They come sliced and sweetened, all ready to thaw and use.

To serve: See Just Fruit Desserts, p. 540, and Fruit-Cup Desserts, p. 542.

SCOTCH PEACHES: In butter or margarine in skillet, sauté drained canned cling-peach halves, topped with generous sprinkling of brown sugar, till piping hot. Serve this dessert hot, topped with pour cream. Really marvelous.

HOT PEACH MARLOW: Fill peach halves with canned crushed pineapple; top with marshmallows; broil until golden.

GLAZED PEACHES: Top peach or pear halves, rounded sides up, with melted currant jelly.

PEACHES DE LUXE: In each chilled, peeled peach half, place spoonful of brandy; drizzle on honey; top with whipped cream.

PEACH-SHERBET CUP: Fill fresh or canned

peach halves with seedless grapes; top with raspberry sherbet.

FROSTY PEACHES: Top fresh, thawed frozen, or canned peach slices with Ice-cream Sauce, p. 536.

BERRY PEACHES: Boil down syrup from canned cling peaches with 1 teasp. vanilla extract until quite thick; add 1 pkg. just thawed frozen raspberries. Pour over peaches.

PEACH BROIL: Arrange drained canned cling-peach halves on cookie sheet; top each with a marshmallow dipped in peach syrup; brown under broiler.

PEACH 'N' BERRIES: Combine canned or thawed frozen peach slices with slightly thawed frozen raspberries and serve very cold.

STEWED PEACHES

6 ripe peaches	1 cup water
¼ cup granulated sugar	4 whole cloves (optional)

Peel fruit; halve and pit if desired. Simmer sugar, water, and cloves 5 min. Add peaches; simmer, covered, 10 min., or until just tender. Refrigerate.

Serve topped with Fruit Sauce, p. 536; whipped cream cheese; cottage cheese; or commercial sour cream. Nice at breakfast too. Makes 6 servings.

To Vary: Substitute ¼ cup white wine for ¼ cup water, or a small piece of stick cinnamon for cloves.

BUTTERY BAKED PEACHES OR PEARS

½ cup granulated sugar	1 cup boiling water
2 tablesp. lemon juice	3 peeled ripe peaches or pared pears,
2 tablesp. butter or margarine	halved
	Currant or mint jelly

Start heating oven to 350°F. Simmer sugar, lemon juice, butter, boiling water 5 min. Arrange fruit in 1½-qt. casserole; add syrup. Bake, covered, 45 min., or until tender; refrigerate; place a little jelly on each.

Serve with whipped cream. Or drain and use as meat garnish. Makes 6 servings.

SPICED: Omit lemon juice, jelly; sprinkle with nutmeg or sherry.

CHOCOLATE FROSTED PEARS: Bake pared pears, whole, as above — about 55 to 60 min., or

until tender. Add a little vanilla extract, if desired. At serving time, stand each pear in a sherbet glass; then pour favorite hot chocolate sauce over top. (Or arrange pears in a large glass bowl, and pour hot sauce over and around them.) For very special touch, put layer of vanilla or coffee ice cream into each sherbet glass, before topping with pear and hot chocolate sauce.

NOTE: For a quicker, but de luxe, version, use canned pears.

CHRISTMAS PEAR PYRAMID: In 3-qt. covered casserole, bake 8 pared whole pears as at left. Repeat with 8 more, using same syrup; refrigerate the 16 pears. At serving time, arrange pears pyramid-fashion, in compote dish. Pour on Holiday Sauce, p. 537. Decorate with 15 to 20 citron strips. Makes 16 servings.

PEARS

To Buy, to Store: Fresh pears, of one variety or another, are available the year round. Their peak is August through October. Varieties of pears include:

BARTLETT: In season from July through October. Bell-shaped; soft yellow; sweet; juicy

BOSC: In season September through February. Russet variety, with long tapering neck

COMICE: In season October through February. Green skin. Famous for size, superb quality, beauty

ANJOU: October through May. Green skin, fine grain, spicy

NELIS: February through June. Russet variety. Very sweet, luscious

When buying pears to eat, check softness by pressing slightly near stem end. If they are not quite soft, let ripen at room temperature in paper bag or fruit bowl. When ripe, store in refrigerator. Slightly underripe pears are best for cooking.

To Prepare: Pears need no peeling. Just wash. Or halve, core, and slice. (To slice and hold before serving, coat with lemon juice or French dressing, to prevent darkening.)

THE CANNED KIND: Canned pears come whole,

quartered, sliced, or as halves. Some are pickled or spiced. They're wonderful!
To serve: See Just Fruit Desserts, p. 540.

ROSY PEAR SAUCE

Cut 4 large pears in halves; remove cores. In saucepan, combine ¾ cup granulated sugar, 1½ cups water, ½ teasp. cinnamon. Bring to boil, stirring. Gently cook 2 or 3 pear halves at a time, in syrup, until tender; remove; cook rest of pears.

About 10 min. before all pears are cooked, add 1 cup fresh cranberries; cook till tender. Pour syrup and cranberries over pears; cool; then refrigerate. Makes 4 servings.

PEAR ELEGANCE

8 canned pear halves, drained	½ cup heavy cream, whipped
¼ cup cocoa	¼ cup confectioners' sugar
1 egg yolk	1½ teasp. brandy

Night before: In center cavity of each of 4 pear halves, place 1 tablesp. cocoa. Top each filled half with inverted unfilled half, making "whole" pears; refrigerate.

Just before serving, in small bowl, beat egg yolk; fold into whipped cream with confectioners' sugar and brandy. In each of 4 individual dessert dishes, arrange one "whole" pear; top with some of whipped cream. Makes 4 servings.

BUTTERSCOTCH PEARS

2 1-lb.-14-oz. cans pear halves	½ teasp. salt
Soft butter or margarine	2 cups packaged bite-size shredded rice cereal
¾ cup light-brown sugar, packed	½ teasp. nutmeg
	Cream (optional)

About 30 min. before serving:
1. Drain pears, reserving and refrigerating syrup.
2. Lightly butter 9" pie plate. Start heating oven to 425°F.
3. In large bowl, with large fork or spoon, toss together 5 tablesp. soft butter, sugar, salt,

cereal, and nutmeg until all are well mixed.
4. Sprinkle some of cereal mixture over bottom and sides of pie plate. Layer 8 or 9 pear halves over bottom of pie plate; sprinkle with some of cereal mixture. Then repeat layers, heaping pears in center of plate. Sprinkle any remaining cereal mixture over top of pears.
5. Bake 8 to 10 min., or until pears are hot. Serve warm, passing reserved syrup or cream, if desired. Makes 8 to 10 servings.

✤ **FOR THE SMALLER FAMILY:** Make half of above for 4 or 5 servings.

PERSIMMONS

To Buy, to Store: Persimmons are in season October, November, and December. Orange-red in color, their pulpy fruit is soft, rich, and very sweet when ripe. Refrigerate.

To Prepare: Wash. Use whole or in halves.
To serve: See Just Fruit Desserts, p. 540.

PINEAPPLE

To Buy, to Store: In season all year long, fresh pineapple is at its peak from March through June. Quality fruit is heavy for its size and has no signs of decay or mold at bottom or around eyes. When ripe, fruit has sweet fragrance, golden-yellow flesh; center leaves loosen easily when pulled. Keep, wrapped, in refrigerator.

To Prepare: Cut off crown and stem ends. (If using only part of pineapple, cut off as much as is needed.) Stand fruit on one end on board. If using only top end, grasp by crown; if lower end, insert fork into core; hold firmly. Cut off rind all around, from top down, following curve of fruit. Remove eyes with pointed knife. Then complete as below:
Slices: Cut into ¼" to ½" crosswise slices. Remove cores with small biscuit cutter or small sharp pointed knife.
Cubes: Cut cored slices into small or large cubes.
Sticks: Stand pared, eyed, whole pineapple

upright on board. Cut lengthwise into eighths. Cut out core from each wedge; cut each wedge into 3/4" lengthwise strips, then in half crosswise; refrigerate. Serve as first course or dessert.

THE CANNED KIND: Packed as sliced, crushed, tidbits, chunks, or spears, canned pineapple lends itself to many tasty, everyday uses.

THE FROZEN KIND: Pineapple chunks come frozen in cans.
To serve: See Just Fruit Desserts, p. 540, Fruit-Cup Desserts, p. 542, Gay Fruit Centerpieces to Eat, p. 541.

PINEAPPLE RING: Set a fresh pineapple in center of tray. Circle with hollowed-out pineapple halves (cut lengthwise), leaning, slightly elevated, against center pineapple, with green tops pointing toward it. Fill halves with prepared fruits in season; top with sprinkling of snowy flaked coconut or sparkling pomegranate seeds; see p. 556.

FROSTED PINEAPPLE: Toss canned or thawed frozen pineapple chunks with slightly thawed frozen orange-juice concentrate and snipped mint.

COCONUT PINEAPPLE: Sprinkle thin slices of fresh pineapple or split canned pineapple slices, with flaked coconut.

POLKA DOTS: In sherbet glasses, arrange, in layers, canned-jellied-cranberry-sauce cubes, canned or frozen pineapple chunks, and chopped walnuts.

PINEAPPLE SOPHISTICATE: Halve a fresh pineapple lengthwise through green top; then cut each half into thirds. Remove cores; cut between shell and flesh to free, but not remove it. Cut flesh into 1/4" crosswise slices. Push first slice so it extends slightly over edge of shell. Push next slice so it extends slightly over edge on opposite side. Repeat.
Serve each with a lime wedge; garnish with mint. Makes 6 servings.

FRESH PINEAPPLE AND STRAWBERRY SUPREME: Pare 1 small ripe pineapple; slice thinly; cut into wedges. Marinate wedges in dry white wine; refrigerate. Arrange undrained pineapple wedges in sherbet glasses, or fruit saucers. Pour a little more wine over each; garnish with fresh strawberries. Makes 3 or 4 servings.

PLUMS AND FRESH PRUNES

To Buy, to Store: Fresh plums are in season June through October; fresh prunes are available July to November. Choose those that are plump and yield slightly to pressure. Refrigerate. About 12 to 15 equal 1 lb.

To Prepare: Wash; eat raw, as is. Or cook whole, pricking with fork or needle beforehand, as in Stewed Plums or Fresh Prunes, below.

THE CANNED KIND: These come, packed whole, in syrup.

TWO-TONE PLUM BOWL: Pour 1/2 cup sherry and drained 1-lb.-13-oz. can purple plums over a chilled 1-lb.-13-oz. can greengage plums with syrup.

STEWED PLUMS OR FRESH PRUNES

Select firm plums or fresh prunes. Wash; prick skins; place in saucepan; half cover with water. Simmer, covered, 20 to 25 min., or until soft. Add sugar to taste; cook, uncovered, 5 min. Refrigerate.
To serve: Top with lemon sherbet; sprinkle with nutmeg, flaked coconut, or canned slivered almonds.

HOT FRUIT COMPOTE A LA MODE

2 cans flaked coconut	1 1-lb.-4-oz. can pineapple spears
3 to 4 pt. vanilla ice cream	2 tablesp. lemon juice
2 1-lb.-13-oz. cans purple plums	3/4 teasp. nutmeg
1 1-lb.-13-oz. can unpeeled whole apricots	1/4 cup honey
	1 tablesp. salad oil or fat

1. *Do ahead:* Toast half of coconut in 325°F. oven 10 min., stirring occasionally; cool. Form ice cream into balls; roll half in toasted coconut, rest in plain coconut; freeze.
2. *About 15 min. before serving:* Drain plums, apricots, and pineapple. Arrange plums in center of 10" or 12" skillet.
3. Arrange apricots and pineapple on either side of plums. Sprinkle on lemon juice, then nutmeg. Drizzle on mixture of honey and salad oil.
4. Heat until fruit is warm, occasionally

spooning over them the syrup that seeps from fruit.

5. Serve hot over ice-cream balls. Makes 10 to 12 servings.

POMEGRANATES

To Buy, to Store: Pomegranates are in season September into December. About the size of an orange, they have a red-brown, leathery rind. The seeds, crimson juice, and pulp are all eaten. Refrigerate.

To Prepare: Halve. Eat with spoon; or use as garnish.

RHUBARB

To Buy, to Store: Rhubarb is in largest supply from January through July, and is at its peak May and June.

Early rhubarb has light-pink stalks; later-rhubarb stalks are dark reddish-green. Buy fresh crisp stalks; store in cool, dry place.

To Prepare: Before cooking, trim ends; discard leaves (they are not edible); wash well. Don't peel unless rhubarb is tough, stringy. THE FROZEN KIND: This comes, sweetened, packed in boxes; prepare as label directs.

RHUBARB SAUCE

1½ lb. fresh rhubarb	½ to ⅔ cup gran-
½ cup water	ulated sugar
⅛ teasp. salt	

SAUCEPAN METHOD: Wash rhubarb; cut off root and leaf ends; cut into 1" or 2" pieces, without peeling. In saucepan, combine all ingredients; simmer, covered, 10 min., or until tender, stirring gently once or twice. Refrigerate.

DOUBLE-BOILER METHOD: Prepare rhubarb as above. Omit water. Place rhubarb in double boiler with salt and sugar. Cook, covered, 25 min., or until tender, occasionally stirring with 2-tined fork.

OVEN METHOD: Start heating oven to 375°F. Reduce water to 1½ tablesp.; increase sugar to 1 cup. Place all ingredients in 1½-qt. casserole. Bake, covered, 30 to 40 min., or until tender, stirring once.

Serve with or without whipped cream. Also nice as breakfast fruit. Makes 4 or 5 servings.

RHUBARB-STRAWBERRY DELIGHT: Use ¾ cup sugar. Just before removing from heat, add 1 pt. halved, hulled strawberries. Makes 6 to 8 servings.

WITH PINEAPPLE: Just before serving rhubarb sauce, add ¾ cup drained canned or fresh pineapple wedges. Also see Fruit-Cup Desserts, p. 542.

TANGERINES

To Buy, to Store: Tangerines, from California, Arizona, and Florida, are in season from November through May. December and January are their best months. Their deep-orange skin is loose and puffy, and peels easily. Refrigerate.

To Prepare: Select firm, heavy fruit for fruit bowls and to eat out of hand. Use sections in salads, fruit cocktails, etc. Juice and grated rind may be substituted for orange juice and rind.

To serve: See Just Fruit Desserts, p. 540.

TANGERINE DELIGHT

8 medium tangerines	5 2" cinnamon
1½ cups water	sticks
½ cup granulated	6 whole cloves
sugar	2 tablesp. lemon juice

Day before: Wash, peel, and section tangerines; place peel from 3 tangerines in saucepan. Remove all white fiber from fruit; add fiber to peel, along with water, sugar, spices, lemon juice. Bring to full, rolling boil; boil, uncovered, 10 min. Remove peel; add tangerine sections; bring to boil again; boil 1 min.; cool. Refrigerate.

Serve with cream cheese and crackers. Makes 4 servings.

SPICY HOT FRUIT COMPOTE

1 1-lb.-13-oz. can cling-peach halves	1 3″ cinnamon stick
1 cup canned pitted Bing cherries	6 thin lemon slices
	2 tangerines, sectioned, peeled
6 whole cloves	1 cup seedless grapes

Day before or early in the day: In 1½-qt. covered casserole, place half of peaches and syrup. Top with drained cherries, plus 1 tablesp. cherry juice, cloves, cinnamon stick, and lemon slices. Top with rest of peaches and syrup. Cover; refrigerate.

At dinnertime: Start heating oven to 400°F. While eating main course, let fruit compote bake 30 min., or until hot; remove. Add tangerine sections and grapes. Serve from casserole. Makes 6 servings.

WATERMELONS

To Buy, to Store: Watermelon is available from May through September. Large watermelons, weighing 20 to 40 lb., vary from round to long cylindrical types and are green to light green, with stripes.

When ripe, underside is turning yellow, not light green; flesh is crisp, juicy, red. Your best guide to ripeness is to buy watermelon in halves or quarters, since a great many markets now sell them by the pound.

The small refrigerator-size watermelon, sometimes called New Hampshire midget, is available April to September. It may weigh 3 to 5 lb., and resembles a cantaloupe in size and shape. Color may vary from light to very dark green, usually with stripes. It ripens close to rind, has texture like that of larger watermelon. Refrigerate until served.

To serve: See Just Fruit Desserts, p. 540.

WATERMELON SCOOPS: From half a large watermelon, if for a party, or from a small melon, if for a twosome, scoop out balls of melon with ice-cream scoop. Arrange, rounded side up, in serving dish or on individual plates. Sprinkle with nutmeg, grated orange rind, a little sherry, or pineapple juice. Nice for either beginning or ending course.

DRIED FRUITS

PACKAGED DRIED PRUNES, APRICOTS, PEACHES, PEARS, APPLES, ETC.: These fruits are so deliciously tender they can be eaten out of hand — directly from the package. (They are partially cooked and pasteurized.) They don't need sugar and their cooking time is cut down too; see label directions. Store them in refrigerator.

To Chop Dried Fruits: Use kitchen scissors, just snipping meat from around pits, if there are pits.

FIVE WAYS TO PLUMP AND COOK PRUNES

To get soft whole prunes for breakfast, dessert, or recipe use, finish plumping by one of these methods.

BOILING WATER METHOD: Cover 1 lb. prunes with 1 qt. boiling water. Soak, covered, 24 hr. in refrigerator. The longer they soak, the plumper they get; their juice will be "light-bodied."

SOAK AND COOK METHOD: Soak prunes overnight. Bring to a quick boil; lower heat; simmer them 3 to 5 min. Juice will be thick and syrupy.

JUST COOK METHOD: In saucepan, cover 1 lb. of prunes with 1 qt. water; bring to boil; simmer gently 10 to 20 min. Let stand overnight in their own liquor. Prunes will grow plumper and the juice richer.

STEAMING METHOD: Set colander of dried prunes over tea kettle or pan of boiling water for 30 min., or till plumped. There's no syrup this way.

COLD WATER METHOD: Put 1 lb. prunes in jar or bowl; cover with 1 qt. cold water. Cover; let soak 24 hr. Then tuck plumped prunes in refrigerator, ready to use in baking or cooking other dishes.

To Vary: Before cooking dried fruit, add a little grated orange or lemon rind, a clove or cinnamon stick, a few raisins, or lemon or orange slice.

CANNED COOKED PRUNES: Several packers market ready-to-serve canned cooked prunes.

DATES

Dates are an excellent energy food containing small amounts of the B-vitamins and iron. They are very low in sodium.

Packaged dates come pitted and unpitted from the Middle East and California — some in plastic containers. Delicious eaten as they are, they are also fine for salads, on cereals, in breads and cakes, cookies, etc.

There are also chopped dates — small pieces, rolled in powdered sugar, for easier handling — all ready to use in favorite bakings.

DRIED FIGS

All American dried figs are grown and packed in California. They are available in the several varieties below. Try them all, then pick your favorite:

BLACK MISSION (BLACK): Equally delicious as confection, for stewing, and other dishes

CALIMYRNA (LARGE, LIGHT BROWN): Delicious as a confection, for stewing, and for a wide variety of other dishes. Especially favored for eating out of hand

KADOTA (LIGHT BROWN): Usually sold canned or fresh

To serve: See Just Fruit Desserts, p. 540.

RAISINS

All of America's fine raisins come from the grapes of the San Joaquin Valley in Central California. Some are sun dried, others are specially dried indoors. They are ready to use straight from the package as a recipe ingredient or for eating out of hand. The most popular consumer-size packages are the 15-oz. and 1½-oz. cartons.

To Store: Modern packaging methods offer sufficient protection for the normal use of raisins in the home. And since they are available the year round, one can buy as one needs them, keeping the package on the pantry shelf, away from direct heat.

To Plump Raisins: If your raisins have become over-dry through improper storage, cover them with water, bring to a boil, remove from heat, then let stand 5 min. before draining. For added flavor, you may soak the raisins in brandy, wine, or fruit juice.

To Chop Raisins: Raisins won't stick to your chopping knife if you sprinkle each cup of raisins with 1 teasp. cooking oil or melted butter or margarine.

DREAMY DESSERTS

Dessert gives you one more chance to fill the day's quota of milk, eggs, fruit, etc. How to choose it? The rule is simple: Keep the rest of the meal in mind when you plan its finale.

If the meal is light, a hearty dessert such as pie or bread pudding will round it out nicely. Fruit gelatin or other light fare can end the very satisfying meal.

Does dinner feature a vegetable main dish? Then include an egg dessert, such as custard or tapioca cream. Is luncheon short of potatoes, macaroni, or other starchy foods? Top it off with rice or bread pudding, or a cake dessert. Plan to bake a dessert right along with your oven dinner; then serve it nice and warm.

If every second counts, become familiar with some of the fix-and-serve wonders on your grocer's shelves. Just a few seconds, early in the day or just before serving, and the dessert is ready.

Next time company comes, dazzle them with one of our fabulous creations.

Before using these recipes, refer to How To Use Our Recipes, p. 3. Always use standard measuring cups and measuring spoons; measure level.

QUICK AND SO GOOD

Fruit Desserts

Fruit desserts are so quick and easy. All are so good for you, too. For many delightful family and company top-offs browse through Wonderful Ways with Fruits, p. 539; Top-Offs, p. 542; Just Fruit Desserts, p. 540; and Fruit-Cup Desserts, p. 542.

Pudding Desserts

Vanilla, chocolate, butterscotch, caramel, coconut cream, lemon, toasted coconut, banana cream, dark 'n' sweet, and chocolate fudge are only a few of the delectable puddings which can be made so speedily with today's packaged pudding and pie-filling mixes. All make creamy fillings for pies and cakes as well as sauces or toppings for gelatin desserts, ice cream, fruit, or cake squares.

There are two types — the kind you cook, which needs only to be brought to a boil with milk (some come in a large size); and the

559

instant puddings to which cold milk is added, with no cooking. Here are ways of varying them.

If Vanilla:

Swirl spoonful of melted semisweet chocolate through each serving.

Serve warm, topped with ice cream.

Alternate pudding layers with sweetened fresh, canned, or thawed frozen berries or fruit.

Flavor with almond, sherry, or brandy to taste; fold in ¼ cup heavy cream, whipped.

Add 1 tablesp. instant coffee powder to pudding mix. Before serving, fold in ½ cup heavy cream, whipped.

Top with chocolate or butterscotch sauce.

Flavor with almond extract; fold in drained, canned, crushed pineapple.

Top with your favorite preserves or canned cranberry sauce.

If Chocolate:

Add ⅓ cup semisweet-chocolate pieces or 1 sq. unsweetened chocolate before cooking; steps up flavor.

Substitute 1¼ cups coffee beverage for milk in making.

Flavor with sherry, rum, or brandy to taste, and top with fine grated coconut.

While still warm, stir in ½ pt. coffee ice cream.

Any Flavor:

Top with scoop of ice cream.

Fold in a few miniature marshmallows while still warm.

Top with whipped cream or dessert topping to which cocoa or instant coffee has been added.

Dietetic Puddings: See p. 86.

RICE CHANTILLY

1 pkg. vanilla pudding and pie-filling mix	½ cup heavy cream, whipped
⅓ cup packaged precooked rice	2 tablesp. confectioners' sugar
Pinch salt	½ teasp. vanilla extract
Milk	Nutmeg

In saucepan, combine pudding, rice, salt, and amount of milk pudding label calls for; cook as label directs, then refrigerate, placing wax paper directly on surface to prevent formation of "skin."

Into cooled rice mixture, fold whipped cream, sugar, and vanilla. Spoon into 6 sherbet glasses; sprinkle with nutmeg; refrigerate. Also nice spooned over almost any fresh, frozen, or canned fruit. Makes 6 servings.

EASY CREME BRULEE

1 pkg. vanilla pudding and pie-filling mix	toasted almonds
	Orange sections
1½ cups milk	Banana chunks dipped in lemon
1½ cups heavy cream	juice
Foil	Thin slices fresh
½ cup light-brown sugar, packed	pineapple
	Tiny bunchlets grapes
¼ cup slivered	as garnish

1. *Day before:* Make vanilla pudding as label directs, substituting 1½ cups milk and 1½ cups cream for the 2 cups milk label calls for. Pour into 1½-qt. shallow baking dish, then lay a piece of foil directly on surface of pudding; refrigerate.

2. *An hour or two before dessert time:* Preheat broiler (rack removed), 10 min., or as manufacturer directs. Meanwhile, remove foil from pudding. Sift brown sugar over top of crème; then sprinkle almonds in a ring, 1″ in from edge. Set crème on broiler rack, 3″ from heat; broil *just* until sugar melts, making a shiny caramel top. Refrigerate.

3. *At serving time,* center crème on a large platter, with fruits arranged attractively around it. Hostess serves fruit with crème spooned over it. Or if it's a buffet, guests help themselves. Makes 8 servings.

PICCADILLY TRIFLE

1 pkg. vanilla pudding and pie-filling mix	½ cup syrup drained from canned pears
3 cups milk	1 1-lb.-13-oz. can pear halves, drained
Sherry to taste	⅔ cup heavy cream, whipped (optional)
2 6″ bakers' sponge-cake layers	Candied cherries (optional)
⅔ cup seedless black-raspberry jam	

Early in day: For custard sauce, prepare pudding as label directs, using 3 cups milk; cool; add sherry. In attractive 2-qt. bowl, set 1 cake layer. Spread with half of jam. Sprinkle with

¼ cup pear syrup. Top with half of pears; gently crush them with 2-tined fork. Pour on half of custard sauce. Repeat. Refrigerate. *To serve:* Spread whipped cream on top of cake; garnish with cut-up cherries. Cut into wedges; over each, spoon some of sauce left in bowl. Makes 9 servings.

TAPIOCA SPECIALS

For luscious tapioca cream, just follow the directions on a package of quick-cooking tapioca, or one of the tapioca-pudding mixes — lemon, orange, chocolate, or vanilla. Then dress it up in one of the ways below if you wish.

RIPPLE-STYLE: Fold in any of these:

Whipped cream or dessert topping, or miniature marshmallows
A little chocolate or butterscotch sauce, and a few salted nuts
Drained canned Bing cherries
Drained fresh, frozen, or canned peach slices or pineapple tidbits, or banana chunks
Raspberry, strawberry, or peach preserves

PARFAIT-FASHION: In sherbet, parfait, or tall glasses, alternate layers of tapioca cream with one of these:

Melted currant jelly, tossed with flaked coconut
Canned crushed pineapple, flavored with mint extract, then tinted green
Canned whole-cranberry sauce, as is or mixed with slivered almonds
Melted semisweet-chocolate or butterscotch pieces and chopped nuts
Cut-up oranges and snipped fresh mint
Fresh blueberries, fresh peach slices, and halved strawberries

SUNDAE BEST: Spoon tapioca cream into sherbet glasses; top with one of these:

Just thawed frozen raspberries, strawberries, or pineapple chunks
Bright jelly, sprig of mint
Flaked coconut tossed with grated orange rind
Crushed peanut brittle or peppermint candy
Chocolate sauce, or butterscotch sauce, then whipped cream
Just thawed frozen orange- or grape-juice concentrate
Vanilla, chocolate, or strawberry ice cream
Snipped, pitted dates or dried figs and chopped nuts, moistened with thawed frozen orange-juice concentrate
Pink rhubarb sauce

DE LUXE RENNET CUSTARD

Choose your favorite flavor of packaged rennet-custard dessert. Make as label directs, substituting light cream for milk. Add a de luxe touch as below:

TOPPINGS: Toasted flaked coconut, orange sections, canned pineapple tidbits, fresh or frozen raspberries or strawberries, or hot canned peach slices.

CHOCOLATE-ALMOND: To chocolate rennet, add ¼ teasp. almond extract.

RUM-MOCHA: To chocolate rennet, add 1 teasp. instant coffee and rum to taste.

TRIFLE: Sprinkle bakers' poundcake slices with rum, sherry, or brandy. Pour vanilla or lemon rennet over slices. Refrigerate till set.

Fruit Gelatin Delights

One of the beauties of packaged fruit-flavor gelatins is that they take so little kitchen know-how to turn out. And their refreshing fruit flavors and versatility give them universal appeal to all ages — little folks, school-age set, and on up.

For your convenience some of these gelatins now come both in the regular 3-oz. and a large 6-oz. size. And there are a dozen or more flavors, including raspberry, cherry, strawberry, orange, lemon, lime, black cherry, black raspberry, blackberry, orange-pineapple, peach, mixed fruit, lemon-lime, etc., to choose from. One brand adds vitamin C.

While molded gelatins will always be favorites, you can vary them in ways sure to please your family and guests. Try these.

1. *For a perky flavor* substitute a carbonated beverage like ginger ale for the cold water you usually use in making up the gelatins.

2. *For a dessert resembling Spanish Cream,* use milk for part of the water the label calls for.

3. *For a jelly whip,* wait till gelatin starts to thicken, then set in bowl of ice water, beat with hand beater till thick and frothy, then spoon into sherbets.

4. *Make jelly flakes* by refrigerating gelatin mixture in a shallow pan until firm. Then run a fork through it or force it through a sieve.

Serve, topped with custard sauce, fruit, or dessert topping. Or fold into chilled vanilla pudding.

5. *Make jelly cubes* by reducing cold liquid you add by ¼ cup for every cup used. Refrigerate in shallow square pan, till firm. Then cut into cubes with knife dipped in warm water. Arrange with favorite fruit, in sherbets. Or mix 2 flavors of cubes. Or serve topped with soft ice cream. Or use to garnish top of another dessert.

6. *Make jelly cut-outs for the young-one's birthday.* Prepare gelatin as in jelly cubes above, but cut into animal or other shapes with cutters. Serve topped with pour cream or whipped cream. Use as garnish for another dessert.

7. *For layered gelatin,* "sandwich" a fruit-gelatin layer between two layers of Bavarian cream. In doing this, chill each layer just until set, but not quite firm, before adding next layer.

8. *For a fruited mold,* it helps to remember that fresh apple, pear, peach, banana, and grapefruit slices, as well as strawberries, all float in the gelatin. Canned fruits, as well as grapes, orange sections, and plums, on the other hand, are "sinkers." So pour liquid gelatin into molds and add fruit that sinks; then add floating fruit, and chill until firm.

9. *For a soft-set jelly — really delightful* — increase the cold water you usually add to regular-size package of gelatin by ½ cup. Serve with pour cream, or layer of fruit and top with soft vanilla ice cream.

Dietetic Gelatin Desserts: See p. 86.

JIFFY JELLIED FRUIT

1 3-oz. pkg. favorite fruit-flavor gelatin	1 unthawed 12-oz. pkg. frozen raspberries, sliced strawberries, or sliced peaches
1 cup hot water	
½ cup cold water or fruit juice	
1 tablesp. lemon juice	1 cup seedless grapes

Dissolve gelatin in hot water; add rest of ingredients. Refrigerate, stirring occasionally, until frozen fruit thaws and gelatin sets — about 30 min. for soft jelly, about 1 hr. for firm jelly. Spoon into sherbet glasses. Top

with custard sauce or dessert topping. Makes 6 servings.

DATE-NUT: Substitute ½ cup chopped walnuts and ½ cup snipped, pitted dates for grapes.

PINE-MALLOW: Substitute drained canned pineapple chunks for grapes. When gelatin is slightly thickened, fold in 4 snipped large marshmallows.

CHERRY-SHERRY JUBILEE

1 1-lb.-13-oz. can pitted Bing cherries	½ cup sherry
	⅓ cup slivered toasted almonds
1 3-oz. pkg. cherry-flavor gelatin	

Drain cherries. Add enough water to cherry syrup to make 1¾ cups. Heat syrup; pour over gelatin; stir until dissolved. Add cherries, sherry, almonds. Refrigerate till set. Then break up gently with fork; spoon into sherbet glasses. Serve with custard sauce, whipped cream, dessert topping, or ice cream. Makes 6 servings.

ORANGE-JELLY BAGATELLE

1 3-oz. pkg. orange-flavor gelatin	sauce (2½ cups)
	⅛ teasp. nutmeg
½ cup hot water	2 teasp. grated orange rind
1 17-oz. can apple-	

In bowl, stir gelatin into hot water until completely dissolved. Add applesauce, nutmeg, orange rind. Pour into 9″ x 5″ x 3″ pan; refrigerate until set.

To serve: Cut jelly into 1″ squares; heap in 4 sherbet glasses. Top with dessert topping or whipped cream; sprinkle with more grated orange rind and nutmeg. Makes 4 servings.

FRUIT-WINE JELLY

1 cup Chianti wine	1 3-oz. pkg. raspberry-flavor gelatin
1 cup orange segments, sweetened	1 cup hot water

Pour wine over oranges; let stand a few minutes. Dissolve gelatin in hot water; cool. Stir in oranges and wine. Leave in bowl; or turn into individual molds or custard cups. Refrigerate until firm.

Serve spooned into sherbet glasses; or unmold. Top with whipped cream, or dessert topping if desired. Makes 5 servings.

CAKE DESSERT QUICKIES

CHARLOTTE RUSSE: Line sherbet glasses with ladyfingers. In each, place mound of sweetened whipped cream; top with maraschino cherry. Serve at once. Or refrigerate; then serve.

COCONUT FINGERS: Butter bakers' poundcake slices; cut into fingers; sprinkle with flaked coconut. Broil till toasted.

TOASTED JAM CAKE: Broil or sauté sponge- or angel-food-cake slices until golden. Spread with jam; top with chopped nuts or flaked coconut.

FRENCH-TOASTED SLICES: Dip bakers' poundcake slices into French-Toast mixture, p. 497. Sauté in butter or margarine till golden. Serve with jelly or maple-blended syrup.

SPUR-OF-THE-MOMENT SHORTCAKES: Fill, then top bakers' dessert shells, or sponge- or angel-food-cake slices, with:

Berries and/or sliced peaches; commercial sour cream
Whipped cream or marshmallow cream; chocolate sauce; salted nuts
Orange cubes and banana slices; sprinkling of sherry; flaked coconut
Orange sherbet; whipped cream
Sprinkling of rum; ice cream; sliced strawberries or butterscotch sauce
Spiced applesauce or canned crushed pineapple
Sweetened, sliced strawberries with pineapple chunks or sliced bananas
Thawed frozen peach slices; almond-flavored whipped cream
Choco-whipped cream (add a little chocolate sauce and instant coffee to cream before whipping it)

MAKE-YOUR-OWN SHORTCAKES: Provide bakers' dessert shells and poundcake slices; plain or whipped cream; sliced peaches or bananas, blueberries, or strawberries. Guests make their own shortcakes.

ORANGE FLUFF: Whip 1 cup heavy cream; add 1 cup flaked coconut, 2 tablesp. orange juice, 1 teasp. grated orange rind. Heap on warm cake squares, made from packaged mix.

APRICOT CREAM TORTE: Crush 1½ cups drained canned apricots with 2 tablesp. sugar. Spoon onto sponge- or white-cake layer. Circle top of layer with whipped cream.

DOUGHNUT DECKERS: Put split doughnut halves together with melted semisweet chocolate as filling.

SPEEDY PEACH CAKE: To 2 tablesp. melted butter or margarine, in 8" x 8" x 2" pan, add 3 tablesp. brown sugar. Arrange 1 pkg. thawed frozen peaches in pan. Cover with sliced bakers' poundcake. Bake at 450°F. 15 min. Serve warm, with cream. Makes 4 servings.

CUSTARDS AND PUDDINGS

CARAMEL-CUSTARD MOLD

1 cup granulated sugar	¾ teasp. salt
6½ cups milk	2 teasp. almond extract
9 eggs	Boiling water
5 egg yolks	¾ cup heavy cream
½ cup granulated sugar	½ cup sliced blanched almonds

Day before:

1. In heavy 10" skillet, place 1 cup sugar; cook over low heat, stirring constantly, until a golden-brown syrup forms. Then remove from heat at once, and carefully pour into bottom of 2½-qt. heatproof soufflé dish (in cold weather, first heat dish with hot water to prevent its cracking).

2. Start heating oven to 325°F. In kettle (about 6 qt.), scald milk. Meanwhile, place eggs and egg yolks in large bowl; add ½ cup sugar; with electric mixer at medium speed, beat till blended. While stirring, quickly pour eggs, all at once, into milk; add salt and almond extract. Set soufflé dish in small roasting pan; place on rack in oven; fill roasting pan with boiling water to within ¾" of its top.

3. Remove 1 cup custard mixture; pour rest of mixture into soufflé dish; carefully pour in reserved 1 cup.

4. Bake custard 80 min. Then insert silver knife in center; if knife comes out clean, custard is done. Remove at once from water and cool slightly on wire rack. Refrigerate overnight.

At serving time next day: Run spatula all around custard in soufflé dish. Place rimmed serving plate, upside down, on top of it; invert; lift off dish (caramel will collect around custard). Whip cream. Spoon up ¼ cup caramel syrup from base of custard and fold into whipped cream. Surround custard with sliced almonds; pass whipped-cream sauce. Makes 12 servings.

You may omit caramelizing (step 1). Instead, serve the custard as is or topped with maple or maple-blended syrup and/or whipped cream, or with peach slices and whipped cream or dessert topping.

SEMISWEET-COFFEE CUSTARDS

¼ cup milk	pieces
¼ cup granulated sugar	1 egg, unbeaten
⅛ teasp. salt	1 teasp. vanilla extract
1 6-oz. pkg. semi-sweet-chocolate	1 cup milk

1. In saucepan, combine ¼ cup milk, sugar, salt; bring to boil; remove from heat. Add chocolate pieces; stir briskly until they are melted smooth. With hand beater, beat in egg and vanilla. Gradually stir in 1 cup milk.
2. Into 4 ungreased 6-oz. custard cups, pour mixture; cover tightly with foil. Set cups in ½" hot water in 10" or 12" skillet. Then cover with lid or foil, and simmer gently 30 min. Serve warm right from cups; or chill and then unmold. Top with Coffee Whipped Cream, p. 649. Makes 4 servings. Nice late-evening refreshment.

BRAZILIAN COFFEE CUSTARDS
(Flan de Café de Mocha)

3 cups milk	1 teasp. vanilla extract
1 cup light cream	
6 to 8 tablesp. instant coffee	1 teasp. almond extract
2 teasp. grated orange rind	½ teasp. salt
	Nutmeg
4 eggs	1 cup chopped Brazil nuts
1 egg yolk	
½ cup granulated sugar	1 egg white
	3 tablesp. guava jelly

Start heating oven to 325°F. In saucepan, scald milk with cream; add coffee and orange rind; stir well; cool 10 min. Meanwhile, in small bowl, with electric mixer at low speed, slightly beat eggs with egg yolk and sugar. Now slowly add coffee mixture, then extracts

and salt; blend well; strain through fine strainer. Pour into 6 custard cups; sprinkle each with nutmeg. Place cups in shallow baking pan; fill pan with cold water up to ¾" from top of cups. Bake 1 hr., or until knife, inserted in center, comes out clean. Remove from water; cool; refrigerate.

Just before serving: With small spatula, remove each custard from cup and arrange, upside down, on serving dish. Sprinkle with chopped nuts. Beat egg white quite stiff; then beat in jelly until stiff. Swirl over nut-topped custards. Makes 6 servings.

SMALL FRENCH-CHOCOLATE CUSTARDS
(Petits Pots de Crème au Chocolat)

4 sq. unsweetened chocolate	¼ cup water
	5 eggs, separated
⅔ cup granulated sugar	2 teasp. rum or cognac

Day before, or early in day:
1. In double boiler, melt chocolate; add sugar, water; cook, stirring, until sugar is dissolved.
2. With hand beater, beat yolks well. Stirring *vigorously*, slowly pour yolks into chocolate mixture. Remove from heat; stir in rum; cool 5 min.
3. Beat egg whites stiff. Fold in chocolate mixture. Pour into 6 custard cups. Refrigerate several hours or overnight. Serve topped with whipped cream if desired. Makes 6 servings.

RUM-PUMPKIN CREAM CUSTARDS

⅓ cup granulated sugar	2 tablesp. light rum
1 cup light cream	⅔ cup canned pumpkin
¼ cup granulated sugar	2 eggs, slightly beaten

Make day before:
1. Start heating oven to 325°F. In small skillet, over medium heat, melt ⅓ cup sugar, stirring, till it's a caramel-like syrup. Pour at once into 4 buttered custard cups.
2. Meanwhile, in saucepan, scald cream; with hand beater, beat in ¼ cup sugar, rum, pumpkin. Beat some of this mixture into eggs; return all to saucepan; beat till blended.
3. Then slowly pour pumpkin mixture into custard cups; set in shallow baking pan, and

place on oven rack. Fill pan with hot water to within 3/4″ of top of cups.

4. Bake about 45 min. Near end of baking time, insert silver knife in center of one custard. When knife comes out clean, remove custards; cool; refrigerate.

Twenty minutes before serving:

1. Remove custards from refrigerator; let stand 15 min.

2. Then run spatula all around inside of each cup; invert on individual dessert plate. If desired, pass rum at table to spoon over custards. Makes 4 servings.

CREAMY BAKED RICE PUDDING

1 qt. milk	margarine
1/4 cup granulated	1/4 teasp. salt
sugar	1/4 teasp. nutmeg
1/4 cup uncooked reg-	1 teasp. vanilla extract
ular white rice*	1/2 cup light or dark
1 tablesp. butter or	raisins (optional)

Start heating oven to 325°F. In greased 1 1/2-qt. casserole, combine milk, sugar, rice, butter, salt, nutmeg, vanilla. Bake, uncovered, stirring often, 2 1/2 hr., or until rice is done. Add raisins after first hour.

Serve warm or cold, with pour cream, whipped cream, custard sauce flavored with rum, fudge sauce, caramel sauce, berries, fruit, or maple sugar. Makes 4 to 6 servings.

For thicker pudding, increase the rice to 5 tablesp.

FRUITED CREME BRULEE

3 cups heavy cream	1 teasp. vanilla extract
6 egg yolks	1/2 cup light-brown
6 tablesp. granulated	sugar
sugar	Choice of fruits

Day before, or early in day: In bottom of large double boiler, heat cream till scalded. In top of same double boiler, with hand beater, beat yolks and granulated sugar till blended; then slowly stir in scalded cream. Cook over hot, *not boiling*, water, stirring constantly, till as thick as heavy cream. Add vanilla; pour into 1 1/2-qt. shallow glass baking dish; refrigerate.

Several hr. before serving: Preheat broiler, with rack removed, 10 min., or as manufacturer directs. Meanwhile, carefully sift brown

sugar over top of brûlée; set it on broiler rack, 3″ from heat, and broil about 4 to 5 min., or till sugar melts, making a shiny caramel top. Return to refrigerator.

To serve: Set icy-cold dish of brûlée on a tray; around brûlée or radiating from it, place one or more of these: sweetened fresh strawberries; fresh, thawed frozen, or canned pineapple chunks; raspberries; fresh or canned peach halves; canned or cooked pears; orange chunks; or tender pitted prunes. Over each serving of fruit, hostess spoons brûlée; or guests help themselves. Makes 6 servings.

CHOCOLATE-CREAM BREAD PUDDING

7 1/2 cups milk	extract
6 sq. unsweetened	1/2 teasp. almond
chocolate	extract
1 teasp. salt	10 slices stale bread,
6 eggs	cut into 1/4″ cubes
1 3/4 cups granulated	Shaved unsweetened
sugar	chocolate
2 tablesp. vanilla	

Make early in day:

1. Start heating oven to 400°F. In saucepan, heat milk with 6 sq. chocolate and salt, over low heat, until chocolate is melted; then beat with hand beater until blended.

2. In large bowl, place 4 whole eggs and 2 egg yolks (put 2 egg whites in small bowl). Slightly beat eggs with yolks, then stir in 1 1/2 cups sugar. Next, gradually fold in melted chocolate mixture well. Add vanilla and almond extracts, then bread cubes, and let stand about 10 min.

3. Now turn chocolate mixture into a 3-qt. casserole; set it in pan of hot water that comes halfway up on side of casserole. Bake 1 hr.

4. Beat the 2 egg whites until foamy. Then add 1/4 cup sugar, gradually, while beating, until sugar is well blended in. Then continue beating until meringue stands in stiff peaks.

5. Now lightly pile meringue in mounds, as a border, around top edge of pudding. Return pudding to oven for 5 to 10 min., or until a delicate brown. Then remove from oven and sprinkle meringue lightly with a little shaved unsweetened chocolate.

Serve pudding warm or cool, with or without pour cream. Makes 8 to 10 servings.

♣ FOR 4: Make pudding as above, using 3 3/4

cups milk, 3 sq. unsweetened chocolate, ½ teasp. salt, 2 eggs, 2 egg yolks, ¾ cup granulated sugar, 1 tablesp. vanilla extract, ¼ teasp. almond extract, and 5 slices stale bread. Bake in 1½-qt. casserole at 400°F. 1 hr. Then top with a meringue made from 2 egg whites and ¼ cup granulated sugar and bake 5 to 10 min. longer.

KITCHENETTE CARAMEL PUDDING

1 cup dark-brown sugar, packed	1 cup milk
3 slices buttered fresh white or raisin bread, cut into ½″ squares	Dash salt
	½ teasp. vanilla extract
	Ice cream or whipped cream
3 eggs	

Generously butter inside of double-boiler top; pour in brown sugar; then add bread squares. Beat eggs with milk, salt, vanilla; pour over bread; don't stir. Cook over boiling water, covered, 1 hr.

Serve warm, with ice cream. Makes 4 servings.

KITCHENETTE CHOCOLATE PUDDING: Melt 1 sq. unsweetened chocolate in buttered double-boiler top. Stir in brown sugar, ¼ cup of milk above. Stir over boiling water until sugar dissolves. Add bread, then eggs beaten with remaining ¾ cup milk, salt, vanilla; *don't stir.* Cook as above.

DESSERTS TO BAKE 'N' SERVE

DUTCH PLUM CAKE

1 cup sifted all-purpose flour	into eighths; or 16 pitted, halved prune plums
1½ teasp. double-acting baking powder	1 teasp. cinnamon
½ teasp. salt	¼ teasp. nutmeg
6 tablesp. sugar	3 tablesp. melted butter or margarine
¼ cup shortening	⅓ cup currant jelly or apricot jam
1 egg	
¼ cup milk	About 1 tablesp. hot water
5 pitted plums, cut	

Start heating oven to 400°F. Sift flour, baking powder, salt, 3 tablesp. sugar. With 2

knives, scissor-fashion, or pastry blender, cut in shortening until like coarse corn meal. With fork, stir in combined egg and milk.

Spread dough in greased 12″ x 8″ x 2″ baking dish. On top, arrange plums, slightly overlapping, in parallel rows, with pointed edges down. Sprinkle with combined cinnamon, nutmeg, 3 tablesp. sugar, butter. Bake 35 min., or until plums are tender.

Beat jelly with enough hot water to make syrup; brush over fruit when it's done.

Serve warm, cut into squares, as is or with Sunshine Foamy Sauce, p. 538; Vanilla Sauce, p. 538; or Ice-Cream Sauce, p. 536. Makes 6 servings.

♣ **FOR 2:** Use 1 egg; halve rest of ingredients. Use greased 8″ pie plate. Bake 20 min.

DUTCH APPLE: For plums, substitute 3½ to 4 cups sliced, pared, cored cooking apples.

DUTCH MEDLEY: For plums, substitute 2 sliced, peeled, ripe peaches; 3 sliced, pitted plums, and a few seedless grapes. Cover one third of dough with each fruit. Or use all grapes.

DUTCH PEACH: For plums, substitute 5 thinly sliced, peeled ripe peaches.

QUICK DUTCH PLUM: For dough, add 3 tablesp. sugar to 1 cup packaged biscuit mix; stir in 1 egg, beaten slightly with ¼ cup heavy cream.

OLD-FASHIONED PEACH DUMPLINGS

Flaky Pastry for Two-Crust Pie, pp. 584–587	1 cup hot water
	2 tablesp. butter or margarine
6 ripe peaches, peeled	1 tablesp. grated lemon rind
2 tablesp. currant jelly	
	3 tablesp. lemon juice
Granulated sugar	1 egg white

1. Roll pastry ⅛″ thick; cut into six 7″ squares. Halve and pit peaches. Place peach half in center of each pastry square; fill each hollow with 1 teasp. currant jelly; top with second peach half; sprinkle each with 2 tablesp. sugar. Moisten edges of squares with cold water; bring points up over peaches; press edges together. Place in well-greased 12″ x 8″ x 2″ baking dish. Start heating oven to 375°F.

2. Combine hot water with ¼ cup granulated sugar, butter, and grated lemon rind and

juice; heat until sugar dissolves; pour into dumpling baking dish. Brush dumplings with slightly beaten egg white; sprinkle with sugar. Bake 40 min., or until tender.

Serve warm, with pour cream; whipped cream; Hard Sauce, p. 537; Lemon Sauce, p. 538; or Ice-Cream Sauce, p. 536. Makes 6 servings.

APPLE DUMPLINGS:
1. Use 6 pared, cored, medium cooking apples (save parings) instead of peaches. Instead of jelly, mix ½ cup granulated sugar with 1 teasp. cinnamon; use to fill apples; then dot each with bit of butter or margarine (1 tablesp. in all). Wrap in pastry, and place in baking dish as on p. 566; then refrigerate.
2. Pour 1½ cups boiling water over apple parings; simmer, covered, 20 min. Drain parings; stir liquid with 2 tablesp. sugar, ¼ cup butter or margarine, ¼ teasp. cinnamon, 1 tablesp. grated lemon rind, and 3 tablesp. lemon juice until sugar dissolves. Pour into dumpling dish. Bake at 375°F. 40 min., or until apples are tender.

QUICK APPLE DUMPLINGS: Make Apple Dumplings, using ¼ cup butter or margarine to dot apples. Omit syrup.

BISCUIT APPLE DUMPLINGS: Make Apple Dumplings, substituting Hot Baking-Powder Biscuit dough, p. 475, or dough made from 2 cups packaged biscuit mix for pastry. Roll into rectangle 21" x 14"; cut into six 7" squares. Omit syrup. Bake as directed.

CARAMEL APPLE DUMPLINGS
About 1 hr. and 30 min. before serving:
1. Prepare 1 pkg. piecrust mix as label directs; roll ⅛" thick. With pastry wheel, cut out 3 7" squares, 6 strips (6" long and ¾" wide), and 3 1" circles, rerolling dough as needed. Start heating oven to 350°F.
2. Wash, pare, core 3 medium baking apples; place one on each of the 7" squares. Turn all 4 points of dough up to top of each apple, forming 4 "ears," pressing edges lightly together. Now, over each dumpling, lay two strips of dough, crosswise, then top with a pastry circle.
3. Brush dumplings with 1 beaten egg, then place in medium-size, shallow baking dish. In

small saucepan, combine ½ cup caramel sauce (from jar), 2 tablesp. butter, ⅓ cup dark-brown sugar, and ¾ cup water; bring to boil, while stirring, then pour over apples. Bake 40 min., or until apples are just tender, spooning caramel sauce over them occasionally.
4. Just before serving, sprinkle ¼ cup canned toasted, slivered almonds over dumplings. Makes 3 servings. If desired, cut dumplings in half for smaller portions and 6 servings.

PEAR-BUTTERSCOTCH CRISP

1 1-lb.-13-oz. can pear halves, drained	¼ teasp. salt
½ cup brown sugar, packed	¼ teasp. cinnamon
½ cup flour	¼ cup butter or margarine

Start heating oven to 425°F. Arrange pear halves, cut sides down, in greased pie plate. Mix sugar, flour, salt, cinnamon; with fork or pastry blender, work in butter until crumbly. Sprinkle thickly over and around pears. Bake 15 to 20 min., or until crumbs are golden brown. Serve warm, with cream, ice cream, or chilled custard sauce. Makes 4 servings.

APPLE BROWN BETTY

⅓ cup melted butter or margarine	brown sugar
2 cups fresh bread crumbs	½ teasp. nutmeg
6 cups sliced, pared, cored cooking apples	¼ teasp. cinnamon
½ cup granulated or	1 tablesp. grated lemon rind
	2 tablesp. lemon juice
	¼ cup water

Start heating oven to 375°F. Toss butter with crumbs; arrange one third of this mixture in greased 1½-qt. casserole. Cover with half of apples and half of combined sugar, nutmeg, cinnamon, and lemon rind. Cover with one third of crumbs, rest of apples, and rest of sugar mixture. Spoon on combined lemon juice and water. Top with rest of crumbs. Bake, covered, ½ hr. Uncover; bake ½ hr. longer, or until apples are done.

Serve warm, with pour cream; whipped cream, sprinkled with cinnamon or grated cheese; Hard Sauce, p. 537; Sterling Sauce, p. 538; cream cheese softened with a little milk; or ice cream. Makes 6 servings.

♣ FOR 2 OR 3: Halve each ingredient; use 1-qt. casserole. Bake, covered, at 350°F. ½ hr.; uncover; bake ½ hr.

PEACH: Substitute peaches for apples.

BANANA-COCONUT BETTY

⅓ cup melted butter or margarine	½ teasp. nutmeg
2 cups fresh bread crumbs	½ teasp. cinnamon
4 bananas, thinly sliced	1 tablesp. grated lemon rind
⅓ cup granulated sugar	3 tablesp. lemon juice
	¼ cup water
	½ cup flaked coconut

Start heating oven to 375°F. Toss butter with bread crumbs. In greased 1½-qt. casserole, arrange one third of this mixture. Cover with half of bananas and half of combined sugar, nutmeg, cinnamon, and lemon rind. Cover with one third of crumbs, rest of bananas, and rest of sugar mixture.

Spoon on combined lemon juice and water. Combine remaining crumbs and coconut; use to top mixture. Bake, covered, ½ hr. Uncover; bake 5 to 10 min. longer, or until coconut mixture is golden.

Serve warm, with pour cream or whipped cream sprinkled with cinnamon. Makes 6 servings.

TOPAZ TAPIOCA

3 large apples, pared, cut into eighths	1 cup light-brown sugar, packed
2 tablesp. butter or margarine	¾ teasp. salt
1 teasp. mace	2 tablesp. lemon juice
⅓ cup quick-cooking tapioca	2¼ cups water
	Light cream

Forty-five minutes before serving:
1. Start heating oven to 375°F. Arrange apple slices, in even rows, in 9″ x 9″ x 2″ baking dish. Dot with butter or margarine, and sprinkle with mace.
2. In saucepan, combine tapioca, brown sugar, salt, lemon juice, and water; bring to a boil, while stirring.
3. Pour hot tapioca mixture over apple slices; bake 20 min., then remove from oven.
4. Serve hot, or warm, with light cream. Makes 6 servings.

CARAMEL PEACH CRUNCH

½ cup all-purpose flour	½ teasp. salt
1 cup uncooked rolled oats	½ cup melted butter or margarine
¾ cup dark-brown sugar	1 1-lb.-13-oz. can cling-peach halves or slices, drained
1 teasp. cinnamon	Vanilla ice cream

1. Start heating oven to 400°F. In bowl, combine flour, oats, sugar, cinnamon, salt; add butter; mix well.
2. In 9″ pie plate or 10″ x 6″ x 2″ baking dish, arrange peaches; over all, sprinkle oats mixture. Bake 25 to 30 min., or until done. Serve warm, topped with ice cream. Makes 6 servings.

HURRY-UP APPLE "PIE"

½ cup brown sugar, packed	1 1-lb. can applesauce (2 cups)
1 cup packaged pie-crust mix	1 tablesp. lemon juice
½ teasp. cinnamon	Light cream or ice cream
½ teasp. nutmeg	

Start heating oven to 375°F. Grease 8″ pie plate. Combine sugar, piecrust mix, cinnamon, and nutmeg until crumbly. In pie plate, place applesauce; sprinkle with lemon juice; spread with crumbly mixture. Bake 25 to 30 min., or until tender. Serve warm, with cream. Makes 4 servings.

CRANBERRY-CRUNCH A LA MODE

1 cup uncooked rolled oats	½ cup butter or margarine
½ cup sifted all-purpose flour	1 1-lb. can cranberry sauce (jellied or whole)
1 cup brown sugar, packed	Vanilla ice cream

Start heating oven to 350°F. Then grease an 8″ x 8″ x 2″ pan. Mix oats, flour, sugar; with 2 knives, scissor-fashion, cut in butter until crumbly. Place half of mixture in pan. Cover with cranberry sauce; top with rest of oat mixture. Bake 45 min. Serve hot, cut into squares; top with ice cream. Makes 6 to 8 servings.

RHUBARB CRUNCH: For cranberry sauce, substitute 3 cups diced, unpeeled young rhubarb mixed with 1 tablesp. flour, ½ cup granulated sugar, 1 teasp. cinnamon, ⅛ teasp. salt, and 1 tablesp. water.

CAROLYN'S APPLE PANDOWDY

1 cup brown sugar, packed	¾ cup milk
¼ cup flour	5 cups sliced, pared, cored cooking apples
¼ teasp. salt	
1 teasp. vinegar	¼ teasp. cinnamon
1 cup water	Dash nutmeg
1 cup sifted all-purpose flour	1 teasp. lemon juice
2 teasp. double-acting baking powder	1 teasp. vanilla extract
¾ teasp. salt	2 tablesp. butter or margarine
3 tablesp. shortening	

In saucepan, mix sugar, ¼ cup flour, ¼ teasp. salt; stir in vinegar, water; cook over low heat, stirring, until thickened. Set this sauce aside.

Start heating oven to 375°F. Sift 1 cup flour, baking powder, ¾ teasp. salt. With 2 knives, scissor-fashion, cut in shortening until size of peas; add milk; stir until moistened but still lumpy.

Arrange apples in greased 12″ x 8″ x 2″ baking dish. To sauce, add cinnamon, nutmeg, lemon juice, vanilla, butter; pour over apples. Drop dough on top of apples. Bake 40 min., or until topping is brown.

Serve warm, with pour cream, commercial sour cream, ice cream, or cream cheese thinned with milk. Makes 6 servings.

FRUITFUL COBBLER

1 qt. sliced, peeled peaches; sliced, pared, cored cooking apples; or sliced pitted plums	½ cup corn syrup or honey
	1 cup packaged biscuit mix
½ teasp. salt	2 tablesp. sugar
1 tablesp. flour	½ cup milk or water
	1½ teasp. sugar

Start heating oven to 425°F. In 1½-qt. casserole, toss peaches with salt, flour, corn syrup. Mix biscuit mix with 2 tablesp. sugar, milk. Pour over peaches; top with 1½ teasp. sugar. Bake, uncovered, 40 min., or until golden and tender. Makes 8 servings.

CHERRY: Substitute 1 qt. drained canned pitted red sour cherries for peaches. Use honey instead of corn syrup.

BUTTER-NUT PANDOWDY

1 cup packaged biscuit mix	fruit
	¾ cup brown sugar, packed
½ cup coarsely chopped walnuts	2 tablesp. butter or margarine
½ cup milk	Heavy cream
1 cup water or syrup drained from canned	

Start heating oven to 375°F. Next grease 10″ x 6″ x 2″ pan. Combine biscuit mix, nuts, milk; spread in pan. Bring water, brown sugar, butter, to boil; pour over dough. Bake 30 min. Serve warm, with pour or whipped cream. Makes 6 servings.

RUM-BUTTERSCOTCH: Omit biscuit mix, walnuts, milk. Arrange 1 can refrigerated biscuits in 10″ x 6″ x 2″ pan. Bake at 375°F. 6 min. Pour on hot mixture of water, brown sugar, butter, 1 teasp. rum extract. Bake 30 min.

KATHY'S PECAN-DATE WEDGES

½ cup soft butter or margarine	1 cup snipped pitted dates
1 cup granulated sugar	1 teasp. vanilla extract
2 egg yolks	2 egg whites, stiffly beaten
2 teasp. milk	Cinnamon
½ cup coarsely broken pecans	Whipped cream

Start heating oven to 350°F. In large bowl, mix butter, sugar, yolks, and milk well. Fold in pecans, dates, vanilla, and egg whites. Turn into greased 9″ pie plate. Sprinkle with cinnamon. Bake about 35 min., or until silver knife inserted in center comes out clean. Serve warm or cold, cut into wedges and topped with whipped cream. Makes 8 servings.

BRAZIL BETTY

2 8-oz. cans pineapple chunks, drained	½ cup chopped Brazil nuts
	¼ teasp. cinnamon
10 graham crackers, crumbled	⅓ cup honey
	2 tablesp. butter or margarine

Preheat broiler 10 min., or as manufacturer directs. In greased 10″ x 6″ x 2″ baking dish, arrange pineapple chunks. Combine cracker crumbs with nuts, cinnamon; sprinkle over pineapple. Drizzle on honey; dot with butter. Broil 9″ from heat for 5 to 6 min., or until browned. (If you can't place broiler pan this low, turn heat control to 400°F.) Makes 6 servings.

PEG'S PUDDING PIE

1 tablesp. corn-muffin mix	½ teasp. vanilla extract
2 eggs, unbeaten	¾ cup snipped pitted dates
½ cup granulated sugar	½ cup finely chopped pecans
½ cup brown sugar, packed	½ cup whole pecan halves
1 tablesp. undiluted evaporated milk	Vanilla and coffee ice-cream balls
½ cup corn-muffin mix	

1. Start heating oven to 325°F. Grease a 9″ pie plate; dust with 1 tablesp. corn-muffin mix.
2. In large bowl, place eggs, granulated sugar, brown sugar, milk, ½ cup corn-muffin mix, vanilla, dates, chopped pecans; with electric mixer, beat together until light and fluffy. Turn into pie plate; top with pecan halves. Bake 45 min. Cool.

At serving time: With spatula, loosen pie around edge; slip onto cake stand; serve with ice-cream balls.

To Freeze: This dessert may be made ahead, freezer-wrapped, then frozen. Thaw at room temperature 1 hr. before serving.

STEAMED PUDDINGS

To save work on busy days, make these puddings ahead; then reheat them at serving time as directed. Of course, they can be made and steamed just before serving, too.

For a Flaming Pudding: For large pudding, heat ½ cup brandy till lukewarm; for individual puddings, heat 2 teasp. brandy per pudding. Immediately pour brandy over and around hot pudding. Touch lighted match to brandy; carry to table ablaze.

Or soak cubes of sugar in lemon extract; place around pudding; immediately light with match.

CRANBERRY HOLIDAY PUDDING

3 cups raw cranberries	purpose flour
	3 teasp. baking soda
¾ cup light or dark raisins	¾ cup light molasses
	½ cup hot water
2¼ cups sifted all-	

Rinse cranberries and raisins; drain; place in mixing bowl. Sift flour, soda, over fruit. Add molasses, water; stir until batter is smooth. Turn into 2 1-lb. greased, lightly sugared coffee cans; replace covers. Place on trivet in deep kettle. Add enough boiling water to come halfway up sides of cans. Steam, covered, 1¼ hr., or until done.

Serve with Butter-Cream Sauce, p. 535. Makes about 12 servings.

To Do Ahead: Make pudding several days ahead. After steaming it, remove from cans; cool; wrap; refrigerate. Or see To Freeze Puddings, p. 707. To serve, wrap pudding in foil; bake at 325°F. about 45 min., or until hot. Or steam in same coffee cans about 1 hr.

FLUFFY STEAMED FIG PUDDING

1 lb. dried figs	sugar
1¾ cups milk or liquefied nonfat dry milk	1 teasp. nutmeg
	1 teasp. cinnamon
	¾ teasp. salt
1½ cups sifted all-purpose flour	3 eggs
	1½ cups ground suet
2½ teasp. double-acting baking powder	1½ cups fresh bread crumbs
	3 tablesp. grated orange rind
1 cup granulated	

With scissors, snip stems from figs. Into double boiler, snip figs in small pieces; add milk; cook, covered, 20 min. Sift flour, baking powder, sugar, nutmeg, cinnamon, salt. In bowl, beat eggs; add suet, bread crumbs, rind, fig mixture, then flour mixture; mix well.

Turn into well-greased 2-qt. mold; cover tightly. Place on trivet in deep kettle. Add enough boiling water to come halfway up sides of mold. Steam, covered, 2 hr., or until done. Let stand 2 min. before removing from mold.

Serve with Hard Sauce, p. 537, or soft vanilla ice cream. Makes about 10 servings.

To Do Ahead: Make pudding several days ahead. After removing it from mold, cool; then refrigerate. Or see To Freeze Puddings, p. 707. To serve, wrap pudding in foil; bake at 325°F. about 1 hr., or until hot. Or steam in same mold about 1 hr.

BLANCHE'S STEAMED CURRENT PUDDING

1 1-lb. loaf sliced bread	1½ teasp. salt
2 11-oz. pkg. dried currants	1¾ teasp. cinnamon
	1¾ teasp. nutmeg
2 eggs, beaten	¾ teasp. allspice
1½ cups ground suet	¾ teasp. ground cloves
2 cups granulated sugar	Hard Sauce, p. 537

Day before: Over bread slices, in large bowl, pour enough cold water just to moisten bread; drain bread well, pressing out moisture with spoon. Break bread into very small pieces. Wash currants; drain. Toss bread well with currants, eggs, suet, sugar, salt, spices. Turn into buttered 2-qt. pudding mold with tight-fitting cover.* Refrigerate, with cover in place.

About 2½ hr. before dessert time: Place pudding on trivet in deep kettle. Into kettle, pour boiling water to come halfway up sides of pudding; cover; steam 2½ hr. Unmold onto serving dish; serve *hot,* spooning some of Hard Sauce, over top and passing rest. If desired, garnish with orange sections, green grapes. Makes 8 servings.

**Or use 2 buttered 1-lb. coffee cans; steam 1½ hr.*

GRANDMOTHER'S PLUM PUDDING
(double-boiler style)

2 cups packaged dried bread crumbs	1½ cups milk or liquefied nonfat dry milk
1 teasp. cinnamon	½ cup diced candied
1 teasp. allspice	citron or mixed preserved fruit
¼ teasp. ground cloves	
1 cup finely ground suet	1 15-oz. pkg. seeded raisins
¾ cup molasses	1 tablesp. flour
2 eggs, unbeaten	

In large bowl, combine crumbs, cinnamon, allspice, cloves, suet, molasses, eggs, milk, blending well after each addition. Then toss together citron, raisins, flour; stir into batter.

Turn batter into well-greased 2-qt. double boiler top. Cook, covered, over boiling water (adding more water as needed) 5 hr. Run spatula around pan and unmold pudding.

Serve hot, with Hard Sauce, p. 537. Makes 8 servings.

To Do Ahead: Make and steam pudding day before; then refrigerate. To serve, reheat in double boiler about 1 hr.

WINTER BREAD PUDDING
(almost a plum pudding)

8 very thin stale white-bread slices	died citron
	½ cup slivered candied orange peel
6 tablesp. soft butter or margarine	½ cup slivered candied lemon peel
Granulated sugar	
Cinnamon	1 egg
Nutmeg	1 cup milk
Allspice	1 teasp. vanilla extract
½ cup currants	1 cup water
½ cup raisins	1 stick cinnamon
½ cup slivered can-	

1. Start heating oven to 325°F. Spread each slice of bread with butter; cut slices into thin strips.
2. In bottom of greased 1½-qt. casserole, place single layer of bread strips so they're almost, but not quite, touching. Sprinkle with 1 teasp. sugar, dash each of cinnamon, nutmeg, allspice; 2 tablesp. each of currants, raisins, candied citron, orange peel, and lemon peel.
3. Repeat layers in step 2, 3 times more.
4. Then, in small bowl, beat together egg, ½ cup milk, vanilla, and 2 tablesp. sugar; pour over pudding; bake 1½ hr., or until brown. Three or four times while pudding is baking, press down on it firmly with back of spoon, and add more milk (about ½ cup altogether).
5. When pudding is nearly baked, make this sauce: In small saucepan, mix together water, 1 cup sugar, and stick cinnamon. Bring mixture to boil and cook rapidly until thick and syrupy. Serve pudding hot with this sauce. Makes 6 servings.

PANTRY-SHELF STEAMED PUDDINGS

Delicious plum, date, and fig puddings come canned, in small and large sizes. Just open them; place in colander; set over boiling water, and steam, covered, until piping hot. Serve with your favorite sauce.

DO-AHEAD REFRIGERATOR DESSERTS

OLD-FASHIONED BLANCMANGE
(Chocolate-Almond Cream)

2 cups milk	⅛ teasp. almond
2 tablesp. cocoa	extract
¼ teasp. salt	½ teasp. vanilla
¼ cup sugar	extract
1½ tablesp. corn-	½ cup heavy cream,
starch	whipped
1 egg, well beaten	

In double boiler, scald 1¾ cups milk. Combine cocoa, salt, 2 tablesp. sugar, cornstarch. Mix with ¼ cup milk till smooth; stir into scalded milk. Cook, stirring, until smooth and thickened.

Combine egg with 2 tablesp. sugar; slowly stir in chocolate mixture. Return to double boiler; cook, stirring, until smooth and thickened — about 2 min. Cool. Fold in extracts, then half of whipped cream. Turn into serving dish or sherbet glasses. Top with remaining whipped cream. Refrigerate until served. Makes 4 to 6 servings.

FEATHERY MARBLE SPONGECAKE

1 env. unflavored	3 sq. unsweetened
gelatine	chocolate, melted
½ cup cold water	½ cup boiling water
4 egg yolks	4 egg whites
1 cup sifted confec-	1 baker's 7″ sponge-
tioners' sugar	cake layer
1½ teasp. vanilla	Fresh grapes (op-
extract	tional)
½ teasp. salt	

Day before, or early in day:
1. Have ready a 9″ by 5″ by 3″ loaf pan. Cut two strips of wax paper, one 16″ x 8¼″, the other 20″ x 4¼″. In loaf pan, fit 16″ strip crosswise and 20″ lengthwise, so there will be a 3″ overhang on all sides.
2. Sprinkle gelatine on cold water. In medium bowl, with mixer at medium speed, beat egg yolks till thickened; gradually beat in sugar until thick and smooth, then vanilla and salt.
3. Now beat in melted chocolate; blend well. Stir boiling water into softened gelatine until gelatine is dissolved; then add gradually to chocolate mixture, beating until smooth, scraping beaters and sides of bowl often.

4. In small bowl, with mixer at high speed, beat egg whites until stiff but not dry; gently fold into chocolate mixture.
5. Pour about 2 cups chocolate mixture into paper-lined pan. Break cake layer in half; break one of halves into about 1½″ pieces, then poke them down into chocolate mixture, being sure chocolate covers cake pieces completely.
6. Make second layer in pan as in step 5, being sure cake is pressed down into mixture. Pour any remaining chocolate mixture into pan and level off, or turn into custard cups. Refrigerate all for 5 hr., or till set.
To serve: Lift out of pan; peel off paper. Garnish with grapes; serve sliced, topped with whipped cream. Makes ten ¾″ slices.

RICE-PEACH MELBA

⅔ cup packaged pre-	½ cup heavy cream,
cooked rice	whipped
2 cups milk	1 1-lb.-13-oz. can
⅓ cup granulated	cling-peach halves,
sugar	drained
½ teasp. salt	⅓ cup currant jelly,
⅛ teasp. nutmeg	melted
⅛ teasp. cinnamon	

1. In saucepan, combine rice, milk; bring to boil; boil gently, loosely covered, 15 min., fluffing rice occasionally with fork.
2. Remove rice from heat; add sugar, salt, nutmeg, cinnamon. Cool 5 min. Chill in a special ice-cube tray, p. 610, 20 min. (don't freeze).
3. Fold rice mixture into whipped cream. Pile into 6 sherbet glasses; top with peaches, cut sides down. Pour on jelly. Makes 6 servings.

MACAROON RUSSE

14 ladyfingers, split	½ cup chopped
⅓ cup sherry	toasted almonds
½ cup soft butter or	2 cups macaroon
margarine	crumbs
1 cup confectioners'	2 egg whites
sugar	1 cup heavy cream,
2 egg yolks, unbeaten	whipped
1 whole egg	

Day before:
1. Line bottom and sides of 2-qt. bowl or mold with half of split ladyfingers; sprinkle with 2 tablesp. sherry.

2. In large bowl, with electric mixer at medium speed, beat butter with sugar until light and fluffy. Beat in egg yolks, one at a time, then whole egg; add almonds, crumbs, remaining sherry.

3. Beat egg whites until stiff; fold into creamed mixture; then fold in whipped cream.

4. Turn half of this mixture into prepared bowl; top with rest of split ladyfingers, then rest of mixture. Refrigerate.

To serve: Unmold onto serving plate. Garnish, if desired, with mounds of whipped cream and slivered almonds. Makes 8 to 10 servings.

STRAWBERRY-CHEESE COUPE

½ cup canned crushed pineapple	¼ teasp. almond extract
½ cup heavy cream	1 10-oz. pkg. frozen sliced strawberries, thawed
1 cup cottage cheese	
¼ cup granulated sugar	2 tablesp. grenadine syrup

1. Drain crushed pineapple very well. Whip cream. In bowl, combine pineapple, cottage cheese, whipped cream, sugar, and almond extract. Refrigerate.

2. Mix strawberries and grenadine syrup. Refrigerate.

3. To serve, alternate layers of cottage-cheese mixture and strawberries in sherbet glasses. If desired, top each serving with a strawberry. Makes 6 servings.

♣ FOR 3: Halve ingredients.

JELLIED MARSALA FRUIT CUP

2 env. unflavored gelatine	Few drops red food color
1 cup water	1 cup cubed, pared fresh pears or apples
½ cup lemon juice	
¼ cup currant jelly	
½ cup granulated sugar	1 cup halved, seedless green grapes
1½ cups Marsala wine	Slightly sweetened whipped cream

In saucepan, sprinkle gelatine on water to soften; add lemon juice, jelly, sugar. Stir over low heat until melted and clear; add wine and food color. Refrigerate until mixture begins to set; then stir in fruit. Turn into 5-cup mold. Refrigerate about 4 hr., or until firm.

Carefully unmold; serve at once, with or without whipped cream. Makes 8 servings.

SPANISH CREAM

1 env. unflavored gelatine	3 eggs, separated
½ cup granulated sugar	3 cups milk
	1 teasp. vanilla extract
¼ teasp. salt	

1. In double-boiler top, mix gelatine, ¼ cup sugar, salt. Stir in egg yolks; then slowly stir in milk. Cook over boiling water, stirring, until mixture coats spoon.

2. Refrigerate mixture until slightly thicker than unbeaten egg white; stir in vanilla. Beat egg whites until they form moist peaks when beater is raised; gradually add ¼ cup sugar, beating until stiff. Fold in gelatine mixture.

3. Leave in bowl; or turn into 12 individual molds or custard cups. Refrigerate until set.

To serve: Spoon into sherbet glasses or unmold. Serve plain or with Easy Chocolate Sauce, p. 634; Butter-Caramel Sauce, p. 536; Butterscotch Sauce, p. 534; crushed strawberries or raspberries; or whipped cream. Makes 12 small molds, or 6 generous servings.

♣ FOR 2 OR 3: Use 2 eggs; halve rest of ingredients.

TWO-LAYER: If you prefer Spanish Cream that separates into 2 layers (custard on top, jelly below), do not chill gelatine mixture, step 2. Add vanilla and fold in beaten egg whites while gelatine is still hot.

BAVARIAN CREAM

1 env. unflavored gelatine	1¼ cups milk
Pinch salt	1 cup heavy cream
6 tablesp. granulated sugar	1 teasp. vanilla extract; ½ teasp. almond extract; or rum to taste
2 eggs, separated	

Day before, or early in day: In double-boiler top, combine gelatine, salt, 2 tablesp. sugar. Stir in egg yolks; then slowly stir in milk. Cook over boiling water, stirring, until mixture coats spoon. Remove at once. Refrigerate until slightly thicker than unbeaten egg whites.

Beat egg whites until they form moist peaks when beater is raised; gradually add ¼ cup sugar, beating until stiff. Fold into yolk mixture, along with whipped cream, vanilla. Leave in bowl; or turn into 1½-qt. mold, or 6 to 8 custard cups or molds. Refrigerate till served. *To serve:* Spoon into sherbet glasses or unmold. Nice as is, or topped with flaked coconut and green crème de menthe; crushed strawberries or raspberries; sliced peaches; canned Bing cherries, flavored with brandy; Hot Fudge Sauce, p. 537; Rum-Butter Sauce, p. 536; or Bing-Cherry Sauce, p. 535. Makes 6 to 8 servings.

BAVARIAN CHARLOTTE: Line bowl, mold, or custard cups with spongecake strips or ladyfingers; spoon in Bavarian Cream mixture.

COFFEE BAVARIAN: To milk, add 1 to 2 tablesp. instant coffee.

GRENADINE BAVARIAN: Refrigerate Bavarian Cream mixture in bowl. To serve, heap in sherbet glasses, spoon on bottled grenadine syrup.

MOLDED CHEESE BAVARIAN

2 env. unflavored gelatine	2 teasp. grated lemon rind
1 cup granulated sugar	3 tablesp. lemon juice
¾ teasp. salt	3 cups cottage cheese
2 eggs, separated	1 cup heavy cream
1 cup milk	Halved, peeled orange slices and small bunch grapes

1. *Evening before:* In double-boiler top, mix gelatine, sugar, salt. Beat egg yolks with milk; stir into gelatine. Cook over boiling water, stirring constantly, until mixture thickens and coats spoon.
2. Cool mixture. Add lemon rind and juice, cheese; with hand beater, beat until very well blended. Refrigerate until mixture mounds slightly when dropped from spoon.
3. Beat egg whites stiff. Whip cream. Fold gelatine mixture into egg whites; fold in cream. Turn into 2-qt. mold or 8 sherbet glasses. Refrigerate until firm.
4. *To serve:* If mold, unmold onto large dessert plate. Garnish with orange slices and grapes. Makes 8 to 10 servings.

♣ FOR 4: Halve ingredients. Turn into 1-qt. mold.

GREAT BAVARIAN: Just double recipe for 8 to 10 servings, above; mold half of mixture in 1½-qt. ring mold, rest in fluted mold of about 2-qt. capacity. Unmold ring mold; then unmold fluted mold on top of ring mold. Makes 16 to 18 servings.

TOASTED SNOW SQUARES

1 env. unflavored gelatine	2 egg yolks
1 cup granulated sugar	⅓ cup melted butter or margarine
1¼ cups boiling water	1 tablesp. grated lemon rind
3 egg whites, unbeaten	2 tablesp. lemon juice
¼ teasp. salt	⅓ cup heavy cream, whipped
1 teasp. vanilla extract	1 cup graham-cracker crumbs

Several hr. ahead:
1. In mixing bowl, blend gelatine with ⅔ cup sugar. Add boiling water, while stirring until dissolved; let cool slightly.
2. In large bowl, place egg whites, salt, and vanilla. Add gelatine mixture; then, with mixer at high speed, beat till mixture has consistency of thick cream.
3. Turn into a 9″ by 9″ by 2″ cake pan, and refrigerate till firm.
About 1 hr. before serving: Make following butter sauce: Beat egg yolks until thick and lemon-colored. Gradually add ⅓ cup sugar, continuing to beat. Now blend in melted butter, grated lemon rind, and lemon juice. Fold in whipped cream; refrigerate.
At serving time: Cut gelatine mixture into 1″ squares; roll each square in graham-cracker crumbs. Heap in 8 to 10 sherbet glasses; then top with butter sauce and serve. Makes 8 to 10 servings.

COFFEE JELLY

1 env. unflavored gelatine	sugar
½ cup cold water	⅛ teasp. salt
⅓ cup granulated sugar	1 cup hot coffee*
	1 teasp. lemon juice

In medium bowl, sprinkle gelatine over cold water to soften. Add sugar, salt, hot coffee; stir until gelatine dissolves; stir in lemon juice. Leave in bowl; or pour into 3 or 4 individual molds or custard cups. Refrigerate until set.

Serve, spooned into sherbet glasses, or unmold. Top with cream; whipped cream; Custard Sauce, p. 537; sliced bananas or peaches;

Eggnog Sauce De Luxe, p. 537. Makes 3 or 4 servings.

If using instant coffee, dissolve 1½ tablesp. instant coffee in 1 cup boiling water.

COFFEE CREAM: Refrigerate coffee jelly until consistency of unbeaten egg white. Fold in ½ cup heavy cream, whipped, and ¼ teasp. almond extract. Pour into sherbet glasses. Refrigerate until set.

COFFEE-RUM JELLY: Double ingredients in Coffee Jelly. Pour mixture into a 4-cup mold or 6 ⅔-cup individual molds. Refrigerate until set. Unmold and serve with Rum Sauce, p. 538. Makes 6 servings.

COFFEE-MARSHMALLOW REFRIGERATOR CAKE

2 tablesp. instant coffee	mallows
1 cup hot water	1½ cups heavy cream
½ lb. large marsh-	18 ladyfingers
	Chocolate curls

Day before: In saucepan, dissolve coffee in hot water. With scissors, snip marshmallows into hot coffee. Cook over low heat, stirring, until marshmallows are melted. Refrigerate until slightly thickened. Whip 1 cup cream; fold into coffee mixture. Separate ladyfingers; use half to line the bottom of a 10" x 8" x 2" baking dish or 9" torte-and-cake pan (with 9" round insert in place); cover with half of coffee mixture. Repeat. Refrigerate.

To serve: Top with ½ cup heavy cream, whipped, curls (shred semisweet-chocolate square with vegetable parer). Makes 8 servings.

TWIN ANGEL PIES

1 10" angel-food cake	raspberries, thawed
1 env. unflavored gelatine	4 teasp. lemon juice
½ cup cold water	2 egg whites
2 pkg. frozen sliced strawberries or	⅛ teasp. salt
	1 cup heavy cream
	2 cups flaked coconut

Cut angel-food cake crosswise into 2 even layers. Hollow out cut side of both layers, leaving shells not quite 1" thick. Place each shell on serving plate. Fill in tube hole in each with bits of cake.

Sprinkle gelatine over cold water to soften; stir over hot water until dissolved; stir into berries with lemon juice; refrigerate until partially thickened. Beat egg whites with salt until stiff. Fold into fruit mixture with cream, whipped. Refrigerate a few min.; then heap in cake shells. Refrigerate several hr.

To serve: Decorate tops of pies with coconut. Makes 16 to 18 servings.

LEMON-LIME "BALI HA'I"

1 env. plus 2 teasp. unflavored gelatine	1 cup lemon juice
½ cup cold water	2 cups heavy cream, whipped
1½ cups granulated sugar	Lime-Milk Sherbet, p. 621*
½ teasp. salt	Lime slices
2 teasp. grated lemon rind	Green grapes, peeled, halved
2½ cups boiling water	

About 24 hr. ahead:

1. In large bowl, sprinkle gelatine onto cold water; add sugar, salt, lemon rind, and boiling water; stir till gelatine and sugar are dissolved. Stir in lemon juice.

2. Refrigerate, stirring often, until almost set. Then, with hand beater or electric mixer, beat until frothy. Fold in whipped cream. Turn into 2-qt. mold. Refrigerate. Make sherbet.

At serving time:

1. Set mold, almost to rim, in warm water about 10 sec., *no longer;* remove. With knife, loosen edges; place serving dish, upside down, over mold; invert; lift off mold.

2. Arrange 10 Lime-Milk-Sherbet balls around dessert; garnish with lime slices and grapes. Makes 8 to 10 servings.

Or buy 1 qt. orange, raspberry, or orange-pineapple sherbet. Or make sherbet from favorite mix.

STRAWBERRY CHANTILLY

1 env. unflavored gelatine	beaten
3 tablesp. lemon juice	1 egg white
2 cups milk	1 cup heavy cream, whipped
¼ cup uncooked regular white rice	2 pkg. frozen sliced strawberries, thawed
2 egg yolks, slightly	

1. Soften gelatine in lemon juice; then set over hot water and stir until dissolved.

2. In milk, in double boiler, cook rice until tender. Now stir a small amount of this mixture into egg yolks; return this to rice mix-

ture and cook, over hot water, till thickened. Stir in gelatine; then cool over ice water till mixture mounds.

3. Beat egg white till stiff. Fold into rice mixture with whipped cream, then strawberries. Refrigerate till serving time. Spoon into serving bowl or sherbet glasses. Makes 6 servings.

STRAWBERRY CREAM CAKE

1 env. unflavored gelatine	1 pkg. frozen sliced strawberries, thawed
½ cup cold water	1 cup heavy cream, whipped
2 tablesp. confectioners' sugar	2 7″ bakers' sponge-cake layers
½ teasp. almond extract	1½ cups flaked coconut

In double boiler, sprinkle gelatine over cold water to soften; heat over hot water until dissolved; stir in sugar, extract, berries. Refrigerate until slightly thickened. Then fold in whipped cream; refrigerate until stiff enough to spread.

Use to fill and frost spongecake layers. Sprinkle with coconut. Refrigerate until served. Makes 8 servings.

CHARLOTTE RUSSE

2 env. unflavored gelatine	⅓ cup brandy
¾ cup granulated sugar	9 ladyfingers, split
¼ teasp. salt	2 cups heavy cream
4 eggs, separated	Whipped cream
2 cups milk, scalded	9 maraschino cherries, drained

1. In double-boiler top, combine gelatine, sugar, salt. Stir in egg yolks; then slowly stir in milk.

2. Cook mixture over boiling water, stirring, until it coats spoon. Cool. Add 3 tablesp. brandy. Refrigerate until mixture mounds slightly.

3. Sprinkle remaining brandy on ladyfingers; use to line side of 2-qt. fluted tube mold or a 3½″-deep 9″ tube pan.

4. In large bowl, beat egg whites until stiff but not dry. Whip 2 cups cream.

5. Fold gelatine mixture into egg whites; fold in whipped cream.

6. Turn into mold. Refrigerate until firm. To serve, unmold onto serving platter. Garnish

with more whipped cream and maraschino cherries, cut to resemble poinsettias. Makes 9 to 12 servings.

See also Ice Creams and Sherbets, p. 604.

A BOW TO COMPANY

CHOCOLATE-CINNAMON TORTE

2¾ cups sifted all-purpose flour	1 sq. unsweetened chocolate
2 tablesp. cinnamon	2 sq. semisweet chocolate
1½ cups butter	4 cups heavy cream
2 cups granulated sugar	2 tablesp. cocoa
2 eggs, unbeaten	12 candied cherries
	12 walnut halves

Several days ahead, make these "cookies":

1. Start heating oven to 375°F. Grease, line bottom with wax paper, then grease again, two or three 9″ layer-cake pans. Sift flour with cinnamon.

2. In large bowl, with mixer at medium speed, mix butter with sugar, then with eggs, until very light and fluffy. Then, at low speed, mix in flour mixture, a little at a time, until smooth.

3. With spatula, spread ⅓ cup "cookie" dough in a very thin layer in each layer-cake pan. Bake, at one time (place on two racks, making sure pans are not directly over one another), about 8 to 12 min., or until golden.

4. Then immediately and carefully remove each "cookie" from pan to wire rack, and cool. Continue baking "cookies" until all dough is used, making at least 12. Store, carefully stacked, in tight container.

About 1 hr. before serving:

1. Grate unsweetened chocolate medium fine; with vegetable parer, shred semisweet chocolate into curls; whip cream.

2. Place one "cookie" on flat cake plate; then spread with ¼ to ⅓ cup whipped cream. Continue building the layers in same way until you have a 12-layer torte.

3. Now fold cocoa and unsweetened chocolate into leftover whipped cream; heap over top of torte.

4. As a finishing touch, decorate top edge of

torte with cherries and walnuts; then heap chocolate curls in center.

5. Refrigerate torte for about ½ hr. before serving, so it will be easy to cut into 12 wedges.

FORGOTTEN TORTE

6 egg whites	⅛ teasp. almond
¼ teasp. salt	extract
½ teasp. cream of	1 cup heavy cream,
tartar	whipped
1½ cups granulated	1 pkg. frozen berries
sugar	or other fruit,
1 teasp. vanilla extract	thawed

About 2 hr. before its overnight "baking":
In large bowl, let egg whites stand at room temperature 1 hr. Butter bottom, not sides, of 9″ tube pan. Start heating oven to 450°F. To egg whites, add salt, cream of tartar. With electric mixer at medium speed, beat until foamy; gradually add sugar, 2 tablesp. at a time, beating well after each addition. Add extracts; continue beating until meringue makes stiff, glossy peaks. Spread evenly in tube pan. Place in oven. *Turn off heat at once.* Let stand in oven overnight. Next morning, loosen edge of torte with sharp knife. Turn onto serving plate; let stand until needed.

To serve: Frost torte with whipped cream; top with fruit; serve in wedges. Makes 8 to 10 servings.

SWEDISH NUT TORTE

4 egg yolks	½ teasp. double-
¾ cup granulated	acting baking
sugar	powder
1½ cups finely ground	4 egg whites
walnuts, packed	¼ cup confectioners'
½ teasp. packaged	sugar
dried bread crumbs	Half recipe Mocha
	Cream, p. 645

Make several days ahead, if desired:
1. Start heating oven to 375°F. Grease, then line with wax paper, bottom of 9″ layer-cake pan.
2. In small bowl, with electric mixer at high speed, beat egg yolks with granulated sugar until light and fluffy. With rubber spatula, fold in ground walnuts, bread crumbs, baking powder, then egg whites, stiffly beaten.

3. Pour batter into layer-cake pan. Bake 25 to 30 min., or until torte springs back when touched lightly in center. Cool in pan; then remove from pan to wire rack.
4. When cool, set torte, bottom side up, on cake plate. Sift confectioners' sugar over top. Then, with cake decorator and tube no. 3, filled with Mocha Cream, make a scalloped border around top of torte. Refrigerate.

At serving time: Remove torte from refrigerator, and cut into wedges. Makes 8 to 10 servings.

GATEAU SAINT HONORE

¼ cup butter	1 teasp. vanilla extract
1 tablesp. sugar	1 stick pkgd. cream-
5 egg yolks	puff mix
¾ cup sifted all-	3 egg whites
purpose flour	3 tablesp. granulated
2½ teasp. unflavored	sugar
gelatine	½ pt. heavy cream
1½ cups milk	2 tablesp. Cointreau
½ cup granulated	⅔ cup granulated
sugar	sugar
6 tablesp. flour	Dash cream of tartar
½ teasp. cornstarch	7 glacéed cherries

Early in day:
1. Make pastry: In small bowl, with electric mixer at high speed, mix butter, 1 tablesp. sugar, and 1 egg yolk until light and fluffy. With mixer at low speed, mix in ¾ cup flour until just blended; sprinkle with ½ teasp. water if pastry seems too dry and crumbly.
2. On lightly floured wax paper, roll pastry into a 9¼″ circle; set inverted 9″ layer-cake pan on it; then cut around it with sharp knife; remove dough trimmings; lift off pan. Invert pastry circle on cookie sheet; peel off paper; prick pastry all over with fork; refrigerate.
3. Make filling: Sprinkle gelatine on 2 tablesp. water to soften. In saucepan, scald 1¼ cups milk. In medium bowl, blend ½ cup sugar with 6 tablesp. flour, cornstarch, 4 egg yolks. Stir in ¼ cup cold milk, then about ½ cup scalded milk; return to rest of scalded milk in saucepan; stir in softened gelatine; then bring to rolling boil, stirring constantly. Remove from heat; cool; add vanilla. Pour into large bowl; cover tightly with foil; refrigerate till like unbeaten egg white — about 1 hr.
4. Complete gâteau: While filling refrigerates, start heating oven to 375°F. Prepare cream-

puff mix as label directs. Spoon it into large pastry bag with no. 6 large plain tube. With it, form cream-puff edging around top of pastry circle. Also make 6 small cream puffs on the same cookie sheet. Bake all 25 min., or till pastry is golden and cream puffs firm; cool.

5. Then, in small bowl, with mixer at high speed, beat egg whites till foamy; gradually beat in 3 tablesp. sugar; continue beating until peaks form. Fold into gelatine mixture; refrigerate.

6. Place cooled pastry shell on flat cake plate. Spoon in filling; refrigerate.

7. Whip cream; stir in Cointreau. Use some in pastry bag with star pastry tube no. 6 to fill partially split cream puffs. Refrigerate puffs and rest of whipped cream.

8. In small skillet, combine ⅔ cup sugar, ½ cup water, and cream of tartar. Bring to boil, stirring; then simmer until amber-colored. Dip tops of 6 cream puffs in this syrup; cool on rack; then arrange around edge of filling.

9. Using same pastry bag and tube and more whipped cream, make mounds of cream between cream puffs and in center; top each with a cherry. Refrigerate until served. Makes 6 generous servings.

MERINGUES GLACEES
(ice-cream-filled meringues)

6 egg whites	1 teasp. vinegar
⅛ teasp. salt	1 teasp. vanilla extract
2 cups granulated sugar	

Day or so before:
1. Let egg whites stand out at room temperature at least 1 hr.
2. Then add salt to egg whites. With electric mixer at high speed, beat whites until stiff enough to hold shape.
3. At low speed, add sugar, about 2 tablesp. at a time, beating about 2 min. after each addition (this takes about 30 min.)
4. Start heating oven to 275°F.
5. To meringue, add vinegar and vanilla; at high speed, beat 10 min. longer.
6. Drop by heaping spoonfuls onto buttered cookie sheet.
7. Bake 45 min.; reduce heat to 250°F.; bake 15 min., or until creamy white and firm. Remove to rack; cool.

8. Cover meringues lightly with wax paper, saran, or foil; store in covered container until needed — they keep well.

To serve: Break each meringue apart like a biscuit. Fill lower part with ice cream or whipped cream; replace top; add spoonful of fruit or chocolate, butterscotch, or caramel sauce. Makes 18 to 24.

MERINGUES GLACEES—BRANDIED STRAWBERRIES: Serve ice-cream-filled meringues with Brandied Strawberries, p. 535.

CREPES

2 eggs	½ cup sifted all-purpose flour
⅔ cup milk	
1 tablesp. melted shortening	¼ teasp. salt
	1 teasp. sugar

Beat eggs thoroughly. Add milk, shortening. Sift flour with salt and sugar; add to egg mixture; with hand beater, beat until smooth. On griddle or in chafing dish, heat a little salad oil or shortening. Drop crepe batter, in 5″ rounds, on griddle; cook, turning once, until a light brown on both sides.

For dessert: Roll up; sprinkle with sugar; serve with lemon wedge.

Or spread with jelly or jam; roll up; sprinkle with sugar.

Or serve, unrolled, in piles of 3, with sweetened strawberries between; cut into wedges.

For main dish: Omit sugar.

STRAWBERRY-CREAM CREPES: Prepare crepes. Just before serving, spoon sweetened halved strawberries, then a level tablespoonful of whipped cream down side of each crepe. Roll up; place, seam side down, on serving platter. Sprinkle with confectioners' sugar. Serve 2 crepes per person.

CREPES SUZETTE

Crepes, above	2 tablesp. granulated sugar
6 sugar lumps	
1 orange	¼ cup Cointreau or curaçao
1 lemon	
⅓ cup orange juice	2 tablesp. rum or Benedictine
½ cup butter or margarine	⅓ cup brandy or Grand Marnier

Make crepes; fold each in half, then in quarters; keep warm. Rub lump sugar on rinds of orange and lemon; add them to orange juice; crush until dissolved.

In chafing dish, melt butter; add orange-juice mixture and granulated sugar; heat. Lift crepes into this sauce; ladle sauce over crepes until saturated. Mix Cointreau and rum; pour over crepes; then pour on brandy but do not stir. When mixture is heated, tilt pan to flame, so sauce catches fire. Spoon flaming sauce over crepes. Serve crepes and sauce on heated plates. Makes 6 servings.

BAKED APPLE PANCAKE

Butter or margarine	Granulated sugar
3 tablesp. all-purpose flour	2 egg yolks
	3 tablesp. milk
¼ teasp. double-acting baking powder	1 cup finely diced, pared apples
	1 tablesp. lemon juice
Dash salt	1 teasp. cinnamon
2 egg whites	Lemon wedges

1. Start heating oven to 400°F. Butter a 10" griddle well; wrap handle in foil; place in oven to heat.
2. Sift flour with baking powder and salt. In bowl, with hand beater, beat egg whites until foamy; then gradually add 3 tablesp. sugar, while beating stiff. In medium bowl, with beater, beat yolks; beat in milk, flour; fold in apples, lemon juice, egg whites. Turn all of it onto hot griddle; spread evenly to edge. Mix 2 tablesp. sugar, cinnamon; sprinkle on pancake.
3. Bake 10 min., or until glazed and baked through. To serve, cut hot pancake into 4 to 6 wedges, then top each with a lemon wedge. Makes 4 to 6 servings.

ZABAGLIONE

3 egg yolks	lemon rind
¾ cup granulated sugar	5 teasp. lemon juice
	½ cup sherry or
2 teasp. grated	Marsala wine

In double-boiler top, beat egg yolks slightly. Add rest of ingredients. Cook over boiling water, beating constantly with hand beater, until as thick and fluffy as whipped cream. Remove from water at once.

Serve hot or chilled, in parfait, sherbet, or champagne glasses. Makes 4 servings.

FRUITED: Ladle, hot, over strawberries; raspberries; peach slices; drained canned fruit cocktail; or pineapple, orange, or banana chunks in sherbet glasses. Serve at once. Makes 6 servings.

PECHES SULTANES FOR TWO: Use 2 egg yolks, 3 tablesp. sugar, and 2½ tablesp. white wine (Chablis); omit lemon juice and rind. Add 1 teasp. Cointreau, if desired, before cooling. Set double-boiler top in ice water; beat until cool. Serve, chilled, over peach slices.

BABA AU RHUM

1 pkg. active dry, or cake, yeast	⅓ cup cut-up citron or currants, or a combination of both
1¼ cups warm water	
2 cups sifted all-purpose flour	¾ cup granulated sugar
3 large eggs, beaten	2 thin orange slices
⅓ cup melted butter or margarine	2 thin lemon slices
	¼ to ½ cup white rum
2 tablesp. granulated sugar	⅓ cup apricot jam
½ teasp. salt	1 tablesp. lemon juice

1. Sprinkle or crumble yeast into ¼ cup warm water in measuring cup; stir until dissolved. Meanwhile, into large bowl, measure flour. Stir up yeast; stir into flour; let stand 5 min.
2. Now stir in eggs; with spoon, beat dough 5 min. (If you sit down, 5 min. won't seem so long.) Let dough rest for 30 min.
3. Next, gradually stir in melted butter. (Dough will ooze butter, but don't worry.) Then stir in 2 tablesp. sugar, salt, citron. Now, with spoon, "knead" dough in bowl 5 min.; although it is soft and sticky, don't add more flour. Pat dough into greased 9" tube pan. Let rise in warm place (80°F. to 85°F.) until triple in bulk and ½" from top of pan. Then bake baba at 375°F. 35 to 40 min., or till a rich brown.
4. Meanwhile, in small saucepan, covered, simmer ¾ cup sugar and 1 cup water, with orange and lemon slices, 5 min. Cool sauce; add rum to taste.
5. Remove baba from pan and place on cake rack. When slightly cooled, set on plate, with bottom side up, and spoon rum sauce over it. Let stand 2 hr. Just before serving, if desired, press apricot jam through strainer;

combine with lemon juice; spread over top of Baba au Rhum.

Serve, cut into 1″ wedges as a dessert.

PETITE BABAS: Make dough as for Baba au Rhum; use to fill 18 greased 2½″ muffin cups one third full. Let rise till doubled in bulk; then bake at 375°F. 15 to 18 min. Arrange babas in deep serving dish or on individual dessert plates. Spoon rum sauce, in step 4, over each baba. Serve warm or cold as dessert.

PETITE BABAS WITH FRUIT: Make Petite Babas, omitting rum sauce. Serve topped with thawed frozen strawberries and whipped cream cheese or sour cream, as dessert.

PETITE BABAS WITH ICE CREAM: Arrange one Petite Baba on each dessert plate; pour rum sauce, in step 4, over each; then place small scoop of strawberry ice cream beside baba.

BREAKFAST BABAS: If desired, serve half of babas with rum sauce, for dessert. At breakfast, the next morning, reheat remaining babas in 375°F. oven 3 min.; serve with jam or split and butter, then toast in broiler.

LARGE BABA AU RHUM: Double all ingredients. Place in greased 4″-deep 10″ tube pan or a 4-qt. mold. Bake at 375°F. 40 to 45 min.

To Freeze: See p. 705.

DE LUXE CHEESECAKE

1 cup sifted all-purpose flour	5 8-oz. pkg. soft cream cheese
2 cups granulated sugar	¼ teasp. vanilla extract
1 teasp. grated lemon rind	½ teasp. grated orange rind
¼ teasp. vanilla extract	3 tablesp. flour
½ cup soft butter or margarine	¼ teasp. salt
3 egg yolks	½ teasp. grated lemon rind
	5 medium eggs
	¼ cup heavy cream

COOKIE CRUST MIXTURE: Mix 1 cup flour, ¼ cup sugar, 1 teasp. grated lemon rind, ¼ teasp. vanilla. With pastry blender or 2 knives, scissor-fashion, cut in butter and 1 egg yolk. Shape into ball; wrap in wax paper; refrigerate 1 hr. Start heating oven to 400°F. Roll about one third of dough between floured pieces of wax paper into a 9½″ circle. Place on bottom of 9″ spring-form pan; trim to fit. Bake at 400°F. about 10 min., or till golden; cool.

Grease side of spring-form pan; fit over filled base. Roll rest of dough into 15″ x 4″ rectangle; cut in half lengthwise; use to line side of pan, patching if necessary.

CHEESE FILLING: Increase oven temperature to 500°F. With electric mixer or spoon, beat cheese until fluffy. Combine 1¾ cups sugar with ¼ teasp. vanilla, orange rind, 3 tablesp. flour, salt, ½ teasp. lemon rind; slowly add to cheese, beating till smooth. Add eggs and 2 yolks, one at a time, beating after each addition. Stir in cream. Turn into lined pan. Bake at 500°F. 12 min., or till dough is golden. Reduce oven temperature to 200°F.; bake 1 hr. Cool on rack away from drafts. Remove side of pan; refrigerate until cold — for 24 hr., if possible.

To serve: Sprinkle cake with chopped, toasted nuts. Or cover with ¼″ layer of commercial sour cream; refrigerate.

Or spread strawberry, peach, apricot, or cherry jam or preserves on top.

Or top wedges with canned crushed pineapple, canned, fresh, or thawed frozen sliced peaches, or fresh or thawed frozen strawberries. Makes 12 servings.

CHEESECAKE DIVINE

1 6-oz. pkg. zwieback	1 teasp. lemon juice
½ cup soft butter or margarine	2 teasp. vanilla extract
Granulated sugar	Grated rind of 1 lemon
⅛ teasp. nutmeg	1 cup heavy cream
1 env. unflavored gelatine	Fresh or frozen sliced strawberries, or
Cold water	canned cling
3 eggs	peaches or pine-
2 8-oz. pkg. soft cream cheese	apple chunks

Make day before, or early in day:

1. Start heating oven to 400°F. With rolling pin, crush zwieback into fine crumbs; mix well with butter, ¼ cup sugar, and nutmeg. Then use three fourths of this mixture as a crust to firmly line bottom and half of the way up side of a 9″ spring-form pan. Bake 10 min.; cool.

2. Meanwhile, sprinkle gelatine over ½ cup cold water. Blend 3 egg yolks, ½ cup sugar, ½ cup water, till smooth; cook over very low heat, *stirring constantly,* until it thickens — about 10 min. Stir in gelatine until dissolved.

3. Into cream cheese, in bowl, with electric mixer at medium speed, gradually beat gelatine mixture; then add lemon juice, vanilla, and grated lemon rind.

4. Now blend in cream, lightly whipped, then the 3 egg whites, stiffly beaten.

5. Turn mixture into zwieback-lined springform pan; top with rest of crumbs. Refrigerate till set; remove from pan.

6. Serve in wedges, as is, or topped with fresh or thawed frozen sliced strawberries, or canned cling-peach slices or pineapple chunks. Makes 6 to 8 servings.

FABULOUS SOUFFLES

HOT CHOCOLATE SOUFFLE

Butter	¼ teasp. salt
Granulated sugar	4 eggs, separated
1 cup milk	1 teasp. vanilla
2 sq. unsweetened	extract
chocolate	¼ teasp. almond
⅓ cup flour	extract

1. Start heating oven to 425°F. With butter, liberally grease 1½-qt. casserole; sprinkle bottom and sides with a little granulated sugar until coated.

2. In double boiler, heat ½ cup milk with chocolate until chocolate is melted; with hand beater, beat till smooth.

3. Stir rest of milk into flour and salt; stir into chocolate. Cook, stirring, until very thick. Remove from heat; beat till smooth.

4. To chocolate mixture, add egg yolks, one by one, beating after each addition until smooth. Cover; let stand.

5. With electric mixer or hand beater, beat egg whites until they form peaks when beater is raised; slowly add ⅓ cup sugar, continuing to beat until stiff. Fold in yolk mixture and extracts. Pour into casserole.

6. Bake, uncovered, 22 to 27 min. When 22 min. are up, insert silver knife part way into center of soufflé; if it comes out clean, soufflé is done. If any soufflé adheres to knife, bake 5 min. more.

Serve at once with Ice-Cream Sauce, p. 536; Holiday Custard Sauce, p. 537; pour cream; or whipped cream. Makes 6 servings.

✦ FOR 8 SERVINGS: Increase milk to 1½ cups, chocolate to 3 sq., flour to ½ cup, salt to ⅜ teasp. Use 6 eggs, ½ cup sugar, 1½ teasp. vanilla extract, ½ teasp. almond extract. Bake in greased 2½-qt. casserole for 32 to 37 min. Serve at once, as at left.

HOT COCONUT SOUFFLE

Butter or margarine	¾ teasp. lemon
⅓ cup quick-cooking	extract
tapioca	¼ teasp. salt
⅓ cup granulated	3 tablesp. flaked
sugar	coconut
2 cups milk	Whipped cream, fla-
3 eggs, separated	vored with sherry
1 3½-oz. can flaked	or rum
coconut	

About 1 hr. before serving:

1. Start heating oven to 350°F.

2. Cut a 28″ length of foil, 6″ wide. Wrap foil around outside of round glass casserole which measures 4 cups to brim, so it stands 3″ above rim. Fasten with cellophane tape.* Press foil over casserole ears. Butter inside of foil collar, but do not grease dish.

3. In double boiler, combine tapioca and sugar; add milk, then cook over boiling water about 10 min., stirring occasionally, or until thickened. Meanwhile, beat egg yolks until thick and light in color. Wash hand beater to remove all traces of yolk.

4. Remove tapioca mixture from heat. Stir in 2 tablesp. butter, contents of can of coconut, and extract.

5. Beat egg whites until foamy. Add salt and beat until stiff but not dry.

6. Into coconut mixture, lightly fold yolks until just blended; turn into large bowl. Fold in whites until just blended.

7. Turn into prepared casserole. Sprinkle with 3 tablesp. flaked coconut.

8. Bake 45 min. Carefully run small spatula between soufflé and foil, snip string or tape, remove collar, and serve immediately with whipped cream flavored with sherry or rum. Makes 6 servings.

For pictured soufflé, prepare a china soufflé dish, 5 cups, measured to brim, as in step 2; tie tightly with string. Then make soufflé, increasing tapioca to ½ cup. Bake 1 hr. Makes 6 to 8 servings.

HOT SOUFFLE GRAND MARNIER

3 egg whites	2 egg yolks, beaten
Butter or margarine	⅛ teasp. cream of
Granulated sugar	tartar
2½ tablesp. flour	Grand Marnier
Dash salt	Whipped cream
¾ cup milk	

1. In medium bowl, let egg whites stand, at room temperature, 1 hr. Butter well, then sprinkle with granulated sugar, a 1-qt. soufflé dish or casserole. Start heating oven to 450°F.
2. In saucepan, melt 2 tablesp. butter; remove from heat. Stir in flour, salt, and milk; cook, stirring, over medium heat until thickened and smooth. Stir in 3 tablesp. sugar; cool slightly; add beaten egg yolks.
3. In medium bowl, beat egg whites until foamy; add cream of tartar; continue beating until whites form stiff peaks when beater is raised.
4. Into whites, gently fold yolk mixture and 3 tablesp. Grand Marnier. Turn into soufflé dish.
5. Set soufflé dish in 1″ hot water in pan; bake 10 min.; then reduce heat to 325°F., and bake 15 min.
6. Serve at once with chilled whipped cream and more Grand Marnier to pour over. Makes 2 or 3 servings.

TOP-STOVE HOT CHOCOLATE SOUFFLE

1⅓ cups milk	¼ teasp. salt
⅔ cup granulated	1 teasp. vanilla extract
sugar	4 eggs, unbeaten
2 sq. unsweetened	
chocolate	

1. In double boiler, heat milk with sugar, chocolate, salt, and vanilla until chocolate melts. With hand beater, beat until smooth. Break eggs into cup; add to chocolate, beating 1 min.
2. Cook, covered, over boiling water 1 hr. 10 min., without removing cover.
3. Serve hot or cold in sherbet glasses, as is or with pour cream. Makes 8 servings.

✦ FOR 4 SERVINGS: Halve all ingredients. Make as directed. Cook 35 min.

COLD LEMON SOUFFLE

2 env. unflavored	8 eggs
gelatine	1 teasp. salt
½ cup cold water	2 cups granulated
2 teasp. grated lemon	sugar
rind	2 cups heavy cream
1 cup lemon juice	

Early in the day, if desired:

1. Fold a 30″ piece of foil in half lengthwise; tie around outside of 1½-qt. soufflé dish as a collar.
2. Sprinkle gelatine over cold water to soften. Grate lemon rind; then extract juice. Separate egg yolks from egg whites.
3. In double-boiler top, combine egg yolks, lemon juice, salt, and 1 cup sugar. Cook over boiling water, stirring constantly, until slightly thickened and custardy. Then stir in gelatine and lemon rind; turn into 3-qt. bowl, cool.
4. Beat egg whites until they hold a shape, then gradually beat in 1 cup sugar, continuing to beat until mixture holds peak.
5. Whip cream until stiff. Now on top of lemon mixture pile stiffly beaten egg whites and cream; gently fold mixtures together.
6. Pour into prepared soufflé dish; refrigerate at least 3 hr., or until firm but spongy. Remove foil. Makes 10 to 12 servings.

P.S. If desired, serve topped with whipped cream, sprinkled with toasted slivered almonds, and surrounded with fresh strawberries.

COLD MARBLE-BAVARIAN SOUFFLE

3 env. unflavored	flour
gelatine	1 qt. milk
1 cup cold water	4 sq. semisweet
8 eggs, separated	chocolate
1 cup granulated	4 tablesp. cocoa
sugar	About 6 drops yellow
1 tablesp. vanilla	food color
extract	2 cups heavy cream
¼ cup all-purpose	¼ teasp. salt

Day before, or early in the day:

1. Sprinkle gelatine over cold water to soften.
2. In large saucepan, combine egg yolks with ¾ cup sugar, vanilla extract; blend in flour, stirring smooth; now add milk, blending well. Cook over low to medium heat, stirring constantly, until custard coats back of spoon. Remove from heat.
3. Add gelatine mixture, stir to completely

dissolve. Refrigerate, stirring occasionally, until small amount mounds when dropped from spoon.

4. Meanwhile fold a 35″ length of foil, 12″ wide, in half lengthwise; wrap around outside of china soufflé dish, which measures 10 cups to brim, so a collar 3″ high stands above rim; fasten with cellophane tape. Melt semisweet chocolate in small saucepan set over hot, *not boiling*, water.

5. Divide cooled custard mixture in half, placing each half in large bowl. Into one half, stir melted, semisweet chocolate and cocoa, until smooth. In other half, stir yellow food color.

6. Whip cream. Beat egg whites with salt until they form soft peaks; then gradually add 1/4 cup sugar, while beating until stiff.

7. Into chocolate mixture, fold half of whipped cream and half of beaten egg whites. Into yellow mixture, fold rest of cream and egg whites.

8. Into soufflé dish, alternately spoon yellow and chocolate mixtures. Then, with rubber spatula, cut through mixture several times, swirling light and dark batters in marbleized effect. Refrigerate several hours or overnight. *Before serving:* Carefully remove foil from soufflé. Makes about 16 servings.

✚ FOR 6 TO 8 SERVINGS: Make half above recipe, using 5-cup china soufflé dish with foil collar, or an 8-cup glass serving dish, omitting foil collar.

COLD RASPBERRY-CREAM SOUFFLE

Day before, or early in the day:
1. Fold 30″ length of foil, 12″ wide, in half lengthwise; wrap around outside of china soufflé dish, which measures 7½ cups to brim, so a collar at least 3″ high stands above rim; fasten with cellophane tape.

2. In medium saucepan, slightly crush with fork 4 10-oz. packages frozen raspberries, slightly thawed. Reserve 9 to 10 raspberries for later use (wrap in foil, return to freezer). To rest of berries, add 1/4 cup granulated sugar, 2 tablesp. lemon juice, 3 env. unflavored gelatine. Stir over medium heat till gelatine dissolves.

3. Chill over ice cubes, while stirring constantly till mixture *just* mounds when dropped from a spoon; remove to 3-qt. mixing bowl at once. Sprinkle 2 teasp. unflavored gelatine onto 1/4 cup water; dissolve over hot water.

4. Meanwhile, in large bowl, beat 7 egg whites with 1/4 teasp. salt to soft peaks; then gradually add 1/4 cup granulated sugar while beating stiff. In another large bowl, combine 4 cups heavy cream, gelatine, 2 tablesp. granulated sugar; beat stiff.

5. Into cooled raspberry mixture, fold egg whites and half of whipped cream. Refrigerate 1 cup whipped cream. Spoon some raspberry mixture into soufflé dish, even with rim. Spread half of remaining whipped cream, next half of remaining raspberry mixture, then rest of remaining whipped cream, and finally rest of raspberry mixture. Refrigerate 1 hr.

6. Now put refrigerated whipped cream in decorating bag with large pastry tube no. 6. Carefully remove foil collar. Press out 4 evenly spaced "commas" from top edge to center of soufflé. Press out one rosette in center, one between every two "commas." Refrigerate.

Just before serving: Arrange reserved raspberries on rosettes. Makes about 16 generous servings.

PIES THAT PLEASE

In the last analysis, the success of your pie depends on good pastry. Top-notch ingredients and streamlined techniques make it possible to turn out masterpieces "as easy as pie." You can start from scratch or use one of the excellent packaged mixes. There's no guesswork if you follow our recipes below.

Before using these recipes, refer to How To Use Our Recipes, p. 3. Always use standard measuring cups and measuring spoons; measure level. Also see Shortenings, p. 100.

Remember, an 8″ pie makes 4 or more servings; a 9″ pie makes 6 or more servings.

Freezing Pies

Pies — double crust, chiffon, and deep-dish fruit, etc. — freeze beautifully. See p. 706.

THE ALL-IMPORTANT PASTRY

FLAKY PASTRY I*

2¼ cups sifted all-purpose flour	shortening (except butter, margarine, or salad oil)
1 teasp. salt	
¾ cup plus 2 tablesp.	⅓ cup cold water

If Two-Crust Pie:

TO MAKE PASTRY:

1. In bowl, mix flour and salt. With pastry blender or 2 knives, scissor-fashion, cut two thirds of shortening into flour until like corn meal — for tenderness. Cut in rest of shortening until like large peas — for flakiness. (Or cut in all of shortening *at once* until like coarse meal.)

2. Sprinkle water, 1 tablesp. at a time, over different parts of mixture, tossing quickly with fork until particles stick together, when pressed gently, and form a dough that clings to fork. (Use only enough water to make flour particles cling together — dough should not be wet or slippery.)

3. With cupped hands, lightly form dough into smooth ball. (If very warm day, wrap in wax paper, saran, or foil and refrigerate up to ½ hr.) Then divide dough in half; form into 2 balls. Makes enough pastry for one 8″ or 9″ pie.

TO MAKE BOTTOM CRUST:

1. On lightly floured surface, place one of balls of pastry. With stockinet-covered rolling pin, flatten gently. Then roll lightly from center out to edge, in all directions, forming circle about

Also makes 2 8″ or 9″ pie shells.

584

1½″ wider all around than inverted 8″ or 9″ pie plate (11″ to 12″ in diameter).

2. Be sure to lift rolling pin near edge of circle, to keep edge from splitting or getting thin. If edge splits, pinch cracks together. If pastry sticks, loosen gently with spatula; then lift and lightly flour surface.

3. Fold pastry circle in half; lift onto ungreased pie plate, with fold at center; unfold. Use bent right index finger to fit pastry gently into plate. (Be sure there are no cracks or holes for juices to seep through.)

TO MAKE TOP CRUST:

1. Roll top crust as in steps 1 and 2 of To Make Bottom Crust, p. 584. Arrange filling in lined pie plate. Trim bottom crust even with edge of plate. Now fold top crust in half; with knife, make several slits of your own design near center fold, so steam can escape.

2. Moisten edge of lower crust with water (use fingers). Lay top crust over filling, with fold at center; unfold. (Or roll pastry circle over rolling pin; then unroll onto filled pie.)

3. With scissors, trim upper crust ½″ beyond edge of plate; fold edge of upper crust under edge of lower crust; press together. Finish pastry edge as in Handsome Edgings, p. 587.

4. To insure nicely browned crust, glaze top of pie as in Pretty Pietops, Glazed, p. 587. Then bake as specific recipe directs.

If Baked Pie Shell:

1. Use 1 cup plus 2 tablesp. sifted all-purpose flour, ½ teasp. salt, 7 tablesp. shortening, and 2 tablesp. plus 1 teasp. water. Make pastry as in If Two-Crust Pie, p. 584, forming it into 1 ball.

2. On lightly floured surface, place ball of pastry. With stockinet-covered rolling pin, flatten gently. Then roll lightly from center out to edge, in all directions, forming circle about 1½″ wider all around than inverted 8″ or 9″ pie plate (11″ to 12″ in diameter).

3. Be sure to lift rolling pin near edge of circle, to keep edge from splitting or getting thin. If edge splits, pinch cracks together. If pastry sticks, loosen gently with spatula; then lift and lightly flour surface.

4. Fold pastry circle in half; lift onto ungreased pie plate, with fold at center; unfold. Use bent right index finger to fit pastry gently into plate. (Be sure there are no cracks or holes for juices to seep through.)

5. Trim pastry about 1″ beyond edge of plate. Flute, or finish pastry edge as in Handsome Edgings, p. 587. With 4-tined fork, make pricks, close and deep, on bottom and side. Refrigerate ½ hr.

6. Bake at 450°F. 12 to 15 min., or till golden. Peek after 5 min.; if bubbles appear, prick again at once with fork. Cool before filling.

If Unbaked Pie Shell:

For pie in which filling is baked in shell, omit pricking and baking in If Baked Pie Shell, left. Rather, fill and bake pie as specific recipe directs.

CHEESE PASTRY: After cutting shortening into flour in Flaky Pastry I, p. 584, add ½ to 1 cup grated process Cheddar cheese.

FLAKY PASTRY II*

2¼ cups sifted all-purpose flour	shortening (except butter, margarine, or salad oil)
1 teasp. salt	
¾ cup plus 2 tablesp.	5 tablesp. cold water

If Two-Crust Pie:

TO MAKE PASTRY:

1. In bowl, mix flour and salt. With pastry blender or 2 knives, scissor-fashion, cut in shortening until size of peas.

2. Blend ⅓ cup of this flour-shortening mixture with water. Add to rest of flour mixture; with fork or fingers, mix until dough holds together.

3. Shape into flat round. (If very warm day, wrap in wax paper, saran, or foil and refrigerate up to ½ hr.) Then divide in half; form into 2 balls. Makes enough pastry for an 8″ or 9″ pie.

TO MAKE BOTTOM AND TOP CRUSTS: Make as in To Make Bottom and Top Crusts, in Flaky Pastry I, pp. 584–585.
Also makes 2 8″ or 9″ pie shells.

If Baked Pie Shell:

1. Use 1½ cups sifted all-purpose flour, ½ teasp. salt, ½ cup shortening, 3 tablesp. water. Make pastry as in If Two-Crust Pie, above, forming it into 1 ball.

2. Make 8″ or 9″ pie shell as in If Baked Pie Shell, Flaky Pastry I, at left.

3. Bake at 450°F. 12 to 15 min., or till golden. Peek after 5 min.; if bubbles appear, prick at once. Cool before filling.

If Unbaked Pie Shell: See If Unbaked Pie Shell, Flaky Pastry I, p. 585.

FLAKY PASTRY III*

¾ cup plus 2 tablesp. shortening (except butter, margarine, or salad oil)
¼ cup boiling water
1 tablesp. milk
2¼ cups sifted all-purpose flour
1 teasp. salt

If Two-Crust Pie:

TO MAKE PASTRY:

1. Put shortening in medium bowl. Add boiling water and milk; with 4-tined fork, break up shortening. Tilt bowl; then, with fork, beat, in rapid cross-the-bowl strokes, until mixture is smooth and thick, like whipped cream, and holds soft peaks when fork is lifted.
2. Sift flour and salt onto shortening. With vigorous round-the-bowl strokes, stir quickly, forming dough that clings together and cleans bowl. Pick up dough and work into smooth flat round. Then divide in half; form into 2 balls. Makes enough for one 8″ or 9″ pie.

TO MAKE BOTTOM AND TOP CRUSTS: Make as in To Make Bottom and Top Crusts, Flaky Pastry IV, right. (Or if you prefer, pastry may be rolled out on lightly floured surface rather than between sheets of wax paper.)
**Also makes 2 8″ or 9″ pie shells.*

If Baked Pie Shell:

1. Use ½ cup minus 1 tablesp. shortening, 3 tablesp. boiling water, 1 teasp. milk, 1¼ cups sifted all-purpose flour, and ½ teasp. salt. Make pastry as in If Two-Crust Pie, above, forming it into 1 ball.
2. Make 8″ or 9″ pie shell as in If Baked Pie Shell, Flaky Pastry IV, right.
3. Bake at 450°F. 12 to 15 min., or till golden. Peek after 5 min.; if bubbles appear, prick again at once. Cool before filling.

If Unbaked Pie Shell: See If Unbaked Pie Shell, Flaky Pastry I, p. 585.

FLAKY PASTRY IV*

2 cups sifted all-purpose flour
1 teasp. salt
½ cup salad oil
3 tablesp. cold water

If Two-Crust Pie:

TO MAKE PASTRY:

1. In bowl, mix flour and salt. Blend oil in thoroughly with fork. Sprinkle all of water over mixture; mix well.
2. With hands, press dough into smooth ball. (If too dry, mix in up to 2 tablesp. salad oil, a little at a time.) Then divide dough almost in half; form into 2 balls. Makes enough for one 8″ or 9″ pie.

TO MAKE BOTTOM CRUST:

1. Wipe table with damp cloth (so paper won't slip). Place larger half of pastry, flattened slightly, between 2 12″-square sheets of wax paper. With rolling pin, roll out gently until pastry circle reaches edge of paper. Then peel off top sheet of paper. If pastry tears, mend by pressing edges together; or press piece of pastry lightly over tear.
2. Lift bottom sheet of paper and pastry by far corners (they will cling together). Place, with paper side up, in ungreased 8″ or 9″ pie plate. Carefully peel off paper. Gently ease and fit pastry into plate.

TO MAKE TOP CRUST:

1. Roll top crust as in step 1 of To Make Bottom Crust, above. Arrange filling in pastry-lined pie plate. Trim bottom crust even with edge of plate. Lay top crust, with paper side up, over filling. Gently peel off paper.
2. Trim upper crust to about ½″ beyond edge of plate; fold it under edge of lower crust; press together. Finish pastry edge as in Handsome Edgings, p. 587. Cut 3 or 4 small slits near center. Bake as specific recipe directs.
**Also makes 2 8″ or 9″ pie shells.*

If Baked Pie Shell:

1. Use 1⅓ cups sifted all-purpose flour, ½ teasp. salt, ⅓ cup salad oil, and 2 tablesp. cold water. Make pastry as in Flaky Pastry IV, above. (If too dry, mix in up to 2 tablesp. salad oil, a little at a time.) Form dough into 1 ball.
2. Roll and fit into 8″ or 9″ pie plate as in steps 1 and 2 of To Make Bottom Crust, above.
3. Trim pastry about 1″ beyond edge of plate. Flute or finish pastry edge as in Handsome

Edgings, below. With 4-tined fork, prick thoroughly, close and deep, on bottom and side.
4. Bake at 450°F. 12 to 15 min., or till golden. Peek after 5 min.; if bubbles appear, prick at once. Cool before filling.

If Unbaked Pie Shell: See If Unbaked Pie Shell, Flaky Pastry I, p. 585.

SARDI'S PASTRY

½ cup soft butter
8 teasp. granulated sugar
⅔ cup soft shortening

3⅓ cups sifted all-purpose flour
1½ teasp. salt
⅓ cup cold water

1. In large bowl, with mixing fork, beat butter with sugar until creamy; then blend this mixture well with soft shortening.
2. Combine flour and salt; with fork, blend with butter mixture.
3. With fork, gradually stir in water until mixture cleans side of bowl. Then, on lightly floured surface, knead dough until just well mixed. Use for pie shells as in Flaky Pastry I, p. 585. Makes 2 9″ or 10″ pie shells, with fluted edges.

PACKAGED PIECRUST

You can make delicious, uniformly excellent pastry, quickly and easily, with national brands of packaged piecrust mix or sticks. Just add water or milk as label directs; mix quickly, roll out as label directs or as in If Two-Crust Pie or To Make Baked or Unbaked Pie Shell, Flaky Pastry I, pp. 584–585.

One package makes pastry for 1 8″ or 9″ two-crust pie, or 2 8″ or 9″ pie shells. You can use half of package and store the rest for later use — see directions on label.

HANDSOME EDGINGS

COIN (for one-crust pie): Trim overhang even with edge of plate. From trimmings, cut penny-size pastry rounds (about 45 rounds for 9″ pie). Moisten pastry rim. Place rounds on rim, overlapping them slightly; press lightly with finger tips.

FLUTED (for one- or two-crust pie): Fold overhang under; turn pastry up to make stand-up rim. Firmly place right index finger on inside of pastry rim; with left thumb and index finger,

pinch pastry at that point. Repeat every ¼″. Leave flutings rounded or pinch into points.

SCALLOPED (for one- or two-crust pie): Make Fluted edging, left, leaving ½″ between flutes; don't pinch into points. Flatten each flute with floured 4-tined fork, forming scallop.

FORK (for one- or two-crust pie): Fold overhang under; turn pastry up to make stand-up rim. With floured 4-tined fork, press pastry to plate rim at ½″ intervals.

ROPE (for one- or two-crust pie): Fold overhang under; turn pastry up to make stand-up rim. Press right thumb into pastry rim *at angle*. Then pinch pastry between this thumb and knuckle of index finger. Repeat around edge.

PRETTY PIETOPS

DOUBLE TRELLIS OR TWISTED LATTICE (for two-crust pie): Line pie plate with pastry as in To Make Bottom Crust, Flaky Pastry I, p. 584; fill. Trim overhang to 1″. Roll rest of pastry into 12″ circle; cut into ½″ strips.

Moisten rim of bottom crust with water. Attach 1 pastry strip to this rim; press; twist strip across filling; attach to pastry rim on opposite side; press firmly. Repeat with 4 strips about 1¼″ apart. Repeat with 5 more strips, placed across first ones to make trellis design.

Turn bottom-crust overhang up over rim and ends of pastry strips; with fingers, press firmly all around to seal strips tightly to rim. Make Fluted edge, left, or press with floured fork. Brush pastry rim and strips with melted butter or cream. Bake as specific recipe directs.

SINGLE TRELLIS (for two-crust pie): Make as for Double Trellis, above, using 7 twisted ½″ pastry strips, placing all in same direction.

LATTICE: Make as for Double Trellis, above, leaving pastry strips untwisted.

WEDGE (for one-crust pie): With knife or pastry wheel, cut 8″ pastry circle into 6 wedges. Prick. Bake wedges while shell bakes. Place wedges on top of such fillings as fresh strawberry, peach, or cream.

GLAZED: Before baking two-crust pie, brush top with one of these: Slightly beaten egg white; undiluted evaporated milk; cream; ice water; salad oil; or melted butter, margarine, or shortening. For sparkling effect, sprinkle with granulated sugar.

FRUIT TWO-CRUST PIES

BETTER-THAN-EVER APPLE PIE

Flaky Pastry for Two-Crust Pie, pp. 584–587

4 or 5 cooking apples, pared, cored, diced

¾ to 1 cup granulated sugar

2 tablesp. flour

½ teasp. cinnamon

4 canned pear halves, drained, crushed

2 tablesp. white rum

2 tablesp. butter or margarine

Start heating oven to 425°F. Line 9″ pie plate with bottom pastry crust; roll out top crust. Combine apples, sugar, flour, cinnamon. Arrange pears in lined 9″ pie plate; sprinkle with rum; top with apple mixture; dot with butter. Adjust top crust. Bake 40 to 50 min., or until filling is tender and crust nicely browned. Serve warm or cold. Makes 1 9″ pie.

APPLE-CHEESE PIE

Flaky Pastry for Two-Crust Pie, pp. 584–587

3 to 4 lb. cooking apples, pared and sliced (about 7 cups)

½ cup granulated sugar

½ cup brown sugar, packed

3 tablesp. flour

¾ teasp. cinnamon

¼ teasp. nutmeg

½ lb. process cheese, sliced

2 tablesp. butter or margarine

Start heating oven to 425°F. Line 9″ pie plate with bottom pastry crust; roll out top crust. In large bowl, toss apples with sugars, flour, cinnamon, and nutmeg. Fill lined pie plate with half of apple mixture. Top with sliced cheese; add rest of apples; dot with butter. Adjust top crust; glaze, if desired, as on p. 587. Bake 40 min., or until filling is tender and crust nicely browned. Serve warm. Makes 1 9″ pie.

SPEEDY APPLE PIE

Today's canned apple slices are all ready to use in a fine 8″ apple pie. Make as label directs.

FRESH PEAR PIE

Make Susan's Fresh Apple Pie, p. 127, substituting sliced, pared fresh pears for apples.

PRUNE-AND-APRICOT PIE

Flaky Pastry for Two-Crust Pie, pp. 584–587

2½ cups cooked dried prunes and apricots, pitted (1¼ cups each)

½ cup prune-and-apricot liquid

1 tablesp. cornstarch

½ cup granulated sugar

Dash salt

¼ teasp. cinnamon

¼ teasp. nutmeg

2 tablesp. lemon juice

1 tablesp. butter or margarine

Start heating oven to 425°F. Line 9″ pie plate with bottom pastry crust; roll out top crust. Arrange prunes and apricots in lined pie plate. Heat fruit liquid; stir in cornstarch mixed with sugar, salt, cinnamon, nutmeg; boil, stirring, until clear and thickened. Add lemon juice, butter; pour over fruit. Adjust top crust. Bake 40 to 50 min. Makes 1 9″ pie.

FRESH BERRY PIE

Flaky Pastry for Two-Crust Pie, pp. 584–587

⅔ to ¾ cup granulated sugar

2 tablesp. flour; or 1½ tablesp. quick-cooking tapioca

½ teasp. grated lemon rind

1 to 2 teasp. lemon

juice

¼ teasp. nutmeg

½ teasp. cinnamon

⅛ teasp. salt

4 cups fresh blueberries, blackberries, raspberries, loganberries, or boysenberries

1 tablesp. butter or margarine

Start heating oven to 425°F. Line a 9″ pie plate with bottom pastry crust; roll out top crust. Combine all ingredients but berries, butter. Arrange half of berries in lined pie plate; sprinkle with half of sugar mixture; repeat. Dot filling with butter; adjust the top crust; glaze, if desired, as on p. 587. Bake 40 to 50 min., or until filling is tender and crust nicely browned. Serve warm or cold. Makes 1 9″ pie.

PEACH OR PLUM PIE: Substitute sliced, peeled peaches or sliced plums for berries.

OLD-FASHIONED MINCEMEAT PIE

3 cups prepared mincemeat

1½ cups coarsely broken walnuts

½ cup brown sugar, packed

½ cup brandy

Flaky Pastry for Two-Crust Pie, pp. 584–587

4 tablesp. soft butter or margarine

1 tablesp. light cream

Soft vanilla ice cream

Several days in advance: Combine mincemeat,

walnuts, brown sugar, and brandy; refrigerate to allow flavors to mingle.

Early on the day: Roll out pastry for bottom crust; spread with 2 tablesp. butter; fold into thirds; refrigerate until well chilled; repeat with top crust.

Now start heating oven to 425°F. Roll out pastry; line 8″ or 9″ pie plate with bottom pastry crust. Fill with undrained mincemeat mixture; adjust top crust; brush top with light cream. Bake 30 min., or until nicely browned.

Serve pie, slightly warm, topped with soft vanilla ice cream. Makes 1 8″ or 9″ pie.

FRESH RHUBARB PIE

Flaky Pastry for Two-Crust Pie, pp. 584–587
1½ cups granulated sugar
2 tablesp. grated orange rind
¼ teasp. salt
4 to 6 tablesp. flour, or 2 to 4 tablesp. quick-cooking tapioca
4 cups fresh rhubarb, in 1″ pieces
2 tablesp. butter or margarine

Start heating oven to 425°F. Line 9″ pie plate with bottom pastry crust; roll out top crust. Combine all ingredients except rhubarb, butter. Arrange half of rhubarb in lined pie plate; sprinkle with half of sugar mixture; repeat. Dot with butter. Adjust top crust; glaze, if desired, as on p. 587. Bake 40 to 50 min., or until filling is tender and crust nicely browned. Serve warm or cold. Makes 1 9″ pie.

STRAWBERRY-RHUBARB PIE: Make and bake as above, reducing sugar to 1¼ cups, omitting rind, using 5 tablesp. flour, and substituting 2 cups hulled fresh strawberries for 2 cups rhubarb. Serve warm, topping each wedge with commercial sour cream.

DE LUXE RED-CHERRY PIE

Flaky Pastry for Two-Crust Pie, pp. 584–587
2 1-lb.-4-oz. cans pitted red sour cherries, packed in water, drained (3½ cups)
Red food color (to tint cherries red)
2 tablesp. quick-cooking tapioca
1 cup granulated sugar
⅛ teasp. salt
¼ teasp. almond extract
1 tablesp. butter or margarine, in bits

Tint cherries a delicate red. Combine with all ingredients but pastry; let stand about 15 min.

Start heating oven to 425°F. Line a 9″ pie plate with bottom pastry crust. Roll out top crust. Turn cherry mixture into lined pie plate; adjust top crust, or make Double Trellis Pie-top, p. 587; glaze if desired. Bake 40 to 50 min., or until filling is tender and crust nicely browned. Makes 1 9″ pie. For 8″ pie, halve ingredients.

CRAN-APPLE PIE

Flaky Pastry for Two-Crust Pie, pp. 584–587
¾ cup granulated sugar
3 tablesp. cornstarch
¼ teasp. salt
¾ cup corn syrup
¼ cup water
1½ cups washed cranberries
1½ teasp. grated orange rind
2 tablesp. butter or margarine
1½ cups chopped, pared, cored cooking apples

In saucepan, mix sugar, cornstarch, salt; gradually add corn syrup, water. Cook, stirring, until mixture thickens slightly and boils. Add cranberries; cook till skins break. Add orange rind, butter; cool. Start heating oven to 425°F. Line 9″ pie plate with bottom pastry crust; roll out top crust. Add apples to cranberry mixture; pour into lined 9″ pie plate. Adjust top crust. Bake 40 to 50 min. Makes 1 9″ pie.

TOPPINGS FOR FRUIT PIES

If the occasion calls for a special topping on your fruit pie, try:
Soft vanilla ice cream, sprinkled with cinnamon or nutmeg
Sharp Cheddar, Swiss, or Gruyère cheese
Whipped cream, dessert topping, or pour cream
Danish blue cheese plus a little cream
Whipped cream cheese plus a little nutmeg
Commercial sour cream
Hard sauce or shaved maple sugar

Storing Leftover Fruit Pies

Fruit pies are best when fresh. So, assuming that what's left won't last longer than a day or two, cover pie well and store on pantry shelf. Freshen by warming it a few minutes at 325°F.

If you want to store pie in refrigerator, its crust will taste better if pie is removed 20 min. before serving, then warmed at 325°F.

DEEP-DISH PIES

DEEP-DISH PLUM PIE

Flaky Pastry or Cheese Pastry for Baked Pie Shell, p. 585	3 tablesp. flour
	⅛ teasp. salt
	¼ teasp. almond extract
2½ lb. plums, halved, pitted (4 cups)	2 tablesp. butter or margarine
1¼ cups granulated sugar	

Start heating oven to 425°F. Roll pastry ⅛" thick to fit top of 10" x 6" x 2" (1½-qt.) baking dish with ½" overhang; fold in half; cut several slits at center fold.

Arrange plums in baking dish. Mix sugar with rest of ingredients; sprinkle over plums. Unfold pastry over filling; turn overhang under; press firmly to side of dish; flute or mark with floured tines of fork. Glaze, if desired, as on p. 587. Bake 45 to 50 min. Serve warm. Makes 6 servings.

APPLE: Make in 2-qt. casserole, using 6 to 8 pared cored medium cooking apples, cut into eighths. Over them pour 1 tablesp. cornstarch mixed with 1 teasp. cinnamon, ¼ teasp. nutmeg, ¼ teasp. salt, ¼ cup sugar, 1 teasp. grated lemon rind, 1 teasp. lemon juice, ¼ cup melted butter or margarine, and ½ cup corn syrup. Top, then bake at 450°F. 45 min., or till done.

LUSCIOUS ONE-CRUST PIES

FRENCH APPLE PIE

Make unbaked 9" Pie Shell, pp. 584–587, with Fluted edge, p. 587. Start heating oven to 425°F. Fill pie shell with Susan's Fresh Apple Pie mixture, p. 127. Sprinkle with Crumbly Topping or Coconut Streusel, right. Cover with foil or another 9" pie plate. Bake 20 min.; uncover; bake 20 min. longer, or until fruit is tender. Serve warm with cream or ice cream. Makes 1 9" pie.

CRUMBLY TOPPING: With fork, blend together ½ cup brown sugar, packed, ¼ cup butter or margarine, ⅓ cup sifted all-purpose flour, and ¼ teasp. cinnamon.

COCONUT STREUSEL: Make Crumbly Topping, adding ½ cup each chopped walnuts and flaked coconut.

ELSIE'S GRATED-APPLE PIE

1 cup sifted all-purpose flour	½ teasp. vanilla extract
½ teasp. double-acting baking powder	4 large, tart apples, pared
⅛ teasp. salt	2 tablesp. grated lemon rind
¼ cup butter or margarine	2 tablesp. lemon juice
2 tablesp. granulated sugar	1 cup granulated sugar
1 egg	1 egg

Start heating oven to 350°F. Into bowl, sift together flour, baking powder, and salt; with pastry blender or 2 knives, cut in butter until very fine. With fork, beat together 2 tablesp. sugar, 1 egg, and vanilla; stir into butter mixture. With finger, press this cookie-crust mixture to bottom and sides of 9" pie plate, forming small rim.

Using fine grater, grate apples. Add lemon rind and juice, 1 cup sugar, and 1 egg; mix well. Turn into lined pie plate. Bake 50 to 60 min. Cool on wire rack. Top with 1 or more cheese cutouts (use cookie cutter and packaged process Cheddar-cheese slices), or serve with ice cream. Makes 1 9" pie.

WONDERFUL WALNUT OR PECAN PIE

Unbaked 9" Pie Shell, pp. 584–587	¼ cup corn or maple-blended syrup
½ cup light-brown sugar, packed	½ cup milk or light cream
½ cup soft butter or margarine	1 cup coarsely chopped walnuts or pecans
¾ cup granulated sugar	½ teasp. vanilla extract
3 eggs	¼ cup broken walnuts or pecans
¼ teasp. salt	

1. Start heating oven to 350°F.
2. In double-boiler top, with electric mixer at medium speed (or with spoon), mix brown sugar and butter until well blended.

3. Add granulated sugar; mix well. Add eggs, one at a time, beating, after each addition, to blend. Add salt, corn syrup, milk; mix well.

4. Cook over boiling water, stirring, 5 min. Remove from water; stir in 1 cup nuts and vanilla. Pour into lined pie plate.

5. Bake 1 hr.; scatter broken nuts on top of pie; bake 5 min. Cool. Makes 1 9″ pie.

NOTE: Pie puffs during baking and shrinks slightly during cooling.

PEANUT PIE: Substitute salted peanuts for coarsely chopped walnuts. Bake 1 hr. 5 min., omitting extra nuts on top. Serve, topped with small mounds of whipped cream and a few peanuts.

PRIZE PRUNE PIE

Unbaked 9″ Pie Shell, pp. 584–587	sugar
	⅛ teasp. salt
2¾ cups cooked dried prunes, pitted	1 tablesp. lemon juice
1 egg	½ cup prune juice
⅓ cup granulated	Crumbly Topping, p. 590

Start heating oven to 425°F. Arrange prunes in pie shell. Beat egg with sugar, salt, lemon juice, and prune juice; pour over prunes. Sprinkle with Crumbly Topping. Bake 40 min. Makes 1 9″ pie.

CHOCOLATE-CHIP-WALNUT PIE

Unbaked 9″ Pie Shell, pp. 584–587	⅔ cup walnut halves
3 eggs	1 6-oz. pkg. semi-sweet-chocolate pieces (1 cup)
⅛ teasp. salt	
1 teasp. vanilla extract	Green grapes or orange sections
½ cup granulated sugar	½ cup heavy cream, whipped
1¼ cups white corn syrup	Walnut halves

Early in afternoon:

1. Start heating oven to 375°F.

2. In medium bowl, beat eggs slightly with fork; add salt, vanilla, sugar, corn syrup, beating just till well blended. Stir in ⅔ cup walnut halves and chocolate.

3. Pour mixture into unbaked pie shell and bake 45 min., or until top is evenly puffed up and starts to crack.

At dinnertime:

1. Cut warm pie into 8 wedges. Then, on large serving plate, arrange wedges in a circle, with green grapes or orange sections heaped in the center.

2. Top each wedge with whipped-cream dollop and walnut if desired. Makes 1 9″ pie.

To Freeze: Freezer-wrap cooled pie; freeze as on p. 706. To serve, unwrap pie; thaw at room temperature. Or heat foil-wrapped, unthawed pie at 350°F. about 15 min.

PILGRIM PUMPKIN OR SQUASH PIE

Unbaked 9″ Pie Shell, pp. 584–587	½ teasp. allspice
	½ teasp. ground cloves
1 cup granulated sugar	1½ cups canned pumpkin or thawed frozen squash
½ teasp. salt	
1½ teasp. cinnamon	
½ teasp. ground ginger	1⅔ cups evaporated milk, undiluted
½ teasp. nutmeg	2 eggs, well beaten

Refrigerate pie shell several hours. Then start heating oven to 425°F. Combine sugar, salt, spices; add pumpkin, milk, eggs; beat till smooth. Pour into shell. Bake at 425°F. 15 min.; reduce heat to 350°F. and bake 35 min., or until custard is set. Cool.

Serve in wedges, each topped with whipped cream or dessert topping, and honey, chocolate curls, or drained canned crushed pineapple in center. Or top with spoonfuls of ice cream. Or top with whipped cream cheese and chopped nuts.

NUT-PUMPKIN PIE: About 10 min. before pie is done, sprinkle with ½ cup sliced Brazil nuts, almonds, filberts, peanuts, pecans, or walnuts.

HEAVENLY HONEY-WALNUT PUMPKIN PIE

Unbaked 9″ Pie Shell, with high fluted edge, pp. 584–587	1 cup heavy cream
	¼ cup butter or margarine, melted
4 eggs, separated	1 tablesp. cornstarch
1 cup light-brown sugar, packed	⅓ cup honey
	⅓ cup chopped walnuts
½ teasp. cinnamon	
½ teasp. nutmeg	¼ teasp. vanilla extract
½ teasp. allspice	
2 cups canned pumpkin	

Afternoon before, or early in the day:

1. Start heating oven to 450°F. In large bowl, with electric mixer at high speed, beat egg yolks

till thick and lemon-colored. At low speed, beat in sugar, cinnamon, nutmeg, allspice, then pumpkin, 1/3 cup heavy cream, and melted butter.

2. Beat egg whites till frothy; gradually add cornstarch, beating until stiff but not dry; fold into pumpkin mixture. Turn into pie shell. Bake 15 min., then reduce oven heat to 350°F. and bake 30 to 40 min., or until knife, inserted in center, comes out clean. Cool; refrigerate.

3. At serving time, mix honey and nuts; spread on pie. Whip 2/3 cup heavy cream with vanilla; pass. Makes 1 9" pie.

MAX'S SUPER CHEESE PIE

Unbaked 8" Graham-Cracker Crumb Crust, p. 594	1/2 cup granulated sugar
1½ 8-oz. pkg. soft cream cheese	1/2 teasp. vanilla extract
2 eggs	1 cup commercial sour cream

Start heating oven to 350°F. With electric mixer at high speed, or hand beater, beat cheese, eggs, sugar, and vanilla until smooth and creamy. Turn into crumb crust. Bake 35 min. Spread sour cream on top; cool. Serve as is. Or top each wedge with sliced fresh or frozen strawberries or canned or frozen peach slices.

CHERRY- OR PINEAPPLE-CHEESE PIE: Omit sour cream. Top cooled cheese pie with cool Cherry or Pineapple Glaze.

Cherry Glaze: Mix 2½ teasp. cornstarch with 2 tablesp. sugar; slowly stir in 1/2 cup liquid drained from canned pitted red sour cherries, packed in water; simmer until clear and thickened. Add 1 cup drained pitted cherries, 1 teasp. lemon juice, 1/4 teasp. almond extract, few drops red food color. Cool.

Pineapple Glaze: Combine 1 cup canned crushed pineapple and 1 teasp. cornstarch. Simmer until clear and thickened; add 1 tablesp. lemon juice. Cool.

MINCE-CHEESE PIE: Substitute Unbaked 9" Pie Shell, pp. 584–587, for Graham-Cracker Crust. Spread 1⅓ cups prepared mincemeat in bottom of shell. Bake at 450°F. 10 to 12 min. to brown crust lightly; remove from oven. Top with cheese-and-egg mixture, then bake at 350°F. 35 min. Omit sour-cream topping.

PINEAPPLE SUPER CHEESE PIE: Omit sour cream. Drain 2 1-lb.-4½-oz. cans pineapple tidbits, reserving 1/2 cup juice; on paper towels, dry tidbits. Arrange tidbits, in overlapping rows, all around and over top of cooled pie, pressing tips of tidbits into pie surface. In small bowl, combine reserved juice with 1/2 teasp. unflavored gelatine; set over hot water and stir until dissolved. Set this bowl of gelatine mixture in bowl of ice; stir constantly until slightly thickened. Use to brush surfaces of pineapple tidbits; spoon rest over top of pie. Refrigerate until set.

FRUIT-GLAZED CHEESE PIE: Substitute 1 teasp. each grated lemon rind and lemon juice for vanilla extract. Omit sour cream. Pour 1 cup boiling water over 1 3-oz. pkg. blackberry- or black-cherry-flavor gelatin; stir to dissolve; add 1 cup juice drained from 1 1-lb.-4-oz. can blackberries or Bing cherries. Refrigerate gelatin mixture until it begins to thicken. Then arrange 1 cup drained blackberries or cherries over cooled pie top; spoon 1/2 cup gelatin mixture over them. (Do not cover crumb rim.) Refrigerate until firm. (Refrigerate rest of gelatin to serve later.)

MACAROON PIE

12 saltines	1 teasp. almond extract
1 doz. pitted dates	1 cup granulated sugar
1/2 cup pecans	3 egg whites
1/4 teasp. double-acting baking powder	

Start heating oven to 350°F. Finely crush saltines; finely snip dates; finely chop pecans. Combine all with baking powder, almond extract, and sugar. Beat egg whites until stiff; gently fold in date mixture. Turn into well-greased 9" pie plate. Bake 30 min. Cool. Serve, in wedges, with unsweetened whipped cream. Makes 1 9" pie.

To Freeze: Double recipe; bake mixture in 2 9" pie plates; then cool, freezer-wrap, and freeze one or both baked pies. See To Freeze and Serve Pies, p. 706.

WALNUT MERINGUE PIE: Substitute 1⅓ cups finely crushed, round, buttery crackers for saltines. Omit dates. Substitute 1 cup chopped walnuts for pecans. Increase baking powder to 2 teasp. Serve, topped with whipped cream and thawed frozen mixed fruits.

LEMON LAYER PIE

1 pkg. piecrust mix
2 teasp. unflavored
   gelatine
1/3 cup lemon juice
3 eggs, beaten
1 1/4 cups granulated
   sugar

1 1/2 tablesp. butter or
   margarine
Grated rind 1 lemon
1 cup heavy cream,
   whipped

Start heating oven to 475°F. Prepare piecrust as label directs, then make 9″ baked pie shell with half of dough. Roll rest of dough into two 6″ rounds; place on cookie sheet; prick; bake, in same oven with pie shell, 8 to 10 min.; cool.

Soften gelatine in lemon juice. In saucepan, mix gelatine with eggs, sugar, butter, and rind. Cook over low heat until mixture mounds slightly when dropped from spoon; cool. Fold half of whipped cream into filling. Spread 1/3 of filling in baked pie shell; top with a baked pastry round, half of remaining filling, second baked pastry round, rest of filling. Garnish with whipped cream and more lemon rind. Refrigerate at least 1 hr. Makes 1 9″ pie.

LEMON MERINGUE PIE

Baked 8″ or 9″ Pie
   Shell, pp. 584–587
1 cup granulated
   sugar
1/4 cup cornstarch
1/8 teasp. salt
1 1/4 cups warm water
Grated rind 1 lemon

1/4 cup lemon juice
3 egg yolks, slightly
   beaten
1 tablesp. butter or
   margarine
Pie Meringue (3 egg
   whites), right

In double boiler, combine sugar, cornstarch, salt. Slowly stir in water, then lemon rind and juice, egg yolks, butter. Cook, stirring, until smooth, and thick enough to mound when dropped from spoon. Remove from heat. Cool thoroughly. Start heating oven to 350°F. Spoon filling into cooled pie shell. Top with meringue. Bake 12 to 15 min.

To Freeze: See Lemon Meringue Pie, p. 706.
LEMON SNOW: Fold meringue into hot filling. Turn into shell. Refrigerate until set.
ORANGE MERINGUE: Reduce sugar to 3/4 cup, water to 1/2 cup, lemon juice to 1 tablesp. Substitute grated rind of 1 orange for lemon. Add 1 cup orange juice with water.
PINEAPPLE MERINGUE: Reduce sugar to 3/4 cup, lemon juice to 1 tablesp. Add 2/3 cup well-drained canned crushed pineapple to hot filling.
QUICK LEMON: For pie filling, use packaged lemon pudding and pie-filling mix, as label directs. To hot filling, add 1 tablesp. each butter or margarine and grated lemon rind. Complete as in Lemon Meringue Pie at left.

HURRY-UP LEMON MERINGUE PIE

Baked 8″ Pie Shell,
   pp. 584–587; or
Baked Crumb Crust,
   p. 594
1 1/3 cups canned
   sweetened con-
   densed milk

1 teasp. grated lemon
   rind
1/2 cup lemon juice
2 egg yolks
Pie Meringue (2 egg
   whites), below

Start heating oven to 350°F. Blend sweetened condensed milk with lemon rind, juice, and egg yolks until thickened. Pour into shell. Top with meringue. Bake 12 to 15 min.
HURRY-UP LIME: Substitute lime rind and juice for lemon.

PIE MERINGUE

	9″ PIE	8″ PIE
Egg whites	3	2
Salt	1/4 teasp.	Pinch
Vanilla extract	1/2 teasp.	1/4 teasp.
Granulated sugar	6 tablesp.	4 tablesp.

1. Have eggs at room temperature. (Whites beat to greater volume if somewhat warm.) Start heating oven to 350°F.
2. Place whites in medium bowl; add salt and vanilla; with electric mixer at high speed, or with hand beater, beat until frothy throughout (don't wait until whites begin to stiffen).
3. Add sugar, a little at a time, beating well after each addition. (Since sugar dissolves better, this method helps prevent beading.)
4. Continue beating until stiff peaks are formed. To test, slowly withdraw beater and hold up; meringue should form pointed peaks that are so stiff they stand upright and don't curl over.
5. With spoon, place mounds of meringue around top edge of filling; spread so it touches inner edge of crust *all around,* to prevent shrinking. Heap rest of meringue in center; push out to meet meringue border.
6. With back of spoon, pull up points on meringue, to make attractive top. Bake 12 to 15 min.*

**Or bake meringue at 425°F. about 4 min. if preferred.*

7. Cool on rack *away from drafts.* To cut meringue neatly when serving, first dip sharp knife into water; then shake off excess drops.

MOCHA ANGEL PIE

3 egg whites	sweet-chocolate
¼ teasp. cream of	pieces (2 cups)
tartar	1 tablesp. instant
Dash salt	coffee
¾ cup granulated	1 cup heavy cream,
sugar	whipped
1 12-oz. pkg. semi-	1 teasp. vanilla extract

Early in day or day before: Start heating oven to 275°F. Beat egg whites until quite stiff; gradually add cream of tartar, salt, and sugar, beating until stiff and satiny. Spread about two thirds of this meringue over bottom and sides of well-greased 8″ pie plate. Drop remaining meringue, in mounds, along rim of plate, pulling each mound up into points. Bake 1 hr., or until shell is light brown and crisp. Cool on wire rack, away from drafts.

In double boiler, over hot, *not boiling,* water, melt chocolate pieces. Combine instant coffee and ¼ cup boiling water; stir into melted chocolate. Cool 5 min., stirring now and then; fold into whipped cream with vanilla. Pour into meringue shell. Refrigerate. Makes 1 8″ pie.

REFRIGERATOR PIES

BAKED CRUMB CRUSTS

KIND OF CRUMBS	CUPS OF CRUMBS	GRANU-LATED SUGAR	BUTTER OR MAR-GARINE
Graham crackers* (16)	1⅓	¼ cup	¼ cup
Vanilla wafers (24 2″)	1⅓	none	¼ cup
Chocolate wafers (18 2¾″)	1⅓	none	3 tablesp.
Ginger-snaps (20 2″)	1⅓	none	6 tablesp.
Corn or wheat flakes (3 cups)	1⅓	2 tablesp.	¼ cup

Let butter soften. Place long piece of wax paper on pastry board; stack crackers, or pour cereal, along center. Wrap, making double fold in paper; tuck ends under. Roll fine with rolling pin. Or roll out in plastic bag.

In 2-cup measuring cup, with fork, mix 1⅓ cups crumbs, sugar, and soft butter until crumbly. Set aside 3 tablesp. mixture. With back of spoon, press rest to bottom and side of 9″ pie plate, forming small rim. Bake at 375°F. 8 min. Cool; fill as specific recipe directs; top with reserved crumbs.

NUT-CRUMB: Reduce crumbs to 1 cup; add ½ cup finely chopped walnuts, pecans, almonds, or Brazil nuts.

MARBLE-CRUMB: Reduce crumbs to 1 cup. Add 2 sq. grated unsweetened chocolate.

UNBAKED CRUMB CRUSTS

GRAHAM CRACKER:* Mix till crumbly 1⅓ cups graham-cracker crumbs, ⅓ cup brown sugar, ½ teasp. cinnamon, ⅓ cup melted butter or margarine. Set aside 3 tablesp. mixture. With back of spoon, press rest to bottom and side of well-greased 9″ pie plate; do not spread on rim. Chill well. Fill as recipe directs; top with reserved crumbs. Refrigerate.

PRETZEL: With rolling pin, crush enough pretzel sticks to make ¾ cup *coarse* crumbs. In 9″ pie plate, blend crumbs with ¼ cup soft butter or margarine and 3 tablesp. sugar. Press to bottom and side of plate; chill; then fill as recipe directs.

Finely rolled graham-cracker crumbs come in a 13¾-oz. pkg. — enough for 3 generous 9″ pies.

NUT CRUST

Mix 1 cup finely ground Brazil nuts, pecans, walnuts, blanched almonds, or peanuts with 2 tablesp. granulated sugar. With back of spoon, press to bottom, side of 8″ or 9″ pie plate; *do not spread on rim.* Bake at 400°F. about 8 min. Cool. Fill as recipe directs.

TOASTED NUT CRUST

Butter 9″ pie plate; line bottom with circle of wax paper; butter it. Use medium blade of food grinder to grind 1½ cups Brazil nuts, walnuts, or pecans. Mix nuts well with ¼ cup granulated sugar and $\frac{1}{8}$ teasp. salt, then with 1 egg white, beaten until it forms soft peaks. Press firmly to bottom and side (not rim) of pie plate. Bake at 375°F. 12 to 15 min., or till light brown. With small spatula, carefully loosen around sides; let stand 10 min. Lift crust to slip out paper; let cool. Fill.

COCONUT CRUSTS

TOASTED COCONUT CRUST: Spread 2 tablesp. soft butter or margarine evenly in 8″ or 9″ pie plate. Pat $1\frac{1}{2}$ cups flaked coconut evenly into butter. Bake at 300°F. 15 to 20 min., or until golden. Cool.

BUTTERY TOASTED COCONUT CRUST: In bowl, toss $2\frac{1}{2}$ cups flaked coconut with 7 tablesp. melted butter or margarine, till well blended. In layer-cake pan, spread $\frac{1}{3}$ cup coconut mixture. With fork, cover bottom and side, including rim, of 9″ pie plate, with remaining coconut; press into place. Bake both at 300°F. until light golden — about 20 min. Use extra toasted coconut to garnish pie.

CHOCOLATE-COCONUT CRUST: Grease 8″ or 9″ pie plate. In double boiler, melt 2 sq. unsweetened chocolate with 2 tablesp. butter or margarine; stir until blended. Combine 2 tablesp. hot milk or water and $\frac{2}{3}$ cup sifted confectioners' sugar; stir into chocolate mixture. Add $1\frac{1}{2}$ cups snipped flaked coconut; mix well. Press to bottom and side of pie plate. Refrigerate 1 hr.

QUICK TOASTED-COCONUT CRUST: Combine 1 pkg. moist toasted coconut (about 2 cups) with $\frac{1}{4}$ cup melted butter or margarine. Press evenly over bottom and side of 8″ or 9″ pie plate. Refrigerate until firm — about 1 hr.

UNBAKED COCONUT CRUST: Combine $1\frac{1}{2}$ cups packaged fine grated coconut with $\frac{1}{2}$ cup confectioners' sugar. Gradually stir in 3 tablesp. melted butter. Evenly press over bottom and side of oiled 8″ or 9″ pie plate. Refrigerate until firm.

MERINGUE CRUST

1 cup granulated sugar	$\frac{1}{4}$ teasp. cream of tartar
	4 egg whites

Start heating oven to 275°F. Sift sugar with cream of tartar. With electric mixer or hand beater, beat egg whites until stiff but not dry.

Slowly add sugar mixture, beating until meringue makes stiff, glossy peaks. Spread over bottom and up side, just to rim, of *well-greased* 9″ pie plate, making bottom $\frac{1}{4}$″ thick, side 1″ thick. Bake about 1 hr., or until light brown and crisp to touch. Cool away from drafts (don't worry if meringue cracks and falls in center — it's supposed to behave that way).

BUDGET MERINGUE CRUST: Halve ingredients; bake in 8″ or 9″ pie plate.

CAFE-AU-LAIT PIE

Add 1 teasp. instant coffee to Budget Meringue Crust, above, baking it in 8″ or 9″ pie plate. Fill cooled shell with 1 qt. vanilla ice cream. Top with thawed frozen or canned cling-peach slices and flaked coconut.

TOASTED COCONUT PIE

Make one of Toasted Coconut Crusts, left; fill with ice cream or fruit; top as in Sundae Pies, p. 614. Serve at once.

Or fill with filling for any of the following pies, then refrigerate until set.

1. CHIFFON PIES: Lemon, Orange, or Lime Swirl, pp. 597–598.

2. BAVARIAN PIES: Chocolate Flake, Frosted Coffee, Strawberry, or Coconut, p. 600.

3. CREAM PIES: Satin Smooth, Banana, Chocolate, p. 596, or Butterscotch, below.

BUTTERSCOTCH CREAM PIE

Baked 9″ Pie Shell, pp. 584–587	3 egg yolks
$\frac{3}{4}$ cup light-brown sugar, packed	3 tablesp. butter or margarine
$\frac{1}{3}$ cup all-purpose flour	1 teasp. vanilla extract
$\frac{1}{4}$ teasp. salt	Pie Meringue* (3 egg whites), p. 593
2 cups milk	

In double boiler, combine $\frac{1}{2}$ cup brown sugar, flour, salt. Gradually stir in milk. Cook, stirring, until thickened. Cook, covered, stirring occasionally, 10 min. longer. Beat egg yolks with $\frac{1}{4}$ cup brown sugar; stir in a little sauce; add to rest of sauce in double boiler. Cook, stirring, 2 min., or until mixture mounds when dropped *Or omit meringue. Top with $\frac{1}{2}$ cup heavy cream, whipped; sprinkle with shaved chocolate.*

from spoon. Add butter, vanilla; cool. Start heating oven to 350°F. Turn filling into shell. Cover with meringue. Bake 12 to 15 min. Refrigerate pie till serving time. Makes 1 9″ pie.

BUTTERSCOTCH-DATE: With vanilla, add ½ cup sliced, pitted dates. Omit meringue. Just befor serving, top with whipped cream.

CHOCOLATE CREAM: Substitute ½ cup granulated sugar for light-brown sugar. Make as above, combining ¼ cup sugar and 2 to 2½ sq. unsweetened chocolate, cut up, with flour and salt. When chocolate is melted, beat with hand beater until smooth. Beat egg yolks with ¼ cup sugar.

SATIN-SMOOTH CREAM PIE

Baked 9″ Pie Shell, pp. 584–587; or Baked Crumb Crust, p. 594	2 tablesp. butter or margarine
1 pkg. vanilla pudding and pie-filling mix	¼ teasp. vanilla, lemon, rum, or almond extract
2 cups milk	½ cup heavy cream, whipped

Prepare pudding as label directs, using the 2 cups milk; add butter, extract. Cover surface of pudding with wax paper. Refrigerate till cold.* Then, with spoon, beat till smooth. Turn into pie shell, refrigerate.

To serve: Top with whipped cream. Garnish with grated chocolate or orange rind, chopped nuts, banana slices dipped into citrus-fruit juice, toasted coconut, crushed peanut brittle, or chopped chocolate mints. Makes 1 9″ pie.

NOTE: You may reduce milk to 1½ cups; fold whipped cream into beaten cold filling.

**If time is short, omit wax paper and chilling. Cool filling 5 min.; then pour into shell.*

DE LUXE TOPPED: Add 1½ teasp. instant coffee or cocoa to cream while it is being whipped.

MERINGUE TOPPED: Omit whipped cream. Add 2 egg yolks to milk. Top with Pie Meringue (2 egg whites), p. 593, sprinkling meringue with flaked coconut or nuts before baking it. Or spread filling with 1 cup sieved, stewed apricots before topping with meringue.

BANANA: Arrange ½″ layer of banana slices in shell just before filling. Circle whipped cream with banana slices dipped into citrus-fruit juice, then, if desired, with toasted coconut.

COCONUT: Fold ½ cup flaked or grated fresh coconut into hot filling. Sprinkle whipped cream, or Pie Meringue, p. 593, before baking, with ¼ cup coconut. Or garnish pie with any canned, fresh, or frozen fruit. Packaged coconut-cream pudding and pie-filling mix makes delicious pie, too.

BLUEBERRY: In saucepan, place 1 scant cup blueberries; add 1 tablesp. cornstarch combined with 2 tablesp. granulated sugar, 1 tablesp. each grated lemon rind and juice. Cook over low heat, mashing and stirring, until mixture thickens and is clear. Add 1 cup blueberries; cool slightly; carefully spoon over cool cream filling in pie shell. Refrigerate until served.

PINEAPPLE TOPPED: Combine 1 cup drained canned crushed pineapple with 2 tablesp. juice from pineapple, 1½ teasp. cornstarch, 1 tablesp. granulated sugar, 1½ teasp. grated lemon rind, and 1½ teasp. lemon juice. Cook over low heat, stirring, until thickened and clear; cool slightly. Spoon over cold filling in pie shell. Refrigerate until serving time.

CRANBERRY TOPPED: Combine 1 cup canned whole-cranberry sauce with 1½ teasp. cornstarch, 1 tablesp. granulated sugar, 1½ teasp. grated lemon rind, and 1½ teasp. lemon juice. Cook over low heat, stirring, until thick and clear; cool slightly. Spoon over cold filling in pie shell. Refrigerate until serving time.

Warning: It is most important that cream, custard, and whipped-cream pies be stored promptly in the refrigerator before and after serving to avoid any possibility of food poisoning.

CHOFFEE PIE

Baked Crumb Crust of Chocolate wafers, p. 594	1 pkg. instant vanilla pudding
1 pkg. instant chocolate pudding	1½ cups milk
	1 pt. soft coffee ice cream

In large bowl, with electric mixer at medium speed, beat chocolate and vanilla puddings with milk until smooth and thickened — about 2 min. Add coffee ice cream and continue beating until blended.

Pour into the crust. Refrigerate at least 4 hr. before serving. Makes 1 9″ pie.

P.S. Any leftover pie should be refrigerated; it's nice the next day.

PEACH OF A PIE

Baked 9″ Pie Shell, pp. 584–587
1 8-oz. pkg. soft cream cheese
3 tablesp. sugar
¼ teasp. salt
1 tablesp. milk
½ teasp. vanilla extract
¾ cup granulated sugar
2 tablesp. cornstarch
1½ cups strawberries, hulled, crushed
2 tablesp. lemon juice
1½ cups strawberries, hulled, halved
1 1-lb.-13-oz. can cling-peach halves, very well drained

1. In medium bowl, thoroughly blend cream cheese with 3 tablesp. sugar, salt, milk, and vanilla extract. Using back of teaspoon, carefully spread this cheese mixture over bottom and side of pie shell, bringing it well up on the side.
2. In saucepan, blend ¾ cup sugar and cornstarch; add crushed berries, lemon juice; cook over medium heat, stirring constantly, until clear and thickened; cool, stirring occasionally. Carefully stir in halved strawberries.
3. Into cheese-lined pie shell, spoon about half of strawberry mixture. Then, on strawberry mixture, carefully arrange peach halves, with rounded side down and tilted slightly. Over and around peaches, spoon remaining strawberry mixture. Refrigerate until serving time. Makes 1 9″ pie.

FRENCH STRAWBERRY PIE

Baked 9″ Pie Shell, pp. 584–587
3 3-oz. pkg. soft cream cheese
3 cups fresh strawberries or peach slices
¾ cup currant or apple jelly

Mash cream cheese; beat smooth. Use to line baked pie shell. Fill with berries; gently press onto cheese. Melt jelly over low heat; stir smooth; cool; spoon over berries. Refrigerate ½ hr. Makes 1 9″ pie.

STRAWBERRY TRIUMPH PIE

Baked 9″ Pie Shell, pp. 584–587; or Baked Crumb Crust, p. 594
1 qt. hulled strawberries
3 tablesp. cornstarch
1 cup granulated sugar
2 tablesp. lemon juice
½ cup heavy cream, whipped

With fork or pastry blender, crush half of strawberries; stir in cornstarch, sugar, lemon juice. Cook over medium heat, stirring, until clear and thickened; cool. Cut rest of berries in halves; fold into cooled mixture. Turn into crust. Refrigerate until well chilled. Serve, garnished with whipped cream. Makes 1 9″ pie.

CHERRY-JUBILEE PIE

Baked 9″ Pie Shell, pp. 584–587
1 1-lb.-13-oz. can Bing cherries, pitted
1 3-oz. pkg. cherry-flavor gelatin
½ cup sherry wine
1 cup heavy cream
⅓ cup canned slivered, toasted almonds

Early in day: Drain cherries, saving juice. To juice, add enough water to make 1¾ cups liquid; heat. Add gelatin; stir until dissolved. Add sherry; refrigerate until as thick and syrupy as unbeaten egg white. Fold in drained cherries, ½ cup cream, whipped, and almonds. Refrigerate until stiff enough to hold its shape. Turn into baked pie shell. Refrigerate.
To serve: Garnish with remaining ½ cup cream, whipped, plus a few almonds if desired. Makes 1 9″ pie.

LEMON CHIFFON PIE

Baked 9″ Pie Shell, pp. 584–587; Baked Crumb Crust, p. 594, or Unbaked Crumb Crust, p. 594
1½ teasp. unflavored gelatine
⅓ cup granulated sugar
4 egg yolks
1 tablesp. grated lemon rind
¼ cup lemon juice
⅓ cup cold water
4 egg whites
¼ teasp. salt
½ cup granulated sugar
½ cup heavy cream, whipped

Combine gelatine, ⅓ cup sugar. In double-boiler top, beat egg yolks; stir in lemon rind and juice, water, then gelatine mixture. Cook over boiling water, stirring, 5 min., or till thickened; *remove from heat.* Beat egg whites with salt till fairly stiff; gradually add ½ cup sugar, beating until stiff; fold in lemon mixture. Turn into shell; refrigerate until set.

Serve, spread with whipped cream or dessert topping. Garnish with blueberries, sliced strawberries or bananas. Makes 1 9″ pie.

ORANGE: Reduce lemon juice to 1 tablesp.; to juice, add ¼ cup thawed frozen orange-juice concentrate. Reduce the ½ cup sugar, beaten with whites, to ⅓ cup.

LIME-SWIRL PIE: Omit the ⅓ cup sugar. Substitute 1 teasp. grated lime rind for lemon rind, lime juice for lemon juice. Swirl whipped cream through filling in shell. Top with ½ teasp. grated lime rind.

SILVER CREAM PIE: Spoon whipped cream in circle on top of pie; sprinkle with silver *dragées.*

PEACH GLACE PIE

Baked 9″ Pie Shell, pp. 584–587	¼ cup sherry
1½ teasp. unflavored gelatine	Pinch salt
2 tablesp. cold water	1 1-lb.-13-oz. can cling- peach halves, well drained
1 cup apricot pre- serves	½ cup heavy cream, whipped

Sprinkle gelatine over cold water to soften. Bring preserves to boil; stir in gelatine until dissolved; then add sherry, salt. Cool mixture until it begins to thicken. Place peach halves in pie shell, with cut sides down; pour on cooled mixture. Refrigerate till set.

Serve, garnished with whipped cream, dessert topping, vanilla ice cream, or small bunches of seedless grapes. Makes 1 9″ pie.

PEACH MERINGUE PIE

Unbaked 9″ Pie Shell, pp. 584–587	1½ to 2 tablesp. quick-cooking tapioca
1 teasp. grated lemon rind	4 cups sliced, peeled peaches
1 tablesp. lemon juice	1 tablesp. butter or margarine
⅔ cup granulated sugar	Pie Meringue (3 egg whites), p. 593
⅛ teasp. salt	
⅛ teasp. cinnamon	

Start heating oven to 425°F. Combine lemon rind and juice, sugar, salt, cinnamon, and tapioca. Place half of peaches in pastry-lined 9″ pie plate; sprinkle with half of sugar mixture. Top with rest of peaches; sprinkle with rest of sugar mixture. Dot butter over peaches. Bake 35 min., or till peaches are tender. Remove pie from oven; decrease oven temperature to 400°F. Make Pie Meringue; pile it on peaches. Bake 10 to 12 min. Remove from oven; cool on wire rack, *away from drafts;* then refrigerate. Makes 1 9″ pie.

APRICOT CHIFFON PIE

Buttery Toasted Coconut Crust, p. 595	2 env. unflavored gelatine
1 1-lb.-14-oz. can whole unpeeled apricots	1 12-oz. can apricot nectar
	¼ cup lemon juice
	3 egg whites, un- beaten

Early on the day:
1. Drain juice from whole apricots, reserving it. Cut apricots in half; refrigerate.
2. Onto ½ cup apricot juice, in 2-qt. bowl, sprinkle gelatine. Heat apricot nectar to boiling; add to gelatine mixture, stirring until gelatine is completely dissolved. Then stir in remaining apricot juice and lemon juice; refrigerate until stiff enough to mound when dropped from spoon — about 1 hr. 30 min. — stirring occasionally after first hour.
3. Now add unbeaten egg whites. Then, with mixer at high speed, beat till light, fluffy, and a delicate apricot color. Refrigerate till stiff enough to hold shape.
4. Now, with rubber spatula or spoon, fold syrup, if any, at bottom of bowl of apricots into apricot mixture until just blended. Then spoon into coconut crust. Refrigerate 30 min., then, on top, arrange 12 apricot halves in pairs; refrigerate till served — at least 3½ hr. *Just before serving:* Garnish pie with small mounds of toasted coconut. Pass rest of apricot halves, if desired. Makes 1 8″ pie.

CHOCOLATE-MOUSSE PIE

Baked 9″ Pie Shell, pp. 584–587; or Baked Crumb Crust of Chocolate wafers, p. 594	1 egg
	2 egg yolks
	1 teasp. rum
	2 egg whites
1 6-oz. pkg. semi- sweet-chocolate pieces (1 cup)	1¼ cups heavy cream
	½ sq. unsweetened chocolate

Melt semisweet-chocolate pieces over hot, *not boiling,* water. Remove from water. Beat in whole egg and yolks, one at a time; add rum. Beat whites till they form peaks when beater is raised; fold in 1 cup cream, whipped, and egg yolk mixture. Spoon into shell. Refrigerate until well chilled.

Hot Coconut Soufflé, p. 581

Serve, topped with ¼ cup cream, whipped; shave on unsweetened chocolate. Makes 1 9″ pie.

MARVEL: Substitute Meringue Crust, p. 595, for the shell. Halve all filling ingredients except the 1 egg. Refrigerate 12 to 24 hr. before serving.

FROSTED-DAIQUIRI PIE

Baked 9″ Pie Shell, pp. 584–587	½ cup lime juice
1 env. unflavored gelatine	1 teasp. grated lime or lemon rind
1 cup granulated sugar	Green food color
½ teasp. salt	⅓ cup light rum
3 egg yolks	3 egg whites
¼ cup cold water	Whipped cream
	Red cellophane straws

1. In double-boiler top, combine gelatine with ⅔ cup sugar and salt; add egg yolks, water, lime juice; with hand beater, beat until blended. Cook over boiling water (or in saucepan over low heat), stirring until mixture coats spoon. Remove from heat; add rind; then tint pale green with food color.

2. Cool mixture; stir in rum; then refrigerate until slightly thicker than unbeaten egg white. In large bowl, beat egg whites until they form moist peaks when beater is raised; then add ⅓ cup sugar, 1 tablesp. at a time, beating until stiff. Fold in gelatine mixture.

3. Turn mixture into pie shell; refrigerate several hours. Top with whipped cream, sweetened if desired; decorate with short pieces of cellophane straws. Makes 1 9″ pie.

LIME-SNOW PIE

Baked 9″ Pie Shell, pp. 584–587	¼ cup granulated sugar
¾ cup granulated sugar	3 tablesp. grated lime rind
7 tablesp. flour	6 tablesp. lime juice
2 tablesp. cornstarch	3 egg whites
½ teasp. salt	¼ teasp. salt
2¼ cups boiling water	6 tablesp. granulated sugar
3 egg yolks	

Early in day: In double-boiler top, combine ¾ cup sugar with flour, cornstarch, and ½ teasp. salt. Slowly stir in boiling water. Cook over boiling water until smooth and *thick*. Beat yolks with ¼ cup sugar; slowly stir in hot mixture, blending well. Return to double boiler; cook

over boiling water, stirring occasionally, 5 min. Add lime rind and juice. Remove from heat at once; cool. Beat egg whites with ¼ teasp. salt until frothy; gradually add 6 tablesp. sugar, a little at a time, beating well after each addition. Continue beating until stiff peaks are formed. Fold this meringue into cooled lime mixture. Turn into baked pie shell. Refrigerate at least 5 hr. before serving. If desired, garnish with few raspberries. Makes 1 9″ pie.

PINEAPPLE-SNOW PIE: Reduce ¾ cup sugar to ⅔ cup. Substitute lemon rind for lime rind, 2 tablesp. lemon juice for lime juice. When folding in meringue, also fold in ⅔ cup well-drained canned crushed pineapple.

PUMPKIN OR SQUASH CHIFFON PIE

Baked 9″ Pie Shell, pp. 584–587	2 egg yolks, slightly beaten
1 env. unflavored gelatine	1 cup undiluted evaporated milk
¾ cup dark-brown sugar, packed	½ cup cold water
½ teasp. salt	1¼ cups mashed cooked or canned squash or pumpkin or thawed frozen squash
½ teasp. nutmeg	
½ teasp. cinnamon	
¼ teasp. ginger	
	2 egg whites

Day before:
1. Combine gelatine, ½ cup brown sugar, salt, and spices.
2. In double-boiler top, mix egg yolks with milk, water, squash, and gelatine mixture. Cook over boiling water, stirring, 10 min.
3. Refrigerate, stirring occasionally, until as thick as unbeaten egg white.
4. Beat egg whites until soft peaks form when beater is raised; gradually add ¼ cup brown sugar, beating until very stiff; fold in squash mixture. Turn into shell. Refrigerate until serving time.
5. Serve, topped with whipped cream, if desired. Makes 1 9″ pie.

ORANGE VELVET PIE

Baked 9″ Pie Shell, pp. 584–587	cheese
1 3-oz. pkg. orange-flavor gelatin	¼ cup granulated sugar
1 cup hot water	¼ cup orange juice
1 8-oz. pkg. cream	1 teasp. lemon juice
	1 cup heavy cream

1. Dissolve orange gelatin in hot water.

Wonderful Fudge Pie, p. 601

2. With electric mixer, beat cream cheese until smooth; beat in sugar, orange and lemon juices; then gradually beat in gelatin mixture. Refrigerate until almost set.

3. With electric mixer, whip cream; quickly beat into gelatin mixture; turn into baked pie shell. Refrigerate until set. Makes 1 9″ pie.

CRANBERRY-FLUFF PIE

Baked 9″ Pie Shell, pp. 584–587	⅛ teasp. salt
1 env. unflavored gelatine	1 tablesp. lemon juice
	1 teasp. almond extract
¼ cup cold water	1 cup heavy cream
½ cup granulated sugar	½ large can whole-cranberry sauce
⅓ cup cold water	1½ teasp. cornstarch
2 egg whites	

Early in day: Sprinkle gelatine on ¼ cup cold water to soften. Boil sugar and ⅓ cup water till mixture forms soft ball (235°F. on candy thermometer); stir in gelatine until dissolved. Beat egg whites till quite stiff, then slowly pour syrup over them, beating. After all syrup is added, beat 1 min. longer; then add salt, lemon juice, almond extract. Whip cream; fold into gelatine mixture; turn into baked pie shell. Refrigerate until set. In saucepan, combine cranberry sauce, cornstarch; heat till thickened; cool; spread on pie, in star shape. Refrigerate thoroughly before serving. (You may thicken 1 can cranberry sauce with 1 tablesp. cornstarch and spread over entire pie top.) Makes 1 9″ pie.

CHOCOLATE-FLAKE BAVARIAN PIE

Baked Crumb Crust, p. 594; Nut Crust, p. 594; or Baked 9″ Pie Shell, pp. 584–587	3 egg yolks
	1¼ cups milk
	1 teasp. vanilla extract
	3 egg whites
1 env. unflavored gelatine	½ to 1 cup heavy cream, whipped
½ cup granulated sugar	¼ teasp. nutmeg
⅛ teasp. salt	½ sq. unsweetened chocolate

Combine gelatine, ¼ cup sugar, salt. In double-boiler top, beat egg yolks; stir in milk, gelatine mixture. Cook over hot, *not boiling*, water, stirring, until custard coats spoon. Stir in vanilla. Refrigerate, stirring occasionally, until mixture mounds when dropped from spoon. Beat until *just* smooth.

Beat egg whites till fairly stiff; gradually add ¼ cup sugar, beating until stiff; fold in custard, whipped cream. Turn into shell; sprinkle with nutmeg. Refrigerate until set. Serve with shaved chocolate on top. Makes 1 9″ pie.

NOTE: If preferred, use whipped cream as topping rather than folded into filling.

FROSTED COFFEE BAVARIAN PIE: Add 2 tablesp. instant coffee to egg whites before beating. Omit whipped cream and shaved chocolate. Melt ¾ cup semisweet-chocolate pieces over hot, *not boiling*, water; stir in ¼ cup water; drizzle on top of pie.

To vary: With egg whites, fold in ½ cup sliced, pitted dates and ¼ cup chopped pecans. Omit semisweet-chocolate topping; sprinkle with cocoa.

STRAWBERRY BAVARIAN PIE: Fold 1 cup sliced strawberries into filling. Garnish with berries instead of shaved chocolate.

NESSELRODE PIE: Substitute 2 tablesp. rum for vanilla. With whipped cream, fold in ¼ cup diced, mixed preserved fruits.

EGGNOG PIE: Omit chocolate. For vanilla, substitute brandy or rum to taste. Increase nutmeg to 1 teasp. Especially nice in Unbaked Pretzel-Crumb Crust, p. 594.

COCONUT BAVARIAN PIE: Omit nutmeg. With whipped cream, fold in ½ cup flaked coconut. Try, too, with grated fresh coconut, adding ¼ teasp. almond extract with vanilla.

CRANBERRY BAVARIAN PIE: Substitute almond extract for vanilla. Use ½ cup heavy cream. Omit nutmeg and chocolate. Heat 1 can whole-cranberry sauce with 1 tablesp. cornstarch till clear and thickened; cool; spread on pie when filling is set.

BLACK-BOTTOM PIE: Make Gingersnap Crust, p. 594. Then make filling, left, stirring in 2¼ teasp. cornstarch with egg yolks. When gelatine has melted in custard, stir 1½ sq. melted unsweetened chocolate and vanilla into half of it. Beat smooth; cool till it just mounds; pour into crust; refrigerate.

While other half of custard chills till it just begins to set, beat egg whites with sugar, as directed; fold into chilled custard with 1 tablesp. white rum; pour in, over chocolate filling, as much as shell will hold. Refrigerate a few minutes; pour rest on top. Omit nutmeg; refrigerate till set. Top with whipped cream. Shave ½ sq. unsweetened chocolate on top.

STRAWBERRY-GLAZED BAVARIAN PIE: In saucepan, mix ¼ cup granulated sugar with 1 tablesp. plus 1 teasp. cornstarch. Drain juice from 1 10-oz. pkg. frozen sliced strawberries, thawed (about ⅔ cup); reserve berries. Slowly stir juice into cornstarch until smooth. Cook, stirring occasionally, until thickened. Cool. Stir in berries. Spoon over cooled pie.

BANANA BAVARIAN PIE: Before pouring filling into shell, line shell with sliced bananas.

CHOCOLATE-COCONUT BAVARIAN PIE: Make Chocolate-Coconut Crust, p. 595. For filling, make coconut variation, p. 600. To serve, garnish with ½ cup flaked coconut, combined with ½ sq. unsweetened chocolate, grated.

HOLIDAY BAVARIAN PIE: Use 9″ baked pie shell. Substitute 2 tablesp. rum for vanilla. Increase nutmeg to 1 teasp. Just before serving, top pie with whipped cream. Drizzle grenadine syrup or melted currant jelly over cream. Omit shaved chocolate.

WONDERFUL FUDGE PIE

½ pt. vanilla ice cream	½ teasp. instant-coffee powder
Half recipe Chocolate Chews, p. 663	1 tablesp. canned chocolate syrup

Make early on day or 1½ hr. ahead:
1. Pack vanilla ice cream in custard cup; freeze. Start heating oven to 325°F.
2. Make half recipe for Chocolate Chews mixture. Pour into greased 6″ glass pie plate; bake 30 min. Cool. Mix instant-coffee powder with canned chocolate syrup.
At serving time: Dip custard cup of ice cream in hot water a few seconds; then, with small spatula, loosen ice cream from sides of cup and invert on Fudge Pie. (Or if desired, spoon ice cream directly from container onto pie.) Pour chocolate syrup over top. Makes 2 or 3 servings.
For a party of 8: Make as above, using three times amounts of ingredients listed; bake pie in a greased 9″ pie plate. Pack ice cream in a small bowl.

FIX 'N' SERVE FROZEN PIES

There are a number of delicious frozen dessert pies — fruit and cream — which you can buy and keep on hand in your freezer — some large, others individual. Follow label directions closely for preparing and serving them.

TARTS AND TURNOVERS

PRETTY TART SHELLS

Make Flaky Pastry I, II, or III for Two-Crust Pie, pp. 584–586, or use packaged piecrust mix, p. 587. Roll out; then shape as below. Prick well. Refrigerate ½ hr. Bake (set on cookie sheet if desired), at 450°F. 10 to 15 min., or until golden brown. Cool; carefully lift from pan.

PETAL: For each petal tart shell, cut 6 2¼″ pastry rounds. Place 1 round in bottom of each custard cup, or 2¾″ muffin cup. Wet edge of round; press 5 rounds to side and bottom of cup, overlapping rounds slightly.

BIG FLOWERET: Cut 5″ pastry squares. Snugly fit 1 square inside each 3″ muffin cup, letting corners stand upright.

LITTLE FLOWERET: Make Big Floweret, using a 4″ pastry square in each 3″ muffin cup.

PLEATED: Invert muffin pan. With piece of cord, measure one of cups — up one side, across bottom, down other side; cut cord to this length. Cut desired number of pastry rounds, using a saucer or small pie plate, with diameter equal to length of cord, as guide. Fit pastry round over outside of 1 inverted muffin cup, pinching it into pleats to fit snugly. Repeat on alternate cups.

QUICK FRUIT TARTS

Just before serving, fill baked Pretty Tart Shells, above, with:
Sliced berries or peaches — fresh, frozen, or canned
Sliced or cut-up oranges, or sliced bananas, dipped into citrus-fruit juice
Pineapple chunks — canned or frozen
Applesauce or apple butter
Fruit cocktail — canned, as is, or tossed with fresh fruit
Grapes, or grapes with cut-up oranges
Apricots or prunes — canned or stewed dried

Then top them with:

Sweetened whipped cream or dessert topping (flavored, if desired, with grated orange rind, vanilla or almond extract, sherry, brandy, or rum).

Vanilla ice cream, with chopped nuts, cinnamon, flaked chocolate, or flaked coconut.

Commercial sour cream, whipped cream cheese or cottage cheese, sprinkled, if desired, with cinnamon sugar.

Or about 1 hr. before serving, glaze fruit tarts with one of these; then refrigerate.

1. Heat ¼ to ½ cup currant or apple jelly with 1 tablesp. water till melted. Spoon over fruit. Glazes 8 to 10 tarts.

2. Blend 1 tablesp. cornstarch with 1 tablesp. water. Stir into ⅔ cup juice from canned or cooked fruit. Boil till clear; add 1 teasp. lemon juice. Glazes 8 to 10 tarts.

SCRUMPTIOUS FILLED TARTS

Several hr. ahead: Fill baked Pretty Tart Shells, p. 601, with any one of these pie fillings:

Pumpkin Chiffon Pie, p. 599.
Lemon or Orange Chiffon Pie, p. 597.
Chocolate-Flake, Strawberry, Frosted Coffee, or Coconut Bavarian Pie, p. 600.
Lemon, Orange, or Pineapple Meringue Pie, p. 593.

GAY CHESS TARTS

10 baked Petal Tart Shells, p. 601	¼ cup lemon juice
2 eggs	1 cup dark or light raisins
½ cup butter or margarine	1 teasp. vanilla extract
Pinch salt	½ cup coarsely chopped walnuts
1 cup granulated sugar	½ cup heavy cream, whipped

In saucepan, beat eggs with fork; stir in butter, salt, sugar, lemon juice, and raisins. Bring to full boil over low heat, stirring constantly. Refrigerate.

At serving time: Into raisin mixture, stir vanilla and nuts. Spoon into tart shells. Top with whipped cream. Makes about 10 tarts.

GAY TOUCHES: Make these tarts look like sundaes: Top whipped cream with different garnishes — whole or chopped walnuts, bits of citron and preserved orange rind, thin slices of dates, candied or maraschino cherries (whole, sliced, or chopped).

RASPBERRY-CREAM TARTS

6 3½" baked Pretty Tart Shells, p. 601	1 10-oz. pkg. frozen raspberries, unthawed
1 3-oz. pkg. raspberry-flavor gelatin	1 pt. vanilla ice cream
1 cup boiling water	

Dissolve gelatin in boiling water. Stir in raspberries and ice cream. Refrigerate till mixture mounds; spoon into shells. Refrigerate till set.

Serve with vanilla ice cream on top, if desired. Makes 6.

SHERRY-PRUNE TARTS

6 to 8 baked Big Floweret Tart Shells, p. 601	3 lemon slices
	¾ cup sherry
	1 tablesp. cornstarch
2 cups large dried prunes	1 tablesp. water
	½ cup heavy cream

Cook prunes with lemon as label directs; drain. Boil down prune liquid to ¾ cup; add sherry; pour over prunes; refrigerate 4 hr. Drain liquid into saucepan; stir in cornstarch mixed with water. Cook, stirring, until thick and clear. Add pitted prunes. Refrigerate till well chilled. Spoon into tart shells; top with whipped cream. Serve at once. Makes 6 to 8.

PECAN TARTS

8 or 9 unbaked Petal Tart Shells, p. 601	2 eggs, slightly beaten
¼ cup butter or margarine	½ teasp. vanilla extract
¼ cup granulated sugar	Dash salt
⅓ cup white corn syrup	1 cup whole pecan meats
2 tablesp. maple or dark corn syrup	½ cup heavy cream, whipped (optional)

Start heating oven to 325°F. Cream butter; gradually add sugar, while mixing until creamy. Slowly stir in corn and maple syrups. Add eggs, vanilla, salt; stir to blend. Spoon into unbaked tart shells. Sprinkle nuts on top, pushing them down so filling covers them slightly. Bake 45 min., or until pastry is golden and knife inserted in center comes out clean. Let tarts cool in pan. Then run spatula between pastry and pan and remove tarts right side up. Serve topped with a dot of whipped cream or dessert topping. Makes 8 or 9.

SHORTCAKE TARTS

Make any Flaky Pastry, pp. 584–587; or use packaged piecrust mix. Cut into 3½″ pastry rounds; with 1½″ biscuit cutter, remove center from half of rounds. Arrange on ungreased cookie sheet. Bake at 450°F. 10 to 15 min. Cool. For each tart, put 2 rounds (1 solid and 1 cutout) together, with filling of apple butter, sweetened peaches, berries. Or use filling for Lemon Meringue Pie, p. 593, Satin-Smooth Cream Pie, p. 596, or Strawberry Triumph Pie, p. 597. Top with whipped cream, dessert topping, or whipped cream cheese.

QUICKIE FRENCH TARTS: Use 3½″ pastry rounds; bake as above. Spread baked rounds with soft cream cheese. Pile favorite fruits on cheese. Glaze with currant jelly, or apricot preserves, heated with a little water.

DELECTABLE TURNOVERS

Make Flaky Pastry I or II for Two-Crust Pie, pp. 584–585; or use packaged piecrust mix. Roll pastry ⅛″ thick. Cut into 4″ squares or 4½″ rounds.

Place 1 tablesp. of any filling, below, in corner of each square (or on half of each round). Moisten pastry edges with water; fold from corner to opposite corner so edges come together. Firmly seal edges with floured fork. Slit top; or prick with skewer. Glaze, as on p. 587. Bake at 450°F. 15 min., or until golden. Serve with cheese cubes. Makes about 12.

FILLINGS:

1. Mix 1 cup finely chopped pitted dates, or cooked dried prunes, with ¼ cup chopped walnuts and ¼ cup orange juice.
2. Use orange marmalade mixed with chopped nuts.
3. Mix apple butter or applesauce with chopped nuts or raisins.
4. Use strawberry, raspberry, peach, cherry, or apricot jam.
5. Mix ½ cup each cooked dried pitted prunes

and apricots with ¼ cup granulated sugar, 1 tablesp. cornstarch, ¼ teasp. salt, and 1 tablesp. lemon juice.
6. Use prepared mincemeat, plain or mixed with chopped apple.

AUSTRIAN ALMOND-CHEESE PASTRY CRESCENTS

1 cup sifted all-purpose flour	1 tablesp. grated lemon rind
⅛ teasp. salt	1 tablesp. lemon juice
½ cup butter or margarine	½ teasp. almond extract
½ 8-oz. pkg. cream cheese, in small pieces	1 cup ground, blanched almonds
2 egg whites	1 egg
¼ cup granulated sugar	Sugar

Day before, if desired: Into bowl sift flour, salt. With pastry blender or two knives, scissor-fashion, cut in butter and cheese till they are all well blended. Shape this cheese pastry into ball; wrap in wax paper, saran, or foil; refrigerate till well chilled.

Early on the day or 2 hr. ahead: Start heating oven to 400°F. In bowl, with electric mixer at high speed, beat egg whites till stiff; then beat in sugar, lemon rind and juice, extract; fold in almonds.

On floured surface, roll out one third of cheese pastry ⅛″ thick. Cut into 10″ circle; cut circle into 8 wedges; remove trimmings. In center of wide end of each wedge, place rounded teaspoonful of almond mixture. Starting at wide edge, lightly roll up each wedge; place, center point down, on lightly greased cookie sheet; curve ends into crescent. Repeat with remainder. Brush with beaten egg; sprinkle with sugar. Bake 10 to 12 min.; cool. Makes about 2 doz.

APRICOT-CHEESE PASTRY HEARTS: Cut pastry with 3¼″ x 2½″ heart-shaped cookie cutter. Remove trimmings; reroll and cut out once or twice again. In center of each of half of cutout pastry hearts, place one teaspoonful of apricot preserves. Brush edges with beaten egg; cover each with another cutout heart. Then, with fork, press edges together. Brush with egg and sprinkle with sugar. Bake as above. Makes 2 doz.

ICE CREAMS AND SHERBETS

Ice cream is popular the year round. Whether you buy it or make your own, serve it plain or dress it up, it is always a favorite dessert — perfect for afternoon or evening refreshments, too.

Before using these recipes, refer to How To Use Our Recipes, p. 3. Always use standard measuring cups and measuring spoons; measure level.

When You Buy Ice Cream

Ice cream quality is affected by texture, flavor, richness, and sweetness. Finding your favorite quality of ice cream is largely a matter of taste testing.

Texture: Stabilizers and emulsifiers are added to ice cream to keep ice crystals small. A high percentage of butterfat will make it especially creamy.

Flavor: In fruit ice creams, the higher priced ones will be labeled fresh fruit. Artificial flavors are permitted by law.

Body: The amount of air, called overrun, incorporated during the making of ice cream increases its volume and lightness. Good quality

604

ice cream should be firm, but not solid or rubbery; also when melted, it will have a creamy, rather than a watery, appearance.

Price: Generally you will save money if you buy half-gallon or gallon containers for your home freezer.

Price is an index of richness — the higher the butterfat the more expensive the ice cream is going to be.

Special Ice Creams

ICE MILK, sold like ice cream, contains less milk fat, more protein and other non-fat solids, and fewer calories.

DIABETIC ICE CREAMS are made with artificial sweeteners and have a low insulin requirement for digestion. They are not necessarily much lower in calories than regular ice cream.

To Store Ice Cream at Home

THE FREEZER is the place to keep ice cream in quantity — a month's supply if you wish. Store unopened containers in coldest part of freezer. Reseal opened containers tightly to prevent loss of flavor and formation of ice crystals. Store away from freezing surface to keep nearer serving consistency.

IN A REFRIGERATOR-FREEZER COMBINATION, the freezer temperature will be close to 0°F. when the temperature control is at the normal setting. Pints, quarts, or even half gallons of ice cream may be stored up to a month if necessary. Keep partly used cartons tightly covered.

IN CONVENTIONAL REFRIGERATORS, you may be able to store ice cream in its original carton for brief periods of time.

Ice cream stays firmer when it is removed from the carton and turned into an ice-cube tray. But be sure it's a tray you keep just for ice cream. (See Make Your Own Tray-Type Ice Creams, p. 610.) Cover tray with wax paper or foil; place where it's in contact with the freezing surface. If necessary turn control to a colder setting, but return it to normal as soon as possible or fresh food may freeze. Use ice cream within a few hours.

P.S. See your refrigerator or freezer instruction booklet for more detailed information on storing ice cream.

WAYS TO SERVE ICE CREAM YOU BUY

Serve it straight from the carton. Or, even better, convert it into some of our production numbers. Don't use wet spoons or scoops in serving ice cream from a large package that will be returned to the freezer for storage; drops of water cause ice crystals to form rapidly throughout the ice cream.

ICE-CREAM INSPIRATIONS

Top each canned cling-peach half with vanilla ice cream, then thawed frozen raspberries, or heated canned whole-cranberry sauce; sprinkle with flaked or fine grated coconut.

Spoon some thawed frozen mixed fruits into each sherbet glass. Top with a scoop of lime sherbet, flaked coconut.

Thin marshmallow cream with cold water till saucelike. Spoon over coffee, chocolate, or pecan ice cream.

Heap tiny lemon sherbet and vanilla ice cream balls in each glass. Top with cold custard sauce and several chocolate curls.

Spoon canned crushed pineapple over vanilla ice cream, then sprinkle with powdered cinnamon, nutmeg, or mace.

Garnish each serving of orange sherbet with cut-up sections of orange, then sprinkle generously with flaked coconut.

Crumble several chocolate-covered peppermint patties over the top of big scoops of coffee or chocolate ice cream.

Spoon your best hot spiced applesauce over vanilla ice cream. Garnish with dessert topping or whipped cream.

Center each canned pineapple slice with a scoop of vanilla ice cream; then pour on Melba sauce.

Spoon hot black coffee over vanilla ice cream. Or make it a favorite jelly such as black raspberry, guava, or apple.

Pit four or five cooked prunes for each serving. Arrange in glasses with some prune juice. Top with vanilla ice cream.

Drizzle maple-blended or buttered syrup on top of vanilla ice cream, then top with toasted corn flakes. Or add snipped raisins to the syrup.

Sauté drained canned pears in melted butter till hot. Top with soft vanilla ice cream, flavored with a little rum.

Spoon warm prepared mincemeat over vanilla or coffee ice cream. Top with chopped walnuts, Brazil nuts, or almonds.

Try sugar-frosted strawberries on lemon sherbet.

Sprinkle grated chocolate over your favorite ice cream.

Crumble a candy bar over vanilla or chocolate ice cream.

Try a sprinkling of sugar-coated cereal on top of almost any flavor of ice cream.

Top toasted frozen waffles with thawed frozen raspberries, strawberries, or blueberries plus ice cream.

STRAWBERRIES ROMANOFF

1 qt. strawberries, cleaned and hulled	or curaçao
	½ cup heavy cream
2 tablesp. brandy	½ pt. vanilla ice
2 tablesp. Cointreau	cream

Ten minutes before serving: In a well-chilled bowl marinate (soak) berries in brandy and Cointreau or curaçao, or all three. Whip cream.

In another pretty chilled bowl, stir ice cream till softened; top with cream. Carry berries and cream to the table and fold them together before your guests' eyes. Then ladle into nappy or sherbet dishes. Makes 4 to 6 servings.

PEACH MELBA

Top each serving of vanilla ice cream with a canned or ripe fresh peach half; pour on Melba Sauce, p. 538.

QUICK: Fill canned or fresh peach halves with vanilla ice cream. Top with thawed frozen raspberries.

Sundae Toppings

TOP VANILLA ICE CREAM WITH:

Applesauce, warmed, then nutmeg or cinnamon

Canned whole-fruit apricot nectar and flaked or toasted coconut

Banana slices and nutmeg

Bing-Cherry Sauce, p. 535

Heated canned Bing cherries

Easy Caramel Sauce, p. 534

Chocolate-Peppermint Sauce, p. 534

Cocoa or crème de menthe

Coconut, tinted green, and lemon wedges

Coconut, tinted pink, and lime wedges

Cranberry-juice cocktail and melon balls

Canned whole-cranberry sauce, mixed with drained canned crushed pineapple and a bit of peppermint extract

Hot fudge sauce, then crumbled pretzels

Frozen grape-juice concentrate, slightly thawed; seedless grapes; sprinkling of cinnamon

Crumbled macaroons or chocolate wafers

Maple or maple-blended syrup, warmed, and a sprinkling of salted almonds, peanuts, etc.

Prepared mincemeat, heated

Honey or Easy Chocolate Sauce, p. 534, mixed with crunchy peanut butter or salted nuts

Frozen orange- or tangerine-juice concentrate, slightly thawed; sprinkle of grated chocolate

Orange marmalade, or berry or apricot jam, heated

Peanut brittle, crushed

Fresh, frozen, or canned peach slices and cinnamon; heated canned peaches with cinnamon are especially nice

Chocolate-covered peppermint patties, crumbled

Frozen pineapple-juice or lemonade concentrate, slightly thawed; cinnamon or nutmeg

Praline Crunch, p. 616

Pitted stewed prunes, ground cloves

Rum-Butter Sauce, p. 536

Frozen strawberries or raspberries, slightly thawed

Drizzle of molasses

TOP CHOCOLATE ICE CREAM WITH:

Canned crushed pineapple

Chocolate sauce and crumbled pretzels

Honey, mixed with crunchy peanut butter

Grated orange rind, mixed with a little sugar

Hard peppermint candy, crushed

Peanut brittle, crushed

Butterscotch Sauce, p. 534

Easy Chocolate Sauce, p. 534, mixed with crunchy peanut butter and a little corn syrup

Marshmallow cream, thinned to sauce consistency, and grated chocolate

Chocolate-Peppermint Sauce, p. 534

Butter-Caramel Sauce, p. 536

Toasted flaked coconut

TOP COFFEE ICE CREAM WITH:

Peanut brittle, crushed

Prepared mincemeat, warmed

Custard sauce and shaved chocolate

Sliced peaches and custard sauce

Easy Chocolate Sauce, p. 534, mixed with crunchy peanut butter and a little corn syrup

Maple or maple-blended syrup; few salted nuts

Marshmallow cream, thinned to sauce consistency, and sprinkling of grated chocolate

Praline Crunch, p. 616

Hot Fudge Sauce, p. 537

Chocolate-Peppermint Sauce, p. 534

Rum-Butter Sauce, p. 536

TOP ORANGE OR
LEMON SHERBET WITH:

Grated orange rind, mixed with sugar

Whipped cream, plus drained crushed berries

Slightly thawed frozen raspberries or orange-juice concentrate

Canned crushed pineapple and mint sprigs
Seedless grapes and cut-up oranges or pine-
apple
Crème de menthe or triple sec

ICE-CREAM-CAKE SUNDAES

MELBA: Spoon 1 pt. ice cream onto sponge
cake layer or square; top with 6 canned pear
or peach halves; then spoon on Melba Sauce,
p. 538.

CHOCOLATE-RIPPLE: Spoon 1 pt. pistachio or
vanilla ice cream onto devil's-food-cake layer
made from cake mix; drizzle chocolate sauce
over ice cream. Serve, cut into wedges.

SPEEDY: Top squares or wedges of warm yellow, white, or devil's-food cake, made from
packaged cake mix, with ice cream and your
favorite sauce.

ICE-CREAM CUPCAKES

TOP HAT: From center of each cupcake, cut out
cone-shaped piece; fill cupcake with ice cream.
Top with "cone" and chocolate sauce.

BLACK AND WHITE: Split chocolate cupcake
into 3 layers. Spread vanilla ice cream between
layers; top with fudge sauce.

FRUIT AND ICE CREAM

BANANA SPLIT: For each serving, split 1 peeled
banana lengthwise; place halves, with cut sides
up, on plate. Top with 3 scoops of vanilla ice
cream. Top 1 scoop with drained canned
crushed pineapple, 1 with chocolate sauce, 1
with crushed strawberries. Sprinkle with nuts.

STREAMLINED BANANA SPLIT: For each serving, slice part of a banana into each sherbet
glass. Top with favorite ice cream or sherbet
and thawed frozen strawberries or raspberries.

FROSTED PINEAPPLE: For each serving, top 1
drained canned pineapple slice with raspberry
sherbet and a spoonful of thawed frozen strawberries or raspberries.

CHOCOLATE PEARS: For each serving, top 1
drained canned pear half with vanilla ice cream
and a spoonful of chocolate sauce; sprinkle with
chopped walnuts.

PINEAPPLE SPLIT: For 6 to 8 servings, halve
fresh pineapple lengthwise through green top;
hollow out. Fill with ice cream; sprinkle with
flaked coconut and pineapple bits.

ICE-CREAM SHORTCAKES

INDIVIDUAL: For each serving, put 2 thin slices
toasted or plain angel, sponge, or white cake together with ice cream. Top with Hot Fudge
Sauce, p. 537, or Butterscotch Sauce, p. 534, or
fresh, frozen, or canned fruit.

BERRY LAYER: On serving plate place 1 8"
white or yellow cake layer. Spoon on about 1 pt.
lemon or other ice cream and several spoonfuls of strawberries or raspberries. Top with
second cake layer, another 1 pt. ice cream, then
more berries. Garnish with whipped cream.
Serve, cut into wedges.

LUXURO: Split 1 spongecake layer into 2 layers.
Fill with favorite ice cream. Sprinkle top with
chopped salted pecans or almonds. Serve in
wedges; pass Hot Fudge Sauce, p. 537.

SPONGE BERRY: Split 2 spongecake layers to
form 4 layers. Fill with sweetened berries.
Serve, cut into wedges and topped with ice
cream, whipped cream, or custard sauce.

APPLESAUCE A LA MODE: For each serving
toast a plain- or raisin-poundcake slice. Spread
sides with soft butter or margarine; sprinkle
with cinnamon. Spoon on canned applesauce;
sprinkle with cinnamon. Place a big scoop of
vanilla ice cream on side.

CAKE LAYER: Try a slice of brick ice cream
between two thin slices of sponge, chiffon, or
poundcake. Spoon apricot preserves on top.

EASY ICE-CREAM CAKES

FROZEN LADYFINGERS: Pack a special ice-cube
tray, p. 610, two thirds full with vanilla ice
cream. Split ladyfingers; sprinkle generously
with rum; arrange crosswise on ice cream, flat
sides down. Freeze until firm. To serve, spread
whipped cream or dessert topping over ladyfingers; then slice.

BUTTER-ALMOND SLICES: Line bottom of a special ice-cube tray, p. 610, with strips of bakers'
poundcake or cake from cake mix. Spread with
1 pt. vanilla, coffee, or chocolate ice cream.
Freeze until firm. Serve sliced, with butterscotch sauce and toasted almonds.

CHOCOLATE CHARLOTTE: Line bottom and
sides of a special ice-cube tray, p. 610, with ¼"-
thick spongecake slices. Sprinkle with 2 tablesp.
sherry; then spread with ½ pt. chocolate ice
cream. Top with layer of spongecake slices,
1½ tablesp. sherry, and another ½ pt. choco-

late ice cream. Freeze until firm. Serve sliced, with whipped cream.

FROZEN TRIFLE: In a special ice-cube tray, p. 610, alternate layers of spongecake strips with vanilla, coffee, chocolate, butter-pecan, or strawberry ice cream, ending with cake. Sprinkle with 1/4 cup rum. Freeze until firm. Serve sliced, with crushed berries and custard sauce, flavored with rum.

ICE-CREAM ANGELS

FROZEN: Hollow out a 9″ or 10″ angel cake this way: Cut down into cake along top, all the way around, about 1/2″ to 1″ in from outer edge (don't cut through to bottom). Then repeat all the way around, cutting same distance in from center edge of cake. Gently pull out cake between cuts, leaving deep trough all around.

Fill cake with 2 or 3 pt. pistachio or other ice cream; frost entire cake with Orange Butter Cream, p. 645. Freeze till frosting is set; freezer-wrap; freeze. To serve, thaw in refrigerator about 1 hr. Cut into wedges.

BLACK AND WHITE: Make Frozen Angel above, filling with chocolate ice cream. Just before serving, frost with whipped cream.

FROZEN LAYER: Split angel cake into 3 layers. Fill with ice cream. Freezer-wrap; freeze to use later. Or serve at once, cut into wedges, with chocolate sauce.

DOUBLE CHOCOLATE: Make or buy 9″ or 10″ angel cake. With fork, tear off large, irregular pieces. Alternate cake pieces and spoonfuls of chocolate ice cream in 9″ x 5″ x 3″ loaf pan, pressing them into pan to form loaf shape. Freezer-wrap; freeze. To serve, thaw in refrigerator about 1 hr. before unmolding. Slice; pass chocolate sauce.

ONE-APIECE SPECIALTIES

Serve any of these ice-cream treats at once to eat out of hand. Or freezer-wrap; then freeze for later use. Nice served from basket or large plate.

COOKIE SANDWICHES: For each serving, spread 2 graham crackers or large chocolate, sugar, or ginger cookies with jelly or with chocolate or butterscotch sauce. Put together, sandwich-fashion, with slice of firm ice cream.

ICE-CREAM BARS: Place 1 slice ice cream between 2 slices cake, sandwich-fashion; cut in half crosswise.

SUNDAE CONES: Fill ice-cream cones with ice cream; dip tops into chocolate or butterscotch sauce; then dip into nuts, flaked coconut, or chocolate sprinkles. Try:

Peach ice cream, chocolate sauce, slivered almonds

Coffee or vanilla ice cream, butterscotch sauce, chocolate sprinkles

Chocolate ice cream, fudge sauce, flaked coconut

Vanilla ice cream, butterscotch sauce, and chopped nuts

KIDDIES' CONES: Fill ice-cream cones with favorite ice cream; make faces on it of tiny candies, raisins, nuts, or semisweet-chocolate or butterscotch pieces; make hair with flaked coconut.

ICE-CREAM PUFFS

TWIN FROZEN: Make Petite Cream Puffs, p. 125. When puffs cool, split from top almost to bottom; fill half of puffs with one flavor of ice cream, rest with another. Carefully pack puffs in containers; freeze.

Just before dinner: Place 2 puffs on each dessert plate; let stand in refrigerator 20 to 30 min. To serve, top with Hot Fudge Sauce, p. 537. Makes 12 to 15 servings.

ICE-CREAM PUFFS OR ECLAIRS: Fill Susan's Cream Puffs, p. 125, or Eclairs, p. 125, with favorite ice cream. Freeze as above; then serve with favorite sauce.

P.S. Cream puffs or éclairs may be filled with ice cream, topped with sauce, and served at once if preferred.

ICE-CREAM AND SHERBET SNOWBALLS

With big spoon or ice-cream scoop, spoon or scoop out balls of ice cream. Roll each in coating, then top with sauce, fruit, or jelly, as below.*

1. Roll in fine cake crumbs; top with Hot Fudge Sauce, p. 537.
2. Roll in grated fresh, flaked, or fine grated coconut; top with Easy Chocolate Sauce, p. 534.
3. Roll in chopped walnuts, pecans, or almonds; top with Rum-Butter Sauce, p. 536.

4. Roll in crumbled sugar-coated cereal flakes or flaked coconut; top with Hot Fudge Sauce, p. 537.

5. Roll in grated chocolate; top with thawed frozen, canned, or fresh peach slices.

6. Roll in tinted or toasted coconut; top with favorite sauce.

7. Roll in flaked coconut; top with canned whole-cranberry sauce.

8. Roll in salted peanuts; top with Butterscotch Sauce, p. 534.

9. Roll tiny scoops of lemon or lime sherbet in sugar-coated cereal; top with crushed fresh or thawed frozen berries.

10. Roll in semisweet chocolate; top with custard sauce.

11. Roll in crushed peppermint candy; top with Easy Chocolate Sauce, p. 534, or hot semisweet-chocolate sauce.

12. Roll in flaked coconut; top with grape juice.

13. Roll in crushed peanut brittle or chopped nuts; top with favorite sauce.

14. Roll balls of chocolate ice cream in flaked coconut tossed with a little instant coffee.

15. Roll vanilla ice-cream balls in salted peanuts. Top with vanilla-caramel sauce, which comes in glass jars.

16. Toss bits of drained maraschino cherries with chopped walnuts. Sprinkle over vanilla ice-cream balls.

17. Roll chocolate ice-cream balls in crushed peppermint candy.

If you have a home freezer or combination refrigerator-freezer, you can make ice-cream balls (without topping) ahead; then freezer-wrap and freeze them. Or make them several hours ahead; arrange on tray; freeze.

COCONUT-LIME BALLS

Scoop vanilla ice cream into each sherbet glass. Top with generous fluff of flaked coconut; then tuck in 2 good-sized lime wedges. Guest squeezes lime juice over the ice cream as he eats it.

RIPPLED ICE CREAM

Turn temperature control of refrigerator to coldest setting. Turn 1 pt. ice cream, slightly softened, into a special ice-cube tray, p. 610. Fold in, or swirl through ice cream, one of fla-

vors below. Freeze until firm; then reset temperature control. Makes 4 servings.

COFFEE-RUM: Melt ½ cup chocolate-rum wafers over hot water; add 2 tablesp. hot water, 1½ teasp. rum. Swirl through coffee or vanilla ice cream.

FUDGE: Melt ½ 6-oz. pkg. semisweet-chocolate pieces (½ cup) over hot, *not boiling*, water; add 4 teasp. boiling water, 2 tablesp. milk; stir till smooth. Cool, but don't refrigerate. Swirl through vanilla ice cream.

BERRY: With fork, swirl 1 cup slightly crushed fresh or just-thawed frozen strawberries or raspberries through vanilla ice cream.

QUICK BISCUIT TORTONI: Combine ⅓ cup fine macaroon crumbs, 2 tablesp. diced candied cherries, and ¼ cup chopped salted almonds. Fold into vanilla ice cream. (May also be frozen in small paper cups.)

SNAP: Fold 1 cup coarsely broken gingersnaps or chocolate wafers into vanilla ice cream.

APPLE SURPRISE: Mix ½ cup applesauce, 1 tablesp. lemon juice, and ¼ teasp. cinnamon. Swirl through vanilla ice cream.

FRUITY ICE CREAM: Crumble leftover fruitcake into slightly softened vanilla ice cream. Serve immediately. Or store in a special ice-cube tray, p. 610, till served.

PEPPERMINT-VANILLA ICE CREAM: In large glass bowl sprinkle crushed pink-and-white peppermint candies over vanilla ice cream.

MAPLE SWIRL: Swirl maple-blended or buttered syrup into slightly softened ice cream.

PEANUT VELVET: In small bowl, with electric mixer, beat vanilla ice cream with 5 tablesp. peanut butter *just* until blended. (Don't let ice cream melt.) Quickly fold in 3 tablesp. chopped salted peanuts. Freeze in special ice-cube tray, p. 610, until firm enough to spoon out. Serve with chocolate or butterscotch sauce.

HOLIDAY SWIRL: Ripple ready-to-use mincemeat through vanilla ice cream.

FROZEN PUDDING: Into slightly softened vanilla ice cream, fold coarsely chopped walnuts and some mixed preserved fruits.

A RAINBOW OF PARFAITS

You don't have to own parfait glasses to serve this impressive dessert! Just use sherbet, pilsner, or small iced-tea glasses instead. Or make half-size parfaits by using fruit-juice glasses.

FRUIT: Alternate layers of vanilla ice cream with crushed sweetened berries or fruit. Garnish with whipped cream, shaved chocolate.

SUNDAE: Alternate layers of 2 ice creams such as vanilla and coffee or chocolate. Or coffee or vanilla and orange sherbet. Layer with fudge, marshmallow, or other sauce, p. 534.

COCKTAIL: Alternate layers of vanilla ice cream with chilled canned fruit cocktail mixed with seedless grapes and grated orange rind.

RAINBOW: For each parfait, alternate layers of vanilla ice cream and two or more favorite jellies. Top with whipped cream.

GRAPE: Thaw a can of frozen grape-juice concentrate. Layer with vanilla ice cream in each glass. Top with almonds.

BANANA SPLIT: Line each parfait glass with banana strips. Fill with vanilla ice cream and thawed frozen strawberries, in layers.

CRANBERRY: Layer vanilla ice cream and chilled canned whole-cranberry sauce in each glass. Top with miniature marshmallows.

LEMON-PRUNE: For each parfait, alternate pitted cooked prunes and lemon sherbet.

PINEAPPLE-MINT: Alternate layers of drained, canned minted pineapple chunks and chocolate ice cream.

RED AND WHITE: Alternate layers of raspberry-flavor gelatin with vanilla cream; sprinkle with cinnamon.

CHOCOLATE: Make layers of chocolate ice cream, whipped cream, and canned crushed pineapple.

ORANGE: Alternate vanilla ice cream with orange sections, strawberry jam, or berries.

HOT JAM: Heat your favorite jam or preserve; then layer it with vanilla ice cream in parfait glasses or sherbets. Especially nice with orange marmalade.

SPRING PARFAIT: In each parfait glass arrange consecutive layers of strawberry ice cream, dessert topping, sliced strawberries, vanilla ice cream, then dessert topping again; garnish with whole strawberries.

CINNAMON POLKA DOT: Sprinkle tiny cinnamon candies between layers of lemon sherbet.

CARIBBEAN COOLER: Spoon a little rum over each layer of orange sherbet in parfait glasses.

MAKE YOUR OWN ICE CREAMS
(tray-type)

In making tray-type ice cream in your freezer, be sure to invest in one or two new ice-cube trays and to keep them just for ice cream and other foods. When trays are used interchangeably for ice cubes, ice cream, and other foods, it has been found that in washing trays their finish is destroyed, so that ice cubes are no longer easily released.

Remember, too, that it is preferable to freeze home-made ice-cream mixtures in a freezer or a refrigerator-freezer combination, rather than in a conventional refrigerator.

FROZEN STRAWBERRY CHEESE

2 3-oz. pkg. soft cream cheese	2 pt. soft strawberry ice cream
2 tablesp. heavy cream	Wedges of honeydew melon

1. In large bowl, with electric mixer at medium speed, beat cream cheese with cream until smooth.
2. Quickly beat in ice cream until blended; turn at once into a special ice-cube tray, above. Store in freezer until firm. Serve in melon wedges. Makes 6 to 8 servings.

FROZEN CHOCOLATE RUSSE

1 teasp. unflavored gelatine	½ cup canned chocolate syrup
4½ teasp. cold water	1 doz. small ladyfingers or sponge-cake strips
1 cup heavy cream	

Sprinkle gelatine on cold water; let soften 5 min. Scald ⅓ cup heavy cream; remove from heat; add gelatine, stir until dissolved; cool. Whip ⅔ cup heavy cream until almost stiff. Add gelatine mixture and chocolate syrup, very slowly, beating constantly until well blended. Line bottom and sides of a special ice-cube tray, above, with split ladyfingers; pour chocolate mixture over them. Place rest of ladyfingers on top; freeze, without stirring, until firm. Makes 4 servings.

FROZEN CHOCOLATE RUSSE WITH SHERRY: Make as on p. 610, sprinkling 2 tablesp. sherry on the ladyfingers.

WILLIE MAE'S FRESH CRANBERRY SHERBET*

1 env. unflavored gelatine	2½ cups water
½ cup cold water	2 cups granulated sugar
4 cups fresh cranberries	⅓ cup lemon juice

Sprinkle gelatine on ½ cup water to soften. Cook cranberries in 2½ cups water, covered, until skins pop open; force through sieve; then add sugar, gelatine. Heat until gelatine dissolves; cool. Add lemon juice.

Turn into a special ice-cube tray, p. 610; freeze until firm. Turn into chilled bowl; with electric mixer or hand beater, beat until thick and mushy. Quickly return mixture to tray; freeze until just firm enough to spoon out. Makes 4 servings.

Especially nice with meats or poultry.

CHOCO-NUT TORTONI

1 egg white	½ 6-oz. pkg. semi-sweet-chocolate pieces (½ cup)
2 tablesp. granulated sugar	1 teasp. shortening
1 cup heavy cream, whipped	¼ cup canned finely chopped, toasted almonds
2 tablesp. granulated sugar	
1 teasp. vanilla extract	

Beat egg white until fairly stiff; gradually add 2 tablesp. sugar, beating until stiff. Combine whipped cream, 2 tablesp. sugar, vanilla; fold into beaten egg white. Turn into a special ice-cube tray, p. 610; freeze until frozen ½" in from edges of tray. Melt chocolate with shortening over hot, *not boiling,* water. Turn frozen mixture into chilled bowl; stir until smooth but not melted; quickly fold in melted chocolate, then almonds. Turn into 8 2-oz. paper cups; freeze until just firm. Makes 8 servings.

MOCHA-NUT TORTONI: Double egg white, sugars, cream, and extract. Make as above, adding 2 beaten egg yolks and 2 tablesp. instant coffee when folding into egg whites. In melt-

ing chocolate omit shortening. Turn into 12 custard cups or 16 2-oz. paper cups. Freeze.

ORANGE CRYSTAL CAKE

2 tablesp. cornstarch	1 cup orange juice
½ cup granulated sugar	2 tablesp. grated orange rind
1 cup milk	18 ladyfingers, split in half lengthwise
3 egg yolks, slightly beaten	3 egg whites
1 tablesp. butter or margarine	1 cup heavy cream

Week ahead, if desired:

1. In double boiler, combine cornstarch and sugar; stir in milk, egg yolks, and butter. Cook over boiling water, stirring constantly, 5 min., or until mixture thickens and clears.
2. Stir in orange juice and rind, cook 2 min.; cool.
3. Meanwhile, line a greased, wax-paper-lined 8" x 8" x 2" pan with ladyfinger halves, rounded side against pan — ten on the bottom and eight, placed end to end, around sides.
4. When orange mixture is cool, beat egg whites until stiff; fold in orange mixture.
5. Spread half of orange mixture over ladyfingers in bottom of pan; top with rest of ladyfingers as before. Top with rest of orange mixture.
6. Freeze cake until firm; freezer-wrap; freeze.

To serve: Thaw unwrapped cake in refrigerator about 3 hr.; unmold on serving plate. Then whip cream, and use to frost top of cake. Makes 9 servings.

RUBY ICE

1 10-oz. pkg. frozen raspberries	1 10-oz. pkg. frozen sliced strawberries
	2 egg whites

Early in day: In saucepan, over medium heat, completely thaw berries. Press through sieve; discard pulp and seeds.

With hand or electric beater, beat egg whites until they form soft peaks when beater is raised; gradually add sieved berries, continuing to beat until egg whites and berries are well blended. Turn into a special ice-cube tray, p. 610; freeze, stirring once, until firm enough to spoon into sherbet glasses.

Serve with tea and a wedge apiece of spongecake. Makes 8 servings.

APRICOT SHERBET

1½ cups canned apricot nectar	2 tablesp. kirsch or 2 teasp. almond extract

Combine nectar and kirsch; pour into a special ice-cube tray, p. 610, and freeze, stirring occasionally, until mushy. Serve at once. Makes 6 servings.

LIME MILK SHERBET

1 env. unflavored gelatine	2 tablesp. grated lime rind
2 cups milk	¼ cup lemon juice
½ teasp. salt	½ cup lime juice
1⅓ cups granulated sugar	Green liquid food color
2 cups light cream	Thin lime slices

About 5 hr. before serving:
1. Sprinkle gelatine onto ½ cup milk in bowl; let soften 5 min. Then set bowl over boiling water; stir until gelatine dissolves.
2. Combine salt, sugar, 1½ cups milk, cream, lime rind, lemon juice, and lime juice; stir in gelatine, then enough food color to tint delicate green. (If mixture curdles, don't worry; it disappears during freezing.)
3. Turn mixture into a special ice-cube tray, p. 610; freeze until frozen 1″ in from edge of tray. Turn into chilled bowl; beat with hand beater until smooth but not melted.
4. Return mixture to tray; freeze until just firm enough to spoon out for serving.
At serving time: Spoon sherbet into sherbet glasses. Garnish each with lime twist, maybe a strawberry or two. Makes 5 or 6 servings.
LIBBY'S LEMON SHERBET: Substitute ¾ cup lemon juice for lime juice and 1 teasp. grated lemon rind for lime rind.

Ice-Cream-Mix Tricks

Don't fail to scan your grocer's shelves for those packaged mixes you can so easily whip up into ice creams and sherbets. The vanilla flavor can be used as a basic mix and varied in a number of interesting ways as suggested on the label. Also try the chocolate and strawberry.

Children love the ready-to-freeze orange, lemon-lime, cherry, and grape pop bars which come in transparent wrappers that serve as molds for freezing them. Keep some on hand in the freezer. Slice them over fruit compote; or mash with fork, then spoon over ice cream or grapefruit halves.

Raspberry, lime, and orange sherbet mixes speak for themselves. For tastiest results, always follow label directions to the letter.

ICE-CREAM TOPOFFS

STRAWBERRY-VANILLA SAUCE: Mix thawed frozen strawberries and soft vanilla ice cream till saucelike. Spoon over canned peach slices.
COFFEE-CACAO SAUCE: Thin coffee ice cream with some crème de cacao. Spoon over vanilla ice cream on poundcake slices.
BING SAUCE: Heat canned, pitted Bing cherries; spoon over strawberry ice cream.
SPICY PEACH SAUCE: In small saucepan, combine a 1-lb.-13-oz. can cling-peach slices with their syrup and ½ teasp. cinnamon. Heat, then spoon over vanilla ice cream.
PEPPERMINT-PINEAPPLE SAUCE: Combine ¾ cup white corn syrup with one 9-oz. can crushed pineapple, ¼ teasp. peppermint extract, and a few drops green food color. Cover and chill thoroughly before serving. Especially nice on vanilla ice cream.
PINEAPPLE-ORANGE SAUCE: To 1 6-oz. can thawed frozen orange-juice concentrate, add 1 9-oz. can crushed pineapple. In glasses, alternate layers of vanilla ice cream and some of sauce.
MOCHA-WALNUT SAUCE: Combine a 10-oz. jar chocolate-caramel sauce with 1 tablesp. hot water, and ½ cup chopped walnuts or pecans. Serve over vanilla ice cream.

IN CRANK FREEZER
(hand-turned or electric)

OLD-FASHIONED VANILLA ICE CREAM

1½ cups milk	2 eggs; or 3 egg yolks
¾ cup granulated sugar	1½ teasp. vanilla extract
2 tablesp. flour	1½ cups heavy cream
Few grains salt	

In double boiler, scald milk. Mix sugar, flour, salt; stir in enough milk to make smooth paste.

Stir into rest of milk in double boiler. Stir until thickened; cook, covered, 10 min. Beat eggs slightly; stir in milk mixture; return to double boiler; cook 1 min. Cool; add vanilla, cream. Freeze in 2-qt. or larger crank freezer until difficult to turn, using 8 parts crushed ice to 1 part ice-cream salt.

To Ripen: When ice cream is firm, draw off water from freezer; wipe off and remove lid. Take out dasher; plug opening in lid. Pack ice-cream mixture down; re-cover. Repack freezer as follows: If serving within 2 hr., use 1 qt. crushed ice to each 1 cup ice-cream salt; if holding ice cream longer, use 2 qt. ice to each 1 cup salt; cover with a heavy cloth. Makes 1¼ qt.

BISQUE: Substitute 3 tablesp. sherry for vanilla. When ready to freeze mixture, add 1 cup fine macaroon crumbs.

BURNT ALMOND: Caramelize half of sugar as on p. 4. Stir into scalded milk until caramel dissolves. Just before freezing mixture, add ¼ lb. finely chopped, toasted, blanched almonds.

BUTTER-PECAN: In ¼ cup hot butter, margarine, or salad oil in skillet, sauté 1 cup broken pecan meats until golden. Add, with ¼ teasp. salt, just before freezing.

CHOCOLATE: Add 2 sq. unsweetened chocolate to milk before scalding. When chocolate is melted, with hand beater, beat till smooth.

COFFEE: Substitute ¾ cup cold strong coffee beverage for ¾ cup milk.

FRENCH VANILLA: Substitute 6 egg yolks for eggs.

PEACH: Just before freezing mixture, add 1½ cups sieved fresh peaches combined with ¼ cup additional sugar (or enough to sweeten) and few drops almond extract.

PEPPERMINT: Omit vanilla; add 1 drop oil of peppermint. Or add 1½ cups very finely crushed peppermint-stick candy to milk before scalding; omit sugar. Tint delicate pink or green with food color.

PINEAPPLE: Substitute 1 tablesp. lemon juice for vanilla. Just before freezing mixture, add 2 cups well-drained canned crushed pineapple.

PISTACHIO: With vanilla, add ¾ teasp. almond extract and ½ cup chopped, blanched pistachio nuts. Tint delicate green with food color.

RASPBERRY: Just before freezing mixture, add 1½ cups crushed raspberries mixed with about ¼ cup additional sugar, and a few drops almond extract.

STRAWBERRY: Reduce milk to 1 cup. When milk-and-egg mixture has cooled, add 1 qt. washed, hulled strawberries, mashed and sweetened with ¼ cup additional sugar; blend well. Then add cream.

CIDER ICE

4 cups cider	1 cup orange juice
1 cup granulated sugar	½ cup lemon juice

Simmer cider with sugar 5 min. Add orange and lemon juices. Freeze in 2-qt. or larger crank freezer until difficult to turn, using 8 parts crushed ice to 1 part ice-cream salt. Ripen as at left. Makes about 1½ qt.

LEMON: Simmer 4 cups water with 1½ cups granulated sugar 5 min. Add ¾ cup lemon juice, 1 tablesp. grated lemon rind, ¼ teasp. salt, and a few chopped mint leaves (optional). Cool. Freeze. Makes about 1½ qt.

ORANGE: Simmer 2 cups water with 1 cup granulated sugar 5 min. Add 2 cups orange juice; ¼ cup lemon juice; ⅛ teasp. salt; 1 tablesp. grated orange rind. Freeze. Makes 1½ qt.

PINEAPPLE: Simmer 2 cups water with ½ cup granulated sugar 5 min. Add 1 1-lb.-4-oz. can pineapple juice; ⅓ cup lemon juice; and ⅛ teasp. salt. Freeze. Makes about 2 qt.

RASPBERRY, STRAWBERRY, OR LOGANBERRY: Simmer 1 cup granulated sugar with 2 cups water 5 min. Pour over 2 cups crushed berries; cool. Rub through sieve. Then add 1 tablesp. lemon juice (or lemon juice to taste). Freeze. Makes about 1 qt.

ICE-CREAM CREATIONS

BAKED ALASKA

Thanks to the freezer, Baked Alaska is no longer a last-minute dessert. If you have a freezer, or a refrigerator freezing compartment with a separate control, you can prepare Baked Alaska a few days ahead. Arrange chilled cake and *firm* ice cream on a paper-covered cookie sheet; cover with meringue; freeze. Remove; bake; serve — calmly, coolly!

Or store wrapped ice-cream-topped cake in freezer; unwrap, then cover it with meringue just before baking.

COMPANY BAKED ALASKA

1 9″ yellow-cake layer	8 egg whites
1 qt. vanilla ice cream	1 cup granulated
1 qt. raspberry sher-	sugar
bet	

A few days ahead:

1. Cut out piece of heavy brown paper at least ½″ larger than cake layer; place on 14″ x 10″ cookie sheet. Center cake on paper; place in freezer to chill.

2. Line a 1½-qt. mixing bowl with wax paper or foil; along bottom and sides, pack vanilla ice cream. (It's easy if ice cream is slightly soft and you use a wooden spoon.) Then fill center with raspberry sherbet (use same wooden spoon). On top, place sheet of wax paper; then, with palms of hands, press top flat. Freeze until firm.

3. When ice cream is firm, make this Meringue: With electric mixer or hand beater, beat egg whites until they stand in moist, drooping peaks when beater is raised. Slowly add sugar, 2 tablesp. at a time, beating until stiff and glossy.

4. Now pull off paper; quickly invert bowl of firm ice cream onto cake, centering bowl about 1″ in from cake edges; then lift off bowl; pull off paper. With spatula, quickly spread meringue over entire surface of ice cream and cake, right down to brown paper; meringue should be at least 1″ thick. Return to freezer.

About 15 min. before serving: Start heating oven to 500°F. Remove Alaska from freezer, and promptly bake 4 or 5 min., or until a delicate brown. Remove from oven; place next to a chilled serving plate; then slip 2 pancake turners between Alaska and paper and carefully transfer it to plate. Serve, cutting into 16 wedges.

NOTE: The Alaska may all be made and baked at the last minute — but you have to work quickly. Choose your cake base. Make meringue. Top cake with ice cream. Frost cake and ice cream. Pop into oven and proceed as above.

MORE ALASKAS

IGLOO: Use bakers' spongecake layer as base. Pile ice cream on top, leaving ½″ free around edge. Cover with ½ recipe for Meringue in step 3, left; bake at 500°F. 4 or 5 min.

BROWNIE: Use panful of uncut brownies as base. Top with brick ice cream; cover with ½ recipe for Meringue as in step 3, left; bake at 500°F. 4 or 5 min.

LITTLE BAKED: Make ½ recipe for Meringue in step 3, left. Use 6 bakers' dessert shells as base. Top each with well-drained canned pineapple slice. Place scoop of ice cream on each; cover with Meringue; bake at 500°F. 4 or 5 min.

TRADITIONAL: Use 1 piece of thin spongecake, 8″ x 6″ x 1″. Top with brick ice cream; cover with ½ recipe for Meringue in step 3, left; bake at 500°F. 4 or 5 min.

FROZEN CAFE PIE

18 round chocolate-	⅔ cup evaporated
sandwich cookies	milk
½ cup melted butter	1 tablesp. butter or
or margarine	margarine
2 sq. unsweetened	1 qt. coffee ice cream
chocolate	Whipped cream
½ cup granulated	Chopped walnuts
sugar	

Roll cookies *fine*; blend with melted butter in 9″ pie plate; press to bottom and up to rim of same pie plate; refrigerate.

In double boiler, melt chocolate with sugar, evaporated milk, and 1 tablesp. butter, stirring to smooth sauce; cool. Into cookie crust spoon ice cream; top with chocolate sauce; freeze firm.

Serve topped with whipped cream, then chopped nuts. Makes 8 to 10 servings.

To Freeze Ahead: When pie is frozen firm, freezer-wrap; freeze for about a week.

SUNDAE PIES

1. *Make a baked pie shell* — any on pp. 584–587.

2. *At serving time* fill with one, two, or three flavors of ice cream — 1 to 2 pt. for an 8″ pie shell, 2 to 3 pt. for a 9″ shell.

3. *Top with* shaved unsweetened chocolate,

plain or toasted flaked coconut, chopped nuts, or one of Sundae Toppings, p. 606. Serve in small wedges.

We suggest:

Baked Crumb Crust, p. 594; vanilla ice cream; chocolate sauce; whipped cream

Baked Crumb Crust made with gingersnaps, p. 594; vanilla ice cream; canned crushed pineapple

Chocolate-Coconut Crust, p. 594; coffee ice cream

Baked Pie Shell, p. 585; peach ice cream; Melba Sauce, p. 538

Meringue Crust, p. 595; vanilla ice cream; sliced peaches, strawberries, raspberries, or canned whole-cranberry sauce

Toasted Coconut Crust, p. 595; vanilla ice cream; canned crushed pineapple

Unbaked Pretzel-Crumb Crust, p. 594; vanilla ice cream; favorite topping

FROZEN SUNDAE PIES: Make and fill as above. Freezer-wrap; freeze. To serve, unwrap; let set in refrigerator until easy to cut.

SUNDAE TARTS

Fill Pretty Tart Shells, p. 601, with your favorite ice cream; top as in Sundae Pies, p. 614. Serve at once.

Or fill tart shells with ice cream; top, then cover completely with Pie Meringue (2 eggs), p. 593. Bake at 500°F. about 2 min.

ICE-CREAM BOMBE

Fill 1-qt. mold with 1 qt. ice cream. With back of spoon, smooth ice cream so it lines bottom and sides of mold evenly, leaving center hollow. Spoon 1 pt. sherbet into hollowed center, packing it down. Freezer-wrap; freeze. Try any of these combinations:

Chocolate or coffee ice cream; orange sherbet or green-tinted, mint-flavored whipped cream in center

Vanilla ice cream; orange sherbet in center

Pistachio ice cream; lemon sherbet in center

Strawberry ice cream; raspberry sherbet in center

To serve: Dip mold into cool water 5 to 10 seconds; unmold.

SNOWY ORANGE CUPS

4 large oranges	Light rum (optional)
2 pt. orange sherbet, slightly softened	Canned flaked or grated fresh coconut
1 pt. fresh strawberries	12 lemon leaves
Sugar	

Day before or early on the day:
1. Slice top from each orange about one third of the way down. With sharp knife, cut out all orange sections, reserving them for later use. Then, if desired, make a pretty, saw-toothed pattern around top edge of each orange shell.
2. Now fill each orange shell with sherbet, pressing it down into shell so it fills saw-toothed edge and rounding it high in center. Set orange cups, side by side, in a shallow pan; place in freezer. Freeze.

Early on serving day:
1. Wash strawberries. Refrigerate 12 of nicest ones, with their green hulls, for garnishing.
2. Cut remaining strawberries into *small* pieces; add sugar to taste; then sprinkle with rum, if desired. Refrigerate until needed, stirring occasionally.

About 15 min. before serving: With teaspoon, make *small* cavity down through center of sherbet in each orange cup. Fill with cut berries; sprinkle top generously with coconut. Arrange on plate with garnish of lemon leaves and 3 whole strawberries; serve at once. Makes 4 servings.

CHRISTMAS IN JULY

6 eggs	About 1½ cups sliced strawberries or peaches, or raspberries or blueberries
⅓ cup granulated sugar	
2 cups heavy cream	
1 cup sherry	
½ gal. container vanilla ice cream	Nutmeg

Early on the day, if desired:
1. Separate eggs, placing whites in large bowl and yolks in 3-qt. bowl.
2. With electric mixer at high speed, beat egg whites until they form soft peaks; add sugar gradually, continuing to beat until they stand in stiff peaks.
3. Beat cream stiff.
4. Now beat egg yolks until blended; stir in sherry. Top with whipped cream and beaten

whites; then carefully fold together until just blended. Refrigerate this eggnog mixture.

Just before serving:

1. Let container of ice cream stand out till just soft enough to serve. Slit container; peel away from ice cream; stand ice cream on end in punch bowl.

2. Next, if eggnog mixture has separated, fold it together again until just blended; pour it around cylinder of ice cream. Top with most of berries and a sprinkling of nutmeg. Sprinkle remaining berries on eggnog mixture.

3. Serve in mugs or nappy dishes, giving each guest a portion of ice cream and berries; then ladle on some eggnog mixture. A wonderful dessert. Makes 12 servings.

PRALINE ICE-CREAM RING

½ cup butter or margarine	½ cup broken pecans or walnuts
1 cup brown sugar, packed	2½ cups corn, bran, or wheat flakes
	Ice cream

Chill 1¼-qt. ring mold. In saucepan, boil butter with sugar *just 2 min.* Add pecans, corn flakes; with fork, toss to coat. Press lightly into mold. Refrigerate 10 min.; unmold onto serving dish. Place spoonfuls of your favorite ice cream, with rounded sides up, in center. Makes 6 servings.

PRALINE CRUNCH: Make Praline Ice-Cream Ring mixture; cool; then crumble. Serve over vanilla or coffee ice cream.

WALNUT MERINGUE TORTE

3 egg whites	3 cups heavy cream
1½ cups granulated sugar	1 pt. slightly soft butter-pecan or pistachio ice cream
32 walnut halves	

Day or so before:

1. Draw a 9″ circle on each of two pieces of wax paper; grease paper lightly. Place each piece of paper on a cookie sheet. Start heating oven to 300°F.

2. Beat egg whites until stiff enough to hold their shape. Gradually add ¼ cup sugar, while continuing to beat; then, with rubber spatula, gently fold in ½ cup sugar, a little at a time.

3. With this soft meringue mixture in decorating bag, and pastry tube no. 6, make a 1″-wide ring around inner edge of one of the drawn circles. Then top ring with a crisscross pattern of meringue, having 3 parallel lines going in one direction, and 3 more crossing them in the opposite direction.

4. Repeat step 3 on circle on other cookie sheet.

5. Bake both meringue rings in same oven for 30 min., or until light brown, exchanging lower cookie sheet with upper one after 15 min. When done, with spatula, remove *at once* from wax paper to cake rack. Then cover meringues lightly with wax paper and carefully store in a covered container until needed.

6. Butter a piece of wax paper. In small skillet, over medium heat, melt ½ cup granulated sugar until it forms a golden-brown syrup, stirring it occasionally with a fork.

7. Then drop walnut halves, a few at a time, into syrup, coating all sides. With fork, place two walnut halves together, lifting them carefully to buttered wax paper to dry; repeat with rest.

About 30 min. before serving:

1. Whip heavy cream until stiff; fold in ¼ cup granulated sugar.

2. On large, round cake plate, spread one third of whipped cream in a circle of same size as one of the meringue-lattice rings.

3. Cover whipped cream with one of the meringue-lattice rings. Now *evenly* spread all the ice cream over this ring, then top it with the second meringue-lattice ring.

4. Place half of remaining whipped cream in decorating bag and, with large pastry tube no. 6, fill each of the 16 holes in the lattice pattern with a swirling mound; top each swirl with a glazed walnut.

5. With rest of whipped-cream mixture make large rosettes around sides of cake. Makes 12 servings.

COCOA-CREAM RING

10 vanilla ice-cream balls	2½ cups packaged cocoa-flavored rice or corn cereal
1 4-oz. bar German sweet cooking chocolate	Jar of chocolate-caramel sauce
1 cup broken walnuts	

Refrigerate a 1¼-qt. ring mold. Form ice-cream balls; freeze. In double boiler, over warm, *not hot,* water, melt chocolate; add nuts and cereal. Toss until uniformly coated with chocolate. Press lightly into well-chilled ring mold. Refrigerate 20 to 25 min.; then unmold on serving dish. Heap ice-cream balls in center; drizzle with sauce. Makes 6 servings.

SHERBET-CREAM CAKE

1½ pt. raspberry sher- | 2 cups coarsely
bet | chopped semisweet-
1½ pt. orange sherbet | chocolate pieces
1½ pt. pistachio ice | 1 pt. heavy cream
cream | Green food color
3 qt. vanilla ice cream | 1 pt. fresh strawber-
2 cups chopped pe- | ries
cans

Day or week ahead, if desired:
1. With a no. 20 ice-cream scoop, make eight balls from each of raspberry, orange, and pistachio flavors (total of 24 balls). Arrange balls in chilled jelly-roll pan or on foil-covered heavy cardboard, and freeze very firm.
2. Chill 10″ angel-cake pan in freezer.
3. In large bowl, with wooden spoon or electric mixer, beat 1½ qt. vanilla ice cream until it is like a heavy batter; stir in 1 cup chopped pecans, 1 cup chopped chocolate.
4. Spoon enough softened vanilla ice cream into chilled angel-cake pan to make 1″ layer. Quickly arrange raspberry, orange, and pistachio balls on top, alternating them against center tube and side of cake pan. Spoon rest of softened ice cream over balls. Return to freezer.
5. Now soften 1½ qt. vanilla ice cream as in step 3; add rest of pecans and chocolate.
6. Continue alternating the raspberry, orange, and pistachio balls and covering with softened

vanilla ice cream until cake pan is full. Cover with foil. Return to freezer.
Early on the day:
1. Cover a 10″ circle of cardboard with foil.
2. Remove angel-cake pan from freezer; run knife around edges of pan and inner tube.
3. Quickly dip cake pan in and out of lukewarm water. Lay foil-covered cardboard circle (or serving plate that fits in freezer) over top of pan; invert pan and circle; then lift off angel-cake pan. Return ice-cream cake to freezer.
Two hours before serving:
1. Whip cream, adding a few drops of green food color, to tint delicate green.
2. Remove ice-cream cake from freezer. Quickly frost with tinted whipped cream; then return to freezer.
To serve: Place cake on serving plate, if not done earlier. Garnish base and top center with strawberries and a few ivy leaves, if desired. Makes 10 to 12 servings.

BUFFET ICECAPADES

Two or three days ahead: Get out a large glass snifter, punch bowl, crystal vase, or oversize salad bowl — its size depending on the number you are serving. Also, with no. 16 scoop, make balls from as many ice cream and sherbet flavors as you wish; freeze balls, side by side, on foil-covered cardboard or cookie sheets.
About 15 min. before serving: Quickly fill snifter, alternating ice-cream and sherbet balls and interspersing thawed frozen strawberries and raspberries and green grapes. Set where guests can serve themselves.

OUR BEST CAKES

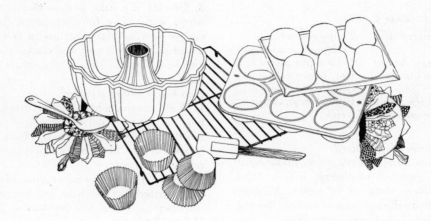

To bake a good cake, you must have a fool-proof recipe. No matter what kind — creamed, quick-method, chiffon, angel, sponge — the cake should be tender, high, rich in flavor — and should invite immediate sampling. Our carefully checked recipes will give you such cakes, but you must follow our directions to the letter.

TO MAKE A GOOD CAKE

1. First read carefully How To Use Our Recipes, p. 3.

2. Next read cake recipe all the way through. Then assemble the necessary utensils and ingredients. Always use standard measuring cups and measuring spoons; measure level.

3. Follow directions; otherwise, even the best recipes can go wrong.

A. *Use pans that are the exact size and depth indicated.* (Read Measuring Pan Sizes, p. 15.) Bigger, smaller, or shallower pans than those called for can cause a cake to fail. If pans aren't the right size, fill only half full with batter, so cake will rise to, but not over, top of pan; use rest of batter for cupcakes.

B. *Be sure aluminum cake pans are bright and shiny inside and out,* so cakes will brown evenly, delicately. Dull, dark pans cause cakes to brown too fast, too unevenly. To keep cake pans shiny, clean with steel-wool soap pads.

If you're using oven-glass cake dishes, and your cakes are overbrowning, try reducing oven temperature 25°F.

C. *Follow recipe exactly.* No substitutions of ingredients, *no* changes in amounts, *no* changes in directions are allowed.

D. *Use exact ingredients called for* — double-acting baking powder, cake flour, etc. This can mean the difference between a masterpiece and a mediocrity.

E. *Bake at the temperature and for the time period specified.*

4. Do these little jobs before you mix a cake:

A. *If cake pans are to be lined with paper,* set pan on large piece of wax paper. Trace around bottom of pan with point of scissors or sharp knife. Cut out; place in bottom of cake pan. Paper should fit snugly. Making several liners at once saves time. You can also buy cake liners, already cut.

B. *If cake pans are to be greased,* apply thin film of salad oil or soft shortening with paper or pastry brush.

618

c. *If cake pans are to be floured*, sprinkle each greased pan with a little flour; then shake pan to coat it evenly. Remove excess flour by gently knocking inverted pan on work surface.

D. *Start heating oven in time* to have it heated to specified temperature when cake batter is ready.

E. *Chop nuts, prepare fruit, etc., ahead.*

F. *Sift flour just before you measure it.*

5. Most cake-making troubles can be traced to:

A. *Not using ingredients called for*. Substitutes are not the same, even though they may look so.

B. *Not using accurate, level measurements*. Small variations in amounts of ingredients may affect volume, texture, or crust.

C. *Not baking in right pan, at right temperature, for right time.*

If You Live at a High Altitude

The cake recipes in this chapter have been perfected for use at sea level. They probably need no modification up to an altitude of 2500 or 3000 feet. Above that, it is often necessary to adjust slightly the proportions of flour, eggs, leavening, sugar, etc. These adjustments, however, vary from recipe to recipe, and only repeated experiments can give the most successful proportions for each.

If high altitude seems to be causing trouble with your baking and cooking, write to the following sources for recipes developed especially for, and perfected at, high altitudes.

General Foods Kitchens
250 North Street
White Plains, New York

Colorado Agricultural Experiment Station
Colorado State University
Fort Collins, Colorado

University of Wyoming
Agricultural Experiment Station
University Station
Box 3354, Laramie, Wyoming

Your local utility company

Your state extension service

When using cake mixes at high altitude, *be sure* to check label for specific baking directions. Some mixes are manufactured especially for use at high altitudes.

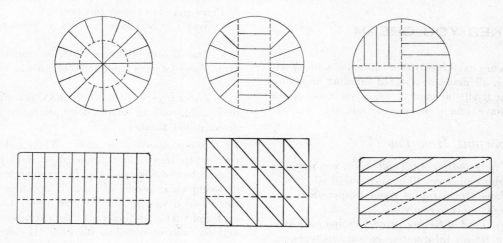

To Cut a Cake

ANGEL, CHIFFON, OR SPONGECAKE: For fluffy, high wedges, use a cake breaker or 2 forks to pull pieces apart gently. Or "saw" cake lightly with very sharp knife.

LAYER CAKE: Use long, thin, sharp knife. Cut with gentle sawing motion; don't press down. If cutting cake in kitchen, after each cut, wipe off crumbs clinging to knife; rinse knife in hot water.

CUTTING WAYS: To cut your cake to best advantage, try one of ways diagrammed above. Dotted lines show first cuts to be made.

To Store Cakes

Any cake is at its best served the day it's made. However, if it's stored well, it will still be delicious the second and often the third day. Keep these pointers in mind:

1. *If cake has a cream or whipped-cream filling*, or is frosted with whipped cream, serve at once. Or store in the refrigerator until served, and after serving — it's the safest place.

2. *Wrap fruitcake tightly* in wax paper, saran, or foil; then refrigerate. If desired, brush occasionally with fruit juice, cider, port, sherry, or brandy. Or you may saturate a cloth with brandy, etc., and wrap cake in it first.

A home freezer is ideal for storing fruitcake; just be sure cake is freezer-wrapped.

3. *Store all other plain or frosted cakes* in clean, covered box, or in a "cake keeper" that has a roomy cover which fits over plate or tray. Or invert large, deep bowl over cake so that bowl rests on cake-plate edge.

4. *After serving cake, keep unserved portion* fresher by covering cut surface with strip of wax paper held in place with a few toothpicks. As a rule, frosted cakes keep more moist than unfrosted layers or squares.

5. *To freeze cakes*, see p. 707.

CAKES YOU CREAM

Here are cake favorites — all made with shortening, all made by the old familiar creaming method, all the kind of cake you make when you have time to enjoy every minute.

Important How-Tos

1. *Where shortening is called for*, you may use any shortening you like except salad oil.

2. *Have shortening at room temperature*, soft enough to mix in easily.

3. *Use kind of baking powder* recipe indicates. See p. 93 for information on various types.

4. *Measure sifted flour, baking powder and/or soda, salt, and spices into sifter;* sift onto large piece of wax paper or into bowl; repeat as recipe directs.

5. *When cake recipe calls for milk*, use milk, diluted evaporated milk, or liquefied nonfat dry milk.

6. *If you have an electric mixer — regular or portable —* cakemaking is a special joy. Set dial on mixer at speed recipe suggests. Beat for time indicated, using a timer so you won't underbeat or overbeat. With rubber spatula, scrape bowl and beaters as needed.

7. *If you prefer to mix cake with a spoon*, here's an easy way:

A. To soft shortening, add sugar in thirds, beating with spoon after each addition until *very light and fluffy*.

B. Then, if whole eggs or egg yolks are to be added, drop them in, *unbeaten*, one at a time, beating thoroughly after each addition. Batter should be *very creamy*.

C. Now, unless otherwise directed, add, alternately, flour mixture in fourths and combined milk and extract in thirds, stirring only until batter is smooth. *Do not overmix* at this point; overmixing reduces volume, causes poor texture. Scrape down batter in bowl with rubber spatula as needed; scrape spoon.

D. When recipes call for beaten egg whites, nuts, or raisins, they are usually folded in last. See Fold In, p. 5.

8. *Pour batter into prepared pan or pans*, dividing it equally if you're using more than one pan. Spread evenly with rubber spatula.

9. *Place cake in oven in this position:*

A. *Single cake:* Bake on rack in center of oven.

B. *Two layers:* Bake on rack in center of oven. Don't let pans touch sides of oven or each other.

C. *Three layers:* Bake on 2 racks, placed so they divide oven in thirds; don't place one pan directly over another.

10. *To test doneness of cake:* When baking time is up (not before), open oven door just enough to test cake quickly. Insert cake tester or toothpick in center of cake; if it comes out clean and dry, cake is done. Or lightly touch center of cake with finger; if cake springs back and no imprint remains, it's done. If cake is not quite done, bake it a little longer; test again.

11. *To cool cake:* Set it, in pan, on cake rack for 10 to 15 min., depending on size and tenderness of cake. Then, with spatula, loosen cake around edges. Place rack over top of cake; invert pan and rack together; then place rack on

table. Lift off pan; peel off paper, if any. Place second rack lightly on cake; invert both racks with cake to turn cake right side up. Finish cooling.

ONE-EGG CAKE

2 cups sifted cake flour	1 medium egg, unbeaten
2½ teasp. double-acting baking powder	1 cup minus 2 tablesp. milk
¾ teasp. salt	1 teasp. vanilla extract; or 1 tablesp. grated orange or lemon rind
⅓ cup soft shortening	
1 cup granulated sugar	

Start heating oven to 350°F. Grease, then line with wax paper, bottom of 8″ x 8″ x 2″ pan. Sift flour with baking powder, salt, 3 times.

In large bowl, with electric mixer* at medium speed, mix shortening with sugar, then with egg, until *very light and fluffy* — about 4 min. altogether. At low speed, beat in alternately, *just until smooth,* flour mixture in fourths and combined milk and vanilla in thirds. Turn into pan. Bake 45 to 50 min. Test for doneness, then cool as in steps 10 and 11, p. 620.

This cake may be baked in:

2 1¼″-deep 8″ layer pans at 375°F. 25 min., or until done.

1 9″ x 9″ x 2″ pan at 375°F. 30 min., or until done.

To mix with spoon, see step 7, p. 620.

FROSTINGS: Choose Harvest Moon, p. 646; Jiffy Chocolate, p. 648; Dreamy Coffee, p. 645; or Orange Butter Cream, p. 645.

Or fill with Clear Orange or Lemon Filling, p. 642; frost with Snow-Peak, p. 647.

NUT: Substitute ¼ teasp. almond extract for vanilla. Quickly fold into batter 1 cup *very finely chopped* walnuts, pecans, Brazil nuts, almonds, or black walnuts. Bake in 8″ x 8″ x 2″ pan. Frost with Quick Fudge Frosting, p. 647, or Harlequin Frosting, p. 645.

CHOCOLATE LAYER: Split 2 layers to make 4 layers. Fill and frost with Bittersweet Frosting, p. 644. Or fill and frost 2 layers with Easy Fudge Frosting, p. 646.

MOCHA SPICE: With flour, sift 2 teasp. cinnamon, ½ teasp. allspice, 1 teasp. nutmeg, and ¼

teasp. ground cloves. Frost with Mocha Butter Cream, p. 645.

PRALINE: Bake in 9″ x 9″ x 2″ pan. While cake is still warm, frost with Broiled Praline Topping, p. 647.

CARAMEL FUDGE: To egg mixture, add 2 sq. unsweetened chocolate, melted. Bake in 2 1¼″-deep 8″ layer pans. Fill and frost with Quick Caramel Frosting, p. 647.

CHOCO-NUT: Combine ⅓ cup semisweet-chocolate pieces, melted; 1⅓ cups snipped flaked coconut; and ¼ cup water. Turn half of cake batter into prepared 9″ x 9″ x 2″ pan. Sprinkle with half of chocolate mixture; top with rest of batter, then with rest of chocolate mixture. Bake at 375°F. 35 min., or until done.

DOUBLE FUDGE CAKE

1 cup sifted all-purpose flour	½ cup dark corn syrup
½ teasp. salt	1 egg
1 teasp. baking soda	1 teasp. vanilla extract
⅓ cup soft shortening	1 sq. unsweetened chocolate, melted
⅓ cup granulated sugar	¾ cup buttermilk

Start heating oven to 350°F. Lightly grease 8″ x 8″ x 2″ cake pan. Sift together flour, salt, and baking soda.

In large bowl, with electric mixer at medium speed, mix shortening and sugar thoroughly. Add corn syrup and mix well; then add egg, vanilla, and chocolate and continue mixing until very creamy. Then beat in alternately, *just until smooth,* flour mixture in fourths and buttermilk in thirds. Turn mixture into pan. Bake 45 min. Test for doneness, then cool as in steps 10 and 11, p. 620.

FROSTING: Split cake into 2 layers; fill, and frost top, with Real Fudge Frosting, p. 648.

FLUFFY TWO-EGG YELLOW CAKE

3 cups sifted cake flour	1¾ cups plus 2 tablesp. granulated sugar
2½ teasp. double-acting baking powder	2 large eggs, unbeaten
1 teasp. salt	1¼ cups milk
½ cup plus 2 tablesp. soft shortening	1½ teasp. vanilla extract

Start heating oven to 350°F. Grease, then line with wax paper, bottoms of 2 1½″-deep 9″ layer pans. Sift together flour, baking powder, salt.

With electric mixer* at medium speed, thoroughly mix shortening with sugar, then eggs, until very light and fluffy — about 4 min. altogether. Then, at low speed, beat in alternately, just until smooth, flour mixture in fourths and combined milk and vanilla in thirds. Turn into pans. Bake 30 to 35 min., or until done. Test for doneness, then cool, as in steps 10 and 11, p. 620.

This cake may also be baked in 13″ x 9″ x 2″ pan, at 350°F., 35 to 40 min.

To mix with spoon, see step 7, p. 620.

FROSTINGS:

Orange Whipped-Cream Frosting, p. 649; Princess, p. 646; Penuche, p. 646.

CHOCOLATE-SUNDAE CAKE

1½ ¼-lb. bars German sweet chocolate	¾ cup soft vegetable shortening
3 tablesp. water	2¼ cups granulated sugar
3 tablesp. light cream	6 eggs, unbeaten
4½ cups sifted all-purpose flour	1½ cups milk
4½ teasp. double-acting baking powder	1½ teasp. vanilla extract
1½ teasp. salt	Chocolate Glaze II, p. 649
¾ cup butter or margarine	

1. Start heating oven to 350°F. Grease, then flour only bottom of 10″ tube pan.
2. In double boiler, over hot, *not boiling*, water, melt chocolate with water until very smooth, stirring occasionally. Remove from heat; blend in light cream.
3. Sift together flour, baking powder, and salt.
4. In large bowl, with mixer at medium speed, cream butter with shortening; gradually add sugar, continuing to beat until light and fluffy — at least 5 min.
5. Now beat in eggs, one at a time, beating 1 min. after each addition.
6. Combine milk and vanilla. With mixer at low speed, add sifted dry ingredients alternately with milk, starting and finishing with dry ingredients and beating thoroughly after each addition. Batter will be quite thick.
7. Now turn about one fourth of batter into prepared tube pan; then drizzle with a layer of about one third of melted-chocolate mixture. Repeat with 2 more alternating layers of batter and chocolate mixture; then top with rest of batter.
8. Bake 70 to 80 min. Test for doneness, then cool as in steps 10 and 11, p. 620. (A crack on top is normal; don't worry.)
9. When cake is cool, spoon Chocolate Glaze II along top edge of cake, letting it run down sides.

BUNDT-CAKE STYLE: Grease and flour entire cast aluminum bundt-cake pan, 10″ x 4½″. Make and bake cake as at left. When cake tests done, turn off oven; let cake remain in closed oven 15 min. Remove to wire rack; cool 15 min.; remove from pan; cool. Drizzle Chocolate Glaze II along top edge of cake.

PECAN CAKE

2 cups pecan meats	¼ teasp. salt
1 cup seedless raisins	3 egg whites
½ cup sifted all-purpose flour	⅓ cup granulated sugar
2 teasp. nutmeg	½ cup soft shortening
½ cup bourbon	¾ cup granulated sugar
1 cup sifted all-purpose flour	3 egg yolks, unbeaten
1 teasp. double-acting baking powder	20 pecan halves

Make day before: Start heating oven to 325°F. Grease, then line with wax paper, 3½″-deep 9″ tube pan. Finely chop pecans; snip raisins; mix both with ½ cup flour. Add nutmeg to bourbon. Sift 1 cup flour with baking powder, salt.

In small bowl, with electric mixer* at high speed, beat egg whites until quite stiff; gradually add ⅓ cup sugar, beating until stiff. Set aside.

In large bowl, at medium speed, mix shortening with ¾ cup sugar and egg yolks until *very light and fluffy* — about 4 min. altogether. At low speed, beat in alternately, in 2 parts, *just until smooth*, bourbon and flour mixture. Fold in nut mixture, then beaten whites. Turn into pan; decorate with pecan halves. Bake 1¼ hr. Test for doneness, as in step 10, p. 620. Cool in pan on wire rack 30 min.; remove from pan; peel off paper. Keeps well. Needs no frosting. Nice served with grapes.

To mix with spoon, see step 7, p. 620.

COMPANY SPICECAKE

3 cups sifted cake flour	2 cups granulated sugar
3 teasp. double-acting baking powder	4 egg yolks
1½ teasp. nutmeg	1 cup water
2 teasp. cinnamon	1 teasp. dark rum
1 teasp. allspice	1 cup walnuts, very finely chopped
¼ teasp. salt	4 egg whites
½ lb. butter or margarine (1 cup)	

Make day before, or early in day:

1. Start heating oven to 375°F. Grease, then line with wax paper, bottoms of 2 1½"-deep 9" layer pans. Sift together flour, baking powder, nutmeg, cinnamon, allspice, and salt.
2. In large bowl, with electric mixer at medium speed, cream butter while gradually adding sugar; beat until smooth. Then beat in egg yolks, all at one time.
3. Now alternately beat in flour mixture and water, blending well; add rum and walnuts. Beat egg whites until stiff but not dry; fold into batter.
4. Turn into pans. Bake 30 min. Test for doneness, then cool as in steps 10 and 11, p. 620. If cake is to be frosted next day, wrap layers in foil, and store overnight.

FROSTING: Fill with Spicy Cream Filling, p. 643. Frost with Fluffy Rum Frosting, p. 647.

FABULOUS CHOCOLATE CREAM CAKE

2½ cups sifted cake flour	1 cup shortening
1 teasp. baking soda	2 cups granulated sugar
½ teasp. salt	4 egg yolks, unbeaten
1 ¼-lb. bar German sweet chocolate	1 teasp. vanilla extract
½ cup boiling water	1 cup buttermilk
	4 egg whites

1. Start heating oven to 350°F. Grease, then line with wax paper, bottoms of 3 9" layer cake pans. Sift flour, baking soda, and salt.
2. Melt chocolate in boiling water; cool.
3. In large bowl, with electric mixer* at medium speed, mix shortening with sugar till very light. Add egg yolks, one at a time, beating after each addition. Add vanilla and melted chocolate; mix to blend.
4. Add flour mixture alternately with butter-
To mix with spoon, see step 7, p. 620.

milk, beating till smooth. Fold in egg whites, stiffly beaten.
5. Pour batter into layer cake pans.
6. Bake 30 to 35 min. Test for doneness, then cool as in steps 10 and 11, p. 620.

This cake may be baked in 2 9" x 9" x 2" cake pans, lined on bottom with wax paper, at 350°F., for 40 to 45 min.

FROSTING: Fill and frost with Coffee Whipped Cream, p. 649.

DEVIL'S-FOOD CAKE

2 cups sifted cake flour	2 medium eggs, unbeaten
1 teasp. baking soda	3 sq. unsweetened chocolate, melted
¾ teasp. salt	1¼ cups minus 2 tablesp. milk
½ cup soft shortening*	1 teasp. vanilla extract; or ¼ teasp. peppermint extract
1⅓ cups granulated sugar; or 1½ cups brown sugar, packed	

Start heating oven to 350°F. Grease, then line with wax paper, bottoms of 2 1½"-deep 9" layer pans. Sift flour, soda, and salt 3 times.

In large bowl, with electric mixer† at medium speed, mix shortening with sugar, then with eggs, until *very light and fluffy* — about 4 min. altogether; mix in chocolate. At low speed, beat in alternately, *just until smooth,* flour mixture in fourths and combined milk and vanilla in thirds. Turn into pans. Bake 25 to 30 min. Test for doneness, then cool as in steps 10 and 11, p. 620.
With butter, margarine, or lard, decrease milk to 1 cup.
†*To mix with spoon, see step 7, p. 620.*

FROSTINGS: Fill and frost with Quick Fudge, p. 647; Snow-Peak, p. 647; Mocha Butter Cream, p. 645; Dreamy Orange, p. 645; or Penuche, p. 646.

CHOCOLATE-NUT: Quickly fold into batter ¾ cup *very finely chopped* walnuts, pecans, or other nuts. Bake as above.

Or bake in greased pan, 13" x 9" x 2", lined with wax paper, at 350°F. 45 min., or until done. Frost with Quick Caramel Frosting, p. 647.

CHOCOLATE-ALMOND: Split each layer into 2 layers; fill with Whipped-Cream Frosting, p. 648; frost with Velvety Frosting, p. 644; top with chopped, toasted almonds.

SILVER WHITE CAKE

2½ cups sifted cake flour
3 teasp. double-acting baking powder
1 teasp. salt
4 medium egg whites
1½ cups granulated sugar

½ cup soft shortening
1 cup plus 2 tablesp. milk
1 teasp. vanilla extract
¼ teasp. almond extract (optional)

Start heating oven to 375°F. Grease, then line with wax paper, bottoms of 2 1¼"-deep 8", or 2 1½"-deep 9" layer pans. Sift flour, baking powder, and salt 3 times.

In small bowl, with electric mixer* at high speed, beat egg whites until foamy. Gradually add ½ cup sugar, beating only until mixture holds soft peaks. Set aside. In large bowl, with mixer at medium speed, mix shortening with 1 cup sugar until *very light and fluffy* — about 2 min. altogether. Next, at low speed, beat in alternately, *just until smooth*, flour mixture in fourths and combined milk and extracts in thirds; then thoroughly beat egg-white mixture into batter. Turn into pans. Bake 25 min., test for doneness, then cool as in steps 10 and 11, p. 620.
To mix with spoon, see step 7, p. 620; beat, then fold egg-white mixture into batter last.

FROSTINGS: Fill and frost with Mocha Butter Cream, p. 645, or Hungarian, p. 644. Or fill with Almond Creamy Custard Filling, Quick Chocolate Cream Filling, or Clear Lemon Filling, p. 642; frost with Snow-Peak, p. 647.

THREE-LAYER COCONUT: Double recipe. Bake in 3 1½"-deep 9" layer pans at 375°F. 30 to 35 min., or until done. Fill and frost with Princess Frosting, p. 646.

LADY BALTIMORE: Fill and frost 2 1¼"-deep 8" layers with Lady Baltimore Frosting, p. 646.

CHOCOLATE MARBLE: Blend 1 sq. melted unsweetened chocolate with 1 tablesp. sugar, 2 tablesp. water, and ¼ teasp. baking soda; cool. Add to one third of Silver White Cake batter, mixing only enough to blend. Alternate plain and chocolate mixtures, by tablespoonfuls, in layer pans. With knife, cut carefully through batter in wide zigzag, to give marbleized effect. Bake at 375°F. 30 to 35 min., or until done. Serve as is; or frost with Jiffy Chocolate Frosting, p. 648.

LANE CAKE

3¼ cups sifted all-purpose flour
3½ teasp. double-acting baking powder
½ teasp. salt

1 cup butter or margarine
2 cups granulated sugar
1 teasp. vanilla extract
1 cup milk
8 egg whites

1. Start heating oven to 375°F. Grease, then line with wax paper, bottoms of 4 1½"-deep 9" layer pans.
2. Sift flour, baking powder, salt.
3. In large bowl, with electric mixer* at medium speed, mix butter with sugar until *very light*. Add vanilla.
4. At low speed, alternately beat in flour mixture in fourths and milk in thirds, just until smooth.
5. In large bowl, beat egg whites until they form stiff peaks. Then gently fold in batter.
6. Turn batter into the 4 layer pans to a depth of about 1". Bake 15 to 20 min. Test for doneness, then cool as in steps 10 and 11, p. 620.
To mix with spoon, see step 7, p. 620.

FROSTINGS: Fill with Lane Filling, p. 642; frost with Lane Frosting, p. 647.

OLD-DOMINION POUNDCAKE

8 large eggs, separated
2¼ cups sifted all-purpose flour
¼ teasp. baking soda
2¼ cups granulated sugar
1½ cups butter, just

soft enough to be worked easily
2 tablesp. lemon juice
2¼ teasp. vanilla extract
⅛ teasp. salt
1½ teasp. cream of tartar

1. Let eggs stand at room temperature 1 hr. before using. Meanwhile, butter well, then flour a cast-aluminum bundt-cake pan that measures 10" x 4½".
2. Sift together flour, soda, and 1¼ cups granulated sugar. Start heating oven to 325°F.
3. In large bowl, with electric mixer at low speed, just barely blend butter with flour mixture, then with lemon juice and vanilla. Now, still at low speed, beat in egg yolks, one at a time, just until yolks are blended.
4. In large bowl, with mixer at high speed, beat egg whites until frothy; add salt, then gradually 1 cup granulated sugar with cream

of tartar, beating well after each addition. Then beat all until soft peaks form.

5. Now gently fold beaten egg whites into cake batter; turn into prepared pan. Then, using a rubber spatula, gently cut through the cake batter 1 or 2 times.

6. Bake cake 1½ hr., or until a cake tester, inserted in center, comes out clean. (*Do not peek at cake during first hour of baking.*)

7. Now turn off oven heat; let cake remain in oven 15 min.; then remove to wire cake rack. Cool cake for 15 min. more.

8. Remove cake from pan; finish cooling it on rack. Then wrap in foil, saran, or wax paper, or store it in cake box until it's time to be served. Nice served with Brandied Apricots, p. 545.

GERMAN GOLD CAKE RING
(Napfkuchen)

3½ cups sifted cake flour	1 cup butter or margarine
1½ teasp. double-acting baking powder	2 cups granulated sugar
⅛ teasp. salt	6 egg yolks
	2 teasp. vanilla extract
	1 cup milk

Start heating oven to 350°F. Sift together flour, baking powder, salt. Grease, then flour, 3-qt. fluted ring mold.

In large bowl, with electric mixer at high speed, mix butter with sugar, then with egg yolks, and vanilla, adding them gradually until *very light, fluffy*. At low speed, beat in alternately, until smooth, flour mixture in fourths, milk in thirds. Turn batter into ring mold. Bake 1 hr. Test for doneness, then cool as in steps 10 and 11, p. 620. Fill center with scoops of ice cream, drizzle with caramel sauce, if desired.

WALNUT-CHIP POUNDCAKE

2 cups sifted cake flour	chocolate pieces
¼ teasp. salt	1 cup soft shortening
1 teasp. double-acting baking powder	1 cup granulated sugar
¼ teasp. mace (optional)	5 eggs, unbeaten
1 6-oz. pkg. well-chilled semisweet-	1 teasp. vanilla extract
	½ cup chopped walnuts

Start heating oven to 300°F. Grease, then line

with wax paper, 10″ x 5″ x 3″ loaf pan. Sift flour, salt, baking powder, mace. Finely grind chocolate, 3 or 4 pieces at a time, in food chopper.

In large bowl, with mixer* at medium speed, mix shortening with sugar until *very light and fluffy*, then with eggs, one at a time, until very creamy — about 8 min. altogether. At low speed, beat in flour mixture, vanilla, walnuts, and chocolate just until smooth. Turn into pan. Bake 1½ hr. Test for doneness, then cool as in steps 10 and 11, p. 620. Needs no frosting.
To mix with spoon, see step 7, p. 620.

LUXURY LOAF: Use ungreased wax-paper-lined 10″ x 5″ x 3″ loaf pan. Substitute sifted all-purpose flour for cake flour; increase salt to ½ teasp. Add grated rind of 1 orange and ¼ cup orange juice alternately with flour mixture; reduce nuts to ¼ cup. Bake at 300°F. 1 hr. 40 min., or until done.

SPICY GINGERBREAD

2½ cups sifted all-purpose flour	½ cup soft shortening
1½ teasp. baking soda	½ cup granulated sugar
½ teasp. ground cloves	1 medium egg, unbeaten
1 teasp. cinnamon	1 cup molasses
1 teasp. ginger	1 cup hot water
¾ teasp. salt	

Start heating oven to 350°F. Grease, then line with wax paper, bottom of 9″ x 9″ x 2″ pan. Sift flour, soda, cloves, cinnamon, ginger, salt.

In large bowl, with electric mixer* at medium speed, mix shortening with sugar, then with egg until *very light and fluffy* — about 4 min. altogether; beat in molasses. At low speed, beat in alternately, *just until smooth*, flour mixture in fourths and hot water in thirds. Turn into pan. Bake 50 to 55 min. Test for doneness, then cool as in steps 10 and 11, p. 620.
To mix with spoon, see step 7, p. 620.

FROSTINGS: Choose Dreamy Chocolate, p. 645; "Four Minute," p. 646; or Broiled Praline Topping, p. 647. Or split cake to make 2 layers; fill with spicy applesauce; top with whipped cream.

QUICK GINGERBREAD: There are excellent packaged gingerbread mixes on the market. Simply add liquid; then bake as directed.

JIM'S APPLESAUCE CAKE

2 cups sifted all-purpose flour	½ teasp. cinnamon
1½ teasp. baking soda	½ teasp. ground cloves
¾ teasp. salt	½ teasp. nutmeg
¾ cup snipped, pitted dates	½ teasp. allspice
¾ cup light or dark raisins	2 tablesp. cocoa
¾ cup chopped walnuts or pecans	1½ cups granulated sugar
½ cup soft shortening	2 eggs, unbeaten
	1½ cups canned applesauce

Make day or so before: Start heating oven to 350°F. Grease 3-qt. ring mold on bottom and sides. Sift flour, soda, salt. Toss 2 tablesp. flour mixture with dates, raisins, nuts.

In large bowl, with electric mixer* at medium speed, mix shortening, cinnamon, cloves, nutmeg, allspice, cocoa. Gradually add sugar, beating until fluffy. Add eggs, one at a time, beating well after each addition. At low speed, beat in alternately, *just until smooth*, flour mixture and applesauce. Stir in date mixture. Turn into ring mold. Bake 55 to 60 min. Test for doneness, then cool as in steps 10 and 11, p. 620. Nice as is or frosted with Orange Butter Cream, p. 645.
*To mix with spoon, see step 7, p. 620.

BUTTERY ORANGE-RAISIN CAKE

4 cups sifted all-purpose flour	2½ cups granulated sugar
2 teasp. double-acting baking powder	¼ teasp. almond extract
2 teasp. baking soda	2 cups seedless raisins
½ teasp. salt	1½ cups milk
Juice from 2 medium oranges; reserve rinds	2 tablesp. vinegar
	1 cup soft butter or margarine
	4 eggs

1. Start heating oven to 350°F. Grease a 3-qt. cast-aluminum bundt-cake pan. Sift flour, baking powder, baking soda, salt. Combine ½ cup strained orange juice with ½ cup granulated sugar; mix until sugar is dissolved; add almond extract; refrigerate. Using fine blade of food grinder and being careful not to have long "strings" of raisins, grind reserved orange rind and raisins alternately; set aside. Combine milk and vinegar.
2. In large bowl, with electric mixer at high speed, cream butter; gradually beat in 2 cups sugar. At medium speed, add eggs, one at a time, mixing well after each addition. At medium speed, beat in alternately, *just until smooth*, flour mixture in fourths and milk mixture in thirds. Fold in orange-raisin mixture, in small amounts, until thoroughly blended. Pour into prepared pan.
3. Bake 60 to 70 min. Test for doneness, as in step 10, p. 620. Remove cake from oven; turn off heat. Spoon 6 tablesp. reserved orange syrup over top and between cake and sides of pan. Return cake to turned-off oven for 1 hr.
4. Then, with small spatula, loosen cake from pan; invert on cake plate to cool; store, covered.

Serve warm or cold with extra syrup as sauce. Makes 12 to 14 servings.

JUNIOR BUTTERY ORANGE-RAISIN CAKE: Halve all ingredients; bake in greased 2-qt. mold at 350°F. 45 to 50 min. Makes 6 to 8 servings.

HARVEST PRUNE CAKE

2¼ cups sifted all-purpose flour	1½ cups granulated sugar
2¼ teasp. double-acting baking powder	3 medium eggs, unbeaten
¾ teasp. baking soda	¾ cup buttermilk
1 teasp. salt	1¼ teasp. vanilla extract
½ cup soft shortening	1¼ cups *finely cut, drained cooked prunes*
½ cup soft butter or margarine	

Start heating oven to 375°F. Grease, then line with wax paper, bottoms of 2 1½"-deep 9" layer pans. Sift flour, baking powder, soda, salt.

In large bowl, with electric mixer* at medium speed, mix shortening and butter with sugar, then with eggs, until *very light and fluffy* — about 4 min. altogether. At low speed, beat in alternately, *just until smooth*, flour mixture in fourths and combined buttermilk and vanilla in thirds. With spoon, quickly stir in prunes. Turn into pans. Bake 35 to 40 min. Test for doneness, then cool as in steps 10 and 11, p. 620.
*To mix with spoon, see step 7, p. 620.

FROSTINGS: Fill and frost with Harvest Moon, p. 646, or Whipped-Cream Frosting, p. 648. Or top wedges with whipped cream to which packaged flaked or fresh grated coconut has been added.

RUM CAKE DE MAISON

2 cups sifted cake flour
2 teasp. double-acting baking powder
¼ teasp. salt
¼ teasp. baking soda
½ cup butter or margarine
¾ cup granulated sugar
2 egg yolks, unbeaten
1 teasp. grated orange rind
½ cup orange juice
White rum
¼ teasp. almond extract
¼ teasp. vanilla extract
2 egg whites
¼ cup granulated sugar
1½ cups walnuts, chopped

Make 24 hr. ahead:

1. Grease, then line with wax paper, bottoms of 2 9″ layer cake pans. Start heating oven to 350°F.
2. Sift flour, baking powder, salt, baking soda; set aside.
3. In large bowl, with electric mixer at medium speed, mix butter until light; add ¾ cup sugar gradually, mixing until very light and fluffy.
4. Add egg yolks, one at a time, beating well after each addition; add orange rind.
5. With mixer at low speed, add flour mixture alternately with orange juice combined with 3 tablesp. rum; add extracts.
6. In medium bowl, beat egg whites until soft peaks form. Gradually add ¼ cup sugar, beating constantly until stiff peaks form.
7. Gently fold batter into egg whites until well combined; turn into prepared pans. Bake 25 min. Test for doneness, then cool as in steps 10 and 11, p. 620.
8. Split cooled cake layers crosswise to make 4 layers in all. Sprinkle each with 2 tablesp. rum.

FROSTING: On cake plate, assemble 4 layers with Whipped-Cream Filling, p. 643, between layers. Frost top and side of cake with Chocolate Frosting, p. 644; generously sprinkle walnuts all around side of cake. Refrigerate at least 24 hr. before serving.

QUICK RUM CAKE: Prepare 1 pkg. yellow-cake mix as label directs, substituting ½ cup orange juice for ½ cup of the water called for. Add 1 teasp. grated orange rind. Bake in 2 9″ layer cake pans. Proceed as directed in step 8, then frost as in Frosting, above.

QUICK-METHOD CAKES

These shortening cakes are made by a quick-and-easy, one-bowl method that produces especially fine-grained, rich, and tasty cakes. Never try to make cakes that call for creaming by this quick method.

Important How-Tos

1. *Have all ingredients at room temperature.* Take eggs, milk, etc., out of refrigerator an hour or so ahead of time. (In hot weather use eggs and milk right from refrigerator.)
2. *Where "shortening" is called for,* use one of shortenings that come in 3-lb. or 1-lb. cans and whose labels recommend use in quick-method, one-bowl, or quick-mix cakes. Store such shortenings on pantry shelf. Do not use butter, margarine, or lard unless so directed.
3. *Use exact kind and amount of baking powder called for.* To identify kind, check can label.
4. *Use pans that are of exact size and depth indicated.* See 3a and b, p. 618.
5. *If you're using an electric mixer — regular or portable —* set dial at speed recipe suggests. Beat for time indicated, using a timer so you won't underbeat or overbeat. With rubber spatula, scrape bowl and beaters as needed.
6. *If you prefer to mix cake with a spoon,* while turning bowl, beat briskly with sweeping, round-the-bowl strokes for same time periods as for making cake with an electric mixer. Allow 150 full, round-the-bowl strokes per min. End each stroke with a strong upward movement; take time out to scrape down batter as needed, but count only actual beating time and strokes.
7. Fill pans; bake cake; then cool as in steps 8 through 11, p. 620.

SIMPLICITY ONE-EGG CAKE

1¼ cups sifted cake flour
¾ cup granulated sugar
2 teasp. double-acting baking powder
½ teasp. salt
⅓ cup soft shortening,
step 2, above
½ cup milk
1 teasp. vanilla extract, or 1 tablesp. grated orange or lemon rind
1 medium egg, unbeaten

Start heating oven to 375°F. Grease, then line with wax paper, bottom of 8″ x 8″ x 2″ pan.

Into large bowl, sift flour, sugar, baking powder, salt. Drop in shortening; pour in milk, vanilla. With electric mixer* at low to medium speed, beat 1½ min., scraping bowl and beaters as needed. Add egg; beat 1½ min. Turn into pan. Bake 25 min. Test for doneness, then cool as in steps 10 and 11, p. 620.

To mix with spoon, beat briskly for same time periods as above, allowing 100 full, round-the-bowl strokes per minute.

FROSTINGS: Choose Broiled Honey-Coconut, p. 647, Dreamy Orange, p. 645, or Penuche, p. 646.

CHOCOLATE-WALNUT: Substitute ¼ teasp. almond extract for vanilla. Into batter, fold ½ cup *very finely chopped* walnuts. Frost with Dreamy Chocolate Frosting, p. 645.

TWO-EGG GOLDEN CAKE

2¼ cups sifted cake flour	½ cup soft shortening, p. 627
1½ cups granulated sugar	¾ cup milk
1 teasp. salt	1½ teasp. vanilla extract
3 teasp. double-acting baking powder	¼ cup milk
	2 medium eggs, unbeaten

Start heating oven to 350°F. Grease, then line with wax paper, bottoms of 2 1½"-deep 9" layer pans.

Into large bowl, sift flour, sugar, salt, baking powder. Drop in shortening; pour in ¾ cup milk, vanilla. With electric mixer* at medium speed, beat 2 min., scraping bowl and beaters as needed. Add ¼ cup milk, eggs; beat 2 min. Turn into pans. Bake 25 to 30 min. Test for doneness, then cool as in steps 10 and 11, p. 620.

This cake may be baked in 13" x 9" x 2" pan at 350°F. 35 to 40 min., or until done.

To mix with spoon, see step 6, p. 627.

FROSTINGS: Fill and frost with Marshmallow "Seven Minute," p. 646, or Easy Fudge, p. 646.

SPICECAKE: With flour, sift 1 teasp. cinnamon, ½ teasp. ground cloves, ¼ teasp. allspice. When you drop in shortening, pour in 1 tablesp. molasses. Bake in 2 1½"-deep 9" layer pans at 375°F. 25 min., or until done. Or bake in 13" x 9" x 2" pan at 375°F. 35 min., or until done.

Fill and frost with Lemon Butter Cream, p. 645, or Quick Caramel Frosting, p. 647.

FRESH ORANGE: With flour, sift ¼ teasp. baking soda. Substitute 1 teasp. grated orange rind for vanilla, ¼ cup unstrained orange juice for ¼ cup milk. Bake in 2 1½"-deep 9" layer pans at 350°F. 25 to 30 min.

Fill with Quick Orange Cream Filling, p. 642; frost with Snow-Peak Frosting, p. 647. Or fill and frost with Tropical Whip Frosting, p. 649.

CHOCOLATE POUNDCAKE

2¾ cups sifted cake flour	Milk*
¾ teasp. cream of tartar	1 teasp. vanilla extract
½ teasp. baking soda	3 medium eggs, unbeaten
1½ teasp. salt	1 egg yolk, unbeaten
1¾ cups granulated sugar	3 sq. unsweetened chocolate, melted
1 cup soft shortening, p. 627	Confectioners' sugar

Start heating oven to 350°F. Line with wax paper bottom of a 3½"-deep 9" tube pan.

Into large bowl, sift flour, cream of tartar, soda, salt, and sugar. Drop in shortening; pour in milk, vanilla. With electric mixer† at low to medium speed, beat 2 min., scraping bowl and beaters as needed. Add eggs, egg yolk, chocolate; beat 1 min. Turn into pan. Bake 1 hr. 10 min. Test for doneness, then cool as in steps 10 and 11, p. 620.

Just before cutting: Spoon confectioners' sugar into ridges on top of cake.

With butter, margarine, or lard, use ⅔ cup milk; with other shortenings, use 1 cup minus 2 tablesp. milk.

†*To mix with spoon, see step 6, p. 627.*

CHOCOLATE-NUT: Into batter, fold ¾ cup *finely chopped* walnuts, pecans, or other nuts.

BANANA CREAM CAKE

2¼ cups sifted cake flour	½ cup soft shortening, p. 627
1¼ cups granulated sugar	2 medium eggs, unbeaten
2½ teasp. double-acting baking powder	4 or 5 ripe bananas, well mashed (1½ cups)
½ teasp. baking soda	1 teasp. vanilla extract
½ teasp. salt	

Start heating oven to 375°F. Grease, then line

with wax paper, bottoms of 2 1¼″-deep 8″ layer pans.

Into large bowl, sift flour, sugar, baking powder, soda, salt. Drop in shortening, eggs; add ½ cup mashed bananas. With electric mixer* at low to medium speed, beat 2 min., scraping bowl and beaters as needed. Add 1 cup mashed bananas, vanilla; beat 1 min. Turn into pans. Bake 25 min. Test for doneness, then cool as in steps 10 and 11, p. 620.

*To mix with spoon, see step 6, p. 627.

FROSTING: Fill and frost with Whipped-Cream Frosting, p. 648. Garnish with thin slices of fully ripe bananas dipped into fruit juice.

BANANA-SPICE LAYER: With flour, sift ⅛ teasp. ground cloves, 1¼ teasp. cinnamon, ½ teasp. nutmeg.

NOTE: To mash bananas, slice them; then beat with fork, hand beater, blender, or electric mixer until smooth and creamy.

HARVEST RIBBON CAKE

2½ cups sifted cake flour	½ cup milk
1 teasp. salt	5 egg whites, unbeaten
1⅔ cups granulated sugar	Yellow food color
⅔ cup soft shortening, p. 627	1 tablesp. grated orange rind
¾ cup milk	½ teasp. cinnamon
4½ teasp. double-acting baking powder	⅛ teasp. ground cloves
1 teasp. vanilla extract	⅛ teasp. baking soda
	2 tablesp. cocoa
	2 tablesp. water

Start heating oven to 360°F. Grease, then line with wax paper, bottoms of 3 1¼″-deep 8″ layer pans.

Into large bowl, sift flour, salt, sugar. Drop in shortening; pour in ¾ cup milk. With electric mixer* at low to medium speed, beat 2 min., scraping bowl and beaters as needed. Stir in baking powder. Add vanilla, ½ cup milk, egg whites; beat 2 min.

Divide batter into three parts. For *yellow layer,* add a few drops yellow food color and grated orange rind. For *chocolate layer,* add cinnamon, cloves, soda, and cocoa, blended with water. Turn the batters into 3 layer pans. Bake 20 to 25 min. Test for doneness, then cool as in steps 10 and 11, p. 620.

*To mix with spoon, see step 6, p. 627.

FROSTING: Fill and frost with Harvest Moon, p. 646.

CHRISTMAS RIBBON: Substitute red food color for yellow, ½ teasp. almond extract for orange rind. Fill and frost with "Seven-Minute" Frosting, p. 646, tinted green.

ELEGANT DEVIL'S-FOOD CAKE

2 cups sifted cake flour	1 teasp. salt
1¾ cups granulated sugar	¾ cup soft shortening, p. 627
¾ cup cocoa	¾ cup milk
1¼ teasp. baking soda	1 teasp. vanilla extract
½ teasp. double-acting baking powder	½ cup milk
	3 medium eggs, unbeaten

Start heating oven to 350°F. Grease, then line with wax paper, bottoms of 2 1½″-deep 9″ layer pans.

Into large bowl, sift flour, sugar, cocoa, soda, baking powder, salt. Drop in shortening; pour in ¾ cup milk, vanilla. With electric mixer* at low to medium speed, beat 2½ min., scraping bowl and beaters as needed. Add ½ cup milk, eggs; beat 2½ min. Turn into pans. Bake 35 min. Test for doneness, then cool as in steps 10 and 11, p. 620.

*To mix cake with spoon, beat briskly for same time periods as above, allowing 100 full, round-the-bowl strokes per minute.

FROSTINGS: Fill and frost with Princess, p. 646, or Dreamy Coffee, p. 645.

LUSCIOUS COCONUT LAYER CAKE

2¼ cups sifted cake flour	¾ cup milk
1½ cups granulated sugar	1 teasp. vanilla extract
4 teasp. double-acting baking powder	¾ teasp. orange extract
1 teasp. salt	4 medium egg whites, unbeaten
½ cup soft shortening, p. 627	¼ cup milk

Start heating oven to 350°F. Grease, then line with wax paper, bottoms of 2 1½″-deep 9″ layer pans.

Into large bowl, sift flour, sugar, baking powder, salt. Drop in shortening; pour in ¾ cup milk and extracts. With electric mixer* at low to medium speed, beat 2 min., scraping bowl and beaters as needed. Add egg whites and ¼ cup milk; beat 2 min. Turn into pans. Bake 20 min. Test for doneness, then cool as in steps 10 and 11, p. 620.

*To mix with spoon, see step 6, p. 627.

FROSTINGS: Fill and frost with Princess, p. 646. Or fill with Clear Lemon Filling, p. 642, or Quick Pineapple Cream Filling, p. 642; frost with Snow-Peak, p. 647; sprinkle with coconut.

CARNIVAL CAKE

2¼ cups sifted cake flour	½ cup milk
1½ cups granulated sugar	1 teasp. orange extract
2½ teasp. double-acting baking powder	½ teasp. almond extract
1 teasp. salt	3 medium eggs, unbeaten
¾ cup soft shortening, p. 627	¼ cup milk

Start heating oven to 375°F. Grease, then line with wax paper, bottoms of 2 1½"-deep 9" layer pans.

Into large bowl, sift flour, sugar, baking powder, salt. Drop in shortening; pour in ½ cup milk, extracts; add 1 egg. With electric mixer* at low to medium speed, beat 2 min., scraping bowl and beaters as needed. Add ¼ cup milk, 2 eggs; beat 2 min. Turn into pans. Bake 25 min. Test for doneness, then cool as in steps 10 and 11, p. 620.

*To mix with spoon, beat briskly for same time periods as above, allowing 100 full, round-the-bowl strokes per minute.

FROSTINGS: Fill and frost with Penuche, p. 646, or Quick Caramel, p. 647.

SPONGE, ANGEL-FOOD, AND CHIFFON CAKES

All the members of this family are wonderfully light and lovely — sure to please all members of your family.

Important How-Tos

1. *Be sure to use ungreased cake pan* if recipe so directs. Then batter can cling to sides of pan, and rise to its full, glorious height. It is important to keep pans well scrubbed and free from grease.

2. *About 1 hr. before using, remove eggs from refrigerator* and separate. (If you're not using egg yolks, cover with water; refrigerate. If you're not using egg whites, just refrigerate.) Whites beat up more easily and produce a finer-textured, lighter cake when at room temperature, so let warm up.

3. *Use type of baking powder* recipe indicates. Also see p. 93.

4. *For correct way to fold one ingredient into another,* see Fold In, p. 5.

5. *To test chiffon, sponge, or angel cake for doneness* at end of baking time, see step 10, p. 620. When cake is done, remove fom oven immediately.

6. *To cool cake,* invert it and let hang in tube pan for 1 hr., or until cold, resting pan on center tube, which protrudes above top edge of pan, or on side "ears." If pan has neither "ears" nor extended center tube, place inverted tube over funnel or neck of a bottle. Or rest edges of inverted pan on other pans to allow air to circulate. Cake will shrink if removed from pan while warm.

7. *To remove cooled cake,* turn pan right side up. Insert spatula between cake and side of pan until tip touches bottom. Then press gently against side of pan, cutting away clinging cake. Pull spatula out; repeat all around edge and tube. (Use slender knife to loosen cake from center tube.) Then invert cake on cake rack and lift off pan.

Serving Sponge, Angel-Food, and Chiffon Cakes

If tube cake:

1. Frost with Snow-Peak Frosting, p. 647.

2. Or sprinkle with confectioners' sugar mixed with a little mace or nutmeg.

3. Or serve cake wedges topped with Ice-Cream Sauce, p. 536; custard sauce; crushed berries; sliced fruit; or fudge or butterscotch sauce.

If cake layers, or tube cake split into 2 or 3 layers:

1. Fill and frost with Whipped-Cream Frost-

Snowy Orange Cup, p. 615

ing or a variation, p. 648. Sprinkle with grated chocolate, chopped nuts, drained canned crushed pineapple, or flaked coconut.

2. Or fill with jam or jelly; frost with whipped cream or Snow-Peak Frosting, p. 647.

3. Or fill with crushed berries; Clear Lemon Filling or a variaton, p. 642; or Dark-Chocolate Filling, p. 642. Frost with whipped cream.

Follow Susan's step-by-step recipe for ANGEL-FOOD CAKE and variations, p. 134.

SARDI'S SPONGECAKE

1½ cups plus 2 tablesp. sifted all-purpose flour*	1 cup granulated sugar
5 teasp. cornstarch	½ teasp. vanilla extract
10 eggs	¼ cup cooled, melted butter

Make early in day, or day or so before:

1. Start heating oven to 350°F. Grease and flour 3 8" layer pans, 1½" deep. Sift flour with cornstarch.

2. Place large bowl in larger pan or bowl of hot, *not boiling*, water. Into bowl, turn eggs; add sugar. With electric mixer at high speed, or with hand beater, beat egg mixture until just slightly warm. Remove from hot water.

3. Continue beating until egg mixture fills bowl. Beat in vanilla.

4. Over egg mixture, sift one third of flour mixture at a time. Carefully fold in each addition till blended (wire whisk makes this easy). Then quickly fold in butter.

5. Turn into prepared pans. Bake 20 min., or until, when lightly touched in center, no imprint of finger remains. Turn out *at once* onto racks; cool, store. Makes 3 layers.

Or use 1¾ cups sifted cake flour, omitting cornstarch.

CHOCOLATE LAYER CAKE: With sharp knife, carefully split one of the spongecake layers into 3 thin layers. (Store rest of layers for later dessert.) Make Chocolate Butter Cream, p. 645; reserve 1 cup. Sprinkle each layer with about 1 tablesp. sherry; fill and frost them with Chocolate Butter Cream. Use reserved frosting and large rosette tube no. 213 to decorate cake. Press ½ cup macaroon crumbs around sides of cake. Refrigerate till served. Makes 12 servings.

JELLY ROLL

4 eggs	¾ cup granulated sugar
¾ cup sifted cake flour	1 teasp. vanilla extract
¾ teasp. double-acting baking powder	Confectioners' sugar
¼ teasp. salt	1 cup tart jelly or jam

1. *About 1 hr. ahead:* Set out eggs.

2. When ready to make cake, start heating oven to 400°F. With wax paper, line bottom of 15½" x 10½" x 1" jelly-roll pan. Sift flour, baking powder, salt.

3. In small bowl, with electric mixer at high speed (or with hand beater), beat eggs until foamy. Beat rapidly, adding sugar slowly; continue beating until *very thick and light-colored*. With rubber spatula or spoon, fold in flour, vanilla. Turn into pan, spreading batter evenly. Bake 13 min., or until light brown.

4. Lightly dust clean dish towel with confectioners' sugar. When cake is done, with spatula, loosen it from sides of pan; invert onto towel. Lift off pan; carefully peel off paper; with very sharp knife, cut crisp edges from cake. Roll up cake very gently, from narrow end, rolling towel up in it (this prevents cake's sticking). Cool about 10 min.

5. Unroll so cake will be on towel. Spread cake with jelly to within ½" of edges. Start rolling up cake from narrow end by folding edge of cake over, then tucking it under; continue rolling cake, lifting towel higher and higher with one hand as you guide roll with other hand. Finish with open end of cake on underside. Wrap towel tightly around roll to shape it. Finish cooling jelly roll on wire rack. Sprinkle with more confectioners' sugar.

Serve, cut into 1" crosswise slices, just as is or topped with vanilla ice cream. Makes 6 to 8 servings.

CRANBERRY CAKE ROLL: Leave jelly roll rolled up until cold. Meanwhile, make Cranberry Filling: Combine 1 cup canned whole-cranberry sauce with ½ unpeeled orange, ground fine, and ¼ cup granulated sugar. Sprinkle 2 teasp. unflavored gelatine over 2 tablesp. cold water in glass measuring cup to soften; place over hot water until gelatine dissolves; then stir into cranberry mixture. Refrigerate until firm. Unroll jelly roll; spread with cranberry mixture; roll up. Refrigerate, with open end on underside, until served (no longer than 1 hr.). At serving time, frost top with whipped cream or 1 8-oz. pkg. cream cheese, softened.

STRAWBERRY-CREAM ROLL: Leave jelly roll, in step 4, rolled up until cold; unroll. Whip 1 cup heavy cream; fold in ¼ cup granulated sugar and ½ teasp. vanilla extract. Spread on cake; sprinkle with 2 cups sliced strawberries (about 1 pt.). Roll up. Refrigerate, with open end on underside, until served (not longer than 1 hr.). At serving time, sprinkle with confectioners' sugar.

LOVELIGHT CHIFFON LAYER CAKE

2 eggs, separated	baking powder
1½ cups granulated sugar	1 teasp. salt
2¼ cups sifted cake flour	⅓ cup salad oil
	1 cup milk
3 teasp. double-acting	1½ teasp. vanilla extract

1. *About 1 hr. ahead:* Set out separated eggs.
2. When ready to make cake, start heating oven to 350°F. Grease generously, then dust with flour, 2 1½"-deep 8" or 9" layer pans.
3. Beat egg whites until frothy. Gradually beat in ½ cup sugar; continue beating until stiff and glossy enough to stand in peaks.
4. Into large bowl, sift remaining 1 cup sugar, flour, baking powder, salt. Pour in oil, half of milk. With electric mixer* at medium speed, beat 1 min., scraping sides and bottom of bowl as needed. Add remaining milk, egg yolks, extract; beat 1 min.
5. Fold beaten egg whites into batter. Turn into pans. Bake 30 to 35 min. Cool in pans on wire racks about 10 min. Remove from pans; cool on racks.

   This cake may be baked in 13" x 9" x 2" pan at 350°F. 35 to 40 min., or until done.
To mix with spoon, see step 6, p. 627.
FROSTINGS: Fill with Clear Orange Filling, p. 642; frost with Snow-Peak, p. 647; sprinkle generously with flaked coconut. Or split each layer into 2 layers; fill with Luscious Cream Filling, p. 642; frost with Yummy Chocolate, p. 643.

CHOCOLATE TWO-EGG CHIFFON LAYER: Decrease flour to 1¾ cups. Substitute ¾ teasp. baking soda for baking powder. Decrease salt to ¾ teasp. Substitute buttermilk for milk. Omit

extract. With egg yolks, add 2 sq. melted unsweetened chocolate. Bake in 2 1½"-deep 8" or 9" layer pans as at left.

   Or bake in 13" x 9" x 2" pan at 350° F. 40 to 45 min. Split each layer into 2 layers; fill and frost with Chocolate Fluff, p. 649.

MOONLIGHT CAKE WITH STRAWBERRIES: Bake in 13" x 9" x 2" baking dish. Serve in squares with thawed frozen strawberries or raspberries spooned over each.

BIG ORANGE CHIFFON

5 medium egg yolks, unbeaten	baking powder
	1 teasp. salt
7 or 8 egg whites	½ cup salad oil
2¼ cups sifted cake flour*	3 tablesp. grated orange rind
1½ cups granulated sugar	¾ cup orange juice
	½ teasp. cream of tartar
3 teasp. double-acting	

1. *About 1 hr. ahead:* Set out yolks, whites.
2. When ready to make cake, start heating oven to 325°F. Into large bowl, sift flour, sugar, baking powder, salt. Make well in flour mixture; pour salad oil in well. Add egg yolks, orange rind, orange juice. With electric mixer at medium speed (or with spoon), beat until smooth.
3. Pour egg whites into another large bowl; add cream of tartar. With mixer at high speed (or with hand beater), beat whites until they hold *very stiff peaks. Do not underbeat.* (They should be stiffer than for angel-food cake or meringue.)
4. Slowly pour egg-yolk mixture over whites, folding in mixture gently with rubber spatula or spoon. *Do not stir.* Continue folding until mixture is just blended.
5. Turn batter into *ungreased* 4"-deep 10" tube pan. Bake at 325°F. 55 min., then at 350°F. 10 to 15 min., or until cake tester inserted in center comes out clean. Cool and remove as in steps 6 and 7, p. 630.
You may substitute 2 cups sifted all-purpose flour for cake flour; if so, use 7 egg yolks instead of 5.

FROSTINGS: Serve unfrosted; or frost with Orange Butter Cream, p. 645. Or serve as on p. 630.

ALMOND CHIFFON: Substitute 1 teasp. each vanilla and almond extract for orange rind, water for orange juice.

LEMON GOLD: Use 6 egg yolks and 6 egg whites. Substitute 1 teasp. grated lemon rind and 2 teasp. lemon juice for orange rind, water for orange juice. Bake at 325°F. 1 hr. 10 min. Frost with Lemon Butter Cream, p. 645.

BANANA CHIFFON: Substitute 1 cup mashed, ripe bananas (2 or 3 bananas) for 3/4 cup orange juice. Substitute 1 tablesp. lemon juice for grated orange rind.

PINEAPPLE CHIFFON: Substitute 2 teasp. grated lemon rind for orange rind, 3/4 cup pineapple juice for orange juice. Just before pouring batter into pan, fold in 1 cup flaked coconut.

LITTLE ORANGE CHIFFON

2 egg yolks	1/2 teasp. salt
4 egg whites	1/4 cup salad oil
1 cup plus 2 tablesp. sifted cake flour	1 1/2 tablesp. grated orange rind
3/4 cup granulated sugar	1/4 cup plus 2 tablesp. orange juice
1 1/2 teasp. double-acting baking powder	1/4 teasp. cream of tartar

Make as in Big Orange Chiffon, p. 632; bake in one of cake pans below as directed:

1 8" x 8" x 2" pan at 350°F. 30 to 35 min., or until done.

1 9" x 9" x 2" pan at 350°F. 30 to 35 min., or until done.

1 3 1/2"-deep 9" tube pan at 325°F. 50 to 55 min., or until done.

SUGAR BUSH WALNUT CAKE

7 eggs, separated	3/4 cup cold water
2 1/4 cups sifted all-purpose flour	1 teasp. vanilla extract
1 1/2 cups granulated sugar	1 teasp. maple extract
3 teasp. double-acting baking powder	2/3 cup finely chopped walnuts
1 teasp. salt	1/2 teasp. cream of tartar
1/2 cup salad oil	

1. *About 1 hr. before using:* Remove eggs from refrigerator, then separate.
2. Start heating oven to 325°F. In large bowl, place flour, sugar, baking powder, salt, salad oil, cold water, egg yolks, and extracts. With electric mixer at medium speed, beat until mixture is smooth; stir in walnuts.
3. In large bowl, beat egg whites for a moment at high speed. Now add cream of tartar, then continue beating until whites are *very stiff*.
4. Next gently fold *(never stir)* stiffly beaten egg whites into batter.
5. Pour batter into *ungreased* 4"-deep 10" tube pan. Bake cake 55 min., then turn oven heat up to 350°F. and bake 20 min. longer. Test cake by gently pressing top with finger; if it does not spring back, bake 5 min. longer. Cool and remove as in steps 6 and 7, p. 630.
6. Store cake, wrapped in foil or saran. Nice topped with Autumn Mist Topping, p. 649, or served as is.

COFFEE CLOUD CAKE

1 tablesp. instant coffee	2 cups granulated sugar
1 cup boiling water	6 egg yolks
2 cups sifted all-purpose flour	1 teasp. vanilla extract
3 teasp. double-acting baking powder	1 cup finely chopped walnuts
1/2 teasp. salt	Coffee Butter Cream Frosting, p. 645
6 egg whites	1 1/2 cups coarsely chopped walnuts
1/2 teasp. cream of tartar	

1. Stir coffee into boiling water until dissolved, then cool. Start heating oven to 350°F.
2. Sift together flour, baking powder, and salt.
3. In large bowl, beat egg whites with cream of tartar until soft mounds begin to form; then add 1/2 cup granulated sugar, 2 tablesp. at a time, continuing to beat until very stiff, and straight peaks are formed. *Do not underbeat.* Set aside.
4. In large bowl, beat egg yolks until blended; then gradually beat in 1 1/2 cups granulated sugar and vanilla. Now beat at high speed until thick and lemon-colored, 5 to 10 min.
5. Then to egg-yolk mixture, add flour mixture alternately with cooled coffee, beginning and ending with flour mixture. Fold in finely chopped walnuts.
6. Into stiffly beaten egg whites, fold egg-yolk mixture, one fourth at a time, using no more than 15 strokes for each addition. After last addition, continue folding just until evenly blended.
7. Pour batter into ungreased 10" tube pan.

Bake 60 to 70 min., or until cake springs back when touched lightly with finger.

8. Cool and remove as in steps 6 and 7, p. 630.

9. Now make frosting. Frost top and sides of cake generously with it. Cover top and sides with 1½ cups coarsely chopped walnuts, sprinkling them on top and pressing them into sides.

LUSCIOUS FRUITCAKES

ETHEL'S FRUITCAKE

4 cups sifted all-purpose flour	½ lb. blanched almonds, finely chopped
1 teasp. baking soda	½ lb. pecans, coarsely chopped
1 teasp. nutmeg	1 15-oz. pkg. light raisins
2 teasp. cinnamon	
1 teasp. ground cloves	2 1-lb. pkg. seeded raisins
1 lb. dried figs, finely snipped	
1 lb. pitted dates, finely snipped	1 lb. soft butter or margarine
1 lb. preserved pineapple, diced	2 cups brown sugar, packed
¼ lb. each preserved orange rind, preserved lemon rind, and citron, diced	12 egg yolks
	½ cup canned pineapple juice
1 lb. candied cherries, snipped	½ cup light molasses
	12 egg whites

Make a month or so ahead, early in day: Sift together flour, baking soda, nutmeg, cinnamon, and cloves. In large bowl, thoroughly mix figs, dates, pineapple, orange and lemon rinds, citron, cherries, almonds, pecans, and raisins; add 2 cups of the sifted flour mixture. With wax paper, snugly line 1 well-greased 5½″ x 3″ x 2¼″ loaf pan; 2 6″ x 3½″ round tea or coffee cans; 2 7½″ x 3½″ x 2¼″ loaf pans; and 1 2-qt. casserole. Lightly grease wax paper.

Start heating oven to 275°F. In large bowl, with electric mixer at medium speed, beat butter and brown sugar until fluffy. Next, mix in egg yolks. Then mix in alternately, just until smooth, remaining flour mixture, juice, and molasses. Turn mixture into large kettle; then stir in fruit mixture by hand. Now beat egg whites until they form soft peaks; fold into cake mixture. Turn mixture into prepared pans, filling two thirds full. Bake 3 loaf cakes 2 to 2½ hr.; bake 2 round cakes 2½ to 3 hr.; bake casserole cake, covered, 2 hr.; then uncovered, 45 min.

Test for doneness as in step 10, p. 620. Completely cool cakes in pans; then remove paper. Wrap cakes tightly in saran or foil; then refrigerate. If desired, unwrap occasionally and brush with cider, port, sherry, or brandy.

To freeze: These cakes freeze well; see To Freeze Cakes, p. 707.

BRAZIL-NUT SENSATION

¾ cup sifted all-purpose flour	zil nuts (3 cups shelled)
¾ cup granulated sugar	2 pkg. pitted dates (about 1 lb.)
½ teasp. double-acting baking powder	1 cup *well-drained* maraschino cherries
½ teasp. salt	3 eggs
2 lb. unshelled Bra-	1 teasp. vanilla extract

Start heating oven to 300°F. Grease, then line with wax paper, 9″ x 5″ x 3″ loaf pan. In sifter, place flour, sugar, baking powder, salt.

In large bowl, place shelled nuts, dates, cherries; sift flour mixture over these; with hands, mix until nuts and fruit are well coated. Beat eggs until foamy; add vanilla; stir well into nut mixture; spread evenly in pan. Bake 1 hr. 45 min. Test for doneness, then cool as in steps 10 and 11, p. 620. Wrap in foil. Refrigerate. Keeps 5 or 6 weeks.

FRUITCAKE CONFECTION

½ cup sifted all-purpose flour	2 tablesp. orange juice
½ teasp. salt	3½ cups pecan halves
½ teasp. double-acting baking powder	1 cup diced preserved pineapple
⅛ teasp. allspice	½ cup diced preserved orange peel
⅛ teasp. nutmeg	
⅓ cup soft shortening	½ cup diced preserved lemon peel
3 tablesp. brown sugar	¼ cup diced preserved citron
3 tablesp. honey	1 cup candied cherries
2 eggs, unbeaten	White corn syrup

Start heating oven to 300°F. With 2 thicknesses wax paper, line 1¼″-deep 8″ layer pan; then grease. Sift flour, salt, baking powder, allspice, nutmeg.

In large bowl, with electric mixer* at medium speed, mix shortening with sugar, then
To mix with spoon, see step 7, p. 620.

with honey and eggs, until *very light and fluffy* — about 4 min. altogether. Then, at low speed, beat in alternately, *just until smooth,* flour mixture and orange juice.

Spread one third of batter in cake pan. To remaining batter, add pecans and next 5 ingredients, reserving a few pecans and cherries; spoon onto batter in pan, packing down batter and leveling top. Decorate with reserved nuts and cherries. Cover with brown paper; tie securely. Set in shallow pan of hot water (water should be only one fourth depth of layer pan). Bake 1 hr.; remove from water; bake 1 hr. longer. Test for doneness as in step 10, p. 620. When cake is done, brush top with hot corn syrup. Cool completely in pan on wire rack; remove from pan; peel off paper. Keeps up to 2 months wrapped in foil and refrigerated.

DARK CHRISTMAS FRUITCAKE

1 cup currants	lengthwise
3 cups light or dark raisins	2 cups sifted all-purpose flour
½ cup diced preserved orange peel	1 teasp. nutmeg
½ cup diced preserved lemon peel	1½ teasp. cinnamon
1½ cups diced preserved citron	1½ teasp. ground cloves
1 cup halved candied cherries	½ teasp. baking soda
	1 cup soft shortening
1 cup diced preserved pineapple	1 cup brown sugar, packed
1 cup pecan halves	6 eggs, separated
1 cup blanched almonds, halved	½ sq. unsweetened chocolate, melted
	¼ cup lemon juice
	¼ cup orange juice

Thoroughly grease 3½″-deep 9″, or 4″-deep 10″, tube pan. Cut heavy wax paper to fit bottom and sides of pan. Line pan with wax paper (be sure paper fits snugly), and lightly grease paper. Or use foil without greasing. In large bowl, thoroughly mix currants, raisins, peels, citron, cherries, pineapple, and nuts with 1 cup flour until all are coated with flour. Start heating oven to 300°F. Sift remaining 1 cup flour with spices and soda.

In large bowl, with electric mixer at medium speed, blend shortening with sugar *until light and fluffy.* Add egg yolks, one at a time, beating thoroughly after each addition. Then add melted chocolate. At low speed, beat in alternately, *just until smooth,* flour mixture and fruit juices.

When mixture is thoroughly blended, stir by hand into fruit mixture. Beat egg whites until stiff; fold into cake mixture. Turn into tube pan. Bake 2 hr. 20 min. Test for doneness as in step 10, p. 620. Cool completely in pan; remove paper; then store as on p. 620.

HOLIDAY WHITE FRUITCAKE

2 cups sifted all-purpose flour	1 cup slivered blanched almonds
1 teasp. double-acting baking powder	1 cup diced preserved citron
¼ teasp. salt	½ cup diced preserved orange peel
1 cup soft shortening	1½ cups halved candied cherries
1 cup granulated sugar	1½ teasp. grated lemon rind
5 medium eggs, unbeaten	½ cup sifted all-purpose flour
1 tablesp. lemon juice	

Start heating oven to 300°F. Grease, then line with wax paper, bottom of 10″ x 5″ x 3″ loaf pan. Sift flour, baking powder, salt.

In large bowl, with electric mixer* at medium speed, thoroughly mix shortening with sugar, then with eggs, until *very light and fluffy* — about 4 min. altogether. At low speed, beat in flour mixture and lemon juice; then add almonds combined with rest of ingredients, beating just until mixed. Turn into pan. Bake 1¾ hr. Test for doneness, then cool as in steps 10 and 11, p. 620. Store as on p. 620.
To mix with spoon, see step 7, p. 620.

GOLDEN FRUITCAKE

2 cups light raisins (or half dark raisins)	1 cup halved, blanched almonds or pecans or walnuts
1 cup diced preserved citron	4 cups sifted all-purpose flour
1 cup diced preserved lemon peel	½ teasp. salt
1 cup diced preserved orange peel	2 teasp. double-acting baking powder
½ cup diced preserved pineapple	1 cup butter or margarine
½ cup halved candied cherries	2 cups granulated sugar
1½ cups snipped dried figs	6 eggs, unbeaten
1 cup snipped pitted dates	1 teasp. lemon or orange extract
½ cup currants	1 cup sherry or orange juice

Make several weeks ahead:

1. Line 4″-deep 10″ tube pan with foil. Start heating oven to 300°F.

2. In large bowl, combine fruits and nuts. Over them, sift flour, salt, baking powder; toss lightly until fruits and nuts are well coated.

3. In large bowl, with electric mixer* at medium speed, mix butter with sugar, then with eggs and extract, until *very light and fluffy* — about 4 min. altogether. Then, with spoon, stir in fruit mixture alternately with sherry just until mixed.

4. Turn batter into tube pan. Bake 3 hr. Test for doneness as in step 10, p. 620. Cool in pan on cake rack; remove foil used for baking, then store as on p. 620.

*To mix with spoon, see step 7, p. 620.

FROSTING: Frost with Golden Frosting, p. 647.

CAKES IN LESS TIME

Turn to a cake mix when you must save time but still want to make a luscious cake. Tube cakes, layers, squares, sheets, or cupcakes can be made with mix. In fact, with cake mix and Fillings and Frostings, pp. 641–650, it's pretty hard to tell whether or not you started "from scratch." It really is your cake, for you've baked it.

The array of mixes on your grocer's shelves is positively staggering. You'll find:

SHORTENING-TYPE CAKES — namely, golden yellow, fluffy white, rich devil's food, fragrant spice, marvel marble, yummy burnt sugar, luscious chocolate mint, cherry and lemon and coconut, black walnut, milk chocolate, toasted coconut and toffee swirl, pink lemonade, fudge coconut, sugar maple, lemon flake, etc., etc.

OLD-TIME FAVORITES — pound cake, apple and raisin, butter pecan, fudge nut, cherry almond, date nut, orange, banana, etc.

CAKES WITH BAKED-ON TOPPINGS — such as apple, cinnamon, butterscotch crumb, cinnamon raisin, cinnamon streusel, etc.

A WONDERFUL VARIETY OF ANGEL-FOOD CAKES — such as fudge swirl, lemon custard, orange-pineapple, chocolate-chip, pineapple-lemon, pink lemonade, raspberry sundae, confetti, Hawaiian, regular angel food, etc. And these have been joined by lemon and orange chiffon cake mixes, etc.

P.S. If your family is small, there are small-size packages of mixes in many flavors. Or make up a regular-size package of mix; bake half of the cake batter as a layer, the rest as cupcakes. Then refrigerate or freeze the cupcakes you don't need that night, for serving in a different way a day or so later.

Quick Tricks with Cake Mixes

With a number of "tricks" up your sleeve, the number of potential cake desserts from cake mixes becomes endless. Your family may vote for one of the ideas below.

BATTER PLUS

1. Fold 1 or 2 sq. unsweetened chocolate, grated, into devil's-food, yellow, white, or black-walnut cake-mix batter. Or alternate layers of grated chocolate and angel-food batter.

2. Fold 3 tablesp. grated orange rind into yellow, lemon, white, or coconut cake-mix batter.

3. Add 1 tablesp. instant coffee to liquid in angel-food cake mix. Or add 4 teasp. instant coffee powder to the dry white, yellow, or chocolate cake mix.

4. Fold ½ cup *finely chopped* walnuts into devil's-food, chocolate-mint, marble, pound, or angel-food cake-mix batter. Or sprinkle top of batter with ⅓ cup finely sliced, blanched almonds or flaked coconut.

IN BETWEEN

1. Blend soft cream cheese with currant jelly and confectioners' sugar. Spread between baked cherry, chocolate-mint, black-walnut, or fudge-coconut cake layers.

2. Combine peanut butter with drained crushed pineapple to spreading consistency. Use between baked spice, yellow, or white cake layers.

3. Spread apricot preserves, mixed with

chopped raisins, between baked white, burnt sugar, or lemon-flake-coconut cake layers.

OVER THE TOP

1. Spoon fudge sauce over slices of devil's-food, marble, chocolate-mint, chocolate-chip, yellow, or angel-food cake.
2. Heat marmalade with some orange juice; spoon over squares of yellow cake or slices of pound cake.
3. Spice applesauce with cinnamon and nutmeg; spoon over slices of spice, burnt sugar, or yellow cake.
4. Fold fresh or thawed frozen strawberries into whipped cream; spoon over slices of angel-food or orange or lemon chiffon cake.

MOCHA ANGEL SPECIAL

1 pkg. angel-food cake mix	2 cups heavy cream
Mom's Mocha Filling, p. 643	1 tablesp. instant coffee

Make day before: Start heating oven to 375°F. Prepare angel-food cake batter as label directs; bake in 2 10″ x 5″ x 3″ loaf-cake pans for 35 to 40 min., or until done. Cool and remove, as in steps 6 and 7, p. 630. Freeze one of the cakes as on p. 707.

Invert second cake; cut into 4 even layers; spread Mom's Mocha Filling between layers; refrigerate overnight.

Several hr. before serving: Combine cream and instant coffee; whip until stiff; spread over top and sides of cake. Refrigerate at least 3 hr.; slice. Makes 8 to 10 servings.

SKY-HIGH CHOCOLATE CREAM

1. Using fine grater, grate 1 sq. unsweetened chocolate.
2. Prepare 1 pkg. angel-food mix as label directs; fold in chocolate; turn into ungreased 10″ tube pan. Bake and cool as directed.
3. Make Chocolate Fluff Frosting, p. 649. Cut cooled cake into 3 even layers; fill and frost with chocolate frosting. Refrigerate until serving time. Makes 16 servings.

MARBLE ANGEL FOOD

Sift 2 tablesp. flour mixture from envelope in 1 pkg. angel-food cake mix with 3 tablesp. cocoa. Use balance of flour with egg-white mixture to prepare angel-food batter as label directs. Place half of batter in second bowl, and gently fold in cocoa mixture till blended.

Alternately spoon white and dark batters into 10″ angel-food pan; with rubber spatula, cut through mixture several times, swirling light and dark batters for a marbleized effect. Bake and cool as label directs. Cut into large wedges to serve.

CREME DE CACAO ANGEL FOOD

1 pkg. angel-food mix	½ cup crème de cacao
2 tablesp. light cream	

Day before, or early in day: Make, bake, cool, remove angel food as package directs.

About 2½ hr. before serving:
1. Turn cake back into pan. Combine light cream with crème de cacao.
2. Using a wooden skewer about 5″ long, make many holes, of varying depths, down through top of cake. Into holes, pour half of cream mixture; let stand in pan 2 hr.; refrigerate all.

Just before serving:
1. Onto serving plate, invert cake, crust side down. Down through top of cake, make more holes.
2. Into these holes, pour remaining crème de cacao mixture. Serve in wedges.

RIBBON POUNDCAKE

Split a poundcake (frozen, from mix, or bakers') lengthwise into 4 layers. Fill layers with 1 cup semisweet-chocolate pieces, melted over hot, *not boiling*, water, or with one or more favorite jams. Slice crosswise to serve.

BITTERSWEET GINGERBREAD

Bake 1 pkg. gingerbread mix as label directs. While it's still warm, cut into 3″ squares, then split each square across middle. Spoon hot or cold chocolate-caramel sauce (comes in jars) over bottom halves; replace tops; spoon on more. Top with dessert topping or whipped cream, if desired.

CUPCAKES UNLIMITED

Children love cupcakes. Cupcakes tote well, store well, and are suitable for just about every occasion. Whether you start from scratch or use your favorite mix, you can individualize each one.

Important How-Tos

1. *Grease and flour just the bottoms of cupcake-pan cups.* This helps keep cupcakes from running over pans.
2. *Or buy and use packaged paper liners* for cupcake cups. They do away with greasing, scouring, and sticking. Peel them off when cupcakes are cool.
3. *Never fill cupcake cups more than half full,* unless directed otherwise. Don't guess. Fill 1 cupcake cup with water; measure water; use half this amount of batter for each cupcake. To pour batter, use cup from graduated measuring-cup set.

ONE-EGG CUPCAKES

Make One-Egg Cake, p. 621, reducing milk to 3/4 cup. Pour batter into cupcake cups, prepared as above. Bake at 375°F. 20 min., or until cake tester, inserted in center, comes out clean. Makes 24 2 1/2" cupcakes.

SPICE: With flour, sift 1 teasp. allspice, 2 teasp. cinnamon, and 1 teasp. nutmeg. Reduce vanilla to 1/2 teasp.

OLD-FASHIONED WHITE CUPCAKES

2 1/2 cups sifted cake flour	4 1/2 teasp. double-acting baking powder
1 2/3 cups granulated sugar	5 egg whites, unbeaten
1 teasp. salt	1/4 cup plus 2 tablesp. milk
3/4 cup soft shortening, p. 627	1 teasp. vanilla extract
3/4 cup milk	

Start heating oven to 375°F. Prepare 24 3" cupcake-pan cups as above.

Into large bowl, sift flour, sugar, salt. Drop in shortening; pour in 3/4 cup milk.

With mixer* at low to medium speed, mix until all flour is dampened; then beat 2 min., scraping bowl and beaters as needed. Stir in baking powder. Then add egg whites, 1/4 cup plus 2 tablesp. milk, vanilla; beat 2 min. Fill cups half full. Bake 20 min., or until cake tester, inserted in center, comes out clean. Makes 24 cupcakes.
To mix with spoon, see step 6, p. 627.

DEVIL'S-FOOD CUPCAKES

1 cup sifted cake flour	1/4 cup soft shortening, p. 627
1/2 teasp. double-acting baking powder	1/4 cup water
1/2 teasp. salt	1/2 teasp. vanilla extract
1/2 teasp. baking soda	1/4 cup plus 2 tablesp. buttermilk
1/4 cup cocoa	1 egg, unbeaten
3/4 cup granulated sugar	1 egg yolk, unbeaten

Start heating oven to 350°F. Prepare 12 2 1/2" cupcake-pan cups as at left.

Into large bowl, sift flour, baking powder, salt, soda, cocoa, sugar. Drop in shortening; pour in water, vanilla, 2 tablesp. buttermilk.

With mixer* at low to medium speed, beat 2 min., scraping bowl and beaters as needed. Add remaining 1/4 cup buttermilk, egg, egg yolk; beat 1 min. Fill cups half full. Bake 25 min., or until cake tester, inserted in center, comes out clean. Makes 12 cupcakes.
To mix with spoon, see step 6, p. 627.

SHERRY CHRISTMAS CUPCAKES

3 cups sifted all-purpose flour	1 cup diced mixed preserved fruits
1 1/4 teasp. baking soda	1 cup chopped walnuts
1/2 teasp. salt	1 cup soft shortening
1/2 teasp. cinnamon	1 1/2 cups granulated sugar
1/2 teasp. nutmeg	2 eggs, unbeaten
1/4 teasp. ground cloves	1 cup sherry
1 cup light or dark raisins	1/2 cup honey

Start heating oven to 325°F. Grease bottoms of 25 to 30 3" cupcake-pan cups. Sift flour, soda, salt, cinnamon, nutmeg, cloves; stir in raisins, preserved fruits, walnuts.

In large bowl, with electric mixer* at medium speed, mix shortening with sugar, then with eggs, until *very light and fluffy* — about 4 min. altogether. At low speed, beat in alternately, *just until smooth,* fruit mixture, sherry, honey. Fill cupcake-pan cups two thirds full. Bake 50 to 60 min., or until cake tester, inserted in center, comes out clean. Dip into sugar; top with pieces of preserved fruit, if desired. Makes 25 to 30 cupcakes.

To mix with spoon, see step 7, p. 620.

DOUBLE-CHOCOLATE MINIATURE CAKES

1 3-oz. pkg. cream cheese, softened	¾ teasp. baking soda
1 egg, unbeaten	¾ cup water
1 egg yolk, unbeaten	⅓ cup salad oil
Granulated sugar	1 egg white
Salt	1 tablesp. vinegar
½ cup semisweet-chocolate pieces	1 teasp. vanilla extract
1½ cups sifted all-purpose flour	¾ cup canned toasted, slivered almonds, chopped
¼ cup cocoa	

Make early in the day, or day before, if desired:

1. Start heating oven to 350°F. Place paper liners in 12 3" cupcake-pan cups.
2. In small bowl, with mixer at medium speed, beat cream cheese, egg, egg yolk, ¼ cup granulated sugar, and dash of salt until smooth; then stir in semisweet-chocolate pieces. Set aside.
3. Into large bowl, sift together flour, 1 cup granulated sugar, cocoa, baking soda, ½ teasp. salt.
4. Combine water, salad oil, egg white, vinegar, and vanilla; beat well with fork. Then add, all at once, to dry ingredients; stir with spoon until well combined.
5. Fill each prepared cupcake-pan cup about half full with cocoa batter. Onto center of each cupcake-pan cup of batter, spoon 1 tablesp. of cream cheese mixture.
6. Now generously sprinkle tops with about 1 tablesp. granulated sugar, then with almonds.

Bake 25 to 30 min., or until cake tester, inserted in the center, comes out clean and cupcakes are golden. Cool in pans 10 min., then remove to rack to finish cooling. Makes 12.

To serve: Peel paper liners off cupcakes. Nice with fruit.

TRICKY CUPCAKES

From your favorite cake or cupcake mix, make cupcakes as label directs. Top as follows:

CHOCOLATE BUTTERFLIES: With paring knife, remove cone-shaped piece from top center of each chocolate cupcake. Fill hollow with whipped cream, ice cream, or Snow-Peak Frosting, p. 647. Cut cake cone in half; press into filling to look like butterfly wings.

HONEYCOMB: Dip top of cupcake into honey; sprinkle with finely chopped nuts or grated orange rind, or nuts and rind combined.

LACY COCOA: Cut out small cardboard pattern of star, tree, etc. Place on top of each cupcake; sift cocoa over top; gently lift off pattern.

NUGGET: Just before cupcakes are done, gently press nut-meat half into top of each; or sprinkle with chopped nuts. Finish baking.

SHADOW: Drizzle melted unsweetened chocolate over frosted or unfrosted cupcakes. Sprinkle with finely chopped nuts, if desired.

SNOWBALL: Frost cupcakes with whipped cream or Snow-Peak Frosting, p. 647. Sprinkle sides generously with flaked coconut, alone or with snipped candied cherries added.

HALF AND HALF: Cut white and chocolate or gingerbread cupcakes vertically in halves. Spread cut surfaces with Butter Cream or Mocha Butter Cream, p. 645. Before frosting sets, press 2 contrasting halves together. Or frost top and cut side of chocolate half with Butter Cream; frost top of white half with green-tinted Butter Cream; press together.

PINEAPPLE-CREAM: Split each cupcake into 3 layers. Fill with Quick Pineapple Filling, p. 642. Sift confectioners' sugar on top. Or top with whipped cream and bit of drained canned crushed pineapple.

BROILED PRALINE: Top each cupcake with Broiled Praline, p. 647, omitting nuts. Broil as directed.

ANGEL CUPCAKE TRIPLETS

1 tablesp. instant coffee	pecans
	¼ teasp. cinnamon
1 pkg. angel-food mix	⅛ teasp. nutmeg
⅓ cup flaked coconut	⅛ teasp. ground cloves
⅓ cup finely chopped	

Start heating oven to 375°F. Line about 4 doz. cupcake-pan cups with paper liners. In bowl in which cake is to be mixed, dissolve coffee in water called for on angel-food-package label. Complete mixing angel food as label directs.

Spoon about one third of batter into about 16 cupcake-pan cups, filling cups about two thirds full; sprinkle with coconut. Divide remaining batter in half. Into one half, fold nuts;

spoon into 16 more cupcake-pan cups. To remaining half, add spices; spoon into rest of cupcake-pan cups. Bake 12 to 15 min., or until done. Makes about 4 doz. cupcakes.

KENTUCKY CUPCAKES

2 sq. unsweetened chocolate	2 eggs, separated
1 teasp. allspice	¾ cup buttermilk
¼ teasp. cinnamon	2 tablesp. fruit juice
1½ teasp. baking soda	½ cup seedless black raspberry preserves
1½ cups sifted all-purpose flour	½ cup light or dark raisins
⅓ cup shortening	½ cup currants
½ cup granulated sugar	½ cup chopped walnuts
½ cup brown sugar, packed	

1. Start heating oven to 350°F. Line 16 3″ cupcake-pan cups with paper liners.
2. Melt chocolate and cool. Sift together allspice, cinnamon, baking soda, and flour.
3. In large bowl, with electric mixer at medium speed, mix shortening with sugars, then with egg yolks, *until very light and fluffy* — about 4 min. altogether.
4. Combine buttermilk and fruit juice. At low speed, add these to egg-yolk mixture, alternately with flour mixture, beginning and ending with flour mixture, *just until smooth.* Add preserves and melted chocolate; blend thoroughly.
5. Fold in raisins, currants, and walnuts. Beat egg whites until stiff but not dry. Fold into batter; pour into prepared cupcake-pan cups. Bake 25 to 30 min., or until cake springs back when lightly touched with finger. Remove from pans and cool on cake racks.

FROSTING: Make up 1 pkg. fluffy white frosting mix as label directs. With yellow food color, tint it yellow. Use to swirl on top of cupcakes. From an uncooked dried prune, snip a long narrow piece; with fingers, shape it into curved piece; set in place on top of one of cupcakes as mouth. Cut 2 small circles from a prune; set in place as eyes. Cut 1 small circle from a prune; set in place as nose. Repeat with more prunes until all cupcakes are decorated. Makes 16.

CANDLE CUPCAKES

RAINBOW: Dip tip end of each almond into melted semisweet chocolate; let dry. Or use Jordan almonds. Tuck tiny candle into top center of each pastel-frosted cupcake; group 3 or 4 almonds around it.

IN THE PINK: Top each white-frosted cupcake with red maraschino or candied cherry; then insert white candle in cherry.

RINGLING: Top each pastel-frosted cupcake with 2 hard round candies with holes in center, placing one on top of other. Insert yellow candle in center of candies.

FLOWERET: Split 2 or 3 small red gumdrops. With fingers, shape into petals. Insert candle into center of each white-frosted cupcake. Surround with gumdrop petals.

BIRTHDAY STYLE: Make, bake, frost cupcakes, using favorite cake and frosting. At serving time, cut firm brick ice cream into ½″ slices. Dip a biscuit cutter, slightly larger than base of cupcakes, into very hot water; use to cut hole from center of each ice-cream slice. Set cupcake in each, with lighted candle on top.

CAKE DECORATING

There's no one, young or old, who doesn't love to celebrate a special occasion with a wonderful, fanciful cake — the kind that's so pretty and gay, you almost hate to cut it.

In *Good Housekeeping's Book of Cake Decorating,* which you will find in your bookstore, we have included 64 color photographs, hundreds of other illustrations, plus everything you need to know to make dozens and dozens of exciting decorated cakes, cupcakes, and cookies, too. Anniversaries, showers, graduations, birthdays, children's and teen-agers' parties, Father's Day, Christmas, St. Valentine's Day, Easter, and all the holidays have been remembered.

And illustrated pages describe all the decorating tubes and what they do, as well as special cake pans and cookie cutters you can buy.

CAKES TO BUY

We're blessed, today, with an unusually fine selection of ready-baked cakes — some baked, waiting for you on your grocer's shelves, others in his freezer. If you have not made the acquaintance of the frozen cake family, do so; they are wonderful to have on hand in your freezer at all times.

FILLINGS AND FROSTINGS

Little people love to clean out the frosting bowl. Big and little people will consider even the simplest cake a wonderful treat when it's frosted with one of our frostings below.

Be sure to read the detailed How-To section below. Remember that frosting is always at its best the day it goes on the cake. For storing leftover egg yolks or egg whites, see p. 358.

Before using these recipes, refer to How To Use Our Recipes, p. 3. Always use standard measuring cups and measuring spoons; measure level.

How to Fill and Frost a Cake

SQUARE, LOAF, SHEET, OR TUBE CAKE:
1. If you plan to use a butter frosting, cool cake well before frosting; otherwise, frosting may melt. If an egg-white frosting is your favorite, cake may be slightly warm when frosted.
2. Brush or rub off loose crumbs; trim ragged edges with scissors.
3. Place cake, with top side up (if tube cake, place bottom side up), on flat cake plate or tray that extends about 2″ all around cake.

4. To keep cake plate clean while frosting cake, cover outer top area of plate with strips of wax paper, extending them beyond edge of plate.
5. So cake can be turned as you frost, set cake plate on rim of mixing bowl, with plate extending at least 1″ beyond rim of bowl; or place plate on platform of electric mixer (if it's a big cake, detach mixer head).
6. Use a spatula to spread frosting.
7. Working quickly, frost sides of cake first, using upward strokes.
8. Pile rest of frosting on top; spread out in attractive swirls to meet sides. Spread naturally and irregularly, not painfully smooth.
9. Let frosting set slightly; then carefully pull out wax-paper strips.

LAYER CAKES:
1. If there is any difference in height of layers make the thicker layer the bottom layer; use smooth, crusted layer on top. Place 1 layer, upside down, on cake plate. Adjust strips of paper on plate, as above.
2. Spread filling on bottom layer, almost to edge (if filling is soft, spread only to 1″ from edge). Adjust second layer, with top side up, so edges are even and cake is of uniform height.

641

If top layer slides, insert wire cake tester or slender knitting needle through both layers to anchor them. Remove cake tester before frosting top.

3. Frost as in steps 5 through 9, p. 641.

FOR VERY SPECIAL CAKES: It pays to frost cake first with thin, smooth layer of frosting, to hold down crumbs. Let this layer set; then final frosting will spread more easily.

Also see Cake Decorating, p. 640.

FILLINGS

CREAMY CUSTARD FILLING

⅓ cup granulated sugar	¾ cup scalded milk
2 tablesp. flour	1 teasp. vanilla extract
⅛ teasp. salt	½ cup heavy cream, whipped
1 egg, slightly beaten	

In double-boiler top, mix sugar, flour, salt. Stir in egg, then milk; blend thoroughly. Cook over boiling water, stirring constantly, 5 min. Cook, stirring occasionally, 5 min. longer. Refrigerate until cold. Add vanilla, then fold in whipped cream.

Fills 2 8″ or 9″ cake layers.

ALMOND: Use ½ teasp. vanilla extract and ½ teasp. almond extract. To cold filling add ½ cup chopped, toasted almonds.

CREAM PUFF: Double ingredients. Fills 8 cream puffs.

CLEAR LEMON FILLING

1 cup granulated sugar	2 tablesp. grated lemon rind
3 tablesp. cornstarch	½ cup lemon juice
½ teasp. salt	2 tablesp. butter or margarine
1 cup boiling water	

Combine all ingredients. Bring to full, rolling boil, stirring occasionally. Turn down heat; boil 1 min., stirring. Let cool at room temperature. Before using, beat with hand beater. Fills 2 8″ or 9″ layer cakes.

LIME: Increase boiling water to 1¼ cups. Substitute grated lime rind for lemon rind, ¼ cup lime juice for lemon juice.

ORANGE: Reduce boiling water to ¾ cup. Substitute grated orange rind for lemon rind, ¾ cup orange juice for lemon juice. Add 1 tablesp. lemon juice.

LANE FILLING

8 egg yolks	3½-oz. can flaked coconut
1¼ cups granulated sugar	1 cup cut-up candied cherries
½ cup butter or margarine	⅓ cup whisky or wine
1 cup chopped pecans	1 cup finely chopped seeded raisins
1 cup grated fresh coconut, or 1	

1. In saucepan, beat egg yolks slightly. Cook with sugar and butter over low heat, stirring, about 5 min., or until slightly thickened.
2. Add pecans and rest of ingredients. Cool. Fills 4 9″ cake layers.

DARK-CHOCOLATE FILLING

1 egg yolk	1 sq. unsweetened chocolate
½ cup granulated sugar	1 tablesp. butter or margarine
3 tablesp. light cream	

Combine all ingredients. Cook over medium heat, stirring, until mixture bubbles around edges. Remove from heat. Beat till thick. Fills 2 8″ or 9″ cake layers.

LUSCIOUS CREAM FILLING

Fix 1 pkg. vanilla pudding and pie-filling mix as label directs, reducing milk to 1½ cups; lay piece of wax paper on surface of pudding; refrigerate. When pudding is chilled, remove paper; fold in ½ cup heavy cream, whipped. Flavor with a little vanilla or almond extract. Fills 2 8″ or 9″ cake layers.

QUICK ORANGE: Substitute 1½ cups orange juice for milk. With cream, add 1 tablesp. grated orange rind.

QUICK PINEAPPLE: Instead of cream, fold in ½ cup drained canned crushed pineapple.

QUICK CHOCOLATE: Substitute 1 pkg. chocolate pudding and pie filling for vanilla pudding. Make as label directs, reducing milk to 1½ cups. Into hot filling, stir 2 tablesp. brown sugar. Omit cream, if desired.

QUICK BUTTERSCOTCH: Substitute 1 pkg. butterscotch pudding for vanilla pudding. Make as label directs, reducing milk to 1½ cups. Into hot filling, stir 2 tablesp. brown sugar and 3 tablesp. melted butter or margarine. Omit cream, if desired.

QUICK LEMON: Substitute 1 pkg. lemon pudding and pie filling for vanilla pudding. Make as label directs. Omit cream.

WALNUT FILLING

Combine 1 cup ground walnuts, ½ cup light cream, ⅔ cup granulated sugar, ¼ teasp. salt, 2 egg yolks. Cook over low heat, stirring, till mixture thickens and turns brown. Add 2 teasp. butter or margarine. Cool at room temperature. Fills 2 8″ or 9″ yellow or white cake layers.

RICH PINEAPPLE FILLING

¾ cup granulated sugar	1 tablesp. lemon juice
2½ tablesp. cornstarch	3 egg yolks, slightly beaten
⅛ teasp. salt	¾ cup canned pineapple juice
1 teasp. grated lemon rind	2 tablesp. butter or margarine

In double-boiler top, thoroughly mix sugar, cornstarch, salt. Stir in lemon rind and juice, then rest of ingredients. Cook over boiling water, stirring constantly, until smooth and thickened — about 15 min. Refrigerate till cold. Fills 2 8″ or 9″ cake layers.

RICH ORANGE FILLING

½ cup granulated sugar	1 tablesp. grated orange rind
3 tablesp. flour	¾ cup heavy cream, whipped
1 egg yolk	
⅓ cup orange juice	

In double boiler, blend sugar with flour, egg yolk, and orange juice; add rind. Cook over boiling water until thickened. Chill; then fold in heavy cream. Fills 2 7″ or 8″ spongecake layers, split.

WHIPPED-CREAM FILLING

2 teasp. unflavored gelatine	½ cup confectioners' sugar
2 tablesp. cold water	⅓ cup white rum
2 cups heavy cream	

1. Sprinkle gelatine over cold water; heat mixture over hot water until gelatine is dissolved; cool slightly.

2. In medium bowl, set in bowl of ice, beat cream with sugar until fairly stiff; gradually beat in rum. Add gelatine slowly, beating till just stiff enough to hold its shape. Keep in bowl of ice till ready to use. Fills 4 9″ yellow or white cake layers.

MOM'S MOCHA FILLING

1 cup butter or margarine	2 egg yolks
1⅔ cups sifted confectioners' sugar	2 sq. unsweetened chocolate, melted
Dash salt	⅓ cup water
1 teasp. vanilla extract	2 teasp. instant coffee
	2 egg whites

Cream together butter and confectioners' sugar until blended. Add salt, vanilla, egg yolks; beat thoroughly. Add chocolate, water, coffee; beat well again; fold in egg whites, stiffly beaten. Fills 1 10″ x 5″ x 3″ angel-food loaf cake, split into 4 layers.

SPICY CREAM FILLING

½ cup heavy cream	¼ teasp. nutmeg
Dash salt	½ teasp. cinnamon

Beat cream until stiff; fold in salt, nutmeg, and cinnamon. Fills 2 9″ cake layers.

UNCOOKED FROSTINGS

YUMMY CHOCOLATE FROSTING

1 cup sifted confectioners' sugar	½ teasp. vanilla extract
1 egg; or 2 egg yolks*	4 sq. unsweetened chocolate, melted
¼ cup milk	1 tablesp. soft butter or margarine

Combine sugar with rest of ingredients. With electric mixer or hand beater, beat until stiff enough to spread — about 5 min. (If weather is warm, set bowl of frosting in bowl of ice, and beat. Or refrigerate frosting a short while before beating.)

Fills and frosts 2 9″ cake layers; or frosts 8″ x 8″ x 2″ cake. So nice on Devil's-Food Cake, p. 623, with chopped walnuts on side.

Yolks make deeper-colored frosting.

To Vary: Substitute almond extract for vanilla.

YUM-YUM CHOCO-MALLOW FROSTING

3 cups sifted confec-
tioners' sugar
½ cup evaporated
milk, undiluted
5 sq. unsweetened
chocolate, melted

¼ cup soft butter or
margarine
1 teasp. vanilla extract
1 teasp. almond ex-
tract
½ cup miniature
marshmallows

In small bowl, blend sugar with evaporated
milk. Add melted chocolate; mix till blended.
Add butter, extracts; mix till smooth and
creamy. Fold in marshmallows. Fills and frosts
2 8″ or 9″ cake layers, or 2 9″ x 9″ x 2″ cake
layers.

CHOCOLATE FROSTING

4 sq. unsweetened
chocolate
1 cup confectioners'
sugar

2 tablesp. hot water
2 eggs
6 tablesp. soft butter
or margarine

1. In double boiler, over hot, *not boiling*, water,
melt chocolate; remove from heat.
2. With spoon or electric mixer, gradually beat
in sugar and hot water.
3. Then beat in eggs, one at a time, beating
very well. Beat in butter, 2 tablesp. at a time;
beat till smooth. Frosts top and sides of 2 9″
cake layers.

CHOCOLATE EGGNOG FROSTING

3 sq. unsweetened
chocolate
1½ cups sifted con-
fectioners' sugar
2 tablesp. hot water

1 egg, unbeaten
¼ cup soft butter or
margarine
Rum extract to taste

In double boiler, over hot, *not boiling*, water,
melt chocolate. Remove from heat. Blend in
sugar, water (mixture will thicken). Add egg,
butter; with spoon, beat well. Add extract. Let
stand until thick enough to spread. Fills and
frosts 2 8″ cake layers.

CONTINENTAL CHOCOLATE FROSTING

4 sq. unsweetened
chocolate
2 egg whites

1½ cups confection-
ers' sugar
½ lb. butter or mar-
garine

1. In double boiler, over hot, *not boiling*, water,
melt chocolate squares.

2. In small bowl, with electric mixer at medium
speed, beat egg whites till stiff but not dry; then
slowly add confectioners' sugar, while beating
until thick.
3. In another small bowl, beat butter until soft;
then slowly add egg-white mixture, while beating. Now add melted chocolate and beat until
a thoroughly-blended chocolate-butter-cream
mixture. Fills and frosts 2 8″ or 9″ cake layers.

BITTERSWEET FROSTING

2¾ cups sifted con-
fectioners' sugar
¼ cup hot water
9 sq. unsweetened
chocolate, melted
3 eggs

½ cup plus 2 tablesp.
butter or margarine
Dash salt
1½ teasp. vanilla ex-
tract

Combine sugar, water, melted chocolate; stir
only enough to dampen sugar. Add eggs, one
at a time, beating vigorously with spoon until
smooth. Add butter; beat till melted and smooth.
Add salt, vanilla. Fills and frosts 2 8″ cake
layers, split to make 4 layers.

HUNGARIAN FROSTING

3 sq. unsweetened
chocolate, melted
1½ cups sifted con-
fectioners' sugar

2½ tablesp. hot water
3 egg yolks, unbeaten
¼ cup soft butter or
margarine

Combine melted chocolate, sugar, hot water.
Add egg yolks, one at a time, beating with electric mixer or spoon after each addition. Add
butter, 1 tablesp. at a time, beating until thick
enough to spread. Fills and frosts 2 8″ or 9″
cake layers; or frosts a cake 8″ x 8″ x 2″ or
10″ x 5″ x 3″.
NOTE: You may substitute 1 whole egg for 3
egg yolks; reduce water to 2 tablesp.

VELVETY FROSTING

1 6-oz. pkg. semi-
sweet-chocolate
pieces (1 cup)

½ cup soft butter or
margarine
2 eggs, unbeaten

Melt chocolate over hot, *not boiling*, water;
cool slightly. Mix butter with eggs. Add chocolate, beating with spoon until smooth and
creamy.

Fills and frosts 2 8″ cake layers or tops of
2 9″ layers.

QUICK-AS-A-WINK FROSTING

1 6-oz. pkg. semi-
  sweet-chocolate
  pieces (1 cup)

1 cup sifted confec-
  tioners' sugar
⅓ cup evaporated
  milk, undiluted

Melt chocolate over hot, *not boiling*, water. Add sugar, evaporated milk. Beat until smooth.

    Frosts tops of 2 8″ cake layers. Nice on Susan's Frosted Brownies, p. 137.

DREAMY FROSTING

2 3-oz. pkg. soft cream
  cheese
2 tablesp. evaporated
  milk, undiluted

4¾ cups sifted con-
  fectioners' sugar
Dash salt
1 teasp. vanilla ex-
  tract

Blend cheese with milk. Slowly stir in sugar, then salt, vanilla. Blend well.

    Fills, frosts 2 8″ or 9″ cake layers. Halve recipe to frost 8″ x 8″ x 2″ or 9″ x 9″ x 2″ cake.

CHOCOLATE: To cheese, add 2 sq. slightly cooled, melted unsweetened chocolate; increase milk to 3 tablesp.

ORANGE: Substitute orange juice for milk, 1 teasp. grated orange rind for vanilla.

COFFEE: With sugar, add 4 teasp. instant coffee.

BUTTER CREAM

⅓ cup soft butter,
  margarine, or short-
  ening
⅛ teasp. salt
About 3 cups sifted

confectioners' sugar
About ⅛ to ¼ cup
  milk or light cream
1½ teasp. vanilla ex-
  tract

With electric mixer at medium speed (or with spoon), thoroughly mix butter with salt and 1 cup confectioners' sugar until light and fluffy. Add rest of sugar and milk alternately, beating till very smooth and of spreading consistency; add vanilla.

    Fills and frosts 2 8″ or 9″ cake layers; or frosts 9″ x 9″ x 2″ cake.

LEMON: Substitute lemon juice for milk. Omit vanilla.

MOCHA: Increase sugar to a 1-lb. pkg.; sift with ½ cup cocoa. Substitute ⅓ cup hot coffee for milk. Decrease vanilla to ½ teasp.

ORANGE: Use ½ cup soft butter, ⅛ teasp. salt, 3½ cups sifted confectioners' sugar, 2 un-beaten egg yolks, 1 teasp. grated orange rind, about 2 tablesp. milk. Make as at left, adding egg yolks and rind before adding rest of sugar and milk.

ORANGE COOKIE FROSTING: Make ½ recipe for Orange Butter Cream, omitting egg yolks. Substitute orange juice for milk. Use for Brazil-Nut Triple-Layer Bars, p. 661.

BROWNED: Lightly brown butter in heavy skillet before blending it with salt and sugar.

CHOCOLATE: Increase butter to ½ cup. Before adding rest of sugar and milk, add 2 unbeaten egg yolks and 3 sq. melted unsweetened chocolate.

PEPPERMINT: Substitute few drops peppermint extract for vanilla.

HARLEQUIN: Make Butter Cream. To half of frosting, add 2 sq. melted unsweetened chocolate. Cut 8″ x ″8 x 2″ cake into quarters. Frost top and crust sides of 2 quarters with chocolate frosting, 2 with plain frosting. Assemble in checkerboard pattern. Decorate top of cake with walnut halves, sides with chopped walnuts.

COFFEE: Increase butter to 9 tablesp., sugar to 6¾ cups, milk to 7 tablesp.; omit salt and vanilla. Add 2 tablesp. instant coffee.

CREAMY FROSTING: Make Butter Cream, using 4 to 5 tablesp. hot light cream for milk. Use for Frosted Chocolate-Nut Drops, p. 655.

ORNAMENTAL FROSTING
(a very hard type — for special occasion cakes)

2 1-lb. pkg. confec-
  tioners' sugar
1 teasp. cream of
  tartar

6 egg whites
1 teasp. vanilla or
  almond extract

Sift sugar and cream of tartar through very fine sieve. Add egg whites; mix, using electric mixer, slotted spoon, or wire whip. Add vanilla. Beat until so stiff that knife drawn through mixture leaves clean-cut path. (On damp days, you may need to beat in more sugar to stiffen frosting.) Use to cement together the tiers of a 3-tiered wedding cake; then spread thinly over entire cake to set crumbs. Make second batch of frosting to refrost cake and make simple decorations. Use leftover frosting to decorate cake. For decorating ideas see *Good Housekeeping Book of Cake Decorating*, available in any book store.

ORANAMENTAL COOKIE FROSTING: Reduce sugar to 1¼ cups, cream of tartar to ⅛ teasp. Use 1 egg white and ¼ teasp. vanilla extract. Make as on p. 645.

COOKED FROSTINGS

"SEVEN-MINUTE" FROSTING

2 egg whites	1 tablesp. white corn
1½ cups granulated	syrup
sugar	½ teasp. salt
½ cup water*	1 teasp. vanilla extract

In double-boiler top, combine all ingredients except vanilla. With electric mixer at high speed, beat about 1 min. to blend; then place over *rapidly boiling* water, and beat till mixture forms peaks when beater is raised (don't be surprised if this takes more than 7 min.). Remove from boiling water (for smoothest frosting, empty into large bowl). Add vanilla; continue beating until thick enough to spread.

Generously fills and frosts 2 8" or 9" cake layers; or frosts 10" sponge, angel, or chiffon cake, or 13" x 9" x 2" cake, or 2 doz. cupcakes. *For crusty surface, reduce water to ⅓ cup.*

CHOCOLATE: When frosting is done, gently fold in (don't beat) 2 or 3 sq. cooled, melted unsweetened chocolate.

HARVEST MOON: Substitute 1½ cups brown sugar, packed, for granulated sugar. While frosting is still soft on cake, you may sprinkle it with chocolate curls or chopped nuts to form 1" border around top.

LADY BALTIMORE: To one third of completed frosting, add ⅓ cup snipped light or dark raisins, ⅓ cup snipped dried figs, 6 tablesp. chopped walnuts; use to fill 2 8" or 9" white cake layers.

Frost cake with remaining plain frosting. Sprinkle with snipped candied cherries, if desired.

MARSHMALLOW: With vanilla, add 1 cup snipped marshallows.

PEPPERMINT: Substitute ¼ teasp. peppermint extract for vanilla. Tint frosting pink with red food color.

PRINCESS: Substitute 1½ teasp. vanilla, ½ teasp. orange, and 1 teasp. almond extracts for

vanilla. Sprinkle filled and frosted cake with packaged fine grated or flaked coconut, or grated fresh coconut.

"FOUR MINUTE": Halve each ingredient, using 1½ teasp. white corn syrup. Make as directed, cooking mixture about 4 min., or until it forms peaks when beater is raised; then complete.

Fills and frosts 2 8" layers; or frosts cake that measures 8" x 8" x 2" or 9" x 9" x 2".

If making variations at left, halve ingredients.

EASY FUDGE FROSTING

3 sq. unsweeteend chocolate	6 tablesp. evaporated milk, undiluted,
2 tablesp. butter or margarine	or light cream
	Dash salt
2¼ cups sifted confectioners' sugar	1 teasp. vanilla extract

Melt chocolate with butter over boiling water; blend. Add 1½ cups confectioners' sugar, milk, and salt, all at once; with spoon, beat until smooth. Cook over low heat, stirring, until mixture bubbles well around edges. Remove from heat. Add vanilla and remaining sugar in thirds, beating until smooth after each addition. Set in bowl of ice water until thick enough to spread, stirring occasionally.

Fills and frosts 2 8" cake layers or frosts 2 8" square cakes.

PENUCHE FROSTING

1½ cups light-brown sugar, packed	¼ cup shortening
1½ cups granulated sugar	¼ cup butter or margarine
2 tablesp. white corn syrup	¼ teasp. salt
¾ cup milk	1 teasp. orange extract
	1 cup chopped nuts

In large saucepan, combine sugars, syrup, milk, shortening, butter, salt. Bring slowly to rolling boil, stirring constantly. *Boil briskly* 2 min. Cool till *lukewarm*. Add extract; beat* until thick enough to spread. Add nuts.

Fills and frosts 2 8" or 9" cake layers; or frosts 8" x 8" x 2" cake or 9" x 9" x 2" cake. *This frosting takes a while to beat. Let your electric mixer do it. It's worth the effort.*

SNOW-PEAK FROSTING

1¼ cups white corn syrup	Pinch salt
2 egg whites	1 teasp. vanilla extract

In small saucepan, heat corn syrup till boiling. With electric mixer at high speed, or with hand beater, beat egg whites until they form soft peaks when beater is raised. Add salt. Slowly pour in syrup, continuing to beat until frosting is fluffy and forms peaks when beater is raised. Fold in vanilla.

Fills and frosts 2 8" or 9" layers.

LANE FROSTING: Substitute 1⅓ cups dark corn syrup for white corn syrup. Frosts top and sides of 4 filled 9" cake layers.

FLUFFY RUM FROSTING

1 cup plus 2 tablesp. dark corn syrup	Dash salt
3 egg whites	1 tablesp. dark rum

1. In saucepan, cook corn syrup to 240°F. on candy thermometer, or until a little mixture, dropped in cold water, forms soft ball.
2. Meanwhile, beat egg whites until frothy; add salt; beat until stiff but not dry. Now gradually add syrup, while beating. When all syrup has been added, add rum; continue beating until mixture hangs in peaks when beater is raised.

Frosts sides and top of a 9" two-layer cake.

BROWNED-BUTTER ICING

¾ cup butter or margarine	3 tablesp. evaporated milk, undiluted
3 cups sifted confectioners' sugar	1½ teasp. vanilla extract

In heavy skillet, lightly brown butter (watch carefully to prevent burning). Blend in sugar, evaporated milk, and vanilla. Use to frost Raisin-Nut Cookies, p. 652.

GOLDEN FROSTING

In saucepan, combine 1½ cups granulated sugar; 1½ cups dark-brown sugar, packed; 1½ tablesp. butter or margarine; 1¼ cups plus 2 tablesp. light cream. Bring to boil over medium heat, stirring constantly; then cook to 234°F. on candy thermometer, or until a little mixture, dropped into cold water, forms soft

ball. Cool till lukewarm; then beat until stiff enough to spread. Fold in ¾ cup finely chopped walnuts, ¾ teasp. vanilla extract.

Frosts a 10" tube cake.

QUICK CARAMEL FROSTING

½ cup butter or margarine	¼ cup milk
1 cup brown sugar, packed	1¾ to 2 cups sifted confectioners' sugar

In saucepan, melt butter. Add brown sugar; boil over low heat, stirring constantly, 2 min. Add milk; stir until mixture comes to boil. Remove from heat; cool. Slowly add confectioners' sugar, beating well with spoon after each addition, until thick enough to spread.

Fills and frosts 2 8" or 9" cake layers; or generously frosts an 8" x 8" x 2" or 9" x 9" x 2" cake.

COOK-ON TOPPINGS

BROILED PRALINE: Blend ⅓ cup melted butter, margarine, or shortening with ½ cup brown sugar, packed; ¼ cup milk; pinch salt; ½ teasp. vanilla extract; 1 cup snipped flaked coconut; ½ cup chopped nuts.

Spread mixture over top of hot 9" x 9" x 2" One-Egg Cake, p. 621. Broil *slowly* until golden — about 5 min.; don't burn.

BROILED HONEY-COCONUT: Combine ⅓ cup honey, ¼ cup melted butter or margarine, 1 cup flaked coconut. Spread and broil as in Broiled Praline, above.

MINT PATTY: Place 12 large, chocolate-covered peppermint patties on top of hot 8" x 8" x 2" One-Egg Cake, p. 621. Return cake to oven for 2 min.; then spread softened patties over cake, or leave as is.

QUICK FUDGE FROSTING

2 6-oz. pkg. semi-sweet-chocolate pieces (2 cups)	3 cups sifted confectioners' sugar
	¼ cup soft shortening
	½ cup hot milk

Melt chocolate over hot, *not boiling*, water. Add rest of ingredients. Remove from heat. With spoon, beat until smooth.

Fills and frosts 2 8" or 9" cake layers; or frosts 9" x 9" x 2" cake.

JIFFY CHOCOLATE FROSTING

2 sq. unsweetened chocolate	1 tablesp. water
1 can sweetened condensed milk	¼ teasp. almond extract; or ½ teasp. vanilla extract
Dash salt	

In double boiler, combine chocolate, milk, salt, water. Cook over *rapidly boiling* water, stirring often, till thick — about 10 min. Remove from heat. Cool. Add extract.

Fills and frosts 2 8″ cake layers; or frosts a 9″ x 9″ x 2″ cake.

SARDI'S CHOCOLATE BUTTER CREAM

1⅔ cups sweet (not salted) butter	½ teasp. vanilla extract
1 cup egg whites	¾ cup sifted cocoa, or 2 sq. unsweetened chocolate, melted, cooled
1 cup plus 2 tablesp. granulated sugar	

Just before frosting cake:

1. In large bowl, let butter stand until slightly soft, *but still cold*. Then beat at medium speed until smooth and creamy.
2. In double boiler, over boiling water, with hand beater, beat egg whites with sugar about 2 min., or until *just slightly warm*. Beat in vanilla.
3. Now, while beating with electric mixer at medium speed, pour egg whites, in thin stream, into creamy cool butter; then beat at high speed until well blended — about 5 min.
4. Beat in cocoa (for very light-colored frosting use chocolate). Use at once to frost and decorate cake.

Fills and frosts and decorates 3 thin 8″ spongecake layers.

VANILLA BUTTER CREAM: Make as directed, omitting cocoa or chocolate.

WHITE FUDGE FROSTING

½ cup butter or margarine	1¼ to 2 cups sifted confectioners' sugar
1 cup granulated sugar	1 teasp. vanilla extract
¼ cup milk	

In saucepan, melt butter. Add granulated sugar, milk; stir until blended. Then bring to boil, stirring occasionally; cool. Gradually add confectioners' sugar until thick enough to spread, beating well after each addition. Add vanilla; blend.

Fills and frosts 2 8″ or 9″ cake layers; or frosts 13″ x 9″ x 2″ cake.

REAL FUDGE FROSTING

2 sq. unsweetened chocolate	Salt
½ cup heavy cream	1 tablesp. corn syrup
¼ cup milk	1 tablesp. butter or margarine
2 cups granulated sugar	1 teasp. vanilla extract

In saucepan, combine chocolate, cream, and milk; cook over low heat, stirring, until chocolate is melted. Add sugar, pinch salt, and corn syrup and continue cooking, stirring constantly, until mixture comes to a boil. Boil hard 5 min.; remove from heat. Drop bit of mixture into cold water to see if it forms soft ball. (If not, continue to cook until it does form soft ball.) Now add butter and vanilla, then let frosting stand 15 min. Then beat it until thick enough to spread; if it seems to lose its gloss and gets too thick, beat in small amount of heavy cream.

Fills and frosts top of 2 8″ cake layers.

WHIPPED-CREAM FROSTINGS

WHIPPED-CREAM FROSTING

½ teasp. unflavored gelatine	Speck salt
2 tablesp. cold water	2 tablesp. confectioners' sugar
1 cup heavy cream	½ teasp. lemon juice

Sprinkle gelatine over cold water in small bowl to soften. Scald 2 tablesp. cream; pour over gelatine, stirring till dissolved. Refrigerate until consistency of unbeaten egg white. Then, with hand beater, beat until smooth. Whip remaining cream; add salt, sugar, lemon juice; fold in gelatine mixture.

Fills and frosts top of 2 8″ or 9″ cake layers; or frosts 10″ angel cake or spongecake. Stands up well, even in warm weather.

CHOCOLATE: Omit lemon juice. After folding

in gelatine mixture, fold in 1 6-oz. pkg. cooled, melted semisweet-chocolate pieces (1 cup).

COFFEE: To remaining cream, add 1 teasp. instant coffee.

ORANGE: Substitute 1 teasp. grated orange rind for lemon juice.

TROPICAL WHIP FROSTING

1 cup flaked coconut	2 tablesp. orange or
1 tablesp. grated	pineapple juice
orange rind	1 tablesp. lemon juice
¼ cup granulated	1 cup heavy cream
sugar	

Mix coconut, orange rind, sugar, fruit juices. Let stand 15 min. Whip cream; fold in coconut mixture.

Fills and frosts 2 8″ cake layers.

AUTUMN MIST TOPPING

1 cup heavy cream	1 tablesp. sugar
1 tablesp. instant	½ teasp. vanilla ex-
coffee	tract

In bowl, with hand beater, beat cream, coffee, sugar, and vanilla until stiff enough to spread.

Tops cake baked in 10″ tube pan.

P.S. Double recipe to fill and frost 3 9″ cake layers or 2 9″ x 9″ x 2″ cake layers.

CHOCOLATE FLUFF FROSTING

In chilled bowl, with electric mixer or hand beater, beat 2 cups heavy cream with 1 cup sifted confectioners' sugar, ½ cup cocoa, and dash of salt until thick enough to spread.

Fills and frosts 2 8″ or 9″ cake layers, split to make 4 layers. Or it fills and frosts a 10″ tube cake, cut into 3 even layers.

FIX 'N' SERVE FROSTINGS

On your grocer's shelves you'll find a wonderful choice of fine packaged frosting mixes. In no time you can have creamy caramel, fudge, vanilla, milk chocolate, caramel fudge, toffee fudge, or chocolate malt frosting, to name a few.

Or you may choose one of the luscious fluffy frosting mixes — white, cherry, lemon, pink lemonade, fudge sundae, etc. Use these plain, or fold in chopped nuts, grated chocolate, or chopped cherries. Or sprinkle with cocoa, instant coffee, flaked coconut, or cinnamon.

GLAZES

CHOCOLATE GLAZE I: Melt ½ 6-oz. pkg. semisweet-chocolate pieces (½ cup) over hot, *not boiling*, water; stir in 1 tablesp. white corn syrup; cool slightly.

CHOCOLATE GLAZE II: In double boiler, over hot, *not boiling*, water, melt 1½ ¼-lb. bars German sweet, cooking chocolate with 2 teasp. vegetable shortening, stirring until smooth. Drizzle along top edge of Chocolate Sundae Cake, p. 622.

CHOCOLATE GLAZE III: Over hot, *not boiling*, water, melt 2 cups semisweet-chocolate pieces; stir in ¼ cup milk. Use to glaze Party Butter Cookies, p. 660.

DECORATING GLAZE: Into 2 egg whites, in bowl, gradually stir 4 cups confectioners' sugar till mixture is smooth; cover with wax paper.

FRUIT GLAZE: In small saucepan, boil 2 tablesp. white corn syrup with 2 tablesp. butter or margarine 3 min.; brush onto Susan's Walnut Cake, p. 135. Decorate with slivered citron and candied cherries, pressed gently into place.

LEMON GLAZE: In saucepan, heat 3 tablesp. milk with 2 tablesp. butter or margarine. Stir into 2 cups sifted confectioners' sugar until smooth. Blend in 1 teasp. grated lemon rind, 3 tablesp. lemon juice. Spread thinly on Lemon-Glazed Date Sticks, p. 662.

SNOWY GLAZE: Mix 1 cup sifted confectioners' sugar with 2 to 3 tablesp. warm milk, ¼ teasp. favorite extract. Use for Lebkuchen, p. 666.

SUGAR GLAZE: Mix ¾ cup sifted confectioners'

sugar, ½ teasp. vanilla extract, and 3 to 4 teasp. water until smooth and of frosting consistency, adding a few more drops of water if needed. Tint with food color if desired. Makes nice thin frosting for cookies; Danish Pastry, p. 509; French Doughnuts, p. 490.

VANILLA GLAZE: In small bowl, blend 1½ cups sifted confectioners' sugar with 1 tablesp. soft butter or margarine, ¼ teasp. vanilla extract, ⅛ teasp. salt, and 2½ tablesp. light cream. Use for Glazed Fresh Apple Cookies, p. 653.

THIN CHOCOLATE COATING

2 tablesp. butter or margarine
2 sq. unsweetened chocolate
2 tablesp. hot water
1 to 1½ cups sifted confectioners' sugar

Melt butter with chocolate and hot water over boiling water. Remove from heat. Blend in sugar. With spoon, beat till smooth but not stiff.

Frosts top of 8″ or 9″ layer cake. Nice on Boston Cream Pie, p. 134; Chocolate Eclairs, p. 125, etc.

FOR THE COOKIE JAR

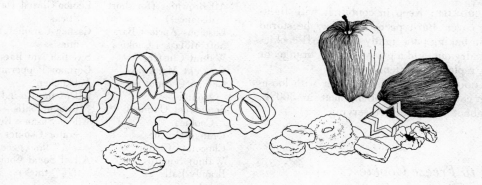

Even Grandmother will enjoy your reputation as a baker. Modern cookie recipes cut time and effort to a minimum, produce the maximum in goodness. Cookies you make from packaged mixes have a homemade flavor. Now, too, you can buy refrigerated slice 'n' bake rolls of cookie dough in a variety of flavors. They are so handy to have in the refrigerator — look for them in the dairy section. And packaged, ready-to-eat cookies hold their delicious own — just as they come or dressed up. Perhaps the only real problem about cookies is keeping the cookie jar filled.

Before you make any of our cookies, refer to How To Use Our Recipes, p. 3. Be sure to use standard measuring cups and measuring spoons; measure level.

Helps for the Cookie Maker

1. *For the soft shortening* called for in some of our cookie recipes, use any shortening that is in condition to be creamed easily. If necessary, let it stand at room temperature until soft enough.

2. *With an electric mixer* (portable or on a stand), you can whisk a batch of cookies together in no time. Just follow our recipes, using medium speed for mixing shortening, sugar, etc., and low speed for dry ingredients, unless otherwise directed.

3. *If you're mixing with a spoon,* use a wooden one with a comfortable long handle so you can mix, stir, and beat effectively.

4. *For evenly baked cookies, use cookie sheets about 2" narrower and shorter than your oven,* to allow space around edges for heat circulation. If you bake one sheet at a time, place oven rack in center of oven; if two sheets, place racks so they divide oven into thirds.

5. *If cookie sheet is to be greased,* do it lightly. Also, you'll avoid hard-to-wash brown patches if you grease or oil only the spots where dough is to drop, allowing space for spreading.

6. *If you need extra cookie sheets,* inverted baking pans may be used. Or cut piece of foil to fit your one and only cookie sheet. While cookie sheet of cookies bakes, drop more dough onto foil; then place foil on cookie sheet as soon as it comes from the oven and is emptied.

7. *No danger of overbaking cookies* if you use

a timer clock to warn you when baking time is up. Then, with a broad spatula, immediately slip baked cookies onto one or more wire cake racks to cool. Never overlap cookies, or place them on top of one another, until they are cold.

Storing Cookies

SOFT COOKIES: Keep in container with tight-fitting cover. Bar-type cookies may be stored right in baking pan, tightly covered. If cookies tend to dry out, add a piece of apple, orange, or bread, replacing it often.

CRISP COOKIES: Keep in container with loose-fitting cover. If they soften, heat in 300°F. oven about 5 min. before serving.

How to Freeze Cookies:

See p. 707.

How to Pack Cookies for Mailing

When you send cookies, use a good-sized box and fill it well. Here's how to be sure they arrive as cookies, not crumbs.

1. Bake travel-wise cookies that can stand a few knocks, such as long-lived soft drop cookies, and packable bars and squares. See list that follows.

2. Use sturdy cardboard packing box. Line it with wax paper. Place cushion of crumpled wax paper or cellophane straw on bottom.

3. In saran, wrap flat cookies in pairs, back to back, with wax paper between. Wrap others individually; tape well.

4. Snugly arrange layers of cookies in straight rows in box, with heavy cookies at bottom; tuck enough ready-to-eat sugar-coated cereal or unbuttered popcorn into each nook and crevice to keep cookies from jiggling. Top with crushed wax paper or folded paper towels. Repeat to within ¼″ of top.

5. Add final generous cushioning layer of wax paper. Tape box shut (use broad brown-paper tape if available). Print address on box. Wrap in heavy brown paper; tie securely.

6. Label front with printed address and return address; cover with clear tape. Add "Fragile, Handle with Care" stickers and correct amount of postage.

7. For overseas mailing, use air parcel post if possible. Metal or wooden containers are best.

Some Good Cookie Travelers*

All Brownies (for short distances)
Luscious Apricot Bars
Soft Molasses Cookies
Walnut Clusters
Crescent Meltaways
Golden Coconut Mounds
Semisweet Oatmeal Cookies
Orange Crispies
Chocolate Chews
Walnut Squares
Brandy Balls
Lemon-Glazed Date Sticks
Cashew-Caramel Yummies
Swedish Nut Bars
German Peppernuts
Lebkuchen
All of the No-Bake Cookie Balls
All of Susan's Refrigerator Cookies (¼″ thick)
All of Sugar Cookies (¼″ thick)

*See Index for page references.

DROP-AND-BAKE COOKIES

RAISIN-NUT COOKIES

1 cup evaporated milk, undiluted	¼ teasp. nutmeg
1 tablesp. vinegar	½ cup soft shortening
2 cups sifted all-purpose flour	2 cups brown sugar, packed
1 teasp. baking soda	2 eggs, unbeaten
½ teasp. salt	3 cups dark or light raisins
1 teasp. cinnamon	1 cup chopped walnuts
1 teasp. ground cloves	Browned-Butter Icing, p. 647
1 teasp. ground allspice	

Start heating oven to 350°F. Into evaporated milk, stir vinegar; set aside. Sift flour with baking soda, salt, cinnamon, cloves, allspice, and nutmeg. Mix shortening, brown sugar, and eggs until light and fluffy. Blend in evaporated-milk mixture, then flour mixture. Stir in raisins and nuts. Drop level tablespoonfuls of dough, 2″ apart, onto greased cookie sheets. Bake about 15 min., or until done. Cool; then frost with Browned-Butter Icing. Makes about 6 doz.

PINEAPPLE-SPICE DROP COOKIES

2 cups sifted all-purpose flour
1 teasp. double-acting baking powder
1 teasp. baking soda
1 teasp. salt
½ cup soft shortening
½ cup granulated sugar
½ cup brown sugar, packed
1 teasp. cinnamon
½ teasp. nutmeg
¼ teasp. ground cloves
1 egg, unbeaten
⅔ cup drained canned crushed pineapple

Start heating oven to 375°F. Sift flour with baking powder, baking soda, and salt. Mix shortening, granulated sugar, brown sugar, cinnamon, nutmeg, ground cloves, and egg until creamy. Blend in pineapple, then flour mixture. Drop rounded tablespoonfuls of dough, 2" apart, onto ungreased cookie sheets. Bake 12 to 15 min., or until lightly browned. Makes about 3½ doz.

SALTED-PEANUT COOKIES

1½ cups sifted all-purpose flour
½ teasp. double-acting baking powder
¾ teasp. baking soda
½ teasp. salt
½ cup soft butter or margarine
1¼ cups brown sugar, packed
1 egg, unbeaten
¼ cup milk
1½ cups whole-wheat flakes or bran flakes (with or without raisins)
¾ cup salted peanuts, chopped

Start heating oven to 375°F. Sift flour with baking powder, baking soda, salt. Cream butter until light and fluffy, gradually adding brown sugar. Add egg; beat well. Add flour mixture alternately with milk, mixing well after each addition. Stir in cereal and peanuts. Onto greased cookie sheets, drop level tablespoonfuls of dough. Bake 8 min., or until done. Makes 4½ doz.

ORANGE-OATMEAL COOKIES

2 cups sifted all-purpose flour
2 cups granulated sugar
4 teasp. double-acting baking powder
1 teasp. salt
1 teasp. nutmeg
1 cup soft shortening
2 eggs, unbeaten
4 tablesp. grated orange rind
2 tablesp. orange juice
3 cups uncooked quick rolled oats

Start heating oven to 375°F. Into large bowl, sift flour with sugar, baking powder, salt, nut-

meg. Add shortening, eggs, rind, juice; blend well. Stir in oats. Onto greased cookie sheets, drop level tablespoonfuls of dough, 2" apart. Bake 15 min., or till done. Makes 4 doz.

SEMISWEET OATMEAL COOKIES

¾ cup sifted all-purpose flour
½ teasp. baking soda
½ teasp. salt
½ cup soft butter
6 tablesp. granulated sugar
6 tablesp. brown sugar
½ teasp. vanilla extract
¼ teasp. water
1 egg
1 cup uncooked rolled oats
1 6-oz. pkg. semisweet-chocolate pieces (1 cup)

Start heating oven to 375°F. Sift together flour, soda, salt; set aside. Blend together butter, sugars, vanilla, and water. Beat in egg. Add flour mixture; mix well. Stir in oats and chocolate pieces. Drop by rounded half-teaspoonfuls on greased cookie sheets. Bake 10 to 12 min. Makes 4 doz.

GLAZED FRESH-APPLE COOKIES

2 cups sifted all-purpose flour
1 teasp. baking soda
½ cup soft shortening
1⅓ cups brown sugar, packed
½ teasp. salt
1 teasp. cinnamon
1 teasp. ground cloves
½ teasp. nutmeg
1 egg, unbeaten
1 cup chopped nuts
1 cup finely chopped, unpared apple
1 cup dark or light raisins, chopped
¼ cup apple juice or milk
Vanilla Glaze, p. 650

Start heating oven to 400°F. Sift flour with baking soda. Mix shortening, brown sugar, salt, cinnamon, cloves, nutmeg, and egg until well blended. Stir in half of flour mixture, then nuts, apple, and raisins. Blend in apple juice, then remaining flour mixture. Onto greased cookie sheets, drop rounded tablespoonfuls of dough, 2" apart. Bake 11 to 14 min., or until done. While cookies are still hot, spread thinly with Vanilla Glaze. Makes 3½ doz.

ORANGE CRISPIES

1 cup soft shortening
½ teasp. salt
Granulated sugar
1 egg, unbeaten
1½ teasp. orange extract
1½ cups sifted all-purpose flour

Start heating oven to 375°F. Cream shortening

with salt until light and fluffy, while gradually adding 1 cup sugar. Add egg; beat well. Blend in orange extract, then flour. Onto ungreased cookie sheets, drop rounded tablespoonfuls of dough, 2″ apart. Bake 10 min., or till edges are light brown. Let stand 1 or 2 min. before removing. If desired, while cookies are warm, sprinkle with granulated sugar. Makes 4 doz.

MOLASSES SNAPS

2 cups sifted all-purpose flour	½ cup light-brown sugar, packed
1 teasp. baking soda	½ cup light molasses
½ cup soft shortening	1 egg, unbeaten
½ teasp. salt	Cinnamon and granulated sugar
1 teasp. cinnamon	
1 teasp. ginger	21 blanched almonds, split

Start heating oven to 350°F. Sift flour with baking soda. Mix shortening, salt, cinnamon, ginger, brown sugar, molasses, egg until well blended; stir in flour mixture. Drop level tablespoonfuls of dough, 2″ apart, onto greased cookie sheets; stamp lightly with a flat-bottomed glass, covered with a damp cloth. Sprinkle cookies with a mixture of cinnamon and granulated sugar; then press almond half in center of each. Bake 12 to 15 min. Makes about 3½ doz.

CHOCOLATE-OAT MEDALLIONS

½ cup butter or margarine	¼ cup chopped walnuts
¾ cup granulated sugar	½ teasp. rum extract
1½ cups uncooked quick rolled oats	¼ cup finely chopped semisweet-chocolate pieces
½ cup heavy cream	

Make several days ahead:
1. Start heating oven to 375°F.
2. In small bowl, with electric mixer at high speed, mix butter with sugar until very light and fluffy; with spoon, fold in rolled oats.
3. By heaping measuring teaspoonfuls, drop them 3″ apart, on greased cookie sheets, making 36 to 40 in all. Bake 8 to 10 min., or until golden around edges. Remove from oven; let stand on cookie sheet about 1 min., or until firm enough to remove to wire racks and cool. Store in tightly covered cookie jar.
Just before serving: Put cookies together in

pairs, with filling of whipped cream mixed with walnuts, rum extract, and semisweet-chocolate pieces. Or fill with Chocolate Butter Cream, p. 645. Makes about 1½ doz.

ALMOND WINE BISCUITS

1 cup sifted all-purpose flour	½ teasp. grated lemon rind
⅛ teasp. salt	½ cup coarsely ground almonds
½ cup soft shortening	¼ cup sherry
⅓ cup granulated sugar	⅓ cup coarsely ground almonds
2 egg yolks	
¼ teasp. anise extract	

Start heating oven to 400°F. Sift together flour and salt. Mix, until creamy, shortening, sugar, and yolks. Add anise, rind, ½ cup almonds; mix. Mix in sherry alternately with flour mixture. Drop by tablespoonfuls onto ⅓ cup almonds; toss until well coated with nuts. Lay, 1″ apart, on greased cookie sheet; shape with spoon into 1½″ rounds, ½″ thick. Bake 12 to 15 min., or until golden. Makes 1 doz.

CHOCOLATE BRAZIL-NUT COOKIES

½ cup soft butter or margarine	2 sq. semisweet chocolate, melted
¼ teasp. salt	¾ cup sifted all-purpose flour
1 cup granulated sugar	½ cup finely chopped Brazil nuts
1 egg, unbeaten	
1 teasp. vanilla extract	

Start heating oven to 325°F. Cream butter with salt until light and fluffy, gradually adding sugar. Add egg; beat well. Blend in vanilla and chocolate. Mix in flour, then nuts, until well blended. Drop level tablespoonfuls of dough, 2″ apart, onto greased cookie sheets. Stamp lightly with a flat-bottomed glass, covered with a damp cloth. If desired, sprinkle a few Brazil-nut slivers over the top of each cookie. Bake about 15 min., or until done. Cool. Makes 3 doz.

GOLDEN COCONUT MOUNDS

2 eggs	3 3½-oz. cans flaked coconut (3 cups)
1 cup granulated sugar	¼ cup sifted all-purpose flour

Make several days before, if desired:
1. Start heating oven to 350°F. Lightly grease

two cookie sheets. In large bowl, with mixer at high speed, beat eggs with sugar *just until well blended* — about 1 min.; then fold in coconut and flour all at once.

2. Onto cookie sheets, drop mixture, about 2 tablesp. at a time, and 2" apart; shape into peaked mounds. Bake 10 to 18 min., or till golden on tops and bottoms. (Cookies will be soft to touch, but will firm up when they cool.)

3. Cool on racks, then store in tight container until needed — flavor develops upon standing. Makes 1¼ doz.

SOFT MOLASSES COOKIES

2¼ cups sifted all-purpose flour	½ cup granulated sugar
1 teasp. ginger	½ cup molasses
1 teasp. cinnamon	1 egg
¼ teasp. salt	6 tablesp. cold water
2 teasp. baking soda	½ cup seedless raisins or chopped walnuts
2 tablesp. hot water	
½ cup soft shortening	

Start heating oven to 400°F. Sift together flour, ginger, cinnamon, and salt. Dissolve soda in hot water. Mix shortening with sugar, molasses, and egg until creamy; mix in flour mixture alternately with cold water; then mix in soda and all but a few raisins. Drop by rounded tablespoonfuls, 2" apart, onto greased cookie sheet. Sprinkle with remaining raisins. Bake 12 min., or until done. Makes about 2 doz.

ALMOND ROLLS
(lace cookies)

⅔ cup canned blanched almonds, finely ground	½ cup granulated sugar
½ cup butter or margarine	2 tablesp. milk
	1 tablesp. flour
	Sifted confectioners' sugar

Start heating oven to 350°F. Grease, and flour well, two cookie sheets. In large skillet, combine all ingredients except confectioners' sugar; heat, stirring, over low heat until butter is melted and mixture is mushy. On prepared cookie sheets, drop by heaping teaspoonfuls, 3" apart. Bake, 1 sheet at a time, about 5 or 6 min., or until golden. Remove, one at a time, from cookie sheet; quickly roll up around handle of wooden spoon; cool. To serve, dust lightly with confectioners' sugar. Makes about 2½ doz.

PECAN KISSES

2 egg whites	1 teasp. vanilla extract
2 cups sifted confectioners' sugar	2 cups pecan halves
1 teasp. vinegar	

Start heating oven to 300°F. With electric mixer or hand beater, beat egg whites until stiff but not dry. Gradually beat in sugar, vinegar, and vanilla; fold in pecans. Drop teaspoonfuls of dough, 2" apart, onto greased cookie sheets. Bake 12 to 15 min., or until firm. (Cookies should remain light.) Remove from sheets at once; cool. Makes 3½ doz.

FROSTED CHOCOLATE-NUT DROPS

1¼ cups sifted all-purpose flour	1 teasp. vanilla extract
¼ teasp. baking soda	½ teasp. salt
½ cup soft shortening	½ cup buttermilk or 7 tablesp. milk plus 2 teasp. vinegar
1 cup brown sugar, packed	
1 egg, unbeaten	1 cup walnuts, coarsely chopped
2 sq. unsweetened chocolate, melted	Creamy Frosting, p. 645

Start heating oven to 350°F. Sift flour with baking soda. Mix shortening, brown sugar, egg, chocolate, vanilla, and salt until well blended. Stir in flour mixture, then buttermilk. Stir in nuts. Onto greased cookie sheets, drop level tablespoonfuls of dough, 2" apart. Bake 12 to 15 min., or until top springs back when lightly touched. Cool; then frost with Creamy Frosting. Makes 3 doz.

WALNUT CLUSTERS

½ cup sifted all-purpose flour	½ cup granulated sugar
¼ teasp. double-acting baking powder	1 egg, unbeaten
½ teasp. salt	1½ teasp. vanilla extract
¼ cup soft butter or margarine	1½ sq. unsweetened chocolate, melted
	2 cups broken walnuts

1. Start heating oven to 350°F. Sift together flour, baking powder, and salt.

2. In large bowl, with mixer at high speed, mix butter, sugar, egg, and vanilla until *very light and fluffy*.

3. With mixer at low speed, mix in chocolate, then flour mixture; fold in walnuts.

4. Drop by teaspoonfuls, 1″ apart, on greased cookie sheet. Bake 10 min. — no longer. Makes 2½ doz.

SHREWSBURY DROPS

1¼ cups sifted cake flour	1 whole egg
2 teasp. double-acting baking powder	1 egg white
⅛ teasp. salt	1 tablesp. granulated sugar
½ cup soft shortening	¾ teasp. cinnamon
½ cup granulated sugar	15 blanched almonds, split lengthwise

Sift together flour, baking powder, and salt. Mix, until creamy, shortening, ½ cup sugar, and whole egg; mix in flour mixture. Refrigerate ½ hr.

To bake: Start heating oven to 375°F. Drop dough by tablespoonfuls, about 3″ apart, onto greased cookie sheet; flatten each slightly with back of spoon or bottom of glass covered with damp cheesecloth. Brush with egg white; sprinkle with 1 tablesp. sugar and cinnamon, combined; top with almonds. Bake 10 to 12 min., or until golden. Makes 2 doz.

MUFFIN-PAN CRISPIES

½ cup soft butter or margarine	1 teasp. vanilla extract
⅔ cup light-brown sugar, packed	1½ cups uncooked rolled oats
¼ teasp. salt	1 tablesp. milk
½ teasp. double-acting baking powder	¼ cup hot water
	¼ teasp. cinnamon
	Dash nutmeg

1. Start heating oven to 350°F. With electric mixer at medium speed, mix ¼ cup butter or margarine with ⅓ cup light-brown sugar, salt, baking powder, vanilla extract, until mixture is smooth. Stir in rolled oats, then milk, and mix until well blended.
2. Into each of 12 ungreased muffin-pan cups, measuring 2″ across bottom, lightly pile about 1½ tablesp. of rolled-oats mixture; with fork, *very gently*, level off top of each. Bake 15 min.
3. Meanwhile, in saucepan, melt ¼ cup butter or margarine; stir in ⅓ cup brown sugar, hot water, cinnamon, nutmeg. Heat about 2 min., stirring constantly.
4. At end of 15 min., remove cookies from oven and spoon about 1½ teasp. butter-brown-sugar sauce over each. Return to oven for 15 min.
5. With a thin-bladed spatula, *very* carefully loosen edges of each cookie from pan edge all around, pressing gently toward center. Cool 5 min., then gently remove from pans, and finish cooling on paper towels on a wire rack. Store, tightly covered; they keep well. Makes 1 doz.

To Freeze: See To Freeze Cookies, p. 707.

ROLL-AND-CUT COOKIES

SUGAR COOKIES

4 cups sifted cake flour	1½ cups granulated sugar
2½ teasp. double-acting baking powder	2 eggs, unbeaten
½ teasp. salt	1 teasp. vanilla extract
⅔ cup soft shortening	4 teasp. milk

1. Sift flour, baking powder, salt. Mix shortening with sugar, eggs, and vanilla until *very light and fluffy*. Mix in flour mixture alternately with milk.
2. Refrigerate dough until easy to handle (you can hasten this chilling by placing dough in freezing compartment).
3. Start heating oven to 400°F. On lightly floured surface, roll a half or a third of dough at a time, keeping rest in refrigerator. For *crisp* cookies, roll dough paper-thin. For *softer* cookies, roll ⅛″ to ¼″ thick.
4. With floured cutter or cardboard pattern, cut into desired shapes, keeping cuttings close together.
5. With broad spatula, arrange cookies, ½″ apart, on lightly greased cookie sheet. If desired, brush with cream or with egg white diluted with a little water. Then, if desired, sprinkle with white or colored sugar, chopped nuts, flaked coconut, cut-up gumdrops, silver *dragées*, cinnamon and sugar, bits of candied fruit, etc.
6. Bake 9 min., or until delicate brown. Then cool. Makes about 6 doz.

BUTTERSCOTCH-PECAN: Substitute 2 cups brown sugar, packed, for granulated sugar. Add 1 cup finely chopped pecans with flour mixture.
CARAWAY: Substitute 3 tablesp. brandy for va-

nilla and milk. Add 1½ teasp. caraway seeds to sugar. Dust cookies with confectioners' sugar.

CHOCOLATE: Add 4 sq. melted unsweetened chocolate to shortening mixture. Add 1 cup chopped walnuts (optional) to flour mixture.

COCONUT: Add 1 cup snipped flaked coconut with flour.

LEMON: Substitute 4 teasp. lemon juice and 2 tablesp. grated lemon rind for vanilla.

PAINTBRUSH COOKIES: In step 5, brush unbaked cookies with this Egg-Yolk Paint: With fork, blend 1 egg yolk with ¼ teasp. water. To portions of this mixture, in small custard cups, add food color as desired. For more colors, make more paint. Using a small new paintbrush for each color, paint designs on unbaked cookies. (If Egg-Yolk Paint thickens on standing, add a few drops of water.) Then bake cookies at 400°F. 6 to 8 min., or until set, but not brown.

Two Short Cuts: To save time needed to roll out Sugar-Cookie dough, you may do this:

1. Drop level or rounded spoonfuls of well-chilled dough, 2" apart, onto greased cookie sheet. Flatten by pressing with fork or bottom of tumbler dipped into sugar.

2. Or cut rolled-out dough to fit greased shallow baking pan. Bake as directed. While cookies are still hot and in pan, cut into squares or "fingers."

CRESCENT MELTAWAYS

1 8-oz. pkg. creamed cottage cheese	¾ cup light-brown sugar, packed
½ lb. butter or margarine (1 cup)	Dash cinnamon
2 cups sifted all-purpose flour	¾ cup finely chopped walnuts
¼ cup melted butter or margarine	1 egg yolk
	2 tablesp. water

Make day before, or early on the day:

1. In medium bowl, with pastry fork, blend cottage cheese with 1 cup butter. Sift in flour, then blend until dough forms a ball.

2. Start heating oven to 400°F. Grease three cookie sheets.

3. Divide dough into thirds. On lightly floured, cloth-covered board, roll out one third of dough ⅛" thick and circular in shape.

4. Brush with some of melted butter; sprinkle with ¼ cup brown sugar, a little cinnamon, ¼ cup chopped nuts.

5. Cut circle into 16 pie-shaped pieces. Beginning at outer edge, roll up each piece tightly, then place, point side down, on cookie sheet. Repeat with rest of pieces.

6. Beat egg yolk with water, then use to brush tops of cookies. Bake about 20 min., or until golden.

7. Repeat with other two thirds of dough. Makes 4 doz.

DANISH TOFFEE COOKIES

3½ cups sifted cake flour	1 cup granulated sugar
2 teasp. double-acting baking powder	1 large egg, unbeaten
⅔ cup soft butter or margarine	2 tablesp. very strong coffee
½ teasp. salt	1½ tablesp. dark rum
	½ cup finely chopped blanched almonds

Sift flour with baking powder. Cream butter with salt until light and fluffy, gradually adding sugar. Add egg, then coffee, then rum, beating well after each addition. Blend in flour mixture, then almonds. Refrigerate about 2 hr., or till dough can be easily handled.

To bake: Start heating oven to 375°F. On floured surface, roll dough ⅛" to ¼" thick. Cut with floured 2¼" cutter. On ungreased cookie sheets, bake 10 to 12 min., or until done. Makes about 4 doz.

MOLASSES-COOKIE CUTOUTS

2 cups sifted all-purpose flour	½ teasp. nutmeg
½ teasp. salt	½ cup soft shortening
½ teasp. baking soda	½ cup granulated sugar
1 teasp. double-acting baking powder	½ cup light molasses
1 teasp. ground ginger	1 egg yolk
1 teasp. ground cloves	Ornamental Cookie Frosting, p. 646
1½ teasp. cinnamon	

Start heating oven to 350°F. Sift flour with salt, baking soda, baking powder, ginger, cloves, cinnamon, and nutmeg. Mix shortening, sugar, and molasses until creamy. Add egg yolk; beat well. Blend in flour mixture. On lightly floured surface, roll out dough ⅛" to ¼" thick. With floured cutters, cut out gingerbread man, Scotty, pony, etc. Or with your own cardboard patterns, cut out place cards in gift box or other shapes. On ungreased cookie sheets, place ½" apart. Bake 8 to 10 min., or until done; cool.

Then, with Ornamental Cookie Frosting in paper cone or cake decorator, decorate cookies in your own way. If desired, trim with colored sugar, candies, nuts, chocolate sprinkles, silver *dragées*, or raisins.

COOKIE SANDWICHES

2½ cups sifted all-purpose flour	2 teasp. vanilla extract
¼ teasp. double-acting baking powder	½ cup sifted confectioners' sugar
½ teasp. salt	2 tablesp. milk
1 cup soft shortening	Top milk
	Blanched almonds
	Currant jelly

Sift flour, baking powder, salt. Mix shortening, vanilla, and sugar until *very light and fluffy*. Mix in flour mixture, 2 tablesp. milk. Refrigerate till easy to handle.
To bake: Start heating oven to 350°F. On lightly floured surface, roll dough ¼" thick. Cut into 2½" rounds. Cut ¾" circle from center of each of half of rounds; brush with top milk; shave on a few almonds. Place, 1" apart, on ungreased cookie sheet. Bake 15 min., or till done; cool. Place 1 teasp. jelly in centers of flat sides of whole rounds; top with rings, with right sides up. Makes 1 doz.

CREAM WAFERS

1¼ cups soft butter or margarine	¾ cup sifted confectioners' sugar
⅓ cup heavy cream	1 egg yolk, beaten
2 cups sifted all-purpose flour	1 teasp. vanilla extract
Granulated sugar	

Mix 1 cup butter, cream, flour until well blended; refrigerate until well chilled.
To bake: Start heating oven to 375°F. On lightly floured surface, roll out dough ⅛" thick (roll only a third of dough at a time, keeping rest refrigerated). Cut into rounds with 1½" cutter. Transfer rounds to wax paper covered with granulated sugar. Turn each round so that both sides are coated with sugar; place on ungreased cookie sheets. With fork, prick each about 4 times. Bake 7 to 9 min.; cool.

Meanwhile, make filling: In small bowl, beat confectioners' sugar gradually into ¼ cup butter until light and fluffy; beat in egg yolk and vanilla; refrigerate. To serve, put cookies together in pairs with filling between. Makes about 4 doz. filled cookies.

WILLIE MAE'S FILLED OATMEAL COOKIES

1 teasp. vinegar	1½ cups granulated sugar
½ cup milk	5 cups uncooked quick-cooking rolled oats
1 cup sifted all-purpose flour	
1 teasp. baking soda	1 cup snipped pitted dates
1 cup soft shortening (part butter)	1 teasp. lemon juice
¼ teasp. salt	¼ cup water

Stir vinegar into milk; set aside. Sift flour with baking soda. Cream shortening with salt until light and fluffy, gradually adding ¾ cup sugar. Blend in half of flour mixture, then milk, then remaining flour mixture. Stir in rolled oats. Refrigerate at least 4 hr.

Meanwhile, for filling, in saucepan, combine dates, ¾ cup sugar, lemon juice, and water; bring to boil; cool.
To bake: Start heating oven to 350°F. On well-floured surface, roll dough ⅛" thick (roll only one third of dough at a time, keeping rest refrigerated). Cut with floured 2" round cutter. Spread 1 teaspoonful of date mixture on each of half of cookies. Top with remaining cookies. Place on ungreased cookie sheets; bake 10 to 12 min.; cool. Makes about 3 doz.

COOKIE BALLS

WALNUT-BUTTER BALLS

1½ cups sifted all-purpose flour	2 teasp. instant coffee
½ cup granulated sugar	1 cup butter or margarine
¼ teasp. salt	¾ cup walnuts, coarsely chopped

Start heating oven to 300°F. Into medium bowl, sift flour, sugar, salt, and coffee. With pastry blender, or 2 knives used scissor-fashion, cut in butter until it's the size of small peas. Press dough together. Shape into small balls; roll in walnuts. Place, 2" apart, on ungreased cookie sheets; flatten with bottom of glass dipped in sugar. Bake about 20 min., or until edges are very lightly browned. Cool slightly; remove to wire rack. Makes about 3 doz.

COCONUT BUTTERBALLS

1 cup soft butter or margarine	2 cups sifted all-purpose flour
¼ cup sifted confectioners' sugar	1½ cups flaked coconut
1 teasp. vanilla extract	Sifted confectioners' sugar

Cream butter until light and fluffy, gradually adding sugar, then vanilla. Blend in flour, then coconut. Shape into 1″ balls; place on ungreased cookie sheets; refrigerate about 15 min. *To bake:* Start heating oven to 350°F. Then bake cookies 15 min., or until delicately browned. While cookies are still warm, roll each in sifted confectioners' sugar. Makes about 4 doz.

PEANUT PUFFS

¾ cup soft shortening	2¼ cups sifted all-purpose flour
½ cup peanut butter	¾ cup salted peanuts, finely chopped
½ teasp. salt	Sifted confectioners' sugar
½ cup sifted confectioners' sugar	
1 teasp. vanilla extract	

Start heating oven to 375°F. Cream shortening with peanut butter and salt until light and fluffy, gradually adding ½ cup confectioners' sugar. Blend in vanilla, then flour. Stir in peanuts; mix well. Shape dough into small balls. On ungreased cookie sheets, bake 12 min., or until golden brown. Roll immediately in confectioners' sugar. If desired, reroll cookies, when cool, in more confectioners' sugar. Makes 4 doz.

KING-SIZE GINGERSNAPS

2 cups sifted all-purpose flour	¾ cup soft shortening
½ teasp. salt	1 cup granulated sugar
1 teasp. ground cloves	1 egg, slightly beaten
1 teasp. ground ginger	¼ cup light molasses
1 teasp. cinnamon	Granulated sugar
3 teasp. baking soda	

Start heating oven to 350°F. Sift flour with salt, cloves, ginger, cinnamon, and baking soda.

Cream shortening till light and fluffy, gradually adding 1 cup sugar. Blend in egg and molasses; then stir in flour mixture until well blended.

Shape dough into 1½″ balls; roll in granulated sugar; place, 3″ apart, on ungreased cookie sheets. Flatten with fingers; sprinkle with more sugar. Bake 8 to 10 min. Let stand a minute before removing from sheets. Makes 18. These keep wonderfully in airtight container.

CHOCOLATE-ALMOND BUTTERBALLS

⅓ cup semisweet-chocolate pieces	2 teasp. vanilla extract
1 tablesp. milk	2 cups sifted all-purpose flour
¾ cup soft butter or margarine	½ cup chopped blanched almonds
½ teasp. salt	Granulated sugar
½ cup granulated sugar	

Start heating oven to 350°F. Melt chocolate with milk over hot, *not boiling*, water; cool. Meanwhile, cream butter with salt until light and fluffy, gradually adding ½ cup sugar. Blend in vanilla and cooled chocolate mixture. Mix in flour, then almonds until well blended. Shape dough into 1″ balls; roll in granulated sugar. On ungreased cookie sheets, bake 12 to 15 min. Makes about 3½ doz.

THUMBPRINTS

COOKIES:

½ cup soft butter or margarine	purpose flour
½ teasp. salt	2 tablesp. milk
1 teasp. vanilla extract	¼ cup semisweet-chocolate pieces, chopped
½ cup brown sugar, packed	Sifted confectioners' sugar
1½ cups sifted all-	

CHOCOLATE FILLING:

¾ cup semisweet-chocolate pieces	2 tablesp. white corn syrup
1 tablesp. shortening	1 tablesp. water
	1 teasp. vanilla extract

Start heating oven to 375°F. Mix butter, salt, vanilla, and brown sugar till light and fluffy.

Blend in flour, milk, and chopped chocolate pieces. Shape into 1″ balls; place on ungreased cookie sheets; with thumb make depression in each. Bake 10 to 12 min. Roll in sugar; cool.

Meanwhile, over hot, *not boiling*, water, melt semisweet chocolate with shortening, stirring. Cool slightly; add corn syrup, water, and vanilla. Heap this filling in centers of cookies. Makes 3 doz.

CRINKLES

2¼ cups sifted all-purpose flour	1 teasp. ginger
1 teasp. salt	¾ cup soft shortening
2 teasp. baking soda	1 cup brown sugar, packed
1 teasp. cinnamon	1 egg, unbeaten
½ teasp. ground cloves	¼ cup molasses
	Granulated sugar

Sift flour, salt, soda, cinnamon, cloves, ginger. Mix shortening with brown sugar and egg until *very light and fluffy*. Mix in molasses, then flour mixture. Refrigerate 1 hr. or longer.
To bake: Start heating oven to 375°F. Shape dough into walnut-size balls; dip one side of each into granulated sugar. Place, with sugar sides up, 3″ apart, on greased cookie sheet. Sprinkle each cookie with 2 or 3 drops water. Bake 12 to 15 min., or until done. Makes 4 to 5 doz.

PUMPKINS: Before sprinkling cookies with water, flatten each ball with fork; press bit of citron into top, for stem.

SLICE-AND-BAKE COOKIES

PARTY BUTTER COOKIES

¾ cup soft butter or margarine	½ teasp. vanilla extract
½ cup granulated sugar	2 cups sifted cake flour
1 egg yolk, unbeaten	Chocolate Glaze III, p. 649

Cream butter, gradually adding sugar. Add egg yolk and vanilla; beat well. Gradually blend in

flour. Refrigerate about 2 hr., or until dough can be easily handled. Shape into 2 rolls, 1½″ in diameter; wrap each in wax paper and refrigerate overnight or longer.
To bake: Start heating oven to 400°F. Slice dough ⅛″ thick; on ungreased cookie sheets, bake 8 to 10 min., or until edges are golden. Cool; then dip half of top of each cookie into Chocolate Glaze III. If desired, while chocolate is still soft, sprinkle with chopped nuts, flaked coconut, or chocolate sprinkles. Makes about 6 doz.

COCONUT-OATMEAL REFRIGERATOR COOKIES

1½ cups sifted all-purpose flour	2 eggs, unbeaten
1 teasp. baking soda	3 cups uncooked quick-cooking rolled oats
1 teasp. salt	½ cup chopped pecans
1 cup soft shortening (part butter)	1½ cups flaked coconut
1 cup brown sugar, packed	
1 cup granulated sugar	

Sift flour with baking soda and salt. Cream shortening until light and fluffy, gradually adding sugars. Add eggs; beat well. Blend in flour mixture, then rolled oats gradually. Stir in pecans and coconut. Shape dough into 3 rolls, 2″ in diameter; wrap each in wax paper; refrigerate at least 24 hr.
To bake: Start heating oven to 375°F. Slice dough ⅛″ to ¼″ thick; on ungreased cookie sheets, bake 10 min., or until done. Makes about 6 doz.

MELTAWAYS

1 cup soft butter or margarine	⅔ cup sifted confectioners' sugar
¼ teasp. salt	2 cups sifted all-purpose flour
½ teasp. almond extract	Colored granulated sugar or chopped nuts
½ teasp. vanilla extract	

Cream butter with salt and extracts until light and fluffy, gradually adding confectioners' sugar. Blend in flour gradually. Refrigerate ½ hr., or until dough can be easily handled.
To bake: Start heating oven to 400°F. Shape dough into rolls about ¾″ in diameter; cut

each roll into ¾″ lengths. Place, on ends, on ungreased cookie sheets; stamp lightly with a flat-bottomed glass, covered with a damp cloth; decorate with colored sugar. Bake 10 to 12 min. Makes about 5 doz.

PECAN CRISPS

1 cup soft butter or margarine	2 cups finely chopped pecans
⅛ teasp. salt	1½ cups sifted all-purpose flour
½ cup sifted confectioners' sugar	Confectioners' sugar
2 teasp. vanilla extract	

Start heating oven to 325°F. Cream butter with salt until light and fluffy, gradually adding ½ cup confectioners' sugar. Blend in vanilla, pecans, then flour. On lightly floured surface, shape portions of dough into rolls, about ½″ in diameter; slice off 1½″ pieces. On ungreased cookie sheets, bake 15 to 20 min. While cookies are warm, roll them in confectioners' sugar. Makes about 6 doz.

RIBBON COOKIES

2½ cups sifted all-purpose flour	1 egg, unbeaten
1½ teasp. double-acting baking powder	1 teasp. vanilla extract
½ teasp. salt	¼ cup snipped candied cherries
1 cup soft shortening	1 sq. unsweetened chocolate, melted
1¼ cups granulated sugar	2 tablesp. poppy seeds

Sift flour with baking powder and salt. Cream shortening until light and fluffy, gradually adding sugar. Stir in egg and vanilla; beat well. Blend in flour mixture. Divide dough into three parts; add cherries to one part, chocolate to second part, and poppy seeds to third part. Into bottom of wax-paper-lined 9″ x 5″ x 3″ loaf pan, pack cherry mixture evenly; next, pack in chocolate mixture, then poppy-seed mixture. Cover with wax paper; refrigerate at least 24 hr.

To bake: Start heating oven to 400°F. Remove dough from pan; cut in half lengthwise, then crosswise into ¼″ slices. On ungreased cookie sheets, bake 8 to 10 min., or till very light brown. Makes 6 to 7 doz.

BARS AND SQUARES

CASHEW-CARAMEL YUMMIES

¾ cup sifted all-purpose flour	¾ cup brown sugar, packed
½ teasp. double-acting baking powder	½ cup chopped salted cashew nuts
¼ teasp. salt	2 tablesp. melted butter or margarine
2 eggs, slightly beaten	1½ tablesp. light cream
½ cup granulated sugar	⅓ cup chopped salted cashew nuts

Start heating oven to 350°F. Sift flour with baking powder and salt. Into eggs, stir granulated sugar and ½ cup brown sugar. Then blend in ½ cup nuts and flour mixture. Turn mixture into greased 9″ x 9″ x 2″ pan. Bake 20 to 25 min., or until crust springs back when lightly touched with finger. Meanwhile make this Cashew Topping: Into butter, stir ¼ cup brown sugar, cream, ⅓ cup nuts. Spread this mixture immediately on baked cookie mixture, covering top completely. Then place under broiler about 1 min., or until topping bubbles and is light brown. While cookies are warm, cut into bars; cool thoroughly in pan. Makes about 3 doz.

BRAZIL-NUT TRIPLE-LAYER BARS

¼ cup soft butter or margarine	½ cup flaked coconut
½ teasp. salt	1 teasp. vanilla extract
1 cup sifted all-purpose flour	2 tablesp. flour
2 eggs, well beaten	Orange Cookie Frosting, p. 645
¾ cup brown sugar, packed	Coarsely chopped Brazil nuts
1 cup finely chopped Brazil nuts	

Start heating oven to 375°F. With wooden spoon, thoroughly blend butter with ¼ teasp. salt and 1 cup flour. With spatula, press this mixture evenly into greased 9″ x 9″ x 2″ pan; bake 15 min. Meanwhile, into eggs, blend brown sugar, finely chopped nuts, coconut, vanilla, ¼ teasp. salt, 2 tablesp. flour. Spread this mixture evenly over baked layer; bake 15 min. Cool; then frost with Orange Cookie Frosting. Sprinkle with coarsely chopped Brazil nuts. Cut into bars or diamonds. Makes about 2 doz.

LEMON-GLAZED DATE STICKS

1¼ cups sifted cake flour
1¼ teasp. double-acting baking powder
½ teasp. salt
2 eggs
1 cup granulated sugar
1 tablesp. butter or margarine, melted
1 tablesp. hot water
2 cups finely cut pitted dates
½ cup coarsely cut walnuts
Lemon Glaze, p. 649

Start heating oven to 325°F. Sift flour with baking powder and salt. Beat eggs well, adding sugar gradually. Blend in butter and water. Stir in dates and nuts, then flour mixture gradually, mixing thoroughly. Turn mixture into 2 greased 8" x 8" x 2" pans; bake 30 to 35 min.; cool. Spread tops thinly with Lemon Glaze; then cut into small sticks. Makes about 4 doz.

WALNUT SQUARES

½ cup sifted all-purpose flour
½ teasp. salt
⅛ teasp. baking soda
1 egg
1 cup brown sugar, packed
½ teasp. vanilla extract
1 cup chopped walnuts

Start heating oven to 325°F. Sift flour with salt and baking soda. With hand beater or an electric mixer, beat egg until foamy. Add brown sugar and vanilla; beat well. Stir in flour mixture, then walnuts. With spatula, spread mixture in well-greased 8" x 8" x 2" pan. Bake 25 to 30 min., or until top has dull crust. While warm, cut into 2" squares; then cool before removing from pan. Makes 1⅓ doz.

LUSCIOUS APRICOT BARS

⅔ cup dried apricots
½ cup soft butter or margarine
¼ cup granulated sugar
1⅓ cups sifted all-purpose flour
½ teasp. double-acting baking powder
¼ teasp. salt
1 cup brown sugar, packed
2 eggs, well beaten
½ teasp. vanilla extract
½ cup chopped walnuts
Confectioners' sugar

1. Rinse apricots; cover with water; boil 10 min. Drain; cool; chop. Start heating oven to 350°F. Grease 8" x 8" x 2" pan.

2. Mix butter, granulated sugar, and 1 cup flour until crumbly. Pack into pan. Bake 25 min.

3. Sift ⅓ cup flour, baking powder, and salt. In large bowl, with mixer at low speed, gradually beat brown sugar into eggs; mix in flour mixture, then vanilla. Stir in walnuts and apricots. Spread over baked layer. Bake 30 min., or until done; cool in pan. Cut into 32 bars; then roll the bars in confectioners' sugar. Makes 2⅔ doz.

ORIENTAL CRUNCH

1 cup butter or margarine
2 tablesp. instant coffee
½ teasp. salt
½ teasp. almond extract
1 teasp. vanilla extract
1 cup granulated sugar
2 cups sifted all-purpose flour
1 6-oz. pkg. semi-sweet-chocolate pieces (1 cup)
½ cup canned almonds, coarsely chopped

Start heating oven to 375°F. Then blend together butter, instant coffee, salt, extracts. Gradually beat in sugar, then flour; add chocolate. Spread in ungreased 15½" x 10½" x 1" pan. Sprinkle nuts over top, press them in. Bake 20 to 22 min. Cool; then break into irregular pieces. Makes 1¾ lb.

BRAZIL-NUT COFFEECAKE BARS

2 cups sifted all-purpose flour
1 teasp. double-acting baking powder
1⅓ cups granulated sugar
4 teasp. cinnamon
½ cup soft butter or margarine
½ cup soft shortening
1 egg
1 egg, separated
1 cup chopped Brazil nuts

Start heating oven to 350°F. Into bowl, sift flour, baking powder, 1 cup sugar, and 3 teasp. cinnamon; add butter, shortening, whole egg, egg yolk. With electric mixer at low speed (or with spoon), mix well. Turn into jelly-roll pan 15½" x 10½" x 1"; spread evenly with spatula. With fork, beat egg white slightly; brush over dough. Combine remaining ⅓ cup sugar, 1 teasp. cinnamon, and nuts; sprinkle over top of dough. Bake 25 min., or until nuts are golden. Cool in pan; then cut into 75 2" x 1" bars. Makes 6¼ doz.

DOUBLE-DECK BROWNIES

⅔ cup sifted all-purpose flour
½ teasp. double-acting baking powder
¼ teasp. salt
2 eggs
1 cup granulated sugar

⅓ cup melted butter or shortening
⅓ cup flaked coconut
½ teasp. almond extract
1½ sq. unsweetened chocolate, melted

Start heating oven to 350°F. Sift flour with baking powder and salt. With hand beater, or electric mixer at medium speed, beat eggs well, gradually adding sugar. Stir in melted butter, then flour mixture, blending well. Into small bowl, pour one fourth of batter; blend in coconut and almond extract. Into remaining three fourths of batter, blend chocolate. In well-greased 8" x 8" x 2" pan, spread this mixture evenly. Onto this mixture, carefully spoon coconut batter; spread carefully to form a thin, even layer. Bake 35 min., or until done. Cool; then cut into squares or bars. Makes about 2 doz. If desired, increase coconut to ¾ cup; stir into batter before dividing.

COFFEE BROWNIES

¾ cup sifted all-purpose flour
½ teasp. double-acting baking powder
¼ teasp. salt
2 tablesp. instant coffee
2 sq. unsweetened chocolate

⅓ cup butter or margarine
2 eggs, unbeaten
1 cup granulated sugar
1 teasp. vanilla extract
½ cup chopped walnuts

1. Start heating oven to 375°F. Grease a pan 8" x 8" x 2". Sift together flour with baking powder, salt, coffee.
2. In double boiler, over hot, *not boiling*, water, melt chocolate with butter; cool.
3. In bowl, beat eggs with sugar until very light and fluffy; add to chocolate mixture; blend well.
4. Stir flour mixture into chocolate mixture until blended; add vanilla and nuts and gently mix. Pour into prepared pan.

5. Bake 25 min., or until center springs back when lightly pressed with finger; cool; cut into 2" squares. Makes 11⅓ doz.

CHOCOLATE CHEWS

2 eggs, slightly beaten
1 cup granulated sugar
½ teasp. vanilla extract
½ cup butter or margarine

2 sq. unsweetened chocolate
½ cup plus 1 tablesp. sifted all-purpose flour
½ to 1 cup chopped walnuts or pistachio nuts

Start heating oven to 350°F. Grease baking pan 11" x 7" x 1½". Mix well eggs, sugar, vanilla. Melt butter with chocolate. Cool a bit; mix with egg mixture. Add flour; mix well. Turn into pan; top with nuts. Bake 35 to 40 min., or until done. Cool in pan; cut. Makes 24 squares.

TEA BROWNIES: Use 2 8" x 8" x 2" pans. Bake 15 to 20 min. Cool in pan; cut with small fancy cutters. Or put layers together with Orange Cookie Frosting, p. 645; then cut.

FUDGE CUTS: Bake as for Tea Brownies; cut into 32 2" squares.

CHOCOLATE HALFWAY BARS

1 cup sifted all-purpose flour
⅛ teasp. salt
⅛ teasp. baking soda
½ teasp. double-acting baking powder
½ cup soft shortening
¼ cup granulated sugar

¾ cup brown sugar, packed
1 egg, separated
1½ teasp. water
½ teasp. vanilla extract
½ cup semisweet-chocolate pieces

1. Start heating oven to 375°F. Grease baking dish 12" x 8" x 2".
2. Sift flour, salt, baking soda, and baking powder. Mix shortening, granulated sugar, and ¼ cup brown sugar till *very light and fluffy*. Add egg yolk, water, and vanilla; mix well. Mix in flour mixture thoroughly. Pat into baking dish; top with chocolate pieces.
3. Next, beat egg white till stiff; gradually beat in ½ cup brown sugar. Spread over chocolate. Bake 25 min., or till done. Cut into 32 bars while warm. Cool in dish. Makes 2⅔ doz.

COOKIES FROM OTHER LANDS

SCOTCH SHORTBREAD

2 cups sifted all-purpose flour	¼ teasp. salt
¼ teasp. double-acting baking powder	1 cup soft butter or margarine
	½ cup confectioners' sugar

Sift flour with baking powder and salt. Mix butter or margarine with sugar until *very light and fluffy*. Mix in flour mixture. Refrigerate until easy to handle.

To bake: Start heating oven to 350°F. On lightly floured surface, roll dough ¼" thick. Cut into squares, triangles, etc. Place, 1" apart, on ungreased cookie sheet. Bake 20 to 25 min., or until done.

Or pat unchilled dough into 9" x 9" x 2" pan; bake as above; cut into desired shapes while warm. Or, if desired, before baking, sprinkle with cinnamon-and-sugar mixture. Makes about 2½ doz.

WALNUT: Substitute ⅔ cup brown sugar, packed, for confectioners' sugar. Add ¾ cup finely chopped walnuts. Decorate cookies with walnut halves or candied cherries. Bake at 300°F. 20 to 25 min.

ENGLISH TEACAKES

1¾ cups sifted all-purpose flour	¾ cup granulated sugar
1½ teasp. double-acting baking powder	1 egg
¼ teasp. salt	3 tablesp. milk
¼ cup soft shortening	½ cup chopped citron
¼ cup soft butter or margarine	½ cup currants or raisins
	1 egg white, slightly beaten
	Granulated sugar

Sift together flour, baking powder, and salt. Mix, until creamy, shortening, butter, sugar, and egg. Add milk, citron, currants, and flour mixture; mix well. Refrigerate.

To bake: Start heating oven to 400°F. Roll dough into balls the size of walnuts. Dip tops in egg white, then sugar. Place, sugared sides up, 2" apart, on greased cookie sheet. Bake 12 to 15 min., or till golden. These keep well. Makes about 3 doz.

FRENCH TUILES

¾ cup (5 or 6) egg whites, unbeaten	¼ cup lukewarm melted shortening
1⅔ cups granulated sugar	1 cup sifted all-purpose flour
¼ teasp. salt	¾ cup finely chopped blanched almonds
¾ cup lukewarm melted butter or margarine	

Start heating oven to 350°F. Beat egg whites with sugar and salt until sugar is dissolved, mixture thick. Add butter and shortening; beat well. Add flour and almonds; mix well. Drop by level tablespoonfuls, 5" apart, onto ungreased cookie sheet. Bake 8 to 10 min., or until done. Let stand ½ min.; then quickly and gently remove, one at a time, and mold into half circle over rolling pin. Makes about 5 doz.

NOTE: Bake only a few cookies at a time. If they harden before you can mold them, soften them in oven. These keep a week or so.

ESTER'S SPRITZ COOKIES
(Ester's Spritsar)

2 cups sifted all-purpose flour	¾ cup granulated sugar
1 teasp. double-acting baking powder	1 egg yolk, unbeaten
⅛ teasp. salt	1 teasp. almond extract
1 cup soft butter or margarine	

1. Sift together flour, baking powder, and salt.
2. In large bowl, with electric mixer at medium speed, or with wooden spoon, cream butter. Gradually add sugar, beating until *very light and fluffy*. Add egg yolk and almond extract, beating until well blended.
3. With mixer at low speed, gradually add flour mixture, beating just until well mixed. Wrap in wax paper. Refrigerate until easy to handle — about ½ hr.

To bake: Start heating oven to 350°F. Onto cold, ungreased cookie sheet, force dough through star disk of cookie press,* forming S, O, and U shapes. Bake 8 to 10 min., or until edges are golden brown. These may be stored in a tightly covered container, or wrapped in

A cookie-press set can be purchased in a housewares department.

foil and refrigerated up to 2 weeks. Makes about 7 doz.

SWEDISH NUT CRESCENTS

1⅓ cups sifted all-purpose flour	1¼ cups granulated sugar
2 teasp. salt	1 egg
1 teasp. double-acting baking powder	2 tablesp. milk
¼ cup soft shortening	1 teasp. vanilla extract
	1 cup chopped pecans

Start heating oven to 325°F. Sift together flour, salt, baking powder. Thoroughly mix shortening with ¾ cup sugar, egg, milk, and vanilla. Mix in flour mixture. Spread ¼ cup dough very thinly, evenly on greased inverted 9″ x 9″ x 2″ cake pan. Sprinkle with some of combined nuts and ½ cup sugar. Bake, 1 pan at a time, 10 to 12 min., or until golden. While hot, cut into 4½″ x ¾″ strips; shape each over rolling pin. Repeat, 1 pan at a time, until all dough is used. If strips become too brittle to shape, soften in oven. Makes 9 doz. These are delightfully salty.

GERMAN PEPPERNUTS
(Pfeffernuesse)

4 cups sifted all-purpose flour	8 oz. citron
1 teasp. baking soda	2 tablesp. butter or margarine
½ teasp. salt	2½ cups very fine granulated sugar
1 tablesp. cinnamon	5 eggs, separated
1 teasp. ground cloves	1½ teasp. grated lemon rind
1 teasp. nutmeg	
¼ teasp. black pepper	1½ cups confectioners' sugar
1 tablesp. ground cardamom seeds	About 3 tablesp. milk
1 teasp. anise seeds	
4 oz. candied orange peel	

Several days ahead:
1. Sift flour with baking soda, salt, cinnamon, cloves, nutmeg, and black pepper. Add cardamom, anise, then orange peel and citron, ground coarsely.
2. In large bowl, with mixer at high speed, mix butter with granulated sugar, then yolks, rind, till well blended. With spoon, blend in flour mixture. Then fold in egg whites, stiffly beaten. Refrigerate 1 hr.
3. With floured hands, shape dough into small balls; place on ungreased cookie sheet; let stand, uncovered, 12 hr. at room temperature. *To bake:* Start heating oven to 350°F. Bake 15 min., or till done. Cool. Glaze with confectioners' sugar blended with milk. Then, if desired, toss in sifted confectioners' sugar. Makes about 7 doz.

NORWEGIAN SUGAR COOKIES

2 cups sifted all-purpose flour	1 cup granulated sugar
2 teasp. double-acting baking powder	1 egg, well beaten
¼ teasp. salt	3 tablesp. brandy
½ cup shortening	1½ teasp. caraway seeds
	Powdered sugar

Sift together flour, baking powder, salt. Work shortening with a spoon until fluffy and creamy. Then gradually add sugar, while continuing to work until light. Beat in egg. Stir flour mixture and brandy into shortening mixture. Stir in caraway seeds. Refrigerate until firm enough to handle easily.
To bake: Start heating oven to 350°F. Then roll out cookie dough, on floured board, to ⅛″ thickness, or thinner. Cut into small stars, circles, etc. Place, ½″ apart, on greased cookie sheets; sprinkle with powdered sugar. Bake 6 to 8 min., or until a light brown. Makes about 12 doz. 1½″ cookies.

SWEDISH NUT BARS

6 eggs, separated	3½ cups finely ground walnuts
1¼ cups granulated sugar	3 teasp. almond extract

1. Start heating oven to 325°F.
2. Line bottom of 9″ x 9″ x 2″ cake pan with wax paper; grease paper.
3. Beat egg yolks until thick and tripled in volume. Add sugar slowly, beating until thick — about 10 min.
4. Slowly fold in nuts and extract.
5. Beat whites until stiff but not dry; blend into yolk mixture.
6. Pour into pan. Bake about 1 hr. Cool 10 min.; turn out; remove paper; cool. Cut as needed (nut bars keep well in refrigerator). Makes about 2½ doz.

ANISE COOKIES

⅓ cup anise seeds
3⅔ cups sifted all-purpose flour
⅛ teasp. baking soda
1 cup soft butter or margarine
1 cup granulated sugar

1 cup light-brown sugar, packed
1 egg, unbeaten
3 tablesp. light molasses
⅓ cup undiluted evaporated milk

With sharp knife, chop anise seeds very fine. Sift flour with baking soda. Cream butter until light and fluffy, gradually adding sugars. Stir in egg, molasses, milk, chopped anise seeds; beat well. Blend in flour mixture. Refrigerate, covered, 1 hr. Then shape into rolls 1¼" in diameter. Refrigerate at least 12 hr.

To bake: Start heating oven to 375°F. Slice dough ⅛" to ¼" thick. On ungreased cookie sheets, bake 9 to 11 min., or until done. Makes about 12 doz.

LEBKUCHEN

2¼ cups sifted all-purpose flour
½ teasp. salt
1 teasp. double-acting baking powder
½ teasp. ground cloves
1 teasp. cinnamon
1 cup coarsely broken walnuts

2 4-oz. jars diced mixed preserved fruits
3 eggs
1 egg yolk
1½ cups dark-brown sugar, packed
½ cup strong coffee or sherry
Snowy Glaze, p. 649

1. Start heating oven to 375°F. Sift flour, salt, baking powder, cloves, cinnamon; mix with nuts, fruits. Grease 15½" x 10½" x 1" jelly-roll pan.
2. With electric mixer at high speed, or with hand beater, beat eggs and egg yolk until thick and lemon-colored; gradually beat in sugar. With spoon, thoroughly blend in coffee and flour mixture. Turn into pan.
3. Bake 25 min., or until cake tester, inserted at several points, comes out clean. Cool in pan on cake rack.
4. Frost with Snowy Glaze. Before frosting dries, with wet knife, mark into 2" x 2½" bars; when it's dry, cut. Store in tight container with an apple to keep bars soft. Makes about 2½ doz.

To Freeze: See To Freeze Cookies, p. 707.

NO-BAKE COOKIES

BRANDY BALLS

2 7¼-oz. packages vanilla wafers, rolled into fine crumbs
½ cup honey

⅓ cup brandy
⅓ cup white rum
1 lb. shelled walnuts, finely ground
Granulated sugar

1. Mix together vanilla-wafer crumbs, honey, brandy, rum, and ground walnuts.
2. Shape into round, bite-size balls; roll in granulated sugar. Wrap each in saran. The flavor improves with holding! Makes about 5 doz. delicious balls.

WALNUT BOURBON BALLS

About 5 doz. packaged vanilla wafers, finely crushed (2½ cups)
2 tablesp. cocoa
1 cup confectioners' sugar

1 cup finely chopped walnuts, or walnuts and flaked coconut
3 tablesp. corn syrup
¼ cup bourbon
Confectioners' sugar

Mix well wafer crumbs, cocoa, 1 cup confectioners' sugar, nuts. Add corn syrup, bourbon; mix well. Form into 1" balls; then roll in confectioners' sugar. Store in covered container a day or so to ripen; these keep very well. Makes 3½ doz.

NO-BAKE COOKIE BALLS

1 6-oz. pkg. semi-sweet-chocolate pieces (1 cup)
3 tablesp. white corn syrup
2 teasp. instant coffee
⅓ cup hot water

3½ cups sifted confectioners' sugar
1 cup chopped walnuts
About 3 doz. packaged vanilla wafers, finely crushed (1¾ cups)

1. Over hot, *not boiling*, water, in double boiler, melt chocolate; remove from heat.
2. Stir in corn syrup, coffee dissolved in hot water, 3 cups sugar, walnuts, and wafer crumbs.
3. Form into 1" balls; roll in ½ cup sugar.
4. Store for a day or so in a covered container, to ripen. Makes about 5 doz.

CHOCO-ORANGE BALLS: Substitute ⅓ cup orange juice for instant coffee and hot water.

SURPRISE BALLS: Cut 1 large nutted candy bar into 4 doz. small pieces. Around each piece of candy, form some of chocolate mixture into 1″ ball; complete as directed.

NO-COOK CHOCOLATE COOKIES

¼ cup butter or margarine, melted	Dash salt
½ cup white corn syrup	1 cup coarsely chopped nuts
⅔ cup cocoa	⅔ cup flaked coconut
1 cup sifted confectioners' sugar	6 oz. candy-coated puffed wheat (4½ cups)

In large bowl, blend butter with corn syrup, cocoa, sugar, salt. Add nuts, coconut, cereal; with large fork, stir mixture until cereal is well coated. Pack this mixture firmly into greased 13″ x 9″ x 2″ pan; refrigerate several hr., or until firm. Cut into squares. Makes 3 to 4 doz.

COCONUT-DATE PORCUPINES

¾ cup granulated sugar	1 cup chopped walnuts
1 cup snipped pitted dates	1 cup cornflakes
2 eggs, well beaten	1 cup sugar-coated toasted rice cereal
1 teasp. vanilla extract	1½ cups flaked coconut

In skillet, blend sugar with dates and eggs. Cook over medium heat, stirring constantly, until mixture pulls away from sides of pan (about 5 min.); remove from heat. Stir in vanilla and walnuts; then carefully stir in cereals; cool slightly. With hands, moistened in cold water, shape mixture into small mounds; roll each in coconut. Refrigerate until served. Makes 2 doz. NOTE: If desired, omit coconut and dip each in melted semisweet chocolate.

DATE BALLS

2 cups bran flakes, wheat flakes, or cornflakes	1 tablesp. butter or margarine
¾ cup pitted dates, chilled	2 teasp. lemon juice
½ cup pecans	Sifted confectioners' sugar
2 tablesp. honey	Pecan halves

Put cereal, dates, pecans through food chopper. To this mixture, add honey, butter, lemon juice; knead until well blended. Shape dough into small balls and roll in confectioners' sugar. Top with pecan halves. Makes 2½ doz.

FUN-TO-FIX COOKIES

Waiting for you in your grocer's dairy case are rolls of refrigerated slice 'n' bake cookie dough — butterscotch nut, coconut, peanut butter, chocolate chip, sugar, raisin, oatmeal, brownie, fudge-mint, ginger-molasses, etc. — all ready to slice and bake as label directs. Keep a roll or two ahead in your refrigerator, on one of the shelves — *never on the inside of the door.*

On your grocer's shelves, too, you'll find an all-purpose cookie mix that you can make up in at least nine different ways, also that famous chocolate-chip cookie mix, another for coconut macaroons, another for date bars, a fudge brownie and a mint-fudge mix, also butterscotch squares, and that old favorite gingerbread mix for your ginger cookies. And packaged biscuit mix with its several cookie variations will be there, too.

What fun! And they're all so good!

TAKE YOUR PICK

ORANGE-COCONUT BARS: Slice 1 roll refrigerated slice 'n' bake coconut-cookie dough about ¾″ thick; then quarter each slice. Press quarters, side by side, into ungreased 13″ x 9″ pan. Sprinkle with 1 cup chopped walnuts mixed with 1 cup flaked coconut, 2 tablesp. grated orange rind, and 1 tablesp. orange juice; lightly press into dough. Bake at 375°F. 20 to 25 min., or until golden brown. Cool; cut into bars. Makes about 3 doz.

PEANUT-BUTTER SPARKLERS: Slice 1 roll refrigerated slice 'n' bake peanut-butter-cookie dough, as label directs. Cut each slice in half, roll into a ball, then roll in granulated sugar. Bake on ungreased cookie sheets at 375°F. 6 to 8 min., or until light brown. Now, into each ball, press lightly 1 or more semisweet-chocolate pieces or miniature marshmallows. Bake 2 min. longer. Cool 1 min., then remove from sheets.

CHOCOLATE-TIPPED CRESCENTS: Slice 1 roll refrigerated slice 'n' bake sugar cookies ¼″ thick. Mold each slice into crescent. Bake, on ungreased cookie sheet, at 375°F. 8 to 10 min., or until golden brown. Cool 1 min.; remove. Now melt ½ cup semisweet-chocolate pieces over hot, *not boiling*, water. Then spread one tip end of each crescent with chocolate, then dip it into finely chopped nuts. Makes about 3 doz.

CHOCO-ROLL COOKIES: Slice your favorite refrigerated slice 'n' bake cookies thin. Spread each slice with melted semisweet-chocolate pieces, roll up like jelly roll, then bake as label directs. Or spread melted chocolate between every two cookie slices, then bake.

OATMEAL LOLLIPOPS: Shape 1 roll refrigerated slice 'n' bake oatmeal cookies into 16 balls; lay on ungreased cookie sheet. Flatten each with bottom of glass, dipped in flour; insert wooden skewer in each. Bake at 375°F. 10 min.; cool. With frosting, attach semisweet-chocolate pieces for eyes, bit of gumdrop for nose, cinnamon candies for mouth, yellow flaked coconut for "hair." Makes 1⅓ doz.

SO-BIG COOKIES: Start heating oven to 375°F Slice two rolls refrigerated slice 'n' bake cookie dough — two favorite flavors — ¼" thick. For each cookie, overlap five slices in circle on cookie sheet, leaving 1" hole in center. Bake 10 min., or until done. Sprinkle with sugar and nutmeg; cool on cookie sheet 2 to 3 min.; remove with large spatula. Makes 1 doz.

PRALINE COOKIES

1 pkg. favorite pie-crust mix	¼ cup light- or dark-brown sugar, packed
2 tablesp. butter or margarine	½ cup chopped pecans

1. Start heating oven to 450°F. Prepare piecrust as label directs. On lightly floured surface, roll out pastry into 9" x 6" rectangle. With 2 broad spatulas, carefully transfer pastry to cookie sheet.

2. In small bowl, with spoon, thoroughly cream butter; add brown sugar and beat until light and fluffy. Spread mixture evenly over pastry. Sprinkle with pecans. Mark pastry into 24 squares. Bake 15 to 20 min. Cool on wire racks. Makes 2 doz.

READY-TO-EATS

No chapter on cookies could be complete without a big bow to the superb variety of luscious packaged cookies and crackers that the grocer has on his shelves. You may always feel proud when they play a part in your hostess plans.

SWEETS TO MAKE

If you or your family have a "sweet tooth," serve candy as dessert. It satisfies a natural craving for sweets at the proper time and so does not spoil one's appetite for other foods. Many varieties supply many important food values — the energy of sugar, corn syrup, chocolate, etc.; the proteins, calcium, and B-vitamins of fluid, condensed, or evaporated milk; the additional body-building properties of nuts, fruits, etc. — in a universally popular form. It enables parents to serve this treat to youngsters in sensible quantities.

Whether you choose a traditional recipe or one that takes advantage of today's easy-on-the-cook ingredients, you can turn out wonderful candy for gift giving or home serving merely by obeying the rules. In this chapter we've omitted elaborate candies that call for special equipment and skill.

Before using these recipes, refer to How To Use Our Recipes, p. 3. Always use standard measuring cups and measuring spoons; measure level.

EASY AND SO GOOD

HEAVENLY HASH

3 6-oz. pkg. semi-sweet-chocolate pieces	1 6¼-oz. pkg. (4 cups) miniature marshmallows
2 tablesp. butter	1 cup broken walnuts

1. In double boiler, over hot, *not boiling*, water, partially melt chocolate pieces plus butter.
2. Remove from heat, and stir till smooth.
3. Blend in marshmallows and nuts till coated with chocolate.
4. Spread in buttered 8″ x 8″ x 2″ pan. Refrigerate till firm; cut into 16 2″ squares. Makes 1¾ lb.

CRUNCHY BRIDGE BITES

Melt 1 6-oz. pkg. semisweet-chocolate pieces (1 cup) over hot, *not boiling*, water. Meanwhile, crumble enough corn chips to make 1½ cups; add to chocolate; stir until chips are thoroughly covered; drop by spoonfuls onto wax paper. Refrigerate until chilled.

CONFETTI

1 6-oz. pkg. butter-scotch pieces	sweet-chocolate pieces
1 6¼-oz. pkg. miniature marshmallows	1 4-oz. pkg. potato chips
1 6-oz. pkg. semi-	1 qt. popped popcorn

In large serving bowl, toss all ingredients together. Makes about 4 qt. as nibbler.

SCOTCH PEANUTS

Combine salted peanuts and packaged butterscotch pieces as nibbler for your bridge party.

SEMISWEET-FUDGE BALLS

1 6-oz. pkg. semisweet-chocolate pieces (1 cup)	¼ teasp. cinnamon (optional)
¾ cup evaporated milk, undiluted	½ cup finely chopped walnuts
	½ cup chocolate shot

Melt chocolate over hot, *not boiling,* water; stir in milk, cinnamon. Cook, stirring often, 20 min. (mixture should be very thick). Refrigerate 1 hr., or until easy to handle. Shape into ¾″ balls; roll some in walnuts, some in chocolate shot (or in fine grated coconut, instant-cocoa mix, or instant coffee). Makes 3 doz.

FRENCH FUDGE

2 6-oz. or 1 12-oz. pkg. semisweet-chocolate pieces (2 cups)	Few grains salt
	1 cup chopped walnuts (optional)
¾ cup canned sweetened condensed milk	1 teasp. vanilla extract (or rum or rum extract to taste)

Line 9″ x 5″ x 3″ loaf pan with wax paper. Melt chocolate over hot, *not boiling,* water. Stir in condensed milk, salt, nuts, vanilla. Pour into pan. Cool a few hr.; when firm, cut into squares. Makes 1¼ lb.

TRUFFLE BALLS: Cool French-Fudge mixture until easy to shape into ¾″ balls. Dip each ball into fine grated coconut, chopped nuts, instant-cocoa mix, instant coffee, or chocolate shot. Or make fudge without nuts; mold around filberts, or press pecan or walnut half into each ball.

TEN-MINUTE MARSHMALLOW NUT FUDGE

1⅔ cups granulated sugar	1½ 6-oz. pkg. semisweet-chocolate pieces (1½ cups)
2 tablesp. butter or margarine	¼ lb. large marshmallows, snipped
½ teasp. salt	½ cup chopped walnuts
⅔ cup evaporated milk, undiluted	1 teasp. vanilla extract

In 2-qt. saucepan, combine sugar, butter, salt, milk; bring to boil over medium heat; boil 5 min., stirring constantly. Remove from heat. Add chocolate and rest of ingredients. Beat vigorously until marshmallows melt. Pour into greased 8″ x 8″ x 2″ pan; sprinkle with more nuts, if desired. Cool; cut into small squares. Makes about 5 doz. squares.

CHOCOLATE-RUM STICKS

2½ cups semisweet-chocolate pieces	Dash salt
	2 teasp. rum extract
1 cup canned sweetened condensed milk	1½ cups chopped walnuts

1. In double boiler, over hot, *not boiling,* water, melt chocolate. Stir in condensed milk and salt; remove from heat; then beat it with electric mixer until it is smooth.
2. Stir in extract and walnuts; then pour into wax-paper-lined 7″ x 3″ x 2″ loaf pan. Refrigerate 24 hr. to mellow.
3. Next, cut into ½″ slices; then halve each slice lengthwise. Store in airtight container. Makes 1¾ lb.

DREAM NUT FUDGE

1 3-oz. pkg. cream cheese	½ cup chopped almonds, walnuts, or Brazil nuts, or flaked coconut
2½ cups sifted confectioners' sugar	
½ teasp. almond extract	Pinch salt

With electric mixer at medium speed (or with spoon), beat cream cheese until soft and smooth. Slowly blend in sugar, extract, nuts, salt. Press into greased 9″ x 5″ x 3″ loaf pan. Refrigerate until firm; cut into squares. Makes about 2½ doz. squares.

CHOCOLATE-NUT: Reduce sugar to 2 cups. Add 2 sq. unsweetened chocolate, melted. Substitute vanilla extract for almond extract, walnuts for almonds.

PEANUT BUTTER: Substitute 2 tablesp. peanut butter for almond extract, ¼ cup chopped salted peanuts for almonds.

TING-A-LINGS

1 6-oz. pkg. semi-sweet-chocolate pieces (1 cup)
1 cup cornflakes
½ cup snipped flaked coconut

1 teasp. vanilla extract
½ cup salted peanuts, cut-up pitted dates, or seedless raisins

Melt chocolate over hot, *not boiling*, water; stir until smooth. Remove from heat. Stir in cornflakes, coconut, vanilla, peanuts. Drop by teaspoonfuls onto wax paper. Refrigerate until firm. Makes 2 doz.

COCONUT PEAKS

¼ cup butter or margarine
2 cups sifted confectioners' sugar
3 cups snipped flaked coconut
¼ cup light cream

1 6-oz. pkg. semi-sweet-chocolate pieces (1 cup)
2 teasp. shortening (not butter or margarine)

In saucepan, slowly heat butter until golden; gradually stir in sugar, coconut, cream. Drop by teaspoonfuls onto wax paper. Refrigerate till easy to handle; then shape into peaks. Over hot, *not boiling*, water, melt chocolate with shortening; stir until smooth. Dip bottoms of peaks into chocolate; harden on rack covered with wax paper. Makes 3 doz.

NOUGAT BARS

3 tablesp. butter or margarine
½ lb. marshmallows
4 cups puffed corn cereal
½ cup flaked coconut

¼ cup coarsely chopped walnuts
½ teasp. salt
¾ 6-oz. pkg. semi-sweet-chocolate pieces (¾ cup)

In double boiler, melt butter with marshmallows; stir until smooth. Remove from heat. Add cereal, coconut, nuts, salt; press smooth into greased 9″ x 9″ x 2″ pan. Melt chocolate over hot, *not boiling*, water; spread over candy. Cool till firm; then cut. Makes 2½ to 3 doz.

To Vary: Omit chocolate topping.

COCONUT MALLOWS

Over hot, *not boiling*, water, melt 1 6-oz. pkg. semisweet-chocolate pieces (1 cup) with 1 tablesp. shortening (not butter or margarine); stir until smooth. Drop in large marshmallows, one at a time, turning until well coated. Lift out; roll in chopped nuts or toasted, white or tinted, snipped flaked coconut. Refrigerate on wax paper till well chilled. Makes about 2½ doz.

CHOCOLATE-PEANUT POPCORN

2 tablesp. butter or margarine
1 6-oz. pkg. semi-sweet-chocolate pieces
12 large marshmallows

1 tablesp. water
1 3½-oz. pkg. popped popcorn
1 7-oz. can salted cocktail peanuts

Several days ahead:
1. In a large saucepan, over *low* heat, melt butter; add chocolate pieces, marshmallows, and water. Stir constantly until all are melted and mixture is smooth.
2. Add popcorn and toss until all are coated. Spread out in shallow baking pan and let cool.
3. Then toss popcorn mixture with salted peanuts. Makes about 2 qt.

APRICOT-COCONUT BALLS

1 cup dried apricots
1 cup flaked coconut
¼ cup confectioners' sugar
1 teasp. grated orange rind

1 teasp. grated lemon rind
1 tablesp. lemon juice
Granulated sugar

Put apricots and coconut through food grinder, using fine blade. Mix in confectioners' sugar, rinds, lemon juice. Form into small balls. Roll in granulated sugar. Let ripen in refrigerator at least a week before serving. Makes 2 doz.

NUTTED CARAMEL-POPCORN BALLS

1. *Day before:* In covered double boiler, heat 2 ½-lb. pkg. dairy caramels with 2 tablesp. hot water, stirring often until smooth.
2. Meanwhile, in a large bowl, toss 2 to 2½ qt. popcorn with 1 cup mixed salted nuts and ½ cup salted peanuts.

3. Pour melted caramels over popcorn; toss until well coated. With buttered hands, form at once into about 17 2½″ balls or 35 1¼″ balls. Insert wooden skewers, lollipop-fashion, if desired. Wrap each in saran; store at room temperature till served next day.

PEANUT CHIPPEROOS

1½ cups peanut butter	½ teasp. grated lemon rind
1 7¼-oz. pkg. pitted dates, snipped	1 teasp. lemon juice
½ cup snipped flaked coconut	¾ cup confectioners' sugar
	¾ cup finely crushed potato chips

Night before, if desired: Combine peanut butter, dates, coconut, lemon rind, and juice. Sift sugar over mixture; blend well. Shape between palms of hands into large marble-size balls.
Just before serving: Roll balls in potato chips which were crushed with rolling pin. Makes 3 doz.

CHOCOLATE-APPLE NIBBLES

1 6-oz. pkg. semi-sweet-chocolate pieces	4 medium red apples, washed, dried
	Toothpicks

Several hr. before serving:
1. In double boiler, over hot, *not boiling*, water, melt chocolate.
2. Meanwhile, core unpared apples; then cut into eighths. Insert a toothpick in skin side of each apple section.
3. Remove melted chocolate from heat. Holding each apple section by toothpick and tilting double-boiler top, dip apple in chocolate, leaving skin side uncoated.
4. Lay apple sections on buttered cookie sheet; store in refrigerator until time to serve. Makes 32.

CARAMEL APPLES

1 1-lb. pkg. dairy caramels	6 medium red apples, washed, dried
3 tablesp. hot water	6 wooden skewers
	Chopped walnuts

Several hr. before serving:
1. In double boiler, over boiling water, melt caramels with water, stirring frequently, until a smooth sauce.

2. Meanwhile, remove stems from apples. Then insert a wooden skewer part way into stem end of each apple.
3. Remove sauce from heat. Now, holding each apple by skewer and tilting double-boiler top, quickly twirl apple in caramel sauce. Remove from sauce; continue twirling to allow sauce to spread smoothly over apple.
4. Next quickly dip bottom or completely roll each apple in the chopped walnuts; then place, skewer side up, on lightly buttered cookie sheet, and refrigerate until serving time. Makes 6.

WITH A CANDY THERMOMETER

Buy a good candy thermometer! For, when making the candies that follow in this group, it is important, for best results, that you use a dependable candy thermometer (a paddle-shaped thermometer with 2-degree graduations). Be sure to stand thermometer in candy mixture before you start to cook and leave it in during cooking. The bulb must be completely covered with boiling syrup, yet must not rest on bottom of pan.

When reading the thermometer, your eyes should be on a level with the mercury. When mixture is ready to be removed from heat, take out thermometer and lay it where it can cool before washing; otherwise it may break.

Cold-Water Test: If you have no candy thermometer, the cold-water test is the next best thing. Drop about ½ teasp. of cooking candy mixture into 1 cup cold water. (Be sure water is really cold.) Let it stand 1 min., then note firmness of mass with fingers as indicated in recipe. Remove candy from heat while making test — it can so quickly overcook.

To Avoid Graininess: Once you're through stirring candy mixture to dissolve sugar, rinse and dry spoon. It's also a good idea to rinse it after cold-water tests, especially if mixture is stirred infrequently.

Don't Short-Cut Cooling: With such creamy candies as penuche and Old-Fashioned Fudge, be sure to cool mixture to 110°F. (or until outside of saucepan feels lukewarm to hand) *before starting to beat at all.* Don't move or jar saucepan. If mixture is stirred while hot, large sugar crystals form, and candy becomes grainy.

Don't Scrape Pan: When candy mixture is ready to be turned into pan, hold it close to pan, and pour quickly. Don't scrape out cooking pan — leavings may be sugary.

SUPERB PLANTATION PRALINES

2 cups granulated sugar	2 tablesp. butter or margarine
1 teasp. baking soda	2⅓ cups pecan halves
1 cup buttermilk	⅔ cup perfect pecan halves
Pinch salt	

1. In large kettle (about 8 qt.), combine sugar, baking soda, buttermilk, salt.
2. Cook over high heat 5 min., or to 210°F. on candy thermometer, being sure to stir frequently and to scrape bottom and crevices of kettle.
3. Add butter and 2⅓ cups pecans. Cook, stirring constantly and scraping bottom and sides of kettle, to 230°F. on candy thermometer (about 5 min.), or until a little mixture, dropped into cold water, forms very soft ball.
4. Remove from heat, and cool 1 to 2 min.
5. With wooden spoon, beat till thickened and creamy; immediately drop by tablespoonfuls onto wax paper, foil, or greased cookie sheet.
6. Then dot top with ⅔ cup pecans. Makes 7 large pralines.

MERRY CHRISTMAS FUDGE

3 cups granulated sugar	1½ teasp. vanilla extract
1½ cups milk	½ cup marshmallow cream
¾ teasp. salt	¾ cup sliced candied cherries or orange peel
3 tablesp. butter or margarine	

1. In heavy saucepan, combine sugar, milk, and salt. Over medium heat, stir mixture constantly till sugar dissolves and mixture comes to a full boil.
2. Cook to 234°F. on candy thermometer, or till little of mixture, dropped into cold water, forms soft ball.
3. Remove from heat immediately; then add butter. Allow to cool to lukewarm; then add vanilla.
4. Beat with spoon until mixture begins to

hold its shape. Add marshmallow cream; beat till thick, glossy. Quickly stir in cherries, and turn into a buttered pan. When fudge is cool, cut into squares. Makes 1¾ lb.

COFFEE-CHIP FUDGE

2 tablesp. instant coffee	3 tablesp. butter or margarine
3 cups granulated sugar	1 teasp. vanilla extract
⅛ teasp. salt	½ cup chopped walnuts, pecans, or almonds
½ cup light cream	
2 tablesp. white corn syrup	1 6-oz. pkg. semi-sweet-chocolate pieces (1 cup)
1 cup milk	

In 3-qt. saucepan, combine coffee, sugar, salt, cream, corn syrup, milk; stir over low heat until boiling. Then cook gently, without stirring, to 236°F. on candy thermometer, or until a little mixture, dropped into cold water, forms soft ball. Remove from heat; add butter, vanilla; *do not stir.*

Cool, without stirring, to 110°F., or until outside of saucepan feels lukewarm to hand. With electric mixer at medium speed (or with spoon), beat until candy loses gloss and small amount dropped from spoon holds its shape. Add nuts, then chocolate. Turn into greased 8″ x 8″ x 2″ pan (don't scrape saucepan; leavings may be sugary). Cool; cut. Makes about 3 doz. squares.

OLD-FASHIONED FUDGE

2 cups granulated sugar	2 tablesp. white corn syrup
1 cup milk; or ½ cup evaporated milk, undiluted, and ½ cup water	2 tablesp. butter or margarine
	½ teasp. vanilla extract
½ teasp. salt	½ cup chopped nuts
2 sq. unsweetened chocolate	

In saucepan, combine sugar, milk, salt, chocolate, corn syrup; stir over low heat until sugar dissolves. Cook gently, stirring occasionally, to 238°F. on candy thermometer, or until a little mixture, dropped into cold water, forms soft ball. Remove from heat; drop in butter; *do not stir.*

Cool, without stirring, to 110°F., or until outside of saucepan feels lukewarm to hand. Add vanilla. With spoon, beat until candy loses gloss and small amount dropped from spoon holds its shape. Add nuts. Turn into greased 9″ x 5″ x 3″ loaf pan (don't scrape saucepan; leavings may be sugary). Cool; cut. Makes 1¼ lb.

CHOCOLATE MARSHMALLOW: Pour half of fudge into pan. Cover quickly with 1 cup miniature marshmallows; top with rest of fudge. Or add 1 cup miniature marshmallows to fudge just before turning it into pan.

PEANUT BUTTER: Substitute ¼ cup peanut butter for butter, adding it after candy cools to 110°F.

DIVINITY DROPS

2⅓ cups granulated sugar	2 egg whites
⅔ cup white corn syrup	½ cup chopped Brazil nuts or walnuts (or flaked coconut)
½ cup water	½ teasp. vanilla or almond extract
¼ teasp. salt	

In 2-qt. saucepan, combine sugar, corn syrup, water, salt; stir over low heat until sugar dissolves. Cover; boil 1 min., or until all sugar crystals on side of pan have dissolved. Uncover; cook gently, without stirring, to 265°F. on candy thermometer, or until a little mixture, dropped into cold water, forms almost brittle ball.

Meanwhile, in large bowl, with mixer at high speed (or with hand beater), beat egg whites until stiff. Slowly pour on syrup, beating, until mixture loses gloss and small amount dropped from spoon holds its shape. Add nuts, vanilla. Drop by teaspoonfuls onto greased shallow pan (don't scrape saucepan; leavings may be sugary). If desired, sprinkle with chopped nuts, chocolate shot, or tinted coconut. Makes about 1½ lb.

DIVINITY FUDGE: Pour mixture into a greased 9″ x 9″ x 2″ pan. Cool; cut into squares.

BRAZIL-NUT TOFFEE

1¼ cups butter or margarine	1¼ cups coarsely chopped Brazil nuts
1⅔ cups granulated sugar	2 4-oz. bars milk chocolate
4 teasp. corn syrup	¾ cup finely chopped Brazil nuts
¼ cup water	

1. In heavy saucepan, melt butter; add sugar, corn syrup, and water.

2. Cook over medium heat, stirring frequently, to 300°F. on candy thermometer, or until a little of candy mixture, dropped into cold water, becomes hard and brittle.

3. Immediately remove from heat; stir in coarsely chopped Brazil nuts; then spread in buttered 15½″ x 10½″ x 1″ pan.

4. Refrigerate till thoroughly cooled.

5. Then turn sheet of toffee out on wax paper by inverting pan and gently tapping its corners.

6. In double boiler, over hot, *not boiling*, water, melt chocolate bars; spread over toffee. Sprinkle with finely chopped nuts. Refrigerate to firm up chocolate; break into pieces. Makes 1¾ lb.

NUT PENUCHE

2 tablesp. butter or margarine	1½ cups granulated sugar
¾ cup liquid (half milk and half heavy cream)	1 teasp. vanilla extract
1 cup light-brown sugar, packed	¾ to 1 cup chopped walnuts or pecans

In 2-qt. saucepan, melt butter; grease side of pan well. Pour in liquid; bring to boil; stir in sugars until dissolved. Cover; boil 1 min., or until all sugar crystals on side of pan have dissolved. Uncover; cook gently, to 238°F. on candy thermometer, or until a little mixture, dropped into cold water, forms soft ball.

Cool, without stirring, to 110°F., or until outside of saucepan feels lukewarm to hand. Add vanilla, nuts. With spoon, beat until mixture loses gloss and small amount, dropped from spoon, holds its shape. Pour into greased 8″ x 8″ x 2″ pan or 9″ x 5″ x 3″ loaf pan (don't scrape saucepan; leavings may be sugary). Cut while warm. Makes about 2½ doz. squares.

NUT BRITTLE

2 cups granulated sugar	Pinch salt
1 cup brown sugar, packed	¼ cup butter or margarine
½ cup white corn syrup	1¼ cups walnuts, peanuts, Brazil nuts, pecans, or blanched almonds, in small pieces
½ cup water	
⅛ teasp. baking soda	

In saucepan, combine sugars, corn syrup, water. Cook, stirring, until sugar dissolves. Continue cooking, without stirring, to 300°F. on candy thermometer, or until a little mixture, dropped into cold water, becomes very brittle.

Remove mixture from heat; add soda, salt, butter; stir *only enough* to mix. Add nuts; turn at once into greased 12″ x 8″ x 1″ pan (don't scrape saucepan; leavings may be sugary). After 1 min. or so, take hold of candy at edges; lift from pan onto greased surface; pull quite thin. When cold, break up. Makes about 1½ lb.

SPICED WALNUTS

1 cup granulated sugar	¼ cup boiling water
½ teasp. nutmeg or cinnamon	½ teasp. vanilla extract
⅛ teasp. cream of tartar	2 cups walnut halves

In saucepan, combine sugar, nutmeg, cream of tartar, and water. Cook to 246°F. on candy thermometer, or until a little syrup, dropped into cold water, forms firm ball. Add vanilla, walnuts; stir until nuts are completely coated. Turn out onto greased cookie sheet or wax paper. With 2 forks, quickly separate nuts; cool. Makes 3 cups.

GINGER ALMONDS: Substitute 1 teasp. ground ginger for nutmeg, 2 cups unblanched almonds for walnut halves.

SHERRY WALNUTS

1½ cups granulated sugar	½ teasp. cinnamon
½ cup sherry	2 to 3 cups walnut halves

Boil sugar and sherry to 240°F. on candy thermometer, or until a little mixture, dropped into cold water, forms soft ball. Remove from heat. Add cinnamon and walnuts; stir until cloudy. Turn out onto well-buttered cookie sheet; separate nuts.

PENUCHE NUTS

½ cup brown sugar, firmly packed	½ teasp. vanilla extract
¼ cup granulated sugar	1½ cups walnut, pecan, or Brazil-nut meats
⅓ cup milk or light cream*	

In saucepan, combine brown sugar, granulated sugar, milk. Cook over low heat, stirring constantly, until sugars are dissolved. Then cook to 240°F. on candy thermometer, or until a little syrup, dropped into cold water, forms soft ball. Remove from heat.

Add vanilla and nuts; stir until mixture begins to coat nuts; quickly turn out onto wax paper. With 2 forks, quickly separate nuts; cool. Makes 2 cups.

You may substitute ¼ cup commercial sour cream for milk.

SPICED MIXED NUTS

¾ cup granulated sugar	1 egg white, slightly beaten
¾ teasp. salt	2½ tablesp. water
1 teasp. cinnamon	1 cup walnut halves
½ teasp. cloves	1 cup pecan halves
¼ teasp. allspice	1 cup Brazil-nut halves
¼ teasp. nutmeg	

Prepare same day, or several days ahead:
1. Start heating oven to 275°F.
2. Combine sugar, salt, cinnamon, cloves, allspice, nutmeg. Stir in slightly beaten egg white and water till blended.
3. Add nuts, about ½ cup at a time. Stir with fork till coated; then lift out, draining off excess syrup; place, nut by nut, on greased cookie sheet.
4. Bake 45 min., or till golden and crusty. Store in covered container. Makes 3 cups.

To Vary: Substitute 3 cups whole walnut halves for the three varieties of nuts.

CRISP COCONUT BALLS

4 cups sugar-coated wheat cereal	¼ cup white corn syrup
½ cup granulated sugar	⅛ teasp. salt
½ cup light molasses	1 tablesp. butter or margarine
¼ cup light cream	1 cup snipped flaked coconut

In shallow pan, in 350°F. oven, lightly toast cereal 10 min. In 3-qt. saucepan, combine rest of ingredients except coconut; stir over low heat until sugar dissolves. Boil, stirring occasionally, to 248°F. on candy thermometer, or until a little mixture, dropped into cold water, forms firm ball. Remove from heat. Quickly mix in cereal, coconut. Quickly and gently shape into 2″ balls. Makes 2½ doz.

COCONUT SQUARES: Pack mixture into greased 8″ x 8″ x 2″ pan; when firm, cut into squares.

POPCORN CAPERS

CHRISTMAS POPCORN BALLS: In large bowl, mix 3 qt. popcorn, ½ lb. cut-up candied cherries. In 2-qt. saucepan, combine 2 cups white corn syrup, 1 tablesp. vinegar, 1 teasp. salt; cook, stirring occasionally, to 250°F. on candy thermometer, or until a little mixture, dropped into cold water, forms hard ball. Add 2 teasp. vanilla extract. Slowly pour over popcorn, tossing until coated. Quickly and gently shape into 3″ balls. Makes about 15.

MOLASSES POPCORN BALLS: In large bowl, mix 1½ qt. popcorn or puffed cereal with ¼ teasp. salt. In 2-qt. saucepan, combine ½ cup light molasses, ½ cup corn syrup, 1½ teasp. vinegar; cook, stirring occasionally, to 240°F. on candy thermometer, or until a little mixture, dropped into cold water, forms soft ball. Continue cooking, stirring constantly, to 270°F. on candy thermometer, or until a little mixture, dropped into cold water, is slightly brittle. Remove from heat. Add 1½ tablesp. butter or margarine, stirring only enough to mix. Pour over popcorn, tossing until coated. Quickly and gently shape into 2½″ balls. Makes about 10.

PULLED MOLASSES-MINT TAFFY

2 cups light molasses	⅛ teasp. salt
2 teasp. vinegar	½ teasp. baking soda
1½ tablesp. butter or margarine	7 drops oil of peppermint

In 3-qt. saucepan, mix molasses, vinegar. Cook gently, stirring, to 260°F. on candy thermometer, or until a little mixture, dropped into cold water, becomes brittle. Remove from heat. Add butter, salt, soda. Stir until foaming stops; pour into greased 12″ x 8″ x 1″ pan.

When candy is cool enough to pull, drop peppermint into center. Lift corners; draw to center; press together. Pull, using thumbs and fingers; fold. Repeat until light in color and slightly firm. Pull into 2 long ropes, ¾″ thick; twist. With scissors (dip often into hot water), cut into 1″ pieces; wrap in wax paper, saran, or foil. Makes about 6½ doz. pieces.

MOLASSES TAFFY: Omit oil of peppermint.

CANDIED FRUIT PEEL

CANDIED GRAPEFRUIT PEEL: Cut peel from 2 grapefruit into 4 lengthwise sections. (If white membrane is very thick, remove some of it; otherwise, leave intact.) Cover peel with cold water; bring to boil. Boil 10 min.; drain. Repeat 3 times. Cut peel into thin strips.

In 3-qt. saucepan, combine 1 cup granulated sugar, ½ cup white corn syrup, 1 cup water; stir over low heat until sugar dissolves. Add peel; boil gently, uncovered, about 40 min., or until most of syrup is absorbed. Drain in coarse strainer or colander. Roll peel, a few pieces at a time, in granulated sugar. Arrange in single layer on wax paper or pan; let dry about 2 days. Store in covered container. Makes about ½ lb.

CANDIED ORANGE PEEL: Substitute 6 thick-skinned oranges for grapefruit; boil peel 5 min. each time instead of 10 min. Increase sugar to 2 cups. Decrease corn syrup to 2 teasp. Makes about 1½ lb.

DRINKS—HOT AND COLD

A CUP OF GOOD COFFEE

There's no trick at all to making good coffee. Just follow our rules every time you put the pot on. And make enough to fill those requests for seconds.

Start with a Clean Pot: A stale pot makes poor coffee. So:

1. Wash coffeepot in hot sudsy water, occasionally using a special brush for valves, spouts, tubes, etc.

2. If water is hard, add a water-softener compound or use a dishwashing detergent.

3. Remove stains on aluminum coffeepots and parts with soap-filled steel-wool pads.

4. Do not scour plated interiors; instead, clean them with products made especially for that purpose, such as Maid-Easy Coffee Stain Remover and Dip-It.

5. After washing pot, rinse it thoroughly with very hot water; dry well.

Use Only Fresh Coffee: Oxygen in the air destroys coffee flavor, produces staleness. To be sure your coffee is fresh:

1. Buy it in a vacuum-sealed can.

2. Or, if it's not vacuum-packed, be sure it was roasted and ground within the last few days.

3. Don't stock coffee unless it's in a vacuum-sealed can.

4. After opening can or bag of coffee, *use it up within a week* if possible.

5. If a little coffee is left over at end of week, don't mix it with a fresh supply.

6. Store coffee in the refrigerator, in a tightly lidded can or a glass jar with screw-on top.

What Grind to Use: We have found that a drip grind is a good "medium" grind and makes good coffee in all types of coffee makers. However, if the manufacturer specifies a different grind for his coffee maker, try it and compare.

Measure Coffee Level: Regardless of the coffee maker — drip, vacuum type, percolator, etc. — use 1 Approved Coffee Measure (2 level measuring tablesp.) of coffee to 6 oz. (¾ cup) of water. Use a ½-pt. or 1-pt. measuring cup to measure water. If you do not own the Approved Coffee Measure, use a set of measuring spoons, leveling off each spoonful of coffee with spatula. (The Pan-American Coffee Bureau and The Coffee Brewing Institute, Inc., both at 120 Wall Street, New York City, distribute the Approved Coffee Measure device for 2 level tablesp.)

Use Right Size of Coffee Maker: Modern coffee makers give best results when filled to capacity. They make from 1 to 10 servings (5 to 6 oz. each). So if your family drinks 4 cups of coffee at a meal, buy a coffee maker for 4 servings. For entertaining, choose at least an 8-serving size. Or buy both a small and large size. A coffee maker should *never* be used at less than ¾ capacity.

Ways to Make It

There are 4 types of coffee-making devices — the old-time coffeepot, drip coffeepot, percolator, and vacuum-type coffee maker. A popular trend is the automatic coffee maker, in either the percolator or vacuum type. It brews for the proper length of time, then automatically switches to a lower "keep warm" heat.

IN AN OLD-TIME COFFEEPOT

1. Measure drip-grind coffee into coffeepot, allowing 1 Approved Coffee Measure (2 level measuring tablesp.) coffee to each ¾ cup (6 oz.) water.
2. Add water — cold, hot, or boiling.
3. Place over heat; stir well. Just bring to boil; stir again; remove. Add dash of cold water to settle grounds. (Don't let coffee boil — aroma and flavor will escape.)
4. Let coffee stand over *very low heat* for about 5 min.; then strain through fine cheese-cloth into another utensil. Serve hot.

IN A VACUUM-TYPE COFFEE MAKER

1. Use a drip-grind coffee, allowing 1 Approved Coffee Measure (2 level measuring tablesp.) coffee for each ¾ cup (6 oz.) water — unless manufacturer directs otherwise.
2. Measure water into lower bowl; start heating.
3. Adjust filter (it may be a cloth, stainless steel, or glass-rod type). Measure coffee into upper bowl; place snugly on lower bowl.
4. When water in lower bowl is heated, most of

it rises to upper bowl. When all but a small amount of water has risen, or when water in upper bowl starts to bubble vigorously, turn off heat. Stir once to mix coffee and water.
5. Let coffee maker stand with heat turned off until brew returns to lower bowl — 5 to 7 min.
6. To keep filter cloth clean, rinse it out well after each use. Keep in cold water until used again, or as manufacturer directs.

IN A DRIP COFFEEPOT

1. Measure drip-grind coffee into coffee section of drip pot, allowing 1 Approved Coffee Measure (2 level measuring tablesp.) coffee for each ¾ cup (6 oz.) water. (If filter paper is used, adjust before putting in coffee.)
2. Pour rapidly boiling water into water section.
3. Immediately put pot over low heat and let water drip through. *Do not let it boil.*
4. Remove coffee and water sections from pot; stir coffee well; serve at once.
5. If coffee cannot be served at once, place pot over *low heat. Do not let it boil.*

IN A PERCOLATOR

1. Measure drip- or percolator-grind coffee, allowing 1 Approved Coffee Measure (2 level measuring tablesp.) coffee for each ¾ cup (6 oz.) water.
2. Pour cold water into bottom of percolator; place coffee in basket.
3. If you're making 6 or more servings, percolate coffee not less than 6 and not more than 8 min. after it has begun to "perc" quite definitely. If you're making less than 6 servings, reduce time to 7 min., so coffee will not get bitter.
4. Remove coffee basket as soon as percolating is completed; grounds absorb flavor, aroma.

INSTANT COFFEE

Instant coffee is a dry soluble extract, obtained by removing the water from a strong coffee brew. Practically all widely distributed brands on the market today consist of just the dehydrated coffee brew, with no added ingredients. Whatever type or brand you use, *make as label directs.*

When only a few cups of coffee are needed,

it is convenient to make the coffee right in the cup. However, when several cups are to be served, make it, all at once, in a pot, then let the brew stand over very low heat for 4 or 5 min. Then you can pour it either in the kitchen or at the table.

DECAFFEINATED COFFEE

Decaffeinated coffee is coffee from which practically all the caffein has been removed. It comes in two forms: One you prepare as you would regular coffee, the other as you would an instant type. Follow label directions.

CEREAL BEVERAGES

For those who do not drink coffee or who prefer other types of hot drink, there are cereal beverages. They come in two forms: One you prepare as you would regular coffee, the other as you would an instant type.

DEMITASSE, OR AFTER-DINNER, COFFEE

Make hot coffee, allowing 6 Approved Coffee Measures (12 level measuring tablesp.) coffee to each 3 cups (24 oz.) water. Serve hot in demitasse cups, with sugar and cream if you wish. Makes 4 6-oz. or 6 4-oz. servings.

ESPRESSO

A drip pot may be used, but a *macchinetta* is better. Use 8 tablesp. Italian-roast coffee to 1½ cups water. Serve with sugar — never with cream. Espresso coffee comes in instant form, too.

CAFFE CAPPUCCINO

Make *espresso* coffee. Combine steaming coffee with equal quantity of steaming milk. Pour into tall cups. Top with cinnamon or nutmeg.

CAFE ROYAL

Place sugar lump in an after-dinner-coffee, regular, or flaming-brandy spoon. Pour on cognac; set ablaze. Stir melted sugar into coffee.

CAFE A L'ORANGE

Add a bit of orange curaçao to each cup of strong black coffee. Provide cinnamon-stick stirrer.

CAFE AU LAIT

To make this breakfast drink of France, use a pot of hot coffee and equal amount of hot, rich milk. Pour simultaneously into large cups.

ITALIAN-STYLE COFFEE

Serve strong, hot coffee in demitasse cups or 4-oz. glasses with a twist of lemon peel and sugar.

VIENNESE COFFEE

Make extra-strength coffee; sweeten to taste. Top with *Schlagobers* (Viennese for whipped cream).

CAFE DIABLE

In chafing dish, place 6 pieces lump sugar; 8 cloves; 1″ cinnamon stick; 1″ strip lemon peel, cut up; 3 oz. cognac. Do not stir. Ignite cognac with match; stir. In a minute, slowly stir in 1 qt. strong coffee; ladle into cups. (There's a gourmet mix on the market, too.)

DELICIOUS ICED COFFEE

DO-AHEAD KIND: Make hot coffee as on p. 677, allowing 1 Approved Coffee Measure (2 level measuring tablesp.) coffee for each ¾ cup (6 oz.) water. Pour into pitcher or other warm container. Cool not more than 3 hr. Serve with ice cubes in tall glasses. Or to avoid dilution of coffee flavor, use coffee ice cubes made by freezing extra coffee in special ice-cube tray, p. 610.

HOT FROM THE POT: Make hot coffee as on p. 677, using half as much water to your usual quantity of coffee, that is, 2 Approved Coffee Measures (4 level measuring tablesp.) coffee to each ¾ cup (6 oz.) water. Pour, hot, into ice-filled tall glasses.

QUICK STYLE: For pitcher or glassful of truly delicious iced coffee, use instant coffee or instant decaffeinated coffee as label directs.

SERVING ICED COFFEE

With iced coffee, pass cream and sugar or small pitcher of white corn syrup. Or serve in one of these ways:

SNOW-CAPPED: In each glass, blend 1 cup cool regular-strength coffee with 2 tablesp. chocolate syrup. Add ice and cream. Top with whipped cream.

TOPKNOT: To ½ cup heavy cream, add 1 teasp. sugar and ½ teasp. cinnamon or a few drops of mint extract. Beat till stiff. Use to top iced coffee.

FLOATS: Into each tall glass, put 1 or 2 scoops of coffee or chocolate ice cream. Fill with cool regular-strength coffee. Stir; sweeten.

A CUP OF GOOD TEA

You can count on tea to your taste — fragrantly full-bodied every time you make it — when you follow these directions *to the letter*.

Pick Your Tea: Black, green, and oolong teas are sold loose, in packages, or in tea bags. Always keep tightly covered.

BLACK TEA owes its full flavor to the fermenting process the leaves go through before they are heated and dried. Black tea — principally from India, Ceylon, and Indonesia — is by far the most popular in this country.

FLAVORED AND SPICED TEAS are often made from black teas; they are delightfully refreshing, too.

GREEN TEA comes from Formosa and Japan. The leaves are not fermented.

OOLONG TEA, from Formosa, is fermented only a short time.

ORANGE PEKOE indicates a particular size and type of leaf, not a kind or quality of tea.

INSTANT TEA. Some instant teas are just the dried extract of freshly brewed tea; some are composed of equal parts of the dried extract and carbohydrates added to protect the flavor. Use as label directs.

Use a Clean Teapot: Wash it in heavy suds, but be sure to rinse it out thoroughly. Next, heat teapot by filling it with hot water. The hotter the pot, the better it keeps the brew warm. The brew should never come in contact with copper, brass, or iron.

Have Water Boiling Hard: For water, use freshly drawn cold water from the tap, to avoid a metallic taste. Bring to full, rolling boil. The high temperature of boiling water extracts the flavor from the tea leaves. Just very hot water will not do; reheated water will also make tea taste flat.

Measure Carefully: Whether you use tea leaves or tea bags, the rules are the same: Allow 1 teasp. tea, or 1 tea bag, per ¾ measuring cup (6 oz.) water. One teaspoonful of tea is equivalent to 1 tea bag.

Time the Brewing: Pour boiling water directly over tea leaves or bags. Then let tea brew (stand) no less than 3 min. and no more than 5 min. *by the clock.* Remember, overbrewing causes bitterness. *Never boil tea.*

Do not judge strength of tea by its color. Some strong teas brew light; some weak teas brew dark. After brewing, stir and serve.

If you like weak tea, you should still follow the rules above for making a cup of good hearty tea; then, after the tea flavor has been extracted from the leaves, weaken it with hot water.

The Serving: Tea experts prefer milk in tea to cream; with milk, you get the full, rich flavor of the tea. But your family may prefer one of our Glamour Touches, p. 681.

SPARKLING ICED TEA

To Please Everyone: For delicious iced tea, follow our basic rules for making tea, left, adding 50 per cent more tea to allow for ice dilution. In other words, use 6 teasp. loose tea, or 6 tea bags, for 4 measuring cups boiling water. To serve, pour hot tea into ice-filled iced-tea glasses; add lemon or sugar to taste. Fills 4 glasses.

When There's Company: To make iced tea in quantity for home use, put 1 qt. cold water in saucepan and bring to full, rolling boil. Remove from heat; immediately add 15 tea bags, or ⅓ cup loose tea; brew 4 min. Stir; strain into pitcher containing 1 qt. cold water. To serve, pour into ice-filled iced-tea glasses. Serve with lemon and sugar to taste. Makes 8 to 10 servings.

P.S. Don't refrigerate hot brewed tea; refrigeration may cause it to cloud, though its flavor will not be impaired. Cloudy tea can be cleared by adding a little boiling water; it brings back the tea's clear amber color.

INSTANT KIND: Use instant tea as label directs. Pour into ice-filled glasses.

READY-TO-SERVE ICED-TEA MIX: It comes with lemon and sugar right in the tea mix. All you do is add water and ice cubes.

GLAMOUR TOUCHES
(for hot or iced tea)

To Add When Brewing:
Bit of grated orange rind
Rose-geranium leaf or few whole cloves
Few crushed mint sprigs
Cinnamon stick

To Add When Serving:
Lemon, lime, or orange slices or wedges studded
  with cloves if desired
Lemon, lime, pineapple, or orange juice, passed
  in small pitcher
Strawberry or red-cherry garnish, if iced
Lemon rind, cut into corkscrew shape
Pineapple spears or chunks
Mint sprigs, dusted with sugar
Pineapple chunks and strawberries, strung on
  sippers, if iced
Cinnamon stick, as stirrer
Garnished Ice Cubes, right, if iced
Flavored Ice Cubes, p. 682, if iced
Tiny scoops of lemon sherbet, if iced

COCOA, HOT CHOCOLATE
(see When You Go Marketing, p. 91)

HOT COCOA

6 tablesp. cocoa	4½ cups milk; or
6 tablesp. granulated	2¼ cups evaporated
sugar	milk, undiluted,
Few grains salt	plus 2¼ cups water
1½ cups water	Few drops vanilla ex-
	tract (optional)

In saucepan, mix cocoa, sugar, salt, water.
Bring to boil over low heat; boil gently 2 min.,
stirring. Add milk; heat thoroughly, but do *not*
boil. Just before serving, beat with hand beater
until smooth and foamy; add vanilla. Makes
9 servings.

SPEEDY HOT COCOA: Use either sweetened
cocoa mix or instant sweet milk cocoa as label
directs. Serve in mugs.

CHOCO-MINT FLOAT: To 4 cups hot instant
sweet milk cocoa add ½ teasp. mint extract;
top with vanilla ice cream; dust with a little
nutmeg.

ICED COCOA: Cool cocoa; pour over ice in 5 or
6 glasses. Stir well. Top with whipped cream;
dust with nutmeg or cinnamon if desired.

RICH, REAL FRENCH CHOCOLATE

½ cup semisweet-	¼ cup water
chocolate pieces	1 teasp. vanilla extract
½ cup white corn	1 pt. heavy cream
syrup	2 qt. milk

Prepare early on day, or 1 hr. before serving:
1. Over low heat, blend chocolate pieces with
syrup and water until chocolate is melted. Pour
into cup; refrigerate till cool; add vanilla.
2. In large bowl, with mixer at medium speed,
beat cream while gradually adding chocolate
syrup. Continue beating until mixture just
mounds, then spoon into crystal serving bowl;
refrigerate.
Just before serving:
1. Scald milk; pour into heated coffeepot. Arrange on tray, with bowl of chocolate whipped
cream, cups and saucers.
2. In serving, spoon some chocolate whipped
cream into each guest's cup, then fill the cup
with hot milk. The guest stirs the two together
before sipping. Most delicious as a companion
to tea at a large afternoon tea — in fact any-
time! Makes 16 servings.

COOLERS

Tall cool drinks are the very symbol of summer refreshment. Here are cool drinks, for any
hour of a summer's day or evening, for any
occasion from a morning pickup for the youngsters to a full-scale party.

THE ICE

JUST ICE: Ice cubes are a must for fruit drinks.
Keep an extra supply in a plastic bag or box
in home freezer.

GARNISHED ICE CUBES: If you're having a
party, fill special ice-cube tray, p. 610, about
two thirds full with water (boiled water may
aid clarity); then let cubes freeze. Now place
one, or a combination of several of the following, on top of cubes; then pour on just
enough water to cover. Complete freezing.
Orange, lemon, or lime slices, in small wedges
Red or green maraschino cherries, halved or
  sliced

Canned pineapple tidbits, drained
Fresh mint sprigs
Purple grapes, halved, or whole green grapes
Fresh raspberries, blueberries, or halved unhulled
   strawberries
Dried apricot halves
Fresh sweet cherries
Fresh cranberries
Melon balls

FLAVORED ICE CUBES: Into small special ice-cube tray, p. 610, empty thawed contents of 1 can frozen lemonade or limeade, or orange-, tangerine-, or grape-juice concentrate; set ice-cube section in place; slowly fill tray with water. Freeze.

TINTED ICE CUBES: For concentrate and water, substitute water delicately tinted with green or red maraschino-cherry juice, grenadine, or food color.

PINEAPPLE JUICE: Freeze canned or reconstituted frozen pineapple juice. Add no water.

GOLDEN: Combine 1 cup orange juice, 1 cup lemon juice, 1 cup corn syrup, and 2 cups cold water. Pour into special ice-cube tray, p. 610, with ice-cube section in place. Freeze.

FROSTY RIMS: To "frost" the rims of your tall glasses, lightly dip top edge of each glass into lemon or orange juice, to a depth of 1/2"; then dip it into plain or tinted granulated sugar. Refrigerate until sugar looks dry and frosty. Fill glasses carefully.

Fresh Fruit Juices

For best flavor, squeeze such fruits as oranges, grapefruit, lemons, or limes just before using, as loss of flavor is rapid. The vitamin C content is not lost so readily; in fact, if the juice is refrigerated, the vitamin C loss is extremely slow in 24 hr. Covering juice helps retain flavor.

Don't strain pulp from juice — it contains valuable minerals and vitamins.

If a recipe calls for both juice and grated rind, it's easier to grate rind first, then squeeze juice.

Chilled orange and grapefruit juices are available in your grocer's cooler or dairy case, in 1-qt. or 8-oz. containers. They are either fresh or reconstituted frozen fruit-juice concentrates. Keep refrigerated. Use within 2 or 3 days.

TAMPA TEA

1 cup boiling water	sugar
2 teasp. tea; or 2 tea bags	4 cups ice water
	1/2 cup lime juice
1/2 cup granulated	2 1/2 cups orange juice

Pour boiling water over tea; let brew (stand) 3 min.; strain. Stir in sugar until dissolved. Add ice water and fruit juices. Pour into 8 tall ice-filled glasses. If desired, garnish with lime slices and fresh cherries. Makes 8 servings.

Off-the-shelf Coolers

Keep on hand some of today's fine branded canned or frozen fruit juices, ades, and fruit drink bases. They provide healthful, vitamin-rich beverages. The variety you can serve is endless. Just scan the partial list that follows; also read our hints for keeping them at their best.

CANNED JUICES:
Straight Juices: Apple, grape, grapefruit, loganberry, orange, pineapple, prune, tangerine, etc.
Nectars: Apricot, apricot-pineapple, peach, pear, pear-pineapple, etc.
Juice Blends: Orange-grapefruit, grapefruit-pineapple, etc.
Juice Drinks, Drinks, Punches, Ades: Apple-grape, breakfast orange drink, cranberry juice cocktail, grape drink, orange-apricot juice drink, orange-banana drink, pineapple-grapefruit juice drink, pineapple-orange juice drink, prune-date-fig drink, tropical punch, etc.

FRUIT DRINK BASES: There are also liquid and powdered fruit drink bases in a variety of fruit flavors. Some contain less than 15 per cent natural fruit juices, others are entirely synthetic. Many are labeled "low calorie"; some are "breakfast" drinks (orange and grapefruit flavor).

FROZEN JUICES:
Concentrated: Berry punches, fruit punch, grape, grapefruit, orange, orange-banana, orange and grapefruit, pineapple-orange, pineapple, tangerine, lemonade, limeade, orangeade, pink lemonade, pineapple-grapefruit, etc.
NATURAL STRENGTH: Lemon juice — bottled, canned, and frozen.

Handle Unopened Canned Juices with Care: The best storage place for canned juices is the coolest, driest spot you have. This way, canned juices will keep their fresh flavor and vitamin content for months. Never store them near a range, pipes, or radiator.

Keep Unopened Frozen Juices in Freezer: Get frozen fruit juices home and into freezer or freezer of combination refrigerator-freezer as quickly as possible; they'll keep many months at 0°F.

If frozen juices are stored in freezing compartment of conventional refrigerator, they'll keep several weeks. Never let unopened cans of frozen juice stand at room temperature — they may burst.

When You Open Canned Juices: Shake can well to mix juice. Puncture top with regular three-cornered puncture-type opener. Make second opening on other side; then juice will pour easily. If it's a concentrate, reconstitute as label directs.

To Reconstitute Frozen Juices: Follow label directions. To bring out juice's full fresh bouquet, be sure to shake or stir briskly and thoroughly before pouring. For best flavor, use within 24 hr. after reconstituting. If using un-reconstituted juice as an ingredient in recipes, let it thaw until just soft enough to be stirred well; then measure.

LEFTOVERS: Of course you can keep opened cans of juice on hand in your refrigerator — it's perfectly safe. For best results, see p. 90.

FROZEN JUICE COOLERS

LEMONADE PLUS: To lemonade, add cranberry juice, grape juice, bottled grenadine, or maraschino-cherry juice to taste. Or add bit of mint extract.

ADE DUET: Mix limeade with orangeade or lemonade. Float a few raspberries, plump red cherries, or strawberries in glasses.

LIMEADE-GRAPE: To limeade, add grape or pineapple juice to taste.

ORANGE-MINT: To orangeade, add a little canned crushed pineapple, a few snipped mint leaves.

ORANGE SCOOP: Float small scoop of vanilla ice cream in orangeade.

GRAPEFRUIT SIP: Reconstitute frozen grapefruit juice with ginger ale; top with twist of lemon peel.

TANGERINE SPARKLE: Mix tangerine juice with some sparkling water or pineapple juice.

GRAPE SPARKLE: Reconstitute frozen grape juice with grapefruit juice, ginger ale, sparkling water, or lemonade. Add lime or lemon juice and sugar to taste.

GRAPE ICE: Add scoop of lemon or lime sherbet to grape juice. Or use half-and-half grape juice and ginger ale.

ORANGE-MILK: Reconstitute frozen orange juice with milk instead of water; beat well.

FROM CANNED OR FROZEN JUICE

PINEAPPLE NECTAR: Mix equal parts pineapple juice and canned apricot nectar.

PINEAPPLE ALE: Mix 2 parts pineapple juice with 1 part ginger ale. Tint delicate pink with maraschino-cherry juice. Or float raspberry sherbet on top.

PINEAPPLE CREAM: To pineapple juice, add few drops peppermint extract, bit of green food color, then small scoop of vanilla ice cream.

ORANGE DUET: Mix equal parts of orange juice and one of these: grapefruit juice, pineapple juice, lemonade, ginger ale. Top with mint sprigs.

PINEAPPLE DASH: Add refreshing tartness to pineapple juice by adding grapefruit juice.

CRANBERRY COCKTAIL: Combine cranberry-juice cocktail with twice as much or equal amount of pineapple juice. Float vanilla ice cream on top if you wish.

APPLE SPICE: Sprinkle apple juice with nutmeg or cinnamon.

APPLE TANG: To apple juice, add lemon or lime juice.

APPLE-MINT: Top apple juice with snipped mint leaves.

PRUNE FLIP: Pep up prune juice with lemonade or orange, lemon, or lime juice to taste; top with twist of peel.

PRUNE CREAM: To prune juice, add small spoonful of vanilla ice cream.

ORANGE FLOAT: Into each glass, pour equal parts of orange juice and ginger ale. Float vanilla ice cream or orange sherbet on top.

CRANBERRY PITCHER PUNCH

1 chilled can jellied cranberry sauce	juice
2¼ cups cold water	1 teasp. almond extract
½ cup lemon juice	
¾ cup chilled orange	1 cup chilled ginger ale

With fork, crush cranberry sauce in can; turn into large bowl. Add water; beat until smooth. Stir in juices, extract, ginger ale, and a few ice cubes. Pour into 6 tall glasses. If desired, garnish with mint and clove-studded lemon circles. Makes 6 servings.

ORANGE-JUICE HIGHBALL

Add 2 cups ginger ale and 1 cup water to 1 6-oz. can frozen orange-juice concentrate.

LEMONADE

HOMEMADE: Combine 2 cups lemon juice, 4 teasp. grated lemon rind, 1½ cups granulated sugar. Pour into glass jar; cover. Keep on hand in refrigerator.

To serve: Allow ¼ cup syrup for each glass. Fill with ice cubes and water. (Nice tinted pink with bottled grenadine.) Makes 2⅔ cups syrup.

JIFFY: Just open can of frozen or canned lemonade or pink lemonade concentrate; add water and ice as label directs; enjoy a pitcherful of luscious lemonade in no time at all.

LIMEADE: Substitute fresh lime juice for lemon juice in Homemade Lemonade, above. Or make limeade as label on can of frozen limeade concentrate directs.

APPLE-LIMEADE

½ cup granulated sugar	½ cup lime juice
½ cup water	2 cups bottled apple juice
12 snipped mint leaves	¼ teasp. salt
	Sparkling water

1. Boil sugar and water together 8 min.; pour over mint; cool.
2. Add fruit juices, salt. Divide among 6 tall ice-filled glasses. Fill with sparkling water. Makes 6 servings.

FRESH MINT TINKLE: Substitute 1¼ cups grapefruit juice for 2 cups apple juice.

MINT-ORANGEADE COOLER

2 cups orange juice	¼ cup lime juice
½ cup granulated sugar	1½ cups chilled sparkling water
12 snipped mint sprigs	

Bring 1 cup orange juice to boil. Add to sugar and mint; cool; strain. Add 1 cup orange juice, lime juice. Just before serving, add sparkling water. Pour into 4 tall ice-filled glasses. Makes 4 servings.

OLD ENGLISH SPICED CIDER

1 teasp. whole allspice	2 qt. bottled cider
2 2″ sticks cinnamon	⅔ cup brown sugar, packed
12 whole cloves	Ground nutmeg

Tie allspice, cinnamon, and cloves together in cheesecloth. In large saucepan, combine cider, brown sugar; heat. Add spice bag; simmer 10 min., or until cider is spicy enough to suit taste. Remove bag.

Serve piping hot in mugs, with dash of nutmeg in each. Makes 7 to 8 servings.

ICED SPICED CIDER: Make hot spiced cider; chill before serving.

CARIBE COOLER

Among 4 tall glasses, divide 2 cups slightly sweetened, cut-up, mixed fresh fruit (berries, peaches, oranges, bananas, etc.). To each portion, add ¼ cup each pineapple and orange juice and 1 big scoop of vanilla ice cream. Fill glasses with chilled sparkling water. Makes 4 servings.

Ice-cream Coolers

HOME SODA FOUNTAIN

A smart mother keeps the makings of ice-cream drinks on hand and lets the youngsters mix their own. Grownups love them too.

Place your favorite ice cream or sherbet in tall glass; add one of flavors below, then one of chilled coolers. Stir well; insert straws; sip away.

FLAVORS:	COOLERS:
Chocolate or maple-blended syrup	Ginger ale
	Root beer or cola

Fresh or frozen berries, peach slices, etc.
Canned whole-cranberry sauce
Molasses or prepared mincemeat
Milk or cream
Coffee (made from instant coffee)
Canned or frozen fruit juice or lemonade

ROOT-BEER SPARKLE

In tall glass, mix ½ cup chilled root beer and 1 tablesp. milk. Add 1 big scoop of vanilla or chocolate ice cream; fill glass with root beer. Makes 1 serving.

NECTAR FREEZE

With temperature control of refrigerator at coldest setting, in special ice-cube tray, p. 610, freeze 2 cups canned apricot nectar until half frozen. Turn into bowl; add ½ pt. vanilla ice cream; beat until light and fluffy. Pour into 3 tall glasses; sprinkle with nutmeg. Makes 3 servings.

PRUNE VELVET

1 chilled jar strained prunes (baby pack)
⅓ cup chilled orange juice
1 cup cold milk
Pinch salt
1 teasp. lemon juice
1 tablesp. sugar
1 big scoop vanilla ice cream
Orange peel

Mix prunes, orange juice, milk. Add salt, lemon juice, sugar, ice cream. Beat to blend; pour into glasses. Top each with twist of orange peel. Makes 2 large or 4 small servings.

FOUR-FRUIT FROST

1 cup orange juice
½ cup lime juice
¼ cup lemon juice
1 cup pineapple juice
⅔ cup granulated sugar
1 pt. vanilla ice cream

Chill juices. Mix in sugar; add ice cream; beat to blend; pour into 4 glasses. Garnish each glass with thin slice of orange, lemon, and lime, with slices touching. Makes 4 servings.

FLIP-FLOP

In tall glass, place 1 scoop of orange sherbet, 1 teasp. jam, then 1 scoop of vanilla ice cream. Repeat till glass is three fourths full. Fill glass with chilled ginger ale. Eat with spoon. Makes 1 serving.

Milk Coolers

Remember, everyone in the family, from the youngest to the oldest, needs plenty of milk every day. Here's one way to get each one to drink it: Serve these milk tempters. Use regular, diluted evaporated, or liquefied instant nonfat dry milk. An electric blender or mixer makes quick work of whipping up the drinks.

MOCHA FLOAT

6 tablesp. canned chocolate syrup
3 cups hot or cold strong coffee
Sugar (optional)
4½ cups cold milk
⅛ teasp. salt
1 pt. vanilla ice cream

Blend chocolate syrup with coffee; add sugar to taste if desired; chill. Blend thoroughly with milk and salt. Pour into 6 tall glasses; top with ice cream. Makes 6 servings.

BANANA SMOOTHIE

Beat 4 peeled ripe bananas until smooth. Add 3 cups cold milk, ½ cup heavy cream, 2 teasp. vanilla extract; beat until well mixed. Pour into 4 glasses. Float 1 scoop of vanilla ice cream on each. Place banana slice on edge of each glass. Makes 4 servings.

BANANA MILK SHAKE

For each tall serving, slice 1 fully ripe banana into bowl; beat until smooth and creamy. Add 1 cup cold milk; beat well. Pour into glass.

If desired, top with whipped cream or dessert topping (or spoonful of ice cream) and grated unsweetened chocolate; or top with sprinkling of cinnamon or nutmeg. Garnish edge of glass with banana slice. Serve at once.

BROWN COW: With milk, add 1½ to 2 tablesp. chocolate malted-milk powder (or homemade or canned chocolate syrup) and ¼ teasp. vanilla extract. Top with ice cream.

PINEANA: Substitute pineapple juice for ¼ cup milk.

CHOCOLATE MILK

Today there's more than one way to make quick work of mixing chocolate milk. In fact, here are four start-offs to which you need only add milk.

Instant sweet milk cocoa

Chocolate-malted-milk powder
Canned chocolate syrup
Melted semisweet-chocolate pieces

Or use chilled Hot Cocoa, p. 681, or bottled chocolate-milk drinks.

STRAWBERRY MILK

Children love milk flavored with instant strawberry-flavored beverage powder.

FOUR CHOCOLATE MILK DRINKS

MOCHA: For each serving, beat 1 cup milk with 2 tablesp. chocolate syrup and 2 teasp. instant coffee.

CHOCO-NOG SPECIAL: For each serving, slowly stir 1 cup chilled milk into 3 tablesp. chocolate syrup; add 1 well-beaten egg. Beat or shake well.

FROSTED CHOCOLATE: For each serving, beat 1 cup milk with 2 tablesp. chocolate syrup and small spoonful of ice cream.

CHOCOLATE FLOAT: Make Frosted Chocolate above, floating spoonfuls of ice cream on top.

MILK TINGLERS

For each serving, into 1 cup cold milk, slowly stir any of the following. If desired, top with dab of whipped cream or dessert topping, marshmallow cream, or a spoonful of ice cream.

¼ cup canned crushed pineapple
¼ cup sweetened, crushed raspberries or strawberries or the frozen kind
2 to 3 tablesp. maple or maple-blended syrup
1 to 2 tablesp. molasses
2 to 3 tablesp. strawberry, raspberry, or apricot jam
2 to 3 tablesp. thawed frozen grape-, orange-, or pineapple-juice concentrate
Vanilla or almond extract
Cinnamon, nutmeg, or mace

TWO BUTTERMILK COOLERS

1. Sprinkle cold buttermilk with paprika and salt.
2. Fill each glass halfway with thawed frozen sliced strawberries; fill to top with buttermilk; stir.

AMBROSIA SHAKE

4 fully ripe bananas, sliced
⅓ cup orange juice
6 tablesp. honey
Pinch salt
¼ teasp. almond extract
1 qt. cold milk

Beat bananas until smooth and creamy. Beat in orange juice, honey, salt, extract. Add milk; beat well. Garnish with whipped cream or dessert topping and flaked coconut. Makes 6 servings.

CHOCO-MINT FLUFF

1 qt. cold milk
⅓ cup chocolate syrup
¼ cup heavy cream
¼ teasp. peppermint extract
2 tablesp. crushed peppermint candy
⅓ cup heavy cream, whipped

Combine milk, syrup, ¼ cup cream, extract; beat well until blended. Pour into 5 glasses. Fold crushed peppermint candy into whipped cream; use to top each drink. Makes 5 servings.

COFFEENOG

1 egg, beaten
4 teasp. instant coffee
2 tablesp. granulated sugar
Dash salt
2 cups cold milk
⅛ teasp. vanilla extract

Combine beaten egg, coffee, sugar, salt; beat until coffee and sugar dissolve. Add milk, vanilla; beat well. Refrigerate. Makes 2 servings.

EGGNOG: Omit coffee; increase vanilla to ½ teasp.

FROM THE PUNCH BOWL

Drinks from the punch bowl make it a festive occasion.

Party Punch Pointers

CONCOCTING THE PUNCH:

Ginger Ale or Soda: Chill well; always add just before serving.

For Quick Service: Fill cups in kitchen; pass filled cups on trays; serve refills from punch bowl.

For Extra-Quick Service: If punch does not contain sparkling water, you can fill cups ahead and refrigerate them on trays. Chill rest of punch in bottles.

Ice: Use small block rather than cubes; remember, ice dilutes flavor.

Leftover Punch: Freeze in special ice-cube tray, p. 610. Use to chill fruit juices or iced tea. Or when making gelatine dessert, use unflavored gelatine; omit sugar; substitute leftover punch for liquid.

The Punch Bowl: Circle bowl with ring of smilax, ivy, blueberry, or laurel leaves. Or cover sides of bowl with wire; tuck roses, ferns, into holes. If you have no punch bowl, use big wooden salad bowl or gay mixing bowl, with soup ladle and paper cups. Tie perky bow on ladle.

GAY GARNISHES (TO TOP PUNCH):
Melon balls or strawberries
Lemon, orange, or lime slices
Twists of orange or lemon peel
Thick banana slices
Summer blossoms and ivy leaves
Small scoops of sherbet or ice cream
Strawberry or tiny bunch of grapes in each cup

ICE FLOAT: Half fill large loaf pan (not glass) with water; freeze. Arrange washed unhulled strawberries on top of ice; cover well with water; finish freezing. Use special pan for this purpose, because freezing water may force pan out of shape.

Or freeze water or canned fruit cocktail or pineapple chunks (plus juice) in 8″ x 8″ x 2″ pan, heart-shaped pan, or ring mold.

To unmold ice block, just dip pan in hot water until block slips out easily. Float in punch bowl. Top with tiny bouquet for bride; roses for sweet sixteener; or lemon, orange, or lime wedges. Or make Christmas wreath of mint leaves and maraschino cherries.

HOLLY-WREATH ICE RING: In ¼″ of water in a 5-cup ring mold, arrange whole fresh cranberries and lime rind cut to resemble a bow. Freeze firm. Fill to top with water; freeze again. Unmold as in Ice Float, above.

CHRISTMAS WREATH: Wash excess color from 13 red and 13 green maraschino cherries. Arrange cherries, alternating colors, in bottom of 1¼-qt. ring mold. Pour on just enough boiling water to cover cherries; freeze solid. Fill to top with cold boiled water; freeze solid. Unmold as in Ice Float, at left.

ICED FRUITS FOR PUNCH

Frozen whole fruits are especially nice "icers"; they do the same chilling job that ice rings or ice cubes do, but are more colorful, do not dilute punch, and can be eaten later.

Grapes, peaches, nectarines, plums, pears, apricots, lemons, cherries, and strawberries all freeze successfully. Of these, grapes and cherries stay close to the bottom of the punch bowl, while rest float on top. So always freeze one or two large bunches of grapes; then you can anchor smaller frozen fruits beneath them.

Before freezing, wash and dry fruits. Arrange on foil, then freeze overnight or till frozen. At serving time, arrange in chilled punch bowl, and add punch. Remember — don't use too much of the fruits or it may be difficult to ladle your punch.

SANTA CLAUS PUNCH

1 pkg. raspberry instant soft-drink mix	2 cups bottled cranberry-juice cocktail
½ cup granulated sugar	6 cups ice cubes plus water

In punch bowl, combine drink mix with sugar, cranberry juice, and ice cubes plus water. Stir till drink mix and sugar are dissolved. Makes 16 half-cup servings.

CRANBERRY PUNCH, SWEDISH STYLE

1½ cup unblanched almonds	1 stick cinnamon
1 cup light or dark raisins	1 qt. water
Peel from 2 oranges	4 1-pt. or 2 1-qt. bottles cranberry-juice cocktail
1 teasp. whole cloves	
½ teasp. whole allspice	2 1-lb.-4-oz. cans pineapple juice

In saucepan, place almonds, raisins, peel. Tie cloves, allspice, and cinnamon in cheesecloth; add with water to almonds. Simmer, uncovered, 15 min.; cool; discard spice bag and peel.
Just before serving: Combine cooled mixture with cranberry and pineapple juices.

Serve cold, over ice in punch bowl. Or serve hot, adding claret or port to taste, if desired.

Spoon a few raisins and 1 almond into each serving. Makes about 24 punch-cup servings.

HOT SPICED CITRUS PUNCH

1 qt. boiling water	2 6-oz. or 1 12-oz. can
2 teasp. instant tea	frozen orange-juice
2 cups water	concentrate
¾ cup granulated	1 6-oz. can frozen
sugar	grapefruit-juice con-
1 teasp. whole cloves	centrate
1 3″-piece stick cin-	Cloves
namon	Orange slices

Add boiling water to tea in large bowl; set aside. Simmer 2 cups water with sugar, 1 teasp. whole cloves, and cinnamon 10 min. Strain into tea. Reconstitute frozen juices; add to tea. Reheat. Serve in bowl with clove-studded orange slices. Makes 30 punch-cup servings.

HAWAIIAN COOLER

1 can frozen pine-	concentrate
apple-grapefruit-	1 28-oz. bottle ginger
juice concentrate	ale, chilled
1 can frozen pine-	Pineapple chunks
apple-orange-juice	Green cherries

Reconstitute frozen juices as labels direct. Pour over ice in large punch bowl. Add ginger ale. Top with pineapple and cherries. Makes 19 half-cup servings.

SHERBET-TEA PUNCH

2 cups strong hot tea	½ cup lemon juice
1 cup granulated	1 pt. chilled ginger ale
sugar	1 pt. orange sherbet
1 cup orange juice	

Pour hot tea over sugar; stir until sugar dissolves; add juices. Refrigerate till chilled. Then pour into punch bowl. Add ginger ale. Spoon on sherbet. Makes 16 punch-cup servings.

LEMON-STRAWBERRY PUNCH

1½ cups strawberries	lemonade concen-
½ cup granulated	trate
sugar	1 qt. chilled ginger
3 6-oz. cans frozen	ale
	Block of ice

Wash and hull berries; crush. Add sugar; let stand ½ hr. Reconstitute lemonade; blend with berries.

Just before serving: In punch bowl, place berry mixture, ginger ale; mix well. Add ice. Makes 32 punch-cup servings.

GOLDEN-MINT RECEPTION PUNCH

30 to 35 mint sprigs	1 qt. chilled ginger
2 cups granulated	ale
sugar	1 qt. chilled spar-
2 qt. boiling water	kling water
2⅓ cups lemon juice	12 mint sprigs
2 qt. orange juice	1 cup thinly slivered
1 1-lb.-4-oz. can pine-	lemon rind
apple juice	

Wash mint. In 4-qt. saucepan, place 30 to 35 mint sprigs, sugar, water. Simmer, uncovered, 10 min. Refrigerate, along with rest of ingredients.

Just before serving: Strain mint syrup. Add lemon, orange, and pineapple juices; ginger ale; sparkling water. Top with 12 mint sprigs and rind. Serve at once. Makes 50 punch-cup servings.

LAVENDER PUNCH

1 cup water	½ cup lime juice
2 cinnamon sticks	Block of ice
¼ teasp. whole cloves	2 qt. chilled ginger ale
3 cans frozen grape-	Seedless grapes
juice concentrate	

In saucepan, combine water, cinnamon, cloves; bring to boil. Remove from heat; let stand 5 min. Chill; strain.

Just before serving: Combine chilled mixture with grape and lime juices; mix well. Pour over ice in punch bowl; add ginger ale. Garnish with grapes. Makes 30 punch-cup servings.

ANNIVERSARY PUNCH

6 tea bags	1 6-oz. can frozen
5 cups cold water	limeade concentrate,
Preserved kumquats	undiluted
1 lime	¼ cup honey
1 6-oz. can frozen	1 qt. chilled carbon-
orange-juice con-	ated water
centrate, undiluted	1 cup light rum
	(optional)

Day before: Place tea bags in 3 cups cold water; refrigerate. For ice rings to float on punch, use 3 to 12 one-third-cup ring molds. In each arrange kumquat, cut into six slices, or lime slice cut into six wedges. Fill with water; freeze.

At partytime: Strain tea into punch bowl; stir in concentrates, honey, 2 cups cold water till honey is dissolved.

Just before serving: Add carbonated water, rum. Unmold, then float ice rings on top. Makes 30 half-cup servings.

CHRISTMAS PUNCH

Mix 2 6-oz. or 1 12-oz. can each of frozen limeade, lemonade, and orange-juice concentrate with 2 qt. cold water. Pour over ice cubes in punch bowl. Add 2 qt. chilled ginger ale. Garnish with twisted lime slices. Makes 60 half-cup servings.

SILLABUB

2 cups white wine	1/3 cup lemon juice
1½ cups granulated sugar	3 cups milk
	2 cups light cream
5 tablesp. grated lemon rind	4 egg whites
	Nutmeg

Early on the day:

1. In medium bowl, combine wine with 1 cup sugar, grated lemon rind, and lemon juice; stir until sugar is completely dissolved. Refrigerate.

About 20 min. before serving:

1. In large bowl, combine milk and light cream. While stirring, gradually pour chilled wine mixture into milk-cream mixture; beat with hand beater until frothy; pour into 2½-qt. punch bowl.

2. Beat egg whites until frothy; continue to beat, while gradually adding ½ cup sugar, until stiff but not dry. Drop by spoonfuls onto top of cream mixture in punch bowl. Sprinkle with nutmeg. Makes 16 to 18 half-cup servings.

CHRISTMAS-WREATH PUNCH

2 6-oz. cans frozen limeade concentrate	2 1-lb.-4-oz. cans pineapple juice
2 6-oz. or 1 12-oz. can frozen lemonade concentrate	3 1-qt. bottles ginger ale, chilled
	1 qt. water
2 1-lb.-4-oz. cans unsweetened grapefruit juice	3 qt. chopped ice
	Christmas Wreath, p. 687

In punch bowl, blend undiluted limeade and lemonade, grapefruit and pineapple juices. Just before serving, stir in ginger ale, water, ice.

Then unmold Christmas Wreath on top of punch. Makes about 50 punch-cup servings.

CHAMPAGNE-PUNCH FRUIT BOWL

4 cups fresh strawberries	1 cup cognac
½ cup granulated sugar	Iced Fruits for Punch, p. 687
1 4/5-qt. bottle sauterne	4 4/5-qt. bottles chilled champagne

At least 2 hr. before serving:
In large bowl, sprinkle strawberries with sugar. Add sauterne, cognac; refrigerate at least 2 hr.

At serving time:

1. Arrange iced fruits in punch bowl, "trapping" nectarines, plums, and strawberries beneath one or two large bunches of grapes.

2. Pour in berries with their liquid, then slowly add champagne. Serve a strawberry in each cup of punch. Makes 36 half-cup servings.

FRUITED CHAMPAGNE PUNCH

1 cup water	¼ cup grenadine
2 cups granulated sugar	1 4/5-qt. bottle cognac
3 cups lemon juice	Iced Fruits for Punch, p. 687
3 cups orange juice	2 4/5-qt. bottles chilled champagne
1½ cups curaçao	

In advance: In saucepan, bring water and sugar to boil; cool. Combine this simple syrup with lemon and orange juices, curaçao, grenadine, and cognac; refrigerate.

At serving time: Arrange Iced Fruits in punch bowl. Pour in grenadine mixture; slowly add champagne. Makes 22 punch-cup servings.

WINE CHAMPAGNE

Combine equal parts of chilled sauterne and sparkling lemon-flavored beverage or sparkling water. Serve at once in cold glasses.

GRANDMOTHER RANDOLPH'S EGGNOG

12 eggs, separated	1½ cups whisky
1 cup granulated sugar	¼ cup peach brandy
	1½ qt. milk
½ cup brandy	1¼ teasp. nutmeg

Day before: In large bowl, beat egg yolks until thick; gradually add sugar, beating until thick and lemon-colored. Add ½ cup brandy, drop by drop, beating. Then add whisky and peach brandy same way. Refrigerate overnight, along with egg whites.

Next day: Stir in milk and nutmeg. At serving time, beat egg whites in large bowl until peaks form when beater is raised; fold into milk mixture. Nice with shortbread, pound- or fruitcake, etc. Makes 16 punch-cup servings.

P.S. Today's eggnog, in bottles or cartons, is delightful as is or with your added touch.

WASSAIL BOWL

1 gal. apple cider	orange-juice con-
1 cup light- or dark-	centrate
brown sugar,	1 tablesp. whole
packed	cloves
1 6-oz. can frozen	1 tablesp. whole all-
lemonade concen-	spice
trate	1 teasp. ground
1 6-oz. can frozen	nutmeg
	24 cinnamon sticks

1. In large kettle, combine cider, brown sugar, and undiluted lemonade and orange juice.
2. Tie cloves and allspice in cheesecloth; add to cider, along with nutmeg. Simmer, covered, 20 min. Remove and discard bag.
3. Serve hot, in punch cups, with cinnamon stick in each. Makes 24 punch-cup servings.

COFFEE ROYAL

Just before serving: In punch bowl, combine 2 qt. chilled coffee, ½ cup Jamaica rum, and 2 qt. vanilla ice cream.

Stir until most of ice cream has blended into coffee and rum. Small bits of ice cream serve as garnish. Makes 30 punch-cup servings.

FLUFFY ORANGE EGGNOG

6 egg yolks	1 cup orange juice
Salt	2 cups heavy cream,
9 tablesp. granulated	whipped
sugar	6 egg whites
1 cup heavy cream	Grated orange rind
2 cups milk	Nutmeg

Beat egg yolks with pinch of salt, 3 tablesp. sugar, till lemon-colored. Beat in 1 cup cream, milk. *Slowly* stir in orange juice. Fold in 2 cups cream. Beat egg whites stiff with pinch of salt and 6 tablesp. sugar; fold into eggnog. Top with grated rind, nutmeg. Makes 24 half-cup servings.

MOCHA PUNCH

1 cup heavy cream	1 qt. chilled coffee
½ teasp. almond ex-	1 qt. chocolate ice
tract	cream
Few grains salt	¼ teasp. nutmeg

Whip cream; add extract, salt. In cold punch bowl, blend coffee and half of ice cream until smooth. Fold in whipped cream, rest of ice cream. Top with nutmeg. Makes 16 punch-cup servings.

WHEN THERE IS WINE

The superb wines produced abroad and in this country can brighten your meals, bring new zest to your cooking, add new smartness to your entertaining.

What Is Wine?

Wine is the fermented juice of freshly gathered, ripe grapes.

The many different species of grapevine grown in different parts of the world, the great variations in soil, aspect, and climate of the various vineyards, and the varying methods of vine growing and wine making result in many different kinds of wine. Even the quality of the grape juice from the same vine differs from year to year according to the weather that prevails during the growth and ripening of the grapes.

In the United States wine is made in 27 states; California produces 85 per cent of the wines produced in this country. California's 8 viticultural sections are planted almost exclusively in European wine grapes. The other states that also produce wines (chiefly New York and Ohio) do so principally from native American grape varieties.

When You Buy Wines

If you are not too well acquainted with different wines or what you should pay for them, talk to a reliable wine dealer. Let him suggest good wines, notable vintage years for imported wines, etc., in keeping with your tastes and budget. Also study the Wine Dictionary, p. 696.

Store and Keep Wine Properly

Storing Wine: Ideally wine should be stored in a wine cellar at an even temperature of 50° to 60°F. If this is impossible (as it often is today), the wine bottle can be laid on its side on a pantry shelf. It is especially important that bottles of table and sparkling wines, which are corked, be kept on their sides, so that the corks are kept moist and, therefore, airtight. If the bottle has a screw cap, it may remain upright.

When Wine Is Left Over

Appetizer and Dessert Wines: Once opened, these wines keep well for weeks unless they are exposed to air for very long periods.

691

Table Wines: Because of their lower alcoholic content, table wines are perishable after opening. Contact with air and heat makes them "go off" (spoil). Care for them as follows:

1. If it's a fifth bottle of wine, cork it tightly; refrigerate; use the next day. If it must be held longer than a day, pour into clean smaller bottles; close with conical cork from drugstore; refrigerate. Plan to use within a week.

2. If it's a gallon jug of wine, pour what is left into clean smaller bottles; cork tightly, refrigerate. Plan to use within a week.

3. If you intend to use leftover wine for cooking, it need not be refrigerated. Just add enough olive oil to form a thin film on wine; then close bottle with conical cork. Such wines are best used in meat and fish cookery, not in desserts or with fruit.

COOK WITH WINE

Wine adds a decided zest to cooking. As the cooking progresses, the wine alcohol evaporates but the delicious flavor remains and mellows. The alcohol vaporizes considerably before the boiling point of water is reached. Actually it is cooked out in just the simmering stage.

IN SOUPS

Wine makes many favorite soups taste even better.

CANNED CONSOMME: Add 1 tablesp. dry sherry or white table wine to each cup of soup.

BROWN SOUPS: Soups such as oxtail, lentil, black bean, etc., taste all the better if 1 tablesp. dry or medium sherry is added for each cup of soup.

MEAT AND VEGETABLE SOUPS: Soups such as minestrone are improved by the addition of 1 tablesp. red or white table wine for each cup of soup.

IN MEAT AND FISH DISHES

BRAISED BEEF, POT ROASTS, ETC.: A few tablespoonfuls of any red table wine, added to beef as it cooks, improves both meat and gravy. Allow about ¼ cup of wine to each pound of meat. Let it replace an equal amount of water.

LAMB AND MUTTON: Pouring ½ cup of any white table wine over a shoulder or stuffed breast of lamb or mutton before starting to cook it, and spooning wine over meat during cooking, makes it a delicacy.

VEAL AND CHICKEN DISHES: You can perk up sauces for these dishes with a spoonful or more of any white table wine, as in Sautéed Chicken, p. 266.

STEWS: A small amount of any red or white table wine gives an added lift to dishes such as lamb stew, beef stew, etc. Try substituting ¼ cup wine for same amount of water in your stew recipes.

FISH: White table wine provides a pleasing foil for the flavor of fish. See Fresh Tuna or Swordfish Provençal, p. 301, Fillets of Fish Dugléré, p. 307, etc.

GAME: Marinating gamey meat, such as venison, in any red table wine 24 hr. or longer removes most of the gaminess, objectionable to some people. The mild acid of the wine also helps to tenderize the meat.

IN SALAD DRESSINGS

FOR TOSSED GREEN SALADS: Use red table wine for part of vinegar in French dressing.

COLD ASPARAGUS AND CHICORY: Dress with a light French dressing in which white wine replaces vinegar. This is a French classic when served with broiled chicken.

IN SAUCES

One of the best-known cooking uses of wine is in the preparation of sauces. Some sauces using wine include:

Bordelaise Sauce, p. 531
Custard Sauce De Luxe, p. 537
Fine Herb Sauce, p. 533
Game Sauces, p. 336
Holiday Sauce, p. 537
Fluffy Hard Sauce, p. 537
Zabaglione, p. 579

IN DESSERTS

Wine adds the master touch, the "French atmosphere," to many desserts, especially to cut-up fruit. Dry-tasting (not sweet) and sweet-tasting table wines (which often eliminate the need for sugar), as well as dessert wines and liqueurs, may be used.

STRAWBERRIES, PEACHES, AND PEARS: These fruits—fresh, canned, or frozen—are often served in port.

BANANAS: Sliced bananas are good in red wine.

COOKED UNSWEETENED RASPBERRIES WITH COOKED DRIED PRUNES: Add a little port and brown sugar to make a compote men like. Serve it with "Devonshire" Cream, p. 349.

FRUIT COMBINATIONS: Combine pitted cherries, sliced peaches, mangoes, blackberries. Add sweet sauterne. Chill.

Or try sliced or diced melon, seedless grapes, and sliced or diced pears tossed with the thinnest julienne strips of orange peel. Add sweet sauterne or inexpensive sparkling wine plus, if desired, 1 liqueur glassful of triple sec. Chill.

SHERBET: Heap firmly frozen lemon sherbet, stuck with sprigs of mint, in bowl packed in ice. Pour over it any cold, cut-up fruits—melon, cut into balls; grapes; pears and unpeeled plums, quartered. Just before serving, pour 1 or 2 wineglasses of light wine, or your favorite liqueur, over all.

Cooking Wines

Two kinds of wine labeled "cooking wine" are found on grocers' shelves in some parts of the United States. They are:

1. Salted wines which are unsuitable for beverage purposes.
2. Wines purposely made with a lower alcoholic content than wines of that type usually contain.

The salted wines may require a slight adjustment in the amount of salt in standard recipes. The difference in alcoholic content will not influence flavor to any great extent.

SERVE WINE AS A BEVERAGE

Wine is as easy to serve correctly as tea or coffee. For greatest enjoyment, there are certain amenities to be observed, but there is no mysterious ritual. These few points should tell you all you need to know.

The Glasses

Unless you go in for elaborate entertaining, 3 standard glass sizes are all you need.

FOR APPETIZER AND DESSERT WINES: The typical sherry glass is conical in shape.

FOR RED AND WHITE TABLE WINES: Use 6- to 8-oz. wineglass.

FOR SPARKLING WINES: If available, flute glasses are often preferred. Or use saucer or hollow-stemmed champagne, water goblet, or high sherbet glass.

Wine will taste best if you fill glasses only one half to two thirds full. Space left in glass permits you to enjoy wine's aroma.

What Wine To Serve When

It's perfectly correct to serve any wine any time you wish. However, if you want the wine-and-food combinations that many people prefer, here they are:

Alone, as Appetizer: Before the meal, serve either of these appetizer wines:

Sherry   Vermouth

Serve it slightly chilled, living-room style.

With Hors d'Oeuvres or Soup: Serve dry sherry, slightly chilled.

With Sea Food, Chicken, Omelet, or Other Light Dishes: Serve one of these delicate white table wines; their characteristic acidity enhances such foods.

Sauterne	Rhine wine
Sauvignon blanc	Riesling
Semillon	Traminer
Chablis	Sylvaner
Pinot chardonnay	White Chianti
Pinot blanc	Rosé

Refrigerate 2 hr. or more; or chill by standing wine in water containing ice. Never put ice in any wine (except in mixed wine drinks, such as spritzes and claret lemonade).

With Steak, Roast, Chops, Game, and Cheese, Spaghetti, or Macaroni Dishes, etc.: Serve one of these red table wines. Their slight tartness goes especially well with red meats.

Burgundy	Zinfandel
Pinot noir	Cabernet
Red pinot	Grignolino
Gamay	Red Chianti
Barbera	Rosé
Claret	

Serve all except rosé at room temperature. Let wine stand in dining room until it takes on temperature of room (unless your room is over-heated). *Do not* warm it up quickly. Chill rosé several hours before serving.

P.S. Although some people prefer rosé with red meats, this pink wine's preferred usage is with chicken and other light dishes.

With Fruit, Nuts, Cookies, Cheeses: Serve one of these dessert wines:

Port	Tokay
White port	Angelica
Tawny port	Sweet sherry
Muscatel	Madeira

Serve chilled or at cool room temperature.

P.S. Table wines have dessert uses too. Sweet-tasting white table wines, such as sweet sauterne or sweet Semillon, go best with fruit or a sweet dessert.

Sweet-tasting white table wines also make delicious punches, wine cups, or iced drinks.

With cheeses, the red table wines, as well as port, are favored choices.

With Appetizer, Main Course, or Dessert: Depending on the degree of sweetness, these festive, effervescent wines are served before, during, and after meals:

Champagne	Sparkling Burgundy
Pink champagne	Sparkling muscat

The dry sparkling wines are appreciated best before and during the meal. Sweet champagnes and sparkling muscats are reserved for dessert time or between meals.

Serve very well chilled.

Flavored Wines

A new type of wine is being produced in this country in response to many Americans' preference for sweeter wines; these new beverages are usually as sweet as dessert wines, and all have added natural flavors, varying from orange and lemon to vanilla. Serve them for afternoon or evening refreshment, chilled or at room temperature and with or without food. They are also useful in fruit punches.

The Order of Serving Wine

The order in which wines should be served varies with individual taste and the food.

For informal meals, when one wine is served throughout, it should be chosen to harmonize with the main course as suggested on p. 693.

For more formal meals, the classic order is:
1. *With oysters:* Chablis or champagne (dry)
2. *With soup:* pale sherry or dry Madeira
3. *With fish:* champagne (dry) or dry white table wines
4. *With entrées:* claret
5. *With roast or game:* Burgundy
6. *With sweets:* champagne (sweet) or sweet sauterne
7. *With cheese:* port, sweet sherry, or Madeira

Serve Wine with Style

At the simple one-wine dinner, bring on the wine with the main course. Pour it just before, or at the same time as, the main dish is served. Then everyone can enjoy a sip after his first taste of the food.

Here's How: Before meal begins, have wine bottle on small tray on table. (It's good practice for host to sample the wine beforehand, to be sure of its quality.) Host pours a bit of wine into his glass, to make certain no pieces of cork remain in bottle. Then he goes from person to person, filling glasses. Or let bottle pass from hand to hand, in the age-old European manner.

Here's Why: Guests enjoy knowing the wine they are drinking. So they can examine the label, pass the bottle as is or, if it's chilled, with a cloth wrapped around the lower part only. Wrapping the bottle completely makes guests feel they are expected to guess what the wine is or to believe the wine is better than it is.

SOME NOTES ON IMPORTED WINES

ALSATIAN: These are white wines from the vineyards on the left bank of the Rhine, from Mulhouse to Strasbourg. Serve as Rhine Wine, p. 697.

WHITE BORDEAUX (graves and sauternes): Graves and sauternes are white wines from Bordeaux. Some are fairly dry, others rather sweet. Serve as Sauterne, p. 697.

BURGUNDY: There are many wines—red and white, still and sparkling—known as Burgundy. They are made in *départements* of France that were formerly part of the old province of Burgundy. The Côte d'Or produces the choicest red Burgundies, particularly in the northern part. To the south, the Saône-et-Loire district produces lighter though pleasing, less expensive wines.

The best known white Burgundy is Chablis. The white wines of the Côte d'Or are finer but also more expensive.

CHAMPAGNE: Champagne is a sparkling wine made from grapes grown within the former boundaries of the ancient province of Champagne. It is always blended, each producer having his own particular blend of old and new wines. A vintage champagne is one bearing the date of the particular year when the grapes from which it was mainly, if not entirely, made, were gathered.

CHIANTI: Chianti is the best-known Italian red wine. It's light and fairly dry. There are also a few white Chiantis of good quality.

CLARET: Claret is the red wine of Bordeaux. In color it should be a brilliant ruby red, never black or pink. It differs very much in bouquet and flavor according to the species of grape, the soil, and aspect of the vineyard, the method of pressing the juice, and length of time it has been kept.

HOCK: Hock is Rhenish white wine, deriving its name from Hochheim on the river Main.

MADEIRA: Madeira is a fortified wine made and matured on the island of Madeira. It is fortified and matured in a different way from port and sherry. The fermented grape juice, or new wine, is subjected to heat and is then racked and rested, after which it is fortified by the addition of cane spirit. At this stage the wines are blended together and left for some years to mature.

MALAGA: This is one of the best sweet wines of Spain.

MARSALA: This is the best, and best-known, dessert wine of Italy.

MOSELLE: Moselle comes from vineyards on the river Moselle. Serve as Rhine Wine, p. 697.

MUSCATEL: This is a white wine made in Spain and Italy from muscat grapes.

PORT: Port is a fortified wine made from grapes grown in the Upper Valley of the Douro River in Portugal and shipped from Oporto. It is fortified by brandy, added at time of pressing grapes. There are a number of different types: red, white, or tawny in color, and different in style, age, strength, and sweetness.

A vintage port is the best; that is to say, red port, made from the grapes of a vintage (good and sunny) year. The grapes must also be perfectly sound and ripe when picked. The wine is shipped from Oporto eighteen months to two years afterward, and bottled in England soon after landing. Then it must be given time, twelve to fifteen years or longer, to mature.

SHERRY: Sherry is a wine made from white grapes grown in the south of Spain, in the Jerez district. It is allowed to ferment in its own way and may be fortified by the addition of brandy at a much later stage of its existence.

The vintage of sherry does not count for much, nor does any individual vineyard; what matters is the shipper. Sherry is a blend of wines, similar in style but made from grapes of different vineyards and wines of different years. They are blended together to maintain the standard set by the different sherry shippers.

TOKAY: This is the best, and best-known, wine of Hungary.

BRIEF U.S.A. WINE DICTIONARY

WINE	CHARACTERISTICS	WHEN TO SERVE	TEMPERATURE
Appetizer Wines:			
SHERRY	Appetizer or dessert wine, with nutty, or *rancio*, flavor. Color ranges from pale to dark amber. Made dry, medium dry, and sweet. Dry sherry is the most popular appetizer wine	*Dry sherries:* Before meal as appetizer *Sweet sherries:* Usually served with dessert, with between-meal refreshments, or with biscuits, crackers, etc.	Chilled or at room temperature
VERMOUTH	Appetizer wine flavored with aromatic herbs. There are two kinds: *Sweet* (Italian type) is dark amber. *Dry* (French type) is pale amber	Before meal as appetizer	Well chilled
White Table Wines:			
CATAWBA	Made in Eastern and Midwestern states from native hybrid grapes that give it characteristic flavor and aroma. Both dry and semisweet	Same as sauterne	Well chilled
CHABLIS	Straw-colored wine, similar to Rhine wine but less tart than most wines in that group, and with fruit flavor and body	With main course. Especially good with fish, shellfish, poultry, veal, lamb, etc.	Well chilled
DELAWARE	Made from Delaware grapes grown in Eastern states	Same as Rhine wine	Well chilled
FOLLE BLANCHE	Chablis type. Made from folle blanche grapes	Same as Chablis	Well chilled
LIGHT MUSCAT	Dry or semisweet. Also called dry muscat. Light wine of muscat grapes with characteristic muscat flavor and aroma	*Dry types:* With white meat or sea food *Semisweet types:* With or after dessert; or with between-meal refreshments	Well chilled
PINOT BLANC	Chablis type. Made from pinot blanc grapes	Same as Chablis	Well chilled

RHINE WINE (*Hock or Moselle*)	Thoroughly dry. Sometimes on acid side, with delicate pale-gold, slightly greenish color. Eastern Rhine wines are flowery, fruity	With main course, especially white meats or sea foods	Well chilled
RIESLING	Rhine-wine type made from Riesling grapes	Same as Rhine wine	Well chilled
SAUTERNE	*Golden-hued wines*, sometimes dry but often semisweet. *Very sweet sauternes*, also labeled haut sauterne or frequently chateau sauterne. *Eastern sauternes*, often less sweet, with characteristic aroma and grape taste	*Dry:* With white meats and sea food *Sweet:* With dessert, between meals, or with white meats and sea food *Very Sweet:* After dessert, often with meals	Well chilled
SEMILLON	Sauterne-type wine made from semillon grapes. Either dry or semisweet	Same as sauterne	Well chilled
SYLVANER	Made from sylvaner (also called Franken Riesling) grapes. Rhine-wine type, but fruitier and more fragrant. Resembles Alsatian wine	Same as Rhine wine	Well chilled

Red Table Wines:

BARBERA	Heavy-bodied—typical Italian type. Made from, and with distinct flavor and aroma of, barbera grapes. Strong in flavor. Burgundy type	With main course. Delicious with highly seasoned food, rice and spaghetti dishes, etc.	Room temperature or slightly chilled
BURGUNDY	Dark ruby in color, stronger in flavor, body, and bouquet than claret. (Made from a number of grape varieties.) Eastern Burgundy has characteristic "grapy" perfume and flavor of Eastern native grapes	With main course, especially red meats, turkey, or dark-meated birds	Room temperature or slightly chilled
CABERNET	Made from cabernet sauvignon grapes, famous Bordeaux grape of France and one of the best red wine grapes of California. Has distinctive flavor. Stronger flavor and body than most clarets, sometimes heavier than California Burgundy. Harsh when young, very fine cabernet becomes really great with age.	Same as claret	Room temperature or slightly chilled

BRIEF U.S.A. WINE DICTIONARY *(continued)*

WINE	CHARACTERISTICS	WHEN TO SERVE	TEMPERATURE
CHIANTI	Medium-bodied, ruby-red wine, strongly flavored, dry, fruity, slightly tart	Same as claret	Room temperature or slightly chilled
CLARET	Medium-bodied, with tasty dryness. Often less expensive than other red wines	With steaks, roasts, chops, spaghetti, game	Room temperature or slightly chilled
GAMAY	Made from gamay grapes. Light in body. Often made into rosé wine	Same as Burgundy	*Red:* room temperature *Rosé:* chilled
PINOT NOIR	Made from famous pinot noir grapes (Burgundy type). Varies greatly with amount of this grape present (by law, at least 51 per cent). Finest are velvety to taste, beautiful red in color. Can be aged into wonderful wine in bottle	Same as Burgundy	Room temperature or slightly chilled
ROSÉ	Lightest of red table wines, being light in color, body, and alcoholic content. Dry, fruity wine	Ideal for luncheon or picnic	Chilled
ZINFANDEL	Claret type. Made from, and has distinct taste and aroma of, zinfandel grapes. Somewhat coarse, fruity, medium-bodied	Same as claret	Room temperature or slightly chilled
Dessert Wines: ANGELICA	Sweet; straw- or amber-colored; mild and fruity in flavor; originated in California	With or after dessert, or with between-meal refreshments	Room temperature or chilled
MADEIRA	Deep amber. Semisweet. Resembles sherry, but is sweeter and darker. Drier than Tokay	With or after dessert, or with little cakes as refreshments	Room temperature or chilled
MARSALA	Deep amber. Resembles sherry but is sweeter and darker. Usually sweeter than Madeira but drier than Tokay. Medium-bodied	With or after dessert, or with cheese and nuts	Room temperature or chilled

MUSCATEL	Has distinctive flavor, aroma, and sweetness of muscat grapes from which it is made. Ranges in color from golden to amber. Medium-bodied	With or after dessert, or with between-meal refreshments, biscuits, crackers, or cheese and nuts	Room temperature or chilled
PORT	Rich, heavy-bodied, sweet wine, ranging from deep-red to tawny color	With or after dessert. Especially good with cheese and nuts	Room temperature or chilled
TOKAY	Amber-colored, sweet dessert wine. In no way resembles Hungarian Tokay in flavor. Usually made by blending angelica, port, and sherry	With or after dessert; or with fruit cake, nuts, raisins; or as between-meal refreshment	Room temperature or chilled
WHITE PORT	White dessert wine. Usually straw-colored. Sweet, heavy-bodied	With or after dessert, or with between-meal refreshments	Room temperature or chilled
Sparkling Wines:			
CHAMPAGNE	Made sparkling by secondary fermentation of finished wine, creating natural effervescence. Comes dry, usually labeled brut; or semidry, labeled dry, extra-dry, or sec. There are pink champagnes	*Dry type:* As appetizer. Or with main course—especially poultry, game, sweetbreads, fish *Sweet type:* With dessert	Very well chilled
SPARKLING BURGUNDY	Red wine made naturally sparkling by same process as champagne. Smooth, slightly sweet, light-bodied	With main course—especially poultry, game, sweetbreads	Very well chilled
Flavored Wines:			
	As sweet as dessert wines, with added natural flavors varying from orange and lemon to vanilla	For afternoon or evening refreshments, with or without food. Useful in fruit punches too	Chilled or at room temperature

FREEZING, CANNING, AND JELLY MAKING

Here are the essentials you need to know about freezing food in a home freezer. You will also find helpful the instruction booklet that comes with your freezer, and the bulletins from the U.S. Department of Agriculture and your state college of agriculture. Write, too, to the state extension service in your state for the names of the best varieties of fruits and vegetables for freezing.

Selecting the Right Home Freezer

You'll have to choose from dozens of makes and sizes. If you have no previous experience to draw on, you may find it helpful to talk to friends and neighbors who own freezers.

What Type? Most freezer manufacturers are reputable, so there's little risk if you choose a well-known make. However, you'll have to choose among three types of freezers:

1. *Upright type*, with shelves like a refrigerator.
2. *Chest type*, with baskets or dividers.

3. *Combination refrigerator-freezer*, with freezer space varying from 2 to 10 or more cubic feet.

The type you should choose depends on the amount of floor or wall space you have available and on which type seems to offer you the most convenience.

When you are about to replace your refrigerator, if you need only limited freezer space or if you don't have room for separate appliances, the combination may be your choice. In a true combination refrigerator-freezer, where the freezer temperature averages about 0°F., you can keep foods fresh and flavorful for months just as in a true home freezer.

Caution: Not all freezer compartments in refrigerators maintain zero. At higher temperatures, home-prepared foods freeze more slowly and may be inferior in texture and flavor. Storage times of commercially frozen food should be limited to a week or two in such freezing compartments.

What Size? The answer to this question depends entirely on what use you hope to make of your freezer. Do you grow your own fruits and vegetables? Do you plan to market infrequently and to buy in large quantities? Do you intend to cook and freeze whole meals? All these projects take space, so choose a size large enough to handle all your freezing requirements.

Cutting Food Costs with a Freezer

Here are the ways a freezer can help you cut food costs:

1. You need never waste a scrap of food.
2. You can cook at your leisure and so spend time concocting less expensive, but time-consuming dishes.
3. You'll have fewer leftovers, because you can package food in amounts to suit your family.
4. When you shop, you can take advantage of every special buy that comes along, whether it's a basket of peaches or a leg of lamb.
5. You can contact the grocer, butcher, locker plant, and nearby farmers about buying in quantity. For example, some stores give quantity discounts on commercially frozen foods. However, when buying large amounts, you should be even more careful about a food's quality, because the supply will last so long.
6. You can freeze your own garden produce.

Using Your Freezer

Freeze Only Food of Good Quality. While freezing does retain the flavor, texture, and color of food to a remarkable degree, it does not improve quality.

Freeze Foods Promptly. If this cannot be done, refrigerate them a short time. Don't let food stand at room temperature.

Freeze Foods in Small Amounts. Don't buy or prepare more food than can be frozen at one time. Consult your freezer instruction booklet on this point, for overloading results in slow freezing.

Use Only Special Freezer Wrapping Materials. The low temperatures of a freezer tend to draw moisture from foods, causing them to lose flavor, volume, and texture. So home-frozen foods need the special types of moisture-vapor-proof packaging material described at right.

Commercially packed frozen foods need no additional wrapping.

SHEET WRAPPINGS: There is a wide variety to choose from — foil, saran, cellophane, polyethylene, and heavy paper impregnated with wax or lined with film. When you use these sheet wrappings, remember that edges must be folded over several times and sealed with freezer tape.

BAGS: Polyethylene or paper freezer bags are quick and easy to use. Often they can be reused.

GLASS JARS: These jars are handy for storing soups, fruit juices, other liquid foods. They are made in pint and quart sizes, have wide mouths, straight sides, screw caps.

CONTAINERS: Many types of containers are available for packing fruits, vegetables, cooked foods, shellfish, etc.

Containers made of aluminum or aluminum foil can be used for both freezing and reheating foods. Others are clear plastic, with plastic lids that seal tight (these can be used for refrigerator storage too); heavily waxed paper cartons, which come in many sizes and shapes; paper cartons lined with moisture-vapor-proof material.

Label and Date All Packages: Labeling is important because it's very hard to identify food once it's frozen. The date will prompt you to use food before it loses quality.

Freeze Packages Quickly: Do not let packaged food stand; place in freezer promptly. Check your instruction booklet to see where you should place packages in freezer.

Storage Time for Frozen Foods: No one can tell you exactly how long you can keep foods in a freezer. Time limits depend on the temperature, kind of food, care taken in packaging, and the original quality of the food. These are general time limits at 0°F. or below.

Beef, lamb, veal	up to 1 year
Chopped beef	up to 2 or 3 months
Fruits and vegetables	up to 1 year
Pork (fresh), poultry, fish	4 to 6 months
Ham	up to 1 month
Cooked and baked foods	1 to 3 months
Franks	up to 1 month
Sandwiches	2 weeks
Ice cream	up to 1 month

Long storage causes loss of flavor. Use your freezer every day, so that when you serve a food it's still as fresh as the day on which it was frozen.

Don't Refreeze Thawed Foods: As a general rule, avoid refreezing foods. If food is left standing after it thaws, it may begin to spoil, and you might refreeze it without realizing this. Also, refreezing almost always results in loss of texture and flavor. So whenever food is thawed, refrigerate it and use it promptly.

Partially thawed food (except sea food) can be refrozen as long as it still contains ice crystals. Remember this if your freezer is accidentally disconnected or the power fails.

Exception to This Important Rule: You can thaw uncooked food, cook it completely, then refreeze it. For example, if you roast a frozen turkey, you can freeze the leftovers — if you package and freeze them quickly.

FRUITS

TO FREEZE FRUITS

General Pointers: Freeze only sound, fully ripe fruits. You can pack them in dry sugar, sugar syrup, or a combination of sugar syrup and corn syrup. (For the last, follow directions given by manufacturer of corn syrup.) Some fruits can be packed unsweetened.

Fruits can be packaged in any liquid-tight container. Leave 1″ at top for expansion.

To Pack Fruit in Dry Sugar: Mix sugar and fruit gently.

To Pack Fruit in Sugar Syrup: Add enough sugar syrup to cover fruit in container.

To Make Sugar Syrup: Heat water with sugar in proportions below until dissolved. Chill well before using.

Light syrup	2 cups sugar per 1 qt. water
Medium syrup	3 cups sugar per 1 qt. water
Heavy syrup	4¾ cups sugar per 1 qt. water
Extra-heavy syrup	7 cups sugar per 1 qt. water

To Keep Fruit from Darkening: To each 1 qt. sugar syrup (or 1 cup dry sugar), add ½

teasp. ascorbic acid; or add a commercial preparation made just for this purpose. Either will also help protect flavor.

APPLES: Peel; core; slice. If apples are to be served as is, add medium syrup. If they're to be used in cooking, add ½ cup sugar per 1 qt. apples. Add ascorbic acid.

APRICOTS: Wash; peel; pit; halve or slice. Add syrup or sugar as for apples. Or to freeze unpeeled whole apricots, drop fruit into boiling water ½ min., then into ice water until chilled. Add medium syrup. Add ascorbic acid.

BLUEBERRIES: Sort; wash. For fruit cup, etc., add medium syrup. For pies, pack unsweetened.

CHERRIES: Wash; pit if desired. If sweet, add medium syrup. If sour (for pies), add ¾ cup sugar per 1 qt. fruit. Add ascorbic acid.

CRANBERRIES: Put unopened packages of fresh cranberries in freezer. When ready to use, rinse frozen berries in cold water and drain. Use as you would fresh berries. Don't thaw them. Berries are easier to chop or grind while still frozen.

GRAPEFRUIT AND ORANGES: Peel; seed; section. Drain off juice; pack, covering with juice mixed with heavy syrup — about 1 part juice to 3 parts heavy syrup. Add ascorbic acid.

GRAPES: Wash; remove stems. If they're to be used in making jam or jelly, pack unsweetened. For fruit cups, etc., remove seeds; add medium syrup.

MELONS: Remove seeds; pare; slice or cube. Or make balls. Add light syrup. Several kinds of melon can be packed together, for fruit cups.

PEACHES: Peel; slice. Add medium syrup. Or add ⅔ cup sugar per 1 qt. peaches. Add ascorbic acid. To keep fruit submerged, place crumpled wax paper on top of it.

PINEAPPLE: Pare; remove core and eyes; slice or cube. Pack unsweetened. Or add light syrup.

RHUBARB: Wash; trim; cut. Pack unsweetened for pies. Or make rhubarb sauce as usual; then freeze.

STRAWBERRIES: Sort; wash; hull. Slice if large. Add ¾ cup sugar per 1 qt. berries (increase or decrease sugar depending on tartness of berries). Or cover with medium or heavy syrup.

TO THAW FROZEN FRUITS

Thaw fruit in container — in refrigerator, at room temperature, or under running cold water — until fruit separates but is still ice-cold. Serve promptly.

FROZEN FRUIT JELLIES AND JAMS

See Jams and Jellies, p. 714.

VEGETABLES

TO FREEZE VEGETABLES

General Pointers: Freeze garden-fresh, tender vegetables. Avoid damaged or bruised vegetables.

Before freezing, vegetables must be heated in boiling water to reduce the action of enzymes, and to preserve flavor and appearance. Then they must be quickly chilled. (Heating in steam is recommended by some authorities. For directions and time periods, see U.S. Department of Agriculture bulletins.)

To Heat: Boil 1 gal. or more of water in large kettle; keep heat high at all times. Add vegetables (1 lb. prepared vegetable per gal. of water); cover; start timing as indicated under each vegetable. Heat thick pieces or stalks longest time indicated.

To Chill: Plunge heated vegetables into ice water; let stand until cold — about the same number of minutes as directed for heating. Drain well; then pack in any convenient container.

ASPARAGUS: Break off tough ends; wash; sort into narrow, medium, and thick stalks. Cut into pieces; or leave as spears. Heat 2 to 4 min. Chill.

BROCCOLI: Use compact, dark-green heads. Wash; trim. Cut lengthwise, making heads 1½" wide. Heat 3 min. Chill.

BRUSSELS SPROUTS: Trim, removing coarse outer leaves. Wash thoroughly; sort for size. Heat 3 to 5 min. Chill.

CORN ON THE COB: Use young, tender ears of corn. Husk; wash; sort for size. Heat small ears 7 min., medium ears 9 min., large ears 11 min. Chill. Pack in cartons; or wrap individually.

CORN, WHOLE KERNEL: Use young, tender ears of corn. Husk, wash. Heat 4 min. After chilling, drain; cut off kernels (avoid cutting into cob).

GREEN BEANS: Wash; remove ends. Cut into lengthwise strips or 1" or 2" pieces. Heat 3 min. Chill.

GREEN LIMAS: Shell; sort for size; discard any over-mature, white beans. Heat 2 to 4 min. Chill.

GREEN PEPPERS: Wash; remove stems and seeds; cut into halves or slices if desired. Heat halves 3 min., slices 2 min. Chill. If peppers are to be stuffed, freeze whole, without heating.

MUSHROOMS: Sort for size; wash; trim stem ends. Slice mushrooms if they're larger than 1". Let stand in 1 pt. water with 1 teasp. lemon juice 5 min.; then heat whole mushrooms 5 min.; slices 3 min. Chill.

PEAS: Shell; discard immature or tough peas. Heat 1½ min. Chill.

SPINACH: Wash; remove tough stems and older leaves. Heat 1½ to 2 min. Chill. Then chop if desired.

SQUASH: If you're freezing summer squash, wash; cut into ½" slices; heat 3 min.; chill. If it's Hubbard squash, wash, cut up, remove seeds. Cook till soft as on p. 430; then remove pulp and mash it. Chill by setting pan in cold water.

TO COOK FROZEN VEGETABLES

Do not thaw any vegetable except corn on the cob. Drop frozen vegetable into small amount of salted water; cook, covered, until just tender. Remember that frozen vegetables take about half as long to cook as fresh ones.

MEAT

TO FREEZE, THAW, AND COOK MEAT

General Pointers: Because meat is usually the most precious food in a freezer, it requires special, careful attention. Follow these important rules.

1. *Package* in amounts convenient for your family.

2. *Wrap tightly* in freezer-wrapping materials

or containers; seal securely with freezer tape. See p. 701.

3. *Label clearly*, noting date, kind of meat, cut, and weight or number of servings.

4. *Thaw meat completely* before cooking in most cases. For 1 lb. meat, allow 5 to 6 hr. in food compartment of refrigerator, 2 to 3 hr. at room temperature, or 1 to 1½ hr. in front of electric fan. If meat is thawed at room temperature, cook it as soon as it's thawed but while it's still icy cold; or refrigerate and cook as soon as possible.

ROASTS:

To Freeze: Trim off excess fat. Pad sharp bone edges with fat, to avoid puncturing wrapping. Pack in bag or sheet wrappings; seal.

To Cook: Thaw, wrapped; roast as usual. If necessary to cook meat unthawed, roast at usual oven temperature until meat thaws sufficiently to let you insert roast-meat thermometer (test first with a skewer); then roast to same internal temperature as you would for a regular roast. (Check Timetables.) A roast-meat thermometer is the only reliable guide to the doneness of any roast, and especially an unthawed one.

STEAKS AND CHOPS:

To Freeze: Trim as desired. Package together, in bag or sheet wrapping, as many steaks or chops as you'll need for one meal. If there's more than one layer of meat, separate layers with film or foil so they'll come apart more quickly when thawing. Press wrapping flat against meat; seal edges securely with freezer tape.

To Cook: Thaw, wrapped (unwrap if packed in layers); cook as usual. To cook unthawed, allow about twice the usual cooking time; be sure to check for doneness by making small cut close to bone.

CHOPPED MEAT OR CUT-UP MEAT FOR STEWS:

To Freeze: Use only freshly cut or ground meat. Package chopped meat in bulk or in patties in any convenient freezer wrapping material or container, separating layers of meat with film or foil. Pack meat for stews in recipe amounts in any freezer material.

To Cook: Thaw, wrapped (unwrap if packed in layers); cook as usual. To cook unthawed patties, broil or pan-broil them, sprinkling them with seasonings as they cook.

POULTRY

TO FREEZE POULTRY

BROILER-FRYER CHICKENS: Clean thoroughly. Halve, quarter, or cut up for broiling or frying. Package compactly in bag or sheet wrapping, separating halves, quarters, or pieces with foil or film to speed thawing. Wrap giblets separately.

STEWING CHICKENS: Clean, cut up, and package as for broiler-fryer chickens. (You may wish to package pieces with special uses in mind, putting together pieces for fricassee, necks and gizzards for stock, breasts for a party dish, etc.) Or leave cleaned birds whole; then package as for roasting chicken.

ROASTING CHICKENS OR TURKEYS: Clean birds as for roasting. Wrap giblets separately; place in body cavity or under wing. Tie wings and legs close to body of bird to make it compact. Package in bag or sheet wrapping.

TO COOK FROZEN POULTRY

Thaw poultry, wrapped. Then cook as usual (see Poultry, p. 259). Or if stewing chickens, unwrap; then cook, unthawed.

SEA FOOD

TO FREEZE SEA FOOD

FISH: Wrap cleaned whole or halved fish, fillets, or steaks individually in sheet wrapping; then place in freezer bags or cartons.

SCALLOPS, OYSTERS, AND CLAMS: Pack washed scallops or shucked oysters or clams in freezer containers. Cover with salt solution, using 1 tablesp. salt per cup water; or substitute their own liquor for part of salt solution. Leave 1″ head space for expansion.

SHRIMP: Pack cooked or uncooked, shelled or unshelled, in freezer containers.

CRABS AND LOBSTERS: Cook as usual; then cool. Remove meat from shells; pack tightly in freezer container.

TO USE FROZEN SEA FOOD

Thaw sea food in wrapping or container only

enough to separate. Use promptly. Serve or cook as usual.

EGGS

TO FREEZE EGGS

Place convenient recipe amounts of whole eggs, yolks, or whites in any freezer container (see p. 701) as below. Store up to 6 months. Be sure to label the number of eggs in each container.

WHOLE EGGS: Break into measuring cup. If eggs are to be used for sweet dishes such as desserts, cakes, etc., add 1 tablesp. sugar or corn syrup per 1 cup eggs. For other kinds of cooking, add 1 teasp. salt per 1 cup eggs. Stir to mix, but do not beat.

YOLKS: Freeze as for whole eggs, adding 2 tablesp. sugar or corn syrup, or 1 teasp. salt, per 1 cup yolks.

WHITES: Freeze without adding salt or sugar.

TO USE FROZEN EGGS

Thaw in container in refrigerator; use promptly. Substitute for fresh eggs in recipes as follows:

2½ tablesp. whole eggs for 1 egg
1 tablesp. yolks for 1 egg yolk
1½ tablesp. whites for 1 egg white

OTHER DAIRY PRODUCTS

BUTTER: Butter may be frozen in original wax carton. To store longer than 1 month, over-wrap with sheet wrapping.

CHEESE: See To Freeze Cheese, p. 344.

HEAVY CREAM: This is the best type of cream to freeze. Freeze in original carton. Or whip; pack in container. Or drop spoonfuls of whipped cream onto foil; freeze; then wrap. Store up to 1 month.

To serve, thaw cream in container until it can be spooned out. Unwrap spoonfuls of whipped cream; place on dessert; let thaw 15 to 20 min. before serving.

ICE CREAM: It's an economical buy in 1-gal. or ½-gal. packages. Freeze in original carton. After opening, keep surface of ice cream covered with wax paper. Store up to 1 month.

BREADS AND COFFEECAKES

TO FREEZE BREADS

KINDS TO FREEZE: Biscuits, muffins, fruit-and-nut bread, brown bread, plain and sweet rolls, tea rings, English muffins, popovers, waffles, yeast bread (white, rye, and whole-wheat, etc.).

BAKERS' BREADS: If they come wrapped, freeze in original wrapper; limit storage to 2 weeks. If unwrapped, place in bag; or wrap in sheet wrapping. Store up to 3 months.

HOMEMADE BREADS: Make and bake as usual; cool.

Place loaf breads in bag; or wrap in sheet wrapping.

Place rolls, biscuits, muffins, or popovers in bag or container.

Place pan rolls on foil-covered cardboard or in paper or foil pie plate; then wrap in sheet wrapping.

TO USE FROZEN BREADS

LOAF BREADS: Thaw, wrapped, at room temperature 1 to 3 hr.

SLICED BREAD: Toast, unthawed (simply drop into toaster, frozen). Or thaw a little if slices cannot be separated easily.

ROLLS, BISCUITS, DOUGHNUTS, ETC.: Place, unthawed, on baking sheet; heat at 400°F. 10 to 15 min. Or thaw, wrapped, at room temperature 30 to 35 min.; then serve.

FROZEN WAFFLES: See Speedy Waffles, p. 489.

TO FREEZE COFFEECAKES

HOMEMADE COFFEECAKE: If frosted kind, don't frost until just before serving. Cool; freezer-wrap (see pan rolls above); then freeze.

BAKERS' COFFEECAKE: Store-wrapped coffeecakes from the grocer's shelves may be frozen the same as Bakers' Breads above. Coffeecakes in foil pans may be frozen up to 3 months.

TO USE FROZEN COFFEECAKES

Let thaw, wrapped, several hours at room temperature; then frost if recipe so directs. Or if not already wrapped in foil, rewrap frozen coffeecake in foil; heat through in 400°F. oven (about 15 min. for individual rolls and buns, 30 min. to 1 hr. for larger coffeecakes).

SANDWICHES

TO FREEZE SANDWICHES

You can prepare them whenever you have the makings on hand, at any convenient time. They'll keep 2 or 3 weeks.

To Freeze: Spread each bread slice with soft butter or margarine. (We often season butter with a little chili sauce, prepared mustard, horse-radish, seasoned salt, or pimento.) Avoid spreading with mayonnaise, salad dressing, or jelly — these soak into bread.

Now fill sandwiches with that leftover, sliced roast beef, lamb, chicken, turkey, or baked ham, etc. Or use pantry shelf items such as canned luncheon meat or tongue. Or make up favorite salad fillings with any of these meats, or with tuna, salmon, shrimp, etc. — just be sure to cut down on the mayonnaise. If egg-salad filling is your choice, leave out egg whites.

Omit lettuce, celery, carrots, tomatoes, etc.; they lose their crispness in freezing. Plan to add them just before eating.

If you're wrapping a variety of sandwiches, be sure to label each kind. For easy storage, pack a number together in a box. If you're freezing only a few, arrange in one of your special ice-cube trays, p. 610. Be sure to label and date sandwiches.

TO USE FROZEN SANDWICHES

Pack lunch-box sandwiches frozen — they'll be thawed in time for lunch. Or thaw, wrapped, 2 to 3 hr. at room temperature, 5 to 6 hr. in refrigerator.

PIES

TO FREEZE AND SERVE PIES

Use any regular pie plate, including glass. Or use special paper pie plate.

CHIFFON PIES:

To Freeze: Make as usual; let set. Omit whipped-cream topping. Freeze. Then place in freezer bag; or wrap in sheet wrapping.

To Serve: Unwrap frozen pie; let stand in food compartment of refrigerator 1 to 1½ hr. Top with whipped cream.

CREAM OR CUSTARD PIES: These pies do not freeze well.

TWO-CRUST FRUIT OR MINCE PIES:

To Freeze: Make as usual. Some juicy fruit pies may require more thickening than usual — ¼ cup flour per pie is about enough to thicken the juiciest fruit. Then bake, cool, and freeze; or freeze unbaked. If pie is unbaked, do not slit top crust.

Place baked or unbaked pie in freezer bag; or wrap in sheet wrapping.

NOTE: If pie seems too tender to handle, freeze before wrapping. For extra protection, cover pie with paper or foil pie plate; wrap.

To Serve: If pie is unbaked, unwrap, frozen; slit top crust; bake at 425°F. 40 to 60 min.

If it's baked, unwrap, frozen; heat at 375°F. 30 to 50 min., or until center is bubbling hot.

FRESH FRUIT FILLINGS:

To Freeze: Combine 1 qt. fresh fruit (strawberries, blueberries, sliced peaches or apples, etc.) with 3 tablesp. tapioca, ¾ to 1 cup granulated sugar, ¼ teasp. salt, 1 to 2 tablesp. lemon juice. With such fruits as peaches, pears, or cherries, stir about ½ teasp. ascorbic acid into sugar before combining with fruit. (Or use a commercial product to prevent browning of fruit; follow label directions.)

Line 8″ pie plate with heavy duty foil, freezer paper, or several layers of saran, letting it extend 5″ around rim. Add 1 qt. of filling. Loosely cover filling with lining. Freeze until firm. Then tightly seal lining over filling. Remove from pie plate; return to freezer at 0°F.

NOTE: Double, triple, or quadruple the filling recipe. (If you have more than 4 times the amount of fruit, make the recipe several times. Otherwise, you may have more mixture than you can handle easily.)

To Serve: For each pie, prepare Flaky Pastry for 2-crust 9″ pie, pp. 584–587. Line 9″ pie plate with pastry; trim. Remove freezer wrapping from *frozen pie-shaped filling;* place in pastry-lined pie plate. Dot with 1 tablesp. butter. Adjust top crust as directed. Bake in 425°F. oven about 1 hr., or until syrup boils with heavy bubbles that do not burst.

LEMON MERINGUE PIE:

To Freeze: Make Lemon Meringue Pie, p. 593 (we have found this recipe best for freezing), omitting meringue topping. Then wrap as in Chiffon Pies, p. 706.

To Serve: Spread meringue on unwrapped frozen pie. Bake at 350°F. 20 to 25 min.; let stand 1 hr. before serving.

PUMPKIN PIE:

To Freeze: Make and bake pie as usual; cool. Then wrap as in Chiffon Pies, p. 706. Or pour unbaked filling into liquid-tight freezer container.

To Serve: Thaw baked pie, unwrapped, at room temperature 1 to 2 hr. To use unbaked filling, thaw and pour into unbaked pie shell; bake as usual.

PIE SHELLS:

To Freeze: Freeze pie shells, baked or unbaked, before wrapping. Then place in freezer bag; or wrap in sheet wrapping. (Frozen, unbaked shells can be stacked before wrapping if you place crumpled wax paper between them.)

To Use: If pie shell is unbaked, unwrap; bake at 450°F. 5 min. Prick; bake about 15 min. longer. If pie shell is baked, unwrap. Heat at 375°F. 10 min.; or thaw at room temperature.

PASTRY:

To Freeze: Make as usual; roll into circles if desired. Stack unbaked pastry circles, placing 2 sheets of wax paper between them. Then place in freezer bag, or wrap in sheet wrapping. If dough is unrolled, wrap in sheet wrapping.

To Use: Thaw at room temperature; then use as usual.

CAKES

TO FREEZE CAKES

KINDS TO FREEZE: Angel-food and chiffon or lovelight cakes, spongecakes, butter cakes, poundcakes, fruitcakes (any flavor freezes well). Bake as loaf, layers, or cupcakes. Or bake 2 layers; use one layer, freeze other.

UNFROSTED CAKES: Make and bake as usual; then cool. Wrap in sheet wrapping. For extra protection, place in cardboard box.

FROSTED CAKES: Make and bake as usual. Set cake on cardboard covered with film or foil. Freeze until frosting is set; then wrap. (Butter Cream, p. 645, and Penuche Frosting, p. 646, freeze well.)

TO USE FROZEN CAKES

Unwrap frosted cakes. Leave unfrosted cakes wrapped. Thaw on cake rack at room temperature. Cupcakes thaw in about 30 min.; cake layers in 1 hr.; other cakes in 2 to 3 hr.

COOKIES

TO FREEZE COOKIES

KINDS TO FREEZE: Molded or cookie-press, drop, refrigerator, bar, and roll-and-cut cookies.

COOKIE DOUGH: Form refrigerator-cookie dough into a roll or a bar; then wrap in sheet wrapping, p. 701.

Pack other cookie doughs in freezer containers.

BAKED COOKIES: Make and bake as usual; then cut if necessary; cool thoroughly. Arrange on cardboard covered with wax paper or foil; then place in plastic bags. Or pack gently in any freezing bag, box, or container of convenient size. Use a sturdy container for fragile cookies — metal or plastic box, or coffee can if you wish. Cushion cookies with crumpled foil or wax paper.

TO USE FROZEN COOKIES

Thaw refrigerator-cookie dough in refrigerator about 1 hr., or until it slices easily. Bake as usual.

Thaw any other kind of cookie dough till it can be handled easily; prepare and bake as usual.

Thaw baked cookies, unwrapped, about 15 min. at room temperature.

STEAMED PUDDINGS

TO FREEZE STEAMED PUDDINGS

General Pointers: After steaming, remove from mold, cool, wrap in foil. You can refrigerate it for several days, or freezer-wrap in foil and freeze for several months.

To Heat: Thaw in refrigerator overnight. Bake, wrapped, at 325°F. for about 1 hr., or until hot.

COOKED FOODS

TO FREEZE COOKED FOODS

See chart, p. 709, for directions on freezing and serving specific cooked foods. Here are some general pointers to guide you.

To Cook Before Freezing:

1. Undercook rather than overcook dishes that will be reheated before serving.
2. When making gravies and sauces for freezing, be sure to beat them until smooth. This helps prevent separation during freezing.
3. Chill hot mixtures quickly before packaging and freezing them. Do this by setting pan, dish, or casserole in cold water or in refrigerator.

To Wrap:

1. If cooked foods are to be baked or reheated in oven before serving, pack in pie plates, baking dishes or pans, or aluminum or foil freezer boxes. Then food can go directly from freezer to oven. (If a container does not have its own cover, use foil.)
2. If cooked foods are to be reheated on top of the range, pack them in straight-sided containers. Then frozen food can be removed from container easily, by dipping container into warm water until contents slip out. (Some paper containers can be peeled off and contents removed.)

TO USE FROZEN COOKED FOODS

1. Don't forget that most cooked foods are perishable; therefore, the way you thaw frozen cooked foods is most important.

If a food is to be reheated or baked before serving, place it in the oven or on top of the range without thawing whenever possible. (Exceptions to this rule are large pieces of meat and deep casseroles in which the outside layer of food would become dry before the center was heated through; thaw these.)

If a food is to be thawed and served without heating, thaw in refrigerator or at room temperature; then refrigerate immediately to keep cold until served.

2. Unless otherwise directed, thaw frozen cooked foods wrapped, whether thawed in refrigerator or at room temperature.

TO FREEZE AND SERVE COOKED FOODS

BREADS, SANDWICHES, SOUPS, AND SPREADS

IF YOU WANT	FREEZE THEM THIS WAY	SERVE THEM
Breads	See p. 705.	See p. 705.
Lunch-Box or Picnic Sandwiches	Spread bread with butter or margarine (don't use salad dressing or jelly). Fill with sliced meat or a spread. (Omit lettuce, celery, tomatoes, hard-cooked egg white.) Wrap individually.	Pack frozen — they'll be thawed in time for lunch. Or thaw, wrapped, 2 to 3 hr. at room temperature, 5 to 6 hr. in refrigerator.
Party Sandwiches	Cut day-old bread into shapes as desired; stack and wrap in sheet wrapping. Or make as lunch-box sandwiches, above; stack in layers, with sheet wrapping between layers; wrap.	Thaw bread or sandwiches, wrapped, 1 to 2 hr. in refrigerator. To use bread, make into sandwiches as desired. To use sandwiches, unwrap and serve while still cold.
Soups, Chowders	When making, cut down on water if possible. Omit milk, potatoes. Cool. Freeze in straight-sided freezer jar (or container).	Run warm water over jar. Slip out frozen block. Heat slowly. Add omitted liquid. If potatoes are to be added, cook them first in this liquid.
Spreads (for sandwiches or nibblers)	Make favorite mixture of meat, fish, etc., as usual, but omit raw vegetables (celery, carrots, lettuce, etc.). Pack in freezer container.	Thaw several hours in refrigerator.

MAIN DISHES

Chicken, Fried	Brown pieces as usual; omit final cooking; cool. Wrap in sheet wrapping or freezer bag.	Unwrap frozen chicken; place in shallow baking dish; bake, uncovered, at 350°F. 30 to 40 min.
Chili con Carne	Make; then cool. Freeze in straight-sided freezer jar or container.	Heat as for soups.

TO FREEZE AND SERVE COOKED FOODS—(continued)

MAIN DISHES

IF YOU WANT	FREEZE THEM THIS WAY	SERVE THEM
Creamed Dishes	Make as usual, but omit any hard-cooked egg white. Cool. Pack in freezer container.	Thaw enough to remove from container; heat in double boiler.
Frankfurters	Franks are cooked when you buy them. To store them 2 weeks or less, leave in original package. Otherwise wrap in sheet wrapping.	Use frozen if they can be separated. Or thaw and heat as desired.
Gravy, Meat Stock	Make; then cool. Skim off fat. Pack in straight-sided freezer container or jar.	Heat as for soups.
Ham, Baked	Leave in large pieces if possible. Wrap in sheet wrapping, using foil if ham is to be heated in oven.	Thaw about 5 hr. per lb. in refrigerator; then use as desired. Or heat small foil-wrapped packages, unthawed, at 350°F. 30 min. to 1 hr.
Macaroni and Cheese, Baked	Make as usual. Place in casserole, but do not bake. Cool; cover.	Thaw about 8 hr. in refrigerator; then bake as usual. Add a little milk toward end of baking period if mixture seems dry.
Meat Balls, Swedish	Make as usual; then cool. Arrange meat balls and gravy in pie or cake pan close to size of your skillet; cover with freezer material.	Set pan in hot water long enough to loosen contents; slip mixture into skillet. Cover and heat slowly — about 25 min.
Meat Loaf	Package, baked or unbaked, in foil or covered loaf pan or baking dish. Or place layer of baked slices on foil; cover with gravy or canned tomato sauce; fold foil over tightly.	Thaw about 8 hr. in refrigerator. Then serve cold; or heat or bake as usual. Or, if they're slices, reheat, unthawed, in foil package at 400°F. 40 min.
Peppers, Stuffed	Fill uncooked pepper shells with desired mixture; cool. Wrap or place in freezer container.	Bake, unthawed, in covered baking dish at 350°F. until tender.

IF YOU WANT	FREEZE THEM THIS WAY	SERVE THEM
Pies — Chicken, Beef, etc.	Pour hot filling into large or individual baking dishes; cool. Add top crust; cover.	Thaw large pies about 8 hr. in refrigerator; then bake as usual. Bake individual pies, unthawed, at 425°F. about 30 min.
Potatoes, Baked, Stuffed	Make as on p. 411, but do not brown; cool; place in shallow baking dish; cover.	Bake, unthawed and uncovered, at 350°F. 25 to 35 min., or until hot and slightly brown.
Potatoes, Candied Sweet	Make candied sweets as usual; cool in baking dish. Cover; or pack in freezer container.	Heat, thawed or unthawed, in double boiler or in covered baking dish at 350°F.
Rice, Cooked	Pack tightly in freezer container or greased baking dish; cover.	Thaw several hours at room temperature; then heat in double boiler. Or heat, unthawed, in covered baking dish at 350°F.
Roast Meat — Beef, Lamb, Veal, Pork	Sort into large pieces, slices, and bits. Pack tightly in freezer container; pour on gravy or broth to protect flavor. Large pieces may be wrapped in sheet wrapping.	Thaw 4 to 8 hr. in refrigerator. Heat; or serve cold. Small containers of meat in gravy may be heated without thawing at 350°F.
Sauces — Spaghetti, Creole, or Barbecue	Make 2 or 3 batches at a time; pack as for soups.	Heat as for soups.
Stews — Beef, Veal, Lamb	Brown and cook meat in usual amount of liquid until tender-firm. Omit all vegetables; or just omit potatoes. Cool. Pack in freezer container.	Thaw about 8 hr. in refrigerator. Add vegetables in time to simmer till tender (add water if needed).
Swiss Steak Braised Veal Chops Pork Chops Veal Scaloppine Spareribs	Make as usual, but cook only until tender-firm. Cool. Pack in shallow baking dish; cover.	Thaw about 8 hr. in refrigerator; then heat. Or heat, unthawed, in covered baking dish at 350°F. about 1 hr., or until tender and hot. (Time depends on quantity.)
Turnovers — Ham, Chicken	Make as usual, but do not bake. Freeze; then wrap.	Bake, unthawed, unwrapped, on baking sheet at 400°F. 15 min. if bite-size, 25 to 30 min. if dinner-size.

TO FREEZE AND SERVE COOKED FOODS — *(continued)*

DESSERTS

IF YOU WANT	FREEZE THEM THIS WAY	SERVE THEM
Applesauce	Make as usual without adding spices; cool. Pour into freezer container.	Thaw several hours at room temperature; add desired spices.
Baked Alaska	See p. 614.	Bake, unthawed, as recipe directs; serve immediately.
Brown Betty Fruit Cobbler	Make as usual; cool. Leave in baking dish; cover.	Heat, unthawed, covered, at 350°F.
Cakes, Cookies	See directions on p. 707.	
Eclairs, Cream Puffs	Make cream puffs or éclairs (see p. 125); cool. Slit; fill with ice cream; wrap.	Unwrap; serve at once with sauce.
Ice-Cream Sundaes (in quantity)	For a party, early in day, set paper dishes on tray and fill with scoops of ice cream. Set level in freezer.	Remove tray from freezer and spoon sauce or fruit over ice cream; serve at once.
Other Ice-Cream Desserts	See Ice Creams and Sherbets, pp. 604–617.	
Pies — Chiffon, Fruit, Mince, Pumpkin, Lemon	See pp. 706–707.	
Steamed Puddings	See p. 707.	

CAN FROZEN FOODS BE SAFELY REFROZEN WHEN THEY HAVE:

	Only partially thawed out?	*Completely thawed out, but still feel very cold?*	*Completely thawed out and warmed up to room temperature for only a short and known time (never more than two to three hours)?*	*Completely thawed out, warmed up to room temperature, and remained there for a prolonged or unknown time?*
FROZEN UNCOOKED FOOD				
Fruits	Yes	Yes	Yes	Probably safe — may be inedible due to fermentation.
Fruit Juice Concentrates	Yes	Yes	Yes, but flavor may be poor, and reconstituted juice will probably separate.	No. Fermentation may have proceeded too far — can may explode. Discard.
Vegetables	Yes	Yes	Yes	Questionable. Safer to discard.
Meat	Yes	Yes	Yes	Yes, if odor is normal. If there are "off" odors, discard.
Variety Meats (liver, kidney, heart, etc.)	Yes	Yes	Yes, if odor is normal. If there is the slightest "off" odor, discard.	No. Discard.
Poultry	Yes	Yes	Yes, if odor is normal. If there is the slightest "off" odor, discard.	No. Discard.
Fish and Shellfish	Yes	Yes	Yes, if odor is normal. If there is the slightest "off" odor, discard.	No. Discard.

FROZEN PREPARED AND PRECOOKED FOOD

Meat, Poultry, and Fish Pies, "Dinners," and Similar Prepared Dishes	Yes	Yes	No. Discard.	No. Discard.
Soups	Yes	Yes	No. Discard.	No. Discard.
Fruit Pies	Yes	Yes	Yes	Questionable. Safer to discard.
Ice Creams and Sherbets	Yes	Yes, but texture will be affected — less if you can beat once or twice during refreezing.	Yes, but texture will be affected — less if you can beat once or twice during refreezing.	No. Discard.

Again, remember: Refrozen foods will never have the same quality they had originally.

HOME CANNING

Canning Fruits and Vegetables: Detailed instructions for canning fruits and vegetables in glass jars or tin cans are included in the U.S. Department of Agriculture's Home and Garden Bulletin No. 8, "Home Canning of Fruits and Vegetables." Individual copies can be obtained for 20¢ by writing to the Division of Publications, Office of Information, U.S. Department of Agriculture, Washington 25, D.C.

Canning Meats and Poultry: Detailed instructions for canning pork, beef, and other lean meats (lamb and veal), as well as poultry, rabbit, and small game, are included in the U.S. Department of Agriculture's Home and Garden Bulletin No. 6, "Home Canning of Meat." Individual copies can be obtained for 10¢ in the same manner described in Canning Fruits and Vegetables above.

Additional Sources: Manufacturers of home-canning equipment offer the following booklets, which also give detailed canning procedures:

"Ball Blue Book" (25¢ per copy); Ball Brothers Co., Inc., Muncie, Indiana.

"Bernardin Home Canning Guide" (25¢ per copy); Bernardin, Inc., P.O. Box 725, Evansville 1, Indiana.

"Kerr Home Canning Book" (25¢ per copy); Kerr Glass Mfg. Corp., Dept. 238, Sands Springs, Oklahoma.

JAMS AND JELLIES

Making jams and jellies the old-fashioned way is quite uncertain, because fresh fruits vary so in the proportions of natural fruit pectin and acid they contain.

However, with Certo, today's liquid natural fruit pectin, and Sure-Jell, today's powdered natural fruit pectin, all the guesswork and hard work have been taken out of jelly making. You can make delicious, full-flavored fruit jellies and jams each and every time — and in so much less time!

So, follow carefully the many perfected recipes which come on each package of Certo or Sure-Jell. Don't fail to try, too, the new, no-cook jellies and jams which, after making, you can refrigerate for use within 3 weeks, or freeze for use over several months.

And if you need other jam or jelly recipes, just write to General Foods Kitchens, General Foods Corporation, 250 North Street, White Plains, N. Y., listing your fruits and the types of jams or jellies you wish to make.

COOKING FOR A CROWD

The job of chairman of the food committee of your club or church group can be as simple as serving guests in your own home. Having a crowd of 25 or more guests for tea, luncheon, or dinner at home seems like a large undertaking. Organizing the work and spreading responsibility is the secret. "Many hands make light work" will prove true, provided each pair of hands knows exactly what to do.

Your Responsibilities as Chairman

1. Call on 2 or 3 other club members to work with you on your committee.

2. Decide on meals to be served during your term.

3. Estimate number to be served at each meal.

4. Decide on purpose of each meal — social, money raising, or both.

5. Appoint a director for each meal. Let her choose her assistants.

6. Plan to co-operate with each director.

Decide Where and How to Serve

Before you do much else, decide how and where you can best handle the serving. If plenty of room is available, you may choose to serve the guests at tables. If space is limited, it may be simpler to serve buffet style, as on p. 60, or to serve plates in the kitchen and pass them to guests, who stand or sit, depending upon available facilities.

Next Choose Your Menu

After deciding on the manner of serving, choose the menu. To help you decide what to serve, see our quantity recipes and quantity chart for serving 50, p. 726. Also consider these points: *If you're serving an expensive main dish,* such as a roast, serve a low-cost vegetable and salad. *If a low-cost casserole is to be your main course,* a more expensive vegetable and salad may be featured. One high spot in the meal — whether it's the main course, salad, or dessert — makes for success.

Experience of Helpers

Willing hands aren't always capable, so steer clear of complicated dishes.

Available Equipment

Don't have a complete oven meal if you've only a limited amount of oven space. Try to spread the work load to all the equipment at your disposal.

Figure What You'll Charge

1. Estimate the total cost of the food.

2. To this total, add 4 to 6 per cent more, to cover any unpreventable loss in handling. This will help keep you on the safe side of the ledger.

3. Now compute the cost per person by dividing the total cost by the actual number of paying guests. Add to that figure if you wish to make a profit.

4. If you're aiming for a profit, check these:
What will all the donated food cost?
What will labor — serving and cooking help — cost?
Will you use paper plates and cups? There are lovely ones for all occasions.
Will you be charged overhead — fuel, light, rent?
Will you have laundry charges?
How much will paper napkins cost?
Will flowers be furnished, or will you buy them?
What extras will be classified "miscellaneous"?
Will you have a guaranteed number of paying guests to depend on, whether they come or not?
Or must you allow for possible losses from canceled reservations?
How many nonpaying persons must be fed?

When You Make Up Your Marketing List

When deciding total amounts of food you'll need, refer to Quantities to Serve Fifty Persons, p. 726. For 25 persons, divide amounts called for by 2. For 100 persons, multiply by 2.

Order all staples well in advance, buying them in wholesale lots, if possible, from school lunchrooms, wholesale dealers, or retail stores willing to quote special prices on large-quantity purchases.

Once you have figured out how large each portion should be, make sure those who serve are not overgenerous — but not skimpy. Otherwise, your profits will disappear.

Check These Items, Too

What about china, silver, etc.? Be sure to check on table linen, silver, china, glass, and other table appointments, to make sure you'll have enough of everything. List all needed items in a little notebook, checking each off as you get it lined up. If the occasion is an anniversary, wedding reception, or the like at your own home, friends and neighbors will usually be happy to lend their appointments.

You can mix china patterns, so don't worry if, to accommodate all guests, you have to use two china patterns and two glass patterns on your tables. Just alternate the patterns at each cover, and your table will have an attractive orderliness.

If you're using flowers, discuss your table centerpiece with the florist ahead of time, so he will be sure to have just what you want.

List cooking utensils you'll need. Plan to buy or borrow any extra utensils needed to take care of the large amounts of food.

Clear the decks. Look around your kitchen and pantry; temporarily put away any unnecessaries, so you'll have more work space.

Make refrigerator space. You will need every bit of storage space your refrigerator affords. So remove any foods that can be safely left out for this period. Have plenty of refrigerator bags, bowl covers, wax paper, foil, saran, etc., on hand for wrapping and storing foods.

Don't Forget These Points

Do as much as possible the day before. For instance, if you're preparing hot breads, mix together the dry ingredients the day before. Make gelatin desserts and salad dressings the day before, too; refrigerate.

If you're roasting meat, don't crowd pans. Leave 2″ to 3″ between roasts. Plan roasting time so roasts can be taken from oven 30 to 40 min. before serving time; then make gravy.

Start carving about 20 min. before serving; stack 10 to 12 portions in pile in heated shallow pan; place in warm oven with heat turned off. See Roasts for a Crowd, p. 721.

Keep soups, vegetables, etc., warm. If you do not have a steam table to hold food a few min. before serving, fill large roasting pans with hot water; set over low heat. Set kettles of soup, vegetables, etc., in these pans.

If you're serving salads on individual plates, arrange about half of them just before serving time; arrange the rest while first guests are being served.

When you're serving dessert, cut pie or cake 1 hr. before serving; refrigerate it if it has a cream or custard filling or frosting. Whip cream 1 hr. before serving; refrigerate.

If you're serving buffet- or cafeteria-style, on serving table, arrange foods (in serving dishes), with proper serving silver, in this order: meat, gravy, potatoes, vegetable, rolls, butter (if not placed on tables in advance), salads, desserts, coffee (optional).

If you're serving a sit-down meal, let kitchen assistants form kitchen assembly line: Each person serves one item and passes plate to next person. When plates are filled, they are placed on tray, which waitress carries to dining room. For very large crowds, arrange two assembly lines, ending both at table where waitresses pick up trays. A waitress with a little experience can handle 18 to 20 guests.

Cleaning Up

Make arrangements for cleaning up in the very beginning. Have your clean-up committee alerted, so that you don't get left with a mess.

Beware of Food Poisoning

Tragic cases of food poisoning at picnics, community suppers, and institutions have been traced to failure to keep refrigerated such perishable food mixtures as meat, fish, or chicken, etc. (for sandwich fillings and salads), as well as fillings for cream puffs, layer cakes, etc. Cool such mixtures quickly by setting container for a short time in sink with cold water running; or set in bowl of crushed ice. Then store mixture *immediately*, while warm, in refrigerator. Keep refrigerated until served.

FOR THE MAIN COURSE

MELLOW HAM LOAVES

7 eggs	5 cups 2-day-old ½″ bread squares
1½ teasp. salt	
¼ teasp. pepper	2¼ cups nonfat dry milk
4½ lb. uncooked (cook-before-eating) ham, ground	2¼ cups water
	1½ cups brown sugar, packed
1½ lb. veal shoulder, ground	¼ cup vinegar
1½ lb. pork shoulder, ground	1 tablesp. dry mustard

About 2 hr. before serving: Start heating oven to 325°F. Lightly beat eggs, salt, pepper. Gently mix in ham, veal, pork. Add bread squares, dry milk, water. Mix lightly but well. Pack into 3 10″ x 5″ x 3″ loaf pans. Bake 30 min. Then mix brown sugar, vinegar, mustard; boil 1 min.; spoon over loaves. Bake loaves 40 to 45 min. longer, or until firm. Pour off excess juice; let stand 15 min. before slicing. When serving, pass juice. Makes 25 servings.

CALICO HAM CASSEROLE

4 10-oz. or 2 16-oz. pkg. frozen mixed vegetables	6 cups milk
	1 medium onion, grated
1 cup butter or margarine	½ to ¾ lb. process sharp Cheddar cheese, grated (2 to 3 cups)
3 cups ½″ fresh bread squares	
1 cup all-purpose flour	2 lb. fully cooked ham, cut into strips about 1½″ long and ¼″ wide
1 teasp. salt	
¼ teasp. pepper	
2 teasp. dry mustard	
2 teasp. Worcestershire	

Day ahead: Cook vegetables as label directs. Meanwhile, in large kettle, melt ¼ cup butter; add bread squares; toss well. Remove buttered squares; set aside.

In bowl, mix flour with salt, pepper, mustard, Worcestershire; slowly stir in about 2 cups milk. Heat rest of milk in same large kettle used for squares; then stir in flour mixture and ¾ cup butter. Cook over low heat, stirring often, until smooth and thickened; add onion and cheese. Cook, stirring often, until cheese is melted. Add drained vegetables and ham. Pour into 2 12″ x 8″ x 2″ baking dishes. Refrigerate along with bread squares.

About 1 hr. before serving: Start heating oven to 350°F. Sprinkle top of each baking dish with buttered squares. Bake, uncovered, 40 min., or until hot. Makes 25 servings.

MACARONI AND CHEESE, FRANK STYLE

2 lb. elbow macaroni	Cheddar cheese,
2 qt. milk	grated (2 qt.)
¾ cup butter or margarine	¼ cup minced onion
1 cup all-purpose flour	2 teasp. Worcestershire
1 tablesp. salt	25 tomato slices,
1½ teasp. dry mustard	sliced ¼″ thick
2 lb. natural sharp	3 lb. franks, halved lengthwise (about 25)

About 1½ hr. before serving: In large pot, cook macaroni as label directs; drain. Meanwhile, in double boiler, heat milk. In large kettle, melt butter; stir in flour, salt, mustard; cook, stirring often, 10 min. Stir in heated milk; cook, stirring constantly, until thickened. Add cheese, onion, Worcestershire; stir gently until cheese is melted. Remove from heat; stir in macaroni.

Start heating oven to 400°F. Pour macaroni mixture into 2 shallow pans, 15″ x 11″ x 2″. Bake them, uncovered, 20 min. On top of macaroni in each pan, arrange tomato slices, then franks. Bake 15 to 20 min. longer, or until franks are golden brown. Let stand about 5 min. before serving. Makes 25 servings.

MACARONI AND CHEESE: Just omit franks.

BARBECUED FRANKS

¼ cup butter or margarine	1½ cups catchup
1 cup minced onions	1½ cups water
½ teasp. salt	¼ cup vinegar
⅛ teasp. pepper	1½ tablesp. Worcestershire
2 teasp. dry mustard	⅛ teasp. Tabasco
3 tablesp. brown sugar	6 lb. franks (about 50)

About 1¼ hr. before serving: In saucepan, melt butter; add onions; cook slowly until tender. Add salt and rest of ingredients except franks. Cook slowly, uncovered, 30 min. Start heating oven to 350°F. Arrange franks in 1 layer in shallow open pans; pour on sauce. Bake, uncovered, 25 min., turning franks occasionally. Serve from pans. Makes 25 servings.

SIMMERED CHICKEN
(for creamed chicken, à la king, salad, etc.)

How Much to Buy: One 4½-lb. stewing chicken or bro-hen (see p. 260) yields about 3 cups cooked meat. One 16-lb. ready-to-cook turkey, quartered, yields about 6½ lb. cooked meat (13 cups medium-sized diced meat).

The Simmering:
1. Cook whole chicken or quartered turkey in covered kettle or Dutch oven. For each 3½- to 7-lb. stewing chicken, add water to one half the depth of chicken; for each 16-lb. turkey, add warm water to cover. Also add 1 clove-studded onion, 1 carrot, 3 celery tops, 3 teasp. salt, and 1 bay leaf. Simmer chicken, covered, as label directs. Or simmer about 2½ to 4½ hr., or until fork-tender. Simmer turkey, covered, about 2 to 3½ hr., or until fork-tender.
2. When chicken or turkey is cooked, cool quickly. Lift bird from broth to wire rack to cool. Cool kettle of broth in cold water in sink, changing water and stirring broth often.
3. Now remove meat from bones in as large pieces as possible; leave meat as is, or cut into pieces as recipe directs. Wrap meat. Refrigerate meat and broth at once until ready to use.

LEMON-BARBECUED CHICKEN

The Sauce:

3 medium cloves garlic	3 cups lemon juice (use 15 lemons, or use frozen or canned juice)
3 teasp. salt	
1¾ cups salad oil	1 tablesp. pepper
¾ cup minced onions	1 tablesp. dried thyme

The Chickens:

6 to 7 2- to 2½-lb. broiler-fryers, quartered	Fat or salad oil for frying

Day before: Combine all ingredients for sauce. Refrigerate along with chickens.

About 3 hr. before serving: In medium saucepan, heat 1½″ fat to 350°F. on deep-fat-frying thermometer as on p. 6. Fry chickens, 3 pieces at a time, until golden — about 5 min. Drain on paper towels. Place in layers, with skin sides up, in 1 large, or 2 medium, baking pans. Start heating oven to 325°F. Pour sauce over chicken pieces. Bake, uncovered, 1½ to 1¾ hr., or until tender, basting 3 times with sauce.

To serve: Arrange chicken on individual plates or platter. Pass extra sauce. Makes 24 to 28 servings.

CHICKEN CURRY ON PARSLEY RICE

4½ to 5 qt. large pieces cooked chicken or turkey*	¾ cup all-purpose flour
1½ cups butter or margarine	Salt
	⅛ teasp. pepper
4 lb. mushrooms, sliced ¼″ thick	2 tablesp. curry powder
1⅓ cups minced onions	3 cups milk
	3 cups chicken broth
4 cups diced, pared, cored cooking apples	12 cups hot, cooked rice
	¾ cup snipped parsley

Day before: To cook chicken and prepare broth, follow directions in Simmered Chicken, p. 718, then refrigerate.

About 1½ hr. before serving: In ¾ cup butter, in large double-boiler top over direct heat, or in kettle, sauté mushrooms, about 1 lb. at a time, until browned; remove mushrooms; set aside. In another ¾ cup butter, in same double-boiler top, sauté onions and apples until tender.

Remove double-boiler top from heat; stir in flour, 4 teasp. salt, pepper, curry. Slowly stir in milk and chicken broth. Cook over boiling water, stirring, until thickened. Cook, covered, 20 min. longer.

Meanwhile, cook rice as package label directs; toss with parsley. Then add mushrooms and chicken to curry mixture; heat thoroughly.

To serve: Spoon chicken over rice. Makes 25 servings.

*You may substitute canned chicken or turkey for cooked chicken.

'TATER-DIPPED CHICKEN

8 eggs, slightly beaten	8 cups instant-mashed-potato flakes (2 8-serving pkg.)
1 cup water	
2½ tablesp. salt	1 lb. butter, margarine, or shortening
1 teasp. pepper	
50 chicken pieces	

Start heating oven to 400°F. Combine eggs, water, salt, and pepper. Dip chicken pieces in egg mixture; roll in potato flakes. Meanwhile, melt butter in 2 15″ x 11″ x 2″ baking pans. Place 1 layer of coated chicken pieces, skin side up, in each pan of melted butter. Then

bake, uncovered, for 30 min. Turn and bake 30 min. longer. Makes 50 servings.

CHICKEN, TETRAZZINI STYLE

4½ to 5 qt. large pieces cooked chicken or turkey*	3 lb. sliced mushrooms
	Chicken broth
1¼ cups butter or margarine	3 8-oz. pkg. fine noodles
¾ cup all-purpose flour	½ cup melted butter or margarine (optional)
Salt	
¼ teasp. pepper	2 tablesp. lemon juice
½ teasp. nutmeg	⅔ cup grated Parmesan cheese
2 qt. chicken broth	
1 cup heavy cream	

Day before: To cook chicken and prepare broth, follow directions in Simmered Chicken, p. 718, then refrigerate.

About 1¼ hr. before serving: In large double-boiler top over direct heat, or in kettle, melt ½ cup butter; stir in flour, 5 teasp. salt, pepper, nutmeg. Now stir in 2 qt. chicken broth, cream. Cook over boiling water, stirring occasionally, until thickened.

In ¾ cup butter, sauté mushrooms, about 1 lb. at a time, until brown. Bring to boil any remaining chicken broth plus 2 tablesp. salt and enough water to make 8 qt. liquid. Add noodles; cook until tender — 10 to 15 min.; drain; if desired, add ½ cup melted butter; season with more salt and pepper if needed. To sauce, add chicken and mushrooms; heat.

To serve: Add lemon juice to chicken mixture. Arrange noodles on dinner plates; top with chicken; sprinkle with cheese. Makes 25 servings.

*You may substitute canned chicken or turkey for cooked chicken.

NEW ENGLAND BOILED DINNER

22 to 25 lb. corned beef brisket	10 lb. carrots
1 lb. onions, sliced	12 lb. medium potatoes
15 lb. cabbage	

1. *About 5½ hr. before serving:* Wash brisket. Place in 17-qt. kettle, cutting brisket into pieces, if necessary, to fit; add onions. Cover with cold water; simmer, covered, 5½ hr., or until fork-tender.

2. Meanwhile, cut cored cabbage into wedges; peel carrots, potatoes.

3. *About 40 min. before brisket is done:* Add potatoes; simmer, covered, until meat and potatoes are tender.

4. *About 25 min. before brisket is done:* Cook carrots, till tender, in boiling salted water to cover, in 8-qt. covered kettle.

5. *About 12 min. before brisket is done:* Cook cabbage wedges, till tender, in boiling salted water to cover, in an 8-qt. uncovered kettle.

6. Serve sliced brisket with vegetables. Pass chili sauce, mustard, pickles, or horse-radish. Makes 50 servings.

♣ FOR 100 SERVINGS: Double all ingredients; prepare as above.

ALMOND CHOP SUEY

Shortening or salad oil	½ teasp. pepper
5 lb. cubed, boned lean pork loin	10 1-lb. cans Chinese vegetables
5 lb. cubed, boned lean veal shoulder	1¼ cups cornstarch
1¼ lb. onions, chopped (1 qt.)	1 cup cold water
3 to 4 bunches celery, sliced (4 qt.)	1¼ cups soy sauce
Liquid from canned Chinese vegetables	Hot fluffy rice (see Quantities to Serve Fifty Persons, p. 728)
5 teasp. salt	5 4½-oz. cans toasted almonds (2½ cups)

1. In each of 2 14-qt. kettles, heat ¼ cup shortening or salad oil; then, in shortening, quickly brown half of meat, a layer at a time, removing it after browning. (Add more shortening if needed.) After all meat is brown, in same fat, sauté onions till golden, tossing often.

2. In one of kettles, put browned meat, onions. Add celery, liquid from Chinese vegetables, plus enough water to make 3 qt. in all. Add salt, pepper. With long-handled fork, toss till well combined. Then cover; bring to boil; simmer till meats are fork-tender — about 40 min.

3. Add Chinese vegetables; mix well; bring to boil.

4. In large bowl, combine cornstarch, water, soy sauce; gradually stir into meat mixture. Cook until thickened.

5. Meanwhile, cook rice as package label directs. On each heated dinner plate, arrange 1 cup rice; top with generous ¾ cup chop suey; garnish with almonds. Pass soy sauce. Makes 50 servings.

♣ FOR 100 SERVINGS: Make 2 batches of chop-suey mixture and rice.

ITALIAN SPAGHETTI MODERNO

1 cup salad oil	1½ cups snipped parsley
6 lb. chuck, ground	
6 medium onions, sliced	1½ lb. spaghetti, broken into thirds
6 cloves garlic, minced	3 qt. tomato juice
	3 cups chili sauce
1 teasp. orégano	3 6-oz. cans sliced mushrooms
7 teasp. salt	
1½ teasp. pepper	Parmesan cheese

About 1¼ hr. before serving: In large kettle, heat oil; add beef, onions, garlic; cook until meat is browned, stirring, with two-tined fork, as little as possible so meat stays in rather large pieces. Add orégano, salt, pepper, parsley, spaghetti, tomato juice, chili sauce, and mushrooms with juice; stir gently with fork. Cook, covered, over low heat, stirring occasionally, about 45 min., or until spaghetti is done.

Serve buffet-style. Let each person help himself to Parmesan cheese. Makes 25 servings.

NOTE: If you have an electric roaster, it's so easy to make and serve this dish. Set roaster at 500°F. Make, as above, in inset pan, but do not add spaghetti until after tomato juice, chili sauce, etc., have been added and have come to a boil. Stir to blend; then reduce heat to 350°F. and cook, covered, as above.

SPAGHETTI WITH MEAT SAUCE

1 cup salad or olive oil	4 8-oz. cans tomato sauce
2 cups minced onions	4 1-lb.-4-oz. cans to-matoes (10 cups)
4 lb. chuck, ground	2 tablesp. salt
8 cloves garlic, minced	2 teasp. pepper
8 3-oz. cans sliced mushrooms	1 teasp. sugar
	6 lb. spaghetti
1 cup snipped parsley	1 lb. sharp Cheddar cheese, diced
2 cups sliced stuffed olives	2 2-oz. jars grated Parmesan cheese

Day before: In hot oil, in large kettle, simmer onions 5 min. Add beef, garlic; cook, stirring, until beef is slightly browned. Add undrained mushrooms, parsley, olives, tomato sauce. Force tomatoes through sieve; add to beef, with salt, pepper, sugar. Simmer, covered, 1 hr. Uncover; simmer 2 hr. longer, stirring occasionally. Cool; then refrigerate.

About ½ hr. before serving: In very large pot, cook spaghetti as label directs; drain. Meanwhile, heat sauce; add diced cheese; heat, stirring occasionally, till cheese is melted.

To serve: Arrange spaghetti on individual plates or platters; pour on sauce; top with grated Parmesan cheese, or pass grated cheese in small bowls. Makes 25 to 30 servings.

ROASTING SCHEDULE FOR BEEF
(beef refrigerated until roasting time)

WEIGHT	OVEN TEMPERATURE	APPROXIMATE ROASTING TIME	MEAT-THERMOMETER READING
STANDING RIBS			
4 RIBS			
(10 to 11 lb.)	325°F.	4½ hr.	140°F. *(rare)*
		5 hr.	150°F. *(medium)*
5 RIBS			
(13 to 14 lb.)	325°F.	5 hr.	140°F. *(rare)*
		5½ hr.	150°F. *(medium)*
7 RIBS			
(20 to 22 lb.)	300°F.	4¼ hr.	130°F. *(rare)*
		5 hr.	140°F. *(medium)*
ROLLED RIBS			
(11½ lb.)	300°F.	5¼ hr.	130°F. *(rare)*
		6 hr.	140°F. *(medium)*
		6½ hr.	150°F. *(well done)*

ROASTS FOR A CROWD

If you're serving roast lamb, pork, veal, or turkey, or baked ham, be sure all roasts are approximately the same weight, so that they'll be done at the same time. Always follow carefully our roasting directions and times. (See Index.)

If you're roasting extra-large standing or rolled ribs of beef, follow roasting directions on p. 175, but use roasting schedule at left. Use shallow open pans; add no water; do not baste. Don't crowd pans. Leave 2″ to 3″ between roasts. Plan roasting time so roasts can be taken from oven 30 to 40 min. before serving time; then make gravy. Start carving about 20 min. before serving; stack 10 to 12 portions in pile in heated shallow pan; place in warm oven with heat turned off.

Because roasting time periods can only be approximate, always use a roast-meat thermometer; insert thermometer into largest roast being cooked.

SCALLOPED POTATOES

9 qt. thinly sliced, pared potatoes
¾ cup all-purpose flour
2¼ cups butter or margarine
4 tablesp. salt
1½ teasp. pepper
3 qt. hot milk

Start heating oven to 325°F. Boil potatoes 2 min., drain. Arrange potatoes in layers in baking pans, sprinkling flour over each layer; fill pans ⅔ full. Combine butter, salt, pepper, and milk; stir until blended. Pour mixture over potatoes in pans; cover. Bake 1½ hr., or until done. Remove covers. Continue to bake till brown — about 20 min. Makes 50 servings of about ½ cup each.

CANDIED SWEET POTATOES

16 lb. sweet potatoes, cooked, peeled
¼ cup butter or margarine
2½ lb. brown sugar
1 tablesp. salt
½ cup pineapple juice

Start heating oven to 350°F. Slice potatoes lengthwise into ¾″ slices. Arrange in single layer in baking pans. Melt butter in large saucepan. Stir in sugar, salt, juice. Cook over low heat, while stirring, until sugar dissolves and syrup is formed. Pour over potatoes. Bake 45 min., basting occasionally. Serve hot. Makes 50 portions.

NOTE: Orange juice may be substituted for the pineapple juice.

LIKABLE SALADS

CHICKEN SALAD DE LUXE

3 qt. plus 1 to 3 cups large pieces cooked chicken or turkey*	2 tablesp. butter or margarine
1 bunch scallions, snipped (1 cup); or 1 cup finely minced onions	3 cups cooked salad dressing or mayonnaise
About 2 bunches celery with tops, sliced (6 cups)	½ cup wine vinegar
1 doz. eggs	1½ cups milk or chicken broth
1½ cups coarsely chopped walnuts	2 teasp. salt
	¼ teasp. pepper
	2 heads lettuce
	½ bunch water cress

Day before: To cook chicken, follow directions in Simmered Chicken, p. 718; then refrigerate. Prepare scallions. Prepare celery (slice through bunch on angle, crosswise, without separating stalks; then wash in strainer). Simmer eggs, in water to cover, 20 min.; cool in running cold water; shell; chop. Refrigerate all.

At least 2½ hr. before serving: Sauté nuts in butter until crisp and golden — 5 min. Drain on paper towels; cool. Combine salad dressing, vinegar, milk, salt, pepper. Toss with chicken meat, eggs, nuts, scallions, celery. Refrigerate until serving time.

To serve: Arrange salad on beds of lettuce; garnish with water cress. Makes 25 servings.

*You may substitute canned chicken or turkey for cooked chicken.

SUMMERTIME TUNA SALAD

9 6½- or 7-oz. cans tuna (9 cups)	all) or diced celery
6 cups raw spinach leaves	1½ teasp. salt
	¾ teasp. pepper
1½ cups snipped scallions (tops and	2 cups French dressing
	6 heads lettuce

Early in day: If using solid-pack tuna, drain well; then break into pieces. Wash spinach; remove stems; drain well; reserve about 1 cup tiny crisp leaves to use as garnish. Toss tuna with 5 cups spinach, rest of ingredients except lettuce. Refrigerate. Clean lettuce and separate leaves; drain. Refrigerate until needed.

About ½ hr. before serving: Arrange salad in lettuce cups on large platters. Garnish with reserved spinach leaves. Makes 25 servings.

ELLEN KERN'S POTATO SALAD

7 lb. potatoes, unpared	sliced (4 cups)
1 big bunch parsley, snipped (3 cups)	1 qt. cooked salad dressing
½ cup snipped chives	½ cup vinegar
1 big bunch celery,	2 tablesp. salt
	1 teasp. pepper

About 8 hr. before serving: Start boiling potatoes. Prepare parsley and chives (snip onto separate sheets of wax paper). Prepare celery; set aside in bowl. Mix salad dressing with vinegar. When potatoes are just tender, peel.

Now slice layer of hot potatoes into large bowl or kettle (about 8 qt.); sprinkle with some of salt and pepper; then add, in order, thin layers of parsley, chives, celery, and salad-dressing mixture. Repeat all layers, starting with potatoes, salt, and pepper; continue until all are used. Then, with clean hands, quickly and lightly turn salad upside down in bowl (about 2 turns). Refrigerate 5 to 6 hr. Makes 20 servings.

GREEN-PEPPER COLESLAW

12 lb. trimmed crisp cabbage (4½ medium, or 4 large, heads)	sugar
	3 tablesp. salt
	1½ teasp. pepper
12 green peppers	1½ teasp. paprika
3 cups vinegar	3 cups cooked salad dressing or mayonnaise
3 cups granulated	

Several hr. before serving: Chop or shred cabbage very fine. Cut green peppers into fine strips. Refrigerate both.

About ½ hr. before serving: Mix vinegar, sugar, salt, pepper, paprika; add to cabbage; let stand 15 min.; then drain. Mix green peppers with cabbage; then add salad dressing, tossing lightly.

Serve as relish in large bowl; or garnish with lettuce and serve as individual salads. Makes 50 servings.

TOMATO-OLIVE ASPIC

1 46-oz. can tomato juice (5¾ cups)	flavor gelatin
Dash pepper	2¼ cups sliced stuffed olives
2 bay leaves	2 heads lettuce
1 small onion, minced	1 pt. cooked salad dressing
3 3-oz. pkg. lemon-	

At least 6 hr. ahead: Simmer 2 cups tomato

juice with pepper, bay leaves, onion; strain. Pour over gelatin, stirring until dissolved. Add rest of tomato juice. Refrigerate till slightly thickened. Add olives. Pour into 2 9" x 5" x 3" loaf pans. Refrigerate until set.

To serve: Unmold salads; cut each into 7 slices; then halve each slice crosswise. Serve each slice in lettuce cup, garnished with 1 tablesp. dressing. Makes about 25 servings.

TOSSED VEGETABLE SALAD

2¼ qt. cooked peas (5 10-oz. pkg. frozen, or 5 1-lb.-4-oz. cans)	¼ cup minced onion
	1 tablesp. salt
	1 teasp. pepper
	½ cup vinegar
2 qt. diced, cooked carrots	1 qt. sliced celery
	About 6 heads lettuce
1½ qt. cooked green beans, in ½" pieces (3 lb. fresh, 3 14-oz. pkg. frozen, or 3 1-lb.- 4-oz. cans)	3 cups salad dressing
	1 cup pimento or green pepper, cut in strips

One hour before serving: Toss peas with carrots, green beans, onion, salt, pepper, and vinegar, then chill. Just before serving, add celery. Arrange cleaned lettuce on individual salad plates; top each with ½ cup of the pea mixture. Top with salad dressing and strips of pimento or green pepper. Makes 50 ½-cup portions.

CUCUMBER MOLD

3 3-oz. pkg. lemon-flavor gelatin	¾ cup mayonnaise or salad dressing
1 tablesp. salt	3 cups drained, pared, finely chopped cucumber
2 cups boiling water	
⅓ cup vinegar	
1 tablesp. grated onion	2 cucumbers, fluted, sliced
1½ pt. commercial sour cream	Water cress

Early on the day:

1. Put gelatin and salt in large bowl; pour on boiling water, stirring until gelatin is completely dissolved.

2. Now stir in vinegar and onion; refrigerate until mixture has consistency of unbeaten egg white. Then, with hand beater, beat in sour cream and mayonnaise; stir in finely chopped cucumber. Pour into 2½-qt. tube mold; refrigerate 3 hr., or till firm.

At serving time:

1. Quickly dip mold in and out of hot water up to ½" of top. Invert serving plate on top of mold; invert both; gently shake cucumber mold till it slips out.

2. Arrange fluted, sliced cucumbers around base of mold, and water cress in top center.

3. Nice served in wedges, with chilled cooked frozen Alaskan-crab legs or drained, thawed frozen or canned King-crab meat on salad greens — and assorted hot breads. Makes 10 to 12 servings.

JELLIED PEAR-AND-CHEESE SALAD

4½ qt. pear juice plus water	strawberry-flavor gelatin
6 1-lb.-13-oz. cans small pear halves (50)	1¾ lb. cream or cottage cheese
8 3-oz. or 4 6-oz. pkg.	Salad greens

At least 2 hr. before serving, or day before: Drain juice from pear halves; measure and add water to make 4½ qt. Heat. Pour over gelatin, and stir until dissolved. Chill until slightly thickened. Pour thin layer of slightly thickened gelatin over bottom of shallow pans (use 6 8" x 8" x 2" pans, or enough pans to obtain 50 portions, each portion about 2½" square). Mash cheese and season with salt if necessary. Fill centers of 50 pear halves with cheese and arrange, stuffed side down, on gelatin layer on bottoms of pans. Pour rest of slightly thickened gelatin mixture over pears. Chill until firm. To serve, unmold on large plates or trays; cut in portions, allowing 1 pear to each; then place on bed of lettuce or other greens, cheese side up. Garnish with Ginger Dressing, below. Makes 50 individual salads.

FRENCH DRESSING

1 cup lemon juice	Dash cayenne
½ cup sugar	2 cloves garlic, thinly sliced
2 tablesp. salt	
1 tablesp. paprika	3 cups salad oil

Combine all ingredients except salad oil. Let stand ½ hr. Strain out garlic. Add oil slowly, beating vigorously. Store in jar. Beat or shake well before using. Makes about 1 qt. — enough for 50 servings.

BLUE-CHEESE DRESSING: Add ½ lb. Danish blue cheese, crumbled, to French Dressing.

GINGER DRESSING: Add 1 cup cut-up or ground candied ginger to French Dressing.

FRUIT-AND-NUT MOLD

3 1-lb.-13-oz. cans
  sliced peaches
8 3-oz. or 4 6-oz. pkg.
  lemon-flavor gelatin

¾ qt. sliced bananas
1 cup broken nut-
  meats
1 qt. heavy cream

Early in day or day before: Drain juice from sliced peaches; measure juice and add water to make 4 qt.; heat, pour over gelatin, and stir until dissolved. Chill until slightly thickened; then pour thin layer over bottoms of shallow pans (use 6 8″ x 8″ x 2″ pans, or enough pans to obtain 50 portions, each portion about 2½″ square). Lay peach slices over gelatin; arrange bananas over peaches. Pour rest of gelatin over fruit, and sprinkle nuts on top. Refrigerate until set. Cut into squares for serving. Garnish with cream, whipped. Sprinkle with additional nuts, if desired. Makes 50 portions.

SANDWICHES FOR 50
(see Production-Line Techniques, p. 516)

Choose a Bread and Spread:

Thin sliced (about 1 lb.) — 4 to 5 loaves
Regular sliced (about 1 lb.) — 6 to 7 loaves
Butter or margarine — 1½ lb.
Mayonnaise (as spread for bread) — 1 qt.

Choose a Filling:

PINEAPPLE-HAM: Mix 2 lb. coarsely ground cooked ham, 2 lb. soft cream cheese, 2 1-lb.-4-oz. cans crushed pineapple, drained.

HAM SALAD: Mix 3 lb. coarsely ground cooked ham, 2 cups minced celery, 1 cup minced green peppers, 1½ cups pickle relish, 2 cups mayonnaise, 2 tablesp. Worcestershire.

HAM AND CHEESE: Mix 1½ lb. coarsely ground cooked ham, 1½ lb. coarsely grated process Cheddar cheese, 1 cup undiluted evaporated milk, 1½ cups pickle relish, 2 teasp. dry mustard, 1 teasp. salt, ¼ teasp. pepper.

CHICKEN SALAD: Mix about 8 cups diced cooked chicken (3 4-lb. stewing chickens or 2 32-oz. cans boned chicken), 3 cups diced celery, 2 to 3 cups mayonnaise.

TUNA SALAD: Substitute 8 6½- or 7-oz. cans tuna (8 cups) for chicken in Chicken Salad, above.

EGG SALAD: Substitute 40 chopped hard-cooked eggs for chicken in Chicken Salad, at left.

SLICED TURKEY OR HAM, TOMATO, AND BACON: Use 1 30-lb., or 2 18-lb., turkeys or 6 to 8 lb. canned ham, sliced; 3 heads lettuce; 6 to 7 lb. tomatoes, sliced; 5 to 6 lb. crisp cooked bacon. For each sandwich, arrange, in layers, between 2 bread slices.

CREAM CHEESE: Mix 4 lb. soft cream cheese with one of these:
2 lb. crumbled crisp bacon
3½ cups chopped stuffed olives
2 cups chopped nuts

PEANUT BUTTER: Mix 3 lb. peanut butter with 2 lb. crumbled crisp bacon or 1 qt. minced cooked ham.

CREAM CHEESE OR PEANUT BUTTER AND JELLY: Use 4 lb. soft cream cheese or 3 lb. peanut butter and 1 qt. jelly or preserves.

SLICED MEAT — COLD OR HOT: To serve cold sandwiches, use 3 heads lettuce and one of the following meats. To serve hot sandwiches, substitute 7 qt. gravy for lettuce.

Ready-cooked meats (salami, liverwurst, etc.)	7 to 9 lb.
Roast beef, rolled rib (weight, bone in)	20 to 25 lb.
Roast leg of lamb	25 lb.
Roast veal	20 to 25 lb.
Smoked tongue	20 lb.
Roast turkey (ready-to-cook weight)	1 30-lb. bird, or 2 18-lb. birds

PERFECT ENDINGS

DEEP-DISH APPLE PIE

18 lb. apples, sliced,
  pared (10 qt.)
1½ cups water
1 teasp. salt
2½ teasp. cinnamon
1½ teasp. nutmeg

2¾ lb. granulated
  sugar (1½ qt.)
⅓ cup butter or mar-
  garine
5 pkg. piecrust mix

Start heating oven to 400°F. Arrange sliced apples in shallow baking pans or casseroles. Pour water over apples. Mix 1 teasp. salt with cinnamon, nutmeg, and sugar; sprinkle evenly over apples. Dot with butter.

Roll out piecrusts ⅛″ thick on slightly floured board. Cut openings for escape of steam. Lay over apples, pressing on to edges of pans. Trim excess pastry from edges. Bake 30 to 40 min., or until apples are soft and pies slightly brown. Cut into 50 squares. Garnish with whipped cream, ice cream, or hard sauce. Makes 50 portions.

NOTE: For homemade piecrust, use 1¼ qt. sifted all-purpose flour, 1 teasp. salt, 3⅓ cups shortening, and about ⅓ cup cold water. See The All-Important Pastry, p. 584.

CHERRY CHIFFON PIE

9 baked 9″ pie shells, pp. 584–587
3 qt. juice (from canned sour red cherries) plus water
9 3-oz., or 4 6-oz. plus 1 3-oz., pkg. cherry-flavor gelatin
1½ qt. drained, canned pitted sour red cherries, chopped
18 egg whites
1½ cups granulated sugar

Heat cherry juice and water. Add cherry gelatin and stir until dissolved; add cherries. Refrigerate until cold and syrupy. Beat egg whites until stiff; add sugar gradually, while continuing to beat until stiff peaks are formed. Fold into thickened gelatin mixture. Turn into baked pie shells. Refrigerate until firm. Garnish with sweetened whipped cream, if desired. Cut each pie into 6 pieces. Makes 54 servings.

APPLE BROWN BETTY

4 qt. fresh bread crumbs (16 cups)
2 cups melted butter or margarine
18 lb. apples, pared, sliced (12 qt.)
4 cups granulated sugar, or brown
sugar, packed
4 teasp. nutmeg
2 teasp. cinnamon
½ cup grated lemon rind
¾ cup lemon juice
4 cups water

Start heating oven to 350°F. Mix bread crumbs and melted butter. Arrange ⅓ of this mixture in 2 greased 16″ x 9″ x 2½″ baking pans. Cover with half of sliced apples. Combine sugar, nutmeg, cinnamon, and lemon rind; sprinkle half over apples. Cover with ⅓ crumbs. Add rest of apples, then rest of sugar mixture. Top with rest of crumbs, then pour combined lemon juice and water over all. Bake 1 hr.

Serve warm with Hard Sauce, below. Makes 50 servings.

HARD SAUCE

½ lb. butter or margarine
2 tablesp. boiling water
3 cups plus 5 tablesp. confectioners' sugar
1 tablesp. lemon extract

Cream butter; add boiling water, and stir until light. Gradually add remaining ingredients. Beat until fluffy. Refrigerate until ready to serve. Makes 50 servings.

BEVERAGES, OF COURSE

STEEPED COFFEE

½ lb. drip-grind coffee (2 cups plus 6 tablesp.)
4¼ qt. boiling water

Tie coffee loosely, bag-fashion, in fine cheese-cloth or muslin. Drop into boiling water in kettle. Cover; turn heat very low; let steep (stand) 15 min., moving bag around in kettle often. Then remove bag. Serve as much coffee as is needed. Keep remaining coffee hot, *but not boiling*, over low heat. Makes 25 average coffee-cup-size servings.

P.S. Coffee for a crowd can be made easily and quickly with instant coffee. Follow label directions. Let instant coffee brew, then stand over low heat, for 4 to 5 min.

HOT COCOA FOR A CROWD

1 to 1¼ cups cocoa
1 cup granulated sugar
¾ teasp. salt
1½ qt. water
4 qt. milk
1 tablesp. vanilla extract

In saucepan, blend cocoa, sugar, salt; stir in water slowly until smooth; boil 10 min. Meanwhile, scald milk in large double boiler. Stir in cocoa mixture. Let stand, covered, over low heat ½ hr. to "mellow." Add vanilla. Serve with dash of cinnamon or whipped cream. Makes 25 servings.

✤ FOR 50: Double ingredients.

PARTY ICED TEA

1½ qt. freshly drawn   Ice
    cold water   Sugar
¼-lb. pkg. loose tea   Lemon
5 qt. cold water (not
    iced)

In a saucepan, bring 1½ qt. water to a full rolling boil. Remove from heat; while the water is still bubbling, immediately add the tea, all at one time. Stir to immerse leaves. Brew 5 min.

Strain into 5 qt. cold water (not iced). Serve in ice-filled glasses with sugar and lemon, if desired. Makes 30 to 35 servings.

P.S. Tea for a crowd can be made quickly, without boiling and cooling, with instant tea. Follow label directions.

FROM THE PUNCH BOWL

Turn to p. 686 for punches for small or large groups.

QUANTITIES TO SERVE FIFTY PERSONS

(Note: For 25 persons, divide amount indicated by 2. For 100 persons, multiply by 2.)

FOOD AS PURCHASED	APPROXIMATE AMOUNT FOR 50 SERVINGS	SIZE OF EACH SERVING
BEVERAGES AND DRINKS		
Coffee, instant	1½ small jars	¾ cup
Coffee, regular	1¼ lb.	¾ cup
Cream for coffee	1 qt. and ½ pt.	1½ tablesp.
Fruit-juice concentrates, frozen	9 6-oz. cans or 5 12-oz. cans	½ cup
Fruit or tomato juice, canned	4 46-oz. cans	½ cup
Half-and-half cream	1 qt. and 1 pt.	2 tablesp.
Lemon for tea	5 large	1 thin slice
Lemonade concentrate, frozen	13 6-oz. cans	8 oz.
Punch	2 gal.	⅔ cup
Sugar, lump	1⅛ lb.	2 lumps
Tea	¼ lb.	¾ cup
MEAT, POULTRY, FISH		
Bacon	6 lb.	2 slices
Beef, rolled rib roast	25 lb. before boning	3 oz. cooked
Beef, standing rib roast	35 lb.	4 oz. cooked
Chicken, to roast	35 to 40 lb.	¾ lb.
Chicken, stewing, for cut-up, cooked chicken	20 to 25 lb.	
Frankfurters	100	2
Fish fillets, frozen	13 1-lb. pkg.	¼ lb.
Ham, canned, boned	1 14-lb. can	¼ lb.
Ham, bone in, to bake	22 to 25 lb.	3 oz. cooked
Hamburgers	12½ to 15 lb.	2½ to 3½ oz. cooked
Lamb, leg to roast	25 lb.	3 to 4 oz. cooked
Meat, chopped, for meat loaf	12 lb.	2 to 3 oz. cooked
Oysters, for scalloped oysters	6 qt.	½ cup cooked
Oysters, for stew	6 qt.	2 cups
Pork, chops (3 to 1 lb.)	17 lb.	1 chop, ¾" thick
Pork, loin to roast	25 lb.	4 to 5 oz. cooked

QUANTITIES TO SERVE FIFTY PERSONS, *(continued)*

(Note: For 25 persons, divide amount indicated by 2. For 100 persons, multiply by 2.)

FOOD AS PURCHASED	APPROXIMATE AMOUNT FOR 50 SERVINGS	SIZE OF EACH SERVING
MEAT, POULTRY, FISH		
Sausage, bulk or links	12½ lb.	2 to 3 oz. cooked
Turkey, for dishes using cut-up, cooked turkey	16 lb.	
Turkey, to roast, to slice	35 to 40 lb.	½ to ⅔ lb.
*Precooked boneless turkey roll	6½ lb. solid pack for cold slices	2 oz.
	9-lb. roll in broth for hot dishes	2 oz.
Uncooked boneless turkey roll	2 4½- to 5-lb. rolls	2 oz.
VEGETABLES		
Any canned vegetable	14 1-lb. cans; or 11 1-lb.-4-oz. cans; or 2 6½- to 7-lb.-5-oz. cans	½ cup
Asparagus spears, canned (medium-sized)	11 1-lb.-4-oz. cans	4 to 6 spears
Asparagus, market fresh	20 lb.	4 or 5 stalks
Cabbage (in eighths)	15 lb.	
Carrots	16 lb. (tops off)	⅓ lb.
Cauliflower	15 lb. (flowerets only)	¼ lb.
Corn on the cob	50 ears	1 ear
Frozen vegetables	13 to 17 pkg. (10 to 12 oz. each) or 7 to 8 16- to 24-oz. size	About ½ cup
Green beans (or wax), market fresh	12½ lb.	¼ lb.
Onions, for creaming	15 lb.	½ cup (3 or 4)
Potatoes, for creaming	12½ to 15 lb.	½ cup
Potatoes, frozen French fries	16 9-oz. pkg. or 8 16-oz. size	
Potatoes, mashed	25 lb., or 2 family-size and 1 regular pkg. instant mashed potatoes	½ cup
Potatoes, to scallop	12½ lb., or 10 pkg. scalloped-potato mix	½ cup
Potatoes, sweet, glazed	25 lb.	1 potato
RELISHES AND SALADS		
Cabbage, for slaw	12 to 15 lb.	⅓ cup
Catchup	3 14-oz. or 2 20-oz. bottles	1 tablesp.
Chicken salad	6¼ qt.	½ cup
Chili sauce	4 to 5 12-oz. bottles	1 tablesp.
Cranberry sauce, jellied	6 1-lb. cans	½″ slice

Order in advance from meatman or from local hotel and restaurant supplier.

QUANTITIES TO SERVE FIFTY PERSONS, *(continued)*

(Note: For 25 persons, divide amount indicated by 2. For 100 persons, multiply by 2.)

FOOD AS PURCHASED	APPROXIMATE AMOUNT FOR 50 SERVINGS	SIZE OF EACH SERVING
RELISHES AND SALADS		
French dressing	1 to 1½ qt.	1½ to 2 tablesp.
Fruit salad	9 qt.	¾ cup
Lettuce, for lettuce hearts	12 medium heads	⅕ head
Lettuce, leaf, for salad	6 heads	2 or 3 leaves
Mayonnaise or salad dressing	1 qt.	1 tablesp.
Olives	2 qt.	2 olives
Pears, for salad	7 1-lb.-13-oz. cans	1 pear half
Pickles	2 qt.	2 small pickles
Potato salad	6¼ qt.	½ cup
Salmon, for salad	8 1-lb. cans	⅓ cup salad
Tuna, for salad	16 6½- or 7-oz. cans	⅓ cup salad
Tomatoes, for salad	30 medium	3 slices
SANDWICHES		
Beef, roast, sliced	4 lb. 12 oz.	1 slice
Bread, sandwich	2 3-lb. loaves	2 slices
Ham, baked, sliced	4 lb. 12 oz.	1 slice
Swiss cheese, sliced	3 lb. 2 oz.	1 slice
MISCELLANEOUS		
Apples, cooking, for sauce	25 lb.	½ cup
Applesauce, canned	14 1-lb.-4-oz. cans	½ cup
Brown bread, canned	8 11-oz. cans	1 slice, ½″ thick
Bread (about 1-lb. loaf)	5 loaves	1½ slices
Butter or margarine	1 to 1¼ lb.	1 pat, ½″ thick
Cling-peach halves, canned	7 1-lb.-13-oz. cans	1 peach half
Crackers	1 lb.	2 crackers
Cream, heavy, to top desserts	1 qt.	1 rounded tablesp., whipped
Fruits, frozen, to top ice cream	13 to 17 pkg. (10 to 12 oz.)	¼ to ⅓ cup
Ice cream, brick or bulk	2 to 2½ gal.	about ⅙ qt.
Jelly	8 8-oz. glasses	about 1 tablesp.
Noodles	8 6-oz. pkg.	½ cup, cooked
Pies	9 pies	⅙ pie
Rice, packaged precooked	6 15-oz. pkg.	¾ cup, cooked
Rice, regular white	3 qt. 1 cup	¾ cup, cooked
Rolls or biscuits	6½ doz.	1½
Soup, canned, condensed	20 10½-oz. cans	1 cup
Soup, mix	10 env.	about ¾ cup

Other Sources of Quantity Recipes

For further recipe and menu helps when cooking for a crowd, we suggest that you write to the Consumer Service Department of any of the following food companies:

Campbell Soup Company, 375 Memorial Drive, Camden 1, New Jersey

American Institute of Baking, 400 East Ontario Street, Chicago 11, Illinois

Kraft Cuisine Service, 500 Peshtigo Court, Chicago 90, Illinois

National Live Stock and Meat Board, 407 South Dearborn Street, Chicago 5, Illinois

National Canners Association, 1133 20th Street, N. W., Washington 6, D.C.

Accent International, Skokie, Illinois

Armour & Company, P. O. Box 9222, Chicago 90, Illinois

The Quaker Oats Company, Merchandise Mart Plaza, Chicago 54, Illinois

H. J. Heinz Company, Pittsburgh 30, Pennsylvania

THE BOUNTIFUL BARBECUE

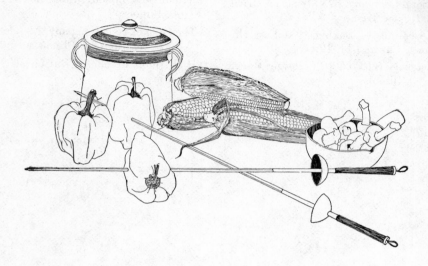

The best place in the world to entertain these days is outdoors. Whether you cook in your own back yard or away from home, charcoal cooking is fun. And it's a wonderful solution for hot weather family meals.

Things to Remember

1. *Choose a menu to suit the grill's space.* Plan meal so the first grilling feeds everyone. Try out your menu on the family before inviting guests.
2. *Take meat out of the refrigerator* not more than 1 hr. before grilling. Trim, leaving a minimum of fat, to avoid fat's flaming.
3. *Wrap food* in 2 thicknesses general household foil or 1 thickness heavy-duty foil, when grilling food in foil.
4. *Provide table space near grill* for board on which chef can carve meat.
5. *Time contributions from the kitchen* so they're ready when the grilled food is done.
6. *Serve some help-yourself appetizers* so the chef can carry on unmolested.

7. *Have steel-wool soap pads handy.* They make scouring picnic pots and grills easy.

For Safety's Sake
1. *Never heat canned food in unopened can.* Can may burst and cause serious burns.
2. *If you are going any distance, invest in some kind of insulated container.* Fill it with ice if directed to do so. In it, carry all perishables — cream-filled cakes and pies, cream puffs, éclairs, meats, salads, sandwiches, etc.

HORS D'OEUVRES FROM THE GRILL

Form a shallow oblong pan from foil, turning up edges all around and mitering corners. Place on grill over fire, puncturing it in several places. Use to hold shrimp dipped in garlic butter, bite-size sandwiches filled with deviled ham or other mixture, cocktail sausages wrapped in bacon, pickled onions, etc., and let them heat up for serving.

MEATS—ALL KINDS

BIG STEAKS

To Buy: Buy steak at least 1" thick — sirloin, porterhouse, or T-bone if you like 1 large steak, club or rib if you prefer individual steaks. (For details see p. 177.) Allow ½ to 1 lb. or more per serving.

Preliminaries: Take steak out of refrigerator not more than 1 hr. before grilling. Trim, leaving minimum of fat. Gash edges.

Special Send-Offs: Rub with garlic. Or rub with mixture of 1 tablesp. flour, 1 tablesp. prepared mustard, ⅛ teasp. pepper, ¼ teasp. salt. Or spread with prepared mustard.

To Grill: Place on greased grill or in folding wire broiler. Grill 3" to 5" from glowing coals (5" for thick or well-done steak), turning at least once with tongs. To test doneness, cut near bone and note color.

To Serve: See Seasoning Touches, p. 178.

SALT-GRILLED SIRLOIN STEAK

Buy 2"- or 3"-thick sirloin steak. Moisten salt with water to form stiff paste. Spread ½"-thick layer on top of steak. Cover with 2 dampened paper towels. Place in folding wire broiler, with paper side down. Repeat salting, papering, on other side. Grill 5" from glowing coals, turning at least once. To test doneness, cut near bone and note color. When steak is done, lift off salt and paper.

SALT-GRILLED STEAK — NAVIN: While steak grills, as above, melt ½ cup butter or margarine with 1 teasp. dry mustard, ¼ teasp. dried marjoram, ¼ teasp. dried tarragon, ¼ teasp. garlic powder, and 1 tablesp. catchup. Use for dunking steak slices before serving.

"DOWN UNDER" BUCKET STEAKS

6 to 12 large, double-spread sheets of newspaper (not colored or rotogravure)	1 long-handled folding wire grill
	1 galvanized bucket, 10" high, 12" at top
4 10-oz. top sirloin steaks, 1" thick, seasoned	Soft Danish blue cheese (optional)

About 20 min. before serving: Crumple each sheet of newspaper into a tight enough ball to keep ball shape. Arrange steaks in center of folding grill. Drop a paper ball into bucket; light it; then lay grill across top of bucket. When paper has almost burned, lift off grill; drop in next ball; turn grill over; replace it. Repeat this turning and burning of balls, using about 6 balls for medium rare steak. Serve hot steaks, spread with mashed Danish blue cheese. Makes 4 servings.

CHARCOAL-GRILLED KING STEAK

Buy sirloin steak at least 2½" thick (9 lb. serves 8). Let stand 1 hr. in ⅓ cup salad oil mixed with 3 cloves garlic, minced. Then place steak in folding wire broiler. Sprinkle with salt, pepper; grill over glowing coals 6 to 10 min. — 1 min. at a time on each side. Then remove steak from wire broiler and place right on glowing coals till charred — at least 6 min. per side.

Slice steak ¾" thick (meat will look raw). Meanwhile, in roasting pan, heat 1 or 2 cups water with 1 cup butter or margarine. Place steak slices in pan. Simmer 30 sec. (for rare meat, 15 sec.) per side, not longer. Lift out; serve as is or in buns.

FILET OF BEEF AFLAME

4- to 6-lb. whole beef tenderloin	Pepper
Salt	¼ cup cognac

Meat from a lower grade of beef will have less fat and grill better. Have meatman roll it as for rolled rib roast, but without added fat.

About 2½ hr. before serving: Start fire. Rub meat with salt and pepper; adjust it on spit and insert barbecue thermometer as manufacturer directs. Over coals, with drip pan in place, start spit revolving. (If 8" from coals, filet takes about 1½ hr. to cook rare — 140°F. on thermometer.) When filet is done, place it, still on spit, on a heatproof platter (or copper or aluminum tray) on table. In small pan, warm cognac slightly; carefully light with a match. Stand an elbow's length away and pour it, flaming, over beef. When flame dies down, remove spit, slice meat. Makes 8 to 10 servings.

GEOFF'S BARBECUED CHUCK ROAST

2½ lb. chuck roast, 2″ thick	¼ cup brown sugar, packed
Instant meat tenderizer, p. 101	1 tablesp. lemon juice
	¼ cup bourbon
1 5-oz. bottle soy sauce	1 teasp. Worcestershire
	1½ cups water

Early in day: Sprinkle chuck with meat tenderizer, as label directs. In 12″ x 8″ x 2″ baking dish, blend soy sauce with rest of ingredients; refrigerate chuck in this sauce for at least 6 hr., turning once.

About 2 hr. before serving: Start fire. Grill chuck about 5″ from hot coals, for 30 min. on each side, or to desired rareness, often spooning on marinade.

To serve: Don't slice meat; rather, divide it into individual servings. Makes 4 servings.

LITTLE STEAKS

MINUTE STEAKS: In a little hot fat, in large skillet, sauté minute steaks (¼″ thick) about 1 or 2 min. on each side. Serve with Seasoning Touches, p. 178.

GRILLED CUBE STEAKS: Buy ⅓″-thick top-quality sirloin, round, or chuck steak. Have it scored. Or buy frozen cube steaks. Let stand 15 min. in barbecue sauce or in ½ cup soy sauce mixed with 1 minced clove garlic; or sprinkle with brandy. Grill 15 to 20 min.; or let guests cook their own on long forks or pointed green sticks.

STEAK SANDWICHES: Serve grilled minute or cube steaks or steak slices in toasted rolls or on toast, with thin onion slices. Or grill frozen sandwich steaks.

LONDON BROIL: See p. 182.

SPECIAL BARBECUED STEAKS: Trim off fat, then gash edges of 4 individual club, boneless loin, or rib steaks, 1½″ thick. Place steaks on greased grill, about 3″ from hot coals. Brush generously with bottled barbecue sauce or French dressing. (Or try spreading steaks with ½ cup crumbled Roquefort cheese mixed with ¼ cup soft butter or margarine and a few drops of Worcestershire.) Grill steaks, turning

and brushing at least once, 18 min. for rare, or until of desired doneness.

SHORT RIBS OONA LOA

3 lb. lean beef short ribs, cut in 6 pieces	¼ cup water
	¼ cup soy sauce
Instant seasoned meat tenderizer, p. 101	1½ teasp. ground ginger
1 1-lb.-4-oz. can pineapple slices	1 tablesp. brown sugar
	¼ cup honey

Night before: Sprinkle ribs evenly with seasoned meat tenderizer (½ teasp. per lb. of meat); then, with kitchen fork, generously pierce ribs on all sides. In 12″ x 8″ x 2″ baking dish, arrange ribs; cover them loosely; refrigerate.

On the day: In bowl, combine juice drained from pineapple slices, water, soy sauce, ground ginger, brown sugar, and honey; pour over ribs; refrigerate 4 to 5 hr., turning once.

About 1½ hr. before serving: Start fire. Drain short ribs; grill them 3″ above hot coals, about 15 min. Then turn ribs; spoon on some sauce; grill second side till browned. A few minutes before meat is done, brush pineapple slices with sauce; grill till golden.

To serve: Spoon leftover sauce over ribs. Makes 6 servings.

BARBECUED FLAPJACKS

Butter or margarine	1½ teasp. salt
¼ cup minced onion	¼ teasp. pepper
1 tablesp. bottled thick meat sauce	¼ teasp. dried savory
	¼ teasp. dried thyme
½ teasp. Worcestershire	1 cup packaged pancake mix
1 cup catchup	¼ cup grated Parmesan cheese
1½ lb. chuck, ground	

In advance: In 3 tablesp. butter, in small pan, sauté onions till golden; add meat sauce, Worcestershire, catchup; refrigerate. Lightly toss chuck with salt, pepper, savory, and thyme; form into 6 4″ patties; refrigerate.

About 1¼ hr. before serving: Start fire. Start heating sauce. On foil, 3″ from coal, grill burgers to guests' taste. Meanwhile, on heated electric griddle or skillet, cook 9 pancakes, prepared as label directs, sprinkling 1½ teasp. cheese on each, before turning.

To serve: On each plate, place a pancake; top with a burger, a big pat of butter, and a little sauce; repeat layers; then top all with a third pancake and more sauce. Makes 3 servings.

CHILI-FRANK BURGERS

1 15½-oz. can chili con carne with beans	½ cup grated sharp Cheddar cheese
½ cup canned tomato juice	2 lb. chuck, ground
	¼ cup minced onion
1 tablesp. vinegar	2 teasp. salt
1 teasp. brown sugar	½ teasp. pepper
½ teasp. dry mustard	½ teasp. monosodium glutamate
½ teasp. chili powder	4 franks, cut into thirds

Early in day: Combine chili, tomato juice, vinegar, brown sugar, mustard, chili powder, and cheese. Lightly toss together chuck, onion, salt, pepper, and monosodium glutamate; divide this mixture into 12 portions; mold each around a piece of frank, tapering ends. Refrigerate all.

About 1 hr. before serving: Start fire. About 3″ above hot coals, start heating chili topping; grill burgers rare, about 8 min., turning once. Serve each guest a burger with chili topping. Makes 12.

BARBECUED SPARERIBS

Cut 4 lb. spareribs into 2 or 3 rib portions. Pressure-cook (half at a time) in 1 cup water at 15 lb. pressure 20 min., or as manufacturer directs. Then grill over glowing coals, turning and basting with Bert's Superb Barbecue Sauce, p. 531, until deep brown — about 10 min. Makes 5 or 6 servings.

HEAVENLY HAMBURGERS

Place Our Best-Ever Hamburgers, pp. 190–191, in folding wire broiler; grill over glowing coals 4 to 5 min. on each side, or till done as desired.

Or form a shallow foil pan and place on grill over fire. Broil hamburgers, hot dogs, fish, etc. (The food will not fall through the grate!)

HOT FRANKS

GRILLED: Grill franks on green sticks or in frank roaster, over glowing coals till brown.

SAUTEED: In hot butter or margarine (with a little barbecue sauce or plain, herb, or horse-radish-flavored prepared mustard added), in skillet, gently sauté franks till brown.

WRAPPED IN FOIL: Wrap franks in foil; heat over glowing coals 10 min.

IN BACON: Cut lengthwise slit in each frank (don't cut completely through). Smear slit with prepared mustard or catchup; stuff with thin sticks of tangy cheese, canned pineapple, or grated sharp cheese with grated onion or pickle relish added. Wrap each frank, spiral-fashion, with bacon strip; secure with toothpick. Grill over glowing coals, turning, till bacon is crisp and franks are hot.

BARBECUED BOLOGNA ROLL

Use 3-lb. piece of bologna, warmed to room temperature. Remove casing; halve crosswise; deeply score surfaces.

Spread with plain or horse-radish-flavored prepared mustard; dot with whole cloves. Put each half on 2 long skewers; grill over glowing coals, turning and basting often with barbecue sauce, until brown and thoroughly heated. Cut into thick or thin slices. Makes 12 servings.

GRILLED HAM

HAM-BANANA ROLL-UPS: Halve peeled bananas lengthwise, then crosswise. Roll each piece in thin slice canned or cooked ham; insert toothpick. Grill in folding wire broiler over glowing coals, turning. Also nice cooked indoors in broiler.

GLAZED HAM OR CANADIAN-STYLE BACON: Use ¼″ slices cooked or canned ham, cooked smoked boneless shoulder butt, or uncooked Canadian-style bacon. Grill over glowing coals, brushing with one of these:

Barbecue sauce
½ cup pineapple juice mixed with ¼ cup garlic vinegar, ½ cup brown sugar, and 1 tablesp. prepared mustard
⅓ cup orange juice mixed with 2 tablesp. peanut butter

GRILL-BARBECUED CHOPPED HAM: Cut 1 can chopped ham or luncheon meat into slices. Grill over glowing coals, basting frequently with barbecue sauce. Place in split hamburger buns or between toasted bread slices.

BARBECUED-HAM SLICES: Before grilling ham

slices, make pineapple-vinegar sauce, p. 733. Use to brush on ham slices as they grill.

LAMB AND BEEF ALFRESCO

BARBECUED SHORT RIBS: Cut meat from bones of 3 lb. beef shortribs; cut into serving pieces; pound pieces to flatten. Grill to desired rareness over glowing coals, turning and brushing with ½ cup soy sauce mixed with ½ teasp. ground ginger, or with barbecue sauce, till brown. Makes 4 servings.

BARBECUED BREAST OF LAMB: Grill 3 lb. lamb breast over slow fire, turning and basting with barbecue sauce till tender and nicely browned. Makes 4 to 6 servings.

BARBECUED LAMB SHANKS: Season 4 lamb shanks. Cook in pressure cooker at 15 lb. pressure 30 min. as manufacturer directs. Or simmer, covered, in 2 cups water 1½ hr., or till almost tender. Then grill shanks over glowing coals, turning and brushing often with barbecue sauce, till brown. Makes 4 servings.

MINTED LAMB, ROTISSERIE STYLE

2 racks of lamb (uncut rib chops)	1 teasp. crushed dried rosemary
½ cup mint jelly	Salt
¼ cup lemon juice	Pepper
	Cut cloves of garlic

Have meatman crack ribs about 3″ from ends. Before starting fire, heat jelly with lemon juice and rosemary. Sprinkle lamb with salt and pepper. Insert garlic in a few gashes in the meat. At 1″ intervals, tie twine around racks; let them stand out till fire is ready.

About 2½ hr. before serving: When coals are hot, adjust racks of lamb on spit; insert barbecue thermometer as manufacturer directs. Over coals, with drip pan in place, start spit revolving. About 10 min. before lamb is done (175°F. on the thermometer is pink), brush mint sauce over it.

To serve: Slice a 2-chop portion for each guest; spoon on a little sauce. Nice with grilled baked potatoes in foil, topped with butter and chopped sweet onion. Makes 8 servings.

KABOBS

To Assemble: String any combination, right, on 12″ to 24″ metal skewers. (If you don't have skewers, use medium steel wires. Cut 1 end of each obliquely to make sharp point; bend other end to form handle. Or use green branches.) Sprinkle kabobs with salt, pepper.

To Grill: Grill kabobs over glowing coals, turning and brushing as directed, or with barbecue sauce, or with melted butter or margarine and lemon juice, until done as desired.

To Serve: Rest end of each skewer on plate or in buttered, toasted, split roll; with knife, push food off skewer. Pass barbecue sauce, prepared mustard, chili sauce, Worcestershire, Tabasco, catchup, or bottled thick meat sauce.

SALAMI: 1″ chunks of lamb steak (from leg), 1½″ chunks of salami.

FRUIT: Canned cling-peach, pineapple, and banana chunks.

SEA FOOD: Deveined, shelled raw shrimp; raw scallops; bacon squares.

FOR COMPANY: 1½″ chunks of sirloin or veal steak, cooked tiny onions, tomato chunks, mushrooms — each on a separate skewer.

TEEN RAGE: Chunks of franks and canned pineapple or apple.

MAIN DISH: Chunks of pickles and franks spread with prepared mustard; cooked tiny potatoes; tomato wedges.

CALIFORNIA: Chunks of canned luncheon meat or franks, bacon squares, pitted ripe olives.

BRUNCH: Cubes of calf liver or chicken livers (frozen), bacon squares, mushroom caps.

TROPICAL: Chunks of canned luncheon meat, pineapple, and banana.

MEDITERRANEAN FRANKS: Cut skinless franks into thirds, wrap in strips of pimento; alternate on long skewers with pitted ripe olives, beginning and ending with piece of green pepper. Brush with oil and vinegar dressing.

SMOKY BOLOGNA: Alternate 1″ cubes of bologna with canned onions and 1½″ lengths of sour or sweet pickles. Brush with Italian dressing.

CHICKEN LIVERS EN BROCHETTE: Wrap each half of a fresh or thawed frozen chicken liver in a half strip of bacon; alternate on skewers with canned onions, beginning and ending with piece of green pepper. Brush with Italian dressing blended with a few drops of Tabasco.

DONIGIAN'S SHISH KABOB

1 leg of lamb (5 to 7 lb.), boned	7 24″ metal skewers
½ cup olive oil	14 not-too-ripe small tomatoes
1 teasp. salt	14 whole short, fat, green and red peppers
¼ teasp. pepper	
1 clove garlic, minced	
1 washed, unpared medium eggplant	14 small white onions

Cut lamb into 1½″ chunks. Let stand in oil mixed with salt, pepper, and garlic about 1 hr. Cut eggplant into 2″ chunks. On each of the 24″ skewers, string 1 tomato, 1 pepper, 2 chunks eggplant, 1 onion, 5 or 6 chunks lamb, 1 onion, 1 chunk eggplant, 1 pepper, 1 tomato. Grill over glowing coals until tender. Push off onto plates. Serve with Pilaf, p. 373. Makes 5 to 7 servings.

SUREN'S SHISH KABOB: See p. 221.

TURKISH SHISH KEBAB

1 5- to 7-lb. leg of lamb	¼ cup olive or salad oil
3 medium onions, finely chopped	8 13″ metal skewers
1 teasp. salt	6 to 8 not-too-ripe tomatoes, in large wedges
½ teasp. pepper	
2 teasp. dried orégano	2 green peppers, cut into 2″ chunks

Day before: Cut lamb into 1½″ chunks; trim off gristle and most of fat. Place lamb in large bowl; add onions, salt, pepper, orégano, and oil, tossing well. Refrigerate, covered, turning lamb occasionally.
About 1½ hr. before serving: Start fire. Alternate, on metal skewers, lamb, tomatoes, and green peppers, allowing ¼″ between pieces; lightly brush vegetables with oil. Grill shish kebab, 5″ above hot coals, about 30 min., turning frequently and brushing with enough oil to keep them moist.
To serve: With fork, push shish kebab from a skewer onto each plate. Pass bowl of rice cooked in chicken broth with raisins and nuts. Makes 8 servings.

POULTRY AND FISH

CHARCOAL-GRILLED CHICKEN

1. Halve or quarter a 2- to 2½-lb. broiler-fryer. Or if it's quick-frozen, thaw as label directs. Or buy fresh or quick-frozen chicken parts — breasts, thighs, etc.
2. Break hip, knee, and wing joints (some cooks remove wing tips, too) to keep bird flat during grilling.
3. Season as in Special Touches, p. 263.
4. When coals are glowing, arrange bird, with cut sides down, on greased grill or in folding wire broiler. Grill slowly, turning with tongs and basting with barbecue sauce, about 25 min., or until tender. When bird is done, knife cuts easily into thick part of leg, and no blood shows at bone.

CHARCOAL-GRILLED TURKEY: Buy small (3½- to 6-lb.) ready-to-cook turkey, quartered. Grill as above, allowing about 45 min.

PINEAPPLE-BARBECUED CHICKS

1 9-oz. can crushed pineapple	Salt and pepper
¾ cup brown sugar, packed	2 2½- to 3-lb. broiler-fryers, halved
1 teasp. dry mustard	Soft butter or margarine
1 tablesp. prepared mustard	4 fully cooked ham slices, ⅛″ thick (optional)
Juice of 1 lemon	
1½ teasp. vinegar	

In a jar, combine pineapple, brown sugar, mustards, lemon juice, vinegar, and dash of salt and pepper. Through length of each bird, insert a skewer to keep it flat. Spread birds with butter, sprinkle them with salt and pepper, wrap them and ham in foil, and refrigerate all.
About 1¼ hr. before serving: Start fire, unwrap, grill birds, cut side down, 4″ above hot coals, 30 min., turning and brushing often with butter. About 8 min. before birds are done, grill ham — 4 min. per side — and spoon some of pineapple sauce over cut side of birds. Let birds grill a few minutes; then turn them and carefully spoon on rest of sauce. Makes 4 servings.

CHARCOAL-GRILLED DUCKLING

Remove neck, wings, and backbone from 3½- to 4-lb. ready-to-cook duckling; then quarter.
Grill as in Charcoal-Grilled Chicken, above,

30 to 40 min., or till tender, brushing occasionally with mixture of ¼ cup honey, 2 teasp. bottled sauce for gravy, and ½ teasp. each salt and ground ginger. Or brush with barbecue sauce. Makes 3 to 4 servings.

FISH FRIES AND BARBECUES

BARBECUED SWORDFISH, SALMON, OR HALIBUT STEAKS: Cut 3 lb. of fish steaks (¾" thick) into 8 pieces. Place in shallow dish; onto fish, pour combined juice of 1 lemon and ¼ cup salad oil. Refrigerate ½ hr.

Arrange fish in folding wire broiler; brush well with hot barbecue sauce. Grill close to glowing coals (cook fish quickly to prevent drying) about 3 min., or until golden brown. Brush with sauce; turn; grill until easily flaked with fork but still moist. Brush with sauce again; serve. Makes 8 servings.

BACON-GRILLED TROUT: Wrap cleaned trout in bacon. Grill in folding wire broiler over glowing coals, turning. When bacon is done, serve.

SHELLFISH ALFRESCO

ROAST CLAMS OR OYSTERS: Scrub 1 doz. raw cherrystone clams or oysters in shell per person. Place on grill or wire screening laid across glowing coals. Or wrap in foil; place on coals; turn occasionally. When shells open, serve as in Steamed Clams, p. 316.

STEAMED CLAMS: See Steamed Clams, p. 316.

GRILLED LIVE LOBSTER: Have lobster split, cleaned. Place, with shell side toward heat, on grill, 3" from heat. Brush with mixture of melted butter or margarine, salt, pepper, snipped parsley, and minced garlic. Grill over glowing coals about 8 min. Turn flesh side toward heat; brush again; grill about 6 min.; brush. Serve with lemon wedges and melted butter or margarine.

GRILLED ROCK-LOBSTER TAILS: (See To Buy, p. 321.) Thaw; snip off thin undershell. To prevent curling, bend shell backwards and crack in one or more places. Or insert metal skewers the whole length of the tail. Grill as in Grilled Live Lobster, above.

LEMON-BARBECUED ROCK-LOBSTER TAILS: Grill tails as above, brushing with ½ cup melted butter or margarine blended with 1 small clove garlic, crushed, ½ teasp. salt, ½ teasp. pepper, and ¼ cup lemon juice.

VEGETABLES, TOO

BEST CORN EVER

BOILED: Husk, then boil fresh corn on grill, over glowing coals, as you would on indoor range (don't boil more than 5 or 6 min.). For easy eating, break ears into thirds.

GRILLED: Butter hot boiled ears of corn; quickly toast on grill over glowing coals. Or each guest grills his own on skewer.

ROASTED IN HUSKS: About 10 min. before eating, place first round of fresh corn, in husks, on grill over glowing coals. (Some cooks like to plunge corn into salted water first.) Roast, turning often, until husks are steaming hot — about 10 min.; then husk and serve.

FOIL-ROASTED: If husks are left on, pull back and remove silk; brush with melted butter or margarine, then sprinkle with seasonings. Replace husks; wrap in foil, twisting ends to secure. If husks are removed, spread corn with softened butter or margarine, and season. Wrap in foil, double-wrapping if fire is very hot or if corn is to be placed on coals. Roast for about 25 min., turning 2 or 3 times.

Final Touch: See To Serve Corn on Cob, p. 400.

THE POPULAR SPUD

FROZEN FRENCH FRIES OR CANNED SHOESTRING POTATOES: Empty potatoes into corn popper; shake over glowing coals till hot; season. Or heat bit of shortening or salad oil in heavy skillet; add potatoes and toss till hot.

BAKED IN FOIL: Scrub baking potatoes; wrap each in foil. Place on glowing coals. Bake, turning occasionally, 1 hr., or till done. Unwrap; cut deep cross in top of each; press ends firmly till savory white potato bursts through cross; season. (Peeled whole small onions with seasonings added may be baked in same way.)

BOILED: On grill, boil new potatoes in coffee or shortening can, covered, until fork-tender.

FRIED WITH BACON: In heavy skillet, fry 4 bacon slices until crisp; remove; crumble. Pare 4 large potatoes; slice very thin; place in bacon drippings. Add 1 teasp. salt, ¼ teasp. pepper. Fry till almost tender and quite brown. Move to edge of grill; add bacon bits; cover; cook till tender. Makes 4 to 6 servings.

BAKED POTATOES AMERICAN: Before wrapping

in foil, rub skins of potatoes with butter. Bake until done, about 1 hr., then make cross in top of each as in Baked in Foil, p. 736. Season fluffy center with butter, salt, and pepper; pass shredded Cheddar cheese, crumbled crisp bacon, and snipped chives to sprinkle on top.

POTATOES IN ENVELOPES: Arrange individual portions of pared sliced potatoes and onions and shredded carrots, green pepper, or pimento on squares of foil. Season, add butter and a little top milk to each. Seal and cook over grill about ½ hr. Turn once or twice.

SWEET POTATOES

BAKED IN FOIL: Follow directions for Spuds Baked in Foil, p. 736, baking sweet potatoes about 45 min., or till tender.

GRILLED: Halve peeled, cooked sweet potatoes lengthwise. Spread with soft butter or margarine. Grill in folding wire broiler over glowing coals, turning often, till bubbly. Top with butter or margarine, salt, pepper.

GEOFF'S ROSIN-BAKED POTATOES

About 2 hr. before dinner: Over deep bed of coals in grill (set up fire in a safe spot where it won't be disturbed), place a 3-gal. bucket half full of pure gum rosin (rosin is usually available at most large hardware stores). Heat rosin to 275°F. on deep-fat thermometer. Then carefully slip in about 6 large white or sweet potatoes. When they rise to the surface of rosin, they are about two thirds done; cook 20 min. longer.

Remove thermometer. With a long-handled, slotted spoon, remove and wrap each potato in a 12″ square of heavy-duty foil or heavy paper. Let potatoes stand at least 10 min.; then, through foil in center top of each, cut an x; press ends so that fluffy potato bursts through slit.

Serve with lots of butter; or from a large wooden tray, let guests top their potatoes with a choice of crumbled Danish blue cheese, sharp-cheese spread, seasoned commercial sour cream, sliced ripe or chopped stuffed olives, snipped chives, or crisp bacon bits.

NOTE: Allow rosin to cool and harden. It can be used over and over again before you need to replenish your supply.

MIXED-GRILL PARTNERS

Grill or sauté fruits or vegetables in skillet over glowing coals, turning, until brown. (See Mixed Grill, p. 180.)

MUSHROOMS IN FOIL: Wash 1 lb. mushrooms. Slice or leave whole. Place on foil. Top with 2 tablesp. butter or margarine, and some seasoned salt. Wrap, folding edges of foil under. Place on grill. Cook about 10 to 15 min. Makes 4 generous servings.

FRESH VEGETABLES: Arrange individual portions of vegetables on squares of foil; add seasonings, butter or margarine. Bring up foil over food in tight package; grill over fire, turning once or twice. Try corn, cut-up tomatoes and green peppers; thinly sliced zucchini and onions; thinly sliced mushrooms and tomatoes.

CANNED BAKED BEANS, PEAS, CORN, MUSHROOMS, ETC.: Pour one third of contents of 2 cans of vegetables into a third empty can. Heat all 3 cans on grill over glowing coals, stirring now and then, until piping hot. Add seasonings and a little monosodium glutamate for zest.

FROZEN VEGETABLES COOKED IN FOIL: Place frozen vegetables on foil. (Or make individual packets.) Add salt, pepper, butter or margarine. Shape into long, flat package, with edges of foil tucked under. Place on grill; cook over glowing coals about 5 min. longer than label directs. If fire gets too hot, move package to edge of grill. Serve from foil, with edges folded back. Or try new frozen-vegetable combinations.

GRILL YOUR BREADS

SAVORY FRENCH OR ITALIAN BREAD

Use yard-long or junior-size loaf of French or Italian bread, or frank rolls. Slash diagonally into thick slices, cutting almost to bottom. Or halve lengthwise; then slash. Between slices and on top, spread one of spreads in Savory French Bread, p. 493. Prop loaf on 2 empty cans on grill or on glowing coals, and grill until hot and toasted. Or wrap loaf in foil and place on grill or coals; or use long skewer to hold loaf over coals. Grill, turning often, until hot or toasted.

CHUNKS: Spread chunks of French bread with one of spreads in Savory French Bread, p. 493. Toast on skewers. Or wrap in foil; heat on grill.

GRILL-BAKED BREADS

CAMP BISCUITS: Use cans of refrigerated biscuits; or make 1/4"-thick biscuits as in Hot Baking-Powder Biscuits, p. 475; or use biscuit mix. In butter or margarine, in skillet, sauté biscuits over low coals, covered, till brown on bottom; turn and brown top. Uncover; stand biscuits on sides till brown.

WAFFLES: Use frozen waffles. (Or make Waffles, p. 489, indoors at your leisure. Refrigerate waffles a day or two; or freeze if storing them for a longer period.) Heat in folding wire broiler over glowing coals. Serve as bread, with butter or margarine.

ROLLS AND MUFFINS

HOT FROM THE GRILL: Place rolls or muffins in covered coffee can. Place can on side on the grill or glowing coals; roll can occasionally till bread is heated.

Or place rolls in skillet on grill. Sprinkle with a few drops of water. Heat, covered, shaking skillet occasionally.

TOASTED: Split rolls or muffins; top with one of spreads in Savory French Bread, p. 493; toast in folding wire broiler or on skewer. Or sauté in butter or margarine, in skillet, over glowing coals. (English muffins and crumpets are good this way.)

HOT CRUSTY ROLLS: Spread split rolls with garlic, herb, or plain butter; wrap in double thicknesses of foil; place on grill; heat 20 min., turning once.

GARLIC-BUTTERED SLICES

Spread white-bread slices with butter or margarine; sprinkle with garlic salt. Put together sandwich-fashion. Wrap in foil; or place in covered can. Toast on grill over glowing coals, turning often. Use as hamburger rolls.

GRILL SANDWICHES, TOO

BARBECUE SANDWICHES: Slice cold or hot roast meat or turkey, baked ham, smoked boneless shoulder butt, or meat loaf; tuck into grilled split buns. Spoon hot barbecue sauce over meat.

WELSH RABBIT IN HAND: Brush outside of cheese sandwiches with melted butter or margarine. Toast in skillet or folding wire broiler over glowing coals.

TOASTED PEANUT BUTTER: Toast peanut-butter sandwiches (plain or with honey, raisins, or catchup) in skillet or folding wire broiler over glowing coals.

BACON-CHEESE BUNS: Spread one side of split frankfurter buns with prepared mustard, other side with butter or margarine. Tuck chunk of cheese in each bun. Wrap in bacon; fasten with toothpicks. Grill in folding wire broiler over glowing coals.

CHILI BURGERS: Let guests make their own sandwiches with hot, canned chili con carne, soda crackers or large saltines, plus process Cheddar-cheese slices, onion rings, or lettuce.

SCRAMBLED-EGG SANDWICHES: Provide scrambled-egg mixture in pitcher. Let chef scramble eggs. Let guests toast buns and fill them with eggs, crisp bacon, then catchup or snipped scallions.

CRACKER SANDWICHES: Make cracker sandwiches (use round scalloped crackers, rye wafers, saltines, or soda crackers) with cheese, peanut butter, etc. Toast in corn popper.

DESSERTS FROM THE GRILL

CARAMEL ROAST APPLES: Place crisp apples on grill; toast over glowing coals, turning occasionally, till apples' skins burst. Peel; roll in brown sugar. Grill till caramelized.

Or core apples, fill centers with sugar, spices, and a little butter. Wrap in foil, and grill over fire about 30 min., or until tender.

WALNUT ROAST *(nice with fruit):* Roast unshelled walnuts in corn popper over glowing coals.

TEEN-AGE DELIGHTS

FRIED MARSHMALLOWS: In small skillet, over glowing coals, melt butter or margarine. Slowly cook 8 large marshmallows until brown on one side. Turn; brown other side. Use to top soda crackers.

DATE-MARSHMALLOW KABOBS: Alternate pitted dates and large marshmallows on stick; toast over glowing coals.

SHORE-FRONT BAKED BANANAS: For each serving, slit unpeeled banana lengthwise, part-way through, to within 1/2" of ends. Tuck in sweet-chocolate-bar pieces or 1 or 2 miniature marshmallows. Toast bananas, with cut sides up, on green sticks over coals till peel chars and center is soft, hot. Cool slightly; peel.

MARSHMALLOW TREATS: Toast 2 large marshmallows over coals until gooey and crisp. Place on graham cracker or thin gingerbread slice. Top with piece of sweet-chocolate bar; cover with graham cracker or thin gingerbread slice. Eat sandwich-style.

GRILLED BANANAS: About 10 min. before serving, grill unpeeled ripe bananas, without turning, till fork-tender — about 8 min. Then remove top half of peel from each banana; salt bananas lightly; serve.

CAMPFIRE PEACHES: Drain 1 1-lb.-13-oz. can cling-peach halves. In skillet, over hot coals, heat peaches with 3/4 cup canned whole-cranberry sauce and 3 tablesp. butter or margarine, stirring occasionally, till hot. Makes 5 to 7 servings.

STRAWBERRY SHORTCAKE, GYPSY STYLE

2 cups packaged biscuit mix
2 tablesp. sugar
1/2 cup milk
1/4 cup shortening, melted
2 tablesp. butter or margarine
2 pt. fresh strawberries
Dessert topping

Night before: In medium bowl, with fork, stir together biscuit mix, sugar, milk, melted shortening. Beat briskly until blended; turn onto pastry board, dusted with flour or biscuit mix. Knead gently until smooth; cut into halves. Pat one half of dough into 9" metal or disposable foil pie pan; dot with butter; on top pat other half of dough. Cover shortcake with a second well-greased 9" metal or disposable foil pan. Wrap in double thickness of foil, making fold across top; press two ends of foil down around pie pan. Set wrapped shortcake in freezer.

About 1 1/2 hr. before serving: Remove shortcake from freezer. Start fire. Open up foil ends of shortcake package. Place it on grill 4" to 5" above glowing coals; bake 30 min.; then remove from heat; remove foil; invert pans so baked side of shortcake is on top. Bake 10 min., or till done. Meanwhile, wash, hull, then slice strawberries lengthwise; crush and sweeten some of them if you wish; refrigerate. When shortcake is done, remove from grill. Lift off top pie pan; then, with sharp knife, split shortcake in half horizontally, setting top half in other pie pan. Top bottom half of shortcake with 1 or 2 layers of strawberries. Replace top half; then cover with rest of berries. Garnish with whipped dessert topping; serve in wedges. Makes 4 to 6 servings.

INDEX

741

Creamy mustard sauce, 532
Creamy potato soup, 160
Crème
brulèe, 543, 560, 565
de cacao angel-food cake, 637
vichyssoise, 169
Crenshaw melons, 550
Creole-stuffed green peppers, 194
Crêpes, 578
strawberry-cream, 578
suzette, 578–579
Crescent(s), 501
meltaways, 657
specials, 479
Crinkles, 660
Crisp artichoke salad, 450
Crisp-coated fish fillets, 302
Crisp coconut balls, 675
Crisp onion relish, 439
Crispy new potatoes, 413
Crookneck squash. *See Summer squash*
Croquettes, 257
deep-fat-frying, 7
Croustades, 497
Croustadin, 243–244
Croutons, 8
cheese, 344
Crowds, cooking for, 715–729.
See also For a crowd
Crown roast of lamb
described, 219
roasting timetable, 220 (*chart*)
Crown roast of pork, 199
roasting timetable, 200 (*chart*)
Crowning glory orange soufflé, 124–125
Crunchy bridge bites, 669
Crunchy crab and shrimp cocktail, 142
Crunchy creamed turkey, 291
Crunchy kidney-bean salad, 451
Crunchy macaroni, 378
Crunchy stuffed lettuce salad, 450
Crunchy-top coffeecake, 511
Crunchy tuna-rice cones, 312
Crunchy tuna salad, 456
Crushed pineapple relish, 437
Crust. *See Pastry*
Cube, how to, 5
Cube steak, 180

Cube sugar, 101
Cucumber(s), 400
-cream salad, 463
in sour cream, 450
marketing for, 423 (*chart*)
mayonnaise dressing, 469
mold, 723
-radish flowers, 524
sauce, 529–530
slices, 118–119
slimmer nibbler, 157
sticks, 119
Cumin, uses, 95
Cup, equivalent measures, 17
Cupcake(s), 638–640
angel triplets, 639–640
broiled praline, 639
candle, 640
devil's food, 638
double-chocolate miniature cakes, 639
fruit cakelets, 136
half and half, 639
honeycomb, 639
ice cream, 607
Kentucky, 640
lacy cocoa, 639
nugget, 639
old-fashioned white, 638
one-egg, 638
pans, 16
pineapple-cream, 639
shadow, 639
sherry Christmas, 638–639
snowball, 639
sponge, 134
tricky, 639
Cups, measuring, described, 13–15
Currants, 549
Blanche's steamed pudding, 571
-mint sauce, 527
-nut French dressing, 469
serving, 540
Curry(ied)
apple-curry savory rice, 370
apricots, 437
-avocado soup, 162–163
beef, 186–189
oxjoint ragout, 198
cabbage, 397
chicken
deviled eggs, 364
different chicken, 278
fried chicken, 265
liver sauté, 275
omelet, 362

Curry(ied), *continued*
chicken, *continued*
on parsley rice, 719
salad, 458
soup, 161
coconut, 441
crab-meat salad, 458
eggs, 361, 364, 367
four-fruit bake, 437
frank curry bake, 246
French dressing, 469
haddock fillets, 302
Hollandaise, 531
lamb, 224, 255–256
stew with poppy-seed noodles, 222
mayonnaise, 470
Nancy's curried spaghetti, 381
of the seas, 309–310
olives, 147
onions sauté, 408
peach halves, 437
pears, 437
pineapple rice, 371
sauce, 528
potato soup, 162
pot roast, 184
powder, uses for, 95
rice, 371–372
pea salad and, 452
raisin-, 371
sandwiches, 520–521, 523
sauces, 143, 527–528, 533
scalloped potatoes, 413
scallops, 324–325
sea food salad, 457–458
shrimp, 142, 330, 458
cocktail, 142
tomato curry dip, 155
tuna, 145–146, 311, 488
pancakes, 488
turkey-olive, 288
veal paprika, 228–229
vegetable salad, 451
waffles, 489
white sauce, 533
Cushion shoulder lamb roast, described, 219
roasting timetable, 220 (*chart*)
Cushion shoulder pork roast, roasting timetable, 200 (*chart*)
Custard(s). *See also Puddings*
baked caramel coconut, 131
baked maple, 131

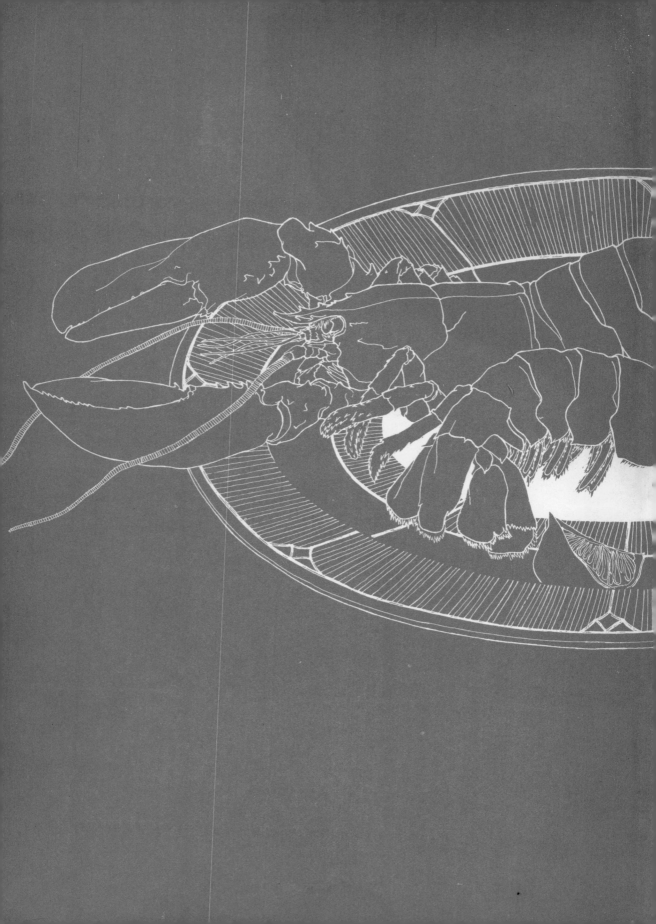